THE OXFORD HANDBOOK OF
SILENT CINEMA

THE OXFORD HANDBOOK OF
SILENT CINEMA

Edited by
ROB KING
and
CHARLIE KEIL

OXFORD
UNIVERSITY PRESS

Oxford University Press is a department of the University of Oxford. It furthers
the University's objective of excellence in research, scholarship, and education
by publishing worldwide. Oxford is a registered trade mark of Oxford University
Press in the UK and certain other countries.

Published in the United States of America by Oxford University Press
198 Madison Avenue, New York, NY 10016, United States of America.

© Oxford University Press 2024

All rights reserved. No part of this publication may be reproduced, stored in
a retrieval system, or transmitted, in any form or by any means, without the
prior permission in writing of Oxford University Press, or as expressly permitted
by law, by license, or under terms agreed with the appropriate reproduction
rights organization. Inquiries concerning reproduction outside the scope of the
above should be sent to the Rights Department, Oxford University Press, at the
address above.

You must not circulate this work in any other form
and you must impose this same condition on any acquirer.

Library of Congress Cataloging-in-Publication Data
Names: King, Rob, 1975– editor. | Keil, Charlie, editor.
Title: The Oxford handbook of silent cinema / [edited by] Rob King and Charlie Keil.
Description: New York, NY : Oxford University Press, [2024] |
Identifiers: LCCN 2023024944 | ISBN 9780190496692 (hardback) |
ISBN 9780197630327 (epub) | ISBN 9780190496715
Subjects: LCSH: Silent films—History and criticism.
Classification: LCC PN1995.75 .O94 2024 | DDC 791.4309—dc23/eng/20230810
LC record available at https://lccn.loc.gov/2023024944

DOI: 10.1093/oxfordhb/9780190496692.001.0001

Printed by Integrated Books International, United States of America

Contents

Acknowledgments ix
List of Contributors xi

1. Introduction: The History of the History of Silent Film 1
   ROB KING AND CHARLIE KEIL

PART I ORIGINS: FROM INVENTION TO MEDIUM

2. The Invention of Cinema 17
   TOM GUNNING

3. Early Cinema and the Emergence of Television:
   An Archaeology of Intertwined Media 38
   DORON GALILI

4. The Right to One's Own Image: Animism,
   The Student of Prague, and Legal Doctrine 55
   STEFAN ANDRIOPOULOS

5. Copying Technologies: Two Pirates, Two Centuries 72
   JANE M. GAINES

PART II INTERMEDIALITY: GENRE AND AESTHETICS IN SILENT FILM

6. The Unfinished Business of History: Defense and Illustration
   of the Concept "Cultural Series" 95
   ANDRÉ GAUDREAULT AND PHILIPPE MARION

7. Reviewing *Maple Viewing* (*Momijigari*, 1899) 116
   DAISUKE MIYAO

8. African American Film History Beyond Cinema:
   William Foster and the Legacy of Black Theatrical Comedy   130
   ALLYSON NADIA FIELD

9. Picture, Shadow, Play: Ontology, Archaeology, Ecology   159
   WEIHONG BAO

10. Biograph 1904: The Invention of Chase Comedy   184
    ROB KING

11. Storied Spaces: Staging and Editing in Early American Feature Films 204
    MIRIAM SIEGEL

12. Salon Tango: Hollywood Pictorialism and the Beaux-Arts Tradition 225
    TOM PAULUS

13. Symbolist Impressions: Modern Theater, Germaine Dulac, and
    the Making of an Art Cinema in Belle Époque France
    (or, the False Ideal of the Cinema against Theater)   251
    TAMI WILLIAMS

PART III PEDAGOGICAL FORMATIONS: NON-THEATRICAL CINEMA AND THE USES OF FILM

14. *Popular Science Monthly* and the Uses of Moving Pictures   283
    GREGORY A. WALLER

15. Cinema and Science in the Silent Era   305
    SCOTT CURTIS AND OLIVER GAYCKEN

16. Cinema on the Move: Museum-Sponsored Expedition
    Film in the Silent Era   332
    ALISON GRIFFITHS

17. Babies and Brochures: Public Service Pamphlet Films of
    the US Children's Bureau (1919–1926)   354
    JENNIFER HORNE

18. Curiosity Seekers, Morbid Minds, and Embarrassed Young Ladies:
    Female Audiences and Reproductive Politics Onscreen   375
    SHELLEY STAMP

PART IV HOLLYWOOD, INC.: THE INSTITUTIONS OF MASS CULTURE

19. Unlikely Allies: Crafting Hollywood as Institution and Invention — 397
    CHARLIE KEIL AND DENISE MCKENNA

20. A System of Thorough Cooperation: Technology, Service, and the Film Labs of Hollywood — 420
    LUCI MARZOLA

21. A Prologue to Hollywood: Sid Grauman, Film Premieres, and the (Real-Estate) Development of Hollywood — 440
    ROSS MELNICK

22. Franchising as a Strategy of National Feature Distribution in the 1910s: The Case of the Triangle Film Corporation — 460
    DEREK LONG

23. Paramount Pictures, National Advertising Agencies, and the Conspicuous Distribution of First-Run Feature Films in the United States — 481
    PAUL S. MOORE

PART V NATION, EMPIRE, WORLD: THE SPACES AND TIMES OF MODERNITY

24. Going Silent on Modernity: Periodization, Geopolitics, and Public Opinion — 505
    GIORGIO BERTELLINI

25. Empire • State • Media — 526
    LEE GRIEVESON

26. Dandyism, Circulation, and Emergent Cinema in Iran: The Powers of Asynchrony — 546
    KAVEH ASKARI

27. *The Covered Wagon*: Location Shooting and Settler Melodrama — 569
    JENNIFER LYNN PETERSON

28. Scandinavian Cinema, Location, and the Discourse of Quality in 1920 — 594
    ANNE BACHMANN

29. Running Late: The Silent Serial, the Cliffhanger, and
    the Exigencies of Time, 1914–1920 618
    RUTH MAYER

PART VI CINEMATIC PUBLICS: CRITICS, FANS, COMMUNITIES

30. The Silent Film Criticism of Siegfried Kracauer 641
    JOHANNES VON MOLTKE

31. The Decline of Middlebrow Taste in Celebrity Culture:
    The First Fan Magazines 662
    SUMIKO HIGASHI

32. The Many Genders and Sexualities of American and
    European Silent Cinema 684
    LAURA HORAK

33. Art, Anti-Art, and Poetic Cinema:
    Revisiting *Un Chien andalou* (Luis Buñuel, 1929) 714
    BREIXO VIEJO

34. Coda: Silent Film after Sound 738
    DONNA KORNHABER

Index 757

Acknowledgments

This volume has been in the making for more or less a decade. We are immensely grateful for the patience and commitment shown by all our contributors and by the team at Oxford University Press, including Norm Hirschy, Brendan O'Neill, Madison Zickgraf, Laura Santo, Jayanthi Dineshkumar, and Joellyn Ausanka. All of them saints. We would also like to thank Justin Morris for extremely helpful assistance with citations and images when we were facing one of many crucial deadlines, and Shayla Anderson for lending her photographic expertise to securing a properly reproduced cover image.

Rob King would like to thank Charlie Keil, who came on as coeditor once the project was already under way. He should also apologize to Charlie's family for editorial chores that spilled over into many family vacations. Sorry, Cathy. But, again, thank you, Charlie: you've been the most valuable support I've had in my career, not just on this project. Rob would also like to acknowledge, guiltily, all those who tolerated his pestering emails over the years it took to bring this volume to completion. Final thanks, as always, are to his wife, Inie Park, who is currently hard at work on her forthcoming collection, *The Oxford Handbook of Surviving Your Partner's Book Projects*.

Charlie Keil would like to thank Rob King, who invited me to participate in this project at a relatively early stage; if email records are to be believed, we have been working on this together since 2016. I leapt from the fat of *A Companion to D. W. Griffith* directly into the fire of this *Handbook*. But Rob kept the singeing to a minimum. May everyone have the opportunity to work with a coeditor as discerning, as generous, and as collaborative as Rob King. His only fault is a regrettable tendency to complete every task in about a tenth of the time it takes mere mortals to do the same thing. His editorial acumen and unassailable work ethic have guaranteed this volume's success. Charlie would also like to thank all of the contributors, and especially those whom he counts as friends, assuming that they still are his friends now that the editing process is complete. And, of course, the aforementioned Cathy Vine, who has listened to far more nattering about the vagaries of silent cinema research than any non-film specialist should have to tolerate and has always done so with grace and affection.

Contributors

Stefan Andriopoulos is Professor of German and co-founder of the Center for Comparative Media at Columbia University. His book *Possessed: Hypnotic Crimes, Corporate Fiction, and the Invention of Cinema* (2008) analyzes anxieties about the agency of invisible corporate bodies and the power of hypnotism in literature, law, medicine, and silent film. It won the SLSA Michelle Kendrick Award for best academic book on literature, science, and the arts. Andriopoulos has also published *Ghostly Apparitions: German Idealism, the Gothic Novel, and Optical Media* (2013), which reveals the constitutive role of spiritualism for the history of philosophy and technology and which was named a book of the year in the *Times Literary Supplement*. His current book project engages in a short and selective history of the constitutive links between rumor, media, and the credence created by new modes of circulation.

Kaveh Askari is Associate Professor and Director of the Film Studies Program at Michigan State University. He is the author of *Relaying Cinema in Midcentury Iran: Material Cultures in Transit* (2022). He has also written *Making Movies into Art: Picture Craft from the Magic Lantern to Early Hollywood* (2014) and co-edited several volumes, including a special issue of *Film History* titled *South by South/West Asia: Transregional Histories of Middle East–South Asia Cinemas* (2021) and *Performing New Media, 1890–1915* (2014). He has collaborated with curators and archives to preserve films made in Iran in the 1950s and 1960s. These preservations have screened at venues including Il Cinema Ritrovato and the Museum of Modern Art.

Anne Bachmann is Assistant Professor of Fashion Studies and Film Studies at Stockholm University and at DIS Study Abroad in Scandinavia. She has published research at the intersection of Scandinavian studies and film studies, often working on transmedia questions ranging from costume design, print design, and small-scale models to online participatory practices. Her work has appeared in *Scandinavica*, *Early Popular Visual Culture*, and *Importing Asta Nielsen* (2013). She also serves on the editorial board of *Journal of Scandinavian Cinema*. Her current research interests concern historical visual culture and consumer culture.

Weihong Bao is Associate Professor of Film and Media at UC Berkeley. She is the author of *Fiery Films: The Emergence of an Affective Medium in China, 1915–1945* (2015), which received honorable mention for the Best Book Prize by the Modernist Studies Association in 2016. She has co-edited two special issues on Media/Climates (for *Representations* in 2022) and Medium/Environment (for *Critical Inquiry* in 2023). She is currently completing a new book, *Background Matters: Set Design and The Art of Environment*. She is editor-in-chief of *The Journal of Chinese Cinemas* and co-edits the Film Theory in Media History book series published by Amsterdam University Press.

Giorgio Bertellini is Professor in the Department of Film, Television, and Media at the University of Michigan. He is the author and editor of the award-winning volumes *The Divo and the Duce: Promoting Film Stardom and Political Leadership in 1920s America* (2019, Italian translation 2022), *Italian Silent Cinema: A Reader* (2013), and *Italy in Early American Cinema: Race, Landscape, and the Picturesque* (2010). His other books include a monograph on Sarajevo-born film director Emir Kusturica, published in Italian (1996, 2011), English (2015), and Romanian (2017). With Richard Abel and Matthew Solomon, he is the editor of the book series Cinema Cultures in Contact for the University of California Press. A contributor to Italy's daily newspapers (*Corriere della Sera, Il Foglio*), he was awarded a Guggenheim Fellowship in 2022.

Scott Curtis is Associate Professor in the Department of Radio/Television/Film at Northwestern University and in the Communication Program at Northwestern University in Qatar. The author of *The Shape of Spectatorship: Art, Science, and Early Cinema in Germany* (2015) and editor of *Animation* (2019), Curtis has published extensively on the scientific and medical uses of moving-image technology.

Allyson Nadia Field is Associate Professor of Cinema and Media Studies at the University of Chicago. She is the author of *Uplift Cinema: The Emergence of African American Film and the Possibility of Black Modernity* (2015). She is also co-editor with Marsha Gordon of *Screening Race in American Nontheatrical Film* (2019) and co-editor with Jan-Christopher Horak and Jacqueline Stewart of *L.A. Rebellion: Creating a New Black Cinema* (2015). Field was named a 2019 Academy Film Scholar by the Academy of Motion Picture Arts and Sciences and is a member of the National Film Preservation Board.

Jane M. Gaines is Professor of Film at Columbia University. She has been awarded the Society for Cinema and Media Studies Distinguished Career Award and an Honorary Doctorate from the University of Stockholm. She is author of the award-winning books *Contested Culture: The Image, the Voice, and the Law* (1991), *Fire and Desire: Mixed Race Movies in the Silent Era* (2001), and *Pink-Slipped: What Happened to Women in the Silent Film Industries?* (2018).

Doron Galili is Senior Lecturer in Film Studies at the University of Gothenburg and a Research Fellow in the Department of Media Studies at Stockholm University. He is the author of *Seeing by Electricity: The Emergence of Television, 1878–1939* (2020), as well as co-editor of *Corporeality in Early Cinema: Viscera, Skin, and Physical Form* (2018), and, most recently, of a special issue on media archaeology for *Early Popular Visual Culture*.

André Gaudreault is Professor in the Department of Art History and Film Studies at the University of Montreal and holds the Canada Research Chair in Film and Media Studies. He is the founder of the Laboratoire CinéMédias, under which he heads/codirects the CINEXMEDIA International Research Partnership, the International Research Partnership on Cinema Technology (TECHNÈS), and the Groupe de recherche sur l'avénement et la formation des identités médiatiques (GRAFIM). His books include *From Plato to Lumière* (2009 [1988]), *Film and Attraction: From Kinematography to Cinema* (2011 [2008]), and, with Philippe Marion, *The End of Cinema? A Medium in Crisis in the Digital Age* (2015 [2013]). Gaudreault's research has earned him several prizes and distinctions, including the Guggenheim Fellowship (2013), the Léon-Gérin Prize (2017), and the Killam Prize in the Humanities (2018). He was named an Officer of the Order of Canada in 2022.

Oliver Gaycken is Associate Professor in the Department of English and a core faculty member of the Cinema and Media Studies and Comparative Literature Programs at the University of Maryland, College Park. He is the author of *Devices of Curiosity: Early Cinema and Popular Science* (2015). His articles have appeared in *Historical Journal of Film, Radio, and Television*, *Science in Context*, *Journal of Visual Culture*, *Early Popular Visual Culture*, *Screen*, and the collection *Learning with the Lights Off* (2011).

Lee Grieveson is Professor of Media History at University College London. He is the author of the award-winning *Cinema and the Wealth of Nations: Media, Capital, and the Liberal World System* (2017) and *Policing Cinema: Movies and Censorship in Early-Twentieth-Century America* (2004). His other books include seven co-edited volumes, among them *The Silent Cinema Reader* (2004), co-edited with Peter Kramer; *Inventing Film Studies* (2008), co-edited with Haidee Wasson; and two anthologies devoted to issues of film and empire, co-edited with Colin MacCabe.

Alison Griffiths is Distinguished Professor of Film and Media Studies at Baruch College, The City University of New York, and a member of the doctoral faculty in Theatre at the CUNY Graduate Center. Her research focuses on early cinema, non-traditional spaces of film exhibition, new media, and medieval visual studies. She is the author of the multiple award-winning *Wondrous Difference: Cinema, Anthropology, and Turn-of-the-Century Visual Culture* (2002), *Shivers Down Your Spine: Cinema, Museums, and the Immersive View* (2008), and *Carceral Fantasies: Cinema and Prison in Early Twentieth-Century America* (2016), as well as more than fifty journal articles and book chapters. Her research has been supported by a Guggenheim Fellowship, a Fulbright Distinguished Chair, and grants from the NEH, ACLS, The Waterhouse Family Institute, the Institute for Citizens and Fellows, and the Huntington Library in Los Angeles, among others. Her latest book, *Nomadic Cinema: A Cultural Geography of the Expedition Film*, is forthcoming from Columbia University Press.

Tom Gunning is Professor Emeritus in the Department of Cinema and Media Studies at the University of Chicago. He is the author of *D. W. Griffith and the Origins of American Narrative Film* (1994) and *The Films of Fritz Lang: Allegories of Vision and Modernity* (2000), as well as more than 150 articles on early cinema, film history and theory, avant-garde film, film genre, and cinema and modernism. In 2009 he was awarded an Andrew A. Mellon Distinguished Achievement Award and in 2010 was elected to the American

Academy of Arts and Sciences. With André Gaudreault he originated the influential theory of the "Cinema of Attractions."

Sumiko Higashi is Professor Emerita in the Department of History at the College at Brockport, SUNY. She is the author of *Virgins, Vamps, and Flappers: The American Silent Movie Heroine* (1978), *Cecil B. DeMille and American Culture: The Silent Era* (1994), *Stars, Fans, and Consumption in the 1950s: Reading* Photoplay (2014), and essays on women in the media, film as historical representation, and film history as cultural history. She has served on the editorial boards of *Cinema Journal* and *Film History*. At the Society for Cinema Studies conference in 1992, she co-founded the Asian Pacific American Caucus in a Pittsburgh coffee shop.

Laura Horak is Associate Professor of Film Studies at Carleton University and director of the Transgender Media Lab and Transgender Media Portal. She investigates the history of transgender and queer film and media in the United States, Canada, and Sweden. She is co-curator of the ninety-nine-film Blu-ray set *Cinema's First Nasty Women* (2022), the author of *Girls Will Be Boys: Cross-Dressing Women, Lesbians, and American Cinema, 1908–1934* (2016), and co-editor of *Silent Cinema and the Politics of Space* (2014), *Unwatchable* (2019), an issue of *Somatechnics* on cinematic/trans*/bodies, and a section of the *Journal of Cinema and Media Studies* on "transing cinema and media studies."

Jennifer Horne is Associate Professor of Film and Digital Media at the University of California Santa Cruz. Her research focuses on American non-theatrical film history, specifically the history of government filmmaking and bureaucracy-based documentary film history. Her publications include chapters in *Useful Cinema* (2011), *Beyond the Screen: Institutions, Networks, and Publics of Early Cinema* (2012), and *The Documentary Film Reader* (2016), and articles in *The Moving Image* and *Historical Journal of Film, Radio, and Television*.

Charlie Keil is Professor in the Cinema Studies Institute and Department of History at the University of Toronto, where he is also Principal of Innis College and a member of the President's Teaching Academy. He has published approximately fifty journal articles and book chapters and is the author and/or editor of seven books, the most recent of which are *Editing and Special/Visual Effects*, co-edited with Kristen Whissel (2016), and *A Companion to D. W. Griffith* (2018). His teaching has been recognized with the SCMS Distinguished Pedagogy Award, as well as the Faculty of Arts & Science Outstanding Teaching Award and the President's Teaching Award at the University of Toronto.

Rob King is Professor of Film and Media Studies at Columbia University's School of the Arts. He is the author of *Hokum! The Early Sound Slapstick Short and Depression-Era Mass Culture* (2017) and the award-winning *The Fun Factory: The Keystone Film Company and the Emergence of Mass Culture* (2009). He has also edited/co-edited the volumes *Cornell Woolrich and Transmedia Noir* (2023), *Beyond the Screen: Institutions, Networks, and Publics of Early Cinema* (2012), *Slapstick Comedy* (2011), and *Early*

Cinema and the "National" (2008). King's latest monograph, *Man of Taste: The Erotic Cinema of Radley Metzger*, is forthcoming from Columbia University Press.

Donna Kornhaber is Professor of English at the University of Texas at Austin, where she teaches film. She is the author of *Charlie Chaplin, Director* (2014), *Wes Anderson: A Collector's Cinema* (2017), *Nightmares in the Dream Sanctuary: War and the Animated Film* (2019), and *Silent Film: A Very Short Introduction* (2020). In 2016 she was named an Academy Film Scholar by the Academy of Motion Picture Arts and Sciences.

Derek Long is Assistant Professor of Media and Cinema Studies at the University of Illinois Urbana–Champaign, where he teaches courses on cinema history and historiography, media production, film theory, and animation. His work has appeared in *Film History, The Moving Image, Velvet Light Trap, Historical Journal of Film, Radio, and Television*, and *[in]Transition*, among other journals. His book on the history of film distribution practice in early Hollywood is forthcoming from the University of Texas Press in 2024.

Denise McKenna is Lecturer in the Cinema Program at Palomar College. Her research explores the gender and class politics of the early American film industry's social and economic integration with Los Angeles and Hollywood's emergent studio culture. She has published work on film extras, gender, and labor stratification in Hollywood's formative years and on the class politics of editorial cartoons in film trade and fan magazines and has edited a special issue on labor for *Feminist Media Histories*. Her current research interests include feminist film historiography, the rhetoric and aesthetics of the film uplift movement in the 1910s, and the relations between cinema and the development of California's regional identity in the early twentieth century.

Philippe Marion is Professor Emeritus in Information and Communication Sciences at the School of Communication of the Catholic University of Louvain (UCL). Co-founder of l'Observatoire due récit médiatique (ORM) and the Groupe interdisciplinaire de recherches sur les cultures et les arts en mouvement (GIRCAM), he is also director of the Media Analysis Research Unit at UCL and administrator of the Collectiana Foundation. As a visiting professor at the University of Paris Sorbonne and the University of Neuchâtel, Professor Marion has been principal investigator since 2018 of the EOS (Excellence of Science) research project on The Magic Lantern and Its Cultural Impact as Visual Mass Medium (1830–1940). A specialist in media narratology and visual culture, he is the author of several books, including *Schuiten, filiation* (2009) and, with André Gaudreault, *The End of Cinema? A Medium in Crisis in the Digital Age* (2015 [2013]).

Luci Marzola is Lecturer and Program Coordinator in Cinema and Media Studies at University of Southern California's School of Cinematic Arts. She is the author of *Engineering Hollywood: Technology, Technicians, and the Science of Building the Studio System* (2021) and co-editor of the forthcoming *Hollywood Unions* (Rutgers University Press). Her research on technology, infrastructure, craft, and labor in Hollywood has been published in *Film History, Historical Journal of Film, Radio, and Television, Velvet Light Trap, American Cinematographer,* and *IndieWire.*

Ruth Mayer is Professor of American Studies at Leibniz University, Hannover, Germany. Her research focuses on modernity, seriality, temporality, and gender. Her work has appeared in the *Journal of Cinema and Media Studies, Modernism/modernity, Screen,* the *Journal of Modern Periodical Studies,* and *Velvet Light Trap.* She is the author of *Serial Fu Manchu: The Chinese Super-Villain and the Spread of Yellow Peril Ideology* (2014) and the co-edited volume *Modernity and the Periodical Press* (2022). She is currently directing a research project titled "Multiplication: Modernity, Mass Culture, Gender."

Ross Melnick is Professor of Film and Media Studies at University of California, Santa Barbara. He is the author of *Hollywood's Embassies: How Movie Theaters Projected American Power Around the World* (2022) and *American Showman: Samuel "Roxy" Rothafel and the Birth of the Entertainment Industry* (2012); co-editor of *Rediscovering U.S. Newsfilm: Cinema, Television, and the Archive* (2018); and co-author of *Cinema Treasures* (2004). His articles have appeared in journals such as *Cinema Journal, Film History, Historical Journal of Film, Radio and Television,* and *The Moving Image* and in numerous edited collections. He was named an Academy Film Scholar and an NEH Fellow for his work on global film exhibition and he is the co-founder of the exhibition history website Cinema Treasures (https://www.cinematreasures.org).

Daisuke Miyao is Professor and Hajime Mori Chair in Japanese Language and Literature at the University of California, San Diego. He is the author of *Japonisme and the Birth of Cinema* (2020), *Cinema Is a Cat: A Cat Lover's Introduction to Film Studies* (2019), *The Aesthetics of Shadow: Lighting and Japanese Cinema* (2013), and *Sessue Hayakawa: Silent Cinema and Transnational Stardom* (2007). Miyao is also the editor of the *Oxford Handbook of Japanese Cinema* (2014) and co-editor of *Transnational Cinematography Studies* (2017), with Lindsay Coleman and Roberto Schaefer.

Paul S. Moore is Professor of Communication and Culture at Toronto Metropolitan University. His writing on early cinema in North America focuses on the relation between audiences and newspaper publicity, appearing in *Film History, Canadian Journal of Film Studies,* and the book *Mapping Movie Magazines: Digitization, Periodicals and Cinema History* (2020). With Sandra Gabriele, his book *The Sunday Paper: A Media History* (2022) recounts the weekend supplement's intermedial relations to magazines, cinema, and radio.

Tom Paulus is Professor of Theatre and Film Studies at the University of Antwerp. He is co-founder of the Visual Poetics Research Group. With Rob King he edited the collection *Slapstick Comedy* (2010) for Routledge/AFI Film Readers. His work has appeared in numerous edited volumes, including *Jewish Aspects in Avant-Garde* (2017), *Ozu International* (2015), and *The Philosophy of Michael Mann* (2014).

Jennifer Lynn Peterson is Professor and Chair of the Media Studies program at Woodbury University in Los Angeles. She is the author of *Education in the School of*

Dreams: Travelogues and Early Nonfiction Film (2013). Her work has been published in journals such as *Representations, Journal of Cinema and Media Studies, Feminist Media Histories, Moving Image,* and *Camera Obscura*. She has published chapters in numerous edited volumes, including *Ends of Cinema* (2020), *Hollywood on Location: An Industry History* (2019), *New Silent Cinema* (2015), and *Learning with the Lights Off: Educational Film in the United States* (2012). She is presently completing a book on US film history and the environment in the 1920s–1940s.

Miriam Siegel is a PhD candidate in the Cinema Studies Institute at the University of Toronto. Her research focuses on the relationship between storytelling, style, and genre in American popular cinema. Her essay on Guy Maddin's *My Winnipeg* was published in *Canadian Cinema in the New Millenium* (2022).

Shelley Stamp is Professor of Film and Digital Media at the University of California, Santa Cruz, where she has twice won the Excellence in Teaching Award. She is author of the award-winning books *Lois Weber in Early Hollywood* (2015) and *Movie-Struck Girls: Women and Motion Picture Culture after the Nickelodeon* (2000); curator of the award-winning disc set *Pioneers: First Women Filmmakers* (2018); and founding editor of the journal *Feminist Media Histories*. She is at work on a comprehensive history, *Women and the Silent Screen in America*, co-authored with Anne Morey.

Breixo Viejo is an Assistant Professor of Film Studies at Hofstra University, New York. He previously held teaching and research positions at Barnard College, Columbia University, and University College London. He has co-edited with Jo Evans *Luis Buñuel: A Life in Letters* (2019) and is the author of the books *Film Books: A Visual History* (2016) and *Música moderna para un nuevo cine: Eisler, Adorno y el Film Music Project* (2008).

Johannes von Moltke is Professor of Film, Television, and Media and of German Studies at the University of Michigan. His work on film, media, and critical theory has appeared in the journals *New German Critique, Screen, October, Cultural Critique,* and *Cinema Journal*, among others. He is the author of *No Place Like Home: Locations of* Heimat *in German Cinema* (2006) and *The Curious Humanist: Siegfried Kracauer in America* (2016). He has co-edited several books on Kracauer: *Siegfried Kracauers Grenzgänge: Zur Rettung des Realen* (2019), *Culture in the Anteroom: The Legacies of Siegfried Kracauer* (2012), and *Siegfried Kracauer's American Writings: Essays on Film and Popular Culture* (2012). Von Moltke is a past president of the German Studies Association and Vice President of the American Friends of Marbach.

Gregory A. Waller is Provost Professor of Cinema and Media Studies in the Media School at Indiana University. He is the editor of *Film History: An International Journal*. His recent publications have focused on the institutionalization of education film, the discourse concerning moving pictures in popular magazines and specialized periodicals, and the use of film in the service of advertising and public relations. His books include *Beyond the Movie Theater: Sites, Sponsors, Uses, Audiences* (2023).

Tami Williams is Associate Professor of English and Film Studies at the University of Wisconsin–Milwaukee, and President of Domitor, the International Society for the Study of Early Cinema. She is the author, editor, and/or co-editor of several books, most recently, *Provenance and Early Cinema* (2020), *Germaine Dulac: What Is Cinema?* (2019, 2020 CNC Prix du livre), *Global Cinema Networks* (2018), *Performing New Media, 1895–1915* (2014), and *Germaine Dulac: A Cinema of Sensations* (2014), as well as a special issue of *The Moving Image* on "Early Cinema and the Archives" (2016). She also serves as a board member of Women Film History International.

CHAPTER 1

INTRODUCTION
The History of the History of Silent Film

ROB KING AND CHARLIE KEIL

REVISIONIST scholarly interest in silent cinema has now lasted longer than the silent era itself. This introduction to *The Oxford Handbook of Silent Cinema* explores the various stages and development of that scholarship the better to see how silent film research positions itself today. Some forty-plus years after the revisionist turn, what has the history of the history of silent cinema been?

***

For a field of inquiry so suspicious of origin myths, it is no small irony that silent film history has one of its own. The legendary thirty-fourth congress of the International Federation of Film Archives (FIAF), held in Brighton, England, in May 1978, is the oft-cited ground zero for what came to be called the "New Film History," which initially focused on the medium's very earliest years. At Brighton, participants systematically viewed nearly two hundred films produced prior to 1906, in the process renouncing long-ingrained assumptions of cinema's first decade as a supposedly "primitive" stage awaiting the maturity subsequently bestowed by the innovations of D. W. Griffith and the development of the feature film. On this telling, Brighton stood as a turning point that sparked repudiation of an older tradition of "informed connoisseurship" (in the words of Brighton participant Jan-Christopher Horak): the next generation of film historians would take their cue from archival holdings, using paper documents and preserved prints as the basis for their claims.[1]

But the question immediately arises: What was the "old" film history against which the "new" defined itself? What was this stupefying tradition, the dead weight of which was finally being sloughed off? Was it Terry Ramsaye's *A Million and One Nights* (1926)? Benjamin Hampton's *A History of the Movies* (1931)? Maybe Georges Sadoul's multi-volume *Histoire générale du cinéma* (1946–1950)? But these are survey histories that, by the time of Brighton, were in the earliest cases already more than fifty years old and could hardly have constituted a meaningful tradition or opponent to be vanquished.

One is tempted to propose that the old film history never really existed, as least not as a meaningful disciplinary formation; that is, that within the academy there has never been anything *but* the New Film History. Nor, moreover, should we presume that the battle cry of "revisionism" was first shouted from the seats of the Brighton Theatre during the springtime of '78. Even if we look only to the pioneering figures of that moment—archivists Eileen Bowser (Museum of Modern Art), David Francis (British Film Institute), and Paul Spehr (Library of Congress), and historians André Gaudreault, Tom Gunning, and Charlie Musser—we find that Gaudreault was already independently in contact with Bowser and Musser the previous year, just starting his research on Edwin S. Porter's *Life of an American Fireman* (1903). We also need to extend our horizon to consider other important conferences that pre-date the events in Brighton: the thirtieth FIAF congress of 1974, titled "Film Archives and Audiovisual Techniques/The Methodology of Film History"; the thirty-first Edinburgh International Film Festival of 1977, which included a colloquium on "History/Production/Memory"; and the Second Annual Purdue Film Conference in 1977 at Purdue University—all of which featured scholarly presentations expressing discontent with traditional models of film historical writing.[2]

But if all this is the case, we will need to look for the Brighton "break" elsewhere, less, perhaps, as a break within an academic tradition of *film history* specifically than as a collective sense of fresh scholarly vistas within the then still-nascent trajectory of academic *film studies* in general. Here, the evidence is somewhat clearer, as Tom Gunning would himself recall a decade after the fact, speaking of Brighton at the 1989 FIAF Congress in Lisbon. "The main direction in American film study during that period had been towards theory, and away from history," Gunning remembered. "I thought theory was important, but films were more important. So to be able to look at films, using theory, but reaffirming the importance of the films themselves was very, very important to me. Brighton gave me that opportunity."[3] We would do well to remember, for example, that Gunning's "Cinema of Attraction" essay—one of the New Film History's founding documents—was, from the outset, a critique of some of the assumptions underwriting theory's dominance within film studies of the 1970s. "What precisely is the cinema of attraction?" Gunning asked there. "First, it is a cinema that bases itself on [. . .] its ability to *show* something. Contrasted to the voyeuristic aspect of narrative cinema analyzed by Christian Metz, this is an exhibitionist cinema."[4] Theoretical claims about spectatorship informed by psychoanalysis now found themselves vying with new models derived from historical study. Viewed thus, the New Film History was a first turn away from the perceived overreach of Marxist, psychoanalytic, and structuralist models that defined what has since come to be called the "apparatus theory" of post-1968 film studies.

One can push too hard on this point, as though the break in question was simply driven by the will to wriggle free from the "dogma" of theory and into the liberating pastures of empiricism. Not that such accusations haven't been leveled: in 2001, no less a figure than Slavoj Žižek traced what he perceived as the political failure of present-day film studies through the career of Ben Brewster, once a hardline Althusserian, subsequently a "pure" film historian working on cinema before 1917, or, as Žižek put it, "significantly, prior to the October Revolution."[5] A similar note was sounded by Patrice Petro, who, in 2002, read the "revisionist" turn in film history symptomatically as a retreat from the polemical analysis of 1970s feminist theory.[6] Such characterizations presume ungenerously that empiricism equates with political retreat—as though, for example, the formidable research into the class and ethnic background of nickelodeon audiences in these years did not touch on fundamental questions of the politics of mass culture.[7] But these critiques also miss how the energies flowing out of Brighton ultimately resulted less in a retreat from theory than in a new way of thinking about history and theory in tandem. Nowhere was this more evident than in a subsequent body of scholarship, first coalescing in the early 1990s, that began to theorize cinema's development in its first decades via the historical optic of *modernity*.

***

An admission: both of the editors of the current volume have, over the years, challenged various particulars of what its critics have labeled the "modernity thesis"—the position that seeks to comprehend cinema's development against the social, cultural, and sensory context of late-nineteenth/early-twentieth-century modernity.[8] But we both also acknowledge the extraordinary reach of the modernity thesis as a catalyst for theoretical and historiographic insight. Scholarly engagement with modernity has constituted one of the few "schools" of thought within film studies—in this case, the "Chicago School," that extraordinary cadre of silent film scholars, headed by Tom Gunning and Miriam Hansen, that came together at the University of Chicago in the 1990s.[9] It switched out 1970s-era film theory's stringent investment in avant-garde "counter-cinema" for a renewed sensitivity to the utopian dimensions of the popular arts. It also represents, to date, the most productive path for thinking beyond the false binary of theoretical obtuseness and apolitical historicism so often mobilized in reductive accounts of film studies' post-Brighton development. As Ben Singer memorably put it in his spirited defense of the approach, in *Melodrama and Modernity* (2001): "The appeal of this concept [i.e., the modernity thesis] derives partly from the hope that, after the exhaustion of *Screen*-style film theory and the pendulum's swing to hard-nosed empirical film history, it seems to offer the possibility of a commodious middleground of theoretically informed history and/or historically informed theory."[10]

How might we characterize this approach? Its basic premise is on first sight a modest and, as Singer notes, appealing one; namely, that we can explain the distinctive formal and spectatorial properties of early cinema in relation to the sensory environment of turn-of-the-century metropolitan experience. As Gunning argued in 1989:

> Attractions trace out the visual topology of modernity: a visual environment which is fragmented and atomized; a gaze which, rather than resting on a landscape in contemplation, seems to be pushed and pulled in conflicting orientations, hurried and

intensified, and therefore less coherent and anchored. [. . .] *The attraction in film consists of a specific relation between viewer and film that reveals aspects of the experience of modernity.*[11]

This is an elegant and potent formulation, whose richness was such that even its detractors seemed only to strengthen modernity's hold on the field. One critique, for instance, concerned the issue of film's stylistic development during the early period. Even if we allow that the cinema of attractions takes its shape from the culture of modernity, the argument went, how then to explain the brute fact of stylistic change in the years that followed, when cinema moved away from an attractions-based aesthetic toward greater narrative integration? Did modernity's influence somehow cease following the attraction era? Did modernity itself come to an end?

The only sensible answer to the last question is: *of course not*. But that answer had the effect of unlocking the silent era more broadly to the explanatory force of modernity, so that a hypothesis first formed in relation to the cinema of attractions quickly began to bleed beyond its initial temporal framework. Modernity's salience as the *explicans* of early film was now extended forward into the 1910s and 1920s, with modernity construed in diverse ways that vastly exceeded its founding *explicandum*. One could now read D. W. Griffith's Biograph films (1908–1912) in relation to the "systematic nature of the modern world"; define movie stars of the postwar years as "idols of modernity" whose star images negotiated a "distinctly modern" array of changes in American life; and even approach color film of the 1920s in the light of a "chromatic modernity" that characterized a "pivotal period of cosmopolitan exchange."[12] Perhaps most impactful of all was a pair of essays by Miriam Hansen, "The Mass Production of the Senses" and "Fallen Women, Rising Stars, New Horizons," published in 1999 and 2000 respectively. These works expanded the application of modernity even further: first, to encompass classical Hollywood cinema, which Hansen described as a "vernacular modernism" that engaged "the impact of modern technology on human experience"; second, to include film cultures outside of the West (specifically, the Shanghai cinema of the 1920s and 1930s, the subject of the "Fallen Women" essay).[13]

But what, ultimately, was this "modernity" at whose door so much of silent film culture was suddenly laid? No doubt there were risks in thematizing history this way. As Fredric Jameson cautioned long ago, "History can be apprehended only through its effects, and never as some reified force."[14] The approach's proponents needed a methodological framework that would avoid positing modernity as such a "force," as though the varied dimensions of silent film culture were somehow "caused," billiard-ball fashion, by the demands of modern life; at the same time the approach had to retain some framework for ascertaining modernity's "effects." This was found in the concept of "experience" (*Erfahrung*) as elaborated in a tradition of twentieth-century thought that had been almost completely neglected by 1970s-style apparatus theory; namely, the intellectual tradition of the Frankfurt School, associated with writers such as Ernst Bloch, Walter Benjamin, Siegfried Kracauer, and Theodor Adorno. Benjamin's pointed suggestion from his celebrated "Work of Art" essay (1935–1939) became the watchword for this newly phenomenological bent in film historiography: "The mode of human sense perception changes with humanity's entire mode of existence."[15]

A host of conceptual terms were mined from this neglected theoretical seam: the "optical unconscious," the "mimetic faculty," "innervation," and many others—all capturing the perceptual and aesthetic forms that defined film's import in mediating human subjectivity's relation to the modern world. Innervation, for example, was the neurophysiological term Benjamin had used to describe how the human sensorium assimilates the experience of modern technology. The mimetic faculty (Benjamin) and mimesis (Adorno) meanwhile referred to practices of embodied mimicry through which such innervation occurs.[16] But how far do these considerations really take us beyond the framework of the apparatus theory that early film historians first sought to challenge? True, the emphases of the two theories are in a sense diametrically opposed: apparatus theory sought, in the words of Christian Metz, to "disengage the cinema-object from the imaginary and win it for the symbolic," to leverage an understanding of cinema away from our common-or-garden experience of it toward a "knowledge" of its ideological functioning, while modernity theories reverse this to restore analysis to the level of the senses (the imaginary).[17] Yet both approach cinema as a means of constituting the filmgoer as a subject, whether that subject be understood as the *ideological* subject of state apparatuses (as per apparatus theory) or the *modern* or *sensory* subject of cinema's experiential calisthenics (as per the modernity thesis). It was as though the wheels of scholarly revisionism had turned full circle: the New Film History that broke with the theory-driven scholarship of the 1970s had fueled a new theoretical paradigm that, on a number of points, resembled the very positions that the historical turn had meant to leave behind.

***

The completion of that circle has a geographical location, too, this time on the Pacific Coast, where the First International Berkeley Conference on Silent Cinema occurred in February 2011—shortly after the untimely passing of Miriam Hansen and shortly before the posthumous publication of her magisterial *Cinema and Experience: Siegfried Kracauer, Walter Benjamin, and Theodor W. Adorno* (2011). This sad circumstance ensured that the event, dedicated to Hansen's memory, inevitably acquired a retrospective edge as something of an unplanned tribute, even as the conference's official theme ("Cinema across Media: The 1920s") enacted a different orientation. For what the preplanned panels primarily displayed was less a focus on the sensory context of modernity than a new concern with the materiality of media forms themselves. Presentations provided an understanding of "Media" that included a range of technologies (photography, the phonograph, radio, etc.), the physical materials for artistic expression (celluloid film, print, bodies in motion), and the larger media ecologies in which films were produced and circulated.

To be clear, we are not talking about incompatible research fields sharing the same conference: the Frankfurt School writings on cinema that Hansen's work explored had always primarily been a theory of *media* in mass culture, rather than a theory of film per se. Nor do we mean to imply that the "Cinema across Media" rubric was in any way new in 2012, since the concept of *intermediality* had been on the critical scene since the 1990s. Despite all of that, the Berkeley conference looms large, if only because of how explicitly, if unwittingly, it traced a shift from silent cinema as (and in relation to) *experience* to silent cinema as (and in relation to) *media*. That shift occasions some of the more recent lines of innovation within the field of film historiography represented in the present volume. As a roadmap for the essays included here, we categorize these new directions as follows:

Media Archaeology: The first—and, as we will see, most paradoxical—of recent developments concerns the impact of *media archaeology* on the historiography of silent film. An object-centered style of history focused on technological assemblages and their cultural effects, media archaeology can trace its origins to the archaeological method of Michel Foucault and the media writings of Friedrich Kittler—the former for his interest in the discursive construction of knowledge, the latter for his hardware materialism. Accordingly, what we are talking about is a Foucauldian approach where the role of *discourse* in the constitution of knowledge and culture gets supplanted by that of the *materials* and *materiality* of media technologies. As an idiosyncratic practice of cultural history, it stresses the "media-epistemological differences" that technology creates, or the "difference that media make in cultural construction," to quote theorist Wolfgang Ernst.[18] The media archaeologist focuses not on discursive or representational elements in dealing with the past (not on the symbolic order, in Lacanese), but rather on material ontologies (that is, the real)—on, for instance, photography as a matter of engraving light beams onto a chemically sensitive surface, or on relations between recording and transmission as distinct media operations.

Why describe this media archaeological turn as a paradoxical move for silent film history? Because, as the late Thomas Elsaesser noted, the New Film History that emerged post-Brighton might *already* be considered a form of media archaeology *avant la lettre*.[19] Many of the historiographic principles advocated by the most visible of today's media archaeologists—scholars like Erkki Huhtamo, Jussi Parikka, and Siegfried Zielinski—were already there, in incipient, less self-conscious form, in the scholarship that emerged in Brighton's wake. The revisionist impetus to rethink the technological conditions of cinema's emergence, the project of situating cinema within broader media formations, the resistance to teleological film histories that had designated cinema's earliest years as "primitive": all of this is a harbinger of media archaeology's call for a mode of registering the past that would neutralize traditional historical narratives the better to allow the objective operations of technological media to appear.

Yet media archaeology's subsequent development into a recognized—if still-contested—research field has created a situation in which silent film historiography now stands to be renewed by the very methods it helped spawn, like an aging parent tended by its offspring. What does it mean, exactly, when media archaeology "comes home" like this? Perhaps the most significant consequence is a greater sensitivity to the interactions—either converging or differentiating—between old *and* new media across film and moving-image history. As Elsaesser argued, the successive phases of cinema's technological development, as well as cinema's relation to subsequent visual media, like television, video art, and digital imaging, can now be "mapped on the matrix of particular processes of 'ontologization'" over a broader span of media history.[20] Freed from the temptation of narrative continuity and teleology, the medium's history *qua* technology can now more readily fashion itself as a matter of nonlinear developments, breaks, recursions, and dead ends, which form the focus of Part I ("Origins: From Invention to Medium") of this volume.

Tom Gunning's essay begins the collection by raising a key question about the relation between technology and medium ontology: should we understand the "invention" of cinema as a series of specific technological developments or in terms of the broader apparatus that constitutes cinema (that is, as a system for the production and display of moving images whose technological foundations are nonetheless fluid and ever-changing)? A focus on this relation can even undermine the differences between media whose historical trajectories we customarily define as discrete: Doron Galili's chapter shows how ontological distinctions between moving-image *storage* (an affordance of cinema) and moving-image *transmission* (an affordance of television) cannot be sustained within the complex ecology of the late nineteenth-century mediascape in which both television and film share their roots. The issue of storage in turn leads to what Jane Gaines calls "copy technologies" and the legal consequences that photographic media raised for issues of ownership and copyright—explored in this volume first by Stefan Andriopoulos in relation to the German legal doctrine of the "right to one's own image," then by Gaines as recursive problems in media history extending into our digital present.

Intermediality: Media archaeology encourages approaches to silent cinema that look backward and forward across media technologies. But we can also look sideways, studying film as an emerging medium in terms of its surrounding media ecologies. According to André Gaudreault and Philippe Marion's principle that "it is through intermediality [. . .] that a medium is understood," scholarship on silent cinema today understands its object less as a "seventh art" with its own autonomous lines of development than as part of various mediascapes that include all manner of entertainment venues as well as non-entertainment purposes for the cinematograph.[21]

At the risk of an overly reductive schematism, we see two methodological options informing the assessment of cinema's significance vis-à-vis these constellations. On the one hand is an approach that would examine cinema's place within the sphere of art and entertainment, broadly construed. This forms the focus of Part II of the collection, "Intermediality: Genre and Aesthetics in Silent Film," which addresses the intermedial constitution of cinema as an aesthetic/cultural practice. One of the key themes that emerges in this section concerns the shifting relations of dependency and autonomy informing cinema's recognition as a medium of cultural expression. For some of the contributors, cinema was initially an instrument for extending pre-existing cultural practices—a container of sorts, into which were poured the representational practices and aesthetic norms of other "cultural series," to borrow Gaudreault and Marion's formulation. Such a perspective would consider a work like Georges Méliès's *Le Royaume des fées* (1903) as an extension of the conventions of the fairy play into film, which Gaudreault and Marion argue. But it applies equally to the supposed first Japanese film, *Maple Viewing* (1899), which Daisuke Miyao understands less as a film in its own right than as a record of a Kabuki performance, or to traditions of racial performativity from the stage, which Allyson Nadia Field shows opened a pathway for Black filmmaking in the silent era.

Other contributors, meanwhile, address the conceptual implications of early cinema's changing place within broader media contexts. Weihong Bao, for instance, looks to turn-of-the-century Chinese art and entertainment to rethink media history in terms of Heideggerian ontology: the question of what a medium *is* here becomes less a matter of that medium's fixed attributes and properties than of its place within the structuring positions that define a given media ecology. Rob King, meanwhile, theorizes the emergence of the first film genres (in his case, the chase film) in terms of the mutations that cinematic technology introduced into pre-existing entertainment practice. Three concluding essays in this section together suggest how, even in the halting passage toward classicism (the topic of Miriam Siegel's essay), filmmakers continued to innovate approaches to staging and composition inspired by aesthetic trends in the other arts (as discussed in the US and French contexts by Tom Paulus and Tami Williams, respectively).

On the other hand, an intermedial methodology also invites consideration of what historians term "nontheatrical" film (i.e., films made for purposes other than commercial theatrical release), which the volume's third section, "Pedagogical Formations: Non-Theatrical Cinema and the Uses of Film" addresses. Just as cinema was a new medium for the representational forms of, say, theater and the like, so also did it promise to remediate the representational practices and agenda of scientific, charitable, governmental, and/or educational institutions. Here, the issue of cinema's broader role and function within the public sphere comes into view: what, in the years before Hollywood's global hegemony, was cinema to be? In its infamous 1915 decision on *Mutual Film Corporation v. Industrial Commission of Ohio*, the US Supreme Court provided its answer to this question, ruling that the "exhibition of moving pictures" was to be considered a "business, pure and simple," "not to be regarded [. . .] as part of the press of the country, or as organs of public opinion."[22] The high court here drew a critical line in the sand, serving at once to legalize the states' rights to prior restraint and to delimit mainstream cinema's public role to that of culturally affirmative entertainment. In a meaningful sense, a federal mandate thus underwrote the transition to classical Hollywood cinema.[23] Greg Waller's contribution to the section examines this trajectory through the particular lens of the American periodical *Popular Science Monthly*, noting how the journal's initial investment in scientific applications of the new medium (in time-lapse records of solar activity, for example) gradually yielded to "behind-the-scenes" articles on camera techniques and special effects within the commercial film industry.

Given that the *Mutual* ruling was a judicial issue of interstate commerce, it applied solely to the commercial film industry and, of course, had no bearing in other countries where, as Scott Curtis and Oliver Gaycken's essay shows, a thriving culture of scientific filmmaking was often tightly woven into the idea and experience of cinema. Even in the US, meanwhile, continued investment in instructional film saw the development of institutionally specific genres, such as the museum-sponsored "expedition film" that Alison Griffiths discusses through the example of the American Museum of Natural History. A final pair of essays in this section explores the points of contact between pedagogical and commercial imperatives, through a shared focus on filmmakers and organizations that sought to educate a primarily female audience. Shelley Stamp discusses a number of birth control films that received commercial exhibition in the mid-1910s—most famously, Lois Weber's 1916 *Where Are My Children?*—to show how that audience often challenged and repudiated the films' typically regressive moral stances on premarital sex and abortion. Jennifer Horne's contribution, meanwhile, details the efforts of the Department of Labor's Children's Bureau to find its place within the media context of instructional film of the 1910s and the Bureau's attempts to navigate the kind of message interference that resulted from commercial collaborations.

Political Economy: One of the most significant developments in recent film history has been a turn to the political economy of film and media industries during the silent period. Writing from a present marked by unprecedented consolidation among telecommunications and media industries, a growing cohort of scholars—Lee Grieveson, Haidee Wasson, and Giorgio Bertellini prominent among them—demonstrates the need to trace the roots of this dominant form of political economy, and the role of the media within it, back to developments under way in America after World War I. The final decade of the silent era, it has become clear, marks a period in which the *film* industry began to morph into an interconnected *media* industry, with many studios investing in or owning broadcast networks, music publishing and recording divisions, and radio stations and/or programs. As Grieveson has suggested, "a corporate media industry was [being] established, and then synchronized with finance capital and other large technology and telecommunications companies, as part of a corporate-dominated consumer economy."[24]

With this understanding, however, has come a mandate for a film history that would clarify cinema's role in the orchestration of media empires and the intersecting axes of labor, public relations, and corporate financing that sustained them. This politically engaged history shares a longheld interest in the social significance of "Hollywood" as an ascendant hub for American filmmaking by the mid-1910s. But whereas earlier histories of American cinema—exemplified by the work of Lary May and Robert Sklar, among others—understood "Hollywood" as foundational to a new cultural imaginary, more recent approaches adopt a perspective akin to social theorist Bruno Latour's "Actor-Network-Theory." Accordingly, attention now falls on the particular processes of association and reassembling among the various agents and agencies that built out the material infrastructure of America's cinematic mass culture, as explored in Part IV of the volume, "Hollywood, Inc.: The Institutions of Mass Culture."[25] The first three essays in this section examine how the idea of "Hollywood" was crafted out of a series of institutional alliances on the West Coast involving protective organizations and studio management (as discussed by Charlie Keil and Denise McKenna), real-estate speculation and development (Ross Melnick), and a growing technological service sector (Luci Marzola). Two further essays shift the focus to the East Coast, where the studios' New York head offices explored various strategies for integrating regional exhibition circuits into a nationwide "mass" market, whether in early experiments with a "franchise" distribution model (Derek Long) or by coordinating distribution with national advertising campaigns (Paul Moore).

Global Networks: The first wave of revisionist film historians strove to differentiate the field of "early cinema" from the broader sphere of silent cinema in general. As Giorgio Bertellini shows in this volume, that demarcation was initially linked to the activities and discourses of Domitor, the International Society for the Study of Early Cinema (established in 1985), which set a loose cut-off date of around 1914 to establish the outer limits of its research agenda. This periodization was *prima facie* justifiable in terms of a range of variables—for instance, as the beginning of the Great War, whose influence on the world's film industries would be enormous, or as a tipping point in the ascendancy of the feature film and cinema's mass cultural dominance. It also served as a catalyst for a number of periodizing concepts that in turn informed new research agendas—for instance, Gunning's famous distinction between the "cinema of attractions" and a "cinema of narrative integration" or Gaudreault's contrast between the period of "kin-attractography" and that of "institutional cinema," with Gaudreault seeing the rough period of 1908–1914 as a thick border between the two.[26] That "thick border" in turn became a subject of increasing investigation in the 2000s, which saw the popularization of the term "transitional era" as a new hermeneutic for historical research.[27] How do we conceptualize the shifts that took place during these years? In terms of the development of storytelling norms and filmic continuity (as implied by Gunning's framework)? In terms of the consolidation of cinema's institutional frameworks (as foregrounded in Gaudreault's)? And how does our choice of framework affect logics of periodization?

Such debates tend to neglect how their frames of reference exclude those cinemas—primarily non-Western—whose developments don't easily fit established periodizations in the first place. What scope could an institution like Domitor give to the study of a cinema such as Iran's, for example, given that the first silent feature in Iran was not produced until 1930 (*Abi and Rabi*, directed by a Russian Armenian émigré, Ovanes Ohanian)? By restricting its initial purview to the pre-1914 period, the New Film History had the effect of reducing great swaths of non-Western film cultures into simply so many sites for the distribution and exhibition of Western-produced films. The resulting lesson is clear: as the map of silent film scholarship becomes more complex, so also must its chronology.

Part V of the volume, "Nation, Empire, World: The Spaces and Times of Modernity" demonstrates this point in a series of essays attuned to what Kaveh Askari, in his contribution, describes as the "powers of asynchrony" unleashed in cinema's uneven global circulation throughout the silent era, as well as to the presence of local modernities that negotiated American cinema's global ubiquity. These essays do not necessarily dispute Fredric Jameson's insistence on reading modernity as a "singular" phenomenon—that is, as a code word for capitalism and its consequences—but they do dispute that we can productively understand this singular phenomenon in singular terms.[28] Accordingly, Giorgio Bertellini, in his essay, posits a distinction between what philosopher Charles Taylor identified as "cultural" versus "acultural" conceptions of modernity to expose the geopolitical blind spots that plague the dominant periodizations of film history. Lee Grieveson's chapter locates the early history of documentary within competing paradigms of territorial versus economic imperialism in the early twentieth century. And Jennifer Peterson's and Anne Bachmann's essays explore the ways in which an arguably *anti*-modern investment in filmic representations of "untamed" wilderness served projects of nation-building that were informed, respectively, by America's settler colonialist past and intra-Scandinavian cultural politics. In the process, all these contributions demonstrate how cultural histories of modernity need to proceed from an awareness of the *plurality* of capitalist formations (imperial, extractive, protectionist, settler, etc.) shaping the geopolitical imaginaries of modernity. A final essay by Ruth Mayer complements this emphasis by exploring the plurality of *temporal* frameworks that informed modernity, as activated in the spectacular incoherence of the motion-picture serial.

Publics: According to social theorist Michael Warner, a public is the "social space created by the reflexive circulation of discourse."[29] A public, per this model, does not simply signify a relation among people but a relation among people *as constituted by the continual circulation of texts over time*. Any material understanding of the filmgoing public, from this perspective, needs to proceed not *deductively* from abstractions like the "mass public" but from an *inductive* examination of the textual relays that addressed people as filmgoers, which is the topic of the volume's final group of essays: "Cinematic Publics: Critics, Fans, Communities." Johannes von Moltke's contribution begins the section with a focus on the silent-era writer who was among the first to theorize the "masses" as a term of cinematic culture: Siegfried Kracauer, whose conception of the mass audience, von Moltke shows, emerged from his hundreds of film reviews for the *Frankfurter Zeitung* before it became a term of his media theory. What further made Kracauer unique, within this context, was his resistance to any condescension that would charge the masses with the putative polluting of "true" art or culture. Bucking an entire tradition of social theory that, beginning with Gabriel Tarde's 1890 *Les lois de l'imitation* and Gustave Le Bon's 1895 *Psychologie des foules*, denigrated the masses for their irrationality and suggestibility, the German critic saw them as the true subjects of a medium that, he believed, could counter their alienation by making it visible to them.

Few were so sanguine at the time. Efforts to gentrify the medium as a handmaiden for "refined" social and aesthetic values never abated during the silent era—albeit with unpredictable consequences, as the following two essays make clear. Sumiko Higashi uses the case study of US film magazines to show how those efforts may have paradoxically smoothed the passage to a modern celebrity culture. Laura Horak, meanwhile, demonstrates how "sophistication" in film entertainment was often braided with queer themes and representations that provoked censorship. In the process, moreover, Horak invites us to think of cinema's publics not simply in terms of the class anxieties that the "masses" invoked but in relation to issues of sexuality and the cultural visibility of alternate sexual identities. Wrapping up this section of the volume, Breixo Viejo's contribution further redefines the notion of publics away from the sphere of reception (film-going publics) toward that of production (publics of artists), to look at the networks of social relations fostering avant-garde filmmaker Luis Buñuel's aesthetic practice.

***

The volume closes with an epilogue by Donna Kornhaber that explores the history of silent film *after* the advent of sound at the end of the 1920s: how have the aesthetic tendencies of silent cinema remained a resource for filmmakers up to the present day? Yet, without wishing to preempt that epilogue, we would like to end this introduction by suggesting a somewhat different way silent film history might have implications for the present: namely, that it has come to serve as a whetstone for new historiographic approaches that now look both backward and forward, to find in cinema's silent past not a "foreign country" but a terrain for reassessing film's origins as part of the broader mediascape in which we find ourselves today.

All of the essays collected here, to one degree or another, are animated by the impulse to subsume silent film history, narrowly conceived, into a media history that does Benjamin one better by announcing the convergence of aesthetics, capital, technology, and politics into various species of media-technological configurations (of culture, of governmentality, of transnational exchange, of gendered labor, etc.). Without wishing to imply that these recent trajectories constitute anything as cogent or self-conscious as a "school," we feel that they share a commitment to what we would call—with due homage to MIT's program of the same name—a *comparative media* approach. Comparative media, as the name implies, suggests a perspective attuned to relations among media forms, technologies, and institutions as frameworks for manifold strategies of historical analysis. The pertinence of this approach is hardly limited to the silent era but serves rather as a generalizable hermeneutic for rethinking media history in terms of processes of technological change and media convergence rendered familiar to us by the present. And perhaps this might stand as one way that today's scholarly work on silent cinema fulfills its promise as a source of intellectual renewal—through the achievement of a set of methods that ultimately no longer needs silent cinema as its historic reference point.

Notes

1. Jan-Christopher Horak, "FIAF Brighton 1978," *Archival Spaces: Memory, Images, History*, June 8, 2018, https://www.cinema.ucla.edu/blogs/archival-spaces/2018/06/08/fiaf-brighton-1978 (accessed November 20, 2018).
2. Philippe Gauthier, "The Brighton Congress and Traditional Film History as Founding Myths of the New Film History" (paper presented at the Society for Cinema and Media Studies Conference, Boston, March 2012), 2.
3. Alain Lacasse, "FIAF Conference, Lisbon, 1989: The Brighton FIAF Conference (1978): Ten Years After," *Historical Journal of Film, Radio and Television* 11, no. 3 (October 1991): 279–292.

4. Tom Gunning, "The Cinema of Attraction(s): Early Film, Its Spectator and the Avant-Garde" (1986), reprinted in Wanda Strauven, ed., *The Cinema of Attractions Reloaded* (Amsterdam: Amsterdam University Press, 2006), 382.
5. Slavoj Žižek, *The Fright of Real Tears: Krzyztof Kieslowski between Theory and Post-Theory* (London: BFI Publishing, 2001), 13.
6. Patrice Petro, *Aftershocks of the New: Feminism and Film History* (New Brunswick, NJ: Rutgers University Press, 2002), 169–173.
7. See, for instance, Robert C. Allen, "Motion Picture Exhibition in Manhattan, 1906–1912: Beyond the Nickelodeon," *Cinema Journal* 18, no. 2 (Spring 1979): 2–15; Russell Merritt, "Nickelodeon Theatres, 1905–1914: Building an Audience for the Movies," in Tino Balio, ed., *The American Film Industry* (Madison: University of Wisconsin Press, 1976), 59–82; and Ben Singer, "Manhattan's Nickelodeons: New Data on Audiences and Exhibitors," *Cinema Journal* 34, no. 3 (1995): 5–35.
8. See, for instance, Charlie Keil, "'To Here from Modernity': Style, Historiography, and Transitional Cinema," in Keil and Shelley Stamp, eds., *American Cinema's Transitional Era: Audiences, Institutions, Practices* (Berkeley: University of California Press, 2004), 51–65; Rob King, "'Uproarious Inventions': The Keystone Film Company, Modernity, and the Art of the Motor," *Film History* 19, no. 3 (2007): 271–291.
9. It was not only at Chicago that this line of thought coalesced (other non-Chicago affiliates played crucial roles, such as Giuliana Bruno, Anne Friedberg, Lynne Kirby, Lauren Rabinovitz, Mark Sandberg, and others), but it was only at Chicago that it became a bedrock of departmental identity. There is nonetheless a risk in conflating a department's academic and pedagogical objectives with (questionable) labels attached to the scholarly output of key figures associated with that department: the so-called Madison School is a case in point.
10. Ben Singer, *Melodrama and Modernity: Early Sensational Cinema and Its Contexts* (New York: Columbia University Press, 2001), 99.
11. Tom Gunning, "The Whole Town's Gawking: Early Cinema and the Visual Experience of Modernity," *Yale Journal of Criticism* 7, no. 2 (Fall 1994): 194, 196 (emphasis added).
12. Tom Gunning, "Systematizing the Electric Message: Narrative Form, Gender, and Modernity in *The Lonedale Operator*," in Keil and Stamp, eds., *American Cinema's Transitional Era*, 27; Patrice Petro, "Introduction: Stardom in the 1920s," in Petro, ed., *Idols of Modernity: Movie Stars of the 1920s* (New Brunswick, NJ: Rutgers University Press, 2010), 4; Joshua Yumibe and Sarah Street, eds., *Chromatic Modernity: Color, Cinema, and Media of the 1920s* (New York: Columbia University Press, 2019).
13. Miriam Bratu Hansen, "The Mass Production of the Senses: Classical Cinema as Vernacular Modernism," *Modernism/modernity* 6, no. 2 (April 1999): 59–72, and "Fallen Women, Rising Stars, New Horizons: Shanghai Silent Film as Vernacular Modernism," *Film Quarterly* 54, no. 1 (Autumn 2000): 10–22.
14. Fredric Jameson, *The Political Unconscious: Narrative as a Socially Symbolic Act* (Ithaca, NY: Cornell University Press, 1981), 102.
15. Walter Benjamin, "The Work of Art in the Age of Mechanical Reproduction," in Hannah Arendt, ed., *Illuminations* (New York: Schocken, 1968), 222.
16. On these terms and concepts, see Miriam Bratu Hansen, *Cinema and Experience: Siegfried Kracauer, Walter Benjamin, and Theodor W. Adorno* (Berkeley: University of California Press, 2011).
17. Christian Metz, *The Imaginary Signifier: Psychoanalysis and the Cinema*, trans. Celia Britton, Annwyl Williams, Ben Brewster, and Alfred Guzzetti (Bloomington: Indiana University Press, 1982), 3.

18. Wolfgang Ernst, "Let There Be Irony: Cultural History and Media Archaeology in Parallel Lines," in Jussi Parikka, ed., *Digital Memory and the Archive* (Minneapolis: University of Minnesota Press, 2013), 49, 53.
19. Thomas Elsaesser, "The New Film History as Media Archaeology," *Cinémas: Revue d'études cinématographiques* 14, nos. 2/3 (Spring 2004): 75–117.
20. Ibid., 110.
21. André Gaudreault and Philippe Marion, "The Cinema as a Model for the Genealogy of Media," *Convergence* 8 (2002): 15.
22. *Mutual Film Corp. v. Industrial Comm'n of Ohio*, 236 U.S. 230 (1915), https://supreme.justia.com/cases/federal/us/236/230.
23. On this topic, see Lee Grieveson, *Policing Cinema: Movies and Censorship in Early-Twentieth-Century America* (Berkeley: University of California Press, 2004), chap. 5.
24. Lee Grieveson, *Cinema and the Wealth of Nations: Media, Capital, and the Liberal World System* (Berkeley: University of California Press, 2018), 1.
25. Robert Sklar, *Movie-Made America: A Social History of American Movies* (New York: Random House, 1975); Lary May, *Screening out the Past: The Birth of Mass Culture and the Motion Picture Industry* (New York: Oxford University Press, 1980). On Actor-Network-Theory, see Bruno Latour, *Reassembling the Social: An Introduction to Actor-Network-Theory* (New York: Oxford University Press, 2005).
26. On the passage from the "cinema of attractions" to the "cinema of narrative integration," see Tom Gunning, *D. W. Griffith and the Origins of American Narrative Film: The Early Years at Biograph* (Urbana: University of Illinois Press, 1994). For a discussion of the concepts "kine-attractography" and "institutional cinema" see André Gaudreault, *Film and Attraction: From Kinematography to Cinema*, trans. Timothy Barnard (Urbana: University of Illinois Press, 2011).
27. See, for instance, the essays in Keil and Stamp, eds., *American Cinema's Transitional Era*.
28. Fredric Jameson, *A Singular Modernity: Essay on the Ontology of the Present* (New York: Verso, 2002).
29. Michael Warner, *Publics and Counterpublics* (New York: Zone Books, 2005), 90.

PART I

ORIGINS
From Invention to Medium

CHAPTER 2

THE INVENTION OF CINEMA

TOM GUNNING

The Question

The question of the invention of cinema inevitably leads us to the primal question haunting film history and film theory: what *is* cinema? Let's distinguish cinema as an institution from its technological base. As an institution, cinema exists as a social practice, including not only the production of films but their reception. Cinema became the dominant form of storytelling and entertainment in the twentieth century, as well as a major source of information and education. But it would be meaningless to speak of the "invention" of cinema as a social practice. As André Gaudreault has stressed, the institutions of cinema did not appear automatically with the invention of its technical devices.[1]

So the question of cinema's invention must be approached partly as a technological issue, though the question remains complex. The recent transformation of cinema exhibition from a primarily mechanical system to one that is primarily electronic, not to mention the multiplication of platforms on which films are viewed, reminds us that the technology of cinema transforms continually. As film theorist Noel Carroll has observed, "Film is not a single distinctive physical medium, but an array or assembly of media."[2] Accordingly, the invention of cinema cannot be restricted to a *single* machine but rather entails a constellation of various devices and practices. As a technological assembly, cinema is best described as an apparatus, in the most common meaning of this term: "a set of materials or equipment designed for a particular use."[3] Without claiming to be exhaustive, this essay surveys the long process of the convergence of technologies that projects the ever-changing shadow of what we call cinema.

Film theory, beginning in the 1970s, introduced the concept of the cinematic apparatus, primarily describing it as a tool of ideological control. But in the context of the invention of cinema the term apparatus allows us avoid a simple dichotomy between the technical and the social. The assembly of the elements of the cinema—the camera, the projectors, the screen, and viewing devices—created a complex situation, both technical and social, in which viewers interacted with moving images. Central to this situation is the manipulation of viewers' perception so that still images appear to move; these moving images can be presented in a range of sizes and spaces. To understand the complexity of the cinematic apparatus it is useful to review how the "invention" of cinema's history has been presented.

In 1948, Georges Sadoul titled the first volume of his scholarly and carefully researched *Histoire generale du cinema, L'Invention du cinema,1837–1897*.[4] Its first section, "L'Invention des appareils," describes not a single invention but a genealogy that includes optical toys, the development of photography, the chronophotography of Muybridge and Marey, the work of Émile Reynaud, and finally the achievements of Edison and Lumière. The task of constructing a genealogy of cinematic inventions preceded Sadoul and ultimately reaches back as far as Edison's first patents cases. In recent years dedicated researchers such as Jacques Deslandes, Deac Rossell, Charles Musser, Paul Spehr, Marta Braun, Martin Loiperdinger, Luke McKernan, Stephen Herbert, and especially Laurent Mannoni in his magisterial work, have corrected some of Sadoul's details. Nonetheless the genealogical approach to cinema's invention remains in place. In this essay, I depend greatly on the researchers named, as well as others, and even on the history as outlined by Sadoul. But as many scholars have demonstrated of late, this genealogy can no longer be seen as moving progressively toward the invention of cinema. The invention of cinema constitutes a process of contingent convergence rather than the achievement of an ideal goal. Creating a list of devices that develop inevitably into "cinema" embodies not only a teleological prejudice but a basic error: defining cinema in terms of an essence, when actually the nature of cinema changes dramatically over the years (and is changing as I write). Approaching cinema as an apparatus that includes the viewer, rather than simply a machine to be perfected, allows us to understand how the nature of cinema transforms in tandem with the situation of the apparatus.

Producing a Moving Image

Our inquiry must begin with the production of a moving image. This technical effect relies on a perceptual phenomenon described scientifically as "apparent motion."[5] Thus these devices operate not simply on images but affect human perception. This may seem obvious, but stressing it highlights the central role of a human viewer within the cinematic apparatus. The technological moving image triggers an aspect of human perception through mechanical control of time and motion. Human vision possesses physical and psychological factors that cause it to synthesize a perception of motion when presented with a rapid succession of images or forms in closely related positions. The simplest moving-image device, the flipbook, shows this clearly. Our vision merges a succession of images showing slightly differing positions; when rapidly flipped by a thumb, the pages create a perception of motion.

The phenomenon of visual perception has been investigated systematically and experimentally since the seventeenth century, beginning with the examination of the physiology of the eye and its relation to sight by Enlightenment figures such as René Descartes and Johannes Kepler.[6] Cinema could be said to begin around 1830 with devices designed by Peter Mark Roget, Michael Faraday, Simon Stampfer, and Joseph Plateau, for the observation of certain visual motion phenomena. Roget and Faraday had observed the effects of viewing the revolving spokes of a wagon wheel through the slats of a fence. Faraday created "a simple arrangement of cut-out sectored discs," known as the Faraday Wheel, to study this phenomenon.[7] Aware of Faraday's invention, but working independently, Stampfer and Plateau in 1833 developed devices that produced the first technological moving images, exploiting the stroboscopic effect Faraday had demonstrated. A revolving disc with slits functioned as a shutter, creating the stroboscopic flicker. The spectator looked through the shutter at a disc on whose perimeter a carefully designed series of figures portraying the successive phases of an action had been drawn, such as a dancer performing a pirouette. As the shutter and disc revolved, each individual drawing appeared through the shutter in a brief flash. Once a certain speed of revolution was achieved, the images merged into a flow, a continuous motion. With their basically identical devices, Stampfer's Stroboscope and Plateau's Phenakistiscope, the technological moving image was invented.

The nineteenth century witnessed a variety of motion picture devices after Plateau and Stampfer opened the floodgates. The conditions for technological motion pictures are simple. A series of images must portray closely related phases of an action. A viewing device displays this image series, using a revolving shutter to transform the individual static images into flickering appearances, which our perception fuses and transforms into movement. The spectator forms an essential part of this apparatus; it is human perception that generates apparent movement when a device creates certain conditions of viewing. Numerous nineteenth-century devices produced moving images: the flipbook, patented in 1868, in which rapidly flipped bound pages created a primitive shutter effect; the Zoetrope (claimed by various inventors, but first published under the name the "Daedeleum" in 1834 by William Horner), which replaced the Phenakistiscope or Stroboscope discs with a revolving slotted drum through which a strip of images was viewed; Émile Reynaud's Praxinoscope from 1877, which used a prismatic circular arrangement of mirrors to create the stroboscopic effect; and Ottomar Anschütz's Electrotachyscope, which employed an electrical Geissler tube to trigger the stroboscopic effect by flashing light briefly through a revolving transparent image.[8] Most of these devices were initially designed to demonstrate scientifically the apparent motion effect in human perception but were soon marketed as toys or amusements. They nonetheless continued to be used by scientists to observe processes in motion, such as the flight of birds studied by physiologist Étienne-Jules Marey by means of a Zoetrope.[9]

From the viewpoint of later cinema, these early devices had limitations. With the exception of the Praxinoscope and the Electrical Tachyscope, observers looked through a shutter to see the moving images, which degraded the visibility of the moving images. Further, the disc or strip of images could not exceed the circumference of the disc or drum, and consequently the actions portrayed had to be brief or repetitive. To expand visibility beyond individuals, T. W. Naylor, Franz Uchatius, Louis Jules Duboscq, and others adapted the Phenakistiscope to projection by the magic lantern.[10] Somewhat more complicated projection systems, such as C. W. Beale's Choreutoscope and Henry Heyl's Projecting-Phenakistiscope, also appeared around the middle of the nineteenth century.[11] These devices used a transparent disc with drawn figures and a revolving shutter in combination with a powerful magic lantern projector to show moving images to large audiences.

The production of a moving image through a device that includes images and a shutter in a systematic engagement forms one aspect of the invention of cinema, arguably the most distinctive. But there are two other strains of the cinematic apparatus that are also often considered essential to "cinema," even though both have independent histories. One is projection, the other the invention of photography. Our dominant image of the cinema includes both: photographic images projected on a screen. But moving-image devices need not involve projection, nor need they be photographic. To define either of these aspects as essential to the cinema introduces many questions, but to ignore their roles in the invention of the cinema would be perverse. The moving-image devices preceding what we now call cinema remind us of the role of perception in the production of a moving image and the focus such devices allowed on enigmas of human vision.

THE PROJECTED IMAGE

Projection plays a complex and fascinating role in the history of the cinema. The moving image can exist without projection, and, likewise, projection exists without moving images. The history of the projected image begins in medieval and Arabic optics with the study of the ability of parabolic mirrors and the camera obscura to project images onto a surface.[12] The invention of the magic lantern in the seventeenth century initiated a new era in projection. The magic lantern consists of a light source housed in a compartment that channels its light in one direction. Originally the light came from a lamp or candle, and much of the technical history of the magic lantern consists of modifications to its light source, making it brighter and/or safer, moving from a candle to the oil-fed Argand lamp, to the brighter limelight, to various gas sources, and eventually to electricity. The light source was given direction by a concave mirror serving as a reflector and an aperture into which a glass slide was placed. Light penetrated the glass and projected the image on the slide onto a surface. Crucially, this image was focused by a lens, which allowed it to appear sharply defined on a surface. The size of the image was determined by both the type of lens and the distance (or throw) of the projector from the surface. The glass slides were initially hand-painted and could be easily exchanged, so showmen could present different images, which could be arranged in sequences to tell stories or illustrate topics. The magic lantern was first publicized and described by the Jesuit polymath Athanasius Kircher in the 1675 edition of his work on optics, *The Great Art of Light and Shadow*, which led earlier scholars to credit Kircher with its invention. But historian Laurent Mannoni and others now credit the invention to Dutch humanist Christian Huygens around 1659.[13] By the early eighteenth century, showmen throughout Europe gave magic lantern exhibitions, sometimes using the device to inspire fear or a belief in supernatural apparitions. The lantern traveled around the world, as Jesuit missionaries brought it to the New World and Asia.

Projection by the magic lantern produced images with an ambiguous materiality. Composed of projected and reflected light, these images could be neither touched nor grasped. The spatial distance between the lantern and the screen not only determined the size and intensity of the image but also rendered the relation between image and source mysterious (especially when, as was often done, the lantern was concealed). The projected image was formed and carried by light and, like the medieval stained-glass window, became endowed with the aura of illumination.

The magic lantern became a major visual medium and transformed the nature of the image, endowing it with a seemingly ghostly or visionary immateriality, which explains an early name for the device: "the lantern of fear."[14] This uncanny aspect of the magic lantern was exploited especially by the Phantasmagoria ghost shows of the late eighteenth century, which were designed to thrill spectators with eerie illusions of visual transformation.[15] Elaborate mechanical lantern slides, coupled with levers, slipping layers of glass, or rack and pinion mechanisms, allowed elements of the slide to move or rotate, producing a variety of special effects.

Initially, limited illumination constrained the projection of early magic lanterns to smaller images in intimate spaces, but by the nineteenth century, improved light sources and complex lenses transformed the lantern from an eerie visual entertainment into a form of mass media, offering entertainment, education, and propaganda. Lanterns with two or three lenses were manufactured, allowing quick changes of slides as well as visual effects, such as dissolving images into each other. Producing the slides, initially painted by hand individually, became an industry rather than an artisanal process, as images were printed on glass by various methods.[16] By the mid-nineteenth century, photographic images could be transferred to lantern slides, bringing the documentary values associated with photography.[17]

In the mid-nineteenth century, the magic lantern, especially in England and the Americas, projected images in large venues (such as London's Polytechnic Institution, whose lantern shows began in 1840, using a screen that measured nearly twenty-five feet across in an auditorium seating five hundred).[18] In contrast to the individual viewer of moving-image devices such as the Phenakistiscope, the enlarged scope of magic lantern projection allowed an extensive audience. The lantern could be a mass medium, rather than a toy for individuals. Thus the lantern introduced a different sort of apparatus situation and a different spectator experience. Lantern slides told stories, presented comic gags, illustrated travelogues, promoted religions, argued political and social causes, advertised commodities, and reported current events.

The magic lantern demonstrates the error of constructing a genealogy of the cinema as progressing inevitably toward the projection of moving pictures. The lantern as a technological visual medium had a longer history than the cinema and possessed its own institutions; it did not become simply absorbed and replaced by the appearance of cinema. Rather than an inevitable goal, we might see the apparatus of cinema as resulting from the intersection of two separate media traditions: the projecting lantern and the stroboscopic creation of moving images.

Photographing Time

Photography's status as a medium independent from cinema cannot be questioned, given the important social and aesthetic roles of the still photograph. The necessity of photography to the invention of cinema remains a vexed issue. The production of the moving image did not initially depend on photography, as it first used drawings of the successive phases of an action. Nonetheless, people often think of cinema as a form of photography that recorded motion. During the nineteenth century, the technology and nature of photography underwent enormous transformations, changing its possibilities. This was particularly true of the rate of photographic exposure.

Photography consists of the registering of an image formed by light reflected from objects and then fixing this image so that it does not fade away. The earliest successful photographic images were made in the 1820s, and in 1839 Nicéphore Niépce and Louis Daguerre's process was announced to the world.[19] Early photographs required extended exposure of the sensitive plate to sunlight. Niépce's first exposures may have taken more than a day, and Daguerreotypes could take up to half an hour. William Henry Fox-Talbot's early paper photographs, "calotypes," greatly reduced the exposure time but still required several minutes. Lengthy exposure times initially limited photography to immobile subjects (landscapes, buildings, corpses) and required bright sunlight. Rapid movement either did not appear at all in early photographs or registered as a blur. Changes in the sensitivity of the photographic material, from the wet collodion process to the dry plate in the 1870s, further reduced exposure time. By the 1880s exposures could be as brief as a fraction of a second, which made possible an image that froze a subject in motion.[20]

This instantaneous photography of the late nineteenth century played an essential role in the invention of motion photography. Freezing the action allowed the analysis of motion via a succession of still images, with brief intervals between them. Thus, an image series of the sort essential to the production of a moving image could be produced photographically. The drawings used in moving picture devices such as the Phenakistiscope could only estimate the various positions that constituted an action. A photographic exposure of a tenth of a second or less could reveal an aspect of the mobile world that exceeded the capacity of human vision.

The photographic motion studies of Eadweard Muybridge, Étienne-Jules Marey, and others exploited this new exposure time. In 1878, photographer Muybridge made a wet-plate photograph with an exposure time brief enough to freeze the position of a horse in full gallop. The anecdote that Governor of California Leland Stanford financed Muybridge's photography in order to settle a bet about whether all four hooves of a horse simultaneously left the ground during a gallop may be journalistic fiction.[21] But no question, Muybridge aspired to capture photographically something human sight had never seen. As the telescope and microscope extended the realm of visibility into previously invisible dimensions of space, the instantaneous photograph extended the realm of visible time. Capturing a series of instantaneous phases of motion inaugurated the scientific practice of chronophotography, the photographing of an action as it unfolded in time. Although the primary purpose of chronophotography was the analysis of motion, its capture of motion in a *series* of images brings us to the brink of photographic cinema.

Muybridge photographed horses in motion as they moved past a battery of separate cameras (usually twelve), electronically devised to be triggered as the horse moved past, producing instantaneous photographs of the phases of its motions. Assembling these images into a continual series with brief intervals between each was as essential for the invention of cinema as capturing a fraction of a second in an instantaneous photograph. The resulting photographs clearly showed what human vision could not register: the exact positions a horse assumed as it moved at various speeds—including the ocular proof that at one point during a gallop all four hooves indeed left the ground. The positions that a running horse took, as captured in these photographs, contradicted previous traditional images of horses in painting, drawing, and sculpture. These novel photographic series had many effects. They fascinated the general viewer with both technical innovation and uncanny revelations; they challenged the representations of equestrian painters; and they held important information for zoologists and physiologists about the physical mechanics of locomotion.

Muybridge's images attracted the attention of physiologist Étienne-Jules Marey, who possessed the scientific training and methods Muybridge lacked. Marey had instituted the "graphic method" to scientifically analyze the physical motion of animals and human beings, using sensitive instruments attached to subjects to trace patterns of movements and collect physiological data. Placing rubber pneumatic shoes on a horse, he had already gathered data indicating that a galloping horse lifted all its hooves simultaneously, before Muybridge offered ocular proof. Once Muybridge's photographs were published, Marey realized the additional information chronophotography could offer him.[22]

Muybridge's method changed a bit over the decade he devoted to studying humans and animals in motion, especially during his association with the University of Pennsylvania; there, he adopted dry-plate photography and added a grid to the background of his images.[23] But he maintained his multiple-camera approach, with each photograph shot from a slightly different viewpoint, allowing for easy reassembly of the order of his images.[24] Marey brought scientific rigor to chronophotography and recognized the importance of maintaining a single viewpoint on mobile subjects. Marey's fixed-plate photographs used a revolving shutter and the movement of the subject to capture multiple successive images on a single plate.[25] However, the overlapping images that resulted, while appreciated today for their aesthetic quality, interfered with scientific analysis. Marey sought ways of moving the photographic surface to produce clear separate images. In 1888, he used a sensitive paper film strip manufactured by George Eastman's company, and in 1890 he used newly available celluloid film. Because of his use of flexible film, Marey can be claimed as the inventor of the motion picture camera that employed a film strip, as Laurent Mannoni claims.[26] However, the lack of perforations on his film yielded irregular image registration, which limited the use of the films for reproducing motion.

Can we identify chronophotography with the invention of cinema? Once again, it depends on what we mean by cinema. The first defining cinematic characteristic—the production of a moving image—preceded chronophotography. However, chronophotography supplied the first means of recording motion photographically. Since cinema as an apparatus involves the viewing of moving images by spectators as much as the capture of a moment photographically, identifying chronophotography with cinema remains problematic. The primary mode of presentation for chronophotography remained as a series of still images. This fixity allowed analysis of the stages and the forms of physical motion. Marey later stressed the difference between his chronophotography and the projection of moving images by the Lumières' Cinématographe. Chronophotography, he asserted, supplemented human vision with a scientific instrument of observation. In contrast, Marey claimed, the cinema simply reproduced human vision.[27] The purpose of chronophotography lay in the *analysis* rather than the *reproduction* of motion.

However, it would be a mistake to claim that producing a viewable moving image played no role in chronophotography. The opposition Muybridge initially encountered with his photographs of galloping horses demonstrates this vividly. Muybridge's photographs not only showed all hooves off the ground at one time but portrayed the horse's legs in what seemed ungainly and unaesthetic positions, completely contradicting the way horses had been rendered for centuries. Muybridge's images seemed so unfamiliar that some equestrian painters and art critics denounced them as fakes, products of Muybridge's perverse imagination rather than records of fact. No vision of a moving horse, critics claimed, could be derived from these ridiculous positions. Synthesizing these series of photographs into a moving image would demonstrate that Muybridge's positions were not arbitrary but authentic phases of a movement. Therefore, animating images from his chronophotographs served Muybridge as a means of verification. His Zoöpraxiscope allowed a Phenakistiscope disc to be projected on a screen by a magic lantern. Thus, ocular proof of the veracity of Muybridge's process could be clearly presented to an audience. Perceiving the moving image, the viewer held an important place in this process of verification.

In Marey's case, while he stressed the value of the intense study that his series of still chronophotographs allowed, the reversibility of his process into the production of a moving image yielded both verification and other observations. His use of a large Zoetrope, in which he placed three-dimensional models of the positions of birds in flight (based on his chronophotographs), allowed Marey to move from a stilled two-dimensional image to its appearance in motion and in three dimensions. In the 1890s, Marey sought to create a projector that could return the appearance of motion to his chronophotographic films.[28] Under Marey's guidance, his assistant Georges Demenÿ devised the Phonoscope, a form of projecting Phenakistiscope that allowed slowing, stilling, or presenting the natural motion of chronophotographs of the act of speech, in order to help teach the deaf to lip read. The purpose of this device remained pedagogical and restricted to a limited class of viewers. But Demenÿ recognized that the fascination the moving image generated could appeal to larger numbers of viewers. He broke with Marey in order to explore the possibilities of the Phonoscope as a commercial device, an action Marey found distasteful. Demenÿ eventually created an early form of film projector, thereby illustrating how devices for producing moving images could be retooled through a change from the pedagogical to the entertaining.[29]

It would be hard, therefore, to overstate the importance of chronophotography for the "invention" of cinema. The mastery of motion through its photographic analysis into separate but closely related images constitutes a major component of cinema as it evolved. If cinema consists of the photographic registering of action, we could declare chronophotography as the invention of cinema. Laurent Mannoni, consummate researcher of early cinema and expert on Marey, has declared Marey to be "the real founding father of cinematographic technique."[30] Besides Marey's assistants, such as Demenÿ and Lucien Bull, physiologists in several countries followed in Marey's footsteps in using chronophotography to record aspects of animal or human motion, including Albert Londe, Ottomar Anschütz, and the Romanian Gheorghe Marinescu. A number of these men devised their own chronophotographic mechanisms, often with multiple lenses as a means of capturing the successive phases of motion.[31] However, as the breach between Marey and Demenÿ demonstrates, the move from chronophotography to cinema as a mass medium involved less a technical change than a reconception of the purposes and the situation of the apparatus.

Drawn Narratives and the Image Band

Did cinema depend on the technology of chronophotography? One of the most complex moving-image devices of the late nineteenth century relied not on photography but on painted images: Émile Reynaud's Théâtre Optique, which premiered in 1892 at the Parisian Musée Grévin. Reynaud had invented the Praxinoscope, the moving-image device that employed revolving prismatic mirrors to animate its circular band of drawn images. He then introduced a number of modifications of this device, such as a Praxinoscope Theater that reflected and framed the images within a miniature proscenium and a projecting Praxinoscope that could show the animated images on a screen. The Théâtre Optique, however, was not a tabletop parlor toy like the previous Praxinoscopes but a theatrical spectacle with a novel mechanism.[32] This device moves us from the conception of the moving image as a toy to the possibility of a spectacle presented for an audience. As well as technical considerations, the shift from a repetitive moving image to an evolving narrative plays a key role in this transformation. These motion picture devices did not depend on photography as much as projection and a flexible base for the images.

The circularity of the Phenakistiscope disc or the band of images within the Zoetrope drum was determined by the devices' revolving motion. This circular motion limited the duration of their moving images to a matter of seconds. This favored cyclical actions, movements that could be repeated endlessly and still seem natural (a girl jumping rope, windmills turning, a dancer pirouetting). To create more complex actions required redesigning moving picture devices.

Reynaud's Théâtre Optique tackled this problem by creating an extensive strip of translucent images, resembling the film strip of later cinema. A master of caricature and visual storytelling, Reynaud painted his series of images directly on squares of translucent gelatin held together by a leather band. The band formed a loop but was much longer than the strips in other viewing devices, accommodating several hundred images rather than the dozen or so pictures of previous moving-image devices. This flexible and extensive band of images and the way it moved through Reynaud's apparatus were as ingenious as his delightful drawn gags and brief narratives. The gelatin squares were translucent, allowing light to project the images onto the prismatic mirrors, which produced the stroboscopic motion effect. The moving image was then reflected by a series of lenses and mirrors onto a screen. The movement of the band was controlled by an operator manipulating handles, which could move smoothly backward or forward. A skilled operator could introduce a rhythm of hesitation or repetition into the movement of the drawn figures. The flexible band moved smoothly in a large loop around the revolving wheels Reynaud had designed. This movement of the band was rendered steady (an essential quality for the consistent registration of the successive images as they were projected on the screen) by the engagement of metal perforations placed between each image with pins on the wheels. This engagement of pins and holes moved the images smoothly, anticipating the system of sprockets and sprocket holes that appeared in Edison's motion picture films.

Each of Reynaud's spectacles for the Théâtre Optique lasted several minutes, presenting a number of individual actions and interactions between characters. Essentially gag-driven, the spectacles lacked dialogue but were accompanied by music. Reynaud produced several bands, and they appeared at the Musée Grévin until the novelty of the Cinématographe gradually made them démodé. The importance of the Théâtre Optique must be acknowledged, however, and not only as the "first" animation. The ability to present a coherent story derived directly from the increased number of images the system allowed. This demonstrates the importance of technological innovation to aesthetic forms and genres. Again, a different sort of spectator address emerges here and arguably a new apparatus.

In Thom Anderson's excellent documentary on Eadweard Muybridge, the narrator states at one point that at the end of the nineteenth century any reasonably skilled mechanic could have invented the cinema, and several did.[33] While this statement may be a bit ungenerous and may simplify the problems confronting moving-image pioneers, it does reveal the invention of cinema as the solution of technical problems rather than a stroke of genius. We must avoid seeing the various aspects of cinema as inevitably converging toward the cinema of the twentieth century. This narrative of technological progress distorts the actual process of invention by tracing backward from an established form and reducing earlier forms to the status of predecessors. Reynaud's *Autour d'une cabine* presented in the Théâtre Optique undoubtedly introduces a narrative complexity impossible in the Praxinoscope, but this need not be described as an improvement or achieving an ideal. As wonderful as the Théâtre Optique's little scenarios were, I do not find them superior to the delight of the brief cyclical action of clowns leaping over a circus pony as seen in the Praxinoscope. Rather than seeing one apparatus as replacing another in a linear evolution toward an ideal form, we should acknowledge how their differences allowed these apparatuses to fulfill different needs and delights and to co-exist.

The Celluloid Film Base

None of these considerations reduces the importance of changes in the technical base of the cinema, which offered a variety of affordances and possibilities. As Anderson has claimed, by the late 1880s a number of cinematic elements were in place: the stroboscopic production of a moving image through a shutter device and a succession of images; the centuries-long tradition of the magic lantern-projected images; chronophotography's capture of the phases of motion; Reynaud's flexible band as a support for a succession of images. A number of these elements had been combined, such as the projection of moving images through a magic lantern in Reynaud's projecting Praxinoscope or Muybridge's Zoöpraxiscope. Anderson's claim that putting them all together was in effect a no-brainer carries some weight. But the effect of this assembly was transformative; it should not be approached simply as solving a technical problem but as reconceiving the nature of the apparatus.

In the 1890s, the primary problem to be solved for the appearance of the modern cinema lay in the material support of the image-series. Moving-image devices had used opaque materials, usually some form of paper or cardboard for the discs of the Phenakistiscope or the strips of the Zoetrope or Praxinoscope. The magic lantern used translucent or transparent material, usually glass, through which light projected an image onto a surface. Devices that combined projection and moving images used translucent supports as well. The most obvious constraint on moving-image devices created by the support material lay in duration, since Phenakistiscope or Zoetrope bands offered limited space for images. The novelty of the Théâtre Optique resided as much in the flexible image band as in its innovations in narrative form. While the material base may seem no more than a technical detail, it is worth recalling that "film" has been an enduring name for the medium whose invention we are discussing. Even today when the material it names has begun to disappear, we still speak of seeing or producing a film.

In the 1880s, paper began to be used in still cameras as backing for newly introduced flexible film, a convenient replacement for individual photographic plates. In 1889 George Eastman introduced the first transparent flexible-roll film, with emulsion on a celluloid base.[34] Marey had used a strip of sensitized paper to take successive images of motion in 1888, but by 1889 he switched to transparent film. Flexible film appeared first in cameras; its use in projectors came somewhat later, although Marey had purportedly had some success projecting his film images.[35] In 1888 the Anglo-French figure Louis Le Prince perfected both a camera and apparently a projector using Eastman's paper-backed film and shot two surviving films, *Roundhay Garden Scene* and a view of traffic on Leeds Bridge, although these films were not shown publicly before their inventor mysteriously disappeared.[36] William Friese-Greene and Wordsworth Donisthorp also experimented with projectors using Eastman's paper film.[37]

The projecting Phenakistiscopes of the nineteenth century had primarily used glass discs. With the development of chronophotography, Anschütz and Demenÿ and others adapted the new motion photographs to Phenakistiscope-based projectors. Other devices adapted the glass slides of the magic lantern to motion picture projection using various means of replacing the slides rapidly, such as Pierre Sequin's device from the 1860s, which used a projector with several lenses and a complex carrier of multiple slides.[38] Some inventors attempted to combine the inflexible glass images with flexible bands of fiber or rubber. Le Prince experimented in 1888 with a complex projector involving glass images on flexible bands after his projections with sensitive paper were not entirely satisfactory. Historian Deac Rossell has shown that glass-based projection devices were promoted even after the introduction of celluloid film as a safer alternative to the highly flammable material of cellulose nitrate.[39] However, a flexible base offered new horizons for the cinema, allowing it to expand from short bursts of movements to a continuous flow of duration. The cinema as it developed relied on this sense of expansive movement.

Edison, Dickson, and the Recording of Time

Americans most often name Thomas Edison as the inventor of cinema partly due to the same nationalistic pride that has motivated the French to promote the Lumière brothers, the Germans during the Nazi era to vaunt Skladanowsky, or the English after WWII to promote Friese-Greene. Edison can hardly be named as the inventor of cinema, but to dismiss or minimize the contribution his company made would also be a mistake. Edison was not a pioneer in any of the areas we have surveyed: the production of the moving image, the development of projection, or instantaneous photography. Yet one of Edison's most famous inventions offered an important model to the cinema: the phonograph. Edison introduced the first version of his phonograph in 1877 and released its perfected commercial version in 1888, shortly before he began research on a motion picture machine.[40]

The phonograph achieved a fundamental revolution in human technology: recording a specific moment of time and playing it back. We not only hear a song, speech, or musical performance repeated, we re-experience its original temporality. A phonographic recording does not merely transcribe sound (as forms of shorthand could), nor does it imitate sounds from memory; it *reproduces the time of the sound's production*. A phonographic moment has been preserved from oblivion not simply as an instant, as with still photographs, but as *duration*. The cinema and the phonograph share this unique ability to replay a passing moment of time. Edison stressed this connection in his many statements announcing his new invention, claiming it "w[ould] do for the eye what the phonograph has done for the ear."[41] The capture of time, the replaying of a previous moment—this was a revolutionary possibility that the technology of the cinema and the phonograph shared. As more than a technical device for the perception of the moving image, cinema would become an apparatus for the preservation of the human experience of time.

The phonograph provided more than metaphysical inspiration for Edison's motion picture device. The support Edison and his collaborators initially tried out for their motion picture device directly imitated the phonograph's cylinder, now coated with celluloid to hold a series of microscopic motion photographs in a spiral pattern. This motion picture machine, labeled the Kinetoscope, was a viewing device like the Zoetrope or Phenakistiscope. Viewers watched the rapid succession of these tiny images through an enlarging lens.[42]

The various "inventors" of the cinema came from diverse backgrounds and contexts. Plateau's Phenakistiscope emerged from early nineteenth-century investigations of the physiology of vision; Muybridge was a landscape photographer interacting with institutions interested in the physiology of movement for both scientific and artistic purposes; Marey and his physiological institutions used a variety of instruments and methods to gather data on the movement of bodies; Reynaud came from the culture of the magic lantern and visual novelties, and his Théâtre Optique was designed as such an attraction for a major urban commercial entertainment center, the Musée Grévin.

Thomas Edison was not only an inventor (who publicized his many inventions and patents for electronic and mechanical devices by using the epithet "The Wizard") but a corporate businessman who had organized one of the first industrial research laboratories, where materials, instruments, experts, and artisans were brought together to pursue a range of technical innovations for their potential profitability.[43] The Thomas Edison Company assigned work on the motion picture device that Edison had envisioned to one of his most trusted assistants, William Kennedy Laurie Dickson, possibly due to Dickson's background in photography. Dickson eventually found that the curvature of the cylinder adapted from the phonograph distorted the tiny photographs affixed to its surface. He turned to strips of celluloid film, which George Eastman had begun to market in 1889. Edison and Dickson determined that these strips of celluloid had to be perforated (an idea Edison probably got from the message strips in his automatic telegraph) to move them through both the Kinetograph camera and the Kinetoscope.[44]

Edison was fully aware of his predecessors in the development of motion pictures, and his correspondence or interaction with Muybridge and Marey is well documented. He probably knew of Marey's use of film and possibly of Reynaud's gelatin strip. Although George Eastman was producing flexible celluloid roll film for his company's Kodak cameras and seemed a likely source for Kennedy's experiments for Edison, manufacturing a suitable material was not simple. Historian Paul Spehr has detailed the enormous effort Dickson undertook to adapt this new material to the Edison camera and viewer. Difficulties with adapting Eastman's strips of celluloid to the new devices led Dickson to turn to the Blair Camera Company for the celluloid in the first Edison films.[45] Although there were earlier sporadic uses of celluloid (by Marey especially) in motion pictures, Edison established celluloid film as a standard element of cinema. Edison's motion picture film standardized the spaces between images and used consistently spaced perforations to move the film through both a camera and a viewing device. Even the width of the film that Dickson chose, 1½ inches—35 mm—became standard. We could claim that with Edison/Dickson, motion picture film was established.[46]

Once celluloid film became the base, the design for both a motion picture camera and a viewer could be determined. Edison applied for patents for the Kinetograph camera and the Kinetoscope viewer in 1891. The early history of motion pictures highlights the devices that display motion pictures more than cameras. Muybridge's chronophotography, for instance, depended on conventional still cameras rather than a specially designed motion picture camera. Marey, however, had introduced new forms of motion picture cameras. But since Marey's primary purpose was producing still images for analysis, the consistency of the registration of individual images in relation to one another was not important. Edison's apparatus interlinked a recording device (the Kinetograph motion picture camera) and a playback device (the Kinetoscope), and the importance of playback made the precise registration of images crucial. The Edison Company created an apparatus rather than a single device: a precision motion picture camera registering images designed to be played back as moving images on another device.

These interlocking aspects of the cinematic apparatus had long-lasting influence on the cinema as it developed, perhaps explaining why Edison has so often been named as the inventor of cinema. It is curious, then, that the motion picture device that Edison actually commercialized was so different from the mainstream cinema projectors that followed. Edison's Kinetoscope remained a viewing device with individual spectators peering through an aperture, rather than a projector that could display a spectacle to an audience. It derived essentially from the tradition of Zoetropes and other early viewing devices and bore little relation to the magic lantern.

Flexible celluloid film was essential to the Kinetoscope. Like Reynaud's band, the Kinetoscope's celluloid film formed a loop joined at the ends, held tight by a series of rollers and enclosed in a cabinet. The film moved continuously, steadily propelled by sprocket wheels that gripped the film by its perforations along the edges. Through a magnifying lens at the top of the cabinet, spectators viewed moving images illuminated as they passed over an electrical light source. A revolving shutter created the stroboscopic effect necessary for the apparent motion. Although the Kinetoscope was basically an improved Zoetrope, the improvements transformed the experience of viewing. The images remained small, but the illumination and the arrangement of the aperture made them much clearer and brighter than those glimpsed through the slit of a Zoetrope. Although the loop of film was still of quite limited duration, usually less than a minute, it was much longer than the moving images seen in the earlier devices and smoother in motion. From this point, the production of *films* as much as the invention and manufacture of *machines* defined the cinema. Instead of repetitive actions, Edison's Kinetoscope films presented complex performances: acrobatics and feats of skill and even narrative gags. Today they still exert a visual fascination, a delight in motion, and are frequently amusing or surprising. Dickson designed a special studio for shooting films that was built in early 1893. The Kinetoscope was publicly demonstrated before invited journalists at the Brooklyn Institute in May 1893. Serious film production began in 1894 with celebrity performers, dancers, acrobats, and strongmen trekking to the Edison studio in New Jersey to be filmed, with more than seventy-five films shot in 1894.[47]

The Kinetoscope offered more than a technical device capable of displaying moving images; Edison launched a successful commercial enterprise, even if it lasted for only a limited time. Unlike such predecessors as Le Prince's projectors or Reynaud's Théâtre Optique, which were unique devices that remained in the hands of their inventor, the Kinetoscope was designed for broad public consumption, offering a new mode of visual entertainment rather than a single attraction. Edison contracted to have Kinetoscopes manufactured by 1894 (around a thousand were ultimately made), with the Edison Company responsible for supplying both films and viewing machines to amusement parlors specially opened for their exploitation.[48] In 1894 Kinetoscope parlors had opened in most major US cities, and by the end of the year they started to appear in Europe. These parlors had rows of coin-operated machines into which paying customers inserted a nickel to see a film flit by.

The Kinetoscope was probably the largest commercialized moving-image device that had yet appeared. Unlike the specialized devices of Marey or other chronophotographers, the Kinetoscope aspired to a public presence, albeit the somewhat trivial one of a cheap entertainment. At this point, moving image toys had been marketed for more than a half a century. The magic lantern was a mass medium of entertainment and information throughout the nineteenth century, but its moving-image forms remained fairly marginal before film projection. A gap seemed to exist for the moving images of the Kinetoscope to fill as a commercial attraction. But by 1896, the Kinetoscope business appeared to have exhausted its commercial potential, although a rival peepshow machine, the Mutoscope (which flipped a wheel of individual photographs mounted on cardboard, rather than running a strip of celluloid film through the viewer), appeared in 1897 and had a longer commercial life.[49] While Mutoscopes persisted in penny arcades until the 1930s, their attraction of offering sometimes salacious images for adults or cartoons for children indicates the marginal role that the individual peepshow was designed to fill, even at its origin. Becoming a mass medium rather just a technical novelty depended very much on moving images being grafted onto the already robust medium of the projecting lantern. This would involve a new conception of the cinema as an apparatus with the appropriate technical affordances.

1895: Projection and the Cinématographe

The year 1895 has been memorialized as the date of the invention of cinema, largely due to the Lumière Company's introduction of their Cinématographe. Like most of the late nineteenth-century devices, the Cinématographe owes much to previous inventors. Nonetheless, as with the Kinetoscope, the Cinématographe also offered major innovations. The significance of 1895, however, is not limited to the Lumières' invention. It also marks a growing recognition of the inevitability of wedding the moving image to projection technology, a possibility that the Cinématographe fulfilled most successfully. Projection of moving images onto a screen defines the dominant apparatus of the cinema.

The Lumière Company was a photographic supply company whose dry-plate process, introduced in the 1880s, was especially well suited to the rapid exposure of the snapshot era and whose ease of handling made it attractive to the burgeoning amateur market. Paterfamilias Antoine, a studio photographer, had founded the company, and his two sons, Auguste and Louis, explored a number of new aspects of photographic technology, such as the snapshot and color photography (their Autochromes, introduced in 1907, became one of the first successful commercial color processes). In the 1890s, the company turned to motion photography, inspired by the work of Marey, the apparatus of Reynaud, and, especially, Edison's Kinetoscope. The Lumière Company did not envision an individual peepshow device like the Kinetoscope but a projector that would present moving images to an audience.

The company's background in producing photographic stock facilitated the use of a flexible celluloid-based film in their device, following the Kinetograph model. But in contrast to Edison/Dickson's unwieldy Kinetograph camera, the Cinématographe, weighing only sixteen pounds, seems inspired by the ease of handling that the recent amateur hand camera had brought to still photography. Elegance marked the Cinématographe: the same basic device could be used as both a camera and a projector. The same intermittent mechanism that moved the film past the aperture for taking images could, with a switch in lenses, be used to crank the developed film for projection, once the back was opened and a magic lantern added as light source. With another adjustment, the mechanism could be used to print positive prints from a negative. The conception of the Cinématographe differed sharply from Edison's Kinetoscope, in spite of the inspiration Edison's machine supplied for the perforated film strip and its movement through the camera. The two companies envisioned entirely different modes of exhibition and, presumably, of audience. The Kinetoscope moved its film continuously, while, as a projector, the Cinématographe employed intermittent motion as the film paused briefly in front of the aperture, increasing its illumination and steadiness, qualities vital for the larger projected image on a screen compared to the miniature scene viewed through Edison's peep hole.

Like Edison's original phonograph, the Cinématographe was a reversible apparatus—both a recording and a playback device, a camera and a projector—although the economical design of the Lumière machine made conversion from one function to the other simple, whereas Edison's cinematic apparatus required two different machines. Generally, as film exhibition emerged as a business, the production of motion pictures, as much as the manufacture of cameras and projectors, formed an essential part of the invention of cinema. The perfection of motion picture devices by major industrial concerns like the Edison and Lumière companies allowed the production of films to surpass the very limited number of artisanal and unique works of Le Prince or Reynaud. The origins of cinematic style could be located in the contrasting approach to filmmaking taken by Edison and the Lumières. Guided most likely by his experience with the phonograph, as Charles Musser has pointed out, Edison's filmmaking drew on an already existing entertainment world of dancers, acrobats, and vaudevillians, and, to this end, he created an enclosed studio within his industrial complex in New Jersey.[50] The studio created a dark environment (recalling the blackened backgrounds of the chronophotography of Muybridge and Marey), against which performers were illuminated by controlled sunlight, placing the emphasis on the skilled human body. By contrast, the Cinématographe's greater portability meant that early Lumière films tended to be shot in exterior locations, capturing moments of everyday life, children playing, urban traffic, or industrial processes. One should avoid seeing this strong contrast as an ideological or artistic dichotomy, since each company made some films in both modes. But these early films do establish different orientations for the Lumières and the Edison Company, based on differing models of cinema: a means of recording performances like the phonograph, or a means of recording everyday experience, like amateur photography.

The paradoxes of invention confront us in 1895. Are we seeking the legal issue of priority (who did it first?) or a widespread influence? Outside the commercial success and publicity of the Lumière and Edison machines, there were numerous other small-scale experiments and even public showings of motion pictures in 1895. As Musser has indicated, adapting the Kinetoscope film to the magic lantern was a logical step.[51] A number of showmen or inventors attempted it in 1895, including American rivals to Edison aided surreptitiously by his principal moving-picture expert, W. K. L. Dickson, such as the Latham family with their Eidoloscope. The Lathams' Eidoloscope briefly projected films of prize fights in a storefront theater in New York in April 1895, possibly the first commercial exhibition of projected films, although its short period of operation and comments by journalists seem to indicate the projections were not satisfactory.[52] The Phantoscope projector of Thomas Armat and Francis Jenkins had a commercial premiere at the Cotton States Exposition in Atlanta, Georgia, in September 1895. Max Skladanowsky premiered projected moving images at Berlin's Wintergarten Theater in November of 1895 with a complex system that employed two separate image bands dissolving between images inspired by magic lantern technology. The Phantoscope has been described by Musser as "the first instance of modern commercial cinema—projected moving pictures using an intermittent mechanism," clearly an important event, although its exhibition in 1895 was limited.[53]

The Kinetoscope and Kinetograph established a technical standard for the cinematic base, perforated film with intermittent motion, and the Phantoscope and Cinématographe established a standard model for projection, with intermittent motion, a single lens, and a celluloid film band. With systems for film exhibition in place, cinema moved from an era of invention to one of public reception. One should not assume, however, that this convergence of various traditions into cinema indicates that all the previous strands became absorbed into the new medium and were replaced by it. The magic lantern, optical toys, and chronophotography all persisted as independent forms. Further, the purpose of cinema and the models it would follow remained not only in flux in 1895 but so diverse that the insight of André Gaudreault that cinema was not "invented" as a social institution until several years into the twentieth century makes some sense.[54] But the cinema exists in a constant state of flux as both a technology and an institution—like the moving and transforming image on which it is based. The apparatus of cinema never has assumed a single stable form once and for all—and likely never will—in spite of periods and situations of apparent stability. The recent multiplication of platforms demonstrates the truth of André Bazin's claim in 1948 that "the cinema has not yet been invented."[55]

Coda: Edison's Greatest Wonder: The Vitascope

The year 1895 does represent a key moment in the invention of cinema if we define cinema as the projected commercial image. But 1896 marks the year in which cinema was seen in major metropolises around the world, including colonial Asia and Africa and Japan. Films were projected by Edison, the Lumières, and the newly launched Biograph in high-profile premieres, but a flood of other projectors and cameras also debuted (Mannoni claims more than a hundred apparatuses appeared in 1896).[56] If one wanted to proclaim a year when cinema announces itself as a public visual medium, that year is 1896. Is this the same as cinema's invention? To accent the ambiguities and even the arbitrary nature of "invention," let us close with a consideration of the premiere of the Vitascope projector in April 1896 at New York's leading vaudeville theater, Koster and Bial's Music Hall. The Vitascope was billed as "Edison's Greatest Marvel," projecting his Kinetoscope films life-size on a screen to a theatrical audience.

The Vitascope was not Edison's invention at all but a renamed Phantoscope, perfected by Thomas Armat after his separation from Francis Jenkins. Entertainment entrepreneurs Raff and Gammon, when approached by Armat about exhibiting his invention, realized how much more publicity would be generated if the projector could be associated with the Edison brand. With Edison's approval, the Vitascope appeared under his name. After the Kinetoscope seemed to have exhausted its commercial profitability as a technical novelty, the future of moving pictures clearly lay in projection. Edison began working on a Projecting Kinetoscope but had yet not reached a satisfactory version when Armat offered his machine to Raff and Gammon. In interviews Edison admitted that his own projector was still in process but endorsed the Vitascope.

We should not denounce this event as a hoax but rather understand it as offering a lesson in the many factors that converge in the invention of a complex apparatus like cinema. The question of invention cannot yield a single inventor, a specific date, or even a single device, however attractive such myths may be. But the Vitascope does reveal the diversity of impulses and the range of devices and relations to spectators that compose the cinematic apparatus. As Bazin hinted, technical invention is an ongoing process, and cinema may be best understood as having a history, more than it possesses an essence.

Notes

1. André Gaudreault, *Film and Attraction: From Kinematography to Cinema* (Urbana: University of Illinois Press, 2011), 5–7.
2. Noel Carroll, "Forget the Medium," *Engaging the Moving Image* (New Haven, CT: Yale University Press, 2003), 9.
3. Merriam Webster Online Dictionary: https://www.merriam webster.com/dictionary/apparatus?src=search-dict-box.
4. Georges Sadoul, *Histoire générale du cinéma: L'invention du cinema, 1837–1897* (Paris: Denoel, 1948).
5. Nicholas J. Wade, *A Natural History of Vision* (Cambridge, MA: MIT Press, 1998), 206–210.
6. Jonathan Crary, *Techniques of the Observer* (Cambridge, MA: MIT Press, 1990), 104–113.
7. Wade, *A Natural History of Vision*, 207; Laurent Mannoni, *The Great Art of Light and Shadow: Archaeology of the Cinema* (Exeter, UK: University of Exeter Press, 2000), 213–214.
8. Franz Liesegang, *Dates and Sources: A Contribution to the History of the Art of Projection and to Cinematography* (London: The Magic Lantern Society, 1986), 34–39; Deac Rossell, *Living Pictures: The Origins of the Movies* (Albany, NY: SUNY Press, 1998), 42–48.
9. Marta Braun, *Picturing Time: The Work of Étienne-Jules Marey (1830–1904)* (Chicago, IL: University of Chicago Press, 1992), 30 and passim.
10. Liesegang, *Dates and Sources*, 37–38.
11. Ibid.
12. David Hockney, *Secret Knowledge: Rediscovering the Lost Techniques of the Old Masters* (New York: Viking Studio, 2006), 74–94.
13. Mannoni, *The Great Art*, 38–42.
14. Ibid., 48.

15. Mervyn Heard, *Phantasmagoria: The Secret Life of the Magic Lantern* (Hastings, UK: The Projection Box, 2006), 78–83.
16. Mannoni, *The Great Art*, 288–296.
17. Ibid.
18. Ibid., 264–267.
19. François Brunet, *La Naissance de l'idée photographique* (Paris: PUF, 2012), 27–67.
20. Beaumont Newhall, *The History of Photography from 1839 to the Present Day* (New York: Museum of Modern Art, 1964), 17–49, 83–96.
21. Philip Brookman, *Helios: Eadweard Muybridge in a Time of Change* (Göttingen, Germany: Steidl/Cochoron Gallery of Art, 2010), 78–93.
22. Braun, *Picturing Time*, 228–254; Laurent Mannoni, *Étienne-Jules Marey: la memoire de l'oeil* (Milan, Italy: Mazzott/Cinémathèque Francais, 1999), 149–158.
23. Brookman, *Helios*, 93–97.
24. Braun, *Picturing Time*, 228–253.
25. Mannoni, *Étienne-Jules Marey*, 163–169.
26. Mannoni, *The Great Art*, 340–343.
27. Jacques Deslandes, *Histoire comparée du cinema, Tome I* (Paris: Casterman, 1966), 130.
28. Mannoni, *The Great Art*, 350–353; Mannoni, *Étienne-Jules Marey*, 291–296.
29. Mannoni, *Étienne-Jules Marey*, 277–299.
30. Mannoni, *The Great Art*, 320.
31. Ibid., 346–350.
32. Dominique Auzel, *Émile Reynaud, et l'image s'anima* (Paris: Éditions du May, 1992), 39–61.
33. Thom Anderson, *Eadweard Muybridge, Zoopraxiographer* [film, 1975].
34. Rossell, *Living Pictures*, 65–72.
35. Mannoni, *The Great Art*, 350–352.
36. Stephen Herbert, "Le Prince, Louis Aime Augustin," in Stephen Herbert and Luke McKernan, eds., *Who's Who of Victorian Cinema* (London: British Film Institute, 1996), 82–83.
37. Paul Spehr, *The Man Who Made Movies: W. K. L. Dickson* (Bloomington: Indiana University Press, 2008), 138.
38. Mannoni, *The Great Art*, 249–252.
39. Rossell, *Living Pictures*, 11.
40. Charles Musser, *The Emergence of Cinema: The American Screen to 1907* (New York: Charles Scribner and Sons, 1990), 56–60.
41. Spehr, *The Man*, 200, 203.
42. Ibid., 82–92.
43. Ibid., 61–64.
44. Ibid., 151–152.
45. Ibid., 382; Rossell, *Living Pictures*, 69–74.
46. Spehr, *The Man*, 236.
47. Musser, *Emergence*, 78.
48. Charles Musser, *Edison Motion Pictures, 1890–1900: An Annotated Filmography* (Pordenone, Italy: Le Giornate del Cinema Muto, 1997), 91–165.
49. Spehr, *The Man*, 388; Gordon Hendricks, *The Beginnings of the Biograph; The Story of the Invention of the Mutoscope and Biograph and Their Supply Camera* (New York: The Beginnings of American Film, 1964).
50. Musser, *Edison Motion Pictures*, 40–43; Spehr, *The Man*, 265–267.

51. Musser, *Emergence*, 91.
52. Ibid., 100–104.
53. Ibid., 103.
54. Gaudreault, *Film and Attraction*, 5–7.
55. Andre Bazin, "The Myth of Total Cinema," *What Is Cinema?*, vol. 1 (Berkeley: University of California Press, 1967), 22.
56. Mannoni, *The Great Art*, 464.

CHAPTER 3

EARLY CINEMA AND THE EMERGENCE OF TELEVISION
An Archaeology of Intertwined Media

DORON GALILI

Cinema's dominant role in the mediascape of modernity often obstructs the fact that film was not the only form of moving-image media conceived in the late nineteenth century. The same period also saw the initial speculations about the electrical transmission of moving images. As early as 1877, shortly after the introduction of the telephone, a number of electrical engineers in Europe and the US published technological designs and, in a few cases, even experimented with the construction of various devices that would capture images in one location, convert them to electric signals, transmit them at a distance, and reproduce them in a receiving apparatus. These pioneering efforts to realize image-transmitting media provided the technical and conceptual foundations for what we have come to call television, whose eventual public launch lagged decades behind the coming of cinema.[1] Regular television broadcasts started in the late 1930s and took the form of a mass media practice only in the postwar era. Ultimately, film and television came to typify the media culture of different moments in modernity and are now understood in terms of distinct sets of medium-specific properties. Even so, the same social, cultural, and scientific contexts informed the emergence of both media, rendering the intermedial consideration of their relationship integral to any study of cinema's origins. In this light, my aim in this essay is twofold. On the one hand, by drawing on media archaeological approaches, I wish to excavate, so to speak, an alternative trajectory of the emergence of cinema that highlights early cinema's relation to media of electrical transmission. Particularly, I wish to claim that while instantaneous transmission is commonly understood today as a medium-specific trait of electronic media (from radio and television broadcasting to the internet), in fact it finds itself historically intertwined with the origins of media of recording (such as phonography, and, of course, cinema). On the other hand, in demonstrating this historical interconnection, I shall also offer an assessment of how media archaeology's historiographical precepts may inform the study of early cinema today. I shall begin, therefore, with a short methodological detour.

Media Archaeology: Revolutionizing Film History, Again

Although the fundamental principles of the approach are still being debated, a growing number of studies of the origins of cinema in recent years have been conducted under the moniker of media archaeology. Even considering media archaeology as an approach is not always an obvious choice, as commentators on media archaeology also refer to it as "a bundle of closely related approaches," "a traveling discipline," "a field," and a "method."[2] According to Erkki Huhtamo, one of the method's pioneering practitioners, heterogeneity in approaches and incentives has characterized media archaeological projects from their very beginning. Even if most media archaeologists find themselves influenced by the work of Michel Foucault, they have developed differing interpretations of his archaeological method. Accordingly, it would be antithetical to the very approach to offer here a conclusive definition of media archaeology.[3] Instead, I will point to four principles worth highlighting.

First, media archaeology seeks to construct *non-linear* historical trajectories. It rejects narratives of progress leading from the "past" to the "present" in an evolutionary fashion, highlighting instead multiple points of origin and, correspondingly, multiple media-historical paths. Scholars like Huhtamo, for example, focus on tracing cyclical recurrences of cultural tropes across periods in various media histories, whereas for others, such as Thomas Elsaesser, media archaeology rather concerns historical discontinuities and ruptures.[4] Second, media archaeology examines *non-discursive* aspects of media. In the spirit of Marshall McLuhan, it focuses not on interpreting the messages (texts, films, programs, etc.) but on the material properties of media and the way media technologies interact with users. In recent years, for example, German media scholar Wolfgang Ernst has been pursuing his own variant of "radical media archaeology" that does not narrate media history per se but investigates the intrinsic operative temporalities of media devices.[5] Third, unlike most canonical media histories, media archaeology *rejects medium-specific* historiographies. It rarely revolves around a single medium and seeks instead to highlight intermedial connections, exchanges, and convergences. Finally, media archaeologists also consider among their objects of study *non-existent* media—that is, forgotten or obsolete technologies, failed experimental devices, and imaginary media that existed only in discourses and were never realized. For media archaeology, the conceptual makeup of such imaginary and failed media is productive for the writing of alternative media histories.

As several commentators have already noted, the revisionist aspiration of media archaeology brings to mind the similar ambition of early cinema scholars identified with the "historical turn" and the impact of the now-famous FIAF conference of 1978, which brought together film archivists and film scholars to closely examine films from the turn of the twentieth century and gave rise to an empirically grounded revisionist strand of cinema historiography.[6] There are several striking resemblances between how film scholars working in light of the historical turn have addressed the relationship between past and present media and how today's work in media archaeology frames such concerns. Since the 1990s, media archaeologists have aimed, at least in part, to challenge the notion of "new media" that has governed debates on digital technologies, and they have done so by embedding the discourse of the digital in a richer cultural and technological historical context. More than a decade earlier, scholars of early cinema aimed at undoing the designation of cinema's first decade as "primitive" by doing essentially the same—namely, by shedding light on the cultural context of modernity that gave rise to early cinematic technologies and practices. Similarly, we might understand both projects as driven by a will to explore possible futures of media and "roads not taken" in media history. Significantly, the archaeology metaphor itself was employed in a number of studies of so-called pre-cinema and early cinema years before the current popularization of media archaeology.[7] One might claim that early cinema scholars such as Charles Musser, Tom Gunning, Anne Friedberg, and Vanessa Schwartz had actually performed media archaeology before the fact by exploring cinema's multiple origins and complex intermedial connections.[8] Moreover, a number of commentators have retroactively labeled writings by theorist Walter Benjamin and filmmaker Sergei Eisenstein—two figures who had a significant impact on the theorizing of early cinema—as media archaeological in nature.[9]

What might the recent rise of interest in media archaeology mean for the study of cinema history, four decades after the historical turn? Media-archaeological tendencies are evident in recent scholarship that integrates the history of early cinema with other historical trajectories, the latter often extending to the present era of digital media. For example, Wanda Strauven's "revision of film history from the viewpoint of gaming" places the observer's tactile experience at the center, with cinema situated within archaeologies of the touch screen and of several play technologies, from nineteenth-century optical toys to post-cinematic video games.[10] Likewise, Lauren Rabinovitz, who does not evoke media archaeology explicitly but whose work shares many of the sensibilities of archaeologists, has also contributed to the study of alternative modes of spectatorship: she explores how early cinematic rides such as Hale's Tours correspond to the experience offered by earlier media forms of panoramic displays as well as to later attractions in the form of virtual reality rides.[11] More recently, Colin Williamson's archaeology of magic and the cinema makes an argument for "the long history of cinema as a device of wonder," drawing on "a constellation of 'old' and 'new' discourses, exhibition and reception practices, regimes of belief, and epistemic systems" from eighteenth-century magic shows to digital special effects.[12]

Thus, as the above examples make clear, media archaeology has proven a timely supplement to the study of film history. In the midst of today's growing interest across the humanities in visual culture, media change, and questions of materiality, media archaeology may help film history find a ready readership by incorporating cinema history into a broader and more inclusive historical and intermedial context. No less importantly, media archaeology's mindfulness of contemporary technologies and dynamics in the mediascape can extend the toolkit of the film historian. However, embedding film history in extended contexts that lead to the present state of media also involves a certain methodological risk. As Elsaesser has cautioned, substituting film history with media archaeology "could end up throwing the baby out with the bathwater." Increasingly broad historical frames of reference rooted in today's digital mediascape may, in Elsaesser's words, "bypass cinema altogether or marginalize it even further when focusing [. . .] on the origins and command (*arché*) of the digital media, and therefore concentrate mostly on electricity, electromagnetic waves, mathematics, algorithms as the material and conceptual infrastructures of contemporary media."[13]

Bearing in mind Elsaesser's observation about the potentially undesired implications of the turn to media archaeology, I present the following case study as an archaeological excavation of early phases in the history of electric (and thereby also of electronic and digital) visual media, which aims not to bypass but to *reframe* cinema's origins as they relate to their continuously altering mediascape. By revealing some of the earliest instances of interconnections between cinema and television, I intend this media archaeological exploration to not only shed more light on the media culture of the late nineteenth century but also interrogate some of the fundamental terms we use to conceptualize the distinctions between photographic and electronic moving images.

The Parallel Histories of Cinema and Television

In the late 1870s and early 1880s, when chronophotography pioneer Eadweard Muybridge and innovator of projected animated pictures Émile Reynaud demonstrated their respective media novelties that would later be christened "pre-cinematic," a group of technicians and electrical engineers engaged in a parallel effort to realize technologies for transmitting images at a distance. Readers of the June 1880 volume of *Scientific American*, for example, could find out about Muybridge's demonstration of projected animated photographs with his zoopraxiscope on one page, and two pages later about a new camera for "seeing by electricity," which utilized selenium as a light-sensitive element that could convert images to electric signals. Four years later—and still ahead of the introduction of the kinetoscope and the cinématographe—the key principle of scanning moving images was first introduced, when German inventor Paul Nipkow patented his "electrical telescope." Nipkow's model was based on rapid mechanical scanning of images captured by a camera and their conversion to a sequence of picture elements that, with the aid of a selenium cell, was designed to enable the transmission of moving images. While Nipkow was not able to fabricate a working prototype of his electrical telescope, the first experimental television models that were demonstrated in the mid-1920s relied precisely on such mechanical scanners.

The so-called speculative era in television history (which lasted up to the mid-1920s, when practical experimentation with visual broadcasting apparatuses began) saw the publication of imaginary depictions of moving-image transmission devices in countless utopian and science-fiction novels, cartoons, newspaper reports, and hoaxes.[14] Collectively, these texts articulated a vision of the future properties and utility of televisual media. Perhaps best known among these early fictional works, French author and cartoonist Albert Robida's 1882 novel *The Twentieth Century* is exemplary in conceptualizing a remarkably diverse range of televisual media. Robida envisions not only domestic small-screen sets but also large-screen outdoor public display systems and portable audiovisual devices. In its multiple formulations, television is utilized in the novel for long-distance audiovisual point-to-point communication, transmission of stage plays from theaters all over the world to people's living rooms, instantaneous dissemination of news reports, and display of commercials.[15]

During the previous turn of the century, then, moving-image technology was conceived in two distinct forms: the cinematic, which involved the capturing, inscription, and reanimation of photographs (or other kinds of pictures), and the televisual, which involved the conversion of images to electric signals and their reconstitution at a remote receiver. Commentators who witnessed the development of the two media forms around the turn of the twentieth century often understood them as conjoined or complementary. Yet the vast majority of histories of the coming of cinema and other accounts of nineteenth-century visual culture have not considered the place of early television history in the context of cinema's emergence. Focusing on photographic techniques, projection methods, and devices for animating images in particular, these studies have overlooked the failed experiments with moving-image transmission and the various imaginary formations of television in the nineteenth century, as if television ought to be considered a separate phenomenon altogether and part of a different historical lineage.[16] Even more tellingly, the few notable cases of media historians who have proposed novel historiographic observations about the relations between early cinema and the initial ideas of television ground their claims in a careful distinction between specific ontological traits of the two media.

Two influential works in media historiography merit more detailed description in this context: those of media historian William Uricchio and the pioneering media archaeology of Siegfried Zielinski. In a number of publications, Uricchio has explored the "competing temporalities" of film and television, which he understands to be, respectively, media of storage and of simultaneity.[17] Uricchio's account of the nineteenth-century technological imaginary highlights the cultural fascination with the idea of simultaneity or "liveness," as made evident by early responses to the telephone and the numerous fictional speculations about televisual technology. Having anticipated a medium for instantaneous transmission of images for several decades, Uricchio hypothesizes, the nineteenth-century public might have eventually met the storage medium of cinema with a sense of disappointment, since it fell short of fulfilling the promise of simultaneity that flourished in the media fantasies of electronic transmission. Uricchio thus suggests that instead of considering television as a post-cinematic medium, we may consider cinema as a detour in the history of television.

Zielinski discusses the concurrent projects of cinema and television in his 1989 book *Audiovisions*, one of the first works to propose media archaeology as a historiographic method, which presents itself as a contribution to an "integrated history of the media."[18] More accurately, one might call it "a history of media integration," since it narrates how cinema and television initially developed along parallel lines that started to converge with the rise of digital technologies. But Zielinski too presumes that cinema and television were initially ontologically distinct based on their temporal characteristics. As he puts it, "the two intrinsic targets of the projects were poles apart," since "in contradistinction to the preservation of images for the purpose of processing and presenting them [in the cinema], the lineage of television is concerned essentially with overcoming spatial distance without any loss of time," much as in the case of the telegraph and the telephone.[19] Accordingly, he titles one chapter of *Audiovisions* "Vanishing Point Cinema" and another "Vanishing Point Television?"

The accounts of Uricchio and Zielinski thus revise the standard versions of media histories by attending to the dualistic origins of nineteenth-century moving-image media, even as they invoke material and temporal characteristics to foreground medium-specific distinctions between film and television. In doing so, Uricchio and Zielinski seem to share a fundamental precept with Friedrich Kittler, another key figure in the formation of media archaeology. Kittler, unlike most film theorists who focus on the medium's representational or pictorial aspects, writes of cinema as first and foremost a storage medium. He understands film (along with the gramophone and the typewriter) as one of the modern technologies of inscription that ended the written alphabet's monopoly, allowing for novel ways to register the real—and facilitating new forms of human subjectivity and modes of perception.[20] In this view, cinema is indeed fundamentally distinct from moving-image transmission media such as television, as it belongs to a different technical and epistemic category altogether.

But how definitive are these basic categories for understanding cinema's and television's origins? What if considering these distinctions in fact obscures crucial dynamics at play in the emergence of the two media? Can we—from the perspective of media archaeology's interests in temporality, intermediality, and imagined conceptions of media—revisit these historiographic accounts and think across the dividing lines between storage and transmission, recording and liveness? With respect to contemporary digital media, this seems perfectly feasible. As Wolfgang Ernst notes about the temporality of digital media operations such as buffering transferred data or streaming video-on-demand, "The choice between storage versus transfer, once so useful for the analysis of cultural communication [. . .] becomes obsolescent. It turns out that storage is nothing but a limit value of transfer. Seen from a media-archaeological perspective, transfer and storage are two sides of one coin: storage is a transfer across a temporal distance."[21] Other scholars of digital media, such as Wendy Chun and Matthew Kirschenbaum, have also written about the interplay between storing and communicating data in computer networks.[22] Exploring an earlier historical moment, television historian Anne-Katrin Weber has recently demonstrated how television broadcasting apparatuses from the interwar era made use of film technologies, thereby forming a hybrid medium and violating the distinction between recording and transmission before the age of videotape equipment.[23]

I would argue that media practices that disprove the mutually exclusive dichotomy between storage and transmission existed already in the earliest periods of modern media history. A careful exploration of the nineteenth-century mediascape proves that, even then, media for recording and media for transmission were often integrally linked both in practice and in the discourse that surrounded them. To be sure, I am not suggesting that the storage/transmission and recording/liveness distinctions are false. In terms of media ontologies, they certainly are not. A telephone wire cannot record texts, and a celluloid sheet cannot relay signals at a distance. But when we think beyond the technological basis and consider instead the overall media *systems* in question, we more often than not find hybrid forms or amalgamations of mechanisms and cultural procedures where different technical operations overlap. These instances, in turn, should be taken as challenges to media theory and historiography that demand reconsideration of, among other issues, the origins of cinematic and televisual moving-image media.

Recording and Transmission from an Archaeological Perspective

Take for example, the telegraph and the phonograph, two nineteenth-century media inventions and preeminent technologies of transmission and recording, respectively. The telegraph has been celebrated as bringing about the "annihilation of space and time" with its ability to convey messages at great distances and at unprecedented speed. Telegraph networks for the first time effectively separated communication from transportation and conducted telecommunications by sending along the wires electric signals that represented textual messages.[24] In the nineteenth-century imaginary they were considered analogous to the nervous system, which similarly coordinates seemingly instantaneous transmission of nerve signals in the body.

Nevertheless, as John Durham Peters has shown, the case of the telegraph demonstrates how the media functions of transmission (the overcoming of space) and recording (the overcoming of time) may be seen as interconvertible, since "to send a message across a distance required some means of preserving it from decay."[25] Telegraph transmission networks could not function as efficient long-distance communication if their expansive systems did not incorporate inscription technologies. Early in the history of the medium, it became evident that electric signals grow weaker when sent at a great distance, and so it was impractical to operate transmission lines at great lengths. As a solution, repeater stations that receive and resend messages were required at intermediate points. One of Thomas Edison's first major inventions in electrical communication was an automated telegraph repeater. Designed to spare telegraph services from employing clerks to resend messages at intermediate stations, the Edison repeater recorded telegraphic messages in the form of indentations on a sheet of paper wrapped around a cylinder, which could subsequently be traced by a stylus that resent the identical telegraphic signals. The repeater, therefore, was at once a recording device and a transmission device, which, by means of writing, made long-distance communication possible.

In a similar fashion, Samuel Morse's telegraph system became the most prominent of its kind because of its introduction of a writing mechanism that inscribed traces of the telegraphed message on paper. Known initially as the "recording telegraph," Morse's apparatus included this simple yet advantageous feature, which freed operators from the need to transcribe messages in real time and made it possible to store messages and deliver them at any time. Once again, introducing writing devices to the transmission system proved invaluable. Even the etymology of the word "telegraph" indicates its dual affinity with inscription ("graph") and relaying at a distance ("tele").[26]

Nineteenth-century discourses on telegraphy also drew parallels with recording media such as photography, sometimes referring to them as if they were synonymous. For example, in 1853, protospiritualist author Andrew Jackson Davis wrote about the telepathic connection between a mother and son, noting that "the actual condition of the son is *daguerreotyped* upon the mother's brain—*telegraphed*, so to speak, or impressed, as perfectly as any object can be painted."[27] For the spiritualists, the telegraph was a medium of great importance because of its capacity to transmit imperceptible signals, which in their view challenged the distinction between absence and presence. But as Jackson Davis's comment proves, the telegraph's capacity to inscribe, even if used only metaphorically, also suited the spiritualist discourse.

The phonograph's relation to transmission media has already been extensively commented upon, notably by scholars like Kittler and Lisa Gitelman, who (from very different perspectives) have discussed phonography as the quintessential writing and storage technology. In their accounts, the phonograph's emergence is indebted to Edison's work on transmission devices. As Kittler puts it, the phonograph "was a by-product of the attempt to optimize telephony and telegraphy by saving expensive copper cables."[28] Furthermore, the phonograph itself shortly became part of a transmission apparatus or a communication system on its own. In 1878, a booklet about Edison's invention mentions "long-distance phonographs"—a concept that today sounds plainly impossible but in Edison's mind was an instrument for the amplification of phonographic recordings that intended to enable signal stations and lighthouses to communicate weather warnings regarding visibility conditions. The booklet argued that with this device's ability to project recorded voices, "the words of warning may be distinctly heard, far above the roar of winds and waves, for a distance from four to eight miles."[29] In 1900, a different formulation of long-distance phonographs emerged, this time signifying the employment of the phonograph as a telephonic repeater, which was intended to increase the range of telephone connection by recording spoken messages and resending their reproduction at a distance.[30] In this deployment of phonography, once again, the transmission medium of telephony incorporates a storage medium into an expanded, hybrid media system.

The modern mediascape that gave rise to the cinema was composed, therefore, of various forms of combination and hybridization of storage and transmission technologies. Thus, even if the kinetoscope was invented, according to Edison's famous claim, as a recording medium in order to "do for the eye what the phonograph does for the ear," we must recall that the phonograph itself belonged within entangled historical lineages that affiliated it with transmission media. In light of this, let us turn to an examination of how nineteenth-century notions regarding recording and transmission came into play in some of the earliest ideas about television.

Excavating *The Great Inventions of the Twentieth Century*

The 1893 pamphlet *A Glance at the Great Inventions of the Twentieth Century: The Future of Electrical Television* (*Ein Blick auf die grossen Erfindungen des zwanzigsten Jahrhunderts: Die Zukunft des elektrischen Fernsehens*) is something of an anomaly among the substantial body of texts published about television in the late nineteenth century, being neither a strictly technical text nor a literary work of futuristic science fiction.[31] Written by former Prussian officer Maximilian Plessner on the eve of Edison's first announcement of the kinetoscope, the pamphlet presents itself as a resource that intends to inspire and inform further inventions in the field. It includes reports on past and current scientific experiments with the transmission of images, as well as notes on further possibilities for such media forms. We may thus read Plessner's text as a sort of real-time archaeology of television. It places the emergent medium within the context of its various connections to other existing and imaginary media and offers speculations about its future configurations, including the conversion of television into a recording medium.

Like many other commentators of his time, Plessner starts *The Great Inventions* by imagining television as a complement to the telegraph and the telephone that would work in conjunction with existing networks and add a visual dimension to long-distance communications.[32] In his description of possible iterations of the television apparatus, he similarly refers to telephone technology and several existing schemes for still-image transmission as potential models. Most of all, however, he draws his inspiration from Alexander Graham Bell's subsequent invention of the photophone, a wireless telephony system that used a selenium cell to convert sound to electric current and transmit it in the form of light rays. Following the design of the photophone, Plessner describes a television apparatus that would consist of a camera obscura with a rapidly rotating scanner and a selenium cell at its focal point to convert discrete areas of the captured images into electric signals. Plessner suggests other possible uses of television, including several that depart from the telephonic configuration of two-way point-to-point communication to anticipate mass-media practices like the transmission of news reports, races, and parliamentary debates, as well as medical and law-enforcement applications. Writing before the introduction of the cinematograph and the kinetoscope, he muses on the possibilities of electrical long-distance transmission technologies for democratizing culture and the arts and foresees that in the future the transmission of stage performances from the world's best theaters will reach masses of viewers in every small province. For Plessner, the invention of television thus signifies a possibility to counter the "further depopulation of the provinces and the uncontrollable growth of the cities."[33] When information and culture are simultaneously disseminated everywhere, some of the advantages of modern big-city life will disappear.

Plessner openly admits that his proposals for television technology might fail (and indeed, according to the available historical record, he was not involved in any successful experimentation with television or the other technologies he discusses in this publication). But as he notes, experiments with such technologies are still worth the time and the effort since they will inevitably lead to other technical possibilities along the way. Explicitly holding to a Darwinian perspective on technological developments, he appears to be just as interested in future "ancillary discoveries" and offshoot inventions that might emerge from ongoing experiments with image transmission as in the prospects of television itself—perhaps even more.[34] *The Great Inventions* includes descriptions of no fewer than a dozen futuristic media and technological combinations that employ in novel ways the television apparatus's "seleno-magnetic" principles of converting light into electric current, including several imaginative devices for the conversion of images to sounds and of sounds to images.[35] Yet, what Plessner considers to be the culmination of coming developments in media technology—or, in his words, the "most excellent of all possible manmade instruments"—is a recording apparatus he dubs the hyaloscope.[36]

The purpose of the hyaloscope is virtually identical to that of Edison's kinetophone (a combination of the kinetoscope and the phonograph)—that is, in Plessner's words, "the capturing and unleashing of ephemeral light and sound phenomena."[37] As an addendum to the pamphlet reveals, Plessner was aware of Edison's work and his plan to exhibit a motion picture device at the Chicago Exposition. But the hyaloscope is radically different from Edison's film apparatus. First, it was conceived as a projection device rather than a peep-hole machine like the kinetoscope. Moreover, Plessner did not envision it as a device for capturing and reanimating photographs but rather as a "telectroscopic recording apparatus."[38] The technical principle of the hyaloscope is simple: if television technology allows for visual information to be instantaneously transmitted in the form of electrical signals, then the signals themselves may also be recorded photographically. According to Plessner's description, the hyaloscope—when realized—would consist of a series of selenium cells that convert light impressions to electric signals. Yet instead of transmitting the electrical signals, as in television systems, the hyaloscope would inscribe them in the form of a "spiraling band of lines of varying transparency" on a large glass cylinder coated with photosensitive material.[39] For the retrieval of the visual recordings, the cylinder would be lit from the inside, so that varying amounts of light would shine through the spiraling lines onto corresponding seleno-photographic playback instruments; these, in turn, would reproduce the images and project them onto a polished plate the size of a theater curtain. According to Plessner, this arrangement would be supplemented with a second cylinder, similarly arranged, onto which the hyaloscope would inscribe sound using the same technique. Overall, he notes, the two cylinders could allow for hours of continuous audiovisual recording and display.

The technological design of the hyaloscope, therefore, rejects the use of existing techniques of phonography and serial photography and instead relies on the photoconductive properties of the selenium cell, then in development as part of the early experiments into television technology. The hyaloscope inscribes not the sound or light phenomena themselves but rather sequences of electric signals that represent the recorded audiovisual information. In this sense, Plessner's argument for the superior fidelity of the seleno-photographic method runs counter to the more familiar claims for the truth-value of phonographic sound recording and the photographic image. As Plessner comments about the case of phonographic sound recording, "any playback of sound waves through mechanical means must be considered erroneous, and in its place attempts must be made to utilize an imponderable medium, such as light," because, in his view, the phonograph stylus is too bulky (compared to a ray of light) and, as such, proves inherently defective.[40] The use of the seleno-photographic method, for Plessner, guarantees that the hyaloscope recordings will have "a totally realistic effect," which will satisfy the desire of future generations to see and hear the big events of the past as if reflected in a mirror.[41]

The tone of Plessner's musing on future media reaches its most utopian mode in discussing the possible uses and effects of the hyaloscope. Here, his bold ideas about the democratizing effects of the instantaneous transmission of information and entertainment make way for a celebration of audiovisual storage media. Plessner appears to consider the hyaloscope primarily as a carrier of authentic documentation of the past free from inaccuracies and historical fraud. He predicts that the imaginary medium will be able to store recordings of sound and images for centuries and thereby partake in the shaping of historical consciousness. Tellingly, Plessner illustrates the potential of the hyaloscope by inviting his readers to imagine a scene in which spectators of the future witness a reproduction of the victory parade that marked the end of the Franco-Prussian war of 1871. Showing this particular spectacle on days of remembrance and jubilee events, he writes, "would contribute greatly to keeping the memory alive of the great era of the re-establishment of the German Reich."[42]

Plessner attempts to speculate also on the audience's emotional and ideological response to the spectacle of the hyaloscope projection. He describes their fascination with the recorded sounds of cheers and bells ringing and the sight of all the details of the parade that would appear on the screen, noting how their gaze would move among the images of historical figures such as the Kaiser, his son, the military strategist Helmuth von Moltke, and Chancellor Bismarck. "At this sight," Plessner notes, "indescribable sentiments would move the hearts of the shaken spectators; the anxiety that had troubled their souls would melt away."[43] Ninety years before Benedict Anderson coined the term *imagined community*, Plessner argues that the historical spectacle "would strengthen Germans' sense of belonging to a great unified state, and remind our descendants to develop national feeling into a domineering political instinct."[44] The effect of unification, furthermore, not only connects the audience of the future to their fellow Germans but also to the historical figures on the screen, as "their enthusiastic cheers would unite with the roaring hurrah from the kingdom of shadows (*dem Reiche der Schatten*) to form an overwhelming cry of celebration, in which the voices of the living could no longer be distinguished from those of the dead."[45] Plessner concludes this imaginary description by noting that while "the gaze of the smitten spectators could still revel in the richly decorated boulevard with its swarming and joyous masses," the hyaloscope projection would come to an end with "the intrusion of bright daylight into the enormous space of the dark arena [bringing] them back to the present."[46]

Overall, the discussion of the hyaloscope in *A Glance at the Great Inventions of the Twentieth Century* prefigures a number of arguments that became common in debates about cinema around the turn of the previous century—including, notably, those that are typically made about the properties of the cinematic apparatus itself. Not only does Plessner foreground the vivid and accurate nature of the moving images reproduced by his imaginary medium and suggest synching them with recorded sound, he also claims that the hyaloscope will give its spectators the feeling they are transported by a time machine, as some authors claimed early film would also do.[47] In addition, Plessner stresses the recording medium's importance primarily as a carrier of historical documents from the national past. By elaborating on how the hyaloscope can preserve fleeting moments of note for posterity, Plessner foreshadows discourses about film's historiographic value such as Bolesław Matuszewski's well-known assertion from 1898 that cinema shall become "A New Source of History" that must be preserved for the future.[48] Notably, the reference to the diegetic world of the historical scene as "the kingdom of shadows" also prefigures (in a manner that is apt to be called uncanny) the same trope Maxim Gorky used to convey the alien nature of filmic images in his classic account of his first experience at the cinema.[49]

Plessner, in sum, anticipated a great deal of what concerns the first witnesses of early cinema. Yet, he did not write about a cinematic apparatus as we have come to know it but about an electrical moving-image recording medium that he conceived of as an offshoot of the emerging technology of television and as an auxiliary that could be connected to a television apparatus to increase its capacity. To borrow a term from André Gaudreault and Philippe Marion's discussion of the invention of cinema, the hyaloscope may therefore be considered an *extension* of television.[50] As television historian André Lange suggests, Plessner's writings on the hyaloscope may be the first conception not of film but of what later would become known as the VCR.[51] Therefore, in much the same way that nineteenth-century technologies of recording and transmission were often developed in conjunction with one another, Plessner's text exemplifies how the discourses that surrounded the emergence of television and those that pertained to early cinema did not necessarily belong to distinct media-historical trajectories dictated by their respective materialities. Rather, they prove to be inextricable.

Conclusion

In this essay, I have attempted to make a case for the merit of applying media archaeological approaches to the study of early moving-image technologies in order to reveal early and largely forgotten connections between recording and transmission media. The archaeological approach does not simply call for revealing forgotten alternative media formations and antiquated technologies. More fundamentally, it requires us to take into consideration various different discourses and technologies (including non-visual media) and to be attentive to intermedial exchanges, imaginary conceptions of media, and the material dimensions of media devices. In the case presented here, the archaeological approach effectively challenges existing media historiographies by remapping media contexts and linking the emergence of cinema to the history of television.

In closing, I shall return to Elsaesser's cautionary words cited above. As this essay has shown, rather than marginalizing the place of cinema (and particularly of cinema's novelty period) in favor of the eventual development of digital media, media archaeology offers an opportunity to undermine the break between (photochemical) cinema and (electronic or digital) post-cinema. In doing so, it allows us to better perceive how cinema history is intertwined with various other technical and cultural media histories. As I have shown, although since the 1990s electronic media have come to signify post-filmic technologies that have gradually taken over cinema's dominant position in the modern mediascape, both cinema and electrical transmission media have their origins in the same historical moment. The culture of nineteenth-century modernity gave rise to two independent and competing imaginaries: one driven by an archival impulse and fantasies of perfected and limitless storage, the other by the desire for instantaneity and the annihilation of space and time. Both imaginaries, in turn, informed how different moving-image media devices were conceived. However, as the example of Plessner's text makes clear, there were no clear-cut distinctions between the different media forms: considerations of each might have provided the conditions for the rise of the other. In the complex ecology of the nineteenth-century mediascape, recording and transmission media often—and inevitably—implied the other.[52] In this light, we may view the era's conception of television as a medium for moving-image transmission as one of the many points of origin for the history of cinema. While in his archaeology of audiovisual media Zielinski traces the two respective "vanishing points" of cinema and television, I argue here for a different optical analogy: would it not be more apt to view both lineages of cinema and television simultaneously, as if through a stereoscope, so that the two vanishing points appear blended together, forming a three-dimensional picture of media history?

Notes

1. For a concise account of the earliest technological schemes for moving-image transmission, see George Shiers "Historical Notes on Television before 1900," *SMPTE Journal* 86, no. 3 (March 1977): 129–137.
2. Erkki Huhtamo and Jussi Parikka, eds., *Media Archaeology: Approaches, Applications, and Implications* (Berkeley: University of California Press, 2011), 2–3; Jussi Parikka, *What is Media Archaeology?* (Cambridge, UK: Polity Press, 2012), 2.
3. A considerable number of review essays and programmatic articles, as well as a recent book-length introduction to media archaeology, have already traced insightfully the intricacies of the approach. See Huhtamo and Parikka, eds., *Media Archaeology*; Jussi Parikka, *What is Media Archaeology?*; Michael Goddard, "Opening Up the Black Boxes: Media Archaeology, 'Anarchaeology' and Media Materiality," *New Media & Society* 17, no. 11 (2015): 1–16; Wanda Strauven, "Media Archaeology: Where Film History, Media Art, and New Media (Can) Meet," in Julia Noordegraaf, Cosetta Saba, Barbara Le Maitre, and Vinzenz Hediger, eds., *Preserving and Exhibiting Media Art: Challenges and Perspectives* (Amsterdam: Amsterdam University Press, 2013), 59–80; and Simone Natale, "Understanding Media Archaeology," *Canadian Journal of Communication* 37 (2012): 523–527.
4. Erkki Huhtamo, *Illusions in Motion: Media Archaeology of the Moving Panorama and Related Spectacles* (Cambridge, MA: MIT Press, 2013); Thomas Elsaesser, *Film History as Media Archaeology: Tracking Digital Cinema* (Amsterdam: Amsterdam University Press, 2016).
5. See Wolfgang Ernst, *Digital Memory and the Archive* (Minneapolis: University of Minnesota Press, 2012).
6. Papers presented at the 1978 FIAF conference were published in Roger Holman, ed., *Cinema 1900–1906: An Analytical Study by the National Film Archives (London) and the International Federation of Film Archives* (Brussels: FIAF, 1982). See also Eileen Bowser, "The Brighton Project: An Introduction," *Quarterly Review of Film Studies* 4, no. 4 (1979): 509–538, and Jon Gartenberg, "The Brighton Project: The Archives and Research," *Iris* 2, no. 1 (1984): 5–16. For a later retrospection of the conference's impact, see Tom Gunning, "A Quarter of Century Later: Is Early Cinema Still Early?" *Kintop* 12 (2003): 17–31.
7. See, for example, the special volume of *Quarterly Review of Film Studies* on "Archaeology of Cinema" (Winter 1984) and Laurent Mannoni's influential volume on early visual media, *The Great Art of Light and Shadow: Archaeology of the Cinema* (Exeter, UK: University of Exeter Press, 2000). In addition, Tom Gunning evoked the notion of "the history and archaeology of the film spectator" in a footnote to his seminal article on the cinema of attractions; Thomas Elsaesser discussed early cinema scholarship under the heading "From Linear History to Mass Media Archaeology"; and William Uricchio noted the need to pursue "an archaeology of vision" in the context of early non-fiction film. See Gunning, "The Cinema of Attraction: Early Film, Its Spectator and the Avant-Garde," *Wide Angle* 6, no. 2 (1986): 70n2; Elsaesser, ed., *Early Cinema: Space, Frame, Narrative* (London: BFI, 1990), 1; and William Uricchio, "Ways of Seeing: The New Vision of Early Nonfiction Film," in Daan Hertogs and Nico De Klerk, eds., *Uncharted Territory: Essays on Early Nonfiction Film* (Amsterdam: Stichting Nederlands Filmmuseum 1997), 123.
8. I am referring here, for example, to Charles Musser, "Towards a History of Screen Practice," *Quarterly Review of Film Studies* 3, no. 1 (Winter 1984): 59–69; Tom Gunning, "Doing for the Eye What the Phonograph Does for the Ear," in Rick Altman and Richard

Abel, eds., *The Sounds of Early Cinema* (Bloomington: Indiana University Press, 2001), 13–31; Anne Friedberg, *Window Shopping: Cinema and the Postmodern* (Berkeley: University of California Press, 1993); and Vanessa R. Schwartz, *Spectacular Realities: Early Mass Culture in Fin-de-Siècle Paris* (Berkeley: University of California Press, 1998). Indeed, both Gunning and Musser have recently acknowledged the connections between their respective works and media archaeology. See Gunning, "Hand and Eye: Excavating a New Technology of the Image in the Victorian Era," *Victorian Studies* 54, no. 3 (Spring 2012): 513, and Musser, *Politicking and Emergent Media: U.S. Presidential Elections of the 1890s* (Berkeley: University of California Press, 2016), 170–190.

9. See Huhtamo and Parikka, "Introduction: An Archaeology of Media Archaeology," in Huhtamo and Parikka, eds., *Media Archaeology*, 6–7, and Antonio Somaini, "Cinema as 'Dynamic Mummification,' History as Montage: Eisenstein's Media Archaeology," in Naum Kleiman and Antonio Somaini, eds., *Sergei M. Eisenstein: Notes for a General History of Cinema* (Amsterdam: Amsterdam University Press, 2016), 19–105.

10. Wanda Strauven, "The Observer's Dilemma: To Touch or Not to Touch," in Huhtamo and Parikka, eds., *Media Archaeology*, 148.

11. See Lauran Rabinovitz, *Electric Dreamland: Amusement Parks, Movies, and American Modernity* (New York: Columbia University Press, 2012), 66–95, and "From Hale's Tours to Star Tours: Virtual Voyages, Travel Ride Films, and the Delirium of the Hyper-Real," in Jeffrey Ruoff, ed., *Virtual Voyages: Cinema and Travel* (Durham, NC: Duke University Press, 2006), 42–60.

12. Colin Williamson, *Hidden in Plain Sight: An Archaeology of Magic and the Cinema* (New Brunswick, NJ: Rutgers University Press, 2015), 19.

13. Elsaesser, *Film History as Media Archaeology*, 26.

14. For a more expansive account of television history's speculative era, see Doron Galili, *Seeing by Electricity: The Emergence of Television, 1878–1939* (Durham, NC: Duke University Press, 2020), part 1.

15. Albert Robida, *The Twentieth Century* (Middletown, CT: Wesleyan University Press, 2004).

16. See, for example, Mannoni, *The Great Art of Light and Shadow*, and Deac Rossell, *Living Pictures: The Origins of the Movies* (Albany, NY: SUNY Press, 1998).

17. William Uricchio, "Storage, Simultaneity, and the Media Technologies of Modernity," in Jan Olsson and John Fullerton, eds., *Allegories of Communication: Intermedial Concerns from Cinema to the Digital* (Eastleigh, UK: John Libbey, 2004): 123–138.

18. Siegfried Zielinski, *Audiovisionen: Kino und Fernsehen als Zwischenspiele in der Geschichte* (Reinbek, Germany: Rowohlt, 1989). For the English translation see *Audiovisions: Cinema and Television as Entr'actes in History* (Amsterdam: Amsterdam University Press, 1999).

19. Zielinski, *Audiovisions*, 59.

20. Friedrich Kittler, *Gramophone, Film, Typewriter* (Stanford, CA: Stanford University Press, 1997).

21. Ernst, *Digital Memory and the Archive*, 100.

22. Wendy Hui Kyong Chun, "The Enduring Ephemeral, or the Future Is a Memory," *Critical Inquiry* 35 (Autumn 2008): 148–171, and Matthew Kirschenbaum, *Mechanisms: New Media and the Forensic Imagination* (Cambridge, MA: MIT University Press, 2008).

23. Anne-Katrin Weber, "Recording on Film, Transmitting by Signals: The Intermediate Film System and Television's Hybridity in the Interwar Period," *Grey Room* 56 (Summer 2014): 6–33.

24. For this observation and an overall eye-opening discussion of the telegraph see James Carey, "Technology and Ideology: The Case of the Telegraph," in his *Communication as Culture: Essays on Media and Society* (New York: Routledge, 1992), 155–177.
25. John Durham Peters, "Technology and Ideology: The Case of the Telegraph Revisited," in Jeremy Packer and Craig Robertson, eds., *Thinking with James Carey: Essays on Communications, Transportation, History* (New York: Peter Lang, 2006), 144. See also Peters, *Speaking into the Air: A History of the Idea of Communication* (Chicago, IL: University of Chicago Press, 1999), 137–164.
26. Peters, "Technology and Ideology," 143.
27. Quoted in Simone Natale, "Photography and Communication Media in the Nineteenth Century," *History of Photography* 36, no. 4 (November 2012): 452 (emphasis added).
28. Kittler, *Gramophone, Film, Typewriter*, 27. See also Lisa Gitelman, *Always Already New: Media, History, and the Data of Culture* (Cambridge, MA: MIT Press, 2006), 25.
29. Frederick Garbit, *The Phonograph and Its Inventor Thomas Alva Edison* (Boston, MA: Gunn Bliss, 1878), 15. As Jonathan Sterne has noted, this instrument is unlikely to have existed. See Sterne, *The Audible Past: Cultural Origins of Sound Reproduction* (Durham, NC: Duke University Press, 2003), 401n124.
30. "Long-Distance Phonographs," *The Literary Digest*, January 20, 1900, 82.
31. Maximilian Plessner, *Ein Blick auf die grossen Erfindungen des zwanzigsten Jahrhunderts I: Die Zukunft des elektrischen Fernsehens* (Berlin: F. Dümmler, 1892 [1893]). Although the pamphlet is dated 1892, I follow scholar Nils Klevier Aas in considering it here as an 1893 publication. For Aas's immensely useful abstract and commentary on the pamphlet, see his "Translation, Abstracts and Comments" (2002), http://histv.free.fr/plessner/plessner.pdf.
32. Plessner uses the German word *Fernsehen*, which I discuss here as "television," although the latter word was coined only in 1900.
33. Plessner, *Ein Blick*, 47 (quoted in Aas, "Translation, Abstracts and Comments").
34. Ibid., 48 (quoted in Aas, "Translation, Abstracts and Comments").
35. I discuss these imaginary media inventions in more detail in "Postmediales Wissen um 1900: Zur Medienarchäologie des Fernsehens," *Montage A/V* 25, no. 2 (2016): 187–190.
36. Plessner, *Ein Blick*, 70 (unless noted otherwise, all of the following quotes from Plessner are from an unpublished translation by Alex Bush).
37. Ibid., 70.
38. Ibid., 68.
39. Ibid.
40. Plessner quoted in Aas, "Translation, Abstracts and Comments."
41. Plessner, *Ein Blick*, 69.
42. Ibid., 72.
43. Ibid., 73.
44. Ibid., 72. On the concept of imagined community, see Benedict Anderson, *Imagined Communities: Reflections on the Origin and Spread of Nationalism* (London: Verso, 1991).
45. Plessner, *Ein Blick*, 73.
46. Ibid., 73–74.
47. See, for instance, Brander Matthews's story "The Kinetoscope of Time," *Scribner's Magazine* 18, no. 6 (December 1895): 733–744, and Mary Ann Doane's discussion of it in *The Emergence of Cinematic Time: Modernity, Contingency, the Archive* (Cambridge, MA: Harvard University Press, 2002), 1–3.

48. Bolesław Matuszewski, "A New Source of History," *Film History* 7, no. 3 (Autumn 1995): 322–324. On early cinema and the archival imaginary, see also Paula Amad, *Counter-Archive: Film, the Everyday, and Albert Kahn's Archives de la Planète* (New York: Columbia University Press, 2010), and, for the German context, Anton Kaes, Nicholas Baer, and Michael Cowan, eds., *The Promise of Cinema: German Film Theory 1907–1933* (Berkeley: University of California Press, 2016), chap. 3, "The Time Machine," 74–107.
49. Maxim Gorky, "Last Night I Was in the Kingdom of Shadows," in Colin Harding and Simon Popple, eds., *In the Kingdom of Shadows: A Companion to Early Cinema* (London: Cygnus Arts, 1996), 5–6.
50. André Gaudreault and Philippe Marion, "A Medium Is Always Born Twice . . . ," *Early Popular Visual Culture* 3, no. 1 (May 2005): 3–15.
51. See André Lange's introductory notes to Aas, "Translation, Abstracts and Comments."
52. Peters, "Technology and Ideology," 144.

CHAPTER 4

THE RIGHT TO ONE'S OWN IMAGE

Animism, The Student of Prague, *and Legal Doctrine*

STEFAN ANDRIOPOULOS

IN 1913, the German film industry released two "photoplays," which are often described as the first German "art films."[1] Both movies, Hanns Heinz Ewers's *The Student of Prague* and Max Mack's *The Other*, presented stories about split personalities and sinister doubles to their audiences—stories that can also be read as meta-cinematic reflections on the precarious and contested status of the moving image at that time. Mack's *The Other* (*Der Andere*), which had its opening night in the Berliner Lichtspiele on January 21, was based on a play by the literary author Paul Lindau and generated considerable attention, since an extremely well-known theater actor played the leading role.[2] Albert Bassermann, who worked with Max Reinhardt in the Deutsches Theater, had previously received the most prestigious prize for acting, the so-called Iffland-Ring. Most theater critics seized the opportunity to see the famous stage actor onscreen so that on the days following the opening night, Germany's major newspapers printed film reviews in their art sections for the first time. It was an enormous gain in cultural prestige for the photoplay, even if many critics condemned what they called Bassermann's "escapade" or felt compelled to assert that Bassermann's acting was "art" despite the cinematic medium.[3]

The disreputable status frequently assigned to cinema also comes to the fore in an essay by the conservative cultural critic Hermann Duenschmann, who in 1912—just one year earlier—had demanded: "Whoever has worked for the movies, must be excluded from the actors' guild."[4] Contrasting theater and film, Duenschmann emphasized cinema's "fateful factor of mechanical [. . .] reproduction," which he considered as "all but pernicious for the actor."[5] In strangely nationalist and highly dramatic terms, Duenschmann deplored the movie actor's loss of control over his or her artistic creation, warning that the photoplay's images could be presented to an anonymous, even foreign, crowd of millions: "Anybody who has a heart in his body to feel what it means to exhibit oneself in this way will understand why the actors in the photoplay prefer not to have their names revealed, [. . .] why all of our famous dramatic artists, male or female, reject such offers with indignation, despite steep financial incentives."[6]

The release of *The Other* proved Duenschmann wrong in his assessment that no recognized theater actor would be willing to act in a film, thereby marking an extraordinary success for the so-called Kunst- or Autorenfilm. Yet, the widespread perception that Bassermann sold his soul in signing a film contract was also echoed in a 1913 letter by Franz Kafka to Felice Bauer. After describing to his fiancée film posters from the lobby of a Prague movie theater, Kafka concludes: "B. [. . .] has lent himself to something beneath him." Kafka imagines Bassermann after the shooting of the film as "the unhappiest man." He continues: "The satisfaction of acting is over. [. . .] The film is made. B. himself can no longer influence it in any way. [. . .] Watching the film, [. . .] he grows older, weak, gets pushed aside in his armchair, vanishing somewhere into the mists of time."[7] The letter emphasizes the split between actor and cinematic image, nearly replicating the film's plot of a district attorney who, in a somnambulist state, splits off into a "double being" that commits crimes diametrically opposed to his character.[8]

Albert Bassermann's participation in this motion picture was even more surprising, since in the years before he himself had been vehemently opposed to being filmed or photographed. His biographer Julius Bab describes an "extremely unusual fanaticism in [Bassermann's] fight against being photographed"—an aversion to photography that went so far that Bassermann sued a journalist for secretly taking a picture of him and publishing it without his consent.[9] Claiming the "right to his own image"—*das Recht am eigenen Bild*—Bassermann pursued this case through numerous appeals until he finally succeeded in his demand that all prints of the stolen photo and its negative be destroyed.[10]

The legal doctrine of a specific "right to one's own image" emerged within German legal theory at the very moment when the Lumière brothers first presented the projection of moving images to an astounded audience. The juridical scholar Hugo Keyssner gave two talks on *das Recht am eigenen Bilde* in 1895 before publishing a treatise under the same title in 1896. While he never explicitly mentioned cinema, Keyssner did refer to the technological advances that led to the possibility of instantaneous photographs and vigorously advocated a legal protection against what he called "the electrical light of publicity."[11] At a time when the first moving images were being projected, and shortly after the introduction of snapshot photography and celluloid film had engendered an unprecedented dissemination of photographic portraits, Keyssner maintained that everybody should have complete control over their image.[12]

In the first part of his book, Keyssner conceived of the photographed person as the "author" (*Urheber*) of his or her image, thereby ascribing the property (*Eigentum*) or copyright of the image to the human being from whom it has been "extracted" (*entnommen*).[13] Yet, the subsequent chapters, which proved much more influential on turn-of-the-century legal debates, left behind the discussion of property rights by appealing to categories that belong to the realm of "personality rights" (*Persönlichkeitsrecht*). While the American "right to privacy" was formulated in the

1890s for the same purpose of banning the "unauthorized circulation of portraits," the German *Persönlichkeitsrecht* was defined in terms neither of privacy nor of property or material possession.[14] Instead, juridical theorists invoked an analogy to the "right to one's own name" and even to the "right to one's own body."[15] The right to one's own image therefore referred not to external possessions but to inalienable and possibly immaterial parts of one's own personality.

Yet, what is peculiar about this legal solution for how to establish a "right to one's own image" is that it concurrently introduced a split into the individual, since there must be a distinction between the holder of a right and its object. As Keyssner wrote succinctly: "The ego, as subject, stands in opposition to the personality, the body, as object."[16] And the juridical scholar Josef Kohler described this split in Faustian terms that resemble Jacques Lacan's theory of the mirror stage:

> Today few call the personality right itself into question; we are no longer affected by the scholastic skepticism that holds there can be no right to one's own personality, because the object of the right is lacking, because subject and object coincide. For everybody knows that two souls inhabit our chest and that one constantly confronts one's own ego as a subject. [...] The moment in which the child realizes this distinction and recognizes its own ego is one of the most important steps within the development of individuality. [...] This split can also enter into the law: the subject-ego is sufficient as the legal subject, the object-ego as the legal object.[17]

The distinction between "subject-ego" and "object-ego," made in a legal text from 1903, seems to anticipate psychoanalytic film theory. But in this essay, I would like to juxtapose Kohler's treatise on *Das Eigenbild im Recht* to films such as Ewers's *The Student of Prague* and Mack's *The Other*, which literalize the juridical figure of a split between "subject-ego" and "object-ego" for the purpose of staging stories about dual personalities and sinister doubles. In fact, Kohler's figure of the legal subject facing itself is visualized in a famous scene from Ewers's film. The film, which was based on a script by its director, was released in the summer of 1913 and represents in one sequence how its main protagonist "confronts his own ego." In a medium shot the camera shows Balduin, the eponymous student of Prague, nearly filling the left part of the frame, while on the right side a human-size mirror with his reflection is seen. The student, who is considered the best swordsman of Prague, fences with his reflection before he announces: "My adversary is—my mirror image."[18] The scene not only enacts Kohler's legal distinction of "subject-ego" and "object-ego," it also anticipates a decisive turn in the plot of the film in which Balduin's mirror image falls under the sway of a sinister villain. Yet before engaging in a more detailed analysis of *The Student of Prague*, I wish to further outline the legal discussion on the right to one's own image, which in addition to providing a storyline for *The Student* also anticipated crucial arguments for Walter Benjamin's and Sigmund Freud's theorizations of cinema.

Keyssner's treatise received much critical attention, and an astonishing number of books and essays were published on image rights in the subsequent years. However, instead of yielding consensus, the lively legal debate on the status of the photographic and cinematic image alternated between ascribing control of it to the photographer or granting it to the photographed person.[19] Whereas Keyssner advocated a new law in order to prevent the unauthorized taking and public display of pictures, the renowned juridical theorist Georg Cohn asserted in 1902 that the existing legal restrictions against "defamation" and "violation of honor" were sufficient to prohibit an abusive reproduction and exhibition of photographic images.[20]

In 1907, a compromise was reached through a new law on the protection of art works that, apart from regulating questions of copyright, also contained a number of paragraphs about the right to one's own image. The new legislation was even reported in an American journal, which printed a somewhat exaggerated warning against taking any photos when traveling to Germany: "Tourists who have loaded themselves with rolls of film for use in Europe this summer will have to be careful when they go to Germany. In that thoroly [sic] regulated country a new law goes into effect July 1 prohibiting the photographing of any person [. . .] without his express permission."[21] The article equated the human gaze with that of the camera, arguing that "when one appears in public it is always with the expectation and often with the purpose of being seen, and nowadays [one] must also anticipate being photographed."[22] However, the criticism of the alleged German propensity "to prohibit anything that can be prohibited" ignored one important distinction, since the new law only ruled out the unauthorized reproduction and public display of photographic images, while the mere taking of photos without replicating or exhibiting them was still deemed legal.[23] Furthermore, in contrast to ordinary persons, "figures of contemporary history" (*Figuren der Zeitgeschichte*) were not entitled to the same protection against being photographed, as the law explicitly asserted that the public held a right to be informed about important events by words and images.

While not banning all unauthorized photography, the new law nonetheless marked a success for those legal scholars who had insisted on a special regulation. This accomplishment was achieved against considerable resistance from critics who characterized concerns about the taking and reproduction of pictures as exaggerated or even "primitive." In his previously mentioned text from 1902, which had denied the necessity of instituting new legal rights, Georg Cohn had written: "It is certainly right that primitive people have an aversion to being photographed. Yet, the superstitious conceptions that are the root of that anxiety cannot be taken seriously among civilized people."[24] Josef Kohler seconded in almost identical terms: "There are indeed people who shun even the most decorous rendering of their image. [. . .] This deserves as little consideration as the Oriental who dreads his image because it contradicts his religious conceptions or because he believes such an image to portend his impending death."[25]

These racist comparisons highlight the parallel between "animist" fears of soul theft and juridical texts turning against the unauthorized "extraction" of images. The legal debate thereby invoked anthropological accounts of a "primitive" terror of photography, taken over from ethnographic texts such as James George Frazer's *The Golden Bough*—a book which went through numerous reprints in England and North America after its first publication in 1890. In the third edition from 1911, Frazer wrote about photography in the following terms:

> Portraits [. . .] are often believed to contain the soul of the person portrayed. People who hold this belief are naturally loth [sic] to have their likenesses taken; for if the portrait is the soul or at least a *vital part of the person portrayed*, whoever possesses the portrait will be able to exercise a fatal influence over the original of it. [. . .] Once at a village on the lower Yukon River an explorer had set up his camera to get a picture of the people as they were moving about among their houses. While he was focusing the instrument, the headman of the village came up and insisted on peeping under the cloth. Being allowed to do so, he gazed intently for a minute at the moving figures on the ground glass, then suddenly withdrew his head and bawled at the top of his voice to the people. "He has all of your shades in this box." A panic ensued among the group, and in an instant they disappeared helterskelter into their houses.[26]

As described in these highly fictional ethnographic accounts, animist anxieties about pictures containing "a vital part of the person portrayed" were indeed surprisingly similar to juridical opinions that defined images as an integral part of one's own personality.[27] Yet, instead of dismissing the fears of being "captured" by visual media as "primitive," one can also understand the striking proximity between the discourses of legal theory and anthropology as the surreptitious projection of a Western anxiety onto those "primitive" people who allegedly could not distinguish between reproduction and original.[28]

This suspicion seems to be confirmed by the fact that Georg Cohn, who, in 1902, ridiculed the fear of being photographed, just seven years later gave in to the very same anxiety, when the newer technology of the motion picture gained such an importance that he could no longer ignore it. By the time of his 1909 *Cinema Law*, one of the earliest legal texts on film, the former critic of a specific "right to one's own image" had converted into its advocate, insisting that such a right applied not only to photography but also to cinematography:

> As everybody knows, according to a statute from [. . .] 1907, nobody may be publicly displayed in his image without his consent. Even the reproduction of the image is illegal, if it can be considered as a preparation for public display. If this law already applies to the motionless, still portrait, it must apply even more to the *vue animée*, to the cinematogram; for the latter shows not only the frozen, mute traits of one single moment; instead, it copies man in his motion, in his actions, similar to the theatrical mask adopted by a versatile actor. And like the mime who is not entitled to copy us without our consent, [. . .] the cinematograph which listens in to our actions should not be allowed to publicly ape us, *like a double*.[29]

The unexpected comparison of being filmed and being imitated by an actor ascribes a life and a body of its own to the moving image, which acts "like a double." Cohn's anxiety about the cinematic apparatus with its uncanny capability of copying physical movement all but coincides with that "primitive" fear of photography he himself had derided seven years earlier. The anthropologist Lucien Lévy-Bruhl described the animist dread of visual media as based on an identification of photo and original: "to the primitive's mind, [. . .] the picture is not a reproduction of the original, distinct from it; it is itself."[30] Lévy-Bruhl continued: "No doubt a portrait, a photograph, is a double."[31] Cohn, in comparison, initially distinguished between original and reproduction when referring to motionless photography. Yet, the newer technology of the motion picture proved so overwhelming that he came to conflate image and original in conjuring early cinema's ghostly doubles.

Cohn's colleague Bruno May also approximated an "animist" conception of cinema in the introduction to his legal treatise *Das Recht des Kinematographen* (1912):

> Film, which previously could only attract the interest of children, has become a sorcerer who draws young and old under its spell. The image it summons onto the screen is for the eye of the beholder *more than a mere image* but *breathes life*. For the perfected technological achievement makes us forget that we see only the dead image and makes us believe that reality is within our grasp; so deceptively close does semblance come to reality in this case.[32]

May emphasizes that to the "eye of the beholder" the living photographs of cinema are "more than a mere image." Nonetheless his subsequent discussion of the legal aspects of cinema insists on the distinction between "semblance" and "reality," criticizing Cohn's comparison of filmic image and double by asserting: "The cinematographic images, even if they create by their rapid succession the impression of movement, are nonetheless *always only images*."[33] May therefore rejects the assumption of a qualitative difference between film and photography, insisting that the same legal regulations apply to both. Cohn's text, in contrast, blurs the distinction between original and cinematic reproduction, simultaneously questioning whether the public right to be informed about important events by words and images should indeed subsume not only photography but also film.

After invoking the ominous analogy between the moving image and the "aping double," Cohn turns to the exceptions within the law of 1907, the so-called figures of contemporary history whose images may be publicly displayed, even against their express objection. Dramatically addressing his juridical readership, Cohn presents the disturbing conclusion that all lawyers may be considered figures of contemporary history and therefore may have to face the possibility of being filmed:

> The infinitely vast realm of contemporary history encompasses amongst many others also almost all of us lawyers, whether we judge, argue, or teach. Thus, we ourselves are concerned by this question; *nostra res agitur*. Would all of us have to put up with being presented to the wide audience of the motion picture theater as a *living photograph, as an acting person*? This question has on principle to be answered in the negative. [. . .] It cannot be the legislator's wish that the judge, administering an oath and pronouncing the sentence, that the lawyer, gesticulating in passionate argument,

that the professor climbing up to the lectern, spreading his notes and clearing his throat, are shown on the screen of the movie theater, perhaps immediately after a grotesque scene of the basest nature has been presented at the very same place.[34]

The alarming tone of this passage testifies to the terror of cinematic reproduction. Cohn's passionate call for the protection of his own image shifts from an abstract scholarly discussion to painting a frightening scenario that directly affects himself and his audience: "we ourselves are concerned by this question; *nostra res agitur*." Simultaneously, the text introduces a second anxiety, which is derived from the underlying identification of "living photograph" and "acting person." The appalling fantasy of having one's own image projected onto a film screen, possibly right after a "grotesque scene of the basest nature has been presented at the very same place," invokes the low cultural status of the movie theater as a dark, sexually charged, and licentious site, comparable to a peep show. Yet, in addition to the physical space of the movie theater, Cohn also here refers to editing or montage as a filmic mode of representation that allows for the unwanted insertion of one's own image into a compromising or degrading pictorial sequence—a promiscuous mingling of images, as it were, that affects not only the "double" of the moving image but also the captured "original."

The anxieties provoked by the "living photographs" of cinema are also at the center of Ewers's *The Student of Prague*. Similar to Mack's *Der Andere*, the film appropriates the contemporaneous legal debate on image rights and transforms it into a fantastical story. The plot of the film therefore can also be read as a meta-cinematic reflection on moving images that can be detached from their "original" to assume a life of their own.[35] As mentioned before, Balduin stages the legal split between "subject-ego" and "object-ego" by confronting his own reflection in a mirror. However, the split between Balduin and his "adversary" is taken even further when Balduin enters into a pact with the diabolic figure of Scapinelli. Unknowingly, the student sells his mirror image and thereby loses control over his double, who eventually kills his beloved's cousin.

Balduin's pact with the devil is invoked three times in the film. The opening sequence ends with a handshake between the student, who has complained about his poverty, and Scapinelli, who hints at a way to get to money. The gesture of consent between the two is observed with horror by Balduin's admirer Lyduschka, who is suspicious of the sinister Scapinelli and shown in the background of the scene. That Balduin is lending himself (as Kafka imagined Bassermann doing) "to something beneath him" is shown in more detail in a sequence shot in Balduin's room, where he had previously fenced with his own reflection.

Balduin has just returned from a visit to the Countess Margit, realizing that his social status will prevent him from being with the woman he loves.[36] Suddenly Scapinelli enters the room, which is shown in the same medium shot as Balduin's previous face-off with his mirror image. Scapinelli offers to make Balduin "the wealthiest student"—a proposition that the sorcerer underscores by pouring a seemingly infinite stream of coins from his purse onto Balduin's table, cinematographically realized by a stop-motion trick. An intertitle shows the following contract, held out to Balduin by the sinister merchant:

"I confirm the receipt of 100,000 golden florins. In return I give Mister Scapinelli the right to take from this room whatever he fancies. Prague, May 13, 1820." Balduin points to the meager and humble furnishings of his room and signs the contract, after which Scapinelli announces his claim to Balduin's mirror image. While Balduin stands close to the left frame of the image, reading the contract one more time, Scapinelli steps before the mirror with Balduin's reflection, passing his hands in an enchanting motion over the mirror image. To the horror of Balduin, shown in the left part of the image, the reflection on the right side steps out of the mirror. The double stares at its "original" and then follows Scapinelli, who leaves the room in an almost dancing manner.

In legal terms, Balduin would of course be entitled to withdraw from this contract, since he unknowingly sold his mirror image, so that his consent would have to be qualified as "uninformed" rather than "informed."[37] The film, however, chooses to represent this deal as irrevocably clinched. Consequently, attention is drawn again to the pernicious pact at the end of the film, when Balduin shoots his double, thereby also killing himself. After Balduin has dropped to the floor rather dramatically, a smiling Scapinelli enters his room, acknowledging the cinematic audience by politely lifting his hat toward the camera. Scapinelli produces the contract, shown to the audience in intertitles one more time, and tears the paper to pieces, which he then drops on Balduin's dead body.

In addition to the filmic diegesis, which relies upon a narrative adaptation of juridical concepts, the innovative camerawork deserves equal attention. The special effect of Balduin staring at his own mirror image as it leaves the room under Scapinelli's command was rendered possible by the cinematic trick of double exposure and an imperceptibly split screen.[38] The actor Paul Wegener, who not only played the part of Balduin but also helped devise the film's scenario, later remarked in an essay how he had intended to develop a storyline that "truly corresponded to the technology of the motion picture." Wegener continued: "First of all, we film people have to realize that one has to forget the theater and the novel. [. . .] The real poet of film must be the camera. [. . .] The possibility of constantly changing perspectives for the spectator, the countless tricks through dividing the image, mirrorings, and so on—in short, the technology of film must become important for the choice of content."[39]

Wegener emphasizes that the plot of *The Student of Prague* emerged out of an attempt at a genuinely cinematic mode of representation unavailable to any other medium. The film draws on stories from literary Romanticism such as Adalbert von Chamisso's *The Strange Story of Peter Schlemihl* (1814) or E. T. A. Hoffmann's *The Story of the Lost Mirror Image* (1815) (a contemporaneous review even went so far as to unjustly characterize the film as based on "naked borrowings" from these authors).[40] The seemingly literary figure of the double is, however, transformed by the film into a meta-cinematic reflection on the technology of early cinema itself. As Willy Haas put it in 1922: "The problem of the double, as we know from Wegener's 'Student of Prague,' is the truly demonic, truly spiritual problem of film: the film problem of all film problems."[41]

This structural affinity between the cinematic medium and the figure of the double would be discussed, decades later, by the German media theorist Friedrich Kittler in his insightful essay "Romanticism—Psychoanalysis—Film" (1986). There, Kittler conceives of cinema as an uncanny technology that produces and reproduces "doubles." But in describing the Romantic theory of the subject—"the shadows and mirrorings of the subject"—as "clinically verified" by psychoanalysis and "technologically implemented" by cinema, Kittler presupposes a teleology that turns the emergence of cinema into the goal and fulfillment of a purposeful development.[42] In typological terms, one could summarize Kittler's thesis in the following manner: literary Romanticism around 1800 prefigures the advent of psychoanalysis and film around 1900 in a mode that structurally corresponds to the relation of Old and New Testament. Around 1900, furthermore, psychoanalysis functions as the equivalent of John the Baptist, as it were, while the technology of cinema represents the word becoming flesh: "Silent films implement with technological positivity what psychoanalysis can only conceive of."[43]

But despite this problematic teleology, Kittler is right in pointing out that in the 1910s cinema was conceptualized in analogy to the literary trope of the double. The "dreadful doubleness of representation" (*dieses furchtbare Doppelgängertum der Repräsentation*), to quote an essay by Berthold Viertel from 1910, is thus foregrounded by the second-order special effects in *The Student of Prague*, which highlight the underlying cinematic trick of capturing and duplicating real objects and people.[44] Cinema's seemingly supernatural capabilities are also emphasized in Hugo Münsterberg's *The Photoplay: A Psychological Study* (1916): "It looks magical. [. . .] Every dream becomes real, uncanny ghosts appear from nothing and disappear into nothing."[45] Indeed, film even forms the absent center of Sigmund Freud's conception of the double in his famous essay "The Uncanny," first published in 1919. Freud's disciple Otto Rank had explicitly compared the dreamwork (*Traumtechnik*) to cinematic modes of representation (*Kinodarstellung*) in order to lend legitimacy to his short interpretation of Ewers's film, which served as the introduction to *The Double: A Psychoanalytic Study* (1914).[46] Similar to Rank, who in the latter part of his treatise described the eternal soul as the originary double of the mortal body, Freud considered the uncanny as a resurgence of "animist" notions from childhood, simultaneously comparing the ontogenetic stage of narcissism to animism within the phylogenetic evolution of the human species: "Our analysis of instances of the uncanny has led us back to the old, animistic conception of the world. This [. . .] was characterized by [. . .] the belief in the omnipotence of thoughts and the technique of magic (*Technik der Magie*) based on that belief."[47] Paraphrasing Henri Hubert and Marcel Mauss's *General Theory of Magic*, Freud describes here pre-modern techniques of magic that he had also conceptualized in *Totem and Taboo* (1913).[48] Yet, his German phrase "Technik der Magie" simultaneously invokes the contemporaneous medium of cinema as a modern "technology of magic"—a "magical practice" that surreptitiously pervades his essay without ever being explicitly mentioned.[49]

Freud's citation of "animism" invokes those "primitive" notions inherent to and constitutive of the legal debate on the right to one's own image.[50] Yet, in addition to conceiving of early cinema's animate images as ghostly doubles, the juridical discussion also formulated important insights into the transformative role of technological reproduction, thereby anticipating later theories of media. Thus, Albert Klöckner's essay, "The Mass Problem in Art: On the Essence and Value of Reproduction (Film and Radio)"

(1928), merely repeats notions from this earlier discussion when describing film as a mode of reproduction that can be decoupled from human agency: "Film as a mechanical product, as a representation which can be repeated independently from the will of the original, [. . .] is diametrically opposed to the artistically determined performance by the stage actor or singer."[51]

Klöckner's foregrounding of mechanical reproduction echoes Duenschmann's warning of the "pernicious factor of mechanical [. . .] reproduction" from 1912, a warning that in *The Student of Prague* is transformed into the fantastic plot of Balduin being unable to exert any control over his double. Ewers's film and the astonishingly early legal debate on the status of cinematic images also parallel Walter Benjamin's famous essay on "The Work of Art in the Age of Its Technological Reproducibility" (1935–1939). Benjamin all but summarizes the plot of *The Student of Prague*, when he writes: "The film actor's feeling of estrangement in the face of the apparatus [. . .] is basically of the same kind as the estrangement felt before one's appearance (*Erscheinung*) in a mirror. But now the mirror image (*Bild*) has become detachable from the person mirrored, and is transportable. And where is it transported? Before the public."[52]

Balduin's detached mirror image indeed serves as a meta-cinematic allegory of the technological production and reproduction of filmic images. Yet while Ewers's film transforms the ostensibly literary figure of the double into a self-referential representation of early cinema, Benjamin's essay sets out to conceptualize the potentially endless series of reproductions made possible by photography and film. In the first version of his essay, Benjamin explicitly referred to literary Romanticism: "The film actor's estrangement in the face of the apparatus [. . .] is basically of the same kind as the estrangement of the Romantic before his mirror image—as is well known, a favorite motif in Jean Paul. But now the mirror image has become detachable from the person mirrored and has become transportable."[53] However, the tension between the literary trope of one double versus the potentially infinite number of cinematic images leads Benjamin to drop this invocation of "the Romantic" in the final version of his essay, which seeks to formulate a theory of technical copies that can be reproduced not just once but endlessly. Nonetheless, even in the final version of the essay, Benjamin remains wedded to the notion of a singular original. Accordingly, he deplores the loss of "aura," which he defines as a singular "here and now," exemplified—once again—by contrasting film and stage actor in terms that are surprisingly similar to Duenschmann's and Klöckner's essays. In a footnote to his essay, Benjamin claims: "The poorest provincial staging of Goethe's *Faust* is superior to a film of *Faust*, in that, ideally, it competes with the first performance at Weimar. The viewer in front of a movie screen derives no benefit from recalling bits of tradition which might come to mind in front of a stage."[54]

A nostalgic marker of a seemingly "authentic" image exchange is also to be found within *The Student of Prague*, which contrasts the economic transaction between Balduin and Scapinelli with a different mode of entrusting one's image to somebody— the giving of an image as a gift. Early on in the film, before Balduin has sold his mirror image, he saves Countess Margit from drowning in a lake after she has fallen from her horse. Margit gives her savior a precious token with the words: "Take this locket [. . .]

it holds my image." Thereafter, the locket containing the image of the Countess and Balduin's loss of his mirror image are repeatedly juxtaposed in the film. Balduin looks longingly at the locket before Scapinelli enters his room and makes him sign the fatal contract. Later, after Balduin has been challenged to a duel by the Countess's jealous cousin and fiancé, he again sits at a table looking at Margit's image before he opens a box containing a small mirror that, to his horror and shame, does not reflect his own image.

Balduin, who, by selling his mirror image, has literally lost his singularity, his "here and now," is unable to reciprocate the Countess's gift. He is barred from a mutual "exchange of images," as it is also described by Hugo Keyssner's legal treatise. There, Keyssner draws a sharp distinction between the soulless mechanical "extraction" of images and a loving bestowal: "If a mutual exchange of images takes place, if one is that of a maiden, the other that of a young man, the discovery of the image treasure on both sides enchantingly leads to the happiest moments in life. Gladly, I would dwell on this. [...] Yet such an interpolation might lead too far away from our topic."[55] Similar to Benjamin's notion of "aura," Keyssner's legal text and Ewers's film introduce this seemingly "organic" or "authentic" exchange of images in order to contrast it with the trafficking of images engendered by technological media such as photography or cinema.[56] And while this turn against technological media is not surprising in the case of Keyssner, it seems paradoxical that Ewers's *The Student of Prague*, itself a film, seeks to legitimize itself as "art" by telling a story about the dangers of technological reproduction and cinema's trading in images.[57]

That Balduin's image has become a commodity, which, in contrast to the Countess's gift, can be paid for with the anonymous medium of money, also reminds us of the protagonist in Nabokov's first novel, *Mary* (or *Mashen'ka*), from 1926. In this literary text, Ganin, a Russian emigré, arrives in Berlin, where he is forced by poverty to trade in "every imaginable sort of goods." The narrator continues:

> *Nothing was beneath his dignity*; more than once he had even sold his shadow, as many of us have. In other words he went out to the suburbs to work as a movie extra on a set, in a fairground barn, where light seethed with a mystical hiss from the huge facets of lamps that were aimed, like cannon [*sic*], at a crowd of extras, lit to a deathly brightness. They would fire a barrage of murderous brilliance, illuminating the painted wax of motionless faces, then expiring with a click—but for a long time yet there would glow, in those elaborate crystals, dying red sunsets—our human shame. The deal was clinched, and our anonymous shadows sent out all over the world.[58]

As if Nabokov's novel were quoting Kafka's description of Bassermann, Ganin is characterized as "lend[ing] himself to something beneath him." Furthermore, despite his "shame," Ganin, like Balduin, is unable to withdraw from the contract into which he has entered: "the deal was clinched." And in a rhetorical move that finds its parallel in Georg Cohn's dramatic interpellation of his juridical readership, Nabokov's narrator shifts from the third-person singular to the first-person plural in describing "*our* anonymous shadows sent out all over the world."

Later in the novel, Ganin goes to the movies with his girlfriend. Sitting in the theater, he suddenly realizes that he is "watching something vaguely yet horribly familiar." To quote at length from the novel:

> He recalled with alarm the roughly carpentered rows of seats, the chairs and parapets of the boxes painted a sinister violet. [. . .] Straining his eyes, with a deep shudder of shame he recognized himself among all those people clapping to order. [. . .] Ganin's doppelgänger also stood and clapped, over there. [. . .] There on the screen his haggard image, his sharp uplifted face and clapping hands *merged* into the grey kaleidoscope of other figures; a moment later, swinging like a ship, the auditorium vanished and now the scene showed an aging, world-famous actress giving a very skillful representation of a dead young woman.[59]

This passage from Nabokov's novel may serve as an apt conclusion of this essay, since it recalls several tropes that I have previously analyzed. Just like Ewers's film *The Student of Prague* or Cohn's legal treatise *Cinema Law*, the literary text compares the cinematic image to an animate double whose life is no longer controlled by the "original." Moreover, the novel describes a "merging" of Ganin's image with that of others—first a "kaleidoscope of other figures" and then the image of an "aging world-famous actress giving a very skillful representation of a dead young woman." This degrading mingling of pictures recalls Cohn's anxiety about editing as a filmic mode of representation that allows for the juxtaposition of one's own image with "a grotesque scene of the basest nature." The terror of cinematic reproduction, invoked in the legal debate on the right to one's own image and Ewers's film, thus surfaces also in Nabokov's literary text. Balduin's loss of his reflection may be read as a meta-cinematic representation of the movie actor's relation to his or her image. A similar fantasy haunts Ganin's thoughts after he has left the movie theater and walks home. Even Duenschmann's nationalist phobia recurs in Nabokov's novel. But the chauvinist anxiety about having one's own image presented to a foreign audience is transformed here into a reflection on exile and displacement, since it is Ganin's walking and wandering that is replicated by that of his double: "As he walked he thought how his shade would wander from city to city, from screen to screen, how he would never know what sort of people would see it or how long it would roam around the world."[60]

Notes

1. All translations from the German by the author, unless otherwise indicated. See Heide Schlüpmann, "The First German Art Film: Rye's *The Student of Prague*," in Eric Rentschler, ed., *German Film and Literature: Adaptations and Transformations* (New York: Methuen, 1986), 9–24. See also Friedrich von Zglinicki, *Der Weg des Films. Textband* (Hildesheim, Germany: Olms Presse, 1979), 377.
2. Despite Hanns Zischler's claim in *Kafka Goes to the Movies*, the film is not lost but survives in several copies at the Stiftung Deutsche Kinemathek in Berlin. Hanns Zischler, *Kafka*

Goes to the Movies, trans. Susan H. Gillespie (Chicago, IL: University of Chicago Press, 2002 [1996]).

3. For a positive response see "Film has become worthy of being covered in the art section," *Erste Internationale Film-Zeitung* 5 (February 1, 1913): 4–5, quoted in Helmut H. Diederichs, *Anfänge deutscher Filmkritik* (Stuttgart, Germany: Fischer & Wiedleroither, 1986), 55. For negative reactions that deplore Bassermann's "Seitensprung in den Kintop" see Ulrich Rauscher, "Der Bassermann-Film," *Frankfurter Zeitung*, February 6, 1913, reprinted in Fritz Güttinger, ed., *Kein Tag ohne Kino. Schriftsteller über den Stummfilm* (Frankfurt a.M., Germany: Deutsches Filmmuseum, 1984), 140–142. See also Oskar Kalbus, *Vom Werden deutscher Filmkunst. 1. Teil* (Hamburg, Germany: Cigaretten-Bilderdienst, 1935), 14: "Most of the reviews were negative and all of them contained the objection that an artist like Bassermann degraded himself by signing up for a movie."

4. Hermann Duenschmann, "Kinematograph und Psychologie der Volksmenge," *Konservative Monatsschrift* 69, no. 9 (1912): 920–930, reprinted in Albert Kümmel and Petra Löffler, eds., *Medientheorie 1888–1933. Texte und Kommentare* (Frankfurt a.M., Germany: Suhrkamp, 2002), 85–99, 97.

5. Duenschmann, "Kinematograph und Psychologie der Volksmenge," 97.

6. Ibid.

7. Franz Kafka, *Briefe an Felice und andere Korrespondenz aus der Verlobungszeit*, ed. Erich Heller and Jürgen Born (Frankfurt a.M., Germany: Fischer, 1967), 326.

8. For a more comprehensive discussion of the interrelations of hypnotism, somnambulism, and cinema, see Stefan Andriopoulos, *Possessed: Hypnotic Crimes, Corporate Fiction, and the Invention of Cinema* (Chicago, IL: University of Chicago Press, 2008).

9. See Julius Bab, *Albert Bassermann. Weg und Werk eines deutschen Schauspielers um die Wende des 20. Jahrhunderts* (Leipzig, Germany: Erich Weibezahl, 1929), 101–102.

10. See also von Ziglinicki, *Der Weg des Films*, 378.

11. Hugo Keyssner, "Das elektrische Licht der Oeffentlichkeit," in *Das Recht am eigenen Bilde* (Berlin: Guttentag, 1896), 13. The phrase, which invokes cinema without explicitly naming it, surfaces unexpectedly within the discussion of print media.

12. "The original (*Urbild*) is the master of its copy (*Abbild*)." Keyssner, *Das Recht am eigenen Bilde*, 2.

13. Ibid., 23.

14. On the decisive role of modern media for the formulation of a "right to privacy" see Samuel Warren and Luis Brandeis's seminal essay, "The Right to Privacy," *Harvard Law Review* 4, no. 5 (December 15, 1890): 193–220, wherein is claimed: "Instantaneous photographs and newspaper enterprise have invaded the sacred precincts of private and domestic life; and numerous mechanical devices threaten to make good the prediction that 'what is whispered in the closet shall be proclaimed from the house-tops.' For years there has been a feeling that the law must afford some remedy for the unauthorized circulation of portraits of private persons; and the evil of invasion of privacy by the newspapers, long keenly felt, has been but recently discussed by an able writer" (195). On the transition from the right of privacy to the right of publicity in relation to cinema see Jane Gaines, "*Dracula* and the Right of Publicity," in *Contested Culture: The Image, the Voice, and the Law* (Chapel Hill: University of North Carolina Press, 1991), 175–206. On the "right to privacy" in relation to the circulation of women's pictures see Jessica Lake, *The Face that Launched a Thousand Lawsuits: The American Women Who Forged a Right to Privacy* (New Haven, CT: Yale University Press, 2016).

15. See Karl Gareis, "Das Recht am eigenen Bilde," *Deutsche Juristen-Zeitung* 7 (1902): 412–415, and Karl Gareis, "Das Recht am menschlichen Körper. Eine privatrechtliche Studie," *Festgabe der Juristischen Fakultät zu Königsberg für ihren Senior Johann Theodor Schirmer zum 1. August 1900* (Königsberg, Germany: Juristische Fakultät, 1900), 59–100.
16. Keyssner, "Dem Ich, als Subjekt, steht die Persönlichkeit, der Körper, als Objekt gegenüber," in *Das Recht am eigenen Bilde*, 23.
17. Josef Kohler, *Das Eigenbild im Recht* (Berlin: Guttentag, 1903), 5–6.
18. "Mein Gegner ist—mein Spiegelbild."
19. For further texts that participate in this discussion see Siegfried Rietschel, *Das Recht am eigenen Bilde* (Tübingen, Germany: Mohr, 1903); Hans Schneickert, *Der Schutz der Photographen und das Recht am eigenen Bilde* (Halle a.S., Germany: Knapp, 1903); Gustav Friedrich von Buch, *Das Recht am eigenen Bilde* (Leipzig, Germany: R. Noske, 1906); Leo Koenig, *Das Recht am eigenen Bilde* (Berlin: Thormann & Goetsch, 1908); Ludwig Graf Rüdt von Collenberg, *Das Recht am eigenen Bild* (Heidelberg, Germany: Rössler & Herbert, 1909); Karl Dumont, *Das Recht am eigenen Bilde* (Berlin: O. Schwartz, 1910); and Kurt Letzel, *Inwieweit ist im geltenden Recht ein Recht am eigenen Bilde anerkannt und geschützt?* (Borna-Leipzig, Germany: Noske, 1912).
20. Georg Cohn, *Neue Rechtsgüter: Das Recht am eigenen Namen. Das Recht am eigenen Bild* (Berlin: O. Liebmann, 1902), 44–46.
21. Anonymous, "The Ethics and Etiquet [sic] of Photography," *The Independent* 63 (July–December 1907): 107–108.
22. Ibid., 108.
23. Ibid.
24. Cohn, *Neue Rechtsgüter*, 46n2.
25. Josef Kohler, *Das Eigenbild im Recht*, 9.
26. James George Frazer, *The Golden Bough: A Study in Magic and Religion*, part 2: *Taboo and the Perils of the Soul*, 3rd ed. (London: Macmillan, 1955 [1911]), 96 (emphasis added). This passage of *The Golden Bough* is quoted in George William Gilmore, *Animism or Thought Currents of Primitive Peoples* (Boston, MA: Marshall Jones, 1919), 45. See also Arthur Baessler, "Reisen im malayischen Archipel," *Zeitschrift für Ethnologie* 22 (1890): 493–500, esp. 494–495. Even before the invention of photography, the stereotype of a primitive fear of visual media had already been formulated in regard to painting by George Catlin, who ascribed the "superstitious" notion that "I was to take part of the existence of those whom I painted and carry it home with me amongst the white people" to, as he puts it, "squaws" and "old quack medicine-men." The "chiefs" of the tribes visited by Catlin, however, allegedly did not succumb to the same fear and heeded Catlin's insistence "that my art had no medicine or mystery about it." George Catlin, *North American Indians: Being Letters and Notes on Their Manners, Customs, and Conditions, Written During Eight Years' Travel, 1832–1839*, vol. 1 (Edinburgh, UK: John Grant, 1926), 122–123.
27. Marina Warner, who quotes the very same passage from Frazer's book, develops the compelling argument that the numerous narratives on the primitive fear of photography are a wishful fantasy on the part of anthropologists, missionaries, or explorers who celebrate their (imaginary) power. See her insightful essay "The Camera Steals the Soul" in *Phantasmagoria: Spirit Visions, Metaphors, and Media* (New York: Oxford University Press, 2006), 189–202.
28. One could even argue that the anthropological debate on soul theft already deployed terms borrowed from contemporaneous representations of modern visual media. Edward Tylor's *Primitive Culture* (1871), for instance, defines the soul in a manner that seems to

invoke visual media: "The conception of a personal soul or spirit among the lower races may be defined as follows: It is a thin unsubstantial human *image,* in its nature a sort of vapour, *film,* or shadow." According to the *OED,* "film" was employed to describe a "copy" of a photographic plate as early as 1845. Edward B. Tylor, *Primitive Culture: Researches Into the Development of Mythology, Philosophy, Religion, Art, and Custom,* vol. 1 (London: J. Murray, 1871), 387 (emphasis added).

29. Georg Cohn, *Kinematographenrecht. Vortrag gehalten in der juristischen Gesellschaft zu Berlin am 12. Juni 1909* (Berlin: R.v. Decker's Verlag, 1909), 19 (emphasis added).
30. Lucien Lévy-Bruhl, *The "Soul" of the Primitive,* trans. Lilian A. Clare (London: George Allen, 1928 [1927]), 154. Lévy-Bruhl further complicates his account by emphasizing the logically paradoxical status of the image within "primitive" conceptions: "To the primitive mind the reproduction is one being, the original another: they are two beings, and yet the same being. It is equally true that they are two and that they are one: two in one, or one in two. The primitive sees nothing extraordinary in that, though we think differently" (156).
31. Ibid.
32. Bruno May, *Das Recht des Kinematographen* (Berlin: Richard Falk, 1912), 3 (emphasis added).
33. Ibid., 127. For a shorter version of the same argument, see Bruno May, "Der Kinematograph und das Recht am eigenen Bilde," *Gewerblicher Rechtsschutz und Urheberrecht. Zeitschrift des Deutschen Vereins für den Schutz des gewerblichen Eigentums* 17, no. 11 (November 1912): 324–326, esp. 325.
34. Cohn, *Kinematographenrecht,* 19–20.
35. On the relation of images and animism see also W. J. T. Mitchell, *What Do Pictures Want? The Lives and Loves of Images* (Chicago, IL: University of Chicago Press, 2005).
36. See the intertitle: "Fort mit den Gedanken —Sie, die reiche Erbin— ich ein armer Student" ("Away with these thoughts—she, the wealthy heiress—me, a poor student").
37. In fact, he explicitly tries to withdraw from the contract at the end of the film, desperately exclaiming (in intertitle) "Scapinelli! Take back your gold!"
38. Guido Seeber, the cinematographer of *The Student from Prague,* published a 1927 book on the possibilities of trick film in which he explained how he had succeeded in shooting the sequences of Balduin encountering his own double. See Guido Seeber, *Der Trickfilm in seinen grundsätzlichen Möglichkeiten. Eine praktische und theoretische Darstellung des photographischen Filmtricks* (Berlin: Verlag die Lichtbildbühne, 1927), 54–55: "Using two consecutive takes for the purpose of capturing the double on film was first used as the premise of a film's plot in *The Student of Prague* in 1913. The illusion achieved in that first film with this title was so perfect that even experts could hardly be convinced that the respective scenes were actually shot in two consecutive takes. For the final cinematic image did not allow for perceiving this, despite the magnifying projection."
39. Paul Wegener, "Von den künstlerischen Möglichkeiten des Wandelbildes," *Deutscher Wille (Der Kunstwart)* 30 (1916/17): 13–15, reprinted in Jörg Schweinitz, ed., *Prolog vor dem Film. Nachdenken über ein neues Medium* (Leipzig, Germany: Reclam, 1992), 334–338, 336.
40. See Ernst Wachler in *Bühne und Welt* 24, no. 2 (1913/14): 187–87, reprinted in Ludwig Grewe, Margot Pehle, and Heidi Westhoff, eds., *Hätte ich das Kino! Die Schriftsteller und der Stummfilm* (Stuttgart, Germany: Klett, 1976), 111–112.
41. "Das Doppelgängerproblem—wir wissen es von Wegeners 'Studenten von Prag' her—ist überhaupt das eigentlich dämonische, eigentlich geistige Filmproblem: das Filmproblem aller Filmprobleme." Willy Haas, "Novemberfilme," *Freie deutsche Bühne* 4 (1922/23): 129–134, reprinted in *Hätte ich das Kino!,* 172.

42. Friedrich Kittler, "Romanticism—Psychoanalysis—Film," in *Literature, Media, Information Systems* (Amsterdam: G + B Arts International, 1997), 95.
43. Ibid., 92.
44. Berthold Viertel, "Im Kinematographentheater," *März* 4/20 (October 18, 1910), reprinted in *Kein Tag ohne Kino*, 48–49. On Berthold Viertel's essay see also Klaus Kreimeier, "Die doppelte Verdopplung der Kaiser-Ikone. Berthold Viertel in einem Kino zu Wien, anno 1910," in Thomas Elsaesser and Michael Wedel, eds., *Kino der Kaiserzeit. Zwischen Tradition und Moderne* (Munich, Germany: text + kritik, 2002), 293–302.
45. Hugo Münsterberg, *The Photoplay: A Psychological Study*, ed. Allan Langdale (London: Routledge, 2002 [1916]), 61. On the relationship of early cinema and magic see also Rachel Moore, *Savage Theory: Early Cinema as Modern Magic* (Durham, NC: Duke University Press, 2000).
46. Rank opens his study of the double with an interpretation of *The Student of Prague*—a recourse to film that he justifies by comparing dream work and filmic modes of representation: "Perhaps it will be concluded that the *cinematic representation* (Kinodarstellung), reminiscent in several aspects of the *dream technique* (Traumtechnik), can also, by means of a clear and sensory pictorial language, express certain psychological facts and relations, which retreat from a clear poetic representation in words" (emphasis added). Yet after this remarkable introduction, Rank's text strangely abandons visual media and their specific modes of representation, summarizing instead an extensive body of literary and ethnographic texts. Otto Rank, *Der Doppelgänger. Eine psychoanalytische Studie* (Vienna: Turia & Kant, 1983 [1914/1925]), 7–8.
47. Sigmund Freud, "The Uncanny," in *Writings on Art and Literature* (Stanford, CA: Stanford University Press, 1997), 193–233, 216.
48. Before coining the phrase "Technik der Magie" in "The Uncanny," Freud introduces a similar term, "magische Technik," in his "Animismus, Magie und Allmacht der Gedanken," from *Totem and Taboo* (1913), one page before explicitly referring to Hubert and Mauss: "So we are not surprised to learn that, hand in hand with the animistic system, there went a body of instructions upon how to obtain mastery over men, beasts and things—or rather, over their spirits. These instructions go by the names of 'sorcery' and 'magic.' Reinach (1905-12, 2, xv) describes them as the 'strategy of animism'; I should prefer, following Hubert and Mauss (1904 [142 ff.]), to regard them as its technique." Sigmund Freud, *Totem and Taboo*, in *The Standard Edition of the Complete Psychological Works of Sigmund Freud*, vol. 13 (1913–1914): *Totem and Taboo and Other Works*, trans. and ed. James Strachey, in collaboration with Anna Freud, assisted by Alix Strachey and Alan Tyson (London: Hogarth Press, 1953–74), 79 and 78. Mauss and Hubert themselves describe magic as functionally equivalent to technology: "Magic works in the same ways as our techniques, industries, medicine, chemistry, engineering, etc." Henri Hubert and Marcel Mauss, "Esquisse d'une Théorie générale de la Magie," *L'Année sociologique* 7 (1904): 143.
49. Freud, "The Uncanny," 221. Freud's essay refers in one footnote to *The Student of Prague* but ignores the cinematic medium, since Freud does not call it a film but "poetry" (Dichtung). See "The Uncanny," 269n1.
50. Ibid., 263.
51. Albert Klöckner, "Das Massenproblem in der Kunst. Über Wesen und Wert der Vervielfältigung (Film und Funk)," *Das Nationaltheater* 1 (1928/29): 10–19, reprinted in *Medientheorie 1888–1933*, 299–311, 305.

52. Walter Benjamin, "The Work of Art in the Age of Its Technological Reproducibility" (third version, 1936), in *Selected Writings* vol. 4: 1938–1940, trans. and ed. Howard Eiland and Michael Jennings (Cambridge, MA: Belknap Press, 2006), 261 (translation slightly modified). The parallel between this passage in Benjamin's famous essay and Ewers's film is also emphasized by Heide Schlüpmann. See her "The First German Art Film," 14.
53. Walter Benjamin, "The Work of Art in the Age of Its Technological Reproducibility" (first version, 1935), trans. Michael Jennings, in *Grey Room* 39 (2010): 11–38, 23.
54. Walter Benjamin, "The Work of Art in the Age of Its Technological Reproducibility" (third version, 1936) in *Selected Writings* vol. 4, 271n5. On the relationship between Benjamin's notion of "aura" and Ludwig Klages's notion of "Urbild" in his *Der Geist als Widersacher der Seele*, see Peter M. Spangenberg, "Aura," in Karlheinz Barck et al., eds., *Ästhetische Grundbegriffe. Band 1 Absenz – Darstellung* (Stuttgart, Germany: Metzler, 2000), 400–416, esp. 406–407.
55. Keyssner, *Das Recht am eigenen Bilde*, 28–29.
56. On the convergence of nineteenth-century representations of the circulation of money and photographic images, see John Tagg, "The Currency of the Photograph," in Victor Burgin, ed., *Thinking Photography* (London: Macmillan, 1982), 110–141, and Allan Sekula, *Photography Against the Grain* (Halifax, Canada: Press of the Nova Scotia College of Art and Design, 1984), "The Traffic in Photographs," 96–101.
57. On the linguistic level a similar paradox arises within Keyssner's text, since the predominance of image reproduction leads Keyssner to transform the photographed "original" into something that is already an image by consistently referring to the represented human being as "Urbild" or "Ur-image" (see, for instance, note 12 above). As mentioned in note 54, "Urbild" is also a central term in Ludwig Klages's *Der Geist als Widersacher der Seele*.
58. Vladimir Nabokov, *Mary. A Novel* (1926), trans. Michael Glenny in collaboration with the author (New York: Vintage, 1989), 9.
59. Ibid., 21–22 (emphasis added).
60. Ibid.

CHAPTER 5

COPYING TECHNOLOGIES

Two Pirates, Two Centuries

JANE M. GAINES

THEY all were "pirates." During the first decade after the advent of motion pictures, all of the major US companies were "dupers." Edison, American Mutoscope & Biograph, and Vitagraph bought, duplicated, advertised, and sold one another's moving image prints as their own.[1] Especially subject to duping were the superior European titles made by Lumière, Méliès, and Pathé Frères.[2] But at the time, who was to know or who could tell a "pirated" print from an original one? Had the print of *Cinderella* advertised in 1900 been struck from the Méliès original for *Cendrillon* (1899) (see figure 5.1) or was it a "dupe print," that is, a duplicated copy of a Méliès print struck by another company?

Print duping was industrial practice, albeit an illicit one. However, for nearly a century of motion picture history this early business strategy came to be associated not with industry leaders but with an outlier—the Philadelphia-based Lubin Company. Singled out, manufacturer Siegmund Lubin was called "the Pirate King." Lubin alone was thus held responsible for the surreptitious practices in which all American companies engaged. In a frequently retold story of Lubin's perfidy, he duplicated a print of *A Trip to the Moon* (Georges Méliès, Star Film Co., 1902) and filed a US copyright on the same moving image work that he renamed *A Trip to Mars* (1903).[3]

Lubin even attempted to sell his *Trip to the Moon* "dupe print" to Méliès's brother Gaston, who had opened a company in New York.[4] Clearly, such anecdotes have helped to depict the political economy of the period as that of a legitimate business under attack by an unscrupulous upstart. Yet here is a version of events rigged in favor of the victors if there ever was one. Actually, during the height of piracy, between 1897 and 1907, all companies were in on the game.[5] Later, Lubin employee and industrial spy Arthur D. Hotaling recalled the reciprocity of "piracy" with a joke: "Two of the original firms used to 'dupe' each others' product. After a while it was such an open secret that each used to call on the other and say: 'Now look here, that was a rotten print you gave me; I can't get a good dupe from that.'"[6] The firms in question here could have been any one of the major

FIGURE 5.1 *Cendrillon/Cinderella* (Georges Méliès, Star Film Co., 1899).

companies. But the practice Hotaling describes as an "open secret" has remained a well-kept secret among motion picture historians, even to this day.[7]

They were all "pirates" in the sense that they profited by using a combination of laboratory and mechanical processes to replicate and sell popular titles originally produced by their competitors. But in early twentieth-century usage, "piracy" existed on a spectrum from necessity to opportunity to duplicity to sabotage and even industrial espionage.[8] As wide-ranging as it was, then, the question of illegality in regard to piracy was not so "cut and dried." For a party was never exactly convicted of "piracy" but rather *could* be found guilty of infringing patent or copyright laws protecting proprietary claims. I say "could" because copyright in this emerging entertainment form—before it was "cinema" or even "film"—was in legal limbo and undergoing tests in the courts.[9] Piracy, then, was not exactly a crime for which a company could be convicted; rather, it was a charge, an accusation. Such charges of piracy were everywhere in the trade press, hurled back and forth among motion picture companies—one against another. The Edison Company, taking aim at Lubin, placed this taunt in the *New York Clipper*: "We have purposefully delayed the delivery of our great production 'Jack and the Beanstalk,' until the production could be adequately protected by law, in as much as pirates have been copying our films and have been waiting until the production could be put on sail [*sic*] so that they could duplicate and offer it to the public. Will be ready for delivery July 15."[10] Lubin, as anticipated, bought a print of Edison's *Jack and the Beanstalk* (1902), then duped it and sold those prints to exhibitors at a lower cost. Edison operatives, looking for evidence of infringement to use in court, then schemed to buy one of the duped prints in question.[11] Most likely, Edison lawyer Howard H. Hayes planned to use the telltale print that one

FIGURE 5.2 *Uncle Tom's Cabin* (Lubin Co., n.d.). Theatre Collection. Free Library of Philadelphia.

spy would surreptitiously purchase as part of the company's appeal of a failed copyright case against Lubin.

In *Edison v. Lubin* (1902), Edison had charged Lubin with unauthorized reproduction of their exclusive actuality footage of the German prince's visit to the US, *Christening and Launching Kaiser Wilhelm's Yacht "Meteor"* (1902). The first-level trial court decision in *Edison v. Lubin* (1902) had gone against the Edison Company, and Hayes was strategically working to get that decision overturned on appeal.[12] Meanwhile, Lubin, duping and selling Edison's *Jack and the* Beanstalk, was proceeding as though the question were settled. After the US Court of Appeals found for Edison in 1903, Lubin continued to dupe as well as to remake Edison titles.[13] In answer to Edison's *Uncle Tom's Cabin* release in 1903, Lubin advertised his own *Uncle Tom's Cabin* remake the following week (see figure 5.2).[14]

HISTORICAL FRAMES: HOW WE RELATE PAST EVENTS

But let's stop right here. Before we continue to relate the events of the 1897–1907 period, we have to decide how to tell "what happened" relative to events to which we no longer have empirical access. Further, we need to ask why the courts should matter, especially if their rulings were ignored. "How to tell" entails deciding what to emphasize and what to excise, what to expand and what to shrink, as well as what comes before and after. Here I call attention to what I call the "historical frame" as that set of assumptions that the researcher brings to any investigation by virtue of the moment of writing. Assumptions are the frames that historians use but forget they are using, intent as historians are on presenting past events directly to the reader as "the way it was."[15] For example, piracy practices were downplayed in the first historical frame (1926–1939), marginalized in a second, and today, in a third, reconsidered. To put it another way, in the first period of historical writing, industry apologists took piracy out of the frame.[16] In the 1990s, a second historical revision relegated piracy to the edges.[17] Today we are seeing new interest in copyright history on the part of early cinema historians.[18]

Now when we look back on the frames that earlier downplayed piracy battles, we can ask what our current frame will see or not see, the problem being that we don't yet know what we will have missed. What faces us, then, is also the task of acknowledging our present-day moment as a historical frame, one associated with the terms "digital turn" or "digital media," as we will see. Narrowing the third frame, I consider media industry lawsuits in the early 2000s as a consequence of the attempt to police the vast then-new territory of cloud computing. Our contemporary frame updates entertainment product piracy with the 2011–2014 lawsuits against German "cyberpirate" Kim Dotcom, aka Kevin Schmitz, aka Kim Tim Jim Vestor, founder of Megaupload Ltd., a site made famous by its demonstration of the gigantic storage capacity of cloud-based cyberlockers.[19]

In Dotcom and Lubin, we have two so-called pirates a century apart. Both enter the market early at the moment of a marked shift in forms of entertainment production and distribution: Lubin from stereoscopic pictures and illustrated slideshows to moving pictures; Dotcom from DVDs to online file-hosting services and from purchase to access. Here are two producers who got ahead of the game and were consequently cast as pirates. Or perhaps these are not crooks but two ingenious entrepreneurs who took up dubious practices that were at the time neither legal nor illegal, thus taking advantage of doctrinal uncertainty. Both were defendants in legal cases that hinged, to a degree, on the problem of "what it was" that they were undertaking to do or to make, and how it worked. And finally, Dotcom, like Lubin before him, continued distributing popular entertainment despite lawsuits from major media industries who claimed his company was in violation of their copyrights.[20] Lawsuits were mounted as the "what" remained unresolved, and, not surprisingly, duping and downloading continued.

Here, in this historical comparison, we discern the problem of technological change in theory but also as to-be-codified in common and statutory law. Note that while intellectual property doctrine may impact business in a way that in turn affects consumer use, our academic critical legal theory approach takes a longer view. Comparative media studies, if analyzing legal doctrine in statutory law and precedent in case law, are an exercise far removed from either federal policy-making or legal practice.

Studying technological transition through intellectual property doctrine contends with a built-in gap—a disjuncture in the form of a time lag between invention and statutory codification, a wait in which lower courts often extend outcomes by appeals to higher courts.

Additionally there is the difficulty of defining each new technology prefatory to the regulation of technological development and to do so by means of the legal balancing act that the US courts represent. Legal doctrine, over a century, has had conceptual trouble grasping copy technologies, as evident in the discourse before and after key statutory revisions in 1865 (photographs), 1976 (television), and 1998 (the internet).[21] Intellectual property doctrine has been and continues to be a strange and imperfect descriptor of the technological transformations it is tasked with regulating for the modern market system, one based on treating as property such unproperty-like objects as popular moving pictures.

Though an imperfect descriptor, the law must attempt to grasp a technology in order to control its use. US copyright has historically approached media change by means of broad historical analogy in which the term "like" drops out. Thus, a photograph *is* "a writing"; a phonorecord *is* a "stored performance"; a videotape of a television program is comparable to a phonorecord because it too *is* a "copy" although of an "original" live broadcast "performance." Hence the possibility that an ambiguous if not odd definition of the technology in question will emerge. As legal definition determines "what" can be regulated, a too-vague definition leaves the "what" question subject to challenge or, as seen in *Edison v. Lubin*, vulnerable to the kind of evasion characterized as "piracy." If the 1902 trial court decided that a motion picture was "an aggregation of photographs" (which were not protected as a *single* photograph already was), Lubin could continue to dupe Edison films, which he did until 1903, when the appeals court, overturning the 1902 decision, concluded that motion picture film was "a different type of photograph," not a new medium but still "a picture produced by a photographic process." Strangely, Edison's copyright was affirmed in 1903 because the court decided that a motion picture film *is* a photograph, the medium for which copyright protection had been established.

Without a doubt, copy technologies present a huge challenge to the principle of copyright—that limited-time monopoly grant that allows the holder to stop another company from industrially duplicating and selling products that it passes off as its own. If earlier unexpected challenges came from the mechanical miracle of photographic duplication, the internet, with production and distribution so indistinguishable, has upped the ante. While earlier commentators characterized photography as a "surprise" to copyright, legal scholar Lawrence Lessig calls the internet a more devastating "shock." At the beginning of the current century, Lessig foresaw more total copyrighted material at risk of "theft" than ever before.[22] After all, to download is "to copy." But paradoxically, Lessig also predicted for owners "more control over copyright in cyberspace than they had in real space."[23] So which is it? More theft or more control?

More theft but also more control may seem strange to the reader although it helps if we map this apparent inconsistency onto the most basic principles of US copyright law. These principles follow from a commitment codified in the US Constitution "to promote the Progress of Science and the useful arts [. . .]," which it does by means of a limited term of exclusive rights, a grant understood as copyright for more than three centuries.[24] Following from the idea that "progress" requires creativity, we have copyright's swing between *circulation* and *restriction*. That is, legal *restriction* is supposed to encourage creativity by securing the monetary awards of the author's labor for a limited period, but *circulation* makes creativity possible by freeing up cultural raw materials for new combination. So copyright is expected to historically oscillate between *circulation* and *restriction*, with a stressed provision that the monopoly conferred is for a limited time.

Now think about the comparability of technologies in conjunction with the comparability of times. Already we have in a century of piracy a case of historical contrast—two pirates a century apart—that complicates the methodology of making things comparable. We have seen the oddity of legal comparability entailing use of analogy (a photograph is a "writing"), to which we can add the family tree of precedent, similar cases branching from established case law. More difficult, however, is the broader comparability of times, the past relative to the present, as framed by historical accounts, first in the 1926–1939 period, and again with our contemporary frame beginning after 2000.[25] Even more problematic, since we started with the motion picture—that twentieth-century copy technology epitomizing "newness" for its time—we will want to ask how the cyberlocker represents "newness" for its different moment. An attendant question is whether the goal of historical research is to gain knowledge about the past itself untainted by the present or knowledge for the present, the answer to which the traditional historian usually evades. Not so the contemporary student of media, for whom a remarkable exception foregrounds our historical frame as part of the "digital turn." This is because the appearance of the digital is so often linked to the "death of cinema."[26]

New to Old: "Digital Media" as Key to Early Cinema

The question of "knowledge for whom and at what historical moment?" may be one way of defining the work of "media archaeology." Let's then test Thomas Elsaesser's proposal to use the advent of what he terms "digital media" as an occasion to study historical change in early cinema by exploring metaphors of "emergence" and "transformation."[27] Paramount here is the question, in his terms, of "rupture," which we'll translate into the problematic of the "when new" relative to emergence. We're reminded that, as John Durham Peters remarks, "Technology ... [is] biased towards newness," so in the history of media technology there may be a high expectation of instrumental breakthrough as a kind of "rupture."[28] Then how "new" is the new, we want to know, if corresponding recognition in US courts has been so incremental? For example, in *Edison v. Lubin* (1903), when the judge was pressed to determine whether motion pictures were a new medium or not, he could only decide, because of the rule of precedent, relative to the established case of the still photograph.

Taking our contemporary "digital media" third frame as a starting point, we might then consider the explosion of online file-hosting services in the early 2000s, as, at the time, the ultimate entertainment access for movie fans via cyberlocker online storage systems, "emergent" at this moment. Then, moving from the cyberlocker back to the "emergent" in the 1897 to 1907 piracy period, we ask what comparable late nineteenth-century "technology" was then undergoing transformation, while we remain aware that the term "technology" glosses over the distinction between mechanical and computational.[29] But if we forge ahead anyway, we still must ask "what" technology, since whatever that technology was, it was then in the process of becoming "something other than what it had been."[30] Certainly in 1902–1903, "what" it was could no longer be "*a* photograph," although the court in *Edison v. Lubin* (1903) found, for purposes of doctrinal application, that it *was* "a single photograph of the whole."[31] Then a further problem goes to the heart of historical vantage: our contemporary "digital media" frame invariably relies on current terminology, one example of which is the distinction between hardware and software. Is this how Elsaesser wants us to proceed?

Let's see if, following Elsaesser's suggestion to use "digital media" to study the first decade, the hardware/software distinction works to enlighten us. More than one scholar has used the hardware/software paradigm to explain the distinction that the Edison Company did *not* immediately make between filmstrips and machines, even though they were initiating separate patent and copyright filings in the first years.[32] As early as 1891, Edison's first patent filing was for what *we* would see as "hardware": the "kinetographic camera." W. K. L. Dickson, however, who undertook the first US Copyright Office filing in 1893, did so for what *we* take to be "software": photographs he titled *Edison Kinetoscopic Records*.[33] Providing further evidence that the "what" was at the time unresolved, the earliest published references from 1894 were to what inventor W. K. L. and his sister Antonia Dickson called "kinetoscopic and kinetographic experiments" which, since these were only "experiments," neatly evaded the "what was it?" issue. There was as well the "which was which?" question. As Paul Spehr later observed, the Edison staff was not always clear about "which" machine, confusing "scope" and "graph," alternatively using one term to refer to the viewing machine and the other to the taking machine (camera).[34] It was just as possible that they used the term "kineto." The chapter heading in the Dicksons' 1894 biography of Thomas Edison curiously uses the term "kinetos," which could refer to either the machine or to whatever was threaded though the machine to create the resultant "illusion" of movement.[35] Edison himself so favored the kinetograph writing machine that he concentrated his attention there and apparently took little interest in images of subjects like Eugene Sandow impressed on the strip of what *Edison v. Lubin* (1902) referred to as "sensitized tape-like film."

So a digital media category used to study late nineteenth-century technological transformation may only tell us that the hardware/software distinction had no easy equivalent at the advent of the kinetoscope and that the "tape-like film" was or wasn't considered part of the machine. But no paradigm can keep up with the speed of change that characterizes a century of copying technologies with such varied entertainment systems, each part of an apparatus: Vitascope film projection, film print distribution, televisual broadcasting, VHS-tape store rental, Netflix DVD mail delivery. Studying the old via the new we might posit from this that the delivery system is gradually disappearing. For instance, the OCFH (One Click File Host) access to favorite movies may be so obscured by the cloud delivery system that viewers haven't stopped to think that there would be no video download to watch on their home computers without a hardware/software interface, not to mention that they are likely unaware that giant servers store the data they use.[36] In asking what media contributes to the historiographic project, Elsaesser may call our attention to how devices have been historically reconceptualized, again and again, and not only as the media that they *never were* in the first decade. For as we have seen, it's difficult to separate "what" they might have been from "what" we today need such "kinetoscopic and kinetographic experiments" to point toward—"cinema" as encompassing "digital media." Or today we may need to see a hardware/software distinction in 1891–1894 in an effort to fit photochemical film on a continuum with computational media with no significant rupture.

OLD TO NEW: EARLY CINEMA AS KEY TO THE "DIGITAL MOMENT"

Does Elsaesser really advocate starting with the (new) "digital media" present as a vantage on the (old) 1897–1907 period? Maybe, maybe not. Because later in the same essay Elsaesser reverses his emphasis—from new to old followed by from old to new. After he asks what the present "digital media" bring to bear on media at their first historical "emergence," he then asks if early cinema can be a key to understanding the "digital moment." He wonders: "What can early cinema studies tell us about the kinds of rupture represented by the digital, and thus what does it teach us about our present multimedial, intermedial, hypermedial moment?"[37] We are being asked to examine the historical past for clues as to developments *in the future*. Yet, to expect that the early period can tell us something about the technological present and even, phrased this way, to suggest that it can teach us at all seems a tall order. Still, in comparative historical, as well as, more specifically, comparative *technological* studies, that is what we expect. In academic endeavor, not to mention daily life, "learning from the past" is an uncontested given. We engage in the established tradition of researching the past as explanation for the present state of affairs on the assumption that the past holds the key to how we got here from there, implying that we ended up here *because of* what went before. This is to say, in effect, that we are where we are today because of what "they" did earlier. How often do we say that consequences will be "borne out" later? This is causality delivering "it is what it is because of what went before." Yet Elsaesser also raises strong objections to this. He objects to such historical causality, yes, but still advocates studying the historical conditions of cinema at its emergence.

What we know today about the first decade we may likely have been taught *not* by the historical past alone but by the historical present, as our hardware/software example suggests. The trouble is that we presently know things without even knowing *that* we know them, let alone knowing *when* it was that we learned them. We might better consider the reciprocity of the present interpreting the past which in turn interprets the present which is more or less in line with a Foucauldian "archaeology." Such an approach takes the present to be historical in its own right and is Elsaesser's justification for studying the past in terms of the (historical) present. "Digital media," he says, tests established film history because, in thinking through a given phenomenon, we are fitting the present into the historiographic equation.[38] Better, then, to think of historical *relations*, to recall my argument for a more circular comparability of times.

To clarify: whether studying the old via the new or the new via the old, we are really studying and learning from both *at the same time*. This leads me to think of the relation between Siegmund Lubin and Kim Dotcom as neither parallel nor similar but as a matter of echoes—a bouncing back and forth between two times and two cases. This is to acknowledge, again, the reciprocity of historical *relations* between the present "now" of our analysis and the "before now" of the inaccessible first decade of the last century. Anglo-American intellectual property doctrine serves our purpose as a foil—historical comparison (a photograph is a "writing") in copyright doctrine overlooks properties in order to fit the technologically new into the old slot of precedent. While legal doctrine is historically deferential, our approach is reciprocal.

To bring copyright doctrine up to date, then, today we approach the regulation of copy technologies as a struggle in which the forces of cultural monopolization threaten to win out—first bigger businesses over smaller and later owners over users often engaged in "peer-to-peer sharing."[39] Or again, copyright swings between *restriction* and *circulation*. However, we must be aware of the fact that the two sides don't map perfectly onto *corporations* like Disney (ownership and *restriction*) as opposed to *users* like you and me (availability and *circulation*). For *users* may find themselves on the same side as corporate Google in the case of the cyberlocker in anticipation of a future of ever-easier access for both the search engine and the downloader.[40]

Copying Technology as "Accidental Technology"

The twenty-first century is marked by the piratical distribution of popular moving pictures relative to world regions and culture-in-transit. For the moment, however, let's leave aside the economic boon that piracy of First World entertainment goods represents for the global South.[41] While "piracy" outside the US testifies to the relative absence of regulation, back home the discourse on *restriction* has threatened to drown out that of cultural *circulation*. Thus, Anglo-American legal commentators today largely see piracy as transgression in the absence of regulation and likely to surface with a vengeance in times when property issues are unsettled. However, there is that countervailing force to which I first alluded, which, advocating *circulation*, may today take the side of the pirate (although we should suspect that it is yet another strategy to maximize profits). So how is piracy legally defended today? Ingeniously, some intellectual property scholars have proposed that copyright pirates can be seen as technological "innovators."[42] One sees here a variation on Lawrence Lessig's premise that every technology can expect a piratical period.[43] To his advocacy for *circulation*, however, I want to add a twist based on one contemporary theory—the cyberlocker understood as an "accidental technology."[44]

Remembering that we can't subtract the 1897–1907 period from what we now know, let's see how the contemporary concept of "accidental technology" connects Dotcom to Lubin. Lessig's "piratical period," however, is not based on our 1897–1907 period but on more recent copyright cases involving, most importantly for our cyberlocker example, off-air taping of network television shows.[45] For there is a century of copyright rulings between 1903 and the first decade of the twenty-first century.[46] Prefatory to the Megaupload cases we need to consider the problem that the videotape recorder (VTR) posed for big media industries in the 1980s. Like the Edison Company before them, Universal Pictures banked on copyright law to guard against the mass duplication of their popular entertainment products, a copying that they claimed undercut their profits. But because the videotape recorder was designed for the home market, business competitors were not considered the infringers. The culprits were ordinary people, that is, Universal's very own television broadcast viewers. These viewers could easily copy their favorite programs in possible violation of the monopoly rights that media producers claimed. In other words, in the 1980s, users were the new "pirates."

Crucially, the US Supreme Court decision in *Sony v. Universal Pictures* (1984), known as the "Betamax" case after Sony's VTR model, shifted the blame from users but also from the machine itself.[47] *Sony v. Universal* thus serves as our bridge connecting *Edison v. Lubin* to Lessig's hypothesis about piracy as technological vanguardism since the Betamax case took up the "as never before" potential of the videotape recorder to make copies, copying having moved out of the photographic laboratory and into the home. One of several defenses explored was the alibi that machine copier use was based on an unanticipated feature, one that was not advertised. The machine could be used to copy television programs and store them for later playback, a practice quickly described as "time-shifting." The inadvertent home copier, discovering the wonderful new use of the machine, might claim as a defense: "The machine made me do it." Following from this principle of something akin to "guilt by association" would evolve the concept of "contributory infringement," or "vicarious liability," to which the first of the cases against Megaupload Ltd. returned.[48] We might think here of how the very ease of cyberlocker access would attract a downloader who is an inadvertent infringer and thus how the "vicarious" concept could be used to shift liability to a corporate entity ostensibly more aware of the danger of copyright infringement than an ordinary user.

Let us test the historical application of Lessig's "piracy as media innovation" but, in addition, try to see it, like copyright infringement, as an inadvertent or "accidental" offshoot (albeit suspiciously calculated).[49] Who at the 2005 Megaupload launch could have predicted that a cyberlocker site would grab 4 percent of all internet traffic? Think back further. Who in 1897 predicted the ease of making multiple copies of a competitor's popular film featuring a moon landing? Let's consider Joseph Eckhardt's description as to how in 1897 Siegmund Lubin bought Edison Co. titles in his capacity as Philadelphia sales agent for the company. When these titles still did not meet the demand, Lubin bought a copy of every title from other foreign as well as US manufacturers. Still short on titles, Lubin produced copies by making negatives from which he struck positive prints, producing "dupe prints."[50]

Eckhardt, defending Lubin, interprets the decision to make dupe prints as a solution to the problem of insufficient supply to meet the demand. Duping could be seen as an offshoot of the innovative process of striking multiple prints that the Philadelphia optician stumbled onto.[51] Eerily, Peter Decherney excuses Lubin with an "accidental technology" theory. "Early duping was almost an accident," Decherney says, and then adds a crucial detail to validate this. A specific technical problem had to be overcome: Edison prints could only be made to thread through Lubin's Cineograph projection machines (see figure 5.3) if they were reprinted and perforated with Lubin-design sprocket holes.[52] Duping was the innovative way around this technical limitation given the specifications of the Cineograph projector tooth mechanism.[53]

So here we have motion picture piracy as accidental offshoot of the technologically new in response to an unanticipated consumer demand and as the consequence of a technical quirk. But in the current moment, viewing the cyberlocker industry as an "*accidental* technology" is taking it to be an unanticipated technological development albeit with not-so-unanticipated legal consequences, as legal historians Roman Lobato and Leah Tang argue. First, they define the cyberlocker phenomenon as "accidental," as in having happened not by "design" but by "chance." That is, the discovery that cloud storage could be used for circulating cultural objects like popular motion pictures, video games, and television programs was not immediate. This new cyberlocker use, the authors think, was the offshoot of an earlier technology that began with simpler systems for file exchange like FTP (file-transfer protocol), bulletin boards, or newsgroups, exemplified by Apple iTools or LG, the South Korean technology "webhard" service.[54] RapidShare, the Swiss cloud-storage platform, made the transition from a free storage solution (for files up to 50 MB and transmission of files too large to send via email) to a business facilitating downloads of popular films and television shows.[55] Megaupload, however, beat out RapidShare by increasing file size storage capacity to accommodate feature-length motion pictures. But here is where our case becomes interesting—the accident was "no accident." The Megaupload cyberlocker phenomenon was subject to legal "fallout" *of its own making*. Citing Paul Virilio, Lobato and Tang argue that the cyberlocker, in producing copyright infringement on such an enormous scale, quite contradictorily "produced its own 'accident.'"[56]

Contradictory as it may seem, however, an "accidental technology" theory can turn into a defense against the charge of "willful" or intentional copyright fraud. Infringement, the argument might go, would have to be an "accident" because who

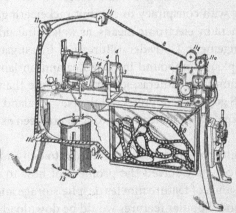

FIGURE 5.3 Lubin's Cineograph advertisement, *The Phonoscope*, October 1897.

would intentionally commit a crime on such a scale? Then again, what company would devise a scheme that was effectively an invitation to "mass infringement" without calculating how *not* to get indicted for "direct civil copyright infringement"? Calculation is the point. That indisputable infringing activity was *only* undertaken by anonymous uploaders *was* no accident, especially since Megaupload reasoned that the company would not be found "vicariously liable" for their members' activity. After all, in an early case, *Perfect 10 v. Megaupload* (2011), the court dismissed the charge of "vicarious liability," reasoning that the company had neither the "right" nor "the ability to supervise and control" infringement since anyone with access to the right URL could download video from the site.[57] The US Department of Justice, however, would not give up on the "vicarious" theory, using it again in their 2012 case against Megaupload, in which they charged the company with "criminal secondary infringement," still untested in the courts at the time.[58]

THE RAID ON THE MEGAUPLOAD COMPOUND

On January 5, 2012, the US government charged Kim Dotcom, his company, Megaupload Ltd., and six colleagues with conspiracy to commit racketeering, money laundering, and copyright infringement by electronic means, as well as the aiding and abetting of criminal copyright infringement. US Federal Bureau of Investigation (see figure 5.4) agents raided the Megaupload compound in New Zealand on January 19, confiscating computers, television monitors, cameras, jewelry, and more than twenty luxury vehicles.[59] But because the US government pressured the New Zealand government to undertake a raid that was illegal there, Dotcom has to date not been extradited to stand trial.[60]

Megaupload supplied a technological means to use the internet to deliver popular feature films as a file-hosting service. They solved the problem of how to provide consumers with easy access to thousands of feature movies despite storage and bandwidth limitations at the consumer end. Popular features would be downloadable but only via links to third-party linking companies accessible from the site.[61] Further, and rather astoundingly, one could make the case that Kim Dotcom, like Lubin before him (who argued that in 1902 moving pictures were not copyrightable because *only photographs were*), was actually compliant with the existing law. And why? Because under the US 1998 Digital Millennium Copyright Act (DMCA), a "host" site, in the words of the statute, has "content immunity from lawsuits when users infringe."[62] The statutory presumption is that the host will immediately take down files when the copyright owner makes a request. Megaupload appeared to comply in that the site was equipped with an "abuse tool," effectively a "take-down" button that would remove pirated files quickly. Here we again recognize Dotcom to be as ingenious a forerunner as Lubin at exploiting legal loopholes. Megaupload was not itself uploading millions of so-called infringing copies of Hollywood films: strictly speaking, company employees were not doing the uploading; its film fan members

COPYING TECHNOLOGIES   85

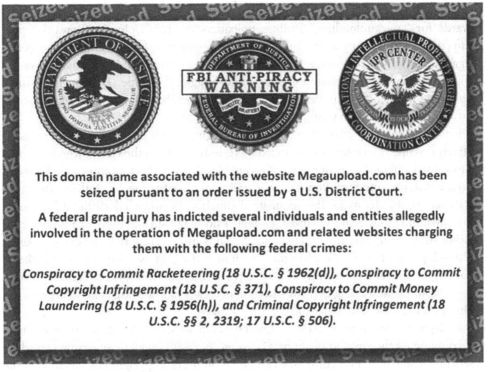

FIGURE 5.4   FBI Anti-Piracy Warning. Megaupload.com website.

were.[63] Further, Megaupload maintained that they operated legally under the provisions of the DMCA that allowed for "safe harbor" from copyright infringement for internet providers. However, they were expected to negotiate the use of an "abuse tool" with copyright holders.[64] But according to the Department of Justice lawsuit, the "take-down" tool button didn't work.

Other means of circumvention a century apart are oddly similar. Cutting off sections of popular movies before posting the films on YouTube reminds us of Lubin's assistant Balshofer inking out trademarks with a brush or, as was likely also his job, snipping off credits from prints before duping them.[65] Lubin used as his defense that he was unaware that he was making copies of Edison titles because there was no evidence of provenance on the strips of film duped in his laboratory (the trademarks or credits having been removed).[66] As Lubin before him, Dotcom could claim that he was unaware of having violated a law. He could plead that he didn't know which film and television titles were linked to Megaupload and that he had no knowledge of copyright violation because the Megaupload site itself did not directly access uploaded files.

In 1902, there was more demand for motion picture product than the first studios could supply. In 2012, there was a "video on demand" expectation before major studios could meet that demand or before subscription services such as Netflix could offer more than a limited number of streamed choices.[67] While the Lubin Company's model was based on "passing off" Edison's product as its own, the Megaupload variation on "passing off" entailed "passing on" the distribution function to users who were offered rewards for "megauploading." Prolific uploaders in the "Uploader Rewards" program could earn as many as five million reward points that would be worth $10,000.[68] Megaupload profits were made from premium subscriptions and advertising, but the key to profitability was volume—truly mind-boggling volume. Leasing forty-three datacenters when it was shut down in 2012, Megaupload had 180,000,000 regular users who averaged fifty million visits per day.[69]

Finally, the property claim that divides "infringing" from "non-infringing use" is effectively invisible, given how far removed this question is from the viewer who just wants to download a digital copy of the most recent blockbuster. Over a century of change in delivery systems, one forgotten feature persists: neither the mechanical nor the computational is able to make the requisite distinction between educational "fair use," "non-infringing use," and the "infringement" said to constitute "theft." Thus Lawrence Lessig's affidavit in support of Megaupload begins by asserting that the cyberlocker is a technology capable of *both* infringing and non-infringing uses. Or, the cyberlocker is a copyright-neutral technology. Here we have it. The assertion of copyright neutrality is tantamount to admitting that the question of piracy has nothing at all to do with the technology itself—not in either 1902 or 2012. And yet.

Yes, legal battles around copy technologies tip us off that culture is property—copyright being the right to profit by exclusion. But with its focus so firmly placed on *restriction*, trained first on companies and then on users, copyright law has missed the technological miracle, time and again. Here is the marvel for which entertainment companies, first moving pictures, then sound recording, then television, have been unprepared. In unguarded moments, media moguls' worst fears slip out. In the documentary *Kimdotcom: Caught in the Web* (2017) (see figure 5.5), the late MPAA president Jack

FIGURE 5.5 Kim Dotcom. Online Advertisement.

Valenti gasps: "Ten thousand copies as pristine as the original." And "if you don't have copyright, you're dead."[70]

Conclusion: What Piracy Tells Us About Copying Technologies Then and Now

I set out expecting to find the Megaupload cyberlocker phenomenon as well as the case against Kim Dotcom to be an aberration from the century before in which Siegmund Lubin defied the Edison Company. Instead, I was struck by eerie echoes beginning with historical market chaos at the advent of new copying technologies—motion picture film production and distribution and digital media reproduction and distribution by file-sharing host sites. Then there is the futility of the legal system engaged as referee in adjudicating disputes on the basis of proprietary claims and copyright lawsuits expected to stand as a warning to those who try to circumvent the system.

A comparative media approach, if nothing else, begins by admitting that at the turns of two centuries the enormity of copying was completely unanticipated by copyright law. Lawsuits against alleged pirates are thus important not so much as indicative of "theft" as of scale—the unprecedented volume of copying due to consumer appetite for even more and ever-cheaper movies. We might then see in "piracy" charges not just the futility of regulation but the promise of copying technologies that can provide increasingly enormous reproductive capacity and ever-speedier delivery. To note a final resonance between Lubin and Dotcom: both thought big and imagined distribution as wider, not to mention product as cheaper.[71]

Copy technologies have historically helped to foil attempts to privatize popular cultural forms as juridical disputes confirm. So let's not then give up completely on mass duplication as a means of resistance to the monopolization of culture or as one more way to critique capitalist expansion into every corner of our social lives. There is, after all, the unbelievable reproductive capacity as seen in the very circulation of favorite titles, from *Trip to the Moon* to the Marvel universe, in unlimited supply, available all the time and possibly forever.[72]

Notes

1. Charles Musser, *Introduction to Thomas A. Edison Papers: A Guide to Motion Picture Catalogs, 1894–1908* (New Brunswick, NJ: Rutgers University Press, 1985), 7, says that the International Film Company as early as October 1896 was selling dupes of Edison Company films. However, the major companies began in 1897 and stopped around 1907.
2. In Jane M. Gaines, "What Piracy Tells Us About Motion Picture Technology That We Didn't Want to Know," unpublished paper delivered at the Domitor Seventeenth International Conference, June 2022, I discuss how Edison Company lawyers checked

with the US Copyright office to determine whether foreign prints they had bought had been copyrighted.
3. Joseph P. Eckhardt, *The King of the Movies: Film Pioneer Siegmund Lubin* (Madison, NJ: Fairleigh Dickinson University Press, 1997), 46, says that the Méliès dupe screened for the angry customer must have been titled *A Trip to Mars* since Lubin had already produced another film titled *A Trip to the Moon* (1899). Eckhardt doesn't give a source for the information about the title of the film in question. Howard Lamarr Walls, *Motion Pictures: 1894–1912* (Washington, DC: US Copyright Office, Library of Congress, 1953), 63, lists *A Trip to Mars* © Siegmund Lubin (4 May 1903), number H31340.
4. Fred Balshofer and Arthur C. Miller, *One Reel a Week* (Berkeley: University of California Press, 1967), 9. Balshofer has confused Georges with his brother Gaston, who opened Star Pictures in New York in 1902.
5. In Balshofer and Miller, *One Reel a Week*, 8, Balshofer had asserted as much: "I had discovered that Lubin wasn't the only one who took part in the shady business of duping. It was common practice."
6. Sumner Smith, "Arthur D. Hotaling Recalls the 'Good Old Days,'" *Moving Picture World*, July 15, 1916, 380–381.
7. Hunter Koch, "Duped History: The Problem of Motion Picture Piracy in the Early Cinema Archive," unpublished paper delivered at the Domitor Fifteenth International Conference, George Eastman Museum, Rochester, New York, June 13–16, 2018.
8. Jane M. Gaines, "Piratical Practices Before 1907: Why Researchers Find Exactly What They Are Looking For," unpublished paper delivered at the Domitor Fifteenth International Conference, 2018.
9. Our 1897–1907 study covers the period before "cinema," the term now widely used to designate the medium's institutionalization from around 1915. André Gaudreault, *Film and Attraction: From Kinematography to Cinema*, trans. Timothy Barnard (Urbana: University of Illinois Press, 2011), 19.
10. *New York Clipper*, July 12, 1902, 444.
11. J. H. White, Manager Film Dept. to Howard H. Hayes, August 29, 1902 (Box 78); James H. White affidavit, October 18, 1902, 1 (Box 77). Edison National Historic Site, National Parks Service.
12. *Thomas A. Edison v. Siegmund Lubin*, no. 25, April Sessions 1902, Circuit Court, Eastern Dist. of Pennsylvania, June 6, 1902.
13. *Thomas A. Edison v. Siegmund Lubin*, US Circuit Court of Appeals, Third Circuit, 122 F. 240; US App. 4757, April 20, 1903.
14. Eckhardt, *King of the Movies*, 46–47. The difference between a dupe and a remake would become important after 1903, such that "Films Pirated and Duped," *Moving Picture World*, September 21, 1907, 451, tried to differentiate between "duped" films and remakes, which they termed "pirated," although this distinction did not catch on.
15. See Keith Jenkins, *Refiguring History* (New York: Routledge, 2003), 39–40.
16. Benjamin Hampton, *History of the American Film Industry from Its Beginnings to 1931* (1931; repr. New York: Dover Publications, 1970), 60, refers to piratical practices as "unbusinesslike"; Terry Ramsaye, *A Million and One Nights* (1926; repr. New York: Simon and Schuster, 1986), 308, analogizes pirates with cattle rustlers and claim jumpers in comparing the first decade with the Wild West; Lewis Jacobs, *The Rise of the American Film* (1939; repr. New York: Columbia University Press, 1975), 62, is more even-handed: accusations of theft and copying multiplied enmities throughout the trades.

17. Charles Musser, *Before the Nickelodeon: Edwin S. Porter and the Edison Manufacturing Company* (Berkeley: University of California Press, 1991).
18. See, for example, the title of the Seventeenth International Domitor Conference: "Copy/Rights and Early Cinema."
19. For more detail see David Fisher, *The Secret Life of Kim Dotcom: Spies, Lies, and the War for the Internet* (Auckland, NZ: Paul Little Books, 2013).
20. *Twentieth Century Fox Film Corp., Disney Enterprises, Inc., Paramount Pictures Corp., Universal City Studios Productions LLLP, Columbia Pictures Industries, Inc., and Warner Bros. Entertainment, plaintiffs v. Megaupload Ltd., Vestor Ltd., Kim Dotcom, Mathias Ortmann, and Bram Van Der Kolk*, https://www.motionpictures.org/wp-content/uploads/2014/04/2014-04-07-Stamped-Complaint.pdf, accessed July 30, 2022. In April 2014, "cyberlocker" Megauploads Ltd., two years after its storage site had been taken down, was charged with copyright infringement by five motion picture producers in the US District Court, Eastern District of Virginia, Alexandria, Virginia. That complaint listed thirty films that had been released by six studios, from older titles like *Ghostbusters* to more recent titles such as *Crazy, Stupid Love*. *Los Angeles Times*, April 7, 2014.
21. Statutory revisions 1865, 1976, 1998. Digital Millennium Copyright Act (DMCA).
22. Lawrence Lessig, *The Future of Ideas* (New York: Vintage Books, 2001), 200. Bernard Edelman, *Le droit saisi par le photographie* (Paris: Maspéro, 1973), if translated as "The Law 'Seized' by Photography," suggests the trouble technology causes this law. The few discussions of this book, translated as *Ownership of the Image: Elements for a Marxist Theory of Law*, trans. Elizabeth Kingdom (London: Routledge and Kegan Paul, 1979), correspond with the appearance of critical legal studies. See Jane M. Gaines, *Contested Culture: The Image, the Voice, and the Law* (Chapel Hill: University of North Carolina Press, 1991), chap. 1.
23. Lessig, *The Future of Ideas*, 202.
24. The United States Constitution, Article 1, Section 8, Clause 8.
25. See Jane M. Gaines, "What Next?": The *Historical Time* Theory of Moving Picture History," in Malte Hegener and Yvonne Zimermann, eds., *How Film Histories Were Made: Materials, Methods, Discourses* (Amsterdam: Amsterdam University Press, 2023), where I discuss the comparability of times relative to Koselleck's concept of "historical time" as it relates to technological "newness." See Reinhart Koselleck, *The Practice of Conceptual History: Timing History, Spacing Concepts*, trans. Todd Samuel (Stanford, CA: Stanford University Press, 2002), chap. 8.
26. See André Gaudreault and Philippe Marion, *The End of Cinema?: A Medium in Crisis in the Digital Age*, trans. Timothy Barnard (New York: Columbia University Press, 2015), for a more complex account.
27. Thomas Elsaesser, "The New Film History as Media Archaeology," *Cinémas* 14, nos. 2–3 (Spring 2004): 75–117.
28. John Durham Peters, *The Marvelous Cloud: Toward a Philosophy of Elemental Media* (Chicago, IL: University of Chicago Press, 2015), 36.
29. Benoît Turquety, "Toward an Archaeology of the Cinema/Technology Relation: From Mechanization to 'Digital Cinema,'" in Annie van den Oever, ed., *Techne/Technology* (Amsterdam: Amsterdam University Press, 2014), explores the historical implications of cinema relative to "technique" or "technology." Equally important, he argues for going beyond the ontological "what is it?" since "digital cinema" is more of a "historical epistemology" question (63).

30. See Rick Altman, *Silent Film Sound* (New York: Columbia University Press, 2014), chap. 3, "Crisis Historiography," on technological identity crises in which "what it is" never appears at first, but emerges after a push and pull between users and producers.
31. *Edison v. Lubin*. US Court of Appeals, Third Circuit. 122 F. 240 April 20, 1903, 3.
32. Charles Musser, *The Emergence of Cinema: The American Screen to 1907* (Berkeley: University of California Press, 1990), sees Edison's attention as focused on machines; Musser, *Before the Nickelodeon*, 44, says that in the first decade, "hardware" was always of more concern than content.
33. Paul Spehr, *The Man Who Made Movies: W. K. L. Dickson* (New Barnet, UK: John Libbey, 2008), 304.
34. Ibid., 84–85.
35. W. K. L. Dickson and Antonia Dickson, *The Life and Inventions of Thomas Edison* (New York: Thomas Y. Crowell, 1891), 297, 299.
36. Lev Manovich, *Software Takes Command* (New York: Bloomsbury, 2013), 114, reminds us that what we thought were "properties" of the image are not even to be found in the data but are dependent on the interface with software; see Tung-Hui Hu, *A Prehistory of the Cloud* (Cambridge, MA: MIT Press, 2015), chap. 3, "Data Centers and Data Bunkers."
37. Elsaesser, "The New Film History as Media Archaeology," 105.
38. Ibid.
39. Nick Marx, "Storage Wars: Clouds, Cyberlockers, and Media Piracy in the Digital Economy," *Journal of e-Media Studies* 3, no. 1 (2013): 9.
40. Ramon Lobato and Leah Tang, "The Cyberlocker Gold Rush: Tracking the Rise of File-Hosting Sites as Media Distribution Platforms," *International Journal of Cultural Studies* 17, no. 5 (2014): 424.
41. See articles in Tilman Baumgärtel, ed., *A Reader in International Media Piracy* (Amsterdam: University of Amsterdam Press, 2015); also important are the recent studies that suggest that piracy be seen as transnational distribution that benefits as well as subverts Hollywood. For example: Laikwan Pang, "Copying *Kill Bill*," *Social Text* 23, no. 2 (83) (Summer 2005): 133–153; Barbara Klinger, "Contraband Cinema: Piracy, *Titanic*, and Central Asia," *Cinema Journal* 49, no. 2 (Winter 2010): 106–124.
42. Ramon Lobato, *Shadow Economies of Cinema: Mapping Informal Film Distribution* (London: Palgrave Macmillan, 2012).
43. Lawrence Lessig, *Free Culture: The Nature and Future of Creativity* (New York: Penguin Press, 2004).
44. Lobato and Tang, "The Cyberlocker Gold Rush," 425.
45. See *A&M Records, Inc. v. Napster, Inc.*; Lessig, *Free Culture*, 73–74: Lessig's analysis of the 2001 court injunction to stop Napster from uploading copyrighted music argues that this was a "war on file-sharing technologies, not a war on copyright infringement."
46. Copyright in the motion picture industry was not established until 1912 as an amendment to the US Copyright Act of 1909, https://www.copyright.gov/history/1909act.pdf, accessed July 30, 2022. For later developments relevant to moving pictures see Peter Decherney, *Hollywood's Copyright Wars: From Edison to the Internet* (New York: Columbia University Press, 2012), chap. 1. On the Motion Picture Patents Company's 1908 solution to piracy, see Janet Staiger, "Combination and Litigation: Structures of U.S. Film Distribution, 1896–1917," *Cinema Journal* 23, no. 2 (Winter 1983): 41–72.
47. *Sony v. Universal Studios, Inc.*, 480 F. Supp. 464 U.S. 417 (1984).

48. *Perfect 10 v. Megaupload, Ltd.* No. 11-cv-0191, 2011 US Dist. LEXIS 81931, at *18 (S.D. Cal. July 26, 2011).
49. See note 44.
50. Eckhardt, *King of the Movies*, 25.
51. Eckhardt attributes to Lubin a more inclusive approach in the first decade and even argues that he envisioned the need for early manufacturers to "pool resources" as a means of jump-starting a new commercial venture. Eckhardt, *King of the Movies*, 25.
52. Peter Decherney, "Copyright Dupes: Piracy and New Media in *Edison v. Lubin* (1903)," *Film History* 19 (2007); reprinted as chap. 1 in Decherney, *Hollywood's Copyright Wars*. On Dickson's design for the Edison 35mm film format, which included four perforations on either side of the frame, see Spehr, *The Man Who Made Movies*, 386–387.
53. An introduction to the ferocity of Edison's patent litigation is Martin Sopocy, "The Edison-Biograph Patent Litigation of 1901–1907," *Film History* 3 (1989): 11–23, 25–27. It is possible to imagine that Lubin built his Cineograph projector by rejigging the component parts of Edison's kinetograph. The proliferation of sprocket hole standards might provide a rationale for making dupe prints and explain entrepreneurial attempts to get around Edison Company patents on the first kinetographic machines.
54. Lobato and Tang, "The Cyberlocker Gold Rush," 425.
55. Ibid.
56. Ibid.
57. *Perfect 10 v. Megaupload, Ltd.* No. 11-cv-0191, 2011 US Dist. LEXIS 81931, at *18 (S.D. Cal. July 26, 2011).
58. Ross Drath, "Hotfile, Megaupload, and the Future of Copyright on the Internet: What Can Cyberlockers Tells Us About DMCA Reform?" *John Marshall Review of Intellectual Property Law* 205 (2012): 217–218.
59. *United States of America v. Kim Dotcom*, 2012 WL 149764 (E.D. Va.), 37–43.
60. As of this writing, the US Dept. of Justice has not been successful in its attempts to have Kim Dotcom extradited from New Zealand to stand trial in the US; see Tracy Withers, "Kim Dotcom Vows to Fight Extradition as Co-Defendants Get Deal," *Bloomberg*, May 9, 2022, https://www.bloomberg.com/news/articles/2022-05-10/kim-dotcom-vows-to-fight-extradition-as-co-defendants-get-deal, accessed July 30, 2022.
61. *United States of America v. Kim Dotcom*, 4. Megaupload used such popular linking sites as: *nnjavideo.net, megaupload.net, megarelease.net, kino.to, alluc.org, peliculasyonkis.com, serisyonkis.com, surfthechannel.com, taringa.net, thepiratecity.org,* and *mulinks.com*. URL links to copies of copyrighted material were stored on Megaupload's servers according to the indictment.
62. Digital Millennium Copyright Act (DMCA), codified at Title 17, U.S. Code, Section 512.
63. Andrew Stevenson, "Another Victory For Kim Dotcom, He's Getting All His Metaupload Data Back," *Neowin*, September 9, 2014, http://www.neowin.net/news/another-victory-for-kim-dotcom-hes-getting-all-megaupload-data-back, accessed July 30, 2022.
64. Digital Millennium Copyright Act (DMCA), codified at Title 17, US Code, Section 512. *United States of America v. Kim Dotcom*, 2012 WL 149764 (E.D. Va.), 5.
65. Balshofer and Miller, *One Reel a Week*, 9.
66. Eckhardt, *King of the Movies*, 25, refers to Lubin's courtroom defense: he did not know what company produced a film when he copied it.
67. Chuck Tryon, *On-Demand Culture: Digital Delivery and the Future of Movies* (New Brunswick, NJ: Rutgers University Press, 2013).

68. *United States of America v. Kim Dotcom*, 2012 WL 149764 (E.D. Va.), 2.
69. Ibid.
70. For the New Zealand-produced documentary *Kim Dotcom: Caught in the Web* (dir. Annie Goldson, 2017) see https://watchdocumentaries.com/kim-dotcom-caught-in-the-web/. Dotcom has also produced his own promotional videos, which appear on his website; the website also includes updates on the company now called Mega: https://www.kim.com.
71. Lubin responded early to the possibilities of motion pictures for the masses, inventing cheaper equipment, undercutting competitors with his pricing, and expanding from production to theater ownership with as many as one hundred theaters by 1910 and a new studio, Betzwood, in 1912. See Linda Woal, "When a Dime Could Buy a Dream: Siegmund Lubin and the Birth of Motion Picture Exhibition" *Film History* 6, no. 2 (1994): 152–165. On Dotcom's empire, see note 19.
72. To get a sense of contemporary scale see Damilola Ibosiola, Benjamin Steer, Albaro Garia-Recuero, Gianluca Stringhini, Steve Uhlig, and Gareth Tyson, "Movie Pirates of the Caribbean: Exploring Illegal Streaming Cyberlockers," *Association for the Advancement of Artificial Intelligence* (2018), http://www.aaai.org, accessed July 30, 2022.

PART II
INTERMEDIALITY
Genre and Aesthetics in Silent Film

CHAPTER 6

THE UNFINISHED BUSINESS OF HISTORY

Defense and Illustration of the Concept "Cultural Series"

ANDRÉ GAUDREAULT AND PHILIPPE MARION

Translated by TIMOTHY BERNARD, unless otherwise indicated

> Wherever there is no personal and even original effort there is not even the beginning of science.
>
> Henri Bergson[1]

THIS chapter,[2] as its title indicates, takes up the concept *cultural series* and, more precisely, its *defense* and *illustration*. If this concept needs to be *illustrated*, it is because, even though the words that make up the term are of common usage, their juxtaposition creates a complex ensemble that is not always easily applied. If it has need of being *defended*, it is because it has met with a fair degree of critical opposition. Despite the resistance to which it may have given rise, the use of the concept "cultural series" has grown exponentially over the past decade in the work of film studies scholars (but not only among them). This is why we thought it useful to return to the issue, with a text that might be seen as a post-scriptum to our earlier work.

The reason the concept has provoked such debate is because it has the merit of its faults! And its principal fault is also, to our eyes at least, its principal merit. Because the notion was conceived in such a supple manner, it leaves room for a kind of indeterminacy. This indeterminacy was palpable from the outset, as could be seen on several occasions in the course of the conference where the concept was initially outlined, more than twenty-five years ago.[3] One of the authors of the present text, who introduced the expression "cultural series" to the field of film studies, wrote the following at the time about the work of Georges Méliès:

> A film such as *Le Royaume des fées* (*The Kingdom of Fairies*, 1903) is a part of the *history of the fairy play* as much as if not more than it is a part of the *history of cinema*. The fairy play and the cinema are two different "cultural practices," and each has as much right as the other to be taken into account by the researcher or historian. They are two different "cultural practices"; or, better yet, they are in a certain sense two different "cultural *series*." A film such as *Le Bourreau turc* (*Decapitation in Turkey*, 1904), on the other hand, is more a part of the history of the magic sketch. The magic sketch and the cinema are two different "*cultural series*," and each has as much right as the other to be taken into account by the researcher or historian.[4]

The expression "cultural series" was thus proposed, initially, to describe different ensembles of recognized cultural practices (*recognized* being important, as we shall see). The fairy play, the magic sketch, the cinema (but also theater, the magic lantern, photography, the café-concert, the shadow play, prestidigitation, pantomime, etc.) are not only (recognized) cultural *practices* but are also, each independently of the other, cultural *series*.[5]

Although seemingly quite varied at first sight, the list above already demonstrates that cultural series can, in our view, involve both representational genres and representational media, meaning media whose vocation is representation. More fundamentally, the equation, the very principle of the concept "cultural series," is thus: *cultural practice = cultural series*. But what is the purpose of such a seemingly straightforward terminological substitution? By introducing the word "series," it becomes possible to view each of the practices under observation from a diachronic perspective, thereby inviting history to surge into the scholar's viewpoint and discourse. For the very idea of "series" makes it possible to connect the different moments experienced by one practice or another in the course of its history, in its evolution and transformations. To speak of a cultural *practice* as a cultural *series* is thus to endow that practice with a historical dimension.

Spread the word, then: in the beginning, a cultural series was just one way of taking a cultural practice out of its phenomenal milieu by assigning it a historical coefficient. The concept "cultural series" thus has a quality of abstraction that enables it to establish connections and continuities and to circulate freely in the world of discourse, whereas the expression "cultural practice" has a more concrete referential nature. The introduction of the concept "cultural series" thus had as its primary vocation to enable us to assume conceptually something that we normally only see empirically, namely, that any cultural practice has a diachronic dimension that can be explored. To use a landscaping metaphor, we would say that the concept "cultural series" invites a topographic perspective that would track the various contour lines, their windings and their turnings, whose presence would be difficult to distinguish by remaining at ground level.

Thus, to return to Méliès, we can see that the notion of a series makes possible something that the notion of a practice does not (or at least not easily): the establishment and recognition of ruptures and continuities *between* series. It is thus possible to argue, for example, that the *filmed* fairy play seems to be in continuity with the *staged* fairy play—as one of the two authors of the present text did twenty years ago, basing his opinion on an authoritative description of the *staged* fairy play published ten years *before* the invention of the Lumière Cinématographe (and thus ten years before the *filmed* fairy play even became possible).[6] We will let readers judge for themselves:

> The fairy play would surely be an adorable entertainment if it were done by a true poet letting himself follow the whims of his imagination freely and capable of delighting the minds of his viewers and amazing their eyes alike. [. . .] A]udiences always crowd into the fairy plays that are served up to them, because they adore this truly magical entertainment that the progress made in staging them has been able to make more enchanting with each new day. [. . .] The fairy play] is staged only where changes of perspective, trick effects, disguises, and apotheoses [can] easily be produced.[7]

This description of the staged fairy play applies so well to the filmed fairy play that one might think its author was Méliès in 1903, the year he made *The Kingdom of Fairies*. And yet this text was published in 1885 by a French theater historian, Arthur Pougin, and of necessity discusses only the live stage. Pougin's book is a dictionary whose title is particularly inspiring for thinking about the concept cultural series: *Dictionnaire historique et pittoresque du théâtre et des arts qui s'y rattachent* (*Historical and Illustrated Dictionary of the Theater and the Other Arts Associated with It*). Thus, in the late nineteenth century, there was the theater and the "other arts associated with it." And what exactly were these other arts? Pougin made no secret of them, because he drew up a prefatory list right on the title page of his book, in the form of a particularly long-winded subtitle: "Poetry, music, dance, pantomime, stage design, costumes, machinery, acrobatics. Sports from antiquity, itinerant shows, staged entertainment, public festivities, popular celebrations, carrousels, races, tournaments, etc., etc., etc." (see figure 6.1). These are "arts" which, with a few exceptions (such as music and dance), are not truly arts; today we would describe them as cultural practices—or, if one prefers, cultural *series*—connected with, but independent of, the theater and which, in addition to having their own autonomous lives, can now and then feed *into* theater.

As can be seen by the example given here, the idea of a cultural series was from the start treated less as a *construct* than as a *given*. A cultural series was not something made up by the thinker or historian but rather something self-evident: in the real world, there are recognized cultural practices, such as the theater, the cinema, literature, and painting, which are divided up in a manner that seemingly owes nothing to the researcher studying them. Naturally, however, this *given* is in reality the result of a social construct, for of course it is "society" that has constructed these series. A cultural series should, in this basic sense, be thought of as a construct that is *perceived* as an apparent given.

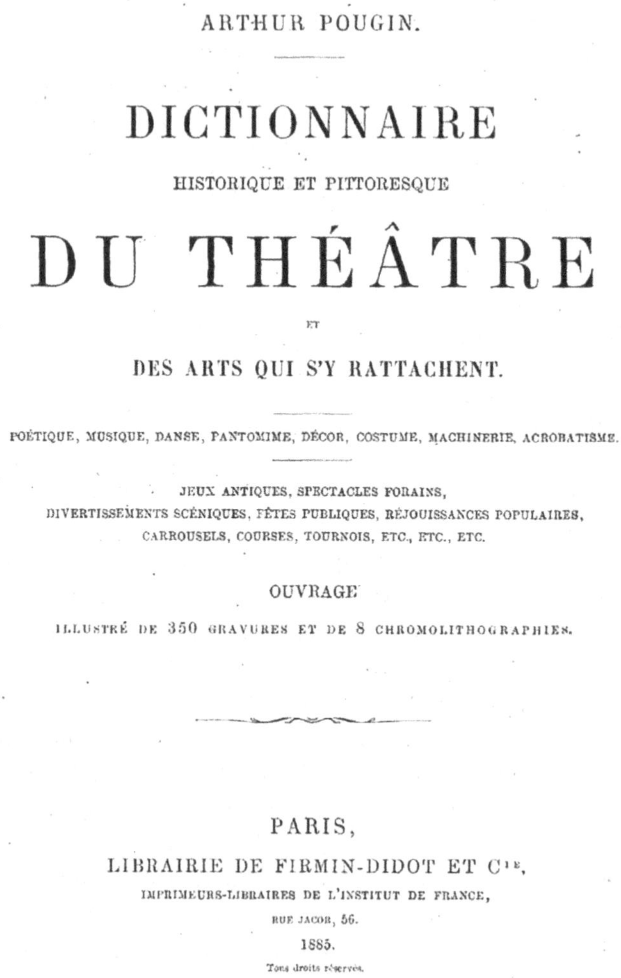

ARTHUR POUGIN.

DICTIONNAIRE

HISTORIQUE ET PITTORESQUE

DU THÉÂTRE

ET

DES ARTS QUI S'Y RATTACHENT.

POÉTIQUE, MUSIQUE, DANSE, PANTOMIME, DÉCOR, COSTUME, MACHINERIE, ACROBATISME.

JEUX ANTIQUES, SPECTACLES FORAINS,
DIVERTISSEMENTS SCÉNIQUES, FÊTES PUBLIQUES, RÉJOUISSANCES POPULAIRES,
CARROUSELS, COURSES, TOURNOIS, ETC., ETC., ETC.

OUVRAGE

ILLUSTRÉ DE 350 GRAVURES ET DE 8 CHROMOLITHOGRAPHIES.

PARIS,
LIBRAIRIE DE FIRMIN-DIDOT ET CIE,
IMPRIMEURS-LIBRAIRES DE L'INSTITUT DE FRANCE,
RUE JACOB, 56.
1885.
Tous droits réservés.

FIGURE 6.1 The title page of Pougin's dictionary.

It is nevertheless the case that historians who are led to view cultural practices from a diachronic perspective (if only by seeing them no longer as *practices* but rather as *series*) will before long encounter a few obstacles in their path. In unspooling the thread of time, historians quickly realize that cultural series are not "eternal." In any event, this is what happens to historians of a relatively recent cultural practice such as cinema. For when film historians examine the earliest years following the supposed "advent" of the medium, they are confronted with problems of method. The first problem is whether it is legitimate for historians to view the practice that came into being with the invention of the Lumière Cinématographe as "cinema," when they discover, in the course of their research, that the word did not exist in the vocabulary of the day. Indeed, the word "cinema" managed to establish itself only over the course of time. In English, people spoke instead, among other things, of the "cinematograph" or "kinematograph." Suddenly there are questions on all sides! Are the *cinema* and the *kinematograph* thus part of the same cultural *practice*? Furthermore, do they belong to the same cultural *series*? Was the invention of the Lumière Cinématographe, patented in early 1895 and often taken as the starting point of the cultural series known as cinema, instead the starting point of another cultural series, that of the kinematograph? For neither the Lumière brothers nor their contemporaries gave the name *cinema* to the cultural practice made possible by the Cinématographe. In fact there are very few occurrences, or none at all, of the word *cinema* in texts published before 1900 (one might expect to see the word mentioned in French texts, considering the term's semantic link with the Cinématographe), and it was only gradually, and fairly slowly, that the word became widespread, around 1910–15, especially in France, but also across the Atlantic.[8] In 1912, the largest publication of the French film industry placed the word "cinema" in scare quotes: "The *cinématographe*, or better yet the '*cinéma*,' or better yet '*ciné*,' as professionals say and as everyone will soon be saying!"[9] The word *cinema* took hold only gradually, in the 1910s, at the very time the new medium was in the process of being institutionalized.

Here is something that will sow confusion in the mind of the unsuspecting historian—especially if that historian is working frantically to show that "cinema" *before*, say, 1912–14 was beholden to a set of representational practices (corresponding, in this case, to "kine-attractography") that were completely alien to cinema *after* this period (corresponding to "institutional cinema").[10] And what, moreover, will this same historian do when they look at the 1890s and realize the incongruity of casting Edison's Kinetograph into the margins of the history of *cinema*, somewhere between "pre-cinema" and "cinema"? What will that historian make of the fact that society in the 1890s recognized, on a daily basis (as can be seen by examining the press of the day), a cultural practice described as "animated photographs" and whose invention preceded that of the Lumière Cinématographe by several years?[11] What will this historian make of the animated photographs shot in the Black Maria studio in 1894 and later, which were not projected on a screen publicly but viewed directly on an individual peep-show device known as a Kinetoscope? By what right would our historian privilege the series *kinematography* over the series *animated photographs*? And by what right might they discredit the series *animated photographs* in favor of the series *cinema*? Because the images from the cultural series "kinematography" belong no less to the series "animated photographs."

And what would this same historian make of the strips in Émile Reynaud's Théâtre optique, which, like those of the Lumière Cinématographe, were "luminous projections" but could not be likened to animated *photographs*, because they were made of drawings painted onto glass plates or gelatin sheets? This tumult of series will only be resolved if the historian concludes in the end that there exists, in a concomitant and concurrent manner, something like a series called *luminous projections* (which enjoyed quite strong social recognition in the final quarter of the nineteenth century), in addition to that other series, *animated photographs*, and that the series *kinematograph* is located at the intersection of these two (see figure 6.2). The *kinematograph* is a part of one as much as the other, because it is made up of *animated photographs* seen by the viewer by means of *luminous projections*. Our historian will also have to acknowledge that the co-existence of concurrent series makes it possible to approach the object of study from a variety of perspectives. At the same time this makes available weapons or tools to counter the monolithic teleology that has held sway until recently in the medium's historiography (but which has also been severely criticized over the past forty years).

Naturally, all these series do not hold the same weight with each researcher. They do not necessarily invite the same social recognition, and not all are equally spotted and listed, nor even spottable and listable (if the reader will permit the expression). Indeed, it would appear that the cultural series *luminous projections* enjoyed less social recognition at the time than the series *animated photographs*, and the latter even less than the series *kinematograph*. Serious documentary research, however, would make it possible to bring the series *luminous projections* out of the shadows. This series links the magic lantern and the optical theater and is perpetuated in subsequent other forms of *luminous projection*, such as the kinematograph and the cinema, not to mention fixed images (slides) or the kinds of visual presentations made by modern lecturers using their laptop computers. Recall, too, that what distinguishes the kinematograph from cinema is not just a matter of terminology. The term *cinema* is a result of the socio-cultural recognition of a visual medium that has become institutionalized. This is not true of the kinematograph. This distinction forms part of our model of the double birth, under which we propose to distinguish, on the one hand, the invention between 1890 and 1895 not of cinema but merely of a device for capturing/recreating moving images (of which the Lumière Cinématographe was the most advanced example) and, on the other, the establishment around 1910–15 of an institution for the production and dissemination of moving images.

Before beginning research to ascertain the level of social recognition of the series *luminous projections*, a film historian may well have certain apprehensions. What will they do if they cannot demonstrate unequivocally that *luminous projections* enjoyed real social recognition? The answer to this question may be surprising: the historian should feel authorized to create this series from scratch. For while the concept cultural series was initially modeled on a variety of *recognized* cultural practices, and the existence of one cultural series or another owed practically nothing to the historian (or to the discourse

THE UNFINISHED BUSINESS OF HISTORY 101

Projections Lumineuses

pour Conférences scientifiques et mondaines

MOLTENI

Chevalier de la Légion d'Honneur

RADIGUET & MASSIOT, Succ^{rs}

44, rue du Château-d'Eau, PARIS (10°)

APPAREILS DE CONSTRUCTION SOIGNÉE

pouvant recevoir tous les éclairages : pétrole, acétylène, lumière oxydriques et oxycalciques, **carburateur sécuritas**, arc électrique, incandescence par le gaz et l'alcool.

Les Appareils et collections de diapositives de **MOLTENI** se trouvent chez tous les Opticiens, Électriciens et les fournisseurs d'appareils photographiques de Province et de l'Étranger.

Exiger la marque : MOLTENI

Location de Vues

Pour la location des Diapositives pour Conférences scientifiques et mondaines, s'adresser au Service de L'Aide du Conférencier, Maison Radiguet et Massiot, *13 et 15, boulevard des Filles-du-Calvaire, PARIS.*

FIGURE 6.2 Period document published by the Radiguet & Massiot company, which in 1899 took over the famous magic lantern manufacturer Molteni.

deriving from his or her research and ideas), since 1999 this has no longer been the case, as proposed that year by one of the two authors of the present text: "The concept 'cultural series' [may also] presuppose a dividing up of the material by the researcher (whether an historian or not), who sets him- or herself the task of constructing *series* of events, *series* of facts, cultural *series*, and then of explaining the connections between them."[12] It was thus in 1999,[13] just a few years after the expression was first introduced (1996–97), that the concept cultural series was broadened in order to authorize, and even encourage, historians to create their own series, thereby becoming a *heuristic* tool in the service of an "exploration method" deriving, as the dictionary definition of "heuristic" would have it, from "successive evaluations and provisional hypotheses."[14]

For a historian of animated pictures, for example, it will be necessary to go beyond the realm of the given, because the given is only given as a construct. And historians must deconstruct the apparent given, must deconstruct every given, in order to see who constructed it, how it was constructed, and at what cost. To answer the question "*Who constructed this given?*" the historian must determine which social actors had an interest in disguising this construct as a given. To answer the question "*How was this given constructed?*" the historian must identify the historical operations carried out by these social actors to construct this apparent given, which has privileged one object over another. To answer the question "*At what cost was this given constructed?*" the historian must rediscover forgotten historical facts that had been buried or overlooked by earlier historians. A cultural series may thus be approached not only as a given (an *apparent* given, as we have just said) but also as, simultaneously, a historical construct. But it may further be a heuristic construct coming from the mind of the researcher, who uses it as a legitimate guide to help divide up cultural phenomena. Taking this logic even further, we might also suggest that the historian's construct may eventually acquire the status of a given for future generations of historians.

We should note, in this respect, that cultural series often sit atop or even encompass cultural practices. A report on a seminar led by Laurent Gerbier on the topic of cultural series makes the following point:

> What is fundamental about this conception of the "cultural series" is that it is not only a cultural practice; it is, above all, a problematic choice on the part of the researcher, who brings into existence a category that appears to make sense. Seen from this perspective, the concept "cultural series" is a research tool that produces the least biased intelligibility possible (meaning the least brutally genealogical possible, because one will have to use the concept cultural series to neutralize the endless question of origins, which operates for science fiction and comics alike as a screen preventing the researcher from working intelligently).[15]

In many cases, then, a cultural series may thus derive from an intellectual construct determined by the point of view of a researcher seeking to develop a category that would make it possible to divide up the historical or phenomenological continuum under study. And to carry this study out, to advance science, film researchers should necessarily, like every other kind of scholar, interpose some sort of heuristic lens between their gaze as observers and the objects they are observing.

Let's take a simple example, one that is dear to us and which has the advantage of clarity, because it has become very widely known: the famous case of the *invention of cinema*. Attributing this invention to the Lumière brothers is a perfectly ordinary notion, as we have been repeating over and over for years. If someone were to express this in casual conversation, it would invite little opposition. But such a thesis should not be admitted into a university setting. As we know, the question "Who invented cinema?" is false: one must first demonstrate that cinema is *something one invents* and that there must have been a patent application for such an invention. And yet of course there never was, anywhere in the world, a patent for the invention of the *socio-cultural phenomenon* known as cinema, which could never be reduced to the mere projection onto a screen of photographic images that give the illusion of movement. The only patents taken out by the so-called inventors of cinema were for devices used to take or project these pictures. To invent a device for projecting or taking pictures is not to invent cinema; it is the invention of a device which, even if it bears the name "Cinématographe," is not cinema. Cinema, as a socio-cultural phenomenon, could not be invented: it was *perfected, constituted, instituted*. Thus, to consider that we owe the invention of cinema to the Lumière brothers is a construct whose fault lies not only in its being a construct; it also has the massive fault of being a construct that *presents itself as a given*. If we wish to succeed in getting anything new out of film history, we must combat such constructs, which abound. And in our view the best way to combat these seeming truths is to contrast them with new constructs that do *not* present themselves as truths and that do not dread letting the truth be known about them—that they are provisional heuristics only and tools of historiographic revision.

The concept cultural series reveals the error in attributing the invention of cinema to the Lumière brothers. Indeed, it provides an opportunity to reshuffle the deck and avoid casting Edison's Kinetoscope into the margins of film history, into the midst of the "pre-cinema" period (another construct that today passes itself off as a given). Should Edison's Kinetoscope—with its perforated celluloid, in continuous use until just recently, and the synthesis of movement it carried out—really be cast into the shadows? We shouldn't believe the moon is made of green cheese, either, even if we do see it in a Méliès film! In the name of what principle and what pseudo-historical truth must we keep Edison and Lumière in opposite camps and incompatible worlds? For Edison and Lumière are easy to reconcile, thanks to the "magic" of cultural series, because they represent, as we said above, two cornerstones of the cultural series *animated photographs*.

A cultural series can thus be a historian's creation. But it is also, inevitably—and this is something we must be aware of—a way of *shining a spotlight* on various phenomena or aspects of a phenomenon. To identify a cultural series is to bring out a "doing [. . .] endowed with a cultural 'identity,'" as a collective of authors around Jan Baetens remarks:

> A cultural series, if we were to try to read this definition as broadly and as openly as possible, is thus a certain kind of doing (for example telling a story or reproducing reality) endowed with a historically identifiable cultural and media "identity" and which can take the most diverse material and media forms (one can tell stories using

words but also with sounds or images, just as one can attempt to reproduce reality, or an aspect or element of reality, through instruments either visual or verbal, analogue or digital, concrete or abstract, and so on).[16]

The construction of any cultural series is based on a principle of continuity. Researchers must ask themselves the kind of question articulated by Pierre Fresnault-Deruelle: "What is placed in series, migrating from medium to medium? Character types (Pierrot, tramps, etc.), a narrative or semantic kernel, themes, genres, decors, mise-en-scène, apparatus, tonality, current events or history, presenters and moderators, actors, etc."[17] The principle of continuity can also be conceived synchronically: how did a motif or cultural element circulate at a given time? An example would be the phenomenon of "buzz": associated with a mode of communication found on the internet and social media, buzz is at one and the same time a kind of marketing, publicity, political communication, viral polemic, artistic expression, and even a kind of aesthetics. This cultural series "buzz" is based on the dynamic of rapid propagation and linking, intensified by the exponential possibilities of the internet and social media. This linking dimension could undoubtedly also be raised up as a more general cultural series capable of incorporating buzz. A cultural series can in this way run through several media synchronously, while a medium or text, conversely, can belong to several series. Baetens and his co-authors provide an illustration of this principle: "The series 'documentary,' for example, can take the form of a journalistic reportage, either illustrated or not, but also the form of a silent film. As for the text of a documentary film, it may not only be a part of the series 'documentary' but also, for example, of the series 'art.'"[18]

But a cultural series truly unfolds in the *diachronic continuity* in which it finds itself. Let's look at a particularly striking example, that of the cultural series provided by the notion *plan* in French, the equivalent in English of both a "shot" in film and of a "plane" (in depth). Or, if one prefers not to lock *plan* into a single cultural series, we could try to understand how the very notion *plan* can be constructed differently according to the various cultural series that traverse it. In cinema, the shot is associated with the overriding question of shot scale, or the plane on which the filmed object is depicted, as determined by the framing and position of the camera. One could certainly carry out a history of this word as part of film vocabulary, but one could also try to trace its origins and follow its evolution beyond the film milieu alone, incorporating the word *plan* into a cultural series that would create connections between the uses of this word in fields other than cinema and before cinema: in cultural practices such as photography, theater, painting, and architecture. A historian studying early kinematography would thus remark upon the following facts:

- In all the above-named cultural practices, *apart from theater*, the word *plan* describes staggered planes of space: in photography, painting, and architecture, *plans* are "every flat surface, perpendicular to the viewer (generally vertical), depicting depth and distance in a real or imaginary scene shown in perspective (in drawings, paintings or photographs)."[19]

- In late-nineteenth-century theater, the word *plan* no longer described flat surfaces perpendicular to the viewer, and thus *vertical*, but rather *horizontal* divisions of the floor of the stage (of the floor itself!). Here is what Arthur Pougin said about the term in 1885:

    PLANS ON THE STAGE—In order both to move sets and block the movements of the characters, it was necessary to divide the floor of the stage into portions—zones of equal size which, on each side, draw a kind of imaginary line named a *plan* and which indicate clearly the division they make. In this way the space between the proscenium arch and the first flat at the back of the stage is called the *premier plan*, the space between the first and second flats becomes the *second plan*, and so on until the backstage curtain, with the final *plan* being the most distant.[20]

- Research carried out recently by one of the present authors on the cultural series *plan* has led to the hypothesis that it was the theatrical sense of the term that dominated in early kinematography, having been introduced through the term *premier plan*, or foreground. Before coming to mean a kind of framing with the camera, for kinematographers it initially meant the position of an actor or character on the floor of the set in which they were acting.[21]

Here, then, is the entirely theatrical origin of the expression *premier plan*, which would crystallize in kinematography and become even more important there than it was originally. Indeed, this expression *premier plan*, which one finds everywhere in scripts and catalogues in the kine-attractography period, was the first element of what would become in institutional cinema the vast nomenclature describing "shot scale," whose other elements (medium shot, medium close-up, close-up, etc., and their equivalents in French) appeared only gradually throughout the 1910s and 1920s. The history of interposed cultural series in this way permits a truly astonishing breakdown of categories. For is it not paradoxical that the origin of the word *plan*, which is thought and said to be a specifically cinematic term (if not *the* specifically cinematic term par excellence: the shot) should be rethought in light of an outside cultural practice such as theater? It would appear we have just answered our own question, as the saying goes.

At this point it is perhaps worth reassessing the distinction between cultural practice and cultural series in view of our understanding of the latter as a hermeneutic construct. One of the great difficulties here concerns how that distinction can profitably be applied to the study of the history, genealogy, or archaeology of media, as the following comment by Frank Kessler demonstrates:

It seems clear enough that a cultural practice is a historically demonstrable phenomenon while a cultural series is a construct of the historian. But beyond that things seem to me to be less clear [...]: when you speak of a filmed opera screened in a movie theatre, you call that a new cultural series. But for me it's a new practice.[22]

Without a doubt, but one must not forget that the notion cultural series was introduced originally to allow for its superimposition onto any cultural practice, whatever its nature, thereby endowing it with a diachronic dimension. It was only later that cultural series constructed from scratch by historians were brought into play, and only later also that such series could exist solely in reference to the historian's work. Filmed opera is certainly a cultural *practice*, but at the same time it may also be a cultural *series* for the historian, researcher, or thinker wishing to divide up cultural reality from the perspective of filmed opera. Moreover, as a cultural series, filmed opera is not as new as one might think. It all depends on whether one approaches the phenomenon in the long or short term. One could limit oneself to the new practice of operas transmitted live in movie theaters, developed around 2006 by the Metropolitan Opera in New York. But we must not forget that there were operas broadcast live in movie theaters as early as 1952. We must also not forget that there exists, in the same family, the cultural series "filmed operas for television" and the cultural series "radio broadcasts of operas," which take us way back. And if, by chance, a historian would wish to encompass all these phenomena, one would need only to propose the cultural series "operas broadcast from a distance," in which we might further include "operas broadcast over telephone," something inaugurated in 1881 by Clément Ader's Théâtrophone, which was marketed until 1932.

What is the value of seeing a *practice* as a *series*? Just this: it adds to the practice continuity and, in so doing, transcends the limitations of a more corporatist or professional perspective. The contours of the series may be confused for a time with that of the *practice*, but its vocation is other: to go beyond that practice by forging other links and other continuities, by prying it free of its status as a *practice*, by "demediatizing" it to give the series a function of heuristic "framing," which is precisely what a cultural series does.[23]

Conversely, we might also imagine that a series hypothesized by a researcher will eventually take concrete form *as* a cultural practice, even if this practice was not yet fully established at the moment the researcher coined the series. If such a theoretical and virtual series were to materialize as a practice at a later date, the researcher's hypothesis would come to bear a forward-looking, visionary perspective from the vantage point of future scholarship. If, for example, we consider the beginnings of the internet and social media, a "cultural series researcher" could have envisioned this new techno-media context through the lens of "linking" described above, thereby predicting its growth potential in future transversal and hypermedia practices. By going back along the thread of the history of this example, a sharp researcher of cultural series could even have interpreted the first publications by Paul Otlet and Henri La Fontaine on their idea of the Mundaneum from the potentially fruitful perspective of this "linking" series.[24]

Or imagine, to take another example, the following situation: a researcher realizes the similarities between magic lantern illustrated song slides and the slides used at the time of early kinematography, without exactly knowing that the cultural series "illustrated songs" well and truly existed—to the point that a weekly French magazine with this title was published at the time (see figures 6.3 and 6.4). He or she then dreams up a cultural series, baptizing it the "illuminated songs cultural series." The historian must then carry out a great deal of research to see whether this is a single series or two complementary

FIGURE 6.3 Cover of magazine *Les chansons illustrées* 90.2 (n.d.), contemporary with early kinematography. (Issues of the magazine were generally undated and one must examine the contents to find indicators with respect to publication dates.)

FIGURE 6.4 Sheet music marketed by the publisher E. Mazo of Paris in 1909 for the serenade *Les quatre âges de Pierrot*.

series that partially overlap, whether they had an equal degree of social recognition, etc. It would then be possible to see how the series relates to cultural practices themselves. Finally, the researcher must try to trace the various elements of continuity or points of rupture that the series encountered with the advent of kinematography.

It is true that the connection between a cultural series and a cultural practice is a field in which we are still working in the dark. For us, it is not necessary that a cultural series have or achieve concrete form in a cultural practice, especially when it serves a heuristic or reframing function. For some, however, this incarnation of a series in practice presents itself as a compulsory feature, as these remarks by Laurent Le Forestier illustrate:

> Each series [. . .] thus takes concrete form in practices. [. . .] These practices can be based on the intersection of several series (this is how I would see the magic lantern). It remains to be seen when and how a practice can become a series, something which is not automatic, because we are moving from the concrete world to the world of ideas. Logically, it becomes a series when it is able to free itself from the here and now, or at least form an element that is sufficiently widespread (geographically) and "timeless."[25]

Be that as it may, and contrary to what is implied in Le Forestier's comments, for us this "becoming a series" is above all a matter for the historian's heuristic determination. More important is that the historian justify the series according to the principle of consistency over time. This dynamic can even take on a reticular dimension. The person we will call the "series maker" is thus also a "connections maker" or, to employ a metaphor in the air today, a *revealer of hyperlinks*, whose relevance and verisimilitude can be proven.

This is in keeping with what might be imagined as a "stream" dynamic, a more or less complex linking in a sequence of operations or components. Cultural practices, which often arise out of a kind of institutionalization, readily adopt the contours of the particular medium into which the cultural series "flows." More precisely, cultural practices concern the social and professional uses that attach themselves to a given medium at a given time and in a given culture. This prompts Baetens and his co-authors to state that:

> Gaudreault and Marion do not limit themselves to saying that media are a function of the way in which putting a medium into operation is institutionalized. [. . . T]hey underscore in particular that the pair medium/media itself can only be understood within a much larger framework, in which we also find an upstream, what they call cultural series, and a downstream, or what we might describe as cultural practices.[26]

One can understand how cultural practices might be said to exist "downstream" with respect to cultural series: with cultural practices, we are examining the evolution of a medium subjected to determined and established cultural uses in different periods, whereas a cultural series approach invites consideration of the unstable equilibrium between series, in a state of constant friction, that a medium introduces as it begins to evolve over time. Nevertheless, we do not believe that this distinction holds up all the way. On the one hand, while cultural series are the result of divisions inaugurated by the historian—who, as we quoted Gerbier above, "brings into existence a category which appears to make sense"—there is no reason for that historian to stay treading water upstream (which too often is confused with a before, with "what preceded," with something prior to a particular media institutionalization). Cultural series, precisely, are made for going through and beyond fixed conceptions of media and genres and to free themselves of institutional crystallizations. They find their dynamic relevance in what comes next, in extending, in continuity in various forms. *Experts in series* can (must) thus address the "post-media" state of the series they examine. As for the downstream of the medium in which cultural practices are fashioned, we could also conceptually locate those practices upstream of the medium in question: often, cultural practices that have become dominant have encouraged or produced a number of media crystallizations and engendered numerous media.

Cultural practices, when they have been established and recognized, can often transfer onto media, in the sense that the latter take advantage of their own expressive singularities to institutionalize a certain number of accepted or even valued cultural practices. In this way, a cultural series, and the deliberate research position it engages, can shine light on a medium and its evolutionary continuity. From this perspective, some might think that our volume *The End of Cinema?* consecrates a research method devoted to the cultural series.[27] Indeed, the book is based on the principle of continuity proper to the series: what, in cinema, persists in the digital age, even if we accept its death as a monolithic or hegemonic medium? For, we repeat, a cultural series never ends at the defined, institutional, and historic borders of a medium. As Édouard Arnoldy has suggested, expertise in cultural series gives the diverse elements that have federated in the medium—always temporarily, in our definition—the freedom to "spread" and to enter into "friction."[28]

While the freedom to establish series may at times appear lax, it is nevertheless governed by various conditions and constraints associated with sound scholarly practices. First, the series obeys the condition of coherence or, if one prefers, of hermeneutical plausibility. On this level, cultural series can extend across a continuum bounded by two extremes that are differentiated by the weak or, on the contrary, strong degree of intervention and construction they bring into play. Thus, at one end of this continuum, the cultural series may, as we have seen, be straightforwardly identified with a given cultural practice, medium, or other existing means of expression (or one that once existed): the researcher, for the needs of the investigation, can view a medium or mediatic *genre* as a cultural series (such as the kinematograph, comic books, or even filmed operas, etc.). At the other end of this continuum, the intellectual construct guiding the putting-in-series can be deployed to show unexpected relations between plural, seemingly scattered elements. The mission of the person putting these elements into series is to bring out the connections in order to open up interpretation (this is the hermeneutic aspect of the cultural series function). Here we share similar ground with Michel Foucault's idea of archaeology: from his perspective, which was also constructivist, the archaeologist has the dual mission of bringing certain aspects of the phenomena out from the shadows while creating connections or continuities among them. An important comment could be made here, again following Édouard Arnoldy: the elements which the "serialist" must shine a light on and relate to one another cannot be truly *scattered* but rather must be *spread*.[29] This is an important nuance, because it indicates that, despite the freedom of choice of the person studying the series, he or she must *bring out* relations that have been obliterated, unsuspected, forgotten, or overlooked by virtue of the very fact of this spreading, which connotes and suggests the task of analysis itself: to highlight a connection which may, in appearance, seem cryptic.

In this connection, Arnoldy also advocates an approach that would pay attention to the contiguity among series rather than the ruptures one might imagine dividing them:

> The concept "series" is thus a useful one, on condition that we *categorically* reject the idea that series are distinct from one another and do not present them as disjointed signifying units (or say that their importance lies more in their always uncertain proximity than in the ways they overlap). If series are the links of a ("cultural") chain, or "sub-ensembles" of a wide-reaching poly-system, we must always keep in mind the permeability and movements of these (sub-)ensembles.[30]

It appears to us in addition that, all things being equal, "putting into series" is most productive when the series are concerned with "doings" which are not (yet) limited to a given medium, or not directly subordinated to a recognized and well-defined cultural practice. Frank Kessler provides us with a good example in his description of the putting-into-series carried out by the media archaeologist Erkki Huhtamo:

> In his exploration of, for instance, what he calls "peep media," [... Huhtamo] in fact establishes a cultural series consisting of a broad variety of practices, machines and spectacles, using as a common denominator the act of peeping, which in a way forms the red thread allowing to align [sic] all these different *dispositifs* according to the same logic. So here, the organising principle is not a cultural practice that manifests itself as an institutionalised form of entertainment (as is the *féerie*, given as an example by Gaudreault with regard to Méliès), but rather one that is based on the more general experience of a specific kind of visual pleasure obtained through a specific type of viewing activity.[31]

The construction of a series of this kind appears to us to be particularly productive, for it dissociates itself from the cumbersome visibility of a medium and does not restrict itself to practices that are well established socially. Positing a cultural series such as this highlights elements that *spread* (rather than being *scattered*) and in the process opens up new research perspectives.

We will conclude with a final example. We have already mentioned the magic lantern and will now say that its characteristic visual motif of "dissolving views" could also constitute a relevant and productive cultural series. In fact it would be stimulating to see how the earliest experiments in dissolving views, by someone such as Étienne-Gaspard Robert as early as the beginning of the nineteenth century, were perpetuated (with numerous modifications) in the "media" phase of the magic lantern as a recognized cultural practice; how the idea of the dissolving view then became subordinated to kinematographic—and later, *cinematic*—practices in different ways; and, at the end of the line (for now), how today these dissolving views can contribute to the success of a modern lecturer's visual presentation from his or her laptop computer...

***

Between the lines of this essay can be detected the signs of a new historiographic paradigm in full expansion for the past several years: media archaeology. By definition our cultural series approach fits well with the general objectives of this "new" archaeology. In this sense our rethinking of cultural practices in terms of cultural series could, without too much effort, be seen as part of this archaeological dynamic. Serial—or serializing—expertise thus prompts us to "demediatize" the phenomena caught in the analyst's viewfinder. To demediatize here means to get free of a well-established medium's institutional grip and its historical over-visibility in order to seek out other connections and other resonances running through the medium without being fully subsumed by it. These links would undoubtedly fly beneath the radar of classical media historiographies, which tend to fall into the false binary of examining their objects either as causes of irreversible rupture and change or as vehicles for already-existing cultural practices. This is an old dichotomy that has swallowed up a great many historical studies, as the late Thomas Elsaesser described: "My 'archeological' perspective was therefore initially intended to distinguish itself both from chronological history (especially the *infancy-adolescence-maturity-decline* narrative) as well as the *nothing new under the sun* approach, where one finds precedents in the past for every innovation in the present."[32]

To a certain extent, and by taking on certain risks of instrumental reduction, we might even see cultural series as constituting a preferred tool for carrying out a media archaeology in general and an archaeology of cinema in particular. Naturally, we must continue this line of thought in order to measure the diversity of media archaeology today, which is anything but monolithic. To illustrate a small corner of this complexity we might also consider that the spirit of cultural series stands apart from that of an archaeology focusing on the differences brought about by media technologies.[33]

To close this defense and illustration of the concept cultural series, we take the liberty of borrowing from Arnoldy the conclusion of the article already quoted, about which we would be hard pressed to say whether it is optimistic or pessimistic:

> The "cultural series" [approach] places the film historian in the presence of an always colossal work project with problematical boundaries. In the face of this task, the film historian, that "digger," may think, as Brecht remarked in the poem spoken by Jean-Luc Godard in his film *Histoire(s) du cinéma* [1988–1998]: "I examine my plan with care. It is unrealizable." This expresses the difficulty of film history in a nutshell; and perhaps, in the end, its impossibility![34]

The two "diggers" who have authored the present text believe—even though the history of cinema may be unrealizable, even if this history were impossible to do—nothing other than that to say it is already to do it. In other words, "saying is doing," Arnoldy may have retorted to a certain philosopher of language.

Who said history should be a finished product?

Notes

1. Henri Bergson, "The Philosophy of Claude Bernard" (1913), in *The Creative Mind: An Introduction to Metaphysics*, trans. Mabelle L. Andison (Mineola, NY: Dover, 2007 [1946]), 172.
2. The research on which the present text is based has benefited from the financial support of the Fonds de recherche du Québec—Société et culture (FRQSC), the Social Sciences and Humanities Research Council of Canada (SSHRC), and the Canada Research Chairs program, through the intermediary of three university infrastructures headed by André Gaudreault: the Groupe de recherche sur l'avènement et la formation des institutions cinématographiques et scéniques (GRAFICS), the Canadian section of the international research partnership TECHNÈS, and the Canada Research Chair in Cinema and Media Studies. The authors would like to thank Frank Kessler and Laurent Le Forestier for the discussions they have had with them, enabling them to refine some of their hypotheses. They would also like to thank Pier-Anne Lussier-Choquette and Kim Décarie for their research assistance prior to the writing of this text, which is an extended version of André Gaudreault and Philippe Marion, "Défense et illustration de la notion de série culturelle," in Diego Cavallotti, Federico Giordano, and Leonardo Quaresima, eds., *A History of Cinema without Names: A Research Project* (Milan, Italy: Mimesis International, 2016), 59–71.
3. The conference in question was on the topic "Georges Méliès et le second siècle du cinéma," August 13 to 22, 1996, at the Centre culturel international de Cerisy.
4. André Gaudreault, "Les vues cinématographiques selon Georges Méliès ou: comment Mitry et Sadoul avaient peut-être raison d'avoir tort (même si c'est surtout Deslandes qu'il faut lire et relire) . . . ," in Jacques Malthête and Michel Marie, eds., *Georges Méliès, l'illusionniste fin de siècle?* (proceedings of the conference "Georges Méliès et le second siècle du cinéma") (Paris: Presses de la Sorbonne Nouvelle, 1997), 121.
5. As the reader can see, the main idea behind the introduction of the concept "cultural series" was, fundamentally, to avoid taking into consideration the emerging practice of kinematography as an island cut off from the rest of the world.
6. Gaudreault, "Les vues cinématographiques," 122–23.
7. Arthur Pougin, *Dictionnaire historique et pittoresque du théâtre et des arts qui s'y rattachent* (Paris: Firmin-Didot, 1885), 360, 364.
8. In French, however, the word *cinématographe* proved quite resistant, as seen in this simple list of books published from 1925 to 1951: G.-Michel Coissac, *Histoire du cinématographe de ses origines jusqu'à nos jours* (Paris: Éditions du Cinéopse, 1925); Georges Potonniée, *Les origines du cinématographe* (Paris: Paul Montel, 1928); Marcel L'Herbier, *Intelligence du cinématographe* (Paris: Corrêa, 1945); and Jean Cocteau, *Entretiens autour du cinématographe* (Paris: André Bonne, 1951).
9. R. Coolus, *Ciné-Journal*, August 31, 1912, quoted by Jean Giraud in *Le lexique français du cinéma des origines à 1930* (Paris: Centre national de la recherche scientifique, 1958), 64 (emphasis added).
10. For a discussion of the concepts "kine-attractography" and "institutional cinema," see André Gaudreault, *Film and Attraction: From Kinematography to Cinema*, trans. Timothy Barnard (Urbana: University of Illinois Press, 2011 [2008]).
11. In the beginning, Lumière films were described in French as "photographies animées" (animated photographs), as seen in this report on a screening in Paris in 1896: "The *animated*

photographs are little wonders. We can see every detail: whirling smoke rising in the air, waves crashing on the beach, leaves rustling in the wind. All these tableaux are arousing Parisians' curiosity, and rightly so." Henri de Parville, *Les Annales*, April 28, 1896, quoted in Bernard Chardère, Guy Borgé, and Marjorie Borgé, *Les Lumière* (Paris: Bibliothèque des Arts, 1985), 99 (emphasis added).

12. André Gaudreault, "Les genres vus à travers la loupe de l'intermédialité ou Le cinéma des premiers temps: un bric-à-brac d'institutions," in Leonardo Quaresima, Alessandra Raengo, and Laura Vichi, eds., *La nascita dei generi cinematografici* (Udine, Italy: Università degli Studi di Udine, 1999), 91.

13. Note that this broadening of the concept cultural series was not present in the text of the conference paper itself, which was given at the Fifth International Film Studies Conference, University of Udine, in March 1998. Rather, the broadening owes much to discussions the authors had with Michèle Lagny onsite at the conference.

14. *Le Petit Robert de la langue française* (2016), digital edition, entry "heuristique."

15. Flaurette Gautier, "Compte rendu de la 2e séance du séminaire 'série culturelle': Laurent Gerbier, 'Naissance d'un genre, naissance d'un medium: les séries culturelles et la question des origines (science fiction et comic books),'" https://intru.hypotheses.org/537. This is a report on a seminar on cultural series given by Laurent Gerbier in 2011 at the Université François-Rabelais in Tours.

16. Jan Baetens, Johan Callens, Michel Delville, Bertrand Gervais, Heidi Peeters, Robyn Warhol, and Myriam Watthee-Delmotte, "Transformations médiatiques: quelques réflexions sur la notion de 'série culturelle' chez André Gaudreault et Philippe Marion," *Recherches en communication* 41 (2014): 224.

17. Pierre Fresnault-Deruelle, *Hergéologie: Cohérence et cohésion du récit en images dans les aventures de Tintin* (Tours, France: Presses universitaires François-Rabelais, 2012), 85.

18. Baetens et al., "Transformations médiatiques," 224–225. This reference to art naturally deserves a more fine-grained discussion than it is possible for us to provide in the limited context of the present article.

19. *Le Petit Robert de la langue française* (2016), digital edition.

20. Pougin, *Dictionnaire historique et pittoresque*, 604–605 (emphasis added).

21. See André Gaudreault, "Les sources inédites de la notion de 'plan' en cinématographie: un coup du (de?) théâtre!" in Vincent Amiel, Gilles Mouëllic, and José Moure, eds., *Le découpage au cinéma, enjeux théoriques et poétiques* (Rennes, France: Presses universitaires de Rennes, 2016), 41–62.

22. Email to the authors, April 12, 2013.

23. On the idea of "framing" in the sense in which we use it here, see Erving Goffman, *Frame Analysis: Essays on the Organization of Experience* (New York: Harper and Row, 1974).

24. At the end of the nineteenth century, Paul Otlet and Henri Lafontaite established the basis of the Mundaneum, whose goal was to "bring together in a single place all world knowledge in every form (books, posters, and newspapers from around the world) in a gigantic and novel Universal Bibliographic Inventory, which can be seen as a forerunner to Google and Wikipedia in the age of paper." See https://fr.wikipedia.org/wiki/Mundaneum.

25. Email to the authors, April 12, 2013.

26. Baetens et al., "Transformations médiatiques," 223.

27. André Gaudreault and Philippe Marion, *The End of Cinema? A Medium in Crisis in the Digital Age*, trans. Timothy Barnard (New York: Columbia University Press, 2015).

28. Édouard Arnoldy, "De la dispersion en histoire du cinéma," *Cinémas* 23, no. 1 (2012): 73–92.

29. Ibid.
30. Ibid., 86.
31.. Frank Kessler, "Notes on the Concept of 'Cultural Series,'" December 2013, http://dspace.library.uu.nl/handle/1874/290013.
32. Thomas Elsaesser, *Film History as Media Archaeology* (Amsterdam: Amsterdam University Press, 2016), 23 (emphasis in original).
33. On this topic, see Wolfgang Ernst, "Let There Be Irony: Cultural History and Media Archeology in Parallel Lines," *Art History* 28, no. 5 (November 2005): 582–603.
34. Arnoldy, "De la dispersion en histoire du cinéma," 87. Here Arnoldy is referring to an interview with Jean-Luc Godard by Serge Daney ("Godard fait des histoires," *Libération*, December 26, 1988), reprinted in Alain Bergala, ed., *Jean-Luc Godard par Jean-Luc Godard, vol. 2, 1984–1998* (Paris: Cahiers du cinéma, 1998), 161–73.

CHAPTER 7

REVIEWING *MAPLE VIEWING* (*MOMIJIGARI*, 1899)

DAISUKE MIYAO

Maple Viewing (*Momijigari*, 1899) is officially considered the earliest extant Japanese film. Photographed by the cinematographer Shibata Tsunekichi (1867–1929), the film records the Kabuki actors Ichikawa Danjurō IX and Onoe Kikugorō V performing in a Kabuki play of the same name. In the play, the samurai Taira no Koremochi (played by Kikugorō V) is invited by beautiful women, including Sarashinahime (Danjurō IX), to a maple-viewing party at Mt. Togakushi. He enjoys sake while watching the women dance. When he falls asleep, a god appears in his dream. The god reveals to Koremochi that the women are in fact monsters in disguise and leaves him a sacred sword. Koremochi wakes up and uses the weapon to dispatch the monsters.

In 2009, the Japanese Ministry of Education, Culture, Sports, Science, and Technology designated *Maple Viewing* to be an Important Cultural Property (*jūyō bunkazai*) under the nation's Law for the Protection of Cultural Properties, making it the first film to receive the designation. Yet, in this chapter, I question the categorization of *Maple Viewing* as the earliest surviving Japanese film.

Of course, the fact that it survives is not under dispute here. Okajima Hisashi, the director of the National Film Archive of Japan, estimates the survival rate for Japanese films of the pre-war period to be only about four percent.[1] As the film curator Irie Yoshirō explains in his 2009 essay, "The Earliest Japanese Movie," filmmaking had already started in Japan in 1897, and the exhibition of Japanese-made films began in 1899.[2] Konishi Honten Company, the photo material merchant, imported a motion picture camera (presumably from the British camera manufacturer Baxter & Wray) in 1897, started filming and developing motion pictures with their cameraman Asano Shirō, and publicly screened the first of those films with the exhibitor Hiromeya in June and July of 1899. Yoshirō meticulously examines newspaper articles, advertisements, memoirs, as well as frame captures from non-extant films that have been published in various forms, to show that Konishi Honten steadily produced films and increased its titles. Hiromeya reliably exhibited the Konishi films, and the two companies jointly initiated "the first industrial model of cinema" in Japan by 1902.[3] However, none of those Konishi films is extant, except a few frames of two photographed by Asano, *Okanesarashi* (*Exposing Clothes to the Sun*; also known as *Nunosarashi*) and *Nagauta Ikioijishi* (*Long Song: Vigorous Lion*), which are preserved at the Tsubouchi Memorial Theater Library of Waseda University. Therefore, it is true that *Maple Viewing* is the earliest "surviving" work. Yet, applying the words "Japanese" and "film" to *Maple Viewing* is more problematic. Can we call *Maple Viewing* "Japanese" simply because it was photographed in Japan by a Japanese cinematographer? If we imagine that it produced for non-Japanese viewers in the context of an Orientalist imagination, what would its classification as "Japanese" amount to? Moreover, we can also question its status as a "film" in turn-of-the century critical discourse. What was *Maple Viewing* understood to be when it was first produced and exhibited?

Is *Maple Viewing* the Earliest Surviving Japanese "Film"?

When *Maple Viewing* was about to receive its 2009 designation as an Important Cultural Property, film historian Aaron Gerow questioned whether the Japanese government considered it to be a film. Gerow argued, "Even in its original production, *Momijigari* was less a film than a recording of a theatrical scene."[4] *Maple Viewing* has its origins in a Noh play turned into a Kabuki dance repertoire by Nakamura Utaemon IV and Kawatake Mokuami. Ichikawa Danjurō IX appeared in it as the princess Sarashinahime for the first time in October 1887. When the play was performed at the Kabukiza Theater in November 1899, Danjurō IX played Sarashinahime again and Onoe Kikugorō V played the samurai Taira no Koremochi.[5]

Gerow speculated that the Japanese government selected *Maple Viewing* "less because it was a film than because it [...] was a record of two illustrious actors."[6] He pointed out, "The actual recommendation [by the Council for Cultural Affairs] to the Ministry of Education in fact categorized the film not as a film but as a 'historical document' (*rekishi shiryo*)."[7] According to Gerow, *Maple Viewing* received the designation because of the cultural properties policy that "privileges pre-modern arts and 'traditional' practices as 'true' Japanese art."[8] In other words, the selection of *Maple Viewing* can be viewed as a substitute designation for the *actors*, who can also be deemed "cultural properties" under the current system.

Gerow's speculation is supported by the fact that Danjurō IX agreed to be photographed only for the purpose of historical documentation. After a November 1899 live performance of *Maple Viewing* at the Kabukiza Theater, Shibata Tsunekichi had hurriedly photographed both Danjurō and Kikugorō V using a Gaumont camera and about two hundred feet of film.[9] The shooting did not take place in the Kabukiza Theater but rather just outside. The official reason was to secure sufficient light. Shibata recalled:

> We set up a backdrop outside, in front of Umebayashi, the teahouse for the Kabuki audience, which was located behind the Kabukiza Theater. We built a stage in front of the backdrop. All supporting actors held the backdrop to prevent it from being blown away by the wind, hoping that Danjurō IX would not change his mind. [. . .] When he performed as Sarashinahime with two fans, Danjurō IX dropped one of them because of a gust. For such an accomplished actor, it was a mistake of a lifetime. But we did not retake the shot. In retrospect, it turned out to be a charming mistake.[10]

According to film historian Ueda Manabu, no retake was done to correct Danjurō IX's mistake because the recording was not meant for exhibition to the general public.[11] Ueda resorts to the testimony of Matsumoto Kōshirō VII, a disciple of Danjurō IX, who suggests that the actor agreed to be photographed "only for the pedagogical purpose" of instructing future Kabuki performers.[12] Danjurō was attracted to photography, argued the Kabuki scholar Kamiyama Akira, only because of its *jitsu*, which means both reality and practicality.[13] In his 1902 book, *Ichikawa Danjurō*, Kamiyama claimed that Danjurō IX "prioritized practicality/reality over beauty" and was bold enough to offer "the ominous image of female impersonation with his old body."[14] The film *Maple Viewing* would, in this way, serve as a historical document that recorded the art of Danjurō and Kikugorō V for a practical purpose. This explains why *Maple Viewing* was not screened for years, except once for the two actors at Danjurō's private residence in Tsukiji, Tokyo, on the evening of November 7, 1900.

The extant 35mm print preserved at the National Film Archive of Japan (from a version struck by Nikkatsu in 1928) is composed of five fixed long shots, following the opening credits.[15] In the first two shots (lasting approximately 136 seconds, with a noticeable film roll change after seventy seconds or so) Sarashinahime (Danjurō IX) performs a fan dance wearing a dark-colored *furisode*, a kimono with long sleeves. Behind him is the trunk of a huge pine tree, with two thinner trees placed diagonally as props in front of a backdrop, onto which trees and a stone garden have been painted. There is also a *kuroko* (stagehand), dressed all in black, sitting before the trunk of the pine tree. He helps Danjurō IX when he drops the fan in the first shot (see figure 7.1). In the third shot (approximately sixty-two seconds), the Mountain God, played by young Onoe Kikugorō VI, dances with a sacred pole while Koremochi (Kikugorō V) sleeps at the right of the frame. In the fourth shot (twenty seconds), Koremochi wakes up, prepares his sword and holds a *mie* pose, a signature posture struck by a kabuki actor to express enhanced emotion. In the fifth shot (fifty-seven seconds), Koremochi and a monster with dark long hair (Danjurō IX) perform a sword-fighting dance together. The stagehand comes forward once to pick up some items dropped on the stage by the actors. Midway through the shot, the actors momentarily pause and look toward the camera, Koremochi raising his sword and the monster holding a *mie* pose. Then they resume their dance. The monster starts swirling her long hair until the shot fades out (see figure 7.2).

FIGURE 7.1 Ichikawa Danjurō IX as Sarashinahime in *Maple Viewing* (*Momijigari*, 1899).

Consisting of just these five shots, *Maple Viewing* might be categorized as part of the "ciné-genre" of "non-continuity" in early film, as coined by the film historian Tom Gunning. According to Gunning, the ciné-genre of non-continuity "consists of a narrative in at least two shots, in which the disruption caused by the cut(s) between shots is used to express a disruption on the story level of the film."[16] Gunning's description of ciné-genres is built upon the theory of filmic narrative proposed by André Gaudreault. In Gaudreault's view, film narrative is "the product of a dialectical combination of the two basic modes of narrative communication: narration and monstration."[17] According to Gaudreault, a one-shot film, such as a Lumière brothers' film, comprises only the "single narrative layer" of monstration, insofar as it shows "no sign of any intervention by the narrator (whose discourse, or narration, comes from the articulation between shots)."[18]

Maple Viewing, however, demonstrates the possibility of "non-continuity" editing that does not presuppose narration. Certainly, the Kabuki play of *Maple Viewing* has a narrative. If the viewer is familiar with the story, it is not difficult to follow the photographed version of *Maple Viewing* across the "non-continuity" cut. However, if the initial purpose of the photographing was simply to record the performance and had nothing to do with storytelling, then it becomes difficult to categorize *Maple Viewing* within any of Gunning's ciné-genres. Its editing serves only as a means of materially

FIGURE 7.2 Taira no Koremochi (Onoe Kikugorō V) fights the monster (Danjurō IX) in *Maple Viewing*.

pasting together five shots despite the fact that those shots indicate some level of narrative articulation. The emphasis is on a *demonstration* of the art of acting.

That said, even if *Maple Viewing* was produced simply as a means of recording Danjurō IX's performance, it is not entirely correct to view it as therefore "not" a film. The point here is not that *Maple Viewing* was not a film because of its non-narrative, documentary orientation. Such a position, after all, would falsely posit an immanent fictive identity for the medium. Rather, the point is that the very notion of "film" (*eiga*) lacked the kind of autonomy or unity that could distinguish it from other media—photography or theater, say—at this stage in Japanese film history. In fact, as Gerow meticulously demonstrates in his 2010 book on the Pure Film Movement, the term *eiga* (映画, "projected pictures") did not even exist as a unified category distinct from other media until around 1910.[19]

Prior to that, following the very first exhibition of Edison's Kinetoscope in Kobe in November 1896, the most common term was *katsudō shashin* (moving photography), which was used in reference to Edison's Kinetoscope (both the viewing device itself and the Kinetoscope films), the projecting Vitascope, and the Cinématographe Lumière, as well as to screenings of Japanese-made films.[20] The machines and the images projected from them were not differentiated as the objects of exhibition. In addition, the Kinetoscope (again, both the device and its films) was sometimes called *shashin katsudō* (photographic movement) and *shashin butō* (photographic dance).[21] Meanwhile, the terms *jidō shashin* (automatic photography),[22] *jidō genga* (automatic phantom picture),[23] *jidō gentō* (automatic magic lantern),[24] and *katsudō genga* (moving phantom picture)[25] were all used to describe the Lumière projections. Moreover, Araki Kazuichi, who imported the Vitascope, called the machine *chikudō shaei* (phonographic projection), since he used Edison's phonographs during screenings.[26]

As these names imply, during its first decade in Japan, cinema was never fully distinguished from other forms of entertainment and technology in newspaper and magazine discourse. While the use of the terms "photography" or "photographic" indicated a consistent emphasis on the medium's technological ontology, the inclusion of other words like "magic lantern" and "dance" point rather to a context of pre-existing entertainments. Gerow claims that "many of the ways of writing and speaking used to discuss the motion pictures existed in Japan before 1896, with cinema first appearing in discourse only as a sign substitutable by other media, and being inserted into an ill-defined subfield within a larger field (such as the *misemono*, or sideshow entertainments) in which all the components were largely equivalent."[27]

An integral part of the urban fabric of Edo-era Japan, *misemono* provides crucial context for understanding cinema's early exhibition. As art historian Marguerite V. Hodge writes: "Set up along major thoroughfares, or inside the grounds of large temple compounds, *misemono* consisted of amusements, attractions, and shows of all manner and variety. These were enormously popular events, drawing huge crowds from all levels and areas of society."[28] Many of the earliest demonstrations of cinema were part of *misemono* shows. For example, Araki Kazuichi, a Japanese promoter of Edison's Vitascope, combined some of his later Vitascope screenings with a demonstration of an X-ray machine, another import from the Edison Company, several months after his initial exhibition of Vitascope. Both Vitascope and the X-ray were thus part of Araki's *misemono* show.[29] According to Gerow, as was the case with other *misemono*, the first film showings in Japan were often described as performances, complete with music and a lecture, in which the presentation of the apparatus was more important than what was represented.[30]

Not even notions of photographic realism and mechanical reproduction served to differentiate cinema from other media in the discourse of this period. The art historian Kinoshita Naoyuki points out that *ikiningyō* (papier-mâché dolls), a popular variety of *misemono*, already anticipated cinema's claims to realism in the mid-1800s. When arranged to recreate scenes from history or literature or introduce views of foreign lands, according to Kinoshita, the dolls were often said to be indistinguishable from the people depicted.[31] He quotes a contemporary observer of *ikiningyō* to the effect that viewing the puppets "was like facing living people."[32] Examining Yasumoto Kamehachi I's 1890 *ikiningyō*, *Two Wrestlers*, Hodge argues that

> The emphatic expression of the wrestlers is characteristic of *iki-ningyō* and is achieved through a paradoxical combination of extreme detail and large scale. The sheer size of the doll produces an arresting physical presence that projects outward into the viewer's space. At the same time, that presence is amplified by increasingly

fine degrees of detail that draw the gaze inward: from the careful modeling of the musculature to the fine textures and colorings of skin, to the glass-inset eyes, individually-shaped teeth—even to the strands of individually inserted, real human hair. All is rendered to achieve a maximum fidelity that is at once confrontational and seductive. In effect, the doll operates in both directions at once, provoking a somatic response on the level both of impact and of intimacy. In this sense, the very materiality of the doll emulates the oscillations—or simultaneity—of wonder and resonance, producing a richly enigmatic aesthetic.[33]

Combining the technical expertise of doll-making, traditional use of raw materials, and an anatomical understanding of human bodies, *ikiningyō* aspired to a level of verimilitude arguably comparable to the photographic representation of a performance.

Of course, the fact that previous media practices had been described as "realistic" does not obviate cinema's unique claim to a specifically *indexical* realism. In this regard, though, it is worth noting a curious paradox when *Maple Viewing* was first publicly screened. On July 7, 1903, *Maple Viewing* was exhibited in a theater for the first time—four years after the recording of the performance by Danjurō IX and Kikugorō V. This was the moment when *Maple Viewing* began to be referenced as the first Japanese-produced film.[34] A 1903 report in the *Osaka Asahi Shinbun* newspaper introduced *Maple Viewing* and *Kyōkanonko musume ninin Dōjōji* (*Dōjōji: A Lover's Duet*, 1899), another film photographed by Shibata, by saying, "The ones that are exhibited at the Nakaza Theater this time are the first Japanese-made motion pictures."[35] Still it is doubtful that the July 7, 1903, audience at the Nakaza Theater in Osaka regarded *Maple Viewing* straightforwardly as a film. The screening was not planned in advance but only as a substitute for a cancelled live performance by Danjurō IX and Kikugorō V at the fifth Domestic Industrial Exposition in Osaka.[36] The cancellation was caused by Kikugorō V's death earlier that year on February 18, leading Danjurō IX to approve the substitute screening of *Maple Viewing*. Alternately, according to the film historian Tanaka Junichirō, the Nakaza Theater needed a program before Nakamura Ganjirō I's Kabuki troop could return from its tour to Kyoto, and approached Inoue Takejirō, the executive of the Kabukiza Theater in Tokyo, who owned the print of *Maple Viewing*.[37] Whichever the case, the screening of *Maple Viewing* was a last-minute substitute for a Kabuki performance. Furthermore, this screening was accompanied by at least two other films produced by a newly established film production/distribution company, Yoshizawa Shōten: *Osaka dai 5 kai hakurankai no jikkyō* (*Report of the Fifth Domestic Industrial Exposition*, 1903) and *Meiyū Onoe Kikugorō no sōshiki* (*Great Actor Onoe Kikugorō's Funeral*, 1903). Ueda Manabu argues that the screening of these three films, with the support of accompanying lectures and orchestra, "jointly formulated the biography of Danjurō IX and Kikugorō V" as the major theme of the event.[38] Thus, at the first public screening, *Maple Viewing* was presented as part substitute for a Kabuki performance (thanks to the medium's verisimilitude, like *ikiningyō*) and part photographic record of the illustrious careers of Danjurō IX and Kikugorō V (thanks to its indexicality).

Five years later, in 1908, *Maple Viewing* was released widely in Tokyo, Osaka, Yokohama, Nagoya, Kyoto, and Kobe by another film company, Yokota shōkai. This, argues Ueda, was when *Maple Viewing* was first treated as "an independent film" that was "decisively severed" from the context of the Kabuki performance.[39] According to Ueda, exhibitions of the film in cities other than Tokyo emphasized theatricality with musical accompaniment, "as if Dangiku [Danjurō IX and Kikugorō V] were actually performing on the stage."[40] It was only during the film's longer runs in Tokyo at the Kinkikan Theater in Kanda (May 8–31, discussed in the introduction to this chapter) and the Fujikan Theater in Asakusa (August 28–October 3) that *Maple Viewing* shed its function as a substitute for a live performance. The Kinkikan Theater was not a movie theater but showed films regularly, whereas the Fujikan Theater was a movie house that opened in 1907. *Maple Viewing* became a "film" because it was one film in a longer list of screenings that included various types of films that Yokota shōkai produced or imported from Pathé. The two films produced by Yokota shōkai were *Kyoto dentō hatsudensho no kaji* (*The Fire at Kyoto Electric Company*, 1908), and *Shimabara tayū no dōchū* (*A Geisha's Walk*, 1908). The Japanese titles of the eleven Pathé films were: *Karadaru no gyōretsu* (*The March of Empty Barrels*), *Shiutome katagi* (*The Mother-in-Law Character*), *Shinan hikōki* (*The Newly Invented Airplane*), *Kettō daishōri* (*The Great Victory in the Duel*), *Kakan nai koi* (*The Cowardly Love*), *Kachiku dorobō no chie* (*The Knowledge of the Cattle Thief*), *Ikita dōzō* (*A Living Statue*), *Kiki kaikai jidō ryōri* (*Mysterious Automatic Cooking*), *Shittatsuri no akiregao* (*The Bailiff's Stunned Face*), *Fushigi no kagami* (*The Mysterious Mirror*), and *Gama no yōjutsu* (*The Toad's Witchcraft*). (It is difficult to identify which Pathé films corresponded to these titles.) To the audience who came to either the Kinkikan or Fujikan theaters, *Maple Viewing* was no longer experienced as part of a *misemono*, especially now that only a limited number of audience members would have had familiarity with the art of Danjurō IX and Kikugorō V.

Tellingly, 1908 was also the year that Yokota shōkai started producing narrative films and joined industrial efforts in the mass production of cinema by other companies, including Yoshizawa shōten, which constructed its first film studio in Meguro, Tokyo, in January of the same year.[41] By the end of the first decade of the twentieth century, film had become a domestic industry in Japan. About the same time, according to Gerow, a unified discourse specific to the cinema began to appear.[42] Thus, *Maple Viewing* arguably became the earliest Japanese "film" for the first time in 1908, when the critical discourse of the time started to recognize "film" as an independent medium.

Is *Maple Viewing* the Earliest Surviving "Japanese" Film?

Yet *Maple Viewing*'s designation as the earliest surviving Japanese film is no less problematic if we now turn from the noun "film" to the adjective "Japanese." It is premature to call *Maple Viewing* a "Japanese" film simply because it was photographed in Japan by a Japanese cinematographer. The film's target audience was not necessarily Japanese, meaning that its content might have been compromised strategically. The Kabuki scholar Kamiyama Akira hypothesizes a very different aetiology for *Maple Viewing* from those discussed above, suggesting that the film was in fact meant for the 1900 Paris Exposition Universelle.[43] In other words, Kamiyama thinks that *Maple Viewing* might have been intended as a film that would represent Japan for the eyes of European spectators, not domestic audiences—that is, a Japanese-made film, but not a film made for the Japanese. Kamiyama says that he discarded the idea because he was not able to find any empirical proof.[44]

But in fact, Kamiyama's speculation has potential validity. According to Kawaura Kenichi, the head of Yoshizawa shōten, which was responsible for the first public screening of *Maple Viewing* in Japan in 1903, "Inoue Takejirō, the head of the Kabukiza Theater, and I discussed [this possibility] and told Shibata to photograph *Maple Viewing* for export."[45] When Shibata filmed *Maple Viewing* in November 1899, the Japanese government was finalizing the selection of products to be exported for the 1900 Paris Exposition Universelle. The governmental policy for the selection focused on publicizing Japan's ascendancy as a modernized nation whose products were competitive on the international market. *Maple Viewing* would have been a perfect fit. It used the modern technology of motion pictures while demonstrating unique characteristics of Japanese art for the purpose of product differentiation. (Notably, Shibata worked for the Lumière Company before he photographed *Maple Viewing*. He was thus an expert in the modern technology of the motion picture camera, the Cinématographe Lumière, even as he captured a unique form of Japanese theatrical tradition in *Maple Viewing*.)

As I have discussed extensively in my monograph, *Japonisme and the Birth of Cinema* (2020), the Lumière Company was overtly interested in travelogues and scenics in Japan.[46] From early on, the Lumières placed their camera in the service of capturing, cataloging, and displaying non-Western subjects—people and sites—and, to this end, sent two prominent cameramen to Japan, one after another—Constant Girel in 1897 and Gabriel Veyre in 1898. Their work resulted in thirty-three films shot in Japan, while the company produced no other films elsewhere in Asia except French Indochina.

While the films that Girel and Veyre photographed in Japan might be thought of as an anthropological and geographic archive of daily scenes in Japan—such as a family having a meal (*Repas en famille* by Girel in 1897) or Japanese women dancing (*Danse japonaise II: Harusame* by Veyer, 1898–1899)—they actually replicated paintings, drawings, and photographs that were already known in the visual archive of "Japonisme" (a term that refers to the influence of Japanese art and culture on European fine art starting roughly in the 1860s). Veyre's *Danse japonaise: II. Harusame* replicated European paintings of geisha by Edward Atkinson Hornel and Charles Wirgman. Effectively, the films revealed the filmmakers' hidden desires to reproduce an exotic, sensual, pre-modern, and timeless image of Japan in a new visual medium. For instance, as Veyre wrote about Japanese women: "In order to fully understand the social status of Japanese women, we need to completely wipe out the sense of Western morality from our minds. [. . .] Japanese girls are extremely attractive because they combine decency and indecency, obedience and obscenity."[47]

As opposed to Girel and Veyre's attempts to reconfine Japan within the exotic image of an atemporal Orientalist space, Shibata's films for Lumière sought rather to document scenes of a modernizing nation. In *Une rue à Tokyo [II]* (1898), for instance, we see a row of three-story Western-style buildings on the street of Ginza. One of them has the name of a store written in the Western alphabet, "Hattori" (now the Seiko Watch Corporation). Japanese people in Western dress and/or with Western-style black umbrellas also appear in this film. Shibata thus included actual images of Japanese daily life, presumably in order to publicize the reality of Japan to Europe. At the same time, however, Shibata was aware of European expectations of exoticism. In *Une avenue à Tokyo* (1898), cherry blossom trees—a Japanese national symbol—are in full bloom on a riverbank, with rickshaws running beneath them, even as crowds of Western-style umbrellas and derby hats worn by men in kimonos create strong contrasts between white blossoms and black objects.

With these Orientalist fantasies in mind, especially during the vogue of Japonisme, one can hypothesize that Shibata considered *Maple Viewing* to be a potential product for the foreign gaze. In fact, recent studies in art history indicate that the story of *Maple Viewing* was first implicitly introduced to a large number of European spectators as early as 1876. In that year, Claude Monet exhibited his painting *La Japonaise* (*Camille Monet in Japanese Costume*) at the Second Impressionist Exhibition in Paris. In this large-scale oil painting completed in the midst of the Japonisme vogue, Monet's wife, Camille, poses in a vivid red kimono in front of a wall filled with a number of Japanese fans. The kimono that Camille wears is identified as an *uchikake*, a formal style worn by brides of the rich merchant class or by high-class geisha during the Edo period, as well as in Kabuki stage performances. The major motif of this particular kimono is a fierce-looking samurai, who is about to draw his sword; additionally, we see a number of maple leaves floating above the figure of the samurai.

According to art historian Yokoyama Akio, the design of the kimono in *La Japonaise* was most likely based on the story of *Maple Viewing*. Yokoyama suggests that the story had been a traditional source for *ukiyo-e* woodblock print motifs since the early eighteenth century, including such works as *Buyū gi Genji: Momijiga, Taira no Koremochi* (*Brave Genji: Taira no Koremochi Celebrating Maple*, 1840s) by Utagawa Kuniyoshi.[48] As Yokoyama points out, the samurai's posture as well as the composition of the maple leaves around him in *Buyū gi Genji* look very similar to those in *La Japonaise*.[49] Even though Monet did not own this particular piece, he did own twenty-three other works by Kuniyoshi, so that, according to Yokoyama, there was a chance he was familiar with *Maple Viewing* motifs as well.[50] Moreover, according to the art historian Mabuchi Akiko, Monet talked about *La Japonaise* to an art dealer and said, "I had a chance to look at an excellent dress and was recommended to paint it. Embroidery is done with golden threads, and some parts are as thick as a few inches."[51] Quite a number of kimonos used by geisha were exported to France during the period of Japonisme, and motifs from *Maple Viewing* presumably came with them. So even if Monet was not familiar with the play or *ukiyo-e* of *Maple Viewing*, one can assume that he saw a kimono with the samurai motif.

In addition, Shibata was also aware that Kabuki dances of samurai and monsters had exotic appeal to foreign viewers. When Constant Girel visited Japan in 1897, four of his eighteen films involved Kabuki actors. In one of them, *Acteurs Japonais: Excercice de la perruque* (1897), which was photographed at Nanchi-Kayūen in Osaka on May 27, 1897, the actor Nakamura Ganjirō I practices the lion dance from the Kabuki play *Shin Shakkyō*, costumed in an extremely long white mane. Like *Maple Viewing*, the performance is demonstrated for the camera in frontal long shot.[52] These films by Girel demonstrate French viewers' interest in Kabuki, in addition to geisha dances.

Even though *Maple Viewing* was not sent to the 1900 Paris Exposition Universelle, the film was possibly made with an awareness of the foreign gaze. If we can call *Maple Viewing* a "Japanese" film, then, we must also acknowledge that the film's evocation of Japaneseness may be part of a lineage of filmic cultivation of Japonisme prevalent at the time of its making. Curiously, when the print of *Maple Viewing* was discovered in 1928 after being lost during the Great Kanto Earthquake of 1923, newspapers claimed the film was "photographed by a foreigner."[53] Even though the information was corrected later, the mistake possibly derives from the film's Orientalist appeal. When the film was screened at the Kinkikan Theater in Tokyo, May 8–31, 1908, as I have noted earlier, it was one of only three films photographed in Japan: the other two were about a fire at an electric company and about geisha. Issues of nationality or cultural specificity were not significant for the former, and the Orientalist appeal for non-Japanese viewers was obvious for the latter. The eleven other films were the ones produced by Pathé.[54] *Maple Viewing* must have blended in sufficiently well with the films shot by European cinematographers that filmgoers could easily have taken it for a foreign-made film. We might even argue that the Kabuki performance in *Maple Viewing* could have been experienced as a reaffirmation of traditional Japanese art by way of a foreign viewpoint, just as the geisha film could have been enjoyed by domestic filmgoers as a depiction of an exotic-looking traditional culture for foreign eyes. If so, *Maple Viewing* should not be simply regarded as a Japanese film for a domestic audience but as the product of two overlapping dynamics: an attempt to export goods that European buyers expected and an opportunity for Japanese filmgoers to experience their own culture through Westernized eyes.

Conclusion

In this essay, I have questioned the status of *Maple Viewing* as the "earliest extant Japanese film" and submitted each of those terms—"Japanese" and "film"—to revisionist pressure. What do we mean by "film," and how can this be squared with the changing medial contexts in which *Maple Viewing* was first encountered? How can we apply a national designation to a film whose production perhaps rather testifies to the global networks and imperializing imaginaries that defined the circulation of moving images at the turn of the century? In this way, I have explored *Maple Viewing* as a case study for querying terms and frameworks that have served as *a prioris* for much of the historiography of moving images. The film's designation as the earliest surviving "Japanese" "film" opens onto a host of historiographic conundrums that have to be reexamined in terms of a properly historicized account of *Maple Viewing*'s production and exhibition.

Rather than confirm or deny a claim to "firsts," I have tried to give a fuller sense of early film culture in Japan. In other words, this chapter has offered a historical analysis of a film that incorporates "a wider scope of pertinent phenomena and [is] more inclusive in its understanding of [...] visual and material culture," to use the words of late film scholar Thomas Elsaesser.[55] In one of his final works, *Film History as Media Archaeology* (2016), Elsaesser encouraged historians to recover the "diversity" and "multiplicity" of trajectories in cinema's past and to explore the medium as one "firmly embedded in other media practices, other technologies, other social uses, and above all as having—throughout its history—interacted with, been dependent on, been complemented by, and found itself in competition with all manner of entertainment forms, scientific pursuits, practical applications, military uses."[56] As I have demonstrated, *Maple Viewing* was embedded in, interacted with, depended on, and was complemented by its diverse relationships with European Japonisme, Kabuki, *misemono*, photography, and cinema as an emerging new medium in the modernizing society of Japan.

Notes

1. All translations are by the author, unless otherwise indicated. Okajima Hisashi, "Japan's Case: Hopeful or Hopeless?" *FIAF Bulletin* 45 (1992): 2.
2. Irie Yoshirō, "Saiko no Nihon eiga ni tsuite: Konishi Honten seisaku no katsudō shashin" ("The Earliest Japanese Movie: Motion Pictures Produced by Konishi Honten"), *Bulletin of the National Museum of Modern Art, Tokyo* 13 (2009): 65–91.
3. Ibid., 89.
4. Aaron Gerow, "Film as an Important Cultural Property," *Tangemania*, March 24, 2009, <http://www.aarongerow.com/news/film_as_an_important_cultur.html>.
5. Tanaka Junichirō, "Satsuei gishu, Shibata Tsunekichi" ("Cinematographer Shibata Tsunekichi"), *Eiga Gijutsu* 4, no. 6 (December 1942): 56.
6. Gerow, "Film as an Important Cultural Property."
7. Ibid.
8. Ibid.
9. Tanaka Junichirō, "'Yunyū kamera dai 1 gō' kō" ("Thoughts on the First Imported Camera"), *Eiga Terebi Gijutsu* 220 (December 1970): 85.
10. Tanaka Junichirō, *Nihon eiga hattatsu shi I* (*History of the Development of Cinema in Japan 1*) (Tokyo: Chūōkōron sha, 1957), 71.
11. Ueda Manabu, *Nihon eiga sōsō ki no kōgyō to kankyaku: Tokyo to Kyoto o chūshin ni* (*Exhibition and Audiences during the Early Period of Japanese Cinema: In Tokyo and Kyoto*) (Tokyo: Waseda daigaku shuppan bu, 2012), 174.
12. Matsumoto Kōshirō, *Geidan issei ichidai* (*Talk on Arts: Once in a Lifetime*) (Tokyo: Ubun sha, 1948), 67.

13. Kamiyama Akira, "Eiga 'Momijigari' zengo to Dangiku igo: 'Edosodachi' to 'kosei' no aida" ("Before and After the Film *Maple Viewing* and After Dangiku: Between 'Growing Up in Edo' and 'Personality'"), *Kabuki Kenkyu to Hihyō* 32 (2004): 7.
14. Ibid.
15. https://meiji.filmarchives.jp/works/01.html.
16. Tom Gunning, "Non-Continuity, Continuity, Discontinuity: A Theory of Genres in Early Films," in Thomas Elsaesser and Adam Barker, eds., *Early Cinema: Space, Frame, Narrative* (London: BFI, 1990), 89.
17. André Gaudreault, "Film, Narrative, Narration: The Cinema of the Lumière Brothers," in Elsaesser and Barker, eds., *Early Cinema*, 73.
18. Ibid.
19. Aaron Gerow, *Visions of Japanese Modernity, Visions of Japanese Modernity: Articulations of Cinema, Nation, and Spectatorship, 1895–1925* (Berkeley: University of California Press, 2010), 25.
20. Tsukada, *Nihon eiga shi no kenkyū: Katsudō shashin torai zengo no jijō* (*A Study of Japanese Film History: Facts around the Time When Motion Pictures Arrived*) (Tokyo: Gendai shokan, 1980), 174.
21. *Kobe Mata Shin Nippō*, November 19, 1896, quoted in Tsukada, *Nihon eiga shi no kenkyū*, 30.
22. Miki Fukusuke's request for a Cinématographe exhibition to the Mayor of Osaka, n.d., preserved at Institute Lumière, Lyon, France.
23. *Kyoto Hinode Shinbun*, March 3 and 4, 1897, quoted in Tsukada, *Nihon eiga shi no kenkyū*, 106–107.
24. *Hōchi Shinbun*, March 3, 1897, quoted in Tsukada, *Nihon eiga shi no kenkyū*, 111.
25. *Otaru Shinbun*, August 31, 1897, quoted in Tsukada, *Nihon eiga shi no kenkyū*, 127.
26. *Osaka Asahi Shinbun*, February 22, 1897, quoted in Tsukada, *Nihon eiga shi no kenkyū*, 169.
27. Gerow, *Visions of Japanese Modernity*, 26.
28. Marguerite V. Hodge, "Enigmatic Bodies: Dolls and the Making of Japanese Modernity," *Nineteenth-Century Art Worldwide* 12, no. 1 (Spring 2013), http://www.19thc-artworldwide.org/spring13/hodge-enigmatic-bodies.
29. *Osaka Asahi Shinbun*, August 22, 1897, quoted in Tsukada, *Nihon eiga shi no kenkyū*, 177, 179.
30. Gerow, *Visions of Japanese Modernity*, 47.
31. Kinoshita Naoyuki, *Bijutsu to iu misemono* (*The Misemono Called Art*) (Tokyo: Heibon sha, 1993), 57–62. See also Gerow, *Visions of Japanese Modernity*, 45–47.
32. Quoted in Kinoshita, *Bijutsu to iu misemono*, 42. Trans. in Gerow, *Visions of Japanese Modernity*, 46.
33. Hodge, "Enigmatic Bodies."
34. "Nihon eiga shi sokō 22" ("Draft of the History of Japanese Cinema 22"), *Kinema Junpō* 575 (May 11, 1936): 82; "Nihon eiga shi sokō 23," *Kinema Junpō* 576 (May 21, 1936): 75–76.
35. Kanoji, "Nakaza no katsudō shashin" ("Moving Photography at the Nakaza Theater"), *Osaka Asahi Shinbun*, July 16, 1903, quoted in Ueda, *Nihon eiga sōsō ki no kōgyō to kankyaku*, 189.
36. Ueda, *Nihon eiga sōsō ki no kōgyō to kankyaku*, 175.
37. Tanaka, "Satsuei gishu, Shibata Tsunekichi," 58.
38. Ueda, *Nihon eiga sōsō ki no kōgyō to kankyaku*, 176–77.
39. Ibid., 181.

40. Ibid.
41. Irie, "Saiko no Nihon eiga ni tsuite," 88.
42. This initial discourse nonetheless regarded cinema primarily as a problem: in response to the sensational popularity of the French crime serial *Zigomar*, which opened in Tokyo in November 1911, education officials and then newspapers started to condemn cinema's capacity to make the fictional seem real and distinguish its nature fundamentally from existing linguistic arts. See Gerow, *Visions of Japanese Modernity*, 40–65.
43. Kamiyama, "Eiga 'Momijigari' zengo to Dangiku igo," 7.
44. Ibid.
45. Nihon eiga terebi gijutsu kyōkai, "Nihon eiga gijutsu shi nenpu No. 16" ("A History of Japanese Film Technology, No. 16"), *Eiga Terebi Gijutsu* 238 (June 1972): 77; Nihon eiga terebi gijutsu kyōkai, "Nihon eiga gijutsu shi nenpu No. 20," *Eiga Terebi Gijutsu* 242 (October 1972): 75.
46. Daisuke Miyao, *Japonisme and the Birth of Cinema* (Durham, NC: Duke University Press, 2020).
47. Gabriel Veyre, *Opérateur Lumière: Autour du monde avec le Cinématographe Correspondance (1896-1900)* (Lyon, France: Institut Lumière/Actes Sud, 1996), 275–276.
48. Yokoyama Akio, "Mone to Nihonshumi sono ichi sokumen: Ra Japonēzu no ishō kara mieru mono" ("A Thought on Monet and Japonisme: What We Can See in the Costume of *La Japonaise*"), *Bijutsushi ronshū* (*Essays in Art History*) 12 (2012): 132, 134.
49. Ibid., 132–33.
50. Ibid., 134.
51. Mabuchi Akiko, *Japonisumu: Genso no Nippon* (*Japonisme: Imaginary Japan*) (Tokyo: Brücke, 1997), 62.
52. Tsukada Yoshinobu, "Jurēru to 'Meiji no Nihon' o megutte" ("On Girel and 'Meiji Japan'"), *Eiga shiryō hakkutsu* 10 (June 15, 1973): 262.
53. Tsukada Yoshinobu, *Eiga shiryō hakkutsu* 18 (July 15, 1975): 1.
54. Ueda, *Nihon eiga sōsō ki no kōgyō to kankyaku*, 185.
55. Thomas Elsaesser, *Film History as Media Archeology: Tracking Digital Cinema* (Amsterdam: Amsterdam University Press, 2016), 25
56. Ibid., 19, 25.

CHAPTER 8

AFRICAN AMERICAN FILM HISTORY BEYOND CINEMA

William Foster and the Legacy of Black Theatrical Comedy

ALLYSON NADIA FIELD

IN October 1913, James S. McQuade's "Chicago Letter" column in the *Moving Picture World* included an account of the visit of William Foster to the trade journal's Chicago office. Foster had recently embarked on a venture in motion picture production featuring African American actors in one-reel comedies—a novelty for McQuade, who identified Foster as "manager and principal director of the Foster Photoplay Company, a concern owned and operated solely by colored people." In a brief notice, McQuade reports that Foster's "riproarious" farce comedies—*The Railroad Porter*, *The Fall Guy*, and *The Butler*— did good business in Chicago's Grand, Phoenix, and States Theaters, all catering to African American audiences on Chicago's South Side, and in New York City's Lafayette Theater, an integrated venue in Harlem. McQuade relates Foster's boast that his films were shown in all of the 214 theaters across the country "owned and operated by colored men."[1]

McQuade's letter is notable as a rare instance of the film industry trade press of this time paying any attention to African American film production. It also contains valuable information. McQuade mentions that Foster shoots his films in the backyard of his office and studio at 3312 S. Wabash Avenue, that he uses no script, that all of the scenarios are written by "colored authors," and that the one-reel comedy *The Railroad Porter* features Lottie Grady, "one of the foremost colored actresses of the present day." Yet what is especially intriguing is McQuade's use of dialect in purporting to quote the filmmaker: "'Ah don't want you to take mah word for it that these comedies are a big hit. Ah jus' want you to come an' see one of them an' laf yo head off,' said Mr. Foster in a most sincere and unaffected manner. From what I can learn, the Foster films thus far issued are laugh makers of a most infectious kind."[2] It's a familiar racist trope of speech attribution, but we can still glean insight from it.

To be clear, there is nothing in Foster's own writing to suggest that McQuade's representation of his speech has any basis in Foster's actual comportment. Quite the opposite; Foster was an accomplished journalist and was deeply critical of "our brother in white" for opportunistically profiting from African Americans while at the same time handling "everything Negro he touches with the roughest kind of glove."[3] Elsewhere, I've suggested that McQuade's quotation is a deliberate misrepresentation of the filmmaker, a joke made at his expense and predicated on a racist perception of the comedic valences of African Americans.[4] This is a familiar kind of reading, but it's one that, as more information comes to light about early African American filmmaking, may be limiting in what it allows us to imagine. What would it mean to take McQuade's dialect at face value and not presume a straightforward misrepresentation? Could we see it as a glimpse of strategy designed by Foster, a deliberate use of racial performativity? What would it mean to give Foster that form of agency and studied action?

McQuade might not have known much of Foster, but Foster would have had significant experience in dealing with figures like McQuade. Aged fifty-three at the time of his visit to the *Moving Picture World*, Foster had already had a long career that began in horseracing paddocks and extended to prizefighting, eventually leading him to journalism, where he became a sportswriter under the pen name Juli Jones (sometimes Juli Jones Jr.) for the Chicago *Defender*, a major African American newspaper. From sports he entered the theatrical world and worked as a publicist for Black musical theater acts, including composers and performers Bert Williams and George Walker and burlesque comedians George Williams and Augustus Stevens; he also opened a booking agency for Black performers. He had a storefront music shop and publishing company that was a popular fixture along the "Stroll," the center of African American entertainment commerce on Chicago's South Side. With this experience, he gained a regular column in another leading African American newspaper, the Indianapolis *Freeman*, to report on the goings on in "Dahomey," the nickname he gave to the South Side theater scene.

With this background, Foster would have been deeply familiar with the concept of racialized performance. And so we might see, through McQuade's suspect quotation, the suggestion of a kind of code switching, an anticipation of the assumptions by McQuade and his readers about what "a concern owned and operated solely by colored people" might—or should—entail. If it was a deliberate strategy on the part of Foster, it worked. Three weeks after McQuade's column was published, *The Railroad Porter* screened at the famed Majestic Theatre in the heart of the Chicago Loop, the city's central business district.

What I provide in what follows, though, is not just a recovery project, a fuller account of an elusive cinematic pioneer. Attending to Foster's career in the aggregate unlocks a vital relationship between stage and screen media, platforms of performance and signification that shared genres, forms, and practices, while also deploying them in distinct ways. As venues shifted, so did meanings. Indeed, Foster's case demonstrates how valences of representation were contingent on the context of performance and reception. The dynamics of race, performance, and audience shaped the Black theatrical world of the end of the nineteenth century—and, in turn, informed the emerging Black cinematic landscape of the early twentieth. Foster played a crucial role in this transition from his work as a manager and promoter of minstrel and vaudeville acts to his work in Black musical theater, to his motion picture productions, to his ever-broader aspirations for the entertainment industry. Through Foster, we get a richer picture of Black theatrical ambitions at a time rife with possibilities for African American creative workers, even while constrained by the racialized hegemonies of the period.

WILLIAM FOSTER AND AFRICAN AMERICAN MUSICAL THEATER

> Build a theatre for the public—no discrimination, and keep it well-stocked up with plenty of good music and comedies in a theatrical rialto and it will be one of the biggest paying investments that could be launched.
> —William Foster, *The Freeman*, March 9, 1907, 6.

Most histories of African American cinema of the silent era still constellate around "Race film" practices—that is, films made by Black and non-Black producers, featuring predominantly Black casts, and made for Black audiences. Emblematized by Oscar Micheaux, a novelist-turned-filmmaker and the most successful and longest working African American producer of Race films, with a career spanning the period from 1919 to 1948, Race films offered an image of Black life that refuted the often demeaning misrepresentations of mainstream cinema. These films took on many forms and subjects, and since the 1970s there has been a proliferation of scholarship exploring the elements that comprised Race filmmaking. Likewise, scholars have brought to light the different ways audiences encountered these films and how they sought to appeal to spectators in varied settings. From the important historical work of scholars like Jacqueline Stewart, we know more about how Black audiences responded to preclassical and classical Hollywood cinema, and the range of raced—and racist—representations these forms produced, as well as the ways audiences negotiated these representations along with those of Race films.

Race film scholarship has largely situated these practices as a "separate cinema"—a parallel industry to mainstream studio film production, yet often working to create contrasts to it.[5] Micheaux's earliest surviving film, *Within Our Gates* (1920), for example, has been understood (correctly) as a direct response—in narrative and form—to the virulent racism of *The Birth of a Nation* (Dir. D. W. Griffith, 1915).[6] Scholars have similarly accounted for other Black filmmakers working before and during Micheaux's career (most notably the Lincoln Motion Picture Company, active 1916–1921), and the uses of motion pictures, by African Americans and white allies, in the service of African American advancement and as a response to the racist affronts of mainstream cinema.

Insofar as he appears in these narratives, Foster is figured as a pioneer. Indeed, most histories of Race filmmaking begin with his production of one-reel comedies of Black life in Chicago, starting with the release of his film *The Railroad Porter* in 1913.[7] Yet with none of these films known to be extant, and with scant surviving evidence of his career, little else has been said about him. By approaching Foster intermedially, my goal is not only to provide the necessary context for his filmmaking projects and ambitions but to address lacunae in the historiography of African American cinema by accounting for the ways in which it emerged from and existed alongside a prior theatrical tradition.

Rather than the separate cinema model that defined Race film, I will argue that Foster's films were aimed to be seen by integrated and even all-white audiences as well. Indeed, we can detect signs of this in McQuade's Chicago letter: Foster's appearance at the industry trade journal's office indicates aspirations to reach broader audiences beyond the growing number of theaters catering to African Americans. What I show here is that this was possible because of Foster's extensive background in and his intersections with the history of Black comedic theatrical performance. Film historians have long understood that the theatrical world of the late nineteenth century profoundly shaped cinema from production to distribution to exhibition. Within the scholarship on African American film, however, such is the power of Micheaux's founding legend that the centrality of Black theatrical performance has been lost.[8] We get a distinctly different picture of early Black filmmaking—its forms and its appeals—if we consider it in relation to Black theater.

Instead of starting with Foster in 1913 and moving forward to Race filmmaking, I aim to move in reverse, using his emergence into cinema as a lens through which to explore his earlier work in and around Black theater. I argue that Foster developed a filmic form of recuperative comedy out of this background in the African American musical theater, one that appealed to Black urban audiences while conforming to popular culture's expectations of the representation of African Americans. Put succinctly, comedy performed to an *intra*racial audience takes on different valences before an *inter*racial, or predominantly white, audience. Indeed, what the dialect in McQuade's letter points to, in its short but unsubtle terms, is the history of a complex mobilization of stereotypes in dynamic relation to audience assumptions. Read within this tradition of theater and theatrical comedy, Foster becomes a figure who both shaped and emblematizes the fraught tensions concerning Black performance, representation, spectatorship, and cinema's negotiation of conflicting desires and taboos.

What is known about Foster is tantalizing. As far as I can determine, he enters the historical record *in media res* in November 1898, at the age of thirty-eight, with an announcement in the *Freeman* that he had accepted a position as Chicago press agent for Bob Cole and Billy Johnson's production of *A Trip to Coontown*, the first full-length musical production created, owned, and staged entirely by African Americans. To be selected for this position meant that Foster must have been sufficiently established in the theatrical world to be so recognized, at least in the Midwest. Perhaps early experience in sports and journalism was enough to earn the respect of the African American theater world.[9] Although there is no record of his precise activities, it's likely that Foster had been working in and around South Side Chicago's entertainment scene by the time of his involvement with *A Trip to Coontown*.

Cole and Johnson's production exemplifies the parameters and stakes of Black theatrical production and entertainment in a mass culture grappling with the shifting terms of racialized performance. I want to go into some detail here, since it's important to see how performers negotiated the demands of their trade. In 1896, Bob Cole had been a writer for Black Patti's Troubadours, the operatic variety company led by famed soprano Sissieretta Jones. When his requests for a raise in compensation for the hits he was writing were denied, he left the show in spring 1897—taking his scripts and songs. As musicologist Thomas Riis notes, the Troubadours' white managers were incensed and quickly spread the word that Cole was "a troublemaker."[10] He was essentially blackballed in the theatrical world, along with around six others who left the show, and limited to performing in Canada. Riis notes it was this "core group of dissidents" from the Troubadours that formed the production team for *A Trip to Coontown*.[11] (The play was named as a spoof on the popular musical *A Trip to Chinatown* [1891] and based on a skit originally written for the Troubadours titled *At Jolly Coon-ey Island*.[12])

Determined to sink the new competition, Black Patti's Troubadours booked their tour route to coincide with that of *A Trip to Coontown*.[13] Possibly in frustration at this campaign, Cole and Johnson broke contract with their booking agent, Michael Leavitt, who subsequently sued: the duo was fined $1,000 by the court.[14] According to Leavitt's attorney, "the reason the defendants in the suit objected was that the same route was mapped out for the Black Patti company two weeks before the 'Coontown' show began its tour."[15] Foster was then engaged as the company began their Midwest tour and joined the show in Chicago at the end of November. He was with Cole and Johnson at least through that season, working as an advance agent and press agent.[16]

A Trip to Coontown opened its Chicago run at the Alhambra Theater on Sunday, November 26, 1898.[17] This was just ahead of the Troubadours—possibly thanks to Foster's intervention—and concurrent with the Chicago run of Will Marion Cook and Paul Laurence Dunbar's *Clorindy, Or, The Origin of the Cake Walk* at the Great Northern Theater.[18] A week later, *A Trip to Coontown* moved to the Academy Theater, then to the Great Northern at the end of January, and finally back to the Alhambra at the end of February and early March.[19] In between these appearances, they traveled to other Midwest cities, including Topeka, Kansas City, and Cleveland. In Cleveland, the company faced "prejudiced white musicians who refused to play with the company's colored orchestra leader." It is not clear how this was resolved, but the Black press reported that "the uncalled for prejudice was overruled however and the last part of the week found the colored man leading and company doing hot work."[20] Because of such incidents, the company was conscious of being a pioneer in many of the theaters where it appeared. *A Trip to Coontown* was the first "colored company" to be booked at the Grand Opera House (see figure 8.1) in New York City, as well as the "only colored show that has been honored by a booking" at the theatre of the same name in Kansas City, Missouri.[21]

A Trip to Coontown's comedy was subversively indeterminate. Krystyn Moon, who recently rediscovered the text of the play, notes that it "played to and against stereotypes of African Americans during the late nineteenth century."[22] For example, the play featured Cole in whiteface as an inebriated tramp—one that David Krasner argues inspired

FIGURE 8.1 Advertisement, *The Sun* (New York), September 11, 1898.

Emmett Kelley and Charlie Chaplin, among others. This makeup, Krasner suggests, had a destabilizing effect on audiences. Cole could perform a gag with a chicken—a cliché of minstrelsy—but performed in whiteface, the target of the humor is deflected away from African Americans.[23] Again, the racial composition of the audience mattered. If whiteface marked Cole's comedy as a performance, this also carried a risk in the context of African American musical theater's general claims to more authentically represent Black life. While contrasting with white-imagined notions of "blackness" formed through decades of minstrel tradition, such play with identity could risk naturalizing the stereotypes on which the comedy depended.

The risk in this gesture was recognized by Foster. In his memoirs of Black theater, written twenty years after his time with the troupe, Foster refers to the period from 1897 to 1908 as "the beginning of a brief but brilliant period in the history of the colored stage." Offering the narrative of Cole's struggles with the Troubadours and his eventual blacklist and forced exile to Canada, Foster writes:

> With his back to the wall Cole issued what might rightly be called the colored actor's Declaration of Independence. "We are going to have our own shows," he declared. "We are going to write them ourselves, we are going to have our own stage manager, our own orchestra leader and our own manager out front to count up. No divided houses—our race must be seated from boxes back." As a means of inaugurating these

principles, Cole organized his "Trip to Coontown" company. The title of the show, by the way, indicates that he did not have the slightest trace of an inferiority complex.[24]

Foster's nod to Cole's choice of title is a little opaque but suggests an appreciation of Cole's subversion of the term "coon" at a time when it was shifting from being a generic marker (e.g., coon songs) to an explicitly derogatory epithet.[25] It was, perhaps, a tension in performance that could only be temporary. By 1905, Cole himself had declared that he would "crusade against the word 'coon'" and relegated his own use of (and benefit from) it to the past, telling the *Freeman*'s chief dramatic critic Sylvester Russell (rather obliquely), "That day has passed with the softly flowing tide of revelations."[26] And in a 1908 critique of a show at the Lincoln Theater on Chicago's South Side, Foster noted, "The word 'coon' has lost its usefulness years ago."[27] This was a period of rapid change not only in racialized signifiers on the stage but also of debates among performers and critics about its terms—"Alas, I gently sighed, how greatly Cole has changed," remarked Russell on Cole's reversal.[28]

Along with the embracing and subverting of stereotype, Cole and Johnson also combined highbrow and lowbrow forms. The effect of this was lauded by the *Plaindealer* as "an agreeable surprise": "A surprise because it had been thought all along that the Negro was not capable of producing any sort of entertainment successfully except that of minstrelsy in its crudest form. While there were several numbers of music on the ragtime order, produced in 'A Trip to Coontown,' there was also enough music suggestive of a very high class of opera."[29] The advance notice in the *Cleveland Gazette*, possibly furnished by Foster, noted: "The Coontown company, of such peculiar name, is the most talked of colored company in this country for many reasons, particularly its clean performance. The only successful colored show that does not do any cake walking or buck dancing."[30] This form of hybrid genre entertainment offered the company a platform that was seen as illustrative of the potential for broader African American achievement. For example, a lengthy review in the African American newspaper *The Illinois Record* lauded the production as "the best Negro entertainment that has ever been presented to the American public":

> And it is no exaggeration to say of this band of merry makers, and others in the same line of work, that they are doing more to break down race prejudice in this country than the race gives them credit for, for as they pass from town to town, from city to city and state to state they not only help to break through the bulwark of American prejudice, but it is also safe to say of them that they are the greatest missionaries of our race that we have before the public today. Their excellent achievement is a bright commentary on the possibilities of American cosmopolitan life. For just to think that our race, a little over a quarter of a century ago in bondage, are today challenging the admiration of the public, treading the stage as colored aristocrats, delighting the colored 400 and the elite of white society, sitting side by side in one of the largest theaters in Chicago. [. . .] "Trip to Coontown" has great merit as a play and does not depend for success alone on race sympathy by delineating the obsequious and illiterate Negro of forty years ago. [. . .] Instead of the burnt cork minstrel of the past to

delight us we have the up-to-date farce comedy of today, in the form of "A Trip to Coontown."[31]

African American newspapers across the Midwest shared this view. As the *Freeman* noted, "A Trip to Coontown has been acknowledged the standard of refined and accomplished Negro talent on the stage."[32]

Yet if Foster, as the company's press agent, did much to frame that reception, he did not seem to unequivocally endorse the model provided by *A Trip to Coontown*. His own comments on the state of Black theater, as they developed over the next decade, varied widely. We can see his contradictory positionings as indicative of the shifting grounds of discourse around Black popular theater at this time—even as constitutive of it.

The range of activities Foster undertook during the first decade of the twentieth century reveal the complexity of the moment. Beyond his work as a promotional agent, he served as business manager and advertising representative for Robert T. Motts's New Pekin Theater, helping to rebuild the theater's stock company with stage veterans like Lawrence Chenault and discovering young talent that would go on to long and distinguished stage and film careers (this included Flournoy Miller, Aubrey Lyles, and Charles Gilpin).[33] Foster even worked with J. Ed. Green, the Pekin's Director of Amusements, to bring a revival of *A Trip to Coontown* to the Pekin for its inaugural season in October 1906.[34] But by 1909, Foster and Motts had had an unexplained falling out, which seems to have rippled beyond the Pekin. Soon thereafter, Elwood Knox, editor of the *Freeman* and Motts's close friend, replaced Foster with Cary B. Lewis as the Chicago theater correspondent.[35] Yet, even then Foster continued as a columnist for the *Freeman*, writing under his nom-de-plume Juli Jones, Jr., and reporting on the goings on in the South Side Chicago theatrical scene.

One incident demonstrates the mutability of Foster's position. At the same time that he was booking the southern tour of burlesque comedians Williams & Stevens, Foster dropped a bomb on Black vaudeville in the Christmas Day issue of the *Freeman* in 1909. In a column titled "Forty Years of the Negro on the Stage in America and Europe," Foster (writing as Jones), unleashed a vitriolic screed against the profession, declaring that with few exceptions, the Negro on stage "has done little or nothing for his race or himself" and that "there is not a real colored act in vaudeville; simply turns and stunts." After chronicling a selective history of Black stage performance derived from early minstrel performances, he regrets that the success of minstrelsy "ruined the Negro's chances of ever becoming an artistic star beyond a black-face, low, ignorant—fool. He has done little or nothing since the day he began until to-day to improve his condition." He places the blame largely on African American song writers who rely on familiar motifs and are unwilling to challenge convention, noting, "The cold fact of the matter is this: there isn't one of the many writers who will take the chance and face starvation to produce plays to challenge 'The Clansman,' and such plays, for fear the white managers would not like such plays." While Black writers and community leaders had critiqued Thomas Dixon Jr.'s 1905 novel and play on which the film *The Birth of a Nation* was based, Foster's focus on Black theater departed from the tone of most of his peers. (Indeed, his call for challenges to *The Clansman* anticipates the African American responses to Griffith's infamous film.)

Foster continues to take aim at writers: "another bush they hide behind is, the managers would not give such a show any time or play them in their houses. This is all rot." With a sharp rebuke, he writes, "The present-day managers would play a show composed of hogs, if the hogs could fill the house." Foster concludes by turning to performers:

> Give the race shows that will have morals, and parts that give us something to go home and think about. Your white and black supporters are tired looking at you in the same old thing, for you have done nothing, nothing, but sing, dance and make a fool of yourself to the people who have been attending your shows in the last forty years. Artistically and financially you have been an absolute failure for forty, forty long years.[36]

This Christmas column surely raised the ire of *Freeman* readers. And it did not go unchallenged, as several published responses soon followed.

A few weeks later, the *Freeman* published an unsigned follow-up column, similarly titled "Forty Years of the Negro on the Stage." This rejoinder to Foster, perhaps even penned by himself, followed a similar historical trajectory, though it provided greater detail and took a more neutral, at times even celebratory tone. Perhaps with Foster's vitriolic lament in mind, the second column concludes by promising a more comprehensive story of the American Negro in show business, conceding that with the lack of a comprehensive written history, "information has to be picked up here and there."[37] This more positive account was followed two weeks later by a sharper response to Foster's Christmas column, written by vaudeville cartoon artist Harry Brown. Rather than offering a full assessment of Foster's column, Brown mainly objected to Foster's singular critique of the emphasis on singing and dancing. Brown also noted that the article came to his attention by "two white performers, and they couldn't understand why such an article should be written by a colored writer." He goes on to lament that the harsh words of "Juli Jones" would be read by "hundreds of white people in and out of the profession" as well as by the "colored readers" of *The Freeman*."[38]

The debate did not end there. Again writing as Juli Jones, Jr., Foster replied in a subsequent column that his critique was of white acts as well as African American vaudevillians, claiming that neither would ever "turn out a real artistic star." Confident in his arguments, Foster nonetheless demonstrated a capacity for self-deprecating humor: "Mr. Brown again said that Juli Jones did not know what he was talking about. Well, Jones agrees with Mr. Brown on this point, and thousands of others are of Mr. Brown's opinion[.] Ha! ha! But the writer will have to borrow from Brooks and Hunter's great song, 'Never Mind the White Man's Teaching.' What Jones knows, he knows. To get at the bottom of this argument one will first have to commence at the beginning with vaudeville, which is the craze of the day and is here to stay." After proffering a genealogy of the vaudeville stage, he concluded emphatically, "Vaudeville is here to stay, no matter what every theatrical or stage writer in the world may say or write. All due respects to everybody in vaudeville. No apologizing to any."[39]

These spats did not occur in a vacuum. At the same time as columnists debated the legitimacy of Black performance on stage, there were discussions about the role of moving pictures in diminishing the opportunities for local and traveling Black performers.[40] As one unnamed columnist lamented, "Here in Chicago, unless something is done or some changes are made, there will not be a decent house for a colored show to plan in."[41] Foster sounded a warning, too, in a column written shortly before his own venture into motion picture production in 1913. "As matters stand to-day, there will not be any cheap vaudeville in two years' time, as moving pictures will take the place of vaudeville. Every day moving pictures are making inroads and taking the place of vaudeville. They are a sure death blow to vaudeville and a boon to managers." Noting the logistical hassles of managing a vaudeville house with rotating and untested acts, he stated, "The pictures of to-day and in the future will take all that worry off their hands and minds, and give a new show every day." He then offered the statistics on 472 licensed theaters, 320 of which were moving picture houses. "In time the supply will be large enough to furnish the small houses. Then good-bye, small acts, white and black, North, South, East and West. The public is tiring of seeing the same old acts, only different faces: same old songs, but a little different tune. Showmen who have not novelties to offer will find themselves out in the cold."[42]

These pressures and debates set the conditions for the emergence of early Black filmmakers. While filmmakers may have been largely galvanized by a desire to refute degrading portrayals with a more uplifting image of African Americans, it was the changing conditions of the theater—and the end of a once-prominent artistic model—that prompted entrepreneurial figures like Foster to venture into motion pictures. And it was the debates on the value of Black performance that gave these early filmmakers a way to think through the promise and danger of their own work.

FOSTER'S MOVING PICTURE VENTURE

> The greatest thing that happened on the Stroll recently was the first appearance of William Foster's genuine Negro moving pictures.
> —Sylvester Russell, *The Freeman*, August 16, 1913, 6.

> Foster saw into the Future.
> —*The Chicago Defender*, November 22, 1913, 6.

When Foster turned to motion picture production in 1913, he was well established not only in the theatrical world—the *Defender* noted that he "has done more than any one man to promote theatrical enterprises"—but in social circles as well.[43] He served, for example, as secretary of the Goats, a group of African American performers first organized as a fundraising endeavor in August 1909. Like the Frogs of New York, which operated as an exclusive club that held "frolics" to support theatrical professionals, the Goats had about a hundred members, including women (called Nanny Goats), and held weekly "rambles" around seven theaters along the Stroll.[44] The combination of community and entertainment informed Foster's approach to filmmaking and the work that he produced in Chicago.

To form his motion picture production company in June 1913, Foster drew on these connections to partner with Joe Shoecraft. Shoecraft was a beloved fixture in the entertainment world of the South Side, serving as manager of the popular nightspot the Pompeii Buffet and Café; was, along with Foster, a member of the Goats; and was a longtime participant and star of the Amateur Minstrel Club, a philanthropic organization. He was also a key figure in Black-owned and operated enterprises that catered to an African American clientele—indeed, when the Pompeii expanded its operations with the erection of a pavilion and Winter Garden, it was lauded in the Black press as marking "a new era in the entertaining line for the Colored people of Chicago."[45]

The partnership between Foster and Shoecraft began in theater. Foster was recognized as an "authority on vaudeville acts and 'stagedom,'" so it made sense that Shoecraft invited him to put together high-profile shows, most notably for the recently opened Pompeii in April 1913.[46] The event was a kind of inauguration of the venue, and many local entertainers were invited to perform, including acts from other houses like the orchestra from the Grand Theater, singers from the Elite Café, Edward Goodbar of the Williams and Walker Company, and a range of singers including Lizzie Hart and Madeline "Kinky Doo" Cooper. Foster organized the entertainment, and Shoecraft, known as one of the funniest men in Chicago, provided the humor as monologist.[47]

The subsequent incorporation of the Foster Photo Play Film Company in Chicago made the industry trade news, which noted the company's capital stock of $2,500 "to manufacture and deal in photo plays" and named Foster, Shoecraft, and Robert Hanson as incorporators.[48] Nothing is known about Hanson, and he wasn't mentioned by the Black press, so he might have been a white investor that Foster or Shoecraft knew through their respective enterprises—perhaps the unnamed "white gentleman" who loaned Foster the money to purchase the equipment.[49] But it is clear that Shoecraft and Foster steered the enterprise, though it is not clear what their financial arrangement was. They began by filming actualities of local events—the dedication of the Wabash Avenue branch of the YMCA and a Chicago American Giants baseball game at Schorling's Park—alongside fictional comedy shorts, beginning with *The Railroad Porter* and *The Butler*.[50] While none of these films has survived, it is clear that the shorts derived their comedy from situations and mishaps extending from recognizable roles familiar to urban Black audiences—the adventures and misadventures of Pullman porters, café waiters, stylish women, and heroic butlers.[51]

Foster's narrative comedies featured accomplished actors formerly associated with the Pekin Stock Company, the most celebrated member of which was Lottie Grady (see figure 8.2), who had appeared with Bert Williams and was a member of the Smart Set Company. The *Defender* celebrated Grady's screen performance: "As a movie artist, Miss

FIGURE 8.2 Lottie Grady, *New York Age*, November 18, 1909.

Lottie Grady is a howling success."[52] Foster capitalized on her popularity: as the films toured, Grady often traveled with them, performing during the reel changes.[53]

Through the summer and autumn of 1913, Foster's comedies and actualities were screened at the major South Side theaters catering to an African American clientele, including the Grand, Phoenix, States, and Pekin, as well as Black theaters in St. Louis, Kansas City, and Birmingham. As the *Defender* reported, "Everybody is pleased with the success of the pictures, and to know we will have the pleasure of seeing the better side of the race on canvas than always seeing some Negro making an ass of himself."[54] But Foster's ambitions were to make films with African American performers that would show in a range of venues to Black, non-Black, and mixed audiences. As his advertisements announced, "they can be shown in anybody's house no matter how small or how big."[55]

Likely through his connections in the entertainment world and Grady's draw as a vaudeville star, Foster was able to screen his films at the recently opened Lafayette Theater in Harlem, a 1,500-seat theater featuring high-class vaudeville and motion pictures (it had three shows daily with changes of bill on Mondays and Thursdays). The Lafayette had a white manager, Benjamin Nibur, who was eager to capitalize on an African American clientele and responsive to the increased booking of Black performers.[56] The theater had desegregated early in 1913, and African Americans were permitted to sit in orchestra seats, instead of being relegated, as they were in other New York theaters, to the balcony.

The importance of the Lafayette's desegregation was noted by *New York Age* arts critic Lester Walton, who wrote a moving column describing the experience of attending a fully desegregated theater. In that article, he says that "all radical advocators of the segregation of the races" should visit the Lafayette where they would "find colored and white theatregoers sitting side by side on the first floor of the theatre peaceably and quietly, thinking not of the dire predictions of calamity howlers who find it to their interest to rave publicly about the bugaboo 'social equality,' but who are industriously engaged in getting their money's worth by watching the vaudeville show." Walton marvels: "How things have changed! Not so very long ago the colored theatregoers were not so warmly received on the first floor of the Lafayette Theatre; in fact, they were not received in that section of the house at all." On the night he attended, Walton noted that about half of the audience in the orchestra was African American, and "the ebony-hued contingent outclassed the whites." He extended his celebration of the integrated theater to the stage as well, noting that "good colored acts are liberally applauded by the white patrons as well as the colored."[57] Walton notes that the headliners were mainly African American acts.[58] Demonstrating the Lafayette's commitment to fostering African American patronage, the *Age* reported, "Manager Benjamin Nibur has made good his promise to replace white female ushers with young colored women. A colored orchestra and colored card boys are now in order at the Lafayette."[59]

The Lafayette's ambitions for a desegregated theater were thoroughgoing. In early March 1913 the theater debuted a stock company, the Negro Players, with Will Marion Cook as the director of the orchestra. Cook had been composer in residence at Chicago's Pekin Theatre for six months in its first season at the same time that Foster was the theater's business manager and advertising representative.[60] Walton reported in advance of the stock company's debut, "The management will continue to present colored and white acts and motion pictures, and the stock company will give an afterpiece at each performance, holding the stage for about thirty minutes."[61] Cook himself described the endeavor: "The founders of this organization aim to put into characteristic [sic], a musical and dramatic form, real pictures of Negro life both of city and plantation. The authors of the playlets will at first treat of the lighter humorous characteristics of their people until Negro actors shall have obtained a surer stage technique. The Negro's talent for music and dramatic expression is now unquestioned. The Negro Players hope to aid in the development and perfection of this talent."[62] Soon thereafter, they were replaced with a new stock company, "unencumbered by any additional references, such as 'Negro,' 'Afro-American' or 'colored,'" called the Lafayette Players, led by Jesse A. Shipp—another veteran of Motts's Pekin Stock Company.[63]

It was in this milieu that Foster's films screened in the second half of the week, showing on September 18–21.[64] In the first half of the week, the vaudeville program had only included one "colored act" on the bill, T. F. Rogers, who was "liberally applauded." The *Age* reported on this, noting, "From now on the patrons will be favored with more colored turns."[65] It's not clear what vaudeville acts were featured with *The Railroad Porter*, but the *Age* complained about aspects of that week's bill, singling out two moments in particular: an objectionable verse from "A Wise Old Mosquito," a song by the famed African American composers Chris Smith and Jim Burris ("Why ridicule the race? We get enough of that from other sources.") and "disgusting" dialogue in an act described as "a cross between a school sketch and a delicatessen store convention." The paper wrote, "if Manager Nibur wants to keep his patrons he had better use more judgment in the future. Because one-third of the house relishes suggestive acts does not give the management license to inflict such stuff on the other two-thirds."[66] It is fascinating that the *Age* points to lowbrow bawdy humor while, apart from "A Wise Old Mosquito," largely ignoring—and even, at one point, praising—the various acts' conventional forms of racialized performance. Indeed, acts featuring racialized comedy, including one with a "pick who works under cork," were actually celebrated.

In this context, *The Railroad Porter*'s somewhat scandalous infidelity plot similarly went unremarked on. Instead, the *Age* reported that *The Railroad Porter*—identified as "The Pullman Porter"—was a "hit" and "a big scream," praising Grady in particular, and requesting that more Foster films should be sent to New York. The paper's summary of the film even relished its impropriety:

> The story of "The Pullman Porter" dealt with a young wife who, thinking her husband had gone out on "his run," invited a fashionably dressed chap, who was a waiter at one of the colored cafes on State street, to dine. However, the husband did not go out, and, upon returning home, found wifey sitting at the table serving the waiter all the delicacies of the season. Mr. Husband proceeds to get his revolver, which he uses very carelessly, running the unwelcome visitor to his home. Then the waiter gets his revolver and returns the compliment. However, nobody is hurt, despite all the shooting, and all ends happily.[67]

The way that the *New York Age* sought to negotiate the competing claims of the varied acts at the Lafayette shows the tensions at play in Black musical theater at this time. While these tensions also inform early motion picture production—not least with Foster—the appearance of his films at the Lafayette is a clear indication that the audience he sought to reach was inter- as well as intraracial.

Success begat success. After screening his films to enthusiastic audiences in South Side theaters and to an integrated audience in New York City, Foster gained entry to two predominantly white theaters in downtown Chicago. The screenings there received attention from national industry trade publications *Billboard* and *The Moving Picture World*, the latter of which was the very notice in which James McQuade (mis)represented Foster's speech.

On Monday October 6, 1913, *The Railroad Porter* was shown at the Pastime Theater, a 460-seat theater at 66 W. Madison St. that showed moving pictures exclusively after 1909.[68] At the center of the downtown business district, the theater drew a large audience of businessmen, especially at the lunch hour.[69] *Billboard* reported favorably on the film's run there (oddly, it suggested that this was the first presentation of the film and that the film was the company's first production—was this in ignorance of its prior screenings, or as a strategic misrepresentation on the part of Foster?). Noting the theatrical bona fides of Lottie Grady and her association with Bert Williams and the Smart Set Company, *Billboard* concluded, "The picture met with a great deal of favor and was considered a splendid production by those present this afternoon."[70]

The Railroad Porter also screened at the Majestic Theatre (see figure 8.3) on Monday, November 17, 1913—possibly for the entire week. The leading vaudeville theater in Chicago, the Majestic was located on West Monroe St., in a twenty-story building erected in 1906—the tallest building in Chicago at the time—with a seating capacity of 1,986, making it the second-largest playhouse in the city.[71] The Majestic Theatre building housed the Western Vaudeville Managers' Association, which managed bookings for performers at theaters, fairs, parks, and cabarets.[72] At this time, the Majestic advertised "distinctive vaudeville," touted itself as the "standard vaudeville theater of America," and offered, in addition to the typical variety of vaudeville acts, "the best of first run motion pictures"—including *Pathé Weekly* films.[73] That Foster was able to show his films at the Majestic is notable; such a venue was a significant departure from the smaller South Side theaters that had previously carried long runs of his films.[74]

The politics of this move were not simple. By law, theaters in Illinois could not be segregated, as the Illinois Civil Rights Act of 1885 forbade discrimination in public facilities and places, including theaters and restaurants. In practice, however, discrimination was rampant.[75] African American newspapers informed theatergoers of their rights and warned them of unscrupulous practices. For example, the *Defender* advised its readers that "it is customary in theatres of cheap caliber and cheap amusement houses to huddle all of our people together. Where this occurs you have good grounds for suit and don't fail to take advantage of such a golden opportunity." While emphasizing theaters of "no class," they also called out the high-class Majestic for known violations.[76] They advised Black theatergoers to hold on to their ticket stubs as ushers and managers were known for the "unfair trick" of switching out orchestra tickets for balcony seats.[77] Indeed, in April 1913 the famous performer Abbie Mitchell, wife of Will Marion Cook, complained of her first-class ticket being changed for a second-class one—a scandal that made the front page of the *Defender* with the assertion that "the State of Illinois has a strong civil rights law which prominent attorneys will quote when seeking redress for Miss Mitchell in the Courts."[78] (While tracking and publicizing affronts, the *Defender* also celebrated successes. A few years after this incident, the paper's society editor was at

FIGURE 8.3 The Majestic Building, *Architectural Record*, June 1906.

the Majestic and witnessed a white woman in the wrong seat refusing to give up her seat for a Black man with the correct ticket. The theater manager insisted she move, leading the paper to celebrate "a well-earned victory" and proclaim that the Majestic "stands for democracy."[79]) Law aside, in practice the Majestic was still known as "the famous White Temple of Vaudeville."[80]

Given the volatile situation among theater patrons, and only six months after the Abbie Mitchell incident, Foster's films were a fascinating event when they screened at the Majestic in mid-November. Though the historical record leaves scant evidence of the exhibition details, we can still create a composite sense of how audiences encountered his films. That particular Monday, for example, marked the first day in a week-long run of a program of mixed vaudeville, headlined by vaudeville star Marie Dressler. Sharing the bill with Dressler were Arenera and Victor, a dance duo from Spain; Paul La Croix, a juggler known as "The Mad Hatter"; Hans Roberts & Co. performing a comedy sketch by Edgar Allan Woolf, "A Daddy by Express"; the Harvey Do Vora Trio, singers and dancers; Ramses, a magician; and Tony Hunting and Corinne Francis, singing and talking comedians performing "A Love Lozenger." These acts were followed by Add Hoyt's Minstrels, with William H. Maxwell as the Interlocutor, Hoyt as Bones, and John Forsman as Tambo. The minstrels were followed by Dressler, and the live program concluded with Louis L. Wills and Charles F. Hassan, equilibrists.[81] Moving pictures were shown at the opening and ending of the program, with a first-run film opening the show and a variety of "latest subjects" closing the bill. Foster's film or films were likely slotted in the latter cluster.[82]

Attendance was reportedly low for the Majestic in the evening, though the matinee did the biggest business seen by the theater in weeks. There was likely some attrition during the show, leaving fewer at the end for the moving pictures.[83] *Billboard*'s review of the Monday matinee show, while mixed overall, was quite appreciative of Hoyt's Minstrels, noting it was "the first minstrel act that we've seen that really succeeded in getting over in a local vaudevil [sic] house in several years. Some of the comedy material is new and the boys have exceptional voices, which win approval in both solo and ensemble renditions. True harmony and a good song repertoire. Novel and pretty setting."[84] This opinion was not universally shared. *Variety* panned much of the program, reserving its harshest words for the minstrel troupe:

> The big flop of the week fell to Add Hoyt's Minstrels, a septet of cork artists who seem to labor under the impression that the windy middle west was discovered in the last six months. Their numbers, all of the past century vintage, could be jerked out and substituted by something modern. The comedy, particularly the closing bit anent [about] the shirt, is absolutely and positively impossible. To be brief, Add Hoyt gave birth to a nifty idea when he schemed out the minstrel plan, but his execution is just a trifle off. The headliner followed. The pictures were good.[85]

This review is particularly interesting: first, the emphasis of the *Variety* writer on the outmodedness of Hoyt's Minstrels and the desire for something more "modern"; and second, the conclusion in which Dressler is elided and a pithy evaluation of the moving pictures is provided—pictures which, as we know, included Foster's. Although it is without much discussion, this adjacency suggests the modern Foster as a kind of answer to the out-of-date Hoyt's Minstrels. In the language of the time race was often coded in temporal terms; indeed, the euphemism "up to date" was used at the turn of the century for African American "coon shouters" to distinguish them from their white counterparts.[86] Understood this way, Black performers' modernness stood in stark relief against the archaism of white minstrels in vaudeville. That the Black performers appeared in moving pictures would have given further evidence of this.

Foster's films can also be seen in relation to the performance of Dressler. A turn-of-the-century star of vaudeville and burlesque, Dressler was famous as an interpreter of "coon songs" and for impersonations. She introduced the character Tillie Blobbs in 1910 and would go on to star in Mack Sennett's *Tillie's Punctured Romance* (1914) and subsequent Tillie films. At the Majestic that November, Dressler performed three numbers, totaling fourteen minutes, a repeat of a performance she had brought to that same venue in June.[87] Reports do not detail which numbers she performed, only that she " 'puts over' her songs in the same old way that has made her justly famous."[88] Of the June performance, *The New York Clipper* reported that she offered "a selection of some of her best known songs," which consisted of "good natured clowning," including her signature number "A Great Big Girl Like Me" "and other wild burlesques." But she then shifted tone, calling for audience silence "while she indulges in pathos."[89]

The act itself seems to have been an affective whirlwind: "She jumped around and shouted, gave imitations and recited; all of which was executed in Dressler style, was liked, and netted her loud and long applause. The offering was mirthful from a burlesque standpoint, but was plenty crude in parts and a part of Miss Dressler's dancing might easily be cut out without being missed. Her serious recitation, in spite of being dramatically given, was entirely out of place, although vaudeville permits a lot of things. But Marie is full of tricks and life, and she was called back again and again, finally giving a little curtain talk, and then she was allowed to go. The act was the most popular event on the bill, judging from the applause."[90] The *Tribune* reviewer commented on her versatility, noting that "it is some achievement to shift precipitately from the grimaces and contortions of buffoonery to the sad stuff, but Miss Dressler accomplishes it and is rewarded by close attention and applause. The versatile lady later gives a travesty on emotional acting, making it easier, thus, for the audience to dry its tears."[91]

There was also the problem of repetition. When she performed in June, *Billboard* reported that the Majestic audiences were "enthusiastic in their approval and Marie left the stage—a hit."[92] However, by November, *Variety*'s chief Chicago critic John J. O'Connor eviscerated the headliner, quipping that Dressler "seems to have hit the toboggan as far as vaudeville is directly concerned. A repertoire of three numbers, one being particularly suggestive and all bound round with a flock of vulgar wiggles, brought the musical comedy star just through with nothing to spare." O'Connor concluded, "remembering the same headliner but a few years back, one must conclude that vaudeville has either gone ahead or Marie Dressler has right-about-faced."[93]

It's not clear if she included numbers from her standard "coon song" repertoire, though plays with ethnic and racial masquerade were at the heart of her stage presence. Some ambiguous evidence can be found in her costuming for the tour, which appears to have been notably eccentric. One theater critic described it as a "mongrel gown," another noted a costume comprising "a weird and wonderful cerise harem skirt, topped by one of those minaret-hoops of black lace, and wearing the Dressler merry-go-round hat."[94]

As Victoria Sturtevant has argued, Dressler's interpretation of "ethnic bodily excess" allowed audiences "to read her as nonwhite."[95] Yet against *The Railroad Porter*, Dressler's non-whiteness would have contrasted with that of Lottie Grady, leaving the white vaudevillian in a kind of racial liminal zone. The presumption of racialized performance, where audiences suspend disbelief to enjoy the burlesque, would be belied by Grady's filmic presence. Indeed, while Dressler performed in the tradition of white-imagined blackness of minstrelsy, Grady had starred as "Lily White" in the Smart Set's "His Honor: The Barber" in the 1910–11 season.[96] Further, Dressler's low-brow comedy depended on a bawdy class-based performance, whereas Grady's stately demeanor as the star of the Smart Set Company and the Pekin Stock Company bent to comedic masquerade in her portrayal of the cheating "wifey" of *The Railroad Porter*.[97] We might even see Grady as not only a refutation of Dressler but a performative inversion. While Dressler sang "coon songs" like "Rastus Take Me Back"—in which she embodies "a transgressive wench" who admits to "gin-drinking, chicken-stealing, policy-playing and husband-beating"—Grady's performance of infidelity seems to have been far more innocent.[98] Such satiric play with race was common on vaudeville stages, but it is not clear if the mixing of Black actors and white performers in racialized roles would have been a familiar effect for most audiences at the Majestic—unlike the mixed-race bills common at theaters such as the Lafayette.

The instability of race as performed on stage was also reflected in audience conduct. As Jacqueline Stewart notes, the (presumed white) audience at the Majestic "so enjoyed Foster's film that they exhibited the kind of 'inappropriate' spectatorial behavior frequently attributed to Black Belt audiences: 'When it was screened patrons jumped up and shouted, some laughed so loud that ushers had to silence them.'"[99] On recounting this response, the *Defender* championed *The Railroad Porter* as the "biggest success of the year at the Majestic" and reported that the theater's manager "states that it contains more wit and humor than any picture ever seen at the house. Foster's 'movies' are a success."[100]

Theater is doubly important here to Foster. First, as I argued above, his background in African American theater was instrumental to his turn to filmmaking, and the way in which his films were shown and received is inseparable from the vaudeville milieu of their exhibition. Second, racialized performance in this period, whether on stage or in film, emerged out of the shared conventions of popular theatrical culture. As Foster developed a form of comedy bound up in and parodying an aesthetics and politics of respectability, he drew on his theatrical experience of comedic ambiguity. Both a product of the stage and a herald of its decline, the "Foster movement," as the *Freeman* declared it, reflects the entanglements and ambiguities of a changing entertainment landscape for African American artists and audiences.[101]

CODA: WILLIAM FOSTER IN HOLLYWOOD

> Heaven only knows how he got to Los Angeles, but he reached there.
> —Associated Negro Press, *New York Amsterdam News*, June 26, 1929, 12

When he was almost seventy years old, Foster added another act to his career. In early 1929 he arrived in Los Angeles with the ambition of entering the mainstream motion picture industry. Much remains unknown concerning Foster's time in California, and it's difficult to differentiate the wishful laudations of his journalist colleagues from the less pleasant realities he encountered in Hollywood. The Associated Negro Press (ANP) reported that upon arriving in Los Angeles, Foster made the rounds of the studios with his scripts. Foster told the ANP journalist, "At Fox's the clerks in the interview offices seemed to take the matter as a joke and at all the other studios I could not get an audience with directors or producers."[102] He finally gained entry to Pathé Studios after befriending the African American gateman there and impressing director Paul Powell.[103] Foster described the encounter thus: "He treated me with the greatest of courtesy, pronounced my work fine and signed me up for ten weeks straight." (Interestingly, Foster also included a somewhat veiled critique: "This man is from Virginia and if there ever was a white man from the South, he is the whitest I have ever met."[104]) Foster's ten-week contract entailed work as a technical director on a series of Black-cast short comedies, working with the Black actors and supervising the "authenticity" of the subjects, with the implication that his own scenarios would then go into production.[105]

Foster's timing was fortuitous. Pathé was hoping to rival Paramount's successful Christie Comedies (featuring, among others, Spencer Williams), which were based on the *Saturday Evening Post*'s "Darktown Birmingham" stories. In March 1929, Pathé purchased the rights to sixteen of Hugh Wiley's *Saturday Evening Post* "Wildcat" stories. Like the "Darktown Birmingham" stories, these were protested by W. E. B. Du Bois and others for their portrayal of African Americans as "superstitious, imitative, lazy clown[s]."[106] The NAACP's Walter White, for example, wrote: "Hugh Wiley writes of a carefree, dice-shooting Wildcat and his goat, Lily, and the average American is all too prone in his ignorance to say, '*There* is the typical Negro!'"[107] But the studios found the stories' caricatured representation of Black dialect and contrived comedic situations perfect fodder for their "colored comedies." After purchasing the source material, Pathé hired Buck and Bubbles, a famous vaudeville duo, for the roles of the Wildcat and his sidekick Demitasse. From April to May 1929, Buck and Bubbles made six "Wildcat" shorts for Pathé (see figure 8.4), at least four of which were directed by Paul Powell: *Black Narcissus*, *High Toned*, *Darktown Follies*, and *Honest Crooks*.[108] So if Foster entered Pathé through Powell, he would likely have worked on those four productions (if not all six in the series). The material, however objectionable it was, would not have deterred Foster. Indeed, he was an ideal intermediary between the white crew and the theater veterans that comprised the nearly all-Black casts.

FIGURE 8.4 Advertisement, *Exhibitors Herald*, July 6, 1929.

Foster appears to have been a conspicuous and anomalous figure in his brief time at Pathé. The ANP reported that the "old man" was a curiosity in the studio among not only the "white property men and helpers" but also the "colored extras," all of whom puzzled about his presence as he "stands or sits about the sets." The ANP journalist wrote: "Occasionally he may be seen in an earnest, quiet discussion with directors and assistants, or with one of the leading colored actors." In these conferences, the ANP reported, "he is unobtrusively suggesting valuable direction."[109] Another report highlighted the significance of Foster's appointment to African American Angelenos: "The news had spread among the people of his Race like wildfire and so many people had congregated around him that it became necessary for him to appeal to the head of the firm to have the gates locked."[110]

Whatever Foster's precise role on set, his work for Pathé earned him laudations in the Black press. Stories about his Hollywood successes were picked up by the syndicated ANP and published across the country. Indeed his presence in the studio was recounted as if legend, as in this June 1929 account: "Foster's stories were read and re-read. Conversations were held with lawyers and finally Foster was sent for—to go to work. He could scarcely believe it himself. Nor could the Negroes whom he was to direct. When he gave them orders they looked at the white men to see if they should do what the Negro director was telling them to do. Powell stuck behind Foster, in spite of criticism from blacks and whites, and now Foster is well in the game. He stuck, and he won."[111] The *Chicago Defender* echoed this assessment, announcing that after his work as a technical director, he was promoted to director with fifty employees beneath him, including six white people.[112]

The realities, not surprisingly, did not match the Black press's celebratory accounts. After the Buck and Bubbles series was completed (and released to poor returns and even poorer reviews), the initial promises dissipated. According to Black press syndicated columnist Sylvester Russell, Foster resigned over disagreements with Powell, having to do with "their method of presenting colored performers."[113] Another account blamed his departure on general racism in the studio and a policy that emphatically barred Black workers from employment.[114] This version suggests that the more successful Foster became within the studio, the more criticism his presence engendered until he was eventually forced out. (It is, I think, the most likely scenario.) And yet he was clearly well connected in Los Angeles, enough so that when Stepin Fetchit's wife died in 1934, Fetchit put Foster in charge of the direction of photographs made of the funeral. (The funeral was covered by Fox newsreel, which raises the question of whether Foster supervised its filming as well.)[115]

There is a curious irony here. While Foster's work was not acknowledged by the studio in any formal capacity, labor was clearly of central concern to him.[116] During his brief time at Pathé, he sought to, as the Black press reported, "learn from the whites for the benefit of his own race's business."[117] He even lobbied to have African Americans apprentice to studio cameramen but reported that "they state that unions would prevent them from working."[118] The press praised his goal of "studying the modern movie game from the inside" in order to open a studio to produce bi-monthly Race films and to professionally train "the small army of Negro movie-tone experts, camera men, developers, etc." required.[119] After his departure from Pathé, he continued to pursue the establishment of his own production company in Los Angeles, hoping to make forays into talking pictures.[120] His goal, he declared, was to ship prints proudly labeled "Produced by Race Men and Women."[121]

After reading a *Defender* article lauding his success in Hollywood, Foster wrote to the paper's publisher, Robert S. Abbott, thanking him for the coverage and reminiscing: "and to think [that] the Defender made me years ago [and is] now making me over again." In this letter—the only known direct account of Foster's time in Hollywood—he tells Abbott, "They say out here that I did the impossible" and that "all want to know how I did it." He provides his own answer, recalling his earlier silent films: "I knew how to make a picture but knew nothing about talking picture [*sic*]. I learnt everything in my ten weeks with Pathe." Dismissing the "negro haters," he exclaims, "They don't know I could take a full crew of colored and make as good picture that was ever made." He concludes his letter with a proclamation: "Let me say right here if the Race wants up to date pictures of themselves [*sic*] they will have to make them. No Race uplift or mixed Race pictures [will get made by the major studios] they are all afraid of the South."[122] Here, Foster corroborates the newspaper accounts of working in the studios and the general skittishness around African American representation that might ruffle Southern white sensibilities. With a tone that suggests a mix of resignation and defiance, Foster gives the last word on the studios' racial animus and reaffirms one of the main premises undergirding Black-controlled film production from its emergence. In fact he echoes words that he had written in 1913: "We must be up and doing for ourselves in our own best way and for our own best good."[123]

Foster's Hollywood ambitions may look like a move away from his home in African American filmmaking, a compromise of sorts. Yet seen through the lens of his long career, it becomes clear that his ambitions always extended to the wider sphere of the motion picture industry. Indeed, what I've tried to show here is that Foster's aspirations were a model for a kind of filmmaking that endeavored to achieve a form of interaction between the mainstream industry and independent Race film. In this way he bears comparison to Noble Johnson, one of the founders of the Lincoln Motion Picture Company—established to make uplifting Race films for Black audiences—who was also a prolific Hollywood actor and independent producer of westerns aimed at a general audience. Indeed, Foster had written to Johnson in 1917 seeking advice about cultivating audiences in "Colored Theatres" as well as producing films that could "become [as] popular from a novelty view in White Theatres as Colored acts are in Vaudeville."[124]

Foster's career also anticipates the trajectory of Spencer Williams (who appears, uncredited, as the "rough'ree" in the Buck and Bubbles Pathé short *High Toned*), who alternated between Race filmmaking and projects in Hollywood. The mobility between independent film production and studio work, however fraught and circumscribed, characterizes the dual appeal of Black stage and screen actors of this period (also including Bert Williams and Charles Gilpin, among countless others), and is similar, albeit on a vastly different scale, to the careers of other entertainers like Duke Ellington and Cab Calloway. If they were celebrated within Black communities for their successes, they were also central to white-operated and -attended theatrical and cinematic endeavors.

The reason for focusing on Foster is that his story makes clear that this dual appeal was constitutive of the earliest African American efforts to produce commercially viable films. It is a vision of cinema at odds with the prevailing narrative about the history of African American film in the first half of the twentieth century, a story of a cinema that operated in its own separate world. As the screening and apparent success of Foster's films at the Lafayette Theater in New York and the Pastime and Majestic theaters in Chicago suggests, Foster saw the potential of a medium on the cusp of industrial transformation—one in which he hoped that African American performers and producers would take on an increasingly large role. A range of factors stymied this ambition, not least of which was the industry itself; Foster's films could play in integrated and predominantly white theaters in northern metropolitan areas, but as studios became increasingly entrenched, the concern over imagined southern outrage greatly circumscribed the possible forms of African American representation. The arc of Foster's career, then, represents not so much a dead end as a historical path not taken—an attempt to realize a vision of filmmaking that, with few exceptions, would remain unprecedented for most of the trajectory of American cinema.

Notes

1. James S. McQuade, "Chicago Letter," *Moving Picture World*, October 25, 1913, 363.
2. Ibid.
3. William Foster, *Freeman*, December 20, 1913, 5.
4. I discuss this episode in Allyson Nadia Field, "The Ambitions of William Foster: Entrepreneurial Filmmaking at the Limits of Uplift Cinema," in Barbara Tepa Lupack, ed., *Early Race Filmmaking in America* (New York: Routledge, 2016), 53.
5. The term "a separate cinema" is used by John Duke Kisch for his collection of Black poster art, the Separate Cinema Archive. See John Duke Kisch, *Separate Cinema: The First 100 Years of Black Poster Art* (London: Reel Art Press, 2014).
6. See, in particular, Jane M. Gaines, *Fire and Desire: Mixed-Race Movies in the Silent Era* (Chicago, IL: University of Chicago Press, 2001).
7. Foster has long been credited by scholars as the first Black filmmaking entrepreneur, though this designation is not entirely accurate. Boston-based filmmaker George W. Broome started making films in 1909. See Allyson Nadia Field, *Uplift Cinema: The Emergence of African American Film and the Possibility of Black Modernity* (Durham, NC: Duke University Press, 2015), chap. 2. African American exhibitors were in operation as early as 1897, screening purchased or rented prints in environments such as churches and lodges. See Cara Caddoo, *Envisioning Freedom: Cinema and the Building of Modern Black Life* (Cambridge, MA: Harvard University Press, 2014). Caddoo also identifies several early exhibitors who either produced or commissioned films for exhibition in the mid-1900s.
8. The exception to this tendency is the important work of Henry T. Sampson, which encompasses African American performance on stage, screen, and in broadcast media

from the mid-nineteenth to the mid-twentieth century. See *Blacks in Black and White: A Source Book on Black Films,* 2nd ed. (Metuchen, NJ: Scarecrow, 1995); *Blacks in Blackface: A Source Book on Early Black Musical Shows* (Metuchen, NJ: Scarecrow, 1980); *The Ghost Walks: A Chronological History of Blacks in Show Business, 1865–1910* (Metuchen, NJ: Scarecrow, 1988); *Swingin' on the Ether Waves: A Chronological History of African Americans in Radio and Television Broadcasting, 1925–1955* (Lanham, MD: Scarecrow, 2005).

9. *New York Age,* April 20, 1940, 4. Foster's obituary has a number of factual inaccuracies, but it offers the suggestion that his early career was spent in New York City in the racehorse and prize-fighting world.

10. Thomas Riis, "'Bob' Cole: His Life and His Legacy to Black Musical Theater," *The Black Perspective in Music* 13, no. 2 (Autumn 1985): 139.

11. Ibid.

12. Krystyn R. Moon, "Finding *A Trip to Coontown,*" *African American Review* 44, nos. 1–2 (Spring/Summer 2011): 7.

13. Riis, "'Bob' Cole," 140. As Riis suggest, this ploy of "tandem booking" was a deliberate strategy to dampen public interest in the upstarts, relying on the Troubadours' fame to outshine the lesser-known company.

14. Riis gets this information from the Plummer Biography, Jewel Cobb papers, unpublished. Ibid., 140. I corroborated this with the *New York Morning Telegraph,* April 5, 1901, 2.

15. *New York Morning Telegraph,* April 5, 1901, 2. While no date is given for when the breach of contract occurred, Leavitt was hired in autumn of 1898 for the 1898–99 tour of the show.

16. See, for example, *Plaindealer,* January 6, 1899, 3: "William Foster, press agent for the 'A Trip to Coontown' company, stopped at the Chiles hotel."

17. *Chicago Daily Tribune,* November 20, 1898, 46; November 27, 1898, 46.

18. *Chicago Daily Tribune,* November 27, 1898, 46. *Clorindy, or The Origin of the Cake Walk* became the first Broadway musical with an all-Black cast and was composed by African Americans Will Marion Cook (music) and Paul Laurence Dunbar (lyrics). It starred Ernest Hogan, considered the father of ragtime, whose 1896 epoch-defining hit with a pernicious title—"All Coons Look Alike to Me"—helped ignite ragtime's popularity. *Clorindy* was managed by George W. Broome, who also served as the American representative and agent for O. M. McAdoo's Minstrels. In addition to working as a manager of minstrel shows, Broome was among the first African Americans to use motion picture technology and to advertise his films for Black audiences, starting in 1909.

19. *Chicago Daily Tribune,* December 5, 1898, 5; January 29, 1899, 32; February 26, 1899, 32. Cole and Johnson presented a revised version of *A Trip to Coontown* in November 1899 at the Great Northern. *Chicago Daily Tribune,* November 12, 1899, 35. The *Tribune* reported that it "has crowded the house to its full capacity at every performance. The light musical farce is being presented by Cole & Johnson. It contains a number of 'coon' songs, some of them catchy, and a variety of ballads, besides possessing a ballet which is at least ambitious in its efforts." *Chicago Daily Tribune,* November 15, 1899, 4.

20. *Freeman,* February 18, 1899, 1.

21. *Freeman,* October 22, 1898, 5; *Plaindealer,* January 6, 1899, 4.

22. Moon, "Finding *A Trip to Coontown,*" 9.

23. David Krasner, "The Genius of Bob Cole," *African American Review* 44, nos. 1–2 (Spring/Summer 2011): 10–11.

24. Foster doesn't mention that he was instrumental in the company's second tour, though his memoirs were compiled by Theophilus Lewis, the editor of the *Interstate Tattler,* under the

title "Pioneers of the Stage," so it is likely Foster's "memoirs" were sketches of reminiscences collected and edited by Lewis. William Foster, "Pioneers of the Stage: Memoirs of William Foster," in Theophilus Lewis, ed., *The Official Theatrical World of Colored Artists* 1, no. 1 (April 1928): 48. Foster's account of Cole's "Declaration of Independence" echoes the writer's own account of "The Negro and the Stage," published in *The Colored American Magazine* in 1902, where he declares that "the greatest dramas of Negro life will be written by Negroes themselves." Bob Cole, "The Negro and the Stage," *The Colored American Magazine*, March 1902, 305.

25. See Lynn Abbott and Doug Seroff, *Ragged but Right: Black Traveling Shows, "Coon Songs," and the Dark Pathway to Blues and Jazz* (Jackson: University Press of Mississippi, 2007), 35.
26. *Freeman*, October 7, 1905, 5.
27. *Freeman*, December 5, 1908, 5. As Lynn Abbott and Doug Seroff trace, the term's usage significantly declined after 1910. *Ragged but Right*, 35.
28. *Freeman*, October 7, 1905, 5.
29. *Plaindealer*, January 6, 1899, 3.
30. *Cleveland Gazette*, February 4, 1899, 3.
31. *Illinois Record*, March 11, 1899, 1–2.
32. *Freeman*, March 4, 1899, 5.
33. Thomas Bauman, *The Pekin: The Rise and Fall of Chicago's First Black-Owned Theater* (Urbana: University of Illinois Press, 2014), 54.
34. Ibid., 161.
35. Ibid., 98.
36. *Freeman*, December 25, 1909, 6.
37. *Freeman*, January 15, 1910, 6.
38. *Freeman*, January 29, 1910, 5.
39. *Freeman*, February 26, 1910, 6.
40. See, for example, "The Outlook for Colored Road Shows: The Moving Picture House Is Taking the Day," *Freeman*, January 15, 1910, 6.
41. Ibid.
42. *Freeman*, February 22, 1913.
43. *Chicago Defender*, August 30, 1913, 6.
44. Bauman, *The Pekin*, 96–97.
45. *Broad Ax*, October 4, 1913, 2.
46. *Freeman*, April 12, 1913.
47. "Joe Shoecraft," *Freeman*, March 15, 1913, 1.
48. *Motography*, August 23, 1913, 150; *Billboard*, November 29, 1913, 92. The *Chicago Examiner* listed the new corporation as having been licensed on August 3 in Springfield by the Secretary of State. *Chicago Examiner*, August 4, 1913, 11.
49. *Chicago Defender*, August 9, 1913, 6. There is no African American named Robert Hanson listed in the Chicago census around this time.
50. For more on the Foster Company's actualities, see Field, *Uplift Cinema*, 193–195.
51. For a complete filmography of Foster's known films, see Field, "The Ambitions of William Foster."
52. *Chicago Defender*, August 30, 1913, 6.
53. *Chicago Defender*, January 3, 1914.
54. *Chicago Defender*, July 26, 1913, 6.
55. *Freeman*, September 27, 1913, 5.

56. *New York Age*, September 18, 1913, 6.
57. *New York Age*, February 20, 1913, 6.
58. Headliners were not always African American acts. See, for example, *New York Age*, September 18, 1913, 6.
59. "The Lafayette Players," *New York Age*, April 17, 1913, 6.
60. Cook was at the Pekin from November 1906 through June 1907. Bauman, *The Pekin*, 52.
61. *New York Age*, February 27, 1913, 6.
62. Will Marion Cook, quoted in "Stock Co. at the Lafayette." *New York Age*, March 13, 1913, 6.
63. "The Lafayette Players," *New York Age*, April 17, 1913, 6; May 8, 1913, 6.
64. *New York Age*, September 18, 1913, 6.
65. Ibid.
66. *New York Age*, September 25, 1913, 6.
67. Ibid.
68. *Moving Picture World*, September 25, 1909, 412.
69. *Moving Picture World*, November 7, 1908, 359.
70. "Films by Colored Actors," *Billboard*, October 18, 1913, 7.
71. It became the Shubert Theater in 1945 and is currently the CIBC Theatre, though the office portion is still known as the Majestic Building.
72. James Langland, ed., *The Chicago Daily News Almanac and Year Book for 1913* (Chicago Daily News Company, 1912), 623.
73. See, for example, *Chicago Tribune*, October 10, 1913, 10; *Chicago Tribune*, October 19, 1913, E4; *Chicago Tribune*, September 12, 1913, 12.
74. In 1913, the Grand Theater was the largest theater on the Stroll, with a seating capacity of around 800. Sylvester Russell, "Musical and Dramatic," *Chicago Defender*, March 18, 1911, 3. The Owl Theatre opened in 1916, with a seating capacity of 944. See James Langland, *The Chicago Daily News Almanac and Year-Book for 1919* (Chicago Daily News Company, 1918), 930; Konrad Schiecke, *Historic Movie Theatres in Illinois, 1883–1960* (Jefferson, NC: McFarland, 2015).
75. See, for example, Jacqueline Najuma Stewart, *Migrating to the Movies: Cinema and Black Urban Modernity* (Berkeley: University of California Press, 2005), 150.
76. "American Music Hall Fined $75 for Drawing Color," *Chicago Defender*, February 11, 1911, 1.
77. "Abbie Mitchell Refused Seat at the Majestic," *Chicago Defender*, April 26, 1913, 1.
78. Ibid.
79. "Real Democracy at the Majestic," May 10, 1919, 14.
80. "Abbie Mitchell Refused Seat at the Majestic."
81. Majestic Theatre program for Week of November 17, 1913, Majestic Theatre, Programs, bound 1906–1913, vol. 2, Chicago History Museum. The Majestic Theatre program lists Hunting and Francis's act as "A Love Lozenger," though *Billboard* reported the "polite little comedy" as "The Love Messenger." Majestic Theatre program for Week of November 17, 1913, Chicago History Museum; "Majestic," *Billboard*, November 22, 1913, 14.
82. Films screened at the Majestic were provided by George Spoor's Kinodrome, an exhibition service based in Chicago that supplied vaudeville managers with films each week. Foster's films were either distributed through Spoor's Kinodrome or directly booked by the theater. This association with Spoor, however tenuous, might account for the otherwise inexplicable mention in a 1929 *Variety* notice about Foster's planned Santa Monica production company that he had "assisted in making a series of colored comedies for Spoor" back in the "old Essanay days." "Coast Negro Company," *Variety*, June 26, 1929, 11.

83. John J. O'Connor, "Correspondence: Chicago," *Variety*, November 21, 1913, 21; *Billboard*'s review notes that less than half of the house was in attendance for the final act, though it is not clear if the house was this empty throughout the matinee or just by the closing. "Majestic," *Billboard*, November 22, 1913, 14.
84. "Majestic."
85. O'Connor, "Correspondence: Chicago,.
86. Abbott and Seroff, *Ragged but Right*, 22.
87. "Majestic."
88. "Majestic," *Billboard*, June 28, 1913, 14.
89. "Vaudeville in Chicago," *New York Clipper*, June 28, 1913, 18.
90. Ibid.
91. "Happenings in and About the Theaters," *Chicago Daily Tribune*, June 18, 1913, 10.
92. "Majestic," *Billboard*, June 28, 1913, 63.
93. O'Connor, "Correspondence: Chicago."
94. "In the Varieties," *New York Tribune*, September 30, 1913, 9; "B. F. Keith's—Marie Dressler," *Washington Post*, October 14, 1913, 10.
95. Victoria Sturtevant, *A Great Big Girl Like Me: The Films of Marie Dressler* (Urbana: University of Illinois Press, 2009), 42. Dressler comes out of a tradition that includes other white women such as May Irwin, Sophie Tucker, Clarice Vance, and Artie Hall who were "coon shouters"—experts in gender and racial masquerade who performed with and without blackface.
96. "At the National Capital," *Freeman*, September 17, 1910, 1; Lester A. Walton, "His Honor, The Barber," *New York Age*, November 3, 1910, 6.
97. "Colored Pictures a Hit," *New York Age*, September 25, 1913, 6.
98. Matthew Kennedy, *Marie Dressler: A Biography; With a Listing of Major Stage Performances, a Filmography and a Discography* (Jefferson, NC: McFarland), 60.
99. Stewart, *Migrating to the Movies*, 298n21. Stewart cites an article in the *Chicago Defender*, November 22, 1913, 6.
100. *Chicago Defender*, November 22, 1913, 6.
101. *Freeman*, August 30, 1913, 6.
102. *New York Amsterdam News*, May 29, 1929, 13.
103. Foster's connection is referred to as a "doorman" in the Black press, but I believe it was the studio gateman, Major Thomas Harris. "Old Pathe Studio Gateman Passes," *California Eagle*, February 16, 1934, 2.
104. *New York Amsterdam News*, May 29, 1929, 13.
105. See, for example, *New York Amsterdam News*, May 29, 1919, 13; *Chicago Defender*, June 1, 1929, 7. The ANP misidentifies Paul Powell as William Powell.
106. Leon Coleman, *Carl Van Vechten and the Harlem Renaissance: A Critical Assessment* (New York: Harland, 1998), 51.
107. Walter White, "The Black Brother," *Nation* 116, no. 3012 (March 28, 1923): 370. The article was reprinted in *The California Eagle*, a Los Angeles–based African American newspaper.
108. The other two shorts, *In and Out* and *Fowl Play*, were directed by Nat Nazarro and Carl Harbaugh, respectively. The series was produced by Monte Brice for Pathé.
109. "Pathe Gives Colored Scenarist Chance to Film Plays," *New York Amsterdam News*, May 29, 1929.
110. "Bill Foster Gets Chance to Enter Movies," *Chicago Defender*, June 1, 1929, 7.

111. *New York Amsterdam News*, June 26, 1929, 12.
112. "Bill Foster Gets Chance to Enter Movies."
113. "Sylvester Russell's Review," *Pittsburgh Courier*, January 4, 1930, A6.
114. "Foster, Movie Producer, Describes Films' Trust," *Chicago Defender*, July 21, 1934, 8.
115. *Chicago Defender*, September 29, 1934, 9; *Baltimore Afro-American*, September 29, 1934, 3.
116. Pathé payroll ledgers of this time do not name assistant directors and second assistant directors. Also, Foster might have been hired directly by Powell and paid by the director rather than through studio payroll. See Pathé Exchange records, Margaret Herrick Library, Academy of Motion Picture Arts and Sciences.
117. "Plans Million Dollar Studio," *Pittsburgh Courier*, June 22, 1929, 3.
118. "Pathe Gives Colored Scenarist Chance."
119. "Plans Million Dollar Studio."
120. Foster Photo-Play Company Incorporation announcement, Microfilm Reel 4, Frame 690–701, George P. Johnson Negro Film Collection, Department of Special Collections, University of California, Los Angeles. I discuss Foster's sound film scenarios in *Uplift Cinema*, 204–205, 241–242.
121. "Foster, Movie Producer, Describes Films' Trust," *Chicago Defender*, July 21, 1934, 8.
122. William Foster to Robert Abbott, June 10, 1929, Box 6, Folder 19, Abbott-Sengstacke Family Papers, Vivian G. Harsh Research Collection, Chicago Public Library.
123. *Freeman*, December 20, 1913, 5.
124. William Foster to Noble Johnson, June 1, 1917, Microfilm Reel 4, Frame 694, George P. Johnson Negro Film Collection, Department of Special Collections, University of California, Los Angeles.

CHAPTER 9

PICTURE, SHADOW, PLAY
Ontology, Archaeology, Ecology

WEIHONG BAO

IN recent years, film studies has experienced a "meta-critical turn" that reflects on the discipline's ontological foundations.[1] Incited by the new possibilities of digital media, these investigations question teleological accounts of medium ontology in order to explore cinema's multiple origins, tortuous passages, missed encounters, and forgotten futures. In effect, this ontological reflection has reoriented how film scholars understand cinema's relation to other media, leading us to discover historical connections between cinema and its surrounding media contexts. More important, we have started to probe cinema's own plurality and heterogeneity, asking meta-critical questions concerning cinema's constitution as a medium within particular historical situations.

Nonetheless, this "media archaeological" approach to the ontology of cinema has often neglected a vast and rich terrain beyond the dominant scope of Europe and North America. By turning to the margins as a site for inquiry, however, I am less interested in mere "inclusion" than in teasing out some of the methodological implications of this onto-archaeological turn. More specifically, I am interested in how cinema's initial appearance in China—where cinema was not subsumed under one name, one media object, or one technical system but rather straddled the capacious concepts of "picture," "shadow," and "play"—reveals the limits of media archaeology and invites a new way of thinking about ontology. Media archaeology's dominant focus on media objects and technical operations, while providing nuanced accounts of cinema's identity in terms of technical specificities, still fails to challenge the reductive notion of ontology understood as material substance and essence. Such an approach, which Martin Heidegger attributes to the tradition of Aristotelian ontology, prioritizes the *ontic*—the facts of entities in isolation. Instead, we can adopt an approach that favors a more phenomenological focus on what Heidegger defines as the meaning of the *being* of entities, the "ground" that constitutes their conditions of possibility.

Applying this to our subject of concern, we can say that descriptions of media and regional specificities concentrating on their material attributes constitute ontical endeavors that do not go far enough. Such descriptions presuppose but do not work out the ontological conditions that enable the entities and their attributes to come into being. Yet ontology in a Heideggerian sense requires both a distinction from, and relation to, the ontic. The latter—the self-evident, everyday appearance of entities—provides us with the proximal and sole access to the underlying structure of their being, as determined by any given entity's involvement with any other. Ontological inquiries thus take place *alongside* ontic ones, yoked as the ontico-ontological.[2] This ontology, which binds existence with appearance, is ecological in method. In other words, we should think of both in terms of the broad "being" of a media environment—as a particular structure of media functions at the ontological level—and the changing media objects that occupy places within that structure at the ontic level. These two dimensions together constitute a *media ecology*. It allows us to reimagine media beyond one-sided technical or cultural determinist accounts, and to put each dimension of media in dialogue with the other.

In the following, I consider these methodological implications via a brief inquiry into where, when, and how cinema came to be in China. I take a slice of the first few years of cinema's inception in China while relocating it within the longer and broader history of visual modernity from the mid-nineteenth century onward. By zooming in and out of this horizontal and vertical span, I am particularly interested in how cinema's ontology was threaded through a series of media analogies: picture, shadow, play. By looking into their historical references, I illustrate how these notions did not correspond to specific media "objects" in a Cartesian sense but instead served as ontological placeholders, hinting at the tremendous transformations in media practice during this period. These ontological constellations, which dissociated media objects from their specific material attributes—the ontic entities—usher in a horizon of involvement that grounds the meaning of media through and as ecology. Together, they contributed to new modes of perceiving, experiencing, and knowing as the condition of possibility for cinema. Such an ontico-ontological inquiry, as I will demonstrate, marks my ontology and archaeology of cinema *in terms of* ecology, which is ultimately a matter of hermeneutics.[3]

On the Name

For film historians, the inception of cinema in China remains a puzzle and a battleground. Not only does the exact date of cinema's introduction remain undetermined, the name for "film" itself has yet to be fixed. Standard narratives of the first showing of what were purported to be Lumière films in 1896 in Shanghai's Xu Garden, a few months after the Lumière brothers revealed their Cinématographe in the Grand Café in France, have recently been challenged by a number of scholars.[4] The main point of confusion has to do with the term *yingxi*, which could refer to a magic lantern performance, a film screening, or even a Western-style play.[5] This term's plural associations make it difficult to determine from historical accounts what constitute the first exhibitions of films in China. Further complicating the question of "what" and "when" is the problem of "where" cinema first took place in China in terms of both the city as well as the specific locales where the screenings occurred: Shanghai or Hong Kong? A teahouse (*chayuan*), a garden, or a Western hotel?

Yet *yingxi*, which has been conventionally translated as "shadow play," is but one of the many names for cinema in China. In addition to *yingxi*, one finds *yinghua* (shadow picture), *dianhua* (electric picture), *yinghuaxi* (shadow picture play), *huodong yingxi* (animated shadow play), *dianguang yingxi* (electric light shadow play), and *dianying* (electric shadow), to name a few of the most commonly seen in historical accounts from the late nineteenth century to the 1920s.[6] These terms, combining varied elements of cinema—picture, shadow, play—have been obscured by existing historiographies which have favored *yingxi* as an indigenous conception that associated cinema with theatrical traditions of popular entertainment.

This theatrical conception of cinema has recently been challenged by a conception indebted to photography, as most eloquently articulated by film scholar Emilie Yeh Yueh-yu, who has spearheaded a collective research project on early cinema in cities beyond Shanghai—in Hong Kong, Guangzhou, Hangzhou, and Tianjin. Combing through an impressive amount of early newspaper material in Hong Kong, Yeh finds evidence to highlight a photographic conception in the early reception of cinema in China, hence joining a more globally shared understanding of cinematic ontology that anchors its specificity in the photographic medium itself and the scene of projection. Parsing through entangled and vague associations linked to *yingxi*, Yeh debunks the historical inaccuracy of contemporary accounts that inform a culturally exoticist, nationalist genealogy. In addition, she focuses on Hong Kong as a specific site of study and cites newspaper data from 1900 to 1924 to highlight both the plural functions and distinct sites of film exhibition: apart from entertainment, early film exhibition in Hong Kong served for religious advocation, colonial and scientific education, and charity. Instead of the more familiar Chinese settings such as teahouses and gardens, new social spaces that she calls "generic Western portals"—YMCAs, public halls, Western hotels and theaters, and, later, movie theaters themselves—provided the sites for the first film exhibitions.

This emphasis on the newness of cinema—its distinct materiality, specific site and mode of exhibition, as well as social function—is coupled with a conscious effort of renaming. Yeh sorts through the plural terms for film and identifies *yinghua* as a statistically more prevalent reference to cinema in Hong Kong. Instead of adopting the common translation of *ying* as "shadow" as in the case of *yingxi*/shadow play, Yeh makes a point of translating *yinghua* as "photo picture" and *yingxi* as "photoplay," so as to detach *ying*, which can mean both "shadow" and "photography," from the discursive "shadows" of Chinese nationalist mythology. Instead, she anchors *ying* assertively in photography, the material technological basis of cinema. Through such historical investigation and naming negotiations, Yeh reframes the scene of early cinema away from Chinese exceptionalism toward a more diverse and internationally shared experience, joining forces with early film studies scholars elsewhere as they set out to acknowledge the multiple sites and functions of film exhibition.[7]

Nevertheless, by identifying the newness of cinema in terms of its materiality and attendant implications for spectatorship, Yeh has unwittingly fallen back into reified dichotomies between China and the West, the traditional and the technological modern. Underlying such binary distinctions is an unwavering assumption of medium specificity that gets reauthenticated and rearticulated through regional specificity. In this instance, colonial Hong Kong serves as the gateway for both modern technology and new social spaces, what she calls the "generic Western portals." This *double specificity* thesis, linking medium and region (Hong Kong), reaffirms Yeh's purist assumption. Despite her interest in diverse screen practices, she questions *yingxi*'s translation as "shadow play," because, she argues, the term yokes together three incongruous media—shadow puppetry, opera, and film—which she considers "different in nature" (*sange xingzhi xiangyi de meijie*).[8] The dichotomy between indigenous tradition and foreign technology thus boils down to the medium distinction between theater and photography, old and new media, with theater associated with the old media of shadow puppetry and Beijing Opera that presumably sustain a nationalist claim. By replacing "play" with "picture" in reference to film, while dissociating "shadow" from the ontological shadows of shadow puppetry, Yeh debunks the myth of origin that "sinicized" the foreign medium by associating it with Chinese settings and cultural conventions. Lifting us from the historical "shadow" of theater and the discursive baggage of *yingxi*/shadow play as a precondition for "understanding Chinese audiences' reception of film," such a demystification simply delivers us back to the medium's photographic associations and familiar accounts of technological novelty and disruption.[9]

Despite Yeh's translation of *yinghua* as "photo picture" to approximate the assumed medium specificity of cinema, the terms "photo" and "picture" also point to two distinct genealogies of cinema in contemporary scholarship. Although film history has for decades been framed as a bifurcated tradition between realism and formalism—from the twin origins of cinema ascribed to Lumière versus Méliès, to the paired legacies of realism versus modernism—our understanding of cinematic ontology has largely been dominated by the realist pole. This photographic ontology found itself bolstered by early film theorists and critical thinkers such as Walter Benjamin, Siegfried Kracauer, Béla Balázs, André Bazin, and Roland Barthes, and revived in conceptions of the time-image (Deleuze) and the recent trend of "slow cinema" that has sustained an enduring faith in the documentary authenticity of the photographic image. Such a photographic conception is often realized by privileging aesthetic choices that maintain the unity of space and the filmed subject, as well as of the qualitative time of duration (Bergson), which, strangely, speaks to a theatrical conception of space and time if we understand theater in terms of such unities. Recent discussions of film in the age of new media, however, have shifted towards a "pictorial" genealogy of cinema. New media scholars such as Lev Manovich have argued that cinema needs to be understood primarily as an art of animation, rather than of reality, by noting the medium's origins in the graphic traditions of proto-cinema devices such as magic lantern slides, the Phenakistiscope, and the Zoetrope.[10] Manovich has extended this painterly ontology into digital cinema, which operates through aesthetic manipulations conditioned by the synthetic processes of new media production (compositing, mapping, editing, paint retouching). No small wonder that animation, a vital but long neglected tradition in film history, is now receiving central attention, given how its rich history and ties to new media help us understand cinema's contemporary transformation.

The lesson we can learn from these shifting ontologies is, again, to rethink the question of ontology from essence to existence, from pure materiality to historically informed yet contemporarily motivated interpretation, from isolation to a horizon of interrelated objects. This is precisely how ontology and archaeology can be rethought in relation to and in terms of ecology. For Heidegger, ontology does not concern the facts of entities, which he calls the ontic, but pertains to the meaning and structuring of the being of those entities. This distinction elucidates two kinds of inquiries: while ontical inquiries are preoccupied with identifying and collecting attributes of the entities, which characterizes positive science operating within a Cartesian tradition, ontological accounts uncover or disclose their ground, the horizon from which meaning arises.[11] In this sense, ontological inquiries are more primordial, as the conceptual a priori to ontical ones. Ontological investigation shifts the emphasis from essence to existence and clarifies the meaning of being in terms of modes of existence.

This movement away from the ontic to the ontological in a Heideggerian sense is not so much to abandon the ontic but to yoke both inquiries together, in an ontico-ontological investigation that de-essentializes media objects and their attributes while concretizing the ground of ontological inquiries. My project thus deviates from that of "fixing" cinema's identity through its proper naming—torn between theatrical and photographic conceptions and their associated labels (*yingxi* and *yinghua*)—toward a better understanding of cinema's emergence in China. I approach this understanding in terms of its shifting grounds—the changing constellations among a number of media entities whose modes of existence were entangled with linguistic, conceptual, and material practices. Within this framework we can interrogate how the terms "picture," "shadow," and "play" and their references—previously associated with various pictorial and performance practices—underwent substantial transformation at the historical moment immediately before and after cinema's arrival in China.

In this sense, cinema's multiple names—*yingxi*, *yinghua*, as well as a host of other terms—testify to the fluid boundary between various media—ontical entities such as lithography, opera, photography, and the magic lantern—whose relationship set the terms for the initial reception of cinema. These designations also problematize the way in which media are defined: do we define them in terms of their material basis, their technological properties, their modes of exhibition, aesthetic conventions, or cultural and discursive construction? My point, however, is not to arrange these operational and perceptual elements—technologies of recording/inscription and reproduction, practices of exhibition involving projection and performance, and the perceptual experience of mediated seeing, hearing, and sensing—as perfect lines of convergence that anticipate and culminate in the technological and institutional novelty of cinema. Instead of exercising the kind of retroactive causality that Thomas Elsaesser warns us against, I would like to consider these elements as entwined, dynamic, and mutually constituted systems out of which cinema emerged, not as a discrete object but as a series of positions within a media environment.¹²

Picture

Among the three terms—"picture," "shadow," "play"—perhaps the most challenging one is "picture." Although we tend to associate "picture" with painting or drawing on a two-dimensional surface, the medium question is sticky. This is not simply because a "picture" does not specify its material basis or technical formation—the conventional understanding of "medium" in the realm of art—but also because a fundamental ambiguity shrouds the notion of picture. A picture seems to oscillate between a physical and a mental image, visual and other forms of sensory perception, object and effect, plus an aggregate of connotations due to historical and social applications. The *OED* provides a basic definition of "picture" as "visual representation" ranging from two- to three-dimensional forms, such as a tableau on stage or in a ballet, a portrait or photograph, film, or more broadly, any "visible image produced by an optical or (in later use) electronic system." In its extended usage, a "picture" can refer to vivid or graphic description either spoken or written, a mental image, a concrete representation of an abstract idea (symbol, figure, type), a person of a certain quality, or a circumstance or situation.¹³ Indeed, the Latin root of the English word "picture," *pictūra*, with triple meanings referring to painting or picture, the action or art of painting, and mental imagery, already suggests the term's ambiguous place between the physical and the immaterial; the term's heterogeneous history certainly contributed to its wide-ranging connotations. In other words, to address a "picture" is to face the mesh of entanglements regarding the term in its literal and physical sense, its globally varied historical and social applications, and its material technical changes and plurality.

In Chinese, the terms for "picture" are multiple, ranging from *xiang* (portraiture), *xiezhen* (sketch from reality), and *hui* (painting, sketching), to two of the most commonly used words, *tu* (picture) and *hua* (painting).¹⁴ In late sixteenth- and early seventeenth-century China, an explosion of commercial publishing facilitated by the improvement of woodcut printing generated a great variety and wide circulation of illustrated books—travelogues, maps, medical illustrations, and various compendiums and manuals—which complicated the notion of the picture, now extended to include "diagrams, charts, maps, portraits," all under the name of *tu* (picture). These pictorial representations opened up "picture" as a spectrum whose cartographical and mimetic poles formed a continuum. As art historian Craig Clunas points out, the generic connotation of *tu* (diagram, chart, map, portrait, picture) makes it possible to subsume another notion of picture, *hua* (painting), as one of its subcategories.¹⁵ In mid-nineteenth-century China, the notion of "picture" underwent another significant transformation. When the Qing government lost the First Opium War in 1842, ceded Hong Kong to Britain, and opened the first treaty ports (Guangzhou, Fuzhou, Xiamen,

Ningbo, and Shanghai), a host of visual media entered China with new means of recording, projecting, and reproducing images. Visuality was henceforth yoked to the violent experience of colonial modernity, with China forced to open its territory as well to new ways of seeing, perceiving, and experiencing.

These explosions of visual media changed the way a "picture" was understood and practiced. Perhaps the most remarkable aspect of this new scene of visual culture was the mutual imbrication between mechanical means of image production and reproduction and manual labor and artistry. Photography entered China in 1842 in the wake of the Opium War, but almost immediately its production and dissemination were entangled with a host of established, concomitant, and new means of pictorial practices. In contrast to our contemporary conception of photography as a medium of mass reproduction, photographs were initially treated as originals that were reproduced in a diverse range of media. Alphonse Eugène Jules Itier (1802–1877), the French photographer who took the earliest extant daguerreotype photographs in China in 1844, had his photographs reproduced as lithographs in his journal in 1848.[16] By the 1870s, when Chinese photography studios took off, the boundaries between photography and other pictorial media were much more fluid and blurred than Yeh Yueh-yu's revisionist history assumes. As Gu Yi's excellent study of early Chinese photography illustrates, photography shared customers, markets, and modes of production with a number of other pictorial media. In the same studio, photographs were copied and enlarged as oil paintings, reproduced on ivory, porcelain, and fabric. In fact, Gu points out, the earliest names of photography—*yingxiang* (portrait or reflected picture), *xiaoxiang* (portrait), *xiaozhao* (small picture)—were terms also used for portrait painting; Wang Tao, a noted member of the nineteenth-century literati, even dubbed photography "Western-style painting" (*xifahua*).[17] These naming practices, by way of analogy, created an intermedial perception bridging photography to painting while changing the meanings of the names themselves. Not only did such commingling of media happen in the same studios and exhibition venues, but elements of painting also came to preside *within* photographs: retouching, calligraphic colophons, and hand coloring were frequently deployed; and visual compositions were often adopted from painterly conventions, resulting in an intimate connection between "brush" and "shutter."[18]

Play

The same question can be posed regarding "play." If the *ying* (shadow) in *yingxi* has historically referred to shadow puppetry, magic lantern shows, and film, what does the element of "play" (*xi*) contain? Instead of understanding play through the problematic term "traditional theater," which is a retrospective, nationalist-modernist construct, I would point to "play's" intimate connection with picture (painting), shadow (photography), and later, cinema.[19]

Before I start, let us revisit the understanding of "play." Despite the term's ready association with theater or a specific genre of theater, an essential part of its meaning resides in the idea of performance, which is the source of *xi*'s ambiguity, insofar as it refers to both performance and play. Furthermore, the Chinese term *xi*, or *youxi* (play), is associated not simply with the specific sense of *dramatic* performance but also with entertainment, playfulness, and execution—performance in a broad sense that can include technological performance.[20] As Christopher Rea points out, this broader notion of play as *youxi* characterized the rise of an amusement culture in the late-nineteenth and early-twentieth centuries. *Youxi* entailed experiment with aesthetic form and modern devices, implying a sense of artistic roving and virtual travel (*you*).[21] New "playthings" (*wanyi*) —cameras, lenses, mirrors, moving pictures, and other gadgets—enabled new types of play encompassing literary games, sports, theater, and magic tricks. Put differently, by considering the plural connotations of play, especially by treating it less as a noun and more as a verb, we can resituate "play" as a corresponding vantage or nodal point that connects photography and cinema. More important, I will return to theater and theatrical performance itself to illustrate how an emerging use of painted scenery as "backgrounds" made theater already a kind of "performed pictures" that shared affinity with both photography and the early productions of cinema. This section thus shifts to the production side to investigate the intimate connection between picture and play where photography constituted not the ultimate vantage point or privileged mediating agent but one of the mutually interactive parts of a media ecology.

A return to the early scene of photography reveals how this broader notion of "play" as *youxi* constitutes an essential element of photography. Whereas I discussed earlier the mutual imbrication of *picture* and *photography* in reproduction and visual aesthetics, another salient aspect of early photography conjoins *picture* and *play* through a dynamic interplay between painted backdrops, props, and human figures. In other words, there was an explicitly performative element in photography in its construction of pictorial space in relation to the human figure. This is particularly the case with studio photography, which, as early as the 1860s, started using painted backdrops that enabled the playful performance of identity.

In China, photography studios were largely operated by Westerners from the 1840s to the 1860s, with the earliest studio traced to 1844 when George R. West opened his business in Hong Kong. By the 1860s and 1870s, Chinese photo studios began to win favor from the locals, who took particular interest in portraiture.[22] The pictorial space for early photography portraiture was rather barebones, with a simple blank drapery or wall and minimal furnishing—such as a chair or flower vase on a stand—modeled after the enduring iconography of portraiture paintings. From the 1880s to the 1930s, the spatial construction in studio photography became increasingly elaborate. A complete set, combining painted backdrop, furniture, and ornamental carpet, adorned the space in front of the camera. Within such a space, photography was less a means to capture a truthful moment of a person or group than a mini-stage for one to perform various personalities, fantasies, and social relations. In other words, photography was practiced both as a medium of indexicality and as one of playfulness and performativity. Such performance defines the human figures in the foreground through their interactions with their environment: a painted background—a landscape of forestry or the seaside, a garden, a domestic interior—delineates the general setting and evokes a certain atmosphere; ornate furnishings such as chairs and flowery carpet convey a sense of wealth and social status. These furnishings often combined Chinese and Western-style domestic objects of consumption: clocks next to flowers on a stand, pens and brushes suggesting one's literary cultivation (see figure 9.1). Sometimes the humans are not simply framed by these realistic or symbolic imageries and objects but physically engage with them: modern vehicles such as a car, an airplane, train, or a steamship (see figure 9.2). In addition, the photographic subject performed multiple identities, propelling the genre of "two-selves pictures" (*erwotu*) with elaborate background, props, costumes, and gestures.[23]

By turning the photography studio into a theatrical space of performance, these practices increasingly converged with the actual stage where a similar dynamic between "picture" and "play" emerged with new styles of theater and performance. From the mid-nineteenth century onward, new forms of theater mushroomed in major treaty ports such as Macau, Shanghai, Tianjin, and Hong Kong.[24] In Shanghai, commercial theater flourished as the city opened its port to the West (1843) and absorbed the internal immigration influx during and after the Taiping Rebellion (1851–1862). This resulted in a productive encounter between Beijing Opera and Western theater, beginning with amateur drama performances. In 1867, the first Western modern theater, the Lyceum Theater (*Lanxin daxiyuan*), built for the Amateur Dramatic Club of Shanghai, opened along with the two earliest Beijing Opera theaters in Shanghai, Dan'gui yuan and Mantingfang. Rarely has it been mentioned that both these Beijing Opera theaters were actually built inside the British-American Concession, followed by dozens of Beijing Opera theaters built on the same street and thirty in total in the Concession.[25] The Lyceum, destroyed by fire in 1871 and rebuilt in 1874, boasted a three-story brick building with two stories of balcony seats, ample stage space, a beneath-the-stage orchestra pool, and layers of painted backdrops that were mechanically manipulated.[26] Although the theater mainly staged Western performance genres such as music, drama, ballet, and opera, the famous Beijing Opera troupe from Dan'gui yuan was invited to the Lyceum in 1874.[27] The Lyceum also allowed circus performances, magic shows, and magic lantern shows. These shows also traveled to the Chinese theater: from May to June 1874, magic performances, including magic lantern shows (*xifa yingxi*), were offered in the Dan'gui Teahouse for nearly a month by a British magician named Wagner, while he also performed at the Lyceum.[28] Despite limited access to the Lyceum, which was largely reserved for Westerners and well-to-do Chinese before the turn of the century, local Chinese visitors, impressed by the theater's architectural design and spectacular stage sets, circulated their impressions through travel accounts and newspaper reports.[29]

Western theater also caught the attention of Chinese travelers abroad, who recorded in detail the impressive stage sets of melodrama and opera. Zhang Deyi, for example, notes in several places his experiences at the theater. At the Louis Theater in Paris, he saw a play about Italy with "mountains, forests, terraces, and buildings, thunder and

FIGURE 9.1 Photograph of a man with Chinese and Western objects of consumption. Rongfang Photography Studio, Guangzhou, 1890s. From Yang Wei, *Liu Ying de beihou: Lao zhaopian zhongde zhaoxiangguan bujing* (Behind the Figures: Backdrops in Old Studio Photographs) (Beijing: Remin youdian, 2017), 40.

lightning, mud slides and earthquakes, and floods and shaken houses, making it impossible to differentiate between true and false."[30] He was similarly impressed by a Swedish theater that staged vivid natural landscapes, street scenes, storms, volcanoes, and icebergs.[31] Again and again, Zhang was enthralled by the stage sets and rarely mentions

FIGURE 9.2 Studio photograph of a man in a painted steamboat. Studio unknown, 1910s. From Yang Wei, *Liu Ying de beihou*, 85.

the plays' narratives. While he paid some attention to the action in the opera *Faust* (1859) at the Grand Theater in Paris, Zhang focused primarily on the sets, whose reproduction of mountains and moons, birds and animals, and rivers and stone bridges fooled his eyes even when he used binoculars. Acknowledging that some of the colorful clouds and flying fairies were painted on paper, he highlights the magical transformation after beholding them for a long time: "the fake water gives ripples, and the paper figurines become human."[32] His interest in this hyperrealism, coupled with an awareness of its artificiality, recurs in his impression of a painting of a shipwreck, in which people on the ship climb the mast and cling to the ropes, struggling with the undulating sea. By focusing his attention on the painting, Zhang writes, he could "hear" the shouts of the people and the crashing of the waves.[33] Other travelogues similarly capture in detail various stage sets and costumes.[34]

In combination, these reports—both from abroad and from Shanghai, both in the news and in travelogues—developed a hyperbolic image of a distinct type of theater that proved influential on the burgeoning local theater culture. Having had a fairly short period of encounter with Beijing Opera, the "Shanghai-style Beijing Opera" (*haipai jingju*), a derogatory label bestowed by the more sophisticated Beijing audience, showed an unabashed penchant for novelty, sensation, and visual display. Less frequently noted is Cantonese Opera, a less prestigious form of opera from Southern China, which entered Shanghai in the mid-nineteenth century. Cantonese Opera allowed novelties such as lantern plays—lanterns made of translucent fabric in the shape of humans, animals, gods, and ghosts—to transform the stage into a fantasy land of colorful moving sets and sceneries. Notably, Tongqing chayuan (1895), the first teahouse devoted to Cantonese Opera, became one of the earliest spaces to show films in 1897. On October 3, the newspaper *Shenbao* advertised the films as "Mechanical Electric Shadow Play" (*jiqi dianguang yingxi*) brought from America by a Westerner. The films, as we learn from the advertisement, were first shown at the Astor House Hotel and were now being shown at the teahouse with reduced prices for three consecutive nights before the Westerner, whose name is not recorded, returned home.[35] The screenings at the Astor House, allegedly the earliest space in Shanghai for showing films according to the revised historiography by Law Kar, Frank Bren, and Huang Dequan, cited by Yeh, pre-date those at the Tongqing teahouse by only three to four months.

Equally important are reforms to the opera stage contemporaneous with the arrival of cinema. In December of the same year, "painted scenery plays" (*huajingxi*) or "plays matched by appropriate painted scenery" (*peijinghua xi*) were presented at Tongqing.[36] The teahouse even broadened its stage in order to accommodate such painted scenery. From the detailed description of various scenes in advertisements, one can surmise that these were early instances of backdrop painting. Notably, the "painted scenery play" was described as a new stage technique from Singapore imported by an opera troupe from Canton, attesting to the transregional traffic in opera performance, scenic design, and stage renovation that intensified the interplay between "picture" and "play." More radical change came about in the 1900s when the negative appellation of *haipai jingju* ceded to more affirmative ones such as Reformed Beijing Opera (*gailiang jingju*) and Reformed New Opera (*gailiang xinxi*).

A similar scenario occurred in Hong Kong during the mid- to late nineteenth century, when the city hosted a medley of Western-style entertainments and Cantonese operas that encouraged mediated exchanges and innovations. The British occupation of Hong Kong in 1841 opened the city to Western performances. From the 1840s to the 1860s, traveling troupes from Britain, Australia, and Europe, as well as military and civilian amateur dramatic clubs, performed in matshed theaters (makeshift theaters usually constructed with bamboo and rattan) and other temporary spaces until the first permanent theater (the Theatre Royal) was built inside the newly constructed City Hall in 1869.[37] The Cantonese Opera had had its own theater space since the 1850s, and three additional permanent theaters are documented after 1867. Although it remains to be confirmed whether the Cantonese theaters furnished painted backdrops and sets like their Shanghai counterparts, the Hong Kong audience had exposure to such modern visual forms through a wide range of entertainment and pedagogical practices. By the last decade of the nineteenth century, as Law Kar and Frank Bren point out, Hong Kong hosted Cantonese Opera alongside circuses, variety and magic shows, professional and amateur theater troupes, boxing tournaments, and concerts. Theaters, clubs, hotels, and the YMCA were the public spaces for these various entertainments and hosted the first film screenings in Hong Kong.[38] Yet if we associate the introduction of cinema with emphatically new, modern, and exclusively Western spaces, we would have to leave out the Cantonese theaters that eagerly incorporated such novel forms of entertainment. Like their Shanghai counterparts, Hong Kong Cantonese theaters started to show films from 1900. By 1903, around ten theaters had shown films either as side shows or as featured programs.[39]

This vast range of theatrical performances transformed the understanding of "play" or performance. Instead of limiting it to narrative-centered drama, "play" came to carry a strong connotation of experiment, frivolity, and wonder, mixing familiarity with strangeness, and exoticism with eroticism (the first Cantonese theaters were near the red-light district). These experiments challenge the linear narrative of media evolution from theater to film: novel forms of theater emerged almost simultaneously with cinema, if not later. Their shared exhibition space and co-evolution also reminds us of *play*'s intricate relationship with painting, photography, and film projection.

SHADOW/SCREEN: A NEW *DISPOSITIF*

Whereas there is a tendency to conflate the notion of a *dispositif* with technical hardware and set-up, the formation of the film *dispositif* in China was not primarily a matter of film projectors or cameras but rather of the emergence of a new spatial and social configuration. The development of this configuration was a gradual process: instead of attributing it to the impact of the magic lantern—which anticipates cinema's key technical elements: projection, magnification, and controlled lighting—we gain a better understanding by linking it to the emergence of a new kind of spatiality, which, interestingly, can be related to a distinct notion of theatricality. In fact, this new form of spatiality *qua* theatricality was defined through the emergence of the *screen*. Relevant here is an argument by William Egginton linking the flattened space of the Renaissance-era stage to the rise of modernity in the West and a new spatial construct of subjecthood.[40] Egginton understands the concept of a "screen" not primarily as a material surface of projection but in terms of a new spatiality—the flattened and abstracted space that demarcates the border between the real and the imaginary. This border "becomes a *screen*, delineating the limits of the stage whereon dramas are acted out for audiences whose attention rather than participation is demanded."[41] More importantly for Egginton, the screen was also an epistemological formation: "The idea of screen, therefore, has nothing to do with the degree of mimesis involved in representation, but rather with the extent to which an audience was capable of projecting an alternate but viable reality onto that border and hence into the abstract space of the stage, and of recognizing in it models or representatives of its own values and modes of behavior."[42]

In other words, the theatricality of the *screen* was not limited to the space of the theater. Instead, we can see modern theater, especially the proscenium stage and its corresponding spatial/social order, as the culmination and institutionalization of a spatiality not exclusive to theater architecture. In that sense and perhaps counter-intuitively, we can view the so-called cinema *dispositif* (apparatus)—including a system of projection, artificial lighting/darkness, spatial division, and the social behavior of the audience—as a continuation of the "screen" *qua* the spatiality of modern performance, rather than as a rupture from it. This section will thus look at *ying* not as an attribute of photography or projection but in terms of the spatial/social construct of the screen as a new *dispositif* that not only provided cinema with its condition of possibility but also imbricated cinema into a broader media network. In this sense, it is important to underscore that this media environment was not a simple symbiosis of these various media but that the boundaries between them had yet to be carved out and that the articulation of such distinctions was part of the exercise of modernity itself.

Whereas one might be able to step out of the ontological shadow of the shadow-puppet play by associating *ying* with photography, image, and projection, as Yeh tries to do, the effort to isolate cinema's supposedly unique spectatorial impact runs into challenges if we consider history more horizontally. Countering historiographical accounts that embed "the primordial scenes of Chinese movies" in the context of "traditional, 'reassuring' Chinese amusements," Yeh posits the newness of cinema against the backdrop of these older forms of entertainment without questioning their "traditional" and "reassuring" quality.[43] This perspective allows her to single out the "unique" *dispositif* of cinema as superseding the magic lantern and optical toys: "Here a film event is enabled by the act of projection, which throws the image on the screen and turns it into a larger than life illusion, whose magic is enlarged by the enclosed, darkened space and the crowd inside that space."[44] Such a claim runs into two challenges: first, amusements provided in the teahouse setting were not necessarily "traditional" and "reassuring"; second, the distinction between the magic lantern and film is less sharp than the antithesis between stillness and motion, and the signature "cinematic" techniques were hardly exclusive to cinema.

Contrary to our common assumptions, Chinese operatic forms such as Beijing Opera and Cantonese Opera were themselves new forms of entertainment that had evolved and mutated after they entered through treaty ports such as Shanghai, Guangzhou, and Hong Kong.[45] The teahouse itself was a newly constructed space for performance rather than one solely devoted to tea drinking; more notably, these teahouses had joined with Western theater and other "generic Western portals" in hosting new forms of entertainment and education such as magic shows, circus performance, and magic lantern exhibitions. For instance, in March 1875, three Beijing Opera teahouses—the Dan'gui, Jin'gui, and Fuchun houses—competed against each other in hosting magic lantern shows from Britain and France to revive their business after the hundred-day performance ban due to the death of the Tongzhi Emperor.[46] Magic lanterns and *dengcaixi*—lantern plays featuring controlled lighting, fireworks, and translucent lanterns shaped like or painted with various figures—increasingly became a major attraction for the opera stage until well into the 1890s.[47]

Such a lively scene of performance-based entertainments cannot be explained away simply in terms of their locations, as though the various media had no other relevance to one another beyond the fact that they shared the same space. Instead, as I have suggested, it emerged from a transformation in how "play" (*xi*) was understood. The variety of plays now commercially available under one roof—from circus (*maxi*), magic (*xifa*), magic lantern (*yingxi*), to lantern plays (*dengxi* or *dengcaixi*)—broadened the notion of "play" previously associated with different spaces and situations, such as religious and ritual plays, shamanism, court drama, and Western forms of entertainment. Their variety and investment in illusion, magic, spectacle, and sensation challenge the hackneyed notion of "traditional" Chinese opera as being minimalist in staging and symbolic in style, a "tradition" that would not become invented and solidified until the early twentieth century.[48]

More important, this new commercial scene of theatrical entertainment, broadly construed, marked the emergence of a new space for the screen that was constructed not only by theater architecture but also by lighting practices and viewing behavior. One crucial factor that empowered the screen for this variety of "plays" was the technological improvement of artificial lighting and, correspondingly, the creation of artificial darkness for visual effects.[49] With gaslight introduced into Shanghai's foreign concessions in 1864, Western and Chinese theaters began to replace candle and oil light. In 1875, the Dan'gui house was already using gaslight for stage performances and magic lantern shows; by the 1880s, major Beijing Opera teahouses were using gaslight, followed by limelight, and eventually electric light, starting in 1884.[50] Interestingly, later technologies of lighting did not entirely replace the earlier ones. Instead, Western theaters and Chinese teahouses took advantage of the different strengths offered by various types of lighting to create more nuanced effects and enhance safety on stage and in the auditorium. These lighting possibilities enabled the creation of darkness as a *theatrical effect*. One example is the late-afternoon staging of a lantern play, *The Mountain of Flames* (*Huoyanshan*) based on an episode from the sixteenth-century novel *The*

Journey to the West. An 1879 *Shenbao* newspaper article describes vividly the manipulation of darkness achieved by closing windows and doors. By deliberately darkening the theater before the lights were turned back on, the theater stunned the audience with the spectacle of a changing landscape on stage and moving lanterns depicting various gods and demons.[51]

The creation of artificial darkness, albeit functioning momentarily as theatrical effect, heightened the centrality of the screen through lighting practices that predated cinematic projection. Whereas the variety of "plays" took place in a range of settings, from proscenium theaters such as the Lyceum to platform theaters typical of teahouse architecture with three-sided seating arrangements, the control of lighting facilitated the transcendence of local space and architecture in ushering in the virtual space of the imaginary.

If the late-nineteenth-century teahouse as an emerging form of modern theater facilitated the rise of the screen as a distinct mode of spatiality, the magic lantern also played an important role. Introduced to China by Christian missionaries in the seventeenth century, the magic lantern had already become a popular and sophisticated form of entertainment and education in China by the mid-nineteenth century. Popular until the late nineteenth century in schools, churches, and teahouses as well as in Western-style theaters, magic lantern shows brought images and events to China from the world over for mass entertainment and enlightenment.

Although recent film scholars in China have identified the magic lantern as the most important media precursor of cinema, we should note that magic lanterns were not the sole agents of progress in this regard.[52] Although reports of magic lantern exhibitions are frequently cited, the fact that many such shows took place in prominent Beijing Opera and Cantonese venues such as the Dan'gui, Fuchun, and Tongqing teahouses has been left entirely unexamined. If we rethink the screen as more than just a material surface for projection, we can easily understand why magic lantern shows in late-nineteenth-century China shared both spaces and techniques with operatic performances in teahouses. Significantly, the same improvement of lighting technologies, from oil to gas-, lime-, and arclight, impacted both theatrical performances and magic lantern shows and was often prominently featured in advertising, reminding us to take these optical exhibitions seriously as live performances.

Along with the presence of the material screen—either in terms of an existing wall or a piece of white cloth coated with water to enhance its reflective quality—controlled lighting played a crucial part in the formation of Chinese screen culture. It served as a fulcrum for the transition from screens as two-dimensional, painted pieces of furniture for spatial and symbolic demarcations to screens in the more modern sense. One telling example is the 1885 magic lantern lecture by the Chinese pastor and scholar Yen Yung Kiung. Between November 21 and December 25, Yen performed at least eight magic lantern shows about his tour of the world in Shanghai's Polytechnic Institute and Reading Rooms (*Gezhi shuyuan*) devoted to Western science and learning.[53] According to one detailed report two days after the first showing, the lecture hall was brightly lit up "as if in broad daylight" while Yen and his assistant arranged the show.[54] The lantern, three- to-four-feet high with a chimney and a burning light inside, sat on a small table facing a Chinese screen on which a piece of "clean white foreign cloth" (*jiebai yangbu*) of the same size was hung.[55] The preparation for the show in this way entailed the replacement of a Chinese screen with a piece of Western, machine-made white cloth. Yet such a transformation from a painted screen to a screen for virtual images could not have occurred without the manipulation of light. Soon after Yen finished the set-up, all the lights went out, and the audience was immersed in complete darkness. Yen stood up and ignited the lantern lamp, projecting onto the screen a round spot of light "as bright as the moon," after which the first image emerged. The contrast between luminosity and sheer darkness not only displaced the Chinese screen by its new material substitute (white cloth) but perhaps more important, performed a ritual transformation that privileged the transition to a distinctly modern mode of spatiality.

If the magic lantern consequently shared screen practices with Beijing Opera in terms of both theatrical and technologized performance through controlled lighting, another important aspect of the magic lantern was its development as a public medium for photography with special effects. By the mid-nineteenth century, glass lantern slides were created by photographic techniques or were used to reproduce photographs. The Yen Yung Kiung exhibition of magic lanterns actually made use of photographs tinted with various colors. It was also not uncommon for magic lanternists to create what one would retroactively recognize as "cinematic" effects of motion, superimposition, dissolves, and iris shots through the use of multiple lenses and revolving or sliding plates. Such effects already appeared in reports on magic lantern shows in Hong Kong in the 1850s and 1860s and in Shanghai as early as 1875, and Yen's own lecture deployed similar techniques.[56] Roberta Wue's meticulous study further illustrates the intricate visual traffic between magic lantern, photography, and lithography when Yen's show was depicted and reported upon with lithographic illustrations in the *Dianshizhai Pictorial*.[57]

In this sense, the "confusing" Chinese terminology for magic lantern shows in fact accurately captures the intimate connections between the magic lantern, photography, and opera performance, as they shared techniques of projection, performance, and image formation. Magic lantern shows were frequently called *yingxi* (shadow play) or *yingxihua* (shadow play picture), without specifying what the references of *ying* (shadow), *xi* (play), or *hua* (picture) were. In the case of Yen's magic lantern performances, the show was consistently described as *huapian* (painted/illustrated page), *tu* (picture), *tuhui* (painted picture), and *xinhui* (newly painted/illustrated). Such wording has led Chinese scholars to assume that the images were drawn rather than photographed, despite the actual use of more than eighty photographs, as clarified by the English-language newspaper report.[58] Yet given that the notions of picture, shadow, and play are sufficiently problematized in this history, the Chinese verbal references are accurate precisely *because* of their "confusion" of these supposedly distinct media and modes of operation. Put another way, the ontical confusions in terms of the mismatch between media objects and their attributes clarify the ontological ground on which "picture," "shadow," and "play" were constituted.

THE SCENE OF CINEMA

We can now finally turn to the first film exhibitions in China and Hong Kong to debunk cinema's myth of superiority and uniqueness.

Frank Bren and Law Kar have presented compelling evidence that the earliest film showing in China occurred in Hong Kong, not Shanghai, sixteen months later than the presumed first film screening at Shanghai's Xu Garden, which may rather have been a magic lantern show. According to their research, the first film screening of the Cinématographe was conducted by a Professor Maurice Charvet, who traveled from San Francisco by ship. From April 28 to at least May 4, 1897, Charvet showed the films at Hong Kong's City Hall for five sessions per day, attracting a large audience, including, at one time, five hundred children from Queen's College.

Rather than focusing on the "firstness" of any particular film screening, we should attend to the fact that the earliest film exhibitions were not limited to one city or one film exhibitor, nor even to a single projection system. Between April 1897 and January 1898, Charvet competed with Harry Welby Cook's Animatoscope in Hong Kong, Shanghai, Tianjin, and Beijing. Both collaborated with the Astor House Hotel's manager Lewis M. Johnson, who served as an impresario, and all three of them crossed one another's paths and sometimes shared the same ship.[59] Nor were these early showings limited to film exhibition, making the novelty of these films more a myth of isolation. Cook's Animatoscope is now considered the earliest film showing in Shanghai. Yet its exhibition, at the Astor House Hotel on May 22, 1897, to a Western audience, was accompanied by magic lantern shows.[60] The *North-China Herald* reported that the Animatoscope was shown in Shanghai at least eight times between May 22 and July 29.

If the origin of cinema in China has been artificially constructed according to the myths of firstness and media isolation, then its technological novelty can be similarly deconstructed by examining the film exhibition reports more closely. An 1897 report from the *Hong Kong Daily Press* of M. Charvet's showing of the Cinématographe on April 28 in the City Hall's Music Room describes it as an "extraordinary tableau." In a private exhibition shown two days earlier, the film was also described as "life-like," with spectators feeling as if they were in the scene.[61]

Yet when the Cinématographe was first shown in Shanghai by Johnson and Charvet at the Lyceum Theater on September 8, the reception was less favorable. The report recognizes the apparatus's "comparative novelty" since "this modern and clever adaptation of photography" had only been shown once before (by Welby Cook); yet the audience could not overcome "the vibration so noticeable and trying to the eyes" at the screening despite the claim that the spectacle attracted a full house.[62] The report describes "twenty views," treating each film as one view and one "plate," many of which were "worn out or defective," plagued by vibration "too plainly and disagreeably in evidence."[63]

> The great drawback to the entertainment was the difficulty in focusing the pictures on the screen, the delay in many instances being very tedious, and if the proprietors intend to give further exhibitions of the Cinématographe they should practice manipulation of the plates so as to secure more prompt production of the moving views. Would it not be possible, by means of a curtain at the back of the screen, to arrange the proper focusing out of view of the audience, and even to throw the picture on the screen as it commences to move? It is so done in London, where the pictures are never shown in a stationary condition even for a moment.[64]

On their second exhibition at the Lyceum Theatre on September 15, Johnson and Charvet were facing "a partially filled house." This time they managed the focus outside of the audience's view, although the report still complained that the "intervals between the pictures were certainly too long." The pair planned to continue the show that Saturday and draw better houses by including some scenes of Shanghai "recently taken for that purpose."[65]

These reports, read against the positive reviews celebrating the wonder of film, suggest several points. First, the film screenings were far from perfect. The audience was keenly aware of the operation of the apparatus, which both fascinated and frustrated them. Instead of the *jouissance* cultivated by the projection system and darkness of the theater space, and in contrast to the hyperbolic claims in advertisements, the newness of film was offset by an awkwardness and imperfection that constantly took the audience out of the magical enchantment. This reaction also challenges Yeh's claim that these first film showings were "an electrifying visual experience, departing significantly from the magic lantern and optical toys such as [the] zoetrope and thaumatrope," and "not to be confused with *standard* entertainments available in *standard* venues."[66] Without an investigation of the historical practices that constituted the screen, assumptions about what constituted "standard" entertainments and venues remain reductive.

Second, it was not simply the technological apparatus of cinema that attracted the audience. Equally important were the content of the images and the specific meanings they conveyed to particular audiences. In the first showing at the Lyceum, the report notes that the film receiving the most enthusiasm was of the jubilee procession in London, which provoked applause and the singing of the British National Anthem: "This was the most striking incident of the evening, and went far to compensate for defects in the exhibition that had been too apparent during the course of completing the program." Whereas such films would resonate with the British expatriates who made up the majority of the audience, scenes shot in Shanghai would speak to the interest of elite Chinese audiences who could afford to attend. These meaningful connections with audiences also underscore the colonial setting of these early film exhibitions.

Third, the discursive tropes for these experiences—life-like motion, the quality of image—repeat those that were already applied to magic lantern shows, photography, lithographic drawing, and the new style of theater. One should not overstress the differences in the way these distinct media were experienced but rather emphasize how these experiences were themselves shaped by existing discursive contexts.

Fourth, when the medium's novelty *was* acknowledged in the press, the reports constantly referred to the films as "photographs" and lantern slide "plates," with each film seen as a single "view." Notably in Cook's first exhibition in Shanghai on May 22, the Animatoscope was shown alongside magic lantern slides to a largely Western audience. While such descriptions confirm what Gaudreault and Marion have called cinema's "two births" —first as an extension of pre-existing media forms, and second as an institution in its own right—we can also see how the technological varieties of cinema, both Cinématographe and Animatoscope, operated in tandem with older media in a new media environment.[67]

Conclusion

Recounting cinema's emergence in the plural scene of visual modernity in China, this essay experiments with a new ontology of cinema in terms of ecology. Its ecological method, as I demonstrate, is enabled by the distinction and relation between the ontic and ontological, which connects the changing media objects and operations at the ontic level with the evolving relationships that shaped the structure and meaning of media at the ontological level. This ecological ontology allows me to reengage media archaeology's attention to technical details while complementing it by addressing the horizon of relevant entities as the condition of possibilities of media. In this sense, against the "anti-" or "post-hermeneutic" trends that characterize media archaeology, my onto-archaeo-ecology recovers hermeneutics by making sense of the meaning and structure of cinema in terms of its media environment.

What we discover in this ecological account is not simply a host of distinct media objects that served as mere context for a new medium. Instead, the media environment operated more like a recursive loop in which media distinctions were constantly reinvented and regenerated as elastic and dynamic intermediaries. In this sense, picture, shadow, and play are not distinct media objects, nor do they correspond to associated attributes of certain media technological devices. Instead of thinking of them as adjectives or attributes, it might be more useful to consider them as simultaneously nouns and verbs, as tangible existences whose modes of operation converge, intersect, and collide.

The historically rich entwinement between picture, shadow, and play helps us understand the emergence of several major elements of spatiality that regulated ways of seeing, perceiving, experiencing, and reacting. These include the technical formation of composite images, the creation of a virtual space enabled by the *screen* as a new mode of modern spatiality, and a broader notion of *play* associated with entertainment, playfulness, and execution that included technological performance. These playful experiments and performances reshuffle the agencies of humans, objects, and technologies through which a picture (photography) could be turned into a mini-stage of performance while the theatrical stage became the place where a painted picture (background) could perform and compete with human agents. In this context, technology is a necessary but insufficient condition for understanding media identity; rather, technology interfaces with cultural practices in ways that each mutually redefines the other.

Similarly, we can rethink regional specificities of cinema by investigating their plurality across the multiple, crisscrossing, and transregional traffic networks and portals that structured human/material flow. Regions, like media, are the products of such encounters, diverse uses, and intersecting traffic, rather than pre-existing givens. In this sense, the plural names by which cinema was coordinated against the concepts of picture, shadow, and play are indices of historical receptions that were ecological in nature.

Such onto-archaeo-ecologies, I would suggest, exercised analogical thinking to make sense of the new in terms of existing patterns of perception, experience, and knowledge. Two decades ago, art historian Barbara Stafford called for a return to analogical thinking, a discovery of resemblance in an age in which overwrought differences blind us to a more nuanced picture of connectedness, of in-betweenness.[68] Analogy, as Stafford proposes, is "the art of sympathetic thoughts" that "forge[s] bonds between two incongruities and span[s] incommensurables."[69] As a "performative rhetoric," analogy entails an active search for similarity-in-difference. It encourages a participatory mode of perception, a reciprocating method that "correlates originality with continuity, what comes after with what went before [. . .] through a *mediating image*."[70] Picture, shadow, and play are precisely the analogies that place cinema in its media environment.

Notes

1. The term is from David Rodowick, "An Elegy to Film Theory," *October* 122 (2007): 91–109.
2. Martin Heidegger, *Being and Time*, trans. John Macquarrie and Edward Robinson (Oxford, UK: Blackwell, 1962), 32–34.
3. Heidegger characterizes his phenomenological approach to ontology as hermeneutic, "in the sense of working out the condition on which the possibility of any ontological investigation depends." Ibid., 62. My emphasis on hermeneutics takes aim at "anti-hermeneutic" tendencies in recent writings on media archaeology. See Hans Ulrich Gumbrecht, "A Farewell to Interpretation," in Hans Ulrich Gumbrecht and K. Ludwig Pfeiffer, eds., *Materialities of Communication* (Stanford, CA: Stanford University Press, 1994), 389–402; David Wellbery, "Foreword" for Friedrich Kittler, *Discourse Networks, 1800/1900*, trans. Michael Meteer and Chris Cullens (Stanford, CA: Stanford University Press, 1990), vii–xxxiii. For more on my critique, see Weihong Bao, "Archaeology of a Medium: The (Agri)cultural Techniques of a Paddy Film Farm," *boundary 2* 49, no. 1 (2022): 25–70.
4. See Huang Dequan, "Dianying chudao shanghai kao" ("On the Arrival of Cinema in Shanghai"), *Film Art* 314 (2007): 102–109; Liu Xiaolei, "'Ying' de jieding yu dianying chuanru Zhongguo yishi" ("Defining 'Ying' and Reexamining the Introduction of Cinema in China"), *Dianying yishu* (2011): 119–125; Hou Kai, "Dianying chuanru Zhongguo de wenti zaikao" ("Re-investigating the Introduction of Film in China"), *Dianying yishu* (2011): 126–129; Sheldon Lu, "Lumière xiongdi dianying zai Zhongguo fangying kao" ("On the Exhibition of the Lumière brothers Films in China"), *Dangdai dianying* (2011): 60–66.

5. See Yeh Yueh-yu, Feng Xiaocai, and Liu Hui, eds., *Zouchu Shanghai: Zaoqi Dianying de Linglei Jingguan* (Beyond Shanghai: The Alternative Landscape of Early Cinema) (Beijing: Beijing University Press, 2016), 15. An updated English volume is now available with additional sections. See Emilie Yeh Yueh-yu, ed., *Early Film Culture in Hong Kong, Taiwan, and Republican China* (Ann Arbor: University of Michigan Press, 2018).
6. I have tentatively translated *ying* as "shadow" to highlight the element of projection. The ambiguous associations of *ying* will be elaborated later in the essay.
7. Yeh, "Yanyi 'yingxi': Huayu dianying xipu yu zaoqi xianggang dianying"("Translating *yingxi*: Chinese Film Genealogy and Early Cinema in Hong Kong") in Yeh, Feng, and Liu, eds., *Zouchu Shanghai*, 19–68. Yeh's essay was informed by exciting new scholarship on early cinema which incorporates non-theatrical exhibition under the rubric of useful cinema. See Marta Braun, Charles Keil, Rob King, Paul Moore and Louis Pelletier, eds., *Beyond the Screen: Institutions, Networks, and Publics of Early Cinema* (New Barnet, UK: John Libbey, 2012).
8. Yeh, "Yanyi yingxi," 52. Yeh makes a stronger argument about medium distinction and incongruity in the revised Chinese version. The earlier English-language essay sought only to debunk *yingxi*'s unlikely association with puppet theater and Beijing Opera. See Emilie Yeh Yueh-yu, "Translating *Yingxi*: Chinese Film Genealogy and Early Cinema in Hong Kong," *Journal of Chinese Cinemas* 9 (2015): 1–34, 18.
9. Yeh, "Yanyi yingxi," 52.
10. Lev Manovich, *The Language of New Media* (Cambridge, MA: MIT Press, 2001), 298–308. I thank Charlie Keil for reminding me of this dichotomy that equally persists in the West.
11. Heidegger, *Being and Time*, 28–31.
12. Thomas Elsaesser, "The New Film History as Media Archaeology," *Cinémas* (2004) 14, nos. 2/3: 75–117.
13. http://www.oed.com/view/Entry/143501?rskey=ZtuIJW&result=1#eid. For a provocative rethinking of images across different conceptual, experiential, and medial categories, see W. J. T. Mitchell, "What Is an Image?" *New Literary History* 15, no. 3 (Spring 1984): 503–537.
14. These words also form compounds such as *tuxiang* and *huihua*; the term *xiezhen* was later adopted in Japanese as the translation for "photography" and reimported in the nineteenth and twentieth centuries to China.
15. See Craig Clunas, *Pictures and Visuality in Early Modern China* (Princeton, NJ: Princeton University Press, 1997), 104–111.
16. See Terry Bennett, *History of Photography in China: 1842–1860* (London: Bernard Quartich, 2009), 2–3; Jules Itier, *Journal d'un voyage en Chine en 1843, 1844, 1845, 1846* (Paris: Dauvin et Fontaine, 1848–53).
17. Gu Yi, "What's in a Name? Photography and the Reinvention of Visual Truth in China, 1840–1911," *Art Bulletin* 95, no. 1 (March 2013): 120–138.
18. Ibid., 123–124. I borrow the term "brush and shutter" from the recent exhibition on early photography in China from 1859 onward held at the Getty Museum (February 8–May 11, 2011). See Jeffrey Cody and Frances Terpak, eds., *Brush and Shutter: Early Photography in China* (Los Angeles, CA: Getty Research Institute, 2011).
19. On the retrospective construction of "traditional theater" in terms of an anti-mimetic modernist aesthetic, see Weihong Bao, "The Politics of Remediation: *Mise-en-scène* and the Subjunctive Body in Chinese Opera Film," *Opera Quarterly* 26, nos. 2/3 (2010): 256–291.
20. Recent scholarship has resituated the origin of Chinese theater from its association with ritual to the broad culture of entertainment. Regina Llamas, "A Reassessment of the Place

of Shamanism in the Origin of Chinese Theater," *Journal of the American Oriental Society* 133, no. 1 (2013): 93–109.
21. Christopher Rea, *The Age of Irreverence: A New History of Laughter in China* (Berkeley: University of California Press, 2015), 40–42.
22. Gu Yi, "What's in a Name?" 121–122. See also Tong Bingxue, *Zhongguo zhaoxiangguan shi, 1859–1956* (History of Photo Studios in China, 1859–1956) (Beijing: Zhongguo sheying chubanshe, 2016).
23. See Zhang Zhen, *An Amorous History of the Silver Screen: Shanghai Cinema, 1896–1937* (Chicago, IL: University of Chicago Press, 2005), 164; H. Tiffany Lee, "One, and the Same: The Photographic Double in Republican China," in Luke Gartlan and Roberta Wue, eds., *Portraiture and Early Studio Photography in China and Japan* (London: Routledge, 2017), 140–155.
24. The earliest Western theaters are now believed to be the Teatro dom Pedro V (1860) in Macau, the Lyceum (1866) in Shanghai, and the Gordon Hall in Tianjin (1890). See Mu Fanzhong, *Dasanba sibainian xilu* (Records of Four Hundred Years of Theater at St. Paul's Church) (Hong Kong: Salian, 2016).
25. Zhao Tingting, "Performative Modernity: Shanghai-style Peking Opera in Pre-War Shanghai: 1872–1937" (PhD diss., Stanford University, 2016).
26. "Xiguo xiyuan luocheng" ("Western Theater Completed"), *Shenbao*, January 27, 1874, 2. The backdrops were called "painted screens" (*hua pingfeng*) in the description. For the history of the Lyceum, see Hu Daojing, "'Lanxin' liushi nian" ("Sixty years of the Lyceum"), in Shanghai tongshe, ed., *Shanghai yanjiu ziliao* (Research Material on Shanghai) (Shanghai, China: Shanghai tongshe, 1935), 487–490.
27. Author unknown, "Xiguo xiyuan heyan Zhongxi xinxi" ("Western Theater Shows New Joint Performance by Chinese and Western Plays"), *Shenbao*, March 16, 1874, 2.
28. Advertisements for Dan'gui Teahouse, *Shenbao*, May 23–June 23, 1874.
29. Wang Tao, for example, documented the Lyceum in his *Yingruan zazhi* (Miscellaneous Jottings on Shanghai) (Shanghai, China: Shanghai guji, 1989 [1875]). For other travel accounts of theater, see Ge Yuanxu, *Huyou zaji* (Miscellaneous Accounts of Shanghai Travel) (Shanghai, China: Geshi xiaoyuan, 1876); Xu Ke, *Qingbai leichao* (Unofficial Categorized Account of Qing) (Shanghai, China: The Commercial Press, 1923), 77.
30. Zhang Deyi, *Suishi Faguo ji: San su qi* (Record of a Diplomatic Visit to France: A Third Account of a Marvel) (Changsha, China: Hunan remin chubanshe, 1982 [1873]), 119.
31. Zhang Deyi, *Hanghai shuqi* (Account of Marvels while Sailing the Sea) (Changsha, China: Hunan remin chubanshe, 1981 [1870]), 99.
32. Deyi, *Suishi Faguo ji*, 238.
33. Ibid., 119.
34. See Wang Tao, *Manyou suilu* (Random Jottings from Wanderings) (Changsha, China: Yuelu shushe, 1985 [1890]), 89; Dai Hongci, *Chushi jiuguo riji* (Diary of a Diplomatic Visit to Nine Countries) (Changsha, China: Yuelu shushe, 1986 [1906]), 358; Wang Zhichun, *Shi e'cao* (Brief Accounts of a Diplomatic Visit to Russia, 1895), reprinted in *Jindai Zhongguo shiliao congkan* (Taipei: Wenhai chubanshe, 1967).
35. *Shenbao*, October 3, 1897, 6.
36. *Shenbao*, December 13–17, 1897, 6.
37. See Law Kar and Frank Bren, *From Artform to Platform: Hong Kong Plays and Performances 1900–1941* (Hong Kong: The Internal Association of Theatre Critics, 1999).
38. Ibid., 22–23.

39. Law Waiming, "Hong Kong's Cinematic Beginnings," in Law Kar, ed., *Early Images of Hong Kong and China: 19th Hong Kong International Film Festival Retrospective Catalogue* (Hong Kong: Urban Culture Council, 1995), 24–25.
40. This notion of theatricality as a historically specific mode of spatiality is conceived in contrast to the emphasis on magical presence in medieval theater in France and Spain and to the idea of dreamscape in medieval China. See William Egginton, *How the World Became a Stage: Presence, Theatricality, and the Question of Modernity* (Albany: State University of New York Press, 2003), 3; Ling Hon Lam, *The Spatiality of Emotion in Early Modern China: From Dreamscape to Theatricality* (New York: Columbia University Press, 2018).
41. Egginton, *How the World Became a Stage*, 108.
42. Ibid., 109.
43. Yeh, "Translating *Yingxi*," 4.
44. Ibid., 6.
45. Beijing Opera originated in the late eighteenth century and did not solidify until around 1845; the origin of Cantonese Opera, still being debated, is estimated to be around the early to mid-nineteenth century. See Joshua Goldstein, *Drama Kings: Players and Publics in the Re-creation of Peking Opera, 1870–1937* (Berkeley: University of California Press, 2007); Li Rixin, "Yueju gainian yu yueju shi guanxi bianxi" ("On the Relationship between the Concept of Cantonese Opera and Its History"), *Xueshi yanjiu* 12 (2007): 154–158.
46. "Dieyan yingxi" ("Repeated Showings of the Magic Lantern"), *Shenbao*, March 23, 1875, 2.
47. On *dengcaixi*, see Xian Jiqing, "Jindai xiqu wutai dengguang zhaoming zhilun" ("On Stage Lighting for the Early Theater"), *Zhongguo xiqu xueyuan xuebao* (2016) 37, no. 2: 118–123.
48. The notion of "Chinese opera" is problematic to start with, given the genre's significant variety and different historical formations; the term "national drama" associated with Beijing Opera was only invented in the 1920s as a product of colonial modernism. For a critique of the invention of such a tradition, see Joshua Goldstein, *Drama Kings*; Weihong Bao, "The Politics of Remediation."
49. On artificial darkness in the history of media, see Noam Elcott, *Artificial Darkness: An Obscure History of Modern Media and Art* (Chicago, IL: University of Chicago Press, 2016).
50. See Xian, "Jindai xiqu," 120–121.
51. "Dengxi xincai," *Shenbao*, June 10, 1879, 2.
52. Li Ming, "Dianying cong huandeng xuedaole shenme" ("What Has Cinema Learned from the Magic Lantern?"), *Beijing dianying xuebao* 4 (2011): 51–59; Tang Hongfeng, "Cong huandeng dao dianying: shijue xiandaixing de mailuo" ("From Magic Lantern to Cinema: Tracing Visual Modernity"), *Chuanbo yu shehui xuekan* 35 (2016): 185–213.
53. For more discussion on Yen's show, see Roberta Wue, "China in the World: On Photography, Montages, and the Magic Lantern," *History of Photography* 41, no. 2 (2017): 171–187; Tang, "Cong Huandeng dao dianying."
54. "Guan yingxi ji" ("Account of the Magic Lantern Show"), *Shenbao*, November 23, 1885, 1.
55. The description uses the word *yangbu*, literally "foreign cloth," a term used after the Opium War to distinguish imported machine-woven fabric from handmade domestic cloth.
56. Dissolving and stereoscopic views were reported in Hong Kong in the 1850s and 60s; see Bren and Law, *Hong Kong Cinema*, 7; Tang, "Cong Huandeng dao dianying," 194.
57. Wue, "China in the World."
58. See Tang, "Cong Huandeng dao dianying," 200; *North-China Daily News*, November 23, 1885, 499.

59. See Bren and Law, *Hong Kong Cinema*, 5, 11–16. Bren and Law found no evidence of the Lumières' presence in Hong Kong in 1897 and suggest that the "Cinématographe" might have been a copycat. The Animatoscope was sometimes advertised as Edison's latest invention, although the credit should probably go to William Wright, who created the projector in February 1896 and founded the United States Animatoscope Company in San Francisco in the same year. James Labosier, "From the Kinetoscope to the Nickelodeon: Motion Picture Presentation and Production in Portland, Oregon from 1894–1906," *Film History* 16, no. 3 (2004): 286–323. For the advertisement, see "H. Wellby-Cooke's Animatoscope," *China Mail*, August 19–21, 1897, 2.
60. "The Animatoscope," *North China Daily News*, May 24, 1897, 4.
61. *China Mail*, April 26, 1897.
62. "The Cinematograph [sic] at the Lyceum Theatre," *North-China Herald and Supreme Court & Consular Gazette*, September 10, 1897, 498.
63. Ibid.
64. Ibid.
65. "Readings for the Week," *North-China Herald and Supreme Court & Consular Gazette*, September 17, 1897, 523.
66. Yeh, "Translating Yingxi," 7 (emphasis added).
67. André Gaudreault and Philippe Marion, "A Medium Is Always Born Twice," *Early Popular Visual Culture* 3, no. 1 (2005): 3–15.
68. Barbara Stafford, *Visual Analogy: Consciousness as the Art of Connecting* (Cambridge, MA: MIT Press, 1999).
69. Ibid., 10.
70. Ibid., 9.

CHAPTER 10

BIOGRAPH 1904

The Invention of Chase Comedy

ROB KING

> The crucial question for media archaeology, then, resides in whether, in this interplay between technology and culture, the new kind of historical imagination that emerged was an effect of new media or whether such media were invented because the epistemological setting of the age demanded them.
>
> Wolfgang Ernst[1]

> At this time, cinema had not yet become an autonomous medium, and the kinematograph was neither more nor less than an instrument, a tool, that made available to anyone cultural practices and genres in vogue at the close of the nineteenth century.
>
> André Gaudreault[2]

THE tension between these two epigraphs provokes questions. What priority do we accord cinema's technological properties within an etiology of the genres of early film? To what extent might those genres profitably be framed as an "effect of new media," or should they be historicized as extensions of genres already "in vogue" elsewhere? In one corner, we have Wolfgang Ernst, a leading figure in the emergent field of German-led scholarship known as "media archaeology"; in the other, André Gaudreault, for decades an agenda-setting scholar of early film. On the one hand, an approach that considers technological factors as catalysts for mutations in cultural practice and discourse; on the other, a position that considers how early cinema initially served as "neither more nor less than an instrument" for extending pre-existing practices (or, to use Gaudreault and Philippe Marion's term, "cultural series"). (See their essay in this volume.) For one, a sensitivity to the *discontinuities* arising from the *mediating effects* of new technologies;

for the other, an insistence on *continuities* in terms of *what was being mediated*—the way in which, say, Georges Méliès exploited cinema as a device for building on the representational norms of stage magic, or how the same filmmaker's *Le Royaume des fées* (1903) extends the conventions of the fairy play into film.[3]

No doubt these binaries are overly schematic. Certainly, they do not summarize a disciplinary state of affairs, as though the protocols of early film historiography have somehow sequestered themselves from the archaeological bent evident elsewhere in contemporary media studies. There are too many excellent works of recent film history that engage the spirit of media archaeology for this to be the case, whether the engagement is explicit (e.g., Noam Elcott's *Artificial Darkness* [2016]) or in everything but name (e.g., Mary Ann Doane's *The Emergence of Cinematic Time* [2002]).[4] Instead, the epigraphs are proposed as poles in a spectrum of possibilities for understanding what Ernst calls the "interplay between technology and culture"—the Scylla and Charybdis between which the film historian must navigate the risks of a reductive technological determinism (where cultural form is simply an "effect of new media") against the equal dangers of assuming a fully determined technology (where a medium is "nothing more nor less than an instrument").[5] Yet, rather than choose dogmatically between a chicken-egg option—which has determinative priority, the medium or that which is mediated?—we should rather heed Raymond Williams's now four-decades-old injunction to think of determination "*not as a single force*" but as a process in which determining factors "set limits and exert pressures, *but neither wholly control nor wholly predict the outcome*."[6] We might seek an understanding of generic formation in early film more profitably in that very margin of unpredictability.

The present chapter takes up this point in relation to the genre for which a media archaeological insistence on the "difference" a medium makes has enjoyed most traction: the chase comedy. Among the genres of early film, few seem so resolutely native to the medium as the comic chase. Whereas other types of early film comedy have been routinely understood in terms of their contextualizing cultural series—as extensions of vaudeville skits or comic-strip humor—the chase comedy seems to have initiated a development arising from specifically filmic affordances, awakening the medium to the possibilities of continuity editing by tracking a single action over a series of shots. However it is framed, whether as "the original truly narrative genre of the cinema" (Tom Gunning) or as a "decisive shift toward fiction 'feature' films" (Charles Musser), the chase comedy is widely viewed as one of the early signposts of cinema's autonomy as a narrative medium: it inaugurates something that both arises from cinema's distinct medial properties and sets cinema apart, although the exact nature of that "something" depends on the historian.[7] To test these claims, I will be focusing on the company that effectively launched the genre in 1904, American Mutoscope and Biograph, and its three chase comedies from that year: *The Escaped Lunatic* (January), *Personal* (June), and *The Lost Child* (October), all directed by Wallace McCutcheon.[8] At the risk of a too-rigid schematism, the argument will proceed by pairing each of the first two films with one of the methodologies here identified—first by applying a "cultural series" reading to *Personal*, then a media archaeological perspective to *The Escaped Lunatic*—before synthesizing the insights reached through those analyses to a reading of *The Lost Child*. In that synthesis we will discover a bridge leading from debates in media historiography to questions of genre formation in moving-image comedy.

"A CLOUD OF FLYING PETTICOATS": *PERSONAL* AND TRADITIONS OF FESTIVE RUNNING

Two English imports, *A Daring Daylight Burglary* and *Desperate Poaching Affray* (both 1903) introduced the chase to the US as a new kind of subject matter, which in the hands of American Mutoscope and Biograph's filmmakers, immediately became comic, first in *The Escaped Lunatic*, and then, more influentially, in the hugely successful and much-plagiarized *Personal*, with which our analysis begins. A headliner at Keith's Union Square for four weeks, *Personal*'s breakthrough was to wed the nascent format of the chase film to the comic display of women running, which the film's subsequent rip-offs—in the form of the Edison company's *How a French Nobleman Got a Wife through the New York Herald "Personal" Columns* and Lubin's *Meet Me at the Fountain* (both 1904)—had the effect of securing chase comedy's first real trope. In all three films, the situation is the same. An impecunious foreign nobleman advertises in the newspaper for a wife. When he arrives at the designated meeting spot (Grant's Tomb in *Personal* and *How a French Nobleman*, a fountain in *Meet Me at the Fountain*), he is beset by a throng of would-be fiancées, and a chase ensues. The chase itself consists of a series of shots (eight in *Personal*, six in *How a French Nobleman*, ten in *Meet Me at the Fountain*) all showing basically the same thing: a man fleeing a pursuing horde, until eventually one of the women catches up and claims her spoils. Almost a decade before the advent of the all-male Keystone cops, the gentrification of chase comedy was initially cast in the spectacle of female pedestrianism: the *Biograph Bulletin* promoted *Personal* for its "cloud of flying petticoats," describing how a "neat little lady with white stockings ... attracts attention as she lifts her fluffy skirts," while a "little fat short-breathed woman ... gets left and finishes a bad last"; and Edison followed suit in exhibitor publicity for the Edwin S. Porter–directed *How a French Nobleman*, outlining how the "fair would-be captors ... [give] merry chase over sand banks, fallen trees, [and] through bushes," while, again, a "stout lady in white bring[s] up the rear."[9] Although the chase genre's success was hardly predicated on it only ever being women doing the running, the trope itself was an unquestionably foundational one, even inspiring later homages, long after the genre's initial popularity, in Ernst Lubitsch's *Die Püppe* (1919) and Buster Keaton's *Seven Chances* (1925).[10]

What, though, was the genesis of this trope? According to Gaudreault's cultural series approach, a first task would be to look for clues within the surrounding context of existing media practice.[11] It is a particularly choice coincidence, then, that just such a search occurred a few months after *Personal*'s initial release, thanks to the lawsuit that Biograph filed against Edison over the latter's remake. As part of that dispute, Edison's side had denied infringement by claiming that both its film and Biograph's shared a basis in a comic strip from the time. According to Edwin S. Porter, testifying under oath, Biograph's *Personal* was "merely the acting of a joke which appeared in a series of pictures in a comic paper" that he had seen "lying on the desk of Wallace McCutcheon" and of which he decided to make his own version too—a claim that was flatly denied by Biograph production head Frank Marion, who, in his rebuttal, asserted that "I never saw such a series of pictures in a comic paper," "I don't believe that they existed," and "the idea was original with me."[12] In the effort to back up Porter's dubious claim—after all, what would a comic strip version of *Personal* even look like?—Edison employee Delos Holden initiated a search for this mysterious comic strip, contacting, among others, the city editor of the *New York World* to see if any of his artists were aware of a "series of pictures" depicting a man "beset by a large throng of enthusiastic females."[13] "None of them remembers seeing such an illustration in a paper," the editor wrote back, before adding that "Several of them . . . tell me that exactly such a scene as you describe is on exhibition in a moving picture series . . . at Keith's"—an amusing circularity in which the effort to excavate a source text for *Personal* ends up unearthing *Personal* itself.[14]

Perhaps, though, we can do one better than Edison's lawyers if we think beyond *Personal*'s surrounding context of media *representations* in order to historicize what is *represented* in the film; namely, running. What happens, for instance, if we try to contextualize these "running films" less in relation to a history of turn-of-the-century media entertainments than within the history of running as *itself* an entertainment? That these films might be historicized in this way was, in fact, sometimes obliquely hinted at in the contemporary discourse—as, for instance, when one newspaper briefly described *The Escaped Lunatic* as an "exciting cross-country chase," as if in continuity with practices of steeplechase or "hare and hounds" running that by the end of the nineteenth century had made the cross-country race a popular athletic pursuit (the first important one in the US was organized by the New York Athletic Club in 1883); or when Biograph itself, a few months after the legal case with Edison, promoted *Tom, Tom, the Piper's Son* (1905) as the "Original Comedy Chase" (see figure 10.1), as though the very format of chase comedy was presaged in an eighteenth-century nursery rhyme recounting a village bad boy's festive flight ("Tom run here / Tom run there / Tom run through the village square"); or, outside of the US, in Alice Guy's *The Obstacle Course* (1906), which appropriates the chase format to the representation of a festive race whose participants dash through barrels and over walls for a chance to win a ham and a bottle of wine.[15]

It is the atavistic orientation of *Tom, Tom, the Piper's Son* that is the really telling clue here. That film's opening shot of village festivities is, of course, best known today in the form of Ken Jacobs's minutely detailed reexamination of the pig's theft in his 1969 structuralist film of the same name. For present purposes, though, what matters is how the shot brings our inquiry into the world of old English fairs, here depicted in a mise-en-scène supposedly "adapted from Ancient Prints of Hogarth" to display "a primitive 'Midway' in full swing" with "a lady tight-rope walker, a clown juggler, a fakir with a

FIGURE 10.1 Cover page from the *Biograph Bulletin*, March 15, 1905. From Kemp R. Niver, *Biograph Bulletins, 1896–1908* (Los Angeles: Locare Research Group, 1971).

shell and pea game, a goose girl, etc."[16] That there existed, from the middle ages through to the late nineteenth century, a festive rural culture in Europe and its diaspora in which running entertainments figured prominently, has been well known for as long as there have been historians and recorders of rural customs; the historian of early film cannot but see in these records a Rosetta Stone for the decipherment of chase comedy. Here, for example, is British writer Montague Shearman, in his 1887 study *Athletics and Football*, describing the prevalence of "ridiculous" and "preposterous" footraces run for wagers during village festivities:

> Luttrell's "Diary" tells us of a wager made by a German of sixty-four years old to walk 300 miles in "Hide Park" in six days, which he did "within the time, and a mile over." In 1780 the "Gentleman's Magazine" tells us that a man of seventy-five years old ran four miles and a half round Queen Square in 58 minutes. Eight years later a young gentleman, with a jockey booted and spurred on his back, ran a match against an elderly fat man (of the name of Bullock) running without a rider. The more extraordinary the wager the more excitement it often caused amongst the public. A fish-hawker is reputed to have for a wager run seven miles, from Hyde Park Corner to Brentford, with 56 lbs. weight of fish on his head, in 45 minutes! Another man trundled a coach-wheel eight miles in an hour round a platform erected in St. Giles's Fields. Another extraordinary match was one between a man on stilts against a man on foot, the former receiving twenty yards start in a hundred and twenty yards. What is more astounding is that the man upon the stilts won the match.[17]

The historian Henning Eichberg has pointed out that popular running, through the nineteenth century, belonged primarily to a festive "culture of laughter"—and no wonder, because all of this reads like a brainstorming session from the Mack Sennett gag room.[18]

This was the village fair world of sack races, hunting the greased pig, and cheese rolling, alongside other non-ambulatory contests like grinning matches and hot hasty pudding eating. It was also, though, the world of the "smock race," which is where the chase comedy trope of female pursuit finds its most vivid genealogical intelligibility. Joseph Strutt's much-cited 1801 study *The Sports and Pastimes of the People of England* gives this definition: "Smock races are commonly performed by the young country wenches, and so called because the prize is a holland smock, or shift, usually decorated with ribbands."[19] There were, of course, other prizes and other forms of footracing that women engaged in during the eighteenth and early nineteenth centuries; none, however, had the festive centrality of the smock race, often held on Whit Tuesday—in May or early June—or in Ireland on St. Patrick's Day, as well as an added attraction in weddings and even cricket matches. Nor did other forms of premodern women's sports go as far in provoking a popular imaginary of semi-dressed female runners, in eighteenth- and nineteenth-century paintings, prints, and poetry that anticipate the chase film both formally and spectatorially (see figures 10.2 and 10.3). The tradition even inspired a poem, in the form of the Reverend James Ward's 1714 "The Smock Race, at Finglas" (near Dublin), which confirms in such sport the same chances for glimpsing

FIGURE 10.2 John Collet, *An Holland Smock to run for, by any Woman born in this County: the best Woman in three Heats*, 1770. © The Trustees of the British Museum.

FIGURE 10.3 Thomas Rowlandson, *Rural Sports: Smock Racing*, 1811.

momentarily revealed undergarments as was promoted two centuries later in Biograph's reference to the "neat little lady [who] lifts her fluffy skirts." The poem begins with a body-by-body enumeration of the three competitors—Oonah, Norah, and Shevan—and ends by imagining victory decided by wardrobe malfunction: "At Norah's Petticoat the Goddess ply'd, / And in a Trice the fatal String unty'd. / Quick stop'd the Maid, nor wou'd, to win the Prize, / Expose her hidden Charms to vulgar Eyes. / But while to tye the treach'rous Knot she stay'd, / Both her glad Rivals pass the weeping Maid." Evidently the kind of "managed irregularity" on which chase comedy thrived—the way the format functioned as a predictable system for generating comically *un*predictable displays of immodestly discombobulated bodies—was shared by its premodern harbingers in festive women's running.[20]

There is no direct evidence, nor is it likely that there could be, that the New York–born Wallace McCutcheon had any inkling of what a smock race was, nor whether *Personal*'s author, Frank Marion, did—although the latter is definitely possible, given Marion's childhood years in Tidioute, Pennsylvania. A small manufacturing town largely populated by immigrants from the north of England, Tidioute seems to have sustained certain village running traditions, albeit adapted to the festive calendar of the United States. Newspaper announcements for Fourth of July ceremonies during Marion's toddler years routinely listed "various amusements... such as, swinging, dancing, climbing the greased pole, catching the greased pig, and taking part in the wheelbarrow and sack races," to quote but one example.[21] No smock races, however, which is not surprising given that the practice had been in decline, in England at least, since the mid-nineteenth century, a casualty of changes in the structure of village life wrought by urban migration and new attitudes toward "decency." As sports historian Peter Radford observes, "by 1840 women running or walking in races was no longer considered 'respectable' and were either not arranged or not reported."[22]

As such, the claims of this section will need to be framed as a hypothesis, rather than a proof: namely, what happens to our understanding of the chase film if we investigate it as part of what Gaudreault would call the "cultural series" *festive running*? Two interim possibilities suggest themselves. The first is that chase comedy, at least at its inception, would appear to have about as much to do with modernity as an egg-and-spoon race. This is not to say that running did not experience its own transfiguration under modernity, but it is to say that that transfiguration is hardly captured in the spectacle of women tumbling down sand banks. Rather, running's modernity is best understood as its conscription to the cultural techniques of precision timekeeping and standardization (such as the synthetic four-hundred-meter track) that formed the preconditions for modern competitive running.[23] If the chase film thrived as a distinctly comedic genre, one explanation, then, might be that it sustained residual traditions of festive running that were being displaced by a modern culture of "Fordist" running that processed new symbolic functions for foot-racing (notably linked to nationalism with the revival of the Olympic Games in 1896, so proximate to cinema's birth).[24] Contrary to Eichberg, who sees the history of running since the nineteenth century as a "one-way street," dominated by an ever-more encompassing emphasis on the "production of results" and the "prevalence of speed," the chase film allows us to catch more recursive counter-imaginaries that preserved the bodily techniques of an earlier moment in running's history, now as a component of screen slapstick's early formation.[25]

A second implication concerns the chase film's place within the historiography of screen comedy. The comic chase can no longer be thought of as a specifically "cinematic" break from one-shot prank comedies derived from vaudeville and the funny papers; rather, it marks a shift in the medium's relation to preexisting cultural series—from single-shot pranks and skits derived from variety acts and comic strips, common as far back as the Lumières' *L'Arroseur arrosé* (1895), to a new style of multi-shot comedy inherited from festive running cultures.[26] Also worth noting is how certain formal peculiarities of early chase comedy are clarified in relation to its premodern precursors. Often noted, for instance, is the chase comedy's somewhat qualified relation to narrative continuity—the way the shots carry little sense of causal consecutiveness or necessity beyond what is given by the spectacle of movement itself—but which makes perfect sense if these films are viewed, formally, not as narratives per se but rather as races or, better yet, as *races with a chase-narrative pretext*. The consensus claim for the chase as a kind of ground zero for filmic narrativity needs, then, to be leavened by the fact that its juxtaposed tableaux have only as much "story" connection as the laps of a race. What may be yet more challenging to this consensus, though, is the fact that the first of Biograph's chase comedies, *The Escaped Lunatic*, was promoted as though it wasn't a narrative film at all, as I next explain.

"Imagining it a comedy scene": *The Escaped Lunatic* and the Pleasures of Indexicality

Aware that Edison's and Lubin's remakes had severely dented *Personal*'s profitability, Biograph's management chose in October 1904 to demote their hit film to a "class B" picture—with a sales price of twelve cents per foot, as opposed to the regular fifteen—and reissue *The Escaped Lunatic* in its place.[27] Commercially understandable, the decision nonetheless had one perplexing wrinkle: the company marketed the reissue as an actuality. To quote the *Biograph Bulletin* of October 10:

> WARNING! A DANGEROUS LUNATIC, who imagines himself to be Emperor Napoleon I, escaped from the Bloomingdale Asylum at 9 o'clock this morning by smashing the iron bars of his cell and leaping to the ground from a third story window. By a miracle he escaped death, and at once started on a mad chase across country, closely pursued by a posse of keepers. [. . .] Fortunately there were a number of Biograph cameras situated about the country in the vicinity of the asylum, and this most astonishing episode was completely covered in moving pictures. The

films are clear, sharp and distinct, and the lunatic's flight is shown in such wonderful realism that every audience which has seen the production has gone into paroxysms of laughter imagining it a comedy scene arranged by actors.[28]

No doubt this is tongue-in-cheek: the final sentence is too obviously a winking betrayal of the conceit. (But not too obvious for everyone, it seems: a writer for the *New York Clipper* was taken in, at least to judge from a brief review in which he paired the film with a genuine Biograph actuality, *At the Foot of the Flatiron* (1903), as two "realistic" pictures playing at Miner's Bowery.)[29] Less obvious, though, is how the *Bulletin*'s writers may also have been making an inside joke referencing the company's concurrent litigation with Edison; for, as we will see, the situation that they here imagined—with cameras fortuitously dispersed "across the country"—closely echoes arguments that were about to have their day in court. Less obvious still is how those arguments imply an etiology for chase comedy that differs radically from the previous section's hypotheses.

To return briefly to the court case: in addition to disputing *Personal*'s originality (the aforementioned comic strip defense), Edison's legal team also sought to query the validity of Biograph's copyright by arguing that only one copyright had been taken to cover what was in fact an "aggregation" of separate "photographs" (i.e., shots). What Biograph's people additionally had to prove, then, was that, despite its several shots, *Personal* should be considered a single entity and could legally be copyrighted as such. They did this by insisting on the continuity of action across shots taken at different locations. As part of his deposition, for instance, Wallace McCutcheon included a document titled "Descriptions of Positions of Camera in Taking Views for Complainant's 'Personal' Photograph," giving precise geographical information on eight separate camera positions and concluding that "These positions were carefully chosen so that, when the impressions were joined in one photograph, *the action would appear continuous and natural*."[30] Biograph's team also contended that the physical relocation of a camera across these various sites should be considered a kind of "camera movement," equivalent, say, to a pan or a tilt: there was, they noted, a basic similarity of method linking a film like Edison's *Kaiser Wilhelm's Yacht Meteor Entering the Water* (1902), which pivots the camera within a single shot to follow the launch, to the mode of production of *Personal*, which shifts the location of the tripod from one position to another. Some months later, on May 6, 1905, Judge Lanning ceded the point, explaining: "I am unable to see why, if a series of pictures of a moving object taken by a pivoted camera may be copyrighted as a photograph, a series of pictures telling a single story like that of the complainant in this case, even though the camera be placed at different points, may not also be copyrighted as a photograph."[31]

Have we found here the cheeky in-joke underlying the *Biograph Bulletin*'s odd claim for the "actuality" of *The Escaped Lunatic*? Both Biograph's publicists (in the promotion of *The Escaped Lunatic*'s reissue) and the company's lawyers (in the legal dispute over *Personal*) imagined filmic continuity in relation to geographic dispersal ("situated about the country" in one case, "placed at different points" in the other). Yet the *Bulletin* absurdly transforms the *temporal sequencing* of camera positions in the case of *Personal* into a *spatial copresence* of fortuitously stationed cameras in the case of *The Escaped Lunatic*. It is as though the *Bulletin*'s copywriter were imagining a situation in which the disputed continuity of a multi-shot action would be entirely unimpeachable: whereas Biograph's argument regarding *Personal* ultimately affirmed continuity as a *filmic* construction ("These positions were carefully chosen so that . . . the action would appear continuous"), the *Bulletin* goes one better to locate continuity on the side of the *profilmic*, that is, in the continuity of a (supposedly) actual event. Indeed, it is on this dichotomy that the conceit of the *Escaped Lunatic*'s publicity turned, toggling between the idea of an "arranged" comedy scene and that of an "astonishing episode" captured on camera and presuming, even in jest, that one might be misrecognized as the other. How could one plausibly deny copyright in the case of a multi-shot film "arranged by actors" if the results were formally indistinguishable from an actuality "covered in motion pictures"?

This is why I have tried to unpack Biograph's perplexing publicity strategies for *The Escaped Lunatic*'s rerelease, because it is in the possibilities and pleasures of that indistinction that an alternate archaeology of the chase film can be proposed—one that seeks understanding not from a "cultural series" approach but rather in terms of the media properties of cinema itself. As I have elsewhere argued, what cinema made uniquely possible—and what no previous medium, not even still photography, could equally sustain—was a new style of comedy based on the conceit of the chance event or funny mishap fortuitously "caught" on camera, many instances of which in fact predate the case at hand.[32] Well before *The Escaped Lunatic*'s rerelease, the conceit had even been the cornerstone of a brief cycle of "What Happened" films, whose pretense was that of a camera having recorded a chance moment to which the viewer becomes privy: *What Happened When a Hot Picture Was Taken* (Biograph, 1898), *What Happened to a Fresh Johnnie* (Biograph, 1900), *What Happened on Twenty-third Street, New York City* (1901), *What Happened in the Tunnel* (Edison, 1903), *What Happened to the Milkman* (Lubin, 1903), and many others. Edison's single-shot *What Happened on Twenty-third Street* is the best known: formally indistinguishable from a straight actuality, the film depicts a man and woman (actors A. C. Abadie and Florence Georgie) walking side by side down the street, whereupon a gust of air from a sidewalk grate lifts the woman's skirt.[33] Despite the claims often made for chase comedy's primacy as the first "cinematic" comedy genre, it is surely here, in the earlier "What Happened" cycle, that we see the initial stirrings of what cinema could uniquely provide to the history of comedy—not just single-shot prank films or canned vaudeville skits but a new cultural paradigm for the production of laughter whose condition of possibility was the ontology of the medium itself. This is comedy, to be sure, but a comedy whose conceit is *not to be a comedy*, to have us imagine that we are witnessing something that simply happened, preserved through the chance presence of a camera.

Viewed in comparison, Biograph's *The Escaped Lunatic* is a far less convincing play on this pretense. The fifteen-shot extravaganza does little to hide its own construction, be it in the obvious use of a set in the film's opening shot, in which the titular lunatic, dressed as Napoleon, paces in his cell, attacks a guard, pries apart his window bars, and leaps out; or in the use of a dummy in the film's subsequent shot, when the lunatic is shown falling from the asylum's third story; or, finally, in *The Escaped Lunatic*'s concluding "coup de cinéma," wherein the fugitive arrives back at the asylum and, impossibly, leaps up to his third-story window (reversing the footage of the original dummy fall). Yet, for all that, we are not quite done with contingency; for, above and beyond the imagined situation of this film's making, the pleasures of chase comedy remain under the sway of a more basic ontology of the film image, what Mary Ann Doane describes as cinema's "unprecedented alliance between representation and unpredictability."[34] The oft-cited reaction of those early spectators who celebrated the breeze randomly rustling the leaves in the trees in the first Lumière films or the pounding of the surf in Birt Acres' *Rough Sea at Dover* (1895) is not too distant from a mode of attention attuned to the "cloud of flying petticoats" of *Personal*. Nor is it far removed from the comic pleasure offered by *The Escaped Lunatic*'s "literally loco" madman, as Jonathan Auerbach calls him, who pursues a bewildering variety of haphazard, back-and-forth trajectories through each frame in the eleven-shot chase (even, at one point, sticking his tongue out at the camera as he runs past).[35] Whereas the runners of *Personal* follow a more or less regular path from distance to foreground, with each character dutifully exiting the frame one after another, the protagonists of *The Escaped Lunatic* tumble their way through a panoply of never-the-same trajectories that keep the entirety of each shot in play as a potential zone of unsystematic motility: the madman runs down a hill to foreground left, but then doubles back to sprint away from the camera (shot three; figure 10.4a), or races out of the frame foreground left, but then circles round to reappear and run off foreground right (shot six; figure 10.4b), or enters in the foreground to find his way blocked by a cliff, which he then daringly ascends (shot eight; figure 10.4c), etc., all the while with the guards struggling to keep abreast of his higgledy-piggledy flight. One way to think about the chase genre, accordingly, is as a formula for producing comically unpredictable variations in the runners' traversals of space (the way in which, for example, one pursuer will leap over an obstacle like a fence, another will crawl under it, another will fall down climbing it, etc.). It is, if you will, a system for producing the unsystematic, a regularity that produces irregularity. Like the "What Happened" cycle that preceded it, it harnesses the medium's receptivity to chance events and converts it into the basis of a comedic genre.

But at this point we seem to have happened upon a détente between the two historiographic models discussed in the introduction. Should chase comedies be viewed from a cultural series perspective that would contain their apparent novelty within the continuity of preexisting cultural practices (here, the village fair tradition of the smock race and other forms of festive running)? Or are they to be comprehended from the vantage point of media archaeology, as testimony to the discontinuities and differences that media forms make in cultural construction (here, in a mode of viewing bound to the contingency of the indexical image)? The foregoing discussion allows us to perceive more clearly why this is a false dichotomy. The fact that any new medium takes shape amid a context of cultural practices by which it is informed hardly obviates the possibility that the medium may also introduce "media-epistemological" differences *within* that context.[36] The former is given in chase comedy's continuity with premodern

FIGURE 10.4 Frame grabs from *The Escaped Lunatic* (1904), with arrows depicting the lunatic's trajectory through three shots of the chase sequence. Courtesy Library of Congress.

traditions of festive running, the latter in the way the chase film exploits the moving image's ontological relation to happenstance. How early filmmakers subsequently innovated new representational schemes around this dialectic would be augured in Biograph's third chase comedy from 1904, *The Lost Child*.

"As ludicrous a situation as anyone could imagine": *The Lost Child* and the Codification of the Chase Genre

"ANOTHER GREAT COMEDY CHASE by the Originators of 'Personal' and 'The Escaped Lunatic' BRIGHTER, FUNNIER AND BETTER THAN THE OTHERS."[37] So claimed Biograph publicity for *The Lost Child*, the third in the studio's chase comedy trifecta that year. Yet behind these unsurprising superlatives, the publicity contained a handful of indications that things were, indeed, different this time around. First, the marketing of the film, much like that of *The Escaped Lunatic*, again asserted a basis in actuality, only this time not as fortuitous *recording* but as *reenactment*. "The story of THE

LOST CHILD," it was claimed, "is founded on a recent happening in Brooklyn. A youngster crawled under a porch and went to sleep. The mother missing it immediately set up a cry of 'Kidnappers,' and soon the whole neighborhood was wild with excitement"—a situation of which Biograph's filmmakers had apparently seen the funny side.[38] Second, on at least two counts, the ensuing plot synopsis hints at a connection with preexisting forms of cultural representation. One of these is melodrama, here invoked ironically in a description of the film's inciting incident.

> The mother [. . .] frantically rushes about the yard searching for the child. It is nowhere to be seen. She hurries out to the street, and there at her very gate is a mysterious man putting something into a large basket. It is the kidnapper, of course! The woman does not hesitate an instant, but assaults him with all the fury of a desperate mother. The astonished man succeeds in breaking away before he is totally demolished, and thinking that the woman is crazy, starts off on a dead run.[39]

A drama of infant kidnapping and maternal struggle is here described in ironic fashion, in recognition of the fact that the moral stakes of melodrama do not actually apply. We know what the woman does not: that the lost child is simply asleep in a dog kennel; that the "kidnapper" is just a passerby; and that the "desperate mother" is, in consequence, acting like a crazy person. The other representational system is that of comedy: in place of *Personal*'s relatively anonymous "cloud of flying petticoats," the pursuers of *The Lost Child* are described according to a more differentiated codification of comic types and stereotypes familiar from comic strips and the variety stage.

> The mother pursues [the suspect] hot-foot. She is joined in the hue and cry by her colored cook and Irish washerwoman. [. . .] Around the corner is a policeman chatting with a nursemaid. A crusty gentleman is being wheeled up and down in an invalid's chair, and a couple of girls are strolling along chatting gaily. The chase bursts into this group full tilt, and everyone joins in, even the old gentleman in the chair. [. . .] Next we see the supposed kidnapper speeding down a country road with the pack in full cry, augmented this time by a dago pushing a junk cart and a one-legged boy hopping along on crutches.[40]

Taken together, these points complete chase comedy's conscription to the emerging conventions of a genre: *The Lost Child* is a *reenactment*, it plays ironic games with *melodrama*, it draws on a familiar repertoire of *comedic* stereotypes. It is self-consciously a representation (in a way that *The Escaped Lunatic* pretended not to be), and, as such, has entered into a system of codifying references to other media representations of the period.

But this codification has a dual effect. On the one hand, it anchors the film's status as comedy by reference to a then-familiar legacy of comedic representation (in this case, parody melodrama and racial/ethnic stereotyping, both common frameworks of turn-of-the-century comicality). On the other hand, the film thereby adds *itself* to that legacy, securing its own innovations as frameworks for subsequent comedic development and imitation, here on at least two counts. The first, evident in the last block quote, is the principle of accretion: the *Lost Child*'s chase *grows*. Passersby, caught in the path of the pursuit, become pursuers in turn—a principle that would come to inform chase comedy on both sides of the Atlantic and that structures the two films often held up as pinnacles of the genre's early development, Pathé's *Le Cheval emballé* (1907) and its quasi-remake by D. W. Griffith, *The Curtain Pole* (1908).[41] The second concerns the role of character mistake as, simultaneously, a plot device and a springboard for intertextual play: a misapprehension of danger not only gets the chase started but also turns the ensuing action into a kind of comedic anti-melodrama. In this, the film looks forward further still, to the terms of chase comedy's revitalization almost a decade later in Sennett's more overtly polemic parodies of Griffithian race-to-the-rescue melodrama, first at Biograph itself, where Sennett headed the comedy unit from 1911, and then, after 1912, at his newly formed Keystone Film Company.[42] In Sennett's 1912 Biograph film *Help! Help!*, a suburban housewife misperceives rustling behind the drapes as evidence of a home break-in, prompting a parallel-edited race to the rescue that uncovers no threat, just a dog playing behind a curtain. In Keystone's *Bangville Police* (1913), directed by Henry Lehrman, a simple country girl mishears a conversation between two farmhands and, mistakenly believing they intend to rob her, barricades herself inside a farmhouse and calls the police: another parallel-edited climax ensues. In *Hide and Seek* (1913)—the Keystone film that comes closest to the plot of *The Lost Child*—office workers mistakenly believe that a child is trapped in a time-locked vault and call the police. Interspersed among subsequent scenes of speeding police trucks, the director, George Nichols, inserts a series of shots that reveal to the audience what none of the characters know: that the little girl has simply wandered off to a nearby playground. Although the revelation of character error is usually withheld in these films until the climax (*Hide and Seek* being a notable exception), it has the same effect of *The Lost Child* in reframing melodramatic iconography as comedic typology: from the perspective of the films' respective conclusions, the country maid of *The Bangville Police* seems more a dimwitted rube than an embodiment of female sanctity, and the suburban wife of *Help! Help!* more a gibbering paranoiac than the "Angel in the House" of sentimental cliché.

The Lost Child is, in all these ways, the visible anticipation of chase comedy's future; it encloses the form's basic indexical pleasures within comedic systems that predict not only Griffith and Sennett but even the relation between the two.[43] A world of difference, after all, separates the decision to film nine women climbing over a fence (in *Personal*) from the comedic intent that, in *The Lost Child*, sends a nursemaid pushing a stroller, a one-legged boy on crutches, an immigrant with a junk cart, and a man in a wheelchair racing down a riverside bluff (a shot described in the *Bulletin* as depicting "as ludicrous a situation as anyone could imagine")—the difference being that which separates the discovery of comic possibilities from their comedic systematization.[44] It can hardly be a coincidence, then, that it was around the point of *The Lost Child*'s release that the chase film really began to effloresce as a comedic genre and that many subsequent entries would contain explicit or tacit reference to the Biograph cycle of 1904. Edison's rip-off of *Personal* would be followed by yet further unacknowledged remakes on that company's part: Porter completed *Maniac Chase*, a version of *The Escaped Lunatic*, in October, and *Stolen by Gypsies*, his remake of *The Lost Child*, in July 1905. Biograph, meanwhile, repeatedly touted subsequent chase comedies as continuations of a studio legacy, as when *Wanted—A Nurse* (1906) was advertised as "A New 'Personal' by the Originators of the Original 'Personal,'" or when *Wanted—A Dog* (1905) was promoted as "Another Exciting and Laughable Chase by the Originators of 'The Escaped Lunatic,' 'The Lost Child,' 'Personal,' etc." (the latter film even tips its hat to *The Escaped Lunatic* by having its fleeing protagonist escape into an asylum).[45] The aporia confronted by Edison's lawyers in searching for a source text for *Personal* is unimaginable as a response to any of the chase comedies produced in the months that followed, so openly do they build upon a snowballing repository of tropes and conventions. It had taken Biograph just three films to transform what was once sold as faux-actuality into a semiotic hall of mirrors.

***

Perhaps we might give that transformation some conceptual traction by reference to what I have elsewhere dubbed "comedification."[46] The term should not be confused with Arpal Szalkolczai's similar "commedification," whose double "m" riffs on *commodification* and which describes the way in which comedy today saturates the late-capitalist public sphere.[47] Rather, comedification names one possible trajectory in the formation of moving-image comedy genres. It describes the process whereby moving-image media's indexical ontology gets converted into the basis for new forms and cycles of comedy. We see it at work not only in cinema's early years (e.g., in the way the "What Happened" cycle leveraged indexicality as the pretext for staged comic vignettes that replicated the form of early actualities) but throughout the history of moving-image media (e.g., in the way the burgeoning genre of reality TV shows since the millennium inspired a wave of "comedy verité" sitcoms like *The Office* [UK, 2001–2003; US, 2005–2013] and *Parks and Recreation* [2009–2015] that mimicked the format of the television "docusoap").[48] In each instance, the pleasure of witnessing some chance mishap or misbehavior caught on camera suggests the possibility of a new style of comedy that deliberately produces or imitates that pleasure. Comedification in this sense names the process whereby indexicality gets harnessed to the representational goals of comedy, or where media ontology suggests comedy.

This essay has reverse-engineered that dynamic out of the case study of the chase film. It has argued that chase comedy coalesced from the intersection of a premodern cultural practice (festive running) and a modern technology (cinema), each of which shared a basis in happenstance, the former as carnival pleasure, the latter as material ontology.

It has also shown how the form's emergent tropes (the rule of accretion, the typology of pursuers, etc.) subsequently worked to further comedify the form, converting indexical representation into ever more intensive and proliferating schemes for the production of mirth-inducing accident. No attempt to unpack that logic can afford to subscribe to the kind of methodological dogmatism that today separates a "media archaeological" emphasis on media *effects* from a "cultural series" focus on mediated *content*: the former wants to treat cinematic representation in terms of the medium's ontological receptivity to uncodified variability and chance; the latter in terms of the codifications and conventions of pre-existing representational forms and cultural practices. But what happens when, as in chase comedy, the indexical effects of the medium both comport with the pleasures of an existing practice (such as festive running) *and* constitute the bedrock of the representational conventions that subsequently unfold? It is at this vanishing point between indexicality and genre, between contingency and formula, that the conditions of comedification are met.

But we need not end on a merely theoretical corrective. For the foregoing has also given us a vantage point from which to appreciate the long-forgotten stature that Wallace McCutcheon briefly enjoyed as a founder of narrative filmmaking. Long before similar claims were made on behalf of D. W. Griffith, McCutcheon was once described in the trade press as "the father of the story film, both comic and pathetic," with reference "principally to such films as 'Personal,' 'The Lost Child,' 'The Chicken Thief' [December 1904], 'Moonshiners' [July 1904]."[49] A few years later, in the wake of Griffith's ascendancy, former Biograph production head Frank Marion penned an open letter to ensure that McCutcheon's stature would not be obscured by the Promethean claims made on Griffith's behalf (usually by Griffith himself). "Without detracting one whit from Mr. Griffith's genius," the 1914 letter proclaimed, "[I submit that] he should instead acknowledge his great indebtedness to Biograph traditions. . . . And in acknowledging what Mr. Griffith has done in a dramatic way, let us not forget the man who made the first dramatic moving picture in America, Mr. Wallace McCutcheon."[50]

I do not mean to end here by reshuffling "firsts," nor, as suggested earlier, do I think that the chase film is usefully framed as a wellspring of film narrative. But perhaps we might read these comments against the grain somewhat, not to reclaim McCutcheon as the "father of the story film" exactly but at least to recover the significance of his films to the broader unfolding of cinema's aesthetic constitution during these years. "Time was when a chase, a fall into water, the upsetting of wagons and pushcarts, the stumbling over sticks and fences, made up a very considerable portion of the funny moving picture," wrote one critic in 1908, looking back on the cycle of chase films that Biograph's innovations had inspired.[51] In transmuting stumbles into system, indexicality into codification, McCutcheon's chase comedy trifecta of 1904 had done more than merely establish a genre; it had established that genre at the heart of a tension that would define both the medium and the methodologies applied to it.

Notes

1. Wolfgang Ernst, "Let There Be Irony: Cultural History and Media Archaeology in Parallel Lines," in *Digital Memory and the Archive* (Minneapolis: University of Minnesota Press, 2013), 42.
2. André Gaudreault, *Film and Attraction: From Kinematography to Cinema*, trans. Timothy Barnard (Urbana: University of Illinois Press, 2011), 67.
3. Ibid., 65.
4. More than that, a case can be made that the so-called revisionist interest in early film, dating back to the famed FIAF conference in Brighton in 1978, was in a sense media archaeological *avant la lettre*, spawning a body of work that anticipated the themes of later German media studies by emphasizing early cinema's role in provoking mutations in cultural discourse and experience. See the introduction to this volume.
5. I am paraphrasing Raymond Williams: "While we have to reject technological determinism, in all its forms, we must be careful not to substitute for it the notion of a determined technology." Raymond Williams, *Television: Technology and Cultural Form* (London: Fontana, 1975), 133.
6. Ibid. (emphasis added).
7. Tom Gunning, "The Cinema of Attractions: Early Film, Its Spectator, and the Avant-Garde," in Thomas Elsaesser and Adam Barker, eds., *Early Cinema: Space, Frame, Narrative* (London: BFI, 1990), 60; Charles Musser, *The Emergence of Cinema: The American Screen to 1907* (Berkeley: University of California Press, 1994), 375.
8. This excludes the ten-shot *The Chicken Thief* (December 1904), which includes chase elements in its second half— the five-shot pursuit of two African American chicken thieves by a white farmer and his son—but hybridizes them with other generic appeals, including an earlier three-minute comic scene of "A Chicken Dinner" in a cabin and a subsequent two-minute scene of black dancing.
9. *Biograph Bulletin* 28, August 15, 1904, in Kemp Niver, *Biograph Bulletins, 1896–1906* (Los Angeles, CA: Locare Research Group, 1971), 121; *Edison Films Supplement*, September 1904, 11, Box 66, Legal Department Records, Edison National Historic Site Archives (hereafter ENHSA).
10. The opening of Richard Lester's Beatles film *A Hard Day's Night* (1964) is part of this lineage too.
11. Rebuttal affidavit of Frank Marion, December 17, 1904, Box 66, Legal Department Records, ENHSA.
12. Ibid.
13. Delos Holden to Henry Romeike, November 25, 1904, Box 66, Legal Department Records, ENHSA.
14. Horace Thurlow to Delos Holden, November 29, 1904, Box 66, Legal Department Records, ENHSA.
15. "About Plays, Players, and Playhouses," *Omaha Illustrated Bee*, January 29, 1905, 2; *Biograph Bulletin* 42, March 15, 1905, in Niver, *Biograph Bulletins*, 149. Information on cross-country racing is taken from Edward S. Sears, *Running through the Ages*, 2nd ed. (Jefferson, NC: McFarland, 2015), 110–112.
16. *Biograph Bulletin* 42, March 15, 1905, in Niver, *Biograph Bulletins*, 150.

17. Montague Shearman, *Athletics and Football* (London: Longmans, Green, 1887), 29–30.
18. Henning Eichberg, *Body Cultures: Essays on Sport, Space, and Identity*, ed. John Bale and Chris Philo (New York: Routledge, 1998), 30.
19. Joseph Strutt, *The Sports and Pastimes of the People of England*, new edition expanded and corrected by J. Charles Cox (London: Methuen, 1903 [1801]), 293. For more on smock races, see Peter Radford, "Women's Foot-Races in the Eighteenth and Nineteenth Centuries," *Canadian Journal of History of Sport* 25, no. 1 (1994): 50–61.
20. Mary Ann Doane, *The Emergence of Cinematic Time: Modernity, Contingency, the Archive* (Cambridge, MA: Harvard University Press, 2002), 192.
21. *Forest Republican*, June 28, 1876, n.p.
22. Radford, "Women's Foot-Races," 57.
23. Although there is little consensus on the term, the concept of "cultural techniques" seeks to capture the material artifacts and human practices that shape the symbolic distinctions orchestrating culture. See in particular Bernard Siegert, *Cultural Techniques: Grids, Filters, Doors, and Other Articulations of the Real*, trans. Geoffrey Winthrop-Young (New York: Fordham University Press, 2015).
24. The notion of "Fordist running" is John Bale's, from *Running Cultures: Racing in Time and Space* (New York: Routledge, 2004), 71.
25. Eichberg quoted in Bale, *Running Cultures*, 21.
26. The principle of multi-shot extension would subsequently fuse with its single-shot counterpart to produce what Tom Gunning has called "linked vignette" comedies that repeat a gag serially across discrete spaces, as in the Edison Company's 1907 *Laughing Gas* or Essanay's 1908 *Mr. Flip*. See Gunning, *D. W. Griffith and the Origins of American Narrative Film: The Early Years at Biograph* (Urbana: University of Illinois Press, 1992), 67–68.
27. Letter to exhibitors, October 4, 1904, in Niver, *Biograph Bulletins*, 130.
28. *Biograph Bulletin* 33, October 10, 1904, in Niver, *Biograph Bulletins*, 132.
29. *New York Clipper*, October 22, 1904, 812.
30. Rebuttal affidavit of Wallace McCutcheon, December 17, 1904, Box 66, Legal Department Records, ENHSA (emphasis added).
31. Lanning quoted in André Gaudreault, "The Infringement of Copyright Laws and Its Effects (1900–1906)," in Elsaesser and Barker, eds., *Early Cinema*, 120. Lanning thus affirmed Biograph's claim to copyright, although he would ultimately conclude the case in Edison's favor, arguing that the framings and locations in *How a French Nobleman* were sufficiently different that Porter could be said to have "worked out [the plaintiff's idea] in a different way." Lanning quoted in Peter Decherney, *Hollywood's Copyright Wars: From Edison to the Internet* (New York: Columbia University Press, 2012), 66.
32. Rob King, "Laughter in an Ungoverned Sphere: Actuality Humor in Early Cinema and Web 2.0," in Paul Flaig and Katherine Groo, eds., *New Silent Cinema* (New York: Routledge, 2015), 294–313.
33. *What Happened on Twenty-third Street* has received the attention of early film scholars for a variety of reasons. Judith Mayne, for instance, reads the film as moving toward a narrativization of the female body as erotic display. Tom Gunning sees it as exemplifying the temporality of the cinema of attractions. For Mary Ann Doane, closest to my position, the film stands for the tension between representational meaning and contingency in early film. See Mayne, *The Woman at the Keyhole: Feminism and Woman's Cinema* (Bloomington: Indiana University Press, 1990), 162–164; Gunning, "'Now You See It, Now

You Don't': The Temporality of the Cinema of Attractions," *Velvet Light Trap* 32 (Fall 1993): 8–9; and Doane, *Emergence of Cinematic Time*, 181–183.
34. Doane, *Emergence of Cinematic Time*, 180.
35. Jonathan Auerbach, "Chasing Film Narrative: Repetition, Recusion, and the Body in Early Cinema," *Critical Inquiry* 26, no. 4 (Summer 2000): 808.
36. Ernst, "Let There Be Irony," 49.
37. *Biograph Bulletin* 36, October 26, 1904, in Niver, *Biograph Bulletins*, 134.
38. Ibid., 135.
39. Ibid.
40. Ibid.
41. Griffith apparently made the latter film on the prompting of Mack Sennett and Billy Bitzer, who had seen the former. On the principle of accretion in chase comedy, see Charlie Keil, *Early American Cinema in Transition: Story, Style, and Filmmaking, 1907–1913* (Madison: University of Wisconsin Press, 2001), 48. The principle became familiar enough to inspire critical mockery at the time, as evident in this tongue-in-cheek 1907 description of the typical chase film: "A man does something he ought not to do. Then a mob gets after him and chases him across about twenty-seven miles of very rough country. He falls down mountains, swims rivers, but the mob is relentless and grows bigger all the time. At last the offender is caught and gets his face punched. That is all." "Trade Notes," *Moving Picture World*, September 7, 1907, 422.
42. For more on Sennett's use of burlesque melodrama, see my *The Fun Factory: The Keystone Film Company and the Emergence of Mass Culture* (Berkeley: University of California Press, 2009), 52–63; and Simon Joyce, "Genre Parody and Comedic Burlesque: Keystone's Meta-Cinematic Satires," in Tom Paulus and Rob King, eds., *Slapstick Comedy* (New York: Routledge, 2010), 49–66.
43. It is further worth noting that Sennett used the working title "The Lost Child" for one of the very earliest of his films to include the "cop chase" finales that would become his hallmark, *The Temperamental Husband* (1912).
44. *Biograph Bulletin* 36, October 26, 1904, in Niver, *Biograph Bulletins*, 134. The shot in question contains an unplanned camera pan when the man in the wheelchair careens off frame right and tips over.
45. *Biograph Bulletin* 44, April 17, 1905, in Niver, *Biograph Bulletins*, 155; *Biograph Bulletin* 83, September 29, 1906, in Niver, *Biograph Bulletins*, 264. Samantha Holland mentions these ads in her essay, "The Thrill of the 'Chase Film': Women, Fairies, and Narrativization in *Jack the Kisser*," *Early Popular Visual Culture* 8, no. 2 (May 2010): 171.
46. King, "Laughter in an Ungoverned Sphere," 301–304.
47. Arpad Szakolczai, *Comedy and the Public Sphere: The Rebirth of Theatre as Comedy and the Genealogy of the Modern Public Arena* (New York: Routledge, 2013).
48. See Brett Mills, "Comedy Verité: Contemporary Sitcom Form," *Screen* 45, no. 1 (2004): 63–78.
49. "News of the Nickolets," *Moving Picture World*, October 12, 1907, 502. On *The Chicken Thief*, see above note 8. A Kentucky-set drama, *The Moonshiners* was part of Biograph's shift to the regular production of one-reel story films in 1904.
50. "Marion Digs Up Some Facts," *Moving Picture World*, September 5, 1914, 1356.
51. W. Stephen Bush, "The Place and Province of Humor in the Moving Picture," *Moving Picture World*, November 28, 1908, 420.

CHAPTER 11

STORIED SPACES

Staging and Editing in Early American Feature Films

MIRIAM SIEGEL

EARLY features occupy an uncertain position in histories of American cinema's transitional era, a term usually taken to refer to the ten-year stretch from around 1907 to 1917, superseding the "attractions" period but prior to the consolidation of classical cinema. Arguing that the transitional period both presented filmmakers with a particular set of challenges and shaped the kinds of solutions they devised, Charlie Keil links the era's distinctiveness first to the industry's adoption of the single-reel narrative film as its principal product. Between 1907 and 1913, he contends, the attempt to tell complex yet comprehensible stories within the limits of the thousand-foot reel spurred filmmakers to experiment with a diverse range of narrational and stylistic conventions. These formal options would only begin to narrow into classicism's limited paradigm of devices in and beyond the transitional era's final years, during which the industry's primary commodity shifted from the one-reel film to the multiple-reel feature. As Keil admits, the question of how to account for the films produced in the four years between 1913 and 1917, between the rise of the feature and the consolidation of classical film language, therefore remains an open one. Yet this tendency for early features to fall outside of any easy classification is not simply due to the fact that their lengthier running times "posed new problems" that demanded new solutions.[1] Rather, because filmmakers continued to experiment with techniques for achieving fundamental representational goals, the storytelling and stylistic strategies they called on in response to these challenges also did not develop in lockstep toward the codification of classical principles. Most notably, the appeal to theater and the novel for models of story construction may well have caused early features to resemble their classical successors on the level of narrative structure; however, filmmakers' ongoing efforts to marshal the representation of space to the task of telling engaging, understandable stories did not always produce a similar affinity on the level of the shot, scene, or sequence.[2]

This task was by no means unique to the years immediately following the transitional era. During the single-reel period, the introduction of new kinds of story material, and the new approaches to cinematic narration that material occasioned, required a fundamental reconceptualization of the relationship between space and story. Early cinema's dedication to spatial unity tended to subordinate the latter to the former. By treating the shot as an integral, homogeneous block of space in which an action simply plays out in front of a similarly singular point of view, narrative events were forced to conform to the area contained by the frame.[3] This approach could allow for the division of the image into narratively significant segments through scenery and props to aid in delivering the brief comic episodes and dramatic vignettes that characterize early cinema.[4] Yet it proved increasingly untenable once filmmakers turned to stories of greater complexity. Narratives founded on a chain of causally connected events driven by the actions of ever more individuated characters required prioritizing unity of action over unity of space. The often anonymous locales of early cinema similarly had to be transformed into multiple, individuated settings tailored to the demands of those events. Cinematic space, that is, had to become narrative space, the shape of which is precisely determined by such demands. It had to become space designed to serve the purposes of narrative, not the other way around.

While the subordination of space to narrational demands typical of classicism may have been the ultimate goal of the formal experimentation during the transitional period, different narrative material made different demands on cinema's storytelling resources. As Keil details, the collective pursuit of goals like "maintaining narrative legibility, and clarifying spatial and temporal relations" did not lead to a single set of strategies: techniques developed to accommodate genres with extensive exterior shooting or fast-paced action, like the western, would simply not serve for the interior spaces and intimate action of domestic dramas.[5] For Keil, however, the transitional period nonetheless was marked by a general shift toward editing as the preferred means of shaping space to narrative ends. Because cutting carries a threat of spatial disorientation and narrative disruption, he notes that filmmakers also produced a host of related spatial strategies that drew on staging, figure placement, and other aspects of mise-en-scène. But as means of mitigating that threat, these strategies seem to serve a supporting role; rather than potential formal resources in their own right, they are the by-product of the development of such cornerstones of the nascent continuity system as shot/reverse-shot, eyeline matches, and intrascene cutting. If the use of these editing figures suggests a step toward the systematization of classicism, Keil is nonetheless careful to note that because transitional-era filmmakers viewed such devices as "innovations to be tested" alongside others, they had yet to achieve the "codified employment" that signals the advent of a fully realized classical cinema.[6] This systematization of favored techniques for the representation of space, he argues, would only take place after 1913, as the experimental ethos that characterizes the period of transition gives way to a "process of honing and refining elements of style" that will find more consistent use under classicism's "deliberately fragmented yet analytically cohesive mode of representation."[7]

Early features certainly display an increasing awareness of the utility of editing as a means of recruiting space to the task of telling stories across five or more reels. The development of cutting as a key formal and narrational resource can therefore hardly be in dispute. Yet to treat these films as an arena for the perfecting of classical principles downplays the continued experimentation with different approaches to the construction of space after 1913. Like the introduction of the single reel, the shift to feature-length narratives necessitated a radical departure from established practices, inviting a wide range of overlapping, occasionally contradictory, but rarely mutually exclusive solutions. An examination of five early features—*Traffic in Souls* (1913), *Tess of the Storm Country* (1914), *The Wishing Ring* (1914), *Joseph in the Land of Egypt* (1914), and *A Fool There Was* (1915)—reveals that filmmakers had yet to establish a preferred set of formal strategies for marshalling space to the service of creating comprehensible and compelling narratives from this array of representational options.[8] As these five features demonstrate, filmmakers instead drew from the full range of available techniques for the narrativization of space in the period. In addition to the possibilities of the cut, they also called on figure placement and depth staging to achieve basic storytelling goals in response to both the greater complexity of story material required to sustain feature narratives and to the proliferation of spaces these stories often entailed.

Far from either relying on staging alone or simply developing toward classical continuity, that is, the five features under examination here continue to work through and redefine the narrational possibilities of both approaches. Core classical values of "organicism, verisimilitude, and self-effacement" may have driven the attempt to arbitrate between different solutions to representational problems both during and after the transitional era.[9] Even so, the representation of space in all five films reveals that achieving these values did not involve a straightforward progression toward a unified set of stylistic devices and spatial logics. Some of the formal practices these films employ suggest an investment in the type of editing figures that would become typical of classicism's creation of multi-shot, syncretic spaces designed to offer the spectator the best view of the unfolding action. Others, however, demonstrate a renewed interest in the narrational potential of scenes enacted in a succession of unified spaces that recalls the spatial strategies of early cinema; at the same time they equally evince a dedication to carefully guiding the viewer's attention in line with classicism's signal goal of ensuring narrative clarity. As a result, they caution us to conceive of the relationship between storytelling and space less in terms of particular techniques as indicative of specified narrational logics than as a dynamic interplay between stylistic resources and narrational goals.

We cannot simply plot the five features on any historical progression from an early cinema, dedicated to the unity of space, to a classical mode, in which filmic space becomes fully tailored to the demands of narration through extended fragmentation. Such an approach is vitiated by the films' tendency to oscillate between enlisting staging and editing to achieve similar narrational tasks. The essential objective of "cueing and guiding [the viewer] to construct a story out of what is presented on the screen" tends to be achieved by both editing and staging, with all five films employing a range of strategies for directing the viewer's attention.[10] While *The Wishing Ring* relies the most on intrascene cutting, it also employs minimally edited scenes and shots of extended duration in which depth staging, figure placement, and performance allow narrative action to unfold in front of a static camera. *A Fool There Was* similarly opts for both closely framed views knitted together through editing and relatively wide shot scales that keep the camera at a distance from the action, relying on performance, staging, and lighting to guide the viewer. *Traffic in Souls* juggles innumerable interior and exterior spaces, often cutting between different actions taking place in different locations; yet it tends to eschew the type of analytical dissection of space employed by *The Wishing Ring*, preferring to take up a single viewpoint on each space. *Tess* shares the resultant emphatic frontality, often staging scenes in tableaux-like arrangements of figures. Yet the film also relies on cut-ins to closer framings and cross-cutting to capture characters' expressions or depict simultaneous action. *Joseph* displays a similar penchant for switching from forcing characters into the foreground to ensure their actions remain clearly visible to cutting in to closer framings. In all five films, that is, editing and staging often serve as functional equivalents; the arrangement of space for narrative clarity between shots works in concert with centering, figure movement, and compositional balance within shots to guide the viewer's eye and to ensure clarity.

We can attribute this amalgam of formal options to multiple factors. In addition to developing new techniques, filmmakers also refined existing compositional strategies as they sought for solutions to the persistent problem of ensuring narrative clarity. Since, as David Bordwell argues, the "most obvious way to highlight a piece of information is to put it smack in the middle of the picture format," centering the primary object of interest became a common means of organizing the image for intelligibility in many fiction films before 1908.[11] All five films often continue to let the center of the image carry the most salient information while arranging characters or elements of décor to ensure that the frame as a whole remains balanced. In some instances, centering helps mitigate the potentially disorienting effects of editing, since the viewer's attention can remain fixed on a single area, reducing the need to scan the image after a cut.

In the process of guiding the viewer's eye, however, centering and decentering a series of actions performed in a single shot can also serve to emphasize shifts in the dramatic trajectory of the narrative. When the squatters in *Tess* return home after framing the heroine's father for murder, for example, the action is played out in a series of lateral arrangements. By employing a tight choreography of bodies around a central axis, the film not only ensures that Tess remains the center of interest but also ties shifts in compositional balance to key narrative moments. Before the squatters enter, Tess is seated in bed in the background at left in front of a large, dark headboard that is balanced on the right by the similarly dark entry to the kitchen behind the squatter mother. This arrangement of figures leaves a small slot of space in the center of the room. When the door opens in the foreground at left, Tess rises and moves forward to look for her father among the returned men; two of them remain by the door while the other walks to the right side of the frame, once again leaving the center of the foreground open. Realizing her father is absent, Tess moves back to the right to speak to the squatters, creating a balanced arrangement of bodies on each side of the frame, with Tess blocking the camera's view of the mother in the middle-ground. When Tess moves back to the left to speak to the other two squatters, the mother is revealed, so that the characters are distributed symmetrically across the frame with two figures on each side delineating a central zone for Tess to occupy.

As Tess is told of her father's arrest, the mother comes forward to stand beside the heroine, lining up all five characters in the same foreground plane. The perfect lateral arrangement of bodies that results creates a moment of compositional stillness that underscores the dramatic turning point of the scene: Tess hopefully assumes that the squatters on the left will assist her but is quickly rebuffed. Their dismissal immediately unsettles the composition, as Tess's attempt to plead for the rightward squatter's help forces her out of the center of the image. The mother takes up Tess's position to redress the compositional imbalance, but she gazes intently at Tess to ensure her newly established pictorial centrality is not confused for narrative saliency. The other characters generally remain stationary for the rest of the scene—save for coming to the heroine's aid when she momentarily falls to the floor in desperation—and Tess retains her position on the right. As a result, the image never regains its strict lateral balancing of figures with the heroine situated at the geometric center. The kitchen door, however, serves to frame Tess's actions, and this, along with her broad gesticulations (which stand in stark contrast to the other characters' relative stillness) helps to keep the viewer focused on her. When Tess finally storms out of the house, pausing for a moment to castigate her fellow squatters, movement, décor, and performance again fix attention on her, even as the mother takes up the central position in the frame, serving to rebalance the shot.

As this careful arrangement of bodies suggests, the representation of space is often driven by the need to capture character actions and reactions in keeping with the nomination of both as the prime motor of the narrative's causal chain. In pursuit of more unified stories, filmmakers built on existing approaches to characterization in order to individuate characters as distinct narrative agents in much the same way that they augmented existing spatial strategies to individuate the spaces these characters occupied as distinct settings for narrative action. Because character actions served as the basic building blocks of transitional-era stories, however, ensuring that they were easily legible remained the chief representational concern.[12] All five films therefore supplement the type of lateral arrangement of bodies and compositional centering employed by *Tess* with strategies that make use of the full depth of the image. Figures may be stacked up in multiple layers or the action staged diagonally so that characters can be brought forward to indicate their importance or to keep their actions in view.

As a result, key causal material is often delivered using foreground staging. For example, early in *A Fool There Was*, the film employs a combination of foreground staging and inserts to deliver necessary story information as Mr. Schuyler arrives at his office to begin the day's work. Like the two-wall sets that became prominent with closer camera set-ups in the late aughts,[13] the office is composed of a single ninety-degree junction. The camera frames the space obliquely so that it seems to point into the corner at rear-left and thus at the door situated on the far end of the short wall. At the beginning of the scene, Mr. Schuyler's secretary is situated at the far right of the frame in a *plan-américain* next to his boss's desk which juts out toward the viewer (see figure 11.1a). The secretary's proximity to the camera allows the viewer to clearly see him rifling with the mail; these messages will soon serve as the center of interest for the scene, but the

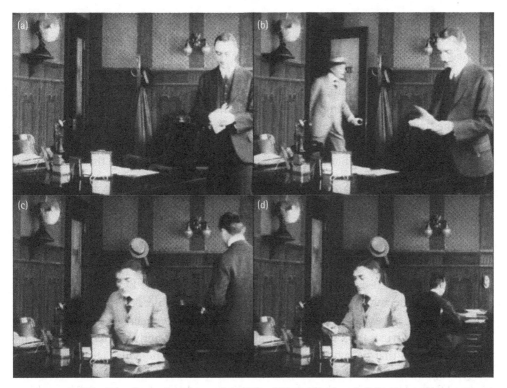

FIGURE 11.1 Mr. Schuyler arrives for work in *A Fool There Was* (1915). Schuyler and his secretary exchange places in the foreground in keeping with the narrative saliency of their actions.

secretary's placement also leaves the space on the left of frame open for Schuyler's arrival. The two figures therefore put the composition in balance when Schuyler enters (see figure 11.1b). The film adopts the common strategy of placing a "piece of furniture in the foreground" as a means of "motivating the movements of characters forward to make important actions more visible."[14] Accordingly, Schuyler approaches his desk and, after a brief exchange with his secretary, sits down to read the newly arrived mail, settling him in center frame (see figure 11.1c). The secretary meanwhile recedes to the background at right to sit at his own desk, turning from the camera in the process. In doing so, he both cedes his previous saliency in the shot to Schuyler, who remains facing forward—relying, in Bordwell's terms, on the fact that "frontality is a magnet for the viewer's eye"—and rebalances the composition.[15] As Schuyler opens the mail, his position in the foreground allows the viewer to easily read his excited expression, the cause of which is soon revealed by an insert of a telegram detailing his appointment to a prestigious government post in England (see figure 11.1d).

Due to its avowed status as a "psychological drama," however, the film relies on a number of strategies to emphasize characters' emotional states beyond simply bringing those characters in closer proximity to the camera. While foreground staging is employed throughout, in some instances the film relies on the simple expediency of cutting in to closer views, culminating in the series of shots of Schuyler reaching desperately through the banister of the townhouse in which he has chosen to live with the Vamp. Abetted by the film's tendency to draw on the dramatic potential of uneven lighting, the banister reduces Schuyler's desperation solely to what can be read from one eye and one outstretched hand within a very discrete portion of the frame. While the use of the banister as an internal framing device suggests that early feature filmmakers continued to assume that close framing alone was insufficient as a means of guiding the viewer's attention, it also testifies to the tendency for single stylistic solutions to solve multiple narrational problems: the banister and the lighting not only organize the frame for intelligibility by directing the viewer's eye to Schuyler, they also serve to reveal aspects of character psychology by visually stripping Schuyler down to "his foolish hide," as the preceding intertitle suggests.

Of the five films, *The Wishing Ring* employs such intrascene cutting to the greatest degree, often dissecting individual spaces into multiple shots. Closer views of characters, however, are similarly combined with depth staging and figure placement to deliver comprehensible scenes, while also making them more effective by contributing to the film's comic rendering of its situations. When Giles's father hires a tutor to continue his son's education, for example, staging and editing work in concert to suggest both the Earl's continued frustration with the young man's behavior and the utter futility of his attempts to curb that behavior. At the beginning of the scene, Giles is situated in the foreground at left idly playing his flute with the rest of the parlor in depth behind him, his head framed by the door that opens onto the veranda (see figure 11.2a). The archway leading to the stairs at the back of frame right similarly serves to frame the Earl as he enters and proceeds forward and left toward his son. The framing in his movement toward the camera allow ample time to capture the Earl's evident frustration with Giles.

Giles's front-facing position in the foreground keeps the Earl's approach out of his son's view. Abetted by the implied volume of Giles's playing, the young man's placement again affords ample time for the Earl to register his impatience with his son and to establish a comedic counterpoint between the two men: initially unaware of his father's presence, Giles's blissful obliviousness simply exacerbates the Earl's palpably growing displeasure.

After the Earl emphatically makes himself known, he snatches his son's flute and throws it into a nearby grate. Giles turns away from the camera in response, clearing the view of the door in preparation for the tutor's arrival in the background of the space. Giles's back remains to the camera as the tutor comes forward so as not to distract attention from the stern exchange between the two older men, which efficiently suggests that the new arrival will demonstrate a similarly harsh attitude toward the young man's behavior (see figure 11.2b). Giles turns around once the Earl provides a chair for his son to occupy, placing the now evidently despondent young man at center frame, flanked by the still severe faces of his father and tutor. After an intertitle indicates the passage of an hour, the film cuts to a closer shot of the tutor and Giles in order to capture the consequences of that temporal gap, as both begin to nod off under the strain of the lesson (see figure 11.2c). This new shot slightly reframes the space, revealing more of the

FIGURE 11.2 The Earl tries to curb Giles's behavior by hiring a tutor in *The Wishing Ring* (1914). Depth staging and editing contribute to the comedic rendering of the scene.

staircase at right but keeping the door to the veranda clearly in view behind Giles in anticipation of the scene's remaining action. Once the young man notices his tutor's lapse in wakefulness, he immediately takes advantage of that ever-present exit. After gingerly extracting himself from his seat, Giles turns from the camera to tiptoe out of the parlor, using the open doorway in the space's depths to make his escape as his tutor continues to slumber in the foreground. When Giles looks back to cheekily wave goodbye to his undisturbed—and therefore unaware—teacher, the door carves out an internal frame, helping to isolate his actions that are now captured at quite a distance from the camera (see figure 11.2d).

Compared to *A Fool There Was* and *The Wishing Ring*, *Traffic in Souls* employs relatively few cut-ins to closer shots, preferring to stage salient actions in the foreground or to direct the viewer's attention to multiple planes of action. When the film does resort to closer framings, editing and staging similarly tend to work in concert to ensure that important moments of character action and interaction remain easily legible while also enhancing their emotional tenor. When the Cadet begins his seduction of Mary's sister in the candy shop, for example, the action is staged in depth, with the sister leaning against the counter that juts toward the camera in the foreground at left. After a cut to the exterior of the shop, the film returns to the same interior set-up. The Cadet enters at foreground right and the sister returns to her position at left—having gone behind the counter and thus out of frame during the cut. With Mary now occupying a position in the middle-ground along the length of the counter, the action is split between two planes. Due to the natural saliency awarded to foreground figures, Mary's concerned expression risks getting lost as the viewer focuses on the interaction between the Cadet and the sister. Their positioning in the foreground, however, transforms the Cadet and the sister into an internal frame around Mary in the middle-ground, directing attention to her without drawing it away from the other two characters. The segment of space that this frame carves out in turn mirrors the following cut-in to Mary, as she continues to gaze concernedly off left, thus helping to clarify the spatial relations between the shots and prepare the viewer for the closer view.

When the film returns to the full view of the shop, the Cadet leans in to talk to the sister, partially obscuring Mary in the middle-ground. In order to ensure that the viewer remains focused on her, the film cuts back to a closer shot of Mary, but this time from a different angle. The reason for the shift in camera placement becomes clear, however, in the subsequent return to the wide shot: Mary has now shifted toward the right, the space she previously occupied having been fully closed off by the Cadet, who has taken up a position directly behind the sister in order to whisper something in her ear. As the scene draws to a close, the film continues to employ this careful arrangement of figures so that both sets of actions remain clearly visible, with the cut-ins to Mary insistently suggesting the danger of the Cadet's seduction.

While the scene's use of depth staging and figure placement to help clarify the spatial relations between shots may suggest a certain lack of faith in the legibility of emerging continuity principles, it is more likely that filmmakers were simply still experimenting with different strategies for connecting spaces across shots. The resultant tendency to oscillate between editing devices that will serve as cornerstones of the classical paradigm and strategies that rely on staging to establish spatial relations is evident from the earliest moments of the film. *Traffic in Souls* begins with a typical series of introductory shots depicting the main characters engaging in emblematic activities in the chain of contiguous spaces that make up the Barton home (see figure 11.3). Mary's maturity and diligence are economically contrasted with her sister's relatively lackadaisical attitude in a quick exchange of shots that show the elder sister in the kitchen ready for work, while the younger has barely risen in an adjacent bedroom. That the two spaces are contiguous is established entirely through eyeline matches: Mary calls off to her sister out of frame left and the younger Barton answers back out of frame right. When the girls' father is introduced tinkering with his inventions in the parlor, however, the film calls on depth staging to establish the room's connection to the rest of the house.

All three spaces employ a similar compositional strategy: each character is situated in the foreground at roughly center frame with the rooms they occupy stretching out in depth behind them. The bedroom is furnished relatively sparsely compared to the other depicted spaces. The kitchen is full of representative décor, including a stove and china cabinet that respectively extend beyond the left and right edges of the frame, giving the impression of a more expansive space. The parlor is crammed full of numerous chairs

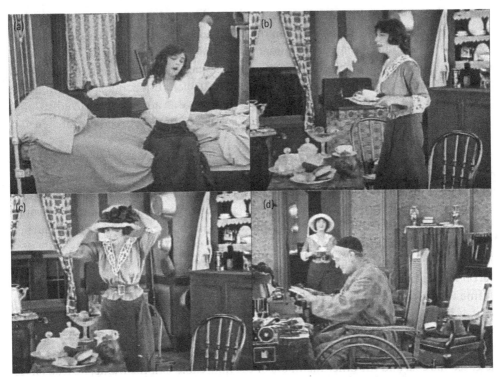

FIGURE 11.3 The Bartons begin their day in *Traffic in Souls* (1913). Emblematic shots of the characters establish their familial roles, while eyelines, depth staging, and décor help create a coherent geography of the Barton home.

and a piano just visible at right to similarly suggest that the space continues beyond the limits of the frame. Notably, the kitchen wall behind Mary is dominated by two large metallic pots that, due to their size and proximity to her in the frame, are markedly conspicuous in shots of that room. The window, which increases the sense of depth in that room by affording a glimpse of an adjacent building, is mirrored in the parlor by the door to the kitchen in the background. The latter room is clearly identifiable by the two pots, which again appear just above the central figure's head, so that the viewer's eye does not have to stray far to notice them. After returning to Mary, who continues to get ready for work while preparing a cup of tea, the film then cuts back to the parlor, as the elder sister appears in the doorway before bringing the tea to her father in the foreground.

This relatively mundane sequence suggests the range of ways in which space could be made to function to achieve narrational goals without relying on a particular formal strategy. Editing, depth staging, décor, and performance work reciprocally to construct a coherent geography of the Barton home while also establishing essential aspects of character psychology. Dividing the two sisters between the kitchen and bedroom helps to emphasize the differences between them due to the two rooms' respective associations with work and leisure. Those differences in turn aid in establishing the connection between the two rooms and then between the kitchen and the parlor: Mary's status as the head of the household (and the attendant associations of responsibility and familial duty) motivates both her chastisement of her sister and attention to her father, and thus the eyeline match and depth staging employed to depict both actions. And while the pots, dishes, and furnishings in the kitchen give the space an appropriately lived-in look, they also offer a visual cue to help cement the spatial relations between the kitchen and the parlor.

In other instances, a similar combination of strategies helps to negotiate the complication of grafting temporal simultaneity onto spatial contiguity while still meeting the demands of delivering causal material. Early in *Joseph*, for example, the film establishes the brothers' growing jealousy of the titular character's status as their father's favored son, as two siblings spy on Joseph and Jacob conversing in the latter's tent. The sequence alternates between shots of the brothers outside the tent—first in a relatively wide shot before cutting in to a closer view to capture their envious expressions—and Joseph and Jacob inside. In both sets of shots, the entrance to the tent holds its position in center frame with each pair of figures flanking the opening. While the panel of fabric immediately behind the brothers flattens out the shots in which they appear, the space inside the tent stretches back into a series of lateral planes, with Jacob and Joseph seated in the foreground and the opening at some distance behind them in depth. After Joseph is gifted his coat and the other members of the household exit the frame, he leans in to talk to his father, partially obscuring the opening. In order to keep the entrance visible in the background and ensure that the viewer's attention is drawn back toward it, the film positions its actors in specific ways: Joseph straightens up, emphasizing a point with a hand gesture before bowing down again and turning from the camera. Having cleared the space in center frame, Joseph makes room for the appearance of his brothers in the background, who surreptitiously open the tent flap to look in on the conversation. By allowing all the characters to be visible at once, the film eliminates any confusion over the spatio-temporal relations between the two sets of shots. Yet in achieving this basic representational task, it also both emphasizes the contrast between the two pairs of men and anticipates the action by mapping the familial dynamic that will soon result in the brothers' betrayal of Joseph onto the space: the brothers are literally left on the outside looking in.

If staging and editing offer alternative, often complementary means for meeting such narrational goals, *Joseph* also points to the potential limits of that complementarity due to the two strategies' respective associations with seemingly contradictory exigencies. In keeping with the implied scale of its status as an entry in the Thanhouser "Big Productions" series of features, *Joseph* stages a great deal of its dramatic action within a series of elaborately mounted locales, each heavily populated with costumed extras. As a result, the frame often has to accommodate not only Joseph and his numerous brothers but also a host of background figures, who afford the requisite degree of spectacular excess needed to justify the film's status as a special production (which would ideally invite lengthy exhibition contracts).[16] Arranging figures in depth using relatively wide shot scales offers an expedient means of displaying the film's expansive cast, but it risks narratively salient actions being lost in the crowd. Cutting into closer shots of the main characters, on the other hand, necessarily excludes a large portion of the film's richly appointed spaces from view.

In the attempt to answer the resultant representational challenge, in some instances the film resorts to momentarily cutting in to closer views in sequences that otherwise rely on wider shot scales. As a result, narrative comprehensibility need not be sacrificed in the name of spectacular display. When Joseph is delivered to Potiphar by the Midianite slavers, for example, the action is initially staged diagonally: Joseph is brought forward from the background at left to be inspected by Potiphar and his wife, who occupy the middle-ground at right. In addition to the principal characters, the space is also fully peopled by Potiphar's guards and staff, arrayed in small groupings in a series of planes similarly receding diagonally from front right to back left. In order to capture these figures along with the arriving crowd of slavers, the camera pans slightly to the right, forcing Potiphar's wife to the upper right corner of the frame. Her placement forms one point of a triangular arrangement of figures that helps direct attention toward Joseph; however, due to her distance from the camera and compositional marginality, viewers may miss her growing attraction to the titular character. The film therefore cuts in to a closer shot to ensure that her eager examination of Joseph is perfectly visible before switching back to the wider view to capture the slavers' exit. The film affords Joseph a number of such closer views at key moments, but it more often relies on staging the action in a series of lateral planes in order to balance the competing demands of spectacle and narrative clarity by pushing salient actions into the foreground and arraying groups of extras in depth.

While less invested in emphasizing the spectacular qualities of its mise-en-scène, the courtroom scene in *Tess* demonstrates a similar reluctance to carve heavily populated spaces into multiple shots (see figure 11.4). The film instead relies on directing the viewer's eye to different zones of action through figure placement and décor. Like *Joseph*, the film resorts to closer views at dramatic turning points in the scene when salient actions would be lost in the wider space of the courtroom. Yet here the cut-ins are triggered by character entrances and dialogue, so that those actions seem to motivate the change of shot. The architecture of the courtroom itself offers an expedient means of breaking down the space into separate points of interest. Filmed at an oblique angle, the bar separating the lawyers' table from the gallery splits the space into dual two-wall sets, the area within the bar encompassed by the rest of the courtroom, with the door visible in the top left. In order to retain this single framing, the film pushes the jury into the extreme foreground with its members' backs to the camera. This eliminates the need for a 180-degree cut to indicate their presence in the room as the judge delivers his charge, while also not distracting attention from Tess's father, situated in the second most proximate plane. After a brief shot of Tess nervously pacing on the train tracks, the film reverts to the same shot of the courtroom as the jury returns. The doors, however, are now thrown open, revealing a crush of eager onlookers whose jockeying for the best view of the proceedings draws the viewer's eye toward that corner of the frame in

FIGURE 11.4 Tess begs the court to spare her father in *Tess of the Storm Country* (1914). Editing, décor, and composition ensure the heroine's actions remain visible in the crowded courtroom.

preparation for Tess's arrival. Because her entrance would be lost in the now-crowded doorway, the film cuts to a closer shot as Tess pushes her way through the throng and is caught by two bailiffs.

When the film returns to the full view of the courtroom, Tess remains framed in the doorway. Her struggle with the bailiffs carries over the cut, and as the entire gallery turns to watch the commotion, the viewer's attention is again drawn to the relatively small portion of the frame she occupies. Tess's position in the background, moreover, brings her head roughly level with both her father's and the judge's halfway down the frame, creating a straight line from left to right that is traced by the molding on the rear wall. While this arrangement of figures draws the viewer's eye across the image, the diagonal arrangement of the foreman, Tess's father, and one of the lawyers in turn points back up toward Tess, creating a triangular array of bodies and heads.

The delivery of the verdict motivates another cut-in to Tess to capture her initial dejection and subsequent attempt to sway the jury with the hymn that serves as a recurring motif of her individuating good-heartedness. The film then cuts back to the full view of the courtroom. Tess's father is now turned from camera, as the titular character comes forward to meet him in center frame. In spite of Tess's relative proximity to the camera, the film again cuts in to a closer view to capture her conversation with the judge, creating another lateral arrangement of faces across the frame. The rest of the scene is played out in the initial framing, with Tess's father and the lawyer again forming a diagonal line of bodies that ends at Tess once she has taken up a position behind the bar. Because Tess's actions ensure that the shifts in shot scale are therefore dramatically motivated, the viewer can form expectations about when a cut is likely to occur, mitigating any potential disruption.

This tendency to justify formal choices as the product of the characters' movement through space or of their reactions to narrative events is typical of the transitional period's attempt to find means of enhancing legibility while also curbing narrational self-consciousness. Enlisting characters to shoulder the burden of narration through a depiction of their actions, however, has implications beyond simply placing added weight on the need to draw the viewer's attention to those actions. In order to foster causal connections between events, character actions similarly require motivation, to be justified in terms of goals, needs, or desires. In other words, filmmakers needed to make viewers aware of what drove characters to act as they did, and this, in turn, forced filmmakers to find adequate means of revealing what characters thought and felt. Such motivic material could be directly relayed using intertitles and inserts, or less narrationally self-conscious texts drawn from the diegesis, like diaries, letters, or telegrams. In addition to these written resources, however, granting the viewer access to what a character sees offered a particularly expedient means of indicating his or her access to narratively salient information, of revealing what a given character knows at any given moment. The result is not simply a greater understanding of characters' inner lives but also a wide range of possibilities for distributing such information. Constructing character-centered narratives, that is, opens up the possibility of creating discrepancies in knowledge, both among characters and between characters and viewers.

While films in the period often eschew "true" point of view shots, as Ben Brewster notes, manipulations of viewpoint allowed for "hierarchies of relative knowledge" by regulating the "relative perceptions and knowledge of the characters" as the narrative develops.[17] As Mary's concerned scrutiny of her sister's seduction in *Traffic in Souls* suggests, however, in addition to experimenting with editing figures in which the viewer and viewed are depicted in separate spaces, early feature filmmakers also pursued compositional options in which both parties occupy the same shot. By dividing the characters between planes rather than between shots, allowing one character to observe another without their knowledge, a single space could be marshalled to manipulate hierarchies of knowledge.[18] While *Traffic in Souls* employs such compositions to forward its narrative of covert criminal operations within a city seemingly lousy with menacing, hidden observers, *The Wishing Ring* often makes use of similar devices for comic effect, as the scene in which the tutor arrives amply demonstrates. In addition to placing viewer and viewed in foreground and background planes, the film also varies the timing of each character's appearance, cueing spectators to form expectations about how a scene's action will play out based on the resultant moment-to-moment manipulations of the flow of knowledge. The film's careful organization of figures to create such unfolding comic situations, however, often calls on editing in order to achieve its full effect.

The Wishing Ring establishes a pattern of enlisting both staging and editing to regulate viewer expectations early in the film. Having engaged in a night of raucous drinking in a local tavern, Giles and his fellow students are suddenly faced with arrest when the militia is called in to break up the festivities. Shifting between the interior and exterior of the tavern as Giles's friends attempt to flee and the neighbors react to the increasing tumult, a flurry of shots captures the ensuing confusion, as Giles ducks under a table to evade capture. When the film returns to the interior of the tavern, the owner and his wife look on anxiously from the background at right while the members of the militia approach the middle-ground, staring intently at something concealed from the viewer by an upturned table. A hand gingerly reaches up over the edge of the nearest tabletop, followed by the appearance of a hat, and, finally, the momentarily trepidatious, and then relieved, face of Giles. Unaware of the militia's presence, he turns to leave, only to be confronted by the contrastingly grim faces of the soldiers, who apprehend the young man and drag him from the tavern out of the door in the background. By obscuring the foreground with the tables and having Giles slowly rise into frame with his back to the militiamen, the film can establish and then gradually develop discrepancies in knowledge, as the viewer is left wondering whom the troops have cornered and then how long it will take Giles to notice their presence. In order to initially keep who is behind the table a mystery, however, the scene relies on the viewer having lost sight of Giles in the initial raid on the tavern. The chaotic rushing of bodies across and through the frame as the soldiers arrive provides ample motivation for the camera's seeming inability to center on Giles, and the relative brevity of the shots leaves the viewer little time to scan the frenzied images for the young man.

This sequence enlists editing to abet the effects of staging in order to create a relatively brief discrepancy in knowledge between characters and the viewer. But much of the film's action is founded on developing more sustained differences in character knowledge, which are also established and maintained by both staging and editing. The film particularly relies on this dual strategy when depicting Giles's attempts to convince Sally that the titular piece of purportedly magical jewelry is granting her the wishes that he is in fact secretly carrying out himself. The film shifts between an approach in which editing works in concert with depth staging and one in which cutting functions on its own to reveal Giles's actions to the viewer while Sally remains unaware and bewildered. When Giles walks Sally home at the end of the date in which he gives her the ring, for example, the film captures the couple saying their goodbyes in front of Sally's garden fence. As Sally retreats to her front door in the frame's depths, Giles slips out of frame right, presumably on his way home. After offering a medium-long shot of Sally sitting on her front porch, however, the film cuts to Giles farther along the fence as he turns and sneaks back into the garden to surprise Sally, who remains visible in depth on the left side of the frame in line with Giles's head. A return to the oblivious Parson's daughter elides Giles's progress, and, in the following shot, the camera reveals Giles stealthily making his way around the corner of the house, entering the frame from the foreground at right, with Sally clearly situated in the background just left of center frame. A tall shrub divides the image in two, and as Giles approaches Sally, he keeps to the right half of the frame to ensure that she remains in view. A dialogue title reveals Sally's wish to be "kissed by [her] true love," again serving to elide Giles's progress while also setting up a specific expectation of what the end point of that progress will entail. When the film returns to the shot of Sally, Giles enters from frame right behind her, perfectly positioned to fulfill the girl's wish and then disappear out of frame right again, leaving Sally at a loss as to who has just kissed her.

When Giles grants Sally's wish for a new dress and shoes, on the other hand, the film simply cuts between Giles shopping for, then delivering the clothes, and Sally wishing for, then excitedly discovering them in her kitchen. Having been made fully aware of the former's actions, the viewer can anticipate how the latter will react once she discovers the gift, much as staging and editing work together to foster expectations in other scenes. By creating and then confirming a series of similar expectations, both from moment to moment and across longer segments of the narrative, the film's efforts to keep the viewer informed of characters' relative degrees of knowledge thus also encourage continued involvement in the unfolding story: as the film arranges and rearranges the distribution of knowledge across its principal characters, the viewer is drawn along through the links in the story's causal chain. *The Wishing Ring*'s articulation of space tends to cue the viewer to formulate accurate inferences about how that story will proceed, creating particular spectatorial effects, usually moving from eager anticipation to delight in the confirmation of expectations.

Editing and staging, however, can also be employed to set up and then refute hypotheses about upcoming action, thus triggering an entirely different set of affective responses. As in *The Wishing Ring*, the construction of space in *Traffic in Souls* serves to set up hierarchies of knowledge and endow the viewer with more information than that possessed by any single character. It does so by both creating a number of layered compositions in which an observer and his unaware quarry appear in the same shot and by affording viewers access to the series of clandestine spaces in which the traffickers conduct their business. Yet in spite of the resultant impression that the viewer shares in the narration's omniscience, the film also manipulates spatial articulations to create false impressions about how the story will unfold.

The film's first moments seem dedicated to providing the viewer with the full range of available information. In addition to introducing the principal characters and establishing crucial causal material, the film extensively explores the workings of the trafficking operation, granting viewers access to a range of personnel operating in seemingly innocuous city spaces as they collect their profits and then set out to meet the Go-Between (see figure 11.5). As the traffickers depart, the film cuts to the Go-Between's office, which is arrayed in three distinct zones of action receding in depth. The primary point of narrative interest, the Go-Between seated at his desk, occupies the foreground of frame right. Once the traffickers begin to arrive, two secondary points of interest are

FIGURE 11.5 The traffickers arrive at the Go-Between's office in *Traffic in Souls*. As gang members enter the room, they are carefully arranged to create distinct zones of space and to cue expectations concerning the action as it unfolds.

delineated, centering on the table in the middle-ground, which takes up the majority of the lower-left portion of the frame, and the door in the background. In addition to suggesting his relative salience, the Go-Between's placement in the foreground forces the traffickers to traverse the entire depth of the frame in order to greet their superior. While such background-to-foreground movement, as Bordwell notes, "became the norm for initiating a scene's action," due to the sheer number of traffickers that come to occupy the space, it also affords the viewer ample "time to identify the participants in the action" as the traffickers arrive.[19] As the first group of gang members enters, two approach the Go-Between, with the leading figure brandishing a newspaper, while the Madame sets herself up at the table. After cutting to an explanatory insert of a newspaper article that details the efforts of Trubus, a social reformer, to curb the white slave trade, the film cuts back to the room at large, with the figures arrayed across the three zones of action.

The film then shifts to the exterior of the building as two more traffickers enter, before returning to the office. The gang members remain in roughly the same places that they occupied before the cut, but the Madame obligingly bends down to count her money, offering a less obscured view of the door. The other two members are then shown climbing a flight of stairs and approaching a door in the foreground of frame left. When the film returns to the office, the pair enters in the background, clearly visible in the slot of space just cleared by the Madame. The newly arrived second Madame—distinguished from her counterpart by her darker clothing—approaches the Go-Between while the others arrange themselves around the table in the middle-ground, again ensuring the door remains visible. The resultant configuration of bodies divides the frame between two points of interest: the continued exchange of money with the Go-Between and the callous disregard for the reform movement efforts represented by the traffickers' continued mocking of the newspaper article in the middle-ground.

The film then takes the viewer to Trubus's home as he meets with his daughter's potential fiancé. A number of critics have argued that such cuts between spaces implicitly connect Trubus with the white slave trade, undermining his carefully protected "separation from his business" while also triggering a certain irony by associating the marriage of his daughter with the more illicit sale of women proceeding in the office.[20] The connection between the two spaces, however, is initially opaque, seemingly motivated by little more than the fact that Trubus is featured in the article. While Trubus is introduced as "the man higher up," the film initially implies that this lofty position is simply within the reform movement, depicting Trubus as he reviews the same article that will later be mocked by the traffickers. There is therefore little reason to suspect any impropriety once Trubus is shown leaving his home, even as the film then cuts back to the office, again hinting at a connection.

Once again, the traffickers have retained their basic positions, arranged in two groups in the foreground around the Go-Between at right and in the middle-ground around the table at left, with changes in position choreographed so that both groups remain clearly visible and neither obscures the door. The film then returns to the landing as another gang member arrives. In order to ensure his entrance is visible in depth, and to make way for his approach forward, when the film cuts back to the office most of the characters obligingly shift positions: the trafficker in the white hat sits down in the foreground left, while the first Madame has turned to a profile view but then walks toward the Go-Between in the foreground, exchanging places with the other Madame, who retreats to the middle-ground to greet another trafficker. This clears the camera's view of the new arrival, who promptly comes forward to take up a position just behind the Go-Between. This movement leaves an unobstructed slot of space leading from the head of the table to the door clearly visible in the background. With the office space seemingly primed for yet another arrival, the film then cuts to two exterior shots of Trubus arriving at the office building. While the first shot represents an entirely new camera set-up—most likely to accommodate Trubus's car, all the traffickers having arrived on foot—the second mirrors the exterior shots that previously captured the traffickers' entries to the building. A brief shot of the office follows, with the figures still keeping the door visible in the background, again suggesting the imminent arrival of another trafficker.

To this point, the editing has established a clear pattern of showing arrivals at the exterior of the building in one shot, followed by a shot of the stairs, before a final shot captures characters entering the office. In that space, a clear path from the background door to the Go-Between in the foreground has been consistently formed and reformed to prepare for each entry. As Trubus moves through the exterior shot and is then shown mounting the stairs, the viewer can reasonably expect that he will follow the traffickers into the office. The film then cuts to the interior, with the door clearly visible in the background and its attendant seemingly primed to admit the reformer, encouraging that expectation. Trubus, however, refuses to appear. When the film returns to the shot of the stairs, Trubus pauses on the landing and looks back toward the office door. This allows the viewer a moment to think through the scandalous implications of the reformer's presence, before Trubus simply continues up the stairs. While the cross-cutting may hint at some illicit connection between Trubus and the traffickers, the sequence's editing patterns and the careful staging of figures in and around the office set up a more explicit set of expectations by tying the construction of space to the process of cueing the viewer to anticipate the action. The prosaic task of articulating spatial relations between shots and arraying figures within them in the interest of presenting a series of clear and comprehensible narrative actions thus also offers opportunities to trigger particular responses to those actions in the interest of rendering them engaging.

Because staging and editing work in concert to achieve these effects, we cannot argue for either strategy's prominence over the other. All five films display a comparable tendency to treat staging and editing as elements of an evolving paradigm of stylistic devices directed at achieving a similarly discrete set of narrational goals. If, as Tom Gunning argues, the transitional period "may distinguish itself from others primarily through its protean nature,"[21] then the treatment of space in these films suggests that cinematic style in the early feature period was no less fluid. Whether the conclusions that we draw from them are applicable to early features per se will therefore require more extensive study. Yet because the five films demonstrate that no single set of formal traits will suffice to definitively characterize the treatment of space in the cinema of the early 1910s, they also point to the limitations of founding any such study on the search for discrete stylistic factors as benchmarks for distinguishing between periods or narrational modes. If we choose to primarily differentiate classical cinema from the transitional period by its approach to spatial organization through editing, then these films can only be conceived as a liminal form. Due to their continued experimentation with the battery of staging options formulated at a time when the thousand-foot film remained the industry standard, and simultaneous exploration of the narrational potentials of editing, they seem to straddle the line between the two eras. Establishing whether or not early features constitute a "unique entity" situated between those eras, as Keil surmises, similarly calls for further study.[22] What is clear, however, is that we must remain attentive to how filmmakers worked through the narrational potentials of both staging and editing in any discussion of transitional-era cinema.

Notes

1. Charlie Keil, *Early American Cinema in Transition: Story, Style, and Filmmaking, 1907–1913* (Madison: University of Wisconsin Press, 2001), 204.
2. For a discussion of the influence of theater and the novel on the development of classical narration, see Kristin Thompson, "From Primitive to Classical," in David Bordwell, Janet Staiger, and Kristin Thompson, *The Classical Hollywood Cinema: Film Style and Mode of Production to 1960* (New York: Columbia University Press, 1985), 157–173.
3. See André Gaudreault, "Temporality and Narrativity in Early Cinema, 1895–1908," in John Fell, ed., *Film before Griffith* (Berkeley: University of California Press, 1983), 311–329.
4. Mark Garrett Cooper convincingly argues that even as rudimentary a narrative as the Lumière brothers' one-shot comedy, *L'Arroseur arrosée*, involves a careful division of the frame into two distinct areas, only one of which is within the unfortunate arroseur's view, and which together create the foundation for the film's sequence of events. See Mark Garrett Cooper, "Narrative Spaces," *Screen* 43, no. 2 (2002): 139–157.
5. Keil, *Early American Cinema in Transition*, 127.
6. Ibid., 12, 204.
7. Ibid., 8–12.
8. Save for *Traffic in Souls* and *The Wishing Ring*, which were selected for their prominence in existing literature on early features, the films were chosen at random. No selection criteria were considered beyond the length of the film and the date of its release.
9. Keil, *Early American Cinema in Transition*, 38.
10. David Bordwell, *Figures Traced in Light: On Cinematic Staging* (Berkeley: University of California Press, 2005), 36.
11. Ibid., 49.
12. The importance of characters to narrative per se is an open question. Narrative theorists generally agree that the presence of a common participant in a series of depicted actions is a requirement for narrativity. Whether those participants or the actions themselves are the basic constituent elements of a narrative is a matter of some debate and will likely depend on the type of narrative being examined. Early cinema features participants that are generally defined by the actions that they perform. In *L'Arroseur arrosée*, the titular waterer and the boy are less individuated characters than types that carry out a specific set of actions: the mischievous prankster and his victim. The participants in early chase films are similarly two opposed types—the pursuers and the pursued—who always perform the same actions. Though the specific participants may vary, the actions do not. Transitional cinema shifts from this type of performed action to actions performed by individuated characters. Rather than the action defining the characters, that is, the characters are increasingly made to motivate the action. This shift is not absolute; character types still appear in transitional films, early features, and their classical successors. Whether the actions performed by these types are attributed to their status as individuated agents is a matter of degree often tied to narrative saliency.
13. Ben Brewster and Lea Jacobs, *Theatre to Cinema: Stage Pictorialism and the Early Feature Film* (New York: Oxford University Press, 1997), 181.
14. Kristin Thompson, "Narration Early in the Transition to Classical Filmmaking: Three Vitagraph Shorts," *Film History* 9, no. 4 (1997): 424.
15. David Bordwell, "*La Nouvelle Mission de Feuillade*; or, What Was Mise-en-Scène?" *Velvet Light Trap* 37 (1996): 14.

16. Ned Thanhouser, "Thanhouser: A Microcosm of the Transitional Era in Silent Films—Why the Studio Never Made It to Hollywood," *thanhouser.org* (2009), https://www.thanhouser.org/Research/Thanhouser-A%20Microcosm%202-27-09-FINAL.pdf, 9.
17. Ben Brewster, "A Scene at the 'Movies,'" in Thomas Elsaesser, ed., *Early Cinema: Space, Frame, Narrative* (London: BFI, 1990), 321–322.
18. For a discussion of such "deep-enfolded view[s]," see Keil, *Early American Cinema in Transition*, 78.
19. Bordwell, *Figures Traced in Light*, 57; David Bordwell, *On the History of Film Style* (Cambridge, MA: Harvard University Press, 1997), 171.
20. Tom Gunning, "From the Kaleidoscope to the X-Ray: Urban Spectatorship, Poe, Benjamin, and *Traffic in Souls* (1913)," *Wide Angle* 19, no. 4 (1997): 52.
21. Tom Gunning, "Systematizing the Electric Message: Narrative Form, Gender, and Modernity in *The Lonedale Operator*," in Charlie Keil and Shelley Stamp, eds., *American Cinema's Transitional Era: Audiences, Institutions, Practices* (Berkeley: University of California Press, 2004), 16.
22. Keil, *Early American Cinema in Transition*, 12.

CHAPTER 12

SALON TANGO

Hollywood Pictorialism and the Beaux-Arts Tradition

TOM PAULUS

ONE of the most iconic moments in movies is the sensational dance scene that introduces the romantic hero, libertine, and aspiring artist Julio Desnoyers, in Rex Ingram's "Million Dollar" super-picture, *The Four Horsemen of the Apocalypse* (1921), a singular box-office hit of the 1920s.[1] Dressed in a "fantasy version of a gaucho's outfit," *rebenque* whip and all, former cabaret dancer Rudolph Valentino soared to stardom and started a new craze for Latin America and the lost art of "el tango."[2] The establishing shot of the Boca tango hall—a port district, "steeped in Old World sin, harboring the dregs of humanity," as a lurid title tells us—boasts a number of pictorial effects typical for the film and Ingram's mise-en-scène in general: tinted a romantic magenta, the smoky basement cabaret is seen in depth through an arch-shaped open wall that separates it from a stark foreground plane, a darkened space where we can barely discern the figures seated at two tables (see figure 12.1). The shot stands out as a composition or a "picture" not only because of its interior framing device—already in evidence in Ingram's earlier films at Metro—but because of the striking separation of the image planes, the shadowy foreground setting off the hazy-bright center and the smoky background in the style of Delacroix's *Liberty Leading the People* (1830), cited explicitly in the "Republican Liberty" sequence later in the film. Although the composition draws attention to itself, it is integrated into a classically edited sequence, with singles, two-shots, reaction shots, and inserts (of the gaucho's unusually long and pointy spurs) intercut with a similarly composed but closer re-establishing shot. Photography, staging, and set design work together in the tango scene to create both an expressive and a pictorial effect within the conventions of the continuity system: I will treat this approach as representative of new conceptions of pictorial mise-en-scène that consolidated near the end of the 1910s.

Cinematic pictorialism of this period can be seen as straddling the old and the new, a reconciliation of the tableau style (carefully composed and staged shots with figures either posed or moving diagonally into the foreground and background) with continuity cutting. In so doing, a filmmaker like Ingram could be seen to balance elements from

FIGURE 12.1 Under the tavern lights. *Four Horsemen of the Apocalypse* (1921).

modern painting (the gentle color schemes and softly brushed contours of Tonalism and Impressionism) with the compositional values of what I will broadly refer to as the "Beaux-Arts tradition," art influenced by the Salons and the classical "Italianist" norms and ideals imposed by the French Académie des Beaux Arts. Cinematic pictorialism, the aesthetic refinement of motion pictures according to the compositional and tonal standards of painting and artistic still photography, had already been a point of debate in the trade press before 1910.[3] However, it was only with the films of Griffith, Ince, DeMille, and Tourneur of the mid-to-late 1910s that we witness a certain systematization and conscious exploitation of artistic value. Ingram, who had actually trained as an artist, was seen to hold an "advanced" position, applying Impressionistic methods to realist ends. In point of fact, he came from an Academic background, which clearly softened the more innovative aspects of his style. Despite Ingram's frequent reference to Manet (absurd, given the flatness and harsh color contrasts of the father of modern painting and the filmmaker's own predilection for roundness and mellow shading) or Rodin (a logical reference given Ingram's training as a sculptor), his style was mainly inspired by the synthesis between Neoclassicism and Romanticism propagated by the French Academy.[4]

We can shed light on this "double-aspectness" of Hollywood pictorialism through a comparison with the original pictorial movement in photography of the beginning of the century. As Kristin Thompson has remarked, "Hollywood craftsmen eager to prove that cinema, too, was an art, were in about the same position in the late 1910s that the pictorial photographers had been in twenty years before."[5] Like Stieglitz and the photographers of the Photo-Secession assembled around the Little Galleries in New York and the journal *Camera Work* (published from 1903 to 1917), Hollywood pictorialists hoped that by imitating earlier, established styles in the other arts they could achieve the same public status themselves. The difference is that while the Photo-Secession was operating in close historical proximity to the Symbolist and Impressionist art it sought to emulate,[6] by the late 1910s, Impressionism and Symbolism were available to Hollywood pictorialists mainly as conventionalized styles, popularized in the decorative arts (Art Deco, Art Nouveau) that shaped widespread book and magazine illustration and poster design and also influenced the movies. If screen pictorialism is indeed, according to Barry Salt's definition, a compositional style "closely based on that used in the painting of *past* periods" (my emphasis), modernist elements are logically absent from the Hollywood art cinema of the 1910s. As I shall show, even the presumably most "modern" of the pictorial directors, the Frenchman Maurice Tourneur, drew his inspiration more from the Salon and the decorative arts than from the contemporary fine arts.

I shall introduce Tourneur as a logical point of comparison, not only because both Ingram and Tourneur were singular in their connection to actual artists—Ingram was close to the sculptor Lee Lawrie, Tourneur, more impressively, to Rodin and the muralist Puvis de Chavannes—but because the case of Tourneur, who was also associated with the naturalist theater of André Antoine, allows me to consider the theatrical background of Hollywood pictorialism. The "New Stagecraft" of Reinhardt and Craig had had an impact on the American theater of the 1910s less at the level of formal innovation than through introducing the idea of an artistically motivated cohesive production style, the unity or "synergy" of every artistic means employed. Reinhardt, elevated in the movie trades as a paragon of artistic sophistication, had also inspired the concern with "mood" and atmosphere in both theater and film (DeMille, for instance, stressed the "mood" of the photography of *The Cheat* [1915]).[7] In the context of Hollywood, however, the synthetic ideas underlying the simplified, quasi-abstract settings of the New Stagecraft largely disappeared, replaced by a more superficial interest in the "realist" possibilities of sparse geometric settings (motivated by sophisticated urban milieus or, as in Tourneur's *The Blue Bird* and *Prunella*, both 1918, by a fairytale setting) and new lighting trends that went beyond the motivation of depth and visibility. As Thompson argues, innovations—already largely confined to specialty divisions and director units—were tolerated in Hollywood only because of the need for product differentiation and accepted only as improvements on the standards of verisimilitude, spectacle, narrative coherence, and continuity.[8] Nevertheless, as Ingram and Tourneur are still regularly portrayed as visionary modern artists who were cast out by the Hollywood system, we can benefit by examining more closely how the harmonization of the Academic and progressive arts, the popular and the experimental, had always defined their practice.

This essay's focus on screen pictorialism and two of its main exemplars, Ingram and Tourneur, aligns with Kaveh Askari's superb study, *Making Movies into Art: Picture Craft from the Magic Lantern to Early Hollywood* (2014). In my previous work on transitional-era "quality" films, I have shared Askari's emphasis on how intellectual networks, institutional publicity, and craft organizations helped to mobilize a critical discourse on craft and pictorialism.[9] This account, however, shifts from considering the influence of these external forces to examining the historical poetics of film creation and inter-artistic influence. In particular, I analyze the stylistic changes that occurred and elucidate what caused those changes. In this, I will closely follow Kristin Thompson's pioneering work on the formulation and adaptability of the classical Hollywood style, specifically in her contributions to *The Classical Hollywood Cinema* (with David Bordwell and Janet Staiger) and her essay on the "Limits of Experimentation in Hollywood" during the silent period.[10] I will also draw on studies by Patrick Keating and Barry Salt on the evolution of cinematographic techniques and on Lea Jacobs's work on the radical shifts in taste during the 1920s.[11]

UNDER THE TAVERN LIGHTS: CHIAROSCURO AND SFUMATO

In her survey of the major technological and stylistic changes in the American cinema of the 1920s, Kristin Thompson singles out the tango-hall shot from *Four Horsemen* as having had a considerable impact on other filmmakers of the period. The film's cinematographer was John F. Seitz, a former chemist and lab assistant who would go on to become the highest-paid cameraman of the 1920s and one of the few whose name was used in advertising.[12] Of course, the low-key schema that separates and layers the different planes of the frame was hardly new in and of itself at the beginning of the 1920s. As has been extensively studied, at Famous Players-Lasky, cinematographer Alvyn Wyckoff, scenic designer Wilfred Buckland, and director Cecil B. DeMille had already been experimenting with "Klieg" arc spotlights and directional lighting in studio interiors in films like *The Cheat* and *The Golden Chance* (1915).[13] Opposing the standard of general overhead illumination by harshly illuminating one image plane only while leaving the rest of the set in darkness, they were looking to achieve not just "mood" and realism but increased dramatic expression and pictorial values through highlighting and shadowing. Of their experiments with "Rembrandt lighting" during the mid-1910s, *Carmen* (1915) was probably the most influential (Ingram himself had closely followed the template set by the DeMille film in his own Universal-Bluebird production *Chalice of Sorrow* [1916]). A comparison of the tango-hall composition from *Four Horsemen* to the famous scene from *Carmen* with a similar chiaroscuro saloon setting, however, reveals a number of important differences that shed light on the evolution of lighting technique and pictorial effects in the five years that separate the two prestige pictures. The most important difference, I will show, can be observed in the relative "hardness" of the respective approaches to lighting: the crisp definition in the earlier film, and the emergence of a more painterly "soft style" in the later one.

The introductory scene at Pastia's tavern, in which Carmen (Geraldine Farrar) seduces Civil Guard officer Don José (Wallace Reid), was famously lampooned by Charlie Chaplin in *Burlesque on Carmen* (1915). But while Chaplin kept Buckland's bustling layout in depth, with a table pushing into the foreground of the shot—a conventional way to make the playing space look larger—he forgot about the "Lasky lighting," the trade press's label for the type of atmospheric low-key effect lighting evident in DeMille's films. Instead, Chaplin shot his *Burlesque* with the same flat illumination typical of most comedy films of the day, one produced by racked mercury vapor lights.[14] DeMille's amber-tinted establishing shot, by contrast, is lit by arc floodlights that create the illusion of solidity and dimensionality, with light dropping off into a flat black plane in the right-hand corner of the frame and the smoke of Pastia's cigarette adding further texture. It is only with Carmen's celebrated entrance in the following (medium) shot, however, that the pictorial inspiration behind "Lasky Lighting" is made explicit: shot from a slightly oblique angle and framed by a doorway, Farrar is lit from one centrally positioned source, as in Rembrandt, resulting in an intense contrast in light and shade that is further heightened by the dark foreground; as she steps forward, she goes almost completely into silhouette.[15]

In the next section, I will address the way silhouetting and the fluctuation in brightness between the different zones in the wide shot are used compositionally in *Four Horsemen*, working together with staging and art design to separate the planes. For now, we need to consider key differences operating purely at the level of photography. For Thompson, the most historically salient aspect of the *Four Horsemen* shot is its "soft" look: while the foreground figures are sharply edged, the background planes drop off noticeably in their degree of contrast.[16] Such softness was completely opposite to the tonalities generally produced by the orthochromatic film stock that was still standard in Hollywood until the mid-1920s, characterized by a sharpness and depth of field further increased by the anastigmat lenses in use at the time.[17] In *Carmen* all the zones of the frame are in crisp focus, from the sprawled-out drunk in the foreground to Pastia in the back: the strong contrast inherent to the orthochromatic stock is brought out further by the sharp shadows cast by the carbon arcs. This was exactly the kind of "contrasty" harshness that Ingram and Seitz, following the lead of Griffith and Bitzer on the groundbreaking *Broken Blossoms* (1919), wanted to eliminate. Despite the painterly use of chiaroscuro in *Carmen*, sharp depth was simply too reminiscent of the "stereoscopic" effect that was still commonly seen as the movie camera's main objective.

Ingram's aspiration toward softness should not be confused with the shot being out of focus. Brewster and Jacobs, for example, mention several instances from the American cinema of the early 1910s where the out-of-focus background is clearly a mistake on the part of the cameraman.[18] On the whole, however, as Kristin Thompson has argued, cinematographers of the period were already quite conscious of f-stops and the depth of field they yielded, so sharpness was not just a default result of the film stock but a desired aesthetic.[19] In the tango-hall shot from *Four Horsemen*, all the planes *are* in focus, but their definition has been softened by intentional manipulation. In his foreword to Victor Freeburg's *Pictorial Beauty on the Screen* (1923), Ingram highlighted the Columbia professor's contention that "in order to be classified among the Arts, the Cinema must become something more than a series of clear photographs of things in motion."[20] Similarly, the photographers of the Photo-Secession had wanted to get away from a too-close adherence to reality produced by the automatism of the camera, by embracing the soft modulating tones of Impressionist painting, the "atmospheric" quality that also typified Whistler's "Nocturnes." Several notable cinematographers like Karl Struss (who developed his own soft-focus lens) and Charles Rosher—but not Seitz—had close ties to the Photo-Secession.[21] The ranks of *Camera Work*, Alfred Stieglitz's journal for art and photography lovers established in 1902, also included the likes of Baron Adolphe de Meyer, a French painter (trained as a child by Monet) and pictorialist photographer whose soft-focus portrait work was widely disseminated via *Harper's Bazaar*, *Vogue*, and *Vanity Fair* (where he was joined by Edward Steichen in the early 1920s) and who influenced Hollywood or was influenced by Hollywood's developing three-point lighting system, as Patrick Keating has argued.[22]

Together with hand-manipulation printing techniques, the pictorial photographers made use of gauze and naturally diffusing elements like mist, fog, and rain to approximate the vaguer outlines and mediated tones of Impressionist and Tonalist painting. By the end of the 1910s, following the triumph of *Broken Blossoms* (for which Griffith and Bitzer had collaborated with portrait photographer Hendrik Sartov), cinematographers had devised similar ways in which contrast could be reduced even in the studio and with orthochromatic film. The first solution was to shoot with larger apertures. Not just lenses with longer focal length (like Sartov's six-inch pictorial lens), but new lenses with higher maximum aperture had become available, and, as Ingram told the *New York Times*, on *Four Horsemen* they opened up the lens on both interiors and exteriors.[23] (Moreover, Ingram planned to shoot all the exteriors he could on dull overcast days in order to use an open lens and get a softer image.)[24] The alternative or additional option was to use optical diffusers like gauzed lamps (softening the edges of the shadows) and coated lenses.[25] In the establishing shot of the scene in the Argentinian tango hall, the thick smoke in the hall also helps to give the central part of the image a softer gradation. Some filmmakers even added mist to the backgrounds, or placed gauzed scrims behind the figures in the background. Although many suspected that Ingram and Seitz had used such background veils, the most important contribution to softening came from the lab work. Seitz, who had begun as a chemist and laboratory man, had been experimenting with developing time since his first film with Ingram, *Shore Acres*, in 1920: by reducing the developing time to about 40 percent from the standard, and thereby under-developing the film and creating less density in the emulsion—possibly also to compensate for the overexposure—he managed to create the soft gradations and subtler shades, the "atmospheric perspective," that would satisfy Ingram.[26] Seitz even provided the laboratory with special chemical formulas to be used in custom-developing separate shots, which explains why the degree of softness changes significantly between shots.[27]

There were a number of reasons for Ingram's turn to the soft look. Somewhat ironically, one was the desire for increased realism. In line with the theories concerning the "retinal" painting of the Impressionists and their source in new developments in nineteenth-century optics, the reasoning seemed to be that soft focus offered a closer approximation of human vision that doesn't see as sharply as an anastigmat lens.[28] The film theorist Jean-Louis Comolli famously argued that the choice for medium focal length lenses (35–50 mm) in the early days of cinema, which had to be stopped down to small apertures and required a lot of light, was dictated by a "realist bias," a presumed analogy to "normal" human vision (at least, as it was projected by the diagrammatic clarity of Renaissance perspective).[29] Comolli's critique was not just aimed at Cartesian perspectivalism but at Bazin's phenomenological understanding of cinematic 'realism' as expressed in deep focus photography (Bazin was, however, much more concerned with the Bergsonian integrity of physical space and time than with the scientific approximation of human vision). In fact, as nineteenth-century optical science had established, human vision is extremely diffused and has a shallow depth of field, corresponding to approximately f1.4, larger than the largest camera aperture in use at the time.[30] But far more important than optical "realism" was a more traditional aesthetic reason: as Ingram told the *Times*, he wanted to "get away from the hard, crisp effect of the photograph," because he wanted "to get something of the mellow mezzotint of the painting; to get the fidelity of photography, but the softness of the old master; to picture not only the dramatic action, but to give it something of the merit of art."[31] Note that the atmospheric effects Ingram was looking for were not inspired by the Impressionists, or by Whistler's halftones, or Rodin's soft contours, or even Turner's swirling shapes and shifting colors, but by Leonardo's sfumato or Rembrandt's rejection of the sharp contrasts of light and dark that had characterized his early work under the influence of Italian Tenebrism.

In his first two films with Seitz, Ingram, given his training as a sculptor, had been mainly concerned with softness, in the sense of creating a more nuanced effect of "modeling" in the lighting of close-ups.[32] Modeling, "obtained by judicious arrangement of light and shade," enabled the filmmaker to give a "stereoscopic" quality to "the soft, mellow-toned close-up."[33] Modeling and "roundness" are antithetical to sharpness and were traditional Academic concerns, implying carefully graded tones of light and shade. Seemingly the only exception to the Academic rule was Ingram and Seitz's quite idiosyncratic experimentation with side-lighting from both directions (cross-lighting) to create more pronounced highlights, hard edges, and deep shadows in the middle of the subject's face. This technique—which approximated the Rembrandt self-portraits of the late period—was used exclusively for more expressionist moments of anguish and high dramatic intensity.[34] In general, Ingram and Seitz were looking to undo the difference between work executed under the studio lights and shooting "on the spot" (*en plein air*) by recreating in the controlled environment of the studio the soft shadows, low definition, and halftones resulting from filtered daylight.

To help us gauge the relative newness of introducing softness in interior long shots, and not just on romantic locations *en plein air*, a final instructive comparison can be drawn to another film with a strong aesthetic pedigree that was in production at almost the exact same time and was directed by a man who would become Ingram's friend: Marcel L'Herbier's Decadentist fantasy *El Dorado* (1921). This Spanish melodrama was famously shot partly on location in Seville and Granada, but the opening scene, set in another smoky "maison de dance et plaisir" and lit in the *Carmen* style, was shot in the Gaumont studios in Paris. The scene features a remarkable—and much commented upon—selective focus effect that sees L'Herbier experiment with gauzy filters over the lens.[35] The differential focus effect, however, is used purely expressively and with limited pictorial effect, despite the film's strikingly decorative style inspired by nineteenth-century Aestheticism. There is no drop-off of focus, definition, or contrast, other than when figures are placed closer than twenty feet from the lens, and even then, the effect does not give the impression of having been controlled in any way. On the contrary, the directional arc lighting, casting sharp shadows, tends to create a rather contrasty look, with dark, undetailed blacks and little tonal variation.[36] The softer, atmospheric look that we tend to associate with cinematic Impressionism since L'Herbier's *Rose-France* (1918) is achieved only in specific—again narratively motivated—moments, mostly by throwing the entire image out of focus. When Sibilla remembers her husband, heavy diffusion is used together with a wide lens aperture to create the kind of image reminiscent of Griffith's *Broken Blossoms*. On the whole, the reigning norm in French cinematography of the 1920s was for sharp focus, and cinematographers were slower to take up lens diffusion than their American counterparts, as Barry Salt has argued.[37] In the films of the Impressionist "avant-garde," the limited use of selective soft focus effects can be attributed to the artistic incentive for expressive, subjective "cinégraphie," as propagated by Symbolist critics like Emile Vuillermoz.[38]

Composing a View: *Contre-Jour* and the Repoussoir

Before the four horsemen ride across the sky in the film's famous ending, Ingram gives us a final pictorial flourish with the shot of Russian socialist Tchernoff, silhouetted high on a steep hill studded with crosses, looking out on a vast military cemetery, the clouds darkened by the orthochromatic film providing an ominous accent. More romantic and hopeful is the closer shot of Julio's sister Chichi and her lover André, silhouetted on the same incline, the French flag fluttering in the wind. *Contre-jour* effects[39] similar to the ones we find in Stieglitz's photographs and in the work of prominent members of the Photo-Secession, like Edward Steichen, Gertrud Käsebier, Clarence White, and Karl Struss, started turning up in the work of cinematographers at the beginning of the 1910s.[40] Mostly silhouettes were utilized as an easily achieved sunlight or (simulated) moonlight effect, often paired with a romantic seaside setting, as in Griffith and Bitzer's coastal melodramas shot in California from 1909 onward. Several historians of the period have clarified that backlighting on exteriors was generally put to use in two ways: as a skyline silhouette with figures outlined against the setting sun or moon (the most common use being the *contre-jour* shot of boats on the sea in Italian and French scenic travel films that often reproduced the picturesque scenery of the lantern slide belonging to the genre of the "vedute" or "voyage pittoresque"), or as a less exalted "open-door" framing with figures shot in an unlighted space against the day-lit exterior.[41] As Barry Salt points out, by 1913 backlighting had become pretty much standard, with many examples found in films from Italy, Denmark, and Russia.[42] One film made a special feature of silhouette shots: Léonce Perret's *Roman d'un Mousse* (1913)—photographed by L'Herbier's cinematographer on *El Dorado*, Charles Specht—includes not only a succession of skyline silhouettes of boats at sea but foreground figures starkly outlined against the setting sun. A similar "marine" effect can be admired at the beginning of *Carmen*, or Thomas Ince's *The Italian* of the same year, both of which juxtapose the protagonist posed on a hilltop overlooking the sea in the background in the manner of the seascape paintings of Caspar David Friedrich (e.g., *Mondaufgang am Meer*, 1822) or the dusk settings of late-period Corot (e.g., *Chevrier Italien*, 1866). The difference lies in the degree of contrast: Perret-Specht's silhouettes were created with the exposure full on the sparkling sea in the background, completely reducing subject detail and creating a starkness that approximates the tonal quality of a Japanese woodblock print.

Although the against-the-light effect can already be found in Ingram's films for Universal-Bluebird, the two skyline silhouettes at the end of *Four Horsemen* were most likely inspired by similar moments in Abel Gance's *J'accuse* (1919), a film rapturously received by American critics.[43] The master of the silhouette in the Hollywood of the late 1910s, however, was another Frenchman, Maurice Tourneur, a former decorator, illustrator, and poster designer who had worked as a scenic artist for André Antoine at the Théâtre de l'Odéon, then started as a filmmaker at Eclair. His first film for Lasky, *Pride of the Clan* (1916), featured effects familiar from *Roman d'un mousse*, notably a profile medium shot of the two leads starkly backlit against a romantically diffuse background of moon and sea (a shot lampooned by Pickford and Tourneur in a publicity photograph collected by Kevin Brownlow).[44] Although silhouette effects are featured in most of Tourneur's films, from his grand-guignol *Figures de cire* (1914) onward, his trademark effect of using *contre-jour* lighting *compositionally*, in depth shots with framing foreground elements, was only systematized in the late 1910s. What Tourneur did, together with his cameramen John van den Broek and Lucien Andriot, was to reverse the standard rule of conventional cinematography by putting more light on the background rather than the foreground of the scene.[45] The trade press, in its contemporary columns on the proper use of cinematography, had also put forward the compositional schema with strong foreground and various intermediate planes between foreground and a distant back view to argue for greater depth and "stereoscopy" in the image.[46] For Tourneur, however, the schema primarily had a pictorial function.

While Seitz's use of silhouetted foregrounds in *Four Horsemen* had been noted[47] (other than in the tango scene, the darkened foreground is a conspicuous feature of the parts of the film set at Marcelo Desnoyers' Marne Valley castle), it was probably under the influence of Tourneur's structurization of the compositional schema in his films of the late teens that Ingram adopted it as a general feature of his own productions. Keating quotes a 1923 article in the *Transactions of the Society of Motion Picture Engineers* suggesting that the illustrator Gustave Doré may have been an inspiration for Tourneur:

"The picture may be given apparent depth, by lighting the background more intensely than the foreground, a familiar trick of Gustave Doré, who seems to have imagined cinematic lighting in the days of the zoetrope."[48] The views from a darkened cave through to sunlight or moonlight beyond, with silhouetted figures against the light, in *The Last of the Mohicans* (1920) certainly resemble Doré, if only because they hark back to the Milano Company's early epic, *L'Inferno* (1911), a film inspired by the illustrator's woodcut engravings for Dante's masterwork.[49] On the other hand, Keating is correct in suggesting that, looking further back, we can note that the technique of shadowed foreground mass had long been associated with French Academic landscape painting, specifically in the arrangements suggested by the seventeenth-century painter Claude Lorrain's pastoral Italianate landscapes that influenced German Romantics like Caspar David Friedrich, The Hudson River School, Turner, and Corot, painters who were often associated with Tourneur's films and with the vogue for the "picturesque" in both painting and photography.[50]

Typical of Claude's perspectival "paysages classiques," often set at dusk, was the contrast between an obstructing foreground bordering the bottom of the frame and the brighter middle ground and distant horizon. These foreground masses were called "repoussoirs," which roughly translates as "push-backs," exploiting the contrast between foreground and background in order to increase the illusion of depth and focus the viewer's attention according to a clear and rational monocular layout. Henry Rankin Poore, whose handbook, *Pictorial Composition and the Critical Judgement of Pictures* (1903), advised artists how to draw observers into a picture, notes the Claudian schema succinctly: "In the first he created sides for the center which were darkened so that the light of the center might gain by contrast. It is the formal Raphaelesque idea. [. . .] The first division is given to the largest mass but usually not the most important. This, if trees or a building are shadow-covered, reserves the more distant mass, which is the most attractive, to gain by the sacrifice of the foreground mass. [. . . T]he light proceeds onwards through an avenue which the sides create."[51] The result is an idealized, geometricalized space that is the complete opposite of the tendency in modern painting toward flattened space. It is certainly not hard to recognize the Claudian arrangement— "the deepest dark [. . .] over which our vision travels"– in the tango-hall shot, although perhaps a more accurate reference would be the repoussoir effect within interiors by the Dutch genre painters of the Delft school (notably Vermeer).[52] Claude had been a point of reference for photographers ever since Henry Peach Robinson's *Pictorial Effect in Photography* (from 1869) and, possibly due to the influence of Poore's handbook, is visible in some of the most noteworthy works of the Photo-Secession, such as the foreground silhouettes of carriages and pedestrians at dusk in Edward Steichen's photograph of *The Flatiron* from 1905. Alfred Stieglitz, too, often employed strong contrast together with soft focus on the background: his 1903 version of *The Flatiron* offsets an atmospheric, dematerialized background diffused by snow and rain with the stark vertical line of a tree in the foreground.

The dark edges of the Claudian frame, represented by (antique) buildings, large trees, or the sides of a cliff, were called "*coulisses*" or "wings," making explicit the theatrical inspiration and layout of these idealized landscapes.[53] They find echoes in the overhanging masses of foliage recalling theatrical curtains that feature noticeably in Tourneur's picturesque compositional schema. Clarence Brown, Tourneur's assistant and editor, had said that on exteriors the crew used to carry branches and twigs around because "Tourneur would always have a foreground."[54] But the principle goes back to the bucolic settings and natural exteriors of Griffith's Biograph days (and to those young directors in thrall to Griffith, like Ford and—later—Stroheim). In *Four Horsemen*, overhanging leafage is prominently employed in the Argentine part of the film (shot at La Brea), in the shots of the French army and villagers fleeing the First Battle of the Marne (reconstructed near Griffith Park), and in the highly pictorial insert shot of the Lourdes Basilica that resembles Alvin Langdon Coburn's photograph *Notre Dame* from 1908.

Through the Arches: Composition and Art Direction

While Ingram's key collaborator was Seitz, he also worked closely with a group of set designers on *Four Horsemen of the Apocalypse*, the most important of whom, Amos Myers, a school friend from Ingram's year of study at Yale, designed the tango hall.[55] In fact, this was a Spanish variation on a Bowery saloon set employed in an earlier film, the Universal Bluebird production *The Pulse of Life*, from 1917 (from which Ingram also borrowed the story idea of an adventurous youth taking a dancer after flooring her partner). *Motion Picture News*, in its elaborate twenty-eight-page spread on *Horsemen*, added in its report on the set—"an exact replica of a pre-War Parisian dance palace"— that construction of Myers's design was overseen by production manager Jacques d'Auray, in charge of the "French technicalities" of the production.[56] Still, editor Grant Whytock told Ingram's biographer Liam O'Leary that the director, a collector of art objects, just like Marcello Desnoyers, would often take control himself: he would repaint sets if he didn't like them, move pictures about on walls, and rearrange everything on the set. Just as with Tourneur, "everything had to make a composition to him."[57] Ingram and his team used architectural framings both on interior and exterior establishing shots, especially in the scenes set in the Marne Valley at the Desnoyers castle, which is consistently framed through an archway portico and by the surrounding hedges.[58] The fact that the castle—as a title tells us—is a "colossal treasure palace" is illustrated by the depth and height of the set and the flanking decorative suits of armor in the foreground.

The function of the foreground arch as proscenium seems to emphasize the theatrical inspiration behind Ingram's staging and framing. Indeed, scenic designers like Ben Carré (the designer of most of Tourneur's films up until *The Last of the Mohicans* and one of the first to assume the new title of art director) and Wilfred Buckland were associated with companies that emphasized theatrical adaptations.[59] Because of their background in opera and theater (Carré worked with Antoine, Buckland with the American Antoine, David Belasco; Tourneur, for his part, was stage manager and scenic designer for Antoine), a lot of attention has been devoted to the inspiration they drew from innovations in theatrical lighting and stage design. But like Ingram, Tourneur and Carré were thinking of painting first: Tourneur was a painter and illustrator, while Carré came from a fine-arts background and had trained as a painter. Carré continued to exhibit his landscape paintings and drawings in the style of Corot at galleries in Los Angeles throughout his life.[60] Buckland, in similar fashion, told *Moving Picture World* that his main source of inspiration was not the realistic theater of Belasco but the evocative paintings of Whistler and Corot. (Corot, who started as an Academic painter and then became more interested in light and atmosphere, thus announcing Impressionism, seems the reference of choice for Hollywood artisans caught between modernist aspiration and more traditional schemas of image composition; Ingram also mentions him in his self-promoting essay "Directing the Picture.")[61] The descriptions in Carré's English-language memoir of how he always tried to work in layers of depth, wanting "to push back" the set, make obvious reference to the principle of the painterly repoussoir.[62] Similarly, the tango-hall shot from *Four Horsemen* is "painterly" before it is theatrical, with the architectonic element of the foreground arches harking back to the Claudian schema where, as trees or columns, it already functioned as attention-guiding proscenium. As a compositional motif in most of Ingram's extant films and in Tourneur's films from the late 1910s, the use of foreground arches goes back not only to Claude but to Renaissance painting in thrall to the Antique. (See the nested archways of Raphael's Vatican Library fresco *School of Athens* [1510–1511], Raphael being, of course, the classical painter most admired by the Neoclassicists). Aptly enough, in Ingram's *Hearts Are Trumps* (1920), the painter John Gillespie (called "John Turner" in the French version I have viewed) is seen copying from a religious painting with an arched interior framing that recalls Veronese.[63] The architectural inspiration behind many of these shots no doubt also came out of Ingram's (one-year) training at the Yale School of Fine Arts with Lee Lawrie, one of the most prominent American architectural sculptors. Lawrie was trained in the Beaux-Arts tradition by assisting the Chicago architects of the White City and by working with fellow Irishman Augustus Saint-Gaudens, dubbed the American Michelangelo.

One aspect of screen pictorialism that can be traced to the New Stagecraft, however, was the radical simplification of stage design in the duo of "experimental" films Carré and Tourneur crafted for the director's own production company in 1918, *The Blue Bird* and *Prunella*—mostly flat painted surfaces and minimally designed built structures that seem to evoke the stylized impressionistic settings theorized by Gordon-Craig and Appia. In fact, there might be a direct inspiration here from the influential staging of Maeterlinck's *Blue Bird* at the Moscow Art Theatre under the direction of Stanislavski (1908). There is also a striking similarity to Ernst Stern's designs for Reinhardt's *Sumurun*, a pantomime that premiered at the Kleines Theater in 1910 before traveling to Paris, where it was likely to have been seen by Tourneur and Carré.[64] Harley Granville-Barker's 1912–13 Symbolist staging of Shakespeare's comedies, characterized by a bare stage offset by draped curtains brightly painted with symbolic designs, is another likely influence, given that *Prunella* was adapted from his and Laurence Housman's 1906 play, *Prunella, or, Love in a Dutch Garden*.

Symbolism was still quite fashionable at the end of the 1910s, especially in the United States, as can be judged not only by the Symbolist-inspired pictorial photographs of Clarence White and George Seeley but by the flavor for allegory in American films of the period, especially in those related to the War (like Ince's *Civilization* from 1916). Tourneur's visual style, in this context, has often been linked to Aestheticism.[65] We would do well, however, to draw a distinction between art-for-art's-sake Aestheticism or "*Décadisme*," firmly associated with the avant-garde, on the one hand, and Symbolism in the Idealist sense, a celebration of the spiritual and the eternal figured by the same mythical or allegorical subjects, on the other. Besides the occasional hint of the grotesque, like the bizarre nightmarish apparition of the demon Mammon at the end of *The Conquering Power* (1921), likely borrowed from Griffith's *The Avenging Conscience* (1914), neither Ingram nor Tourneur was especially interested in "Décadisme."[66] The connection to Symbolism in both painting and theater is most manifest in the emphasis on "suggestion," on mood and atmosphere, a priority picked up by several critics and commentators.[67] The preeminence of suggestion, however, came out of Ingram's idolization of Lee Lawrie and the Academic painter and sculptor John Singer Sargeant, singled out in this regard in "Directing the Picture": "In them we see not the surface but what lies beneath."[68] The association of suggestion with Lawrie and Sargeant shows that Ingram strictly adhered to Symbolism's Neoclassicist undertone and preference for morally or spiritually enlightening tableaux. In fact, the models Julio is seen painting in his Parisian garret in *Four Horsemen*—scantily clad Hellenic nymph figures, the kind one might find in the studio of a Bouguereau—seem to accurately evoke Ingram's aesthetic inspiration (see figure 12.2). (Conversely, the scene of American painter John Gillespie sketching Bull Montana sporting a Roman centurion Galea helmet in *Hearts Are Trumps* reveals Ingram's ironic take on the aesthetic.)[69]

Like Lawrie, many of the new art directors—Hugo Ballin, Robert Brunton, Everett Shinn, and William Cotton—had their architectural roots in the Greco-Roman Revival style. Ballin's case is the most instructive: although he became associated with the sparse, geometric style of contemporary design fashions, Ballin was enrolled in classes in the studio of the portraitist Wyatt Eaton, a prominent alumnus of L'École des Beaux-Arts in Paris. There, Eaton had studied classical techniques and aesthetic ideals of European antiquity and the Italian Renaissance with Neo-Greco master painter Jean-Léon Gérôme. Eaton returned to New York seeking to promote a similar reverence for tradition, craftsmanship, and beauty among other American artists. By bringing the Neoclassicist revival to the United States during the Gilded Age, Eaton and his European-educated peers hoped to advance American art and inspire a new American Renaissance. Before turning his attention to movies, Ballin's specialty was mural decoration, a fact noted by a puff piece in *Motion Picture News* summing up his many awards and credentials.[70]

Mural decoration was also an important source of inspiration for Tourneur, as can be judged from the "delirium" sequence in his 1917 adaptation of Eleanor Gates's play *The*

FIGURE 12.2 The artist's models. *Four Horsemen of the Apocalypse*.

Poor Little Rich Girl (a play with distinct Symbolist leanings), which anticipated the style of *The Blue Bird* and *Prunella*. The scene in which the drugged Gwen (Mary Pickford) dreams of an allegorical netherworld starts with a shot that reappears almost identically in *The Blue Bird*: the presence of a Greek temple in the background of the shot is explained by the superimposed appearance of a group of muse-like figures, dressed in white Grecian tunics, who start dancing around Gwen. The effect recalls Jacques-Dalcroze's Hellerau Neo-Greco settings or Isadora Duncan's art dances but was inspired by two works by the French muralist Pierre Puvis de Chavannes, *Le Rêve* (1883) and *Le Bois sacré cher aux arts et aux muses* (1884–89), part of a suite of murals he designed for the Musée des Beaux Arts of Lyon that was first shown as an enormous oil painting at the Paris Salon.[71] The close connection between Puvis's style and Maeterlinck's *Blue Bird* is also shown by Frederick Cayley Robinson's designs for the 1911 revival of the play in New York City and his illustrations for the published edition. Robinson was a Symbolist artist whose style is highly indebted to Puvis (Robinson's 1904 watercolor *To Pastures New, Dawn* is a virtual copy of Puvis's *Esquisse pour le pauvre pêcheur* from 1879). Puvis was a Salon painter whose two-dimensional "flat" style and pastel palette strongly impressed the Symbolists. The young Tourneur had provided preliminary sketches for the creation of Puvis's famous *The Muses of Inspiration* design for the Boston Library, installed in 1895. Puvis's influence—already looming large, together with that of Corot and Bouguereau, in the mythological-pastoral films in the Gaumont "Films esthétiques" catalogue—can be perceived not just in the allegorical motif of the muses but in the frieze-like composition in which figures seem to occupy multiple two-dimensional planes within three-dimensional space.[72] Although he was included in the Armory show (as was Corot) and was eulogized by Mallarmé (who saw his "modernité" precisely in his classicism), Puvis was a conservative artist, a student of Academic painter Thomas Couture, and a co-founder (with Delacroix) of the Société Nationale des Beaux Arts, who considered himself primarily a history painter. His paintings and murals expressed a deep nostalgia for a Hellenizing golden age. While his characteristic simplification of form, lack of chiaroscuro, emphasis on line and general flattening attracted Symbolists and abstractionists, these techniques can be said to have resulted from the two-dimensionality demanded by wall paintings (inspired by the Greek bas-reliefs and pre-Renaissance frescoes he had studied abroad).[73] As Kaveh Askari has argued, Puvis's style and his methods proved completely adaptable to American museums and other educational institutions, where the more decadent Symbolist traditions were less appropriate.[74]

Ingram and Tourneur's use of the architectural foreground arch also partook of the Orientalist vogue in French nineteenth-century painting, architecture, and the decorative arts. Ingram's update of Balzac's *Eugénie Grandet* (1833), *The Conquering Power* (1921), opens on a sensational Orientalist shot that rivals Lang's vision of Babylon in *Metropolis* (1927). The shot introduces Valentino as a modern-day Charles Grandet, living the high life in a decadent sérail (that turns out to be his own living room), and features skimpily dressed dancers brought on in chalices, framed through the opening of an elaborate Arabic tent that is worked into the design. As in *Four Horsemen*, the shot includes a repoussoir effect, with silhouetted musicians in Arab garb in the foreground, and boasts selective lighting with modulated softness and smoke. Both iconographically and compositionally, the shot looks forward to *The Arab* (1924), a more upscale version of *The Sheik* (1921), starring Ramon Novarro and shot on location in Tunisia at Gabes and Sidi Bou Said. *The Arab* would foster Ingram's lifelong interest in Arabic culture and Oriental artifacts. Ingram was friends with Orientalist painter Étienne (later Nasreddine) Dinet, a student of Bouguereau, who, like the great Salon painters—Delacroix, Ingrès, Gérôme and their successors, such as Paul Louis Bouchard—was in thrall to the Near East. All of these painters' genre scenes of North African or Middle Eastern harems and bathhouses drew on the Neo-Grec style. The influence of Gérôme's *Prayer in the Mosque of Amor Cairo* (1871) and its open arcade of arches can be detected in one of the more striking instances of Tourneur's use of the foreground arch in *The Blue Bird*: in the palace the fairy Berylune is seen silhouetted in the background and framed by a succession of arches that show the horseshoe design typical of Islamic architecture.

The vogue for Islamic pointed arches in the set design of the time can also be attributed to the success of *Sumurun* (both the play and Lubitsch's film from 1920, released in the US in September 1921). But it also resulted from a closely connected Spanish cycle that started with DeMille's *Carmen* and continued with Lubitsch's *Gipsy Blood* (1918) (the German version of *Carmen* released in the US right before *Sumurun*), a trend that certainly motivated Loew to acquire the Blasco Ibáñez property. *Four Horsemen* triumphed, as did the Valentino follow-up *Blood and Sand* (1922), made at

Paramount by the director of the Spanish-Californian fantasy *The Mark of Zorro* (1920), Fred Niblo. At the same time, the Andalusian architectural style with inner courtyards and horseshoe arches could be admired in a more poetic mode in L'Herbier's *El Dorado*, featuring an abundance of highly picturesque silhouetted scenes framed through the arches of the icon of Al-Andalus, the Alhambra. In Hollywood the cycle was supposed to have culminated with Lubitsch's *Rosita* (1923), an adaptation of the 1872 opera *Don César* with scenic work by Sven Gade and William Cameron Menzies, the latter credited with "artistic design." *Rosita* featured arches in the foreground framing both Rosita's family's humble home and an enormous prison courtyard. But the film proved less successful than Ingram's friend Herbert Brenon's version of the same material, *The Spanish Dancer* (1923), starring Antonio Moreno and Lubitsch's Carmen, Pola Negri. Other than with the Argentine chapters of *Four Horsemen*, and his earlier response to the success of *Carmen* with the Universal Bluebird *Chalice of Sorrow* (1916)—a version of *Tosca* transplanted to Mexico to approximate the atmosphere of DeMille–Buckland's Seville—Ingram did not further participate in the Spanish-Moorish cycle. Instead he further developed the Islamic aspect of the Andalusian pictorial style in films like *The Arab* and *The Garden of Allah* (1927).

Paris, As We Picture Her

In her study of the radical change in taste in the Hollywood of the 1920s, *The Decline of Sentiment*, Lea Jacobs quotes the response of the trade and broader press to Tourneur's historical romance, *Lorna Doone* (1922), which was deemed "respectable" but "old-fashioned," despite or perhaps because of the director's signature pictorial effects.[75] As the integration of Hollywood's classical "invisible" style continued, the idea was not to distract the eye too much and keep the focus on the story and the characters. "Restraint" in all aspects of film production was seen as a prime value. Looking for things to praise in *Lorna Doone*, the reviewer for the *New York Times* wrote: "Mr. Tourneur is a storyteller as well as a maker of motion pictures, and he knows the value of restraint as well as that of emphasis."[76] The critic Norbert Lusk praised in this light the designs of Hugo Ballin, who, "for the first time in movies," "eliminated useless detail" and "used large spaces of clear wall with restrained detail."[77] Lusk's colleague Matthew Josephson, in a long essay for *Motion Picture Classic*, "Super-Realism in the Movies," strongly opposed any kind of eye-catching pictorial effect: "When the director orders a certain kind of bedroom, shaped like a gondola, let us say, a bit of fantastic Orientalism, whose formal beauty is created not by the camera, but by the art director, then I protest, and become unhappy."[78] Ingram was one of the directors targeted (Lubitsch and Stroheim were the others) in quips like: "The more high-handed the director becomes [. . .] so much the more stagy dives, cafés and boudoirs do you get. [. . .] You get more and more uncomfortable-looking actors and more blurs and blurs and glazings on the film."[79] The general spaciousness and incredibly high ceilings of the design for the historic Burlesdon Hall set in *The Prisoner of Zenda* (1922), filled to the hilt with objets d'art and framed by the same suits of armor used for the Villeblanche castle in *Four Horsemen*, clearly failed to heed the general recommendation for restraint in art design. Still, it could be said that Ingram simply adhered to the new conventions for the historical swashbuckler established by Fairbanks and Allan Dwan's *Robin Hood* (1922). On the other hand, when the "humble" Grandet household in the "sleepy village" of Noyant in *The Conquering Power* appears designed to accommodate at least twenty, the impression of lavish size and depth reinforced by adjoining spaces at the back and furniture placed close to the camera in the old-fashioned style, one cannot but conclude that Ingram was building them bigger than the norm.

Next to restraint in art direction, the main concern of the advisory discourse of the trades and industry publications was narrative integration. It was during the twenties— a decade during which a new *Blue Bird* was as unthinkable as a second *Intolerance* (although Stroheim certainly gave it his best)—that both Ingram and Tourneur turned to classic adventure stories (*The Prisoner of Zenda*, *The Last of the Mohicans*, Tourneur's *Treasure Island* from 1920), probably to stress the integrative potential of their pictorial style. The theater critic Robert Burns Mantle wrote in *Photoplay*: "Tourneur differs from most directors in that he can achieve great beauty of background without sacrifice of story value, and while he does permit a certain repetition of his favorite shots . . . they seldom interfere with the spectator's interest in the tale."[80] Patrick Keating cites an article John Seitz contributed to *American Cinematographer* in 1923 that offers another variation on the same theme: "In the best of the dramatic productions we often see examples of what is at once the science and art of cinematography—the perfect harmony of the photography with the mood of the story of the players. The story is more than just a causal chain of events that runs through the entire film; it is a generator of dramatic, emotional moments. It is these emotional moments that call for artful cinematography." Instead of a pictorial quality in itself, "mood" has now become story-specific. As Keating writes, "more story means more mood, and more mood means more opportunity for artistry."[81] The most prominent commentator was former pictorialist Cecil B. DeMille, who in a piece in the *Los Angeles Times* from July 1923, "Pictures Secondary in Cinema Success," warns against films becoming too pictorial in a storytelling medium.[82] The article was illustrated with images from Ingram's *Scaramouche* (1923). Askari nevertheless points to the more integrated pictorial mise-en-scène of *Scaramouche*, which sets the action within the pictorial frame (as in the final duel in a wide shot through two nested archways of a Gothic cathedral), instead of relegating composition to the status of ornament. He makes the same point about Tourneur's adventure novel adaptations, which sought out ways to "merge athletic physical performance with conspicuous style, into a kind of swashbuckling pictorialism."[83]

Although swashbucklers were said to be perennial and both *Zenda* and *Scaramouche* were sizable hits, there was a reason why Ingram decided to update his adaptation of *Eugénie Grandet*. *The Conquering Power* came with a disclaimer that aims to establish the film's contemporaneity: "Commercialism tells us that you, Great Public, do not like the costume play. Life is life, so we make our story of today, that you may recognize each character as it comes your way." Although audiences still complained about anachronisms, having forgotten about the modernization the minute the highly sentimental prestige picture got under way, Ingram's move was shrewdly considered. As Lea Jacobs argues, by the middle of the decade the taste for sentimental "hokum" was over, and the call was for modernity and sophistication. The opening shot of *The Conquering Power* seems to respond to this call: while its Moorish trimmings and pictorial softness emblematize the Salon inspiration of Ingram's style, other aspects point ahead to a new, more modern, Gatsby-like accommodation for the Beaux-Arts style. The design of the shot was handled by Ralph Barton, the famous illustrator and poster artist whose work appeared in *The New Yorker* and *Vanity Fair* and in Jazz-Age classics like Anita Loos's *Gentlemen Prefer Blondes* (1925). Barton, another fellow student from Yale, was actually living the kind of fast life in Paris, London, and New York to which the opening shot of *The Conquering Power* alludes. "Paris as we picture her," a title tells us. Paris was seen as the embodiment of such urbanity, now associated less with "la vie de Bohème" of Montmartre and its starving artists and demimondaines—which Tourneur was still bringing to the screen in movies like *While Paris Sleeps* (1920)—than with the bars, nightclubs, and cabarets of Montparnasse, where jazz reigned. Valentino as Armand and Nazimova as Marguerite appeared in the notorious Art Deco version of *Camille* (1921), updated to 1920s Paris, and arguably the crucial linking film between the old—also incarnated by Valentino as Julio Desnoyers in *Four Horsemen*—and the new Parisian cycle. *Camille* possibly motivated the updating of Balzac in *The Conquering Power*, a movie on which former French film journalist Robert Florey served as advisor for "French atmosphere." (He performed the same service on Ingram's next film, *Trifling Women*, a remake of his 1916 Gothic fantasy *Black Orchids*.)

In many ways, "modernity" for American audiences was equated with Paris. American culture was transplanted to Paris during *les années folles* (as recorded by Edmund Wilson's 1922 *Vanity Fair* article, "The Aesthetic Upheaval in France: The Influence of Jazz in Paris and Americanization of French Literature and Art"), but the new Hollywood trend for risqué musicals and "sex comedies" was in turn inhabited by the spirit of, or literally based on, French bedroom farce. The irony was that Ingram and Tourneur, who had made careers out of Parisian "atmosphere," went into decline once the values of the Jazz Age began to take over. Although audiences still flocked to spectacles like *Scaramouche* and *Ben-Hur* (1925, a film Ingram was originally slated to direct at Metro), it was clear that once Chaplin's *A Woman of Paris* (1923) had brought out the Parisian ground-tone of DeMille's divorce comedies of the late 1910s, tastes were changing—and movie style and technique with them.

A Woman of Paris provided the template for the Lubitsch comedies of the mid-1920s which, despite their basis in German/Viennese operetta and farce, were associated far more with Paris than with Berlin. None of these films was a big hit, but the "sophistication" associated with Lubitsch—less a matter of outré sets and clothes as in recent DeMille films than of understated dramaturgy, subtle gestures, and glance-object editing which, together with carefully handled visual motifs, provided the equivalent for the literary wit of the farceurs—set a new industry standard. The films were held to be the acme of cinematic refinement, not only because of their flexible moral values but also because of their scintillating rhythm, a tempo completely at odds with the rather deliberate, "calm" pacing of even a sensational topic like *Four Horsemen*. What interests me is how the employment of pictorialism, with its ties to both proto-modern theatrical and painterly Symbolism and Neoclassical Academicism, survived as a decorative option for cinematographers and designers in a model stressing unobtrusive continuity and a cinema stressing modernity above all. How was pictorial style adapted from historical or fantasy subjects (with their blatantly architectural sets) or horror films and melodramas (for the low-key lighting) and applied to contemporary Jazz Age comedies and romantic dramas? In other words, what happened to the tango-hall shot?

In her monograph on Lubitsch, Kristin Thompson suggests that, after borrowing from Chaplin and DeMille for *The Marriage Circle* (1924), Lubitsch copied from the tango-bar scene in *Four Horsemen* for a nightclub setting in his sophisticated society drama, *Three Women* (1924): the drapes that create a scalloped frame in the foreground recreate Ingram-Seitz's repoussoir effect, reinforced by the contrast between the dark foreground and the softer, brighter background.[84] The movie, photographed by Charles Rosher, is full of such dark foreground zones in darkly lit rooms, a possible influence from Tourneur-Carré. In fact, the shot in *Three Women* is closer *qua* composition to the establishing shot of the Parisian tea-dance scene in *Four Horsemen*, a more sophisticated rehearsal of the Boca tango scene, viewed from a darkened stage area, with the large foreground curtain drawn back to let the viewer into the more brightly lit dramatic space. Although similar use of the darkened foreground is completely lacking in the nightclub scene at the beginning of *Woman of Paris* and is not to be found in any of DeMille's sex comedies (DeMille having opted for a more general illumination of his expensive sets and a less contrast-heavy style), it appears in many of the films that Jacobs discusses as examples of sophisticated comedy in the Lubitsch vein, notably the films of the Constance Talmadge unit at First National, which included the art director William Cameron Menzies and Charles Rosher.[85] A Sidney Franklin film, *Her Sister from Paris* (1925), with art direction by Menzies and a screenplay by Lubitsch's steady collaborator Hans Kräly, provides one such example (see figure 12.3).

The view from the tonally dark orchestra section, through an open wall with decorative borders to the brighter middle ground and background, adheres to a compositional pattern found in many of the Jazz Age comedies but spruces it up with pictorial flourishes. The nightclub setting created opportunities for designers and photographers like Menzies and Rosher to provide not just Art Nouveau or Art Deco stylings but classical pictorialist schemas that would also resurface later in the decade in some of the "naturalist" films by the German-Austrian trio of Stroheim, Sternberg, and Murnau, or in the films of Ford and Borzage at Fox. The diffused contrast on the middle and background planes, in this case, also shows that the soft look had become a generally accepted option independent of genre or degree of artistic independence by the mid-1920s (although Lubitsch generally preferred sharpness and harder edges).[86] Stroheim's director of photography, William Daniels, together with Tony Gaudio, another cinematographer with roots in pictorialist photography, shot Mauritz Stiller's first American

FIGURE 12.3 Under the tavern lights. *Her Sister from Paris* (1925).

film (finished by Fred Niblo), *The Temptress* (1926), another Blasco Ibáñez adaptation that opens in Paris at a masquerade ball. "Spring—and the nights of Paris, Throb with love and desire," the opening art title tells us. After a shot of a Pierrot figure strumming his guitar in the moonlight, we dissolve into a view of the costumed revellers seen in depth from a balcony framed by overhanging theater curtains. As if to accentuate the separation of the darkened foreground from the brighter but softly graded backdrop plane (despite the illusion of a roaming spotlight!) a silhouetted Greta Garbo walks into the foreground. Just as Tourneur and Ingram (and, for a while, Seitz) left for France[87] while the vogue for Parisian sophistication was only really taking off, the pictorialist style was back where, in *Four Horsemen of the Apocalypse*, it had first been promoted, "under the tavern lights."

Notes

1. *The Film Daily* called *Four Horsemen* a "pictorial triumph" and singled out the "Tango Dance in the slums of Buenos Aires" as "possibly the best dance ever put in pictures." *The Film Daily*, February 20, 1921, 3.
2. Gaylyn Studlar, *This Mad Masquerade: Stardom and Masculinity in the Jazz Age* (New York: Columbia University Press, 1996), 168.

3. In a piece on Griffith's pastoral *A Summer Idyl* (1910), titled "Pictorialism and the Picture," the *Moving Picture World* columnist refers to contemporary photographic practice as a standard for the movies: "A photograph may be just a photograph: that is, a cartographical transcript of the original or, in simpler words, a mere map; or it may be a picture; that is to say, it complies with the definite laws of composition, balance, and all the rest of the elements that go to make up a picture of any kind. These are the elements that we desire to see in the moving picture." *Moving Picture World*, September 10, 1910, 566–567.
4. Ingram studied drawing and sculpting at Yale with the sculptor Lee Lawrie. At Yale he learned ("despite inattention") about "the laws that govern perspective, composition, balance, construction, form and the distribution of light and shade." Rex Ingram, "Directing the Picture," in *Opportunities in the Motion Picture Industry* (Venice, CA: Photoplay Research Society, 1922), 29.
5. David Bordwell, Janet Staiger, and Kristin Thompson, *The Classical Hollywood Cinema: Film Style and Mode of Production to 1960* (New York: Columbia University Press, 1985), 292.
6. Alvin Langdon Coburn illustrated Maeterlinck, while his cousin F. Holland Day was co-founder of the publishing firm that put out the American edition of the infamous *Yellow Book* and Wilde's *Salomé* with illustrations by Aubrey Beardsley.
7. See also the role of "Stimmung" in the writings of late nineteenth-century art historians like Alois Riegl and Heinrich Wölfflin.
8. Kristin Thompson, "The Limits of Experimentation in Hollywood," in Jan-Christopher Horak, ed., *Lovers of Cinema: The First American Film Avant-Garde, 1919–1945* (Madison: University of Wisconsin Press, 1995), 67-94.
9. See "Pictorialism and the Picture: Art, Photography, and the 'Doctrine of Taste' in the Discourse on Transitional-Era Quality Films," in Scott Curtis, Philippe Gauthier, Tom Gunning, and Joshua Yumibe, eds., *The Image in Early Cinema: Form and Material* (Bloomington: Indiana University Press, 2018), 249–257, where I discuss the attempt by both the trade press and art institutions to connect film literacy to a discourse on taste in order to preserve a coherent American identity in the face of ethnic diversity and class struggle.
10. Thompson, *Classical Hollywood Cinema*; "Limits of Experimentation."
11. Patrick Keating, *Hollywood Lighting from the Silent Era to Film Noir* (New York: Columbia University Press, 2010); Barry Salt, *Film Style and Technology: History and Analysis* (London: Starword, 1992 [second expanded edition]); Lea Jacobs, *The Decline of Sentiment: American Film in the 1920s* (Berkeley: University of California Press, 2008).
12. Thompson quotes cinematographer Arthur Miller on *Four Horsemen* as one of the most visually influential films of the period: Bordwell, Staiger, and Thompson, *Classical Hollywood Cinema*, 233, 291.
13. See Lea Jacobs, "Belasco, DeMille and the Development of Lasky Lighting," *Film History* 5, no. 4 (December 1993): 405–418.
14. Patrick Keating quotes cinematographer Arthur Miller on his days shooting comedies at Essanay: "My first instructions were that the faces of the actors must be white and the sets fully lit with no shadows." He also quotes a 1923 interview with Seitz in which he distinguishes between the "unobtrusive" style of the comedy cinematographer and the more openly "artistic" work in drama cinematography: *Hollywood Lighting*, 78, 93.
15. Although "Rembrandt lighting" was the sales pitch, the chiaroscuro seems closer to the Academician John Singer Sargent's "Spanish Dancer" paintings from 1880–1881. Keating quotes pictorialist Henry Peach Robinson's dissatisfaction with the term, since it usually

denoted side-back lighting, while Rembrandt favored soft light from above: *Hollywood Lighting*, 31–32.
16. Bordwell, Staiger, and Thompson, *Classical Hollywood Cinema*, 289–290.
17. Patrick Ogle, "Technological and Aesthetic Influences on the Development of Deep-Focus Cinematography in the United States," in Bill Nichols, ed., *Movies and Methods, Volume II* (Berkeley: University of California Press, 1985), 63. Karl Struss, a pioneer of the soft style, was one of the first cinematographers to start experimenting with panchromatic stock on *The Affairs of Anatol* (1921). See Charles Higham, *Hollywood Cameramen* (Bloomington: Indiana University Press, 1970), 122.
18. Ben Brewster and Lea Jacobs, *Theatre to Cinema: Stage Pictorialism and the Early Feature Film* (Oxford: Oxford University Press, 1997), 172–173.
19. Bordwell, Staiger, and Thompson, *Classical Hollywood Cinema*, 222–223.
20. Victor Oscar Freeburg, *Pictorial Beauty on the Screen* (New York: Macmillan, 1923), vii.
21. The Struss Pictorial lens was the first soft-focus lens introduced into the motion picture industry in 1916. In 1919, Struss signed on as cameraman with DeMille.
22. Bordwell, Staiger, and Thompson, *Classical Hollywood Cinema*, 291–292; Patrick Keating, "From the Portrait to the Close-Up: Gender and Technology in Still Photography and Hollywood Cinematography," *Cinema Journal* 45, no. 3 (Spring 2006), 98. Keating has also suggested that while portrait photographers were slow to turn to the artificial lighting techniques used by cinematographers and generally relied on bounced daylight, *Vanity Fair* commercial photographers like Arnold Genthe and Victor Georg had a pronounced influence on the development of the soft style in cinematography: Keating, *Hollywood Lighting*, 39–41.
23. "Ideal Directors," *New York Times* 13 February 1921, quoted in Richard Koszarski, *An Evening's Entertainment: The Age of the Silent Feature Picture, 1915–1928* (New York: Charles Scribner's Sons, 1990), 124.
24. Ibid.
25. Barry Salt points out that while heavy lens diffusion was used for the close-ups in Ingram's *Scaramouche*, in *Four Horsemen* actual diffusion was limited to one or two emotional moments, the filmmakers generally preferring the soft circular vignette mask with the blurred edges of the mask affecting the definition of the center of the frame: *Film Style and Technology*, 154.
26. Liam O'Leary, *Rex Ingram: Master of the Silent Cinema* (London & Pordenone, Italy: BFI and Le Giornate del Cinema Muto, 1993), 65–66.
27. Bordwell, Staiger, and Thompson, *Classical Hollywood Cinema*, 291.
28. O'Leary, *Rex Ingram*, 66.
29. Jean-Louis Comolli, "Technique et idéologie: Caméra, perspective, profondeur du champ," *Cahiers du cinéma*, no. 229 (May 1971).
30. Joel Snyder explains that "the photograph shows everything in sharp delineation from edge to edge, while our vision, because our eyes are foveate, is sharp only at its 'center.'" "Picturing Vision," *Critical Inquiry* 5, no. 3 (Spring 1980), quoted in Martin Jay, *Downcast Eyes: The Denigration of Vision in Twentieth-Century French Thought* (Berkeley: University of California Press, 1994), 131.
31. Koszarski, *An Evening's Entertainment*, 124.
32. Although the manipulation of light to suggest volume and texture is shared by the sculptor and the filmmaker, the assessment in *Motion Picture News* that "much of the notable excellence of 'The Four Horsemen of the Apocalypse' is directly traceable to Director Ingram's

study of sculpture" is certainly an exaggeration that fits in with the promotional use of artistic associations discussed by Kaveh Askari. See "Ingram Film Inspires Sculpture Teacher," *Motion Picture News*, March 26, 1921, 2224.
33. "Directing the Picture" in Ingram, *Opportunities in the Motion Picture Industry*, 31.
34. Barry Salt has called this much harsher contrast-heavy style, leaving shadows in the middle of the subject's face, "core-lighting." See *Film Style and Technology*, 154.
35. Salt mentions that lens diffusion in a selected area of the frame was also used by Jean Epstein: *Film Style and Technology*, 161.
36. Although Moussinac evoked, somewhat predictably, the Tenebrist trio Goya, Velazquez, and Ribera. Richard Abel, *French Film Theory and Criticism: A History/Anthology (1907–1939)* (Princeton, NJ: Princeton University Press, 1988), 253.
37. Salt, *Film Style and Technology*, 130–131, 161.
38. Brewster and Jacobs quote Henri Diamant-Berger's 1919 *Le Cinéma*, in which the filmmaker states that "sharpness of vision should be the same in every plane." See *Theatre to Cinema*, 171.
39. "Contre-jour" (or "against daylight") photography has the camera pointing directly toward the source of light, producing backlighting on the subjects.
40. In its review of the Universal production *A Soul at Stake* (1916), *Moving Picture World* praised the film's "novel effects in black and white chiaroscuro" and its "shapes thrown up against the sun in silhouette," concluding that "the present vogue for silhouette effects among Fifth Avenue photographers has had its reflex at Universal City": October 7, 1916, 66.
41. On the travel films, see Giorgio Bertellini, *Italy in Early American Cinema: Race, Landscape, and the Picturesque* (Bloomington: Indiana University Press, 2010). For more on this style of exterior shooting, see Eileen Bowser, *The Transformation of Cinema, 1907–1915* (Berkeley: University of California Press, 1990), 239–242; Kristin Thompson, "The International Exploration of Cinematic Expressivity," in Lee Grieveson and Peter Krämer, eds., *The Silent Cinema Reader* (London & New York: Routledge, 2004), 261; and Salt, *Film Style and Technology*, 71–73.
42. Salt, *Film Style and Technology*, 71–73.
43. Brownlow also notices similarities between the mobilization scenes in both films. But he notes that since *J'accuse* was not shown in America until 1921, the similarities may be coincidental. Kevin Brownlow, *The Parade's Gone By . . .* (Berkeley: University of California Press, 1968), 535. Nevertheless, the similarity between the famous "sea of crosses" shot in *Four Horsemen* and the "return of the dead" sequence in *J'accuse* is striking.
44. Ibid., i. Charles Rosher, Pickford's steady cameraman at Artcraft, reproduced the marine moonlight effect as a day-for-night shot in *The Love Light* (1921), but with a shot scale closer to Perret than to Tourneur, bringing to mind the skyline silhouettes in the pictorialist photography of Annie Brigman (the naturalist-Symbolist *Dawn* [1913]), rather than, say, the striking foreground silhouettes of Edward Steichen's photograph of another of Tourneur's old mentors, Auguste Rodin, seen in stark relief against the white marble of his "Monument to Victor Hugo" in *Rodin–The Thinker* (1902).
45. Keating points out that many cinematographers of the period relied on a simple guideline: when in doubt, put a little extra light on the foreground: *Hollywood Lighting*, 83.
46. See for instance "Plastic Motion Photography," *Motion Picture News*, August 5, 1916, 816–817.
47. *Motion Picture News* noted that "departures have been made in backlighting effects that will set a new standard for cinema photography": "Production a Distinctive Achievement," *Motion Picture News*, March 26, 1921, 2242.

48. Keating, *Hollywood Lighting*, 88. Ingram also mentions Doré in "Directing the Picture," *Opportunities*, 28. Oddly, the writer and teacher Victor Freeburg's *Pictorial Beauty on the Screen*, also from 1923, and quite focused on *Four Horsemen* (the book has a preface by Ingram), makes no mention of the use of foreground silhouettes in the tango hall scene, noting only the use of smoke to separate the planes.
49. Thompson, "Limits of Experimentation," 74n19.
50. Keating, *Hollywood Lighting*, 88.
51. Henry Rankin Poore, *Pictorial Composition and the Critical Judgment of Pictures: A Handbook for Students and Lovers of Art* (New York: Baker & Taylor, 1903), 164.
52. Ibid., 172. Art historian Svetlana Alpers has pointed out, however, that seventeenth-century Dutch art in general was less committed to the monocular perspective and favored a division of attention over the entire canvas. See *The Art of Describing: Dutch Art in the Seventeenth Century* (Chicago, IL: University of Chicago Press, 1983).
53. As Bertellini notes, the "Claude glass," a slightly convex, opaque, black-tinted mirror that functioned as a portable frame, popularized by Romantic artists, structured a natural landscape into theatrical thirds: "its use of foreground, middle ground, and background compares well to modern theatre's upstage, middle stage, and downstage." See *Italy in Early American Cinema*, 31.
54. The original source for the anecdote is Brownlow, *The Parade's Gone By*, 140.
55. "More building material was used in the making of the picture than was required to erect the Woolworth building," boasted *Exhibitors Herald* in a claim that rivaled those connected to Griffith's epics: January 29, 1921, 48.
56. *Motion Picture News* also called the set and its careful reproduction of the original resort's table space, dance floor, and restaurant "one of the most pretentious of the kind ever constructed for picture purpose": March 26, 1922, 234.
57. O'Leary, *Rex Ingram*, 77.
58. Victor Freeburg noted the use of arches in *Carmen* in his *The Art of Photoplay Making* (New York: Macmillan, 1918), 43.
59. On the arrival of the art director, see Bordwell, Staiger, and Thompson, *Classical Hollywood Cinema*, 147–148. Scenic designers were often credited with creating "art interiors."
60. See Askari, *Making Movies into Art*, 97.
61. "The Scenic Side of the Photodrama" *Moving Picture World*, July 21, 1917, 374–375; Ingram, *Opportunities*, 30.
62. See Askari, *Making Movies into Art*, 98.
63. I want to thank the Belgian CINEMATEK and Nicola Mazzanti and Bruno Mestdagh for letting me view their restoration of this rare Ingram film.
64. Reinhardt had wanted a plain white background with minimal flat designs against which the players could dance and act their pantomime in silhouette, an effect reproduced in *The Blue Bird* in the backdrop of the fairy Berylune's castle, strikingly similar to some of Stern's designs. Stern also created the flamboyant design for Lubitsch's "grotesque," *Die Bergkatze* (1921). That film prominently features arches in its design, but so did *Anna Boleyn* (1920), much more inconspicuously decorated and designed by Kurt Richter in a reasonably historically accurate Gothic style. That designers working in Hollywood liked to flaunt their familiarity with theatrical innovators with whom they were not entirely "au courant," is shown by frequent references to "Rinehardt."
65. Jacobs, *Decline of Sentiment*, 25–26.

66. While the "vision scenes" in *Four Horsemen* and *The Conquering Power* still closely follow the symbolism in Griffith (and the mystical bent he shared with June Mathis), Ingram's adaptation of Somerset Maugham's *The Magician* (1926) veered into Stroheim's world of decadence with its lurid Bacchanalian orgy scene, in which Alice Terry is ravished by a near-naked faun/devil.
67. See for instance "Rex Ingram on 'Atmosphere'" in *Motion Picture* critic Peter Milne's *Motion Picture Directing: The Facts and Theories of the Newest Art* (New York: Falk Publishing, 1922). Ingram explains that, "While good atmosphere gives an air of reality to a picture yet the most convincing and engrossing atmosphere is often far from realistic. This is so because the aim of the director should be to get over the *effect* of the atmosphere he desires, rather than the actual atmosphere which exists in such scenes as he may wish to portray, and which, if reduced literally to the screen would be quite unconvincing." Milne explains that what is at stake is "the principle of creating something by implication and suggestion," 62.
68. Ingram, *Opportunities*, 29. Milne writes in *Motion Picture Directing* that "[Ingram] *suggests* scenes in his pictures and refuses to *label* them. In this respect he is farther advanced than most any director in the art today." Quoted in Koszarski, *An Evening's Entertainment*, 238.
69. Judging from promotional photographs, Lon Chaney's Latin Quarter sculptor Henri Santados can be seen working in the same Beaux-Arts mode in Tourneur's lost film, *While Paris Sleeps* (1920).
70. "The Picture a Medium for Art—Hugo Ballin, Goldwyn Art Director, Has Taken the Photoplay Seriously as Field for Creation," *Motion Picture News*, July 12, 1919, 541.
71. The Symbolist painter Maurice Denis, heavily inspired by Puvis, painted Isadora Duncan as one of the nine Greek muses in a mural for the newly revamped Théâtre des Champs-Elysées in 1913.
72. Barry Salt has argued that Tourneur's idiosyncratic use of a distinctive arch-shaped camera mask is consistently tied to the denotation of fantasy or hallucination and is not used merely for decoration. Given that the mask appears both in Feuillade's "sujets antiques" (like *Le Printemps* 1909) and in Lubitsch's films of the late 1910s and early 1920s, I would argue that its decorative lineage is well established, even as this arched vignette serves to organize the films thematically and structurally. On the one hand, the idiosyncratic masking device refers to the outside circular frame of the *tondo*, inspired by the circular compositions of Leonardo, adapted by Raphael, and secularized by Dutch genre painters like Vermeer, Steen, and De Hooch. The *tondo*—often used in conjunction with interior architectural arched framings—resurfaced in the elaborate borders and ornamental frames that Puvis insisted were integral to specific paintings like *Homère (la Poésie épique)* (1895).
73. Russell T. Clement, *Four French Symbolists: A Sourcebook on Pierre Puvis de Chavannes, Gustave Moreau, Odilon Redon and Maurice Denis* (Westport, CT: Greenwood, 1996); see also Aimée Brown Price, *Pierre Puvis de Chavannes* (New York: Rizzoli, 1994).
74. Askari, *Making Movies into Art*, 95–96.
75. Jacobs, *Decline of Sentiment*, 223.
76. Ibid., 224.
77. Norbert Lusk, "Beauty and the Silversheet," *Picture-Play Magazine*, February 1921, 633.
78. Matthew Josephson, "Super-Realism in the Movies," *Motion Picture Classic*, April 1926, 43, 72, 77.
79. Ibid., 77.

80. Quoted in Thompson, "Limits of Experimentation," 91n19.
81. Keating, *Hollywood Lighting*, 93.
82. Cited in Ruth Barton, *Rex Ingram: Visionary Director of the Silent Screen* (Lexington: University of Kentucky Press, 2014), 122.
83. Askari, *Making Movies into Art*, 126, 108.
84. Kristin Thompson, *Herr Lubitsch Goes to Hollywood: German and American Film after World War I* (Amsterdam: Amsterdam University Press, 2005), 65.
85. On DeMille's style in the 1920s, see Keating, *Hollywood Lighting*, 86.
86. David Bordwell cites cinematographer Joseph Dubray, a regular contributor to *American Cinematographer*, on the general acceptance of photographic softness by 1928: "It is acknowledged by cinematographers in general that the need of absolutely sharp definition is a thing of the past. The dramatic quality of present day cinematography demands a certain softness of contours throughout the whole image." See *Classical Hollywood Cinema*, 342.
87. After the deal went sour on *Ben-Hur*, Ingram left Hollywood for Nice, where he shot most of *Mare Nostrum* (1926) (still nominally an MGM film) at the Victorine studios. He produced two more films for MGM from France—*The Magician* (1926) and *The Garden of Allah* (1927). Tourneur also ran afoul of MGM: he was fired from what would have been his first (part-)talkie, a production of Jules Verne's *The Mysterious Island*. He returned to France in 1928, where he had a long career in sound pictures.

CHAPTER 13

SYMBOLIST IMPRESSIONS

Modern Theater, Germaine Dulac, and the Making of an Art Cinema in Belle Époque France (or, the False Ideal of the Cinema against Theater)

TAMI WILLIAMS

INTRODUCTION

THEATER has long been in the wings of cinema.[1] During the rich and turbulent transitional period, from circa 1908 through World War I, as the early film industry began to expand its reach, setting up movie houses across the globe, the age-old art of Theater and the burgeoning motion picture medium waged local battles on multiple fronts. By the mid-1910s and into the 1920s, in metropolitan cities across the West, the art of the stage fought to maintain dominance, while the new art of the screen sought to achieve moral legitimacy and economic hegemony by asserting its own status as an expressive representational form. In this poignant coming-of-age saga, Theater, cinema's foremost predecessor, with its shared aspects of story, décor, performance, and new urban publics, swiftly became an ideal adversary, or the medium that the Cinema *loved to hate*.

Born out of an intense cinephilia, or love of cinema, this much-touted oppositional narrative, and enduring intrigue, propagated by the 1920s avant-gardes with their rallying cries for "medium specificity," not only elides the early influence of the rapidly modernizing Theater (with a capital "T") or *theaters* in their multiplicity. It also disregards the individual tendencies, the tangible material relations, and the extensive network of associations shared by the turn-of-the century theatrical avant-garde and 1920s cinematic avant-gardes.

This is particularly the case in France, where, during the first decades of the twentieth century, the experimental tendencies of Paris's Belle Époque theaters, and notably those of leading modernist directors and "international impresarios," Naturalist André Antoine and Symbolist Aurélien Lugné-Poë (who premiered the work of Maeterlinck, Bataille, Claudel, Ibsen, Strindberg, and Hauptmann), had an unmistakable impact on early dramaturgical writers, actors, and critics working in the new medium.

These early modernist forms provide key concepts, such as new modes of vision, perception, and authorship, as well as innovative approaches to mise-en-scène and performance. Crucial here, at the crossroads of late nineteenth-century Naturalist and Symbolist dramaturgy, is a *stylistic dualism* or hybridity on the level of structure and visual culture that prefigures that of Germaine Dulac and the Impressionists in its alliance of a pragmatic, *realist* aesthetic foundation and an associative *symbolist* structure. These new dramaturgical forms served as an important model not only for new author-spectator relations but also for the abstraction or minimization of story, décor, and performance for the pioneers of France's first narrative avant-garde, 1920s Impressionist cinema.

Three of the five most prominent Impressionist filmmakers, Dulac (1882–1942), Marcel L'Herbier (1888–1979), and Louis Delluc (1890–1924), each began their artistic careers as playwrights and/or critics during the prewar decade and at the apex of Belle Époque theatrical renovation.[2] Crucially, of the foremost Symbolist dramatists, Aurélien Lugné-Poë, Maurice Maeterlinck, and Paul Claudel, their corresponding muses, Suzanne Desprès, Georgette Leblanc, and Ève Francis, became the early lead actresses of Dulac, L'Herbier, and Delluc, respectively. Of the three critics-turned-directors, between Louis Delluc—an early spokesperson for the movement, and Marcel L'Herbier—the most enduring as a film and television director (1917 to 1961), stands Germaine Dulac—a relentless innovator across the 1920s avant-gardes, from Impressionism and Surrealism to abstraction, who can serve as an illuminating guide.

A trailblazing feminist journalist, theater critic, and amateur playwright (1906–1913), wartime film theorist and director (1917–1918), and steadfast pioneer of the 1920s avant-gardes (1919–1929), Germaine Dulac played a vital role in the development of cinema as an art and social practice. Over the course of her film career (1915–1942), she directed more than thirty fiction films, many marking new tendencies, from figurative to abstract, including what are often considered the first Impressionist film, first "feminist" film (from a woman's psychological perspective), and first Surrealist film: respectively, *La Fête espagnole* [1919], based on an anecdote by Louis Delluc; *The Smiling Madame Beudet* [1923], adapted from the successful avant-garde play by André Obey and Denys Amiel; and *The Seashell and the Clergyman* [1927], from a script by Surrealist poet and disciple of Lugné-Poë, Antonin Artaud.[3] Dulac's 1929 experimental shorts (*Disque 957*, *Arabesque*, *Thèmes et variations*) or "pure films" (based on "visual impressions" of Chopin, Débussy, and classical melodies) serve as corollaries for her ideal of cinema as a form of "visual music" before she shifted to directing newsreels in the 1930s, which she would argue served as the ultimate form of "pure cinema." Yet, as Dulac herself notes in her 1928 essay "La Musique du Silence," inspired by Symbolist playwright, poet, and essayist Maurice Maeterlinck's "Théâtre du Silence": "Story is just a surface."[4]

Theater and Cinema: Debates and New Directions

First, early avant-garde debates, with their enduring discourse of "Theater" as the grand adversary of cinema, merit a brief exploration. As scholars from Richard Abel to Laurent Guido have noted, already, by the early 1910s, a chorus of voices proselytizing cinema's status as a "unique art" could be heard. In France, this rhetorical patronage came from a variety of young cineastes and cinephiles. Early ontological proclamations by Ricciotto Canudo ("Triumph of the Cinematograph," 1908, "The Birth of a Sixth Art," 1911) and Abel Gance ("What Is the Cinematographe? A Sixth Art," 1912), cofounders, with Dulac, of Club des amis du septième art (C.A.S.A.), France's first cine-club, each celebrated the new medium as a "synthesis" of the other arts.[5] Whereas Marcel L'Herbier ("Hermès et le Silence," 1918), if reticent about its artistic status, vaunted the subtle power of this "popular, true and silent" life-printing-machine ("une machine à imprimer la vie"),[6] Louis Delluc decried the use of theatrical décors while applauding the artfulness of Scandinavian adaptations (such as Victor Sjöström's *Terje Vigen* [1917], based on an Ibsen poem), that "t[ook] only the essence" of their literary texts.[7] In this pressing litmus test, amid these early debates, one of the most trenchant calls for "cinematic specificity" or "film purism" came from Dulac, several years before the "pure cinema" debates.[8]

In 1917, during the Great War, and long before André Bazin's treatise on "aesthetic realism," Dulac, in her articles "Mise-en-scène" (1917), "Où sont les interprètes?" ("Where are the Artists?," 1918), and, unreservedly, "Ayons la foi!" ("Have Faith!," 1919), sounded the alarm with clarion calls for cinema to distinguish itself (from a newly dominant US cinema) by using on-location shooting and non-professional actors (including animals and children) and to "have faith" in itself.[9] In 1917, the eloquent protest of musicologist, film critic, and one of Dulac's greatest supporters, Émile Vuillermoz, encapsulates the sentiment behind this realist foundation nicely: "The great defect of current cinematographic technique is to have remained theatrical. Everything is instinctively packed there between an invisible ramp and an imaginary backdrop: you must stretch one and tear the other to let the air in, light and life."[10] In the wake of the Great War, as the disciples of the new art rallied around the "promise of cinema" with lectures, films, and exhibits promoting medium specificity, who dared speak of seeking inspiration from the Theater, its stories, actors, and décors? We have so internalized cinema's demonstrable antagonism toward theater at this time that the question of "Why theater?" or "Which theater?" has scarcely been raised.[11]

Of this historic rivalry and century-long debate, Eric de Kuyper enquires in his aptly titled essay, "Le Théâtre comme 'mauvais objet'" ("The Theater as 'Bad Object'"): [mais] "quel théâtre?" ([but] "which theater?"). As De Kuyper's study highlights, what remains most disturbing is that recurrent representations of theater as a "bad object" are formed almost exclusively around an abstract or monolithic view of "Theater" (with a capital

"T").[12] With regard to Belle Époque France at least, the idea of theater as "bad object" has formed almost singularly around the popular "Théâtre de Boulevard" (Boulevard theater); or, as Michael Corfin has called it, the traditional, bourgeois theater of "mauvaise presse et bon public" (bad press and a good crowd).[13]

This dualistic notion of the Boulevard Theater recalls that expressed by the young and astonished Germaine Dulac in early 1904. Unable to obtain tickets to the Comédie-Française, the twenty-two-year-old future cineaste wrote her mother to recount her transformative experience when attending the *Opéra comique* to see *Le Fils de l'étoile* (*The Son of the Star*), a five-act musical drama (written by Catulle-Mendès and composed by Camille Erlanger, husband of Dulac's future paramour and co-founder of her first film company, DH Films, Irène Hillel-Erlanger). Enthralled by the venue's mixed-class audience donning brightly colored hats and singing the national anthem, "La Marseillaise," Dulac chalked up this mindless diversion as "du pain et des jeux" ("bread and games" or "bread and circuses," from the Latin *panem et circenses*), and announced her commitment to gaining a better understanding of people of distinct social backgrounds and to helping emancipate them through art.[14]

Only two years later, at age twenty-four (and after marrying agricultural engineer, novelist, and theater critic for *La Rampe*, Albert Dulac, in 1905), Germaine Dulac began to answer this calling when she produced her one-act feminist drama, *L'Emprise* (April 1907), and inaugurated a seven-year collaboration (1906–1913) as a journalist and theater critic at the pioneering weekly *La Française* (the journal of the women's progress movement), with an interview of the celebrated theater actress Réjane (December 23, 1906). An early ally of Lugné-Poë, the thespian's Théâtre de la Réjane would become a prime venue for early twentieth-century Symbolist Theater.[15]

The Theatrical Scene: Naturalism and Symbolism

Prefiguring De Kuyper's inquiry, "Le Théâtre ou les théâtres," the title of Dulac's album assembling her prewar review columns at *La Française* evokes the very multiplicity of companies and wide range of directorial approaches that emerged during a period of profound renovation across the Parisian theatrical circuit. Between 1908 and 1913, Dulac wrote reviews of more than 160 plays (by authors from G. Bernard Shaw and Sacha Guitry to Matilde Serao and Colette Willy) and performed in Paris's most prestigious and most popular theaters (from the classical Comédie-Française and Théâtre du Palais Royal to the lively Bouffes-Parisiens and Menus-Plaisirs). She also critiqued the works of independent and mobile theater companies, including those associated with Naturalist André Antoine, founder in 1887 of the Théâtre Libre, and Symbolist Aurélien Lugné-Poë—co-founder in 1893 of the reformist avant-garde company the Théâtre de l'Œuvre—and whom she had met at the association's International Salon in 1907, along with his muse and companion, Suzanne Desprès, star of Dulac's first film (1916's *Soeurs Ennemies*).[16]

In her reviews, Dulac covered a wide diversity of developments of the early twentieth-century stage, as a means of tackling contemporary social issues, addressing everything from story and performance to costumes and décor, and revealing her preferences at this naturalist-symbolist intersection ("carrefour naturalo-symboliste"), to use Alice Folco's expression, for certain types of mise-en-scène.[17] In her early reviews and wartime correspondence, Dulac extolled the portrayal of feminist heroines in myriad Lugnée-Poë productions of Ibsen (featuring Suzanne Desprès, an early interpreter of the "Theater of Ideas").[18] She also lauded the "poetry and truth of symbols" in Maeterlinck's *The Blue Bird* (starring Georgette Leblanc, 1908), Claudel's *L'Annonce faite à Marie* (1912) and *L'Otage* (1914) (each with Ève Francis), and Debussy's 1902 revolutionary symbolist opera, *Pelléas et Mélisande*, based on Maeterlinck's play, which she attended a representation of in the summer of 1915.[19]

Debussy's original and audacious conception of harmony and rhythm, and his dramatic use of sound, silence, and interweaving themes and motifs, created not only an impression of improvisation or instability within continuity but also a new auditory sensuality, whose visual equivalent can be found throughout Dulac's narrative and abstract films (e.g., *La Belle Dame sans merci* [1921], *L'Invitation au voyage* [1927], *Thèmes et variations* [1929], and *Arabesque* [1929]). By late 1915, when Dulac established her first film production company, with the Symbolist poet Irène Hillel-Erlanger, she had also authored over a dozen of her own (mostly unrealized) theater projects, in a variety of genres, from comedies and parodies to historical dramas, that anticipate the diversity and inventiveness of her oeuvre.[20]

The modernization of twentieth-century French theater is largely credited to André Antoine (1858–1943). He not only created an epicenter for realist narration and mise-en-scène in early twentieth-century France but also opened the floodgates for Symbolist experimentation and a new relationship to spectatorship that challenged the theater's relation with "its audience and the world" that directly informed Dulac and her contemporaries.[21] Inspired by the writings of Darwin (*Origin of Species*, 1859), Nietzsche (*Birth of a Tragedy*, 1871), and celebrated novelist and playwright Émile Zola ("Naturalism on the Stage," 1881), Antoine promoted a positivist and social determinist conception of tragedy represented by an "anatomical image," or realist portrayal of the struggle of daily life—a directive that acting, staging, décor, and costume design should follow.[22] Naturalism's visual culture, as Dan Rebellato notes, was based on the creation of "meticulous resemblances of contemporary reality," "contemporary dialogue," and "realistic three-dimensional sets," employing "real objects" and "psychologically detailed action," for "an audience, unacknowledged by the actors, primed to participate in make-believe."[23]

Yet, more than sociological and dramaturgical (or representational) naturalism, achieved through the use of psychologically detailed action, real sets, and real objects (epitomized by his infamous hanging of a side of beef to create *real* smells), Antoine's metaphor of a "fourth wall," or imagined "toile" (or cloth) separating audience and scene, revolutionized theatrical representation. The concept of the fourth wall, proposed by Diderot,[24] coupled with Zola's crucial notion of *art* as a "window onto the world,"[25] delivered something beyond a new mimetic model and a new attention to audience perception of the performance and visual arts. It also provided an essential *catalyst* for theatrical symbolism and abstraction.

In the first decade of Lugné-Poë's Théâtre de l'Oeuvre, the fourth wall was literalized by the Symbolist "scrim" or gauze used to separate the scene in a more oneiric manner, as it would be later by the postwar Impressionist penchant for "effets techniques" (special effects). Moreover, as a perspectival method, the window (from the Old Norse, *vindauga* or "wind-eye")—like the mirror that *gazes back*, looks *out*, *through*, or *into* real as well as imagined spaces (cf. Walker)—provided the Impressionists with both a physical and metaphorical device for the exploration of the Modernist and Symbolist interest in capturing the state of mind ("état d'âme") or spirit.[26]

The eyes, the window, the mirror, and other visual or reflective (and perspectival) devices found in nature (glass, water, wind, light), along with more complex effects and the concomitant design of custom lenses and effects, would prove central for Dulac and her fellow Impressionists, seeking to represent the "inner life" of the "new" or "modern" woman (and man).[27] While both schools were present at the birth of the theatrical avant-garde, as Rebellato asserts, "Naturalism worked to strip the theatre of its decorative self-indulgence; Symbolism restored poetry to the stage and made the theatre into what Maurice Maeterlinck called 'the temple of dreams.'"[28]

Toward a Symbolist-Impressionist Aesthetic: From Theater to Film

In a period that Bettina L. Knapp calls "the reign of the theatrical director," we can characterize Naturalism and Symbolism as an intimate sharing of vision, sentiments, and sensation between *director* and *audience*.[29] This *affective* connection proved crucial to the 1920s cinematic Impressionists and notably to Dulac's early *auteurist* vision of the cinema, in which "suggestion" and "sensation" (transmitted through scenic or filmic technical effects) offered a direct "line of sentiment" between the director and the spectator. In her 1927 essay "Du Sentiment à la ligne," also echoing Nietzsche's idea of a "morale créatrice" (or moral creativity, based on *sensation*, concretized through *will* and *action*), Dulac writes, "The *creative will* must address the receptivity of the audience by a sensitive line that unites them."[30] So, it is at this "Naturalist-Symbolist" crossroads that we also discover the veiled theatrical urge—or to use Robert Bird's expression, Symbolist "temptation"—that stirred the Impressionists.[31] A driving desire to draw on the "imagination"—via what Dulac, like Mallarmé prior, calls "suggestion"—allows the filmmaker to convey or transmit a character's psychology, "inner life," or "soul states."[32]

Dulac's first known film essay "Mise-en-scène" (*Le Film*, November 12, 1917), defining the director as author or "artiste créateur" (artist creator, long before "la politique des auteurs"), adopted a militant tone, as she defended, with strong Symbolist echoes, cinema as "a new means of expression [...a] new form. Perhaps a new form of art." Dulac announced her interest in creating a subtle yet sophisticated technique that, through the "silence of gesture," would allow her to pair the visual culture of Naturalism and Symbolism with the *concrete* and the *spiritual*, asking: "Isn't there a lot to be said when one can exploit the most subtle nuances of light, *make gestures speak*, animate forms, evoke all that which, through our eyes, addresses our spirit, from reality to dream?"[33]

On the eve of the Armistice (November 11), in her October 1918 "Où sont les interprètes?," just prior to release of the Naturalist *La Cigarette* (1919, script by Naturalist Jacques de Baroncelli, shot on location in Paris by wartime newsreel cameraman Louis Chaix), Dulac compares the role of the director (or "artist creator," from her 1917 article) to that of the realist painter, "inspired *directly* from nature." Accordingly, she calls for the use of non-professional actors in secondary roles, and outdoor or "natural decors" (or on-location shooting) that could reveal and express the social reality and 'inner life" of her characters.[34] Of particular interest are the desires for women's liberty, often set in opposition to the anxieties of the dejected male of the postwar period (cf. *La Cigarette, La Fête espagnole, La Souriante Madame Beudet, La Folie des vaillants*).

While decrying the "broad gestures" of the stage in favor of more subtle and "detailed" film acting ("On the screen, we don't need actors. We need artists. We don't need processes. We need truth."[35]), Dulac's crucial cinematic allusion to *direct, natural*, or "realist" representation has a notable precursor in Dulac's theater reviews (1910). The latter praise the realist immediacy of French Symbolist playwright and poet "Henry" Bataille,[36] alongside that of Réjane's paramour, Italian dramatist and screenwriter Dario Nicodemi.[37] In contrast to the work of Sam Benelli and Romain Coolus, written *indirectly*, "d'après la vie" (*based on* or *adapted from* life), the pragmatic realism of Bataille's *La vierge folle* and Nicodemi's *La Flamme* drew praise from Dulac for the ways they operated *directly*, "selon la vie" (*according to* or *as in* life).[38] This appreciation for a realist foundation persists throughout Dulac's work, from her 1920s Impressionist period to her time as as Director of Newsreels at France-Actualités Gaumont (1932–34), when she moved toward proto-Direct cinema.

Yet, central to Dulac's Symbolist approach, as she describes it in her 1927 essay "Visualization" and her 1928 article "La Musique du Silence," is the notion of a "visual idea," which cannot be recounted but that develops in the "silence of the eye."[39] For Dulac, this "visual idea" is exemplified by the early dramaturgical approaches she admired, from the Symbolist adaptations of Nordic realist Henrik Ibsen (1828–1906) by Lugné-Poë (1869–1940) to the "Theater of Silence" of Maurice Maeterlinck (1862–1949) to the mystical Symbolism of Paul Claudel (1868–1955), and which returned to the stage in the postwar period (Ibsen's *Romersholm* and Claudel's *Otage*, both starring Ève Francis). Maeterlinck's "Theater of Silence" (or "Theater of the Soul"), alongside Bataille's "Theatre of Ideas" (and disciple Denys Amiel's "Theater of the Unexpressed," which Dulac adapted to the screen in 1923, like Jean-Jacques Bernard's ensuing "École du Silence"), rejected "literary" theater in favor of "indirect language" or "hidden" exchanges (beyond spoken words), which audiences, given "pregnant pauses" or silent intervals, could access through their imagination.

Dulac's predilection for visual primacy and her aversion to cinematic ventriloquism fit hand in glove with her investment in an Impressionist signifying system, which evolved progressively from figurative to more abstract forms. For Dulac, who would use the designation "Impressionist" in 1921 to describe her own films in relation to the late-nineteenth-century movement in music and painting (and, as we will see, also in reference to Symbolist theater), the term corresponded to a whole system of meaning or a universe of intersecting symbols. Cinematic Impressionism utilized technical effects, but it was above all a culturally specific intermedial and intertextual system of visualization and organization of both performance and mise-en-scène, sometimes augmented by pro-filmic or in-camera effects. Inspired by theatrical Naturalism (and its preference for realist decors and understated acting), as well as poetic and dramaturgical Symbolism (and its use of a symbolic network), Dulac's approach, while drawing on painting, music, poetry, sport, and dance, implied a reconceptualization of performance styles and of spatial and temporal relations, as well as of narrative and looking structures; indeed, it demanded a new kind of critical viewing.[40]

Her 1923 feminist classic *La Souriante Madame Beudet*, based on Amiel's 1921 homonymic avant-garde play, is her most celebrated Impressionist work due to its use of psychological symbolism to visualize the heroine's "inner life"; arguably her 1927 *L'Invitation au voyage*, with its refusal of speech and intertitles, amid a complex network of looking patterns, and, finally, her 1929 abstract films, without stories, decor, or actors, take these ideas a step further.

Crucially, Dulac's analysis of Bataille's *La Vierge Folle* (1910) and Nicodemi's *La Flamme* (1910), alongside the work of Coolus, Benelli, and dramatist and suffragist Héra Mirtel (1868–1931), marks her earliest known reference to dramaturgical "Impressionism," before her use of the term "Impressionist" in 1921 to describe her cinematic approach to *La Belle Dame sans merci*.[41] Comparing the directors' approach to the school of Impressionist painters (in their "synthesis of the modern evolution of our aesthetic aspirations"), Dulac applauds the directors' "notation" and "skillful superimposition" of "sentiments" and "observed facts" as a means of "interpreting abstract ideas." Such comments directly anticipate her own cinematic Impressionism and abstraction in the 1920s and her "purist" ideal of cinema as a "visual symphony," "music of silence," or "music for the eyes."[42]

Much like Lugné-Poë and his close associates, Symbolist poet Stéphane Mallarmé and composer Claude Débussy, Dulac (who visited Bayreuth at a young age) was marked, like the Symbolists, by Wagner's notion of visual equivalences (cf. *Gesamtkunstwerk* or "total work of art," in "Art of the Future," 1849), along with his notion of the artist as a conveyer of the sublime. These also find echoes in the poetry of Baudelaire, a reference point in Dulac's *Beudet* and a source of inspiration for her later *L'Invitation au voyage*. As Baudelaire's conceptual poem and manifesto "Correspondances" (1857) suggests, "hidden analogies of nature" can be transmitted through *synesthesia* or multi-sensory experience (sight, sound, smell, taste, and touch), whereby "all perceptions have a common form."[43]

For Dulac and the Impressionists, cinema (like music for Wagner and Débussy, poetry for Baudelaire and Mallarmé, and theater for the Symbolists or Symbolo-Impressionists) operates through an *associative* rather than a *narrative* logic, as a network of *interconnected* scenes and *interpenetrating* motifs, which percolate into the consciousness of the masses. In this regard, certain elements (e.g., the swans in Dulac's *La Cigarette*, the automobile and the tennis player in *Beudet*, or the ship in *L'Invitation au voyage*), while peripheral to the *outer* action (plot), are crucial to the *inner* action (or character psychology), a strategy that would become vital to Dulac's feminist approach to filmmaking. Yet, with the dawn of the war in 1914 on the Franco-German front, for the cinematic Impressionists the work of French Symbolist dramatists, such as Lugné-Poe, Maeterlinck, and Claudel, would provide a pivotal and more suitable reference.

The Symbolist Theater Scene

Despite widespread discourses of "film purism," as Germaine Dulac's diverse cinematic oeuvre attests, the Symbolist scenography of Lugné-Poë's Théâtre de l'Oeuvre, which he describes in opposition to realism in 1921 as "Synthétiste" (from the French "synthétiser"), constitutes one of the most striking, if largely overlooked, models for 1920s cinematic Impressionism and abstraction.[44] Faced with an official moral discourse of postwar conservativism and pro-natalism, the Nabi-Symbolist aesthetic of "Synthetism," in its alliances with Symbolist poet Mallarmé, composer Débussy, dancer Loïe Fuller, and the bourgeoning Women's Progress movement, provided an opportune visual and scenic model for the socialist and feminist Dulac (and her queer contemporaries Jean Epstein and Marcel L'Herbier), who sought to express progressive social ideals, and more equitable gender and sexual relations, through an aesthetic of "suggestion."

Contextualizing the key aspects of Lugné-Poë's theater proves essential in order to elucidate their influence on Dulac and the 1920s cinematic avant-garde or how they manifest themselves in Impressionist practice. In the spirit of Symbolist intermedial mobility and "collective creation," and after his acting debut at Antoine's Théâtre libre (1888), Lugné-Poë (1869–1940) founded, with poet Camille Mauclair (1872–1945) and post-Impressionist painter, printmaker, and decorator Edouard Vuillard (1868–1940), the reformist and avant-garde Théâtre de l'Oeuvre (1893).[45] Like Antoine, in his own highly charged departure from Paul Fort's Théâtre d'Art in 1893—and stirred by rallying cries for the Symbolist poet Mallarmé, more than Zola—Lugné-Poe and the young Nabi artists of Symbolist Theater broke with scenic illusionism. Collectively, they displayed a fascination with the paranormal and the unconscious and began to implement a "non-mimetic" aesthetic that allied the stillness, silence, and often intimate lighting of quotidian spaces with an enigmatic use of line, surface, and depth. These techniques, which would harmonize with the aims of a modern cinema, were designed to help emphasize or draw attention to the elusive, if not invisible and more expressive, movements and sensations of daily life.

Inspired by Paul Gauguin's use of flat planes and emphatic contours and pointillist Georges Seurat's organization of geometric surfaces, whose elements were united by rhythm, the Nabis also believed that painting must move beyond the easel, and work in the service of all the arts, and especially theater.[46] As Dutch Nabi painter Jan Verkade (1868–1946) famously declared in a rejection of realist perspective: "There are no pictures, only decorations. Give us walls!"[47] The work of the Nabis (meaning "prophets" in reference to and in reverence of Gauguin), marked a new era of collaboration between the artists of the canvas and the stage, inexorably leading the way to the experiments of Italian Futurism and the Ballets Russes before providing a propitious orientation for the 1920s cinematic avant-gardes.

Cinematic Impressionism's move toward visual formalism has a clear precedent in Symbolist scenic design. In contrast to the meticulous reconstruction of social milieux by the Naturalists, Lugné-Poë (see figure 13.1 top) and the Symbolists or dramaturgical "Impressionists," to use Dulac's expression, sought inspiration in the narrative (and decorative) simplification and condensation of Synthetism, offering liberating alternatives for the cinematic Impressionists to express character psychology. In terms of early twentieth-century visual (and narrative) culture, this broader artistic trend proposed to "refine forms," "call on the imagination," and "make [things] understood, without showing [them]."[48] For Lugné-Poë, in concert with Maeterlinck's Symbolist manifesto "Tragedy in Everyday Life," a single, line-like figure—for example, an old man seated beside his lamp—could evoke the "fullness of life experience" and the mysterious forces of the universe more powerfully than any action drama. One finds inspiration for such an exchange of insights in Ibsen's *The Master Builder*, for which Germaine Dulac wrote a film treatment (*Solness, le Constructeur*, 1923–24), and the imagery brings to mind the oneiric mise-en-scène of Dulac's own dreamy heroines (from *Soeurs Ennemies* [see figure 13.1 bottom], *Beudet*, and *L'Invitation au voyage* to *La Princesse Mandane*).[49]

Working with Nabi artists Edouard Vuillard, Maurice Denis, and Pierre Bonnard, with their emphasis on the purity of line, color, and form, Lugné-Poë used low-lit, suggestive, painted decors—along with what he called "spectral narration" (or offstage monotonal recitatives)—to create an atmosphere that could also capture and transmit the emotions or "inner life" of the artist.[50] For the Symbolists, as for the Impressionists later, such means also could "transport the spectator" via stillness and the "inner drama" of immobile characters (or what Maeterlinck called "static theater.")[51] This approach to containing mobility prefigures that of Dulac, who called for stillness of scene and performance. Prefiguring the association between artist and spectator, Dulac privileged the distinction between "exterior" facts or "impressions" reacting against the "inner" movement of the soul, before their expression through physiognomy, or as she writes in reference to her 1921 *Mort du Soleil*, "mobility amidst the immobility of things and the apparent calm of beings."[52]

FIGURE 13.1 Top, *Portrait de Lugné-Poë*, Edouard Vuillard, 1891; bottom, *Suzanne Després*, Vuillard, 1908.

The use of abstract technical effects by Dulac and postwar Impressionists to create a space of sensibility and reverie also has links to Belle Époque Symbolist theatrical abstraction. As mentioned before, Lugné-Poë (following Vuillard's design indications) often placed a green gauze or scrim in the front of the stage, and the actors moved and gestured behind it, prefiguring the Impressionist use of the body as symbol.[53] Further, the filtering of scenic action and character movement through a gauze-like screen (either backlit in the foreground or sometimes as a backdrop) not only imposed an authorial point-of-view but also reconnected with a non-mimetic scenography. Such an approach had an indelible impact on the chromatic and tonal aspects of the play. Not unlike the cinematic "Impressionists," who would later use technical effects, the dramaturgical "Impressionists" did not seek to produce an "illusion of realism" but instead to create a metaphorical, enigmatic, and chimerical space that combined the familiar and strange, a "space of dreams." This push toward formal abstraction provided a crucial model for Dulac and the cinematic Impressionists in the postwar period, who sought to visualize the conscious and unconscious mind through both figurative and abstract forms.

Starting with some of her earliest films from 1917 to 1919 (*Soeurs Ennemies, Ame de fous, Venus Victrix, La Cigarette*), Dulac used atmospheric effects (such as oil lamps, colored lighting, incense, and exotic flowers) to conjure up the reveries of her heroines. Yet, it was during the postwar period, through the principles of Symbolist "Synthetist" scenic design, based on post-Impressionist Nabi painting and décor and its abstraction or two-dimensional flattening of space, that Dulac made a more significant foray into Impressionist scenography.

Edouard Vuillard and Symbolist Scenography

Significantly, during the pre-war period, Lugné-Poë's lead designer, Edouard Vuillard, moved in the same artistic circles as Dulac in his association with the Salon d'Automne (1903–1913), which challenged the older, more academic Salon des Indépendants (f. 1884). During Lugné-Poë's "Ibsenian period," Vuillard had worked closely with Nabi artists (Maurice Denis, Pierre Bonnard, Paul Sérusier, and others), designing sets and programs for the Symbolist scene, including for *The Master Builder*, which, as previously established, Dulac adapted to the screen in the mid-1920s.[54]

In 1903, Vuillard had co-founded the Salon d'Automne, with architect Frantz Jourdain. Dulac's close associates, Fauvist painter Georgette Sembat and her husband, future Socialist Minister of Public Works Marcel Sembat (who worked with Dulac's uncle Raymond Saisset-Schneider at the Assemblée Nationale), each played an important role in its creation and longevity: Georgette Sembat (née Agutte), by assembling its first works in 1903, and Marcel Sembat, in his historic defense of the Salon d'Automne before the National Assembly in 1912. According to Sembat's journal and the Dulac correspondence, the pair hosted Dulac and her husband, Albert, along with the Salon's myriad artists (from Henri Matisse to "that little agile dancer, *la Napierkowska*, whom Germaine [was] crazy about") up through the start of the war.[55]

In this same circle could be found Dulac's future decorator, artist and activist Francis Jourdain, the architect's son, who had made his debut as an extra in *The Master Builder* at Lugné-Poë's Théâtre de l'Oeuvre, alongside Vuillard, before opening his small furniture factory, "Les Ateliers Modernes," in 1912 and his celebrated furniture shop, "Chez Francis Jourdain" (2 rue de Sèze Paris), in 1919. It is in this capacity, as Jourdain attests, that he provided set elements for various films by Dulac, as well as for Louis Delluc's *La Fumee noire* (1919, in collaboration with Van Dongen), *La Fièvre* (1921), and Delluc's minimalist *La Femme de nulle part* (1922), and much later for Jean Vigo's *L'Atalante* (1934), commissioned by Dulac. Jourdain was also close to modernist architect and stage and film designer, Robert Mallet-Stevens (1886–1945), production designer for L'Herbier's 1923 feature, *L'Inhumaine*.[56]

While Francis Jourdain played an important role in delivering and erecting décors for the 1920s Impressionist scene, Vuillard's work provides a long-lost context for its decorative and abstract elements and forms, particularly the formal aspects of Dulac's mise-en-scène. The Synthetist approach to painting, such as the two-dimensional flattening of space and arabesque designs, indicates Vuillard and the Nabis' scenic method, which emphasized natural forms, a purity of line, and sensation. One can trace back to Vuillard the evolution from figurative to more abstract forms in Dulac's work and her predilection for abstract visual and structural motifs, such as the line, circle, and the arabesque, often associated with gender and sexual liberation.

Moreover, Vuillard's work in particular can also be read ideologically, as a class-conscious and feminist model for Dulac and the 1920s avant-garde in general. A staunch Socialist like Dulac, Vuillard provided a foundation for Symbolist mise-en-scène, based on narrative, decorative, and gestural condensation, in a popular context. But he also highlighted gestural figuration in female-coded domestic settings to create an abstract, metaphorical, and phantasmatic space of female reverie, important to Dulac.

As a point of formal comparison, we can first point to the presence of some of these decorative and abstract elements and forms in 1920s avant-garde cinema in general, which sought to upend models of realism in the wake of a horrific war. In their Synthetist combination of natural, realist, yet abstract geometric forms (cf. *Une partie des dames/ A Game of Checkers* [1906]), Vuillard's paintings prefigure the complex spatiality and play between two-dimensional geometric abstraction and cinematic depth of field in the 1920s avant-gardes. They further call to mind some of the perspectival experiments of Dada and "Pure Cinema" or abstract works of the 1920s (cf. the infamous scene of Marcel Duchamp and Man Ray playing chess on a roof, shot from a disconcerting, though different, high-angle, in René Clair and Cubist painter Francis Picabia's *Entr'acte* [1924]).

Moreover, resonant of his Ibsenian period with Lugné-Poë, Vuillard's emphasis on the two-dimensionality of the design to express tensions of surface and depth in his dramatic portraits of middle-class women can be read critically, as a means of emphasizing surface placidity and revealing deeper social conflict. This approach, which placed the body as symbol in relation to arabesque-like decorative forms to express women's complex relationship to their domestic environment, is visible in his women's portraits (*The Reader* [1896], *Intimacy* [1896], *Music* [1899], and *Lay* [1901]) (see figures 13.2). The "thick sensations" of this dense mise-en-scene, combined with its use of color to create flat surface layers, allows the viewer to drift, as Hilton Kramer

FIGURE 13.2 *Figures in an Interior: Intimacy*, Vuillard, 1896 (top left); *Figures in an Interior: Music*, Vuillard, 1896 (top right); *Interior with Worktable, aka The Suitor*, Vuillard, 1893 (bottom left); and *A Game of Checkers/A Game of Draughts*, Vuillard, 1906 (bottom right).

describes it, between decorative impulse and affectionate observation.[57] This approach finds echoes in Dulac's stylistic dualism, the visual cultures of Symbolism and Naturalism, and in the tension between the psychological and the social in her key feminist films, *La Belle Dame sans merci*, *La Souriante Madame Beudet*, and *L'Invitation au voyage*, which employ similar techniques of character blocking, and decorative layering, along with the painterly liberty of matching costumes and settings, to express female subjective relations.

Similarly, for comparison, drawing on the Symbolist approach of body-as-symbol, in L'Herbier's Impressionist films, the actor becomes an element of décor. One sees this in his 1921 *El Dorado* (see figures 13.3a-b), with Claudel's muse, Ève Francis, and the later *L'Inhumaine* (with Maeterlinck's muse, Georgette Leblanc), but also with Jacques Catelain in L'Herbier's wartime ballad, *Rose-France*, from 1919. In these films, actors function sometimes as surface, sometimes as layering. In certain cases, as in *L'Inhumaine* (see figures 13.3c-d), designed by Mallet-Stevens, the figure or face becomes an abstract form, a surface, or a mask (cf. Catelain, and Leblanc as Claire Lescot), eliciting the predilection for puppets by Symbolist dramatists such as Jarry (*Ubu Roi*) and Maeterlinck (*The Blue Bird*).

FIGURE 13.3 Ève Francis as the dancer Sibilla in two screen captures from *El Dorado* (L'Herbier, 1921) (top left and right); Jacques Catelain as Einar Norsen (bottom left) and Georgette Leblanc as Claire Lescot in *L'Inhumaine* (L'Herbier, 1924) (bottom right).

Germaine Dulac and the Synthetist Influence

Dulac and the Impressionists would use similar methods of decorative condensation (and more generally of streamlining of narrative, décor, and performance) to foster spatialized discourse as a form of social critique in their postwar films. For *La Fête espagnole*, whose position as the first "Impressionist" film is tied to its mythical debut of having been written on a napkin or tablecloth at a corner café by the young critic Louis Delluc, simplification of "intrigue" or plot becomes the founding tale of the first narrative avant-garde movement. In this film, Ève Francis stars as Soledad, the object of a fatal dispute between her suitors, wearing a dress expressly designed for its visual effect (see figure 13.5a). The poster for the film similarly condenses the film's allegorical representation of the rift between the joyful liberties of women on the homefront and the miserable suffering of men on the warfront (see figure 13.4).[58]

Delluc's notion of literary adaptation—of taking "only the essence" or "everything that is cinema" and "throw[ing] the rest away"—placed his approach to narrative at the intersection of these intermedial crossroads. Delluc's perspective encapsulates the Symbolist and Dulacian notion of the "visual idea," or "visualization," which consisted of making the idea "felt," to use Nell Andrew's formulation.[59] One could also make the case that Synthetism's basic principles and concepts of visual condensation stand as a precursor to Delluc and Epstein's "photogénie" (based on appearance and vision, respectively), Dulac's "cinegraphie" (writing with cinema), and even L'Herbier's notion of cinema as a "life-printing machine." Amid the diversity of the cinematic Impressionist school, Dulac's ideal of a "pure cinema" made of lines and forms in movement and rhythm becomes a way of visualizing, and a way of seeing.

Penned by her early business partner and paramour, Irène Hillel-Erlanger, Dulac's *La Belle Dame sans merci* (*The Beautiful Merciless Woman* [1921]), a postwar deconstruction of the femme fatale archetype (named for Keats's ballad and the Napoleonic era "vamp"), uses similar techniques of Synthetist visualization, as well as synesthesia. Along with flowers, incense, and other atmospheric elements enveloping its heroine, Lola, Dulac employs decorative patterns in the costume and wallpaper to contribute to the reflexivity of the scene (see figure 13.5b). It is through this Synthetist technique of graphic correspondences that the spectator, like the cuckolded Countess, who arrives on the scene, is encouraged to adopt a state of critical reflection. The approach encourages neither outright criticism of Lola (who is hiding the Countess's husband, while surreptitiously flaunting his cane) nor submission to her charms (through the enchanting ambiance of the studio); instead, the viewer is invited to analyze the visual tension within the scene (created primarily through the rich, matching patterns of Lola's costume and the décor) and thus to call into question and deconstruct (through a series of similar instances) the myth of the femme fatale.[60]

FIGURE 13.4 Poster of *La Fête espagnole* (Dulac, 1920).

268　TAMI WILLIAMS

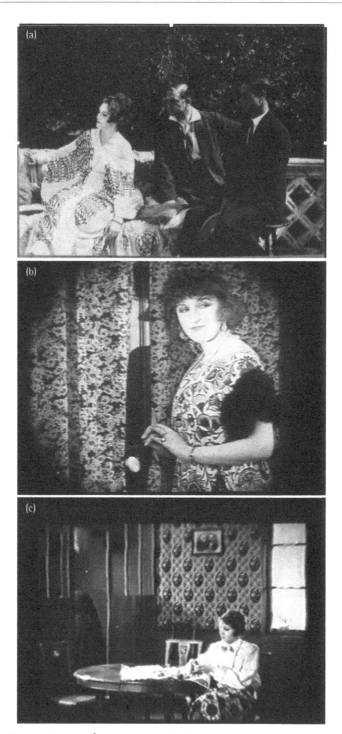

FIGURE 13.5 Top to bottom: Éve Francis with her two suitors in *La Fête espagnole*; Tania Daleyme as Lola in Dulac's *La Belle Dame sans merci* (1921); and Sylvia Mai as the abandoned fiancée Annette in *La Princesse Mandane* (Dulac, 1928).

Similarly, in *La Princesse Mandane* (1928), Dulac employs Synthetist and abstract techniques, along with a brilliant satire of Eisenstein's "Odessa Steps" sequence from 1925's *Battleship Potemkin*, within a broader *mise-en-abyme* structure. After a Saturday night screening of Jules Verne's *Michel Strogoff* (dir. Victor Tourjansky, 1926), one of the film's female characters, Annette, finds herself left at home to tend to household duties; she is shown wearing a dress that matches the decorative wallpaper of the background, capping a critical commentary on her domestic situation (see figure 13.5c). Meanwhile, Annette's fiancé, the misguided explorer Etienne Pindère, weary of his factory work, dreams of rescuing "Princesse Mandane" in "Mingrelia" (Georgia), "the land of the Tartars." In the film within the film, Dulac employs the simple linear figure of an immobile ballerina, a musical signifier of constraint, to signal the princess's social isolation. Yet, in a "coup de théâtre," the cross-dressed princess escapes of her own accord following the Odessa steps satire, saves and discharges her presumptuous rescuer, and, to his shock, departs with another woman. In the film's obligatory ending, of course, the misguided adventurer wakes up to his ever-faithful fiancée.

Dulac uses a more complex anti-mimetic approach, with abstract backgrounds, in her early feminist masterpiece, *La Souriante Madame Beudet*, to convey her heroine's inner desires and reveries. The subtle and restrained acting of Madeleine Beudet (Germaine Dermoz) may well be inspired by and modelled after Lugné-Poe and Dulac's mutual muse, Suzanne Després. Dulac guides Dermoz (see figure 13.6a) in her immobile Symbolist style (asking her not to move and to let her "performance, united with the rhythm of the images," do the work), before setting it in contrast to the agitated (and sped-up) movement of theater and adventure serial actor Alexandre Arquillière, playing Mr. Beudet.[61] Madeleine's modernist style coalesces with her modernist dreams, which are represented in a Synthetist manner, through the image of a car (from her magazine) driving across a two-dimensional painting of a cloudy and uncertain sky (see figure 13.6b).

Madeleine's imagined liberation is also expressed in an abstract manner through the chronophotographic, linear, and arabesque-like movement of a young, modern tennis player, Charlie Adden (played by athlete Raoul Paoli). Adden springs from the magazine page to liberate Madeleine by picking up her overbearing and tradition-bound husband and carrying him out of their home. Set against a black background, Adden enters the living room, his arm extended above his head holding his racquet, which he brings down in a fluid gesture, filmed in a single slow-motion shot (see figure 13.6c). Notably, at the time of her imagined liberation, Madeleine's head falls back in ecstasy. Her posture, in arabesque, rhymes with the Marey and Vuillard-like chronophotographic gesture of the tennis man, aligning this figural representation of the body with its Symbolist and pre-cinema heritage.

These gestures also have a quasi-musical quality (an idea that Dulac develops in subsequent films and writings). In her 1927 article "Du sentiment à la ligne" ("From Sentiment to Line"), a manifesto of sorts for a "pure cinema," made of "life-material itself" in its lines and forms, and in movement and rhythm, Dulac declares, "movement is not only displacement, but also and above all, evolution, transformation."[62]

In an introductory text commenting on the article, she affirms that the "mathematic combinations of movement, thus broken down into rhythms" are linked by "a 'sentimental and suggestive' inspiration, analogous to musical thought that guides the coordination of sounds."[63] Dulac's predilection for the "visual rhythms" of gesture, important to the Symbolists, makes dance an ideal figure in her move toward abstraction. For the film's denouement, Dulac tempers the couple's reconciliation (see figure 13.6d), obliged by distributors and postwar attitudes on marriage, with a Symbolist-style "Coup de Théâtre": a superimposed image of two marionettes appears in a frame (over a rear-projected mask effect) above the couple's head, along with one word: "Theater," with a capital 'T'!

L'Invitation au voyage can be seen as a sequel of sorts to *Beudet*, in which the heroine, a restless housewife (played by Emma Gynt) ventures out to the liberated atmosphere of a cabaret during her husband's absence (see figure 13.7). In this film, heterosexual and homosexual longing, and feminine passivity versus illicit desire are set in opposition and rendered through the intermediality of music, dance, and painting, and aligned metaphors of transport (taxi, ships, dance) and complex looking patterns (homosociality). Echoing Debussy and Maeterlinck's Symbolist musicality, the film

FIGURE 13.6 Germaine Dermoz as Madeleine Beudet (top left); a modern car crosses a 2D painted sky (top right); Raoul Paoli as the tennis player "en arabesque" (bottom left); and the couple's obligatory reconciliation (bottom right), all from *La Souriante Madame Beudet* (Dulac, 1923).

deploys a series of associated techniques (superimpositions, rhythmic editing, and suggestive abstraction).[64] Contributing in its own way to a new mode of vision or perception, like that promoted by Antoine and Lugné-Poë, the film returns to Dulac's preferred paradigm of social reality versus illusion, employing non-mimetic and abstract backgrounds for the introspective sequences, coupled with more dynamic circular camera movements and superimpositions of the heroine's fantasies.

The heroine's imagination and the fluidity of gender are also expressed through the circular motif of a revolving door (when she enters the cabaret), a childhood locket, and a portal window; this motif reappears in Dulac's abstract and musical films, such as *Disque 957* (1929) and *Celles qui s'en font* (1930). Canted angles and the circular movement of the camera add to the destabilization of the space. Yet, it is with the literalization of visual music, during the film's climactic sequence in which the heroine closes her eyes in ecstasy during a dance, that the blurred image of the feet of female couples, distinct from the heteronormative couples on the dance floor, can be read as queer.[65] When she opens her eyes, the illusion, as well as the erotics of the cabaret as a space of fantasy and sexual emancipation, is shattered.

In her search for a "pure cinema," with its three essential qualities of "la matière vie elle-même" (the material of life itself), "movement," and "rhythm," Dulac's abstract films come ever closer to her Symbolist ideal of a cinema without story, décor, or actors. By minimizing plot, staged décor, and performance in favor of rhythm and sensation, Dulac meets and expands on Maeterlinck's ideal of a "Theater of Silence" with that of a "Music of Silence."[66] In 1929, Dulac made three experimental shorts, or "pure" films (*Disque 957*, *Arabesque*, *Thèmes et Variations*), exemplifying her Symbolist ideal of cinema as a "visual symphony" (1925) or "music for the eyes," before turning to the newsreel, which she saw as the "purest" form of cinema. In these films, all inspired by music and nature, human figures, hands, legs, a smile, become a simple line or form of gesture or expressive physiognomy in movement.

In her film *Thèmes et Variations*, which echoes Picabia's "mechanical Symbolist" portrait of Dulac's early paramour, Stasia Napierkowska, the contrasting motion of a dancer (Lilian Constantini) and machine delivers a striking form of rhythmic figuration (see figures 13.8a-b). In Henri Miller's 1930 viewing of the film at l'Oeil de Paris, he aptly praised the film as "another realm of film magic. Thoroughly French, absolutely artistic, unsentimental, and beyond realism."[67] Echoing the Naturalist visual foundation emphasized by Antoine, and the Symbolist abstraction of Lugné-Poë and Maeterlinck, Dulac (as director and "creative artist") aimed to show, through the expressivity of light and movement, and as a visual corollary for music, that the lines and forms of gesture and figuration could move the spectator without actors or characters, or via what she called "La Musique du Silence."

Arabesque resonates with the natural forms and biomorphic, often circular motifs of *Disque 957*, and the winding, curved, interlaced patterns that Vuillard's painterly décors (and those of Bonnard and Denis) and Debussy's musical suites inspire. *Arabesque* features arcs of light, waterspouts, spiderwebs, and burgeoning flowers and foliage (see figures 13.8c-d); we also see a woman's face, arms stretching, and a leg that

FIGURE 13.7 A bored housewife (Emma Gynt) ventures out to the cabaret in Dulac's *L'Invitation au voyage* (1927).

rhythmically moves a rocking chair.[68] Just as Debussy's pioneering work had employed layers of sound (atonal music, orchestral tone-color) and silence to express the ineffable or elements of human consciousness or soul that are beyond language (as articulated in Maeterlinck's "Theater of Silence"), Dulac's abstract films express or serve as "proof of concept" for her own theory of a "Music of Silence." While utilizing photographic techniques such as blurs, masks, dissolves, multiple exposures, and multiple lenses to render the natural elements more abstract, Dulac also incorporates elements from nature, such as light, mirrors, water, and wind, to distort or blur the various elements or to intensify their design. We find tree branches reflected in water, blurred streaks of light on a spinning mirrored globe, the reflection of flowers arched in a mirror (which Dulac refers to as a "dance of tulips"), water jets bouncing off trees, wind blowing a scarf, the reflections of light from the mirrored globe on a scarf, and so on. Recognizable figures give way to more abstract forms.

For Dulac, like the Symbolists, the musical analogy not only provided a footbridge to a non-narrative and non-figurative form of cinema; it also permitted Dulac to qualify the "movement" and "rhythm" essential to cinema, with its intangible or spiritual dimension. In her 1928 article "La Musique du silence," Dulac reminds us of a central Symbolist tenet: "The cinema can certainly tell stories, but one must not forget that the story is

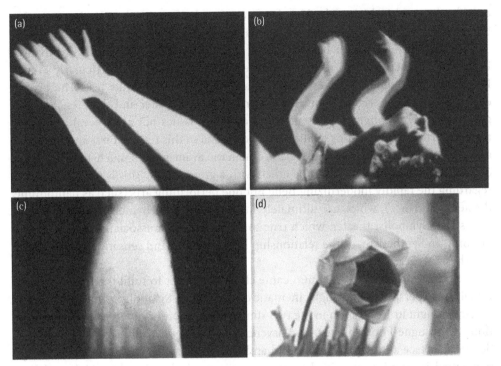

FIGURE 13.8 Lilian Constantini as the ballerina in *Thèmes et variations* (Dulac, 1929) (top left and right); screen captures of fountains and tulips from Dulac's *Arabesque* (1929) (bottom left and right).

nothing. The story is just a surface. The seventh art, the art of the screen, is the depth that extends beneath this surface made perceptible: the elusive musicality (*l'insaisissable musical*)."[69]

"Making the Idea Felt": Synthetism's Challenge to Medium Specificity

As dance scholar Nell Andrew reminds us in her work on the Nabi painters and Loïe Fuller (a key Symbolist reference), "we can no longer think of the abstract developments of Lautrec or the Nabis as indicative of a largely formal desire to reach a purity of medium. Instead, it seems more plausible that the realizations of abstraction in print and decorative work were achieved through a shared interdisciplinary, intellectual, and kinesthetic urge to grasp and to articulate the sensations of immaterial experience, in other words, to make the idea *felt*."[70] To be sure, aligning certain of these corporal and transitory arts with the pictorial and performative in theater shifts our habits of attention—not only for the way in which we look at cinema, as framing, staging, or enacting sensation but also in how we approach and manifest its history.

Given the commonplace understanding of critics-turned-filmmakers as invested in film's difference, we find in the 1920s French avant-garde, and particularly French Impressionist Cinema and Germaine Dulac, an irresistible litmus test. The precise encounters and material exchanges between Symbolist theater and the French avant-garde not only highlight important historiographic issues but also reveal a pressing need to further query and/or qualify historic dogma in this regard. First and foremost, as Dulac's work demonstrates, the 1920s cinematic avant-garde's much-touted dictum of "medium specificity" needs to be taken with a grain of salt. This is particularly true regarding the rapidly modernizing Belle Époque performing arts (such as pantomime, theater, and dance), which are ultimately linked through their musicality, and in this case study, Symbolist theater, which true to its Symbolist or associative nature, insists not only on Synthetism, or the relationship between form and sensation, but also on a "synthesis of the arts."[71]

At a time when the new medium came closer than ever to fulfilling the promise of Renaissance perspective through cinematic depth of field, Symbolist theater, faced with cinema, sought its inspiration in the two-dimensional expressivity of painterly abstraction. And Lugné-Poë's abstract and psychological themes, conveyed through a play between surface and depth, foreground and background, abstract contemplation and perceptual immersion, provided a crucial dramaturgical and spectatorial model for 1920s cineastes. Symbolist scenography also anticipated a wide array of 1920s experimental film tendencies, from Dadaism (René Clair's 1923 *Paris qui dort*) and Surrealism (Dulac's *The Seashell and the Clergyman*) to abstraction, and announced a broader stylistic dualism in French cinema, based on the visual cultures of Naturalism and Symbolism, that extends from Poetic Realism and the French New Wave to New French Extremism.[72]

Despite the allure of the "specificity" discourse, there are many important intersections between cinema and the other arts that mark the medium and shape its expressive forms in central ways. Ironically, the specificity (or "pure cinema") discourse evokes many of the core principles of Symbolist dramaturgy as a theater of ideas, silence, and visuality. In conclusion, as this study has aimed to show, we need to read film histories against the grain of "medium specificity" to consider the relationship between film and the other arts more specifically. In the spirit of Symbolism, let's return to our initial premise: theater has always been in the wings of cinema.

Notes

1. As eloquently phrased by Mirabelle Ordinaire in "The Stage on Screen: The Representation of Theatre in Film" (PhD diss., Columbia University, 2011), 2.
2. Other major cineastes associated with the movement include early poetry critic Jean Epstein, and theater-turned-film actor Abel Gance.

3. As František Deák notes, Artaud not only began his theater career in 1920 with Lugné-Poë but also published his first essay on the director, "Au Théâtre de l'Oeuvre," in the journal *Demain*, that same year. Deák, "Antonin Artaud and Charles Dullin: Artaud's Apprenticeship in Theatre," *Educational Theatre Journal* 29, no. 3 (1977): 345.
4. Germaine Dulac, "La Musique du silence," *Cinégraphie*, no. 5 (January 15, 1928), 77–78, reprinted in Germaine Dulac, *Écrits sur le cinéma (1919–1937)*, ed. Prosper Hillairet (Paris: Paris Expérimental, 1994), 108. While new French and English editions have become available in 2020 and 2021 respectively, I refer to the more widely distributed first edition of Dulac's writings, the "little red book" published in 1994 (and the edition that launched my own research). All translations are mine unless otherwise indicated.
5. See Ricciotto Canudo's "Lettere d'arte. Trionfo del cinematografo," *Il Nuovo giornale* (Florence), November 25, 1908, reprinted by Dotoli in *Filmcritica*, no. 278 (November 1977): 292–296, and his expanded essay, "La Naissance d'un sixième art: Essai sur le cinématographe," *Les Entretiens Idéalistes*, October 25, 1911, 169–179, reprinted as "The Birth of the Sixth Art," in Richard Abel, ed., *French Film Theory and Criticism: A History/Anthology 1907–1939* (Princeton, NJ: Princeton University Press, 1993): 58–66; and Abel Gance, "Qu'est-ce que le cinématographe? Un Sixième Art," *Ciné-journal*, March 9, 1912, 10, reprinted as "A Sixth Art," in Abel, ed., *French Film Theory and Criticism*, 66–67.
6. Marcel L'Herbier, "Hermès et le silence," *Le Temps*, February 23, 1918, reprinted in Abel, ed., *French Film Theory and Criticism*, 147–155.
7. On décor, see Louis Delluc, *Photogénie* (Paris: Maurice de Brunoff, 1920), 64, cited in Nourredine Ghali, *L'Avant-Garde Cinématographique en France dans les Années Vingt: Idées, Conceptions, Théories* (Paris: Paris Expérimental, 1995), 116.
8. Dulac contributes to the core debates on "pure cinema" in *Les Cahiers du mois* and the first and sole issue of her own journal, *Schémas*. Germaine Dulac, "L'Essence du cinéma. L'idée visuelle," *Les Cahiers du mois*, no. 16 (October 17, 1925): 64–65, and "Du Sentiment à la ligne," *Schémas* 1 (February 1927): 26–31, reprinted in Dulac, *Écrits sur le cinéma*, 62–67 and 87–89, respectively.
9. Germaine Dulac, "Mise-en-scène," *Le Film*, November 12, 1917, 7–9; "Où sont les interprètes?" *Le Film*, October 14, 1918, 69–70; "Ayons la foi," *Le Film*, October 15, 1919, 46, reprinted in Dulac, *Écrits*, 21. Her first film essays were signed Germaine Albert-Dulac.
10. Emile Vuillermoz, "Chronique—Devant l'écran," *Le Temps*, February 7, 1917, 3a, cited in Ghali, *L'Avant-Garde Cinématographique*, 115.
11. A notable exception is Sabine Lenk's detailed book-length study, which conversely addresses theater's anti-cinema position, showing that the zeal for autonomy and exclusivity went both ways. Sabine Lenk, *"Théâtre contre cinema": Die Diskussion um Kino und Theater vor dem ersten Weltkrieg in Frankreich*. Reihe Film-und Fernsehwissenschaftliches Arbeiten (Muenster, Germany: MAKS Publishing, 1989).
12. Eric De Kuyper, "Le Théâtre comme 'mauvais objet,'" *Cinémathèque* 11 (1997): 60–72.
13. Michel Corfin, *Le Théâtre de Boulevard* (Paris: Presses Universitaires de France, 1989), 3.
14. Letter from Germaine Dulac to Madeleine Claire Waymel Saisset-Schneider (Dulac's mother), July 14, 1904, DULAC572-B59, Fonds Germaine Dulac, Bibliothèque du film, La Cinémathèque française, Paris.
15. Germaine Dulac, "Réjane!" *La Française*, December 23, 1906, 1. Dulac signed this first article "G. de l'Estang," a pseudonym that she would revive for her theater reviews in *La Française* beginning in late 1908. In the intervening period, she went by Germaine

Albert-Dulac for a series of front-page columns for *La Française* titled "Figures d'autrefois et d'aujourd'hui" ("Figures of Past and Present").

16. Dulac, "Matinée Italienne du Salon International." *La Française,* January 20, 1907, 2. Following a visit to Després's home, at *rue Condorcet*, Dulac notes her discovery of Després as Hilde in Ibsen's *The Master Builder* at L'Oeuvre and compares the actress's industriousness and independence to that of an "Ibsenian heroine." Dulac, "Madame Suzanne Després," *La Française,* November 17, 1907, 1.

17. Alice Folco, "Au carrefour naturalo-symboliste: Zola / Mallarmé," *Etudes théatrales* 56–57 (2013): 145–150.

18. See chapter 2 of my book, *Germaine Dulac: A Cinema of Sensations* (Urbana: University of Illinois Press, 2014).

19. See Dulac's review of Maeterlinck's "L'Oiseau Bleu" and her article "Mary Garden" (*Pelléas et Mélisande*) in "Le Théâtre ou les théatres," DULAC564-B58, 122–123 and 132–133; Letter from Albert Dulac to Germaine Dulac, June 12, 1915 (on *Pelléas*), DULAC419-B32.

20. Among these are a one-act comedy of manners, *Le Bonheur est chose légère* (*Happiness is Frivolous*); a three-act fantasy, *Le Fantôme*, based on a Norwegian legend; a four-act social parody titled *Les Pieuvres* (*The Octopuses*); and an elaborate sixty-one-page, class-conscious comedy, *Le Jardin magnifique*. Germaine Dulac, "Le Bonheur est chose légère," DULAC544-B57; "Le Fantôme," DULAC549-B57; "Les Pieuvres," DULAC554-B57; "Le Jardin magnifique," DULAC551-B57. While these theater projects are undated, her correspondence with Albert Dulac allows us to situate this last work in late 1914 or early 1915, just prior to her first film production. Albert Dulac to Germaine Dulac, September 9, 1914, DULAC418-B31.

21. Dan Rebellato, "Naturalism and Symbolism: Early Modernist Practice," http://www.danrebellato.co.uk/naturalism-and-symbolism (accessed July 7, 2021).

22. Maryse Souchard and Marc Favier, "Le naturalisme, le symbolisme et le populisme: vers la modernité du xxe siècle (1887–1924)," in Alain Viala, ed., *Le théâtre en France* (Paris: Presses Universitaires de France, 2009), 395. Long before André Bazin's post–World War II treatise on aesthetic realism, Antoine's dramaturgical naturalism, or the expression of social causation through realist mise-en-scène, provided a vital foundation for the Impressionists (from Dulac's *Les Soeurs Ennemies* in 1917 to Delluc's *La Femme de Nulle Part* in 1923).

23. Rebellato, "Naturalism and Symbolism," 26.

24. See Denis Diderot, *Entretiens sur* Le Fils naturel, ed. J. Goldzink (Paris: Flammarion, 2005), cited in Alice Folco, Ariane Martinez, and Bénédicte Boisson, *La mise en scène théâtrale de 1800 à nos jours* (Paris: Presses Universitaires de France, 2010), 57.

25. See Colette Becker, *Zola, le saut dans les étoiles* (Paris: Presses de la Sorbonne Nouvelle, 2002), 238, cited in Rebellato, "Naturalism and Symbolism."

26. As Phillip Walker writes, "The window, the mirror, the eye—all those things which intervene between the observer and the object observed, which obstruct light, frame filter, bend, transform it or interpret the data it transmits—are, indeed, among the most central, recurrent, and characteristic motifs of his art." Walker, "The Mirror, the Window, and the Eye in Zola's Fiction," *Yale French Studies* 42 (1969): 52.

27. Dulac created and exhibited camera lenses she designed, along with a large-scale model of a film set, at the 1924 exposition "L'Art dans le cinéma français," curated by Musée Galliera director Henri Clouzot.

28. Henri Dorra, *Symbolist Art Theories: A Critical Anthology* (Berkeley: University of California Press, 1995), 144.
29. Bettina L. Knapp, *The Reign of the Theatrical Director, French Theatre, 1887–1924* (Troy, NY: Whitson, 1988).
30. Dulac, "Du Sentiment à la ligne."
31. Robert Bird, *Andrei Tarkovsky: Elements of Cinema* (London: Reaktion Books, 2008).
32. As Mallarmé writes, "To name an object is to remove three-quarters of the enjoyment of the poem, which is made to become it little by little. To *suggest* it, that is the dream." Stéphane Mallarmé, "Bibliothèque de la Pléiade" (1891), cited in Folco et al., *La mise en scène théâtrale*, 69 (my translation).
33. Dulac, "Mise-en-scène," 7 (emphasis mine).
34. Dulac, "Où sont les interprètes?" 70.
35. Ibid., 69–70.
36. Bataille wrote more than forty plays, including *La Femme Nue* (1908), *Le Scandale* (1909), and *La Vierge Folle* (1910), each of which Dulac reviewed.
37. As Réjane's early lover and secretary, the Italian playwright-turned-screenwriter Dario Nicodemi is considered a key modernizer of Italian theater. He not only composed and translated countless plays for Réjane but later founded the Teatro Valle in Rome in 1921, where he premiered Pirandello's groundbreaking *Six Characters in Search of an Author* that year.
38. See Dulac's composite review of "La Vierge Folle" (Bataille), "La Flamme"(Nicodemi), "Une Femme Passa"(Coolus), "La Beffa" (Benelli, starring Sarah Bernhardt), alongside "Après le voile" (by writer, suffragist, and spiritist Hera Mirtel), published in *La Français*, March 13, 1910, 2, and collected in "Le Théâtre ou les théâtres," DULAC564-B58, 98–101. Romain Coolus staged his first play at Antoine's Théâtre Libre in 1893 and at Lugné-Poë's Théâtre de l'Oeuvre in 1896. Dulac's 1927 *Antoinette Sabrier* (starring Ève Francis) is an adaptation of Coollus's 1903 homonymous play, which she discusses in her 1909 review of his *4 fois 7:28*. "Le Théâtre ou les théâtres," DULAC564-B58, 61.
39. Dulac, "Visualisation," *La Rumeur*, November 29, 1927, in Dulac, *Ecrits*, 97; and Dulac, "La Musique du silence," 78.
40. See chapter 3 of my book, *Germaine Dulac: A Cinema of Sensations*, 106.
41. Dulac, "La Vierge Folle" and "La Flamme" in *La Française*, March 13, 1910, 2, reassembled in "Le Théâtre ou les théâtres," DULAC564-B58, 98–101. Dulac, "Lecture cinématique. La Belle Dame," lecture given at C.A.S.A., Paris, in May 1921, DULAC24-B2, 1. In contrast, David Bordwell writes that Dulac did not identify the "movement as one of 'impressionism'" until 1927, while Georges Sadoul later "name[d] it 'Impressionism,' and suggested some points of stylistic homogeneity." David Bordwell, "French Impressionist Cinema: Film Culture, Film Theory, and Film Style" (PhD diss., University of Iowa, 1974), 4–7.
42. Dulac, on "La Vierge Folle" and "La Flamme," in "Le Théâtre ou les théâtres," 98.
43. Judd D. Hubert, "Symbolism, Correspondence and Memory," *Yale French Studies* 9 (1952): 46–47.
44. Lugné-Poë, "Les deux ecoles dans l'art du décor," press clipping [n.s.], July 26, 1921. Rt. 12.266 ASP 1921, Collection Auguste Rondel, Bibliothèque nationale de France.
45. Folco et al., *La mise en scène théâtrale*, 2.
46. See Lawrence Alloway and Marilyn Huny, *Gauguin and the Decorative Style* (New York: Solomon R. Guggenheim Foundation, 1966).

47. Jan Verkade, *Le tourment de Dieu* (Paris: L. Rouart and J. Watelin, 1923), 93, cited in Susan Houghton Libby, "An Adjustable Means of Expression: A Selection of Édouard Vuillard's Decorative Works of the 1890s," *Studies in the Decorative Arts* 1, no. 2 (Spring 1994): 26.
48. Souchard and Favier [in *Le théâtre en France*, ed. Viala], 396.
49. Maeterlinck, "À Propos de Solness" (Concerning *The Master Builder*), *Le Figaro*, April 12, 1894; revised and included in Maeterlinck's manifesto, "Le tragique quotidien" (1896), in *Le Trésor des humbles* (dedicated to Georgette Leblanc) (Paris: Mercure de France, 1896); reedition: Espace Nord (Bruxelles: Éds. Labor, 1986), 104–105. Lugné-Poë's staging of Ibsen's *The Master Builder* lit the spark for a new scenography that privileged "second level" or internal (vs. external) dialogue, or, as Mireille Losco-Lena suggests, of the alliance between silence and the invisible, central to Dulac's own approach to mise-en-scène during this period. Losco-Lena, *La Scène Symboliste (1890–1896): pour un théâtre spectral* (Grenoble, France: Editions littéraires et linguistique de l'université de Grenoble, 2010), 85; Dulac, "Solness le constructeur [Screenplay. Synopsis]" [n.d.] DULAC 246-B17, Bibliothèque du film, La Cinémathèque française, Paris.
50. As Mireille Losco-Lena notes, Lugné-Poë's "spectacle" is above all a "spectacle de l'ombre" (shadow play). Losco-Lena, *La Scène Symboliste*, 78.
51. Maeterlinck, "Le tragique quotidien," in *Le Trésor des Humbles*, 1986, 104–105; see also Marcel Postic, *Maeterlinck et le Symbolisme* (Paris: Editions A.-G. Nizet), 112.
52. Dulac, "*La Mort du soleil* et la naissance du film," *Cinéa*, February 17, 1922, 14.
53. The Symbolists also separated the narrator from the actors, by hiding the former in the orchestral pit (like musicians of the silent era). Gertrude Jasper, in her account of Vuillard's 1894 staging of Henri de Regnier's Mallarmé-inspired symbolist poem *La Gardienne* (1891), provides a rare description of the technique: "[the reading of the poem] thoroughly disconcerted the audience and critics, as it was recited by actors concealed in the orchestra pit while others, on the stage, behind a green gauze curtain, followed the words in pantomime." Gertrude R. Jasper, "Lugné-Poë and the œuvre," *The French Review*, December 1941, 29.
54. Vuillard's lithographies accompany almost all of Lugné-Poë's Ibsen productions, from *Romersholm* to *The Master Builder*; these works also recall the subtle greys of Dulac's *La Souriante Madame Beudet* (1923), providing an idea of what her unrealized adaptation of *The Master Builder* might have looked like.
55. Sembat makes note of diverse artistic encounters and dinners with Germaine and Albert Dulac during the prewar period. In November 1913, having lectured on symbolist poetry *chez Antoine* (possibly Théâtre Antoine), in his diary, Sembat notes the presence of "a few friends" including "[Albert] Dulac, [Gustav] Kahn, [Henri] Matisse." "Marcel Sembat, "'Les Cahiers noirs' 4éme partie: 1911–1915" (Paris: Office universitaire de recherche socialiste, 1985), November 26, 1912, 27; September 22, 1913, 31; and November [n.d.] 1913, 38, 220.
56. Jourdain and Mallet-Stevens sought to create décors that were both real and poetic, anticipating the work of later Russian emigré set designers, such as Lazare Meerson and Eugenie Lourié. See also "Visite à Francis Jourdain" (interviewed by Marie Epstein), September 28, 1956. CRH75-B4, Fonds Commission de recherche historique, Bibliothèque du film, La Cinémathèque française, 2–3.
57. Hilton Kramer, *The Age of the Avant-garde: 1956–1972* (New Brunswick, NJ: Transaction Publishers, 2011), 195.

58. In this respect, the poster parallels the observation of novelist Henri Barbusse that wartime France had become two countries: "the [war front], out there where too many [men] are miserable, and the *home front here*, where too many [women] are happy." Henri Barbusse, *Le Feu, journal d'une escouade* (Paris: Flammarion, 1916), cited in Françoise Thébaud, *La Femme au temps de la guerre de 14* (Paris: Stock, 1986), 104.
59. Germaine Dulac, "Visualisation," *La Rumeur*, November 19, 1927, in Dulac, *Ecrits*, 97; Dulac, "La Musique du silence," 106–108; Nell Andrew, *Moving Modernism: The Urge to Abstraction in Painting, Dance, Cinema* (New York: Oxford University Press, 2020), 7.
60. As Dulac asked in her 1921 lecture on the film, "Will the Countess also allow herself to be charmed by Lola[?] Will she give up fighting with her rival? These questions are left unanswered. In this way, these things [i.e., the visual elements] show her evolution." "Lecture cinématique. La Belle Dame."
61. Recounting her direction of Dermoz, Dulac says, "Just think and feel without moving any muscles in your face; and you'll see that your performance, united with the rhythm of the images and with your thoughts, will give exactly the real measure of emotions to be exteriorized." She adds, "In Denys Amiel and André Obey's 'La Souriante Madame Beudet,' there is no action or very little: the life of a soul. This film was a big turning point for me." Germaine Dulac, *Qu'est-ce que le cinéma? / What Is Cinema?* Texts assembled by Marie-Anne Colson-Malleville, ed., Clément Lafite and Tami Williams (Paris: Light Cone, 2019), 237 (my translation).
62. Dulac, "Du sentiment à la ligne," 30.
63. Germaine Dulac, "Commentaire et transition," *Schémas* 1 (February 1927): n.p., DULAC408-B26, Bibliothèque du film, La Cinémathèque française.
64. *L'Invitation* also functions intertextually to invoke ideas of forbidden desire by featuring actors from earlier films, such as *Malencontre* and *La Belle dame sans merci*.
65. See, for example, Tami M. Williams, "Dancing with Light: Choreographies of Gender in the Cinema of Germaine Dulac," in Dietrich Scheunemann and Alexander Graf, eds., *Avant-Garde Film* (Amsterdam: Editions Rodopi, 2007), 121–132.
66. See also Tami Williams, "Germaine Dulac: Du Figuratif à l'abstraction," in Nicole Brenez and Christian Lebrat, eds., *Jeune, dure et pure: Une histoire du cinéma expérimental en France* (Paris: Cinémathèque française, 2001), 78–82.
67. Henry Miller, *Letters to Emil*, ed. George Wickes (New York: New Directions, 1989), 63.
68. Remarkably, the literal and abstract motif of the "arabesque" is also mirrored in the film's overall editing structure, much like the Symbolist form of Mallarmé's poems.
69. Dulac, "La Musique du silence," 108.
70. Andrew, *Moving Modernism*, 6–7.
71. Dorra, *Symbolist Art Theories*, 7.
72. Losco-Lena, *La Scène Symboliste*, 83–84.

PART III

PEDAGOGICAL FORMATIONS

Non-theatrical Cinema and the Uses of Film

CHAPTER 14

POPULAR SCIENCE MONTHLY AND THE USES OF MOVING PICTURES

GREGORY A. WALLER

As a wave of recent scholarship has ably demonstrated, the scope and significance of cinema in the United States during the twentieth century expands appreciably when the field is understood to include not only films made for commercial theatrical release but also educational, scientific, government, sponsored, useful, and non-theatrical film.[1] These overlapping categories all point to, I would argue, an understanding of cinema as multi-sited and multi-purposed, variable across time and location, even before the widespread adoption of 16mm and other small-gauge film stocks and portable projectors in the later 1920s and 1930s. Such a claim does not necessarily mean neglecting or underestimating the everyday presence of film as theatrically exhibited commercial entertainment, but it does foreground central questions concerning the first twenty-five years of American cinema history: how were moving pictures discursively and in practice made useful beyond the movie theater, the commercial system of distribution, and the ubiquity of Hollywood's products? For commentators outside the immediate orbit of the film industry, why did non-commercial as well as commercial moving pictures merit attention and what was assumed to be the place of film in relation to the overlapping fields of public media, communication technologies, and modes of image production in the United States?

With these questions in mind, I will view the history of American cinema from the perspective of *Popular Science Monthly* (hereafter *PSM* in the text and notes for the sake of brevity), which began publication in 1872. In the following decades *PSM* was a well-established periodical committed to furthering what it took to be the unquestionably beneficial aims of practical science, broadly understood, while also (before 1915) being driven by a mandate to address an educated audience including, but not limited to, academically affiliated specialists. This magazine had no special investment in championing motion pictures as a new medium and no connection to the film industry, and thus *PSM* affords a vantage point quite different from the contemporary print sources that have deeply informed research in American film history: daily and weekly newspapers, the motion picture/commercial entertainment trade press, fan magazines, and promotional publications. The availability of all *PSM* issues between 1890 and 1920 in a searchable and browsable digital format (thanks largely to the HathiTrust Digital Library) makes it far more manageable now to undertake a comprehensive, issue-by-issue reading of this periodical, attending, in particular, to this magazine's interest in various media and its commitment to making sense of modernity.

I focus here on how consideration of film as medium, commercial enterprise, and research and teaching tool figured against the broader spectrum of material published in *PSM* over two decades, beginning in 1897. This timespan covers the first article *PSM* published addressing what it called "animated photography" in December 1897 and extends just past October 1915, when *PSM* was fully transformed into a less intellectual and more heavily illustrated, streamlined, panoramic compendium devoted to the modern, the efficient, the strange-but-true, the cutting edge of technology, and the ingenuity and effort driving industries large and small. In contrast to the surprising paucity of commentary on moving pictures in *PSM* between 1898 and 1915, the refashioned (and far more widely circulated) version of this magazine in its first year found much worth noting both in the many novel non-commercial uses of what was emerging as a multi-purpose medium and also in cinema's technological apparatus and the logistics of film production, including stunt work, set design, and special effects. These topics would continue to draw considerable attention from *PSM* well into the 1920s and beyond. Rather than track this longer history, I will conclude by discussing how moving pictures figured in *PSM* as it fine-tuned its new format from October 1915 through the following year, which sets the parameters of this study as 1897–1916. This range allows me to examine in detail *PSM*'s coverage of film from the emergence of moving pictures as new media in the late 1890s through the mid-1910s, when a rapidly maturing commercial film industry had made movies and moviegoing a ubiquitous feature of American daily life.

Animated Pictures and the Advance of Science

Published in December 1897, *PSM*'s first account of the still relatively novel phenomenon of moving pictures was a twelve-page article titled "Animated Pictures," by astronomer J. Miller Barr, illustrated with two images of C. Francis Jenkins's Phantoscope (see figure 14.1) and two others showing strips of celluloid (see figure 14.2).[2] Readers of this particular issue of the magazine would have found, under the rubric of "popular science," a quite diverse bill of fare, including articles on phonetics and astronomy, Pacific Coast gulls and geological features of Russia, the relative success of so-called liquor laws,

MACHINE FOR PROJECTING ANIMATED PICTURES ON THE SCREEN. The phantascope, latest model, being an attachment for a J. B. Colt & Co. electric lantern.

FIGURE 14.1 Projecting machine, from the first article on moving pictures in *Popular Science Monthly*, December 1897.

and psychological and sociological studies of contemporary issues. Book reviews covered titles from a host of disciplines. Other regular sections were devoted to summaries of scholarly articles and accounts of new research findings—suggesting the linkage between scientific efforts in the United States, England, and continental Europe. Editorials articulated the more general social, cultural, and political orientation of *PSM*, blaming "parental neglect" for "hoodlumism" in America and insisting that the "true end of education" should be more than simply serving as a "preparation for money-making."[3]

The centerpiece of the December 1897 issue was likely not Barr's introduction to moving pictures but rather the latest installments in two timely, high-profile, continuing series that indicate the parameters of what passed in *PSM* as popular science: the thirteenth article on "Principles of Taxation" by prominent economist David Ames Wells, and the eleventh article in William Z. Ripley's sociological account of the "Racial Geography" of Europe. Ripley's twenty-five-page article relied extensively on photographic evidence of racial types and what then would have been sophisticated maps depicting supposedly "racial" variables, for instance, the "cephalic index" in Sweden and the range of hair pigmentation (i.e., "nigresence") and the density of Scandinavian and Celtic place names in the British Isles.

What looks in hindsight to be the eclectic or catholic reach of the December 1897 issue was fully typical of *PSM*'s editorial strategy for the next eighteen years. This journal's stated aim was "to present fully and accurately the advance of science; to permit the leading men of science to bring their work before the largest public; to set a standard to the popular press in its treatment of science."[4] In practice, such advancement could

FIGURE 14.2 "Animated pictures" as filmstrip, from the first article on moving pictures in *Popular Science Monthly*, December 1897.

take many forms, and science covered a broad spectrum of new and traditional areas of inquiry, with *PSM* regularly publishing articles on astronomy, economics, philosophy, eugenics, history, sociology, art history, the history of science, geography, geology, biology, philology, and medicine.[5] Among contemporary concerns, race, public health, immigration, and the role of higher education figured prominently in *PSM*. In fact, it was in the pages of this magazine that Booker T. Washington's "The Race Problem in the United States" first appeared, along with other notable articles, like William James's "The Moral Equivalent of War" and an early introduction to Freud's theory of the unconscious.[6]

One essential responsibility of the work of science, conceived of as broadly as this, was to guide and shape public debate by making sense of the experience, the promise, and the challenges of modernity.[7] For instance, a *PSM* editorial in the December 1897 issue celebrated the nineteenth century's "onward march of scientific discovery and invention," which had resulted in a "world" (unmistakably Euro- and American-centric) transformed by the "innumerable wonders that science in its practical application has wrought," with photography ranking among the most influential contributions of applied science, on par with electro-chemistry.[8] The question, then, is not simply *when PSM* took notice of moving pictures, but *how* this new medium was understood and assessed by a periodical deeply committed to the notion that progress was fueled by useful technology in the service of multi-faceted applied science.

From the perspective of *PSM*, the promise of film very much depended on the medium's status as a "beautiful invention," which Barr designates explicitly as "a new and wonderful realm in the field of photography." As such, two aspects of animated pictures warrant the attention of *PSM*'s readers: (1) the potential utility of the medium, "whose extent, variety, and richness" held great promise; and (2) the apparatus itself, meaning the mechanism and operation of the motion picture camera and projector, including the prehistory of this "distinctively modern" technology that had "evolved" from "more primitive forms of apparatus" like the Zoetrope and the Phenakistiscope. Barr is confident that the apparatus will further evolve, aiming toward realizing the mimetic "ideal" of projected stereoscopic color moving images with appropriate sound.[9]

While the Kinetoscope and Cinematograph, Barr notes, have found some success in delivering a "form of entertainment," the apparatus is destined to serve grander and "more serious" scientific and instructional purposes. For example, moving pictures of present-day royalty and other "distinguished men and women" will constitute "records" available for future generations. The potential is even greater when it comes to what would later be called time-lapse cinematography, allowing "the general public, not less than the advanced student of science" to see plant growth, for instance, "with a vividness never before realized." Such films, Barr claims, will be "invaluable ... object lessons in botany" that will "produce an effect at once marvelous, unique, and instructive." Likewise, filming the sun in time-lapse images "will enable us to actually see" change and movement that is "invisible to the observer's eye."[10]

Barr predicts that this unprecedented capacity for recording and projecting moving images of otherwise unviewable natural phenomena will make motion picture technology important both for scientific research and also for delivering "instructive entertainment to the public."[11] In contrast to the revelatory potential of time-lapse animated photography, providing "instructive entertainment" might seem like merely a mundane calling, until we note that *PSM* at the turn of the twentieth century—that is, well before the full-scale commercial development of moving pictures in the nickelodeon era—was already worried about the "quicken[ed] pace of life," particularly for the masses of people tempted by "the ever-increasing multiplicity of luxuries and novelties of every kind."[12] "The vast provision made to-day for the entertainment and amusement of the multitude," warned the December 1897 editorial I cited above, "has little educative value and may even tend to the injury of the reflective powers."[13] And to make matters worse, declared another editorial the following year, for an increasingly "self-indulgent" and undiscriminating populace, "amusements are continually being brought to their very doors, and in a hundred ways forced on their attention."[14] Under these troubling and distinctly modern conditions, successfully providing "instructive entertainment to the public" might well constitute a prime strategy for popularizing science, reorienting the masses away from the lure of amusements and even helping to prevent "the actual degeneration of character and intellect."[15] Thus the potentially vast utility of moving pictures as a photographic recording medium for scientists found its corollary, Barr suggests, in the promise of the motion picture projector as a means of public exhibition.

Judging solely from the next eighteen years of *PSM*, however, Barr's prognosis for the future of animated pictures as a potentially influential multi-use medium was ill-founded. A *PSM* article published in 1900 describes attempts to use a Kinematograph to film sound waves caused by an explosion, and another article in 1905 on research at university medical schools claims in passing that "the moving picture . . . has gradually replaced the single view" for the purposes of biological and medical research.[16] But in effect that was the extent of *PSM*'s coverage of motion pictures until 1913, when a brief note titled "The Scientific Origin of Moving Pictures" recounted Eadweard Muybridge's photographic motion studies at the University of Pennsylvania.[17] While praising Muybridge's innovative experiments, *PSM* bemoans the fact that this groundbreaking scientific research project—supported by a university—had led only to the $150 million commercial film industry, whose stock in trade is delivering "crude farces and melodramas." Nevertheless, *PSM* at this date still held out a modicum of hope that "the moving picture show will make possible a democratic development of art and become an educational institution of the greatest possible consequence."[18] This article, however, offered no plan for how the medium might realize its pedagogical potential.

Less than a year later, George Thomas White Patrick, writing on "The Psychology of Relaxation" for *PSM*, was much less sanguine about the prospects for moving pictures, likening the "moving-picture craze" of the 1910s to the "epidemics of the middle ages."[19] Patrick, a professor of philosophy at the State University of Iowa, had long been interested in the social psychology of the masses. He had written for *PSM* in 1900 "The Psychology of Crazes," an anxious account of the dangers posed by easily manipulated group behavior, in which he observes that "crazes of all kinds have found a prolific soil in America. The American mind is highly suggestible. One fad after another rages over the country and in some cases reduces the aggregate mind to a condition of idiocy."[20]

Perhaps even more telling than this hardly unique disdain for the commercial film industry and its mass audience in America are those instances in *PSM* where we might expect to find references to moving pictures but do not. Most notable are articles that recount the remarkable changes that had fundamentally reshaped the terms and conditions of life at the dawn of the twentieth century—changes driven in significant ways by the media and communication technologies and industries that Paul Starr examines in *The Creation of the Media: Political Origins of Modern Communications*, a book that situates moving pictures and radio in the historical context of the press, telegraphy, and telephony.[21] For example, in 1914, Smith College professor of economics and sociology Charles F. Emerick concluded his series of articles on "The Struggle for Equality in the United States" by surveying the status of the American working class and arguing for a greater measure of "popular government" because "the ideals of democracy are permeating all classes of society" thanks to:

> schools and colleges, books, newspapers and magazines, modern transportation and communication, business intercourse, the trade union, political discussion, the numerous clubs and Chautauqua circles, and the growing density of population which brings mind more frequently in contact with mind, are so many agencies for promoting the general enlightenment. Rural free delivery, the telephone, the interurban trolley and the influence of the city are widening the mental horizon of the farmer.[22]

If popular print media for Emerick qualify as "agencies for promoting the general enlightenment," then why not moving pictures? Surely picture shows in rural areas were by 1914 a primary site for spreading "the influence of the city." Perhaps Emerick simply could not imagine moving pictures, however ubiquitous and popular, as furthering this grand civic goal of democratization or "widening" anyone's "mental horizon" in contemporary America. Nor, apparently, could he conceive of moving pictures as a communication medium that facilitated mind-to-mind contact, helping to realize what he saw as America's promise of participation and equality.

While *PSM* after 1897 paid only scant, usually negative, attention to moving pictures even as film increasingly became a commercially driven fixture in everyday life, this periodical devoted considerably more space to what Starr calls "technological networks" like wireless telegraphy and telephony, including a twelve-part series of articles largely focused on the Bell Telephone system, and a six-part series detailing the engineering issues involved in the development of wireless telegraphy.[23] But more than corporate expansion and research practices were at stake. The promise of instantaneous communication across spatial divides via telephone and wireless telegraphy was highlighted in articles that embraced the opportunities available in a world increasingly powered and reshaped by technology. As early as 1899, an author in *PSM* effusively declared that wireless telegraphy "is the nearest approach to telepathy that has been vouchsafed to our intelligence [...] the nerves of the whole world are, so to speak, being bound together, so that a touch in one country is transmitted instantly to a far-distant one."[24] University of Chicago professor Albert P. Mathews went even further in his 1908 *PSM* article, "Science and Morality," confidently asserting that "the evolutionary hypothesis, the germ theory of disease, the telegraph, the telephone, the locomotive, the printing press, the daily paper, wireless telegraphy, these are the great moral apostles of the age, for they knit men together, conquer prejudices and extend our sympathies."[25] Concerned less with moral progress than with the course of empire, Sir George S. Robertson, in an address to the British Association for the Advancement of Science that was printed verbatim by *PSM* in 1901, announced: "measured by time distance ... the world indeed has wonderfully contracted," thanks to improvements in sea and rail transportation as well as to "the postal improvements, the telephones, and perhaps we may soon add the improved commercial utility of wireless telegraphy." Robertson remained optimistic that "in the near future we may anticipate equally remarkable improvements of a like kind, especially in railways, telegraph lines and deep-sea cables, and other scientific discoveries for transmitting man's messages through the water, in the air, or perhaps, by the vibrations of the earth."[26]

These utopian visions of modernity's future hinged on the promise of technologically enabled communication that was networked, interactive, and instantaneous. Robertson, for example, suggests that telephony and telegraphy, by collapsing space and allowing for person-to-person contact, are world-altering innovations. While animated pictures were touted for their unprecedented capacity to record and re-present reality—or were dismissed as simply crowd-pleasing commercial amusement—no contributor to *PSM* imagined that some future iteration of this new medium would be able to facilitate (and even create) instantaneity and interactivity. At the same time, it perhaps was impossible for a commentator like Mathews to conceive of moving pictures as an example of early twentieth-century public media along the lines of newspapers, books, and magazines, because that conception would have required believing that moving pictures somehow were helping to "knit men together," thereby "promoting general enlightenment" (and thereby meriting the protection of the First Amendment). More surprisingly, the new medium even goes unmentioned in a 1909 *PSM* article that references "current means of communication [that] succeed so well in bringing distant lands and deeds within our field of vision that the whole world contributes to the fascination of the passing scene."[27] Vision in this instance seems to be more figurative than literal; there is no indication that the "field" in question might be a movie screen.[28] For *PSM*'s commentators, then, motion pictures did not constitute a "means of communication" and so had no role in driving evolutionary progress, spreading enlightenment, or creating the networks to power national and transnational interconnectivity.

THE USES OF PHOTOGRAPHY AND THE ABSENCE OF MOVING PICTURES

Rather than thinking of moving pictures as a medium of technologically facilitated communication that was fundamentally reshaping—and improving—the experience of life in a new century, *PSM*'s only articles on moving pictures placed film securely within the domain of photography. Recall that Barr lauded the appearance of moving pictures as the "opening" of "a new and wonderful field in the realm of photography," while *PSM*'s brief 1913 article located the "scientific origin of moving pictures" in Muybridge's photographic motion studies. Contextualizing these claims requires considering the role of photographs and photography in a periodical like *PSM*. How frequently and on what grounds did *PSM* claim that photography could serve as a tool for scientific research? What role did photographs play as part of the instructional work of popularizing science—a practice recently examined by Kelley Wilder, who finds that "by the early twentieth century, the presence of photographs in nearly all branches of science was taken as a given?"[29] What might the utilization of photographs in *PSM* suggest about "animated pictures" as a useful medium for the purposes of research and the delivery of information?

For instance, when Barr saw in moving pictures the potential for revelatory time-lapse records of otherwise unseeable solar activity, he was implicitly placing this new resource within the well-established tradition of what *PSM* regularly referred to as "astronomical photography."[30] "For almost ten years," announced an article in 1910, "a sleepless watch" and "continuous exploration" of the heavens "has been kept up by an all-seeing photographic eye with an accuracy of which the world has hardly a conception."[31] Given the purportedly godlike reach and preternatural reliability of the camera, it is not surprising that Edward C. Pickering, then director of the Harvard College Observatory, could declare in 1909 that "the application of photography to the study of the stars" constitutes nothing less than "the second great advance in astronomy."[32]

The combination of camera and microscope—then called "photomicrography"—likewise garnered attention and acclaim from *PSM*. An article in 1898, for instance, provided instructions for how to "easily and quickly" photograph snow crystals, and another in 1902 offered a more extended investigation of this technology, which was said to be capable of producing images with "unmodified and unprejudiced exactness of detail." Once again, the "educational value" was deemed significant, since "photomicrography serves a double purpose. First, it enables the scientific investigator to determine accurately a knowledge of the minute physical structure of matter, and secondly, it provides a means of placing such information before others in a comprehensive manner."[33] Thus, like the new medium of moving pictures as described by Barr, photomicrography here equally serves the aims of research and instruction.

Both purposes have figured in recent scholarship on science and cinema in the early twentieth century, including Hannah Landecker's claim that film's "temporal dimension led to an explosion in experiments with and on film in scientific and medical disciplines from astronomy to psychiatry."[34] Barr's suggestion about filming solar activity surely fits this model, and Virgilio Tosi, in *Cinema before Cinema: The Origins of Scientific Cinematography*, includes "cosmocinematography" as one of many examples of "scientific cinema" ultimately rooted, he argues, in the research "needs" of nineteenth-century science.[35] At the same time, Barr's optimistic predictions about the use of moving pictures as a means of providing "instructive entertainment" that brings science to a mass audience were in some fashion realized in what Oliver Gaycken calls early cinema's "popular-science films." In fact, Gaycken notes that "the time-lapse subject of flowers blooming was a conspicuous hit" at the New York premiere of Charles Urban's Kinemacolor program in 1911.[36] Strips of colored celluloid from Urban's *From Bud to Blossom* were actually featured on the cover of the June 1911 issue of *Popular Mechanics*. But for all of *PSM*'s interest in astronomical photography and photomicrography, the magazine made virtually no mention of contemporary uses of film for either research or instruction.

In contrast, the value of photography as an essential resource for and element of expository, non-fictional, broadly scientific print discourse was demonstrated in virtually every issue of *PSM* during this period, even though the majority of this periodical's articles were not illustrated. Predictably, the articles that warranted the addition of photographs included first-person accounts of expeditions, tours, journeys, and visits to distant localities, ranging from a touristic travel talk like "A Visit to Nassau," which highlights the "wonderful flowers and trees as well as the curious customs of its picturesque natives," to "A Trip around Iceland," a four-part scientifically informed series that follows the travels of L. P. Gratacap of the American Museum of Natural History.[37] This combination of firsthand description and photographic images has much in common with a magic lantern or stereopticon lecture devoted to a particular place of interest, a public presentation format that could and did readily incorporate film sequences, as Rick Altman, Allison Griffiths, and Jennifer Peterson have demonstrated.[38] Yet *PSM* offers no indication that during the first two decades of cinema history, scientists, professional lecturers, and educators had begun to realize the potential of moving pictures, or—more significantly—that the new medium was being deployed for non-fictional purposes, paralleling the functions photographs served in *PSM* articles.[39]

Beyond accounts of travels and expeditions, *PSM* utilized photography in a host of articles devoted to the field experiences of zoologists and anthropologists, as well as to manufacturing and industrial operations, genetic experiments, and race-based eugenics.[40] Serving the purpose of evidence, elucidation, and documentation, the photographs in these articles were always more than merely illustrative, and they point to the vast, broadly "scientific" potential of what Barr in 1897 called the "realm of photography." Particularly given that Barr highlights the promise of animated photography for research and instructional purposes, the extended absence of moving pictures from the pages of *PSM* stands out. That this journal seems to have been unaware of or uninterested in microcinematography and other well-publicized, partly "scientific" uses of film is striking. Equally telling, given its broad understanding of applied science, *PSM* never published articles about a cluster of subjects that were ready-made for examination and commentary: experiments and innovations related to the motion picture apparatus; the highly visible business of producing and circulating films as a commercial enterprise; or the sociological and public health issues raised by the exhibition and reception of increasingly popular motion pictures to a mass audience. In effect, after animated pictures' short-lived and unrealized moment of promise, there was, judging from *PSM,* nothing more worth analyzing or even noting about what cinema was and what it might become. Was this absence based on certain assumptions about *PSM*'s educated readership and its reputation as a high-minded journal of science and ideas? Did the perceived devolution of moving pictures into merely a cheap commercial amusement render it unworthy of attention? No editorial in *PSM* explains why moving pictures as a practice, a tool, and a medium did not merit focused attention, as did, for example, the Bell system of telephony, the technology of the wireless, and the use of photography in the service of zoology, botany, and astronomy.

Popularizing *Popular Science Magazine*

That the absence of any coverage of motion pictures had been an editorial decision became immediately apparent with the October 1915 issue of *PSM*, when everything about this periodical changed. The September 1915 issue had announced that after forty-three years of publication, *PSM* in its current form would be renamed *Scientific Monthly* and would continue its established editorial policies (and—as soon became apparent—its stolid, word-heavy format). The name *Popular Science Monthly* had been purchased to be used as the title for a new "well-illustrated magazine devoted to the popularization of science" and unquestionably aiming at a "wide circulation." Henceforth *PSM* would be combined with *The World's Advance*, a profusely illustrated magazine covering "Electricity Mechanics Invention Science."[41] This decisive bifurcation of serious, academically rooted science and commercially lucrative popularized science attests to the profitability and the high visibility of illustrated monthly magazines in the competitive publishing marketplace of the 1910s, and points to different understandings of science, technology, manufacturing, work, and media—notably including motion pictures.

The change from the old to the new *PSM* is striking, from the full-color cover and table of contents that lists almost one hundred items, to the twenty-page section filled with photographs covering the war and other current events, and columns offering tips for the "home craftsman" and "encouragement to amateurs and experimenters in the field of radio communication." Virtually every page features up to four illustrations (largely photographs), with the layout varying almost page by page. The cover boasts of "Over 200 Pictures," while an announcement declares that the next issue will "contain over 140 pages of illustrated articles and three hundred pictures of the most varied kind." New editor Waldemar Kaempffert (fresh from a fifteen-year stint as managing editor of *Scientific American*) promises readers a magazine "more useful and stimulating than ever," one dedicated to presenting "the new, the practical and the unusual in modern science, mechanics, and electricity. It will strive to be a fascinatingly interesting, easily grasped, and trustworthy monthly record of the latest achievements in science, invention and industry."[42] This record will be composed not of conventional essays or scholarly research findings but largely of easily digestible items reduced to a paragraph or two of text, always illustrated.

PSM's new format derived directly from *World's Advance*, which, in turn, had incorporated or borrowed from magazines like *Popular Electricity* and *Modern Mechanics* that typically had paid more attention to motion pictures than the pre-1915 *PSM*. *Electrician and Mechanic* magazine, for instance, first explored the new medium in an ambitious seven-part series of articles in 1910–11, titled "The Motion Picture," which focused on the theatrical "motion-picture business," detailing, in particular, the workings of the projector and providing much practical advice regarding "the perplexing situations encountered by the motion-picture operator in the daily routine of his work."[43] The same month that this series began to run, *Popular Electricity* published "The 'Inside' of Moving Pictures," its first article on the subject. Rather than addressing projectionists or aspiring projectionists, *Popular Electricity* highlighted various topics that might interest "the patron of a moving picture show"—ranging from the creation of onscreen trick effects to the important role of the Stereopticon and the skilled work that goes on daily in the projection booth.[44] What was then called *Popular Electricity and The World's Advance* began a section called "Motion Pictures" in September 1913; this continued after *Modern Mechanics* was also incorporated into this magazine in July 1914. Within a few years, the coverage of motion pictures in this type of magazine had expanded considerably, often singling out the difficult, dangerous, complex, and/or costly aspects of commercial film production. In January 1915, a typical month, the "Motion Pictures" section of *Modern Mechanics* offered a detailed tour of the Thanhouser studio as well as briefer accounts of aerial stunt work, an elaborate mining camp set, the huge number of extras in *The Birth of a Nation*, and the many injuries suffered by the performers in the serial *The Trey o' Hearts*.[45]

One measure of the distance between pre-1915 *PSM*, disdainful of "picture shows" and for all purposes uninterested in the medium of moving pictures, and its flashy, commercial-minded namesake, was that the new version paid regular attention to motion pictures, initially in the form of a ten-page "Motion Pictures" section. As in the rest of the refashioned *PSM*, the items in this section were heterogeneous and fully illustrated, surveying the "latest achievements" and eye-catching innovations in the field while also providing more detailed accounts of behind-the-scenes filmmaking activity, usually involving some enterprising use of technology. For example, the premiere issue of the new *PSM* covered J. R. Bray's patented "special way" of making of animated cartoons, the various tricks behind "fake war pictures," and the problems to be overcome in filming royalty, as well as information about the production of a major feature film under the elaborate and "efficient" system of artificial lights at Essanay studios, where "factory schedules and factory rules are enforced," and at Selig's studio with its indexing system for keeping track of costumes and bit players. Though this section of the October 1915 issue also included a brief note on the use of films by a lecturer at the Agricultural College of North Dakota, "Motion Pictures" (see figure 14.3) here meant the commercial film industry—more specifically, the fascinating, ingenious, and efficient production of films, notably including newsreels and cartoons, intended for theatrical release. It is worth underscoring that the remade *PSM* cast a broad net in its fascination with and celebration of (largely American and even more largely male) individual and corporate

FIGURE 14.3 "Motion Pictures" section in the reinvented *Popular Science Monthly*, October 1915.

resourcefulness in the service of progress, efficiency, and utility. The October 1915 issue included articles explaining the production not just of films but also of canned tuna, foolproof bank vaults, artificial limbs, torpedoes, and machine guns—all in all a revealing panorama of modern technology at work.

WHAT WAS CINEMA IN 1916?

Only a few months after the rollout of the new *PSM*, a self-congratulatory editorial in January 1916 announced that the updating had proven to be remarkably successful, a testament to a format filled with "as many illustrations as can be crowded" into every page and nonstop "flashing from one subject to the next, superficially unrelated yet having an invisible bond" (not unlike newsreels then screening in movie theaters).[46] By this date, *PSM* had dropped the special "Motion Pictures" section but still featured articles in each issue concerning cinema. Most frequently, the commercial film industry remained the focus, though *PSM*'s coverage differed significantly from trade journals like *Moving Picture World* or fan magazines like *Motion Picture*, focusing not so much on picture personalities, corporate activity, exhibition practices, and promotional material as on the costly, dangerous, labor-intensive, and/or technologically sophisticated aspects of film production. In fact, the first time moving pictures graced the cover of *PSM*—in June 1916—the subject was "Making Moving Picture Thrills" (see figure 14.4), and the full-color image showed an intrepid cameraman filming a Western chase scene while perched precariously on a platform atop a moving car, doing a job at least as thrilling as the performance of horseback heroics by the cowboys and Indians he is filming.

As well as the dangers faced by "the man who was turning the camera-crank," stunt work, far more than star turns, was likely to attract this magazine's attention.[47] Brief items describe stuntmen who parachuted from atop New York's tallest buildings or leaped on horseback off a cliff eighty-three feet down into the water.[48] According to

FIGURE 14.4 Moviemaking on the cover of *Popular Science Monthly*, June 1916.

the article that accompanied the June 1916 cover image of exciting location filming, the "pure dare-deviltry" of performers who actually jump from bridges or drive cars across chasms accounted for many screen thrills, but so too did the "ingenuity of the cameraman and of the cutter" in creating "fake" scenes that comically defy the laws of gravity or suspensefully put characters in apparently life-threatening peril.[49] And along with recounting the dangers of stunt work, *PSM* marveled at underwater filming and staged "automobile smashups," as well as at the sheer magnitude and cost of what it called "spectacular" sets purportedly being built in Jamaica for an unnamed film promising to have a cast including "ten thousand Hindus" and "five thousand British cavalrymen."[50] "It is indeed difficult," declared another article, "for one who is not on the 'inside' of the motion picture business to realize the expense to which a picture company will go to secure effects necessary for the successful filming of a photoplay"—effects designed both to deliver unmatched "cinema realism" and to produce "shivery thrills."[51] At a historical moment often associated with the institutionalization of feature-length, narratively coherent Hollywood cinema, *PSM* rarely if ever mentions stars, storytelling, literary and dramatic pretensions, moral standing, or national systems of distribution; instead it celebrates commercial moving pictures as a cinema of spectacular attractions. This emphasis, which has its roots earlier in the 1910s in the coverage of cinema in magazines like *Popular Mechanics*, *Modern Mechanics*, and *Popular Electricity and The World's Advance*, is a corollary to what Rob King calls "technological spectacle" that "addressed interests that were widely shared in a technocratic society," as evidenced most richly and successfully in the Keystone Film Company's development of inventive comedies filled with stunt work and special effects.[52]

At the same time, the emphasis on how stunts and set design generate "moving picture thrills" satisfies *PSM*'s abiding interest in revealing how things operate or are manufactured and how technology can be put to practical as well as innovative use, a preoccupation equally apparent in articles (all from the June 1916 issue) about the marvels of "trench-digging apparatus" and a new "aerial scenic cableway" across Niagara Falls, X-ray photographs used in legal proceedings, and instructions for building ice-making equipment for the home.[53] Paralleling its coverage of novel devices relying on sound or photographic technology (like "a hand-made hand-played phonograph" or a still camera mounted on a pigeon for military reconnaissance purposes), *PSM* offers instructions on how to build a home-made motion picture camera and describes ingenious inventions that allow for smooth reel changeovers or better synchronize live music accompaniment with projected images.[54]

Significantly, the most extended account of moving picture technology comes in an article on the "revolutionary new motion picture camera" invented by Carl F. Akeley of the American Museum of Natural History. In many respects this camera might stand as the quintessential *PSM* object: the product of an inventor who coupled experience in the field with "technical knowledge," Akeley's remarkably ingenious invention, reports *PSM* (see figure 14.5), "overcomes" the problems and limitations of conventional film cameras

FIGURE 14.5 Celebrating technology advances that enable the greater usefulness of cinema (*Popular Science Monthly*, July 1916).

"with a mechanism entirely new" (which is pictured in elaborate detail). The result is an "instrument"—portable, versatile, and "as easily handled as a rifle"—that has important potential use-value, not solely for the commercial film industry but also for filmmakers working in what *PSM* calls the "diversified fields of motion-picture photography": specifically, naturalists and big-game hunters, as well as newspaper photographers who will now be able to "film every stage of an exciting fire rescue, or a riot, or a sinking ship, or an explosion, or a shooting." In effect, Akeley's invention promises to facilitate cinema's usefulness as a multi-purpose medium.[55]

With less fanfare, *PSM* also regularly took note of instances where film was projected for non-commercial uses outside of movie theaters: to entertain British soldiers and to aid in recruitment drives but also as a means of advertising for an automobile company whose specially equipped car "not only carries the apparatus, but generates the power for the motion picture machine." Another type of projection device attracting the attention of *PSM* was the "specially designed" mobile apparatus used by the Bureau of Commercial Economics to project US government films on the "fair white sides" of the Washington Monument—surely the most striking example of multi-sited cinema noted by *PSM* during 1916.[56]

Conclusion

PSM's accounts of the Akeley camera and the Washington Monument screening point toward significant lines of inquiry that track the uses of moving pictures beyond the ambit of the movies and the movie theater during the 1910s, hinting at a broader, more inclusive history of American cinema in the silent era. At the same time, *PSM* after 1915 paid considerable attention to the commercial film industry, particularly this industry's investment in and privileging of spectacular attractions that relied on set construction, camera and editing tricks, and, especially, dangerous stunt work. *PSM*'s interest in both the creation of these movie attractions and also in the possibilities of multi-purposed, multi-sited cinema are fully in keeping with this magazine's celebratory fascination with novelty and invention as much as with elaborate production processes, applied mechanics, amateurism, and progress fueled by technology. Pre-1915 *PSM* was another matter. While J. Miller Barr's 1897 introduction to "animated photography" welcomed the new medium as a highly promising tool for scientific research and disseminating scientific knowledge, *PSM* for the next eighteen years paid only cursory, usually negative attention to moving pictures. This absence throws into greater relief the media technologies and communication networks that did actually interest *PSM* as a subject (telegraphy, telephony, photography) and as a tool (photographic evidence deployed across a range of topics and disciplines).

Popular Science Monthly, of course, did not stand alone as the voice of popularized science and technophilia in the period. Both the old and the new iterations of this magazine were part of a larger field of American periodicals that included titles like *Popular Electricity*, *Modern Mechanics*, *Popular Mechanics*, and *Technical World*. These periodicals were hardly uniform in their understanding of applied science, useful technology, and the strategy of popularization—and in the extent and focus of their coverage of moving pictures and media more generally. For example, *Scientific American*, published weekly and highly topical in covering what it called in 1897 "practical information, art, science, mechanics, chemistry, and manufactures,"[57] devoted much more attention to motion pictures than did *PSM*. Particularly after 1908, *Scientific American* regularly took note of patents and new products, refinements and adaptations of the motion picture apparatus, and varied uses of moving pictures for the purposes of education and research. Accessible digital archives make it infinitely easier to mine *PSM* and these other magazines for relevant information about specific practices, equipment, and experiments related to film. More broadly, for the purposes of the history of American cinema, the discourse offered across the range of sometimes quite different popular periodicals devoted to science/technology/mechanics collectively provide a perspective on the first quarter-century of motion pictures that is particularly valuable precisely because it is quite distinct from the film industry trade press, fan magazines, and high-circulation general-interest magazines, as well as from the recreation surveys and other progressivist discourse that situated moving pictures in a constellation of cheap amusements.

Notes

1. The scholarship in these areas continues to increase dramatically. Key studies includeTerry Lindvall, *Sanctuary Cinema: Origins of the Christian Film Industry* (New York: New York University Press, 2007); *Films that Work*, ed. Vinzenz Hediger and Patrick Vonderau (Amsterdam: Amsterdam University Press, 2009);*Useful Cinema*, ed. Charles R. Acland and Haidee Wasson (Durham, NC: Duke University Press, 2011); *Learning with the Lights Off: Educational Film in the United States*, ed. Devin Orgeron, Marsha Orgeron, and Dan Streible (New York: Oxford University Press, 2012); Gregory A. Waller, "Locating Early Non-Theatrical Audiences," in Ian Christie, ed., *Audiences: Defining and Researching Screen Entertainment Reception* (Amsterdam: Amsterdam University Press, 2012), 81–95, 248–253; Oliver Gaycken, *Devices of Curiosity: Early Cinema and Popular Science* (New York: Oxford University Press, 2015); Scott Curtis, *The Shape of Spectatorship: Art, Science, and Early Cinema in Germany* (New York: Columbia University Press, 2015); *Films That Sell: Moving Pictures and Advertising*, ed. Bo Florin, Nico de Klerk, and Patrick Vonderau (London: Palgrave, 2016).

2. J. Miller Barr, "Animated Pictures," *Popular Science Monthly (PSM)* 52 (December 1897), 177–188. Barr's article circulated more widely, presented in digest form in the *American Monthly Review of Reviews* 17, no. 1 (January 1898), 102–103; Barr's section on time-lapse cinematography is also quoted at length in "Studying Plant Growth with a Kinetoscope," *Literary Digest* 16, no. 5 (January 29, 1898), 136–137.

3. "The Uses of Education," *PSM* 52 (December 1897), 266–267; "Parental Neglect as a Cause of Hoodlumism," *PSM* 52 (December 1897), 267–269.

4. *PSM* 59, no. 6 (October 1901), ii.

5. See John C. Burnham, *How Superstition Won and Science Lost: Popularizing Science and Health in the United States* (New Brunswick, NJ: Rutgers University Press, 1987), 30, who notes in reference to *PSM* that when "'science' . . . included archeology, economics, history, linguistics, and politics, any cultured person might ideally be a man of science as well as a reader of popularized science, upholding a traditional view of culture, while adding to it." Gaycken provides a succinct overview of how "popular science" has been considered by scholars in the history of science (*Devices of Curiosity*, 5–11).

6. H. W. Chase, "Freud's Theories of the Unconscious," *PSM* 78 (1911), 355–363; William James, "The Moral Equivalent of War," *PSM* 77 (1910), 400–410; Booker T. Washington, "The Race Problem in the United States," *PSM* 55 (July 1899), 317–325.

7. Louise Michele Newman, ed., *Men's Ideas/Women's Realities: Popular Science, 1870–1915* (New York: Pergamon Press, 1985) reprints articles and editorials from *Popular Science* on the "woman question"; Daniel Patrick Thurs, *Science Talk: Changing Notions of Science in American Popular Culture* (New Brunswick, NJ: Rutgers University Press, 2007) considers *PSM* in the context of "the popular diffusion of scientific knowledge," during the later nineteenth century, largely in terms of the discourse concerning evolution. Christine Bold provides a succinct overview of how historians have considered the popularization of science in American periodicals: Christine Bold, ed., *The Oxford History of Popular Print Culture*, vol. 6, *US Popular Print Culture 1860–1920* (New York: Oxford University Press, 2011), 626.

8. "The Scientific Advance," *PSM* 52 (December 1897), 263–266. This view was perhaps most fully developed by George Iles, a frequent contributor to *PSM*, whose book *Flame, Electricity, and the Camera: Man's Progress from the First Kindling of Fire to the Wireless*

Telegraph and the Photography of Color (New York: Doubleday & McClure, 1900), celebrated evolutionary progress and claimed that photography was second only to electricity in its broad import.

9. Barr, "Animated Pictures," 177, 179.
10. Ibid., 184, 186. The same type of claims celebrating new ways of seeing had been made a year earlier in *PSM*, occasioned by the prospect of capturing in photographs the information revealed by X-ray technology. An editorial in May 1896 went so far as to announce that with X-rays "the eye and its wonderful supplement, the photographic plate, now find disclosed what had been deemed forever hidden from sight and light" ("The Röntgen Ray," *PSM* 49 [May 1896], 126). Perhaps even more interesting is that utopian predictions based on the supposedly unprecedented, revelatory capabilities of X-ray photography quickly became the object of parody in *PSM* when David Starr Jordan (then president of Stanford University) published an account of the "sympsychograph," an X-ray camera device used by the "Astral Camera Club" to photograph in complete darkness "psychical images" like the "thought of a cat." David Starr Jordan, "The Sympsychograph: A Study in Impressionist Physics," *PSM* 49 (September 1896), 597–601.
11. Barr, "Animated Pictures," 178.
12. "Scientific Advance," 265.
13. Ibid.
14. "The Upward Struggle of Society," *PSM* 52 (March 1898), 705.
15. "Upward Struggle of Society," 704–705.
16. R. W. Wood, "The Photography of Sound Waves," *PSM* 57 (August 1900), 354–364; Theobald Smith, "Medical Research: Its Place in the University Medical School," *PSM* 66 (1905), 516.
17. A brief note in 1898 reprinted an account of "an episode in the early history of animated photography," an 1870 magic lantern exhibition in Philadelphia using photographs of acrobats and a waltzing couple (complete with orchestral accompaniment). "An Episode in the Early History of Animated Photography," *PSM* 53 (July 1898), 424–425.
18. "The Progress of Science," *PSM* 83 (November 1913), 515–517.
19. George T. W. Patrick, "The Psychology of Relaxation," *PSM* 84 (June 1914), 590–604.
20. George T. W. Patrick, "The Psychology of Crazes," *PSM* 57 (1900), 285–294. After *PSM* had been transformed into *Scientific Monthly*, Patrick again singled out the moving pictures as offering the wrong type of leisure activity, describing moviegoers in a 1919 article as "sitting quiescent in a darkened moving-picture room, gazing spell-bound at a tawdry drama." George T. W. Patrick, "The Next Step in Applied Science," *Scientific Monthly* 8 (February 1919), 121.
21. Paul Starr, *The Creation of the Media: Political Origins of Modern Communication* (New York: Basic Books, 2004), 1–19.
22. Charles F. Emerick, "The Struggle for Equality in the United States," *PSM* 85 (July 1914), 64.
23. Starr, *Creation of the Media*, 153–230. Industry insider Fred de Land's "Notes on the Development of Telephone Service" appeared November 1906–November 1907. He charts the step-by-step creation and commercial roll-out of the Bell Telephone system and is most concerned with the commercialization and what we might think of as the corporatization of practical science in the face of legal challenges and fluctuating economic conditions. J. A. Fleming's "Hertzian Wave Wireless Telegraphy" ran June–December 1903, totaling almost one hundred pages that provided detailed technical information concerning the equipment and processes involved in wireless telegraphy, largely in terms of the contributions

of certain inventors, the working of particular inventions, and the solutions discovered for various engineering problems.
24. John Trowbridge, "Wireless Telegraphy," *PSM* 56 (November 1899), 72.
25. Albert P. Mathews, "Science and Morality," *PSM* 74 (March 1908), 287.
26. Sir George S. Robertson, "The Science of Distances," *PSM* 58 (March 1901), 539.
27. Madison Bentley, "Mental Inheritance," *PSM* 75, no. 12 (December 1909), 458.
28. By way of contrast, consider that in 1910, for instance, *Scientific American* published articles on stereoscopic moving pictures, microcinematography, a new camera for amateurs, legal issues surrounding the Motion Picture Patents Company, and instructions for how to build a motion picture camera in the home workshop: "Stereoscopic Motion Pictures in Natural Color," *Scientific American* 101, no. 15 (October 9, 1910), 256, 269–271; "The Life of the Infinitely Small," *Scientific American* 101, no. 22 (November 27, 1909), 390; "A Motion Apparatus for Amateurs," *Scientific American* 102, no. 23 (June 4, 1910), 463; "Moving Picture Royalties," *Scientific American* 102, no. 13 (March 26, 1910), 270–271; C. J. Harcout. "How to Make a Moving-Picture Camera," *Scientific American* 103, no. 25 (December 17, 1910), 483.
29. Kelley Wilder, *Photography and Science* (London: Reaktion Books, 2009), 15.
30. See, for example, "Growth of Astronomical Photography," *PSM* 53 (October 1898), 854; "Photography of Solar Eclipses," *PSM* 58 (December 1900), 214; George R. Hale, "Stellar Evolution in the Light of Recent Research," *PSM* 60 (February 1902), 290–313.
31. Simon Newcomb, "Chapters on the Stars," *PSM* 57 (July 1900), 229.
32. Edward C. Pickering, "The Future of Astronomy," *PSM* 75 (August 1909), 107. See also his "The Light of the Stars," *PSM* 66 (October 1904), 46–55.
33. W. A. Bentley and G. H. Perkins, "A Study of Snow Crystals," *PSM* 53 (1898), 75–82; Arthur Curtis Scott, "Educational Value of Photomicrography," *PSM* 61 (June 1902), 142–156.
34. Hannah Landecker, "Microcinematography and the History of Science and Film," *Isis* 97 (2006), 122–123.
35. Virgilio Tosi, *Cinema before Cinema: The Origins of Scientific Cinematography*, trans. Sergio Angelini (London: British Universities Film and Video Council), 2005, xi.
36. Gaycken, *Devices of Curiosity*, 69–79.
37. Emma G. Cummings, "A Visit to Nassau," *PSM* 52 (April 1898), 772; L. P. Gratacap's "A Trip around Iceland" ran from October 1907 through January 1908. Among the many other examples are Charles Joseph Chamberlain, "Monte Alba and Mitla as the Tourist Sees Them," *PSM* 73, no. 5 (November 1908), 392–402; and Angelo Helprin's five-part series on Alaska and the Klondike, published from May 1899 through April 1900. On expeditions, see also S. P. Langley, "A Preliminary Account of the Solar Eclipse of May 28, 1900, as Observed by the Smithsonian Expedition," *PSM* 57 (July 1900), 302–309; and S. A. Mitchell, "An Eclipse Expedition to Spain," *PSM* 68 (June 1906), 551–563. On geography and landscapes, see J. E. Kirkwood, "Desert Scenes in Zacatecas," *PSM* 75 (November 1909), 435–451; Laurence F. Schmeckebier, "The National Parks from the Scientific and Educational Side," *PSM* 80 (1912), 530–547; A. M. Reese, "The Home of the Alligator," *PSM* 77 (1910), 365–372; and A. S. Pearse, "Tropical Nature in Colombia," *PSM* 84, no. 3 (March 1914), 290–305. On flora and fauna, see Alice Carter Cook, "Plant Life of the Canary Islands," *PSM* 53 (October 1898), 758–772; B. F. Herrick, "Wild Flowers of the California Alps," *PSM* 51 (1897), 348–357; C. C. Nutting, "The Bird Rookeries on the Island of Laysan," *PSM* 63 (August 1903), 321–332. On sites of geological interest, see G. Frederick Wright, "Glaciers on the Pacific Coast," *PSM* 35 (June 1889), 155–163; J. W. Spencer, "Geological

Water Ways across Central America," *PSM* 53 (September 1898), 577-593; Marlin O. Andrews, "The Swedish Valley Ice Mine and Its Explanation," *PSM* 82, no. 3 (March 1913), 280-288.

38. Rick Altman, "From Lecturer's Prop to Industrial Product: The Early History of Travel Films," in Jeffrey Ruoff, ed., *Virtual Voyages: Cinema and Travel* (Durham, NC: Duke University Press, 2006), 61-76; Jennifer Lynn Peterson, *Education in the Field of Dreams: Travelogues and Early Nonfiction Film* (Durham, NC: Duke University Press, 2013), 23-61; Alison Griffiths, *Wondrous Difference: Cinema, Anthropology and Turn-of-the-Century Visual Culture* (New York: Columbia University Press, 2002), 203-227. No article in *PSM* mentioned the parallel between illustrated lectures and illustrated articles or dealt directly with lantern slides as another "field in the realm of photography."

39. But in fact there are some striking correlations between the articles in *PSM* that rely on photographs and various production trends in early cinema. These correlations become apparent if we compare the illustrated articles in *PSM* with the terrain covered in George Kleine's *Catalogue of Educational Motion Pictures* (1910), which lists more than one thousand non-fiction films.

40. For self-described anthropological articles in *PSM* that relied on photographic evidence, see, for example, Frank Vincent, "Journey in Madagascar," *PSM* 47 (June 1895), 239-248; E. P. Evans, "Semon's Scientific Researches in Australia," *PSM* 52 (November 1897), 17-37; and three articles by George P. Dorsey, who in the mid-1910s produced films of China and Japan for the Field Museum: "A Cruise among Haida and Tlingit Villages about Dixon's Entrance," *PSM* 53 (June 1898), 160-174; "Up the Skeena River to the Home of Tsimshains," *PSM* 54 (December 1898), 181-193; "The Hopi Indians of Arizona," *PSM* 55 (October 1899), 732-750. A sample of illustrated articles on manufacturing and industrial processes include Charles Richards Dodge, "The Possible Fiber Industries of the United States," *PSM* 54 (November 1898), 15-34; Charles E. Munroe, "The Applications of Explosives," *PSM* 56 (1900), 300-312; Hugh M. Smith, "The French Sardine Industry," *PSM* 59 (October 1901), 542-556; Nelson P. Lewis, "Modern City Roadways," *PSM* 56 (March 1900), 524-539; Waldon Fawcett, "Rapid Battleship Building," *PSM* 58 (November 1900), 28-33; and Charles Howard Shinn, "Nevada Silver," *PSM* 49 (1896), 734-756. Articles relying extensively on photographs as evidence for claims about genetics, immigrants, and "mental defectives" include W. E. Castle, "Heredity," *PSM* 76 (May 1910), 417-427; E. M. East, "The Role of Hybridization in Plant Breeding," *PSM* 77 (1910), 342-355; Cyril G. Hopkins, "The Illinois System of Permanent Fertility," *PSM* 84, no. 1 (January 1914), 52-63; Martin W. Barr, "Mental Defectives and the Social Welfare," *PSM* 54 (April 1899), 746-759; Samuel G. Smith, "Typical Criminals," *PSM* 56 (March 1900), 539-546; Alfred C. Reed, "Going through Ellis Island," *PSM* 82 (January 1913), 5-18; and Alfred C. Reed, "Immigration and the Public Health," *PSM* 83 (October 1913), 313-338.

41. "The Scientific Monthly and the Popular Science Monthly," *PSM* 87 (September 1915), 307-309. *World's Advance* in September 1913 had merged with yet another illustrated monthly, *Popular Electricity*, which, in turn, consolidated with *Modern Electrics* and *Electrician and Mechanic* in July 1914 to form *Popular Electricity and Modern Mechanics*. "A Word with Our Readers," *Popular Electricity and Modern Mechanics* 29, no. 1 (July 1914), 1.

42. "Two Important Events for the World's Advance," *PSM* 87, no. 4 (October 1915), 7.

43. Stanley Curtis, "The Motion Picture—Part VII," *Electrician and Mechanic* 22, no. 5 (May 1911), 314.

44. Arney H. Ritchie's "The 'Inside' of Moving Pictures," *Popular Electricity Magazine*, 582.

45. *Modern Mechanics* 30, no. 1 (January 1915), 35–47.
46. "The Vision of a Blind Man Forty-Four Years After," *PSM* 88, no. 1 (January 1916), iv–xii.
47. George F. Worts, "Staging the Celluloid Thriller," *PSM* 89, no. 3 (September 1916), 406.
48. "Risking His Life to Make a Motion Picture Play," *PSM* 88, no. 1 (January 1916), 65; "Some Jobs You Would Not Want," *PSM* 88, no. 4 (April 1916), 579.
49. E. T. Keyser, "Hazards of Motion-Picture Acting: Real and Faked," *PSM* 88, no. 6 (June 1916), 885–889.
50. Worts, "Staging the Celluloid Thriller," 401–406; George F. Worts, "Capturing Jamaica for a Film Play," *PSM* 88, no. 3 (March 1916), 396–397.
51. Arthur Marple, "Expense in Motion Picture Making," *PSM* 88, no. 4 (April 1916), 572; "Catastrophes by the Foot," *PSM* 89, no. 2 (August 1916), 162–164.
52. Rob King, *The Fun Factory: The Keystone Film Company and the Emergence of Mass Culture* (Berkeley: University of California Press, 2009), 189.
53. "Trench-Digging by Machinery," *PSM* 88, no. 6 (June 1916), 830–831; Charles W. Person, "Niagara's New Air Route," *PSM* 88, no. 6 (June 1916), 858–861; "X-Rays and the Law," *PSM* 88, no. 6 (June 1916), 879; Jay F. Bancroft, "Ice Making at Home," *PSM* 88, no. 6 (June 1916), 891–894.
54. "A Hand-Made Hand-Played Phonograph," *PSM* 89, no. 3 (September 1916), 381; "The Pigeon Spy and His Work in War," *PSM* 88, no. 1 (January 1916), 30–31; "Home-Made Motion Picture Camera," *PSM* 88, no. 3 (March 1916), 440; "Ingenious Circuit Saves House Money," *PSM* 88, no. 1 (January 1916), 127; "Making the Music Fit the Screen," *PSM* 89, no. 5 (November 1916), 733–735.
55. Charles W. Person, "As Easily Handled as a Rifle: A Revolutionary Motion Picture Camera," *PSM* 89, no. 1 (July 1916), 77–80. *Moving Picture World* likewise offered a quite detailed description of the Akeley camera, but with no mention of its potential uses; see "The Akeley Camera," *Moving Picture World* (May 5, 1917), 797.
56. "Motion Pictures on the Front Line," *PSM* 88, no. 2 (February 1916), 230; "Recruiting Britain's Army with Motion Pictures, Mirrors and Brass Bands," *PSM* 88, no. 3 (March 1916), 382; "Wandering Motion Pictures," *PSM* 88, no. 3 (March 1916), 382; "Washington Monument as a Motion Picture Screen," *PSM* 89, no. 3 (September 1916), 354.
57. This phrase appears on *Scientific American*'s masthead in 1897 and later was reduced to "A Journal of Practical Information."

CHAPTER 15

CINEMA AND SCIENCE IN THE SILENT ERA

SCOTT CURTIS AND OLIVER GAYCKEN

Our starting point is this image from the front page of the November 5, 1910, issue of *The Illustrated London News* (see figure 15.1).[1] It depicts an event from a few days earlier: a lecture at King's College by Dr. Levaditi of the Pasteur Institute. We see the speaker watching from the wings as an appreciative audience of elite male scholars beholds moving images of microbes. The image prompts questions about the event: Who was Levaditi? What is this film? Where and how was it made? But it also raises questions about cinema and science during this era: How typical was this scene? What did film offer researchers that other media did not?

The screening was one of several organized by Constantin Levaditi, an immunologist at the Pasteur Institute in Paris, during the summer and fall of 1910 (see figure 15.2). For the films, he collaborated with Jean Comandon, a French scientist who specialized in microcinematography and who also worked for Pathé Frères, one of the world's biggest movie studios (see figure 15.3). Comandon's films of microbes and other microscopic subjects were used by scientists but often made their way, via Pathé, to movie theaters worldwide, where they were shown in programs containing dramas, comedies, and other typical entertainment fare. This academic screening presented Comandon's films of trypanosomes and spirochetes, which are microbes associated with a variety of diseases such as sleeping sickness and syphilis. Levaditi investigated both diseases, but since 1908 he had been especially interested in the immune reaction to trypanosomes. In the spring of 1910, he worked with Comandon to create the centerpiece film of the evening's screening: *Mécanisme de la phagocytose des trypanosomes, phénomène de l'accolement* (The Mechanism of Phagocytosis of Trypanosomes: The Attachment Phenomenon). Levaditi took that film and a handful of other Comandon films to screenings in Paris and London.

FIGURE 15.1 "Living Pictures of Bacilli," from *The Illustrated London News*, November 5, 1910.

Our first image, then, opens up a broader history of film and science during this period. The surprise captured by the artist typifies the delight at this genre's novel ways of seeing. Microcinematography, along with time-lapse films, high-speed cinematography, and other relatively new techniques, provided spectators with a distinct vision of the natural world, one that seemed innately scientific but also inherently modern. Theorists ranging from Eisenstein to Epstein to Benjamin commented often on the connection between these kinds of films and this modern mode of vision; for them, science films exemplified the ubiquity of scientific modes of visuality but also the expressive power of cinema itself.[2] This novelty is typical of science films of the silent era, especially around 1910, but even through the 1920s and beyond—throughout the modern era, cutting-edge visualization techniques have sparked or renewed interest in an object of study. Moreover, for most readers before the era of the internet and instant dissemination, news of the latest technique often preceded the visualization itself. Such was the case in 1910, when limited access to the films prompted illustrations such as that of

FIGURE 15.2 Constantin Levaditi (1874–1953). Courtesy Bibliothèque de l'Académie nationale de Médecine, Paris.

The Illustrated London News or newspaper reports that relied on first- or secondhand accounts. Film's novelty, then, helped to propel the dissemination of knowledge, because these accounts not only described the screening but alerted readers to the object of study.

There has always been an inherent duality to science films, equal to or perhaps even more than that of other scientific media, between documenting and projecting, or between research and performance. Motion pictures unlocked mysteries of movement for a wide range of disciplines, but the projected image of that movement offered a deeply moving, spectacular performance of the scientific encounter with the natural world, a performance that held an indisputable but also controversial rhetorical power. The two sides of the scientific mission—investigation and persuasion—correspond roughly to the work of the camera and of the projector, to recording and projecting. Film's particular abilities to capture movement and to manipulate time were matched only by

FIGURE 15.3 Jean Comandon (1877–1970). Courtesy CNC-Archives françaises du film, dépot Louis-Chevalier.

its revelatory projected images of worlds unseen. Our point is that these two sides—recording and projecting, or exploring and explaining, or research and popularization—were never separate in practice.[3] The illustration of the King's College lecture neatly presents this duality: the film is at once a scientific document and an object of wonder. (The difficulty in addressing both the science and the wonder is perhaps why science films remain relatively unexplored.) Indeed, film's epistemic ambidexterity—its ability to function as both objective record and fantastical vision—makes it an especially revealing case from which to explore common historiographic assumptions about popularization, collaboration, and media in science. If the *Illustrated London News* image stages the history of science films, it also challenges the usual historiography of those films.

In the history of science, the "diffusionist model" of science popularization holds that knowledge of the natural world cultivated by elites trickles down in a diluted form to the populace, losing theoretical sophistication and content along the way.[4] This model is unsatisfactory for several reasons, but mostly because it ignores the history of resistance to and reworking of elite science in popular culture. That is, as Roger Cooter and Stephen Pumfrey explain, "popular culture can generate its own natural knowledge which differs from and may even oppose elite science."[5] Popular audiences might come to conclusions different from the orthodoxy, as Anne Secord has shown of nineteenth-century working-class botany, or they might take elite lessons in an entirely unexpected direction.[6] Rather than "watery" metaphors of one-way flow, dilution, and passive osmosis, those of "grafting, appropriation, and transformation" might be more appropriate to the dynamic relationship between popular culture and learned science.[7] Levaditi and Comandon's film provides an excellent example of this dynamic in action. The film had deep scientific significance, but it was also taken up by journalists, writers, and other participants in popular culture for various kinds of knowledge or speculation. That is to say, when non-scientists encountered the film, their understanding of it is best viewed not as misunderstanding or dilution but rather a use that differs from the academic exchange depicted in the *Illustrated News*. This chapter will trace elite and popular appropriations to illustrate the divergent paths to knowledge that film afforded, and even encouraged.

The history behind the image leads us to reconsider other common assumptions about media and science. While Levaditi is the sole scientist pictured, we know that this film was fully a collaboration between him and Comandon. Indeed, the history of scientific representation is a history of collaboration between researchers and craftspeople working together to visualize an event or phenomenon. Each member of the team has specific skills and their own vision of how to render the object of study, so the final illustration requires negotiation and collaboration. A conception of the lone scientist figuring out problems sequestered in a laboratory or of the craftsperson as merely a hired hand is inadequate to this history. But most histories of film and science focus on the researcher rather than the craftsperson. While we may not know all the details of the collaboration between Levaditi and Comandon, we know enough to see it as an equal partnership, so this chapter will emphasize that aspect of the film's history as well.[8]

The motion picture screen dominates the scene in figure 15.1, emphasizing the centrality of film in this narrative, but film was only one medium or technology among many used in the process of knowledge production. Histories of motion pictures and science tend to put film in the spotlight at the expense of other media or technologies, but journal articles, graphs, tables, and, of course, microscopes and petri dishes were all vital to this project as well. In the laboratory, film was part—a rare part during this period, to be frank—of an ensemble of media technologies enlisted to capture the imperceptible and ephemeral features of the natural world (the still camera and the draftsman's pen were much more common at this time). Yet this case also speaks to science's historical readiness to adopt new media technologies for research and outreach, not only as tools to see things differently but also as a means to present the world in a novel way. Film's abilities to capture and present were surprising and unique, so even if film were only a part of the ensemble, it usually garnered the most attention. This is the singular nature of the relationship between moving images and science: film's outsized impact communicated findings more vibrantly than other media of the day. But it did not do that work alone; the popular press communicated knowledge more widely than did film, for example. This specific instance can serve as an emblem of the manifold interactions of media that typify the intersection of cinema and science.

Popularization, collaboration, intermediality: more than historiographical emphases, we could also argue that these concepts are different ways of expressing the interaction among historical agents at all stages of knowledge production, from the production of images by craftspeople and scientists, to the intermedial dissemination of these images, and on to the multiple understandings of those images by a variety of audiences. Films facilitate these exchanges because, like images in general, they are less anchored to specific meanings than words, so they can be adapted more easily across domains. Films are therefore an especially *mobile* form of knowledge. And the spectacular quality of the cinematic image—its ability to vividly portray the world in a way that commands attention from all quarters—accelerates its movement across those domains. With film, especially, this movement across elite and popular spheres was not always frictionless, as we shall see. But if we are to understand knowledge-making as a communicative act, as always part of a larger conversation, then our attention turns from the boundaries between elite and popular culture to the productive interplay between them.[9] Because of these features—their functioning between evidence and wonder, their spectacle and movement, their inherent ambiguity, and their epistemic mobility—science films are an especially rich archive from which to examine the circulation of knowledge across domains, or "knowledge in transit."

We will use the screenings of the Levaditi/Comandon film as a case study to test these ideas and to describe the relationship between cinema and science in the silent era. Shuttling among the lab, the auditorium, and the press, we will explain the scientific context for this partnership while also considering the excitement scientific films generated and the importance of this enthusiasm for both popular and elite scientific knowledge. The first section describes Comandon's research, his films, and their reception, while the second section details Levaditi's research and his interest in working with Comandon. Finally, we will take a close look at the film's role in a larger academic conversation about the immune system. While the film focused on phenomena that were minute and specific, it is representative of both a broader conversation in science as well as a growing trend in the use of scientific moving images that was relatively uncommon at the time but has exploded since the silent era.

COMANDON

Jean Comandon was the most celebrated and accomplished microcinematographer of his time. Through his partnership with Pathé, which provided studio space, technical assistance, and distribution, Comandon made more than four hundred short scientific films from 1909 to 1926, many of which were shown in theaters all over the world (see figure 15.4).[10] Covering a variety of topics, these films ranged from public health shorts

FIGURE 15.4 A Pathé poster advertising Comandon's films and "a glimpse of the infinitely small." Affiche Adrien Barrère, ca. 1910. Courtesy collection Fondation Pathé.

to surgical films for medical instruction to botanical and zoological films. But most of Comandon's films demonstrated his expertise with the microscope, which he acquired during his studies for a doctoral degree in medicine from 1906 to 1909 at the Saint Louis Hospital in Paris. His thesis concerned the clinical use of the ultramicroscope.[11] Unlike a regular microscope, the ultramicroscope collects light at a right angle to the objective lens, rather than from directly underneath it. The light therefore scatters against the microscopic objects, allowing views of particles smaller than the wavelength of visible light. Combined with the technique of dark-field microscopy, in which the background against which the microorganisms appear is black rather than the white of conventional microscopy, the ultramicroscope provides much greater magnification of and resolution for microscopic objects. The ultramicroscope had just been announced in 1903, so Comandon was on the cutting edge of its application.[12] As a medical researcher, he was especially interested in its potential for diagnosis, especially of spirochetes, the spiral-shaped bacteria most associated with syphilis.

During his research, Comandon and his thesis supervisor, Paul Gastou, became intrigued by the possibility of recording the unique movements of these spirochetes. Gastou had attempted a microscope-cinematograph combination, which Comandon pursued further.[13] In the fall of 1908, Comandon and Gastou secured a photomicroscopy system from German manufacturer Leitz as well as help from a Pathé engineer to adapt it to microcinematography. This process was typical for any intrepid researcher hoping to use motion pictures during the silent era: there were no readymade cameras or attachments designed for this kind of precision work, so researchers invariably also had to be tinkerers or team up with manufacturers who helped them with their special requests. Extra work was always necessary to adapt the motion picture camera to scientific tasks. That Pathé lent its engineer signaled the studio's early interest in this work.

The resulting apparatus looked much like the depicted example from 1909 (see figure 15.5). Pictured on the far right of the workbench is a heliostat, which is a special mirror that reflects sunlight in a fixed direction, in this case through a shutter (to regulate its intensity and temperature) and then a bank of lenses (to focus the beam). Consistent with the principles of an ultramicroscope, the light source is perpendicular to the optical axis of the microscope, pictured center left. On top of the microscope is mounted a motion-picture camera, which focuses through the bellows tube and the objective lens onto the stage. At this magnification, any movement of the apparatus can result in a shaky image, so the workbench was designed to be extremely heavy. Comandon's apparatus included several innovations, including a method for constant focusing while shooting, which was necessary to capture the moving microbes, and a shutter system to avoid overheating the specimen.[14] The instrument's potential led to an offer from Pathé in the spring of 1909 to outfit a studio in Vincennes devoted to the production of microcinematographic films.[15] In October 1909, Comandon presented his thesis films to the Academy of Science in Paris, and notices of this event sparked worldwide interest in his views of the infinitesimally small.[16]

Comandon and Gastou were initially interested in the diagnostic potential of cinematography: the varieties of spirochetes can be identified by their unique movements,

FIGURE 15.5 Comandon's microcinematographic apparatus from 1909. Courtesy CNC-Archives françaises du film, dépôt Louis-Chevalier.

so recording them would be a valuable step toward standardizing observation and training experts in the finer points of microscopic diagnosis. But the broader scientific utility of cinematography also became immediately clear: films supplied permanent records of fleeting phenomena usually difficult to capture and study, thereby making these phenomena available to educators and researchers "independent of time and place," as German scientist Paul Ehrlich put it.[17] That meant that educators were no longer dependent on specimens and technology acting properly at the precise time they were needed, and that researchers could use the film record as a substitute for the object, studying it at their leisure and manipulating its temporal register through projection. The filmstrip itself, with its discrete frames, already broke down movement into fixed units, and the ability to analyze this movement systematically was one of cinematography's key features for the scientific community. In this regard, the appeal of motion pictures for Comandon was representative of the larger scientific interest in film.[18]

For Pathé, the appeal was less academic. After the success of F. Martin Duncan's "The Unseen World" series from the UK in 1903, Pathé recognized the commercial potential of scientific film for movie theater audiences.[19] During this period, the cinema program usually comprised a series of short films of different genres emphasizing the spectacular aspect of moving images. Music hall acts, staged train wrecks, actualités from exotic locales, and more—all emphasized display and spectacle. This "cinema of attractions" would soon give way to films that emphasized narrative over display, but the spectacular element never really left entertainment cinema—indeed, it has always been a core feature of cinema and one of the main reasons we go to the movies.[20] Early scientific films, such as time-lapse recordings of plant growth or microscopic views of battles in the blood, were novel, surprising, and spectacular in their own way. Indeed, as Laurent Le Forestier has argued, at Pathé the popular-science film inhabited the niche that the trick film had carved out.[21] Soon, the popular-science film became a staple of the nickelodeon program, as Pathé, Gaumont, and Éclair in France, Charles Urban in the UK, and George Kleine in the US offered theater owners a substantial number of films from which to choose.

Despite Pathé's support of Comandon's thesis work, the dozen or so films that he initially made did not go straight to cinemas. Instead, they first were screened at the French Academy of Science on October 26, 1909. The presentation received positive reviews and led to at least four other academic presentations in December 1909 alone; Pathé then released the films to theaters in January 1910. Comandon, an accomplished and engaging speaker, screened his films for academic and elite audiences throughout his career.[22] Given the science film's checkered history in France—the notoriety of Dr. Eugène Louis Doyen, a French surgeon who enthusiastically filmed his innovative techniques, comes to mind—there may have been some grumbling within the expert community about the scientific and social value of Comandon's films.[23] But the number and frequency of Comandon's subsequent academic presentations can allow us to assume that any reservations were minor. The popular press, however, was not at all equivocal, raving about his films, providing a plethora of fantastic metaphors to describe the novel wonder on view.

The coverage of Comandon's screenings by the press constituted an important relay for popularizing cinema's role in generating microbiological knowledge. "The Battles in the Blood," an elaborate article that appeared in the *St. Louis Post Dispatch*'s Sunday magazine, exemplifies this mode of communication (see figure 15.6).[24] The article combines three sources: the introductory section was written by an unnamed editor for the *Dispatch*; the conclusion contains an excerpt from a piece by "an English journalist" about Élie Metchnikoff, a scientist who made important discoveries about phagocytosis; the majority of the article is a translation of Régis Gignoux's "Les microbes en liberté," an account of a screening of Comandon films at the Hôpital Broca in Paris that took place on December 6.[25] Reprinting news stories was common during this period, but the additional work that went into this piece—the framing commentary, the illustrations, and the translation of a lengthy French source—indicate an exceptional degree of interest in these films and the scientific advances they signaled.

The range of the article's illustrations is also noteworthy. Of the seven illustrations, five are views through the microscope. Some are drawn, some are photographs, and at least one of the images is a set of three frames from a Comandon film depicting the sleeping-sickness parasite (probably *Trypanosoma lewisi*, one of Comandon's thesis films from 1909). Another illustration depicts an often-reproduced image of Comandon's microcinematographic apparatus. The most spectacular illustration by far takes up the upper left-hand corner of the page, depicting two fantastical beasts engaged in mortal

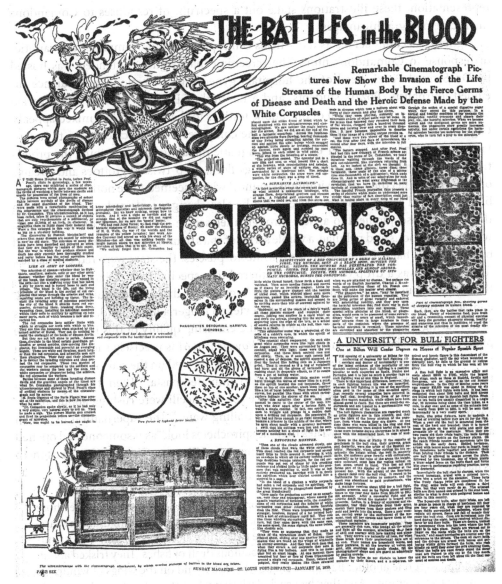

FIGURE 15.6 "The Battles in the Blood," *St. Louis Post Dispatch*, January 16, 1910.

combat. The snake-headed appendages of the one creature evoke trypanosomes; this image represents the battle between, in the *Post Dispatch*'s words, "fierce germs of disease and death" and the "heroic defense made by the white corpuscles." These images correspond, loosely, with the verbal accounts of Comandon's screening in the article, which also move from precise description to metaphorical interpretation. Indeed, rather than seeing a clash between two distinct and even contradictory modes of representation, these illustrations stake out a spectrum of responses to Comandon's microcinematographic images.

Gignoux's account serves as the article's centerpiece, and it exemplifies the varieties of response to Comandon's films. The screening that Gignoux attended was hosted by Dr. Samuel Pozzi, head of the hospital's gynecological section; the audience included journalists, Pozzi's students, and a handful of Parisian socialites. The varied class and gender composition of this public testifies to the science film's mixed appeals. Gignoux's essay swarms with metaphors. He compares the projected image to "a fantastic aquarium," and he later extends the aquatic metaphor by describing the projection as: "A submarine landscape, with strange flora, deep-twisted grottoes and streams of lava" where "needles" are swimming around, "which seemed to be nothing more than bits of seaweed agitated by the waves." But he also changes scale radically, comparing the ultramicroscopic field to a view through a telescope: "Like a chart of the heavens, with constellations and nebulae, a whole series of stars of uniform size, each surrounded by a luminous halo. The nebulae were white corpuscles, the stars were red corpuscles, for the chart was a drop of blood." Untethered to a specific scale, Gignoux compares the white corpuscles to "light clouds in an August sky" that are surrounded by "black confetti" (red corpuscles). Later, the phagocyte, no longer a light cloud, is described as "a devouring monster." (We can note here the enduring quality of this impression; the phagocyte in Richard Fleischer's *Fantastic Voyage* [1966] is precisely such a devouring monster.) The attempt to register the movements witnessed on the screen results in surreal derangements; spirochetes are likened to animated pasta: "Then it seemed as if a bag of vermicelli had burst and all the pieces of vermicelli were rushing about in desperate efforts, as if to escape from a pot of boiling water." The supernatural makes an appearance as well; Gignoux writes that the spirochetes look "as if someone had opened a den of demons." Reacting to a film featuring trypanosomes, Gignoux describes them as having

> a fat, twisted body with a sort of extraordinary rapid tail. They rose like those whirling skyrockets that burst at each turn, but they came down with the same ease, the same speed, the same zigzags, the same twists, like electric eels. They were so numerous that they made us think of the miraculous draft of fishes. They frisked about, sliding over one another like those snakes that are found on the wings of windmills on stormy evenings. And they had such dash that when they struck a red corpuscle they sent it flying like a toy balloon.[26]

The references proliferate, as Gignoux sees skyrockets, electric eels, a school of fishes, an optical effect of rain on the blades of windmills, and a toy balloon.

We might dismiss this account as the result of an untrained eye encountering a novel sight and repeatedly misunderstanding it; the unnamed author/editor for the *St. Louis Post Dispatch* would have agreed, having described Gignoux as "the fanciful French journalist." (Gignoux was also a theater critic, playwright, and novelist.) But such a reading would result in an impoverished understanding of how scientific knowledge circulates. Immediately after the passage just cited, Gignoux writes, "And this is no metaphor but an exact image. At one moment there remained but four or five of these trypanosomes around a single red corpuscle. Exact, twisted and pointed, they really looked like those educated seals in circuses which toss a balloon about with blows of their snouts and play the clown."[27] How might we take this claim of exactitude seriously? One way would be to invoke Yuri Tsivian's concept of early cinema audiences as having a particular "medium sensitivity."[28] Gignoux was seeing something for the first time, and his reaction resembles that of early audiences who were fascinated by all aspects of cinematic projection, from how wind moved the leaves of a tree to such phenomena as billowing smoke and crashing waves. In his reaction to this optical experience, Gignoux was experiencing something novel, and he described the unprecedented sight with as much care and attention to detail as his considerable linguistic gifts could muster. Witnessing a novum, Gignoux was writing in a mode closer to speculative fiction. And, indeed, he references a number of speculative fiction texts to help orient his reader, mentioning Jules Verne, "the prehistoric romances of Rosny" (i.e., J.-H. Rosny aîné), and André Couvreur, author of *Une invasion de Macrobes* (serialized 1909; reprinted/revised 1910). As Laura Forsberg has noted about the Victorian popular reception of the microscope, "Rather than opposing one another, scientific discoveries and fairy fictions reinforced each other's imaginative appeal. By combining scientific observation with fanciful imagination, both the fairy and the microscope produced a sense of wonder."[29] The combination of "scientific observation and fanciful imagination" that Forsberg notes as characteristic of Victorian microscope culture clearly persisted into the early twentieth century. The mixture of figures that accompany "The Battles in the Blood"—scientific photographs and a spectacular drawing of battling creatures—continued the nineteenth-century tradition of illustrating the microscopic world in both observational and imaginative modes.

Ultimately, Gignoux's "fanciful" response to the screening is valuable because fancy (or imagination) has an important role to play in scientific understanding. As Gignoux notes at the beginning of his description of the screening: "Now, one ought to be learned, one ought to know microbology [sic] and bacteriology, to describe microphyter (bacteria) and microzoa (pathogenic protozoa). But we knew nothing, except how to watch. And it was a sight so terrible and so strange that at the moment we did not regret our ignorance, for we saw the 'beasts' better." Gignoux makes a powerful claim about the quality of his attention versus that of a more educated eye. He sees the film with untrained eyes, which results in a heightened attention to the moving images that allows him to convey the experience of the screening in a way that would resonate with a general audience. The *St. Louis Post Dispatch* contributor makes this point, noting how Gignoux "presents a series of pictures which make us understand more vividly than matter of fact description could just what is taking place in every drop of our blood when we are attacked by disease." As this quotation suggests, Gignoux's descriptions coincide with the qualities of the moving image: he presents a "series of pictures" that conveys a vivid impression. The spectacular, sensual aspects of the moving image function in both the register of scientific revelation and popularization. These aspects of the moving image recur in descriptions of both professional and lay audiences. Comandon's films fascinate because either they present phenomena that are either entirely new (for lay audiences) or because their presentation of known phenomena (for professional audiences) has the effect of revealing new dimensions.

As a credentialed and respected scientist with the support of a major film studio to carry out his work, Comandon was in some ways unique: most scientific films did not find their way to the neighborhood movie theater. It should be noted, however, that while many of Comandon's films were made explicitly for commercial theater audiences, others were made for and stayed with specialized scientific audiences, and some found success with both. Comandon's luck with either kind of audience speaks to his special talents as a scientist, a craftsperson, and a popularizer. But it also testifies to the role of spectacle in scientific representation, which can be amplified or attenuated according to taste and goal. Scientific images successful with elite and popular audiences alike tend to be both accurate and spectacular, but spectacle appeals not only to non-elite audiences. Scholars appreciate spectacle, too, albeit in measured doses. Historically, the scientific community has objected when images stray too far from what is actually known or from a more objective standard. Guardians of objectivity have not wanted too much spectacle, fearing readers might be carried away by the image.[30] This, however, is exactly what motion pictures do: they carry us away, they move and move us, so they have always been slightly suspect. Comandon, as an employee of a bastion of popular culture like a film studio, probably had few qualms about the blurry line that his work represented. Others voiced objections more explicitly. Comandon admitted that many within the academy policed the line between elite and popular science—the history of scientific representation tells of the controversies that sometimes ensue from crossing that boundary—and hinted that his own films encountered some opposition early on: "Some people at the time manifested a certain surprise at seeing cast on the screen the till then somewhat mysterious objects of their researches. In the opinion of others, I had appeared almost in the light of a profaner, for the cinema had been considered, so far, as a not particularly intellectual form of amusement."[31] But his many scientific collaborators were apparently not so queasy, precisely because they chose film as their demonstration medium. We can therefore assume that Levaditi came to Comandon because motion pictures would demonstrate his findings not just accurately, but spectacularly, thereby balancing objectivity and imagination.

Effective, accessible, even spectacular presentations are in the interest of researchers, because their primary goal is always to *persuade* their colleagues of their discovery. That their colleagues will accept their innovation or observation is not a foregone conclusion; almost all novel (or even not-so-novel) approaches or findings encounter some level of resistance. Researchers therefore muster the tools and techniques at their disposal to present a persuasive case. Film, as another instrument in the representational toolbox, was perhaps more persuasive than most. Like photography, it represented accurately the patterns and details of the natural world to the extent that it was often mistaken for a completely objective image free of human handiwork. But unlike photography, film moved, and this temporal push from one moment to the next carried spectators along in a rush that was nearly irresistible (and, not coincidentally, the object of much concern and resistance).[32] These two features—detail and movement that can mimic that of the natural world—gave films a rhetorical power that was both respected among academics and feared by those wary of the taint of popular culture. The barrier to entry was high during this period, given the cumbersome technology and the resources required to create a scientific film, but any scientist like Levaditi interested in a persuasive record of movement could not ignore its potential.

LEVADITI

Levaditi was likely present at one of Comandon's academic screenings; at the very least he was aware of them. Something undoubtedly must have clicked for him. Perhaps he was impressed by the screenings' quality: Comandon's films are generally regarded to be the best of their era. But more likely, he saw that Comandon was already making films that coincided with Levaditi's research at the time. Levaditi was a Romanian-born cytologist and immunologist who had been with the Pasteur Institute since 1900; he was head of his own laboratory by 1910.[33] In that position, Levaditi inherited a tradition of engagement with the public, especially via the press, so he might have been intrigued by the potential Comandon's films presented for that part of his mission.[34] His research focused on methods of diagnosis and therapy of infectious diseases, and he had up to 1909 pursued investigations of tuberculosis, leukemia, and especially syphilis.[35] In this connection, Comandon's presentation of *Spirochaeta pallida*, the bacterial cause of syphilis, must have caught Levaditi's attention. From 1908 to 1911, Levaditi was further preoccupied with African trypanosomiasis, also known as sleeping sickness, which is still prevalent in areas of Africa where its carrier, the tsetse fly, is common. The disease is caused by a trypanosome, or a single-celled parasitic protozoan, which is transmitted through the tsetse fly's bite. There are several varieties of this trypanosome, some of which infect only animals. *Trypanosoma brucei*, which Comandon also had recorded for one of his thesis films, is the major cause of sleeping sickness in humans. Finally, around 1909/1910, Levaditi was interested in the mechanism of phagocytosis—the process by which one cell engulfs another—and, according to Gignoux, Comandon's film on *Spirochaeta gallinarum* included a shot of phagocytosis (see figure 15.7).[36]

Levaditi therefore might have seen several points of contact between Comandon's work and his own. Institutional contacts between the two probably cemented this alliance. For example, it is likely that Comandon procured his trypanosome specimens from the Pasteur Institute, given that the Saint Louis Hospital specialized in spirochetes.[37] Another Institute scientist, Félix Mesnil, France's leading expert on trypanosomes, was undoubtedly familiar with Comandon's work and may have helped him procure the specimens for his four other trypanosome films. (Mesnil, who worked alongside Levaditi in Metchnikoff's lab at the Institute, might even have introduced him to Comandon.) In turn, Comandon lent his films to help illustrate Mesnil's May 1910 lecture at the Museum of Natural History in Paris on "Trypanosomes and Their

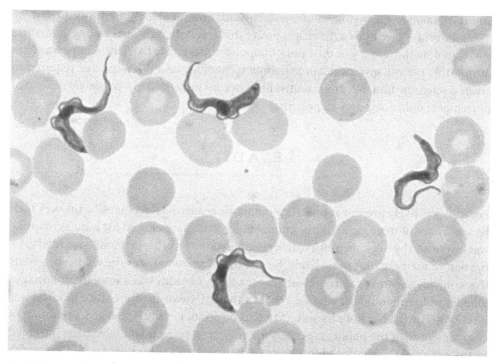

FIGURE 15.7 A modern image of trypanosomes among round red blood cells. Courtesy CDC/ Dr. Myron G. Schultz (1970).

Harmful Effects."[38] The lecture surely included Comandon's 1909 trypanosome films (*Trypanosoma brucei* and *Trypanosoma lewisi*), and perhaps two other trypanosome films Comandon completed in 1910 (*Trypanosoma gambiense* and *Trypanosomes de la grenouille*). The films would have been obviously useful to Mesnil, who hoped to show his public audience precisely and spectacularly what these protozoa looked like.[39]

But Levaditi was after bigger game. Comandon's trypanosome films would have been helpful, of course, and they were likely part of Levaditi's 1910 screenings in Paris and London. More than simply showing the *features* of these protozoa, however, Levaditi was interested in their actions during a particular *process*. Levaditi had been working with colleagues at the Institute, especially Polish microbiologist Stefan Mutermilch, on the mechanism of resistance among *Trypanosoma*, especially the conditions under which a phagocyte might attach to a trypanosome. Understanding this process has obvious implications for an immune response (and potential agents to aid that response). But it also happened that the specific features of this encounter had diagnostic potential, especially for the varieties of *Trypanosoma* that infect livestock, which are harder to identify than the species that infect humans.

Microscopic inspection was and still is the principal way to identify parasites. Yet trypanosomes are difficult to diagnose precisely, because so many varieties look and act alike. When that method no longer suffices, other procedures must come into play.

Around 1905 and 1906, Mesnil and others at the Pasteur Institute developed serodiagnostic techniques for identifying trypanosomes.[40] The blood serum from an animal that has previously been infected by one variety of trypanosome is "active"—meaning that its immune response is triggered by the presence of that parasite—whereas the same serum is not active for other types of *Trypanosoma*. So, if the trypanosome in question is placed in a serum, the properties of the serum can be chemically tested to identify it. Levaditi and Mutermilch noticed, however, that part of this overall response is physical and directly observable: trypanosomes in active serum will attach to the white blood cells as part of the process of phagocytosis. Other kinds of trypanosomes will not attach if the serum is not activated to that variety. Microscopic observation of the parasite's morphology is always the first step in diagnosis; Levaditi and Mutermilch's finding therefore gave technicians another diagnostic tool that could be easily implemented after morphological identification. This technique could even exclude varieties of parasite one by one until attachment was spotted and the correct variety identified.

Mécanisme de la phagocytose des trypanosomes provides a straightforward depiction of this phenomenon. The extant version is five-and-a-half minutes long with six shots of phagocytic activity accompanied by Pathé-branded intertitles that function less as full explanations than as lecture cues. For example, the first title reads, "Trypanosomes—leucocytes de cobaye—sérum de cobaye ordinaire; pas d'accolement" (Trypanosomes—guinea pig leukocytes—ordinary guinea pig serum; no attachment), meaning that onscreen are trypanosomes—easily identified by their fish-like shape and corkscrew undulations—and white blood cells from a guinea pig. The serum is not active, so the parasites pass by the white blood cells with impunity; no attachment is visible. The next title indicates that a specific serum has been prepared that is active to this species of trypanosome, and we then have four shots of the struggle that writers so vividly recalled: trypanosomes attached to white blood cells like eels caught in coral wriggling to get free. The first three shots in this section focus on individual leucocytes—maybe three at a time at most—with their attached trypanosomes. While the third shot shows a large leucocyte with several parasites attached in various stages of engulfment, all the other shots depict attachment only. But the fourth shot offers a climactic scene of swirling chaos as many trypanosomes move and attach to over a dozen white blood cells. Finally, the film ends with a shot of some trypanosomes attaching and others not attaching: those roaming free have been "vaccinated" against the prepared serum, probably by extended serological exposure that reduces the presence of specific antigens.

The film, then, is a spectacular demonstration of how the attachment process can be used to diagnose species of *Trypanosoma*. Levaditi and Mutermilch published their findings in June 1910 and held a screening of the film with Comandon at the Academy of Medicine in Paris in July 1910.[41] In November 1910, Levaditi went to London to present this film and others at various academic venues; in December he and Mutermilch published further findings on the attachment phenomenon.[42] His audiences in all cases consisted of educated medical professionals who were familiar with phagocytosis but who likely had not witnessed it themselves. Based on what we know of these screenings, Levaditi's demonstration of the process was probably very persuasive.

Following in the footsteps of Comandon's efforts to demonstrate the usefulness of cinema as an aid to medical science, Levaditi's screenings also attracted significant attention from the press. The public screening at the Academy of Medicine was reported in the major Parisian daily newspapers *Le Figaro, Le Journal, Le Radical,* and *Le Matin.* These accounts reveal that, while Levaditi's specific focus on phagocytosis was the principal aim of his presentations, there was considerable overlap between his screenings and Comandon's. We can begin by noting that the phenomenon of phagocytosis had already appeared in Comandon's screenings.[43] Furthermore, the press accounts make it clear that Levaditi showed a full program of films in addition to *Mécanisme de la phagocytose*: spirochetes, haemolysis, circulation of the blood in capillaries, and "the slow but sure engulfing motion of amoeboid corpuscles"—all were part of the screening program.[44] So Levaditi was leveraging Comandon's corpus, and, we can speculate, perhaps even using some of Comandon's lecture notes.

Levaditi took *Mécanisme de la phagocytose* and a selection of Comandon's films to London, where he presented them at the Royal Institute of Public Health on November 7, 1910, and at St. Thomas's Hospital on November 9.[45] The screening at the King's College Hospital Medical Society was captured in the illustration created for *The Illustrated London News* with which this paper began (figure 15.1). The image on the screen is from *Trypanosoma lewisi* (1909), a film made with the ultramicroscope of the blood of an infected rat.[46] The standing figure on the far right of the image is Levaditi himself, in a quiet moment when he was not providing commentary. A press account provides a more detailed assessment of his qualities as a lecturer: "In the first few pictures the phagocytes had rather a bad time of it in their battle with the invaders, and, like a general commanding his forces, Dr. Levaditi cried: 'See! They weaken!' [f]ollowing with his pointer the combatants appearing on the screen like weird creatures conjured from a nightmare."[47] The account's description animates the illustration, adding details about Levaditi's running commentary and his use of a pointer to direct the audience's attention. The journalist's coloring of the scene with a martial tone by representing Levaditi as a general as well as the association of the microscopic organisms with the phantasmic are further instances of the powerful metaphorical response that these films evoked.

The image from *The Illustrated London News* also gives us a sense of that most elusive of phenomena, audience reaction. The all-male, formally dressed audience displays a range of responses. Two younger men in the center of the image are conferring—the film has given them something to discuss. One of those men enthusiastically applauds, along with another at the far-right front of the image. A final significant gesture that the illustrator has chosen to depict is the older man's clasped hands in the front left of the image. This posture can be taken as a form of appreciation that suggests reverence. But it is also possible to see the hands as a sign of absorbed concentration. As an account of one of Levaditi's London screenings noted, "it is no exaggeration to say that the films were watched with a remarkable intensity even by those to whom the movements of the organisms were already familiar."[48] The cinematographic projection of views through the microscope, in other words, could have a refreshing, revelatory effect even for practitioners accustomed to such sights. Yet for all the discourse of novelty that these exhibitions generated, some accounts acknowledged the familiarity of microcinematography even in 1910, as when "The Unseen World" was evoked as a precedent: "The projection of many of these films before lay audiences is probably an event shortly to be expected; indeed, we believe already some seven years ago certain films of the circulation of the blood and the typhoid bacillus were shown at the Alhambra."[49]

One account of Levaditi's screenings also mentioned the inclusion of "popular" films that depicted "laboratory scenes," "such as the inoculation of a mouse with the trypanosome of sleeping sickness, and the somewhat humorous pictures of the life of a laboratory ape."[50] The inclusion of these films indicates that Levaditi was navigating the same dynamics between professional science and popularization that characterized Comandon's career. As another account observed, "This film is not only of scientific interest, it is a wonderful instrument of popularization, it will make people love science and perhaps on the steps of the cinema, children interested in this extraordinary spectacle will feel awakening in them a vocation they were far from suspecting."[51] These screenings, as well as their journalistic reverberations, could evidently forge powerful connections between scientific and lay audiences.

Given his expert audience, Levaditi surely would have wanted to show them something they hadn't seen before. Even if attachment and phagocytosis were a familiar sight for some, his goal would have been to add to their understanding in some significant way by providing his audience with a clear takeaway: the ability to diagnose different varieties of *Trypanosoma*, which was a pressing issue, especially for tropical disease experts. But the film also prompted a larger question: how does attachment happen? In their articles on the topic, Levaditi and Mutermilch suggested that the larger process of phagocytosis has two phases, first attachment and then engulfment. Engulfment is initially a mechanical process: one can observe the phagocyte's cell membrane physically extend around the captured parasite. The nature of attachment, however, is more elusive. Levaditi and Mutermilch observed that the pathogen *attaches itself to* and is then engulfed and digested by the phagocyte, thereby reversing the normal understanding of this process:

> The first phase of phagocytosis is therefore a physicochemical phenomenon, at least with regard to leukocytes. *It is not that the white blood cell, attracted by the sensitized trypanosome, goes in search of it: the initial act of attachment results rather from the fortuitous meeting of the phagocyte and the trypanosome, and reflects the existence of a specific affinity of the sensitized antigen for leukocyte protoplasm.*[52]

Their most important point is that attachment is a *physicochemical* process, meaning that the initial "affinity" or attraction between phagocyte and trypanosome was chemical, not mechanical—the phagocyte did not reach out and grab the parasite. Their meeting might have been fortuitous, but something else was going on to allow attachment to occur. Furthermore, they noted that the phagocyte does not even need to be alive for attachment to happen. Under a variety of experimental conditions—with live or dead phagocytes, or with active and inactive serums—attachment occurred predictably. This finding proved that one could detect *through direct observation* both the mechanical *and* chemical processes underlying phagocytosis. The film provided an occasion to explain this significant discovery.

The Debate

To understand why this finding was so important, we must consider then-contemporary debates about the process of phagocytosis. The engulfment process requires a live phagocyte, of course, but that attachment can occur even when the phagocyte is dead also illustrates something we cannot see in the film but which Levaditi certainly explained to his audience: the chemical process that accompanies the mechanical process of phagocytosis. And if they had been paying attention to the news of the Nobel prizes in their field, the members of the audience at King's College Hospital would have nodded their heads in recognition.

In 1908, the Nobel Prize Committee awarded the annual prize in Physiology or Medicine to both Élie Metchnikoff (see figure 15.8) and Paul Ehrlich (see figure 15.9) "in recognition of their work on immunity." The significance of this dual honor requires some explanation. Despite what journalists may have reported at the time, Metchnikoff did not discover phagocytosis, which had been observed many times before. But Metchnikoff, a Russian-born scientist who found a home in France at the Pasteur Institute, recognized something that others did not: the significance of this process for the body's defense mechanism. In fact, he built an entire theory of immune defense based on phagocytosis. He also discovered that phagocytosis played an important role in maintaining an equilibrium between dead and live cells in the body—some phagocytes are assigned not to foreign invaders but to the millions of cells that die within us every day. Phagocytes, according to Metchnikoff, thereby have a vital role in homeostasis, or the stable identity of the organism. For his understanding of the role of specialized cells in large questions about physiology, Metchnikoff is counted as one of the great theorists of nineteenth-century biology.[53]

Metchnikoff's theory of immune defense was built largely on the mechanical process of phagocytosis, which he saw as the answer to most questions. This theory was met with resistance, specifically from the Germans, led by Paul Ehrlich, who was working on the biochemical features of immunity. Ehrlich was the major proponent of the humoral theory of immune response, which focused on the role of antibodies and antigens. The fundamental question at the end of the nineteenth century was whether a particular immune response was innate or adaptive—that is, whether the body is always already primed to attack invaders, or whether each immune response is tailored to the threat before it. Metchnikoff was the major voice for the innate side of the answer: phagocytes are there in the bloodstream and ready to attack. And this is true. Ehrlich, however, developed his side-chain or receptor theory to explain how cells adapt to specific threats.

FIGURE 15.8 Élie Metchnikoff (1845–1916). Photograph by Nadar. Courtesy Wellcome Collection.

He argued that cells are outfitted with a range of receptors, which fit or attract specific receptors on the pathogens like a lock and key. When a cell locks onto a pathogen or antigen with specific receptors, it sends a signal to the body to respond with more of that receptor, or antibody, producing the necessary set of antibodies to counter the threat. This is all true as well. But around 1900, the French-German rivalry was heated, and it was either one or the other: innate or adaptive, Metchnikoff or Ehrlich.[54]

In 1908, however, the wisdom of the neutral Swedes put this all to rest when they awarded the prize to both Metchnikoff and Ehrlich. It is not one or the other: the innate and adaptive systems are complementary in the body's immune response. Levaditi had known this all along. Before he joined the Pasteur Institute, Levaditi worked as Ehrlich's assistant at the Institute for Serotherapy in Frankfurt, where he became familiar with Ehrlich's theories and experiments.[55] He brought these insights to the Pasteur Institute, where he worked directly with Metchnikoff for ten years before becoming head of his own lab. In fact, amid the intensely anti-German chauvinism of the French scientific

FIGURE 15.9 Paul Ehrlich (1854–1915). Courtesy Wellcome Collection.

community, Levaditi was the lone researcher friendly to Ehrlich's theories and the sole proponent of his ideas at the Pasteur Institute.

The film he made with Comandon starts to come into sharper focus now. Having just become head of a laboratory, Levaditi was now free (and perhaps expected) to offer more lectures and public outreach. The encounter with Comandon came at the right time in Levaditi's career and in his research program. Levaditi used the film to demonstrate an aspect of phagocytosis, which was also in the news after the 1908 Nobel Prize. He showed phagocytes attached to trypanosomes and engulfing them. But he also revealed, surprisingly, that attachment does not require a vital phagocyte to occur. How could this be? The only explanation is chemical: that with the right serum vaccine, the trypanosome is irresistibly drawn to the phagocyte, almost as if it were a magnetized key, to modify Ehrlich's lock-and-key metaphor. In the presence of a correct serum, the antibodies of the phagocyte display a literal chemical attraction to the antigens of the trypanosome. That the phagocyte does not even need to be alive for this to happen proves incontrovertibly the presence of receptors and their chemical signals. Levaditi, then, as the mediator between Metchnikoff and Ehrlich, worked with Comandon to demonstrate the complementary elements of the organism's immune response. The King's College audience might have read about the Nobel Prize, but now they understood its significance without a doubt, thanks in no small part to the film's vivid demonstration of the phenomena under consideration.

Conclusion

There are multiple narratives embedded in the image from *The Illustrated London News*. First, we have a story of collaboration between Levaditi and Comandon. Our tendency in the historiography of scientific media to focus on the medium itself must be counterweighted by an equal emphasis on the team or network of craftspeople who contribute to the visualization process. In this case, it is rather straightforward with two main players. But even when the scientist and craftsperson are the same individual, there are always other agents involved in the circulation and reuse of scientific films. Here, the intermedial relay between film and the popular press framed and disseminated the film in a different but still highly significant way.

Second, these narratives of collaboration and intermediality lead us to a story about the entwinement of research and popularization. Seeing popularization as a degraded form of science is unhelpful. We must acknowledge that not all experts are equally expert, so Levaditi's presentation of his new findings required a bit of showmanship even for his academic audiences. Admittedly, the difference between Levaditi's and Gignoux's account of the same film is stark. But even for an expert audience, scientific films do not exist on their own. There is always an entanglement or mutual dependence of text and image. Here, Levaditi's published findings are a necessary key to deciphering the phagocytosis film. But a description such as Gignoux's is also a decoding or interpretation. If the film is in some way a translation of the experimental write-up, then the journalistic account is also a translation of the film. The collaboration, then, is not just between scientist and craftsperson but also includes the journalist and writer, all of whom contribute to our common understanding of the natural world.

This is why scientific images are so central to the history of science: they are ambiguous yet pivotal elements in the transfer or transport of knowledge among expert and lay agents. Levaditi's and Gignoux's descriptions are not at all similar, but they are both disseminations, to different audiences and ends. The ambiguity of films or images—that they are capable of holding multiple meanings and associations—allows different kinds of knowledge transfer to flourish. But viewing descriptions such as Gignoux's as mere entertainment discounts the power of the cinematic image to move and to persuade its audience, an essential feature that scientists such as Levaditi counted on when choosing this medium. Indeed, the nature of the cinematic image—its duality, its rhetorical power, its inherent spectacle of movement—forces histories of science film to account for both the evidence it presents and the wonder it evokes.

Acknowledgments

The authors would like to thank Damien Blanchard of the Bibliothèque de l'Académie nationale de médecine; Béatrice de Pastre and Patrice Delavie of the Centre national du cinéma et de l'image animée; Thierry Lefebvre; and Stéphanie Salmon of the Fondation Jérôme Seydoux-Pathé.

Notes

1. *The Illustrated London News*, November 5, 1910, 685.
2. Hannah Landecker, "Cellular Features: Microcinematography and Film Theory," *Critical Inquiry* 31, no. 4 (2005): 903–937.
3. Admittedly, though, our own work has tended to emphasize this division: Scott Curtis focused on films for research in *The Shape of Spectatorship: Art, Science, and Early Cinema in Germany* (New York: Columbia University Press, 2015), while Oliver Gaycken investigated popular science films in *Devices of Curiosity: Early Cinema and Popular Science* (New York: Oxford University Press, 2015).
4. The classic example of the diffusionist model is John C. Burnham, *How Superstition Won and Science Lost: Popularizing Science and Health in the United States* (New Brunswick, NJ: Rutgers University Press, 1987).
5. Roger Cooter and Stephen Pumfrey, "Separate Spheres and Public Places: Reflections on the History of Science Popularization and Science in Popular Culture," *History of Science* 32, no. 3 (1994): 249.
6. Anne Secord, "Science in the Pub: Artisan Botanists in Early Nineteenth-Century Lancashire," *History of Science* 32, no. 3 (1994): 269–315.
7. Cooter and Pumfrey, "Separate Spheres," 249.
8. On the historiography of craft in scientific culture, see Klaus Hentschel, *Visual Cultures in Science and Technology* (New York: Oxford University Press, 2014). For an account of the creative importance of craft knowledge in a media industry, see Luci Marzola, *Engineering Hollywood: Technology, Technicians, and the Science of Building the Studio System* (New York: Oxford University Press, 2021).
9. James A. Secord, "Knowledge in Transit," *Isis* 95, no. 4 (December 2004): 654–672.
10. Comandon continued to make films, first for Albert Kahn's Archives de la Planète from 1926 to 1929, then at the Pasteur Institute from 1932 to 1966. The best overview of his career is Béatrice de Pastre with Thierry Lefebvre, eds., *Filmer la science, comprendre la vie: Le cinema de Jean Comandon* (Paris: CNC, 2012); see also Paula Amad, *Counter-Archive: Film, the Everyday, and Albert Kahn's Archives de la Planète* (New York: Columbia University Press, 2010) for Comandon's work for Kahn as well as an illuminating consideration of the reception of Comandon's films.
11. Jean Comandon, *De l'usage en clinique de l'ultramicroscope, en particulier pour la recherche et l'étude des spirochetes* (Paris: G. Steinheil, 1909).
12. The classic text explaining the instrument is Henry Siedentopf and Richard Zsigmondy, "Über Sichtbarmachung und Größenbestimmung ultramikoskopischer Teilchen, mit besonderer Anwendung auf Goldrubingläser," *Annalen der Physik* 10, no. 1 (1903): 1–39. For

a history of the instrument, see David Cahan, "The Zeiss Werke and the Ultramicroscope: The Creation of a Scientific Instrument in Context," in Jed Z. Buchwald, ed., *Scientific Credibility and Technical Standards in 19th and Early 20th Century Germany and Britain* (Dordrecht, Netherlands: Kluwer Academic Publishers, 1996), 67–115.

13. Laurent Mannoni, "Jean Comandon technicien," in de Pastre and Lefebvre, eds., *Filmer la science*, 47–59.
14. "Perfectionnements aux dispositifs de prises de vues micro-cinématographiques," French Patent No. 419,305 (October 22, 1909).
15. Stéphanie Salmon, "Le docteur Comandon chez Pathé," in de Pastre and Lefebvre, eds., *Filmer la science*, 401–411.
16. Jean Comandon, "Cinématographie, à l'ultra-microscope, de microbes vivants et des particules mobiles," *Comptes rendus hebdomadaires des séances de l'Académie des sciences*, November 22, 1909, 938–941.
17. Ehrlich was referring to the advantage of dry-stained specimens, as opposed to fresh, but the phrasing is appropriate for recorded media as well. Paul Ehrlich and Adolf Lazarus, "Histology of the Blood: Normal and Pathological," in Fred Himmelweit, Martha Marquardt, and Henry Dale, eds., *Collected Papers of Paul Ehrlich*, vol. 1 (New York: Pergamon Press, 1956), 193.
18. See Curtis, *The Shape of Spectatorship*, 26–31.
19. See Gaycken, *Devices of Curiosity*, 15–53.
20. See Tom Gunning, "The Cinema of Attractions: Early Film, Its Spectator and the Avant-garde," *Wide Angle* 8, nos. 3–4 (1986): 63–70.
21. See Laurent Le Forestier, "Une disparition instructive: Quelques hypotheses sur l'évolution des scenes à trucs chez Pathé," *1895*, no. 27 (1999): 61–73.
22. Thierry Lefebvre, "Jean Comandon conférencier, 1909: les débuts," in de Pastre and Lefebvre, eds., *Filmer la science*, 413–422.
23. For an excellent account of Doyen's engagement with cinema (and other media), see Thierry Lefebvre, *La chair et le celluloid: Le cinéma chirurgical du Docteur Doyen* (Brionne, France: Jean Doyen éditeur, 2004). Lefebvre traces Doyen's various uses of the moving image, beginning in 1898, and he provides a detailed examination of one of Doyen's most infamous films, *Séparation des soeurs xiphopages Doodica et Radica* (1902). The film's explicit purpose—to create a record of the surgical separation of conjoined twins—was an excellent example of Doyen's vision of cinema as an educational device. But this ability to circulate also caused significant problems. Since Doodica and Radica were part of Barnum and Bailey's touring circus, their surgery became the subject of intense media attention, and the second camera operator hired by Doyen to film the operation, Ambroise-François Parnaland, distributed illicit copies of his film to fairground exhibition venues. Although Doyen won an ensuing lawsuit, the unsanctioned appearance of this film in a sideshow exhibition crystallized a concern about cinema held by many members of the medical community. On the reception of Comandon's films at the Academy in 1909, see Comandon, "The Evolution of Micro-Cinematography," *International Review of Educational Cinematography* 4, no. 6 (June 1932): 417.
24. "The Battles in the Blood," *St. Louis Post Dispatch*, Sunday Magazine, January 16, 1910.
25. Charles J. Brandreth, "The Man Who Prolongs Life," *London Magazine* 23, no. 137 (January 1910): 578–584; Régis Gignoux, "Les microbes en liberté," *Le Figaro*, December 7, 1909, 2. The title "Les microbes en liberté" is from this line in Gignoux's article: "all that was nothing beside the magic lantern where we saw the microbes at liberty, microbes at home, that is to say, in us."

26. "Battles in the Blood."
27. Gignoux is describing, probably, the sleeping-sickness film, *Trypanosoma lewisi*: "And these were two views of the blood of a rat, the first after two days of inoculation, the second after four days, with the microbes in full control."
28. See Yuri Tsivian, *Early Cinema in Russia and Its Cultural Reception*, trans. Alan Bodger (Chicago, IL: University of Chicago Press, 1998).
29. Laura Forsberg, "Nature's Invisibilia: The Victorian Microscope and the Miniature Fairy," *Victorian Studies* 57, no. 4 (Summer 2015): 640. See also Stefan Ditzen, "Instrument-Aided Vision and the Imagination: The Migration of Worms and Dragons in Early Microscopy," in Horst Bredekamp, Vera Dünkel, and Birgit Schneider, eds., *The Technical Image: A History of Styles in Scientific Imagery* (Chicago, IL: University of Chicago Press, 2015), 130–137. For more on the constitutive but also controversial role of imagination in the construction of scientific knowledge, see Omar W. Nasim, *Observing by Hand: Sketching the Nebulae in the Nineteenth Century* (Chicago, IL: University of Chicago Press, 2013), esp. 118–121 and 199–206; and Natasha Myers, *Rendering Life Molecular: Models, Modelers, and Excitable Matter* (Durham, NC: Duke University Press, 2015), esp. ch. 3.
30. G. Nigel Gilbert and Michael Mulkay, *Opening Pandora's Box: A Sociological Analysis of Scientists' Discourse* (Cambridge, UK: Cambridge University Press, 1984); Alberto Cambrosio, Daniel Jacobi, and Peter Keating, "Erlich's 'Beautiful Pictures' and the Controversial Beginnings of Immunological Imagery," *Isis* 84 (1993): 662–699.
31. Comandon, "Evolution of Micro-Cinematography," 417.
32. See Curtis, *The Shape of Spectatorship*, esp. chapters 2 and 3.
33. Pierre Lepine, "C. Levaditi (1874–1953)," *Annales de l'Institute Pasteur* 85 (1953): 535–540.
34. For an account of Pasteur's own complex relationship with the public and the press, see Massimiano Bucci, "The Public Science of Louis Pasteur: The Experiment on Anthrax Vaccine in the Popular Press of the Time," *History and Philosophy of the Life Sciences* 19, no. 2 (1997): 181–209.
35. Constantin Levaditi, *Travaux scientifiques* (Paris: Impr. L. Maretheux, 1928).
36. Gignoux, "Les microbes en liberté," 2.
37. Thierry Lefebvre, email message to authors, September 20, 2021.
38. "Vie scientifique universitaire," *Revue scientifique*, May 21, 1910, 665.
39. Another microorganism hindered our ability to conduct primary research during the writing of this chapter; more definitive answers are probably at the Pasteur Institute archives.
40. Alphonse Laveran and André Thiroux of the Pasteur Institute offered a useful survey of diagnostic options in "Identification des trypanosomes pathogènes," *Comptes rendus hebdomadaires des séances de l'Académie des sciences*, February 27, 1911, 487–490.
41. Constantin Levaditi and Stefan Mutermilch, "Mécanisme de la phagocytose," *Comptes rendus hebdomadaires des séances et mémoires de la Société de biologie*, June 18, 1910, 1079–1081; and *Bulletin de l'Academie de Médecine*, July 12, 1910, 72.
42. Constantin Levaditi and Stefan Mutermilch, "Diagnostic des trypanosomiases par le phénoméne de 'l'attachement,'" *Comptes rendus hebdomadaires des séances et mémoires de la Société de biologie*, December 24, 1910, 635–637.
43. Gignoux noted, probably referring to *Spirochaeta gallinarum*: "In the blood of a chicken a white corpuscle has eaten a red corpuscle. We have been present at the phagocytosis described by the great Metchnikoff!"
44. "Moving Pictures in Medicine," *Moving Picture News*, January 21, 1911, 15.

45. "Scientific Notes and News," *Science*, December 2, 1910, 793.
46. *Trypanosoma lewisi*, in de Pastre and Lefebvre, eds., *Filmer la science*, 95.
47. "A Lecture on 'The Mechanism of Phagocytosis,' given by Dr. C. Levaditi of the Pasteur Institute, Paris, at the Royal Institute of Public Health," *San Francisco Chronicle*, November 27, 1910, 48.
48. "The Cinematograph in Medicine," *The Hospital* (London), November 19, 1910, 217.
49. Ibid.
50. Ibid.
51. Docteur X, "La Science au Cinéma," *Ciné-Journal*, August 6, 1910, 4–5. The fact that this professional medical investigator chose to write under the pseudonym "Docteur X" is also worth noting, since it suggests that a connection to the cinema industry was something medical professionals had to approach with caution.
52. Levaditi and Mutermilch, "Mécanisme de la phagocytose," 1080–1081 (emphasis in original).
53. The classic text is Paul de Kruif, *The Microbe Hunters* (San Diego, CA: Harcourt Brace Jovanovich, 1954). See also Alfred I. Tauber, *The Immune Self: Theory or Metaphor?* (Cambridge, UK: Cambridge University Press, 1994) and Tauber, "Metchnikoff and the Phagocytosis Theory," *Nature Reviews Molecular Cell Biology* 4 (November 2003): 897–901.
54. Stefan H. E. Kaufmann, "Immunology's Foundation: The 100-Year Anniversary of the Nobel Prize to Paul Ehrlich and Elie Metchnikoff," *Nature Immunology* 9, no. 7 (July 2008): 705–712.
55. See Levaditi's biography at the Pasteur Institute website: https://webext.pasteur.fr/archives/levo.html.

CHAPTER 16

CINEMA ON THE MOVE

Museum-Sponsored Expedition Film in the Silent Era

ALISON GRIFFITHS

THE 1920s is considered the era of "great expeditions," the last gasp of exploration, when museums and institutions such as the American Museum of Natural History (AMNH) in New York, the Royal Geographical Society in London, and the National Geographic Society in Washington, DC, enlisted cinema within an arsenal of recording devices.[1] By the early 1920s, expedition films were de rigueur in museums of natural history, seen as an important part of their institutional mission (the AMNH established a committee in 1923 to support the "preparation, use and the preservation of motion picture films for scientific purposes"), accomplished either by equipping staff to shoot film or hiring professional cinematographers.[2] However, the fate of expedition film footage once the expedition party returned to the sponsoring institution was far from certain, making expedition filmmaking an unusually complex, enigmatic, and not surprisingly neglected genre of non-fiction filmmaking. Nevertheless, in a manner distinct from written accounts, photographs, and phonographic recordings, expedition films provide compelling glimpses of the interactions between Indigenous peoples and scientists, members of the expedition party and Indigenous laborers, and the impact of the expedition on the global landscape, real and imaginary.

The complicated organizational and personal determinants of expedition cinema emerge from two broad production contexts. The first is the institutionally sponsored expedition, financed by private and public funds, designed to serve several masters and exigencies, and inevitably revealing fissures and tensions among stakeholders.[3] The second is the lone-wolf expedition, shaped less by institutional constraints than by the psycho-social motives of wanderlust, the ego document, and the need to establish scientific credibility.[4] This chapter focuses on one example of the institutionally sponsored expedition film, a neglected, orphan title made as part of the AMNH's 1926 Morden–Clark Central Asiatic expedition, part of a series of expeditions sponsored by the AMNH to Central Asia between 1921 and 1930.[5] The untitled eighteen-thousand-foot film (it is simply known as the *Morden–Clark Expedition*, shortened here to *MCE*), with animated maps and no intertitles, hews closely to some of the characteristic tropes of the expedition genre, including extreme long shots of the traveling party winding its way through a variegated landscape, sequences of ethnographic interest, footage of transportation animals and supplies, and a couple of scenes featuring the expedition leaders.[6] Anthropologist Johannes Fabian's idea of exploration as a series of "events" oscillating between travel as movement and travel as stillness, corresponds quite nicely to the modular sequences of the *MCE*.[7]

But what exactly differentiates expedition filmmaking from early cinema's ubiquitous ethnographic actualities, the genteel travelogues of showmen-travelers such as E. Burton Holmes, Lyman H. Howe, and Frederick Monsen, or safari films made by Paul J. Rainey (*African Hunt*, 1910) and Teddy Roosevelt (*Teddy Roosevelt in Africa*, 1910)?[8] Furthermore, how does expedition filmmaking differ from the 1920s adventure, safari, or romantic ethnographic films made by Robert Flaherty (*Nanook of the North*, 1922), Martin and Osa Johnson (*Simba*, 1928), and Merian C. Cooper and Ernest B. Schoedsack (*Chang*, 1927), or the sound-era exploitation films *Ingagi* (William Campbell, 1930) and *Forbidden Adventure* (Norman Taurog, 1931)? Chronologically situated roughly between the early travelogue and the safari-style adventure features, expedition films share many discursive and aesthetic qualities with both genres, but their institutional raison d'être, credibility leveraged from scientific authorities, and limited public audience distinguish them as a different kind of cinematic undertaking.[9]

The Morden–Clark expedition film serves as a generative case study, helping us engage not only with the wider universe of expedition filmmaking throughout the silent era but also with several still-urgent geopolitical questions relevant to cross-cultural image-making, including the clash of colonial and scientific agendas with hostile landscapes and communities, claims for the camera's objectivity challenged by footage replete with evidence of subjective biases, and the tension between institutional support for expedition footage and the paltry record of public exhibition. The following questions shape my investigation: In what ways is *MCE* typical of an expedition film, and what habits of seeing does it privilege? In what ways does the expedition's extant footage, along with its four thousand field photographs, Morden's four-volume fieldwork diary, letters written by the men to their wives (some of which were published in *Natural History* magazine), dozens of popular articles, and public and professional reception, construct knowledge?[10] How do these informational texts parse and document what Mark Hobart calls the "welter of activities going on around them"? And how do they isolate the pertinent facts from the background noise of the expedition as a massive collecting enterprise?[11] Which elements of the expedition are sublimated into discourses for either public or private use (such as a personal diary or letters)?[12] What kinds of authority does expedition film embody, distinct from other textual and visual media?[13] And what larger lesson about the use-value and patterns of exhibition of silent non-fiction filmmaking can we take from *MCE*, given its scant record of exhibition and relative obscurity?

Institutionally Sponsored Expedition Film: Funding, Logistics, and Informing Optics

> Night after night, I donned white tie and tails and talked Gobi Desert at some one of New York's great houses. Compared to the financial battle, fieldwork was child's play.
> Roy Chapman Andrews, *Beyond Adventure*.[14]

By the mid-1920s, the AMNH was going through a severe financial crisis. In the "Financial and Administrative Report" for 1926, President Henry Fairfield Osborn described the situation as "very grave," a result of a 120 percent rise in operating and administrative costs over the previous decade, with no corresponding increase in either the AMNH's endowment or city appropriations.[15] In response, the Museum cut $43,500 from its scientific and educational budget that year, which meant the "practical suspension of all the exploration and field work, except that provided by special gifts."[16] Even during less lean budgetary times, it was customary for Museum scientists to fundraise for their research expeditions. AMNH's acclaimed naturalist and explorer (and real-life inspiration for Indiana Jones) Roy Chapman Andrews shared the following strategy in his book *Beyond Adventure*: "My best chance is to make it a 'society expedition' with a big 'S.' You know how New York society follows a leader. If they have the example of someone like Mr. J. P. Morgan, for instance, they'll think it is a 'Must' for the current season."[17] It was therefore imperative to secure a wealthy patron, preferably an individual who straddled the amateur and professional worlds of expeditionary travel.

The Morden–Clark expedition adhered to this model of patronage, with the $26,000 budget (the equivalent of $373,258 in 2020) covered by William J. Morden, (1886–1958), the son of a railroad industrialist and Honorary Fellow and Field Associate in mammology at the AMNH, not a salaried position at the museum. Morden was the ideal benefactor: given his significant personal wealth and passion for hunting and adventure, he could forge close ties to several elite scientific organizations. In 1921, Morden led an expedition to the head of the Donjeck River in northwest Canada's Yukon Territory looking for the area's white sheep (a dry run for the *ovis poli* search in the 1926 Morden–Clark expedition), and in 1922 he funded the Morden African Expedition to Kenya, Uganda, and the Sudan. For the 1922 African expedition, Morden hired professional cinematographer Herford Tynes Cowling to shoot footage, testimony to cinema's established place in the arsenal of scientific recording devices expected of a major expedition. Morden made a pitch for the Central Asian expedition to James L. Clark (1883–1969), Head of the Department of Preparation at the AMNH and Director of the New York Explorers Club, in a 1925 letter, where Morden spoke openly and in an unfiltered fashion about needing a companion, since "I don't want to spend another five to six months with just a bunch of savages," and offered to cover what he called all "safari expense."[18] Morden did pay for everything, except for Clark's outbound travel from New York to Bombay and return from Beijing to New York.

The Central Asiatic expedition's primary focus was zoological, tasked with collecting examples of the *ovis poli* sheep (with their long curly horns and white fluffy winter coats), Tien Shan ibex, gazelles, and other smaller mammals for installation as groups in the proposed North Asiatic Hall at the AMNH. Not wanting to be outdone by the Field Museum in Chicago, which boasted an impressive habitat group of *ovis poli* collected by Theodore Roosevelt, the AMNH hoped to install a diorama featuring the sheep in its planned hall.[19] Morden and Clark were aiming to bring home ten *poli*s, although they were encouraged by the locals to hunt at least a hundred.

Morden and Clark had planned to meet up with the Third Asiatic Expedition to Hami, Eastern Chinese Turkestan, led by Roy Chapman Andrews (one of five AMNH expeditions to the region between 1921 and 1930), but the plan was abandoned due to political instability in the region. The idea of traveling as a larger group was in order to "insure greater safety in travel and larger collections of fauna and flora from this almost impossible country."[20] The expedition also carried the flag of the Explorers Club in New York City, a mark of prestige and legitimacy, since to this day, the Club only grants flag-carrying privileges to respected scientific exploration undertaken by active members.[21]

With a few exceptions, Clark himself shot the expedition's film, along with taking a significant number of the photographs and documenting his experiences in several popular-press articles and the book *Good Hunting*.[22] Given his expertise in taxidermy and habitat group preparation, Clark would have been at ease reconciling the needs of zoology with that of popular science/culture, recognizing that both were essential to the creation of illusionistic museum habitat groups. Similarly, he had no difficulty turning scientific field reports into commercial adventure tales for public consumption.[23] Clark used a Bell and Howell Edema, a compact 35mm camera introduced in 1925, and acquired Eastman Kodak film stock along the route.

In January 1926, Morden and Clark sailed from New York to India, traveling via London and Paris to outfit and obtain official travel credentials. Sixty porters were hired in the northern Kashmir city of Srinigar, permitted by law to carry no more than sixty pounds of equipment each, although the weight fluctuated depending on the topography. Paid a government-set rate of one cent per mile, the men worked on as few as one or up to three fifteen-mile legs of the journey, replaced by recruits requisitioned from nearby villages.[24] The expedition party departed Srinigar on March 31, 1926, heading toward the Russian Pamirs by way of the Gilgit-Hunza route, an eight-thousand-mile, eight-month trek along the Silk Road. For the 2,600-mile journey, Morden and Clark relied on modes of transportation virtually unchanged from the time of Marco Polo, including ponies, donkeys, and yaks, either ridden or used to haul wagons, carts, and sleighs (see figure 16.1). For the eight-hundred-mile journey across the Gobi Desert, the men rode Bactrian camels, animals that Clark described as "the railroad trains of Central Asia."[25] Their endeavor hews closely to Peter N. Miller's characterization of an expedition as a "logistical crossword puzzle, in which groups of disparate individuals and their gear are moved along distances for long times in order to tame the unknown."[26]

FIGURE 16.1 James L. Clark, Head of Preparation at the American Museum of Natural History, aboard his "yak-mobile" during the 1926 Central Asian Expedition led by William J. Morden. James L. Clark Photography File 1214.1, courtesy AMNH Special Collections.

Still, we shouldn't ignore the mix of animal and human labor involved, what Fabian describes as "different kinds of bodies and things, each of them with different abilities or requirements [as] regards motion."[27]

Marco Polo also does duty in Clark's book about the expedition, *Good Hunting*, where his mythic quality and stature serve to geographically orient the reader and reinforce the idea of an allochronic landscape and people.[28] The historical resonance of famous travelers and warriors whose paths Morden and Clark followed was not lost on Clark, who described "becoming philosophical as he gazed down at the land of Attila, Marco Polo, and Genghis Khan."[29] Ironically, it may have been easier for Marco Polo to navigate this region in 1271 with his father and uncle than it was for Morden and Clark, since much of Asia in the thirteenth century was under the rule of a unitary Mongol government, a fact that Polo scholar Peter Jackson tells us "greatly facilitated the opportunities for both merchants and missionaries to travel from western Europe across the continent."[30] Moreover, the kidnapping and torture of Morden and Clark by Mongolians during the penultimate leg of the expedition in November 1926 forced them to abandon their route through Mongolia and instead head to Peking by way of Kobdo and the Trans-Siberian Railroad at Biisk in Siberia.[31] The account of their experience mobilized cultural stereotypes, going back to the mid-thirteenth century, of the Mongols as fierce warriors, and even though Morden initially underestimated the danger of the situation—"probably a bit of the 'dominant white man' feeling still remained," he later confessed—the entire event made for excellent copy upon return to New York. Morden defended the Mongols' response, noting that the "outburst of savagery was the natural consequence of suspicion and fear, engendered by our unheralded arrival."[32] The Central Asiatic peoples that Morden and Clark photographed, filmed, and described in their notebooks were no strangers to foreigners, and although the two men may very well have been the first Americans to travel in the region, they followed in a long line of outsiders.

THE MORDEN–CLARK EXPEDITION FILM: IN SEARCH OF *OVIS POLI*

> One cannot search for knowledge and pay attention to the well-being of one's body.
> *Siyar A'lam al-Nubala*, cited in Touati.[33]

The expedition's geographical ambition is presented via a map at the start of the film with an animated black line to mark the route. This is followed by a title card and medium close-ups of Morden and Clark running their fingers through their unkempt hair and wooly beards, authenticating their status as rugged explorers. The camera is restless from the outset, alternately assuming the point of view of an observer standing on the shore in Srinigar looking at the boat, a reverse angle of this shot, and a shot of a crew member seated directly behind an Indian man paddling. Images of Indigenous laborers carrying trunks on their shoulders through the ancient streets offer the first visual clues that we are watching an expedition film—Morden and Clark assembled nothing less than a small army—since footage of the transportation of vast amounts of equipment was a privileged visual trope in expedition films. But a medium-long shot of Indian men being hired as laborers also conveys a sense of the political economy of the enterprise.

Footage of the expedition party negotiating the ancient camel path between Srinigar and Gilgit in Pakistan along the Burzil Pass occupies most of the screen time, and Clark's long shots of the snaking expedition from different camera angles make us feel strangely detached, an omniscient mountain presence immune from the exhaustion, cold, and blizzard conditions affecting humans and animals. A quick succession of shots takes us deep into the mountain and onto the Tragbak rest house on the Burzil Pass. The scale of the human and animal effort involved is powerfully on display in a later sequence in the film showing ponies and donkeys getting stuck on the Murzat Pass across the Tien Shan mountains, an ordeal Clark captured on camera from several angles:

> It was so slippery and rough that no one dared ride his horse because of the deep crevasses and huge potholes ever gaping up at one, ready to swallow one up if he should make a misstep. [. . .] Our animals slipped and fell into deep surface pockets,

where they had to be completely unpacked and helped up to get a better footing, and many times we had to chop stairways for ourselves and our horses over these otherwise impassable, sloping surfaces."[34]

These images assume an analeptic quality, evoking earlier moments in the expedition's narrative while paradoxically signaling its forward progression. Clark frequently filmed the expedition party marching toward and past the camera, a compositional tactic going back to early cinema when cameramen showcased cinema's kineticism by filming marches, parades, trains, and buses. Clark also elevates the camera to obtain a high angle view of the porters and animals on the move and at other times stations himself at the rear of the group, gazing at the backs of the expedition party disappearing into the distance. The repeated image of an isolated strand of laborers that serves as a visual refrain in the film is mentioned in one of Morden's *Natural History* articles, when he writes that among his "most vivid recollections of Himalayan travel is of a long file of gray-clad figures toiling upward through the deep drifts of the Burzil Pass in the dim half-light of early dawn, with snow-clad peaks showing ghostlike against the gray sky."[35]

A poetics of distracted looking comes to define the *MCE*, as the onward march of travel brings new visual treats and oddities, from Morden's and Clark's pith helmets, sunglasses, and nose coverings, a local version of sun protection entailing wrapping one's beard around the face, to the loading of a thirty-foot-long ferry called a scrow with two mapas (carts), eight horses, and forty people to cross the Aksu river near the Tarim Basin in China. The "look at this, now look at that" quality of Clark's sequences resonates with the elliptical narrative structure of travel literature around the world, including early Islamic travel writing that typically jumps from one thing to the next with no warning, as illustrated in thirteenth-century traveler Ibn Fadlan's discussion of "The Chinese and Some of Their Customs" when he hopscotches from talking about carpets, to marriage, to the use of rice as a staple food in a single paragraph. Indeed, as Islamic literature scholar Tim Mackintosh-Smith reminds us, the Qur'an repeatedly tell its listeners to "go about the earth and look," an impulse validating the pleasure of feasting one's eyes on the world's wonders, and one shared by the expedition film and, before that, the travelogue.

Film scholar Ravi Vasudevan argues that these kinds of structural discontinuities, common in amateur colonial films of the period, not only lend an "autonomous status to the different segments" but shore up the camera's indexicality, its ability to capture the "physicality of people and objects and material life in the world."[36] However, beyond providing information about the particular mode of transportation and the logistics of securing the gear to the animals for each leg of the journey (whether pony, yak, or camel), shots of the expedition party merely walking offer scant scientific testimony about local flora and fauna or substantial ethnographic evidence. Instead, they work to imbue the film with a visual poetics and a reminder of what kind of film the viewer is watching, one governed by a reflexive desire to document its coming into being.

Guiding Clark's selection of film subjects was the picture-book aesthetic of habitat groups that he was responsible for constructing back at the AMNH.[37] His footage is also replete with images of posed family groups (a staple of life groups, museum dioramas featuring mannequins), river- or mountain-pass crossings, examples of material culture, and visually arresting cultural practices. For example, perhaps inspired by Robert Flaherty's famous igloo-building sequence from *Nanook of the North*, Clark filmed a yurt being constructed by Kyrgyz people and, to demonstrate its portability, carried by men scurrying across the landscape. The footage of the Kazaks is the most ethnographically rich, presumably because the more hospitable weather at this stage of the expedition made it easier for Clark to be out and about with his lightweight and relatively inconspicuous Eyemo camera. The pattern of brief shots of a new locale is occasionally interrupted by more structured sequences in which a process is demonstrated, such as Kazak bread-making or Kalmuch women shearing sheep and preparing felt.

The *MCE* gives scant indication of the passage of time, and save changes in the topography, modes of animals transportation, and sparse use of the map insert, there's little way to gauge how far the entourage has traveled. As the expedition group advances, Morden turns his attention to its major mission, hunting *Ovis poli* and other rare mammals. He and Clark were pleasantly surprised at the robust *poli* population in the region, reporting that they saw five hundred males and a thousand females over the course of the journey.[38] Morden was delighted with the "excellent pictures" Clark took of the sheep, the first footage of this particular breed. Morden, likely aware that members of the Explorers Club in New York were especially interested in the *poli*, ensured that the expedition captured ample footage of them alive and dead.[39] A long shot of a group of *poli* cuts suddenly to a close-up of one of their heads, the tips of the huge curly horns extending beyond the edges of the frame as Morden rotates it for the camera.[40] This macabre image of the dead sheep's head may have been the limit of what was appropriate for a general museum audience, and yet, for Morden, likely represented the long-awaited money shot.[41] There's also a depiction of an animal being measured in preparation for taxidermy; according to Clark, this was a vital part of the process, since it is "the skeleton that decides the species of an animal, not the skin."[42] There's only a single brief shot of a *poli* being skinned by a Kirghiz hunter—with most of the action partly obscured by something else going on in the foreground—and only one image of the scale of the hunting, a medium shot of a mound of severed *poli* heads about to be loaded onto the pack animals. The largest head Morden obtained measured 57 ½ inches in circumference, significantly shy of the then-world record of seventy-four inches, although Morden was quick to point out that the larger head had not been honorably hunted but was instead a "pick-up" head, one that had been found.[43] After being measured and separated from the bodies, the *poli* heads were recorded being tied to the sides of the pack animals, a surreal image of living beasts of burden transformed into animal hearses (see figure 16.2). Morden offers us clues for understanding the use value of the *poli* footage by describing it, along with still photography, as part of a "series which

FIGURE 16.2 Horns of hunted *ovis poli* sheep secured to the back of a camel for ongoing transportation; yaks were also loaded with horns as seen in the top right of the image. Frame enlargement *Morden-Clark Expedition* film (James L. Clark and William J. Morden, AMNH, 1926).

supplemented the specimens and added to their scientific value."[44] This is a rare explicit justification for expedition film as a form of scientific collection among other artifacts and data points, and the reference to seriality suggests that film was a key component of a triangulated method of knowledge accumulation.

Expedition Film Footage as Visual Small Talk

Since the goals of the expedition were primarily zoological rather than ethnographic, and neither man had any training in anthropological fieldwork, Morden and Clark were engaged in the metaphorical equivalent of small talk in terms of their interactions with Indigenous communities. Small talk is a useful hermeneutic for thinking about the negotiations involved in ethnographic filmmaking: oftentimes, Bronislaw Malinowski's methodological gold standard of extensive fieldwork and linguistic competency was eschewed in favor of a rapid tour of diverse countries and Indigenous groups. (For example, Morden and Clark stayed in no place long enough to learn much about the culture, had very limited linguistic competences, and were preoccupied with obtaining mammalian specimens.) Small talk, then, opens up a discursive space for examining the kinds of cultural interactions and negotiations involved in cross-cultural image making.[45]

As a "discourse of limits," small talk is by definition circumscribed by superficiality and brevity, captured in the ephemeral and often awkward interactions seen in the *MCE*. And yet the incidental and transitory offered advantages over in-depth participatory observation-style research, since it gave Clark the artistic freedom to simply film what caught his eye.[46] If, as literary theorist Sheldon Lu argues, small talk as a mode of storytelling disengages from official historical discourse, operating in the form of whispers and gossip, then it serves as a fitting metaphor for expedition film as an equally marginalized yet insightful source of knowledge.[47] Worrying about how he and Morden would be received by locals throughout the journey, Clark initiated small talk with the help of a phrasebook, using it as a social lubricant, a means of getting what he needed from a situation, or staying out of trouble.

Furtive glances or staring that might precede small talk are conveyed in the film's many close-ups of Indigenous men, women, and children, shots that mobilize discourses of orientalism, self-other negotiations, and seeing the familiar in the unfamiliar. While people's rank, occupation, and gender in part determine the behavior they might feel obliged to display in front of the camera, there are moments when small talk is displaced by a more carnivalesque letting-go, as in a sequence at Kizil Rabat near the Chinese border that begins with shots of Russian soldiers dancing, playing instruments, and saluting the camera. The men are clearly putting on a show for Clark and enjoying every minute of it. A quick cut reveals the same group at twelve thousand feet bathing in a hot spring, protected from the elements and perhaps a display of immodesty by a yurt that has been strategically placed around them (the opening is tied back to give the men and the camera access).[48]

Close-ups of local people staring and smiling at the camera suggest a letting down of one's guard, and a remarkable shot of an old man's wizened face and half-smile reminds us of the long history of travel and cross-cultural encounters in this region (see figure 16.3). The old man might very well have seen it all before, since, as film historian Oksana Sarkisova argues, between 1920 and 1940, Soviet authorities commissioned a large number of films depicting the territories and nationalities representing the "motherland" of the Soviet Union, films that helped codify a visual formula for depicting Indigenous peoples. According to Sarkisova, these films served a didactic function under the broad label of *kulturfilm*, motivated by the twin missions of salvage ethnography and the structuring of space through the establishment of borders.[49] Writing in 1925, Konstantin Oganezov made a compelling case for archiving cultural difference and regional material cultures: "We have to send cameramen to all corners of the USSR, and their footage will be of enormous importance. Many of the poorly studied people are dying out. . . . It is all the more important to preserve them on film."[50] Dziga Vertov's ethnographic documentary *A Sixth Part of the World* was made the same year Morden

FIGURE 16.3 Screenshot of close-up of man's face shot in East Turkestan, *Morden–Clark Expedition* film.

and Clark traveled through the region, and along with *Salt for Svanetia*, shot in Georgia in 1930 by Mikhail Kalatozov, is a key example of the *kulturfilm's* textual practices and ideologies.[51]

Clark's choice of what to shoot seems motivated as much by an attempt to capture the sensory contours of what he witnessed as to construct a scientific record, an experience that infuses his writing about traveling by camel at night: "I can close my eyes and see the dim shapes of our thirty camels looking huge and weird against the background of snow that lay gray in the faint starlight. I can hear the camel bells clanging [. . .] in the darkness, their sounds punctuated, now and then, by the shouts of the caravan men—shouts that end eerily in high falsetto notes."[52] Clark appears to "see" the experience cinematically, even as a multimedia event, with sound as striking as the visuals. Camel riding had a soporific effect on Morden, who confessed to falling asleep atop the animal, although both he and Clark hated riding inside the *johs* (felt-covered wooden constructions slung on either side of the camel), since it gave them terrible motion sickness.[53] (Draping oneself artfully over a donkey's neck during a long night-time trek was the technique favored by porters.)[54] Morden seem to channel Andalusian Sufi poet Abu al-Hasan al-Shustari's sensual experience of camel riding under the cloak of darkness across the Central Asian desert in his thirteenth-century poem:

> Desire drives the camels on the night journey
> When sleep calls out to their eyelids.
> Slacken the reins and let them lead, for they
> Know the abode of the Nijad as well as anyone.[55]

Clark uses the visual power of shots of the long camel march, as well as the rhythmic abstraction of the camel's feet, to evoke the timeless quality of this mode of transportation; there's a quasi-mystical quality to the visual aesthetics of this sequence, something that cinema, like Sufi poetry, is preternaturally disposed to capture. The desert's representation as a place of wonder and bewilderment in Arab poetry finds expression not only in the iconography of narrative feature films set in desert locations but also in Morden's description of the surreal silhouettes of the camels and Clark's medium close-up of their feet. There's an uncanny symmetry in Clark's decision to film the camels walking, echoing the close-up of oxen and human feet commingled at the beginning of the film.

The final fifteen minutes of the film contain some of its most visually striking and eclectic footage, including shots of a day laborer smoking opium, medium-close-up swish pans of children dashing about before the camera, and a man on horseback holding a bird of prey. Gutchenztse is the last re-outfitting post before crossing Mongolia to Urga, where Morden and Clark hired a camel train, a Turkestan guide, and a Mongolian interpreter. It is also the last location before the fateful encounter with the Mongolian police. Information about the thirty-six-hour kidnapping is conveyed via five map inserts with animated pop-up captions: "Captured and tortured by Mongols"; "Preventing carrying out our proposed trip across Mongolia"; "Taken back to Kobdo under armed guard"; "By weapon and sleigh to R.R. [railroad]"; "Christmas Day took train east"; and "Arrived Pekin New Year's Day." Absent from the cinematic record of the expedition, although a dramatic highlight in *all* other accounts, the kidnapping transformed the two men into national heroes for showing American manliness in the face of adversity.

The film concludes with a return to the opening visual polemic of "man versus nature." The incongruity of an image of Morden riding a tiny donkey at the front of a long line of camels across the Dzungarian plains, the line broken up only by another small donkey, could be straight out of a Buster Keaton film, although as Ira Jacknis reminds us, the image of the explorer riding ahead of his caravan, "while the rest blend into a file that gets smaller and smaller until it disappears into the landscape," is a familiar trope of expedition photography and film.[56] One cannot help but think of the closing shots of *Nanook* during this sequence, when the snowstorm transforms the husky sled dogs into abstract sculptures and a shot of Nanook's sleeping face filling the frame foreshadows his death. In the closing moments of the *MCE*, close-ups of the camel's feet trudging through the snow are intercut with repeated extreme long shots of the camel train reduced to dots on the landscape; the heavy snow plays perceptual games, as resting camels begin to resemble the mounds of supplies. By engendering pathos and ennobling the expedition, elevating it into a quasi-spiritual quest, the sequence is among the most memorable of the film, coming closest to imprinting deep impressions of the environment on the spectator's mind. The word "impression," with its nod to indexicality as well as a more ethereal intuition, seems especially appropriate in the context of expedition cinema. At its height, the genre deploys cinema's ability both to capture what Siegfried Kracauer called "life at its least controllable" as well as evoke life at its least inscribable, what Jennifer Fay in *Inhospitable Worlds* calls a "contingent and fragmented reality that film reflects back to us."[57]

Safely Home in New York: The Morden and Clark Expedition in the Media and Museum

Morden's and Clark's return to the United States became a media event, as their kidnapping mobilized discourses of American grit, racial superiority, and imperialist expansion in the national press. The *New York Times* called their expedition "one of the most dangerous and adventuresome trips in modern times," anointing the explorers "the only pure-blooded white men in the wilds of central Asia at the time."[58] Portrayals of marauding Mongolians lying in wait for unsuspecting Americans dominated the headlines: "Explorers Back with Marks of Torture," "Museum Scientists Narrowly Escape Being Shot by Mongols," and "Mongol Savages Torture Museum Hunt Director" all dramatized the human ordeal over the scientific aims of the project.[59] The figure of the fearless globe-trotting scientist was well established in the nineteenth century, supporting claims of credibility, since it is precisely "*because* [explorers] act heroically that their testimonials can be believed."[60] As Justin Marozzi reminds us in *The Way of Herodotus*, drama and tall stories are exactly what audiences expect in a lecture:

> When we're listening to a mountaineer discuss his latest expedition, we want frostbite and arguments in raging snowstorms, we'd like a broken leg, disaster on the summit, an avalanche in the descent, perhaps an abortive rescue mission, maybe a death while we're at it, above all we want triumph and tragedy[,] for this is an intoxicating cocktail. There's nothing worse than the bloodlessly teetotal story that everything went to plan, the expedition was successful and no one was hurt.[61]

However, if equipping expeditions with the tools of filmmaking became commonplace for large museums of science and natural history by the early 1920s, there was less certainty about what to do with the resulting footage. *MCE* was included among a long list of zoological specimens—the 1927 *Annual Report* noted that in addition to a "fine series of skins, complete skeletons, and full scientific measurements," Morden and Clark had amassed a "*complete record of the trip* in motion pictures, still photographs, and field notes."[62] However, unlike the taxidermy specimens that found a prominent home in the Northern Asiatic Hall, the associated film seemed to have no guaranteed audience. Possessing limited resources to explore how motion pictures might be integrated into gallery exhibits, the AMNH fell back on the familiar model of screening brief extracts in public lectures at the Museum, while granting the filmmaker freedom to screen excerpts or the entire film in private and public talks elsewhere. While the AMNH seemed determined not to be left behind in an era of visually centered mass media, the expedition footage they sponsored was turned over to the institution's education department, often with little attention to the content and production circumstances of the footage, and was used primarily to illustrate popular auditorium lectures rather than for research.[63]

The Morden–Clark footage was also used in the manner of home movies, when in April 1927, AMNH president Henry Fairfield Osborn invited Mr. and Mrs. Morden and "some of the younger trustees" to a special dinner and screening at the Osborns' Fifth Avenue home.[64] As expedition sponsor and director, Morden owned the rights to the film, although for tax purposes, he donated it to the AMNH, asking in return that he be allowed to have an *ovis poli* ram for his personal collection.[65] Morden also oversaw arrangements for processing and editing the negative, telling George Sherwood in a series of letters that the negative should be turned over to a Mr. Holland and that the five-hundred-foot containers of "positive cutouts" would be delivered to a Miss Holland.[66] So while the general public had ample access to the expedition photographs that were published in popular magazines, there is little evidence of extensive public exposure of the expedition's filmmaking efforts; based on extant archival material, the film never found an audience beyond a limited public lecture circuit, trustees' homes, the Explorers Club on Manhattan's Upper East Side, and within the AMNH itself.

The limited clues we have about the film's exhibition history include an undated flier (see figure 16.4) for an illustrated Morden lecture with "motion pictures and lantern

Flier for Morden "Across Asia's Snows and Deserts" illustrated lecture

FIGURE 16.4 Flyer for illustrated lecture with lantern slides and motion pictures delivered by William J. Morden, most likely at the Explorers Club in New York City as part of a book tour for *Across Asia's Snows and Deserts* in December 1935. Courtesy AMNH Special Collections, file 1214.1.

slides" that was most likely part of a 1935 book tour, since it shared the book's title, *Across Asia's Snows and Deserts*; a talk given by Clark to a packed house of women at the Explorers Club as part of the "'No-Smoking' Smokers Ladies Night" lecture series on April 8, 1927, in which his "vivid account of the travel" offered sensational details about their "fearful adventures experienced when crossing the interior of Mongolia at the hands of the robbers who ached to become murderers";[67] and a men-only version of the same lecture at an "Explorers Club Outing" to Bayside, Queens, on June 2, 1927, which purportedly made the "hair of his hearers [stand] on end and the blood [run] cold in their veins."[68] Clark lectured with the film into the 1930s, including a talk as part of a new lecture series at the Horace Bushnell Memorial Hall (now the Bushnell Center for the Performing Arts) in Hartford, Connecticut, in 1932.[69] All of this points to the film's circumscribed past in the professional lecture circuit, what Gregg Mitman sees as expedition film's vitality as a material object and cultural artifact, "created for one purpose, archived for another, and resurrected again for quite another reason."[70]

SHAPING A LEGACY: MAKING SENSE OF EXPEDITION CINEMA

What sense we ultimately make of the *MCE* must take into consideration its tonal complexity; in this respect the film negotiates discrete contradictions, including juxtapositions between military-style marching or salutes to the camera; more ludic moments, such as images of Russian soldiers from the military post dancing and splashing around in their makeshift sunken bath; and affectionate close-ups of locals smiling at the camera. The film's position as an empirical record of transportation logistics and cross-cultural exchange stands in uncertain relation to its status as a work of imagination composed of "sense impressions" of people's faces, material culture, and responses to the visual spectacle of the expedition. The expedition film was steeped in the exhibition culture of the late nineteenth-century naturalist tradition of collecting undertaken by "explorer types," a tradition Bell and Hasinoff describe as comprising a spectrum of "'amateur' and 'serious' naturalists—tied together through naturalist unions, explorers clubs, and natural history museums."[71] Lacking the visibility of expedition films such as *Grass* and *Chang*, the *MCE*'s authority and credibility derived from its affiliation with the five Asiatic expeditions led by Roy Chapman Andrews and the personae of Morden and Clark, rather than its ability to succeed as a stand-alone cinematic experience.

Despite the relatively limited circulation of the *MCE* beyond the AMNH itself, the film nevertheless offers some striking lessons. The film testifies to the unavoidably meta and recursive quality of expedition cinema generally, evoked in the repeated shots of the porters and pack animals, the campsite, and expedition leaders. These images shore up the evidentiary power of the film, providing seemingly incontrovertible evidence about the difficulty of traversing great distances by means of primitive modes of transportation. Through Clark's choice of what to film and what to exclude, the experience of the expedition has been submitted to a "regime of censorship, abstention, and discipline" that Johannes Fabian argues transforms the authority of fieldwork's "been there" into institutionalized, disembodied knowledge.[72] And yet this putative objectivity underestimates the film's affective power, its negotiation of ways of seeing that, while influenced by the picturesque optics of the commercial travelogue, is never reducible to a monolithic Western gaze. In some respects, Clark's footage shares some of the behavioral norms of the Arabic concept of *adab*, a way of presenting oneself in public that conforms to high standards of etiquette, good manners, morals, decency, and decorum. The footage rarely offends or shows anything abject (save the hunted animals), and explicit racist attitudes can hardly be gleaned from the footage alone.

Nevertheless, while depicting the arresting landscapes, wildlife, and human populations of Marco Polo's trade routes, the film fails to address the uncomfortable tensions in Morden's and Clark's status as Western observers, although their wealth and privilege are metaphorically inscribed in the scale of the enterprise. Their assumption that their white skin, American passports, permits, and letters of introduction would guarantee them safe passage across politically unstable Outer Mongolia suggests a misplaced confidence in their own position as travelers. Morden's and Clark's small talk, cinematic and otherwise, may have served to lubricate the implicit social contract that permitted their passage and their filmmaking, but it failed to fully obscure the underlying relations of power and privilege fundamental to the encounter. And while Clark's cinematic images of the expedition conjure up a benign and open-minded global adventurer, Morden's diaries tell a different story, revealing his disgust at the Indigenous customs and peoples he encounters and grumblings about the physical and mental ordeal of travel.

MCE also reveals the disposition of expedition filmmakers more generally to display a restless, slightly anxious aesthetic seemingly never quite knowing what to look at or for how long. In Clark's case, he seems to have followed his instincts as a photographer, since 80 percent of the photographs illustrating Morden's 1927 "By Coolie and Caravan" *Natural History* article are also the subjects of motion pictures, taken at the same time and place (we often see the same bystanders and stray dogs in the frames of each). Travel is never simply about pure physical movement but is freighted with cultural significance and inconveniences large and small, everything from the climate to food to standards of personal hygiene. That a film like the *MCE* oscillates between a poetics of amazement and a poetics of the mundane reflects to a large extent the undulating flow of travel, the visual highlights along with moments of monotony. Jane Gaines's characterization of history in the context of polar exploration as "both authoritative *and* mysterious," is an apt description of the ineffable quality of expeditions as well as their significance as geopolitical acts.[73] In this respect, the film negotiates discordant elements, evidence of its status as an empirical record of transportation logistics and cross-cultural exchange as well as a work of the imagination and self-representation that represses as much as it reveals.

Finally, while similar in some respects to the ethnographic travelogue, expedition cinema's economic value as public entertainment, while important, was not its primary reason for existence. For the AMNH and other institutions, expeditions played a key role in collection building, exhibit preparation, professionalizing and popularizing anthropology, and public promotion. As Ira Jacknis observes, expeditions did not simply amass material culture and shape the understanding of the variety of cultural forms but literally spurred the growth of institutions, as new wings were built to house large collections.[74] And while we learn something of the expedition's external landscapes, challenges, and obsessions, and catch glimpses into Morden's and Clark's interiorities from multiple written and visual sources, the expedition film affords some latitude in making sense of the entire endeavor. In fact, given the preponderance of wide shots in their footage, the film evokes the qualities of contemporary VR explorations of exotic landscapes, promising spectators' greater agency in deciding what to look at. As storytelling, the *MCE* has a bare narrative at best, and were it not for the map inserts, the film would read as an assemblage of shots of different modes of travel in different climates with different people helping out or getting caught up in the melee. The expedition was the equivalent of the circus coming to town, a comparison not lost on Lieutenant Jérôme Becker, a member of the 1887 Belgian International African Association Third Expedition to Africa, who Fabian says compared "an expedition's equipment to the props needed for a theatrical performance," a spectacle as well for the local population that came out to see what all the fuss was about.[75] James Clifford's definition of an expedition as a "sensorium moving through space" provides a provocative invitation for us to think more expansively about the visual output of expeditions and to place this material on equal footing with the "amalgams of human, material, technical, and intellectual objects comprising an expedition."[76] As small villages moving through unfamiliar and challenging landscapes, expeditions required and represented enormous institutional power and human ambition, and their scattered filmic record, often buried in the archive for almost a century, now invites the attention and audience it never attained.

Notes

1. Joshua A. Bell and Erin L. Hasinoff, "Introduction: The Anthropology of Expeditions," in Bell and Hasinoff, eds., *The Anthropology of Expeditions: Travel, Visualities, Afterlives* (New York: Bard Graduate Center, 2015), 1.
2. For a useful primer on the expedition film's diverse institutional contexts, see Joshua A. Bell, Alison K. Brown, and Robert J. Gordon, eds., *Reinventing First Contact: Expeditions, Anthropology, and Popular Culture* (Washington, DC: Smithsonian Institution Press, 2013). For more on the AMNH's earliest sponsorship of an expedition to the American Southwest, see Alison Griffiths, *Wondrous Difference: Cinema, Anthropology, and Turn-of-the-Century Visual Culture* (New York: Columbia University Press, 2002), 283–311.
3. The AMNH played a major role in lending its institutional authority (if not significant funding) to sponsored expeditions, underwriting one of the landmark expeditions of the late nineteenth century, the Jesup North Pacific Expedition, among communities on both sides of the Bering Strait.

4. Norwegian ethnologist Carl Lumholtz's expeditions to Mexico (1890–1910) and Borneo (1913–17) are examples of lone-wolf expeditions; for more on the Borneo research, which was captured in the 1920 film *In Borneo, the Land of the Head-Hunters*, see Alison Griffiths, "Through Central Borneo with Carl Lumholtz: The Visual and Textual Output of a Norwegian Explorer," in Eirik Frisvold Hanssen and Maria Fosheim Lund, eds., *Small Country, Long Journeys: Norwegian Expedition Films* (Oslo: National Museum of Oslo Press, 2017), 136–177.
5. For a chronology of the Asiatic expeditions see http://data.library.amnh.org/archives-authorities/id/amnhc_2000167. In a letter to the Chicago Field Museum's president Stanley Field in September 1926, Osborn reported how the Asiatic Expedition had been "completely blocked by General Fung's army" from accessing every route from China into Mongolia. In the wake of three dangerous attempts, Andrews had given up and returned to San Francisco. The success of the Morden–Clark expedition was viewed as something of a consolation in light of the aborted Asiatic Expedition; letter to Field from Osborn, September 1, 1926, File 1214.1 1926-1928 Morden-Clark Expedition, American Museum of Natural History Central Archives [hereafter AMNH-CA], New York, New York. For a brief overview of Andrews's career, see the last section of Roy Chapman Andrews, *Beyond Adventure: The Lives of Three Explorers* (New York: Duell, Sloan, and Pearce, 1962), 145ff.
6. Morden's Field Associate title was an honorific one, and, like the figure of the traveler itself, he was something of a liminal figure at the Museum, present as a funder but not employed in a department or on payroll.
7. Johannes Fabian, *Out of Our Minds: Reason and Madness in the Exploration of Central Africa* (Berkeley: University of California Press, 2000), 39.
8. For more on the travelogue, see Jennifer Peterson, *Education in the School of Dreams: Travelogues and Early Nonfiction Films* (Durham, NC: Duke University Press, 2013).
9. For more on key characteristics of the expedition film, see Alison Griffiths, "The Untrammeled Camera: A Topos of the Expedition Film," *Film History* 25, nos. 1–2 (2013): 95–109.
10. For example, lengthy excerpts from letters Clark wrote his wife on April 24 from Misgar, India, and on May 9 from the Russian Pamirs are included in "The Morden–Clark Asiatic Expedition," *Natural History,* September–October 1926, 432–434. The letters are cast as "interesting side lights on the activities of the expedition"; Clark refers to the cold being of the "mild kind and is not as bitter as that we get at home," and notes that he is taking some interesting pictures (433).
11. Mark Hobart, "Ethnography as a Practice, or the Unimportance of Penguins," *Europaea* 2, no. 1 (1996): 1.
12. Hourari Touati discusses the idea of sublimated discourses in his fascinating chapter "The Price of Travel," in his *Islam and Travel in the Middle Ages* (Chicago, IL: University of Chicago Press, 2010), 94.
13. See James E. Montgomery, "Travelling Autopsies: Ibn Fadlan and the Bulghar," *Middle Eastern Literature* 7, no. 1 (January 2004): 14, 19.
14. Andrews, *Beyond Adventure*, 213. Fund-raising was time-consuming and relentless; according to Andrews, "I haunted Wall Street, spoke at luncheons, went to teas, public lectures in the evenings, wrote four magazine articles and a book. . . . Peary and all the other important explorers had gone through the same ordeal. It was the price one had to pay" (210, 213).

15. New York City's appropriation for maintenance and education in 1926 was $369,737.06, $270,000 less than the amount needed to run educational programs and other vital divisions. The Museum's ability to service New York City schools was hit hard by a massive growth in school-age children between 1915 (1,300,000) and 1925 (5,400,000). The operating costs of the Department of Education rose from $11,478.38 in 1915 to $53,394.50 in 1925, an amount that included a grant of $15,000 from the Carnegie Foundation and $5,000 from the Cleveland H. Dodge Foundation. Press Release "Financial and Administrative Report," Jan. 4, 1926, 1, File 1214.1, AMNH-CA.
16. "Financial and Administrative Report," 1.
17. Andrews, *Beyond Adventure*, 207. Vice President of the AMNH J. P. Morgan donated fifty thousand dollars to the expedition, telling Andrews, "Now you go out and get the rest" (Andrews, *Beyond Adventure*, 210).
18. File 1214.4 1926-1928 Morden-Clark Expedition, AMNH-CA.
19. The goal, Morden declared, was to "get you people [the AMNH] a group of Poli, if they can be found." File 1214.4 1926-1928 Morden-Clark Expedition, AMNH-CA. The Asiatic Hall was one of three new buildings under construction in 1926: the others were the Oceanic Hall (location of the giant whale) and the School Service Building. The construction project operated with a budget of $3,000,000; "Extracts from Minutes," Annual Meeting Feb. 5, 1923 (Jan. 1926), 1, File 1117, AMNH-CA.
20. "News from the Field," *Natural History* (January–February 1927): 108.
21. Based in New York City, the Explorers Club (EC) grew, and in some cases absorbed, membership from the Arctic Club of America (started in 1897, but petering out by the 1920s), the Perry Arctic Club, the Scott Arctic Club, the Women's Geographer's Society, the Audubon Society, and the Angler. Conceived in 1904, the EC viewed itself as a "meeting point and unifying force for explorers and scientists worldwide." It sent out six hundred expeditions a year to land, sea, and space, created archives of 550 million feet, a fourteen-thousand-volume library, and a thousand artifacts, spanning artwork to taxidermy. See *Life: The Greatest Adventure of All Time* (New York: Time Books, 2000). Flag notice from *The Explorer's Journal* 5, no. 1 (January–March 1926): 16. Flag #5 was mailed to Marseilles, France, where it was retrieved by Clark. It was returned to the EC on the evening of April 7, 1927, when Clark gave the illustrated "Ladies Night" lecture. The same flags are passed down from expedition to expedition; there are currently 222 flags at the EC.
22. Clark wrote "Chinese Turkestan," *Natural History* 34, no. 4 (1934): 345–360; "Expeditions to Central Asia," in James L. Clark, *Good Hunting: Fifty Years of Collecting and Preparing Habitat Groups for the American Museum* (Norman: University of Oklahoma Press, 1966).
23. Such groups were often made from life casts of the heads of Indigenous people, sometimes including topographically accurate painted backgrounds copied from photographs, and specimens of material culture that shored up the indexicality of the display. The nuclear family tableaux revealed certain cultural differences between the Western observer and Indigenous peoples. For more on life and habits groups installed at the AMNH, and the debates they engendered around illusion versus science, see Alison Griffiths, *Wondrous Difference: Cinema, Anthropology, and Turn-of-the-Century Visual Culture* (New York: Columbia University Press, 2002), 3–45.
24. Writings by William J. Morden include "By Coolie and Caravan Across Central Asia," *National Geographic Magazine* 52, no. 4 (October 1927): 369–431.
25. Clark, *Good Hunting*, 88. They traveled along the northern edge of the Taklamakan desert, heading into the Tien Shan mountains to shoot spiked ibex and roe deer, and eventually reached Urumchi, the capital of Chinese Turkestan, in October 1926.

26. Peter N. Miller, "Preface," in Joshua A. Bell and Erin L. Hasinoff, eds., *The Anthropology of Expeditions: Travel, Visualities, Afterlives* (Chicago, IL: University of Chicago Press, 2015), lx.
27. Ibid.
28. In light of contemporary debate over Marco Polo's life and writing we must place what Clark says about his ancestral muse within its proper context of epistemological uncertainty. See Marco Polo, *The Travels*, trans. and with an introduction and notes by Nigel Cliff (London: Penguin Classics, 2016). The book goes by the titles *Le Divisament du monde* ("The Description of the World") and *Il milione* by Marco Polo's contemporaries. For scholarship on Marco Polo, see John Larner, *Marco Polo and the Discovery of the World* (New Haven, CT: Yale University Press, 1999); Peter Jackson, "Marco Polo and His 'Travels,'" *Bulletin of the School of Oriental and African Studies* 61, no. 1 (1998): 82–101; and Suzanne Conklin Akbari and Amilcare Inannucci, eds., *Marco Polo and the Encounter of East and West* (Toronto, ON: University of Toronto Press, 2008). Netflix also produced a two-season TV series called *Marco Polo* (2015).
29. Clark, *Good Hunting*, 71.
30. Jackson, "Marco Polo and His Travels," 83.
31. Morden and Clark were presumed to be spies, "the advance party of some invading force." They were subjected to a wrist-binding form of torture used in Mongol jails for thirty-six hours until released and escorted by armed guard out of the region. For a detailed description of events leading up to, during, and in the aftermath of the torture, see Morden, "By Coolie," 425–431. Also see Morden, "Mongolian Interlude," in Frederick A. Blossom, ed., *Told at the Explorers Club* (New York: Albert & Charles Boni, 1931).
32. Karen C. Pinto, "Cartography and Geography," in Richard C. Martin, ed., *Encyclopedia of Islam and the Muslim World*, vol. 1 (New York: Macmillan, 2004), 128; Morden, "Mongolian Interlude."
33. Dhahabi, *Siyar A'lam al-Nubala*, ed. Shu'ayb al-Arna'uti et al., 25 vols. (Beirut: Mu'assasat al-Risalah), 13:265, cited in Touati, "The Price of Travel," 87.
34. Clark, *Good Hunting*, 80.
35. Morden, "How Central Asia," 148–149.
36. Ravi Vasudevan, "Official and Amateur: Exploring Information Film in India 1920s–40s," in Lee Grieveson and Colin McCabe, eds., *Film and the End of Empire* (London: BFI, 2011), 89.
37. Clark trained at the Rhode Island School of Design and spent much of his time as a curator at the AMNH designing and constructing illusionistic groups of taxidermy animals.
38. Clark, *Good Hunting*, 75.
39. Morden, "Marco Polo's Sheep," 488. According to Morden, "telescopes were essential in hunting the wary animals. Only by locating them at great distances, and stalking them very carefully, could they be approached at all" (489).
40. Morden, "By Coolie and Caravan," 387.
41. When Clark wounded a sheep with a "smashed hind leg," he aimed from thirty yards away, "scoring a body shot that tore the lungs to pieces." Still alive, the ram ran another hundred yards before finally collapsing. Though too damaged to mount in an exhibit, the animal was successfully skinned. Morden Field Work Diaries, May 6, 1926, and April 9, 1926, AMNH-CA.
42. The gruesome reality of hunting *poli* is censored in the extant version, which conceals the extensive blood stains and gaping holes in the sheep's bodies that Morden writes about in his diary, in favor of the celebratory iconography of the safari trophy shot of the head and horns. Clark, *Good Hunting*, 82.

43. Clark, *Good Hunting*, 75.
44. Morden, "By Coolie and Caravan," 488. The sound of the Eymo motion picture camera scared the sheep, even though Clark gave the camera to an Indigenous porter to use as he crawled along on his belly toward the herd. Clark, *Good Hunting*, 489.
45. Bronislaw Malinowski, *Argonauts of the Western Pacific: An Account of Native Enterprise and Adventure in the Archipelagoes of Melanesian New Guinea* (London: Routledge & Kegan Paul, 1922).
46. Sheldon Hsiao-peng Lu, *From Historicity to Fictionality: The Chinese Poetics of Narrative* (Stanford, CA: Stanford University Press, 1994), 43, cited in Gang Zhou, "Small Talk: A New Reading of Marco Polo's *Il milione*," *Modern Language Notes* 124, no. 1 (January 2009): 11.
47. Lu, *From Historicity to Fictionality*, cited in Zhou, "Small Talk," 11.
48. Morden and Clark also "indulged in a welcome hot bath" while the temperature outside was below freezing, although there is only footage of the Russians doing so. Morden, "By Coolie and Caravan," 386.
49. Oksana Sarkisova, *Screening Soviet Nationalities: Kulturfilms from the Far North to Central Asia* (London: I. B. Taurus, 2017), 2.
50. Konstantin Oganezov, "Kino i etnografiia," *Sovetskii ekran* 19 (1925): n.p., cited in Sarkisova, *Screening Soviet Nationalities*, 7.
51. For more on Vertov's *Sixth Part of the World*, see chapter two of Sarkisova's *Screening Soviet Nationalities*. Also see Yuri Tsivian, ed., *Lines of Resistance: Dziga Vertov and the Twenties*, trans. Julian Graffy (Sacile/Pordenone, Italy: Le Giornate del Cinema Muto, 2004); and Emma Widdis, *Visions of a New Land: Soviet Film from the Revolution to the Second World War* (New Haven, CT.: Yale University Press, 2003).
52. Morden, "How Central Asia," 153. The camels were exceptionally efficient travelers, loaded with four to five hundred pounds of freight and averaging between two and two-and-a-half miles per hour.
53. Morden, "By Coolie and Caravan," 423.
54. Morden, "How Central Asia," 158.
55. "Desire Drives the Camels." in Abu al-Hasan al-Shushtari, *Songs of Love and Devotion*, trans. and introduced by Lourdes Maria Alvarez (Mahwah, NJ: Paulist Press, 2009): 108–109.
56. Ira Jacknis, "In the Field/*En Plein Air*: The Art of Anthropological Display at the American Museum of Natural History," in Bell and Hasinoff, *Anthropology of Expedition*, 5.
57. Jennifer Fay, *Inhospitable World: Cinema in the Time of the Anthropocene* (New York: Oxford University Press, 2018), 179.
58. Anonymous, "Adventuresome Trip Through Turkestan, Mongolia and Lower Siberia Will Be Theme of Program on Tuesday," *New York Times*, April 3, 1927, X22. The *Times* had contacted the AMNH about an exclusive before the expedition left northern India, hoping for photographs for their Rotogravure Section features, Mid-Week Pictorial, and World-Wide Photos Syndicate (Letter from *New York Times* to George Sherwood, March 20, 1926, File 1214.1, AMNH-CA). C. L. Bowman of Standard Oil also contacted the AMNH, asking for a list of planned expeditions, in the hopes of product placement for their insect repellents (letter October 7, 1926, File 1214.1, AMNH-CA).
59. Press coverage includes: "Morden and Clark Back: Museum Scientists Narrowly Escape Being Shot by Mongols," *New York Times*, February 10, 1927, 25; "Explorers Back with Marks of Torture," *Boston Daily Globe*, February 10, 1927, 10; "Explorers Tell Story of

Torture," *LA Times*, February 10, 1927; and "Mongol Savages Torture Museum Hunt Director," *LA Times*, February 20, 1927, 4.

60. Henrika Kyklick, "Science as Adventure," in Bell and Hasinoff, *Anthropology of Expeditions*, 35, 36. Emphasis added.
61. Justin Marozzi, *The Way of Herodotus: Travels with the Man who Invented History* (Cambridge, MA: DaCapo Press, 2008), 70.
62. "Chief Expeditions for the Year 1927," AMNH *Annual Report* (1927): 18–19. Emphasis added.
63. Jacknis, "In the Field," 84.
64. Letter from Osborn to Sherwood, April 16, 1927, in File # 1150, AMNH-CA.
65. Letter from Sherwood to Morden, 6/13/29; Letter from Morden to Sherwood, 6/15/27; Letter from Sherwood to Morden, 6/20/27, in Box # 1238 UNCL. M-Q 1927, AMNH-CA.
66. There is reference to twenty thousand feet of film in an entry in *The Explorer's Journal* 5, no. 4 (October–December 1926): 15. Letter from Clark to Sherwood, June 15, 1927, in Box #1214.4; and Letter from Clark to Sherwood, June 20, 1927, Box # 1238 UNCL. M-Q 1927, AMNH-CA.
67. James L. Clark, "Across Asia from Bombay to Pekin," *Explorer's Journal* 6, no. 2 (April–June. 1927): 10.
68. Anon., "Notes on This Year's Outing," *Explorer's Journal* 6, no. 2 (April–June. 1927): 9. Museum Director George Sherwood recommended Clark and the *MCE* film to those who contacted the AMNH about quality lecturers, confirming that Clark had "a fine series of pictures" and was an excellent speaker. Letter to William L. Bryant from Sherwood, May 2, 1927, File # 1927 1271c: DP, BOX #750, 1925-1970 Lectures recommended by Museum, AMNH-CA.
69. "Hazards of Trip Across Asia to Be Told at Bushnell," *Hartford Courant*, November 18, 1932, 6.
70. Gregory Mitman, "A Journey Without Maps: Film, Expeditionary Science, and the Growth of Development," in Gregory Mitman and Kelley Wilder, eds., *Documenting the World: Film, Ethnography, and the Scientific Record* (Chicago, IL: University of Chicago Press, 2016), 126.
71. Bell and Hasinoff, "Introduction," 7.
72. Fabian, *Out of Our Minds*, xii.
73. Jane M. Gaines, "The History Lesson in Amundsen's 1910–1912 South Pole Film Footage," in Eirik Frisvold Hanssen and Maria Fosheim Lund, eds., *Small Country, Long Journeys: Norwegian Expedition Films* (Oslo: Nasjonalbiblioteket, 2017), 62, http://www.academia.edu/35241782/Small_Country_Long_Journeys_Norwegian_Expedition_Films.
74. Jacknis, "In the Field," 275.
75. Fabian, *Out of Our Minds*, 122.
76. James Clifford, *Routes: Travel and Translation in the Late Twentieth Century* (Cambridge, MA: Harvard University Press, 1997) cited in Miller, "Preface," lx.

CHAPTER 17

BABIES AND BROCHURES

Public Service Pamphlet Films of the US Children's Bureau (1919–1926)

JENNIFER HORNE

COULD a movie prevent 300,000 American children a year from dying in the first weeks and years of life? What sort of film could mitigate the horrors of death in childbirth and numerous preventable infant diseases on such a tremendous scale? What if a film were publicized through seventeen thousand women's civic activity clubs, potentially reaching more than ten million American women already actively volunteering and energetically involved at the community level across the country? What if a helpful pamphlet were displayed in the film and every viewer who saw the film were handed the document shown in the film free of charge or found it at their public libraries or health department waiting areas? Furthermore, what if those same types of public services arranged film screenings and distributed the depicted brochure free throughout their cities and counties? These were the questions posed by the civil servants at the US Children's Bureau after 1914 and from a perspective definitively marked by their gender-differentiated social experience. Compelled by the growing commercial availability of health and hygiene motion pictures, and the agency's governmental mission to address a growing child mortality crisis, the Bureau's female employees pondered the effectiveness of moving-image media in multimedia civic health communication as a form of statecraft and moved eagerly toward in-house film production.

The establishment of the Children's Bureau within the US Department of Commerce and Labor in 1912 was a particular triumph of Progressive Era coalitions focused on changing conditions created in poverty that affected women's and children's domestic lives. It came after many years of congressional pressuring by elite and high-profile reform groups, including the prominent leaders of church, community, and women's organizations, and with the support of the National Child Labor Committee. Opposition to the legislation that would establish the agency came from predictable foes aligned with anti-labor corporate interests and the conservative National Congress of Mothers.

In the years leading up to the successful petitioning, arguments over the service charges of the Children's Bureau winnowed down the initially more ambitious design (which had included funding mothers' pensions) for a federal Bureau serving the broad interests of domestic workers with childrearing duties. Initially envisioned as an agency with tentacles reaching into education, agricultural sectors, and employment, the Bureau emerged as a leaner and more laissez-faire entity built to lend research guidance to national concerns of childhood health. Political compromises opened the door to a welfare trust and reform agenda that could be increasingly stage-managed by activist social workers, pediatricians and nurses, and leading sociological educators eager to participate in the shaping of public policy.[1] Even as these members of the white elite asserted the need for scientific solutions, their passionate outcries emanated from across the political spectrum, often tinged with nostalgic and sentimental imagery of humanitarian rescue, as they advocated for white middle-class society's social duty to immigrants and the poor. In a move immediately celebrated by women's club leaders and activists, President Taft signed the proposed legislation and named Julia C. Lathrop the Bureau's initial chief, making her the first female appointment at the head of a federal government bureau.[2]

Lathrop, an optimistic yet clear-eyed protégée of Jane Addams, came to her civil service post in Washington after years of anti-poverty work in Chicago. During those years at Hull-House, Lathrop's outlook toward the professional and political lives of healthcare and social workers was shaped by a strong desire to reform how public welfare agencies performed. Such reforms included career training in fields of social work open to educated white women, the standardization of services to the public made possible by embracing new methods of statistical research, and the efficient administration of state social welfare, free of meddlesome private benefaction. In this regard, Lathrop's arrival in Washington represents a critical turning point in the dominance of progressive maternalism's approach to the plight of the poor and a broadening acceptance of managerial roles for white women in child and family welfare services.[3]

The public service mandate for the Bureau was derived equally from moral and ethical ideals claiming "a right to childhood" for all as a fundamental protection owed to children and their parents by the government. This popular child welfare advocacy slogan was taken up by the agency for its publications and used by Lathrop in her public appearances in an explicit attempt to link her work to social justice. It was nebulous as a bureaucratic idea but succinct enough to conjure up just the right images to resonate with the modern practices that sketched visible contours of childhood as a protected domain apart from adulthood: nursery schooling; the building of recreation and play spaces; nutritional standards for infants; and other instruments to guide parental care from outside the family unit. In this way, "a right to childhood" demanded seemingly unassailable state protection for the sanctity of being young. Not only could it foster the Bureau's need to cultivate an imagined culture of happy, cherubic babies and bucolic scenes of kids at play, but the slogan also shifted attention away from feared childhood illnesses such as typhoid, diphtheria, and rickets. However, given the seriousness of such problems, the Bureau's staff would have to frame the protection of childhood in starker terms and develop for its public a program of more actionable civic behaviors in order to demonstrate its bureaucratic utility. How to achieve the balance between the sober and sentimental in government-issued written information was an immediately pressing question for Lathrop and her enterprising staff and a problem that a strategic use of films might potentially solve.

As has been consistently pointed out by her biographers, while Julia Lathrop was otherwise deeply movement-oriented, she was determined to avoid association with any activism that had the potential to brand her work as sympathetic to anti-corporate workplace labor reform.[4] The opportunity to garner public sympathy for hardships experienced by women in acts of *maternal* labor—an image one might think of in this period as a kind of iconic readymade carrying the force of mass pity and melodrama for the nation—was a far safer strategy. Ideally, the focus on child and maternal health could secure more family-minded cooperation from women's clubs and other civic organizations, an orientation that would increase volunteering and participation at the state and community level. Lathrop's decision led her to link this focus specifically to alarming rates of maternal and infant death, a statistical unicorn at a moment when census data or death reporting was scarce or unavailable. In this, and in other ways related to the image-making practices engaged in by her office over the next decade, she was effective and influential. Her legacy included helping to shape the politically volatile and divisive Sheppard-Towner Act of 1921 that significantly altered the clinical administration of maternal health through midwifery education and enabled the medicalization of pregnancy and childbirth on a national scale. In the years leading up to this achievement, guided by Lathrop's determination to make infant mortality legible as a national concern, the agency would produce some of the most widely circulated health information of the period, both onscreen and on paper.

As Molly Ladd-Taylor points out, the confirmation of Lathrop's appointment as chief of the Bureau reflected the bitter irony of women's gender-subordinated association with expertise in maternal caregiving, childrearing, and uncompensated domestic labor. That she was appointed to the position eight years before the vote for white women was granted "suggests both the power of dominant beliefs in women's responsibility for child welfare and the lack of importance attached to the new agency."[5] However, it was also Lathrop's power-restricted line of sight that emboldened her media-savvy approach to government reform. For, as historian Cecelia Tichi has noted, Lathrop's new approach to education took full advantage of both grassroots-movement-level transmission of ideas and the persuasive tools of modern, civically meaningful mass media.[6]

In this regard, the Children's Bureau's novel approach to a "coordinated program" of propaganda, not limited to but including cinema, indicates how Lathrop's public service mission sought to effectively disseminate social-scientific metrics as tangibly meaningful in the operations of her underfunded agency.[7] The earliest and most successful instruments created by the Bureau were serialized print pamphlets dispensing instruction based on the Bureau's gathered data and, in the earliest iteration, its research on infant mortality. Print pamphleting during this period was a medium of contingency and a ubiquitous feature of government information and bureaucratic communication. However, as I discuss below, the use of government pamphlets and informational brochures by the Children's Bureau built on practices of civic organizing, modes of official and grassroots club communications, and serial formats of community education that had a long and established history among charity and service groups, and by women's groups particularly. Lathrop's own authorial voice was in many ways honed as a writer of such publications. During her time at Hull-House, Lathrop had written information pamphlets to assist non-specialist volunteers from the community; these pamphlets functioned akin to handbooks of social-scientific data relaying the conditions of those housed in institutional care (including numbers of deaths, criminal histories, types of physical disabilities, for example).[8] Exactly what these pamphlets signified for women bureaucrats relates to both the widely understood power of political leafleting for the early women's movement and the institutionalizing of a certain type of sisterly comfort offered by a caregiver. As Tichi puts it, Lathrop envisioned her publication, *Suggestions for Visitors to County Poorhouses and to Other Public Charitable Institutions*, as being "welcoming as a hot cup of tea and yet coldly scientific as an evaluation tool."[9] Among the agency's first priorities, and following Lathrop's model, was the publication and distribution of Children's Bureau information in the format of a thorough but readable bifold pamphlet.

Prenatal Care (1913) and *Infant Care* (1914) promoted routine management, whether by calculating menstruation cycles, recommending sleeping and waking times, measuring quantities of food, or putting out supplies necessary for birth. Every aspect of the subject matter—even addressing disturbing states of mind brought on by worry and abuse—could be quantified in numbers of times per day, amounts necessary, appropriate hours. The pamphlets were written by a non-specialist, Mary Mills West, and included an official opening address from Lathrop situating the information as a matter of national and political consequence.[10] Mills's words spoke to the "average" mother, oddly, a tacit acknowledgment that poorer women would find it impossible to follow all of the guidance.[11] Nonetheless, her voice assured those receiving the document that the guidance provided therein was prepared for the public, with the expert help of medical and research specialists. Moreover, the pamphlet served as a manifestation of the right of women to possess full ability to care for their families. Supportive of this discourse, the crafting of these government publications sought to convey to a "collegial" readership of women the newfound view that childcare could become a "profession" underwritten by education and medical knowledge.[12]

Historians of pediatric health have noted that handbills by hygiene associations and state boards of health had long been distributed to the public as newspaper inserts, a modality of public-health instruction specifically used to address increasing infant mortality rates.[13] In some ways, while not disseminated in newspapers, the Bureau's publications were a continuation of a multimedia approach to distribution. As artifacts, however, the pamphlets *Prenatal Care* and *Infant Care* were also manifestations of the Children's Bureau's hard-won political and bureaucratic existence in three critical ways. First, the Bureau fashioned the series of publications as evidence of deeply felt beliefs in the new value of scientific motherhood and the social science disciplines that advanced the tools to study infant and child development. Second, the pamphlets urged the implementation of home practices to mitigate the looming tragedy of infant death and the ongoing population crisis, the very cause that lobbyists and pressure groups had used to justify the Bureau's establishment to lawmakers. Third, the graphic layout of the pamphlets favored lists of supplies and demonstrated tools of time-based recordkeeping to underscore the need for mothers to adopt these methods step by step—mandated processes in a gendered approach to childcare and physical labor in the home. Even more, as a government publication bearing the seal of the Department of Labor, the pamphlet's existence seemed to bear witness to reputable civic work, carrying a whiff of *documenticity*.[14]

Printed and mass-distributed written pamphlets were a standard information vehicle for all manner of official business and, in many ways, a necessary choice of format in early twentieth-century government communication meant to reach a broad audience.[15] What seems at first glance to be a dryly factual or neutral artifact of state propaganda takes on added significance when understood in the context of communicating with masses of women. Women's organizations had developed a deep familiarity with how written pamphlets (and the activity of distributing and receiving them) constructed their civic livelihoods and supported their political agency. More specifically, these types of publications had played a trusted role in organizing and disseminating information to women outside of newspapers and other periodicals perceived as sources of an unrelenting gender-based attack on women's spheres of suffrage and community. In such contexts, print pamphleteering had been central to more conventional means of undergirding social movements and debate, and even a mechanism to spread religious zealotry. Information pamphlets carried strong connotations from other literary forms of character-building and from earlier campaigns for cultural self- and community-improvement that also occurred in burgeoning areas of motion picture regulation and exhibition.

Sixty-three thousand copies of *Infant Care* were distributed the year of its publication, with one-and-a-half million copies circulated by 1921. By 1985 the unsentimental but care-oriented booklet was considered to be the government's biggest blockbuster pamphlet.[16] Reportedly creating a demand for pamphlets too high in number for the Bureau to meet, the publication's success later translated into a significant increase in employees for the Children's Bureau, as Congress increased appropriations, allowing the size of the agency to grow from fifteen to seventy-five by 1920.[17] The "Care of Children" (the name of the series in which *Infant Care* and *Prenatal Care* appeared) pamphlets circulated alongside the periodic transmission of transition-era media culture that included serial films and the "film magazine"-type of non-fiction programmed at neighborhood theaters. To be sure, the primary information ecosystem into which these documents were released was already laden with public health and hygiene advising at the state and regional levels, intermingling and perhaps in conflict with the fair displays, eugenic tracts, and better-baby information women were likely encountering.[18]

For Lathrop, the pamphlets delivered compelling scientific census data that provided evidence of the need for vigilant "baby-saving" measures to the public in the form of a manageable guide. Compiling infant mortality statistics by combining birth and death records had not been done before, but the resulting figures confirmed the as-yet-unsupported claims of infant health advocates, eugenics leaders, and organizations supporting visiting nurses.[19] Citing alarming figures of prenatal death and infant mortality—forty-two percent of newborns in the first year of life in 1911—Lathrop linked the publications to a crisis of national mortality: "The existence of these facts justified the publication of a pamphlet on prenatal care."[20] In this way, prenatal and infant mortality could be presented as a national emergency requiring the public's acceptance of modernized knowledge and participation in the country's first large-scale birth registration initiatives. Using the spectral cause of race suicide, maternalism and advice manuals could function jointly to map the citizenry, relying on traditional discourse about the home while claiming to protect privacy of the family to make the perceived intrusion of government expertise more palatable. Coded references to legitimate birthright were worked into the very first printing of *Infant Care*: its opening line advised mothers to register their birth as a "service to render" to their newborn.

***

Headlining the Bureau's propaganda program, the Children's Bureau's pamphlets met the conventional needs of information that would be supplied nationally through state departments of health and civic organizations. Given the publication's successful dissemination of the Bureau's mission, the potentially broader reach of cinema doubtless motivated Lathrop's openness to other media forms, spurring the agency's interactions with film exhibitors and suppliers of educational film at this time. Lathrop's stamped signature on outgoing letters related to film work in the effort to "get a square deal for children," if only a signifier of top-down leadership and bureaucratic process, demonstrated her literal endorsement of motion pictures as a tool of civic education.[21] She authorized her publicity staff—none of whom had experience in the new fields of sponsored filmmaking—to contract outside filmmakers to produce motion pictures in bolstering birth registration and health reform operations. Lathrop's leadership in this regard gave a particular tone and purpose to the agency's approach to motion picture production that did not continue under her immediate successors. While the Children's Bureau's staff created its multimedia film campaign under Julia Lathrop's "baby-saving" birth certification agenda, after Lathrop's tenure the agency struggled to position itself within the business climate of instructional and industrial filmmaking. Against its attempts to avoid sentimentalizing and patronizing narratives and maintain a coordinated, editorial control over the way the films related to the pamphlets, the Bureau ultimately ceded authority to its sponsored filmmaker.

The Panama-Pacific International Exposition of 1915 in San Francisco marked a turning point for the Children's Bureau, proving the importance of film screenings for its visibility; this experience accelerated the staff and Lathrop's familiarity with the cost of production, issues of projection and rental, and the handling and storage of government-owned film negatives. Although the Children's Bureau had only completed its first civil-service examinations to hire employees in late 1914, by the spring of 1915 the agency was already distributing an infant-health slide lecture and two short films, one of which was produced for the agency by the Edison Manufacturing Co., timed for release at the Exposition site.[22] By no means was the agency the only federal agency projecting its information to the public on large screens. Programs of what Jennifer Zwarich termed "federal films" were installed in one viewing space at the Panama Pacific Exposition and reflected the multiplicity of film bureaus within the US Government after 1914, each one seeking to attach the most modern and often industrialized spectacle to its presentation of service to the American public.[23] Documentary film historians, including Richard Dyer MacCann and Zwarich, write that US federal agencies had been making and distributing documentary and educational film since at least 1908, when the Department of Agriculture filmed its secretary, James Wilson, giving an address at a 4-H meeting.[24] However, the popularity and success of state film reception at the Panama Pacific Exposition "catalyzed the work of federal filmmakers and set a meaningful precedent for the line item funding of federal films[,]" in ways that translated into increased budget allocations through the government exhibits office.[25] (See also Lee Grieveson's essay in this collection.)

The first film produced for the Bureau, *A Day in Baby's Life* (Children's Bureau, 1915; not extant), was displayed at the exposition and faithfully represented onscreen elements of the *Infant Care* publication. The continuity sheets for the film suggest that this first motion picture project at the Children's Bureau began with the title "The most loving act of a mother is to nurse her baby." The medical urgency of the message, consistent with the agency's post-natal and maternal health manuals, reflected the concerns of physicians and public health experts, who tied birthweight, contagious disease management, and milk spoilage, among other variables, to the patriarchal and biopolitical valences of a mother's intimate responsibility to the nation. The other Children's Bureau film shown at the exposition, *When Tom Went to Work* (1915), was intended to help advance the agency's legislative agenda of supporting the reform of federal child labor laws.[26]

***

Under Lathrop, film as an instrument of civic education aligned with the Bureau's new mandate to engage non-professional women more broadly in health concerns, particularly in ways that required local community-level involvement. To engage motion pictures as a trusted instrument of social work and public health information meant throwing off the criticism of cinema's harmful effects by reformers and religious moralists while also developing connections to a national patchwork of leagues, clubs, sewing circles, temperance workers, and charity workers. Attaching film spectatorship to more venerable redemptive traditions of character development and individual improvement provided civic-facing organizations with a necessary rhetoric, a strategy that was used in both white and Black communities.[27] Much of the knowledge and rhetorical skill used to sustain this sort of reform work had grown out of earlier political activity related to the suffrage movement and then in opportunities at settlement houses in particular. Because the most prominent of settlement houses, Jane Addams's celebrated Hull-House in Chicago, had considered select entertainment films and educational short films ideal for engaging settlement community members, and because many of the women's clubs' members who joined the better films campaigns had familiarity with the Hull-House example (and with Julia Lathrop), the public-service potential of educational motion pictures had achieved credibility among clubwomen and their esteemed and powerful leadership.[28]

Of the films produced, four neo- and post-natal and childhood disease-related maternal hygiene films by the New York-based director Carlyle Ellis—*Our Children* (Children's Bureau, 1919), *Well Born* (Children's Bureau, 1923), *The Best-Fed Baby* (Children's Bureau, 1925), and *Sun Babies* (Children's Bureau, 1926)—were among the most widely shown and requested from the agency, traveling internationally with intertitles for foreign-language audiences.[29] Each of these films played a significant role in publicizing the aims of the Children's Bureau. Viewed today, the motion pictures the Bureau produced record and amplify its neglect of economic inequities as well as its white-espoused ideals of natural birthright and implicit endorsement of social separation based on race. As an instance of *civic* film production attuned to the interests of the women's club community and professional organizations, the Children's Bureau's motion pictures spoke directly to a white female constituency in distinct ways. However, as the remainder of this chapter argues, this quartet of films visually registers the rapid diminishment of the strong social linkages that tied the Bureau to the exemplary practices of women's organizing; such practices were central to both the founding of this progressive flagship and the ways that it connected with large, diverse groups of women.

The first film that the Bureau contracted Ellis to make promoted the agency as part of a newly devised media network promoting maternal wellness; it did so by depicting women's collective action in local civic health education and inserting diegetic scenes of women distributing Bureau publications, often in close up. The quasi-documentary *Our Children* delivered viewers information framed via the recognizable civic mechanism of the health conference and served as a desirable invitation for women's groups to participate in aspects of maternally relevant governance. In this way, *Our Children* was also, importantly, a film *about* how to disseminate health information to improve citizens' welfare by means of non-govermental community and women's civic circuits. Even though Carlyle Ellis was aware that the support of women's groups and Better Films advocates led to his affiliation with the Children's Bureau, none of the Ellis-made films depicted groups of women viewing films; instead, the filmic presentation of the Bureau's publications at work in the domestic realm of small-town America implied an engaged media reception tying women's health to women's political activity. Subsequent productions reflect the gradual loosening of the staff's editorial management of the films, negotiated behind the scenes. The diminishment of Bureau control translates into the injection of sentimentally overwrought dialogue into scenes of advising and a reduced presence of pamphlets. These stylistic and informational changes correspond directly with the Bureau's success and administrative growth. It is also possible to connect these changes to Julia Lathrop's departure. Only the first film, *Our Children*, was produced under her management of the agency's policy objectives. The other films were produced while Grace Abbott was the Bureau's chief. Abbott, who was equally revered for her advocacy of labor reform and child welfare, did not have the same relationship to mass media as Julia Lathrop famously did.

From the outset, the new motion-picture production and distribution job fell to the Bureau's head of exhibits, a position designed to oversee the continuity of instructional presentation across all the agency's textual propaganda and graphic presentations. During the first decade of the Bureau's operations, Anna Strong and Ella Latham oversaw and maintained the agency's publicity.[30] These employees handled externally commissioned work for the bureau's numerous publications and displays and corresponded with producers and filmmakers. In 1914, Ella Latham approached the quality films-minded Edison studios with *When Tom Went to Work*, with aims similar to the Thanhouser Corporation's *Cry of the Children* (1911) and Edison's collaboration with the National Child Labor Committee, *Children Who Labor* (1912).

Despite the mutual solicitations to partner with producers such as Edison, Lathrop regularly rejected unsolicited overtures of this type out of a persistent belief in the separation of government work from commerce and private for-profit ventures. A telling example of this principled stance was Lathrop's response to a proposal for a "seven or eight"-reel child welfare-themed film produced by International Harvester Company for the Vanta Clothing Company in 1915.[31] As presented to the Bureau, the film would be offered free of charge to women's clubs for screenings, and plans would be made to screen the film at department stores carrying Vanta's children's clothing with an American Medical Association physician present to answer mothers' questions. Asked whether the Children's Bureau would entertain endorsement as a tie-in arrangement, Lathrop refused the collaboration. Even as this line had been drawn by Lathrop, it was a line less well understood by staff whose job involved receiving and responding to regular requests for movie suggestions. The Bureau had been serving as a *de facto* clearinghouse of health film rental and purchase information, receiving and recommending lists of commercially produced films on a wide range of health topics. Public service films with commercial advertising tie-ins, such as *The Fly Pest* (Urban-Eclipse; Kleine Optical, 1910), the first instance of a public-service interest and motion-picture producer joining forces, regularly appeared on the Children's Bureau's lists of recommended films when the agency was asked for suggestions for health screenings.[32]

Bureau staff members were opening letters daily from the public and from organization leaders asking for informational health films; requests that poured in sought film suggestions, film rental information, and film handling questions. These requests for credible, expert information about maternal health came equally from health departments and nurses' organizations, individuals in cities and community groups in rural areas. Julia Lathrop took to personally signing off (albeit in stamped form) on film rental and circulation information requests as they came in; the Bureau's memos recommended ordering films endorsed by the Russell Sage Foundation as "better films" through distributors such as Beserer Films and Bray Educational Pictures or with a suggestion to write to the National Board of Censorship for Better Films referrals.[33] Among the more oft-mentioned film titles of these stock exchanges were: *The Long vs. The Short Haul: Mother's Milk Best for Baby* (National Motion Pictures, 1915); a widely distributed short-subject motion picture on milk spoilage, *The Man Who Learned* (Edison Mfg. Co., 1910); *Summer Babies* (Essanay, 1911); *From the Field to the Cradle* (Lubin, 1911); *The Error of Omission* (Essanay, 1912); *The Fly Pest* (Urban-Eclipse, Kleine Optical, 1910); and *The Visiting Nurse* (Selig Polyscope, 1911).[34] The regularity with which Lathrop vetoed proposals for commercial co-sponsorship reflected her view that government films were, after all, *government* publications, and guided by policies of publication and exhibit that included oversight for photographic contract work.

In 1918, the Children's Bureau sought ways to increase its visibility through participation in "Children's Year," an unprecedented American public health campaign mounted in partnership with the General Federation of Women's Clubs "to save 100,000 babies and get a square deal for children." The promotional keystone of the Children's Bureau's platform pushed new federal legislation to address the crises of women's and infants' health with the aid of community leaders, regional club activities, and the expansion of baby clinics and visiting nurse programs. Children's Year had the effect of enlarging the Bureau's purchase on the national crisis of child health as a matter being attended to by a massive, domestic female dominion. The National Council of Defense and the General Federation of Women's Clubs marshaled volunteers for this postwar national campaign. They enabled the Children's Bureau's leadership to extend its birth registration conferences and mass public health clinics held at fairgrounds, with a great deal of readymade fanfare. As a mobilizing cause, Children's Year engaged the participation of seven million women, drawing on volunteers for women's groups, the participation of public health associations, and state and federal offices.[35] Maternity education and prenatal healthcare guidelines had been put out to these groups as a domestic "war measure," just short of a declaration of an acknowledged national public health crisis in response to rising infant mortality rates. While increasing birth registration continued to drive Lathrop's public philosophy for child protection, another concern with national defense implications was added to the agenda: the high rates of birth defects and early childhood diseases learned about by the military in their medical examinations that canvassed the wartime draftees for their suitability for service.[36] In addition to the Children's Bureau's pamphlets, articles in women's magazines showing techniques of birthing, regional Better Baby contests across the country, and child health information displays offering nutritional information, American "agitprop"-style trucks were specially equipped to deliver a spectacular "Baby Special" message to rural areas of the country.

* * *

At that same time, the prevalence and visibility of images of motherhood and illness in dramatic films made by major studios and more minor, independent film producers could not help but increase the urgency felt by the Children's Bureau staff members to offer mothers practical, scientific approaches to traditional mothering. In contrast to catastrophically medicalized bodies, such as Alice Guy's phantom limb farce for Gaumont, *Chirurgie fin de siècle* (Guy, 1901), the medical mise-en-scène of childbirth had rarely emerged as a post-traumatic laughing matter for audiences. Within the parallel pseudo-public spheres of entertainment filmgoing, women's and infants' health had remained nearly or completely shunned as an element of popular comedies or humorous sight-gag situations on screen. On occasion, crises of reproductive fitness or damaged or stunted youth had been thematically scenarized into realistic family dramas as a minor plot point or the subject of polite scandalous intimation, as had references to prostitution or out-of-wedlock pregnancy. Miscarriages, abortions, sexually transmitted diseases—all received full-blown screen treatment and eye-raising publicity and arrived on screen as multi-reel films of feature length between 1916 and 1919. No uniform attitude was adopted toward the commercial exhibition of films depicting topics shielded by mores of personal or family shame.

Writing about the context of American exploitation films, film historian Eric Schaefer notes that the climate of progressivist improvement permitted the introduction of otherwise hushed topics to be billed as "social issue" films. A different but centrist strain of Progressive protectionist alarm argued for these films' suppression or pre-distribution censorship.[37] Narratives of paternity and family lineage (*What the World Should Know* [Sunshine Film Co., 1916]), or medical quackery, as in the white race-survival title *The Black Stork* (Wharton, 1917) or *For Those Unborn* (Majestic, 1914) starring Blanche Sweet, depicted sexually transmitted diseases and congenital disabilities as health problems requiring male-only solutions.[38] *The Black Stork*, circulated later with the title *Are You Fit to Marry?* (1919), continued the vernacular tradition of lecture screenings focused on eugenics and was publicized with the sensationalizing tagline "How Unfit Humans Breed." The film was frequently presented with "Dr. Harry Haiselden" present and lecturing in an authoritative role. Writing about the production and circulation of *The Black Stork*, historian Martin S. Pernick notes that Progressive-era welfare advocates and health authorities sometimes tolerated misinformation "as a way to get people to follow expert technical advice without having to use direct state coercion," a point also relevant to widespread fears of state overreach.

Even more notably, sensitively portrayed and artfully directed films such as Lois Weber's *Where Are My Children?* (Universal, 1916) and *The Hand that Rocks the Cradle* (Universal, 1917) offered audiences film plots that framed their characters' pregnancies in terms of social systems of support and included references to the types of information and clinical or non-clinical help to which women were entitled.[39] In her contribution to this volume, Shelley Stamp astutely observes that theater operators willingly toed the lines of protest by announcing such films on their theater marquees. She goes on to suggest that while women's health was not always directly depicted in such films, through the appeal of mainstream narrative filmmaking, women's health activists increased their reach to the public beyond hygiene lectures or other sorts of projected, epideictic instructional media.[40] Finally, presented as more directly informational but no less controversial in their addressing of complications in human reproduction, the emergence of eugenics message films such as *Birth* (Eugenics Film Co., 1917) and advocacy films such as *Birth Control*, also titled *The New World* (B. S. Moss Motion Picture Corp., 1917), indicates that consumers and exhibitors alike sought the incorporation of *something* that resembled actual medical information in films of feature length.

While showing films on women's sexual health was not on the Children's Bureau media agenda, all of the ancillary answers to questions delivered by the new "scientific pediatrics" could potentially be written into lessons depicted on screen. Day after day, personal appeals for help with dangerous and potentially fatal ailments such as infant diarrhea and typhoid were received and responded to by staff. The letters reflected racial lines of trust in government at the time; writers were mainly white middle-class women, but letters also arrived from rural homemakers and urban laboring women, whether they had a doctor, a visiting nurse, or not.[41] Nevertheless, one must take into account the flow of postcards and letters coming into the Bureau—ninety thousand handwritten letters in 1919 and more in subsequent years—to fully grasp the urgency of its desire to reach mass audiences with movies on sensitive subjects.[42]

Lathrop made occasional public appearances with films, such as in the spring of 1916 with a program of baby-themed Paramount films as part of a *Women's Home Companion* magazine's "Better Babies Week" tie-in in New York City.[43] By the time that Lathrop made such appearances, she had already grown comfortable with the new, mediatized brand of public leadership established for her in the spheres of New Womanhood and female-bonded club networks. As attitudes shaped by this new "social feminism" were replacing earlier notions of Republican Motherhood, it was clear that motion pictures could validate ideas of progressive maternalism. Lathrop's appearance at these screenings suggests, in this way, that the Bureau's publicity program was in line with the broader modernizing shift in the direction of increasing the visibility of female civic leaders in American public culture.[44] Women's club members, especially their elite leadership and powerful political lobby, continued to constitute Lathrop's key audience. Members celebrated Lathrop for her decades of transformative settlement work, advocacy for improving conditions for the mentally ill, and social justice education and training. Lathrop's use of media-aided public advocacy for women working in the professional realms of civic service distinguished her from the well-known female progressive leaders of the day such as Sophonisba Breckinridge, Grace Abbott (who followed Lathrop's tenure as chief of the Children's Bureau, appointed in 1921), Edith Abbott, Lilian Wald, and Florence Kelley.[45]

At a time when the government was promoting its newly created opportunities for clerical and non-clerical jobs to the American workforce, Lathrop embodied a different kind of state agent. Significantly, members of the US federal workforce had received their first screen treatment around this same time, with the profession of the civil servant presented as men's work. A film celebrating new career opportunities in civil service, *Won Through Merit* (Edison Mfg. Co., 1915), was made by the US Civil Service Commission to attract workers. This upward-mobility-drama-turned-public-service-announcement showed the career journey of a young man from Michigan, celebrating bureaucratic life in the District of Columbia.[46] Skepticism regarding the degree of authority handed to the Children's Bureau increased the likelihood that practical legislative obstacles could be raised to limit the work of the agency's female leadership in Washington. As Nancy Pottishman Weiss noted in a 1974 study of the agency, employees suffered public derision by male members of Congress and in press coverage: "They were called 'mannish,' 'the third sex,' and 'bespectacled and sharp nose spinsters,' by congressional leaders and publicists who were trying not only to discredit them but to cast aspersions on the programs to which they were linked."[47] Such defaming, sexually limiting caricatures, used to stir up antagonism toward existing public health programs, were in dialogue with the powerful stereotypes projected in the movies of the moment: the intrusive widows and aged scolds of D. W. Griffith's derisive melodramas; the preferences for childish femininity in actors like Mary Pickford; and even the inverted fantasies of unbounded athleticism visible in serial queen adventuring.

All of this, including the celebration of a newly minted US civil service workforce counting a second-class female secretariat in its ranks, and the public's screen-fed appetite for sideways looks at women's collective agency, was the backdrop and significant discursive context for the Bureau's 1919 release of *Our Children*. The symbolic interplays that fashioned the New Woman's urbanized likeness on screen around the personal cost of an educated, middle-class woman's professional independence can in a sense contextualize the very real misogynist caricatures of the Children's Bureau's rank and file. The linkage of child-saving as community-based rescue to women's club membership as patriotic public service are centrally placed themes of Ellis's documentary-style *Our Children*. The celebrated film illustrates how filmgoing and pamphleting were jointly conceived as material mechanisms for "civic efficiency," recruited for the benefit of national birth registration campaigns.[48] Specifically, the staged reenactment of women initiating a health conference in Gadsden during Children's Year over the resistance of male municipal leaders in the film relies on the pamphlets as authorizing the women's collective demand for improved birth records and health information. Crucially for this analysis, the depiction of civic engagement in the campaigns for birth registration in this film, or of the proper care and feeding of infants in the other films Ellis made for the Bureau, were framed in relation to a public health crisis of infant mortality. Accordingly, its subject matter was approached as one answer to a question beginning with "*why?*" This rhetorical framework, the interrogative thread linking the pamphlets and the films, persisted as an echo of Julia Lathrop's mission-leading pleas to understand "Why are babies dying?"

One could say that "why?" or "how?" lies embedded in every educational film, and so, unsurprisingly, this interrogative mode becomes central to the scenarios of Ellis's films for the Bureau. But as the variety of betterment films already mentioned here indicates, we might seek to define the public-serving motion picture as a silent-era film modality categorically distinct from, or a subgenre of, other exploitation one-reels, short educational process films, or straight-ahead advertising pitches. One way of understanding the approach taken to the adaptation of the pamphlet to screen is via the genre of the process film, especially given the screen prevalence of that mode of representing and celebrating modernization. Writing in 1990, Eileen Bowser confirmed the importance of the genre as a screen practice with edifying force, even if the historical record of reception was limited. "Process films—pictures showing steel manufacture or textile weaving or any modern manufacturing process—were frequently produced [around 1910], too, and were admired as highly educational, although I don't know whether they were as widely seen. There was a tradition of audience interest in the manufacturing processes that predates the movies, as illustrated by the model coal mine and breaker with which Lyman Howe toured in the nineteenth century."[49] If the viewer of a process film was simply presented with a chronological "processual representation," then Carlyle Ellis's films, with their dramatized torn-from-real-life scenarios, sentimental appeals to community membership, and reenacted performances, diluted the process appeal considerably by virtue of their conventional social-problem narratives.[50]

Indeed, each of the four films that Carlyle Ellis made for the agency visualized the work of the Children's Bureau's studies and its government health advice in cheerfully picturesque sites, depicting women seeking clinical expertise, and staging views of the modern mise-en-scène of male medical authority over the domestic lives of families and children. The perky observational voice emerging from the intertitles of *Our Children*, with photography credited to James Goebel, describes the documentary scenes as footage from two birth registration conferences held in Gadsden, Alabama: one for the white citizens of Gadsden, and a second, late in the second reel of the film, for "colored folk . . . equally enthusiastic over their conference." *Our Children*, shown nationally and internationally by the Bureau's own account, opened with title cards shifting the film's purpose from birth certification propaganda to preventing an infant mortality crisis (see figure 17.1). The film depicts the work of well-heeled women's club

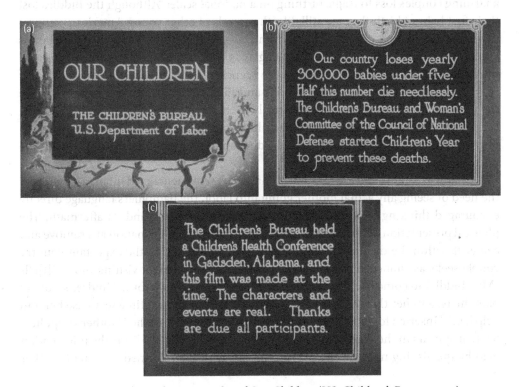

FIGURE 17.1 Screenshots of opening titles of *Our Children* (US. Children's Bureau, 1919).

members as all-white female advocates for birth registration; this method of gaining access to accurate records of births and deaths is also woven into *Our Children*'s indirect address to its audience. As the film depicts the weighing and measuring of the children at the birth registration events, Children's Bureau and Children's Year publicity appears on walls and tables.

Carlyle Ellis's directorial approach is observable in all four of these films, but *Well Born*, *The Best-Fed Baby*, and *Sun Babies*, photographed by Walter Pritchard, entailed increased editorial scrutiny by the employees at the Bureau and stirred up consternation back in Washington as control over medical knowledge collided with Ellis's desire to cater to his perceived audience of white club women. Carlyle Ellis was prominent in educational film circles at the time; by 1926, he had directed over fifty health education films for a variety of organizations, and his association with the Bureau resulted from his excellent reputation among members of the General Federation of Women's Clubs and the Better Films Movement.[51] As a filmmaker, he drew upon his background in literary long-form journalism, expressing a back-to-nature, anti-modern ethos of Progressivism tangible in his film work for the Bureau even as the assignment was to espouse the new science of motherhood.

Four years after *Our Children*, the Bureau signed Ellis to make a film without any quasi-documentary framing but still in the guise of confronting the national infant mortality crises. The opening titles of *Well Born* introduce its characters by coldly equating a farming couple's loss to tragic birthing on a national scale: "Although the Biddles lost their first baby at birth they are still, like thousands of other young Americans, unprepared for the coming of another." The film was intended to build on the tremendous success of *Our Children*, which in spring 1923 was still circulating with translated intertitles beyond US borders. Behind the scenes at the Children's Bureau in June of 1923, memoranda circulated between Ellis and Ella Latham detailing attempts to have the narrative of *Well Born* hew more directly to the popular brochure *Prenatal Care*. In the pamphlet, all of the preparation and childbirth processes are described according to normative ideas about pain tolerance, bleeding and soiling, vaginal discharge, and "the necessity for perfect cleanliness."

If Charlie Chaplin's *The Kid* (First National, 1921) sentimentalized infant care without the need of seeing any actual mother going into labor, the pamphlet's language directly encouraged thinking about the physical suffering of birthing and its aftermath. The physical presentation of the pamphlet could both place the information at a remove and center it within the diegesis: in one version of the film's script, the expectant country couple seeks assistance at a state board of health office where a visiting nurse "[t]ells [Mrs. Biddle] to come back Friday, with specimen. Gives her books, Children's Bureau pamphlets, tells her that she will stop at her house from time to time to advise her and help her."[52] Inserted for emphasis is a close-up (see figure 17.2) of the "Mother's Supplies" list that appears in the Prenatal Care brochure, implying that the list is the information held by the visiting nurse in the two shot of her with the reformed expectant mother

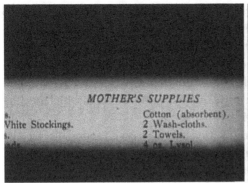 

FIGURE 17.2 Screenshots from *Well Born* (US Children's Bureau, 1923).

conversing astride a car's bumper. That no such scene exists in the final film suggests that even where objections were offered, Ellis's sentimental masculinism ultimately swayed the critics at the Bureau. Even so, his framing received considerable pushback from the Children's Bureau staff. In one particularly lengthy response to the scenario for *Well Born*, the following comment in June 1923 led to a sustained critique and textual edit of the film scenario's misinformed plotting:

> I think that Mr. Ellis' theory that such a movie must be put over as a melodrama is entirely wrong. I also think that his conception of the attitude of the public toward prenatal care and of the character of the public who are likely to see the movie, is mistaken. The public is not antagonistic, but indifferent or ignorant. The audiences who will see the film will not be, except in isolated instances, the very poor, untrained "working women." They will probably be the fairly intelligent, self-respecting wives of the storekeeper, the carpenter, the plumber, the clerk, the salesman, and the many young girls who in a few years will become such wives; they do not need anecdotes, plots, and counterplots. They are interested in mothers and babies and a straightforward representation of the subject would command their respect and attention.[53]

Both of the subsequent Ellis/Pritchard projects, *Best-Fed Baby* (1925) and *Sun Babies* (1926), handling even more candidly medicalized maternity topics—lactation and bottle-feeding in the former and the prevention of rickets in growing toddlers in the latter—generated heated internal discussion between nursing experts and concerned Bureau staff. (Even beyond the film's production, and over the many months in which the Children's Bureau fielded high demand for these films and sought control over the negatives from Ellis, his attempts to control pricing and master prints produced additional frustration.) *Best-Fed Baby* featured the Children's Bureau's pamphlet *Breast Feeding*, as it is received with relief by Jill, the sympathetic and struggling suburban mother. *Sun Babies* removed all pretense of diegetic pamphleting and nearly excised scenes of direct maternal instruction entirely from the picture. The film prescribes to urban dwellers the use of precarious-seeming window boxes to expose young babies to the sun outside their high-floor apartments. It delivers its message anxiously, though, linking skin tone and sun exposure in white and Black children. *Sun Babies* closes with Ellis's characteristic reach for a pastoral cliché—a long shot of an unidentified mountain location where children climb over rocks in a stream, and another shot in which healthy white children are shown frolicking in a sprinkler.

Given that the impetus for this film was eradicating a terrifying childhood disease, the concluding image suggests how at odds Carlyle Ellis was with a public health environment that attempted to recenter information gathering to meet the needs of women and parents who worried over the life and health of their children. The agency employees understood well that their films were being issued into a complicated media ecology where sentimentality and spectacle interfered with the sober reality of a mother's sadness or child's death.

Returning to the broader institutional context out of which these films were created, we can understand them to exist as partial evidence of how managerial control and bureaucratic work operated and evolved. As government-made filmmaking expanded and as the secretarial and clerical roles for women in government changed, the powerful collective advances of clubwomen as a specific driver of public policies in areas of healthcare and medical neediness dim onscreen. So too does the representation of the tools of their public activism and coded incorporation of tactics broadly used in women's movement activities. My analysis forwards the claim that filmmaking and pamphlet production operated in tandem, standing as an occasion when bureaucratic activists were guided by a sense that filmgoing and reading might each produce social transformation. The Children's Bureau is one of the many instances of early state filmmaking at the federal and local level that invite a fuller examination. The example is unique, as it benefits from the compelling interplay between a proto-feminist charismatic figure and a leading non-theatrical auteur, whose interactions point to the tensions inherent to this type of educational government filmmaking. These films, which had widespread circulation, helped shape shifting popular beliefs about childrearing, birth practices, and illnesses, as communities dealt with the systemic and unequal labor of domestic care. They are artifactual (or manuals for instruction, so perhaps the neologism here will become *manufactual*) and isomorphic of the bureaucrats and justice-seeking agents who collectively produced them. Further research will help complete the picture for film historians about how these Children's Bureau films, internationally distributed or locally remediated, were woven into the sponsored media environment. For now, they remain a partial picture of civic media practice, consciously intermedial, and produced out of a need to address women spectators who were, after all, the largest segment of the filmgoing audience of the day.

Notes

1. The author wishes to thank Charlie Keil and Rob King for their productive and generous suggestions during the preparation of this chapter. Molly Ladd-Taylor, *Mother-Work: Women, Child Welfare, and the State, 1890–1930*, Women in American History (Urbana: University of Illinois Press, 1994), 76–81.
2. For a full history of the agency's founding, leadership, and activities in its first years, see the indispensable work by Kriste Lindenmeyer, *A Right to Childhood: The U.S. Children's Bureau and Child Welfare, 1912–46* (Urbana: University of Illinois Press, 1997). Any errors I have made in my account here can be corrected by this authoritative work.
3. Ladd-Taylor, *Mother-Work*, 78–79.
4. Even after all of the compromises that had narrowed the agency's focus to child health, the Children's Bureau's broad description of child protection extended to the following areas: reporting to Congress on the exploitation of young children employed as factory and farm workers, a burdened juvenile court system, orphanage abuses, and scourges of childhood disease across rural and urban communities in the US and its territories.
5. Ladd-Taylor, *Mother-Work*, 78.
6. Cecelia Tichi, *Civic Passions: Seven Who Launched Progressive America (and What They Teach Us)* (Chapel Hill: University of North Carolina Press, 2009), 9.
7. Paul Theerman, "Julia Lathrop and the Children's Bureau," *American Journal of Public Health* 100, no. 9 (September 2010): 1589, https://doi.org/10.2105/AJPH.2009.188185.
8. Julia Clifford Lathrop, *Suggestions for Visitors to County Poorhouses and to Other Public Charitable Institutions* (Chicago, IL: Public Charities Committee of the Illinois Federation of Women's Clubs, 1905).
9. Tichi, *Civic Passions*, 117.
10. A panel of doctors and reviewers later demanded West's name be removed from the opening pages, insisting that the advice seem to come from a synthesis of research, as opposed to a member of the Children's Bureau staff. Judith Reed, "Infant Care, Then and Now," *Children Today*, 1981, 19, https://www.mchlibrary.org/history/chbu/28915a.pdf.
11. Lindenmeyer, *A Right to Childhood*, 257.
12. Ladd-Taylor, *Mother-Work*, 83.
13. See Russel Viner, "Abraham Jacobi and the Origins of Scientific Pediatrics in America," in Alexandra Stern and Howard Markel, eds., *Formative Years: Children's Health in the United States, 1880–2000*, Conversations in Medicine and Society (Ann Arbor: University of Michigan Press, 2004), 36.
14. While the characterization here is borrowed from Roland Barthes's classic description of signification in his *Mythologies* (New York: Hill & Wang, 1983), 125, in which he coins the term *basquity* for the arresting way that "interpellant speech" operates, it connects equally with Zoe Druick's elaboration of the concept of "documentality," initially explored in Hito Steyerl, "Documentarism as Politics of Truth," European Institute for Progressive Cultural Policies. https://transversal.at/transversal/1003/steyerl/en?hl=Documentarism (2003; accessed March 23 2017). Druick sees this quality in the postwar mental health films by the National Film Board of Canada that, like the Children's Bureau's filmmaking, require a more capacious definition of documentary in the context of the state's bio-political aims. Zoë Druick, "Documentality: The Postwar Mental Health Film and the Database Logic of the Government Film Agency," in Joshua Malitsky, ed., *A Companion to Documentary Film History* (Hoboken, NJ: Wiley-Blackwell, 2020), 107–122. Those interested in a

sustained discussion of the meaning of print documents in bureaucratic life should turn to Lisa Gitelman, *Paper Knowledge: Toward a Media History of Documents—Sign, Storage, Transmission* (Durham, NC: Duke University Press, 2014).

15. As the anthropologist Matthew S. Hull notes in his overview of the bureaucratic uses of paper, since at least the early nineteenth century, writing itself had been so thoroughly associated with a highly functional state apparatus that its absence would indicate structural failure. In Hull's terms, writing has been a "central semiotic technology" for the functioning of organizations and is thought of as "isomorphic" for the way that bureaucrats communicate between and beyond the boundaries of their offices. See Matthew S. Hull, *Government of Paper: The Materiality of Bureaucracy in Urban Pakistan* (Berkeley: University of California Press, 2012), 20–21.

16. Ladd-Taylor, *Mother-Work*, 84; Reed, "Infant Care, Then and Now."

17. Lindenmeyer, *Right to Childhood*, 48; Tichi, *Civic Passions*, 120: "[. . .][T]he prenatal and infant care pamphlets of 1913–1914 became runaway successes printed in the multimillions and requested by members of Congress for their constituents."

18. Alexandra Minna Stern and Howard Markel, eds., *Formative Years: Children's Health in the United States, 1880–2000* (Ann Arbor: University of Michigan Press, 2004), 129.

19. Lindenmeyer, *Right to Childhood*, 48.

20. Reed, "Infant Care, Then and Now," 18.

21. United States Children's Bureau, *Save 100,000 Babies. Get a Square Deal for Children . . .*, Children's Year Leaflet, No. 1 (Washington, DC: Government Printing Office, 1918).

22. Lindenmeyer, *Right to Childhood*, 60.

23. Jennifer Zwarich, "Federal Films: Bureaucratic Activism and the U.S. Government Motion Picture Initiative, 1901–1941" (PhD diss., New York University, 2014).

24. Ibid., 32.

25. Ibid., 94.

26. This title, solicited by the Children's Bureau for production by the Edison Manufacturing Company at one time (although it is not clear if Edison ultimately fulfilled the contract), also shows up as *When Willie Went to Work* and was circulated both as lantern slides and a filmstrip.

27. Vernetta D. Young and Rebecca Reviere, "Black Club Women and the Establishment of Juvenile Justice Institutions for Colored Children: A Black Feminist Approach," *Western Journal of Black Studies* 39, no. 2 (Summer 2015): 102–113.

28. See Amy Shore, *Suffrage and the Silver Screen* (New York: Peter Lang, 2014).

29. All four of these films are still archivally extant. Collectively, in conjunction with written correspondence and other day-to-day business communication guiding their production and exhibition, they telegraph the aims of the agency's educational and data-driven missions in cinematic form. Researchers can find the extensive textual records of the Children's Bureau dating back to its formation in 1912 arranged in Record Group 102.2 at the National Archives and Records Administration in College Park, MD. The Record Group 102.3 includes silent 35mm prints of *Our Children* (1919; 2 reels), *The Best-Fed Baby* (1925; 1 reel), and *Sun Babies*, with titles in Spanish (1926; 2 reels). One print of *Well Born* (1923) is held by Library and Archives Canada in Ottawa, ON.

30. Ella O. Latham's signature on countless pieces of correspondence suggests that her job included leadership in areas of intra-agency communication and editorial oversight crucial to the bureau's consistency of messaging. Additionally, part of her organizational remit was to manage the filing system for the entire agency. Of particular note to researchers working

with these materials is the memorandum she left in June 1925 signed "Ella O. Latham, In Charge of Central Files." This document, which remains part of the Finding Aid for the historical records of the agency at the National Archives and Records Administration in College Park, MD, explains the filing and folder scheme for the paperwork, print, and photographic traffic beginning in 1914.
31. "Memorandum from Dr. Grace Meigs to Julia Lathrop," December 21, 1915, Record Group 102, Children's Bureau Central Files 1914–1920, Box 73, Folder 8-1-4-1-4, National Archives II College Park, MD. Internally, this film received the usual reaction: to question the film's synopsis based on factual information. "I feel," wrote Children's Bureau director of the Division of Hygiene, Dr. Grace Meigs Crowder, "the whole film could be made far more useful if someone were directing it with more experience and general knowledge of the subject than Mr. Morris [the director] seems to have." Dr. Grace Meigs was employed at the Children's Bureau until July 1918 and was a specialist in maternal morbidity and obstetrics.
32. Oliver Gaycken, *Devices of Curiosity: Early Cinema and Popular Science* (New York: Oxford University Press, 2015).
33. "Julia C. Lathrop to Mrs. Arthur Bates," February 24, 1916. Record Group 102, Children's Bureau Central Files 1914–1920, Box 73, Folder 8-1-4-1-4, National Archives and Records Administration II, College Park, MD.
34. For a fuller summary of the context of these and other public health instruction films, see Marina Dalquist's chapter, "Health Instruction on Screen: The Department of Health in New York City, 1909–1917," in Marta Braun, Charlie Keil, Rob King, Paul Moore, and Louis Pelletier, eds., *Beyond the Screen: Institutions, Networks and Publics of Early Cinema* (Bloomington: Indiana University Press, 2012), 107–116.
35. Alice Boardman Smuts, *Science in the Service of Children, 1893–1935* (New Haven, CT: Yale University Press, 2006), 81–102.
36. Ibid., 96.
37. See Eric Schaefer, "An Attempt to 'Commercialize Vice,'" in *"Bold! Daring! Shocking! True!": A History of Exploitation Films, 1919–1959* (Durham, NC: Duke University Press, 1999), 16–41.
38. Kevin Brownlow, *Behind the Mask of Innocence* (Berkeley: University of California Press, 1990), 271.
39. Martin S. Pernick, *The Black Stork: Eugenics and the Death of "Defective" Babies in American Medicine and Motion Pictures since 1915* (New York: Oxford University Press, 1996), 125.
40. See Shelley Stamp's article, Chapter 18 in this volume, "Curiosity Seekers, Morbid Minds, and Embarrassed Young Ladies: Female Audiences and Reproductive Politics Onscreen."
41. Smuts, *Science in the Service of Children*, 92.
42. These numbers are in Alice Smuts's section, "Letters to the Bureau;" the numerous handwritten letters, collected in the folders of the agency, are heartwrenching accounts of women's suffering, and are moving to handle as a researcher.
43. "Sifted from the Studios," *Motography* 15, no. 18 (April–June 1916), 1002.
44. A letter to Julia Lathrop in 1916 begins, "I am fully aware that moving pictures is a matter that does not come under the Childrens' [sic] Bureau, but I know that when you were in Chicago you were particularly interested in securing the right sort of pictures..." "Marian Whidden to Julia C. Lathrop," March 17, 1916. Record Group 102, Children's Bureau Central Files 1914–1920, Box 73, Folder 8-1-4-1-4, National Archives and Records Administration II, College Park, MD.

45. Lela B. Costin, *Two Sisters for Social Justice: A Biography of Grace and Edith Abbott* (Urbana: University of Illinois Press, 1983), 120–124. Even as the Children's Bureau clearly operated against the strong winds of systemic sexism, Costin writes in this biography of Grace Abbott of the fierce belief that both Abbott and Lathrop held about non-partisan civil service as offering higher opportunities for advancement for women than did the private sector.
46. A 35mm print of *Won Through Merit* (1915) is held at the National Archives in College Park, MD, https://catalog.archives.gov/id/37619.
47. Nancy Pottishman Weiss, "Save the Children: A History of the Children's Bureau, 1903–1918" (PhD diss., University of California Los Angeles, 1974), 174. These same caricatures are cited by Molly Ladd-Taylor in describing Lathrop's challenge to traditional femininity, noting that Lathrop was portrayed as "statesmanlike and judicious" by her supporters, a testament to her successful rejection of sentimental maternalism. See Ladd-Taylor, *Mother-Work*, 81.
48. Writing in 1915, John Dewey defined "civic efficiency" ("good citizenship") as what would be attained by a proper synchronization of scientific knowledge with social life in the interests of human progress. Arguing in terms that would influence the cultural and Progressive elite at the time, Dewey expressed the need to understand the broader educational mission of society in civic efficiency, writing that the "[a]bility to produce and to enjoy art, capacity for recreation, the significant utilization of leisure, are more important elements in it than elements conventionally associated oftentimes with citizenship." John Dewey, *Democracy and Education: An Introduction to the Philosophy of Education* (New York: The Free Press; Collier-Macmillan, 1966), 120.
49. Eileen Bowser, *The Transformation of Cinema: 1907–1915* (Berkeley: University of California Press, 1990), 44. See also Rick Altman, "From Lecturer's Prop to Industrial Product: The Early History of Travel Films," in Jonathan Kahana, ed., *The Documentary Film Reader* (New York: Oxford University Press, 2016), 16–26.
50. Salomé Aguilera Skvirsky, *The Process Genre: Cinema and the Aesthetic of Labor* (Durham, NC: Duke University Press, 2020).
51. Carlyle Ellis's career biography included stints on the editorial staff at the *Alaska Yukon Magazine*, *Everybody's Magazine*, and with Sinclair Lewis and Theodore Dreiser on other publications. Prior to joining the US Committee on Public Information in 1918, Ellis worked briefly as a title writer and scenarist for Universal. His profile is included in the non-theatrical history written by Arthur Edwin Krows, "Motion Pictures—Noor Theatres" in *Educational Screen* 18, no. 9 (November 1939): 331.
52. *Well Born* correspondence and files, including the Memorandum to Carlyle Ellis referred to here and early script, are found in Record Group 102, Children's Bureau Central File Box 214 (February 1923–October 1923), Folder 8-1-2-4, Motion Pictures, National Archives and Records Administration II, College Park, MD.
53. "Memorandum on the 'Prenatal Care' Movie," June 29, 1923. Record Group 102, Children's Bureau Central File Box 214 (February 1923–October 1923), Folder 8-1-2-4, Motion Pictures, National Archives and Records Administration II, College Park, MD.

CHAPTER 18

CURIOSITY SEEKERS, MORBID MINDS, AND EMBARRASSED YOUNG LADIES

Female Audiences and Reproductive Politics Onscreen

SHELLEY STAMP

IN 1915 the *New Republic* proclaimed "The Age of Birth Control," demonstrating how the fight to legalize contraception had become central to broader discussions about sexuality, poverty, race, and gender equality in the Progressive Era—and how quickly the term "birth control," coined just the previous year, had caught on.[1] Cinema, relatively new to the national media stage, became one of the chief catalysts in these debates, as a diverse range of films engaged moviegoers in matters of human reproduction and family planning. Feature films dramatized sensational stories of unplanned pregnancy and abortion; public health films provided instruction on childbirth and infant care; and birth control activists, including famed radical Margaret Sanger, turned to cinema to promote their cause. Women were the primary audience addressed by these films, for then as now, contraception and reproduction were framed almost exclusively as women's issues, despite benefiting both men and women in heterosexual unions. Whether inexperienced teenagers or married women, newly pregnant or seasoned mothers, white women or women of color, wealthy or working class, female moviegoers were offered a host of ways to navigate reproductive politics onscreen during these years. In fact, regardless of whether they saw films in commercial theaters or educational settings, it is likely no exaggeration to say that many girls and women got much of their information about these topics either at the cinema or in parallel discussions provoked by film screenings.

On the whole, films released during "The Age of Birth Control" exhibited an overwhelmingly conservative approach to matters of reproduction, contraception, and abortion, as scholars like Kay Sloan, Kevin Brownlow, and Martin F. Norden have emphasized.[2] Film plots manifested anxieties about female sexuality outside of marriage—indeed outside of reproduction—and were inclined to sentimentalize motherhood as the pinnacle of female experience. Yet, by looking not only at the films themselves but also the culture in which they were exhibited, promoted, and discussed, it becomes clear that in spite of the guarded messages most films espoused about sexuality, motherhood, and human reproduction, cultures of moviegoing and consumption offered female moviegoers surprisingly varied means of untangling these thorny issues—and in some cases may have furnished tactics for contesting regressive attitudes championed onscreen.

Even with the conservative approach adopted in most films, there was still considerable alarm about the spate of relatively frank films on contraception and abortion that drew female audiences to the cinema. Commentators feared they were among the most explicit and shocking of their day. According to one irate New York City exhibitor in 1916, films on sexuality and reproduction amounted to "the worst lot of pictures" that "the trade had seen in its entire history," among them "abortion pictures so raw as to cause police interferences; birth control pictures which were positively shocking to even men who were not squeamish; love dramas so transparently lustful as to shock and embarrass young *ladies* in the audience."[3] Some theater owners showed these films at screenings reserved exclusively for women, attempting to lend them a cachet associated with "ladies' matinees" that catered to white middle-class patrons, but even this tactic became suspect. Critics worried that woman-only screenings, rather than underscoring refinement and taste, might actually telegraph sensational content. Exhibitors might advertise ladies' matinees for films on human sexuality and reproduction, some cautioned, precisely to hint at salacious content and graphic material. J. E. Hipple, proprietor of the Bijou Theater in Pierre, South Dakota, accused fellow exhibitors of "advertising in the afternoon for women only and throwing the doors wide open at night," surmising that the matinees were just a ruse to generate prurient interest.[4]

Descriptions of promotional strategies used at the time indicate that many theater owners gleefully played up the sensational aspects of these films—so successfully, in fact, that they drew crowds of women. When the anti-abortion film *The Miracle of Life* (1915) opened in Chicago, it was "luridly postered" at the Bijou Dream in the downtown commercial district with advertising that promised "the fallacy of race suicide exposed." Explaining his approach, the Bijou's owner told journalist Kitty Kelly, "It's this sex stuff that goes on State Street. Make it look that way and they swarm in." Kelly reassured her *Chicago Tribune* readers that the picture itself was quite tame but wondered about the number of moviegoers drawn in with "the expectation of seeing something very spicy," imagining they might enter the theater "sneakily propelled by anxiety lest anyone be looking."[5] When *The Unborn* (1916) opened the following year at the city's Bandbox Theater, a three-hundred-seat venue just off La Salle Street in the Loop, the theater front was draped in purple bunting, mourning fabric in honor of "the unborn." "They're dead ones, aren't they?" the theater manager told a curious journalist. Screenings were restricted to women during the film's first week, and the *Tribune* reported "the line of

FIGURE 18.1 A "ladies only" screening of *The Unborn* (1916) in Chicago: "They went in a-tiptoe; they came out weeping." *Chicago Tribune*, October 17, 1916.

women in front of the theater never diminished from 9 a.m. until the closing hour. They went in a-tiptoe; they came out weeping" (see figure 18.1).[6]

Promotions for *Birth* (1917), a quasi-documentary shot in "a great New York hospital," provide an indication of how such ladies-only screenings might complicate traditional sentiments about human reproduction espoused onscreen. Despite the promise of its title, *Birth* included no scenes of childbirth but emphasized infant care, showing doctors resuscitating a newborn, nurses caring for a premature baby, and women recovering from labor and childbirth. As trade reviewer George Gould put it, "urge is laid on all women to prepare themselves or their daughters for that greatest of honors—the bringing forth of a new life."[7] Analyzing the film's "box office angle," *Wid's* recommended that exhibitors "show it to women only" but advised them, "be careful about the wording of your advertising," for "curiosity seekers who figure that they're going to see something they oughtn't to" will be in store for "a sad disappointment," echoing persistent concerns about women-only screenings.[8]

When *Birth* played in Los Angeles in late 1917, shows at the Majestic Theatre were initially restricted to female patrons, as *Wid's* advised, and were "packed with women at practically every performance," according to the *Los Angeles Times*.[9] Located next to Hamburger's Department Store in the heart of the city's downtown shopping district, the Majestic was ideally situated for white, middle-class moviegoers in particular—a fitting audience for a picture produced by the Eugenic Film Company. During the first week of the film's run, theater owners circulated a ballot asking women, "Shall men see 'Birth'?" and pledging "men will be admitted if the majority of women so rule." More than seven thousand women cast ballots and voted overwhelmingly to admit a "husband, father, son, brother or sweetheart." Boasting of this initiative, a large advertisement in the *Times* proclaimed "Women Vote to Admit Men," reproducing a ballot with a handwritten annotation, "I believe men will have a greater realization of the responsibilities

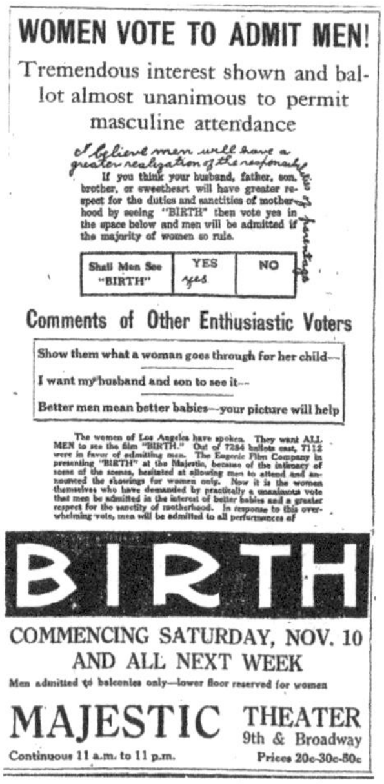

FIGURE 18.2 When *Birth* (1917) played in Los Angeles, theater owners allowed female patrons to vote on whether men should be admitted to screenings. *Los Angeles Times*, November 9, 1917.

of parentage" (see figure 18.2).[10] Men were duly permitted to attend screenings at the Majestic during the second week of the film's run, though some segregated seating remained: men were allowed in the balcony and galleries only; the lower floor would be reserved for women. An advertising gimmick allowing women a "vote" at the height of the national campaign for women's suffrage was highly charged, of course.[11] Indeed, it furnishes an example of how promotional strategies might complicate—or even contradict—a film's conservative message, for the "vote" about whether to allow men into screenings of *Birth*—however gimmicky—achieved a number of things simultaneously. It suggested that white women's views were essential in discussions of reproduction; it converted an outmoded view of womanhood—identified primarily with motherhood—into an ideal of feminine sisterhood, inviting collective action and political engagement; it replaced a sentimentalized view of motherhood with a more inclusive view of "parenthood" that involved male partners; and, finally, it encouraged a level of civic-mindedness that might spill over from a movie promotion into wider debates about reproductive politics.

Like *Birth*, promotions for *Enlighten Thy Daughter* (1917) capitalized on the film's potential to attract female patronage: trade advertisements promised exhibitors it was "a sure-fire matinee booster" and "a positive magnet to women."[12] And that it was. When the film opened at the 1,584-seat Park Theatre in New York City, it drew such crowds that owners opted to show it continuously from 2:30 to 11:00 p.m. each day, dramatically increasing screenings from the three-per-day originally planned.[13] During its subsequent run at the Prospect Theatre in Brooklyn, ads boasted that the "enormous crowds" admitted to see the picture did not come close to "the crowds which have been turned away."[14] Released by Ivan Film Productions, known for their lurid titles and subject matter, *Enlighten Thy Daughter* is typical of many films where abortion featured prominently in cautionary tales about sexuality outside of marriage, contrasting the fates of two young women from wealthy white families: Ruth has been "carefully guarded against the pitfalls which beset young girls," as one reviewer put it; but her cousin, Lillian, under less strict parental supervision, takes up a sexual relationship with Ruth's fiancé, a wealthy millionaire, who abandons her after she becomes pregnant.[15] Lillian's mother, intervening too late, attempts to procure an abortion for her daughter, but the procedure is botched and Lillian dies. Blame is laid squarely on "the neglectful mother who allows her daughter to grow up unenlightened," according to another reviewer.[16] The film's apparently unambiguous message, proclaimed from the outset in its title, encouraged young women be "enlightened" about sexuality and reproduction. To be clear, this was *not* done with the aim of informing them about family-planning options but to *curtail* any and all pre-marital sexual activity.

The film's publicity campaign touted the educational conversations that *Enlighten Thy Daughter* might provoke, simultaneously suggesting that these were discussions mothers ought to have with daughters in the privacy of their homes *and* offering cinema as a space where young women might learn from stories they watched onscreen. Advertisements promised that the film delivered its message "with sledge hammer blows," enacting a story that "every Mother, Father and Brother knows but does not dare to tell." Appealing directly to mothers, another ad proclaimed, "you can't afford to have your daughter miss seeing this great moral play. She'll never forget it and will never forget herself."[17] Director Ivan Abramson told clergy assembled for a special screening of the film in New York, "No mother can leave the Park Theatre without giving serious concern to the fact that she owes her daughter a duty. No daughter can leave the theatre without being deeply impressed by the calamity that befalls Lillian" (see figure 18.3).[18]

At one early showing in New York, cards were distributed asking audience members to discuss whether they agreed with Ruth's decision to break off her engagement with the young millionaire who impregnates her cousin Lillian, specifically inviting viewers to contemplate how they themselves might behave in a similar situation.[19] It is telling that moviegoers were invited to occupy *Ruth's* position—to imagine how they would act in the face of a fiancé's sexual improprieties—not Lillian's position, where they would be asked to ruminate about their own sexual behaviors, unplanned pregnancies, or histories of abortion. Even so, once prompted to picture themselves in Ruth's shoes, what would prevent young women from going one step further and imagining Lillian's fate befalling themselves —unmarried, facing an unplanned pregnancy, and contemplating abortion? If advertisements for *Enlighten Thy Daughter* promised the film's message was delivered "with sledge hammer blows," promotional strategies that prompted audiences to discuss predicaments faced by characters onscreen might significantly complicate how "daughters" could be "enlightened" about sexuality and reproduction.[20]

FIGURE 18.3 A newspaper advertisement for *Enlighten Thy Daughter* (1917) emphasized the importance of conversations between mothers and daughters on matters of sexuality and human reproduction. Unidentified source, Katharine Kaelred Scrapbook, New York Public Library.

What is more, films that catered to young viewers by adopting a modest, even circumspect approach to these matters might provide an unwitting education of another kind. *New York Dramatic Mirror*'s critic ultimately found himself less troubled by events that had been dramatized in *Enlighten Thy Daughter* than what had been *left out* of the film. Topics like pre-marital sex, pregnancy, and abortion had only been alluded to onscreen, never spoken about directly; as a result, the reviewer feared, much had been "left to the imagination of the spectator." Indeed, a "germ" had been "very well planted" in a way that might be "appealing to the morbid mind."[21] No gender was ascribed to the morbid minds the reviewer envisaged, but the film's own marketing campaign made it clear that its intended patrons were young "daughters" who had begun dating and might already be sexually active. Such impressionable viewers might conjure in their own minds details about sexuality and reproduction that had only been hinted at onscreen.

Much like *Enlighten Thy Daughter*, publicity materials for *The Natural Law* (1917) trumpeted the film's educational potential, with advertisements quoting New York–area Rabbi Isaac S. Moses: "I wish every mother would take her young daughter. [. . .] It would spare her the task of trying to teach what every growing girl should know."[22] While this ad suggests moviegoing could stand in for frank conversations between mothers and daughters, *The Natural Law* provides a further example of how discussions provoked by these films might challenge conservative attitudes endorsed onscreen. The first release of France Films, the film treated "the ethics of abortion" with "unusual frankness," according to *Moving Picture World*'s Edward Weitzel, so much so that it was likely to "create a large amount of discussion among the people who go to see it," added *Variety*'s reviewer, who imagined that "after emerging from the theater," patrons would debate the heroine's choices.[23] "The picture will appeal to women more than men," *Motography*'s critic Helen Rockwell proposed, "as it is the sort of subject women love to fuss over, but which men take for granted."[24]

The central character in *The Natural Law*, another Ruth, has an affair with "an athletic college chap" who "makes frequent calls on her, clad in scanty running costume" while her fiancé, a prominent older doctor, is out of town.[25] Soon the young couple "cannot resist the natural law of youth calling to youth" and forget "the bounds beyond which there is sorrow in crossing": the young woman then becomes pregnant.[26] Reviewers, sometimes coy about the circumstances in which Ruth finds herself, explained that she calls upon her doctor beau "for assistance."[27] The scene depicting "the pleadings of the terror-stricken heroine," desperate for an abortion, was the longest in the film and provided its climactic moment. The doctor ultimately refuses Ruth's request, and she marries her younger lover, pregnant with their child.[28] As Helen Rockwell predicted, these events prompted many ethical questions for viewers to "fuss" over: Should the young couple have refrained from sexual activity altogether or should they have had access to contraception? Should the doctor have provided Ruth with an abortion after she became pregnant? So while *The Natural Law* ostensibly offered a chilling admonition about the dangers of sexuality outside marriage, emphasizing the dire consequences for women in particular, viewers discussing the film might arrive at starkly different conclusions. "What every growing girl should know" took on entirely new resonance in this context.

There is a palpable tension, then, in discussions about female audiences at films on reproduction, contraception, and abortion. They manifest, on the one hand, a repeated insistence on the innocence of women attending these films—"embarrassed" young ladies who ought not to be exposed to such material, "daughters" in need of enlightening. Yet, at the same time, one also hears a frank recognition that these very same women might bring to the cinema considerable "curiosity" about these issues, a "morbid" ability to conjure incidents only hinted at onscreen, even some memory of their own sexual exploits, their own need for birth control, and possibly their own experiences of abortion—all accompanied by a desire to discuss and debate choices made by characters onscreen.

The question of whether to speak to young women about sexuality and reproduction—and, if so, how—was a keen topic of discussion in the popular press of this era. Relatively staid outlets like *Ladies' Home Journal* suggested such conversations might provide opportunities to instill a conservative approach to sexuality in young women. In late 1910 and early 1911, the magazine ran a monthly column, "How Shall I Tell My Child?" by Rose Woodallen Chapman, framed as "a little talk as mother with mother." Following several early columns in which she recommended that very young children be given relatively explicit information about human reproduction, Chapman then advanced a much more cautious stance when speaking with teenage girls, whose "creative forces" were "receiving a new impulse." Better to teach young women to uphold "the sacredness of the body" and "the highest ideals of womanhood," than the details of human reproduction, Chapman proposed.[29]

But the closed-lip approach urged by Chapman was challenged in contemporaneous pieces that questioned the "policy of silence" surrounding human reproduction. Dr. Charles W. Eliot, Honorary President of the American Federation of Sex Hygiene, advised *Ladies' Home Journal* readers that all young people "should be systematically taught the natural, normal processes of reproduction"; in an accompanying piece, the Reverend Arthur C. A. Hall, Episcopal Bishop of Vermont, denounced the "criminal reticence" often shown by mothers reluctant to speak with their daughters about matters of sexuality and reproduction. However frank, such conversations ought to underscore conservative principles, both men emphasized. Eliot stressed that mothers could promote the idea that "chastity is perfectly healthy" and that begetting and bearing children are not "sinful or foul processes." Hall suggested that these conversations could emphasize the "dignity" of motherhood in order to ward against other women informing their daughters about how to "avoid the burden."[30] One sees in these articles the rather tortured logic required to counsel chastity for unmarried women, on the one hand, and a hearty embrace of motherhood in marriage, on the other—all the while entirely avoiding any discussion of female sexuality.

Family planning activist Margaret Sanger entered these debates in 1911, penning a series of articles for the socialist newspaper *The Call* under the heading "What Every Mother Should Know, or How Six Little Children Were Taught the Truth," encouraging clear and direct discussions with children about human sexuality. Two years later, Sanger published another series in *The Call* titled "What Every Girl Should Know," tackling much more taboo subjects like masturbation and venereal disease.[31] Conversations that might *not* be happening at home could, she implied, be staged in more public forums like the daily newspaper. Exhibitors publicizing early films on sexuality and reproduction evidently viewed cinemas as another domain where such conversations might take place, as did reviewers like Helen Rockwell, attentive to the "fuss" these pictures might cause. But unlike the highly scripted and cautionary dialogues prescribed by outlets like *Ladies' Home Journal*, early feature films on abortion and birth control had the potential to unleash much more wide-ranging conversations, as female moviegoers debated, dissected, even criticized the choices made by characters onscreen.

If films like *Enlighten Thy Daughter* and *The Natural Law* emphasized the dire consequences of pre-marital sexual activity in narratives intended for young viewers, *The Miracle of Life* epitomizes another group of features focused on married white women who used contraception or had abortions in order to delay childbearing while remaining sexually active. Mutual promoted the film as a simple "plea for motherhood," but speaking more bluntly, *Motography*'s critic dubbed it "a preachment against birth control."[32] The judgment against married women depicted in these films seemed clear in virtually every case, a rigid morality often reinforced in the hectoring tenor of reviews. As Louis Reeves Harrison informed readers in his assessment of *The Miracle of Life*, many a young wife enjoying "the charm of the honeymoon" and the "long-anticipated joys of love," will "revolt" against motherhood.[33] The film's protagonist finds herself unhappily pregnant early in her marriage, procures an abortifacient, but falls asleep before taking the medication. Dreaming of the unfulfilling, lonely life she would lead without children, she wakes up with her mind changed, ready for motherhood. *Motography* summed up the film's message rather baldly: those who "fight against" motherhood would face not only "an unhappy old age, but everlasting punishment after death."[34]

Despite this apparent cautionary tale, there is evidence that women who flocked to see *The Miracle of Life* might have interpreted events onscreen quite differently. *Motion Picture*'s Hazel Simpson Naylor reported overhearing two women leaving a screening, debating a suggestion made in the film that women could keep their husbands faithful by having children. Skeptical of this logic, one woman reportedly quipped to the other, "I've seen men who have children stray from their wife, same as men who haven't."[35] This exchange reminds us that audiences did not always subscribe to the traditionalist sensibilities promoted onscreen and underscored by reviewers—that discussions women had in and around screenings were precisely those moments when they might overturn regressive attitudes toward female sexuality and family planning. Women weighed their own lived experience against oversimplified film plots and readily compared notes with their comrades. Moreover, by reproducing the dialogue she had overheard in *Motion Picture*, the nation's largest-circulation fan magazine, Naylor not only encouraged *further* discussion on these issues among her (largely female) readership but also invited readers to refute the dogmatic attitudes espoused in the film, just as these other women had.

Some exhibitors explicitly pressed moviegoers to debate choices made by characters onscreen, suggesting the complex moral dilemmas surrounding sexuality and reproduction portrayed in movie plots might provoke entirely different responses in real life—that the range of options open to women might extend considerably beyond those shown. Take the example of *The House Without Children* (1919), one of many films that combined plots about married women using birth control or abortion to delay motherhood with plots about "wronged" single women who became pregnant. During the film's popular two-week run at the Erlanger Opera House in Cleveland, four-column advertisements were published in the *Cleveland Plain Dealer* highlighting a series of questions raised by incidents in the film (see figure 18.4). The central female character remains childless over her husband's objections, but when her brother impregnates a young niece, she decides to adopt the baby and present it as her own in order to "save the young girl from disgrace," as one reviewer put it.[36] Ads in the *Plain Dealer* posed a series of questions about these events for moviegoers to ponder: "Should a girl marry her betrayer (whom she hates) to give her child a name? Should a man marry a girl knowing her to have been the innocent victim of a libertine? Should a wife attempt to retain her husband's love by foisting on him a child not their own? And should a husband forgive his wife for denying him the children his heart craves?"[37] These questions opened up for speculation moral stances that the film—and many reviewers—took for granted, encouraging audiences to imagine an array of other choices that might be made, even possibilities that remained unspoken in the advertisement: Is family planning an option for married women? When and how should women delay childbearing? What is the best method for doing so? Is abortion a viable choice in the face of sexual assault?

Citing the *Plain Dealer* advertisements with great enthusiasm and encouraging other proprietors to mount similar campaigns for *The House Without Children*, the *Exhibitors Herald* noted "a question demands an answer. It always gets a hearing."[38] As the queries prompted by *The House Without Children* reveal, the range of topics provoked by films on reproduction and family planning extended far beyond contraception itself to include morality, the sexual double standard, sexual assault, and marital sexuality. And despite the doctrinaire messages espoused by these films, oftentimes reiterated in trade and popular reviews, promotional strategies could help women imagine additional avenues open to them.

Many other films offered similar versions of the plotline sketched in *The House Without Children*, interlacing stories of wealthy white women "avoiding" motherhood with subplots involving younger unmarried women who become unexpectedly pregnant as a result of clandestine sexual relationships. The younger women often come from markedly less privileged circumstances, and their sexual experiences are frequently non-consensual— sometimes they are said to have been "deceived" or "betrayed" by wealthy lotharios, other times the encounters are more plainly described as sexual assault. This formulation is best known from Lois Weber's 1916 sensation *Where Are My Children?*, where the story of society women having serial abortions is set against the tragic death of a housekeeper's daughter, who seeks an abortion when she becomes pregnant after a liaison with her employer's predatory brother.[39] But analogous narratives surface in other films of the period, some obvious knock-offs of Weber's box-office hit, others produced contemporaneously. In *The Question* (1916), a wealthy society

REPRODUCTIVE POLITICS 385

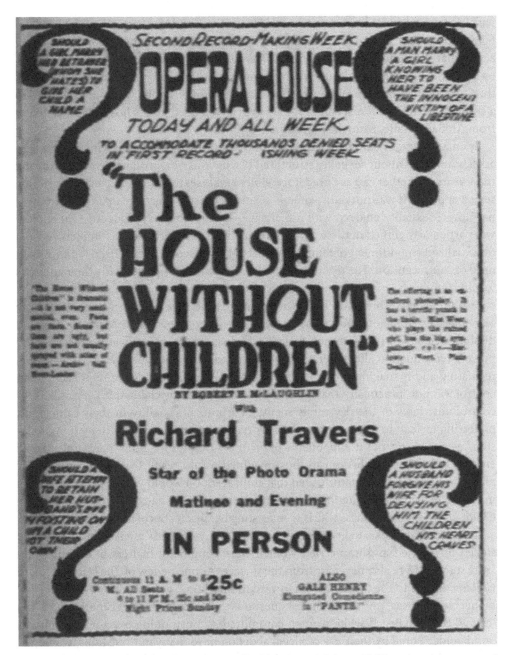

FIGURE 18.4 A newspaper advertisement for *The House Without Children* (1919) encouraged Cleveland moviegoers to ponder questions provoked by the film. *Exhibitors Herald*, September 13, 1919.

wife "deliberately avoiding motherhood" later adopts an infant conceived by her husband and his pretty young stenographer during an "unlawful honeymoon," embracing a maternal ethos she had at first denied.[40] In *The Unborn* a naïve country lass "betrayed" by a wealthy urban sophisticate gives birth to a son who is eventually adopted by his father, for the wealthy man's own wife has "avoided motherhood" with repeated trips to a certain "Dr. Ahlbad." A second plot involves a "wronged girl" who seeks an abortion from Ahlbad but dies from the procedure.[41]

By entangling stories of married and unmarried women, these plots demonstrate how acutely anxieties about sexuality structured discussions of reproductive politics during these years—whether cast as a predatory, violent male sexuality or a debauched feminine sexual appetite. It was not only women's sexuality outside marriage that troubled these narratives; sexuality enjoyed *within* marriage—outside of its reproductive function—was particularly vilified in these plots. In many cases, motherhood was emphasized as a desexualized embodiment of femininity, directly opposed to a sexualized femininity in need of contraception. The reactionary tenor of these films—particularly their attempts to vilify family planning by conflating it with abortion—ran counter to much of the discourse circulated by birth control advocates at the time. One popular 1913 guide, *Private Sex Advice to Women for Young Wives and Those Who Expect to be Married*, aimed to disabuse readers of two common misconceptions: contraception was not designed to prevent reproduction altogether, the guide insisted; rather, its purpose was "governing, regulating and managing the production of human offspring." More important, birth control was not "practically analogous to abortion," as many claimed.[42] Even still, birth control advocates of the day rarely mentioned human sexuality in their campaigns, preferring instead to argue for control over nature by promoting "birth by human design," as one writer put it. Opponents of birth control, on the other hand, relentlessly emphasized the sexual hedonism they imagined would result from accessible family planning.[43] One commentator feared that contraception would yield a world of "sexual indulgence" without limitation—a specter evocatively visualized in *Where Are My Children?* when the childless wife is seen feasting lustily on chocolates.[44]

If anxieties about sexuality—*female* sexuality—lay beneath many film plots where stories of married and unmarried women were combined, matters of eugenics and "race suicide" were also never far from the surface. As one review of *The House Without Children* insisted, "the disinclination toward motherhood, general among the so-called higher classes," was "one of the biggest questions that face the present generation."[45] The "crime" that privileged white women committed by postponing or avoiding motherhood, underscored by their use of illegal abortion in so many of these films, was registered much more intensely when set against stories of impoverished, unmarried women facing unplanned pregnancies. Wealthy white women in these plots were refusing an obligation to "better the race." Adoption plots, such as those in *The Unborn*, went one step further, celebrating privileged white families raising a new generation of white children to ward against an imagined "race suicide." Ideas about eugenics, the pseudo-science of human improvement, were increasingly aligned with the birth control movement during these years, as activists focused more on the health benefits of contraception and less on feminist ideals.[46] Eugenics supplied "a scientific basis" to sentimentalized views of motherhood, historian Linda Gordon has emphasized, for "eugenic thought had always contained the assumption that reproduction was not just a function but the purpose [. . .] of women's life."[47] A racist and classist logic prevailed in eugenics, as these feature films indicate, by placing blame squarely on the shoulders of prosperous white women.

Black moviegoers of this era evidently saw plainly eugenicist features like *The Unborn*, *The House Without Children*, and *Where Are My Children?* when they played in Black theaters on Chicago's South Side after lengthy runs for predominantly white audiences at theaters in the Loop. Advertisements in the city's Black newspaper, the *Chicago Defender*, did not shy away from the controversy surrounding these pictures and, in fact, often emphasized their entanglement with eugenics.[48] When *Where Are My Children?* opened at the seven-hundred-seat States Theater after a fourteen-week run at the LaSalle Theater in the Loop, the *Defender* promised "race suicide and birth control exposed," underscoring the film's eugenicist politics in a way that would likely have had particular valence for Black women.[49] "Don't miss this one," the paper advised in its column "Among the Movies."[50] South Side theaters like the States typically catered to a wide cross-section of patrons from the Black community, as Jacqueline Stewart and Cara Caddoo have emphasized; but female moviegoers, those likely most attentive to matters of human reproduction, were an especially important clientele, for they served, in Stewart's words, as "magnets for other potential patrons across lines of gender, age, and class."[51]

The *Defender* ran a lengthy column on *The Unborn* during its run at the States after a ten-week engagement at the Black Box Theater in the Loop. Describing it as "far and away the strongest message" on birth control yet provided on film, the newspaper suggested *The Unborn* had become "the talk of the town—the topic in every home."[52] As fodder for this "talk," the *Defender* reminded readers that the film's plot resonated with three news stories that had garnered front-page headlines in the city's *Tribune* newspaper that fall: a raid on an abortion practice that revealed some fifteen hundred female clients; the death of a woman from an illegal abortion; and the suicide of a doctor arrested for performing abortions.[53] It is not clear that any of these headline-grabbing events involved Chicago's Black community, but the *Defender* suggested they resonated with its readership to such a degree that Black moviegoers would be keenly interested in stories of the white characters depicted in *The Unborn*—a naïve young woman "betrayed" and impregnated by a wealthy married man; a wife who has repeated abortions; and an unmarried young woman who dies from an unsafe abortion.[54] The *Defender*, in other words, empowered readers not only to talk about incidents depicted in *The Unborn* but to *connect* those incidents to events occurring in their own city—where lack of contraception forced women into unsafe, illegal abortions. Oversimplified, scaremongering film plots might be tempered by consideration of deeper, more structural problems in one's community, the paper suggested. By participating in conversations that linked onscreen narratives to contemporary events in Chicago, Black audiences might also be encouraged to participate in wider debates about reproductive politics in the city, including the eugenicist specter of "race suicide" invariably hovering over stories about abortion and contraception. After all, the *Defender* began its column on *The Unborn* by invoking the banner that had hung over the entrance of the LaSalle Theater when the film played there for largely white audiences: "Knowledge Is Power: Safeguard Your Dear Ones." This slogan likely held a keen resonance for Black Chicagoans of this era, attentive to the role eugenics played in discussions of family planning and keen to "safeguard" their own.

While newspapers like the *Defender* encouraged readers to discuss the birth control pictures they saw and draw connections between events dramatized onscreen and those occurring in their own communities in ways that might challenge conservative attitudes about contraception, abortion, and "race suicide," activists in the campaign to legalize contraception also seized on cinema as a means of spreading word about their efforts and mobilizing new recruits for the cause. Margaret Sanger, the era's best-known activist, released her film *Birth Control* in the spring of 1917, recreating scenes from her storied crusade (see figure 18.5). As Margaret I. MacDonald noted, rather dryly, in her review, Sanger's work "had aroused not a little controversy within the past few months."[55] Indeed, Sanger used the film to redefine herself and her campaign at a key juncture, historians Kay Sloan and Martin F. Norden emphasize, targeting a broad audience by downplaying more radical aspects of her past, accentuating her own martyrdom, and "paying homage to the sanctity of the family and to the traditional role of women," as Sloan put it.[56] The film concludes with a shot of Sanger behind bars and the title, "No matter what happens, the work must go on."[57] By the time the film was released, Sanger

FIGURE 18.5 A trade paper advertisement for Margaret Sanger's *Birth Control* (1917) proclaimed "every woman in the world will demand to see it." *Moving Picture World*, April 21, 1917.

had long been out of prison—in fact, she intended to accompany the film at screenings around the country promoting her cause. Thus, the decision to end with Sanger's imprisonment and a direct appeal to viewers pushed moviegoers to take action in their own communities, their own homes, and their own lives.

Birth Control was advertised to exhibitors as Sanger's "message for the million millions" that "every woman in the world will demand to see."[58] Noting that the film would surely "attract crowds" of "feminines," *Variety*'s critic conveyed some of the film's impact, suggesting that "the average viewer is electrified" by Sanger's "intense convictions" and concluding "if not making everyone who sees the picture a convert to her cause [the film] will certainly make everyone think twice" about the campaign to legalize contraception.[59] When New York City's Park Theatre attempted to screen *Birth Control* in May 1917, patrons packed the venue, hoping to hear Sanger "speak her cause" at the opening, but were "sadly disappointed" when the city's license commissioner stopped the screening, saying movie theaters "ought not to be used to exploit something that is against the law."[60] The film's overt feminist politics—and the use of movie theaters as a space to mobilize female activists with feminist oratory and feminist films—presented a frightening prospect to Commissioner George Bell, who felt it was "going rather far to classify a birth control film as theatrical entertainment."[61] Women in the city closely followed the ensuing legal battle, according to *Billboard*, which reported in its "Tea with the Ladies" column that "New York women have been interested in knowing what would happen" to Sanger's film.[62] The crowds of women drawn to *Birth Control* became an important visual index of support for the campaign to legalize contraception; the even greater legion of women evidently following coverage of the controversy in the press, some perhaps hesitant to show their support in public at movie theaters, hints at the presence of a substantial feminist community garnered in and through screenings of films like *Birth Control*—all the more so, it seems, when those screenings were banned.

At the height of the controversy surrounding Sanger's *Birth Control*, Lois Weber released her second feature on contraception, *The Hand That Rocks the Cradle* (1917), presenting a story clearly drawn from Sanger's well-known campaign and one in which Weber herself plays a birth control advocate jailed for her activism (see figure 18.6).[63] It was not simply Sanger's personal story that Weber adapted in her script, for as reviewer Peter Milne observed, Weber also "molded her picture on facts and propaganda constantly in use by advocates of birth control." The film's titles, Milne reported, "contain facts and figures that startle" and "make one gasp."[64] *The Hand That Rocks the Cradle* emphasizes, in particular, the importance of female voices in debates about reproductive politics, charting the evolution of fictional activist Louise Broome's campaign for what she calls "intelligent childbearing." After first talking privately with her maid and her affluent friends about their own efforts to control reproduction, Broome (played by Weber) adopts an increasingly prominent voice, speaking first to groups of friends in their homes, then later to large crowds, and is eventually jailed for her advocacy. As the film's promotional materials made clear, a woman's class, ethnicity, and race often determined whether she had access to adequate information on family planning: the "great

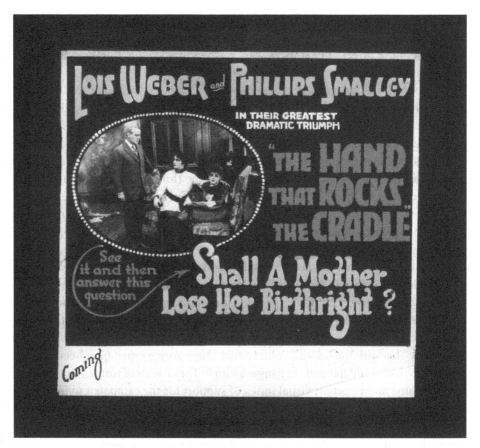

FIGURE 18.6 A glass slide for *The Hand That Rocks the Cradle* (1917), featuring director Lois Weber in her starring role as birth control activist Louise Broome. Author's collection.

secret" of contraception was "an open one to rich women; a closed one to the poor."[65] According to Milne's report, the film "stirred a certain portion of the audience to applause" when Broome points out "if the [male] lawmakers had to bear children they would change the law."[66] What is more, questions about *who* speaks about reproduction and *where* are not confined to the diegetic story in *The Hand That Rocks the Cradle*, for the film ends with an invocation to its audience, asking in a final title, "What do *you* think?," urging viewers to continue their own discussions of the campaign to legalize birth control outside the theater.[67]

Direct appeals to the viewer at the end of both *The Hand That Rocks the Cradle* and Sanger's *Birth Control* remind us how important female movie audiences were in the fight to legalize contraception, how much thinking, discussion, and debate the films would have prompted, and how vital women's voices were in public conversations about reproductive politics during these years. If films made during the "Age of Birth Control" promulgated largely conservative messages about female sexuality (bad), motherhood (good), and abortion (deadly), it is clear that the discourse surrounding these films in promotions, reviews, and commentary invited women in the audience to think beyond these safe parameters, to assess choices made by characters onscreen, to contemplate their own behavior, to connect stories onscreen to events in their own communities, and to seize every opportunity to add their voices to civic debates and political protest.

It is no wonder, then, that the merits of depicting topics like abortion and family planning for female moviegoers prompted considerable controversy during a period when the film industry eagerly courted female patrons. Were movie theaters an appropriate venue for this adult material? Were female-only screenings an appropriate way to dignify this material, framing it under the auspices of a ladies' matinee, or did this practice only telegraph a salacious appeal? Were women seeing things onscreen they ought not to see—scenes depicting birth control clinics or abortion providers, scenes of childbirth, scenes of "seduction" or implied sexual assault, scenes of frank sexual interest between unmarried or adulterous couples? Even worse, were women perhaps tempted to *imagine* such scenes, even when not depicted onscreen? Were women inspired to discuss these matters after screenings in ways that might prompt them to speculate beyond the films' conservative appeals to sexual "purity," motherhood, or "eugenic marriage"? And, finally, could women be mobilized by these films, motivated to advocate in their communities for family planning, for access to safe abortion, or for modern childbirth methods? Female audiences and female-centric subject matter, however much coveted by those eager to uplift cinema's reputation during these years, often introduced unanticipated challenges, as films on reproductive politics demonstrate. The "respectable" white, middle-class female moviegoers imagined by an industry eager for cultural legitimacy did not always materialize. Instead, films on birth control, eugenics, and abortion attracted curiosity seekers, morbid minds, and embarrassed young ladies.

Notes

1. "The Age of Birth Control," *New Republic*, September 25, 1915, 195–197. For information on reproductive politics of this era, see Linda Gordon, *Woman's Body, Woman's Right: A Social History of Birth Control in America* (New York: Viking, 1976), 206–244; Peter C. Engelman, *A History of the Birth Control Movement in America* (Santa Barbara, CA: Praeger, 2011), 75–139; Leslie J. Reagan, *When Abortion Was a Crime: Women, Medicine, and Law in the United States, 1867–1973* (Berkeley: University of California Press, 1997), 80–112; Trent MacNamara, *Birth Control and American Modernity: A History of Popular Ideas* (New York: Cambridge University Press, 2018); Dolores Flamiano, "The Birth of a Notion: Media Coverage of Contraception, 1915–1917," *Journalism and Mass Communication Quarterly* 75, no. 3 (1998): 560–571.
2. Kay Sloan, *The Loud Silents: Origins of the Social Problem Film* (Urbana: University of Illinois Press, 1988), 86–94; Kevin Brownlow, *Behind the Mask of Innocence: The Social Problem Films of the Silent Era* (New York: Knopf, 1990), 47–55; Martin F. Norden, "Reproductive Freedom, Revisionist History, Restricted Cinema: The Strange Case of Margaret Sanger and Birth Control," in Lester Friedman, ed., *Cultural Sutures: Medicine and Media* (Durham, NC: Duke University Press, 2004), 263–279. See also Megan Minarich, "Hollywood's Reproduction Code: Regulating Contraception and Abortion in American

Cinema, 1915–1952 (PhD diss., Vanderbilt University, 2014). For information on public health films of this era focused on motherhood and infant care, see Marina Dahlquist, "Health Instruction on Screen: The Department of Health in New York City, 1909–1917," in Marta Braun, Charlie Keil, Rob King, Paul Moore, and Louis Pelletier, eds., *Beyond the Screen: Institutions, Networks, and Publics of Early Cinema* (New Barnet, UK: John Libbey, 2012), 107–116.

3. "Sunday Pictures Should Draw on Merit," *Motion Picture News*, December 16, 1916, 3805 (emphasis in original).
4. J. E. Hipple, "Exhibitor Kills Sunday Laws," *Motography*, April 7, 1917, 726.
5. Kitty Kelly, "'Miracle of Life' A Motherhood Film," *Chicago Tribune*, October 25, 1915, 12.
6. Mae Tinee, "Next Week It'll Be Your Turn, Men," *Chicago Tribune*, October 17, 1916, 15.
7. George D. Gould, "Birth," *Motion Picture News*, April 28, 1917, 2687. The film does not survive. Further details are available in "Birth," *Moving Picture World*, April 28, 1917, 609; George Graves, "Birth," *Motography*, April 28, 1917, 975; "Birth," *New York Dramatic Mirror*, April 21, 1917, 28.
8. "Many Closeups of Just Kids, With a Few Instructive Scenes," *Wid's*, April 19, 1917, 244–245.
9. "A Eugenic Picture," *Los Angeles Times*, November 11, 1917, III.4.
10. Advertisement in *Los Angeles Times*, November 9, 1917, II.10.
11. White women in California already enjoyed the right to vote in municipal and state-wide ballots, but they were not yet eligible to vote in federal elections. Women were granted voting rights in 1910 in Washington and 1911 in California, though not all women enjoyed the privilege of voting in these states. Voting rights were restricted to those with literacy and fluency in English, rules often used to disenfranchise women of color; and citizenship restrictions on many Asian and Native American women prevented them from voting.
12. Advertisement in *Motion Picture News*, March 10, 1917, 1506.
13. "'Enlighten Thy Daughter' Crowds Park," unidentified newspaper clipping, n.d., n.p., Katharine Kaelred Scrapbook, Billy Rose Theatre Division, New York Public Library for the Performing Arts (hereafter KKS).
14. Unidentified advertisement, n.d., n.p., KKS.
15. Dickson G. Watts, "'Enlighten Thy Daughter,'" unidentified newspaper clipping, n.d., n.p., KKS.
16. Unidentified review, n.d., n.p., KKS.
17. Unidentified advertisements, n.d., n.p., KKS.
18. "'Enlighten Thy Daughter' Crowds Park."
19. "Enlighten Thy Daughter," *New York Dramatic Mirror*, n.d., n.p., KKS.
20. Unidentified advertisements, n.d., n.p., KKS.
21. "Enlighten Thy Daughter," *New York Dramatic Mirror*, n.d., n.p., KKS.
22. Quoted in "The Natural Law," *Exhibitors Herald*, November 17, 1917, 30.
23. Edward Weitzel, "The Natural Law," *Moving Picture World*, November 17, 1917, 1032; "The Natural Law," *Variety*, November 2, 1917, 51.
24. Helen Rockwell, "The Natural Law," *Motography*, November 17, 1917, 1055.
25. Ibid.; and Weitzel, "The Natural Law."
26. "Publicity Campaign for 'Natural Law' by Hesser," *Motion Picture News*, August 11, 1917, 1002.
27. Rockwell, "The Natural Law," 1055.
28. Ibid. The film does not survive. Further plot details were gleaned from the reviews cited above, as well as "Across the Silversheet," *Motion Picture*, February 1918, 128–129.

29. Rose Woodallen Chapman, "How Should I Tell My Child?" *Ladies' Home Journal*, November 1910, 60. See also "How I Told My Children: The Experience of a Mother of Six Children," *Ladies' Home Journal*, May 1912, 28.
30. Charles W. Eliot, "Why I Believe the Policy of Silence to be Wrong," *Ladies' Home Journal*, June 1911, 6; Right Reverend Arthur C. A. Hall, "My Reasons for Believing That Mothers Should Speak Out," *Ladies' Home Journal*, June 1911, 6.
31. Engelman, *A History of the Birth Control Movement in America*, 32.
32. Advertisement in *Reel Life*, December 23, 1915, 33; "Mr. Exhibitor: Miss Fisher [sic]," *Motography*, November 18, 1916, 1137.
33. Louis Reeves Harrison, "The Miracle of Life," *Moving Picture World*, October 9, 1915, 281.
34. "Mr. Exhibitor: Miss Fisher," 1137. See also "The Miracle of Life," *Motography*, October 30, 1915, 937; Kitty Kelly, "'Miracle of Life' a Motherhood Film," *Chicago Tribune*, October 25, 1915, 12.
35. Hazel Simpson Naylor, "As Others See You, or Gleanings from the Audience," *Motion Picture*, May 1916, 178.
36. "The House Without Children," *Motion Picture News*, August 23, 1919, 1683; "The House Without Children," *Exhibitors Herald and Motography*, August 23, 1919, 57.
37. The advertisement is reproduced in "Question Mark Gets Attention," *Exhibitors Herald*, September 13, 1919, 71.
38. "Question Mark Gets Attention."
39. For a more detailed analysis of *Where Are My Children?* see Shelley Stamp, *Lois Weber in Early Hollywood* (Berkeley: University of California Press, 2015), 168–190.
40. Oscar Cooper, "The Question," *Motion Picture News*, March 11, 1916, 1468. Additional plot details from "The Question," *New York Dramatic Mirror*, February 26, 1916, 33; Lynde Denig, "Two Equitable Dramas," *Moving Picture World*, March 4, 1916, 1489; "The Question," *Moving Picture World*, March 4, 1916, 1554; and Tony Langston, "The Question," *Chicago Defender*, April 15, 1916, 5.
41. The film does not survive. Plot details garnered from the following reviews: H. S. Fuld, "The Unborn," *Motion Picture News*, July 1, 1916, 4085; Mae Tinee, "Next Week It'll be Your Turn, Men," 15; "The Unborn," *Chicago Defender*, December 30, 1916, 6.
42. R. B. Armitage, *Private Sex Advice to Women for Young Wives and Those Who Expect to be Married* (Chicago, IL: Advance Thought Publishing, 1913), 128, 129.
43. "The Age of Birth Control," 197.
44. F. W. Peterson, "Joy in Store for the Debauchee," *Harper's Weekly*, October 2, 1915, 331.
45. "The House Without Children," *Exhibitors Herald and Motography*, August 23, 1919, 57.
46. Gordon, *Woman's Body, Woman's Right*, 116–158; Engelman, *A History of the Birth Control Movement in America*, 130–137.
47. Gordon, *Woman's Body, Woman's Right*, 132, 134.
48. "Among the Movies," *Chicago Defender*, December 30, 1916, 9; "Among the Movies," *Chicago Defender*, January 13, 1917, 2; "The House Without Children," *Chicago Defender*, October 23, 1920, 4; "The House Without Children," *Chicago Defender*, November 13, 1920, 4; Tony Langston, "The Question," *Chicago Defender*, April 15, 1916, 5.
49. Advertisement in *Chicago Defender*, October 28, 1916, 4.
50. "Among the Movies," *Chicago Defender*, October 28, 1916, 4.
51. Jacqueline Najuma Stewart, *Migrating to the Movies: Cinema and Black Urban Modernity* (Berkeley: University of California Press, 2005), 136–141; and Cara Caddoo, *Envisioning*

Freedom: Cinema and the Building of Modern Black Life (Cambridge, MA: Harvard University Press, 2014), 82. Quote from Stewart, 139.
52. "The Unborn," *Chicago Defender*, December 30, 1916, 6.
53. See "'Abortion Mill' List of 1,500," *Chicago Tribune*, September 26, 1916, 1; "Abortion Case Death Certificate Forged," *Chicago Tribune*, October 14, 1916, 15; "Arrest Doctor Takes Poison?" *Chicago Tribune*, October 14, 1916, 1; "Arrested Physician Dies at St. Luke's," *Chicago Tribune*, October 15, 1916, A1.
54. Fuld, "The Unborn," 4085; Tinee, "Next Week It'll be Your Turn, Men"; "The Unborn," *Chicago Defender*, December 30, 1916, 6.
55. Margaret I. MacDonald, "Birth Control," *Moving Picture World*, April 21, 1917, 451.
56. Sloan, *The Loud Silents*, 87. See also Norden, "Reproductive Freedom, Revisionist History, Restricted Cinema."
57. Quoted in Brownlow, *Behind the Mask of Innocence*, 48. Further details of the film's plot are available in "Stop 'Birth Control,'" *New York Dramatic Mirror*, May 12, 1917, 32. See also MacDonald, "'Birth Control,'" 451; "Birth Control," *Variety*, April 13, 1917, 27; and "Mrs. Sanger to Tour with Her Film," *New York Times*, March 28, 1917, 11.
58. Advertisement in *Moving Picture World*, April 21, 1917, 388–389.
59. "Birth Control," *Variety*, April 13, 1917, 27.
60. "Birth Control 'Movie' Barred from Public," *New York World*, May 7, 1917, 9.
61. Ibid.
62. "Tea with the Ladies," *Billboard*, June 23, 1917, 25. For more on the troubled exhibition histories of *Birth Control* and *The Hand That Rocks the Cradle*, see my article "Taking Precautions, or Regulating Early Birth Control Films," in Jennifer Bean and Diane Negra, eds., *A Feminist Reader in Early Cinema* (Durham, NC: Duke University Press, 2002), 270–297.
63. No extant print of *The Hand That Rocks the Cradle* survives. The film's screenplay is reprinted in "Continuity and Subtitles: 'Is a Woman a Person?'" *Film History* 1, no. 4 (1987): 343–366. Contemporary reviews and plot summaries confirm that the film was released in this version. See "Hand That Rocks Cradle," *Variety*, May 18, 1917, 26; "The Hand That Rocks the Cradle," *New York Dramatic Mirror*, May 26, 1917, 28; "The Hand That Rocks the Cradle," *Wid's*, May 31, 1917, 349–350; Edward Weitzel, "The Hand That Rocks the Cradle," *Moving Picture World*, June 2, 1917, 1458; Peter Milne, "The Hand That Rocks the Cradle," *Motion Picture News*, June 2, 1917, 3462–3463; and "The Hand That Rocks the Cradle," *Moving Picture World*, June 2, 1917, 1501.
64. Milne, "The Hand That Rocks the Cradle," 3462.
65. *The Hand That Rocks the Cradle* publicity herald, private collection.
66. Milne, "The Hand That Rocks the Cradle," 3463.
67. "Continuity and Subtitles: 'Is a Woman a Person?'" 366.

PART IV

HOLLYWOOD, INC.

The Institutions of Mass Culture

CHAPTER 19

UNLIKELY ALLIES
Crafting Hollywood as Institution and Invention

CHARLIE KEIL AND DENISE MCKENNA

IN 1925, Charles Donald Fox wrote a book about filmdom evocatively titled *Mirrors of Hollywood*. In it, he stresses that Hollywood's status as the center of movie production creates constant confusion between the "real" locale (a quiet Southern California community) and the mythic site (so outside the realm of the ordinary that he calls it a "fairyland"). Throughout Fox's account, Hollywood is a city of profound contradictions, at once a "setting for the brilliance of the motion picture stars, as gorgeous and colorful as the [celestial] stars themselves," and at the same time a place where "white-tiled grocery stores, dairies and meat markets, ten-cent stores, toy bazaars and soda fountains reflect the simplicity of Hollywood life."[1] Many of the book's photo illustrations confirm the contrast: a solemn image of Hollywood High School shares space with publicity stills of stars; a page featuring Thomas Ince's elegant mansion is answered on the flip side by a "typical" Hollywood street (see figure 19.1). As Fox's mirror metaphor suggests, attempts to define Hollywood have often run up against the incongruities embodied by its glaring oppositions of the everyday and the fantastical, collisions between materiality and illusion, structure and artistry.

Another dominant metaphor employed to describe the studio system, the "dream factory," similarly captures the tension inherent to the opposition between reverie and industry. Such contrasts were amplified during the formative years of the "classical cinema" era, as production became increasingly prevalent on the West Coast, and defenses of the rigor and expertise required by film production consistently jostled against discourse that celebrated the industry's casual sociability and freewheeling creativity.[2] These contradictions also became topographical in accounts of filmmaking—as an industry, as an art form, and as a lifestyle—that were written in the wake of the shift to the West Coast and which often merged the industry's cultural malleability with regional boosterism that romanticized Southern California's "Spanish" past and promised a Utopic future.[3] Charles Donald Fox's interrogation of Hollywood is telling because it effectively exposes how this place, from its founding,

A TYPICAL HOLLYWOOD STREET

FIGURE 19.1 Charles Donald Fox, *Mirrors of Hollywood* (New York: Charles Renard, 1925): "A Typical Hollywood Street."

was a site where self-definition operated according to a sliding scale rather than a fixed reality. Throughout *Mirrors*, Fox's metaphor of reflection vacillates between extremes in order to encapsulate the inherent paradox at the core of Hollywood's dualistic identity. At once commonplace and extraordinary, Hollywood, much like the stars it produced, worked to reconcile potentially antithetical ideas about fame and the everyday, glamour and industry, the mythic and the mundane, which effectively transformed contradictory concepts into a potent and malleable image.

"Hollywood" as a cultural byword was born out of a discursive process that was years in the making. The locale itself pre-dated the arrival of the film industry by many decades, with dedicated development of the area beginning in the 1880s; by 1902, when it was officially made a city, Hollywood boasted a population of less than a thousand and the requisite community centers of church, school, post office, and a newspaper. But the histories of West Coast filmmaking and Hollywood's changing municipal fortunes would become intertwined soon thereafter, sometimes dictated by the mundane practicalities of bureaucratic need and sometimes driven by chance. Ongoing sewage problems caused by the area's rainy season forced Hollywood to agree to annexation to the city of Los Angeles in 1910; the boundaries separating Hollywood from Los Angeles were always porous and subject to negotiation. At the same time, West Coast filmmaking did not restrict itself to Hollywood proper, with companies choosing to operate in adjacent communities from Glendale to Culver City. Nothing about Hollywood's origins as one of the many outposts of Los Angeles recommended it as an exceptional site, and one cannot trace the city's anointment as the synecdochal representation of all moviemaking activity to any defining moment or decisive gesture.

Instead, crafting "Hollywood" out of Los Angeles was a process driven by the need to define the filmmaking community against a set of questions that threatened its status as an emergent industry and influential cultural entity. What we identify as the site's functional value to the motion picture industry—its "institutional dualism"—manifested itself in a variety of ways and through numerous discursive agents. If a throughline exists, one can locate it in a desire to assert the industry's stability by aligning it to the reassuring rhythms and identifiable touchstones of small-town life; at the same time, such assertions consistently acknowledged the unruly nature of filmmaking as a creative enterprise. Still, that acknowledgment necessarily contained a multitude of tensions, extending from the manner of characterizing studio leadership to the nature of the filmmaking workforce. Were those charged with making movies part of a pre-existing community or a unique group with separate status? Did the industry function akin to other established businesses, reliant on trade organizations, or did its unorthodox products and processes require equally unusual forms of industrial management? And who should take responsibility for representing an industry whose chief aim was to provide fanciful forms of imagery to the masses? It's little wonder that the symbolic incorporation of all the film industry's ambitions and foibles should be capacious and unwieldy, constantly toggling between the desire to establish clear boundaries and the impulse to break free from all constraints.

As filmmakers aimed for self-determination and self-definition during these turbulent years, we find a case study of a developing institution imposing order on the disorderly process of creativity. Equally, we find a distinctive artistic and industrial community identifying itself in relation to a dubious nation and to its conservative municipal landlords. The process of definition extended to crafting particular images of leadership, where moviemakers could be managers, and to deploying protective organizations to smooth tensions between the industry and its regional overseers. Stoked by challenges to the industry's expanding infrastructure and social acceptability during the teens, filmmakers established intercompany alliances that continued to develop and solidify into the 1920s. Hollywood became the functional center of these efforts, as both a tool and a target in the ongoing cultural wars that coalesced around such moments as the star scandals of the early 1920s and the interstudio coordination of labor and management in the Studio Basic Agreement and the formation of the Central Casting Bureau mid-decade.[4] Moreover, so imbricated was moviemaking in the development of Southern California that Hollywood's emergence also serves as a way to map film production onto changing small-town life: charting the growth of the film industry on the West Coast requires, then, the parallel examination of industrial and urban expansion in Los Angeles County. Accordingly, we set the struggles of studio management next to the ambitions of land developers to understand the ways in which Hollywood's spatial and symbolic potential emerged out of the transactional logic that tied urban development to civic moralism. The resulting discourse culminates in the shifting rhetoric evident in the pages of local newspapers such as the community weekly *Holly Leaves*, and in the increasingly popular industry exposé, a genre exemplified by Fox's *Mirrors of Hollywood*. Ultimately, defining Hollywood entailed styling the city into a complex metaphorical site that blended industry and artistry, and establishing the complex terrain of Hollywood's institutional dualism.

MOVIEMAKERS AS MANAGERS

A central point of contention between filmmakers and their newly adopted city was the need to account for the industry's vast, mobile, and sometimes volatile workforce. The question of how to deal with the rapidly expanding studio labor contingent was a particularly thorny issue in Los Angeles, which was a determinedly anti-union city. Managing the unfolding complications of the industry's labor force was compounded by the unease prompted by an influx of outsiders, anxiety that crystallized in the negative publicity accorded movie extras during the 1910s and 1920s.[5] Conflict over labor agitation and the problems associated with a heterosocial workplace, however, had unexpectedly productive outcomes, insofar as these issues forced the industry to adopt a variety of self-defining strategies that identified key managerial roles, produced cohesion across otherwise competitive interests, and opened up conversations between the filmmaking community and municipal forces.

Advancing an image of professionalism was paramount for an industry eager to promote its legitimacy and to define its processes. Movie magazines, trade journals, and local newspapers filled countless pages interviewing film personnel about their work, which allowed performers, technicians, and managers to explain their roles within the evolving drama of a fascinating new industry. Enlisting creative personnel to affirm their professional bona fides had the added benefit of proving that filmmaking talent could embrace responsible business practices. To represent filmmaking as both an economic enterprise and aesthetic endeavor became the prevailing discursive strategy, one that infused potentially impersonal corporate structures with the dynamism of creative inspiration. Prior to the emergence of film moguls as the public face of the studio system in the 1920s, the director served as the figure who reconciled these contradictory impulses toward creativity and control.[6] A photographic collage in Fox's *Mirrors of Hollywood* literalizes this discourse, depicting the director Frank Borzage casually leaning on a camera as he explains to the author "what is required of those who seek screen fame" (see figure 19.2). Borzage's command of the camera underpins his authority to define the requirements of stardom, while the bottom half of the image, with its rather chaotic image of extras in scanty costumes, reinforces the gendered structure of the studio labor hierarchy. Serving as a visual reminder of Borzage's directorial command over the studio, the collage also invests the combination of director and technology with a power capable of managing the anarchic energy just below the surface of any Hollywood production.[7]

The struggle between these two, seemingly irreconcilable, impulses also plays itself out in correspondence between Cecil B. DeMille and Jesse Lasky during the 1910s, where it assumes a more explicitly financial valence. In various memos to DeMille, Lasky seems unable to decide whether artistry or profits should be given priority, at one point saying "when you wire me to engage a director, I can feel that the main thing to consider is his ability first and his salary second," but at another declaring "While you may not agree with me, my slogan is 'Dividends first and art second.'"[8] As the industry matured, and timely delivery of increasingly longer and more expensive product depended on a systematized production process, one can understand why the preference for factory metaphors conferring efficiency and economy of means might prevail. But Hollywood wasn't mass-producing utilitarian products or even bland educational tracts; rather, it fabricated exotic tales populated by nationally adored stars. Accordingly, the ongoing conflict between artistry (or at the very least a form of imaginative labor) and industry remained an animating tension pervading depictions and definitions of Hollywood. Initially, at least, and certainly in the case of DeMille, that tension could be rationalized by representing the director as a controlling creative force. DeMille's persona, as defined by Famous Players-Lasky's (FPL) advertising material, melded the creative impulses of the director with the managerial sensibility of a studio executive; conveniently, DeMille performed both roles, as FPL's Director General of studio operations on the West Coast. The company's promotional rhetoric contributed to the understanding of the director (dramatized by DeMille) as a public figure; it also depended on fusing an image of authority (sartorial choices included jodhpurs and boots, signifiers of mastering a horse) with artistic deviation from corporate norms (he was typically shown wearing an open-necked white shirt).

Critically, the director's authority as an organizing principle brought into balance conflicting impulses in the emerging studio system, between creativity and control and between talent and management, and provided a workable counterpoint to Lasky's economic imperative of "dividends first." Directors could represent art first and dividends second, and ultimately balance the two, all while performing critical governance functions. Artful oversight becomes the dominant trope in representations of the

FIGURE 19.2 Fox, *Mirrors of Hollywood*.

director's value. Ads for DeMille's films in the 1910s defined him as the "directing genius who aided Jesse L. Lasky in establishing the Lasky Productions as motion pictures of supreme merit."[9] Individual genius merged with company branding, just as East Coast corporate oversight guided West Coast production.

The physical distance separating the two spheres of the film industry, however, inevitably created strain, with DeMille at one point plaintively asking Lasky if the studios in Hollywood were anything more than "branch plants."[10] In this comment, DeMille might well have been alluding to the primary manner in which other California industries had grown. Moviemaking wasn't singular in this regard: the area's second-fastest growing sector, rubber and tires, developed precisely according to this center/periphery model.[11] To placate his star director and studio head, Lasky made periodic visits to the West Coast operation; while ultimately these visits helped to cement the idea that the true center of filmmaking activity was in California, they also affirmed the bifurcated nature of film production. The literal and figurative distance separating Lasky from FPL's Hollywood studios would need to be bridged by more than Lasky's trips to the West Coast, and as a matter of structural efficiency, the film industry had to vest more power in its center of production operations by settling its leaders in Hollywood.

If filmmaking's ingrained institutional paradoxes could be managed by personifying them in the figures of its directors, other rhetorical strategies emerged that emphasized the industry's relationship with its newfound home. In the teens, the director provided a useful figure through which to imagine cinema's social identity, but by the 1920s the movie mogul assumes prominence. A transitional figure such as Thomas Ince proves instructive—launching his career as a director in 1910, Ince moved progressively into the role of producer by the time he developed a massive West Coast production facility dubbed "Inceville" in the early 1910s. As Ince refined the process of dividing filmmaking into craft-specific tasks overseen by a production manager, his organizational acumen easily translated into the commandeering of huge tracts of land to serve as the laboratories for large-scale filmmaking. While the scope of Ince's productions increased, his dedication to a domesticized image for studio manufacture comes to the fore in the main office building constructed to anchor his second filmmaking complex, Thomas H. Ince Studios, initiated in Culver City in 1919. Reportedly modeled after George Washington's home at Mount Vernon, this building, later immortalized as the edifice featured in the Selznick International Pictures title image, has come to be the iconic representation of a mogul's power.

But neither Ince nor DeMille would endure as the dominant figuration of studio control. As the film industry matured, the mogul as (typically Jewish) potentate became the signal representative of upper management, supplanting the director as a rationale for control over production that had expanded beyond studio walls into the amorphous notion of Hollywood as a system and an idea. Jesse Lasky, Carl Laemmle, and Samuel Goldwyn, among others, moved beyond the role of manager, chief, or producer into the more rarefied realm of media magnate. One can see the transformation in the public image of the mogul by comparing two profiles of Jesse Lasky, one from 1921 and the other appearing six years later. In the first, Lasky's home remains hidden from "rubber-neck men who seldom take the trouble to point it out at all."[12] But by 1927, Lasky no longer stays sequestered in his vine-covered hideaway; the profile's author, Terry Ramsaye, describes Lasky as dashing out of his Fifth Avenue apartment every morning to "go briskly and businesslike to his office and clear up that desk."[13] Despite Lasky's deep and expansive roots in the film industry, Ramsaye represents him as a kind of metaphysical media poet rather than a corporate executive, working "incidentally" in the realm of business but living "in the land of far dreams and speculations." That Lasky still works on the East Coast matters less than the symbolic transformation of his livelihood as existing in a land of "dreams" that resides "far" from a normal workaday world.

The famous film moguls interviewed by Ramsaye for *Photoplay* exemplify different styles of studio management, but each harnesses creative chaos to business acumen in ways that allow him to effectively govern his filmmaking empire. Expanding the roster of studio talents, the mogul's genius is corporate, reconciling conflicts between creativity and control with inspired management. But it was also something more alchemical; according to Ramsaye, the mogul was able to harness the power of the motion pictures through "some deep combination of luck, magic, and genius." The movie mogul's mutability is well suited to governing the potentiality of Hollywood as a capacious cultural idea and burgeoning industrial system. Not tied to megaphone or camera, Ramsaye's modern media moguls are also a mysterious sect, able to sell the public "their own state of mind about a shadow on the screen" and yet control the "odd, wild organism" of the film industry with practical skills grounded in banking, investing, and even shipbuilding.[14] Like many of the stars whose contracts they owned, they are described in terms that vacillate between the ordinary and extraordinary, pictured in casual family photos but surrounded by glimpses of luxurious wealth. Furthermore, as Mark Garrett Cooper explains, Hollywood's Jewish mogul could stand in for the history of cinema's progress as an American institution. Movie moguls encapsulated the struggles of ethnic assimilation, winning authority by "overcoming their Jewish difference" while at the same time, paradoxically, the industry was able to become "supremely American through the intuition of foreign Jews."[15]

By the end of the 1920s, the movie mogul's corporate mastery validated Hollywood's success at expanding its imaginative borders, allowing Hollywood to become the nation's foremost cultural industry while retaining its regional identity. Fittingly, the mythologizing of movie moguls occurred at a time when studio ranks had begun to swell with exoticized European screen stars and directors; the shifting terms of insider/outsider dichotomies within the studio helped reinforce the identity of Hollywood moviemaking as a preeminently American institution. Ever adaptable, Hollywood's commitment to its hometown ethos enfolded its ethnically "other" moguls in order to distinguish truly foreign talent from its own jealously protected institutions. Moreover, as the visible face of the labor force seemed ever more remote from—and heedless of—Main Street norms, the need for management heads to assert the values of small-town America became all the more pressing, even if their only claim to this ordinary life was in carefully posed family photos or soft-focus stories that promoted their "brisk" business-like efficiency. But insisting on the normalcy of leadership became only one rhetorical strategy in the industry's ongoing campaign to manage its public image and ward off incipient scandal.

Countering Crisis Through Interinstitutional Alliances

Critics had long argued about cinema's relative merits as an aesthetic medium, but as film's popularity increased, those concerns took a back seat to publicly expressed anxiety about the exploitative dimensions of motion pictures. The controversies roiling around film culture as it developed during this period put the industry on the defensive, both in relation to a national debate over censorship and also to the exploitation of young women in the newly built and increasingly high-profile studios.[16] Indeed, the formation in 1915 and 1916 of Los Angeles–based protective organizations such as the Motion Picture Directors Association, the Motion Picture Conservation Association, the Motion Picture Protective Organization, and the Motion Picture Producers Association should be seen as responses to foundational challenges to the industry's authority. The formation of these various protective organizations served to defend the integrity of directors and producers, but it also had the effect of crafting ideas about industrial hierarchies and the image of studio executives.

As scandal remains synonymous with Hollywood's institutional identity, it seems fitting that the industry's integration with Los Angeles was propelled, in part, by local investigations into the studios and their "immoral" hiring practices. The controversy started in 1915 when a local minister accused unnamed directors of taking advantage of young women looking for work in the studios. Newspapers in Los Angeles followed the crisis with enthusiasm, chronicling meetings, accusations, anonymous letters, and testimony that called the studios into question as reputable institutions. Deputy District Attorney Claire Woolwine demanded further inquiry and a possible Grand Jury investigation.[17] This ominous turn of events was mitigated somewhat by the Deputy DA's confidence that any problems associated with motion pictures and the treatment of female employees could quickly be resolved with the cooperation of industry leaders.[18] Although the official investigation was eventually dropped, directors, managers, and producers figured prominently in stories published throughout the year that chronicled abuses of power and sexual corruption.[19]

Quickly contained, this proto-"casting couch" scandal remained primarily a local story, but the industry's reactions to it, particularly in the formation of professional organizations, contributed to forms of institutional self-definition that exceeded municipal boundaries. Anxiety about the reputational status of film directors, for instance, informed the articles of incorporation for the Motion Picture Directors Association (MPDA), which explicitly connected reputation and behavior, asserting that the organization's purpose was to: "(a) maintain the honor and dignity of the profession of motion picture directors [and] (b) to cultivate the usefulness and exert every influence to improve the moral, social and intellectual standing of all persons connected with the motion picture producing business."[20] Neither a guild nor a union, the MPDA still shared something in common with these types of organizations, and the MPDA's articles listed its aims as fostering more interaction among associates and helping "distressed" members and their wives and families. Such altruism was inevitably coded in paternalistic terms: at a time when the directing field was not yet entirely dominated by men, the formation of the MPDA asserted the collective identity of directors as responsible, respectable, and male.[21] Critically, organizations such as the MPDA helped craft an "official" voice that could speak for the moviemaking business, allowing one director to stand for many during meetings involving the city, women's groups, and business organizations, as the industry worked to contain studio scandals and to promote industry interests.

The MPDA was not a singular organization during this period. The turn to interinstitutional cohesion was further prompted by the Mutual Decision of 1915, which denied the industry protection under the First Amendment and essentially undercut the industry's claims to cultural credibility.[22] Repercussions from the Mutual Decision heightened the national debate about film censorship, drawing studio representatives into dialogue with civic leaders and the Los Angeles business community concerning this issue.[23] Although the Mutual decision was certainly a blow to the industry's uplift agenda and anti-censorship crusade, perhaps more significantly for studios in Los Angeles, the court's condemnation of cinema's "prurient appeal" coincided with the hiring practices scandal already plaguing the city. In response to these external pressures, the Motion Picture Producers Association, or MPPA, brought together representatives from various studios to devise and assert a common agenda. Alongside other groups such as the Motion Picture Protective Organization, a name that overtly declared its defensive posture, and the Motion Picture Conservation Association, the MPPA was conceived in the midst of these twin crises and asserted a professionalized and reputable image for the industry.[24] The MPPA moved quickly to the forefront in negotiations with the city, with members such as Jesse Lasky, D. W. Griffith, and Thomas Ince featured prominently in what was essentially a public relations campaign staged by the studios to deal broadly with the "morals question" plaguing the film world.

As with the MPDA, the formation of the MPPA served to align diverse studios against common threats, and while there were several other identifiable impending crises during this period—labor management, increasing production costs, star salaries—it was the problem of censorship that created a space to unite filmmaking companies.[25] These alignments can be traced through local newspaper accounts of encounters between the city and studio representatives that presented the industry as a unified front regardless of the complex power struggles occurring behind the scenes.[26] So while high-profile hearings about censorship were being conducted in Washington, a series of meetings was held in Los Angeles between city officials and industry representatives that helped to solidify the MPPA's standing as a voice of industry interests. Director D. W. Griffith appeared before the Women's Million Club to discuss "Art in the Motion

Pictures" and the problems of making art "in the face of unnecessary censorship."[27] Thomas Dixon, who had worked with Griffith on *The Birth of a Nation,* met with the city council in the name of producers and exhibitors to protest censorship and to promote the "wizardry and artistry of the screen," promising that it would be possible to bring all the eastern studios to Los Angeles if only the city offered the industry "fair treatment."[28]

In his talk before the Los Angeles Realty Board, Jesse Lasky wielded both a carrot and a stick: according to the *Los Angeles Times,* Lasky presented "an inspiring array of facts and figures" that promised impressive monetary investments in the city. Lasky opined that more than twenty thousand people were steadily employed by the film studios and drawing good salaries, pointing out to his audience of realtors that "a large percentage of them have bought or built homes here." With a prescient nod to the region's burgeoning car culture, he also asserted that untold numbers of studio employees had bought "more automobiles in Los Angeles than any other one class of people." As the *Times* reported, Lasky also claimed to know at least two large East Coast-based companies that were considering the move west. However, after promising even more revenue for the city coffers, Lasky threatened the city with what would become a refrain during the teens—industry retreat. Lasky assured his audience that if Los Angeles continued to make the situation "uncomfortable" for filmmakers, and if their friends in the city did not "rally" to their support, there could be consequences; he reported that "more than one producer has been tempted to pack up and go to some other location." Not surprisingly, the meeting concluded with a unanimous pledge in support of the MPPA and "hearty cooperation" from the Los Angeles Realty Board in promoting the interests of the film industry in Southern California.[29]

Threats that helped the industry coalesce through interstudio alliances also allowed business leaders and organizations in Los Angeles to demonstrate their loyalty to the industry. The newly formed, and apparently short-lived, Motion Picture Conservation Association brought together "prominent citizens" with "picture men" in early 1916 to secure the "mutual co-operation between film producers and civic interests of Los Angeles."[30] Members of the executive committee included representatives from the LA Realty Board, the City Civil Service Commission, and the Chamber of Commerce. The *Los Angeles Times* detailed the vicissitudes of the censorship debate and its impact on the local Censors Board, while editorials in the *Los Angeles Herald* persistently pushed back against censorship legislation.

Beginning in late January, the *Herald* featured articles by prominent filmmakers based in Los Angeles, such as Griffith, Ince, H. O. Davis of Universal, and H. M. Horkheimer of Balboa. The editorials were published under the continuing title "Public Opinion Is Censorship Enough for Motion Pictures" and voiced the industry's talking points about the threats posed by censorship. Local theater owner W. H. Clune argued against restrictions on film as an art, although he also advocated for a single censorship board that would eliminate competing fiefdoms and contradictory standards.[31] In his defense of the motion pictures, Ince argued that censorship amounted to "class legislation" that was unfair and unconstitutional; more pointedly, he argued that the moviegoing audience was able to judge film content for itself.[32] In this he was supported in the *Herald*'s editorial pages, which published a cartoon titled "This Is Practical Censorship," effectively illustrating the industry's argument that if a film was offensive, the audience could speak with its feet (see figure 19.3). And when the push for a federal censorship board encountered procedural problems during its congressional hearings, the *Herald* somewhat prematurely proclaimed victory for the industry in a campaign that had "radiated" from Los Angeles under the "auspices" of the MPPA.[33]

FIGURE 19.3   "This Is Practical Censorship," *Los Angeles Herald*, January 24, 1916.

The mutual need that drove studios to form organizations such as the MPDA and the MPPA was undoubtedly a defensive response to intersecting pressures and had broader implications for the industry's identity, crafting a recognizable and conventional corporate character that could resonate with other local organizations. Additionally, it pulled studios together with the connective tissue of bureaucratic banalities—the committees, the meetings, the articles of incorporation—and routinized procedures that formed the backbone of its institutional cultures. Perhaps of equal importance, such organizational logistics formalized the industry's physical ties to the city and demonstrated a commitment to remaining in Los Angeles, a measure of economic security avidly pursued by the city and consistently used by the industry as a bargaining chip in negotiations with civic leaders throughout the decade. Evidence of the industry's ties to Los Angeles also became part of an evolving narrative about the city's identity as the home to American filmmaking. For instance, in describing the formation of the MPPA, the *Herald* declared in typically self-aggrandizing booster verbiage that the MPPA would be a national organization with headquarters in Los Angeles, the "film capital of the world."[34] Such language inverted the city's historically marginal status on the national stage and promised great financial rewards. As a representative of the MPPA in meetings with city officials, Lasky made this point explicit, declaring that he would "convince the eastern producers that city administration, the merchants and the newspapers of Los Angeles are all for the motion picture industry." With an acute understanding of the city's business interests, Lasky also promised to try and persuade some East Coast manufacturers that they should relocate to Los Angeles.[35] The *Herald*'s valedictory rhetoric, along with what amounted to the endorsement of organizations such as the Merchants and Manufacturing Association, the Realty Board, and regional government agencies, exemplify the kind of local support the industry continued to accrue and suggest the efficacy of interstudio alliances that could personify institutional power and speak with a unified voice.

The "Invisible Empire" of Los Angeles "Reel" Estate

In 1928, despite ranking among the top dozen manufacturing cities in the United States, industrial Los Angeles was described as an "invisible empire." The absence of an identifiable production zone and the horizontal expanse of the city's urban design shrouded its industrial strength in mystery. As a reporter for the *Los Angeles Times* observed, visitors responding to the city's apparent lack of traditional urban markers might be "tempted to declare that Los Angeles has no industry."[36] Much like the cinematic image itself, the film industry and Los Angeles were both predicated on a play between presence and absence: as a seemingly non-industrialized space with an invisible labor force, studios hid their manufacturing reality behind the benign facades of quasi-residential studio buildings while backlots bled into the rural wilds of the Los Angeles environs.[37] In this way studios upheld the political economy of Southern California's regional aesthetic, which depended on the city's physical appeal, not on the evidence of industry. Underlying this synergistic investment in appearances was the common ground that subtended Southern California's business interests and the industry's institutional expansion: real estate.

In a region with few natural, exploitable resources, Southern California's economic survival had been bound up with real-estate speculation since the nineteenth century. Historically, the area had attracted entrepreneurs in farming and food processing and, eventually, oil refining and filmmaking, but the absence of local power sources as well as the long distances required for exporting goods limited most manufacturers to supplying their wares locally: even Los Angeles's major industries (lumber mills, flour mills, and slaughterhouses) were geared primarily to a limited market. Large-scale public works programs such as the dredging of San Pedro Harbor in 1912 and the opening of the Los Angeles Aqueduct in 1913 helped modernize the area's economy, as did the region's exploding population.[38] Indeed, the insularity of the region's economy helps explain the powerful hold that real-estate speculation had over the city, which spawned a resolute and influential culture of boosterism.

LA's practice of self-promotion (along with an adamantly anti-union business ethos) developed to ensure fiscal growth despite the city's reliance on what was essentially a risky real-estate economy. Certainly, the Southland's dependence on a speculative real-estate market could drive the economy in the short term, but with little in the way of natural resources (significantly water, coal, and/or a natural port), the economy was defined by cycles of boom and bust.[39] For the realty market to continue expanding, and for established and emerging industries to reliably find new employees, the area needed ever more residents—and so the drive to expand dominated, motivating government officials and business leaders alike to find ways to boost Los Angeles and its appeal to new homeowners.[40] The film industry's arrival at that time was propitious, bringing as it did a peculiar business model—defined by portable technologies, creative advertising, and an ever-growing payroll of studio talent—that found particularly fertile ground for growth in Los Angeles.

In many ways, the move to California also defined the film industry in terms of a new terrain of possibility, allowing filmmakers to reshape their practice in relation to a different economic and cultural environment. In its first decades, filmmaking had been integrated into the pre-existing urban infrastructure of older American cities like New York and Chicago. The move west did not actually sever these ties, as financial decision-making for most LA studios remained firmly located back east, closely linked to the corridors of banking in New York City. But the West Coast provided an opportunity for a new type of (spatial) identity, one less beholden to established narratives that were tied to the historical complexities of densely populated urban environments. The relatively cheap land and open spaces of the Los Angeles region afforded film companies the opportunity to impose themselves on the landscape in ways that had not been possible on the East Coast. Early attempts at studio-building in California resulted in the creation of stand-alone motion picture towns, like Universal City in 1915, or exotic would-be tourist attractions such as the Selig Zoo.[41] Numerous companies soon purchased sufficient acreage to create studio backlots, an expansionary zeal that perfectly complemented Los Angeles's own investment in significant infrastructure ventures. Such projects would redefine the region's economic future and alter the social fabric of Los Angeles, attracting ever more new inhabitants and helping to bolster local businesses. Moreover, the film industry's growth contributed to, and was symptomatic of, the spread of a distinctive type of West Coast industrialization; such manufacturing growth was characterized by decentralized sprawl and a low-slung aesthetic easily in keeping with the region's city-beautiful ambitions.

Accordingly, throughout the teens and twenties, as the city's industrial possibilities developed rapidly, they aligned with measures designed to retain the region's distinctive "rural" appeal.[42] In this way, regionally defined communities like Hollywood became crucial, not only because filmmaking could be isolated as an enterprise found only in certain areas but also because the "small-town" quality of such communities counter-balanced the sense of Los Angeles's unbridled growth. Always taking into account the rural nature of the areas outside its core, Los Angeles's aspirations to the economic benefits of urbanization were informed by the topographical specificity of its West Coast environs. Despite a desire to compete with larger metropolitan centers such as San Francisco, Chicago, and New York, Los Angeles could not offer the vertical drama of their skylines. By way of contrast, Los Angeles became a city whose iconography was defined by the aerial vista from the Hollywood Hills looking out over the flatlands or, eventually, of the Hollywood sign, floating over the city. As suggested by the expansive clarity of its unbounded spaces, Los Angeles could be promoted as a place where careful strategizing might preclude the problems associated with other urban centers. In 1910, the writer and Progressive developer William E. Smythe prophesized that Los Angeles was going to be a new kind of city, where the "hovel [is] forestall[ed] by the bungalow and the tenement by the Garden City."[43] As an emerging metropolis, one that was self-consciously imagined as a new type of urban environment, Los Angeles differed from the melting-pot cities of the East. This city-beautiful ethos also distanced the region from non-Anglo immigrants, the working classes, and the entrenched union power that defined older urban centers.[44]

Both filmmaking and California experienced phenomenal expansion in the 1910s and 1920s, fueled by a mutual recognition of exploitable resources and economic models built upon real estate and advertising. This expansion also translated into dramatic changes in the city's demographics, keyed to its nascent claims to being the home of American moviemaking. Migration to California throughout the nineteenth and early twentieth centuries had typically been dominated by men who were lured by occupations in prospecting or farming; for women, the possibilities for work were limited to positions as domestic servants, dressmakers, cooks, and schoolteachers.[45] But between 1900 and 1920, the interstate migration of young, single women surged dramatically. During this period, Los Angeles's population growth outpaced all other

Californian cities, for the first time receiving the majority of migrants and inverting historical norms, with female newcomers actually outnumbering men.[46] Connections between this kind of migration and the film industry were unavoidable, as young women arriving at the gates of film studios dramatized the changing nature of life in Los Angeles. The "immorality crisis" that plagued the studios and helped to spur the formation of the MPDA, as described earlier, was tied to these changes in the city's workforce, with young women also providing fodder for social anxieties about the recently arrived film colony, concerns only rivaled by countervailing discourse that celebrated the new industry's economic potential.

During a period of critical growth for the film industry, immigration to the Los Angeles area continued to rise, soaring to a rate of 100,000 people per year in the first half of the 1920s. Greg Hise has estimated that the population of Los Angeles County increased 140 percent during the decade, translating into an influx of "350 newcomers a day for ten years."[47] The population surge drove a concomitant increase in subdivision and construction: as Kevin Starr documents, Los Angeles issued more than 51,000 building permits in 1924 alone.[48] This demand for real estate drove up prices, particularly in Hollywood, and while the real-estate boom segregated neighborhoods socioeconomically, it was lauded as a boon to the city's survival. Starr argues that city boosters tied economic incentives to civic imperatives, espousing the moral advantages of home ownership that would produce a more "committed citizenship." This citizenry of new investors could be expected to advocate for the markers of established domesticity, such as parks, playgrounds, and schools, services typically designed for children. Further rationalizing the moral economy of home ownership, realty board organs such as the *Los Angeles Realtor*, responding to the destabilizing potential of the city's surging populace, argued that local governance could reflect "a higher and finer sense of purpose than possible to mere renters."[49] Attempts to extend the mantle of civic virtue over land ownership can be seen not only in newspaper coverage and booster journals such as *Sunset Magazine* but was also picked up and repurposed in the already-established genre of the film industry exposé. For instance, an appeal to civic normalcy finds its echoes in Fox's *Mirrors of Hollywood*, which speaks of "miles and miles of quiet residential streets, busy shopping centers, well-populated grammar high schools, thriving banks, wealthy churches, [and] beautiful shops."[50]

In another tell-all, "The Truth About Hollywood," Thoreau Cronyn renders explicit the link between employment and home ownership as both aspirational and a leveling agent, claiming that "the crowd came and it sought homes. Transients, finding themselves settled for long sojourns in California, bought or built houses. The trooper, always a nomad, dreaming of a fixed habitation, found his dream coming true. [. . .] There sprung up a feeling of local pride. The actor and his retinue, the director, the scenario writer, the host of others who help make the pictures came to have a love for Hollywood because it was 'their town.' "[51] Cronyn's musings on Hollywood as a domestic and civic idyll may have reassured local boosters, but the constant surge of new residents also required a corresponding expansion of employment. An editorial from the *Los Angeles Times* in 1923 anxiously notes that "the vast hegira of people who are rushing into Los

Angeles must find a way to work and make their living. They can't go on indefinitely supporting themselves by building each other houses and selling lots. As roofs are built to cover their heads, big industries must be developed to give them means to earn money. Whenever population outruns industry, stagnation follows."[52] Rampant expansion may have concerned some city observers, but it was a boon to the film industry, which was ideally suited to its adopted environment: it imported its own resources, amassed large tracts of land and adapted them to LA's horizontal aesthetic, and it benefited from a large population that could supply the film industry's needs for a workforce that was often transient and replaceable.

The co-dependency between population growth, real-estate development, and industrial expansion promoted particular attitudes toward zoning and city-building that resulted in what Gregory Hise has labeled a "dichotomous" perception of the city. It led to a dualistic representation of LA's identity, wherein the importance of industry was acknowledged at the same time that its presence was submerged and sequestered. In Hollywood, this impulse prompted the creation of industrial zones in the late 1910s that Luci Marzola has mapped elsewhere in this volume, while also motivating studio construction that mimicked residential architecture.[53] The region's real-estate imperative also animated rhetorical strategies that culminated in arguments connecting regional prosperity with the profitability of home ownership. A headline in *Holly Leaves*, Hollywood's hometown newspaper, summed up the equation concisely: "Growth of Moving Picture Industry Causes Increase in Local Realty Values."[54] When the Hollywood Business Men's Club made the effort to increase the scope of film-print manufacture in the vicinity, the rationale operated along both economic and civic fronts: "[such expansion] would bring to Hollywood a larger population of business men, skilled craftsmen, scientific men and experts in photography, who would come with their families to make their homes here and to become integral parts of the community."[55]

Fox's *Mirrors of Hollywood* provides another instructive model of how land management merged with industry operations, affirming yet again the pervasive sense of dualism underwriting Hollywood's self-definition. As Fox notes, the film industry stages the mise-en-scène of its adopted home so effectively that one cannot discern where small-town reality leaves off and motion-picture imagery begins: "Framed against the backdrop of Hollywood's hills, the whole city—all the palm-lined streets, with their impossibly picturesque and gaily colored bungalows, forming a veritable riot of color with here and there quaint windows peering sightlessly from air spaces under low roofs—looks more like one of the huge movie sets that have brought it fame than it does like the peaceful city of normal community activities and interests."[56] Fox's conception of the film set imagines a carefully coordinated but still-fabulous space, the organization of imagery blurring the boundaries between reality and fantasy. Here, city and industry are aligned as both the means and the object of representation, and the most resonant metaphor becomes the movie screen, the ultimate agent of reconciliation. Its reflective surface serves both as a repository of blended energies but also a blank canvas for idealized projections.

Epilogue: *Holly Leaves* and the Dynamics of Inclusion

As the preceding account underscores, the fortunes of Hollywood played a significant role in the industrial and financial prospects of the Los Angeles area. And the appeals of "Hollywood" functioned as a synecdoche for regional real-estate boosterism. Yet despite the formation of strategic alliances, integrating the movie colony into the city did not occur quickly or easily. Initially, filmmakers were outsiders in Hollywood, set apart by social prejudice and the itinerant logistics of early film practices, embraced for their financial contributions to the city, yet only slowly accepted into the community. The dynamics of inclusion and exclusion that typified Hollywood's social structure shifted significantly in the twenties to strategically incorporate "film folk," a process one can trace by examining the pages of *Holly Leaves*, a community newspaper. *Holly Leaves* began publication in the mid-teens, as an organ for the Hollywood Art Association. An ardent proponent of city-beautiful programs, the paper featured articles about the constant need for street cleaning, interviews with artistic luminaries and local business leaders, along with full-page ads for rubber tires and housing tracts.[57] *Holly Leaves* gradually integrated film news into its pages, asserting its connections with the most admirable qualities of a select group of industry notables. The paper also found some films worthy of praise, even as it still consistently distanced itself from "filmdom." After the Roscoe "Fatty" Arbuckle scandal and his subsequent acquittal, however, *Holly Leaves* made a more vocal commitment to the motion picture industry, supporting Will Hays for banning Arbuckle from the screen. Acknowledging that "Hollywood's destiny is inseparably linked with that of moving pictures," *Holly Leaves* publisher Orren M. Donaldson made the case that Hays would finally help bring film to a "higher plane"—a rehabilitation that was necessary for decency and for profit in Hollywood.[58]

Further evidence of Hollywood's stability was literalized in the form of Sid Grauman's "massive" Egyptian Theatre, which *Holly Leaves* celebrated with a cover story and praised as a "magnificent temple dedicated to the silent drama" in the "very heart of the picturesque film capital."[59] The religiously tinged description was appropriate, as the Egyptian was designed to create what Kevin Starr has called an "overall effect of mystic reverence."[60] Hollywood's first premiere, the Douglas Fairbanks epic *Robin Hood* (1922) occurred at the Egyptian, and Fairbanks himself, dressed respectably in sober business attire, appeared on the cover of *Holly Leaves* in late 1922, joining such previous neighborhood notables as the high school boys' club treasurer, a local real-estate developer, and the Chamber of Commerce secretary-elect. Mary Pickford, Douglas Fairbanks's recent bride, would also warrant a *Holly Leaves* cover, having already made inroads as a famous citizen of the town when she and Fairbanks purchased studio property there, promising that the neighborhood would remain their "headquarters." Their contributions to Hollywood's prosperity are enumerated in a summary of the impressive costs for filming *Monsieur Beaucaire* (1924) and the estimated expenses for Pickford's *Dorothy Vernon of*

Haddon Hall (1924) at their lot on Santa Monica Boulevard.[61] Pickford's agreement to be the "honorary chairman" for the Hollywood Art Association's city-beautiful "Save the Trees" campaign verified her civic spirit.[62] Similarly, Cecil B. DeMille served as an executive for a local bank and extolled the virtues of real estate as a sound financial investment, advice followed by many of the Hollywood elite, Pickford included. As DeMille put it, "When you old residents with a wide forward vision and a belief in the future of Los Angeles came to us and suggested subdivision of bare acreage, then miles from the center of things, you found in the motion picture colony not scoffers but friends."[63]

Common ground literally forged connections between "the motion picture colony" and "the old residents." With movies stars now bona fide members of the Hollywood community, substantially invested in the real estate that they shared with the town's founders, the dualities of Hollywood could find reconciliation through land and finance. As a *Holly Leaves* editorial opined, "What Hollywood needs above all is unity and comm-unity, and the coming into our population of a large element, bound to the motion picture industry on the one side and incorporated into the community life on the other, might result in successfully bridging the chasm that has so long split Hollywood in two."[64] Ironically, the film industry's search for self-definition, focused on the reconciliation of opposed dualities, found its ideal resolution in the collapsing of all such paradoxes into the singular name of "Hollywood." With the distinction between Hollywood as a prototypical California small town and as filmmaking's symbolic center dissolved, and the community's real-life bungalows merging with their cinematic counterparts, the rhetorical value of "Hollywood" as promotional shorthand had been verified. One also sees the fusion played out in the fate of *Holly Leaves*: by 1926, it had changed its name to the more resonant *Hollywood*, its editorial approach now blending community newspaper and fan magazine in equal measure. And in 1928, when the Academy of Motion Picture Arts and Sciences formed, the organization planned to adopt *Hollywood* magazine as its in-house journal. From this point onward, though scarcely a univocal term, "Hollywood" would operate as an effective shorthand for the power of the movies, a promotional tool whose glittering surface distracted from the socioeconomic contradictions that continued to define the film industry.

Notes

1. Charles Donald Fox, *Mirrors of Hollywood, with Brief Biographies of Favorite Film Folk* (New York: Charles Renard, 1925), 28–29.
2. We expand on the ways in which Hollywood's self-definition depended on the somewhat contradictory notion of "creative collaboration" in "Hollywood: Promoting Collaboration," in Philippa Gates and Katherine Spring, eds., *Resetting the Scene: Classical Hollywood Revisited* (Detroit, MI: Wayne State University Press, 2021), 109–117.
3. For more on how "Spanish" history was used to craft regional identity during this period and to support booster rhetoric about Los Angeles, see William Alexander McClung, *Landscape of Desire: Anglo Mythologies of Los Angeles* (Berkeley: University of California Press, 2000). See also Kevin Starr, *Inventing the Dream: California through the Progressive Era*

(New York: Oxford University Press, 1985); Robert Fogelson, *The Fragmented Metropolis: Los Angeles, 1850–1930* (Berkeley: University of California Press, 1993); and William Deverell, *Whitewashed Adobe: The Rise of Los Angeles and Remaking of Its Mexican Past* (Berkeley: University of California Press, 2004).

4. Heidi Kenaga observes that Central Casting allowed producers to manage bad publicity around the employment of young women. See her "Making the 'Studio Girl': The Hollywood Studio Club and Industry Regulation of Female Labour," *Film History* 18, no. 2 (2006): 129–139.
5. See, as a representative example, Shelley Stamp, "It's a Long Way to Filmland: Starlets, Screen Hopefuls, and Extras in Early Hollywood," in Charlie Keil and Shelley Stamp, eds., *American Cinema's Transitional Era: Audiences, Institutions, Practices* (Berkeley: University of California Press, 2006), 332–351.
6. For an overview of the role of the director in the 1910s, with a focus on DeMille, see Charlie Keil, "Cecil B. DeMille Shapes the Director's Role," in Virginia Wright Wexman, ed., *Directing* (New Brunswick, NJ: Rutgers University Press, 2017), 26–47.
7. Karen Ward Mahar examines how the film industry was rationalized during this period in relation to a patriarchal structuring of studio power that resolved class and gender conflict within a hierarchical production system. See her *Women Filmmakers in Early Hollywood* (Baltimore, MD: Johns Hopkins University Press, 2004).
8. Letter from Jesse Lasky, July 21, 1916, Cecil B. DeMille Papers, Box 238, Folder 14, Tom Perry Special Collections Library, Harold B. Lee Library, Brigham Young University, Utah.
9. Advertisement, *Moving Picture World*, March 30, 1918, 1739.
10. Letter from Cecil B. DeMille, February 8, 1917, Cecil B. DeMille Papers, Box 240, Folder 1.
11. Kevin Starr, *Material Dreams: Southern California through the 1920s* (New York: Oxford University Press, 1990), 90–100.
12. "Not Listed in the Guide Books," *Photoplay*, August 1921, 60.
13. Terry Ramsaye, "Intimate Visits to the Homes of Famous Film Magnates," *Photoplay*, December 1927, 50–51, 131. Included in the interview series are Laemmle, Adolph Zukor, and Marcus Loew.
14. Ibid., 50. Ramsaye uses some of his most florid prose to describe the distinctly wholesome Joseph Patrick Kennedy, who is pictured alongside portraits of his seven children and, "last but not least," his wife, Rose Elizabeth Fitzgerald Kennedy.
15. Mark Garrett Cooper, *Love Rules: Silent Hollywood and the Rise of the Managerial Class* (Minneapolis: University of Minnesota Press, 2003), 185–195. Cooper ties the emergence of the movie mogul to changing conceptions of the managerial classes in the 1920s, particularly as these identities derived from an understanding of national identity in terms of ethnicity, race, and social stratification.
16. For more on the debates and anxieties surrounding early studios, see Stamp, "It's a Long Way to Filmland," and Denise McKenna "The Photoplay or the Pickaxe: Extras, Gender, and Labour in Early Hollywood," *Film History* 23, no. 1 (2011): 5–19. To see how this issue was dealt with in the 1920s, see Kenaga, "Making the Studio Girl."
17. "Rid Plants of Immorality, Slogan of Officials," *Los Angeles Tribune*, December 29, 1915, 1. Woolwine is also quoted as suggesting that women's clubs would come together with those leaders to "eliminate the evils" uncovered during the scandal.
18. "District Attorney Gets Movie Evidence," *Los Angeles Record*, December 29, 1915, 1.
19. "Moving Picture Camp Charges Fall Down," *Los Angeles Tribune*, December 29, 1915, 3.
20. Cited by Lisa Mitchell in "Ties that Bind: Searching for the Motion Picture Director's Association," *DGA Magazine* 26, no. 4 (November 2001). The formation of the MPDA

preceded the public uproar over the "casting couch" scandal by several months, although other instances of directorial misbehavior were regularly documented by local papers.

21. Lois Weber was admitted to the MPDA in 1916 and was the only exception to the organization's roster of male membership for many years.
22. See Garth S. Jowett, "'A Capacity for Evil': The 1915 Supreme Court Mutual Decision," *Historical Journal of Film, Radio and Television* 9, no. 1 (1989): 59–78.
23. Regulating film content was the putative issue under dispute, but it also played out as a power struggle involving the conflict between national and local film boards and their respective regulatory authority. For more on the complex debates over censorship during this period, see Lee Grieveson, *Policing Cinema: Movies and Censorship in Early-Twentieth-Century America* (Berkeley: University of California Press, 2004).
24. "Film Heads to Co-operate," *Los Angeles Record*, December 30, 1915, 2. At a meeting in early January, the studio representatives were identified as the Motion Picture Protective Association *and* as the Motion Picture Producers' Association, although it is not clear from this news report if these were separate entities. It is possible that the Motion Picture Conservation Association, described later in this section, was also present, contributing to the confusion. However, as discussions with the city continued in early 1916, the MPPA came to be more clearly identified as a unified voice for the industry.
25. For more on how a coalition of film industry producers marked an important step in the development of an effective business model for Hollywood as a recognizable regional industry, see Maryann Feldman, Johanna France, and Janet Bercovitz, "Creating a Cluster While Building a Firm: Entrepreneurs and the Formation of Industrial Clusters," *Regional Studies* 39, no. 1 (February 2005): 129–141.
26. Conflicts between studios remained an ongoing issue with the reintroduction of the Hughes Bill, which sought to institute a federally regulated censorship commission, an obvious source of disquiet for the film industry. Kia Afra documents the intense interstudio competition that occurred during the Hughes proceedings, particularly how Jesse Lasky attempted to dictate the terms of the debate to Paramount's advantage. See Afra, *The Hollywood Trust: Trade Associations and the Rise of the Studio System* (Lanham, MD: Rowman & Littlefield, 2016), 33–52. See also Jowett, "Capacity for Evil," 71, and Grieveson, *Policing Cinema*, 188–191.
27. "Griffith to Speak Before Million Club," *Los Angeles Herald*, January 11, 1916, 8.
28. "Fight to Abolish Censoring of Films is Waged in Council," *Los Angeles Herald*, January 24, 1916, 1.
29. "Earnest Plea for Fair Play," *Los Angeles Times*, January 7, 1916, II.2.
30. "Would Boost Film Industry," *Los Angeles Times*, January 6, 1915, II.5.
31. W. H. Clune, "Public Opinion Is Censorship Enough for Motion Pictures," *Los Angeles Herald*, February 3, 1916, 6.
32. Thomas H. Ince, "Public Opinion Is Censorship Enough for the Motion Pictures," *Los Angeles Herald*, February 1, 1916, 6. Griffith, Ince, and Horkheimer, all members of the MPDA, were the prominent voices defending the industry against charges of immoral hiring practices the year before.
33. "Beat Film Censorship; Producers Jubilant," *Los Angeles Herald*, February 10, 1916, 1.
34. "L.A. Film Men Back Big Combine," *Los Angeles Herald*, January 12, 1916, 2.
35. Ibid.
36. R. D. Sangster, "Los Angeles Manufacturing District," *Los Angeles Times*, January 3, 1928, H10. Two explanations for this strange aberration are offered: the first is the dispersed

nature of manufacturing, and the second is the distinctly horizontal style of commercial construction in Southern California.

37. In reality, Los Angeles moved to restrict studio growth to circumscribed industrial zones, established after considerable municipal debate in the late 1910s. But industry discourse tended to favor the notion of the seamless integration of moviemaking into the geography of Hollywood.

38. For a concise history of Southern California's changing economy during this period, see Fogelson, *The Fragmented Metropolis*, 108–134.

39. For more on the regional economy of boom and bust, see Carey McWilliams, *Southern California: An Island on the Land* (Salt Lake City, UT: Peregrine Smith Books [1946], 1973).

40. There is a rich body of scholarship on Southern California's booster history: see, for example, McWilliams, "The Boosters," in *Southern California*, 156–161; Lee M. A. Simpson, *Selling the City: Gender, Class, and the California Growth Machine, 1880–1940* (Stanford, CA: Stanford University Press, 2004); and Starr, *Inventing the Dream*, 72–89.

41. See Brian Jacobson, *Studios Before the System: Architecture, Technology, and the Emergence of Cinematic Space* (New York: Columbia University Press, 2015), 192–197.

42. Arthur Krim links misconceptions about the city's anti-urban ethos to the post–World War I circulation of images of Los Angeles, particularly aerial views and night views. See Krim, "Los Angeles and the Anti-tradition of the Suburban City," *Journal of Historical Geography* 18, no. 1 (1992): 121–138.

43. Quoted in Greg Hise, Michael J. Dear, and H. Eric Schockman, "Rethinking Los Angeles," in Michael J. Dear, H. Eric Schockman, and Greg Hise, eds., *Rethinking Los Angeles* (Thousand Oaks, CA: Sage Publications, 1996), 6. Hise et al. argue, however, that Los Angeles's anti-urban reputation is of a more recent construction, propagated by urban critics and conventional wisdom. As they point out, Los Angeles was designed as a "polycentric urban agglomeration" that was organized around mixed use that became associated with its sprawling expanse. See Hise et al., x–xi.

44. For more on this history, see Deverell, *Whitewashed Adobe*.

45. Growth in white-collar occupations had, however, opened up selected new jobs to some women and affected the shifting migration patterns. The 1900 census data indicates that women were working as stenographers, telephone operators, nurses, and landladies; see Barbara Laslett, "Women's Work in Late-Nineteenth-Century Los Angeles: Class, Gender and the Culture of New Womanhood," *Continuity and Change* 5, no. 3 (1990): 420. Railway expansion in the latter half of the nineteenth century had drawn in more residents, but these were primarily families attracted to the hospitable climate. Los Angeles had not experienced the same influx of women "adrift" because it lacked the light industry, such as the textile mills, dress manufacturing, and shoe factories typical of Northeastern cities and Chicago, which had attracted many single women looking for work. See Joanne Meyerowitz, *Women Adrift: Independent Wage Earners in Chicago, 1880–1930* (Chicago, IL: University of Chicago Press, 1988).

46. Frank L. Beach, "The Effects of the Westward Movement on California's Growth and Development, 1900–1920," *International Migration Review* 3, no. 3 (Summer 1969): 25–28.

47. Greg Hise, "Industry and Imaginative Geographics," in Tom Sitton and William Deverell, eds., *Metropolis in the Making: Los Angeles in the 1920s* (Berkeley: University of California Press, 2001), 18.

48. Starr, *Material Dreams*, 70–71.

49. Ibid.

50. Fox, *Mirrors of Hollywood*, 2.
51. Thoreau Cronyn's "The Truth about Hollywood: With the Film Stars Who Are in the Limelight," *New York Herald*, March 12, 1922, 7. Cronyn published a series of articles from March 19 through April 2, 1922 that documented different aspects of life in Hollywood. The full text is also available online at Bruce Taylor's *Taylorology* 12 (December 1993) at https://silentera.com/taylorology/issues/Taylor12.txt.
52. "Balanced Progress," *Los Angeles Times*, November 18, 1923, II.4.
53. Luci Marzola mentions these zones in her chapter (20) in this volume.
54. "Film World Capital: Growth of Moving Picture Industry Causes Increase in Local Realty Values," *Holly Leaves*, December 4, 1920, 16.
55. "Bridging the Chasm," *Holly Leaves*, March 26, 1921, 22.
56. Fox, *Mirrors of Hollywood*, 3.
57. The publisher of *Holly Leaves*, Orren M. Donaldson, was a Midwestern transplant who was well connected with the arts community in Los Angeles.
58. "Benefactor of Hollywood," *Holly Leaves*, April 22, 1922, 5.
59. "The Master Showman," *Holly Leaves*, September 9, 1922, 20–21.
60. Starr, *Material Dreams*, 100.
61. "Fairbanks to Spend Millions," *Holly Leaves*, November 3, 1922, 15. It is notable that both of these films are adaptations of famous literary material (a play and a novel, respectively), marking them as quality productions.
62. "Mary Pickford Leads," *Holly Leaves*, December 29, 1922, 8.
63. "Bridging the Chasm," 22.
64. Ibid.

CHAPTER 20

A SYSTEM OF THOROUGH COOPERATION

Technology, Service, and the Film Labs of Hollywood

LUCI MARZOLA

HERBERT Kalmus and his partners, mostly recent graduates from MIT, elected to establish the Technicolor Motion Picture Corporation right in their hometown of Boston. In 1915, this seemed as good a place as any to serve an industry with several production centers throughout the region. At the time, the bulk of physical motion picture production had already moved west to California, but those with power, especially to make financial decisions, remained largely on the East Coast, as did most of the technology supplies and services. Given the cumbersome and expensive process for color motion picture production that Technicolor was developing, the major producers were the company's only potential customers, meaning Kalmus soon found himself traveling frequently to New York.[1]

Most people in the business saw Hollywood as little more than a manufacturing outpost—one of many possible locations for motion picture production. As such, Kalmus envisioned a model for his business in which only a small part, the actual taking of the negative, might be performed out of his reach, while print production and processing would stay centered in his home base in Boston. But unlike major corporations such as Eastman Kodak and General Electric, which made motion picture-related products as a part of a larger catalogue of goods, Technicolor was a small business with a singular product to market, so it had a vested interest in establishing a close relationship with the limited number of customers that could actually make use of the company's technology.

When Hollywood filmmakers began to show interest in the company's two-color process, the physical distance between the service firm and its customers became untenable. In 1922, Kalmus sent a few engineers to Los Angeles, and two years later he took the weeklong train journey west to establish offices near the studios and meet with the filmmakers whom he hoped would see the necessity of shooting their pictures in color.[2]

Within two years he was in Boston so seldom that he began noting it along with his other travels, such as his tour of Europe with the Fairbankses in 1926.[3] Kalmus had no doubt come under the thrall of Hollywood, but he had also come to recognize that the only way to cultivate this market, the only significant one for his business, was to live in it.

By the time the company shifted its focus to its now-famous three-strip color process in the early 1930s, it had moved not only much of its processing and print production but also its research laboratory to its Hollywood facilities. The relocation of top engineers to Los Angeles in the 1920s signaled a new orientation for motion picture technology manufacturers. Companies such as Technicolor, which relied primarily on this small market for their business, could no longer remain content to merely sell *to* Hollywood. Now they needed to develop and manufacture *in* Hollywood to remain competitive. Relying on contact only with the New York financial interests of the studios would not allow these companies to adapt to the needs and desires of those using their tools in the studios, which was essential to maintaining a competitive edge.

Technicolor is just one high-profile example of a larger shift in the technological infrastructure that serviced the motion picture studios as the industry grew in size and cultural reach. The establishment of technology service firms in the vicinity of Hollywood was a signal development in the formation of the studio system. From the late 1910s, Los Angeles was the home of a growing sector of film-processing labs, mobile generator companies, lighting suppliers, and special process innovators such as Technicolor and Dunning. The presence of these companies differentiated Los Angeles from other production outposts throughout the country, allowing the Hollywood industry to become more and more independent from established East Coast entities.

The development of this technological service sector designed specifically to cater to the needs of the studios was instrumental in transforming Hollywood from a manufacturing outpost into an integrated economic and industrial zone.[4] In this way, Hollywood can be considered a prototype for what business scholars have termed creative industrial "clusters." Michael Porter effectively defines clusters as "geographic concentrations of interconnected companies, specialized suppliers, firms in related industries, and associated institutions."[5] Importantly, companies and institutions that make up an industrial cluster "compete but also cooperate," as they search for "strategic differences."[6] As the studios grew in the Hollywood area so did the service sector, with several competing companies in the same field, such as processing labs and prop suppliers, all residing within a short distance of one another.

Technology service firms provided products and services that fulfilled the specialized needs of studio production and that could potentially be quickly and widely adopted as standard within the tightly knit production community. These companies built their facilities around the studios and were quick to adapt to the desires of the studio technicians and artists, even when those needs went against guiding industrial principles of efficiency and precision. These companies were more effective in creating mutually beneficial relationships with the studio technicians than their larger, East Coast brethren. At the same time, staffers at the service companies were often connected to these larger corporations, being former employees or members of the East

Coast-based Society of Motion Picture Engineers. In this way, they were instrumental in establishing a motion picture engineering community in Los Angeles and paving the way for stronger links between the studios and the technology industry as a whole.

To establish the production context on the West Coast, I begin with a portrait of Hollywood in the mid-1910s and the technological and creative limitations of operating as a production outpost. Enterprising "lone inventors," both local entrepreneurs and those who traveled west like the producers, saw a market in supplying specialized tools to the studio personnel, who were isolated from their established economic community back East. The independent film-processing laboratories emerged as the first significant sector of technological service firms that recognized a market for alleviating filmmakers' frustrations. Once these businesses established Hollywood facilities, they shifted their marketing and service to those who would actually use their products, courting the studio technicians and creative workers rather than the financial executives back East or the production executives in town. The efforts of these small technology-service companies facilitated Hollywood's transformation from a filming destination into an industrial center that still controls the motion picture business and several other creative enterprises to this day.[7]

A New Customer in Town

As production companies put down more permanent roots in Los Angeles, building massive motion picture plants designed to facilitate multiple steps of the filmmaking process, the requirement to obtain technological supplies and services from across the country constituted a growing problem. The newest studios had been marketed as complete factories, in which, for the first time, the entire process of making moving pictures took place in a single location.[8] Contrary to this narrative, which the producers perpetuated themselves, the studios were not entirely self-sufficient facilities. Unlike the motion picture plants on the East Coast, very few of the new studios in Los Angeles had laboratories for processing negatives.[9] Additionally, though sets, props, and costumes were often manufactured in studio-based workshops, cameras, lights, film stock, and other highly complex tools and supplies had to be bought. Most of the tools of the trade moved from the manufacturers' factories to New York-area distributors, such as Jules Brulatour, Allison and Hadaway, and G. Gennert Camera, from which the Los Angeles technicians and producers had them shipped across the country. These East Coast distributors and their suppliers were perfectly content to maintain this structure, leaving the door open for new entrepreneurs to fill the underserved market.

Personnel at the technology service companies that came to supply the new motion picture industry had unique histories and varied motives. Some of them were former employees of the movie studios who, after the creation of some innovative tool, left studio employ to strike out on their own as independent entrepreneurs catering to their former colleagues. Others abandoned their positions at major technology companies to pursue an interest in motion pictures. And a third contingent pre-dated motion pictures' ascendency in Los Angeles and seized on the new market in their native home. One such innovator was Karl Thalhammer, a man of many trades who took it upon himself to create unique tools to sell to the motion picture workers in town. He was an Austrian inventor, who, according to a 1921 "who's who"-style publication, had brought his Vienna education in "electro-technique" to New York in 1904 "with twenty-five cents in his pocket."[10] After getting into the phonograph business and working his way through Toledo and San Francisco, Thalhammer, likely apocryphally, then rode away from that earthquake-ravaged city in 1906, this time "on a bicycle with a couple of dollars in his pocket." He once again rebuilt his phonograph empire in his new home of Los Angeles, opening a manufacturing business downtown in 1908 and creating, among other inventions, a telephone signal recorder, a self-stop device for phonographs, and a self-photo apparatus.

By 1913, the motion picture industry was making a significant impact in the area, and Thalhammer "applied his inventive genius" to the new industry in town.[11] Thalhammer's first success in the motion picture industry was in inventing and manufacturing a "Vigneting Iris" which, by 1921, was known and used widely by all the cameramen of Hollywood.[12] It was around that time that Thalhammer began advertising his tripod in the pages of *American Cinematographer* and other industry trades, boasting of sturdy leg clamps and a special range head that allowed for shooting straight up or down. Thalhammer applied for five patents for modifications to the tripod and motion picture camera between 1919 and 1920 and continued to innovate in the industry well into the 1950s.[13]

Thalhammer built and marketed specific refinements to the cameraman's tools that could only be created through close and regular contact with his customers and an intimate knowledge of their needs. The ability to tilt a camera 180 degrees was not a refinement of an instrument so much as it was an accommodation to the storytelling desires of the industry professionals. As an *American Cinematographer* article explained:

> Suppose it were desired to take a picture of a man looking through a hole in the ceiling—the same view as that of a person looking straight up at this man. Of course, this could be faked, but would it not be better to get the natural picture?[14]

This was a very different approach to Hollywood than could be seen in the East Coast–based Society of Motion Picture Engineers (SMPE), which was dominated by corporate engineers, executives, and sales agents.[15] In 1918, at a meeting of the SMPE, engineers discussed a lighting method and studio staging that would allow cameramen to obtain "perfect" exposure, as if this were the ultimate goal of filmmaking.[16] As the techniques of the field became more and more artistically motivated, these East Coast engineers were increasingly out of touch. Working in the shadow of the studios allowed firms such as Thalhammer's to understand that technology needed to serve creative ends.

As with Thalhammer and his tripod, many of these small businesses attempted to corner one or two small slivers of the market. For example, Harvey's Motion Picture

Exposure Meter was unrivaled, and Cinema Studio Supply was the only supplier of wind machines. But one area quickly became competitive—the independent film processing labs. By 1922, no fewer than five different laboratories advertised their services in the pages of *American Cinematographer* while several more would join them in the coming years.[17] Like Thalhammer, the independent labs created a market for themselves by catering to the specific, creative needs of the filmmakers and technicians themselves.

The Rise of Independent Laboratories

Laboratory work was an unavoidably necessary aspect of motion picture production—one that was both mechanical and highly specific to individual productions. It was laborious, hazardous, and difficult to do well. Exposed negatives were developed and duplicated by hand well into the 1920s. As late as 1927, in their *Tinting and Toning* guide, Eastman Kodak advocated the "rack and tank" method, in which film was wrapped around large wooden frames, dipped by hand into tanks of chemicals, and then wound around drums for drying.[18] Automatic developing machines were made available to the industry by 1921; however, the cinematographers in particular resisted the use of machines for negative development—limiting them to the duplication of positive prints for distribution.[19]

Through the end of the 1910s, laboratory work was still almost entirely performed on the East Coast. Early motion picture literature rarely mentions laboratory work at all, with such services only occasionally appearing as an additional feature of rental studios for filmmaking.[20] This aspect of production did not gain a notable presence in the trades until the mid-1910s, when the producers began building their "complete" motion picture plants, and, at the same time, concerns about film safety came to the fore. The new motion picture factories of the East and the Midwest offered a vision of completely self-sufficient production unheard of until this time. Trade stories enumerated the technologically advanced facilities of plants such as Lubinville, which included two studios; various machine shops; carpentry, upholstering, cabinet-making, costuming, scenery, and property shops; film laboratories; editorial and publicity departments; and a negative vault.[21]

At the same time that many plants were incorporating film processing into the production-studio spaces, independent labs began advertising their services, indicating that this aspect of the industry was expanding in size and relevance. As Janet Staiger has shown, by the mid-1910s, the motion picture industry had become much more organized and departmentalized in order to provide more complex and coherent narratives for the screen.[22] These moves to more complicated narratives led to more realistic sets and intricate lighting schemes. All of these changes contributed to the increased professionalization of motion picture work. With more labor and skill going into the images being exposed onto the negative, it stands to reason that interest in the quality of processing and printing would likewise intensify.[23]

Processing companies scattered across the northeastern United States, from Boston to Chicago, boasted in the pages of *Moving Picture World* of their safety, promptness, and low cost, such as Philadelphia's Brilliant Film Manufacturing Company's promise of "five cents a foot."[24] There was a consistent narrative of "perfect" development in these ads, addressing conventional concerns about mass production. Advertisements from 1915 for the newly built American Film Laboratories boasted of "quality," "up-to-date, fire-proof printing," and a million-feet-per-week capacity.[25] There was no discussion of creativity and customer needs (or desires); instead, lab work was presented as a necessary aspect of production that in its best form did nothing to alter or degrade the picture taken in the studio.

The proliferation of "up-to-date" massive volume facilities built in New York and elsewhere in the East throughout the 1910s provided the industry with significant lab capacity. For that reason, companies with production outposts in Los Angeles saw little need to build labs in the hinterlands. George Eastman himself had similarly argued against building a Kodak film-stock plant in the West, as it was cost-prohibitive to ship equipment and chemicals on the long train journey across the country.[26] Everyone agreed that it was cheaper and safer to send film stock back and forth from coast to coast, rather than vats of chemicals. Shipping the undeveloped negatives back to New York via train for processing, editing, and printing was the standard process in these early years. This structure had the added incentive of allowing the financial executives to maintain control of the final product shipped to theaters around the world, rather than ceding it to the creative workers in California.

Even as studio-based and independent labs began popping up in Los Angeles in the latter half of the 1910s, it was clear that producers still clung to the idea of laboratory work as best accomplished back East.[27] In April 1916, the Lasky studio added "the most modern and best equipped" film laboratories in the country to its Hollywood studio, but they continued to have a much larger facility on the East Coast.[28] Even Carl Laemmle, the entrepreneur behind the first motion picture "city" in Hollywood with laboratories, invested another half a million dollars into his New Jersey laboratory facilities in 1916, a year after the grand opening of Universal City.[29] Universal's Hollywood lab mostly provided the filmmakers with necessary dailies and toning samples, while printing and distribution continued to be handled on the East Coast.

This bicoastal structure, which kept the Hollywood lab industry small, held for the first decade of Los Angeles production, but the field experienced several major shifts as early as the advent of the war in Europe. The film stock production *and* processing industries were heavily reliant on chemicals manufactured in Germany. Kodak itself quickly turned to American companies such as DuPont for the building blocks of film stock, despite the fact that the latter was working on a competing product.[30] According to *Variety* in 1916, the price of chemicals used in film *processing* that were generally obtained from Germany, such as methanol and potassium, had seen a 2000 percent increase since the beginning of the war.[31] The scarcity and high cost of these essential ingredients led some labs to reuse them past the point of acceptable quality. The producers' concerns with subsequent print quality were quickly addressed in laboratory ads, as with Craftsmen's boast of "no substitute chemicals" and Republic's assuaging fears of "the substitution of cheaper and usually inferior raw materials."[32] Republic went on to assure its customers that the lab only used Eastman Kodak stock and Mallinckrodt chemicals—both American companies.

The chemical scare and increased concerns with print quality ultimately led to a strategic change that saw the laboratories increase their direct appeals to the specific needs and desires of the producers. These needs were often more creative than scientific, something that the labs had heretofore ignored. The rhetoric of "perfection," which was still prevalent, changed in meaning from low costs and efficiency to scientific innovation, and finally, by the end of the decade, to individualized, creative fulfillment. As the industry continued to mature, filmmakers' priorities changed, opening the door to a new type of laboratory with a different relationship to the producers. Trying to get a leg up on the competition in this new environment, Craftsmen offered "individual projection rooms for directors to cut their pictures," providing a level of service "that has so long been conspicuous by its absence."[33]

Perhaps no one took the service ethos further than Watterson Rothacker of Chicago, who generated publicity by journeying to New York to spend two days viewing *Tarzan of the Apes* (First National, 1918) "taking careful notes" so as to decide on the appropriate methods of toning and printing.[34] Rather than aiming for some objective notion of perfection, Rothacker sought to "utilize those particular tints and duo-tones that will intensify the emotional and aesthetic effects aimed at."[35] Labs such as Rothacker and Craftsmen created a new pitch directed at the creative talents of the industry rather than the financial interests, a strategy that would be expanded on in the labs of Hollywood.

Having laboratory work performed in Los Angeles looked all the more appealing when the New York laboratory workers went on strike in 1920. Making matters worse, the New York labs engaged in a public dispute with Eastman Kodak and its distributor, Jules Brulatour, the next year.[36] Brulatour was the intermediary on all sales of motion picture film stock to the producers and laboratories, giving him an outsized role in an industry almost entirely dependent on Kodak's product. Several lab owners had become suspicious that Brulatour planned to open his own lab and thereby create unfair competition. The suspicions were either unfounded or served to thwart his plans, but the public squabble diminished the standing of the New York-area labs. As a measure of protection, they banded together to form the Allied Film Laboratories Association, with William Horsley in Los Angeles and Burton Holmes in Chicago as the only members outside of the New York area. The members began advertising as a coalition, boasting of their long history of reliability and quality.

The Allied Film Laboratories Association's assertion that "[w]e don't need to boost stars, directors, and producers with costly publicity," was a pointed critique of the creative service orientation of Rothacker and the new Los Angeles labs.[37] Rothacker himself had recently expanded his operations into Los Angeles, with plans for new labs in New York and London, but he was not found on the roster of the Association.[38] The creative customer-service ethos he had initiated in Chicago was clearly at odds with the established New York industry, but it would serve him well among the artists and craftsmen of Hollywood.

Conveniently Located in the Heart of Hollywood

From their very first advertisements in the trades in 1916, the independent laboratories of Los Angeles boasted of their advantage in being in the vicinity of the studios. "Have your printing done where the producers can supervise each print," urged Pacific Film Labs, while William Horsley's new laboratory was "conveniently located in the heart of the studio section of Hollywood."[39] With distribution still operating out of the East, the Los Angeles-based labs tended to concentrate on quickly turning around toning samples and daily rushes for the studio producers, directors, and cameramen to peruse. This type of work was not nearly as lucrative as running off dozens of release prints, so Bloom Film Labs urged producers to "have your release prints made where you make the picture."[40] As long as filmmakers had any say in where printing was done, it seems obvious that they would prefer that it be where they could observe and control the completion of their work.

From the advent of their publication *American Cinematographer* in 1920, Hollywood cameramen showed a keen awareness of the fact that their work was completely dependent on the laboratory. Unlike Watterson Rothacker, cinematographers viewed the laboratory less as a creative entity unto itself and more as a place where their work could be destroyed as easily as it could be enhanced. In a 1921 article, William Foster, Lois Weber's cameraman, stated that "the function of the laboratory is not a creative one" but one that held great power over the final product of the "well planned and executed ideas of those higher up."[41] Somewhat self-interestedly, Foster asserted that "few producers have any personal knowledge of the laboratory or of chemistry" while "the cameraman is probably the one who most appreciates competent and conscientious work."[42]

American Cinematographer and the organization that it represented, the American Society of Cinematographers (ASC; founded in 1919), sought to legitimize the profession in the same way that producers had sought to gain respectability for the medium as a whole for years—by championing artistic aspirations.[43] John Caldwell has pointed to the *Cinematographer* and ASC as the "prototype" for critical industrial theory, in which motion picture industry professionals attempt to define themselves through discourse.[44] In a 1922 editorial, *Cinematographer* editor Foster Goss combated the notion of the cinematographer as someone who merely "grinds a crank," emphasizing both the cameraman's artistry and his "scientific knowledge."[45] Another Goss editorial assured the reader that the cinematographer should never be "considered as mechanic [sic]" just because he worked with a machine.[46] While camerawork had been defined by basic technical competence in the early years of the industry, by this time quality cinematographic work had gained a highly artistic definition. As Patrick Keating has shown, in the 1920s, the cinematographer grew from being considered a "mechanic" to gaining a public identity that rested on "good taste, emotional sensitivity, and a deep understanding of dramatic values."[47]

Through editorials in *American Cinematographer*, cameramen likewise asserted their interest in increased involvement in laboratory decision-making as a means of greater control over both the art and the science of their craft. They, as well as the directors, had much to gain, in terms of power over their work, by moving laboratory work to their backyard. For the cinematographers, it was not just a matter of improving on their labor in the studio but also of mitigating carelessness or incompetence that might detrimentally affect their reputations. As William Foster claimed, the finished product "is thought of as the work of the cameraman, when in reality one of the three processes is his responsibility [the taking of the negative], the other two [developing and printing] are the product of the laboratory."[48] This conception of the work of the cinematographer was widespread at the time, as in a later editorial, in which cameraman John Leezer defined photography as both the work of the photographer and "the laboratory force as well."[49] With few Hollywood studios incorporating their own full laboratories, the cinematographers' desire to control their work through post-production created the potential for a significant market.

The cinematographers' rhetoric in *American Cinematographer* gave the independent labs an approach to gaining business in the Hollywood studios by targeting those with knowledge of their technical processes. As early as 1921, a representative of Filmcraft Labs wrote an editorial echoing the need for a closer relationship between cameramen and labs. Using an apt metaphor, he lamented that the man in the dark room is often "in the dark" as to the expectations of the cameraman for his negative, and therefore advocated closer cooperation.[50] The paid content in the magazine used similar language, with a 1921 advertisement for Kosmos Labs claiming:

> Pride in the perfection of your photography needs the support of perfection in the laboratory. No matter what genius you display in photography, your negative will be only as good as the laboratory makes it.[51]

Clune Labs took the motto "Quality and Individual Service," Crouse and Davidge boasted of their "system of thorough co-operation," and Standard strove to bring out "all the artistry of your work."[52] Perfection, as Kosmos defined it, was now an extension of individual genius rather than an objectively clear picture. In stark contrast with the rhetoric of low cost, efficiency, and technical perfection of the East Coast labs of the 1910s, Standard used titles on their 1923 ads in *American Cinematographer* such as "What You Want," "Protect Your Creation," "Protect Your Art," and "Harmony," followed by descriptions of the ways in which their business catered to the cinematographers' creative desires.

Yet Standard was savvy enough about their customers to adjust their marketing to different publications. Their ads in the exhibitor trades used titles such as "Emergencies,"

"Centralized Buying," and "Responsibility."[53] These ads were designed to assure the exhibitors and distributors of the quality of the prints they would receive. Even in Hollywood, the labs existed between the production and distribution branches of the industry and needed to acknowledge the needs of both. If Standard were going to move into the release print business, it would have to appeal to the financial concerns of distributors and exhibitors. But the Los Angeles labs, outnumbered by the New York labs two to one, clearly had a larger stake in wooing the creative side of the business.[54] In addition, their relationship to "every producer in Southern California" was used as a selling point with the exhibitors. Ultimately, Hollywood labs such as Standard built their marketing strategies around creating loyal customers within the studios and then using this relationship as an asset with the exhibitors.

By 1923, the independent labs had created an identity for themselves aligned with the creative workers of the motion picture studios, rather than the executives or the exhibitors. Customer service had become a way of differentiating between studio-based laboratories and independent laboratories; as cinematographer and ASC President James Van Trees argued, only the latter "depends on the ability to satisfy customers."[55] Van Trees described the "ideals" of the two classes of laboratories, showing a clear preference for the independent ethos. While the independents sought to make the cameramen happy, the studio labs were primarily concerned with following "set rules of policy," which Van Trees only found acceptable "if we have reached the point where we don't care to have individuality in our photography."[56] Like the engineers in the SMPE and their earlier claims of "perfect exposure," the in-house operations were portrayed as tone-deaf to the creative impulses of their main clients, the filmmakers.

The cinematographers and producers both generally agreed that the increased competition from the Hollywood labs (and independent labs, in general) fueled improvements in the quality of laboratory work in the early 1920s. As an unintended consequence of the growing attention to and financial investment in the field, the structure of the industry altered, both by the studios expanding and improving their internal laboratory work and by the consolidation of the independent laboratories. In mid-1924 the merger of New York's Craftsmen, Erbograph, Republic, and Commercial Traders, resulting in Consolidated Film Industries, was announced. Several months later Consolidated bought out Los Angeles leader Standard and made that facility its western branch.

Rather than preserving a bicoastal model, which limited its West Coast labs to producing dailies and samples, Consolidated used its dominant position in both markets to begin striking release prints in Los Angeles. With much of the competition eliminated, Consolidated could force the issue whose "consummation will fulfill the desires of many," according to *Cinematographer* editor Foster Goss.[57] But when Consolidated consumed its last major competitor, Rothacker, in 1926, Goss, who had cheered the amalgamation of Standard and Consolidated, expressed concern about the complete elimination of competition. Goss conceded that consolidation could cut down overhead and "enlarge facilities for research and general progress" but also allowed that it diminished competition, which had been the fuel for innovation and increased attention to the needs of the cameramen during the previous half-decade.[58] As James Van Trees had emphasized during their heyday, the independent labs in Hollywood had greatly increased the power of the cinematographers over this aspect of production. But not only did the reduction of competition have the potential to blunt this keen attention to customer desires, it also spurred the studios to double down on investment in in-house developing facilities.

By the late 1920s the major Hollywood studios all had significant laboratory facilities, with Paramount having the "most advanced" developing machines, Universal claiming to have "perfected" its developer, and Fox boasting of their scientifically advanced facilities.[59] Upon the sale of Standard Film Labs, the head of the lab, John M. Nickolaus, chose not to join Consolidated but rather to assume oversight of the laboratory of the newly created Metro-Goldwyn-Mayer, itself a product of a merger.[60] In a promotional film produced in 1925, MGM displayed all the facilities that made up the enormous new plant for this megastudio. Among them was a laboratory that handled "more than 40,000,000 feet of stock" annually.[61] The film shows Nickolaus himself walking into one of the secure "fire-proof" vaults to examine film before the camera. The prominent appearance of Nickolaus, including a title card with his name, would have little meaning outside of the industry, but it served as a signal to those in the business that the studio was investing in the best, even in the less publicly visible aspects of the motion picture industry.

With significant competition among independents all but eliminated, the new dynamic pitted the studios' in-house processing against that of the few customer service–oriented independents. Nevertheless, there would always be production houses too small to manage their own processing facilities, as well as varying needs in the majors that forced them to outsource projects. Independent competition ensured that even in-house technology facilities would need to continue to improve and innovate.[62] Into the 1930s, Consolidated would handle the bulk of negatives and release prints for Universal, RKO, and Reliance, and William Horsley managed Columbia's lab work; meanwhile, Fox, MGM, Paramount, and Warner Bros. mostly worked in-house.[63] Of course, Consolidated's Herbert Yates would eventually move into production with the 1935 creation of Republic Pictures, formed by the purchase of six studios all indebted to his company for lab work fees.

Though the studios wrested back much of the business from the independent labs, the latter's move into Hollywood had been essential to the transferal of lab work to Los Angeles. Had they not seized on the possibility of catering to the creative desires of filmmakers, lab work and print making might have stayed in the East, thus keeping Hollywood on the periphery of the industry. By creating a viable laboratory infrastructure in the area, the mass production required of the distribution side of the business could be shifted in part to the purview of the production studios in Hollywood rather than the financial offices in New York. Additionally, the independent laboratories were a significant sector in the larger community of technological service firms as they began to cluster geographically around the studios. Their independence allowed them to be aligned with this larger technology community as they all sought the patronage of customers from the studios.

These seemingly small shifts in business practices and infrastructural alignment made Los Angeles different from other production outposts. As long as negatives were being sent back to New York or Chicago to be edited, developed, and printed, the finishing and manufacturing aspects of the business resided in these industrial centers of the country, and Hollywood remained an oversized location-shooting destination. But with a permanent service infrastructure, particularly one that shifted the manufacturing of prints to the backyard of the studios, Hollywood moved from the periphery of the industry to its center. As reliant as the studios were on the finances provided from their New York office, their dependence on the technological infrastructure of the country's East Coast manufacturing belt was slowly lessening.

THE HOLLYWOOD SERVICE CORRIDOR

The independent labs, like most motion picture technology service firms, positioned themselves within easy distance of the Los Angeles studios. In the early 1920s, they could be found peppered throughout Hollywood, often falling within the boundaries of the Hollywood motion picture districting areas that had been established in 1919 to keep production out of residential areas.[64] By the latter half of the decade, the technology companies had formed a district of their own, lining Santa Monica Boulevard and its immediate side streets between La Brea Avenue and Gower Street, in the heart of Hollywood. This mile-and-a-half stretch was framed on the west by United Artists' Pickford-Fairbanks Studios and on the east by the massive Paramount Famous-Lasky lot, while Warner Bros., Fox, Metro, RKO, Clune, Columbia, and Chaplin were all within walking distance.[65]

In this tightly packed service corridor (see figure 20.1), the studio workers could walk from door to door for all their equipment needs. A cameraman could rent his lights at Mole-Richardson, Creco, Inc., or the Cinema Equipment Co. and supervise the processing of his negatives at the labs of Roy Davidge, Tremont, or Consolidated. The lab superintendents themselves could buy and repair their developing and printing machines at Barsam-Tollar Mechanical Works or purchase film stock at the Eastman Service Building, Smith & Aller (DuPont dealers), or the Commercial Raw Stock Co. Likewise, the Hollywood-Pioneer Lumber Co., Wholesale Supply Co. (purveyor of paints, dyes, and fireworks), and the Cinema Prop Co. all tailored their businesses to the needs of the studios. The Chicago-based Bell & Howell Camera Co. situated its local sales office in the corridor, while local manufacturer Mitchell Camera built cameras in its factory right on Santa Monica Boulevard.[66]

While looking at Hollywood as an agglomeration, geographer Allen J. Scott describes the advantages of clustering similar businesses into "spatially concentrated labor markets" that tap into "information flows and innovative potentials."[67] Location in such a corridor proved of particular advantage to companies that not only served the studios but also bought film stock and other motion picture equipment from other service firms. For example, Technicolor did not make its own cameras or film

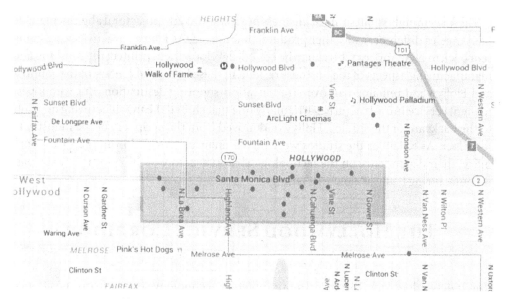

FIGURE 20.1 Map of locations of technology service firms as of 1929, based on advertisements in *American Cinematographer* and *International Photographer*. The shaded square indicates the parameter of the "service corridor." Businesses identified include Barsam-Toller Mechanical Works, Bell & Howell Co., Cinema Equipment Co., Cinema Props Co., Cinema Studio Supply Corp., Commercial Raw Stock Company, Creco, Inc., Roy Davidge Film Laboratories, Eastman Service Building, Wm. Horsley Laboratories, Inc., Mechanical Research Laboratories, Smith & Aller, Tremont Film Laboratories Corp., and The Wholesale Supply Company.

stock, but rather bought them from Bell & Howell, Mitchell, Kodak, DuPont, Agfa, and anyone else willing to sell at a reasonable price. Technicolor then modified the equipment for its own purposes. What could make more sense than residing in the midst of all of your suppliers and down the block from your customers?

When Herbert Kalmus came to Hollywood in 1922, he set up the first Technicolor office on Lodi Street and Santa Monica Boulevard, with his company comfortably nestled between the two major camera companies and the walls of the Paramount lot.[68] The company continued to expand its Boston facilities, adding another laboratory, while the Los Angeles shingle was little more than a sales office, much like that of Kodak at the time.[69] Less than two years later the company built its first plant in Hollywood. Rather than moving to a less congested part of town, Technicolor built just two blocks over, even closer to the center of the technology service corridor. The future growth of the company, including the development of its three-strip process, all happened in this corner of Hollywood, where the company would build several more plants in the coming decades. This section of Hollywood remains a central hub for motion picture technology service firms to this day.[70]

Unlike agglomerations that formed in existing cities such as New York or London, in Los Angeles, producers and firms were able to cluster tightly and easily due to the ample availability of unused, cheap land and resources. Hollywood in the 1910s and Culver City and the San Fernando Valley in the 1920s were suburban or even rural areas undergoing rapid development.[71] As such, the density of the industry was not a result of a densely designed city but rather the competition for convenience to customers. Once the corridor was established in Hollywood, even as many studios dispersed north or west to build bigger studios with soundproof stages, service firms stayed in the area where producers and technicians had become accustomed to venturing for their technology needs. Moving close to Warner Bros.' new studio in Burbank and to Universal City would just push them farther away from Fox and MGM in Culver City. Since the new studios with their sprawling backlots were not built in close proximity to each other, Hollywood remained the most geographically desirable location. In other words, with its smattering of smaller studios and its strategic position between Culver City and the San Fernando Valley, Hollywood became the hub, rather than the home, of the motion picture industry.

The industrial geographic clustering in 1920s Hollywood allowed personnel to move easily between the independent technology firms and in-house operations of major studios. As with John Nickolaus moving from Standard to MGM, technicians who began in independent firms were often brought in to manage the new in-house technology departments, and the movement of labor went both ways. Nickolaus himself had moved West with William Horsley in 1914 to oversee the building of the labs in the new Universal City, the first significant in-house labs in Los Angeles.[72] After several years of supervising both the Universal City and larger New Jersey facilities, in 1918 Nickolaus left for the Triangle Film Corp., before announcing the establishment of Standard in 1920 and making his final leap to MGM in 1924.[73] Horsley himself moved from Universal to Centaur to Christie before starting his own lab in 1918.

Likewise, engineers working in the service firms and laboratories of Hollywood often served as the industry's primary connection to East Coast corporate engineers. Lighting engineer Peter Mole had worked at General Electric prior to his work in Hollywood at Creco and establishing his own Mole-Richardson Lighting Co. He sustained a close relationship with Henry Ritchie of GE, collaborating on the designs of studio lights (using GE bulbs) as he worked for Creco. Mole shared his work with Ritchie and in turn gave feedback on GE lamp designs from the perspective of studio needs.[74] Mole's history and relationship with GE aided his employer Creco and later his own company, while at the same time, he provided GE with firsthand knowledge of studio conditions. This relationship and Mole's company were central to the conversion of the studios to incandescent lighting in early 1928.

Businessmen-engineers such as Peter Mole and Herbert Kalmus benefited from their preexisting relationships to East Coast manufacturing and engineering at the same time that they had an advantage over these companies through their geographic proximity to the studios and their employees. The large manufacturers would come to realize the importance of acknowledging the desires of the producers and technicians in Hollywood by the end of the decade, but the smaller motion picture technology manufacturers didn't have the luxury of waiting so long. Mole's only clients were in the Hollywood studios, as were those of the independent laboratories and innovators such as Technicolor. Their entire business (and often personal) fortunes rested on satisfying these customers whose needs straddled the lines between the creative and the technological. Their recognition of this marriage of art and science in providing tools to Hollywood not only contributed to their success but also to making Hollywood unique as a motion picture production center.

Conclusion

With the establishment of a technological service sector catering to the needs of the motion picture industry, the studios became less wholly dependent on the financial decisions of their executive offices and the innovations of East Coast manufacturers. By the late 1920s the technological and creative agency of Hollywood demanded attention. East Coast laboratories, equipment-sales companies, and corporate manufacturers could no longer view Los Angeles producers as a captive audience, beholden to whatever products and services these companies chose to provide. Technological self-sufficiency in important areas such as film processing allowed Hollywood to increase its creative and industrial agency in key decision-making areas. This was not a phenomenon that went without note in the higher offices of the studios. Rather, when the production executives sought to expand their power through such institutions as the Academy of Motion Picture Arts and Sciences (established in 1927), they made increasing their authority over the technology of the industry a central priority.[75] As evidenced by the example of Technicolor, the last years of the 1920s would see many companies, including Eastman Kodak, and institutions such as the Society of Motion Picture Engineers actively increase their presence in Hollywood so as not to cede further ground to local enterprises.

Through this narrative of problem-solving and adaptation, we can see that the establishment of companies that required both scientifically trained personnel *and* a clear acknowledgment of the needs of studio workers served to connect Hollywood to the networks of professional engineers and to the larger community of motion picture technology companies throughout the country. The efforts of these companies served in the creation of an expanded motion picture industry based on the sharing of technical knowledge. The existence of competent technical service within the geographic region forced an increased presence from those operating at a distance and aided the establishment of a permanent technology and production community. As such, Hollywood became not just a cultural force but also a technological presence demanding recognition. The unique practices innovated for harnessing specialized tools for mass creative production continue to resonate in the hills of Silicon Valley and beyond.

Notes

1. Memoranda (diary) books, March 1916–December 1928, Box 1, Herbert Kalmus Papers, Library of Congress, Manuscripts Division, Washington, DC. (Hereafter cited as Kalmus Papers.)
2. *Memoranda Book* (1924), Memoranda (diary) books, March 1916–December 1928, Box 1, Kalmus Papers.
3. *Memoranda Book* (1926), Box 1, Kalmus Papers. Kalmus traveled with Douglas Fairbanks and Mary Pickford, as well as Doug's brother Robert, throughout April and May 1926. This was a few months after Fairbanks shot *The Black Pirate*, the first Technicolor feature.
4. Less technologically centered service firms such as prop and costume houses also played a role in turning Los Angeles into an industrial cluster. Nevertheless, it is the technology firms that allowed Hollywood to connect to the larger technology industry of the country.
5. Michael Porter, "Local Clusters in a Global Economy," in John Hartley, ed., *Creative Industries* (Malden, MA: Blackwell Publishing, 2005), 264.
6. Ibid., 263.
7. See Allen J. Scott, *On Hollywood: The Place, the Industry* (Princeton, NJ: Princeton University Press, 2005). Scott argues that even as physical production has been largely outsourced through "runaway" production to Canada and other parts of the US, the service firms—from special effects houses to studio lighting manufacturers—are still largely based in Los Angeles.
8. F. H. Richardson, "The Home of Vitagraph," *Moving Picture World* 19, no. 4 (January 24, 1914): 401. See Brian R. Jacobson, *Studios Before the System: Architecture, Technology, and the Emergence of Cinematic Space* (New York: Columbia University Press, 2015) for more on the Hollywood studio facilities.
9. Universal seems to have been the first Hollywood studio to boast in-house labs. "Building Universal City," *Moving Picture World* 22, no. 1 (October 3, 1914): 49.
10. John Steven McGroarty, "Karl W. Thalhammer," *Los Angeles from the Mountains to the Sea: With Selected Biography of Actors and Witnesses to the Period of Growth and Achievement*, vol. 2 (Chicago, IL and New York: American Historical Society, 1921), 334. This publication focused mainly on the pre-Hollywood establishment of Los Angeles—lawyers, clergy, bankers, and those who made their fortunes in oil, minerals, real estate, and railroads. Hollywood is a minor presence in this world, making Thalhammer's inclusion a notable choice.
11. Ibid.
12. "Pans and Tilts: As Time Goes On," *American Cinematographer* 2, no. 22 (December 1, 1921): 8.
13. *USPTO Patent Full-Text and Image Database*, http://patft.uspto.gov/netacgi/nph-Parser?Sect1=PTO2&Sect2=HITOFF&u=%2Fnetahtml%2FPTO%2Fsearch-adv.htm&r=0&f=S&l=50&d=PALL&OS=IN%2Fthalhammer&RS=IN%2Fthalhammer&Query=IN%2Fthalhammer&TD=67&Srch1=thalhammer.INNM.&NextList2=Final+17+Hits.
14. "Pans and Tilts: As Time Goes On," 8. Thalhammer later adapted his tools for the amateur market as it grew in the late 1920s, making his tripod adaptable into a projector stand and opening offices in Chicago and New York. "Thalhammer Openings," *Movie Makers* 4, no. 5 (May 1929): 336.
15. I discuss the relationship between the SMPE and Hollywood technicians at length in "A Society Apart: The Early Years of the Society of Motion Picture Engineers" *Film History* 28, no. 4 (Fall 2016).

16. John W. Allison, "Standardization of the Motion Picture Industry, and the Ideal Studio," *Transactions of the Society of Motion Picture Engineers, Cleveland, Ohio, November 18–20, 1918* (New York: Society of Motion Picture Engineers, 1919), 9.
17. Early motion picture laboratories included Clune, William Horsley, Crouse-Davidge, Kosmos, and Rothacker-Aller.
18. Eastman Kodak Company Research Laboratories, *Tinting and Toning of Eastman Positive Motion Picture Film* (Rochester, NY: Eastman Kodak Company, 1916 first edition; 1927 edition).
19. Kristin Thompson, "Major Technological Changes of the 1920s," in David Bordwell, Janet Staiger, and Kristin Thompson, eds., *The Classical Hollywood Cinema: Film Style and Mode of Production to 1960* (New York: Columbia University Press, 1985), 286.
20. Ad for Miles Bros., *Moving Picture World* 1, no. 23 (August 10, 1907): 400.
21. Thackeray P. Leslie, "Lubin of Lubinville: From Optician to Millionaire Picture Manufacturer," *Movie Pictorial* 1, no. 9 (July 4, 1914): 12.
22. Janet Staiger, "Blueprints for Feature Films: Hollywood's Continuity Scripts," in Tino Balio, ed., *The American Film Industry* (Madison: University of Wisconsin Press, 1976; revised 1985), 173–192.
23. Kristin Thompson, "Initial Standardization of the Basic Technology," in Bordwell, Staiger, and Thompson, *The Classical Hollywood Cinema*, 279–280. Thompson has noted the evident desire on the part of cinematographers in the 1910s and early 1920s to "control" the developing phase as well as a deepening knowledge of this aspect of filmmaking on their part.
24. Ads for New York Film Laboratories, Modern Film Laboratories, Industrial Moving Picture Company, Standard Motion Picture Company, and Brilliant Film Manufacturing Co. from *Moving Picture World* 26, no. 9 (November 20, 1915): 1544, 1548, 1558, 1574.
25. American Film Laboratories ad, *Moving Picture World* 23, no. 11 (March 13, 1915): 1667; *Motion Picture News* 11, no. 15 (April 17, 1915): 132. Louis B. Jennings and Edwin S. Porter of Famous-Players ran the laboratory. After their previous studio burned to the ground, Famous-Players found it wiser to separate out their laboratory business from their new studio. This separation also meant they operated independently and served several studios.
26. George Eastman to A. C. Arnoll, Manager Industrial Department, Los Angeles Chamber of Commerce, November 17, 1919, Eastman Legacy Collection, George Eastman House, Rochester, NY.
27. The first mention of a laboratory being established in Los Angeles appeared in mid-1915, when Fred J. Balshofer, who had come to the area in 1909 with the first Bison crew, proposed to build F. B. Film Laboratories next to his Quality Pictures Corporation at Sunset and Gower. His "up-to-date," "dust-proof" developing, printing, tinting, and toning facilities would be "on a par with the best establishments of the East." It is unclear if this announcement became a reality. "Quality Pictures Corporation: New Metro Ally with Fred Balshofer at the Helm," *Moving Picture World* 25, no. 2 (July 10, 1915): 240.
28. "$150,000 Addition to Lasky Studio," *Motography* 15, no. 15 (April 8, 1916): 807.
29. "Cold Facts," Universal Ad by Carl Laemmle, *Moving Picture World* 27, no. 6 (February 12, 1916): 872. While Universal City did have laboratories, he made it clear that he was not moving a significant portion of the lab work West.
30. See Luci Marzola, "Better Pictures Through Chemistry: DuPont and the Fight for the Hollywood Film Stock Market," *Velvet Light Trap* 76 (Fall 2015): 3–18.

31. "Chemicals Growing Scarcer," *Variety* 42, no. 4 (March 24, 1916): 23.
32. "Craftsmen Film Laboratories Open," *Moving Picture World* 33, no. 1 (July 7, 1917): 112; ad for Republic Laboratories, Inc., *Wid's Daily* 11, no. 45 (February 15, 1920): 20.
33. "Craftsmen Film Laboratories Open," 112.
34. "Rothacker Film Co. Gets Record Order for 'Tarzan' Prints," *Exhibitors Herald* 6, no. 13 (March 23, 1918): 18.
35. Ibid.
36. "Laboratory Workers Continue the Strike in New York," *Motion Picture News* 22, no. 7 (August 7, 1920): 1097; "Laboratory Men Stirred Up, Organize; Fear Eastman—Brulatour Control," *Wid's Daily* 16, no. 60 (May 31, 1921): 1.
37. Ad for Allied Film Laboratories Association, *Exhibitors Trade Review* 11, no. 1 (December 3, 1921): 14.
38. "Rothacker Plant in West Ready in April," *Exhibitors Herald* 12, no. 10 (March 5, 1921): 68.
39. Pacific Film Labs advertisement, *Motion Picture News* 14, no. 3 (July 22, 1916): 491; William Horsley Labs ad, *Wid's Daily* 10, no. 51 (November 23, 1919): 26.
40. Bloom Film Laboratories ad, *Wid's Daily* 10, no. 58 (November 30, 1919): 11.
41. William C. Foster, "The Laboratory," *American Cinematographer* 2, no. 5 (March 1, 1921): 1.
42. Ibid.
43. For more on early attempts to position cinema as art, see: William Uricchio and Roberta Pearson, *Reframing Culture: The Case of the Vitagraph Quality Films* (Princeton, NJ: Princeton University Press, 1993) and Lee Grieveson, *Policing Cinema: Movies and Censorship in Early-Twentieth-Century America* (Berkeley: University of California Press, 2004). For a thorough analysis of the cinematographers' efforts to position themselves as artists, see Patrick Keating, *Hollywood Lighting: From the Silent Era to Film Noir* (New York: Columbia University Press, 2009).
44. John Thornton Caldwell, *Production Culture: Industrial Reflexivity and Critical Practice in Film and Television* (Durham, NC: Duke University Press, 2008): 116.
45. Foster Goss, "The Editors' Corner," *American Cinematographer* 3, no. 8 (November 1922): 10.
46. Ibid., 11.
47. Keating, *Hollywood Lighting*, 15.
48. Foster, "The Laboratory," 1.
49. John Leezer, "Photography and Motion Pictures," *American Cinematographer* 2, no. 15 (July 22, 1921): 1.
50. Frank V. Biggy, "The Value of the Laboratory as Applied to the Cameraman and His Work," *American Cinematographer* 2, no. 7 (April 1, 1921): 2.
51. Kosmos Film Labs ad, *American Cinematographer* 2, no. 22 (December 1, 1921): 7.
52. Clune Film Laboratories ad, *American Cinematographer* 2, No. 23 (December 15, 1921): 13; "The Finishing Touch," *American Cinematographer* 2, no. 24 (January 1, 1922): 4; Standard Film Labs ad, *American Cinematographer* 3, no. 8 (November 1922): 18.
53. Standard Film Laboratories ads, *Motion Picture News* 27, no. 4 (January 27, 1923): 380; *Motion Picture News* 27, no. 5 (February 3, 1923): 502; *Motion Picture News* 22, no. 8 (February 24, 1923): 872.
54. The *Exhibitors Trade Review* in December 1922 lists forty-one labs in its index, including nineteen in the New York/New Jersey area, ten in Los Angeles, five in Chicago, and the rest peppered throughout the Northeast and Midwest. *Exhibitors Trade Review* 13, no. 5 (December 1922).

55. James Van Trees, "Co-Operation Between Cinematographer and Laboratory," *American Cinematographer* 4, no. 9 (December 1923): 6.
56. But he also warned against the extremes of the customer service mentality in which the cinematographer was never to blame for faulty photography.
57. Foster Goss, "The Editors' Lens," *American Cinematographer* 5, no. 6 (September 1924): 10–11.
58. Foster Goss, "The Editors' Lens: Laboratory Consolidation," *American Cinematographer* 7, no. 2 (May 1926): 8–9.
59. "Developer Perfected," *American Cinematographer* 8, no. 11 (February 1928): 17; "Fox's New Laboratory," *American Cinematographer* 9, no. 5 (August 1928): 8.
60. "With Them a Moment In Front of the Camera," *American Cinematographer* 5, no. 9 (December 1924): 25.
61. *MGM Studio Tour*, 35mm, 1925, Library of Congress Motion Picture Archive.
62. "Fox's New Laboratory." Fox's labs were proclaimed in 1928 to be the "last word in the scientific evolution of the photographic art." While Fox would have liked to think that their laboratory was the last word, shutting out the need for further improvement to keep up with the competition, it is unlikely that this was indeed true.
63. File-Technicians' Credits 1935, Academy Archive, Margaret Herrick Library. Information comes from a stack of index cards labeled "Technicians' Credits 1935" in the Academy of Motion Picture Arts and Sciences internal files. Some of the in-house labs also did outside work, as with Paramount handling Walter Wanger's productions and Warner Bros. processing for Cosmopolitan. Technicolor did all of the lab work for films using their process.
64. "Moving Picture Zones," *Holly Leaves* (February 15, 1919): 42. Addresses for businesses were gathered from advertisements in *American Cinematographer*.
65. Studios included Warner Bros. (until 1928, now Capital Studios), Fox Studios (until 1928 when they moved to West Los Angeles), Metro Pictures (later Desilu, now Red Studios), RKO Studios (now part of Paramount), the Clune Studios (now Raleigh), Columbia Pictures (now Sunset Gower Studios), Charlie Chaplin Studios (now Henson), General Service Studios (now Hollywood Center Studios), and Mascot Pictures. The studios clustered on Gower Street became known as Poverty Row.
66. Mitchell moved out of the district in 1928 when the company built a massive factory in West Hollywood. Others, such as the Dunning Process Co. and Max Factor, up north on Hollywood Boulevard and Vitacolor downtown, chose to be outliers.
67. Scott, *On Hollywood*, 7.
68. Address of 1116 Lodi Street found on Technicolor engineer J. Arthur Ball's listing on the membership list of the SMPE in *Transactions of the Society of Motion Picture Engineers, Atlantic City, NJ, May 7–10, 1923* (New York: Society of Motion Picture Engineers, 1923): 8.
69. "Technicolor Adds New Laboratory in Boston," *Motion Picture News* (December 29, 1923): 3078, 3080, 3092, 3094.
70. Exact numbers are difficult to find, but a simple Google Maps search of the area for key terms "production" and "studio" yields well over a hundred service firms, including Studio Depot (Mole-Richardson), Bell Sound Studios, Out of Frame Production Rentals, SonicPool Post Production, Camera Crew Los Angeles, Digital Jungle, The Post Group, Runway Post, Master Key Visual Effects, Anytime Production Rental, Advanced Digital Services, Inc., Quixote Production Supplies, Outpost Sound Mixing, Film Technology Co., Inc., and Mixers Hollywood. The current home of Technicolor is just a few blocks north on Sunset Boulevard.

71. Kevin Starr, *Material Dreams: Southern California Through the 1920s* (New York: Oxford University Press, 1990): 72–76.
72. "John M. Nickolaus Goes to Coast," *Moving Picture World* 19, no. 7 (February 14, 1914): 799.
73. John M. Nickolaus, "Photography—The Mile-a-Minute Art," *Photoplay* 14, no. 6 (November 1918): 34; "Big Laboratory Planned," *Wid's Daily* 13, no. 57 (August 27, 1920): 2.
74. Henry Ritchie, GE Searchlight Engineering Dept. to Peter Mole, Creco, May 1, 1924, Mole-Richardson Company Collection. Mole first came to the decision to try incandescent lights for the productions of Maud Adams through Ritchie's suggestion. Ritchie had shared a GE report on the comparative screen illumination of "Mazda and low and high intensity lamps" but drew a line at sending him photographs of their lamp models. Ritchie also informed Mole of the greater efficiency of incandescents as well as their compatibility with panchromatic film. This predates Mole's founding of Mole-Richardson as an incandescent lighting company by three years and his central role in the Mazda Tests by four.
75. The Producers-Technicians Committee and the Technical Bureau were early efforts of the Academy. I discuss them at length in my dissertation, "Engineering Hollywood: Technology, Technicians, and the Science of Building the Studio System, 1915–1930" (PhD diss., University of Southern California, 2016).

CHAPTER 21

A PROLOGUE TO HOLLYWOOD

*Sid Grauman, Film Premieres, and
the (Real-Estate) Development of Hollywood*

ROSS MELNICK

On the ninetieth anniversary of Grauman's Chinese Theatre, *Los Angeles Times* journalist Kevin Crust devoted nearly half of his breezy, 522-word profile of Sidney "Sid" Patrick Grauman (see figure 21.1) to a long discredited paternity case. Grauman's career, and his influence on Hollywood—the theaters, hotels, banks, and other buildings he helped erect across this iconic neighborhood, as well as the signature premieres he presented that marketed the area's dedication to entertainment, celebrity, and real estate—couldn't even garner three hundred words from his hometown newspaper.[1] This is hardly surprising. Like most silent-era impresarios, Grauman has had his industrial and cultural legacy truncated and obfuscated by time, myth, and, later, disinterest.[2] Instead, showmen like Grauman are often neatly packaged into hagiographic and/or erroneous caricature rather than analyzed more critically for their role in developing the very marketing and infrastructure that built Hollywood as both a place and an institution that has sustained its global lure and identity for the last century.

This chapter examines Sid Grauman's expansive role in developing some of Hollywood's most important early institutions—the Egyptian and Chinese theaters, the Roosevelt Hotel, and the Academy of Motion Picture Arts and Sciences—as well as the glamorous eye-catching premieres that helped redirect the focus of the film industry westward in the 1920s through a combination of film marketing and exhibition and real estate investment and promotion. Arriving a few years after *The Squaw Man* (1914) and other films began shifting film production and the industry to the West Coast, Grauman, in association with Joseph Schenck and others like Charles E. Toberman, became a key figure in the (real-estate) development of Los Angeles, and specifically Hollywood, as the city became more and more synonymous with entertainment. *Variety*

FIGURE 21.1 Sidney Patrick Grauman, ca. 1930.

would, for example, refer to Grauman by March 1926 as "a pioneer of California realty development."[3] Through real estate and showmanship, Grauman helped consolidate the growing national attention on Hollywood as a center of both film production and film exhibition.[4]

His theatrical presentations set the stage for the nation's never-ending adoration of celebrity as he transformed film premieres from special events that once needed the conferral of New York's social and cultural elite to increasingly West Coast affairs that generated a new type of celestial royalty: the movie star. Beginning in 1922, Grauman's theaters and his elaborate premieres in Hollywood at the Egyptian and, later, Chinese theater were central weapons in the local film and real estate industry's efforts to consolidate and reify the westward shift of film production and the global marketing thereof from its base in New York. This was accomplished in part by making these publicized (and broadcasted) events essential tools for the platformed release of new films and by amplifying the stardom of a growing number of Los Angeles-based actors and moguls who relied on the now habitual occurrence of these premieres to generate ongoing radio, print, and newsreel publicity. As more and more stars moved out West, their attendance at Hollywood premieres followed. In essence, Grauman's opening nights, his expansive and popular prologues, and his real estate projects all became part of the machinery of a soon-to-be globalized Hollywood for studio flaks and stars and the fan magazines and other publications that profited from them. The need for stars to be *in* Hollywood to be "seen" became increasingly important. This, in turn, boosted local tourism that benefited from the opportunity to see America's new royalty up close in their natural habitat, out and about at theaters, hotels, nightclubs, restaurants, and other venues across this rapidly developing area. Lary May writes that the movie (and movie theater) boom of the 1920s created a "mass culture legitimized by theaters" that reinforced a "new consumer culture [that] did not erode but reinforced the cultural authority of the wealthy."[5] There were few more conspicuous displays of wealth than a Grauman film premiere, with its luxury cars, designer clothes, and manicured idols catwalking one by one into Grauman's exoticized temples to mass consumption and mass fantasy.

None of this was happenstance. Grauman, through his real estate development projects, redefined the cityscape of downtown Los Angeles in the 1910s and then, in the 1920s, the growing urbanity of Hollywood. First, his theaters transformed downtown Los Angeles from a place of retail, manufacturing, residence, and commerce into one increasingly focused on filmed entertainment and its large-scale, klieg-light promotion. By the late 1910s, Grauman's theaters helped make downtown Los Angeles's own Broadway a competitive film-exhibition rival of New York's, despite being a fraction of the Great White Way's economic and geographical size and scale. Then, during the 1920s, Grauman helped convert a sleepy orchard-filled neighborhood (Hollywood) into a boulevard of Orientalist fantasy and commercial investment. This was accomplished with millions of dollars of real estate development, a cadre of film, bank, and other investors, and growing opportunities to reshape a prospecting town not with a sifter's pan of gold but with the developing allures of twentieth-century American culture.

The 1920s provided an increasingly atomized nation with a common parlance—movies and movie stars—and America's obsession made Hollywood the mythological location of dreams, wealth, fame, sex, vanity, and abject desire. Over the next century, the buildings Grauman and his cohort constructed—and the staging of glamorous premieres and parties promoting all of the above—would lure the world to Hollywood either as a visitor, investor, or as yet another dreamer. As Denise McKenna reminds us, "Los Angeles was, and still is, a city dominated by real estate speculation." But the "emergence of Los Angeles," she writes, "and eventually Hollywood, as the nation's dream-factory, was not the simple accident of location: the arrival of filmmakers in Los Angeles was a boon to a city desperate to promote itself to the world."[6] Grauman, with his financial and artistic investment in Hollywood's key theaters, hotels, and other institutions, was a born marketer and showman, an ethnic outsider working alongside many others to remake America in a new image. Nothing sold that image more than Hollywood's growing numbers of stars and the setting in which they shone so brightly: the klieg-light premiere and afterparty and its ensuing national and increasingly international media coverage.

The Graumans and the Gold Rush: From Kansas to the Yukon to California

Grauman's Los Angeles career reflects the vast changes in the American film industry, its growing vertical *and* horizontal integration, and the way in which independent exhibitors (as well as producers) were increasingly swallowed whole by multinational entertainment companies whose not-yet-divested theater chains quickly consolidated their power. Grauman's career, like Samuel "Roxy" Rothafel's, is emblematic of a period in which even the industry's most powerful impresarios were no match for the scale of bank and other investment capital that made exhibitors surprised pawns in a much larger financial and real estate development game.

Like many who came to Los Angeles and found fame and fortune, Grauman traveled a circuitous route to get there. In the late nineteenth century, his father, David (D.J.), sold train tickets in Kansas City and turned his profits into real estate investments, buying several thousand acres of land which he then sold off in lots. He later packaged up a Georgia Minstrel show and took his family along for a life on the road. The tour took D.J. and his son Sid to the gold rush town of Cripple Creek, Colorado, and then on to Oklahoma City, where the father-son duo reportedly "cleaned up" in gold panning and pilfering.[7] They moved on next to the Yukon and Dawson City in 1897, following the area's gold rush. Sid, now eighteen, sold newspapers in town as well as pies and flowers. He created his first theatrical show there for the benefit of the impoverished newsboys. Jack London, whose novels would later bring him fame, served as publicist for the benefit and even sold tickets for the Graumans. Sid wasn't primarily interested in sales, though; he was enthralled by entertainment and producing.[8] D.J. was the consummate businessman; Sid wanted to be a showman.

The Graumans pocketed their Yukon earnings and headed to San Francisco, where they followed the nickelodeon craze and converted a retail store into their first motion picture theater, the Unique, with "800 kitchen chairs, [a] screen, scenery and piano."[9] To attract more audiences to their ten-cent odeon, they also booked vaudeville acts for the Unique's stage. One of their early bookings was the Musical Laskys, starring Jesse L. Lasky and his sister, Blanche. Jesse was later an investment partner with Grauman and Adolph Zukor at Famous Players-Lasky (FPL). Another talent was Nellie Revell, a future columnist, radio producer, and associate of Rothafel.[10] Louella Parsons would later note that Sid was "a great discoverer of talent." So was D.J. In addition to the Laskys, he also booked Al Jolson for forty dollars per week and discovered a young Sophie Tucker.[11]

The 1906 earthquake and subsequent fire gutted the city of San Francisco and the Graumans' theatrical business. They were not deterred. The Graumans found a safe plot of earth in the city and erected an outdoor theater seating fifteen hundred weary citizens.[12] The theater was dubbed the National and later outfitted into a more permanent structure. The money from the National was later plowed into a new theater on Market Street between Fifth and Sixth streets. This was followed by another Grauman offering, the seventeen-hundred-seat Imperial. They would later add the 2,500-seat Globe Theatre in the city's Mission district.[13] From the ashes of the quake, the Graumans became leading vaudeville and motion picture exhibitors in San Francisco.

Nearly a decade later—with Roxy's Strand and Rialto theaters garnering much press in New York and feature films ascendant nationwide in middle-class viewership and respectability—the Graumans moved away from a mixture of vaudeville and film and into deluxe motion picture exhibition. Soon they'd be moving out of San Francisco as well. In December 1916, Sid announced a $400,000, ten-year lease for a deluxe motion picture theater to be constructed inside a new twelve-story office building at Third Street and Broadway in downtown Los Angeles.[14] The theater was already being given the name "Grauman," but its famous moniker, "Million Dollar," was not yet affixed.[15] By December, however, the adjective had taken hold in the press, no doubt thanks to Grauman's own efforts to publicize the theater's growing costs.[16]

Opening night attendees on February 1, 1918, were a who's who of early Hollywood: (former employee) Jesse Lasky, Cecil B. DeMille, Thomas Ince, Mary Pickford, Sessue Hayakawa, Wallace Reid, Mae Murray, William S. Hart, Lois Weber, Thomas Meighan, Douglas Fairbanks, Roscoe "Fatty" Arbuckle, Charlie Chaplin, Edna Purviance, Dustin Farnum, Constance Talmadge, Mary Miles Minter, Mack Sennett, D. W. Griffith, Hal Roach, Viola Dana, William Desmond, and innumerable others.[17] The *Times*'s extensive coverage noted that onlookers were "[j]ammed together like sardines in a box" along Broadway, stretching from Third Street all the way to Fifth Street "and beyond," "overflowing into the street and on the other sidewalk. This was the sight, unusual even for Los Angeles."[18] Grauman was slowly developing his expertise in event management and publicity. It was his first grand premiere, one of many to follow.

The Million Dollar, with its star-studded debut, opulent prologue—a themed stage show that would prove a central appeal of Grauman's theaters—and evocative architecture, was an instant success, and Grauman became Los Angeles's premiere showman. His list of attendees included virtually everyone who mattered in the burgeoning movie capital of the West. The opening of the Million Dollar meant that Los Angeles and Grauman promised to battle New York, Chicago, and other major cities for movie palace supremacy. Filmmaking had put Los Angeles on the film industry's atlas; now the Million Dollar had made the city a vital hub of film exhibition (and film premieres) as well. The Million Dollar, *Motion Picture News* reported, "will be able to offer an innovation that no other theatre in the country has been able to give, and this is the policy of having the star of the feature appear during at least one showing of the picture." Grauman offered moviegoers an appearance by William S. Hart on his opening bill and promised appearances by increasingly local film stars at all subsequent openings.[19] What better way to advertise the premiere of any given film in Los Angeles than by marketing the appearance of the city's cinematic stars on the Million Dollar's stage (see figure 21.2)? This geographical advantage made Grauman's new theater not just a local sensation but a tourist attraction as well. Years before his Egyptian and Chinese theaters became "must sees" when visiting the city, Grauman's Million Dollar was, according to the *Los Angeles Times* in 1919, already "drawing admiring thousands from all sections

FIGURE 21.2 Charlie Chaplin, Sid Grauman, Mary Pickford, and Douglas Fairbanks at Grauman's Million Dollar Theater. *Exhibitors Herald*, June 19, 1920.

of Southern California."[20] " 'Grauman's Million Dollar Theatre?' says the native of Los Angeles in amazement when accosted as to its location. [. . .] 'I thought everybody in the world knew where Grauman's was.' " *Exhibitors Herald* observed that locals "take pride in it. Sid Grauman [. . .] has made it one of the attractions of Los Angeles, a city of attractions."[21] The trade journal added that the theater was built on a growing brand—the allure of the Grauman name—that was bolstered by marketing, film premieres, and a healthy dose of media buying.[22]

By 1919, the Million Dollar was still *the* picture palace of the moment in downtown Los Angeles, but its fame and acclaim were transitory, as was the early glow of all movie palaces that opened between 1913 and 1932. Rumors of projects in and out of Los Angeles appeared in trade and newspapers throughout the year, including one in *Wid's Daily* that claimed, presciently, that Sid was building a 2,200-seat movie theater seven miles away on Hollywood Boulevard.[23] His first formal announcement, though, came when the Graumans paid a million dollars to buy the city's First Methodist Church on the corner of Sixth and Hill streets downtown. Their plan: to demolish the church and construct a 4,200-seat movie palace—Grauman's Metropolitan Theatre—in its place. The value of the land alone, one observer noted at the time, "proves that Los Angeles is a big city and is destined to become even greater. It shows the big business men, hotel-men and industrial men as well as theatrical men have faith in the growth and importance of Los Angeles."[24] Grauman's latest was financed in part by FPL's substantial investment, as the Metropolitan would later become Paramount's downtown showcase.[25] Grauman's association with FPL expanded further when he purchased a controlling interest in Quinn's Rialto in downtown Los Angeles and it became a second-run venue for Paramount-Artcraft films.[26]

While the Million Dollar had been opened with a weekly change policy, Grauman was now booking feature films far longer, for up to two, three, or even four weeks. The popularity (and expense) of his live entertainment (and specifically his much-lauded prologues) made employing longer runs at the Million Dollar essential in reducing overhead.[27] Grauman would increasingly book fewer and fewer films each year; instead, he would hold them over longer, from weeks to months, buoyed entirely by the growing local and then national appeal of his famous prologues. The time not spent developing and staging new prologues, and synchronizing the other live entertainment, music, and short films he presented nightly, freed him up to secure additional real estate and other investments and projects.[28] Grauman began to look westward, to the growing possibilities in Hollywood.

Hollywoodland: Grauman's Egyptian Theatre and the Development of Hollywood

In February 1920, Grauman purchased a large plot of land at Hollywood Boulevard and MacAdden Place for a theater that would be located a half block from the popular Hollywood Hotel.[29] The hotel was a hot spot for actors and moguls, the *Times* noted, situated "very near the center of gravity for filmland activities," drawing in "members of the profession" and the "large residential population of Hollywood and Wilshire district."[30] The purchase of lots was still infinitely cheaper in Hollywood than in Manhattan, making it a low-risk investment. Even if a lot was not developed, the land could be resold.

Construction on Grauman's new Hollywood theater began during the summer of 1921 after a star-studded launch.[31] "Over there under those orange trees I discovered Anita Stewart, Mildred Harris and other stars, whom I now forget, ready to turn little silver shovels of dirt over as [sic] the ground-breaking ceremony of the Egyptian Theater," Grace Kingsley would later recall. "Sid Grauman stood by and made a speech to a big bunch of film men and exhibitors. A few natives, dwellers in cottages close by, came with the dust of the orchards on their shoes, to watch [the] proceedings."[32] The construction of the Egyptian was funded in part by real estate developer Charles E. Toberman to not only shift film premieres away from downtown Los Angeles but to move other premieres from New York to Hollywood. The focus on Hollywood would, in turn, make all of Toberman's investments up and down the boulevard and beyond far more valuable. The budding Hollywood Chamber of Commerce also worked to make the city the "home of photoplay premieres," and the organization argued that "all pictures made in Hollywood should present their world premieres in this city."[33] This would help boost Toberman's (and Grauman's) plans to develop Hollywood into both a national center of film production *and* film exhibition.[34]

Grauman's new Hollywood theater (see figure 21.3) depended on widespread publicity to draw audiences away from downtown. It would be the first in the western United States to offer a reserved-seat policy, with sales offices opened in both Hollywood and downtown Los Angeles two weeks prior to its debut.[35] When the theater later grew in popularity, more publicity generated ticket sales in far-off Santa Barbara, Long Beach, and San Diego; visitors could even schedule a bus trip from these cities that included lunch or dinner at the Musso & Frank Grill next door.[36] This made the Egyptian a regional, and, later, national tourist attraction. Grauman began touting a star-studded tie-up as well, much like the Million Dollar's, wherein each prologue would include "players who appeared in the picture . . . in their identical roles" on the Egyptian stage, another draw for opening night.[37]

Tickets for the first Egyptian premiere on October 18, 1922—costing five dollars per head—sold out in a matter of hours.[38] A Grauman premiere was already a must for

GRAUMAN'S EGYPTIAN THEATRE, HOLLYWOOD, CALIFORNIA

FIGURE 21.3 Grauman's Egyptian and Sid Grauman (ca. 1922).

moguls and movie stars to see and be seen in. Opening night for *Robin Hood* (1922), the *Los Angeles Times* noted, "resemble[d] a special edition of the blue books of society and the film industry combined" with "[p]ractically every star in the industry" in attendance.[39] The Egyptian premiered with 1,760 seats, an orchestra of fifty musicians, and a bevy of notable presenters. Fred Niblo served as master of ceremonies, and speeches were given by Los Angeles mayor George Cryer, George Eastman, Cecil B. DeMille, Charlie Chaplin, Jesse Lasky, and Toberman, a familiar and increasingly important player.[40] As promised, *Exhibitors Herald* reported, "Players who took part in the filming of the picture appeared on the stage during the pageant prologue, in which they wore the original costumes of the photoplay."[41]

Hollywood was also becoming a center of film *and* broadcasting and the convergence thereof. One month after Grauman's thunderous debut of *Robin Hood* at the Egyptian, he presented De Koven's "Robin Hood" opera over local station KHJ, performed live from the Egyptian theater.[42] Radio was also an additional avenue for promotion of the theater. A few days after the KHJ broadcast, Grauman sold half of his equity in the Egyptian to the West Coast Theaters chain, which already boasted five smaller theaters in Hollywood.[43] In the coming months, Grauman also sold his stakes in the Metropolitan, Rialto, and the Million Dollar in downtown Los Angeles. His sights were now fully on Hollywood and the future possibilities along the boulevard.[44] Grauman, with his growing cash reserves, threw his lot in with Toberman, West Coast Theaters, and the rampant real estate development in Hollywood.

Grauman continued managing the Egyptian Theatre in the years that followed, as the Egyptian's star-studded premieres, famous prologues, and exotic architecture became tourist attractions that spread Grauman's name around the world through images captured by the theater's visitors. The *Los Angeles Times* observed in June 1924:

> Tourists and visitors in Los Angeles are carrying back to their houses in the remote corners of the world kodak [sic] snapshots of Grauman's Hollywood Egyptian Theater and intimate close-ups of the forcourt [sic] [. . .] Attaches [sic] of the Egyptian Theater have questioned many of these kodaking visitors and find that the traveling public has had it impressed upon them by tourists, bureaus, literature and word-of-mouth comment that the Hollywood Egyptian is numbered among the greatest attractions Los Angeles and Hollywood have to offer, hence the almost daily visits of tourists who wax enthusiastic over this bit of old Egypt transferred to Hollywood Boulevard.[45]

Columnist Nellie Revell would later write that the "Egyptian theatre is something no conscientious visitor to Southern California thinks of missing [. . .] from Maine to Mexico."[46] Col. Harry Baine, president of the Hollywood Boulevard Association, remarked that "People not only came from all parts of Los Angeles, but as soon as the fame of its unique architecture and magnificent productions spread, from all parts of the world. Probably no single structure ever erected in the film capital did more to advertise Hollywood to persons in all parts of the country than this palatial theatre."[47] In Baine's estimation lies the intricate relationship between real estate development, theater construction, film premieres, and, ultimately, tourist dollars.

Grauman's premiere for *The Big Parade* (1925) serves as a key example of how he attracted ongoing attention for his theaters, well after their debut, and how the showman created the sort of celebrity-driven extravaganzas that have characterized film premieres ever since. Since much of the nation could not yet visit Hollywood and his theater, Grauman used radio again to sell the Egyptian and Hollywood as *the* location for world premieres. On November 5, 1925, Grauman inaugurated electrified, klieg-light premieres broadcast over radio station KNX. Giant amplifiers were installed in the Egyptian's forecourt so that the crowd gathered outside could hear the same broadcast being sent out over the airwaves. Inside, five microphones were placed throughout the foyer so that the buzz of celebrity arrivals and the opening ceremonies could be reported and broadcast to listeners on the street and at home. "For the first time at an opening performance anywhere," the *Times* reported, "the arrival of screen stars, cinema celebrities and other distinguished guests will be announced over the radio to the entire world."[48] The premiere created the mixed-media model for countless others to follow.

The evening began with a mile-long street parade "furnished by MGM and various civic organizations" with "six [brass] bands, innumerable floats, artillery, fire-fighting apparatus, militia men, police, illumined by blazing red torches at every street corner and escorted by a fleet of airplanes overhead."[49] Hal Cody, star of *The Big Parade*, and Maude Marsh, of MGM's costume design department, were on-air hosts, "announc[ing] the arrival of the stars and broadcast[ing] descriptions of their costumes."[50] *Exhibitor's Trade Review* described the program and evening:

> Upon reaching the theatre the soldiers acted as a special guard lining the entire block in front of the Egyptian. Fifty red, white and blue searchlights stationed on and in front of the theatre made a spectacular electrical display. A loud speaking system told the crowds outside the theatre, which covered the area of a square block, of the arrival of various notables. [...] Never has Hollywood seen such an opening. Everyone from Mary Pickford to Bull Montana was there. With the start of the parade at seven o'clock until one in the morning excitement ran high for local filmdom. Hollywood's entire police force was unable to handle the crowds and a hurry call to Los Angeles for additional men was necessary before traffic could be adjusted.[51]

Grauman's extravagant prologue, featuring 150 performers, was secondary to the parades, lights, movie stars, and broadcasts.[52] *Exhibitor's Trade Review* added that it was "The most sensational premiere ever accorded any picture in the history of the motion picture presentation."[53] The selling of the *The Big Parade*, of the Egyptian, of the boulevard, and, most of all, of Hollywood—figurative fantasyland and logistical movie town—helped disseminate the growing legend of this pastoral area turned into a bustling dream factory. The excitement and attention paid to the Egyptian and its premieres drove up the value of Hollywood's surrounding real estate and the price of those rapidly vanishing lots even further.

The Business of Hollywood: Sid Grauman, Joseph Schenck, and Charles Toberman

Grauman was anxious to build an even greater attraction. Earlier, in July 1924, Grauman had announced the purchase of a large lot on the northeast corner of Hollywood Boulevard and Orange Drive for $850,000.[54] (Land values were climbing fast.) Two months later, Grauman trumpeted the construction of a new theater on that lot, financed in part by Charles Toberman and designed once more by Meyer & Holler.[55] "The location, in close proximity to the Egyptian Theater," the *Times* noted, "will give Hollywood a dominating position as a theatrical center—another step toward making the film metropolis the amusement mecca of the world."[56] *Variety* was already estimating that Grauman's newest theater—to be built in association with his new exhibition partners, West Coast Theaters—would cost two million dollars.[57]

Grauman was also being courted during this period by Joseph Schenck, the newly elected chairman of the board of United Artists, who planned to establish a chain of United Artists theaters across the country. Schenck was a member of the Board of Directors of A.P. Giannini's Bank of Italy, which bankrolled part of Hollywood's larger expansion, and he owned twenty percent of West Coast Theaters.[58] By December 1924, trade journals began reporting that Schenck, in a new association with Grauman, planned to create a chain of twenty deluxe theaters across the country. Each theater would be an "outlet" for United Artists films and would be staged with Grauman prologues—the first time the exhibitor signaled a willingness to disseminate his stage shows beyond one of his own theaters.[59]

Grauman's focus, however, remained on Hollywood, on the prologues and premieres at the Egyptian, and on the construction of a new Grauman theater set to begin there on July 1, 1925.[60] Grauman's latest palace was principally owned by Grauman's Greater Hollywood Theater, Inc., a California corporation owned equally in thirds by West Coast Theaters, Inc., Sid Grauman, and Joseph Schenck.[61] It was "designed, executed and engineered" by Mendel Meyer of Meyer & Holler, working in close association with and based on ideas by Grauman.[62] The venue was part of a boom in theater construction that included Charles Toberman's own El Capitan, Warner Bros.' Warner Theatre, the Music Box, and the Hollywood Playhouse, as well as a number of smaller theaters being built by Schenck's West Coast Theaters.[63] Grauman's new theater was not the only project under development by Schenck and Grauman either. Work was also set to begin on a new $2.5 million "Roosevelt" hotel. That project—across the street from Grauman's new theater—was sponsored by the Hotel Holding Co., a "syndicate," *The Film Daily* reported, that was headed by Schenck and Toberman and supported by principal stockholders such as Louis B. Mayer, Grauman, longtime Schenck manager Lou Anger, and others.[64] (Grauman, Schenck, and Anger were also key investors in San Diego real estate, where $3 million of Hollywood-related money had already found its way by early 1926.)[65] Arthur Ungar remarked in *Variety* that "The name of Schenck is as good as a Federal bank note."[66]

Each of these Grauman businesses was subject to his impressive publicity efforts. So it was then, in December 1925, that Grauman and screen star Anna May Wong drove the first shovels into the dirt to commemorate the start of Grauman's Chinese Theatre. A month later, Grauman and Wong held an official groundbreaking on January 12, 1926, with "Stars of the silver sheet, studio executives and distinguished citizens in all walks of life" standing by, and, for thematic flavor, "high Chinese dignitaries."[67] Even groundbreaking ceremonies had been turned into star-studded events through Grauman's publicity staff and machinery.

The ties between Grauman and Schenck grew in 1926. While the Egyptian attracted ongoing crowds and the Chinese and Roosevelt were still under construction, Grauman traveled in February and March 1926 to look for possible theater sites in New York, Chicago, Philadelphia, and Boston for his and Schenck's burgeoning theater chain.[68] These trips led to the creation of a new company, the United Artists Theatre Circuit Inc. (UATC), which was formally organized in Maryland in May 1926 by Schenck, Grauman, Mary Pickford, Douglas Fairbanks, and theater magnate Lee Shubert.[69] Charlie Chaplin was not involved.[70] The circuit remained a separate company from the Delaware-incorporated United Artists Corporation, but the two entities entered into a ten-year contract whereby UATC would book United Artists films, *Variety* noted, in " 'pre-release' or 'first' runs before they [we]re shown in other motion picture theatres in the same localities."[71] Theaters in the proposed chain would have double features and prologues similar to the Egyptian.[72] Grauman was named president of the new circuit and planned to manage all of the UATC theaters from his base in Hollywood.[73] This would be a marked change from Paramount, Loew's, Warner Bros., and others, all of whom operated their national theater chains from offices in New York City. In November 1926, UATC signaled its growing investment in Hollywood by buying Grauman's remaining one-half interest in the Egyptian and leasing it for twenty-five years. Grauman pocketed the cash and retained, for now, his management of the theater.[74]

Grauman, Hollywood, and 1927

Grauman's attention, despite UATC's expansion in downtown Los Angeles and elsewhere, remained focused on Hollywood, and, in 1927, his role in its continued architectural and institutional development began to reach far beyond his theaters. Grauman was, as previously mentioned, a key investor in the new twelve-story Hollywood Roosevelt Hotel (see figure 21.4) being built across the street from the Chinese. He was joined in the project by Joseph Schenck, Louis B. Mayer, Fred Niblo, and Charles Toberman as business partners.[75] The enormously busy year also included an investment, with Joseph Schenck and Jesse Lasky, in the new Hollywood Olympic Club, a

FIGURE 21.4 Groundbreaking ceremony for the new Roosevelt Hotel in Hollywood. Charles Toberman is fourth from left; Sid Grauman is third from right. *Exhibitors Herald*, June 12, 1926.

million dollar "clubhouse" to be built at Franklin and Highland avenues with 440 rooms in a twelve-story building.[76] Grauman's influence widened further when he was elected to the board of directors of the Federal Trust and Savings Bank of Hollywood. Members of the board included many familiar names from UATC and/or the Hollywood Roosevelt project: Louis B. Mayer, Mary Pickford, Douglas Fairbanks, Norma Talmadge, and frequent Grauman emcee and presenter Fred Niblo.[77] Schenck served as president of the bank while Charles Toberman was chairman of the board, further evidence of the small, intricately linked coterie of names that propped up Hollywood's rapid development.[78] Grauman was highly placed enough, both socially and economically, that he dallied at this time in bank management, though it was short-lived."[79]

Yet another Grauman-linked pillar of Hollywood was erected in 1927: the formation of the Academy of Motion Picture Arts and Sciences (AMPAS). Many of Grauman's business partners were instrumental in its creation, with Douglas Fairbanks serving as its first president and Fred Niblo its first vice-president. Mary Pickford, Louis B. Mayer, and Joseph Schenck were all named to its board of directors, representing the industry's producers, while the organization's initial sponsors included Jesse Lasky and, not surprisingly, Sid Grauman. As *The Film Daily* noted, Lasky and Grauman and other sponsors of the organization "all have been active in the preliminary meetings which have been quietly under way since January."[80]

A week after the formation of AMPAS, the Hollywood Roosevelt Hotel opened on May 15, 1927, financed primarily by Academy members and sponsors. Thus, it was hardly surprising that when the Academy held its first awards dinner two years later that it took place at the Hollywood Roosevelt Hotel. Grauman also performed a historical role as one of four "central" judges of those first fifteen awards of merit.[81] The celebration of American filmmaking *in Hollywood*, not in New York City or in downtown Los Angeles, was also part of the westward strategy of Grauman, Mayer, and others who were inextricably linked to this area through real estate and other investments. Grauman, too often remembered only for his theaters, was a central figure in the formation of some of Hollywood's most important early buildings and institutions as well as a growing, singular focus on making that iconic neighborhood synonymous with motion pictures.

GRAUMAN'S CHINESE THEATRE

Just three days after the opening of the Roosevelt Hotel—as Grauman's attention switched from project to project, opening to opening—his most enduring monument was unveiled. Tickets for the May 18 gala premiere of the Chinese Theatre commanded a hefty sum of eleven dollars. They sold out within forty-eight hours.[82] "Tonight is the night of all nights in the entire history of the motion picture industry," the opening-night program exclaimed.

> It marks the dedicatory premiere of a playhouse whose fame is already spread to the four corners of the world. [...] Governors, mayors, generals, admirals, judges, millionaires, screen and stage stars of the first magnitude, city, county, state and federal executives, producers, directors, authors—they have come—one and all—many crossing the continent just for tonight's festivities—ready to dash back early tomorrow to the shores of the Atlantic. Truly, it is a night of nights."

The rhetoric of the dedication indicated that, by 1927, "screen and stage stars" were key dignitaries of public life, alongside "governors, mayors, generals, admirals, judges." Fred Niblo organized the evening, while D. W. Griffith served as Master of Ceremonies, presenting Will Hays who, in turn, introduced Mary Pickford, the emcee of "the evening's performance."[83]

Excitement for the opening night was ultimately a community affair. The *Los Angeles Times* reported that Hollywood had been transformed in order to celebrate the opening of the theater and its possibilities for new business and tourism. "All merchants are cooperating in the decoration of buildings, street lamps, electric poles, hotels, cafes and places of amusement," the *Times* noted. "[S]treet parades, floats, night celebrations, massed bands, orchestras and a general program of entertainment" could be seen up and down the boulevard with "[a]ll street lamps [. . .] turned into Chinese lanterns along the length of Hollywood Boulevard." The celebratory parade included "a gigantic dragon, several hundred feet in length" backed by "a real Chinese orchestra [that] will play typical Chinese music on a pagoda balcony of the theater while nearly 200 Chinese girls from the Los Angeles Chinatown disport with the dragon."[84] The area's support paid tribute to the draw that Grauman's Chinese would bring in for the century that followed.

The gala premiere drew a crowd of a hundred thousand—roughly 10 percent of the city of Los Angeles—who jammed the streets of Hollywood to catch a glimpse of the new theater and the celebrities who attended its premiere. Five hundred policemen were called in to handle the crowds as automobiles were forced to wade through the throngs, waiting up to an hour to drive one block.[85] William C. DeMille—eldest brother of Cecil B. DeMille—wrote in *Hollywood Saga* that, by then, "to be able to get seats for a Grauman premiere was a mark of distinction and a guarantee of professional standing." Grauman's premieres, De Mille noted, were in stark contrast to those in New York, which drew the titans of *traditional* finance, business, and politics but did not overly privilege movie and other stars: "Premieres have been attempted in New York, but they have never had quite the right flavor. For one thing, New York has never felt that on the night of a premiere the city's traffic must be stopped and the entire police department assigned to protecting stars from the affectionate pressure of their public. . . . The whole scene," he added, "suggested a combination of the French Revolution with the procession of peers in 'Iolanthe.'"[86] De Mille detected that Grauman's premieres and the whole machinery of Hollywood marketing had begun shifting the course of American culture:

> An attitude like this on the part of the public toward its entertainers must be founded on something much deeper than mere publicity or notoriety. Even the President of the United States cannot hold a crowd of thousands waiting for hours just to see him leave his car and enter a theater. [. . .] In its imagination, the public has identified the player with his roles, and glorifies him as a superman. [. . .] The American nation today wants to make some form of drama a vital element in its life. [. . .] We are idealists and sentimentalists; priding ourselves on our materialism, we lose no opportunity to make a hero out of any possible candidate and endow him with every virtue most dear to us. So on stage or screen, drama pleases us as it expresses us to ourselves in heroic terms."[87]

The Chinese was an Orientalist temple, but it was also a shrine where America's secular followers could travel to worship, quite literally, at the feet of their idols. The Chinese's famous footprints—the first pair from UATC, AMPAS, and Roosevelt Hotel partners Mary Pickford and Douglas Fairbanks—helped spread the notoriety of the theater even further, a desire that built fifty ticket offices throughout Southern California to allow patrons to organize their own trips to see the theater and the growing number of corporeal imprints of their favorite stars.[88] Edwin Schallert wrote in the *Times* that the theater was "an Aladdin's wonder palace that will be visited by all who visit Southern California, or dwell here, as an institution."[89] The new Roosevelt Hotel, opened across the street from the Chinese that July, was perfectly poised to meet the overnight needs of out-of-town visitors to the new theater.[90] Harry Baine, president of the Hollywood Boulevard Association, would later note that "[i]t is largely through [Grauman's] efforts that Hollywood boasts of [the] Roosevelt Hotel, a magnificent hostelry that has come to be the rendezvous for famous folk and world travelers who come from afar."[91]

Exit Stage Left

Despite all of his success in 1927, Grauman's control over his own fate, like other exhibitors of the era, was illusory. The rise of corporatization and consolidation had made the independent exhibitor an increasingly tenuous figure in major markets. In September 1927, UATC bought out West Coast's interests in the Chinese, giving Schenck et al. controlling interest and an outsized role in decision-making.[92] Grauman still held a one-third interest in the Chinese and a long-term contract as managing director, but it was now *Grauman's* Chinese with an asterisk.[93] Over the next two years, between its opening on May 18, 1927, and June 20, 1929, Grauman's Chinese exhibited only seven different feature films. Grauman's extended-run policy, ironically, made his day-to-day management far less important than his role as a producer of premieres and prologues.[94] In May 1929, Grauman sold his remaining stake in the Chinese to the newly merged *Fox West Coast Theaters* and announced his retirement.[95] As he left the building, so, too, did his famous prologues, though he and they would return sporadically.[96] The coming of sound offered many efficiencies for large theater circuits, most profitably the reduction or outright dismissal of labor in musical accompaniment and other performers in those expensive stage shows.

What remained for the next century, instead, were the celebrated Hollywood premieres that Grauman had inaugurated down the street at the Egyptian and expanded on at the Chinese. Cinematic evidence of their power and popularity can be seen in the coverage of Grauman's own premiere of films such as *Grand Hotel* (1932) and in their celebrated treatment in films such as *Singin' in the Rain* (1952).[97] For journalist Edwin Schallert, Grauman's premieres—and their growing proliferation—were far more impactful than his famous prologues, which had largely vanished from the scene after his departure. "Grauman has been the impresario extraordinary of the operatic type of film entertainment," he wrote, but it was "his premieres [that] have had an irresistible glamour. They have been unsurpassed as shows."[98] Despite all of the work Grauman had put into his prologues, which often lasted months at his theaters, it was his staging of premieres, which lasted only one night, that would have the longest and most pronounced resonance in Hollywood and beyond. The premiere had become a signature marketing event that ensured stars and moguls remained relevant, photographed, and adored. For Hollywood's real estate and entertainment investors, the Hollywood premiere reiterated the retail, commercial, and real estate value of the area, especially as more and more of the entertainment industry's infrastructure moved West, decentering its origins from New York City to the very real and mythological *Hollywood*. That value and mythology has helped raise the price per square foot ever since.

Grauman's focus on stars, publicity, and premieres to sell his real estate, theatrical, and other ventures is only one aspect of a much larger story about his role in Hollywood's development. Examining Grauman's connections with local developers, financiers, stars, hotels, banks, and industry organizations and companies provides a window into the small number of key players in Hollywood's early development and how Grauman's Egyptian and Chinese, the Hollywood Roosevelt Hotel, and other local entities became essential parts of Hollywood's growth as an iconic place for global commerce, entertainment, and tourism. That nexus became a central draw of Hollywood and crystalized the name Grauman as one synonymous with a specific attention to entertainment, celebrity, fantasy, and the klieg-light wattage of a star-studded evening.

NOTES

1. Kevin Crust, "Chinese Theatre Turns 90," *Los Angeles Times* (hereafter *LAT*), May 18, 2017, E1.
2. The one book dedicated to Grauman's work—Charles Beardsley's *Hollywood's Master Showman*—contains no bibliography or endnotes. An extensive study certainly seems overdue. Charles Beardsley, *Hollywood's Master Showman: The Legendary Sid Grauman* (New York: Cornwall Books, 1983).
3. "Investments By Film Men At San Diego," *Variety*, March 3, 1926, 26.
4. "Hollywood Club Moves To Make City Home Of Premieres," *Exhibitors Herald* (hereafter *EH*), September 30, 1922, 22.
5. Lary May, *The Big Tomorrow: Hollywood and the Politics of the American Way* (Chicago, IL: University of Chicago Press, 2000), 127.
6. Denise M. McKenna, *The City That Made the Pictures Move: Gender, Labor, and the Film Industry in Los Angeles, 1908–1917* (PhD diss., New York University, 2008), 24, 32.
7. "Colorful Career Of Grauman; Greatest Picture Showman," *Variety*, May 11, 1927, 10.
8. Grace Kingsley, "Struggle For Success Sees Fulfillment," *LAT*, January 26, 1923, 119.
9. "Colorful Career Of Grauman; Greatest Picture Showman."
10. Ibid.
11. Louella O. Parsons, "Film Veteran's Name Magic In Hollywood," *Los Angeles Examiner*, March 6, 1950, clipping files, Academy of Motion Picture Arts and Sciences-Margaret Herrick Library (hereafter AMPAS-MHL), Los Angeles, CA.
12. "Sid Grauman's Theatre History," *Motion Picture News* (hereafter *MPN*), July 27, 1929, 349.
13. J. C. Jessen, "New Theatre Crowns Grauman," *MPN*, March 2, 1918, Grauman Section–3.
14. "Grauman Leases Theater Building in Los Angeles, *San Francisco Chronicle*, December 30, 1916, 13; "Unusual New Los Angeles House," *Motography*, February 3, 1917, 227.
15. "Grauman's New Theater to Open in January," *LAT*, December 16, 1917, III.15.
16. "New Los Angeles Movie," *The Billboard*, December 29, 1917, 59; "Sid Grauman's House Nearing Completion," *Moving Picture World* (hereafter *MPW*), January 5, 1918, 66.
17. G. P. Harleman, "Grauman's Theater Opens Auspiciously," *MPW*, February 23, 1918, 1106; "Opening's Brilliant Of Million-Dollar Theater," *LAT*, February 2, 1918, II.3.
18. "Opening's Brilliant Of Million-Dollar Theater."
19. "Paramount-Artcraft Pictures Seated," *MPN*, March 2, 1918, Grauman Section–11, 14.
20. "Screen: Thrill And Touch; Films Of Fun And Power And Loveliness," *LAT*, February 3, 1918, III.1.
21. "A Builder Of Entertainment Is Sid Grauman Of Los Angeles," *EH*, December 27, 1919, 125.
22. "Graumans Becomes Institution Through Well Devised Program," *EH*, December 20, 1919, 81.

23. "Grauman's New House," *Wid's Daily*, June 2, 1919, 1.
24. "Two Million Dollars For Great Showhouse Here," *LAT*, August 20, 1919, II.1.
25. "Adolph Zukor Predicts A Year's Run On Broadway," *MPN*, December 11, 1920, 4407.
26. "Big Plan For New Grauman House," *LAT*, October 27, 1919, H8..
27. "Grauman's December Advertising Marks Close Of Progressive Year," *EH*, January 17, 1920, 90; "Grauman At Los Angeles Plans Longer Runs," *MPN*, May 17, 1919, 3190.
28. "Long Runs At Grauman's Rialto," *Wid's Daily*, November 5, 1919, 3.
29. "Grauman in Hollywood," *The Film Daily* (hereafter *TFD*), May 26, 1920, 5.
30. Hy Edwin, "New Picture Palace: Sid Grauman Announces Plans For Great Hollywood Theater," *LAT*, May 21, 1920, 117.
31. "Rush Work On $3,000,000 Grauman Theatre," *MPN*, August 20, 1921, 1002; "Eight Hundred Workmen Build New Metropolitan," *EH*, August 13, 1921, 58.
32. Grace Kingsley "When Hollywood Was a Pasture," *Photoplay*, June 1927, 34.
33. "Hollywood Club Moves To Make City Home Of Premieres," *EH*, September 30, 1922, 22; Renee Beeman, "Live News Of The West Coast," *Exhibitor's Trade Review* (hereafter *ETR*), October 7, 1922, 1237.
34. "Hollywood Club Moves To Make City Home Of Premieres," 22.
35. "New Theater Policies Are Announced," *LAT*, October 8, 1922, III.27.
36. Terry Helgesen, "Grauman's Egyptian Theatre," in *From The Land of the Pharaohs*, ca. 1969, Tom B'hend and Preston Kaufmann Collection, 1866–1990s, 20.f-505, AMPAS-MHL.
37. "New Theater Policies Are Announced."
38. "Everybody Will Be There," *LAT*, October 12, 1922, 19; "Late News Briefs From The Coast By Wire," *MPN*, October 28, 1922, 2151.
39. "Everybody Will Be There."
40. Helgesen, "Grauman's Egyptian Theatre"; "Grauman's New Hollywood Theater Opens," *LAT*, October 19, 1922, 22; "Brilliant Assembly Attends Opening Of Grauman Temple," *EH*, November 14, 1922, 33; "An Egyptian Theater In Hollywood," *ETR*, November 25, 1922, 1660.
41. "Brilliant Assembly Attends Opening Of Grauman Temple," 33.
42. "Robin Hood In Radio Debut: KHJ Program Centers About De Koven's," *LAT*, November 22, 1922, II.3.
43. "Grauman Deal," *TFD*, November 27, 1922, 1; "Famous-Grauman Coast House Sold," *Variety*, March 29, 1923, 25; "Downtown Playhouse Now Sold," *LAT*, March 30, 1923, II.1; "Paramount Taking Over Three Grauman Theaters," *Billboard*, July 21, 1923, 17.
44. "Held At $4,500,000," *TFD*, March 28, 1923, 1;
45. "Use Theater as Background for Cameras," *LAT*, June 8, 1924, 39.
46. "Nellie Revell In Hollywood," *Variety*, March 23, 1927, 39.
47. Col. Harry M. Baine, "Grauman's Vision and Hollywood," *MPN*, July 27, 1929, 350.
48. "Premiere Air Report Promised: 'The Big Parade' Opening to be Broadcast Tomorrow," *LAT*, November 4, 1925, A9.
49. "Big Coast Premiere For 'Big Parade,'" *ETR*, November 14, 1925, 15.
50. "Premiere Air Report Promised."
51. "Big Coast Premiere For 'Big Parade.'"
52. "Premiere Air Report Promised."
53. "Big Coast Premiere For 'Big Parade.'"
54. "Unusual Lease Is Closed," *LAT*, July 6, 1924, A7.
55. "$1,500,000 Will Go Up In Hollywood," *LAT*, September 12, 1924, A1.

56. "Grauman Plans Theater," *LAT*, September 14, 1924, D2.
57. "Grauman's Newest Theatre," *Variety*, November 5, 1924, 24; West Coast Theaters, meanwhile, was expanding rapidly, having bought twenty-three additional theaters in the Southern California area since that January through its newly created Southwest Theaters subsidiary. Harry Hammond Beall, "West Coast Theatres Acquires Number Of New Houses," *Exhibitors Herald*, January 12, 1924, 26.
58. "Radical Amusement Changes Observed by Wm. Morris," *Variety*, March 8, 1923, 41.
59. "Schenck and Grauman to Establish Theatre Chain," *ETR*, December 13, 1924, 15; "Theater Chain in 20 Cities is Plan," *Billboard*, December 13, 1924, 27; "Grauman and Schenck Plan Twenty Key City Theatres," *MPW*, December 13, 1924, 603.
60. "Pictures: Grauman's 2,480-Seater," *Variety*, May 27, 1925, 30.
61. "Bonds For Theater On Sale Today," *LAT*, December 7, 1925, A22.
62. "Final O. K. Placed On Plans For New Grauman Theatre At Hollywood," *MPN*, October 10, 1925, 1732.
63. "Over-Seated Los Angeles Will Have 52,260 Additional Seats," *Variety*, September 30, 1925, 44.
64. "Film Hotel for Hollywood," *TFD*, October 27, 1925, 5.
65. "Investing in San Diego," *TFD*, March 16, 1926, 1.
66. Arthur Ungar, "Joe Schenck As Cal. Sees Him," *Variety*, October 20, 1926, 58.
67. "Stars Officiate When Ground Is Broken For Grauman House," *EH*, January 16, 1926, 36; "Grauman's 'Chinese' Will Have Oriental Garden For Forecourt," *MPW*, February 6, 1926, 58.
68. "Sid Grauman Due East," *Variety*, January 27, 1926, 291; "Sid Grauman Is In New York," *Variety*, March 10, 1926, 30.
69. "Chicago To Get First United Artists Theatre," *MPN*, August 21, 1926, 669.
70. "Chain Of 20 Projected By United Artists Theatres," *MPW*, June 5, 1926, 2.
71. "Pictures," *Variety*, May 19, 1926, 18.
72. "Grauman Chain Prologues," *TFD*, April 28, 1926, 1.
73. "Chain Of 20 Projected By United Artists Theatres."
74. "Schenck To Buy Egyptian," *LAT*, November 12, 1926, A1; "Plans Not Dropped," November 24, 1926, TFD, 1; "U.A.'s Grauman's House $500,000 6% Bond Issue," *Variety*, April 13, 1927, 11.
75. "Showmen's New Hotel In Hollywood, Cal.," *Variety*, May 26, 1926, 5; Wright, Alexander & Greeley advertisement, *The Film Spectator*, July 23, 1927, 24.
76. "Hollywood's Sports Club," *Variety*, August 11, 1926, 50.
77. "Joe Schenck's Bank," *Variety*, January 26, 1927, 17; "Schenck Plans Bank Expansion," *TFD*, 2; Untitled, *The Film Spectator*, June 11, 1927, 20.
78. "Bankers Win Promotion," *Hollywood News*, January 17, 1927 (AMPAS-MHL, Mary Pickford Papers-Clippings).
79. Gregory Paul Williams, *The Story of Hollywood: An Illustrated History* (Austin, TX: B L Press, 2011), 137.
80. "Academy of M.P. Arts and Sciences Formed," *TFD*, May 5, 1927, 1.
81. "Film Efforts Rewarded: Academy Announces Fifteen Awards of Statuette for Elevating Standards of Screen," *LAT*, February 18, 1929: A1.
82. "King Of Kings," *Variety*, May 11, 1927, 63.
83. "Dedication, Grauman's Chinese Theatre Hollywood, Program," May 18, 1927, Tom B'hend and Preston Kaufmann Collection, 1866–1990s, 20.f-487, AMPAS-MHL.

84. "Dedication of Theater to Be Fete: Chamber to Help Make Opening of New Chinese," *LAT*, May 13, 1927, A1.
85. "100,000 Jam Streets For Opening Of Grauman's New Chinese," *Variety*, May 25, 1927, 11.
86. William Churchill De Mille, *Hollywood Saga* (New York: E. P. Dutton, 1939), 90–91.
87. Ibid., 92–93.
88. "Footprints," *LAT*, May 31, 1927, A.4; "Grauman's Chinese Theatre Hollywood," ca. 1927 (*The Circus*), Tom B'hend and Preston Kaufmann Collection, 1866–1990s, 20.f-488, AMPAS-MHL.
89. Edwin Schallert, "'King Of Kings' Impresses," *LAT*, May 19, 1927, A1.
90. Wright, Alexander, & Greeley advertisement.
91. Col. Harry M. Baine, "Grauman's Vision and Hollywood," *MPN*, July 27, 1929, 350.
92. "Schenck Buys Out W. C. In Grauman's Chinese," *Variety*, September 28, 1927, 5.
93. "No Change at Chinese Under U.A. Banner," *TFD*, October 24, 1927, 11.
94. "Films Playing Grauman's Chinese Theater Hollywood." Compiled by Bruce Lalanne, Tom B'hend and Preston Kaufmann Collection, 1866–1990s, 19.f-470, AMPAS-MHL.
95. "Grauman Sells To Fox Chain," *LAT*, May 14, 1929, A.1; "Fox Buys Chinese," *Variety*, May 15, 1929, 31.
96. "Grauman Out," *Variety*, May 29, 1929, 20; Edwin Schallert, "Sid Grauman Retires Today," *LAT*, June 16, 1929, C11.
97. I will note the irony here that *Singin' in the Rain* had its world premiere not at Grauman's Chinese Theatre but at (Roxy's former) Radio City Music Hall in New York, almost exactly a quarter century after the opening of the Chinese in Hollywood. "MGM Field Men to See 7 New Films," *Motion Picture Daily*, March 11, 1952, 2.
98. Schallert, "Sid Grauman Retires Today."

CHAPTER 22

FRANCHISING AS A STRATEGY OF NATIONAL FEATURE DISTRIBUTION IN THE 1910S

The Case of the Triangle Film Corporation

DEREK LONG

Introduction

HISTORIANS have tended to adopt a linear narrative when it comes to charting the development of American film distribution during the silent era. The narrative goes something like this: over the course of roughly twenty years, distribution moved away from being an intensely local enterprise and came under the sway of a centralized regime of control in New York. The story originates with the itinerant exhibitors of the first decade or so of cinema, who purchased films directly from manufacturers and showcased them to local markets one venue at a time across an extended span of time. The story then moves on to the local independent film exchanges of the early one-reel period—with their endless demand for daily product—and then further to the coalescing national distribution systems of the General Film Company, Mutual, and Universal. The narrative's logic asserts that as early as 1910, film distribution in the United States had become a largely rationalized and centrally controlled system releasing one- and two-reel films at a national scale.

Within this same narrative, the handling of longer feature films of four or more reels after 1910 essentially mirrors the pattern of film distribution before the General Film Company (GFC). Distribution of features begins with the state rights system, whereby manufacturers directly sold "special" films to many independent state and regional distribution companies for large sums.[1] It advances to the centralized national systems of the first feature program distributors, which provided theaters with new features on a weekly basis beginning in 1914, and concludes (for the silent period, anyway) with the vertically integrated producer-distributor oligopoly of the 1920s. Michael Quinn's work on Paramount—the first company to successfully distribute regularly released features when they inaugurated a twice-a-week five-reel feature service—carefully details a canonical example of this phenomenon of centralization, concluding that Paramount adapted the GFC's model to multireel features.[2] And Ben Singer writes that "beginning around mid-1914, the feature distribution business underwent a major transformation[,] from a haphazard regional enterprise fragmented among hundreds of states rights firms to a national enterprise dominated by about ten big companies."[3]

As a diachronic pattern of historical change, this narrative is correct in its essential outline. There is little doubt that the various systems of film distribution in the United States in 1920 were more centralized than those of 1914, which were in turn more centralized than those of 1905. However, as a consequence of the linearity of this historiography, the extent to which local concerns and interests continued to determine distribution patterns and practice, particularly for features in the period 1914–19, has been significantly underestimated. This is at least partially a function of the discourse of business efficiency so widely promulgated by the industry itself. The trade press made constant reference to the systematizing of film exchanges in an effort to, as Greg Waller puts it, "conjure up a thriving industry that [was] open to both quick-thinking entrepreneurs and also to ambitious corporations with national business strategies."[4] Scholars in recent years have begun to dig deeper in tracing the importance of regional distribution in the early 1910s. Maureen Rogers, in her article on the state rights system in the early and mid-teens, has valuably emphasized the importance of the regional distribution practices of state rights to the rise of the star system and the centralized program feature distributors of the mid-teens.[5] But to what extent did the influence of state rights and other regional entities continue into the mid-teens and beyond?

This chapter seeks to answer Rogers's call for "greater attention to regional and itinerant distribution practices in the field of film and media history" by examining a hybrid form of national feature distribution, prevalent from the mid-teens until at least the early twenties.[6] This hybrid form, which I will refer to as the franchise system, combined the income and circulation benefits of state rights distribution with the coordination, pricing, and branding advantages of the centralized release program used for shorts in the transitional era. Through a history of franchising practice, as well as a case study based on archival records of the Triangle Film Corporation, a major national distributor that relied extensively on the franchise model in this period, this chapter outlines the rise and eventual marginalization of franchising as a distribution strategy.

Franchising enabled feature distributors to build a national network quickly and without significant capital investment. Furthermore, because local franchisees enjoyed greater control over pricing and booking than would be the case under more centralized distribution, they paid much higher rentals for films than they otherwise might. Like state rights, franchising ultimately became a marginal practice used by Poverty Row distributors, since it delegated too much spatial and temporal control over releasing to local interests and prevented national distributors from maximizing their profits on individual films. Nevertheless, the use of franchising among major distributors in the mid-to-late 1910s complicates our image of early Hollywood's distribution practice as uniformly or inevitably centralized. By bringing distribution structures and practices to greater prominence, it also forces us to nuance conceptions of the relative importance of exhibition and production in the rise of the Hollywood oligopoly, as well as of the relationships between distribution and the other sectors.

Franchising before 1915, outside and within the Film Industry

According to business historian Thomas Dicke, franchising is a system of industrial organization in which "one firm is granted the exclusive right to market the goods or services of another company in a given area." A key aspect of this right is that "producer and distributor are legally independent of one another, and the relationship between them is closely defined and controlled by contract."[7] Dicke distinguishes between two types of franchising: system franchising and product franchising. System franchising, also known as business format franchising, is exemplified by the fast food industry and is the most familiar form of the practice. In system franchising, the fundamental product being sold by the national firm (McDonald's, for example) to its franchisee is not the retailed output itself (hamburgers) but the right to operate a particular branded outlet (a McDonald's location), along with that brand's reputation and a set of standardized production, marketing, and training procedures. From the perspective of the producer in system franchising, the real customer is not the retail consumer but the franchisee, who pays for the use of the producer's standardized methods of marketing and manufacturing.[8]

Product franchising, by contrast, is fundamentally a form of distribution rather than one of selling a manufacturing or marketing format. In product franchising (also known as product distribution franchising), manufacturers use franchise contracts with local entities to build and maintain a national distribution network. The most familiar example of this type of franchising in the United States is the car dealership. Nearly all car manufacturers sell franchise agreements to local dealers or regional dealer chains, who assume the overhead costs of owning and operating the outlet in exchange for the right to retail the cars and to offer maintenance and financing services associated with the manufacturer's brand. As a consequence, the manufacturer is able to minimize distribution and retail costs, outsource sales and marketing strategy to local entities, and roll out new products efficiently on a national basis.

Franchising as an industrial practice is often thought of as a postwar phenomenon, closely associated with chain restaurants and hotels. However, this is true only with regard to system franchising, which, according to Dicke, was not possible in the United

States until the 1920s. Before then, a "well-developed national transportation and communication network" to ensure practical coordination and standardization of system franchising had not yet developed, limiting its viability on a national scale.[9] However, product franchising had been a common strategy for creating national sales networks since well before the 1920s. Dicke notes that product franchising was used as early as the mid-nineteenth century to sell farm implements and sewing machines. By the first years of the twentieth century, the system was commonly employed to sell a variety of high-cost durable goods that were difficult to market locally through the traditional system of manufacturer-controlled agencies.[10] This older agency system, which involved manufacturers contracting with established wholesalers of similar products acting as the manufacturer's legal agents, made the manufacturer and the agent-distributor indistinguishable from a legal standpoint.[11] Auto manufacturers, who early on sold their products through the agency system, increasingly moved toward franchise dealerships in the 1900s and 1910s. This obviated the need to account for the frequently changing local laws regarding automobile sales, while simultaneously allowing the car makers to build national sales networks quickly. It also proved a stable cash flow to the manufacturers, since cars were now sold directly to dealers rather than consigned—at no small amount of risk—to agents.[12]

Given product franchising's advantages for selling durable goods, its utility for film distribution in the 1900s and 1910s might not seem obvious. Positive film prints could hardly be described as a durable product; indeed, during the one-reel period they were rarely conceived of as having value in distribution for more than a few weeks. The widely imitated success of the GFC's model was a result of its conception of film as a low-cost, mass-market generic good, one that could be efficiently moved through the national exhibition market—via exchanges it centrally owned and operated—for modest but predictable profits. Franchising made little sense under this conception, since the main determinant of its profitability was the efficient spatial and temporal coordination of distribution enabled by centralized organization. However, for film manufacturers making less generic, "special" negatives produced in smaller quantities and at considerable cost, product franchising offered a compelling model of distribution for the exact reason that it outsourced distribution and marketing to local entities. In offering something like the filmic equivalent of a durable good, manufacturers could charge their local franchisee-distributors higher prices for that good without having to devote additional resources to the marketing and sales details needed to ensure its profitability at the local level. As Dicke argues, "distributors of non-generic goods were unable to exploit fully the potentials of the economies of speed [that enabled mass marketing in the twentieth century], since the specialized nature of their products forced them to concentrate on a limited product line that did not allow for a large flow of goods through retail outlets. As a result, there was less need to internalize the transactions between the producer and the final distributor and fewer reasons to turn to newer, more elaborate methods of organization."[13]

Product franchising was an attractive option for feature producers in the 1910s in part because the GFC's dominant model of film distribution as of 1910 conceived of cinema as a mass-market generic good rather than a specialized and individuated product. While the GFC was more open to longer, specialized features in the 1910s than is generally acknowledged, it was ill equipped at the local level of distribution to sell such product profitably. As Max Alvarez's work makes clear, the fundamental purpose of local exchanges, both when they acted as independent entities and after many were consolidated under the control of the GFC in 1910, was efficiently managing the physical circulation of films rather than marketing differentiated product to exhibitors.[14] Such marketing was essential to feature makers, but it was also complicated and represented a significant financial risk. Outsourcing marketing to specialized local firms via product franchising was fundamentally a strategy for managing that risk, while the physical circulation of films could, for the most part, continue to employ preexisting models used in shorts cinema.

In its early years, national feature film distribution in the American context is thus better understood as a hodgepodge of external and highly local transactions between manufacturers and distribution entities than as an inevitable march toward centralization and vertical integration. Even though centralization had obvious advantages from the strict standpoint of circulation, marketing feature films nationally required different, or at least hybrid, distribution strategies. The earliest form of such distribution that was clearly influenced by product franchising in other industries was the state rights system, which has been examined by a number of scholars. Under state rights, manufacturers sold exclusive distribution rights for an individual film to many buyers throughout the country on a territorial basis, typically for extended periods (usually five years, according to Quinn). Those buyers could then rent the film to exhibitors, subdivide the distribution rights to other companies, exhibit the film directly, or accomplish some combination thereof—they effectively had complete control over the distribution of their print(s) of the film.[15] As Ben Brewster points out, state rights had its origins in the practice of the exclusive contract used in legitimate theater, which allowed theaters to charge much higher prices for acts over which they had an effective monopoly.[16] The system thus allowed extended runs for individual films and encouraged state rights firms and exhibitors to market films extensively at the local level to build up audience interest in a particular production. This differed significantly from the variety program model of the GFC, where advertising focused on particular brands of program service rather than individual films. Because this model of tailored, exclusive releasing encouraged local companies to pay high (if flat) fees, the state rights system could generate significant profits for the manufacturer on individual films—much greater than was possible in the program system.

Furthermore, state rights distributors tended to contract for exhibition in larger and more prestigious venues like opera houses and legitimate theaters, which could charge higher ticket prices and seat larger audiences.[17] This is one reason why the state rights system was the most common method of feature distribution before 1914: it was more effective at generating the kinds of grosses in exhibition that might recoup the higher costs of specialized feature production. In contrast to the variety program, where the GFC or Mutual circa 1914 might pay a manufacturer $4,000 for forty positives of a one-reel film, the state rights to distribute a single feature could be sold for ten times that much across the country, or even more. As Quinn shows, *Tillie's Punctured Romance* (1914) was produced at Keystone for $9,000, but the manufacturer sold the film to the state rights distributor Alco for $70,000.[18] At Majestic that same year, D. W. Griffith's *The Avenging Conscience* was offered on the state rights market for $6,000 in Illinois and $2,400 in Wisconsin; the rights for just those two states earned back two-thirds of the film's $12,800 negative cost.[19]

In its delegation of distribution authority to local companies independent from the manufacturer, the state rights system was a clear example of product franchising. Indeed, from the teens and throughout the years of the studio system, trade press ads for the state rights of specific features frequently described manufacturers' contracts with territorial distributors as franchises.[20] State rights was the dominant method of feature distribution in the early 1910s, but after 1914, the system began to manifest a number of problems that the modified franchise system sought to remedy. As Quinn points out in his study of Famous Players, despite its profit potential, state rights distribution was simply too haphazard to be practical at a national or programmatic scale. While it worked reasonably well for specialty producers (or for the special productions of a manufacturer that otherwise made shorts), any feature producer hoping to nationally distribute more than a few films through the system faced a number of problems. The most obvious of these was the issue of distribution coordination. Because the rights for each film were sold to territories on an individual basis, manufacturers that used state rights had to deal with many separate territorial distributors at once. A manufacturer wishing to release a film nationally through the system circa 1913 would have needed to maintain relationships with around 150 separate companies. This meant 150 separate negotiations over pricing, release dates, payment schedules, quality control of prints, and so forth. The duplicated costs to the manufacturer of selling individual films to so many distributors blunted the cost advantages of outsourcing distribution in the first place.[21]

Perhaps more important, the haphazard structure of the state rights system tended to give pricing advantages to the regional franchisees in the long term. As Quinn shows, operating a state rights distributor required very little start-up capital, certainly as compared to the amounts needed to actually produce features. This meant that state rights companies were often fly-by-night operations organized to distribute one or two films, and they could generally afford to hold out for lower prices when negotiating with producers for local distribution rights. Feature producers, by contrast, tended to need capital quickly to amortize debts incurred on previous productions, and so had less leverage to bargain over pricing.[22] Furthermore, because producers typically sold their territorial distribution rights for a flat fee, they tended not to share in the profits of unusually successful films.[23]

For these reasons, previous histories have tended to characterize state rights as either a marginalized distribution practice or one that was subsumed into more centralized releasing after 1914, when distributors like Warner's Features and Paramount began offering nationally coordinated feature programs of a certain number of releases every week. However, the state rights system was fundamental to the creation of these centralized national distribution networks. Rogers, building on Quinn's work, has emphasized that the May 1914 combination of Famous Players' exchanges and the exchange holdings of W. W. Hodkinson to form Paramount was only one major step in a more continuous process of coalescence: "Paramount Pictures' national distribution network grew out of the state rights market; in effect, Hodkinson recruited existing state rights franchisees to operate as their exclusive exchanges."[24] Even after this combination, Paramount was not, strictly speaking, a national distributor; as Quinn points out, the company was obliged to sell additional sub-franchises to cover the entire territory of the United States.[25]

The product franchising model of the state rights system continued to be an important norm of feature distribution into the mid-teens. Even as Paramount consolidated its long-term relationships with local state rights franchises ever further to become a centralized producer-distributor—effectively completing that process with Zukor's hostile takeover of W. W. Hodkinson's holdings to form Famous Players-Lasky in July 1916—newer firms relied on the vestiges of state rights to create national distribution networks through modified systems of franchising.[26] As the teens went on, approaches to product franchising in the film industry increasingly coalesced around locally influential exhibition entities as well as state rights companies. These magnates, whose theaters and chains in key cities and territories gave them particular power in their local market, were extremely useful to producers as part of a national product franchising strategy. They tended to represent longstanding businesses rather than fly-by-nights, had an understanding of the idiosyncrasies of their local markets, and perhaps most crucially, could leverage the longstanding reputation of their houses in marketing the new phenomenon of the feature program. The Triangle Film Corporation, to which we now turn as a case study of such an exhibition-centered product franchising system, instantiated both its strengths and its weaknesses.

THE FRANCHISE SYSTEM AT TRIANGLE, 1915–1917

In mid-1915, the bulk of the major manufacturers who had made films for the Mutual Film Corporation, including D. W. Griffith's Majestic, Thomas Ince's New York Motion Picture Company, and Mack Sennett's Keystone Film Company, departed the shorts-oriented national distributor and aligned themselves with a new feature concern, the Triangle Film Corporation, organized by former Mutual heads Harry and Roy Aitken. From the outset, Triangle modeled its feature production strategies on those of Paramount. These included its structuring of contracts with producers to encourage higher-cost filmmaking, its programmatic output of two features and two shorts a week, and its premium price. However, while Paramount refined these strategies over the course of the mid-1910s at the same time that it consolidated its producers and distributor-franchisees, Triangle's distribution model continued to rely to a great extent on the much more decentralized releasing strategies of the state rights system. This was in part out of necessity. After their ouster from Mutual, the Aitkens had to build Triangle's national distribution system quickly. The most straightforward way to do that was to leverage preexisting relationships with the state rights companies that had handled Aitken-produced features like *The Birth of a Nation*. State rights had also proven a lucrative approach in the past, and as we have seen, its cashflow benefits were considerable.

However, Triangle's system was not a simple reversion to state rights. It combined the advantages of a nationally coordinated feature program with the income potential of state rights, in a hybrid franchise system. Distinct from the state rights model, Triangle's entire *program* was franchised, rather than individual films. This enabled the company to coordinate national release dates and advertising—a crucial aspect of the feature program. Triangle's luxurious "model theaters" are often cited as an early example of the vertical integration of the industry into exhibition, but most of Triangle's model theaters were actually the centerpieces of local independent distribution franchises operated by local exhibition magnates.[27] Triangle's contracts with these franchisees put spatial, temporal, and pricing restrictions on the distribution of the company's films. This strategy sacrificed flexibility and control over releasing in order to maximize profitability. Additionally, Triangle operated its own exchanges in most major cities, often alongside independent franchisees, completing its national network while reducing the costs of managing that network. According to Kalton Lahue, this company-owned exchange system cost around $500,000 to initially set up.[28] However, it theoretically ensured that recurring distribution costs to Triangle were limited to those of physically circulating prints, with local marketing and sales expenses mostly taken up by franchisees. In its emphasis on efficient circulation and throughput of product, Triangle's own exchange system was conceptualized according to the GFC model, and the Aitkens hired former GFC distribution head J. R. Naulty to manage it.[29]

In theory, at least, this strategy of separating the circulation and marketing aspects of film distribution eliminated many of the problems of the state rights system while preserving its advantages. The rights to Triangle franchises were a source of significant potential income, which is why well-heeled exhibitors, many of whom were also longtime state rights distributors, were willing to pay handsomely for them.[30] Franchises with well-known exhibitors also served as useful advertising copy for Triangle in the fall of 1915, as the company sought to expand its fledgling distribution and exhibition networks. Trade press ads touted the company's franchises with William Kemble in Brooklyn, S. M. Hexter in Cleveland, the Archer Brothers in Chicago, and E. H. Hulsey in Texas.[31] This advertising benefited franchisees as well by positioning their own theaters as bellwether exhibition sites in their local markets—a clear instance of the "show window" function of first-run theaters in the emerging studio system.

Triangle's November 1915 contract with Harry I. Garson and Pliny P. Craft, owners of the Broadway Strand and Miles theaters in Detroit, outlines the details of their particular franchise with the company. The deal would have been a familiar one for Craft, who was a pioneer in the use of state rights for feature distribution. He had been instrumental in the state rights release of *The Birth of a Nation*, leading one scholar to dub him "the father of the feature."[32] Garson and Craft agreed to pay Triangle $2,000 per week for a year of Triangle service—an incredible sum, given that Paramount service for a theater in a city the size of Detroit would have cost only around $600 or $700 per week during this period.[33] What this hefty price bought, however, was an effective exhibition *and* distribution monopoly on Triangle service in the city. Triangle made Garson and Craft's two theaters their model exhibition spaces for the zone encompassing the entire city, for all of 1916. In addition, the company gave them the authority over all bookings of the Triangle program to subsequent-run theaters in Detroit.[34] All of these sub-rentals were subject to Triangle's approval, and prints were shipped directly from Triangle's own exchanges, but the contract made no provision for additional payments to Triangle as a result of rentals to these subsequent-run theaters.[35] This meant that Garson and Craft were free to charge the theaters whatever they wished for subsequent-run bookings and could keep all of the rental income.

This subsequent-run booking privilege was the key to Triangle's franchise strategy. It justified the high cost of the franchise and provided Triangle weekly cashflow from its releases in franchised territories without the accompanying expenses entailed in selling and contracting for subsequent-run distribution. In its basic form, this franchise system was effectively the state rights model, but applied to programmatic booking. Indeed, Triangle's franchise contracts make clear that some territories it franchised were anticipated to bring in almost as much on a weekly basis as the state rights system might have earned in a single flat payment. Garson and Craft got their Triangle service in Detroit for a relative bargain compared to state rights distributor William H. Kemble of Brooklyn, whose Big "T" Film Corporation paid $4,000 per week for the Triangle franchise covering all of Long Island, with first runs at the Crescent Theatre in Flatbush.[36] The owners of the Southwestern Triangle Film Corporation were so confident in their three-year franchise for all of Missouri and Texas that in their contract with Triangle, they accepted an increase in the price of their service from $3,800 per week for the first year to almost $5,000 per week for the second year, and $6,000 for the third.[37] Compared to the $6,000 flat fee paid to Majestic for the state rights in Illinois for *The Avenging Conscience* in 1914, this was serious money.

The exact terms of each franchise could differ significantly from contract to contract. While Garson and Craft's contract only lasted for a year, others had two- or three-year terms. Some franchise contracts had percentage-based pricing systems rather than weekly flat fees, while others resembled state rights in paying a lump sum. Ernest Fenton's two-year contract for distribution in Canada, for instance, specified no weekly charge but required Fenton to pay Triangle 50 percent of all weekly net rental profits plus 6 cents per foot for all prints of every film sent him.[38] In cities like New York, Chicago, and Philadelphia, where Triangle leased its flagship model theaters and directly profited from ticket sales, the company distributed to subsequent-run theaters in some zones directly, while selling franchises to cover other zones in the same market. In New York as of late 1915, Triangle was distributing directly to Broadway and downtown theaters after showings at the leased Knickerbocker, while selling franchises to the 81st Street Theater (at $750 per week) for the west side of Manhattan, the Classic Theater in Washington Heights (at $500 per week), and David Picker's Berlin Casino in the Bronx ($700 per week).[39] In Philadelphia, Triangle's own exchange, which centered on first-run showings at the Chestnut Street opera house, was less than successful in selling the company's program directly. As a result, in December 1915, the company sold a one-year exclusive franchise for the entire city to Harry Schwalbe's Electric Theatre Supply Company for $250,000, payable monthly (equivalent to about $4,800 per week).[40] Triangle's own exchange continued to handle subsequent-run theaters outside the bounds of the city itself.[41]

Despite being modeled on the state rights system, Triangle implemented a number of centralizing strategies in its distribution. Given the varying terms of the franchise contracts (one to three years rather than the five-year terms common in state rights), Triangle's franchise system may not have been intended as a long-term arrangement, with the company planning to take a more active role in its own distribution after 1916. Indeed, Garson and Craft's Detroit franchise was canceled after four months due to a dispute with the company, and as a result Triangle opened its own exchange in the city.[42] Yet by June 1917, this exchange had been replaced by another franchise controlled by the Orpheum Theater on Lafayette Avenue.[43] Thus, the franchise system proved useful to the company both in building a national distribution network quickly and in mitigating the failures of its own distribution management that would become increasingly apparent in 1916.

Nevertheless, Triangle's franchise contracts imposed certain booking and screening limitations on its franchisees and any subsequent-run exhibitors to whom they sub-rented. These limitations forced a more programmatic, coordinated, and nationally focused structure on the company's releases than would have been possible under state rights. Like Paramount, Triangle offered a full-service program and offered franchisees no option to book films individually. While none of the contracts in the Aitken collection reveal an explicit requirement for Triangle's franchisees to play the company's films exclusively, the program's cost, as well as its booking provisions, effectively made anything but exclusivity impractical for first-run theaters.[44] Crucially, Triangle prevented its franchisees from extending the runs of its films past a one-week maximum. Garson and Craft's Detroit contract obliged them to play Triangle releases at either the Broadway Strand or the Miles Theater, "and not elsewhere, during the first week of each release, and at no other time." Each week's releases—two five-reel features and two two-reel Keystone shorts—had to be screened either as a full fourteen-reel program, or (more commonly) split by showing a particular Griffith/Fine Arts or Ince/NYMP release along with its corresponding Keystone for the first half of the week, and the other feature and short for the second half.[45]

Other stipulations guided franchisees' sub-rentals, the contracts for which had to be expressly approved by Triangle at least a week in advance. Prints for sub-leases came direct from, and were to be returned directly to, Triangle's own exchanges. Most interestingly, sub-leases were generally limited to short runs as well, and always in theaters of at least four hundred seats that charged ten cents admission or more for evening performances. Garson and Craft's contract allowed them thirty-five *one-day* subsequent-run bookings for each Triangle five-reeler—always paired with a corresponding Keystone—and required that all sub-rentals be booked within a four-month window beginning after a thirty-day clearance period from the first run.[46] Thus, while a particular Triangle bill might be in distribution in Detroit for as long as five months, it would only stay in any one subsequent-run theater for a single day. This was not the case in all franchisee contracts; Kemble did not have such a restriction in Long Island, for example. However, Triangle's practice of splitting the program in half this way suggests that for most subsequent-run theaters around the country, Triangle bills lasted three days at an absolute maximum.

The product franchising distribution model used by Triangle differed in a number of important respects from the strategies used at Paramount. First, it was much more decentralized in terms of its pricing, particularly with regard to showings beyond the first run. Since 1914, Paramount had structured its pricing based on the situation of individual exhibitors, particularly the size of the local market and the length of the desired run (which could be as long as two weeks). As Quinn points out, this pricing model was adapted from contemporary legitimate theater, and it applied to all contracts for Paramount service, whether or not a franchisee was involved.[47] Triangle, by contrast, charged its franchisees a lump sum for their contract that was based on a calculation of the value of distributing within their larger territory—the same practice used in state rights. Apart from the physical circulation of prints and the ultimate approval or disapproval of sub-run contracts, Triangle's did not stipulate the rentals that franchisees charged theaters for its service.

Second, Triangle conceived of the value of its product fundamentally at the level of the program as a whole rather than at the level of individual films. This attitude manifested itself in the company's restrictions of both the length of its films' runs and the theaters with which it did business. While Paramount was also program-oriented, it clearly saw the potential of longer runs early on, as evidenced by the fact that its exhibition contracts had a pricing tier for two-week runs. By the end of 1916, the company was already institutionalizing longer and more flexible runs in its Artcraft service. By contrast, Triangle runs could not be extended even by the company's own franchisees, who had paid hefty prices for Triangle product. The company's continued emphasis on the weekly release—if at a more expensive scale—was effectively a direct extension of the variety cinema model devised by the GFC and Mutual. Furthermore, since Triangle effectively forbade theaters under four hundred seats from renting their program regardless of run, they intentionally limited the distribution of their program. This was in keeping with what Rob King has shown to be the company's strategy of appealing to upper-class audiences and tastes; combined with the minimum ten-cent ticket price, the size requirement effectively restricted the Triangle program to newer and more well-appointed houses. However, it was also a model that employed some of the contemporary strategies of the shorts distributors as they attempted to adapt to the arrival of features. As Quinn points out, the GFC had offered a premium "exclusive service" program of two- and three-reel films in 1913, available only to larger theaters charging a minimum price; this approach enabled exhibitors to advertise films in advance while preserving the run structure of normal program service.[48] Triangle's program-oriented distribution employed a similar strategy in its franchise contracts: concentrate the value of short runs by restricting distribution to larger houses and mandating higher ticket prices.

Finally, Triangle's distribution strategy encouraged a different kind of relationship with its producers than was the case at Paramount. Triangle's payments to its three producers in 1915–16 were based on flat fees for each production and also incorporated a percentage payment of rentals past a certain amount. Triangle's three-year contract with D. W. Griffith, signed July 1915, stipulated flat payments to Majestic of $40,000[49] for the negative and twenty-five positive prints of each film, along with 25 percent of the film's gross rentals "after such gross receipts shall have equalled 175% of the cost of such photoplay to [Triangle]."[50] By contrast, Paramount paid its producers through a percentage arrangement of 65 percent of the gross after recouping the distributor's production advance, giving producers a much greater stake in the success of individual films. On top of that, Triangle's contract with Majestic provided that the distributor could, "from time to time," assign its own high-priced theater actors (such as the notorious DeWolf Hopper and Sir Herbert Beerbohm-Tree) to the films at a cost to the producer of $1,000 per week. As with its franchising strategy, Triangle imposed specific contractual restrictions on its producers with the goal of differentiating its films from those of other feature programs.

By attempting to concentrate the value of short runs through the terms of its franchise contracts rather than managing its booking more directly, Triangle was left unable to adapt to the strategy's increasingly apparent problems in 1916–17. Based on the collected evidence of trade press accounts throughout 1916, which make far more frequent reference to franchises than to Triangle's own exchanges, the latter seem to have been ill equipped to sell and market the company's product. While Triangle was successful in centralizing the physical *circulation* of its films—all domestic franchise contracts routed prints through the company's own exchanges—it was unable to structure its *booking* practices efficiently at both local and national scales. In October 1916, Triangle announced in the trade press that it would offer all twenty-one of the key city exchanges it directly owned for sale to "independent exchange men" on the open market.[51] While franchisees had been handling most of the company's booking since the beginning, ostensibly reducing costs, Triangle's own exchange system had been unable to "pay its own keep," according to Lahue.[52] Triangle's films simply did not bring in enough in rentals to defray the overall costs of distributing them. It is telling that as the company began to flounder, the Aitkens thought of their own exchange system not as a crucial part of a strategy to save the company but as an asset to be liquidated.

A large part of the problem stemmed from the relationship between production and distribution at Triangle. While the usual explanation of Triangle's failure is production-based, emphasizing the company's use of highly paid theatrical stars who lacked appeal for cinemagoers, the structural inadequacy of Triangle's franchise distribution system was also an important factor in the studio's downfall. Because Triangle's system encouraged upward pressure on the price of its program as a whole in distribution, its producers were consequently pressured to spend more than was needed in order to keep the perceived quality of the program high. According to Kalton Lahue, "[Triangle's] New York office begged Sennett to spend more money on his comedies and studio manager George W. Stout obliged Kessel and Baumann by raising the salaries of the minor actors."[53] This logic came straight from the received wisdom of the one-reel program: the higher the average production cost enabled by the distribution program, the higher the average quality of that program. This was a common belief among shorts-program producers in the mid-1910s: Biograph's J. J. Kennedy exemplified such a belief in his 1914 claim that under the GFC's system, an increase in the "average quality" of the program tended to lead to more copies (positives) being sold of each film.[54]

Triangle's franchise strategy melded this programmatic logic with the state rights system's assumed suitability for marketing premium films at a local level. Harry Aitken, justifying the sale of Triangle's exchanges, claimed in *Moving Picture World* that the company's new system was a "semi-cooperative plan of distribution which permits the return to active participation in film circulation of the independent exchange man":

> [...] a man in business for himself will invariably give better service to his customers than the same man as a representative of a distant corporation. Not only the producer and the exchange man, but each individual benefits greatly from extra promotion effort on each film. Moreover, the more prints of a film that are bought by exchanges, the better it is possible to make the pictures.[55]

Aitken's discourse here came directly from the logic of the variety program in its emphasis on the local exchange, the purchase of additional prints (rather than extended runs) as an index of success, and its overall characterization of film as a mass-market generic good. Even though Triangle's program was made up of expensive features with highly paid stars, the methods used to distribute it were in keeping with this programmatic logic. Because Triangle service was so expensive for franchisees, the program as a whole—virtually every film—had to be at least a solid performer in exhibition in order to justify that cost. Furthermore, Triangle's pricing system was still based largely on contractually locked-in flat-rate payments, both from franchisees and to producers. As a result, the system as a whole encouraged consistently high costs in production, rather than a separation of productions into distinct cost tiers, as had long been the practice at Famous Players.[56] Thus, when Triangle's product proved less of a draw than its franchisees had hoped, many began renegotiating or canceling their contracts in 1916. A downward spiral in the average cost of Triangle features resulted. At the Fine Arts studios, average negative costs dropped measurably in the second half of 1916, settling around $20,000 rather than $35,000. This was despite their (likely meager) percentage share of rentals; Fine Arts could actually make more money by keeping a portion of Triangle's $40,000 production reimbursement than they could hope to make in new rentals for the program.[57]

These weaknesses in Triangle's franchise model were obvious by the fall of 1916, when the company was forced to change its production and rental policies. In October 1916, in conjunction with the sale of its exchanges, the company allowed its program to be rented on the open market, including exchanges independent from Triangle. This strategy had decidedly mixed results; while it made Triangle's program more widely available to theaters without the intermediary of a franchisee, its high price continued to keep it out of most theaters as a practical matter. Lahue estimates that no more than fifteen percent of all the cinema houses in the United States ever played a Triangle film, even in rerelease.[58] Franchisees also reacted negatively to the revelation that the "exclusive service" they had paid for no longer applied. As King shows, they were particularly annoyed when Triangle replaced the two-reel Keystones with one-reelers on the program, so that the two-reelers could be sold as a separate program; this further soured their relationships with exhibitors and devalued their franchises.[59] In November, the Aitkens finally sold the company-owned exchanges to W. W. Hodkinson for $600,000, who combined them with his own Superpictures, Inc. to form the Triangle Distributing Corporation. The sale cleared some of the Aitkens' debts and helped keep the producing end of Triangle afloat, but Triangle Distributing's status as a more centralized distribution company independent from the Aitkens signaled a clear shift away from the franchise system.

Franchisees continued to handle Triangle's distribution in some US markets at least through the summer of 1917 and in Canada through the end of that year. Well before then, however, it was clear to producers that Triangle's original distribution concept—the high-cost feature program sold to franchisees for select exhibition venues at advanced prices—was no longer feasible. Triangle's payment system to producers was changed to a pure percentage basis in February 1917, suggesting that the company's cash flow was no longer sufficient to pay Ince and Griffith $40,000 per week.[60] A month later Griffith ended his association with Triangle, and by the end of June both Ince and Sennett had sold back their stakes in the company. Around the same time, the Aitkens hired Universal's H. O. Davis to economize production.[61] By 1919, the producing side of Triangle was effectively defunct, though the Aitkens and others would gradually liquidate the remaining elements of the company throughout the early twenties.[62]

Triangle Distributing continued to limp along until early 1920 with the help of William S. Hart and Douglas Fairbanks reissues and other low-cost fare. A vestige of the original franchise system continued to operate there, though less as a coherent strategy of distribution than as a vehicle for personal enrichment. In May 1917, Stephen A. Lynch, who controlled a chain of dozens of theaters throughout the southeastern United States, bought out his partner Hodkinson's shares in Triangle Distributing and took control of the company.[63] Lynch's notorious "dynamite gang" tactics had earned him a reputation as a Paramount franchisee in 1914 and 1915, and his leadership of Triangle took on a similarly disreputable character.[64] According to Lahue, in the second half of 1917, he not only made his own Southern Enterprises company Triangle's franchisee for the Southeast but replaced the Triangle title cards on the prints he distributed, promoting the films as his own. Lynch also instituted a suspiciously flexible booking system that allowed exhibitors to set aside a brand new Triangle release in favor of a cheaper Triangle reissue, or even a film from another company—Famous Players-Lasky, for instance, which Lynch was heavily invested in and whose franchise for distribution in the Southeast he continued to hold.[65] Indeed, three years after the dissolution of Triangle Distributing in the spring of 1920, Lynch would sell that Famous Players-Lasky franchise, as well as his holdings of around two hundred theaters, back to Zukor.[66]

As Eric Hoyt has argued, any discussion of Triangle's mismanagement at any level of the industry, be it production, distribution, or exhibition, must be couched in the knowledge that the studio's leadership ran it on an essentially fraudulent basis.[67] They frequently transferred Triangle's assets to their own private company, Western Import, enriching both themselves and their associates; Triangle's distribution franchise to Australia, New Zealand, and Tasmania was even sold to the manager of Western Import, Hyman Winik.[68] We should therefore be careful not to uncritically characterize Triangle's use of the franchise system as merely a well-intentioned strategy to finance high-cost program production. It may have simply been the easiest way for the Aitkens to perpetrate their schemes, and Lynch certainly manipulated it to his own advantage. Nevertheless, the fact that so many franchisees and exhibitors—not to mention three of the industry's leading production companies—bought into Triangle's franchise system in 1915 demonstrates the extent to which it was perceived as a possible way forward for program feature production. Despite its failure, the initial set-up of Triangle's distribution and production policies for features was structured according to the fundamental assumptions of the variety shorts program and the state rights system. These assumptions were not limited to Triangle—they were intrinsic to the industry's evolving conception of feature service through the mid-1910s.

Conclusion

Triangle was not the only major national feature distributor of the 1910s to use product franchising. The First National Exhibitors' Circuit was incorporated in April 1917 as a combine of more than two hundred of the largest exhibitors in the United States and Canada, many of whom had themselves been Triangle franchisees (including E. H. Hulsey and Harry Schwalbe). First National employed product franchising for reasons similar to Triangle: the system enabled the rapid creation of a national distribution network and simplified the process of booking to thousands of theaters of all sizes. However, First National had much more flexible structures of production financing and sub-run distribution than Triangle. In the early years of the company, each First National franchisee paid a particular percentage for each production, based on its expected rental income in that territory, in exchange for the exclusive right to sub-lease the First National program to local theaters independently.[69] *Moving Picture World* took special note of the fact that First National was not a "closed [exclusive] corporation" and that franchisees could not only purchase any films from any distributor they wished for their own territory, independently of the national organization, but could also distribute First National features to sub-franchisees in any way they saw fit as long as they played all of the company's films.[70] This was in stark contrast to Triangle's program-franchising arrangement, which tended to strictly dictate release timing, run lengths, number of bookings, and the size of theaters franchisees could sub-contract with.

Because First National had no real "program" of its own for its first years—the company distributed only two films in 1917 and a mere sixteen in 1918—those productions were, as a practical matter, booked much more openly and flexibly by the contemporary standards of the weekly feature program. This would eventually change, however, as First National increased the number of productions it released and industry conditions changed. In November 1919, First National underwent a major reorganization to centralize its distribution operations. After two years, it was becoming clear that the company's decentralized model had left First National's franchisees vulnerable to buyouts and takeovers from Famous Players-Lasky, which had become a centrally organized behemoth that was beginning to expand into exhibition, ensuring vertical integration in the process. In addition, the franchise system meant that First National had no uniform national policy of booking or for determining the pricing of the company's releases to franchisees, weakening the organization as a whole.[71] After its reincorporation as Associated First National Pictures, the company effectively eliminated its independent franchises and replaced them with twenty-four affiliated "local companies," which in practice were little more than company-owned exchanges. Unlike the old franchise-exhibitors, who had first-run rights and could distribute to subsequent-run exhibitors any company's pictures they chose (in addition to First National's), the local companies were not allowed to exhibit. Moreover, they dealt only in First National releases, and all contract sales were supervised and approved by the New York office.[72] The company's subsequent coalescence in the 1920s, when it was arguably the second most powerful national distributor prior to the transition to sound, puts the failure of Triangle's franchise strategy in 1915–17 into sharp relief.

First National's reorganization at the end of 1919 was an effort to centralize the company's distribution in an industry whose conception of the relationship between distribution and film quality had changed. At the beginning of the decade, when most films were considered a generic mass-market good, franchise distribution via the state rights system offered a specialized outlet for marketing individuated films of higher value. Even as the new feature companies were obliged to coordinate their releases in various ways according to the demands of programmatic distribution, Triangle's founders clearly believed that distribution franchises were a fast and profitable way to build their national release network. This attitude continued to hold significant sway over the industry well into the teens—at least through 1917, based on the structure of First National at its founding.

In the late teens, however, a number of shifts in distribution practice marginalized the franchise as a viable release strategy for the major distributors. The most important was the rise of so-called open-booking models that decentered the yearlong release program and emphasized more flexible units of distribution, including the star series and individual films. While studios sold these distribution schemes under the moniker of "open" or "selective" booking, the way they were priced to most theaters effectively required bulk sales of films (only the biggest independent first-run theaters had the market clout to leverage truly selective booking of their films). Nonetheless, by freeing distributors from the restricted run and release schedule of the program system, these new forms of block booking encouraged even more attention among the studios to the nationwide marketing of individual films. Distributor-controlled exchanges and centralized sales offices, combined with these new flexible forms of block booking, enabled companies to profitably extend the runs of very successful films and to bury failures quickly in a way that the franchise system simply could not accommodate.

Yet product franchising did not disappear as a method of film distribution. In the 1920s and 30s, the state rights system continued to be a key strategy of independent producers and Poverty Row studios seeking to release their product nationally outside the major distributors' networks. According to Robert Read, the state rights market remained fairly robust through much of the 20s, bolstering such production. Several of the Poverty Row companies of the mid-20s may have had distribution models not unlike Triangle's, combining their own exchanges in the largest key markets with franchise arrangements to enable national releasing.[73] However, much more research is needed on these independent distributors and their relationships with franchisees, both before and after the transition to sound.

By reconsidering the linear historiography that has tended to frame the history of film distribution in the United States, we can see that distribution in the 1910s constituted a set of diverse practices that were recombined from preexisting models in both cinema and other industries. Far from consistently developing these practices into a series of increasingly centralized, coherent, and cinema-specific strategies, distribution firms deployed them in varying combinations (and at varied levels of success) in structuring their industrial conduct in production and exhibition. As the Triangle example shows, these practices could be heterogeneous even within a single company, and they did not always privilege centralized, national control over distribution. Indeed, recent work has begun to advance our understanding of distribution as a set of culturally and industrially imbricated practices that functioned at both national and local scales.[74] Much remains to be discovered about the ways in which the distribution shifts noted here changed the way that studios planned and produced films at scale, for instance, or the extent to which they encouraged regimes of data collection about local markets and theaters. Perhaps the most significant story that remains to be told is about the franchisees themselves—the William Kembles, Harry Schwalbes, E. H. Hulseys, and other local distribution-exhibition entities that exerted significant power during this period of American film history. As work in this field continues, it has become increasingly obvious that local institutions of distribution were crucial in the creation of the Hollywood studio system.

Notes

1. Film historians have frequently described the system as "states rights" or "states' rights." Contemporary sources, particularly the trade press, tended to use the singular—"state rights." I employ the latter usage in this chapter.
2. Michael Quinn, "Early Feature Distribution and the Development of the Motion Picture Industry: Famous Players and Paramount, 1912–1921" (PhD diss., University of Wisconsin–Madison, 1998).
3. Ben Singer, "Feature Films, Variety Programs, and the Crisis of the Small Exhibitor," in Charlie Keil and Shelley Stamp, eds., *American Cinema's Transitional Era* (Berkeley: University of California Press, 2004), 87.
4. Gregory Waller, "Mapping the Moving Picture World: Distribution in the United States circa 1915," in Frank Kessler and Nina Verhoeff, eds., *Networks of Entertainment: Early Film Distribution 1895–1915* (New Barnet, UK: John Libbey, 2007), 98.
5. Maureen Rogers, "'Territory Going Fast!' State Rights Distribution and the Early Multi-Reel Feature Film," *Historical Journal of Film, Radio, and Television* 37, no. 4 (2017): 598–614.
6. Ibid., 600.
7. Thomas Dicke, "Franchising in the American Economy, 1840–1980" (PhD diss., Ohio State University, 1988), 2.
8. Ibid., 5.
9. Ibid., 5–6.
10. Ibid., 6–7.
11. Ibid., 2–3.
12. Ibid., 9–10.
13. Ibid., 27.
14. Max Alvarez, "The Origins of the Film Exchange," *Film History* 17, no. 4 (2005): 431–465.
15. Michael Quinn, "Distribution, the Transient Audience, and the Transition to the Feature Film," *Cinema Journal* 40, no. 2 (2001): 48; Rogers, "'Territory Going Fast!,'" 602.
16. Ben Brewster, "Periodization of Early Cinema," in Charlie Keil and Shelley Stamp, eds., *American Cinema's Transitional Era* (Berkeley: University of California Press, 2004), 67.
17. Sheldon Hall and Steve Neale, *Epics, Spectacles, and Blockbusters* (Detroit, MI: Wayne State University Press, 2010), 24–25.
18. Quinn, "Early Feature Distribution," 116.
19. Letter from Western Import Company to Leading Features Co., November 10, 1914, Griffith Papers Microfilm Edition, Reel 2; Majestic Motion Picture Company Trial Balance, January 31, 1915, Box 33, Aitken Papers, Wisconsin Historical Society, Madison, WI (hereafter Aitken Papers).
20. See ads for *At the Old Cross Roads*, *Moving Picture World*, August 29, 1914, 1283; W. H. Productions, *Moving Picture World*, January 5, 1918, 129; *The Haunted House*, *Moving Picture World*, September 21, 1918, 1666.
21. Quinn, "Early Feature Distribution," 120–123.
22. Ibid., 123.
23. Ibid., 131.
24. Rogers, "'Territory Going Fast!,'" 608.
25. Quinn, "Early Feature Distribution," 133.
26. Ibid., 175–178.

27. Rob King, *The Fun Factory* (Berkeley: University of California Press, 2008), 150–155. We should also note that Triangle was directly interested in only three of these theaters, in New York, Chicago, and Philadelphia, and then only via sub-leases.
28. Kalton Lahue, *Dreams for Sale: The Rise and Fall of the Triangle Film Corporation* (South Brunswick, NJ: A. S. Barnes, 1971), 150.
29. Ibid., 50.
30. As Sheldon Hall and Steve Neale have noted, *Moving Picture World* cited Pliny Craft as a pioneer in the use of state rights for features other than boxing films. *Moving Picture World*, July 11, 1914, 272–73, cited in Hall and Neale, *Epics, Spectacles, and Blockbusters*, 24.
31. "Brooklyn Pays $750,000 for Triangle Plays," *Motion Picture News*, October 23, 1915, 13; "More Wise Men in the Triangle Garden," *Motion Picture News*, October 30, 1915, 18; "Triangle Spells Dollars to These Men," *Motion Picture News*, November 6, 1915, 21.
32. Hall and Neale, *Epics, Spectacles, and Blockbusters*, 24; Tino Balio, *The American Film Industry* (Madison: University of Wisconsin Press, 1985), 110–111; William Paul, *When Movies Were Theater* (New York: Columbia University Press, 2016), 122–123.
33. Quinn, "Early Feature Distribution," 306.
34. November 17, 1915, Contract between Triangle Film Corporation and H. I. Garson and P. P. Craft, Box 11, Aitken Papers.
35. The only exception was for lost or destroyed film, in which case the sub-renting house was required to pay Triangle 20 cents per foot.
36. February 21, 1916, Contract between Triangle Film Corporation and Big "T" Film Corporation, Box 11, Aitken Papers. By 1916, Kemble was a state rights distributor, handling various propaganda films including *The Zeppelin Raids on Verdun and London* (1916), *America Preparing* (1916), which he directed, and *The Men of the Hour* (1918). "Kemble to Handle Big Features," *Motography*, August 19, 1916, 447. The Big "T" Film Corporation would go completely bankrupt in early 1917, angering exhibitors who had paid it deposits for Triangle service. "Exchange Fails—Ties Up Deposits," *Moving Picture World*, March 10, 1917, 1542.
37. October 4, 1915, Contract between Triangle Film Corporation and Southwestern Triangle, Box 11, Aitken Papers.
38. December 27, 1915, Contract between Triangle Film Corporation and Ernest A. Fenton, Box 11, Aitken Papers.
39. "81st Street Gets Triangle," *Variety*, 8 October 1915, 18.
40. "H. Schwalbe Secures Local Triangle rights," *Moving Picture World*, December 18, 1915, 2217.
41. "Christmas Spirit Much in Evidence in Quaker City Film Circles," *Motion Picture News*, January 15, 1916, 220.
42. The dispute stemmed from Craft's sub-leasing of a Triangle film at another theater, the Duplex, for a first-run showing in contravention of the contract. "Duplex Enjoined from Using Triangle Films," *Detroit Free Press*, January 5, 1916, 9. See also "Crafts [sic] No Longer a Franchise Holder in Detroit," *Motion Picture News*, April 22, 1916, 2351; "Local Triangle Office Closed," *Moving Picture World*, April 8, 1916, 297; "Triangle's New Plans for State of Michigan," *Moving Picture World*, May 6, 1916, 1005.
43. "W. S. Hart Stops Over," *Moving Picture World*, June 16, 1917, 1823.
44. Russell Merritt claims that Triangle demanded its theaters "play only Triangle films and none other, according to a fixed release schedule." Triangle did not technically forbid its franchisees from running other programs in any of the contracts I have seen. Exclusivity

was definitely *not* the case for subsequent-run theaters, many of which ran the Triangle program only one or two days a week. Indeed, given the one-day run stipulations in Garson and Craft's contract, none of the subsequent-run theaters in Detroit would even have been able to book the Triangle program exclusively. Russell Merritt, "The Griffith Third: D. W. Griffith at Triangle," in Paolo Cherchi Usai, ed., *Sulla Via di Hollywood* [*The Road to Hollywood*] (Pordenone, Italy: Le Giornate del Cinema Muto, 1988), 262.

45. Contract between Triangle and Garson and Craft, Box 11, Aitken Papers.
46. Ibid. Thirty-five bookings over 120 days averages out to about two subsequent-run bookings every week for a particular film, across the entire city. Triangle's contract with Garson and Craft stipulated nothing about clearance beyond the first run, but it seems likely that they would have built in some form of clearance protection in their dealings with subsequent-run exhibitors.
47. Quinn, "Early Feature Distribution," 188, 306.
48. Exhibitors who purchased exclusive service got a program made up of one-, two-, and occasionally three-reel films, changed three times a week, and clearance protection for ninety days (regular service included no clearance at all). Quinn, "Early Feature Distribution," 76.
49. Unlike Paramount's arrangement with its producers, this lump-sum payment was a reimbursement, not an advance (see Quinn, "Early Feature Distribution," 138). Majestic received $30.000 within a week of the film's release, and the remaining $10,000 within sixty days. Beginning the second year of the contract, Triangle's payment to Majestic increased to $45,000, although this would be renegotiated to a percentage-based payment system in February 1917: Lahue, *Dreams for Sale*, 161.
50. This would seem to contradict Lahue's claim (49) that Triangle producers were reimbursed for their negative costs and then shared in receipts through a 65/35 arrangement (which would have been identical to Paramount's system).
51. "Triangle Plans to Change Its Distributing Scheme," *Motion Picture News*, October 14, 1916, 2347; "New Triangle Exchange Proposition," *Moving Picture World*, October 14, 1916, 214.
52. Lahue, *Dreams for Sale*, 150.
53. Ibid., 133.
54. *United States vs. Motion Picture Patents Company*, vol. 6, Testimony of Witnesses for the Defendants (1914): 3203–3204.
55. "New Triangle Exchange Proposition," *Moving Picture World*, October 14, 1916, 214.
56. Quinn, "Early Feature Distribution," 125–126.
57. These numbers are based on Fine Arts production records for the 4500 Sunset Boulevard studios, held on microfilm reels 7 and 18 in the Aitken Collection, with additional data from Majestic's inventory files held in Box 33 of the same.
58. Lahue, *Dreams for Sale*, 177.
59. King, *The Fun Factory*, 157–158; Lahue, *Dreams for Sale*, 149–150.
60. Lahue, *Dreams for Sale*, 161.
61. Ibid., 165; King, *The Fun Factory*, 26–27.
62. "Aitken's Novel Scheme to Market 2,000 Old Triangles," *Variety*, January 12, 1923, 39.
63. Lahue, *Dreams for Sale*, 167.
64. Quinn, "Early Feature Distribution," 250–251.
65. Lahue, *Dreams for Sale*, 171.
66. Ibid., 182; "Lynch Purchase by Famous Clears Paramount Franchises," *Variety*, January 12, 1923, 39.

67. Eric Hoyt, *Hollywood Vault: Film Libraries Before Home Video* (Berkeley: University of California Press, 2014), 47.
68. Contract between Triangle and Hyman Winik and Henry Brock, December 27, 1915, Box 11, Aitken Papers.
69. See Quinn, "Early Feature Distribution," 339–341, for a breakdown of these percentages by franchise territory.
70. "Big Exhibitors Form Co-Operative Association," *Moving Picture World*, April 28, 1917, 589.
71. Quinn, "Early Feature Distribution," 252–256; Miles H. Alben, "History of First National Pictures Inc.," 20, unpublished manuscript, n.d., Folder 15494A, Warner Bros. Archives, School of Cinematic Arts, University of Southern California, Los Angeles, 23–24.
72. Alben, "History of First National Pictures Inc.," 24–30. The centralization of First National's distribution assets was made feasible by the fact that the company had finally signed enough production contracts to offer a program that could feasibly compete with Paramount; the company would release fifty films in 1920.
73. Robert Read, "A Squalid-Looking Place: Poverty Row Films of the 1930s" (PhD diss., McGill University, 2010), 80–85.
74. Martin Johnson, *Main Street Movies: The History of Local Film in the United States* (Bloomington: Indiana University Press, 2018); Daniela Treveri Gennari, Danielle Hipkins, and Catherine O'Rawe, eds., *Rural Cinema Exhibition and Audiences in a Global Context* (London: Palgrave Macmillan, 2018); Marta Braun, Charlie Keil, Rob King, Paul Moore, and Louis Pelletier, eds., *Beyond the Screen: Institutions, Networks, and Publics of Early Cinema* (New Barnet, UK: John Libbey, 2016); Andrea Comiskey, "The Sticks, the Nabes, and the Broadways: U.S. Film Distribution, 1935–1940" (PhD diss., University of Wisconsin–Madison, 2015).

CHAPTER 23

PARAMOUNT PICTURES, NATIONAL ADVERTISING AGENCIES, AND THE CONSPICUOUS DISTRIBUTION OF FIRST-RUN FEATURE FILMS IN THE UNITED STATES

PAUL S. MOORE

PARAMOUNT Pictures was created in 1914 as a "marketing combine" of distributors for three early feature-film companies—Adolph Zukor's Famous Players (including the films of Mary Pickford), Jesse L. Lasky Productions (including those directed by Cecil B. DeMille), and W. W. Hodkinson's Bosworth Productions of Jack London stories.[1] These together constituted a block program of multiple-reel features with prominent theatrical players, playwrights, and producers. Paramount's first officers were the five regional exchange owners who held the franchise rights to distribute the films; Zukor and Lasky did not gain direct control until two years later.[2] Central to Paramount's initial set-up was a plan to advertise on a national scale, taking advantage of pooled publicity. The firm's inaugural president, W. W. Hodkinson, spent part of the summer of 1914 traveling the country to meet with local managers, putting into action his claim that "we expect to do more for the high-class exhibitor than was ever done before. [. . .] He will be glad to help us in widening the gulf which even now divides the 'movies' from the motion pictures. We will give him the aid of a new and systematic method of national advertising."[3] This campaign was designed by publicity experts, the H. E. Lesan agency. The firm managed contracts for billboard advertising on a national scale and monthly advertisements in the *Saturday Evening Post*, the largest general circulation magazine of the day and self-described arbiter of "a transcendent American consciousness."[4] The ad campaign began with a double-page spread to announce the first releases of the new season on September 5, 1914; other magazines were soon added, as was a parallel campaign in metropolitan newspapers. For the rest of the silent era, Paramount stood out among Hollywood studios for its extensive use of national advertising. Where other studios occasionally promoted new feature films, trademarks, or popular stars, Paramount took a more systematic approach to conspicuously display its feature films as a modern staple of an emerging consumer society. Paramount's trademark commingled with mass-produced brand logos heralding new routines of chain-store-style abundance and conspicuous consumption.

Paramount soon took the parallel with chain-store consumption well beyond its advertising by forging Hollywood's largest chain of US movie palaces, located in almost every metropolitan downtown, and gaining control of exhibition in several regions. The form and function of the studio's national publicity, in a sense, foreshadowed its later pursuit of a vertically integrated business model. Douglas Gomery's pioneering research on Paramount-Publix theaters in the 1920s noted a "chain store strategy" that "advertised widely and developed trade-marks for instant recognition."[5] Even at the time, some called for the film industry to "follow in the footsteps of the chain store" where circuits of theaters "would have one name" so that "no matter where a person happened to be he could drop in to a chain theater and by the sign on its front know that he was getting the same quality of entertainment."[6] The chain-store rationale is most overt in Paramount's own justification in a trade ad that answered the question "Who are the Joneses?" with the tautology, "[T]hey're the great happy 'middle class.' [. . .] Mr. Jones wears Arrow Collars and shaves with a Gillette razor. Mrs. Jones buys Ivory Soap, Heinz's pickles and Campbell's soups. [. . .] They know all about Paramount and Artcraft Pictures, for they read National Advertising."[7] On the other hand, no two feature films were actually the same; therein lay the limits of the chain store analogy, as William Paul has recently noted.[8] The theatrical model adopted with the zone-run-clearance system ensured each feature film could not be seen in two nearby theaters at once. Theaters could be built and operated in standardized ways—this was really the substance of Gomery's essay—but "the picture, unlike any other commodity, cannot be standardized," noted *Motion Picture News* editor William A. Johnston. "Unlike an automobile, or a safety razor, or a package of breakfast food, you cannot make fifty-two pictures just alike in quality. Therefore, you cannot employ general publicity as general publicity is used with other nationally advertised products to create steady, year-around customers."[9] Johnston extended his argument in the next week's editorial, carefully grounding his logic in the characteristics of film distribution as a time-based system: "The peculiar distribution of pictures, the fact that they appear locally only for a few days, makes it impossible for the manufacturer to direct the advertising out of New York. [. . . The picture] must be advertised when and where it appears."[10] A year later, Johnston returned to the issue and acceded that "national advertising campaigns were bound to develop with a product of so universal an appeal [. . . but] the picture will never be uniform in quality like other products. Consequently, the advertising has been largely local. It had to be."[11] Why then did Paramount expend so much more effort and expense on national advertising than other silent-era studios?

Prior research into Hollywood advertising and promotion has not carefully considered its structural place in the industry as a branch of film distribution, an extension of the work of regional exchanges in providing publicity for local adaptation by exhibitors.[12] Neither has much attention been paid to the relation between Hollywood and Madison Avenue, or to such adjuncts as the Associated Motion Picture Advertisers, created in 1916 by the competing heads of advertising and publicity of all the major studios of the day.[13] My own prior research, for example, esteemed newspaper journalism over public relations and conflated all forms of print publicity to define cinema's mass audience as an intermedial reading public.[14] I did not consider how national circulation in newswire items, syndicated stories, and magazine advertising differed from one another and from local efforts relying on handouts and home delivery. I also failed to distinguish between national advertising and nationally syndicated publicity, such as film news columns and serial-film fiction tie-ins. Our historical understanding of the mechanisms for advertising movies is thus incomplete, despite widespread scholarly acknowledgment of the central role publicity played in the classical Hollywood system.[15] Richard Abel, for instance, has described the range of film-related print items as "menus for movieland," to signify advertising's role as both agent and archive of the public's relationship with movies.[16] A grasp of film studios' work with advertising agencies, and those agencies' roles in mediating distributors' commercial relations with exhibitors, should contribute to a broader understanding of the full complexity of Hollywood's practices of public relations.[17]

Let me be clear that studio-run advertising campaigns stand apart from the copious examples of local advertising and publicity. Most movie exploitation was arranged by local exhibitors in their own handbills, sidewalk displays, souvenir programs, or newspaper advertising for their specific theaters—sometimes called "exhibitors' advertising."[18] Theater owners typically paid distributors for posters, lithographs, slides, and other promotional accessories. Exchanges provided press books free of charge to design ads and flyers, but the cost of printing and publishing fell to the exhibitor.[19] Most work of film exploitation remained firmly tied to local theatrical exhibition. The exception came when studios carried the expense of centrally coordinated "national advertising." Campaigns managed centrally by ad agencies allowed film distributors to directly address the public, with only generic, idealized reference to theaters. By isolating advertising campaigns managed by agencies from other forms of publicity, this essay offers a counterpoint to cultural histories of the small-town audience and independent exhibitors' relation to national chains.[20] Because Paramount was synonymous with national advertising, debates over the value and impact of studio-controlled ad campaigns were, in a sense, tangents to disputes over Paramount's business tactics and the legal status of vertically integrated "producer-exhibitors."[21] Distribution was the latent but essential lynchpin of vertical integration, and above all else, national advertising was a conspicuous display of mass distribution.

This reference to Thorstein Veblen's theory of conspicuous consumption as "a means of reputability" is deliberate, and I propose that these advertising campaigns helped establish Paramount's status and prestige among rival studios and with the general public. Veblen also noted the importance of "resorting to the giving of valuable presents" in the process, because gifts established an expectation of reciprocal "aid of friends and competitors."[22] Paramount continually proffered nationwide publicity as a free benefit to local showmen, a bonus begging for the exhibitor's gratitude in contracting with the Paramount program. Some exhibitors were skeptical, complaining that the extravagant expense was implicitly passed on to them in higher film rental rates, that magazine ads mentioned the latest first-run films months before they were available at their theaters, and that publicity designed in New York failed to appeal to regional audiences. National advertising was a classic example of gifts as a totem of servitude, following Marcel Mauss. "One has no right to refuse a gift," he wrote, for doing so would precipitate a break in the existing relationship.[23] Gifts inscribe status and reify inequity, but Pierre Bourdieu went a step further to conflate "the gift, generosity, [and] conspicuous distribution" by defining them all as "operations of social alchemy which [. . .] tend to bring about the transmutation of economic capital into symbolic capital."[24] In the emerging studio system for Hollywood movies, the generosity of conspicuous distribution as displayed in national advertising transformed the deep pockets of Paramount studios into symbolic dominance over exhibitors at a vital time when the company was establishing plans for vertically integrated ownership of first-run theatres.

H. E. Lesan's Campaign for Paramount, 1914 to 1917

By the end of the silent era, the classical Hollywood system of distribution in the United States was entrenched. A relatively small number of first-run movie palaces in metropolitan downtown locations provided an outsized proportion of the profits.[25] Equally important, first-run advertising in those few dozen metropolitan cities approximated national-scale publicity, following patterns of circulation already well developed for popular syndicated features in Sunday newspaper comic and magazine supplements.[26] Hollywood's profits derived from throttling the supply of film prints for any one title while mass producing publicity to stoke demand. In a sense, film distribution condensed to a regional scale the commercial logic of a theatrical circuit, each key city serving as the equivalent of New York for its metropolitan territory. Benjamin B. Hampton later pinpointed the origins of this system in the opening of first-run movie palaces like the Strand on Times Square in 1914. "The new palace theaters became liberal advertisers in newspapers and publishers responded by giving their shows publicity in news columns and reviews. The newspapers in thirty to fifty metropolitan centers throughout the country—key cities—circulate in all neighboring cities and towns, and the advertising and publicity of a first-run in a key city create a demand for the picture in the surrounding district."[27] Adding national advertising was to some extent redundant; this explains why it was used sparingly by most studios. Not Paramount. Beyond affirming an ideology of mass leisure over local culture, Paramount systematically circumvented local theater advertising by addressing audiences directly. The business tactic symbolically asserted the studio's dominance over exhibitors, especially important around 1920 as the studio was establishing its own theater chain. (The assertion was not always just symbolic; in 1927, with vertical integration largely achieved, Paramount took direct control of key city newspaper advertising for its feature film "specials," imposing a proportion of the cost onto first-run exhibitors on the same percentage basis as the contracted box-office split. The move acted as "insurance against a picture taking a nose dive [. . .] to prevent a poor or inadequate advertising campaign in a large city practically killing the business of a picture for an entire territory.")[28]

Hints of the growing importance of first-run theater circuits were already evident by 1914. Marcus Loew's in New York, Nathan Gordon's in New England, and Turner & Dahnken's in California had begun to sub-contract regional states rights for feature films beyond exhibition runs in their own theaters. An industry insider predicted it would be "extremely probable that the day will come when a single concern will be both the producer and exhibitor. [. . .] There are only two roads by which the day of the circuit may arrive. It may come by means of combinations of exhibitors or through a producing company acquiring a chain of theaters."[29] Just a few years later, one path of this fork in the road was taken by several dissatisfied clients of Paramount, who jumped ship to create First National Exhibitors Circuit in 1917, pushing Paramount down the other path of acquiring theater chains in 1919 as a "defensive measure," as Adolph Zukor claimed at the time.[30] The tumultuous competition meant film rental agreements varied dramatically among studios, changing from one season to another. It took several years before a uniform contract existed to arbitrate studios' relations with exhibitors. Richard Maltby neatly summarizes the conditions leading to the 1922 establishment of the Motion Picture Producers and Distributors Association and soon after its Standard Exhibition Contract: "The extreme contractual instability of the distribution industry—and not any goings-on in Hollywood—was the principal source of the industry's reputation as 'a wildcat proposition.' The MPPDA was established in 1922 to address this reputational hazard, to stabilize distributor-exhibitor relations, and to act as 'a clearing house for the problems of the industry,' not to fix a hullaballoo in the Hearst press."[31] Paramount's national advertising also reinforced this need for standardized consistency by effectively equating all theaters playing its films as offering the same experience.

Paramount was not the first film producer to run standardized advertising campaigns in popular magazines or major metropolitan newspapers. Early in 1910, Pathé ran a series of six weekly display ads in newspapers such as the *Detroit Free Press* and the *Chicago Tribune*. This ad campaign spotlighted Pathé's trademarked red rooster as the brand source for a variety of genres of moving pictures.[32] Another major advertising effort came late in 1913 when Mutual Movies placed full-page advertisements in Chicago and other Midwest newspapers, as well as two full-page ads in the *Saturday Evening Post*, a genuine novelty for a film company. Mutual's campaign centered entirely upon associating its "wing-ed clock" with respectable amusement, showing well-dressed, smiling crowds entering theaters displaying Mutual's trademark.[33] Carl Laemmle then turned to national advertising in January 1914 to promote Florence Lawrence, now appearing under the Universal trademark. Unlike the earlier Pathé and Mutual ad campaigns, Universal's Florence Lawrence ads appeared in dozens of smaller-circulation newspapers in addition to metropolitan papers—not just Cleveland and Pittsburgh, but also Akron and Reading.[34] A flood of syndicated newspaper tie-ins also began in 1914. Pages upon pages of syndicated fiction and advertising appeared for serial films in nearly every Sunday edition in the United States, in addition to three nationally syndicated columns of "daily stories" to accompany moving pictures—"Read the Story in the Morning; See it in Moving Pictures at Night!"[35] Amid the saturated burst of syndicated film publicity, Paramount took up national advertising with fervor, asserting its predominance first through conspicuous publicity, before its actual dominance in distribution was established.

One of the first tasks assigned to the H. E. Lesan advertising agency was creating the trademark logo of the snow-capped mountain encircled by stars, accompanied by the phrase "Paramount Pictures" in cursive font (see figure 23.1).[36] In the early phase under the H. E. Lesan agency, 1914 to 1916, Paramount's national advertising quite explicitly emphasized its brand name as an inherent quality that could be trusted no matter where Paramount films were playing. The series began with great hoopla and a double-spread in the *Saturday Evening Post* and continued monthly for a year, later adding other magazines such as *Ladies' Home Journal*, *Woman's Home Companion*, and the *American Sunday Magazine* supplement to Hearst chain newspapers. In September 1915, a parallel campaign began in around three dozen metropolitan newspapers across the country.[37] Approximately every week for four months, each newspaper ad in this series profiled a Paramount star, beginning with Mary Pickford. By 1916, however, the size of these displays had withered to only half-pages in magazines and single columns in newspapers. Having repeatedly promoted the studio's roster of movie stars, the final ads in this series took on a more gimmicky, direct-marketing tone. Many of the ads included cut-out coupons to request free booklets telling *The Story of Paramount* and *Paramount Progress* fan magazines. In the final ads in the series, readers were begged to "Sign This Motion Picture Protest" by cutting out a coupon listing Paramount Pictures and stars, to give to their local theater manager if he wasn't already showing Paramount films. If later commentators, cited below, associated national advertising with hucksterism of the patent-medicine variety, it was surely due to this turn to conflating the company trademark and movie star ballyhoo with coupons for premiums and mock-democratic protests. This phase under H. E. Lesan included just two additional Paramount ads in the *Saturday Evening Post*, months apart, and nothing further in newspapers.

FIGURE 23.1 Movie stars, trademarks, and cut-out coupons clutter early ads for Paramount by H. E. Lesan agency. *Saturday Evening Post*, November 6, 1915.

Standardized national publicity for Paramount features was taken as a clear value at first, especially by first-run exhibitors managing the largest and most profitable movie palaces in the United States. An array of early subscribers to the Paramount program featured in one of the early magazine ads, including many of the key figures in the subsequent creation of First National Exhibitors Circuits just a few years later: Turner & Dahnken in California, Stanley Mastbaum in Philadelphia, the Saxe Brothers in Minneapolis, and John H. Kunsky of Detroit.[38] What was it that eventually soured their commitment to Paramount? One of the factors was centralized publicity. Consider a letter of unusual candor by Kunsky to *Motion Picture News* in November 1918 that cast aspersions on national advertising for being "similar to the fake patent medicine copy we used to read."[39] He argued studios' budgets for advertising should be allocated to the accounts of first-run exhibitors to arrange local newspaper ads. Kunsky complained that the cost and content of national advertising "would have resulted in much greater returns to the exhibitors had the producers been imbued with the thought that a New York desk is not prolific with information about conflicting conditions in the different territories." He repeated the insulting comparison to patent medicines, explaining that "syndicate advertising will not lengthen the run of any production [. . .] set up like a medical ad, with the name of the producer spread all over the sheet."[40]

For this founding member of First National, centrally planned nationwide advertising was a waste because it promoted the brand name over the film title and the local theater. Kunsky wanted the studio to reimburse or subsidize his local advertising as a first-run exhibitor, reasoning that his local ads served the same purposes as national advertising with the added bonus of informing all the other regional exhibitors of his success with the best pictures. He ultimately based his entire argument on moving pictures' inherent difference from other modern branded goods. "Advertising for a motion picture subject must be entirely different from the advertising for a breakfast food or any other staple article [. . .] a trade mark means very little to the public."[41] The commentary provides some insights into the sentiment behind the creation of First National Exhibitors Circuit from the perspective of a key founding member, further confirmed by First National's strategy in magazine ads of offering "news" about its latest releases rather than studio branding.[42] Kunsky's comments struck a nerve and sparked debate and discussion in subsequent months. Especially resonant was the self-serving logic that the cost of national advertising would be more beneficially placed in the hands of first-run exhibitors who best knew their metropolitan publics and better defined the run of a film within the region.[43] On the other hand, Tarkington Baker of Universal Pictures chimed in with the perspective of head office. He explained how "producers are beset daily by solicitors for agencies representing newspapers. These solicitors want the 'producers' advertising.' [. . .] I have been from one end of the country to the other. Everywhere newspaper advertising managers have solicited me for this vague, nondescript, illusory 'general product' advertising."[44] His comments confirm that publishers expected and preferred standardized advertising campaigns. In this context, Paramount's emphatic embrace of modern brand advertising campaigns staked a claim that its entertainment products deserved a prominent place alongside other mass-produced goods.[45]

Hanff-Metzger's Campaign for Paramount, 1917 to 1921

Paramount's efforts at national publicity gained urgency with the competition of First National. A new campaign began in 1917 under a partnership with a new agency, Hanff-Metzger, Inc.[46] The content of this new publicity tapped the homefront zeitgeist in the context of World War I without turning to overt patriotism. An emotional appeal based in storytelling went well beyond branding trademarks and movie star personalities; none of the ads profiled specific stars or movie titles. Instead, the company presented a generic, but idealized, form of moviegoing as a routine part of family life (for white, patriarchal, middle-class, home-owning, newspaper-reading families, to be sure, but depicted with sentimental realism—the consumer society idealized). Rather than cater to America's fifteen million regular moviegoers, Hanff-Metzger announced they would target "the other twenty million" who were "waiting for an invitation—only they don't know it."[47] The advertising industry took special note of the new approach as a first for the film business.

Joseph A. Hanff and George P. Metzger had established their advertising agency in June 1913, with offices at 95 Madison Avenue at a time before that avenue was synonymous with the art of persuasion. The firm specialized in novel approaches that relied on statistical and demographic research and meticulous organizational reflection with its corporate clients. Among its first contracts were the amusement products Tel-Electric Player Pianos and Columbia Phonographs (where Metzger had been advertising manager).[48] Noted as "rather a departure" among advertising agencies, the firm made an unusual effort to explain its philosophy and practices to the general public as well as prospective clients by advertising routinely in New York newspapers.[49] The company widely promoted its specialized "Maplan," which borrowed the tools and format of architectural schematics to create an elaborate wall-sized diagram for each client. The flowchart served as "a merchandising blueprint [that] presents in graphic form the interrelations of all the elements and efforts involved [. . . and might be] as large as fourteen feet in length."[50] An illustrated article on the approach emphasized how the rational veneer of the Maplan primarily served to improve communication with clients by prodding them to imagine their own businesses in a new light: "a blueprint 6 feet long by 3 feet wide, imagine with what pleasure you could unroll that before some stubborn director, and tell him to take it away with him, spread it on his desk or tack it up on his wall."[51] Its "technical department" also offered basic but then-novel branding and marketing principles, for example a flowchart with a choice branched in two from the phrase "If you manufacture," showing on the one hand "a staple – advertise – your trade-mark," and on the other "a specialty – advertise – the article."[52]

This prompts a vital question: were moving pictures a staple or a specialty? The earlier ad campaign under H. E. Lesan more clearly aimed to use the Paramount trademark and stars to transform occasional filmgoing for specialty films into habitual moviegoing, whatever the title. The later campaign by Hanff-Metzger worked more subtly to show the specialty article in realistic action—the story of a family going to the movies, the fantasy of make-believe when watching a Paramount film. Without mentioning a specific star or film title, the ads conveyed how the experience of entertainment as a habitual staple retained the selection of a specialty in the moment: a particular film, a specific movie star.

With the switch to Hanff-Metzger in 1917, Paramount escalated the frequency of its national ads, returning to full-page displays in the *Saturday Evening Post*; the campaign also now included monthly pages in movie fan magazines. Other publications were used judiciously at first, until a ramped-up effort in 1919 following the war.[53] Hanff-Metzger facilitated Paramount's use of quarter-page display ads in up to three hundred newspapers across the United States, well beyond the scope of H. E. Lesan's 1915 campaign. The first ads to run in newspapers in October 1917 included significant rebranding: newly stylized letterhead with Paramount's and Artcraft's twinned trademarks profiling "Famous Players–Lasky Corporation"; an instruction that there were "Three Ways to Know" those trademarks (through local newspaper ads, theater displays, and at the start of the films themselves); and a freshly-minted slogan, "Famous Stars, Superbly Directed, in Clean Motion Pictures" (see figure 23.2).[54]

The newspaper publishing business took note of the new direction, and a lengthy review in *The Fourth Estate* offered praise for the canny use of sentiment and story to achieve a wide appeal. The first ad "was the talk of the town for an entire week. [. . .] In make-up, illustration, text and spirit, it represents quite the highest degree of motion picture publicity. [. . .] There was a time when Paramount Pictures were rather crudely advertised. Tons of electros were sent to papers all over the country. They were about as inspired and as inspiring as the plated matter then sent to further the sale of soap or beans."[55] The review of the campaign singled out Richard Culter's accompanying illustration, which showed two couples in a dimly-lit motion picture theater, adding a subtle gesture to the war while depicting a timeless scenario:

> Grandmother in her plain gown and fluffy cap has managed to find Grandfather's hand in the darkness and is holding it—very tightly. Near them, the second couple is equally absorbed in the picture—a pretty girl and her soldier sweetheart. And they are holding hands. It's all very sweet and natural and interesting, even to the hurried reader of a daily paper—in New York. The caption reads: "And there you will find your old sweetheart!" The copy is quaintly convincing: "Come—drop that newspaper for tonight! Maybe she's tired of a paper wall and silence and the width of a lighted table between you." [. . .] There is a sense of being talked to—intimately. The text rings true. The big, blustry press-agent type of publicity grab is entirely missing. [. . .] There has been entirely too little of genuine sentiment in newspaper advertising copy.[56]

This ad was the first of a type developed by Hanff-Metzger, tapping into "John-Smith interest" as opposed to journalistic human interest, "something warm enough to make

FIGURE 23.2 Illustrator Richard V. Culter depicted a family using Paramount and Artcraft trademarks in the newspaper directory to plan a night out. "What do we see tonight?" *Saturday Evening Post*, August 3, 1918.

the reader think he wrote it himself. Full of understanding of the reader and of his personality. Your reader is not merely a human. He is John Smith, and he lives at Number 123 Jones Street. And you've got to reach him right there!"[57] This approach was used in about three-quarters of Paramount's national advertising between 1917 and 1922, altogether animating the story of an idealized evening out at the movies, from start to finish. Each illustration derives an idealistic value from the story of an enjoyable evening, as, for example, in the early ad, "Keeping the Family Together," which explained that "the real cementing influence, as many parents have found, is for the family to enjoy itself together, as it does at the motion picture theatre."[58] Taken collectively, the twenty ads illustrated by Culter paint the picture of that story in remarkable detail. First, the family asks "What's on tonight?" and turns to the newspaper's amusement listings. "Sometimes it's the man of the house and sometimes it's the woman that starts the ball a-rolling. An eventful evening two or three times a week is an important part of the art of enjoyable home life."[59] In more than one, Dad and children help wash the dishes after dinner—"Six hands now and a good seat that much sooner!"—or it could be "Father's turn home tonight" to mind the baby.[60] Out the door and onto the trolley car, "Let us off at that Paramount sign."[61] Early-career Norman Rockwell pictured the family smiling at the box office, "Four, please! Multiply the pleasure by sharing it!" (see figure 23.3)[62] Others show the imagination at play while watching the film, such as a trio illustrated by Willy Pogany that turned to metaphor to depict motion pictures as an Aladdin's Lamp or crystal ball—"You gaze into it and you see life"—or a curtain drawn back to see dreams come to life, "unveiling the thoughts, loves, passions and ideals of humanity."[63] Finally, the family is happier than ever on the way home, because "when the show is over—the last touch of Paramount-Artcraft magic vanished—you stroll away richly content. A fitting end for a perfect day."[64]

One of the ads stumbled on what became Paramount Pictures' slogan for several decades. A Culter-drawn businessman arriving at a hotel front desk asks, "What's the Best Show in Town?" to the concierge, who points across the street to a theater marquee. "Not only in the palatial theatres of the big cities, but in the leading theatres of several thousand cities and towns in every state in the union, Paramount-Artcraft Pictures are regarded as the 'best show in town.' [. . .] Go by that name and you'll go right!"[65] In February 1921, Hanff-Metzger transformed the year-old phrase into a new catchphrase added to every ad: "If it's a Paramount Picture, it's the Best Show in Town." Curiously, the ads do not reflexively include national advertising—*the ads themselves*—within the idealized story of moviegoing. Rather, they show how *local* newspaper ads played an essential role in that idealized practice, as important as the theater itself, as the film itself.[66] In that sense, Paramount's national advertising did not directly contradict Kunsky's argument that the advertising that mattered was local exhibitors' listings in newspapers. Advertising in magazines served a distinct purpose, and a distinctly ideological one, in framing the norms of the ordinary practice, while excluding itself from that quotidian realm. To some extent, the national-scale ads occupied a contradictory position by depicting how local newspaper movie directories were key to planning a night out at the movies, even as they circumvented the role of local exhibitors in promoting

FIGURE 23.3 Going to the theater as a "family affair." Norman Rockwell pictures the family buying tickets to a Paramount feature. "Four, please," *Saturday Evening Post*, April 5, 1920.

Paramount Pictures. This paradoxical position helps frame the importance of another genre of national advertising begun in 1918: an annual Paramount Week launching each September's season of new feature films.

ADVERTISING PARAMOUNT WEEK, 1918 TO 1927

Across the United States, each Labor Day throughout the 1920s marked the arrival of Paramount Week, prominently lauded on city billboards, banners, and posters outside theaters, and especially by advertising in magazines and newspapers. Paramount's national advertising had detractors who deemed the costly branding exercise a wasteful distraction from the basic function of publicizing which films were playing at what local theatres.[67] Annual ads promoting Paramount Week counteracted that criticism by combining a branded national campaign designed by Hanff-Metzger with a local showtime directory. The campaign's boast of "celebrating better pictures at *all* the better theatres" was not entirely hyperbole.[68] For the third annual campaign in September 1920, Paramount claimed to have purchased more than a million dollars in newspaper advertising in all 434 US cities with a population exceeding ten thousand. The ads for most cities included nearby theaters in smaller towns, altogether listing nearly every one of the estimated six thousand theaters booked to exhibit Paramount films across the United States that week. For the fifth annual Paramount Week in 1922, a majority of the nation's fifteen thousand theaters participated, with an estimated fifty million people attending a theatre exhibiting a Paramount Picture, nearly half the US population.[69] In her analysis of Paramount's magazine ads, Kathryn Fuller-Seeley focuses on an early instance in which the Strand on Broadway was equated with the theater in "your own town" by virtue of showing the same Paramount pictures.[70] The national campaign only rarely returned to this point after Hanff-Metzger took over, focusing instead on the generic story of family entertainment. On the other hand, each September's Paramount Week from 1918 to 1927 conspicuously underscored the relation between first-run chain theaters and independent theaters. Downtown movie palaces in metropolitan cities played the newest releases on Paramount Week; these were listed top-and-center—usually in larger font and with more details. Distant small-town theaters played year-old subsequent-run releases and were listed on the margins of the page, matching their location in the periphery of the marketplace.

Other studios experimented with national advertising for first-run engagements, but never on a wide scale simultaneously promoting thousands of theatres playing their films.[71] Internally, the annual Paramount Week campaign marked a sales competition among exchange branches and set a deadline for sales agents to ink new contracts for each Labor Day's new season. Such sales competitions had begun at Paramount in 1915 for its second season but became attached to Paramount Week in 1919.[72] Sales contests would have required careful centralized accounting of Paramount Week contracts throughout the territory, submitted by a certain date to be counted in the competition—exactly the accounting and documentation needed to compile and arrange the listing of theaters and films shown in the various newspaper ads across the territory. Hanff-Metzger coordinated the publishing contracts for hundreds of newspaper ads.[73] The content was laid out locally by each newspaper, combining details from the regional exchange's list of contracts with advertising material from a special press book. More than a few Paramount Week ads went to press still including the bracketed instructions to compositors at the newspaper: "[Insert here the name of your city] joins in the national demonstration of the better motion pictures."[74] For the next decade, thousands of theaters acted as a unified circuit on Paramount Week, in a hierarchy according to the age and currency of their Paramount features. These annual listings were the only times many smaller, urban neighborhood theaters obtained newspaper publicity and were small-town theaters' only notice in their metropolitan regional newspapers.

This first Paramount Week was planned hastily by Arthur O. Dillenbeck, in charge of the Paramount account at Hanff-Metzger.[75] The model came from a regional version organized by Paramount's New York exchange for the first week of July 1918, which "doubled their ordinary receipts" and centered on a collective display ad in *The New York Telegram*—far from the leading paper in the city—listing dozens of theaters playing Paramount and Artcraft films. Finding great success in New York, Dillenbeck quickly planned an expanded version across the country for the opening of the season in September. The idea lasted the rest of the 1920s. Several other studios even mimicked the success of Paramount Week with their own sales-focused efforts to concentrate on bookings for special promotional periods: Universal Joy Week, Metro Week, and Fox Week, among others.[76] None of these, however, was accompanied by national advertising or anything beyond exhibitors' mentions of Goldwyn Week or First National Month in their own local advertising. Paramount Week was deemed so successful a paradigm for structuring distribution sales that Paramount created quarterly versions in 1921 and 1922, inventing seasonal reasons to book a national-ad-supported Paramount-only week, culminating with "Paramount's 10th Anniversary Week" in March 1922.

Neighborhood and small-town exhibitors were essential to Paramount Week's conspicuous display of national reach in film distribution, especially for the regional promotions that depended on quantities of theaters listed to give the impression of a saturated mass market. Some exhibitors welcomed the effort and reported box-office gains. For example, among the thousands of locations listed in Paramount Week ads in 1922 was F. E. Sabin's Majestic Theater in Eureka, Montana, which reported to the *Exhibitors Herald*'s "What the Picture Did for Me" column: "*Behold My Wife, Always Audacious, The Testing Block, The Gilded Lily*—These constituted my Paramount Week program and every one was a success, first in entertainment and second in box office receipts. What more could I ask?"[77] Such praise contrasted with reports from such small-town showmen as R. C. Buxton, who complained of a "costly slip up" at his Strand Theater in Ransom, Kansas, listed within the *Topeka Capital*'s 1922 regional Paramount Week display ad. His opening night film was replaced last minute. "What did it do for me? Simply this: Last year, I did $120 in three nights Paramount Week. This year, $34. [. . .] No more Paramount Weeks for yours truly."[78] Buxton's was not the only reported mishap. J. L. Meyers' Liberty Theater in Ivesdale, Illinois, was part of the regional list of a dozen theaters advertised in the *Decatur Herald*. Among his two Paramount films booked that week, Meyers showed *The Ghost in the Garret* starring Dorothy Gish. "Picture arrived late, causing the smallest crowd of the year. Am through with these 'weeks.'"[79] His resolve didn't last long; the Liberty in Ivesdale was listed again in the seventh annual Paramount Week regional ad in Decatur, showing Gloria Swanson in *Bluebeard's Eighth Wife* on September 6, 1924. The draw of taking part in Paramount Week's annual national advertising tie-in was one day's free publicity in a nearby city's weekend paper, but the need to coordinate publicity regionally, well in advance, exposed the drawbacks of centrally managed advertising for these independent theatre owners.

By 1922, Paramount was conducting promotional weeks on a quarterly basis and many other studios were using similar sales pitches. Some independent exhibitors became weary and skeptical of the gimmick. G. W. Yeaton, manager of the Ioka Theater in Exeter, New Hampshire, wrote a wry assessment of the situation to the *Exhibitors Herald*: "A salesman calls upon us and says such a week has been set aside as Witchcraft Film Week. If you will book this week solid with Witchcraft pictures, you will be doing him a personal favor. [. . .] We fall for it as usual, although no reduction in prices is ever offered during this week. Only once in a while, a little free advertising, which does them more good than us, as it seldom advertises anything except Witchcraft Week."[80] Paramount's national advertising (see figure 23.4) may have worked well to elevate the motion picture to a mainstay of mass, middlebrow consumption, but a contradiction lay exposed. The rhetoric relied on conspicuous distribution to almost all theaters, almost everywhere, but the campaigns also spotlighted the relative importance and profitability of first-run metropolitan movie palaces. And, of course, Paramount possessed a controlling or direct interest in many of these same premiere theaters.

From 1917 for half a decade, Paramount advertising had illustrated how to make movies an everyday entertainment, and Paramount Week advertising had charted the hierarchy of film distribution. Together, these ad campaigns represent a genuinely remarkable achievement of modern promotion and conspicuous distribution, but the costly effort was never adopted systematically by other film studios, and even Paramount soon changed emphasis for its ads. After 1922, Hanff-Metzger's national advertising campaign for Paramount more or less abandoned its illustrations of idyllic family moviegoing. Instead, magazine ads focused on the roster of movie stars and specific new feature films. Some ads profiled first-run palaces and regional chain showmen but no longer illustrated the generic story that bound together all sites of moviegoing. Paramount Week continued to use newspaper advertising extensively for a few more years but by 1928 stopped including lists of participating local theaters showing Paramount films.

Paramount's early use of advertising agencies nonetheless illustrates the vital role of publicity in the classical Hollywood system. Advertising designed and circulated by H. E. Lesan and Hanff-Metzger was as important as studio policy in creating and

FIGURE 23.4 Advertising for the fourth annual Paramount Week in Minneapolis focused on downtown first-run movie palaces but listed dozens of theaters across its entire metropolitan region. *Minneapolis Tribune*, September 4, 1921.

standardizing Paramount's brand. The Lesan Agency designed its trademark; Hanff-Metzger displayed its predominance as a cornerstone of middle-class life. On a smaller scale, other studios conducted advertising campaigns in magazines and metropolitan newspapers. National advertising and publicity for Hollywood movies soon became a routine part of commercial radio and television broadcasting. In conclusion, let me reiterate how national advertising acted as a totem of servitude for exhibitors—a gift that couldn't be refused—a symbolic parallel to corporate control that paralleled the agglomeration of Hollywood-owned theatre chains. National publicity extended the work of film production into a direct address to the mass moviegoing public, extending the work of distribution into the realm of exhibition. National-scale ad campaigns may have been proffered as a free gift to assist the work of local exhibitors, but the indirect costs included symbolic dominance under the studio trade-mark. Mass-marketing films through the conspicuous display of their wide distribution benefitted the brand of the producer above all.

Notes

1. "Will Distribute Films," *New York Times*, May 21, 1914, 11; "Feature Firms Form Marketing Combine," *Motion Picture News*, May 30, 1914, 33. On Paramount's early years, see Mark Lynn Anderson, "The Historian Is Paramount," *Film History* 26, no. 2 (2014): 1–30; Douglas Gomery, "What Was Adolph Zukor Doing in 1927?" *Film History* 17, nos. 2–3 (2005): 205–216; Michael J. Quinn, "Paramount and Early Feature Distribution, 1914–1921," *Film History* 11, no. 1 (1999): 98–113.
2. Hodkinson would distribute Paramount features in the Western states; Vice-President James Steele held the rights for much of the Midwest; Secretary-Treasurer Raymond Pawley controlled the rights for mid-Atlantic states; two other directors, William L. Sherry and Hiram Abrams, held the rights for New York and New England, respectively. "Feature Firms Form Marketing Combine," *Motion Picture News*, May 30, 1914, 33.
3. "Hodkinson on Visit to Coast," *Moving Picture World*, July 25, 1914, 579.
4. Jan Cohn, *Creating America: George Horace Lorimer and The Saturday Evening Post* (Pittsburgh, PA: University of Pittsburgh Press, 1989), 9; Louise Appleton, "Distillations of Something Larger: The Local Scale and American National Identity," *Cultural Geographies* 9, no. 4 (2002): 423.
5. Douglas Gomery, "The Movies Become Big Business: Publix Theatres and the Chain Store Strategy," *Cinema Journal* 18, no. 2 (1979): 27.
6. Bert Moran, "Away from Beaten Paths," *Exhibitors Trade Review*, September 23, 1922, 1099.
7. "Who Are the Joneses?" *Motion Picture News*, December 14, 1918, 3435.
8. William Paul, *When Movies Were Theater: Architecture, Exhibition, and the Evolution of America Film* (New York: Columbia University Press, 2016), 351. For a contemporary critique of metaphors equating Hollywood with other big businesses, see William Marston Seabury, *The Public and the Motion Picture Industry* (New York: Macmillan, 1926), 37.
9. William A. Johnston, "National Advertising: When Exhibitors Shouted 'Hooray,'" *Motion Picture News*, January 25, 1919, 525.
10. William A. Johnston, "National Advertising II: Reasons Why the Exhibitor Is Nucleus of Advertising," *Motion Picture News*, February 1, 1919, 678.
11. William A. Johnston, "The Newspaper and the Picture," *Motion Picture News*, May 1, 1920, 3815.
12. Janet Staiger, "Announcing Wares, Winning Patrons, Voicing Ideals: Thinking about the History and Theory of Film Advertising," *Cinema Journal* 29, no. 3 (1990): 3–31; Jane

Gaines, "From Elephants to Lux Soap: The Programming and 'Flow' of Early Motion Picture Exploitation," *Velvet Light Trap* 25 (1990): 29–43.

13. "Movie Ad Men in Association," *Fourth Estate*, August 5, 1916, 12.
14. Paul S. Moore, "Advance Newspaper Publicity for the Vitascope and the Mass Address of Cinema's Reading Public," in André Gaudreault, Nicolas Dulac, and Santiago Hidalgo, eds., *A Companion to Early Cinema* (Malden, MA: Wiley-Blackwell, 2012), 381–397; Paul S. Moore, "Subscribing to Publicity: Syndicated Newspaper Features for Moviegoing in North America, 1911–1915," *Early Popular Visual Culture* 12, no. 2 (2014): 260–273.
15. Advertising and promotional gimmicks have especially received attention in relation to the feminized character of movie fandom. See Kathryn H. Fuller-Seeley, "Dish Night at the Movies: Exhibitor Promotions and Female Audiences during the Great Depression," in Jon Lewis and Eric Smoodin, eds., *Looking Past the Screen: Case Studies in American Film History and Method* (Durham, NC: Duke University Press, 2007), 246–275; Moya Luckett, "Advertising and Femininity: The Case of 'Our Mutual Girl,'" *Screen* 40, no. 4 (1999): 363–383; Charlie Keil, "Studio Girls: Female Stars and the Logic of Brand Names," in Sofia Bull and Astrid Söderbergh Widding, eds., *Not So Silent: Women in Cinema Before Sound* (Stockholm: Acta Universitatis Stockholmiensis, 2010), 278–285.
16. Richard Abel, *Menus for Movieland: Newspapers and the Emergence of American Film Culture, 1913–1916* (Berkeley: University of California Press, 2015).
17. On the history of advertising agencies, see Liz McFall, "What About the Old Cultural Intermediaries? An Historical Review of Advertising Producers," *Cultural Studies* 16, no. 4 (2002): 532–552; Stephen Fox, *The Mirror Makers: A History of American Advertising and Its Creators* (Urbana: University of Illinois Press, 1997).
18. For example, in the column "Exhibitors Advertising: A Department of Motion Picture Exploitation," *Exhibitors Herald*, March 1920 to December 1921.
19. For example, "Exhibitor's Accessories" in the *Paramount Press Books* for 1919 notes costs of ten to ninety cents for promotional lithographs, photographs, slides, printing cuts, and layouts, but newspaper-use mats and half-toned photographs were free, as were cuts of studio trademarks.
20. Jeffrey Klenotic, "From Mom-and-Pop to Paramount-Publix: Selling the Community on the Benefits of National Theatre Chains," in Karina Aveyard and Albert Moran, eds., *Watching Films: New Perspectives on Moviegoing, Exhibition and Reception* (Bristol, UK: Intellect, 2013), 189–208; Gregory A. Waller, "Imagining and Promoting the Small-Town Theater," *Cinema Journal* 44, no. 3 (2005): 3–19.
21. Terry Ramsaye summarized succinctly: "The formation of First National [. . .] set in action a counter movement of distributors, notably Famous Players-Lasky Corporation, toward theater control. The war began to be fought in terms of theater seats quite as much as in stars and pictures." Ramsaye, "The Romantic History of the Motion Picture," *Photoplay*, March 1925, 118. See also "What Do You Think?" *Wid's Film Daily*, December 1, 1918, 1; and "Battle Starts," *Wid's Film Daily*, June 9, 1920, 1.
22. Thorstein Veblen, *The Theory of the Leisure Class* (Amherst, NY: Prometheus, 1998), 75.
23. Marcel Mauss, *The Gift: The Form and Reason for Exchange in Archaic Societies* (New York: Routledge, 1990), 52.
24. Pierre Bourdieu, *Outline of a Theory of Practice* (New York: Cambridge University Press, 1977), 192.
25. William Marston Seabury, *The Public and the Motion Picture Industry* (New York: Macmillan, 1926), 42. See also Robert Sklar, "Hub of the System: New York's Strand

Theater and the Paramount Case," *Film History* 6, no. 2 (1994): 197–205; Douglas Gomery, "The Picture Palace: Economic Sense or Hollywood Nonsense?" *Quarterly Review of Film Studies* 3, no. 1 (1978): 23–36.

26. The syndicated *Associated Sunday Magazine*, for example, boasted a combined circulation of more than a million copies weekly in 1907, from distribution in just nine Sunday newspapers, whose territory collectively included eighty-nine percent of the US population in thirty-nine states. "Kernels No. 6 Distribution," *Detroit Free Press*, July 9, 1907, 10.

27. Benjamin B. Hampton, *A History of the Movies* (New York: Covici-Friede, 1931), 173. Hampton anchors this explanation in newspaper circulation and the regional reach of metropolitan newspapers far beyond their nominal cities of publication.

28. "Par's Publicity For B.O.," *Variety*, November 16, 1927, 5.

29. George D. Proctor, "The Circuit—Its Growing Importance," *Motion Picture News*, February 28, 1914, 19.

30. Adolph Zukor, "Action of Exhibitors Themselves Forced Famous Players to Acquire Theatre Chain," *Moving Picture World*, June 19, 1920, 1568.

31. Richard Maltby, "The Standard Exhibition Contract and the Unwritten History of the Classical Hollywood Cinema," *Film History* 25, nos. 1–2 (2013): 144. Maltby is referring, of course, to the Roscoe "Fatty" Arbuckle scandal.

32. Abel, *Menus for Movieland*, 47. Pathé Frères advertisements began with an overview "The Rooster Stands for Quality," *Chicago Tribune*, February 6, 1910, II.5.

33. Abel, *Menus for Movieland*, 48–50. The Nichols-Finn Agency of Chicago handled Mutual's pioneering ad campaign late in 1913. "Tips for the Ad Manager," *Editor & Publisher*, November 1913, 438.

34. Abel, *Menus for Movieland*, 60. The Witt K. Cochrane Agency of Chicago handled Universal's national advertising. "Big Advertising Campaign," *Editor & Publisher*, November 1913, 438.

35. Paul S. Moore, "Everybody's Going: City Newspapers and the Early Mass Market for Movies," *City & Community* 4, no. 4 (2005): 339–357.

36. See, H. E. Lesan, "How the Paramount Trade-Mark was Made," *Paramount Pep-O-Grams*, May 15, 1931, 3, reprinted from *Printers' Ink*, April 1931.

37. Abel, *Menus for Movieland*, 55–56. "Paramount Pictures Campaign," *Editor & Publisher*, August 28, 1915, 286; Frank Leroy Blanchard, "Photo-Play Makers are Spending a Million a Year in Newspapers," *Editor & Publisher*, October 30, 1915, 529.

38. "We Show Paramount Pictures," *Saturday Evening Post*, February 6, 1915, 28.

39. John H. Kunsky, "Hot Shots from a Hot Town!" *Motion Picture News*, November 30, 1918, 3195.

40. John H. Kunsky, "National Advertising Idea," *Motion Picture News*, December 7, 1918, 3353.

41. Ibid., 3353–3354.

42. Detroit theaters later became a legal test case in 1922 when Paramount began providing Kunsky its pictures, reneging on an existing competitor's exclusive franchise of the Paramount program. "No First Choice under Famous Players Franchise," *Variety*, August 11, 1922, 38.

43. For example, Leon H. Grandjean, director of publicity for the Saenger Chain in New Orleans, "On National Advertising; Hurray for Kunsky!" *Motion Picture News*, December 28, 1918, 3861.

44. Tarkington Baker, director of publicity for Universal, "National Advertising," *Motion Picture News*, February 1, 1919, 680.

45. Jason Rogers, *Building Newspaper Advertising: Selling the By-Product of the Newspaper* (New York: Harper & Brothers, 1919); William H. Rankin, "Rankin Advocates for Advertisers," *Editor & Publisher*, June 5, 1919, 14–16, reprinted widely as Rankin, "National Newspaper Advertising: How, When and Where to Use it," *Washington Star*, July 18, 1919, 6, and elsewhere.
46. The company's first dealing with the film industry was an emergency consultation with General Film Company in December 1913. "Mutual Publicity Campaign Jolts Competitors to Life," *Variety*, December 12, 1913, 13.
47. Hanff-Metzger, Inc., "The Other Twenty Million," *New York Times*, September 28, 1917, 6.
48. "New Hanff-Metzger Agency," *Printers' Ink*, July 3, 1913, 12.
49. "Mainly About Advertising People," *Advertising News*, December 1, 1916, 23.
50. Hyman L. Roth, "The Application of Statistics to Advertising and Marketing," *Publications of the American Statistical Association* 15, no. 116 (1916): 465.
51. "Blue Printing a Sales and Advertising Campaign," *Advertising & Selling*, April 1914, 36; see also Hanff-Metzger Inc., "To a Manufacturer," *New York Herald*, June 11, 1920, 9. The company was certainly on par in technique with J. Walter Thompson (and located on Madison Avenue earlier). See Peggy J. Kreshel, "Advertising Research in the Pre-Depression Years: A Cultural History," *Journal of Current Issues and Research in Advertising* 15, no. 1 (1993): 59–75.
52. Hanff-Metzger Inc., "To a Manufacturer," *New York Herald*, May 14, 1920, 3.
53. A total of twenty-one magazines are listed with a combined circulation of twelve million copies in "F. P.-Lasky Campaign Starts," *Motion Picture News*, December 13, 1919, 4284. At least three hundred different ads were printed in the twelve years spanning 1917 to 1928, only 220 of them in *Saturday Evening Post*.
54. "Artcraft" was formally a separate distributor of specialty features, but the distinction quickly became blurred. The 1917 term "Paramount and Artcraft Pictures" became hyphenated "Paramount-Artcraft" in 1919, then simply "Paramount Pictures" in January 1920. The "Artcraft" trademark was cast off entirely in 1921.
55. W. Livingston Larned, "Putting Over The Big Campaigns: Motion Picture Industry Discovers The Great Power of Newspaper Publicity," *Fourth Estate*, December 1, 1917, 33.
56. Ibid., referring to the Paramount ad, "And There You Will Find Your Old Sweetheart Again," *New York Times*, November 17, 1917, 9. The ad had appeared weeks earlier, for example, in *New York Evening World*, October 22, 1917, 4, and was also published in *Saturday Evening Post*, December 8, 1917, 32.
57. Hanff-Metzger Inc., "What Advertising Word is Most Abused?" *New York Herald*, June 10, 1920, 24.
58. "Keeping the Family Together," *Saturday Evening Post*, March 23, 1918, 32.
59. "What's on Tonight?" *Saturday Evening Post*, January 11, 1919, 41.
60. "Out of the Kitchen into the World," *Saturday Evening Post*, February 22, 1919, 56; "It's Father's Turn Home Tonight," *Saturday Evening Post*, May 17, 1919, 56.
61. "Let Us Off at That Paramount Sign" *Saturday Evening Post*, July 10, 1920, 58.
62. "Four, Please!" *Saturday Evening Post*, April 5, 1920, 43.
63. "Aladdin's Lamp," *Saturday Evening Post*, October 4, 1919, 39; "The Crystal of Life," *Saturday Evening Post*, September 21, 1918, 60; "The Curtain of Life," *Saturday Evening Post*, March 22, 1919, 88.
64. "The End of Perfect Day," *Saturday Evening Post*, July 26, 1919, 37.
65. "What's the Best Show in Town?" *Saturday Evening Post*, October 18, 1919, 57.

66. Paul S. Moore, "'It Pays to Plan 'Em': The Newspaper Movie Directory and the Paternal Logic of Mass Consumption," in Richard Maltby, Daniel Biltereyst, and Philippe Meers, eds., *Companion to New Cinema History: Audiences, Reception and Experience* (New York: Routledge, 2019), 365–377.
67. In 1923, *Exhibitors Herald* reported extensive results to a survey asking "Is National Advertising Helping You?" The headline stated the consensus clearly: "Exhibitor Sentiment Strongly Against National Advertising," *Exhibitors Herald*, May 26, 1923, 31–38.
68. "Celebrating..." from Paramount Week advertisements in hundreds of newspapers across the United States, August 31 to September 5, 1922.
69. Summary figures from Paramount Week Trade Advertisement, *Motion Picture News*, July 24, 1920, 688; "Movie Season Opens with a Paramount Week," *Louisville Courier-Journal*, September 3, 1922, 19. These figures are clearly for publicity purposes, even the specificity of 434 cities with populations above ten thousand in 1920. Ayer's 1920 Annual listed more than 750 such cities. *American Newspaper Annual and Directory* (Philadelphia, PA: N. W. Ayer & Sons, 1920), 19–30.
70. Kathryn H. Fuller, "'You Can Have the Strand in Your Own Town': The Marginalization of Small Town Film Exhibition in the Silent Film Era," *Film History* 6, no. 2 (1994): 166–177.
71. Other experiments with national advertising of first-run engagements included ads timed to correspond with local exhibitions or listing first-run theatres. See "Goldwyn Expands Exploitation," *Motion Picture News*, November 1, 1919, 3327; ad for Paramount's *Peter Pan*, *Saturday Evening Post*, December 27, 1924, 76–77.
72. "Los Angeles Wins Famous Players' Prize for Paramount Week Showing," *Wid's Film Daily*, November 12, 1919, 2.
73. "F. P.-L. Making Big Arrangements for 7th Annual Paramount Week," *Moving Picture World*, August 30, 1924, 696.
74. For example, *Wellington* (KS) *News*, September 2, 1921, 8; *Charlotte* (NC) *News*, September 3, 1922, 14; *Mansfield* (OH) *News*, September 2, 1923, II.7.
75. "Dill—One of Us," *Paramount Pep*, March 27, 1922, 3.
76. "Metro Week is to be an Annual Event," *Moving Picture World*, February 19, 1921, 945; "Solid Booking, Solid Gold is Slogan for Goldwyn Week," *Moving Picture World*, July 30, 1921, 527; "September 11 to 17 Is Announced as Fox Film Week for This Year," *Moving Picture World*, July 30, 1921, 537; "First National Week Set for February 18 to 25," *Moving Picture World*, January 28, 1922, 385; "Special Plans Made for Holiday Season," *Moving Picture World*, November 4, 1922, 57.
77. "What the Picture Did for Me," *Exhibitors Herald*, October 14, 1922, 76.
78. "A Costly Slip Up," *Exhibitors Herald*, October 21, 1922, 74.
79. "What the Picture Did for Me," *Exhibitors Herald*, December 30, 1922, 157.
80. "How about 'Exhibitors' Week'?" *Exhibitors Herald*, February 18, 1922, 62.

PART V

NATION, EMPIRE, WORLD

The Spaces and Times of Modernity

CHAPTER 24

GOING SILENT ON MODERNITY

Periodization, Geopolitics, and Public Opinion

GIORGIO BERTELLINI

Let us assume two consecutive periods taken out of the uninterrupted sequence of the ages. To what extent does the connection which the flow of time sets between them predominate, or fail to predominate over the differences born out of the same flow?

Marc Bloch[1]

The study of early cinema must always serve as a challenge to film history, not simply the study of a specific period, but a challenge which constantly causes us to re-examine the terms of film history: the nature of cinema and periodization itself.

Tom Gunning[2]

IN her groundbreaking essay on modernity in early Latin American cinema, Ana M. López has warned against the dangers and pitfalls of "directly superimpos[ing] the developmental grid of US and European film history [. . .] on the Latin American experience."[3] To understand modernity in the Latin American context, she claims, one should not just point to a convergence of novel industrial, social, and cultural developments. Instead, one should also look at these developments *dialectically*, as made up of dramatic and persisting conflicts such as national versus foreign cultures, city versus countryside, and urban and cosmopolitan versus non-urban and vernacular. While following her sound advice of avoiding facile comparisons and projections, scholars working on areas that are distant from Euro-American centers may nonetheless be tempted to elaborate notions of *alternative modernities*.[4] This may be a necessary first step, particularly in terms of framing and assessing initial research findings, but it comes with the risk of granting Euro-American modernity a modeling role that turns all other versions into subordinate and tributary ones—*alternative*, that is.

López's essay, I would argue, invites another, more radical possibility, one that, given the structural transatlantic framework of Latin American history in terms of sovereignty, commerce, and culture, looks at the established articulation of early cinema's modernity from a global, geopolitical perspective. What was occurring in New York or Paris was also structurally interwoven with other, remote contexts. Or, phrasing it differently, if we take seriously a critical framework that insists on "a heightened geocultural sensibility for local and even peripheral *placedness*," to use one of López's phrases, we ought also to challenge past and recent tendencies to celebrate the modernity of early Euro-American cinema as a universal center and mode. Modernity's idealistic quality may in fact lie in an apparent obliviousness to its own distinct cultural underpinnings, including its selective Western metropolitan placedness. What López's argument ultimately stimulates is an epistemological revision of universalist claims often attached to both early and late twentieth-century accounts of cinema and modernity.

In a recent essay on theories of modernity, philosopher Charles Taylor has offered a productive framework to think through said epistemological shift. Without having film studies in mind, Taylor sets out to distinguish between "cultural" and "acultural" formulations of modernity.[5] A cultural approach, he argues, sees modern transformation as the rise of a new, distinct culture with its specific understanding of personhood, social relations, and morality. An acultural theory of modernity, instead, "describes modern transformation in terms of some culture-neutral operation [. . .] that is not defined in terms of the specific cultures it carries us from and to, but is rather seen as of a type that any traditional culture could undergo."[6] At the heart of this acultural framework is praise for a broad "growth of reason," associated with the development of a scientific consciousness, a secular outlook, and an instrumental rationality, all resulting from increased mobility, urbanization, and industrialization. As a whole, these dynamics are not perceived as relative to a *specific cultural constellation* but instead emerge as *universal*, namely as prone to be the subject of experience within every culture. When read through this perspective, the acultural dimension of the cinema/modernity argument becomes apparent in the way it underplays distinct cultural markers, such as class, racial, and ethnic differences, in a celebration of technological spectacle and progress.[7]

In one of the most enlightening recastings of the cinema/modernity argument, Ben Singer appears first to contradict López's charge when he describes the distinct circumstances of modernity's emergence by way of, to use Taylor's language, an appealingly *cultural* description. "The emergence of cinema," he argues, "was predicated on a *specific* convergence of modern technology (mechanical engineering, chemistry, optics, electricity, etc.); on systems of speculative investment and industrial rationalization applied to the efficient manufacture and distribution of amusement; on massive urbanization; on the subsequent coalescence of a mass audience [in possession of] a modicum of expendable income [. . .]; on the cultural permissibility of heterosocial public circulation [. . .]; on extensive transportation and communications networks."[8] At closer inspection, however, this apparently culturally specific combination of technological advancements and attendant social changes is attributed to an unspecified yet transnational Western universe that is nonetheless charged to define an epoch. The statement that "cinema *was* only possible in the modern era" appears then as an obvious sequitur to an implicitly universal inventory of modern phenomena.[9] In this narrative, modernity's impact is indicative not just of a "growth of reason" but also—and I am complicating Taylor's diagnosis here—of an intensification of corporeal effects. In Singer's account, the same rationalization of urban and public life, including the novelty of the "film-viewing experience," prompts a range of distinct bodily reactions (i.e., shock, thrills, and a heightened perceptual intensity of daily experience), which altogether turn cinema into "the mirror of modern life."[10] In Singer's account, the diagnosis of what modernity entails seamlessly advances from a specific (and selective) identification of enabling historical circumstances to a broad, acultural assessment. Scholars have variously deployed this comprehensive formulation of modernity to address adaptive modes of representation and narration in conjunction with new forms of film exhibition and their resulting modes of cultural consumption and experience. A universalizing language of corporeal effects has informed scholarly diagnoses of modernity against other cogent and potentially disruptive counter-narratives centered on issues of social difference (e.g., gender, race, and class).[11]

A few critics of this so-called modernity thesis have questioned its epistemological foundation in relation to its idealizing penchant for an epochal logic, claim of a radical change in human perception, or devaluing of geographical differences and spatial politics.[12] Others have questioned its heuristic value for American cinema in relation to the broad set of representational, narrative, and institutional changes grouped under the expression "transitional period."[13] Drawing on Taylor's "cultural" formulation, I wish to articulate a different critical approach. To address and challenge the modernity discourse of early Euro-American cinema, I look at the rarely discussed issue of periodization.[14] The apparently contingent question of dates, I argue, provides a platform to expose tacit historiographical stipulations that mask the geographical placedness of dominant constructions of modernity. For the study of film history, revisiting the familiar periodizing distinction between "early" versus "silent" cinema may enable us to unveil the methodological penchants informing acultural constructions of modernity. For instance, only rarely does the modernity argument extend its reach to 1920s America or 1920s Europe. Instead, when addressing the postwar years, it goes silent, as if the phenomena that in the earlier years had prompted radical and unprecedented transformations of moviegoers' lives had found closure and resolution.

Periodization

Once again, I wish to return to López's essay. In one important passage, it identifies the period "roughly 1896–1920" as encompassing "the early years of the silent cinema in Latin America."[15] To scholars working on US film culture, the association of this time span with the essay's titular reference to "early cinema" constitutes a slight incongruity. In American film studies, "early cinema" customarily refers to pre-1914 productions, as opposed to the subsequent period, variously described as "early Hollywood," "late silent cinema," or just "the 1920s." The six-year difference between the two dating frameworks, "1896–1914" versus "1896–1920," is not an inconsequential, antiquarian quibble: it includes one of the most extraordinary events in twentieth-century western history—World War I. What is the reason for such a notable difference in periodization?

The institutional history of "early cinema," as deliberately distinguished from "silent cinema," is largely linked to the activities and discourses of Domitor, the International Society for the Study of Early Cinema, established in 1985.[16] I asked two Domitor founders, Stephen Bottomore and Paolo Cherchi Usai, to clarify the rationale of the association's target periodization, specifically the criteria for early cinema's end-term. They graciously responded to my query with a matching response. Bottomore promptly replied: "The Domitor cut-off date was set at about 1914, which seemed to make sense with the beginning of WWI, a war that almost from the outset had a huge effect on film industries *globally*."[17] Paolo Cherchi Usai fully concurred with Bottomore on the crucial importance of the Great War for the ways Domitor framed this chronological divide (*ante quem*). He also added that other critical variables arose during the discussions—including the emergence of feature films, the consolidation of cinema as an industry, and the decline of the so-called cinema of attractions.[18]

I find their replies enlightening. At the time of the organization's founding, Domitor members did not ignore or deny the importance of the Great War for the global development of motion pictures. On the contrary, they saw it as paramount. Yet, *because of it*, they decided to keep the war out of consideration in the study of the early period. This decision has had a major critical impact. Discussions about the modernity of motion pictures, in fact, have often followed Domitor's historical periodization. While nowadays US film historiography does not advance a single, agreed-upon reason for the now customary separation between early and silent cinema, it commonly refrains from hailing the war as a key divider. The result has been consequential. If the category of "early cinema," in fact, identifies the chronological boundaries for reading cinema in terms of modernity, at least within film studies, and if the framework of early cinema does not conventionally include the war as its constitutive end-term, the resulting formulations of modernity do not regard the war as one of its constitutive features. For the proponents of a link between cinema and modern experience, the war appears to be playing no relevant role, as if its allegedly accidental significance to film history made it morphologically extrinsic to the phenomenon of modernity. Yet for film historians working on American cinema who do *not* engage with the modernity thesis, the war has often assumed the status of momentous cultural divider, functioning as a launch pad for US cinema's global hegemony. The constitutive processes of that reach have in consequence been underexamined in relation to the processes detailed in the modernity thesis.[19]

Given the war's dramatic relevance for European film production and consumption, a truly *culturalist* conception of modernity that were to regard the war as a key phenomenon would have to make distinctions between the European and the American experience. Since considerations about the war are absent from discussions of early cinema's modernity, so are differentiations between the European and the American contexts. One has therefore to conclude that, both because of choices in periodization and the attendant exclusion of the world conflict, the conception of modernity that is being presented as "defined in terms of the specific cultures," to borrow again from Taylor, is in reality being applied in culturally unspecific terms.

This may explain a highly selective use of scholarly sources, particularly European ones. Singer's eloquent conceptual exposition of the key characters of Euro-American modernity abounds with European sources of evidence—from Ricciotto Canudo to several German and French commentators.[20] Yet, his omission of any reference to European writings about the wartime experience (1914–1918) should surprise, particularly in light of the growing body of work that over the years has explored the striking effects of the conflict on art in general and on avant-garde movements in particular.[21] Historian Emilio Gentile has described the total impact of such effects as amounting to the "apocalypse of modernity."[22]

Furthermore, Singer makes extensive use of terms and concepts (i.e., "shock" and "sensorium") derived from the work of the key interpreter of the modernity discourse, Walter Benjamin. Yet, Singer, like many of the proponents of the "dynamic model of the cinema-modernity nexus," does not acknowledge that for Benjamin, the experience of the war "had a decisive effect" on his worldview, as Martin Jay has noted, in that it provided "the traumatic background to [his] culture theory."[23] In fact, Benjamin's work on the tragic crisis of modern experience in response to the war's unprecedented scale of physical and perceptual violence may be more aptly referencing the European context, rather than the American one. Given that the war was fought "over there," and that the actual US war engagement lasted only eighteen months, the American experience of modernity may not be read through the lens of Benjamin's war-inflected view of the modern crisis of human experience (*Erfahrung*). Incidentally, in the postwar years American film historians Vachel Lindsay and Terry Ramsaye also insisted on how differently Europe and the US had experienced the war.[24] Running this argument to its logical conclusion, one would have to maintain that if the war provided a key cultural divider between Europe and America, any conceptualization of Euro-American modernity ought to make this distinction quite explicit, since such differences supply critical markers of *placedness*.

Geopolitics

The study of America cinema between 1914 and 1927 has customarily been concerned with identifying the period's key phenomena as the emergence of Hollywood, the standardization of new labor divisions, and the consolidation of the country's national imagery. Scholars have repeatedly stressed the period's key *modern* occurrences (e.g., women's voting rights and new public relevance; expanded interclass consumerism; pervasiveness of star discourse), without necessarily framing their accounts as updates or expansions of the modernity argument. Further, and similarly to early cinema inquiries, historians of late 1910s and 1920s Hollywood have generally *not* identified in the world conflict a crucial facet of Western cinematic modernity. What would a modernity argument look like for silent American cinema if it were to include the war and its effects upon American and global cinema from the late 1910s on? Without fully developing such an argument in the present essay, I would like to draw some of its general contours.

First, a discussion of *silent* cinema/modernity cannot entail the mere redeployment of an emphasis on expanded spectatorial experience—even an upgraded one. Instead, it ought to look at the war as a catalyst of dramatic global economic and cultural changes, variously affecting American film expression, reach, and standing on *both* national and international grounds, in ways that exceed questions of formal representation and international distribution. In this sense Ruth Vasey's 1997 *The World According to Hollywood* has been groundbreaking.[25] Building on Kristin Thompson's 1985 research into American film distribution in the silent period, Vasey's institutional study of post–World War I Hollywood shows how the industry organized its financial, studio, and political operations domestically and abroad into an "industry policy" that was much more impactful than the contingent adjustments prescribed by the Production Code.[26] By the late 1920s, she argues, the film industry managed to accommodate the demands of "big business, the political process, isolated lobby groups, or governments of other nations" in a way that ensured that Hollywood's output "could be distributed domestically and abroad with a minimum of disruption through censorship action or consumer resistance."[27] Vasey also shows how Hollywood's ensuing "Big Picture" homogenized the depiction of ethnic minorities in the US and of foreigners around the world into picturesque exotica and celebrated the democratic and corporate fabric of the US. Largely free from political and social contentiousness, but bursting with sublimated sexual imagery, the result was a "deliberate packaging of salable elements" that accustomed people in America and beyond to identify with the world of American motion pictures.[28]

My perspective does not contradict Vasey's narrative but seeks more cogently to read such broad processes, to use Amy Kaplan's words, as the "effects of the war on the internal bonds of national unity and the changing relations between the domestic and the foreign."[29] What I would call for would be a study of the domestic and global impact of the war on Hollywood's hegemonic practices and on their subsumption into, and contribution to, US imperial culture.

Admittedly, such endeavors are no easy scholarly task, due to the nationalistic inertia of film historiography and obvious linguistic barriers, resulting in the absence of a comparative analysis of cinema history during World War I.[30] Still, the first step in moving past familiar historiographical paths and recognizing, beyond representational references, the national/global reach of American cinema's modernity, is to acknowledge the non-negligible practical effects of the war *in* and *for* America.

Compared to some European countries that experienced the war's devastating consequences for more than four years, the US participation in World War I was considerably shorter and never involved US territory. Still, it entailed significant human and material costs, including those related to the influenza pandemic that hit the US nearly as hard as it did Europe.[31] The US Government mobilized about four million soldiers, ranking just behind Italy in total number, and spent about 17 billion dollars against the 20 and 23 billion dollars spent respectively by Germany and the UK. Beyond the mere scale of the military and material investments, the American cultural mobilization was colossal and pervasive. It was prompted by the newsworthiness of the events, the implications of the so-called war preparedness during the months preceding President Wilson's declaration of war, and the country's response to the government's countless policy initiatives. The final result was an exacerbation of the process of Americanization of US film culture, or "exaltation of nationness" in López's analysis, that found expression within the multi-national (yet ultimately American-dominated) domestic film market and which surpassed the earlier nationalistic manifestations so well described by Richard Abel for the pre-war years.[32]

The intense association of patriotism with cinematic newsworthiness during America's involvement should be underscored, since it countered the transnational dimension of filmic attractions with the appeal of nationalistic consensus. Battles had to be covered, either through heavily censored newsreels, reenactments, or fictionalized versions. Over the course of almost two years, Hollywood and such government agencies as the Committee on Public Information (CPI) produced patriotic fiction films, from *The Little American* (Mary Pickford Co./Artcraft, 1917) to *America's Answer* (US Army Signal Corps/CPI, 1918), as well as weekly newsreels aimed at supporting the morale of American spectators at home and US military men abroad.[33] The CPI also devised exceptional prowar initiatives, including the Four-Minute Men, consisting of short scripted speeches uttered by volunteers in movie theaters ahead of the shows. Similarly, the Treasury Department launched the Liberty Bonds Campaigns, starring iconic Hollywood figures (i.e., Mary Pickford, Douglas Fairbanks, Charles Chaplin, etc.). Such mobilization granted political import to stars, whose broad cultural resonance outside movie screens enabled Hollywood to appreciate its own exceptional power in shaping national public opinion, at home and abroad.[34]

When viewed from an international perspective, Hollywood's postwar film distribution benefited from broader structural changes in the global commercial and financial markets. The US was already controlling colonial outposts in the Atlantic and Pacific Oceans, but the Great War, even before the US intervention, brought unique opportunities as Europe was experiencing growing logistical and financial challenges.

For instance, American companies began increasing their investments in Cuban sugar, Chilean copper, and Argentine meat-packing, thereby partnering with countries that had long been within the British orbit of influence.[35] Even more important, American financial institutions, beginning with J. P. Morgan & Co., Dupont, and Kuhn, Loeb & Co., among others, began bankrolling the Allied war efforts by becoming their major supplier of goods and credit. Before the war was over, the US managed to shift from a "debtor nation to being the world's number one creditor," with New York replacing London as the center of world finance.[36] Likewise, the conflict favored US film distribution companies in Europe by cutting off France from Central and East-European markets and Germany from the Allied film circuits. Even before April 1917, Hollywood's rising world hegemony had reached such a level that the industry "ceased to focus so exclusively on Europe, both as a market and as a point of world distribution."[37] A few months before the US entered the conflict, in fact, Hollywood was no longer administering its international distribution to such distant locations as the Far East and South America from its London offices, as it had been up to that point, but from New York City.

Film historians have recognized how the destruction of European production facilities and the drying up of continental film financing enhanced Hollywood studios' domestic hegemony and unprecedented domination of foreign markets. In 1931, Benjamin B. Hampton wrote about the war events as securing "American conquest of the screens of the world," while a few years later, Lewis Jacobs stressed how the conflict had made Hollywood the "international production center for movies."[38] For a long time, as Ruth Vasey noted in 1997, researchers "largely overlooked the *influence* of the foreign market on Hollywood production," and seldom took into serious consideration "the extent to which Hollywood tailored its products to the requirements of its international audiences."[39] This still rather persistent historiographic neglect is particularly surprising given that, on the basis of data drawn from the US Department of Commerce, major film companies "derived an average of 35 percent of their gross revenue from the foreign field"—a proportion of international revenues larger than most American export industries.[40]

In the 1920s, Hollywood's international power was no secret, but it was often framed as *representational plasticity*. In his 1928 history of Adolph Zukor's Paramount Pictures, Will Irwin noted that "the more ambitious films were all produced with an eye to the export market," and that "specialists on foreign races edited and cut export films to fit the tastes, prejudices, and government regulations of fifty nations."[41] But beyond profitably tailoring narratives to foreign markets, there were other aspects to Hollywood's growing global reach that Irwin, despite being a former CPI foreign department chief, did not touch on. During the war, in fact, Hollywood films did not go abroad alone, nor did they just "naturally" achieve success by filling the vacuum of wartime entertainments with narrative adjustments mostly pertaining to heroic characterizations and happy endings. Without displaying the visual and narrative range of the postwar years, the American cinema of 1917–1918 significantly expanded its reach with the support of the CPI, which enhanced, promoted, and often forced the distribution of both educational and commercial American films into markets around the world. On the one hand, the CPI used the power that Hollywood had already established in foreign nations to market its own propaganda work and frame Hollywood's appeal as typically American: as the CPI's former director, George Creel, wrote in the 1920s about the successful and openly patriotic alliance between celebrated film stars and the CPI's less exciting feature film productions, "Charlie Chaplin and Mary Pickford led *Pershing's Crusaders* and *America's Answer* into the enemy's territory and smashed another Hindenburg line."[42] On the other hand, Hollywood gained in standing, both at home and abroad, through its association with the highest office in the land and authoritative identification with American values. The postwar history of the alliance between the US State Department and the Motion Picture Producers and Distributors of America (MPPDA)—established in 1922 to replace the failing National Association of the Motion Picture Industry—further expanded on the collaborative wartime template of power and persuasion and contributed to a commercial domination that was exceptionally profitable for Hollywood.[43] Rather than functioning merely to change Hollywood's public image in the face of the many scandals, "the MPPDA's original bylaws," as Kristin Thompson has noted, "charged it to represent the industry's interest abroad."[44] And represent it did. After establishing relationships with both foreign representatives of film companies and officials of the Departments of State and Commerce, the MPPDA facilitated American global economic preeminence by turning cinema into a sales agent for US commodities.[45] In turn, the alliance between private Hollywood firms and the government secured tremendous advantages for the industry's hegemonic aims, including regular and detailed information about foreign markets and critical advice in negotiations concerning foreign countries' protectionist policies.[46]

By war's end, industry and government had begun to learn to do public relations for each other's global ambitions by masking contingent geopolitical ambitions in the name of the universality of both the medium and American values. Supplying the industry's most coveted testimonial, President Wilson sold the pro-America alliance between the CPI and Hollywood on the ground of motion pictures' alleged expressive *universality*. Such a term provided a most conveniently acultural description of motion pictures' modernity, one that matched Wilson's own ideas about universal democracy. "The film has come to rank as the very highest medium for the dissemination of public intelligence," he was repeatedly quoted noting in 1918, "and since it speaks a *universal language*, it lends itself importantly to the presentation of America's plans and purposes."[47] Four decades later, the MPPDA's first and long-serving head, Will Hays, was still combining the same chauvinistic, sermonizing, and acultural registers in his justification of Hollywood's global ambitions. "There is a special reason why America should have given birth and prosperous nurture to the motion picture and its world-wide entertainment," Hays argued in his memoirs through the very recognizable rhetoric of universalism, democracy, and American exceptionalism. "America in the very literal sense is truly the world state. All races, all creeds, all men are to be found here."[48]

Beyond the convergence of economic and technological developments enhancing the experience of motion pictures as new and democratic, US participation in World War I provided a new primary scene of modernity. The novel appreciation of how the film industry could manage popular consensus served the intertwined interests of the country's political and economic power centers—at home and abroad—thereby binding Hollywood with America's liberal capitalism. A discussion of the modernity of late 1910s and 1920s Hollywood should therefore account for the industry's transition into one of the most effective conveyors of the country's ideals and purposes.[49]

I wish now to look closely at this transition by briefly considering a specific case, that of banker and film financier Otto Kahn, whose archival holdings allow us to see how postwar cinema's newly discovered power of mass persuasion, enhanced by financial consolidation and celebrity culture, could serve the converging aspirations of financial dominance and cultural influence. Kahn's case will allow me to return, and expand on, the vexed question of cinema and modernity in my conclusion.

Modern Finance and Public Opinion

The story is familiar. As studios competed with one another and sought to gain an advantage by acquiring control of stars and exhibition venues, they began to turn to investment and commercial banks to raise funds or secure loans. A few financial institutions had been quite active during the war and were seeking ways to invest capital derived from their European loans. Beginning in 1919, a new era of movie financing began. While J. P. Morgan did not enter the film business in the years immediately following the war, other banks did, including Kuhn, Loeb & Co. from New York City. A February 1920 *Variety* article spoke of an "invasion" to describe the unprecedented incursion of Wall Street's financing power into Hollywood's commercial sovereignty.[50] At the helm of Kuhn, Loeb & Co. was Otto Kahn, a popular personality, arts benefactor, and eloquent public speaker. His activity and public pronouncements may shed light on the relation between cinema and finance, not just in terms of investments and returns but also through the no less calculable function of shaping public opinion.[51]

Let us first consider the financial side. As several sources indicate, in 1919, Kuhn, Loeb & Co. financed Zukor's Famous Players-Lasky with a ten-million-dollar loan, which within three years enabled the company to purchase about three hundred first-class, first-run movie theaters.[52] The bank's bold financial decision was based on careful consideration of both domestic and international factors. Before proceeding, Kuhn, Loeb & Co. had commissioned a complete study of Famous Players-Lasky for H.D.H. Connick, vice president of the Morgan-controlled financial firm American International Corporation.[53] Filled with statistics and financial figures related to imported/exported films, box-office receipts, and number of foreign movie theaters, the study ended with a surprising conclusion: the studios' largest return was in *exhibition*, not manufacturing. Addressing the widespread perception that stars' salaries were one of the industry's major problems, the report instead described compensation as a matter of supply and demand, and identified performers' vital role in the industry's exhibition and financial prospects.[54] The report praised Famous Players-Lasky's roster of stars and directors, which gave tangible value to the company's films but also suggested, in an overt recognition of publicity, "a more aggressive sales campaign" to increase domestic and foreign rental returns.[55] As both a banker and an industry advocate, Kahn fully appreciated the novel extent to which the motion-picture business could, beyond contingent financial gains, mold public opinion through aggressive publicity. As a frequent speaker at public events, he did not hesitate to vouch for the unique cultural and political opportunities that motion pictures enjoyed by virtue of their modern power of mass persuasion.

In an address, titled "The Motion Picture," delivered at the Paramount Sales Convention Banquet (Washington, DC) on May 2, 1928, Kahn intertwined praise for cinema's soundness as a business with recognition of its democratic value as a shaper of public sentiments.[56] To best explain how motion pictures took hold of "the emotional impulses of the people" and represented the most effective democratic factor in American life, even ahead of the automobile and the radio, he told of a curious historical coincidence. He recounted how two public Individuals, Rudolph Valentino and the former Harvard University president Charles William Eliot, died on the same day, August 23, 1926, and how the reactions of the American media and the American people to these deaths differed dramatically.[57] For the Harvard man, Kahn remarked, "public opinion rendered respectful and reverential tribute," mostly in short pieces placed on newspapers' internal pages.[58] For Valentino's death, conversely, front-page titles "brought forth a veritable flood of popular grief, expressing itself in almost hysterical demonstrations as his body was transported across the country." To those who denounced the disparity of merits and reactions, not to mention the questionable taste of public demonstrations, Kahn objected by pointing out what today might seem obvious—cinema's unique capacity to arouse national mass participation. Rather than a morbid fad, he argued, to many millions Valentino, even in death, represented "the very embodiment and symbol [of] romance, beauty, grace, chivalry, and youth," for "his art and personality on the screen had endowed, enriched, and beautified their lives."[59] In Kahn's estimation, Valentino's death revealed motion pictures' American triumph as a modern phenomenon. If, from a business perspective, "the credit facilities [. . .] are ample [and] their securities have a ready market," from a cultural standpoint, cinema had expanded its reach so dramatically that it ought to be taken seriously as a legitimate phenomenon. Kahn invited his audience of business investors not to linger on high-minded or moral objections, but to consider that "the public taste has advanced and become more discriminating." His apology for motion pictures was also an apology for Americanism.[60] As both an art and an industry, Kahn concluded, motion pictures "present a striking parallel to that dualism of the spiritual and material which I consider as one of the most notable and distinguishing characteristics of America." Cinema, in other words, represented that most American combination, "in fifty-fifty proportion," of "hard-headed business capacity and deep-seated idealism."[61] The modern cinematic alchemy of the period, he concluded, in a display of Wilsonian rhetoric, was exactly the matching of an idealism of universal cultural values with commercial and geopolitical interests. "The American film," he ultimately argued, "is an advertising medium of remarkable effectiveness in making known all kinds of American products throughout the world, and a powerful agent in stimulating their sale."[62]

In addition to his more recent role in financing Paramount, Kahn's wartime experience of coupling financial return with propaganda made him a credible public advocate of postwar cinema's comparable development—namely an alignment of commercial success with cultural influence. American cinema could play a pivotal role in realizing goals of commercial and cultural expansion, because, in his words, it "is an advertising medium of remarkable effectiveness."[63] Within this novel framework, motion pictures were not just modern mass entertainment but an efficient operation of mass publicity, shaping public opinion.[64] Kahn's speech was spelling out *and* embracing what a few public intellectuals, who were skeptical of the utopian rhetoric of mass appeal, had also noticed. One of them was the influential editorialist and *New Republic* co-editor Walter Lippmann.

In his 1922 *Public Opinion*, Lippmann had come to view cinema and image-making in general as a most effective, pervasive, and at times pernicious medium of mass experience. His starting point was a critical assessment of democratic participation that depended on the distorting manipulation of ordinary human knowledge. In the past, Lippmann argued, individual subjects directly experienced the outside world and acted on such knowledge. In the modern, "hurried and multifarious" life of his time, human knowledge resulted from an interaction with "prejudices," or "pictures in our heads," and thus from "the insertion between man and his environment of a pseudo-environment" to which "his behavior is a response." As a result, Lippmann observed, "the analyst of public opinion must begin by recognizing the *triangular relationship* between the scene of action, the human picture of that scene, and the human response to that picture."[65]

The expressions "mental pictures" and "pictures in our heads" were obviously not original to Lippmann but had a wider and often different currency, which brings us back to cinema as a form of knowledge. A September 1918 *Photoplay* editorial, titled "War and the Fifth Estate," self-servingly praised cinema for providing Americans with an understanding of what the war implied. "As they gained a first-hand knowledge of events from the physical pictures on the screens," the editorial read, "their *mental pictures of the war* broadened into a true perspective of its overwhelming importance."[66] In Lippmann's analysis, however, photography and motion pictures' powers of realistic visualization, namely their "authority over imagination," acquired a troublesome resilience outside the confines of the movie theater and served as an agent of public-opinion manipulation. To support his argument, he turned to the most successful film of the silent period, D. W. Griffith's racist blockbuster *The Birth of a Nation*, released in 1915, between the end of the early film period and the US intervention in World War I:

> The shadowy idea becomes vivid; your hazy notion, let us say, of the Ku Klux Klan, thanks to Mr. Griffiths [sic], takes vivid shape when you see the *Birth of a Nation*. Historically it may be the wrong shape, morally it may be a pernicious shape, but it is a shape, and I doubt whether anyone who has seen the film and does not know more about the Ku Klux Klan than Mr. Griffiths [sic], will ever hear the name again without seeing those white horsemen.[67]

The realism of the photographic or cinematic image, Lippmann added, did not just set the new medium apart from newspapers but affected what the press tended to cover. "There can be little doubt," he admitted, identifying a powerful feedback loop phenomenon, "that the moving picture is steadily building up imagery which is then evoked by the words people read in their newspapers."[68] Four decades before Daniel Boorstin introduced the notion of "pseudo-events," Lippmann's description of pseudo-environments allowed him to denounce the fallacy of modern human knowledge and, with it, of modern democratic life.[69] With a diametrically opposite attitude, a few years later Kahn arrived at a very similar conclusion: modern citizens in the US and elsewhere cannot always make judgments about the world based on first-hand knowledge. They have to rely on mental images, or advertisements of remarkable effectiveness that have been created for them. Whether judged positively or negatively, the radical modernity of postwar American cinema, I would argue, rested in films' increasingly sanctioned power to shape the perception of events, individuals, and even cinema itself, on both a domestic and international scale.

* * *

In conclusion, the conventional cleavage between early and silent cinema has had profound effects on film historiography—some productive, others much less so. Periodizing per se is not the problem. One of the heuristic gains of distinguishing between early and silent cinema has been the promotion of the category of "transitional cinema," which has been quite productive to the study of the changing relationship between film form and commerce. Discussions of cinema's modernity that do not consider the culturally specific impact of World War I, however, have resulted in a focus on technologically informed experiences that have often gone hand in hand with celebrations of democratic ideals of consumer access and civic progress. The adoption of a different historical periodization, one that accounts for the short- and long-term impact of the Great War, would recast the notion of modernity so that it includes critical assessments of Hollywood's partnering of its domestic and global hegemony with the country's financial and cultural leadership.

Admittedly, this is not wholly uncharted territory. One of the most influential contributions in assessing Hollywood's modernity beyond the early film period has been Miriam Hansen's 1999 essay on "vernacular modernism." With the goal of analyzing the nexus between modernity and modernism, Hansen historicizes classical Hollywood cinema as a set of modernist aesthetic practices and forms that altogether represent a distinctly American response to the economic and cultural changes of modern life. In her view, Hollywood's modernism, mislabeled "classical," best exemplifies the expansive recasting of Americanism into a globally dominant convergence of business practices, advanced technology, and mass consumption.[70] But by foregrounding the acultural terms of what she calls, following Benjamin, the "new sensorium," Hansen sidesteps Hollywood's—and thus America's—powerful contribution to the global spreading of a liberal economy. Spurred during the American involvement in the war, the alliance of the film industry with the US government and Wall Street made filmmakers, producers, government officials, and journalists realize that cinema could be a shaping force of public opinion, and thus a distinctly powerful vector of social governance, both in America and, especially, overseas. Within a research perspective that includes other geographical and economic contexts as part of a *relatable global history*, post-WWI American cinema may emerge as not just a successful exemplar of a global sensory experience but also a catalyst of national influence, international hegemony, and inevitable attritions.

The modernity of post-WWI American cinema may well have relied on the standardization of production and reception practices related to the division of labor, film genres, stars' on- and off-screen charisma, and the promises of mass consumption. But it also depended on another standardization, linked to the cultural and transnational synergy of press coverage, economic interests, and political goals. The emergence of the Hollywood dream factory meant the transformation of a Southern California outpost into a national paragon of both efficient storytelling and hegemonic public opinion management.

Two recent studies point the way for assessing the impact of this multi-dimensional convergence of media, finance, and politics in the interwar years. I view them as foundational for future research, even though my argument would insist on seeing World War I as the primary moment for the emergence of the phenomena they describe. Kathryn Cramer-Brownell has shown how in the early 1930s, in conjunction with US presidential and gubernatorial elections, a novel partnership emerged between Hollywood's vastly recognizable narratives and personalities and the political process.[71] The culturally expanded mobilization of Hollywood's machine gave celebrities a political clout and taught politicians to regard their electors as movie audiences and radio listeners. Similarly interested in the pervasive convergence of Western politics and media practices, Lee Grieveson has examined the way states and corporations came to use educational and non-fiction films to facilitate the establishment of a transnational liberal political economy.[72]

Rather than insisting on claims of a sensory vernacular, these works highlight the modern configuration of hegemonic practices of mass governance. To reconnect with López's post-colonial framework for the study of cinema and modernity, we can profitably return to what Hollywood learned from the events of WWI: the film industry's mass appeal, coupled with global commerce, facilitated a hegemonic strategy cloaked in the universalist ethos of peace, progress, and profit. On a domestic level, suffice here to mention President Coolidge's consistent availability for newsreels (despite his notorious aloofness), Herbert Hoover's proclivity for publicity stunts, and the film industry's unprecedented mobilization for Franklin Roosevelt's 1932 presidential campaign. Roosevelt's victory relied on film studio executives' turning a formerly rare practice of political advocacy into a repeated custom. Over time showmanship became an essential quality of his government. On a broader level, the film industry's adoption of the "Good Neighbor" policy from the late-1930s onward, evident in more respectful representations of South American settings and characters, sought to ease the country's tense relationship with south-of-the-border governments to "maintain hemispheric unity as a bulwark against foreign invasion," at a time of growing threat of war with Germany.[73]

In this sense, the study of modernity in post-WWI cinema needs to take into account both the development of practices of mass persuasion in the US and the competing reactions of defeated and non-Western nations—including Fascism's mastery of public promotion and, more broadly, authoritarian governance.[74] While Thomas Carlyle argued in 1833 that the invention of the printing press would make democracy inevitable, a century later Walter Benjamin alleged the inescapability of totalitarian brutality in association with mass-mediated artforms and communications.[75] "*Fiat ars—pereat mundus*" ("Let art be created, though the world perish") was one of Fascism's maxims, Benjamin noted, before closing his most famous essay by recognizing that the ideologies of Fascism and Communism—both inherently linked to the shockwaves of World War I—relied on the engineered mass circulation of aesthetic and political formulas.[76]

NOTES

1. I am grateful to Charlie Keil and Rob King for their careful, repeated readings of this essay and for their most constructive suggestions. One could not hope for better editors. For earlier drafts I also benefited from Richard Abel's always productive and detailed feedback. Thanks, too, to Stephen Bottomore and Paolo Cherchi Usai for promptly responding to my questions about the founding of Domitor and for granting me permission to publish excerpts from their answers. This essay reworks a paper I delivered at the Society for Cinema and Media Studies Conference (Montreal, March 25–29, 2015) for the panel "Early Cinema and Modernity in Latin America: Fifteen Years Later." I wish to thank Laura Isabel Serna for inviting me to contribute to the panel. This is for Leila. Marc Bloch, *The Historian's Craft*, trans. Peter Putnam (New York: Knopf, 1962 [1953]), 28–29.
2. Tom Gunning, "A Quarter of a Century Later: Is Early Cinema Still Early?" *KINtop. Jahrbuch zur Erforschung des frühen Films* 12 (2003): 30.
3. Ana M. López, "Early Cinema and Modernity in Latin America," *Cinema Journal* 40, no. 1 (Fall 2000): 50.
4. See, for instance, Dilip Parameshwar Gaonkar, *Alternative Modernities* (Durham, NC: Duke University Press, 2001) and Bruce M. Knauft, ed., *Critically Modern: Alternatives, Alterities, Anthropologies* (Bloomington: Indiana University Press, 2002).
5. Charles Taylor, "Two Theories of Modernity" *Hastings Center Report* 25, no. 2 (March–April 1995): 24–33.
6. Ibid., 24.
7. In 1987 Raymond Williams recognized exactly this issue. If we acknowledge "the imperial and capitalist metropolis as a specific historical form," as he put it, then we ought to discard the notion that the cultural practices that emerged out of Western metropolitan centers "were universals not only in history but as it is were above and beyond it." Williams, "When Was Modernism?" (1987) in his *Politics of Modernism: Against the New Conformists* (London: Verso, 1989), 47
8. Ben Singer, "The Ambimodernity of Early Cinema: Problems and Paradoxes in the Film-And-Modernity Discourse," in Klaus Kreimeier and Annemone Ligensa, eds., *Film 1900: Technology, Perception, Culture* (New Barnet, UK: John Libbey, 2009), 39 (italics mine). The essay juxtaposes two strands of cinema's relationship with modernity: on the one hand, an "ambimodern" framework, encompassing a "dynamic model [...] characterized

in terms of novelty, velocity, mobility, instability, flux, contingency, transformation, attraction, shock, distraction, disconcertion, hyperstimulus"; on the other, a neo-Romantic counter-impulse, equally modern (although appearing arguably anti-modern), associated with cinema's magical and metaphysical ability to peer "beyond the veil into the noumenal realm where objects exist in their pure, ideal, essential form" and thus closer to the realms of the occult, supernatural, and metaphysical (38 and 46–47).
9. Ibid., 39 (italics in the original).
10. Ibid., 42 and 39. Singer's work builds on the theoretical foundations laid out by Miriam Hansen in several essays and in her monograph *Babel and Babylon* (Cambridge, MA: Harvard University Press, 1991).
11. Jennifer Bean claims the centrality of gender difference for discussions of the modernity of early cinema in "Technologies of Early Stardom and the Extraordinary Body," *camera obscura* 16, no. 3 (2001): 9–57. The best scholarly works on African American film culture have articulated a space for "black modernity" that complicates and enriches the conventional formulation of the modernity argument, without ever challenging it. See Jacqueline Stewart, *Migrating to the Movies: Cinema and Black Urban Modernity* (Berkeley: University of California Press, 2005) and Allyson Nadia Field, *Uplift Cinema: The Emergence of African American Film and the Possibility of Black Modernity* (Durham, NC: Duke University Press, 2015).
12. For more on the modernity thesis and its critics, see Ben Singer, *Melodrama and Modernity: Early Sensational Cinema and Its Contexts* (New York: Columbia University Press, 2001), especially 102. Among the opponents, see David Bordwell, *On the History of Film Style* (Cambridge, MA: Harvard University Press, 1997), 141–146; and, with an emphasis on issues of migration, space, and geography, my *Italy in Early American Cinema: Race, Landscape, and the Picturesque* (Bloomington: Indiana University Press, 2009) and Jennifer M. Bean's "Introduction," in Bean, Anupama Kapse, and Laura Horak, eds., *Silent Cinema and the Politics of Space* (Bloomington: Indiana University Press, 2014), 1–13.
13. Charlie Keil, "'To Here from Modernity': Style, Historiography, and Transitional Cinema," in Keil and Shelley Stamp, eds., *American Cinema's Transitional Era: Audiences, Institutions, Practices* (Berkeley: University of California Press, 2004), 51–65.
14. For a productive discussion of the issue of periodization for the historian's craft, see Laurence Basserman, "The Challenge of Periodization: Old Paradigms and New Perspectives," in Basserman, ed., *The Challenge of Periodization: Old Paradigms and New Perspectives* (New York: Garland, 1996), 3–28.
15. López, "Early Cinema and Modernity," 48.
16. From the Domitor site: "Domitor was launched in October 1985 in Pordenone, Italy, during the silent film festival 'Le Giornate del Cinema Muto' by its five founding members: Stephen Bottomore of the United Kingdom, Paolo Cherchi Usai of Italy, André Gaudreault of Canada, Tom Gunning of the United States, and Emmanuelle Toulet of France" (https://domitor.org/about/). One of the organization's most cogent conceptual urgencies was to frame the study of the inception of motion pictures in terms that did not duplicate the decades-long prejudicial charge of "primitive cinema."
17. Bottomore also added that the 1914 date was already deployed in early film histories: "For example, books and articles often set 1914 as a limit date. A typical example is FIAF's 'Union catalogue of books and periodicals published before 1914 held by the film archive members of the International Federation of Film Archives,' published in 1967." Email to the author, February 27, 2015. Without referring specifically to Domitor, another of its

founding members, Tom Gunning, briefly addressed the periodization question in a 2003 essay reflecting on the revisionist impulse set off by the 1978 Brighton Conference. While the "*terminus a quo* of the origins of the medium is precisely a field of discussion, not a set date," he argued, "the *terminus ad quem* seems somewhat clearer [...] based on a contrast with the Classical Hollywood Cinema (the volume by Bordwell, Staiger and Thompson set its origins in 1917)." Gunning, "A Quarter of a Century Later," 28. More recently, Charles Musser has drawn a different account of the emergence of the "early cinema" paradigm in *Politicking and Emergent Media: US Presidential Elections of the 1890s* (Berkeley: University of California Press, 2016), 180–185. His genealogy maps the efforts to legitimize the study of pre-Griffith cinema. As for the endpoint of early cinema, Musser notes that it "was apparently up for grabs" (185).

18. When I brought up the issue of the war, Cherchi Usai replied, "I agree that World War I played a crucial role in Domitor's articulation of chronological parameters. We were all flexible about dates—I for one would have accepted 1915 as well. I would not be surprised, however, if the definition 'early cinema' were to be subject to further revisions in the next few decades. The question is paramount: in a century, what would 'early' mean in relationship to cinema? Already today I hear scholars speaking of 'early cinema' when referring to the 1920s." Email to the author, March 2, 2015 (my translation).

19. Interpreters of American cinema's transitional era—the period, roughly 1908-1917, in which cinema acquired "the visual grammar and industrial structures" that it would retain for decades to come—have similarly neglected the Great War (including America's intervention in 1917–1918) as a consequential moment for the global development of motion-picture culture. As Charlie Keil and Shelley Stamp posit, the transitional era of US filmmaking stands between "the earliest motion picture work at the turn of the twentieth century and the rise of classical filmmaking models in the late 1910s." Keil and Stamp, *American Cinema's Transitional Era*, 1. In the same volume, Ben Brewster has delineated "three broad phases" within early cinema in Europe and the US, mainly under an industrial and aesthetic perspective, from the variety-theater/fairground period to the feature-film one. Brewster, "Periodization of Early Cinema," *American Cinema's Transitional Era*, 70–71. Moving beyond the mid-1910s, in his overview of American film culture from 1915 to the end of the silent period, Richard Koszarski similarly does not hail the war as a critical moment in the development of the industry, whether in terms of corporate organization, production, distribution, or star marketing. Even with selected references to global markets, his framework remains mostly domestic. Koszarski, *An Evening's Entertainment: The Age of the Silent Feature Picture, 1915-1928* (Berkeley: University of California Press, 1990).

20. Admittedly his text also relies on Brazilian and Australian sources.

21. For instance, Richard Cork has noticed how "advanced modernist abstraction soon proved an inadequate starting point for developing a viable approach to the conflict." Richard Cork, *A Bitter Truth: Avant-Garde Art and the Great War* (New Haven, CT: Yale University Press, 1994), 9. This body of literature started immediately after the end of the conflict with works such as Albert Eugene Gallatin, *Art and the Great War* (New York: Dutton, 1919) and has continued over the decades, for instance with Barbara Jones and Bill Howell, *Popular Arts of the First World War* (London: Studio Vista, 1972), and Matthias Eberle, *World War I and the Weimar Artists: Dix, Grosz, Beckmann, Schlemmer* (New Haven, CT: Yale University Press, 1985). Works published after Singer's own contribution include the catalog of an exhibition held at the Getty Research Institute Gallery, edited by

Gordon Hughes and Philipp Blom, and published with the very Benjaminian title *Nothing But the Clouds Unchanged: Artists in World War I* (Los Angeles, CA: Getty Research Institute, 2014), and David M. Lubin, *Flags and Faces: The Visual Culture of America's First World War* (Berkeley: University of California Press, 2015).

22. Emilio Gentile, *L'apocalisse della modernità. La Grande Guerra per l'uomo nuovo* (Milan, Italy: Mondadori, 2008).

23. Martin Jay, "Walter Benjamin, Remembrance, and the First World War," in Helga Geyer, Ryan Paul Koopman, and Klaas Yntema, eds., *Benjamin Studies I: Perception and Experience in Modernity* (Amsterdam: University of Amsterdam/Rodopi, 2002), 189.

24. In the chapter introducing the 1922 edition of his 1915 *The Art of Moving Pictures*, Vachel Lindsay did not view the war as important enough to force him to modify his previous account. Vachel Lindsay, *The Art of the Moving Picture* (New York: Liveright, 1970 [1922]), 17. Similarly, in his 1927 *A Million and One Nights*, to take another instance, Terry Ramsaye caustically regarded the conflict as "a chapter of sensational importance—because nothing of importance occurred," since "the motion picture industry had been too busy to pay much attention." Ramsaye, *A Million and One Nights: A History of the Motion Picture* (New York: Simon and Schuster, 1964 [1926]), 777 and 726.

25. Ruth Vasey, *The World According to Hollywood: 1918-1939* (Exeter, UK: University of Exeter Press, 1997).

26. Kristin Thompson, *Exporting Entertainment: America in the World Film Market, 1907-1934* (London: BFI, 1985).

27. Vasey, *The World According to Hollywood*, 6 and 5. More recently, John Trumpbour has looked at European, and not just American, attempts to link film culture and global foreign policy in his *Selling Hollywood to the World: U.S. and European Struggles for Mastery of the Global Film Industry, 1920-1950* (New York: Cambridge University Press, 2002).

28. Vasey, *The World According to Hollywood*, 227.

29. Amy Kaplan, *The Anarchy of Empire in the Making of U.S. Culture* (Cambridge, MA: Harvard University Press, 2002), 147.

30. As Uli Jung and Martin Loiperdinger have pointedly remarked, "A concise comparative analysis of cinema history during World War I does not yet exist." See "World War I," in Richard Abel, ed., *Encyclopedia of Early Cinema* (New York: Routledge, 2005), 702. A still remarkable overview is Kevin Brownlow's *The War, the West, and the Wilderness* (New York: Knopf, 1978), which looks at American film culture during wartime as well as the contemporaneous film cultures of France, Germany, and Russia.

31. Richard Koszarski, "Flu Season: *Moving Picture World* Reports on Pandemic Influenza, 1918-19," *Film History* 17, no. 4 (2005): 466-485.

32. López, "Early Cinema," 61; Richard Abel, *Americanizing the Movies and "Movie-Mad" Audiences, 1910-1914* (Berkeley: University of California Press, 2006).

33. On the patriotic investment in filmic reportage and newsreel production, prompted by both government agencies and commercial studios, see James R. Mock and Cedric Larson, *Words that Won the War: The Story of the Committee on Public Information, 1917-1919* (Princeton, NJ: Princeton University Press, 1939), 136-137; Raymond Fielding, *The American Newsreel, 1911-1967* (Norman: University of Oklahoma Press, 1972), 70-108; and Richard Wood, ed., *Film and Propaganda in America: A Documentary*, vol. 1, World War I (New York: Greenwood Press, 1990).

34. In the following pages I am indebted to the work of Leslie Midkiff DeBauche, who has devoted numerous studies to Hollywood and the Great War, including *Reel Patriotism: The*

Movies and World War I (Madison: University of Wisconsin Press, 1997). On World War I stardom, see Sue Collins, "Star Testimonials and Trailers: Mobilizing during World War I," *Cinema Journal* 57, no. 1 (Fall 2017): 46–70.

35. Mary Nolan, *The Transatlantic Century: Europe and America, 1890-2010* (New York: Cambridge University Press, 2012), 64.
36. See Robert H. Zieger, *America's Great War: World War I and the American Experience* (Lanham, MD: Rowman & Littlefield, 2000), 16, 30.
37. Thompson, *Exporting Entertainment*, 91. The volume's third chapter, "Cashing in on Europe's War, 1916–18," provides the best-researched overview of the period.
38. Benjamin Hampton, *History of the American Film Industry from Its Beginnings to 1931* (New York: Dover, 1970 [1931]), 349; Lewis Jacobs, *The Rise of the American Film: A Critical History* (New York: Harcourt, Brace, 1939), 263.
39. Vasey, *The World According to Hollywood*, 7. For a rare recent intervention, see Peter Miskell, "International Films and International Markets: The Globalisation of Hollywood Entertainment, c. 1921–1951," *Media History* 22, no. 2 (2016): 174–200.
40. Vasey, *The World According to Hollywood*, 7.
41. Will Irwin, *The House that Shadows Built* (Garden City, NY: Doubleday, 1928), 237.
42. George Creel, *The Complete Report of the Chairman of the Committee on Public Information, 1917: 1918: 1919* (Washington, DC: Government Printing Office., 1920; reprinted New York: Da Capo Press, 1972), 7.
43. By 1925, American films made up to ninety-five percent of the total shown in Great Britain, seventy percent of the total shown in France, sixty-five percent in Italy, and sixty percent in Germany. William Victor Strauss, "Foreign Distribution of American Motion Pictures," *Harvard Business Review* 8, no. 3 (April 1930): 309.
44. Thompson, *Exporting Entertainment*, 111.
45. In 1926 Hays persuaded the Department of Commerce to create a Motion Picture Section within its Bureau of Foreign and Domestic Commerce. The MPPDA also fostered a close alliance with the State Department that proved instrumental in enabling the industry to negotiate directly with foreign governments over quota legislation. As Vasey put it, with these powerful government allies, "the MPPDA itself proclaimed the role of the movie as a sales agent for American goods." Vasey, *The World According to Hollywood*, 43.
46. On the close relationship between American cinema and the US Department of Commerce, see Trumpbour, *Selling Hollywood to the World*, 18–19, 64.
47. The same quote appeared on both sides of the Atlantic. In the UK, it was published in "Helping the Moving Pictures to Win the War," *Bioscope*, July 18, 1918, 8, quoted in Thompson, *Exporting Entertainment*, 94. In the US it appeared in a Chicago-based educational film journal, *Reel and Slide*, September 1918, 2. I thank Richard Abel for sharing this second reference.
48. Will Hays Papers, Rutgers University, microfilm division, II, reel 19, frame 1167ff., quoted in Trumpbour, *Selling Hollywood*, 19.
49. The literature on American mass culture vis-à-vis other nations' cultural sovereignty is conspicuous. See Victoria de Grazia's broad discussion in *Irresistible Empire: America's Advance Through Twentieth-Century Europe* (Cambridge, MA: Belknap Press, 2005), especially chap. 6 ("the Star System").
50. "Wall Street Battle Seen in Finance's Film Invasion," *Variety*, February 6, 1920, 57.
51. Theresa M. Collins, *Otto Kahn: Art, Money, and Modern Time* (Chapel Hill: University of North Carolina Press, 2002).

524 GIORGIO BERTELLINI

52. Mae D. Huettig, *Economic Control of the Motion Picture Industry: A Study in Industrial Organization* (Philadelphia: University of Pennsylvania Press, 1944), 36; and Koszarski, *An Evening's Entertainment*, 75.
53. With fictitious names for both Connick and Famous Players-Lasky, the study was later published as "Gilmore, Field and Company: Investment Bankers," in Howard T. Lewis, ed., *Cases on the Motion Picture Industry, with Commentaries* (New York: McGraw Hill, 1930), 61–79.
54. "Gilmore, Field," 68; see also Janet Wasko, *Movies and Money* (Norwood, NY: Ablex, 1982), 42nn4, 18.
55. "Gilmore, Field," 73.
56. The printed speech, titled *The Motion Picture*, is now included as "77—The Motion Picture" in the Otto Kahn Papers, Princeton University, "Pamphlets 73–82," Box 300, Folder 5.
57. Eliot had actually died a day before, on August 22, 1926.
58. Kahn, *The Motion Picture*, 7.
59. Ibid., 7, 8.
60. Ibid., 12.
61. Ibid., 13.
62. Ibid., 15.
63. Kahn's understanding of the role stars played as the nation's best advertising testimonials revealed more than industry officials were keen on publicly acknowledging. See Robert H. Cochrane, "Advertising Motion Pictures," in Joseph P. Kennedy, ed., *The Story of the Films* (New York: Shaw Company, 1927), 233–262.
64. As both a profession and a set of practices, publicity was the subject of a special section of *Moving Picture World*, dated July 20, 1918, which featured numerous contributions from industry insiders. I thank Richard Abel for bringing it to my attention.
65. Walter Lippmann, *Public Opinion* (New York: Free Press, 1997 [1922]), 10, 57.
66. Editorial, "War and the Fifth Estate," *Photoplay*, September 1918, 17.
67. Lippmann, *Public Opinion*, 61.
68. Ibid., 60, 61.
69. Ibid., 59; I am obviously referring to Daniel Boorstin's bestseller *The Image: A Guide to Pseudo-Events in America* (New York: Vintage, 1962).
70. Miriam Hansen, "The Mass Production of the Senses: Classical Cinema as Vernacular Modernism," *Modernism/modernity* 6, no. 2 (1999): 59–77.
71. Kathryn Cramer-Brownell, *Showbiz Politics: Hollywood in American Political Life* (Chapel Hill: University of North Carolina Press, 2014).
72. Lee Grieveson, *Cinema and the Wealth of Nations: Media, Capital, and the Liberal World System* (Berkeley: University of California Press, 2018).
73. Allen L. Woll, "Hollywood's Good Neighbor Policy: The Latin Image in American Film, 1939–1946," *Journal of Popular Film* 3, no. 4 (Fall 1974): 279.
74. I do not mean to posit a clear-cut opposition between the US and other nations on this count. My own *The Divo and the Duce: Film Stardom and Political Leadership in 1920s America* (Berkeley: University of California Press, 2019) examines the convergence of Italian Fascist propaganda and American publicity practices in the 1920s.
75. The original quote reads as follows: "He who first shortened the labor of copyists by device of *Movable Types* was disbanding hired armies, and cashiering most kings and senates, and creating a whole new democratic world: he had invented the art of printing." Thomas

Carlyle, *Sartor Resartus: The Life and Opinions of Herr Teufelsdröckh* (Oxford, UK: Oxford University Press, 2008 [1833–34]), 31.
76. Walter Benjamin, "The Work of Art in the Age of Mechanical Reproduction," in *Illuminations*, ed. Hannah Arendt, trans. Harry Zohn (New York: Schocken Books, 1969), 242.

CHAPTER 25

EMPIRE • STATE • MEDIA

LEE GRIEVESON

CINEMA emerged in the late nineteenth century and was quickly deployed for the fusion of economic, state, and geopolitical logics that powered the intensification of capitalist imperialism. Early forms of display and spectacle mutated into propaganda in the coverage of complex US imperial wars beginning in 1898. The imbrication of cinema with globalizing capital and state is evident also in state practices of media-making promoting global trade and the "development" of peripheral regions. One example is a series of films made beginning in 1913 by the United States Department of Agriculture—probably the first state-run film unit in history—focused on the completion of the Panama Canal as symbolic of the "infrastructural power" of the US state and its newly central position within the geopolitical and economic world order.[1] By the point the canal was completed, in 1914, Europe was convulsed in an intra-imperial conflict, lasting until 1918, and the US became for the first time a net exporter of capital. Responding to this, the British state abandoned the "imperialism of free trade" that had been integral to its global hegemony in the nineteenth century, opting instead for a walled-off protectionist imperial economy.[2] One epiphenomenon of this doomed effort to shore up geopolitical and economic hegemony was the creation of a state-run film unit as part of the Empire Marketing Board (EMB) in 1926. Established by the self-declared "founding father" of documentary cinema, John Grierson, the EMB unit consecrated the union of cinema and imperialist interests. "Documentary film" emerged directly from the imperatives of imperialism. My essay explores some of this history of how cinema in its non-fictional, didactic, and propagandistic forms was put to work to facilitate imperialism and the dynamics of capital accumulation that structure the modern world system.

"ACCUMULATION BY DISPOSSESSION"

Our definitions of "documentary" must expand, clearly, but I have no interest here in further meta-theoretical debate about the term or practice, which sometimes seems to be only ever a paragraph away in scholarship on documentary cinema. Better to take leave of film-specific issues to first reflect on the broader context of imperialism that shaped media practice. Broadly speaking (and laying my definitional cards on the table), I understand the accelerated imperialism and wave of capitalist globalization in the latter years of the nineteenth century, from something like 1870–1914, to be driven principally by the expansionist logics of capital and its fusion with liberal state interests and geopolitical strategy.[3] To speak of *capitalist imperialism* brings into focus the expanding logics of capital that drove the division of the world system into core, semi-peripheral, and peripheral zones. Such divisions created an exploitative international division of labor, facilitating the extraction of materials from the periphery that came to be used in the industrial processes of the center and, from there, circulated globally via newly created infrastructural networks.[4] Liberal capitalist states in particular played dominant roles in this process because such states have historically taken their remit to be the expansion and protection of property rights and capital.[5] Liberal imperatives to foster so-called free trade and the Open Door have been constitutively enmeshed with imperialism because both were (and are) shaped by the logics of capital and its expansion across the world system. *Empire* is an extractive and circulatory system requiring both the development of new infrastructures in terms of transport and communication and the global deployment of military forces capable of securing strategic interests.

But we must always understand these logics and dynamics in their historical specificity, a sketch of which I offer now. The global circulation of British capital deriving from the Industrial Revolution and related state-infrastructural expenditures was facilitated by the innovation of the Gold Standard. And that standard established fixed exchange rates and tied monetary and banking systems into an international system, beginning in the 1860s. Growth in European trade from that point motivated imperial expansion and the creation of a global order enabling the unprecedented worldwide circulation of capital in the years 1880–1914.[6] Parts of that capital were invested in the US in the 1860s, specifically to fund the building of transcontinental rail lines. The building of the railways necessitated the confiscation of land from indigenous populations and its transformation into "property."[7] One can see this clearly as a process of "accumulation by dispossession," to use David Harvey's updating of Marx's concept of "primitive accumulation," and consistent with the enclosure of common lands that was central to early capitalist accumulation.[8] Capital became infrastructure to facilitate the further circulation of capital. And in turn, these developments in new forms of capital allocation sped up the development of the institutions and practices of finance capital in the US.[9] Bankers played significant roles thereafter in the explosion of business mergers during the 1890s that produced a number of large, globally oriented corporations.[10]

Capital that expanded through the financing of infrastructure and the growth of a corporate-dominated economy was exported globally in the turn-of-the-century period. I will come back to the specific dynamics of that process in a moment, but overall, it gave shape to the imperative of accumulation that produced a new round of brutal colonial conquest in Africa, the Middle East, and Asia in the midst of the long economic depression of 1873–1896. Peripheral and semi-peripheral regions of the world economy were exploited in this process for cheap or slave labor and mined for the energy and mineral resources needed to sustain the "second-stage" industrial revolution predicated on developments in chemistry and electricity. Quite clearly, the intensification of capitalist imperialism and the geographical scope of the system melded territorial and economic "logics of power," as Harvey, among others, has shown.[11] The fusion of capitalist and state imperatives produced interstate rivalries that straightforwardly led to war.

I end this conceptual and historical sketch of the dynamics of imperialism and the capitalist world system roughly where I began, then, with the late flourishing of a spurt of territorial plunder by the US in the complex global wars beginning in 1898 that were among the very first pictured by the new technology of moving-picture cameras. Indeed, the many war films produced principally by the Edison Manufacturing Co. and the American Mutoscope & Biograph Co. were so wildly popular with American audiences that the preeminent historian of that period, Charles Musser, has suggested that they played a significant role in entrenching the popularity of cinema itself in the US.[12] Edison, both a film producer and exemplar of the new technology corporations of the second-stage industrial revolution, issued a special War Catalogue of films. Most of them were "actualities," a form—or mode—that dominated early film production until around 1903: brief snippets of real life, frequently a static single shot, conceived as a form of display. The cinema was born principally as a non-fictional form. War actualities displayed the military and technological might of the US. Films such as *U.S. Cruiser "Raleigh," U.S. Battleship "Indiana,"* and *Troop Ships for the Philippines* (all Edison, 1898) demonstrated and made visible the naval ships that were built in the early 1890s as the US military was "professionalized" to help facilitate geopolitical strategy.[13] Such films *document* the birth of the modern US military as one part of the imperative to *exhibit* state power that has been integral to imperialism. Cinema as a mobile display mechanism was quickly put to work to depict and reinforce the technological advancement essential to both imperialism and the mechanized mass medium that was cinema itself.

But what underpinned this imperative to display new forms of mechanization, technology, and state strength? The answer necessarily takes us into an effort to understand which wars the US began fighting in 1898 and why. This period of conflict is often perceived simply as that of the Spanish-American War, but the situation was more complex than that, incorporating actions against Filipino resistance fighters in the Philippines (up to 1902) and the annexation of Puerto Rico, the islands of Guam and Hawaii, and parts of Cuba. The separate conflicts were principally fought to enshrine trade routes and establish a global infrastructure of naval bases, treaty ports, shipping lanes, and coaling stations that enabled the US to achieve a territorial foothold and access to commodities, markets, and labor in Latin America and Asia through control of seaways in the Caribbean and Pacific.[14] In fact, the US had been planning for the conflict against the rump Spanish Empire since 1894 and used the fighting between Cuban rebels and the Spanish as an opportunity to send a naval ship to Cuba to protect US interests, particularly in sugar.[15] (The ship was sunk in an incident that historians tend to call "mysterious," rather than a "false flag" operation, although Cuban radical José Julián Martí Pérez had predicted that the US would provoke war with Spain and that Cuba would thus pass from one imperial power to another.)[16] The control of the deep port at Guantanamo Bay on Cuba was essential to the control of seaways and the Panama Canal, and the Bay was "leased" from Cuba in 1903, after the Platt Amendment of 1901 effectively ensured US dominance over a nominally independent Cuba.[17] Obviously, this speaks to the long arc of US militarized imperialism, a subject to which I shall return.

Edison's War Catalogue of films displayed the advanced technology of weapons of mass destruction, showing troops leaving from Florida to Cuba and the Philippines, some reenactments of key battles, and the victorious battleships returning home to celebratory marches in New York City (see figures 25.1 and 25.2). These films documented imperial conflict and expansion, as well as the relatively easy victory of the technologically advanced US Navy, which had quickly destroyed the older wooden ships of the Spanish in ports in the Philippines and Cuba. Indeed, the films stand now as remarkable historical documents of a conflict between historical and emergent imperial powers, and the birth of a US imperialism that thereafter radically transformed the global system. Blink and you will miss the moment that imperial control of infrastructure and circulation shifted from Europe to the US. Charles Musser has shown how the films were frequently connected in exhibition programs to narrate the story of the conflict from troop movement to battle to return home. Beginning, middle, and end—*a creative treatment of actuality*, to use Grierson's well-known definition of "documentary"—suturing narrative form and imperial conflict.[18] *Documenting* imperial expansion was important to the birth of cinema as a mass medium, and the cultural work of cinema was quickly assimilated to the sustenance of imperializing capital.

FIGURE 25.1 *U.S. Battleship "Indiana"* (Edison Manufacturing Co., 1898). Edison's "War Catalogue" described the ship as "the most powerful fighting machine in the world to-day."

FIGURE 25.2 *Troop ships for the Philippines* (Edison Manufacturing Co., 1898). Ships departing from San Francisco bound for Manila during the Spanish-American War.

"Helping Negroes"

Vessels from the newly professionalized US naval militia, fleetingly visible in these films, were also deployed in Colombia in 1903, part of a process designed to create the state of Panama via the building of the isthmian canal, which radically reshaped global trade flows. (The US warship *Nashville* protected Panamanian rebels from Colombian troops, and the Canal Zone was thereafter leased back to the US, with work beginning in 1904: this and the Cuban episode are textbook examples of what used to be called "gunboat diplomacy.")[19] By the time the Canal was nearing completion, in 1913, Congress made available funds for an exhibit at the forthcoming Panama-Pacific International Exposition. On display would be "such articles and materials as illustrate the function and administrative faculty of the Government of the United States[,] tending to demonstrate the nature and growth of our institutions, their adaption to the wants of the people, and the progress of the Nation in the arts of peace and war."[20] Quickly after the release of funds, in late 1913, the United States Department of Agriculture (USDA) began a series of "experiments to determine the feasibility of taking motion pictures and the educational and promotion [sic] value of these motion pictures" that led to the purchase and construction of the materials necessary for film production and the establishment of what seems to have been the first-ever state-run "documentary" film unit.[21]

Over time, the USDA film unit produced significant films about (broadly speaking) the modernization of agriculture. But the unit was also charged with making films for other state bureaus and departments for the 1915 Panama-Pacific Exposition. Government planners, that is, marshaled and utilized film as part of the imperative to display the "infrastructural power" and technological advancement of the state. Greg Waller has shown that non-theatrical pedagogical film was widely displayed at the Exposition, including both films made by the state and those produced by large corporations like Ford and International Harvester.[22] Various forms of the infrastructural circulation fundamental to imperializing capital were thus celebrated together at the Exposition. Here, for example, is a picture of the giant telephone built by the powerful Morgan-financed corporation, AT&T, to celebrate the first transcontinental

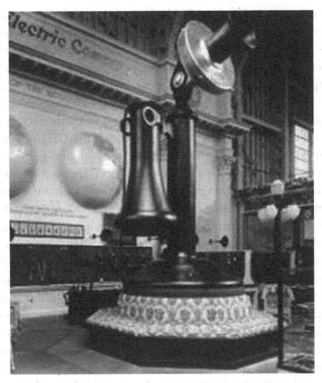

FIGURE 25.3 Giant Western Electric/American Telephone and Telegraph Co. telephone displayed at the Panama Pacific Exposition in 1915.

telephone call and the long-distance telephonic network integral to the sped-up circulation of information at the dawn of the American century (see figure 25.3).

The Canal was partly financed through the same House of Morgan, thereby exemplifying the complex alliances between finance capital and the state that deepened in this period.[23] Because of its centrality in financing the Canal, the House of Morgan became the chief financial conduit for the new state of Panama.[24] "JP Morgan," writes noted journalist Ed Vulliamy, "led the American banks in gradually turning Panama into a financial centre – and a haven for tax evasion and money laundering—as well as a passage for shipping, with which these practices were at first entwined when Panama began to register foreign ships to carry fuel for the Standard Oil company in order for the corporation to avoid US tax liabilities."[25] Capital courses through Panama, still, as does a significant part of the flow of global trade.[26] Cinema produced by purpose-built state film units and exhibited inside the built space of the Exposition celebrated this global flow at the dawning of a new era of US-led economic imperialism.

That such a film unit would have originated within the USDA was in no way arbitrary but rather a natural evolution of the agency's operations. Set up by the federal government in the 1860s, the USDA emerged in the midst of massive transcontinental rail construction and related investments in agricultural colleges and higher education to stimulate economic productivity. By the latter years of the nineteenth century, the Department wielded scientific knowledge to develop crop management and animal husbandry and promoted the mechanization of farming to facilitate growth and productivity. It thereby offers an instructive example of how liberal governments invested in pedagogic approaches and institutions to facilitate economic growth. Rationalizing rural practices in this way was a common goal of modern states as they exploited the legitimacy of science and technology to convert land formerly occupied by migratory people into property.[27] By the early twentieth century, the USDA developed a system of "agricultural extension" that harnessed the network of land-grant state universities and agricultural colleges alongside a system of model farms and mobile instruction to disseminate knowledge about farming and economic management.[28] Broadly speaking, the Department invested in cultivating knowledge that would facilitate food production and thereby sustain the country's populace, which is a crucial foundational task of states.[29] But the USDA focused on other aims as well: to establish a stable rural economy and simultaneously counter the agrarian "Populist" insurgency of the turn of the century by integrating rural workers into a new national economy;[30] to buttress the urban and industrial expansion of the second-stage industrial revolution and sustain an industrial economy on a continental scale;[31] and to enable and sustain a mass economy of abundance that could, among other things, deradicalize working-class opposition.[32]

The role accorded film in this expansive economic, political, and pedagogic project was considerable. By 1934, the unit had produced around five hundred films, many of which documented particular practices—such as how to dip cattle to avoid ticks—but that also tipped over into general advice to rural workers on how to live productively (for example, how to introduce labor-saving devices into the home to facilitate recreation and consumption). Visualizing new productive practices, film was a form of communication that could be persuasive and pedagogical and, to some extent, mobile. It could circulate through the agrarian and extraction-based peripheries of the American South and interior, bringing federal government advice to rural populations in a way characteristic of the liberal state's imperative to facilitate economic productivity and govern from a distance. Indeed, this is one of the ways liberal polities began to use technology to materialize forms of indirect rule.[33]

USDA film circulated initially through the creation and expansion of a network of "extension departments," mostly at land-grant universities that purchased films from Washington and disseminated them through their local communities. By the early 1920s the Department's Bureau of Animal Industry innovated the use of a mobile cinema van that could carry films and newly developed mobile film projectors to ever-more remote peripheral regions. These mobile film units made use of electricity generated from the vans' engines to project films extolling governmental guidance in agricultural and life management to isolated rural populations (see figure 25.4).[34] In the accompanying image, for example, from the cover of the USDA's 1926 publication *Use of Motion Pictures In Agricultural Extension Work*, the department's idealized depiction of such a screening shows an extension cord connecting the USDA's car to a brick-built building, supplying power to a film projector screening a film emblazoned with the USDA logo.[35] The car's

FIGURE 25.4 Cover, *Use of Motion Pictures in Agricultural Extension Work*, USDA miscellaneous circular, no. 78, November 1926.

headlamps and the cone of light provided by the portable film projector outshine the dim moon, as government technology brings illumination to the pre-electrified countryside and metaphorically enlightens its population. Quite simply, the state began to make systematic use of the supposed affective or pedagogic power of film, as well as its mobility. Cinema's status as an emblem of a machine-made economic modernity, and its figural articulation of state oversight, worked in concert to position movie watching as a privileged technique of governmental management.

I shall single out just one of the USDA films to quickly illustrate this argument. *Helping Negroes to Become Better Farmers and Homemakers* (States Relations Service, ca. 1921) was made in some form of cooperation with the Alabama Polytechnic Institute and the Tuskegee Institute. Demonstrating the benefits the extension system brings to tenant farmers in eastern Alabama, the scripted film mixes various registers as is characteristic of non-theatrical pedagogic cinema of the period: partly it documents farming problems (particularly the boll weevil, a pest that destroyed cotton crops), but it connects this to forms of characterization and narrative. Beginning with an introduction to "Rube Collins, typical of many Negro tenant farmers in the South," and his family, the film seeks to root its general story of farm development in the structures of alignment and allegiance that had become by this point central to narrative fiction film. Collins is clearly poor, indicated by the sparseness of his family's shack. But things get worse before they get better. A neighbor appears and tells Collins that he has found a pest in his cotton crop. Collins and his colleague travel to tell their white landlord, who immediately summons the white extension agent, who tells them they have boll weevils. Here a microscopic close-up shows the weevil, as the film inserts informational detail into its story. The agent explains to the two farmers the way to control the boll weevil pest, outlining the methods of early cultivation and crop diversification established by the USDA to counter the damage inflicted on the significant cash crop of cotton.

By following these instructions, with the benign oversight of the white landlord, the problem is solved, and Collins becomes richer. "Two years later," an intertitle tells us, "better farming has given the Collins family a better home, and a local Negro agent to assist the White agent has become necessary." Collins and his family now live in a larger farmhouse, containing several rooms. The contrast is made explicit in a brief sequence starting with the intertitle "The old," followed by a shot of the family's previous shack, and then "The new," showing in a slow pan their more prosperous home: the old ways are superseded by the new, made possible by government intervention. The shift from the old to the new has quite a different valence than in, say, Sergei Eisenstein's contemporaneous film *The Old and the New* (1929), about the collectivization of agricultural practices. Here, instead, the emphasis is on the material benefits brought by government extension, dramatized by a slow pan presenting Collins's new and larger house. But note here also that the articulation of time passing marks the presence of a narrative form that meshes with governmental purpose to show the economic benefits of government-led farming practices. The unstable mix of documentary and fictional techniques common among non-theatrical pedagogic films of the period is directed toward facilitating economic productivity. Collins is made modern and becomes a prosperous homeowner because of the intervention of white extension agents. The film here straightforwardly ignores a longer history of black-led extension and community work, as J. Emmett Winn has astutely shown, to equate governmental agency with white authorities and institutions.[36] Winn's research has in fact suggested the film was more widely shown among white audiences.[37] In this way it may have sought to be equally educational for white landlords, for the film publicizes the power of government to transform not only the economic conditions of black tenant farmers but also the economic potential of white-owned land.

The state orchestrated filmmaking, then, to encourage economic development, particularly of the rural South and the interior. In time, this state process produced new forms of agribusiness that utilized the latest developments in chemistry and mechanization. (Monsanto, to give just one example, was formed in 1901, and the Morgan-financed International Harvester played a central role in fostering mechanization.) But the South remained an "undeveloped" region, an "internal analogue of Latin America," historian Alan Dawley remarks, "producing raw materials and profits for absentee owners."[38] Our conception of "imperialism" needs to expand here to discern the ways in which the state played crucial roles in breaking down the resistance of pre-capitalist societies to capital's dominance and in the elaboration of a productive system characterized by the domination and exploitation of some classes and ethnic groups by others. USDA films performed some of this work, mixing "documentary" with narrative and the delineation of empathetic characters in ways that straightforwardly positioned government intervention as the motor of narrative and progress. Equally significant was the elaboration of a material network for the circulation of these films, as seen in the USDA image of a film screening, and reliant also on a network of "extension departments," at land-grant universities in particular. The state-run film unit innovated new forms of mobile exhibition and new institutional networks to foster the circulation of film to propagandize populations. *Helping Negroes to Become Better Farmers and Homemakers* remains a remarkable document of this process. Populations who were most likely the descendants of slaves forcibly removed from the old world were "educated" in new ways to serve the dictates of capital and state. Cotton, of course, was a key commodity in the broader history of imperialism, slavery, and global capital.[39]

"Making Films for Primitive People"

Cotton can be a useful connecting thread, if I may, for transitioning here to the British imperialism that was still a globally significant political and economic system in the 1920s. British efforts to orchestrate a newly walled-off imperial economy in the early part of that decade eventually produced the Empire Marketing Board in 1926, and it is within that institution that a documentary film unit was established under the direction of Stephen Tallents and John Grierson. "Documentary" is often said to begin here, though I have suggested a far different genealogy that locates this development in a longer history of non-fiction film produced to facilitate the dynamics of capitalist imperialism and the changing dynamics of the world system in the early twentieth century.

The specific history of the establishment of the EMB film unit can further illustrate the point. I have discussed this history in more detail elsewhere, so here I will skip to a summary of the key issues that situate this development in the broader context of global capitalism and push on to explore subsequent iterations of the British use of cinema to sustain imperialism in the 1930s.[40] Broadly speaking, the British state's response to the growing economic power of the US in particular, as well as the devastating cost of WWI and the economic depressions that opened and closed the 1920s, entailed a partial shift in trade policy. Britain moved away from the classical free-trade liberalism that had been the guiding principle of economic strategies since the mid-nineteenth century and toward a policy of protectionism and "imperial preference" that would place a tariff on goods imported from outside the Empire.[41]

Simultaneously, the British government constructed new economic and political structures for the establishment of a Commonwealth bloc.[42] By doing so, state praxis sought to safeguard finance capital and industrial growth as well as lower levels of unemployment and worker disaffection. Recall that imperialism requires class domination domestically—including here the interpellation of working-class populations into imperial commerce—as well as the exploitation of foreign subaltern populations. It behooves us to see those processes as dialectical.

Culture was integral to these governmental efforts to establish a new imperial political economy in various ways, including imperial exhibitions, the creation of the British Broadcasting Corporation (beginning in 1922 and taking its modern shape in 1927), and new state propaganda agencies like the British Council.[43] In the process, film and documentary became one crucial component of the governmental use of culture/media to foster economic and political security. Indeed, the Empire Marketing Board was itself designed with this purpose in mind. It emerged from an Imperial Economic Committee (IEC) set up in 1924 to promote a protectionist economy and closer economic ties with the Empire. In 1925 the IEC recommended that a body be established to produce "continuous publicity on a national scale with a view to spreading and fostering [the idea] that Empire purchasing creates an increased demand for the manufactured products of the United Kingdom and therefore stimulates employment at home."[44] Elite state officials at the Board of Trade and the Colonial Office all supported this suggestion; the executive commission to carry out this economic task was established as the EMB in May 1926. By doing so, the British government created a propaganda institution to foster the idea of intraimperial trade as a part of its broader economic and geopolitical strategies. One can see this as consistent with a number of developments beginning around WWI that increasingly positioned propaganda—or, as it was frequently framed, "education"—as integral to governmental practice: the USDA is one example of that imperative, as was the Panama-Pacific Exposition, as was the BBC, and so on. The point I want to emphasize is that liberal states increasingly came to see "culture" and, especially, media as important to government. And that this intensified further with the expansion of suffrage and mass democracy in the aftermath of WWI.[45]

Documentary was particularly significant to this process. The EMB established a film unit under the direction of Stephen Tallents, a civil servant who had played a central role in orchestrating the state response to the 1926 General Strike.[46] Tallents employed Grierson, initially on an ad hoc basis, and Grierson set about assembling a pool of talent to make films supportive of the broader state goal of creating an imperial market. Grierson spent a good deal of time trying to differentiate "documentary" from previous forms, such as the "actualities" and non-theatricals I have explored here, and became an effective advocate for the term "documentary." But the distinctions were largely specious: all were non-fictional forms, predominantly state-produced, integrated directly into the practices of capitalist imperialism that mandated the "development" of economic regions and their integration into broader economic and political systems in order to foster the security of state and capital.

Key to the EMB films was the celebration of the infrastructural and circulatory networks that were (and are) integral to the operations of empire.[47] The films sought specifically to promote consumption of British Empire produce and materials as part of the strategy to wall off an imperial political economy, particularly from the incursions of the coming American global hegemony. They also sought to explain the benefits imperialism brought to British working-class populations.[48] Such explanations were essential to the maintenance of support for Empire—which of course largely benefited the owners of capital—and to the necessity of warding off any conceptions of worker solidarity outside of the fictions of racial hierarchy integral to imperialism.

Other films produced by the British were addressed more directly to subaltern populations (or, in British imperial parlance, "backwards races") to educate them in the virtues of imperialism and enslavement.[49] I shall concentrate on one influential example mostly located in East Africa in the mid-1930s, by describing the development of what came to be called the Bantu Educational Kinema Experiment (hereafter BEKE). In late 1927, one year after the formation of the EMB, the Colonial Office convened a film conference at which a Colonial Films Committee was formed to discuss, principally, the circulation of British films in the empire, the control of films already circulating, and the production of educational cinema for the "benefit" of the colonized. In the wake of the conference, the Colonial Advisory Committee on Native Education sent the noted biologist Julian Huxley to Uganda, Kenya, Tanganyika, and Zanzibar to "advise upon certain aspects of native education."[50] Huxley took with him a projector and a selection of films supplied by the Empire Marketing Board in his visits to various educational institutions. Leading on from the perceived success of this experiment in cinema as colonial pedagogy, the Colonial Office subsequently supported a plan from missionary John Merle Davis to produce and show films for the populations of the Copperbelt in Central Africa.[51] Davis formed an alliance with Major Leslie Alan Notcutt, a sisal plantation owner in East Africa who himself had previously "thought that an estate cinema might be an effective method to help maintain a contented labor force."[52] Davis secured funding from the Carnegie Institute, as well as other mining operations in the region, and began an experiment to produce and exhibit "cultural, recreation and educational films for the Bantu" people.[53] In this he was supported by a somewhat cash-strapped Colonial Office in London grateful for the utility of American corporate philanthropic money.

What brought the missionary, the plantation owner, corporate American philanthropy, and the British Colonial Office together? If that sounds like the set-up for a joke, the short answer is a little more prosaic—the management of African mobility and labor in the midst of the massive social transformations wrought by large-scale mineral extraction to serve transnational capital. (How is that for a punchline?) Davis's proposed project was motivated by an interest in the social impact on local villages of mass labor migration to (then) Northern Rhodesia's Copperbelt, which was the subject of his influential 1932 report *Modern Industry and the African*. In this sense he was part of the wider shift in the interwar years toward a new conception of colonial "development." Such a conception was clearly predicated on finding ways to educate Africans in their "natural" roles as agriculturalists and to disrupt the drift of African farmers and laborers from land reserves to employment in mines and other jobs in cities.[54] These interventions sought to minimize the deleterious consequences of population movement for colonial rule and the imperial system. Rural development in this way sought to integrate the extraction of materials from Africa into the global market and simultaneously minimize the emergence of political nationalism, contestation over land rights, and an incipient pan-Africanist movement among the migrant laborers. Carnegie and the British colonial state found some common ground in these objectives, and we can see the connections among missionary, state, and American corporate philanthropic capital as one example of an expansive development apparatus to manage the "modernization" of African populations and economies and facilitate their integration into a transnational liberal economy. Violent police reprisals against the 1935 strike of workers in the Copperbelt were the flipside to this project of pedagogical hegemony.

The thirty-five films made by the Bantu Educational Kinema Experiment between 1935 and 1937 included several on agricultural matters, including films about crop rotation, seed selection, soil erosion, and cooperative marketing. BEKE films also advertised the colonial government's departments and services. In the very first film of the experiment, *Post Office Savings Bank* (1935), two African men working on a plantation handle the salaries they've been given differently. One buries his money in the floor of his hut and later has it stolen, while the other agricultural worker takes his straight to the colonial Post Office bank. The structure of wise and foolish choices, usually embodied in character positions, was a common one in the colonial pedagogy produced by state and quasi-state institutions. In this example, it works to support a colonial banking system and so, therefore, the extraction of further profit from colonized labor.[55] Various other BEKE films focused on hygiene and disease prevention. *Tropical Hookworm* (1936), for example, showed the step-by-step process of constructing a pit latrine to avoid the hookworm infection that proliferated in rural areas in sub-Saharan Africa and so constituted "a drag on the fiscal health of the empire."[56] In these direct ways film was integrated with the biopolitical project of managing colonized populations to ensure their productivity.

Quasi-state officials, missionaries, anthropologists, and philanthropists all worked from similar assumptions that there was a unique "African mind" and that education should take these race-based proclivities into consideration. It became axiomatic in these colonial circles that educational films should therefore be minimally edited, should unfold at a slower pace, should remove extraneous material from the frame, and so on.[57] Watching Africans watch movies became an ideologically charged anthropological and state intervention. Part of the British concern was about the effects of commercial American films on subaltern subjects. The BEKE project was "partly designed," Glen Reynolds has argued, "to 'capture' African viewers and correct the 'falsehoods' perpetuated by the Hollywood dream machine."[58] The films were certainly widely disseminated in East and Central Africa, tracking the same migratory patterns exploited by global capital through Kenya and the mining towns of the Copperbelt in Northern Rhodesia, Tanganyika, Nysaland, and Uganda.[59] Mobile vans like that seen in the USDA example above enabled the government to take its message to areas often beyond government supervision—extending the visibility of government at the same time as they expanded the ability of the state to see. Mostly the films were silent, but exhibitions frequently utilized sonic projection, through an early sound-on-disc system, that concluded with the British national anthem accompanying a short film of London and a picture of the King.[60] But, of course, many of these audiences had never seen moving pictures before, and it seems likely that the films themselves came in some ways to stand as metonymic representatives of the technological power of the colonial state—a form of mechanized shock and awe in the service of the biopolitical and economic management of empire.

The BEKE experiment mirrored in some ways that enacted by the USDA in relation to the agricultural periphery of the US. The effort to use cinema to educate rural populations in productive agricultural practices and related ways of living took roughly similar forms and prompted related developments in mobile cinema technology and exhibition.[61] Indeed, we can notice here a significant alliance emerging between the British colonial state and American corporate philanthropy to "develop" resources and populations. US corporations, and their related foundations, were becoming increasingly invested in the resources housed within the British Empire in the interwar years, and this connection, especially as it relates to mineral resources, is intriguing.[62] The US would make the dismantling of imperial preference key to its support for Britain after World War II.[63] Encoded in this was a shift from British territorial empire to US-dominated economic imperialism. One can see this as one of the key shifts in the functioning of empire in the twentieth century: a transition from the territorial logics and protectionist variant elaborated by the British in the interwar years to the economic and free-trade variant pursued by the US thereafter (at least until the latter's recent turn to forms of economic nationalism amid the fracturing of the neoliberal world order after 2008). Continuity can be discerned underneath these shifts, too, though: the interventions of the USDA were frequently designed to manage the descendants of African populations forcibly removed from their homelands to serve transnational capital, just as the British colonial efforts sought to manage displaced African populations while enabling extractive imperialism.

Indeed, one cannot overstate the significance of the sites of these experiments in pedagogy and governance. The discovery of rich copper deposits in Northern Rhodesia, on the border of the Belgian Congo, in the early twentieth century was a crucial economic and political boon to the British, given how important copper was to the wired communicative networks that facilitated imperial governance and economic globalization. AT&T's enormous telephone at the 1915 Panama-Pacific Exposition is one striking example of the growing importance of telecommunications as "capitalism's essential lubricant" to the maintenance of empire.[64] Much of this informational network required resources dug up from African soils by occupying powers. Pedagogical state-produced mobile and mostly non-fiction media sought to facilitate these developments in an effort to sustain imperial governance and facilitate the global flow of information and materials.

***

One can deduce from the history sketched here that cinema was quickly utilized to supplement and facilitate forms of territorial and economic imperialism. Frequently the films involved were non-fictional and crossed the categories of actuality, education, propaganda, and documentary: the borders of those categories are porous. We need to examine closely the establishment and practices of significant institutions that produced, circulated, and showed films to try to influence the belief and conduct of their viewers. But this does not mean that the propaganda always worked. British efforts prove that point: documentary cinema in the UK was integrated within efforts to halt the shifts in the world system that brought the US to its center, but such efforts could only fail. By the time the British had innovated "documentary," US fiction film producers—buttressed by finance capital and working in concert with large companies devoted to technological research and development—had become globally dominant. The commercial corporate American film industry had developed sophisticated and successful infrastructural networks for circulating shiny images of consumer abundance around the world. This approach became central to a new round of imperialism, now more clearly economic than territorial—though always intertwined—and Hollywood relied on support from the US state as well as global trade agreements concerning "intellectual property," to dominate markets. The imperializing work of media shifted to fiction and indeed to the creation of media systems that were fundamentally geared to the generation of capital. One might say, then, that at its inception documentary was to territorial imperialism what fiction became to economic imperialism.

Notes

1. For Priya. I wrote this essay originally as a keynote address for the Sawyer Seminar Series "Documentary and Historical Transformation," held by the Centre for Documentary Research and Practice in the Media School at Indiana University in the summer of 2016. I am grateful for the invitation from Joshua Malitsky and Marissa Moorman; to my friend Greg Waller; and to my co-panelist and friend, the brilliant Priya Jaikumar. My thanks go also in particular to my fabulous, and patient, co-editors, the dynamic duo of Charlie and Rob. Michael Mann, "The Autonomous Power of the State: Its Origins, Mechanisms, and Results," in John A. Hall, ed., *States in History* (Oxford, UK: Oxford University Press, 1986), 109–136. Mann refers to infrastructural power as the positive capacity of the state to "penetrate civil society" and implement policies throughout a given territory. On the building and significance of the Canal see, for example, Julia Greene, *The Canal Builders: Making America's Empire at the Panama Canal* (New York: Penguin Press, 2009).
2. John Gallagher and Ronald Robinson, "The Imperialism of Free Trade," *Economic History Review* 2, no. 6 (1953): 1–15; Philip Williamson, *National Crisis and National Government: British Politics, the Economy and Empire, 1926–1932* (Cambridge, UK: Cambridge University Press, 1992).
3. See, for example, Giovanni Arrighi, *The Long Twentieth Century: Money, Power, and the Origins of Our Times* (London: Verso, 1994); David Harvey, *The New Imperialism* (Oxford, UK: Oxford University Press, 2003); and Alex Callinicos, *Imperialism and Global Political Economy* (London: Polity, 2009).

4. Callinicos, *Imperialism and Global Political Economy*, in particular 25–101; Immanuel Wallerstein, *Historical Capitalism with Capitalist Civilization* (London: Verso, 2011 [1983]); Immanuel Wallerstein, *The Modern World System IV: Centrist Liberalism Triumphant, 1789–1914* (Berkeley: University of California Press, 2011).
5. C. B. Macpherson, *The Life and Times of Liberal Democracy* (Oxford, UK: Oxford University Press, 1977).
6. Karl Polanyi, *The Great Transformation: The Political and Economic Origins of Our Times* (Boston, MA: Beacon Press, 1957).
7. Robert G. Angevine, *The Railroad and the State: War, Politics, and Technology in Nineteenth-Century America* (Stanford, CA: Stanford University Press, 2004); Albert Fishlow, "Internal Transportation in the Nineteenth and Early Twentieth Centuries," in Stanley L. Engerman and Robert E. Gallman, eds., *The Cambridge Economic History of the United States*, vol. 2, *The Long Nineteenth Century* (Cambridge, UK: Cambridge University Press, 2000), in particular 572–594.
8. David Harvey, *Spaces of Global Capitalism: Towards a Theory of Uneven Capitalist Development* (London: Verso, 2006), in particular 69–116.
9. Vincent P. Carosso, *Investment Banking in America: A History* (Cambridge, MA: Harvard University Press, 1970).
10. Mira Wilkins, "Multinational Enterprise to 1930: Discontinuities and Continuities," in Alfred Chandler and Bruce Mazlish, eds., *Leviathans: Multinational Corporations and the New Global History* (Cambridge, UK: Cambridge University Press, 2005), 45–80.
11. Harvey, *The New Imperialism*.
12. Charles Musser, *The Emergence of Cinema: The American Screen to 1907* (New York: Scribner's, 1990), 225–262. The films are also discussed by Kristen Whissel, *Picturing American Modernity: Traffic, Technology, and the Silent Cinema* (Durham, NC: Duke University Press, 2008), in particular 58–60 and 216–219; and James Castonguay, "The Spanish American War in U.S. Media Culture," http://chnm.gmu.edu/aq/war/. A number of the films have been made available online by the Library of Congress at http://memory.loc.gov/ammem/sawhtml/sawhome.html.
13. Paul A. C. Koistinen, *Mobilizing for Modern War: The Political Economy of American Warfare, 1865–1919* (Lawrence: University Press of Kansas, 1997). See also Robert P. Saldin, *War, the American State, and Politics Since 1898* (New York: Cambridge University Press, 2011), 12–13, 32–33.
14. Thomas J. McCormick, *China Market: America's Quest for Informal Empire, 1893–1901* (Chicago, IL: Quadrangle Books, 1967); Walter LeFeber, *The Cambridge History of American Foreign Relations*, vol. 2, *The American Search for Opportunity, 1865–1913* (Cambridge, UK: Cambridge University Press, 1993).
15. The political and economic logics of the Spanish-American war, as well as of the conflicts in the Philippines, China, and East Asia in 1898, are explicated in Thomas Schoonover, *Uncle Sam's War of 1898 and the Origins of Globalization* (Lexington: University Press of Kentucky, 2013). Writes Schoonover: "The conflux of rapid technological change, an aggressive and expansive U.S. political economy, and resistant traditional states in Spain and China ended in conflict. [. . .] The War of 1898 and its aftermath transferred the leadership (unwillingly on the part of Spain, most of Europe, and Japan) in [the] quest for wealth in Asia and the Pacific to the United States" (2).
16. Martí feared that the US planned "to put pressure on the island and drive it to war so as to fabricate a pretext to intervene in its affairs and with the credit earned as guarantor and

mediator keep it as its own." Cited in José M. Hernandez, "Cuba in 1898," https://www.loc.gov/rr/hispanic/1898/hernandez.html.

17. Philip S. Foner, *The Spanish-Cuban-American War and the Birth of American Imperialism, 1895–1902*, 2 vols. (New York: Monthly Review Press, 1972).
18. Musser, *The Emergence of Cinema*. On Grierson, see, for example. Ian Aitken, *Film and Reform: John Grierson and the Documentary Film Movement* (London: Routledge, 1990).
19. John Major, *Prize Possession: The United States and the Panama Canal 1903–1979* (Cambridge, UK: Cambridge University Press, 1993), 34–63.
20. 38 Stat., 63rd Congress, 76, June 23, 1913. The statute appointed a Government Exhibit Board, and this Board made funds available for the production and exhibition of films mostly at the Government pavilion at the Exposition in 1915. The considerable sum of $500,000 was initially set aside.
21. B. T. Galloway to W. O. Thompson, March 9, 1914, 2, RG 16, Records of the Office of the Secretary of Agriculture, General Correspondence of the Office of the Secretary, 1906–1970, Box No. 151, 1914, National Archives and Records Administration II (NARA). (Hereafter NARA materials from state bureaus and departments will be referenced by their Record Group Number [RG] with a corresponding box number, date, and page number where available.) Arthur Edwin Krows, in his expansive history of non-theatrical cinema, describes the USDA unit as "possibly the first government film laboratory in the world." Arthur Edwin Krows, "Motion Pictures—Not for Theatres," *Educational Screen*, January 1942, 14. The film-unit was charged with making films for the Exposition but had broader goals also to modernize agricultural practices.
22. Gregory A. Waller, "Nontheatrical Theaters: The Panama-Pacific International Exposition (1915)," paper delivered at the Society for Cinema and Media Studies conference, Boston, 2012.
23. James Livingston, *Origins of the Federal Reserve System: Money, Class, and Corporate Capitalism, 1890–1913* (Ithaca, NY: Cornell University Press, 1986). The 1913 creation of the Federal Reserve banking system was key here.
24. In 1902, Congress had authorized President Theodore Roosevelt to pay forty million dollars to France to buy its uncompleted assets in the Isthmus of Panama for the construction of the canal. J. P. Morgan, Sr., carried out the financing for what up to that point was probably the largest real-estate transaction in history. Ron Chernow, *The House of Morgan: An American Banking Dynasty and the Rise of Modern Finance* (New York: Atlantic Monthly Press, 1990), 111.
25. Ed Vulliamy, "How a US President and JP Morgan Created the State of Panama—and Turned It into a Tax Haven," *The Observer*, April 10, 2016, 6–7.
26. The subsequent history of the invented state of Panama's place in the global flows of trade and capital is fascinating. In 2016 a large cache of financial records was released that was labeled "The Panama Papers": the papers revealed the offshore tax havens utilized by the wealthy elite and corporations to avoid paying taxes to contribute to the public good. See Bastian Obermayer and Frederik Obermaier, *The Panama Papers: Breaking the Story of How the Rich and Powerful Hide Their Money* (London: Oneworld, 2017). Why were the papers called the Panama Papers? Because the records came from a Panamanian law firm established to make use of the *liberal* regulations regarding tax and economy that were largely set in place when the US created the nation for the purposes of constructing the Canal built in partnership with finance capital.

27. Frieda Knobloch, *The Culture of Wilderness: Agriculture as Colonization in the American West* (Chapel Hill: University of North Carolina Press, 1996). This is one aspect of what political scientist James C. Scott calls the "high modernist ideology" of the liberal capitalist state. James C. Scott, *Seeing Like a State: How Certain Schemes to Improve the Human Condition Have Failed* (New Haven, CT: Yale University Press, 1998), 4.
28. Elisabeth Sanders, *Roots of Reform: Farmers, Workers, and the American State, 1877–1917* (Chicago, IL: University of Chicago Press, 1999), 314–339; Roy V. Scott, *The Reluctant Farmer: The Rise of Agricultural Extension to 1914* (Urbana: University of Illinois Press, 1970); Daniel P. Carpenter, *The Forging of Bureaucratic Autonomy: Reputations, Networks, and Policy Innovation in Executive Agencies, 1862–1928* (Princeton, NJ: Princeton University Press, 2001), 179–254 and 290–325.
29. Ken A. Ingersent and A. J. Rayner, *Agricultural Policy in Western Europe and the United States* (Cheltenham, UK: Edward Elgar, 1999), 1–8; Robert Paarlberg and Dan Paarlberg, "Agricultural Policy in the Twentieth Century," *Agricultural History* 74, no. 2 (Spring 2000): 136–161.
30. Norman Pollock, *The Humane Economy: Populism, Capitalism, and Democracy* (New Brunswick, NJ: Rutgers University Press, 1990), in particular 1–11 and 57–84.
31. Giovanni Federico, *Feeding the World: An Economic History of Agriculture, 1800–2000* (Princeton, NJ: Princeton University Press, 2005), in particular 187–201.
32. Oliver Zunz, *Why the American Century?* (Chicago, IL: University of Chicago Press, 1998), 47–114.
33. Scott, *Seeing Like a State*; Chris Otter, "Making Liberal Objects: British Techno-Social Relations 1800–1900," *Cultural Studies* 21, no. 4 (July/September 2007): 570–590.
34. The testing and development of this mobile technology can be traced in various department memoranda and reports, including "Report to the Secretary of Agriculture on the Work of the Committee on Motion Picture Activities," November 30, 1914, Box 151 RG16, 6; George Wharton, Chairman of the Committee on Motion Picture Activities, "Memorandum to Chiefs of Bureaus, Independent Offices, and to the Committee on Motion Picture Activities," March 3, 1917, RG16 Box 415, 1; and John L. Cobbs, Jr., "Memorandum for the Secretary," April 29, 1921, Box 837, RG16, 4, all NARA.
35. *Use of Motion Pictures in Agricultural Extension Work* (Washington, DC: United States Department of Agriculture, 1926).
36. J. Emmett Winn, "Documenting Racism in an Agricultural Extension Film," *Film and History* 38, no. 1 (Spring 2008): 36–37.
37. Ibid., 39–40.
38. Alan Dawley, *Struggles for Justice: Social Responsibility and the Liberal State* (Cambridge, MA: Harvard University Press, 1991), 123. See also Martin J. Sklar, *The United States as a Developing Country: Studies in U.S. History in the Progressive Era and the 1920s* (New York: Cambridge University Press, 1992), in particular 1–77.
39. See Sven Beckert, *Empire of Cotton: A Global History* (New York: Vintage Books, 2015). Sugar is also relevant here, the control of which sparked the Spanish-American War.
40. Lee Grieveson, "The Cinema and the (Common) Wealth of Nations," in Lee Grieveson and Colin MacCabe, eds., *Empire and Film* (London: British Film Institute, 2011); Grieveson, "Empire Marketing Board" at the website *Colonial Film: Moving Images of the British Empire*, http://www.colonialfilm.org.uk/production-company/empire-marketing-board.

41. P. J. Cain and A. G. Hopkins, *British Imperialism, 1688–2000*, 2nd ed. (New York: Longmann, 2002); Tim Rooth, *British Protectionism and the International Economy: Overseas Commercial Policy in the 1930s* (Cambridge, UK: Cambridge University Press, 1992).
42. Stephen Constantine, *The Making of British Colonial Development Policy, 1914–1940* (London: Frank Cass, 1984).
43. D. L. LeMahieu, *A Culture for Democracy: Mass Communication and the Cultivated Mind in Britain between the Wars* (Oxford, UK: Clarendon Press, 1988); Simon Potter, *Broadcasting Empire: The BBC and the British World, 1922–1970* (Oxford, UK: Oxford University Press, 2012).
44. Quoted in David Meredith, "Imperial Images: The Empire Marketing Board, 1926–1932," *History Today* 37, no. 1 (January 1987): 31.
45. Notably in the British Representation of the People Act of 1918 that extended the franchise to non-property owners and the Nineteenth Amendment to the US Constitution in 1919 extending voting rights to women.
46. Philip Williamson, *Stanley Baldwin: Conservative Leadership and National Values* (Cambridge, UK: Cambridge University Press, 1999), 83–87; and J. A. Ramsden, "Baldwin and Film," in Nicholas Pronay and D. W. Spring, eds., *Propaganda, Politics and Film, 1918–1945* (London: Macmillan, 1982), 133.
47. Some of the EMB films are viewable at http://www.colonialfilm.org.uk/production-company/empire-marketing-board.
48. See, for example, the discussion of the Conservative Party and EMB films in Grieveson, "The Cinema and the (Common) Wealth of Nations," 80–84 and 96–99.
49. Commission on Education and Cultural Films, *The Film in National Life* (London: Allen and Unwin, 1932), 126.
50. Julian Huxley, *Africa View* (London: Chatto, 1931), 1, quoted in Aboubakar Sanogo, "Colonialism, Visuality and the Cinema: Revisiting the Bantu Educational Kinema Experiment," in Grieveson and MacCabe, eds., *Empire and Film*, 231.
51. Tom Rice, "Bekefilm," at *Colonial Film: Moving Images of the British Empire*, http://www.colonialfilm.org.uk/production-company/bekefilm; Rosaleen Smyth, "The Development of British Colonial Film Policy, 1927–1939 with Special Reference to East and Central Africa," *Journal of African History* 20, no. 3 (1979): 437–450.
52. L. A. Notcutt and G. C. Latham, *The African and the Cinema: An Account of the Bantu Educational Kinema Experiment during the Period March 1935 to May 1937* (London: Edinburgh House Press, 1937), 24.
53. Ibid., 25
54. Aaron Windel, "The Bantu Educational Kinema Experiment and the Political Economy of Community Development," in Grieveson and MacCabe, eds., *Empire and Film*, in particular 207–211.
55. Established in 1939, the Colonial Film Unit would subsequently formalize this use of cinema by sending a Savings Bank van alongside its cinema van to encourage local populations to sign up for a new bank account after watching the films. See the details in "The Mobile Cinema Van in the Villages (Contributed by an African)," *Colonial Cinema*, March 1945, 11–14. My thanks to Tom Rice for this reference.
56. James Burns, "American Philanthropy and Colonial Film-making," in Grieveson and MacCabe, eds., *Empire and Film*, 56. The film, together with astute analysis of its context and form by Tom Rice, is available at http://www.colonialfilm.org.uk/node/735.

57. See Tom Rice, "Colonial Film Unit" and "Anti-Plague Operations, Lagos," at *Colonial Film: Moving Images of the British Empire*, http://www.colonialfilm.org.uk/production-company/colonial-film-unit and http://www.colonialfilm.org.uk/node/1526.
58. Glenn Reynolds, "The Bantu Educational Kinema Experiment and the Struggle for Hegemony in British East and Central Africa, 1935–1937," *Historical Journal of Film, Radio and Television* 29, no. 1 (March 2009): 61.
59. Notcutt and Latham, *The African and the Cinema*, 75.
60. Reynolds, "The Bantu Educational Kinema Experiment," 64.
61. Indeed, as the Eisenstein example earlier suggested, this imperative spread out to other state systems too, and Soviet Russia innovated mobile film education quickly after the revolution of 1917.
62. See also Glenn Reynolds, "Image and Empire: Anglo-American Cinematic Interventions in Sub-Saharan Africa, 1921–1937," *South African Historical Journal* 48 (May 2003): 90–108.
63. W. Roger Louis and Ronald Robison, "The Imperialism of Decolonization," *Journal of Imperial and Commonwealth History* 22, no. 3 (1994): 462–511. See also Arrighi, *The Long Twentieth Century*, 58–73; Neil Smith, *The Endgame of Globalization* (London: Routledge, 2005), 53–121.
64. David Trotter, "Representing Connection: A Multimedia Approach to Colonial Film, 1918–1939," in Grieveson and MacCabe, eds., *Empire and Film*, 152.

CHAPTER 26

....

DANDYISM, CIRCULATION, AND EMERGENT CINEMA IN IRAN

The Powers of Asynchrony

....

KAVEH ASKARI

For much of the twentieth century the juncture of dandyism, media, and modernity provided writers, illustrators, and filmmakers in Iran with a wellspring of comic material. Jamshid Vahidi's *Gigolo*, serialized and illustrated in the arts and culture magazine *White and Black* (*Sepid o Siah*, 1954–57), is not the best known dandy text, but it offers a snapshot of Iranian dandyism peerless in its value as an introduction. The character who serves as tour guide and narrator of the story, Mamoosh Pochettian, describes the routines of the gigolo, a 1950s incarnation of dandyism in Iran.[1]

One of the many composite illustrations in the series depicts Mamoosh standing before a mirror describing his elaborate morning ritual, which involves grooming his *Douglasi* (after Douglas Fairbanks) moustache, styling his exaggerated *Corneli* (after Cornel Wilde) pompadour, and powdering his legs so that they will slide into his narrow trousers. He lacks access to new clothing, a troubling situation, as style is his primary concern. He hesitates to remove his jacket in public for fear of exposing the patchwork holding it together.[2] He is careful to conceal the tattered parts of his socks in his shiny loafers, their own riddled soles amended with years of makeshift repairs.[3] His wristwatch is borrowed.

Mamoosh comes of age in the postwar downtown dancehall scene, but he looks back across several decades. The Iranian gigolo's style references the 1920s French gigolo and subsequent adaptations of the character by authors such as Edna Ferber and Noël Coward. He bridges the 1950s rockabilly, the 1930s dancehall denizen, the 1920s modernist artist, and the 1890s aesthete. Mamoosh's modern identity is highly mediated, and these mediations interweave past and present. His clothes are as chronologically mismatched as his abundant film references. His family name refers to the French *pochette*, an accessory associated with feminized Iranian dandies since the early 1920s. His first name is a play on diminutives like "Mamal," a contraction of the common name Mohammad Ali: it combines the first syllable "Mam" with "*moosh*" (mouse) to create a portmanteau name that sounds something like "Mickey Mouse." When Mamoosh spends time with his beloved female dandy, Gigi (another comic "gigolized" name used in popular Iranian films), he discusses "a history of artistic kisses of movie stars" before he sets his own "mise-en-scène" for "filmic kisses."[4] He dances tango and mambo and believes everyone should be able to hum the tune of "Johnny Guitar."[5] He memorizes songs and soundtracks by hanging out outside record stores and cinemas.[6] Throughout this memoir of a life cultivated and mediated, Mamoosh guides the reader through his sartorial tricks, his favorite haunts among the cafés on Istanbul and Lalezar Avenues, and his principles for dealing with the contradictions of living such a high-profile lifestyle on limited means. He refers to these principles, illustrated throughout the text, as his "gigology."[7]

> You might scoff at my strange taste, but do not forget that you are talking to a gigolo. [. . .] Gigolos are committed to loud colours because they attract attention. You will often see a gigolo dressed in brown suede shoes with crepe soles, red socks, blue trousers, a white belt, a green shirt, a brown tie, and a yellow suede coat. It is vital that we follow this fundamental principle. We hold the acts of posturing and making spectacles of ourselves sacred above all else, and we are ready to give our lives for our convictions. For this very same reason, in painting, I am a fan of the movements that create a splash: Cubism, Realism, Surrealism [. . .] basically any style that ends in "ism." The classical style and I are mortal enemies. If a Cubist were to paint a portrait of Gigi and gift it to me, I would readily hang it in the bedroom and enjoy its jumbled lines as much as I enjoy her own lovely face. As a general rule, the gigolo rejects everything that appeals to the public taste. This is why we value modernist poetry, Cubist painting, and the like. We make a show of support for these new forms of art in order to be admired.[8]

These two images (see figure 26.1) illustrating Mamoosh's gigology offer a tongue-in-cheek introduction to the powers of asynchrony in modernist self-presentation. That is, they highlight the imbalanced exchange of goods along global trade routes as well as the forms of detachment and refusal that are available to an ambivalent modernist like Mamoosh. At the same time that Mamoosh is a figure associated with circulating goods and fashions, particularly those associated with cinema, he is also defined by the obstructions to this circulation and his talent in working with those obstructions. As a result, his image is literally a modernist collage. In the illustration on the left, the illustrator has scribbled a Corneli hairstyle and Douglasi mustache over an advertisement for men's fashion. Half of the text's illustrations are like this one. They compile

 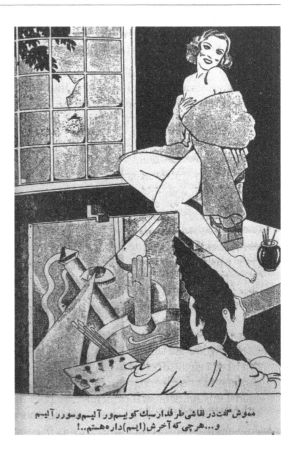

FIGURE 26.1 Mamoosh beholding himself in a mirror (left); a fan of any style that ends in an "ism" (right). Illustrations from Jamshid *Gigolo: A Memoir of Mamoosh Pochettian* (Tehran: Entesharat-e Sepid o Siah, 1957).

and repurpose print material from European magazines and catalogues. In the drawn illustration on the right, Mamoosh is put together in this same wardrobe, which barely conceals that it is assembled out of second-hand finds. He gazes upon the caricature of Surrealist and Cubist tropes in a painting of his beloved, which the illustrator draws in a style different from that used to draw Mamoosh and from the style in which Gigi is rendered as present in the room. "In-person" Gigi, seated as if posing for the painting, is no less stylized than the portrait. She resembles a Hollywood pin-up of the kind that was repurposed, probably from Italian film fan magazines, and printed in color on the back cover of each issue of *White and Black*.[9] The character moves from one stylized citational frame to another. The illustrator of Mamoosh and Gigi incorporates collage and bricolage, just as the characters of Mamoosh and Gigi approach their own modernism as an irreverent juxtaposition of mismatched objects and styles.

If Iranian dandy stories illustrate subcultures that thrive on appropriations of found objects and styles, then these stories offer a cosmopolitan framework through which to reconsider longstanding discussions of subcultural bricolage. In Mamoosh and Gigi's manifesto of style over substance, they engage, like the well-known subcultures that helped to establish cultural studies methodology, in a stylistic refusal of official culture. Their refusal is partly based on repurposing everyday items from that official culture. But in this case, they do so by repurposing found objects with a wider geographical and historical range. The passage quoted above aligns almost point-for-point with the characteristics of subcultural bricolage as Dick Hebdige defines them: dissonant blending of elements, unnatural self-presentation, stylization, spectacularity, and a form of refusal *through* conspicuous consumption.[10] Mamoosh knows that he looks out of place and unnatural. He blends crepe-soled suede shoes (a style developed during British imperial adventures in the Middle East) with gaudy socks and trousers. His taste in art is as mismatched as his pants. He would give his life before giving up his commitment to style, and he loves consumer goods in a manner that contradicts public taste. Each of these elements appears with regularity in many iterations of the Iranian dandy. But as they collectively relate to networks of exchange much wider than those addressed in foundational studies of subcultural bricolage, they warrant a shift in emphasis. Complicated distribution networks simply take more time to function than their streamlined counterparts. When objects and styles trace circuitous paths over long distances, they fall out of sync. They create their own temporal incongruities. The dandy in Iran exaggerates these incongruities and builds a spectacular subcultural style from dissonances between one period and the next as much as between coexistent social spheres.

In what follows, I consider how a cross-media focus on dandyism and asynchrony might help to position a singular silent film within a history of an emergent cinema in Iran. The silent period in Iran witnessed an active film culture formed around imported films and commercial cinemas, but there was very little local production. The film trade through the 1930s was characterized by a series of dramatic disruptions, appropriations, and recalibrations. For these reasons, I address the only surviving silent fiction feature film made in Iran, *Mr. Haji, the Movie Actor* (Ovanes Ohanian, 1934), as part of a dynamic culture of circulation, rather than as the start of a narrative of a national industry. In silent cinema historiography, of Iran and of other early experiments with filmmaking in the Middle East, where uneven circulation of cinema becomes particularly evident, practices of reassembly warrant positive attention.

In *Mr. Haji, the Movie Actor*, bricolage realigns past and present. I address the significance of the film's asynchronies by reading them through theories of the dandy's self-mediation and desire for commodities and alongside the influential play *Jafar Khan Has Returned from the West* (Hasan Moghaddam, 1922). The characters in these stories, like the real-life dandies who created them, navigate a cosmopolitan sphere that offers them promising, but limited, agency and access. In response, they braid asynchrony into their style. Their junk-shop bricolage looks backward even as it pays lip service to consumerist fashion. If the acceleration of global exchange yields the confidence and agency that Rebecca Walkowitz associates with traditional (as opposed to critical) cosmopolitanism, here ambivalence undermines that confidence.[11] These figures emphasize the uneven chronologies of global exchange and the creative adaptations to those chronologies. While I would hesitate to rely on often-comical Iranian dandy texts to bear full responsibility for a critique of globalized consumerism, their practices of asynchronous bricolage, their attitudes of refusal, and their enduring failures should not be excluded from a history of critical cosmopolitanism.[12] The figures in these stories, as well as many of their authors, are aesthete assemblers, modernists who look backward, and avowed attention hounds who nevertheless seek to build coalitions. These ironies offer a way of approaching both the global geographies of dandyism and the shifting geographies of silent cinema studies. Thus an approach informed by the way Iranian dandies enshrine an ambivalent modernism through their asynchrony can draw out, rather than explain away, the ambivalent modernism of a singular film and of early film culture in the region.

Dandy Geographies, Mediations, and Commodities

In developing an understanding of asynchronous dandyism, I am engaging recent theorizations of the dandy as a figure for cosmopolitan exchange. Important here are recurring themes of geographical dislocation, technological mediation, and a fascination with commodities. Jessica Feldman highlights the challenges in locating the dandy when definitions of the type often begin with a gesture abroad. "For the French, dandyism is an English phenomenon, an import. For stylish Londoners 'la mode,' Parisian style, must set the standard. This international proliferation of dandyism suggests the very displacement crucial to 'placing' dandyism: it exists in its purest form always on the periphery of one's vision, often in a foreign language or a text requiring decipherment."[13] For Rhonda Garelick, the dandy emerges alongside the rise of commercial media as "a personality that encompasses its own mechanically reproduced versions, and eventually seems indistinguishable from them."[14] Dandies lent themselves easily to caricature, but their mediaphilia created a symbiosis with even their harshest satirists. They were at home in print and moving-image media as well as in the venues for the industrialization of culture, including dancehalls and cinemas. For this reason, such studies make a point of moving, as I do, between dandies of flesh and blood and those of ink or celluloid.

Elisa Glick sets up two fundamental traditions of reading dandyism across historical periods. The dandy as style, coming from Sontag, emerges as a figure who sees the world as an aesthetic phenomenon and is preoccupied with surface, artifice, and commodity fetishism. The dandy as a figure for political rebellion, following Baudelaire, rejects bourgeois culture, (hetero)sexual norms, materialism, industriousness, and utilitarianism. Rather than pursue one of these elements at the expense of the other, Glick sets them in dialectical relation, beginning with a reading of *The Picture of Dorian Gray* (1890). "Both enchanted and threatened by the commodity dreamworld that engulfs him, Dorian's ambivalent desire for objects is actually a repudiation of value that strives to free the commodity from its mundane existence in the system of exchange."[15] In this formulation, the political dimension of dandyism happens not despite, but by way of, the preoccupation with enchanting surfaces. Most importantly, Glick takes the dandy's relation to the *commodity* as a way to place these elements into dynamic relation.

Dandyism in the Middle East and South Asia intertwines these three elements of geographical dislocation, control over a mediated personality, and the preoccupation with circulating commodities, and amplifies their stakes. If the dandy often depends on something acquired from abroad as a condition for a kind of self-mediation, what happens when these acquisitions cross thousands of miles and depend on multiple trade networks? If the dandy thrives on interaction with media, how does that interaction change when the local publishing infrastructures and imaging technologies have formed through uneasy relationships with those trade networks? If an ambivalent relation to the commodity establishes the agency of the dandy, how might that ambivalence manifest itself differently for commodities routed eastward, traded through secondhand markets, or for commodities on indirect trade routes, say, from England to port cities in India and then through the Persian Gulf to inland cities in the Middle East?

The self-mediating glance abroad, supported by the circulation of commodities, has a reciprocal configuration in this context. Cities in the Middle East and South Asia were relay points for ambivalent collectors. They were producers of the goods used to express an anti-industrial response in the West (among connoisseurs and craft-conscious builders) and at the same time were destination points for colonial goods and open-market commodities (including fashion, automobiles, timepieces, phonographs, and films; more on these specific examples later). The Western dandy collected handmade objects from around the world, especially from the Middle East and South Asia, leveraging an imperialist fantasy to obsessively consider an object's appeal to the senses and to put it at odds with its usual instrumental exchange. The Middle Eastern and South Asian dandies stood in the same circuit of exchange, closer to where many of these objects were made and engaged with objects moving in the opposite direction. Dorian Gray burns "odorous gums from the East" while Mamoosh and Jafar Khan, discussed in the next section, spray themselves with French perfume (which was, itself, sometimes composed of ingredients sourced along some of these same trade routes).[16] While they may not be entirely visible to each other, these dandies' looks abroad are linked through a network of asynchronous exchange. And as Ohanian's filmmaking experiments and Mamoosh's constant film references make clear, for the Iranian dandy, the emerging film culture reinforced these linkages.

If there is an association to be made between the dandy's cosmopolitan consumption and state power within Iran, one could pursue the forms of urban consumption that followed top-down Pahlavi modernization initiatives.[17] These initiatives began with the infrastructural changes and secularization policies of Reza Shah, and then, increasingly during the subsequent rule of Mohammad Reza Shah, associated spectacular consumption with a certain elitist conception of national unity. But, as Golbarg Rekabtalaei points out, this characterization of the powerful cosmopolitan elite elides the experience of everyday life in non-elite, multi-ethnic, and religiously diverse neighborhoods in Tehran. It also obscures the fact that these attitudes formed in a continual process, not as a fixed relation.[18] As a figure of conspicuous consumption, the Iranian dandy certainly reminded some writers of various forms of elitism and new-money consumerism, particularly in the postwar era. Also prominent in these representations, as Mamoosh illustrates, is a kind of outsider relationship to commodities in everyday urban space that runs counter to elite consumerism and one-dimensional conceptions of national modernization. If speed of circulation is essential to the commercial projection of power across space, then the dandy's asynchrony becomes a liability. If both top-down modernization and fashionable consumerism depend on the ability to control attention through print media and the moving image, then the dandy's excesses interrupt this instrumental control with alternative media-savvy appropriations of attention. Making a spectacle of oneself on a downtown sidewalk neither serves the interests of the state nor is it particularly profitable. Mamoosh, proudly superficial as he may be in the story, lacks the personal wealth that would make such superficiality easy to recuperate. His resourceful adaptations to the holes in his jacket, socks, and shoes, commodities that had been in use for a while, indicate an ambivalent relation to the new. In the convenient parallel between perfumes crossing paths along trade routes, it bears repeating that those channels of exchange were defined by obstructions, and by adaptations to those obstructions. When objects of cosmopolitan consumption have lost their luster, they struggle to remain useful in a nationalist project of modernization. These objects serve as a reminder of the forms of friction that have characterized their exchange.[19] Commodities that do not circulate easily, but circulate nonetheless, possess a certain historicity that, in non-Western dandy texts, nags at the fascination with the modern as new and fashionable. These stylish texts dwell in the démodé. In doing so, they call for an approach to circulation that examines the long shelf life of objects and styles typically associated with a cosmopolitan up-to-date-ness. Such an approach might instead highlight the asynchronous bricolage that characterizes the practices of these (actual and fictional) fellow travelers who often cultivate detachment from centers of power, either local or foreign.

JAFAR KHAN ON LALEZAR AVENUE AND IN ALEXANDRIA

Before moving on to *Mr. Haji, the Movie Actor*, I want to briefly discuss perhaps the most significant text in establishing the Iranian dandy type. Hasan Moghaddam's one-act play

Jafar Khan Has Returned from the West influenced later avatars and provided a context in which they would be received. The play would not be adapted for the screen until long after its early performances and printings in the 1920s, but it premiered in a theater/cinema exhibition space and has been referenced in many films. It went through multiple adaptations, including a loose film adaptation made by Ali Hatami in 1985, and some of its language and situations have evolved into everyday expressions. It has been discussed as a foundational work of modern literature and as an illustration of the ambivalence of the Iranian intellectual toward Western modernity.[20] Another look at this famous work, at its historical references as well as the institutions that brought it to the public, can highlight the ways asynchrony characterizes the dandy archetype at one of its foundational moments.

The play portrays the dandy as *fokoli*, a term (adapted in the early twentieth century from the French *faux-col*) literally meaning one who wears a detachable collar, necktie, or bowtie. The title character is a foreign-educated Iranian young man who returns home to his traditional family styled and affected as a fin-de-siècle Francophile aesthete. When Jafar Khan wants to socialize, even with his own family, he insists on imposing exaggerated European customs instead of following Iranian forms of hospitality. He eats his food, including individual grapes, with a knife and fork. He forces his poodle Carotte, who only understands French commands, on his devout uncle and tutor, who fret about the dog's unclean nature but eventually refer to him as *Havij Agha* (Mr. Carrot). Jafar Khan, concerned about microbes and preoccupied with his watch, lectures his family about cleanliness and punctuality. His family is represented as smothering, comically misinformed, and superstitious. Jafar Khan's mother has heard a false rumor that Chartreuse is made from the skin of dead priests. She summons this repellant thought to justify her suspicion of Jafar's contacts in the West: "They are not Muslims. If they were, they would make their liquor from grapes like normal people."[21] His family members consult an almanac, searching for numerological rather than rational guidance for their daily choices. *Jafar Khan*'s world is one of exaggerated satire, but its play with the histories of its stereotypes marks it with the extremity of camp more than the conceit of a socially conservative comedy of manners.

Moghaddam's own work as a coalition builder presents another challenge to reading the story as simple conservative satire. His engaged, self-aware play with types stands in contrast to the crude dandy stereotypes found in nationalist or masculinist parody in the decades that followed. Moghaddam, who played the title role in the first production, himself lived many of the experiences parodied in his play. He was educated in Switzerland, was known for his sartorial refinement, and traveled extensively, working in Cairo and Istanbul. The institutional life of Moghaddam and his collaborators counters the solipsism of dandy caricatures, including his own. He was a coalition builder and one aware of the community formed in downtown coffeehouses and performance spaces. He was a key member of the Young Iran Society in the 1920s, an organization that advocated, in Hamid Naficy's assessment, "a reasoned, selective adoption of important aspects of the West, in other words, a form of syncretic Westernization."[22]

The society met at the café of the Grand Hotel on Lalezar Avenue, a famous gathering place for intellectuals and partial inspiration for the play. The hotel café is featured in the play's narrative, and the hotel's theater space hosted *Jafar Khan*'s first performance. The same theater space also served as a first-run venue and distribution relay point for silent films under the name Grand Cinema. The Grand Hotel complex, a hub for the movement of guests as well as traveling performances and films, offers a prime vehicle through which to consider chronologies of circulation. This choice of location, combined with Moghaddam's own travels and coalitional interests, encourages attention to the multiple forms of asynchrony at work in the play.

Jafar Khan reflects the three elements of the dandy discussed above. He is defined by his geographical dislocation, his self-mediation, and his obsession with objects in circulation. He peppers his speech with bad French, but he is also losing his Persian language skills. Inseparable from his lint brush, atomizer, and toiletries, he undertakes a form of self-presentation that speaks to no one but himself. As part of his hyperactive attention to self-mediation, he makes appointments by presenting his own *carte de visite* instead of following Iranian forms of hospitality. His trademark pochette and watch (objects that would define the Iranian dandy in coming decades) function less as useful tools than as clutter that gets between him and the other characters of the story.

When Jafar Khan's clutter and mannerisms come from is just as important as *where* they come from. Jafar Khan is out of date and unaware. He is less a successful modern cosmopolite than a collector of insufferable affectations of bygone fads. The *carte de visite* may signify Jafar Khan's wholehearted embrace of the West, but not because it showcases the latest fashions. This ostensibly modern custom of mediating one's arrival reads as clueless and démodé, like his mismatched socks and gloves. The same can be said of his expressions, pochette, atomizer, and other articles of grooming. The affectations satirized in this story were not exclusive to Iranian perceptions of Westernized dandies. They were just as common in representations in Western satirical media, many of which would have featured in the imported silent films that screened at the Grand Cinema (the same stage where *Jafar Khan* was first performed). Numerous dislocated traditions overlap in the play, with its satire targeting multiple forms of backwardness.

Moghaddam must have become well versed in these conventions of satire during his travels, as his own authorial voice and role as a performer play with the ironies of "fashionable" affectations that are out of sync. With Naficy's assessment of Moghaddam's syncretism in mind, we may read Jafar Khan's failures less as a cautionary tale about his admiration of Europe than as a result of his one-dimensional understanding of his own success as a cosmopolite. On the surface, this character's dandyism amounts to a kind of comic failure. But Moghaddam's own dandyism steers the tone of the work away from a moralistic high ground. The writing offers multi-dimensional satire whose simple lessons resist being taken literally. Moghaddam's performance of the title character adds another layer of awareness. Jafar Kahn demonstrates a failure to cultivate a capacity for reflection on his own asynchronies so that Moghaddam may give voice to this capacity as author and performer.

Finally, Moghaddam's subsequent role in publicizing the play outside of Iran points to the ways in which his dandy persona helped him to reconfigure the past. Like many Iranian dandies, he played with the idea of the démodé, but he also served as an anti-official guide through the treasures of the distant past. Moghaddam translated the play himself into French and published it under the pseudonym Ali No-Rouze (Ali New Year) in Egypt, in a special issue of the journal *Messages d'Orient* devoted to Iran.[23] Moghaddam guest-edited this special issue and juxtaposed his own modern parody with several illustrated articles written by him and his brother, Mohsen, on the art, architecture, and literature of Iran. Hasan and Mohsen (who went on to an influential career as a professor of art and architecture) also published the mission statement of the Young Iran Society and wrote about how knowledge of the region should come from the region.

In this 1926 publication, a modernist writer, and the dandy figure that he made a household name, intersect with the politically charged history of modern mediation of the ancient Middle East. Under one of his many comical pen names (another being Pierrot Malade), he translates his own satire into French and also presents, in collaboration with his brother, the serious topic of art in Iran for a francophone audience in Alexandria. Hasan takes an unserious posture with *Messages d'Orient*, which provides a welcome distance from the journal's imperial claims to knowledge. And he was not alone. Other notable Iranian dandies followed this pattern of unseriousness in mediating Iran's cultural history. Bahram Kirmani, a self-styled "Balliol man" (where he visited in the 1890s but did not complete a degree), was influential in opening up sites of ancient and Islamic art in Iran to Western visitors in the interwar period. He was known to overdress, to recite Swinburne in everyday conversations, and to profess that "Oscar Wilde was much more the type of guy for me. He was a great friend of mine, so was Mrs. Langtry."[24] In a media environment where representations of histories of the Middle East included official government publicity as well as a range of publications laced with the ideologies of missionaries, settler communities, or energy-extraction companies, the posture of the detached and irreverent mediator allowed dandies to perform the intellectual labor of historical mediation against the grain of some of these other institutions.

Assembling *Mr. Haji, the Movie Actor*

Let me return, now, to *Mr. Haji, the Movie Actor*, relying on these readings of Iranian dandies' engagements with modernity as a way to approach the film's historiographical challenges. The literary works discussed so far mark moments in a history of dandies, both real and fictional, who depended on mediated asynchrony as a means of cultivating detachment. Moghaddam's *Jafar Khan* assembles 1890s clichés in a play printed alongside articles on Iranian literature and art, which are attributed to Moghaddam's ostentatious pseudonym in a volume published for francophone Alexandrians. Mamoosh and

Gigi are presented as collages of movies, clothing advertisements, pin-ups, and anachronistic modernisms in a magazine that reprints, reviews, and advertises each of these elements. All of this material is shaped by powerful institutions as it moves through imbalanced exchange networks, but the dandy cultivates a detached and irreverent attitude toward those institutions. If modern living in Iran meant unavoidable relationships of power, including state modernization and commercial circulation of goods, the dandy navigates those relationships through a form of modernism that is curated but out of step. This modernism conforms neither to official modern nationalism nor to the merely fashionable consumption of goods in circulation.

Cinema figures prominently in the circulation of commodities, star imagery, and modernist styles in Iran. Film prints follow along the same trade routes as natural resources, film publicity fuels the engine of magazine production, and film knowledge provides a common language for syncretic modernization. My approach to *Mr. Haji*, rather than understanding this surviving narrative feature as a single-film origin story of a national cinema, is to discern the traces of circulation that made a film like this possible. And these traces are numerous, moving as they do through Vertov, Richard Talmadge, Maciste, Méliès, knockabout comedy, and the early chase film. Placed next to Mamoosh's irreverent collection of -isms, these multiple uprooted references deserve to be assessed as more than irrelevant bowdlerizations. In other words, if creating more space within the discipline of film studies for non-Western silent cinemas means pulling away from the historiographical narrowing that can occur by nationalizing a singular narrative feature and thus downplaying the reach of its many citations, then following the dandy's asynchronous citations can offer one path to remedy this narrowing. *Mr. Haji* itself is about the process of appropriation. It happens to be a reflexive irreverent film, directed by a dandy, about dandyism, modernity, filmmaking, and moviegoing.

An analysis based solely on *Mr. Haji*'s narrative might contradict a reading of the film as playing with asynchrony. The story has its fair share of heroic certainties. It looks forward to the instrumental possibilities of cinema in a way that lines up with Reza Shah's reforms. The main narrative tension of *Mr. Haji* repurposes a common early cinema trope toward this end: a conservative rube encounters cinema for the first time and is won over by the medium. Mr. Haji (Habibolla Morad) is a religious man, suspicious of cinema, and refuses to allow his daughter Parvin to act in films. Meanwhile, a dandy filmmaker (Ohanian) with writer's block cannot come up with a scenario for his next film. Parvin's fiancé, Parviz, devises a plan by which he and the filmmaker might change Mr. Haji's mind. The family's servant, Pouri, will steal Mr. Haji's watch so that they can film the ensuing chase. The filmmaker will finally have his film, and the young couple will have a pretext to lure Mr. Haji into a cinema. They wager that after recognizing himself on screen, Mr. Haji will have no choice but to accept the new medium, his daughter's chosen profession, and her marriage to a man with the same profession. And in the climactic scene he does just that. This resolution aligns with a nationalist instrumentality and a national film history of pioneers. But given that the narrative is one of the thinnest elements of the film, it provides less of a solid structure than an excuse to pile on variety acts and other filmmaking experiments. To understand this film in line with the forms of dandyism discussed here, we must turn away from its obvious message and move carefully through these elements, first its context of production, and then its layers of asynchronous bricolage.

The production of the film hovered somewhere between the ambitions of coalition building and that of tall-tale showmanship to try to drum up investment. Ohanian did not just want to make films; he wanted to establish a film school involving gymnastic, comedic, and dramatic actor training. Through careful attention to the discussion of the school in the media, he did manage to build a functioning program.[25] He was creative in his fundraising efforts for the school and his film productions, and he did not shy away from dressing his makeshift projects in grand façades. Ohanian established a board of directors for the *Mr. Haji* project and claimed to have convinced Cecil B. DeMille to serve on the board. The DeMille papers do indicate later correspondence with the Shah about making historical epics in Iran, but I have found no record of DeMille's correspondence with anyone in Iran in the 1930s.[26] It helped to oversell these projects in order to attract investors, which Ohanian eventually did by selling shares in the production and small product tie-ins within the film. While the budget and production were modest, the hype surrounding the production was robust. Even as box-office returns ultimately disappointed, Ohanian and journalists used the film's release as an opportunity to reflect on the state of filmmaking in Iran.[27] In practical economic terms, Ohanian's film project was a coalitional effort that borrowed from as many sources as possible.

Ohanian composed the film as a series of episodes: a scene with a quack dentist, a knockabout car chase, a gymnasium scene, a stage performance with a conjurer and a dancer, and a concluding scene that takes place in an outdoor cinema. Each of these episodes was a stand-alone exercise created with the help of students at Ohanian's school. Much of the eclectic footage bears no indication that it was even shot with this particular film in mind before being recycled and edited to appear as diegetic material within the frame story. Although it was a new production, in this way it shares a structure of loose compilation with films that local exhibitors fashioned out of pieces of globally circulating junk prints. André Malraux famously described them thus: "In Persia, I once saw a film that does not exist. It was called *The Life of Charlie*.... The Armenian exhibitors had artfully compiled Chaplin's shorts into a single film. The resulting feature film was surprising: the myth of Chaplin appeared in its pure state."[28] These Armenian exhibitors mentioned by Malraux did not themselves receive original prints. They sourced their second-hand prints from Russia and elsewhere. They were often already reedited for a local audience before being relayed to markets farther south. These practices of compilation, which were not unusual to cinema audiences in Iran, further compel a reading of the film in the context of circulation. As a work of asynchronous bricolage, the film points to the realities of cinema's obstructions in the region—to limited films for exhibitors and limited film stock for filmmakers.

At the same time, Ohanian and some of his collaborators, as former students of the Moscow Film Academy, would have known the compilation films of Esfir Schub and the montage theories of Dziga Vertov and Sergei Eisenstein.[29] *Mr. Haji*'s creators were likely familiar with Soviet films that edited nondiegetic footage so that it appeared to take place within a staged narrative, such as *Chess Fever* (1925) or *A Kiss from Mary Pickford* (1927). The economic factors driving compilation converged in this case with an intellectual tradition that theorized compilation and put into practice an influential aesthetics of reused footage. The film, like so many productions during this period, was a one-off experiment. As such, it does little to foreshadow Iranian industry standards that would develop in the 1950s. As a raw-edged experimental effort of a Soviet-trained instructor and his students, it reveals other historical patterns. From the bodies of the actors to the cutting exercises deployed through the film, we see the influence of Soviet film styles and of Soviet film education.

Vertovian subjects in *Mr. Haji* recur throughout the scenes of daily urban life in Tehran, as do Vertovian techniques of formal parallelism and analysis of trained bodily movement. To my mind, the most noteworthy gesture to Vertov happens at the moment when the chase plot of the film wends its way through Ohanian's film school. Ohanian uses editing to enfold non-diegetic footage of gymnastic performance into the narrative. The sequence echoes Vertov's interest in using slow and reverse motion as tools to analyze the movements of trained bodies. Like the divers in *Kino Eye* (1924), the acrobats in this scene fly in reverse motion from a landing pad to a diving platform. They begin dives in slow-motion handstands from this platform. In reverse motion again, gymnasts levitate onto and spin around a horizontal bar. The scene deploys a Vertovian technique, but it also documents the curriculum of Ohanian's acting school. This footage may not have been staged specifically for *Mr. Haji*'s story. Given the skill of the gymnasts and the fact that the school emphasized gymnastic training, it is likely that the footage came from a filmed demonstration for the students and was resourcefully patched into the feature-length project.

Of course, gymnastic training formed a foundation for the biomechanical acting style, which influenced performances in the films of Lev Kuleshov like *By the Law* (1926) and *The Extraordinary Adventures of Mr. West in the Land of the Bolsheviks* (1924). While not consistent throughout *Mr. Haji*, we see movements derived from this training in the performances of some of the actors. Ohanian's own performance as the director of the film-within-the-film stands out. After an early intertitle that reads "A director in search of a scenario," the director brainstorms scenes from behind his desk. This presents an opportunity for him to run through a lexicon of dramatic poses, which he performs in an articulated series of gestures and short pauses. These serial, punctuated movements, combined with eccentric expressions and diagonal positioning of his shoulders, bear the clearest traces of a performance style seen in actors who came up under Kuleshov's mentorship. Habibolla Morad's performance as Mr. Haji is less kinetically precise than Ohanian's, but his repetitive, dynamic, eccentric positioning of shoulders and arms is not out of place next to the director's movements. These performances do not point to a single pedigree so much as an interlacing of -isms of which the constructivism of biomechanical performance is one important thread.

The editing choices in the film are as eclectic as the performances. The scenes fit together like a series of exercises in film editing, with each change of location offering an opportunity to play with a new form. The sequence that most resembles an exercise, and pushes the limits of continuity in its play with form, is a series of Kuleshov-effect gags with a microscope in a dentist's office (see figure 26.2). After removing one of Mr. Haji's teeth, the dentist places it under a microscope where it reveals fantasy images to each person who looks through the ocular. The views through the microscope recall early scientific films and their fantasy reconfigurations in films like *Les Joyeux Microbes* (Émile Cohl, 1909), a Gaumont film that circulated widely.

Each of these fantasies is filmed from above to suggest the microscope's point-of-view, but these linkages remain loose, as no other techniques to suggest continuity are used. The dentist's look through the microscope is intercut with a progression of bandaged patients holding their jaws. His assistant (played by Zema Ohanian, Ovanes's daughter) looks through the same microscope and sees a man blowing kisses and offering a flower, which then appears before her by way of a match cut and a substitution splice. His male assistant, a strongman who operates a massive winch to remove teeth, glances through the eyepiece to find a barking poodle and falls back against the wall. The dentist's view satisfies his desire for business, the first assistant's for love, and then this expectation is upset by a strongman, a dog, and a pratfall. The microscope scene documents a series of

FIGURE 26.2 A strongman peers through a microscope in a sequence that borrows several elements from early cinema. *Mr. Haji, the Movie Actor* (Ovanes Ohanian, 1934).

experiments with montage to structure a gag with loosely linked images from discontinuous sources.

The film's episodes rework Soviet physical training and montage, but, as the microscope sequence suggests, they also invite us to track the compilations farther abroad and further back into film history. The strongman tooth-puller in the dentist's office also plays on the feats of strength from Maciste films. As Jacqueline Reich has shown, the demonstrations of masculinity in these films developed currency around the world when they were produced in serial form.[30] This was certainly the case in Iran, where Maciste and Albertini serials played successfully at both well-heeled venues like the Grand Cinema and at second-run houses. Strongman films found a ready audience in Iran alongside serial-queen melodramas, but their particular form of masculine (and muscular) heroism resonated with deeply rooted cultural traditions. In a culture long involved with the sport of wrestling, where public displays of brawn and chivalry were ritualized in *zurkhaneh* (house of strength) performances, the strongman film provided unique pleasures of recognition. Ohanian folded this influence into his film and into his pedagogy. His acting school designated displays of strength as one of its areas of specialization.[31] Repeatedly throughout the film, the scenes follow this pattern and overlap elements from a long chronology of silent and early cinema.

Indeed, the entire film's structure is not unlike an early chase film, only with a running time long enough to include episodes that jump from one genre and period to another. The accelerated moments in the chase include a knockabout sequence in an automobile and the most spectacular stunt of the film, the famous acrobat Mirahmad Safavi's leap from the top of a building into a moving truck. In some instances, these stunts garnered comparisons in the press to famous film performers. This was especially the case with the building jump, as it was staged to attract a crowd and thus to generate publicity for the film. Journalists recounted the excitement of the crowd (non-diegetic footage of which also became part of the film), standing behind police barriers. "What's going on up there, officer? And the answer was, 'up on that building is Mr. Safavi, the famous athlete. He is a natural movie star. He is performing in an action scene in the style of Richard Talmadge.'"[32] Each of these references, to recent films and to films of decades past, operates independently of the others; collectively, they comprise nearly the entire film. The episodic chase and the reflexive frame story showcase a compendium of attractions borrowing from Iranian, Italian, Russian, US, and French traditions, different genres, and featuring elements from the 1900s, 1910s, and 1920s.

Such citations are not merely collected as atomized elements in the film. Like the dandy and his bricolage of -isms, the film often comingles its asynchronous attractions. The best example of this blending can be found in the film's magic and dance sequence. Ohanian begins the sequence with a stage performance that recalls Méliès and early dance films and then introduces, in an eccentric manner, elements of straightforward continuity editing and modernist disruptions. Mr. Haji is led to the performance (secretly orchestrated by the director within the film) in hopes that the conjurer might be able to use magic to find his watch. Curtains open and the conjurer appears, through a substitution splice. Dressed in a turban and beads and staged frontally, the conjurer looks like a recycled Méliès character. At the moment he appears, the forms of staging and editing shift to those of an early trick film. The initial phase of the magic show uses a single camera position for its fifty-second series of substitution splices, during which he conjures birds in his hands and releases them into the air. There are no reaction shots or cut-ins. The style of the scene then shifts again. The conjurer walks offstage and sits, at which point the camera tightens to a medium long shot, his movements become more eccentric than they were, and the editing accelerates to construct a dynamic space. His body sweeps through punctuated Kuleshovian movements as he gestures offscreen to conjure additional performers. A three-piece band and a dancer appear in sequential puffs of smoke and begin to perform on stage. Ida Meftahi has discussed the dancer in this scene, Armenian-born Asia Qustanian, as a preeminent example of performers who hybridized ballet and Iranian dance to create the modern genre of "national dance" (*raqs-e melli*) on the Pahlavi stage.[33] Ohanian's editing and camera position complement the asynchronous modernism of Qustanian's style with their own asynchronous modernism. Like the conjurer's performance, the dance sequence begins with one frontal long take reminiscent of the cinema of attractions. But unlike the initial magic performance, the dance scene includes reaction shots, eyeline matches, comic interludes, and interactions with all of the scene's characters in each of their different locations. Once it establishes a continuous space, it shifts again in style to include a series of rapid close-ups of musical instruments in motion, hands, feet, and canted angles of inverted faces. No sooner is the continuous space established in the scene than it is literally turned upside down by these eruptions of Soviet modernist style (see figure 26.3).

In the eighth and final reel, the experimentation accelerates. Previous scenes included brief moments of rapid cutting, but the film's chase culminates in a crescendo of focused experimental montage. Mr. Haji is led into an outdoor cinema in hopes that he will be converted, finally, into a lover of the medium once he sees his own image on screen. He sits next to a fashionably dressed woman with a small lapdog, which creates a comic situation similar to the scene in *Jafar Khan* when the uncle meets Carotte. Mr. Haji is initially agitated both by her dog and by his own image on the screen, but the woman guides him in learning appropriate behavior in the cinema. This conversion takes place in a rapid montage sequence that intercuts highlights from the previous eight reels with Mr. Haji's reaction shots. It accelerates, with twenty-seven cuts in as many seconds, adding fragmented images of spinning wheels and rapid movement to scenes of his adventures.

The name of the cinema where this scene takes place, Luna Park, is apt for a reflexive feature steeped in early cinema. Luna Park was among the most photographed and filmed amusement parks anywhere. By the end of the 1920s it had lent its name to amusement parks in cities around the world. The Luna Park scene in *Mr. Haji* is not so far removed from *Rube and Mandy at Coney Island* (1903). Mr. Haji is a naïve character, who stumbles through a series of eccentric variety acts and whose education culminates

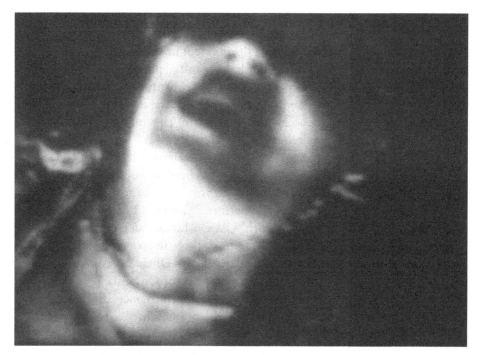

FIGURE 26.3 Modernist camerawork and cutting during a dance sequence. *Mr. Haji, the Movie Actor.*

at an amusement park cinema. This popular plot device of early cinema serves here, as it has elsewhere, as a defining allegory for cinema's modernity, but with a more complicated historical and geographical orientation. It is the conclusion of a rube comedy, within an early experiment in feature filmmaking, produced in the 1930s, culminating in a montage sequence that resembles the crescendo of *Man with a Movie Camera*. This conclusion to an extended chase film brings the film's instances of asynchronous bricolage, from rube films to Maciste, from *Les Joyeux Microbes* to Vertov, together in an real-life aerodrome cinema named after an iconic center for modern amusement. Tehran's Luna Park, part of the global imaginary of Coney Island's Luna Park, serves as an ideal setting for a climactic scene that blends contemporary transnational modernism with a common subject of early cinema.

Before wrapping up my analysis of the film, I want to tie this approach to its style back to my earlier discussion of circulating luxury goods. An analysis guided by conceptions of asynchrony and detachment can also illuminate the curious way the film "advertises" modern technological commodities. Consider the four primary technologies on conspicuous display in the film: the automobile, the wristwatch, the phonograph, and film itself. Each of these technological goods was manufactured abroad, and each indicates a particular pathway in the geopolitics of circulation. All were luxury objects doing brisk business and were ubiquitous in advertising media. Scenes showcasing automobiles in *Mr. Haji* point to the rise of firms like F. A. Kettaneh, a major automobile importer in the Middle East originating in Lebanon, which was selling an increasing number of cars in Iran and would expand its permanent regional headquarters there after the war. At the time of *Mr. Haji*'s production, automobile ads filled the newspapers, not only promoting brands of cars but also the brand of Kettaneh as the rising name associated with the regional presence of these automobiles. The stolen watch that drives the plot is an Omega watch, and in the film we see the logo for this Swiss company on one of the urban storefronts in downtown Tehran. Omega was one of the European watchmakers, along with Zenith and Theil, that had a strong presence in public spaces in Armenia, Azerbaijan, and Iran. Ohanian reportedly received some compensation for this product placement in his film.[34]

The gramophone in Mr. Haji's home, which is presented in close-up during a brief interlude in which Mr. Haji's children and Pouri dance in the courtyard, follows the marketing push of Columbia and RCA records in the Middle East and South Asia. Here the slogan "His Master's Voice" became as known as the brand. And, of course, the film itself, a film about film, should be seen in the context of the importers of Agfa, Lumière, Guillemot, and Mimosa, who supplied photochemicals, paper, and film. These products circulated through the same shipping routes as the imported feature films that contributed to Iran's developing film culture. The representations of these technologies comingle in *Mr. Haji* in a fashion similar to their advertising in newspapers of the time. In the back pages of *Ettela'at* in the early 1930s, Kettaneh, Omega, RCA, Agfa, and local cinemas were the most consistent advertisers. Their logos could often be found on the same page. The film participates in a form of advertisement of modern commodities that parallels the officially sanctioned print publicity of its era.

One could use the didactic message of the film's narrative to read an instrumental optimism about these technologies in the film. That is, the film could be said to showcase technological goods as part of its call to get "up to speed" with a one-dimensional national modernization and fashionable consumerism. But given that, stylistically, the film makes a medley of elements from cinema's past, a richer interpretation might appreciate the asynchronies of the film's advertised technological goods. The gramophone, a popular living-room display item in the region, was valued for its relation to the past as a collectible, while it simultaneously brought fashionable music into the modern home. And the Omega watch, despite being a timekeeping instrument, falls short as a figure for synchronization. It is an object of value, stolen by the gramophone-loving Pouri. While it receives a line in an intertitle about its quality (part of the film's product placement), the line is delivered by Mr. Haji. The Omega watch never marks time for him or anyone else in the film. It is a collectible possession, of indeterminate age, valued by a character who represents backwardness. While both of these commodities on display in the film gesture to a consumerist modernity with a tendency to be suspicious of the past, they also highlight the fact that circulation is a variable process that challenges any simple call to get up to speed.

Indeed, the film itself was at once an innovation and a product of technology that showed its age. This born-old quality of a film with such a didactic gloss on modernity is one of the reasons the film has been so challenging to place historically. Critical discussion of the film when it was released noted the datedness of the filmmaking technology. While another Iranian filmmaker, Abdolhussein Sepanta, went to India to collaborate on the first successful Persian-language sound film, Ohanian shot on location in the streets of Tehran with a Pathé camera from the 1910s. His low-budget asynchrony was noted both in the original press for the film and in later oral histories of the production: "The film has been shot by means of old equipment and a system belonging to some years ago."[35] The hand-crank had been modified with a sewing machine motor and only one of the lenses worked.[36] And when films like this one premiered, they were shown in cinemas where exhibitors displayed kinetoscopes in the lobbies and advertised the age of imported films as evidence that the films were world-traveled. At every stage of *Mr. Haji*'s life, from conception in Soviet training, to production with outdated devices and processes, to exhibition in halls alongside moving-image devices of the distant past, the film challenges a tidy chronology. Gramophones, Omega watches, hand-cranked cameras, and kinetoscopes may have been designed to travel as far and as fast as the market would take them, but the intricacy of their patterns of reuse overshadows the purpose of their design. This is awkward baggage for a film that has been valued as a milestone. Better to take the dandy's cue and shrug off the worries of these contradictions. Datedness is woven into the style of the film, in the objects showcased within it, and in the tools of its very construction. The asynchrony of styles in Ohanian's film parallels the asynchrony of the technology it showcases, as well as of the technologies used to produce it.

Overtaken by the incongruities of its parts, *Mr. Haji*'s confident narrative gives way to the creative practice that I have been tracing through the figure of the dandy. The film's treatment of modern technologies and film styles, simultaneously dated and elevated, aligns with the Iranian dandy's use of asynchronous bricolage to cultivate detachment. This was indeed a feature-length comic car-chase film about a stolen luxury watch made during the early years of a modernization program that included the standardization of national time and the increased circulation of luxury commodities. In one sense, the film's narrative internalizes the Reza Shah's reforms by presenting a narrative where a religious man converts to the medium of cinema and its modernity. But the film's appropriations are also excessive and self-aware. The apparent asynchrony of its components results in a deliberately unfocused impudence. For the film to truly succeed as a simple mirror image of official nationalist modernization, it would require a greater degree of reverence and clarity than it has. The film's aesthetic follows the dandy's: it sets itself at a remove from a faith in traditional cosmopolitanism and thus from the powers such a faith might serve.

Writing Histories of Enduring Failures

Mr. Haji, the Movie Actor's singularity was, from the start, entangled in its failures. Its influences and citations aside, the film owes much of its uneasy place in film history to this tension. Despite its public buildup, it could not draw significant crowds to cinemas. It was overshadowed by Persian-language sound films developed simultaneously in India and by the imported films from which it drew its references. And yet, as an early experiment in local institution-building, it continued to generate discussion in the press and has remained a central historical reference point. In considering the film's fate as one of enduring failure, we can draw once more from the intersecting dandy stories that have shaped my reading of the film. Each of the flesh-and-blood dandy figures discussed in this article met an abrupt, nonproductive, anticlimactic, or undignified end. Moghaddam contracted consumption and lost his life in Switzerland at the age of twenty-seven. Kirmani, the Baliol man, announced that he would drink himself to death in a Tehran slum and then proceeded to do exactly that.[37] Ohanian's career, notwithstanding his perennial optimism, fell far short of the successes of the dandy director he played in his film. According to interviews with those who knew him, which themselves take on the quality of tall tales, he first moved to Ashkabat and tried to set up another acting school there. He then attempted to make Persian-language films in India and landed in a British prison for his political associations with the independence movement. He escaped punishment by fleeing to Russia and then back to Iran. In the 1950s his film projects within the burgeoning Tehran film industry never came to fruition, and he resigned himself to representing a pioneering era of Iranian cinema at occasional film functions like the awarding of an honorary doctorate to Raj Kapoor in 1956.[38] He wound up trading on his remaining notoriety by selling miracle cures for hair loss for years until his fraudulent claims ran him into legal trouble. He was advertised as "Professor Ohanian" in *White and Black*, the same magazine in which *Gigolo* was serialized, alongside film reviews and color pin-ups of Hollywood stars.[39] These pages of the popular arts and culture magazine from the late 1950s not only preserve a serialized caricature of a new iteration of the Iranian dandy but also document the makeshift business ventures of an earlier dandy and founding filmmaker of Iranian cinema, who ended his career selling snake oil.

On these same pages Mamoosh's story ends, too, with a turn away from his neighborhood toward a peripatetic, if not exilic, life. He decides that he will be forever misunderstood in Tehran and continues his mediated life as an emissary of "Point 2x2." This fictional sponsored film company is a burlesque on the Truman administration's Point Four Program, which had a strong presence in postwar Iran's media landscape.[40] He travels to India, where he discusses gigology with Raj Kapoor, and then to Bali and Japan. His journey lands him in US territory. In Hawaii, he lives out a Technicolor Polynesian fantasy popular in mid-century Iran. His experience of Hawaii is entirely mediated by his "memories of Hollywood films and all of their details," as well as pop music. He refers to a popular Hawaiian guitar song as "the anthem of Istanbul Avenue dandies," which he memorized during the hours he spent "in front of the Metro record store in Tehran."[41] This conclusion intermingles Hollywood's Hawaii with postwar American-sponsored documentaries in the fantasies of a cinephile dandy in exile. It nods to the decades of a cinema history in which the films that form its chronology had experienced, long after the coming of sound, more than their fair share of upendings and overshadowings.[42]

Citing the global dimension of dandyism opens up a discussion of *Mr. Haji, the Movie Actor* that expands outward from its fictionalization of a dandy character within the film. It encourages a particular reading of the film, and others like it, that acknowledges its distinctive historical texture. It offers a different way to position a film structured as a patchwork of themes and characters from popular circulating junk film prints. It provides a positive reason to investigate the film's assembly of mismatched historical fragments rather than explaining them away as background noise; as distracting from a history of the instrumental development of a national film industry; as drowning out traces of an indigenous film style; or as merely echoing developments with distinct and distant points of origin. Each of these approaches would correspond to a narrowing historiography that, following the film's own lead, its historians should resist. As we consider new possible periodizations and global geographies of silent cinema history, we might hold up *Mr. Haji's* irreverent junk-shop dandyism and its backward glances as part of an asynchronous aesthetic that finds itself at home among the recent work on intermedial moving-image history, on circulation through institutions, and on the porous boundaries between compilation and creation.

Notes

1. Jamshid Vahidi, *Gigolo: A Memoir of Mamoosh Pochettian, Famous Gigolo of Istanbul Street with the Cornel Wilde Hairdo* (Tehran: Entesharat-e Sepid o Siah, 1957), 126.
2. Ibid., 66.
3. Ibid., 36–40, ill. 18.
4. Ibid., 72.
5. Ibid., 96.
6. Ibid., 76.
7. "Gigology" in the original. Ibid., 81.
8. Ibid., 100–101. The text uses several French words in this passage including "*cadeau*," "*portrait*" (spelled in Persian to indicate the French pronunciation), and "*succés*" (which I have translated in context as "to be admired"). It also mixes affected jargon with phrases that suggest a lack of formal education.
9. These images, which also appeared on the covers of film magazines, were collected by fans, but they were a common target for a variety of critics. Some critiqued recycled pin-up portraits on moral grounds. Others claimed that the magazines' choice to print these images lacked intellectual sophistication, had lowered the taste of film audiences, and thus was partly to blame for artistic stagnation in the film industry in Iran. By rendering Gigi in this fashion, the illustration was designed to call these debates to mind.
10. Dick Hebdige, *Subculture: The Meaning of Style* (London: Routledge, 1981 [1979]), 101–107. It is also worth remembering that Hebdige's chapter on 1970s subcultural bricolage is full of analogies to earlier modernist art, to the "isms" that Mamoosh mentions during his adventures.

11. Rebecca Walkowitz, *Cosmopolitan Style: Modernism Beyond the Nation* (New York: Columbia University Press, 2006), 11–12.
12. Walkowitz's distinction does not discredit practices of bricolage, aestheticism, and syncretism, which are essential for these figures. Ibid., 19.
13. Jessica Feldman, *Gender on the Divide: The Dandy in Modernist Literature* (Ithaca, NY: Cornell University Press, 1993), 2.
14. Rhonda Garelick, *Rising Star: Dandyism, Gender, and Performance in the Fin de Siècle* (Princeton, NJ: Princeton University Press, 1999), 3.
15. Elisa Glick, *Materializing Queer Desire: Oscar Wilde to Andy Warhol* (Albany: State University of New York Press, 2009), 26.
16. Oscar Wilde, *The Picture of Dorian Gray* (1890), ed. Donald Lawler (New York: Norton, 1988), 246.
17. One of the classic discussions of these initiatives and their social effects can be found in Nikki Keddie, *Modern Iran: Roots and Results of Revolution* (New Haven. CT: Yale University Press, 2006 [1981]). For a more recent discussion of Pahlavi modernization in relation to urban planning in Tehran, including the planning of the avenues that were the stomping grounds of the dandy characters discussed in this article, see Azadeh Mashayekhi, "Tehran, the Scene of Modernity in the Pahlavi Dynasty: Modernisation and Urbanisation Processes 1925–1979," in Fatemeh Farnaz Arefian and Seyed Hossein Iradj Moeini, eds., *Urban Change in Iran: Stories of Rooted Histories and Ever-accelerating Developments* (New York: Springer, 2016).
18. Golbarg Rekabtalaei, *Iranian Cosmopolitanism: A Cinematic History* (New York: Cambridge University Press, 2018).
19. See Anna Tsing, *Friction: An Ethnography of Global Exchange* (Princeton, NJ: Princeton University Press, 2004).
20. See Mehrzad Boroujerdi, "The Ambivalent Modernity of Iranian Intellectuals," in Negin Nabavied, ed., *Intellectual Trends in Twentieth-Century Iran: A Critical Survey* (Gainesville: University of Florida Press, 2003).
21. Hassan Mogaddam, *Jafar Khan az Farang Amadeh* (Tehran: Faroos Publishing, 1922 [1301]), 3.
22. Hamid Naficy, *A Social History of Iranian Cinema*, vol. 1, *The Artisanal Era* (Durham, NC: Duke University Press, 2011), 288.
23. *Messages d'orient*, ed. Elian Finbert and E. J. Suares (Alexandria, Egypt: Les Imprimeries Tachydronos et du commerce, 1926.)
24. Conversation between Christopher Sykes and Kirmani quoted in Christopher Sykes, *Four Studies in Loyalty* (London: Collins, 1946), 62. Sykes's main admiration for Kirmani stemmed from the way he pushed against some of the Shah's global political alignments in the buildup to World War II.
25. Newspaper articles advocating for building this gymnasium tended more toward a language of uplift than of the kind of leisure lifestyle of the dandy or the aesthetic preoccupations of the artist. Quoted in their entirety in Jamal Omid, *Ovanes Oganians: Zendegi va Sinema*, Tarikh-e Sinema-ye Iran 2 (Tehran: Faryab, 1984/1363), 55.
26. In Ohanian's archive, he also possessed an autograph of Adolf Zukor addressed to him. Reprinted in Omid, *Ovanes Oganians*, 76.
27. Press articles reprinted in Omid, *Ovanes Oganians*, 49–78.
28. André Malraux, *Esquisse d'une Psychologie Du Cinéma* (Paris: Gallimard, 1946).

29. The extent of Ohanian's Soviet training is not on record (and very well may have been exaggerated by such a showman), but the compilation quality of the film itself offers many clues. Omid, *Ovanes Oganians*, 9.
30. Jacqueline Reich, *The Maciste Films of Italian Silent Cinema* (Bloomington: Indiana University Press, 2015), 115–148.
31. The list of graduates designates "display of strength" alongside drama, comedy, and tricks as an area of specialization. Reprinted in Omid, *Ovanes Oganians*, 26.
32. Omid, *Ovanes Oganians*, 61.
33. See Ida Meftahi, *Gender and Dance in Modern Iran: Biopolitics on Stage* (London: Routledge, 2016), 18–48.
34. Omid cites a much later interview with Habibolla Morad, who indicated that Omid received tie-in money for the placement of a watch in the film. Morad apparently misremembered the brand as a Galo. The watch his character wears and mentions in the film is an Omega. Omid, *Ovanes Oganians*, 76n11.
35. Omid, *Ovanes Oganians*, 65.
36. Ibid.
37. As he announced in a letter, "I have decided to retire to a Tehran slum where I shall devote the few weeks remaining to me, the most wretched of sinners, to drinking myself to death." Quoted in Sykes, *Four Studies in Loyalty*, 65.
38. Interviews compiled in Omid, *Ovanes Oganians*, 84–91.
39. These advertisements appeared in multiple publications. For an example that intersects with the pin-ups and serialized dandy stories discussed earlier, see "Professor Ohanian," *Sepid o Siah* 218, Tehran, October 5, 1959 [12 Mehr 1338], 90.
40. Vahidi, *Gigolo*. Point 2x2, 28–49. For an authoritative account of the Point Four Program in Iran, including an extensive discussion of satirical treatments of the operation, see Hadi Gharabaghi, "'American Mice Grow Big!': The Syracuse Audiovisual Mission and the Rise of Documentary Diplomacy" (PhD diss., New York University, 2018).
41. The scenes of his departure abroad do not seem to exist in book form. They can be found in *Sepid o Siah*, 4:9, 24, 4:14, 24–25, 4:15, 24, 1957. Mamoosh's self-imposed exile is perhaps another callback to earlier dandy texts. The final curtain falls on Jafar Khan as he departs again for Europe despite his family's comic pleas for him to stay.
42. These cycles of overshadowing seem to characterize much of the thinking about Iranian cinema history. *Mr. Haji* was overshadowed from the start by the Persian-language Indian production *The Lor Girl* (*Dokhtar-e Lor*, Ardeshir Irani, 1933), because of its synchronous sound. Then the postwar industry crafted a new paradigm of genre production with some films, like those of Samuel Khachikian, creating a form of prestige cinema. This, in turn, was shattered by a new popular cinema heralded by *Qarun's Treasure* (*Ganj-e Qarun*, Siamak Yasami, 1965). Then, for many, the new wave films of the 1970s (with important precursors earlier in the 1960s) cast suspicion on these popular films of the 1950s and 1960s, only to be upended by the revolution. Often the historical writing on these cycles has carried with it negative implications of failure and resetting. Understanding these cycles of overshadowing as frustrating setbacks, rather than seeing them within a historical texture of experimentation, reflects a tendency to seek out markers of progress or continuities of artist-driven movements.

CHAPTER 27

THE COVERED WAGON
Location Shooting and Settler Melodrama

JENNIFER LYNN PETERSON

> We need to learn to "read" a settler colonial world where we simply see a "normal one."
>
> Lorenzo Veracini, *The Settler Colonial Present*[1]

IN its incongruous appearance near the heart of US finance capital, nothing could have been more modern than the giant electrified covered wagon adorning the Criterion Theatre just off Times Square in 1923. On March 16 of that year, *The Covered Wagon* debuted at New York's Criterion, a nine-hundred-seat movie palace at Broadway and 44th Street. As part of the lavish promotional campaign launched by Paramount-Famous Players, the theater's exterior was decorated with giant electric signs depicting a covered wagon fording a river; the two signs depicted a single wagon in three dimensions, shown from the side and the back.[2] The larger of the signs, on the Broadway side of the building, measured thirty-four by sixty feet and was "illuminated by a flame of incandescents and a battery of flood lights concealed on the canopy. The water effects [we]re produced by six stereopticons operated by electric motors" (see figures 27.1 and 27.2).[3] *The Covered Wagon* narrates a story of white settlers traveling westward from Kansas City along the Oregon Trail. An idealized vision of actual nineteenth-century settler experience, the film is set in 1848, seventy-five years before its release. One of the most commercially successful films of the silent era, *The Covered Wagon*'s significance as a cultural artifact extends beyond the boundaries of film history into the culture at large. The film played an important role in sedimenting the image of the covered wagon as an icon of western expansion and settlement; the electrified signs were no less commodities than the bushels of grain traded four miles downtown on Wall Street.

FIGURE 27.1 Electric signs advertising *The Covered Wagon* at the Criterion Theatre, New York City, 1923.

Unlike a material commodity, however, *The Covered Wagon* (both the film and its signs) functioned primarily as myth: "Manifest Destiny" anchored in a narrative of vehicles traversing a landscape. This ideology derived its potency from the way it bound together several pre-existing themes of American national identity: nature, technology, conquest, and mobility. The electrified covered wagon promised a story of traveling to a better future; at the same time, it naturalized the displacement of Native Americans

Starting out on a long journey on the screen of the Criterion, New York City, "The Covered Wagon" has been given an elaborate sign by Paramount. The photograph above of course does not give the colorings which add materially to the effect of the display. The sign, which is on the Broadway side, is 60 feet long by 34 feet high. The wagon, hub deep in the waters of the many streams forded by the historic caravan about which the play is written, is illuminated by a flame of incandescents and a battery of flood lights concealed on the canopy. The water effects are produced by six stereopticons operated by electric motors. The stereopticons are equipped with 2,000-watt nitrogen lamps especially made for the purpose.

FIGURE 27.2 The larger of the two signs at the Criterion. *Exhibitors Trade Review,* April 7, 1923.

upon which that story depended, disavowing the violence of colonialism. A glowing vision of utopia and death, these signs' material purpose may have been to sell movie tickets, but their mythic power resonated beyond the release of the film. In becoming a spectacle, settler colonialism lodged itself unconcealed at the center of American national ideology.

Wagon trails have long been a popular trope in US cinema. From the Vitagraph serial *The Fighting Trail* (1917) to Kelly Reichardt's *Meek's Cutoff* (2011), filmmakers have returned again and again to the figure of nineteenth-century settlers and their overland journey along westward expansion trails.[4] Whether affirmative or critical, the wagon trail narrative depicts colonialism as a historical phenomenon, located in the past. Yet the nature of settler colonialism is that it continues into the present. As such, I read the cinematic trope of the covered wagon as a fairy tale prefiguring automobile usage, one of many ongoing forms of fossil capitalism causing global warming today.[5] The image of the covered wagon in 1923 lent an air of moral virtue to middle-class consumerism just as the first mass-produced automobile, the Ford Model T, was selling more than a million units a year, and as the federal government was launching a series of vast, decades-long roadbuilding initiatives. Not just a veneration of settlers, *The Covered Wagon* also rationalized new forms of territorialism and consumption appearing in the form of the automobile. In this, *The Covered Wagon* both celebrated settler colonialism and helped pave the way for fossil capitalism. As an archetypal portrayal of white settlers, their wagons, and their trails through the wilderness, this film sketches a blueprint for the modern visualization of settler colonialism through vehicles, roads, and landscape.

Directed by the prolific actor-turned-director James Cruze, *The Covered Wagon* is one of the earliest and most popular iterations of the "trail film." The film earned $3.8 million at the box office, tying for the seventh most profitable American silent film, according to *Variety* in 1932.[6] It was later venerated in film history texts such as John Tuska's *The Filming of the West* (1976) and Kevin Brownlow's *The War, the West, and the Wilderness* (1979), ultimately entering the National Film Registry in 2018.[7] *The Covered Wagon* is being rediscovered in the digital age, too, along with the early sound film *The Big Trail* (Raoul Walsh, 1930), described by one early reviewer as "a noisy *Covered Wagon*."[8] Such epic Westerns demonstrate what Hollywood could accomplish in the silent and early sound eras using location shooting, movie stars, and state-of-the-art film techniques. But from a more critical perspective, these films epitomize interlocking systems of colonialism, patriarchy, and environmental exploitation. This dialectic is crucial: we must understand the utopian appeal of *The Covered Wagon* in order to unpack its ideological force. Indeed, *The Covered Wagon* is particularly relevant now as film history is being reevaluated through decolonial, anti-racist, and environmentalist critique. The film is significant not only as a commercial success but because it served as an archetype for the visualization of settler colonialism in Hollywood films for generations to come.

In this essay, I analyze *The Covered Wagon*'s location shooting as a cinematic technology that worked in the service of naturalizing settler colonialism. I argue that the narrative of the trail—which shares affinity with the narrative of the road movie—constructs the territorial act of settlement and the laying-in of modern infrastructure as both extraordinary and, more important, ordinary. While studio location shooting practices were being standardized in early 1920s Hollywood, this film's extensive location shoot in Utah and California was unprecedented for its time. The beauty and grandeur of the film's landscapes conjure a world and a history beyond the frame. *The Covered Wagon* consolidated a silent-era tendency in which location shooting glorifies the colonization of the West, as though nature itself validates white settlement. By depicting the nineteenth-century American West as a wilderness in need of taming by white farmers, the film uses landscape to anchor its colonialist depiction of history in an aesthetic of pictorial realism, while dramatizing its settler conflicts through the conventions of melodrama.

The Covered Wagon defined the parameters of what I call the "settler melodrama." Drawing from Linda Williams's influential analysis of the "racial melodrama," as well as Peter Brooks's classic theorization of melodramatic narrative, I analyze the film's use of location shooting to show how landscape is incorporated into melodrama to function as more than just setting.[9] The film's location shooting influenced directors such as John Ford, King Vidor, and Raoul Walsh, each of whom made films that further codified the terms of the settler melodrama. An important text in the larger history of the topos of the trail, *The Covered Wagon* initiated a formula for cinematic landscapes that we are still contending with today. This formula hinges on a dynamic of figure-ground relations in which the natural landscape serves not only as a stage for the drama of humans in the foreground but as a moral field with a force of its own.

From Westerns to science fiction, the pioneer fantasy's appeal has endured, and the covered wagon is perhaps the most iconic vehicle to have emblematized it. Humble wood-frame trailers, covered wagons offer a fantasy of escape, of traveling to safety in harsh conditions, of striving for freedom and a brighter future. But in centering settler stories, the pioneer fantasy avoids accounting for the economic and political forces that brought about the conditions for migration and colonization in the first place. *The Covered Wagon* is a migration story, but one that uses the story of pioneers to legitimize structural inequities. While migration and escape have continued to be paradigmatic experiences in modernity, the specificity of wheeled-vehicle land travel took on a consumerist aspect. As I argue, *The Covered Wagon* turned the covered wagon into a nostalgic precursor for the automobile in the 1920s. As an archetypal text, *The Covered Wagon* dramatizes the themes of mobility, landscape, and power that sustain the American pioneer myth.

THE SETTLER MELODRAMA

An academic subfield related to post-colonial studies, settler colonial studies has gained momentum in the past two decades as a methodology for analyzing the forms of imperialism specific to colonial states in which the colonizers remain rather than leave; the United States, Canada, and Australia are three prominent Anglophone examples. As Lorenzo Veracini puts it, "the study of settler colonialism is necessarily premised on the realization that colonialism does not always arrive on boats and that settlers typically act on their own behalf, not as agents of distant metropoles. Settlers characteristically arrive on wagon trains [. . . and] they rarely sail away. [. . .] Settler colonialism is an ongoing phenomenon; writing its history is charged with a presentist preoccupation."[10] Or as Patrick Wolfe famously wrote, "invasion is a structure not an event."[11] Given its unfinished, structural character, settler colonialism continually finds new ways to define, eliminate, and erase Indigenous people, their societies, and their cultures. Analysis of settler colonialism thus aims to clarify how it functioned in the past and to reveal how it has unceasingly remade itself over time, up to and including the present. Cultural expressions of settler territoriality are varied, but the Western genre in film and literature is a particularly rich node for cataloguing the seemingly endless variety of settler narratives and their strategies of Indigenous elimination. The caricatured Indians who appear in Westerns are conjured up to be erased, even as they are sentimentalized in the process.[12] To quote Wolfe again: "We cannot simply say that settler colonialism or genocide have been targeted at particular races, since a race cannot be taken as given. It is made in the targeting. Black people were racialized as slaves; slavery constituted their blackness. Correspondingly, Indigenous North Americans were not killed, driven away, romanticized, assimilated, fenced in, bred White, and otherwise eliminated as the original owners of the land but *as Indians*."[13] In this essay, I am concerned with how landscape as a concept and a visual tradition was harnessed by settler colonial ideology. Because settler colonialism is invested in territory and land use, landscape representations form a significant tradition in its mythology; *The Covered Wagon* modernized settler tropes already established by nineteenth-century landscape painting through its use of location shooting and cinematic melodrama.

The scholarship on Westerns in film and literature is vast, and since the 1980s, following pioneering work such as Patricia Nelson Limerick's *The Legacy of Conquest*, it has focused critically on the imperialist dimension of these stories.[14] Joanna Hearne and Michelle Raheja have centered Indigenous presence in the history of silent-era Westerns, while Scott Simmon and Richard Abel have likewise moved racism and conquest from the background to the foreground of Western genre criticism.[15] As Simmon has written, "we need to *start* from acknowledgment of the genre's racism, rather than arriving at it as if it were a discovery."[16] But while its implications for cinema are vast, the analytic framework of settler colonialism has infrequently been incorporated into cinema and media studies. Peter Limbrick's 2010 book *Making Settler Cinemas* is the most extensive analysis of settler colonialism in film history published to date, covering films set in the US, Australia, and New Zealand. In the American context, Limbrick analyzes the "settler spatiality" of John Ford's Argosy Westerns, demonstrating how "cinema itself has been a privileged site for the construction of settler cultures."[17] Although it is obviously a settler text, *The Covered Wagon* has not been analyzed in a settler colonial context. Often referred to as the first epic of the Western film genre, *The Covered Wagon* should also be understood as an archetypal expression of settler territoriality.

The Covered Wagon's epic scope, conceptualized by producer Jesse Lasky, was a deliberate attempt to match the ambition and box-office success of D. W. Griffith's *The Birth of a Nation* (1915). From the start, Lasky envisioned *The Covered Wagon* in the grand style of Griffith's *Birth*, and there are many similarities between the two films. *The Covered Wagon* extended two cinematic conventions associated with Griffith: the historical period piece and the racial melodrama. While *The Covered Wagon* does not explicitly argue for white supremacy and lynching as *Birth* does, it nonetheless validates the white supremacist ideals of Manifest Destiny. The film disavows the unseemly violence of colonial history by marginalizing Indigenous presence and foregrounding a drama of white settlers. Indeed, *The Covered Wagon* helped produce the ideological sleight of hand in which Manifest Destiny was sold as a triumph of modern progress rather than a marauding dispossession. This sleight of hand operated through a dialectic of promise and disavowal: the promise of land ownership, citizenship, dignity, and a leg up for the white working class overshadowing the Indigenous dispossession on which it rested. The film's homely racism was in lock step with mainstream ideologies of the time: the era from Reconstruction through the 1920s has been called "the nadir of American race relations."[18] In fact, the film's socially acceptable glorification of Manifest Destiny as modern progress proved not only palatable but precisely the ideology that audiences applauded. Just as *Birth* was shown at the White House and praised by President Woodrow Wilson, *The Covered Wagon* was shown at the White House and praised by

President Warren Harding.[19] Educators commended the film for its realism and fidelity to historical truth.[20] Reviewers raved about its depiction of "our great American Empire builders," gushing that "Like the 'Birth,' it is based on historical fact."[21] Audiences flocked to theaters, and the film broke box-office records set by *Birth* eight years earlier.[22]

A key difference between the two films, however, is that *Birth* announced itself as extraordinary in all ways and received tremendous attention, most of it exalting, though some of it coming in the form of protest.[23] *The Covered Wagon*, for all its epic scale, is more invested in a kind of ordinariness. Its grand landscapes and epic story of white migration serve as the backdrop for a sympathetic story of families, romantic love, and the desire to build a home. The film's visual grandiosity, conveyed in extreme long shots of the landscape, is contrasted with the everyday familiarity of its characters: a cast of white settlers who function as democratic, folksy character archetypes. This contrast between grandiose backgrounds and ordinary people in the foreground is a constitutive tension of the film. I argue that this "ordinariness" cannot be separated from the settlers' characterization as white.

In *Playing the Race Card*, Linda Williams analyzes melodrama "not as a genre as many film critics have thought, but a central *mode* of American popular culture."[24] Williams demonstrates the ways in which American racial melodramas such as *Uncle Tom's Cabin* (the novel, popular play, and film adaptations) produce racially defined sympathy for Black characters through the dramatization of their suffering—these she calls "pro-Tom melodramas." In turn, "anti-Tom" melodramas such as *The Birth of a Nation* reverse that dynamic to produce racially defined sympathy for white characters through the dramatization of their suffering at the hands of caricatured Black villains. "Melodrama's sympathy could be described as the feeling of emotional connection to suffering victims," she writes.[25] While Williams is concerned with melodramas of Black and white, her insights also apply to the settler melodrama. *The Covered Wagon* dramatizes a traditional melodramatic quest for moral legibility, focusing on white settlers tested by a series of hardships on the trail to a new home. Home functions in melodrama as a "space of innocence," whereas the trail functions as a space of challenges. Through the work of the narrative, the film draws clear distinctions between moral values, assigning some characters the stamp of virtue and defining others as villains. Trail films construct oppositions between white and Native characters, but in *The Covered Wagon* that conflict is secondary to the struggle between white characters; indeed, the Natives in the film remain alien Others rather than individuated characters, a point I will return to below. While we might think it was outmoded in the jazz age, in fact melodrama was and is profoundly modern, assigning moral values in what Peter Brooks calls a "postsacred" world. Indeed, one of Williams's main points is that melodrama persists through its continual modernization: "melodrama continually decks itself out in the latest trappings of realism in order to command recognition of the world it represents."[26] As we shall see, location shooting is a key "trapping of realism" used to assign moral virtue in melodrama.

The Covered Wagon features a central conflict between two white male characters, Will Banion (played by J. Warren Kerrigan) and Sam Woodhull (Alan Hale), who compete for the love of Molly Wingate (Lois Wilson). The bulk of the film's drama works toward locating the innocence of Banion (accused of theft until the third act) and the villainy of Woodhull (who turns out to be a cowardly scoundrel). As in a road movie, the Oregon Trail provides a series of dramatic trials that provide opportunities to test the characters, such as riding a wild horse, fording a river, and fighting against a band of attacking Indians. Validated as the film's hero, Banion is finally cleared to marry the virtuous Molly and settle into a new life in Oregon. The larger aim of the film is to extol the white pioneers in their struggle to bring civilization to the wilderness.

As a self-conscious epic, some of *The Covered Wagon*'s intertitles offer interpretations of the film's meaning in the manner of a Greek chorus. Before the drama even begins, the film presents an opening intertitle that reads: "The blood of America is the blood of pioneers—the blood of lion-hearted men and women who carved a splendid civilization out of an uncharted wilderness." This intertitle invokes the era's biological notion of racial difference: the pioneers' whiteness is measured in their blood. This discourse on blood eclipses (and does not directly reference) the federal government's notion of "blood quantum" as a measure of Native American status. As Indigenous anthropologist Kimberly TallBear explains, "Since its conception, 'Indian blood' has enjoyed a unique place in the American racial imagination. [. . .] Considered a property that would hold Indians back on the road to civilization, Indian blood could be diluted over generations through interbreeding with Euro-American populations. Indians were seen as capable of cultural evolution (unlike Africans) and therefore of cultural absorption into the white populace. 'Kill the Indian, save the man' was a mantra of nineteenth-century U.S. assimilation policies."[27] The persistent focus on white characters in *The Covered Wagon*, as in many settler narratives, treats Native American characters as part of the background, generalized along with the landscape as threatening if majestic natural forces. The film's second intertitle clearly expresses a moral claim about the virtue of settler colonialism, and by extension the values of progress and modernization, proclaiming, "With dauntless courage, facing unknown perils, the men and women of the 'forties flung the boundaries of the nation westward, and still westward, beyond the Mississippi, beyond the prairies, beyond the Rockies,—until they bounded the United States of America with two Oceans." In depicting the settlers' "dauntless courage" and the "unknown perils" they faced, the film dramatizes settlers as ordinary heroes in an extraordinary land, their virtue conferred through the process of their suffering.

The film's first two photographic images introduce two archetypal characters: a young white boy playing the banjo spits on the ground, and a young white girl sews and sweetly smiles while looking almost directly at the camera. Soon these two will be introduced as Jed and Molly Wingate, son and daughter of the commander of the entire wagon train posse. Between these two opening shots, the film dissolves to sheet music for the song "Oh! Susanna." The stage is set for a story about people on the move, accompanied by a popular song that was historically associated with the Forty-Niners, or gold rush migrants whose historical numbers peaked in 1849. Shot three is an extreme long shot of "Kansas City" in 1848 (actually Baker Ranch in Utah). The bottom half of the frame is composed of water softly rippling along the "Mississippi river" (also Utah). The composition emphasizes horizontality, with wagons and teepees arranged on the riverbank drawing our eyes to center frame, a hilly bank of shrubs behind that, and a cluster of houses along the top of the ridge. People move through this landscape, but the natural setting dwarfs these tiny figures and their spare-looking houses.

A moment later, the film's white patriarch, Jesse Wingate, draws our attention to his plow. Frustrated at having to wait for his wagon train's departure from Kansas City, Jesse exclaims, "I'm just as anxious to git my plow into Oregon soil as anybody." He gestures toward the bottom of the frame, motivating a cut to a medium shot of the plow. This shot initiates a brief narrative aside that efficiently sketches the film's secondary conflict between settlers and Native Americans, expressing the film's larger ideological stakes. After a dissolve to an expository intertitle stating, "Far out on the Westward trail stands another plow that bravely started for Oregon," we see a group of Native Americans standing in semicircle around the same kind of plow, smoke rising in the foreground and teepees receding in the distance. In a medium shot, an unnamed Indian man, wearing braided hair and feathers, gestures broadly and speaks: "'The pale face again crosses the River of Misty Water—always advancing towards the setting sun—.'" A second, older Indian man, hair also in braids, steps forward to say: "'With him he brings this monster weapon that will bury the buffalo—uproot the forest—and level the mountain.'" He points down, echoing Jesse's earlier hand gesture, which motivates a shot of this second plow. With these two plows, the film shows that these Indians have killed a different group of settlers who brought a plow west. The film cuts back to a group shot, and once more the older man speaks: "'The Pale Face who comes with this evil medicine must be slain—or the Red Man perishes!'" Returning to the master shot, the group of assembled Natives closes in around the plow, looking down to examine it. The scene ends with a fade to black, and a fade-in on Jesse's plow returns us to the scene of white settlers about to head west in their wagon train.

In its original context, these opening segments function to establish the film's two plotlines, the main drama of white settlers and the secondary conflict between the settlers and the "natural forces" that challenge them (the wilderness and its "savage Indians"). We might call this the foreground and the background of the film. Classical narrative films often have this double plotline structure (screenwriters refer to these as the "A" story and the "B" story). In this essay I am concerned more with the film's background or second plotline ("natural forces") than its foreground (white settlers) and how the background ("B" story) is held in relationality with the foreground ("A" story). *The Covered Wagon* presents an archetypal settler-colonial structuring of these two plotlines; disaggregating the film's figure-ground relations can help us see how this structure works. We can also observe that this brief narrative aside expressing a (cartoonish) critique of colonial dispossession punctures the direction of the rest of the film and resonates with our current moment of ecological crisis. The "Red Man's" critique is caricatured, yet its inclusion in this paradigmatic settler film betrays a legitimization anxiety that the ideology of Manifest Destiny seeks to overcome. That is the work of the narrative.

I argue that in the settler melodrama, landscape serves to materialize the "moral occult" of settler colonialism. In other words, landscape bears a moral resonance in the romantic European pictorial tradition that *The Covered Wagon* borrows to confer moral validity on the wagon train that moves through it. As Peter Brooks described it, "the 'moral occult' [is] the domain of operative spiritual values which is both indicated within and masked by the surface of reality. [. . .] It bears comparison to the unconscious mind, for it is a sphere of being where our most basic desires and interdictions lie. [. . .] The melodramatic mode in large measure exists to locate and to articulate the moral occult."[28] It is significant, then, that the film's primary plotline turns on the question of who is and is not a thief. When Banion is absolved of guilt for theft at the end of the film, the secondary plotline about land—expressed in the "Red Man's" speech bemoaning territorial dispossession and environmental degradation—is symbolically resolved in such a way that white settlement is also absolved of guilt by association with the heroism of Banion and the other virtuous settlers. Thus, landscape naturalizes the structure of settler colonialism in *The Covered Wagon* and the many films it influenced. This aesthetic strategy is not hidden but open and apparent: the moral forces in this film (and many other Westerns) are simplified and dramatized in the most literal way. The work of analyzing melodramatic landscape is not about uncovering buried ideologies, for melodrama and landscape are both manifestly visible. Rather, I aim to show how the film's dramaturgy materializes its ideology, thereby revealing the dialectical workings of this highly effective story of utopian struggle for white people at a moment when whiteness itself was being constructed in American national identity.

Historian Matthew Frye Jacobson has shown how "whiteness" coalesced in the 1920s as previously separate categories such as Celts, Teutons, or Slavs began to be generalized as white. Jacobson notes that the passage of the Immigration Act of 1924 (the year after *The Covered Wagon*'s release), "mark[s] the beginning of the ascent of monolithic whiteness."[29] Modern whiteness was defined in opposition to a set of other broad racial categories, including Black, Asian, and Native American; the point is that these categories were being redrawn in the 1920s in "a shift from one brand of bedrock racism to another."[30] *The Covered Wagon* is primarily concerned with whiteness, not Indigeneity, but it is significant that 1924 was also the year of the Indian Citizenship Act, which extended US citizenship to all Native Americans and "crowned the assimilationist epoch in Indian affairs."[31] Having been stripped of millions of acres of land and encouraged to live like farming homesteaders with the Dawes Act of 1877, Native Americans may have appeared to many whites as completely assimilated by 1924. "If the pioneer represented the forces of change that had transformed the West, the Indian naturally represented what had been lost," historian Brian Dippie writes.[32] A primary strategy of Native dispossession by the federal government, erasure-by-assimilation was echoed in mass culture by a series of caricatured representations of "Red Men" who signified the mythological "Vanishing Indian" of the past. Such representations were in turn lent a form of cinematic veracity using landscapes shot on location in the American West.

Location Shooting as a Truth Claim

Based on a popular 1922 novel by Emerson Hough, *The Covered Wagon* is a story about cross-country travel, and, in fact, Lasky decided to make the film during a cross-country train trip. Lasky first read Hough's novel as he was commuting by train between the studio's offices in New York and Los Angeles. At this time, Lasky was bothered that despite the success of his production company Famous Players-Lasky, "we had never produced a history-making, cinematic milestone [... T]he seven-year-old challenge of *The Birth of a Nation* still stood."[33] In a moment that seemed magical to Lasky, Hough's novel provided a solution. He describes this moment of inspiration in his autobiography:

> I picked up the book somewhere over the plains of Kansas and became so absorbed in the struggles and adventures of the pioneers [. . .] that for the whole day I became again a child at my grandfather's knee, listening to the most exciting tales a boy ever heard. And every time I glanced out the train window at the rolling prairies, the mountains, the desert, I saw the vast panorama of sky and earth forming a backdrop for those heroic souls whose first wagon train actually took much of the same route three quarters of a century before—a procession that united the West with the East, a migration but for which I myself would not have been born in my beloved California. Superimposing the past on the present by reading about that trek while actually retracing it myself, as I looked out the window of a speeding luxury train at the same scenery my grandfather had viewed from a lumbering Conestoga, was an emotional, almost mystical experience.[34]

Lasky's "emotional, almost mystical" epiphany derives its force not only from the landscape but from the moving train in which he views it. This is the specifically modern, technologized point of view described by Wolfgang Schivelbusch as "panoramic perception," in which "the traveler [sees] the objects, landscapes, etc. *through* the apparatus which [moves] him through the world."[35] Cinema replicates the comfort and safety of panoramic perception, and although he does not mention it, Lasky might well have realized in this moment that shooting on location could provide a similar sensation. Automobiles would soon turn panoramic perception into an oil-powered everyday experience within the reach of the American middle class.

It is not just technology (the railroad, the cinema, the car) that enables panoramic perception; it is the presence of an idea of nature as a moral or spiritual force that activates this "almost mystical experience." Here Lasky was channeling a long tradition in American thought, from the Transcendentalists to conservationists such as John Muir, who valued wilderness as a sacred space for communing with the divine. Lasky had hit upon a cinematic combination—narrative plus landscape—that proved a commercially lucrative formula in *The Covered Wagon*. Finally, the apparent timelessness of the landscape enabled the act of "superimposing the past on the present." Lasky's epiphany hinged on cinema-specific technology: by shooting on location in the landscapes of the west ("the rolling prairies, the mountains, the desert [. . .] the vast panorama of sky and earth"), cinema had a unique power to render the myth of settler colonialism as a "true story," which could in turn be enjoyed from a comfortable distance in the movie theater.

The film was already on the studio's production schedule, slated to be made by a journeyman director with a standard Western budget of $110,000. After this train trip, Lasky decided to produce the film as an epic. He removed the first director and, on the basis of "hearsay" that James Cruze "was supposed to have Indian blood" and "a natural instinct or affinity for the courageous drama of the barren plains," assigned the picture to him instead.[36] Born and raised in Utah, Cruze was familiar with the regions of the location shoot, but the legend about his Native heritage is unsubstantiated and likely false.[37] Lasky wrote to studio head Adolph Zukor that *The Covered Wagon* should only be produced "in a big way, [or] it ought not to be made at all. I think the picture can be made one of our big specials."[38] Although years later in his autobiography, Lasky proudly remembered the proposed budget for his newly elevated film as $500,000 (and this number has been repeated everywhere since), the budget he suggested in this internal studio letter was actually $300,000—which is still higher than the typical budget for a Western at that time. According to his autobiography, the budget eventually ballooned to $782,000.[39] The film earned all that back and much more, because it received a roadshow release with $1.50 tickets, just as *The Birth of a Nation* had been released in 1915.

The film's primary shooting location was a massive property called Baker Ranch, located in the Snake Valley on the Utah-Nevada border, eighty-five miles from the nearest railroad. The ranch was then owned by Otto Meek, a landowner with friends in Hollywood; news stories from 1924–25 explain that Meek owned property not only in Utah but also in Oakland, CA, and Beverly Hills, and that he tried (unsuccessfully) to open a "dude ranch" tourist resort at Baker Ranch after filming on *The Covered Wagon* concluded.[40] The area is still largely undeveloped; an unincorporated community called Garrison is located there today, and nearby Pruess Lake was used as a stand-in for the North Platte River in the film. Cruze and a small crew shot the buffalo hunt sequence on a secondary location at Antelope Island in the Great Salt Lake. Studio publicity claimed that "Nine square miles of waste prairie were burned up for the great Prairie Fire scenes," but the fire scene has not survived in the extant print.[41] In fact, the original ten-reel print ran to 125 minutes, but the print in circulation today runs ninety-eight minutes; about half an hour of footage has been lost. According to one source, the missing footage included the prairie fire scene and "considerable footage of a documentary nature."[42]

Lasky suggested *The Covered Wagon*'s elaborate release plan, urging Zukor to exploit the film outside the usual distribution channels. "I earnestly believe that if 'The Covered Wagon' does not gross four or five million it will be our own fault through not having properly realized its possibilities, and I do not see how we can get such a gross, which the picture is entitled to, unless we use road show methods."[43] In addition to a roadshow release, Paramount promoted *The Covered Wagon* with a lavish publicity campaign. The studio's general manager of distribution, S. R. Kent, explained that the studio had planned "the most sweeping exploitation campaigns ever given a picture." In addition to roadshow engagements in major cities, Paramount's publicity department arranged a cross-marketing campaign with Appleton & Company, publishers of the novel, and a "unique tie-up" with the Union Pacific Railroad.[44] As *Moving Picture World* put it, "For months, under the supervision of John C. Flinn, and with the cooperation of the entire Paramount publicity staff, 'The Covered Wagon' has been kept constantly before the American public [. . .] practically every rotogravure supplement in the country has carried stills from the picture or location scenes."[45] Much of this publicity centered on the vast scale and difficulty of the film's location shoot. Paramount pushed a specific set of numbers: multiple advertisements and printed theatrical programs boasted that "To make 'The Covered Wagon,' 3,000 actors spent three months on a location 80 miles from a railroad. They endured floods, blizzards, zero temperature, and sometimes lack of food. A thousand Indians were used, and the live stock included 600 oxen, 1000 horses, and 500 mules."[46] Adam Hull Shirk, director of publicity at Paramount's West Coast studio, traveled to the Antelope Island and Baker Ranch shoots and reported back in multiple dispatches to the studio's house organ *Paramount Pep.*[47] Shirk describes "Camp Cruze" as a "city" of three thousand, with "some five hundred tents."[48] These numbers are likely an exaggeration; another description from around the same time claims the camp housed one thousand people and contained two hundred tents.[49]

While I have been unable to determine the precise number of people housed there, Camp Cruze was certainly large, and it may well have been the largest-ever location shoot at that time, as the studio asserted. In a dispatch from Camp Cruze written for *Picture Play Magazine,* star Lois Wilson described the cast and crew's living conditions: "The camp, housing the greatest number of people ever taken on location, includes the mess tent, commissary, and small tents for each member of the cast and is laid out like a regular city with a poplar-shaded 'Boulevard' and numerous cross streets. It is built around a lake which becomes a river for us because Emerson Hough put one in his story." Dailies were developed on-site and projected in the mess tent, along with new films sent out from the studio.[50] Shirk's description makes it clear that the camp was organized around a familiar studio division of labor: "A big mess tent, a wonderful kitchen, a commissary, business office, prop, costume, construction and other departments are housed in tents."[51] Indeed, accounts of *The Covered Wagon*'s location shoot demonstrate the extent to which silent-era Hollywood filmmakers attempted to replicate studio production conditions as much as possible on location. As a Paramount theatrical program for the film put it, "A whole studio was practically transported into the desert" (see figures 27.3 and 27.4).[52]

The film's location shooting proved central to its success and was widely praised. Upon its release, a reviewer in the *New York Times* exclaimed that "you may think, at first, that such pictures make themselves."[53] Years later, Kevin Brownlow similarly remarked that *The Covered Wagon* gives the impression of being "a documentary record of an original trek in 1848."[54] A primary function of location shooting is to establish just this impression of realism. Through the indexical reference to actually existing landscapes, Westerns shot on location had been asserting the "truthfulness" of their fictional narratives since the dawn of cinema.[55] This connection between real landscape

FIGURE 27.3 *The Covered Wagon* cast and crew on location at "Camp Cruze." Photo courtesy of the Academy of Motion Picture Arts and Sciences' Margaret Herrick Library.

and historical fiction shores up the ideological force of settler colonialism in the Western genre. The location shooting in *The Covered Wagon* served to assert a particular "truth" about the history of the Oregon Trail, affirming the virtue of settlement and disavowing the violence of the forced removal of Native Americans from their ancestral lands. The land itself does not assert this "truth," but in the transformation of land into cinematic landscape, existing places take on social and political meaning.

Shooting on location created unique compositional challenges for silent-era cinematographers. Simmon has analyzed the landscape techniques in early Westerns, tracing the history of "eastern Westerns" from Edwin S. Porter's *The Great Train Robbery* (1903), shot in New Jersey, to Griffith's Biograph Westerns such as *The Redman and the Child* and *The Girl and the Outlaw* (both 1908), shot in New York State. Simmon argues that the genre's spatial dynamic changed as the film industry shifted westward, and its attitude toward Native Americans became more violent. By the time Griffith shot *The Battle of Elderbush Gulch* in Southern California in 1913, Simmon argues, Griffith and his cameraman Billy Bitzer were beginning to incorporate compositional techniques used by nineteenth-century landscape painters and photographers, such as "the prospect shot from high atop a hill," as a way of framing the larger and wider landscapes of

FIGURE 27.4 *The Covered Wagon* crew at "Camp Cruze." Cruze is standing front and center wearing a heavy fur-collared coat; Dorothy Arzner, who edited the film, is standing third from right wearing a sweater and pants. Photo courtesy of the Academy of Motion Picture Arts and Sciences' Margaret Herrick Library.

the West.[56] Cruze's cinematographer on *The Covered Wagon*, Karl Brown, had served as an assistant to Bitzer on numerous films, including *The Birth of a Nation*.

The Covered Wagon's visual style was central to its popular reception. Victor Freeburg lavished praise upon the film in his 1923 book *Pictorial Beauty on Screen* and included a frame enlargement of the film's famous scene of wagons in an arroyo (see figure 27.5). Freeburg wrote, "James Cruze [. . .] did not bungle his composition. Always the historic wagon train of the pioneers strikes the dominant note of the scene, seeming to compose itself spontaneously into a pictorial pattern which accents the dramatic meaning. This is true even when there is no physical movement. In the arroyo scene, for example [. . .] the wagons, drawn up into formation for a camp, harmonize sternly with the savage-looking cliffs, and their zig-zag arrangement somehow suggests the sharp action of the fight with the Indians which fate holds in store for this very place."[57] As Kaveh Askari has noted, such critical praise contributed to a "public sentiment surrounding Lasky's 1923 production [that] aligned it effortlessly with the aims of pictorial education."[58]

FIGURE 27.5 Victor Freeburg, *Pictorial Beauty on the Screen* (New York: Macmillan, 1923).

Live prologue shows, a staple of film programs in large urban movie theaters at this time, were an important part of *The Covered Wagon*'s roadshow exhibition. At Grauman's Egyptian Theatre, where the film premiered in Los Angeles, there were two prologue shows, one with songs from the 49ers and another with Native American performers. The Egyptian Theatre's program describes "In the Days of '49" as "A Spectacular Prologue on the Oregon Trail, with a Cast of Original Forty-niners." The second prologue show, as described in the program, is "A Stage Presentation of 25 FAMOUS INDIAN CHIEFS Just Off the Reservation, the REAL Americans, with their Squaws and Papooses."[59] This group, who also performed in the film, was photographed for a promotional story in *Paramount Pep*, which describes its members as "a band of Arapahoe Indian chiefs" (see figure 27.6). In a recent article about foreign reception of *The Covered Wagon* and *The Iron Horse*, Patrick Adamson has shown that this troupe of Native American performers also traveled to Chicago, New York, London, and Paris. Adamson rightly connects these performances to the long history of imperial exhibitions of Indigenous people in Europe and North America, explaining that "these introductions worked to frame the film as a deliberate work of historiography and, in particular, one with an overtly educational function."[60] Adamson's argument that the film's prologue show helped to "reframe[e] nationalistic discourse" about the American West into universal themes of migration

FIGURE 27.6 Studio publicity photo courtesy of the Academy of Motion Picture Arts and Sciences' Margaret Herrick Library. A publicity story running a nearly identical (but cropped and lower-quality) image from this same photo shoot captions this scene as: "A band of Arapahoe Indian chiefs who appear in 'The Covered Wagon.' [. . .] Mr. Lasky can be seen holding one of the little Indian girls and next to him is James Cruze. At his left is Major T. J. McCoy, who is responsible for bringing the Indians down from Wyoming to participate in the opening of the production." "Chiefs Call at West Coast Studio," *Paramount Pep*, April 25, 1923.

and settlement can be extended further to account for the film's explicitly racialized approach to history.[61]

The Covered Wagon was not the first Western to use location shooting to make a truth claim about its portrayal of history; it drew on long-established traditions in landscape painting and photography, and within the aesthetic of realism. If realism, as defined by art historian Linda Nochlin, aims "to give a truthful, objective, and impartial observation of the real world, based on meticulous observation of contemporary life," this aesthetic is manifested distinctly in different moments in history and in different art forms.[62] As Joshua Gleich and Lawrence Webb explain in their introduction to *Hollywood on Location*, "[f]ilming locations are physical, material *spaces* that constitute the basic infrastructure of the filmmaking process outside the studio. They are also *places* with culturally constructed uses and meanings that interact with the story material and resonate for the audience in complex ways. Locations are transformed, through the filmmaking process, into the manufactured place of mise-en-scène: they become cinematic landscapes."[63] Location shooting in the spectacular landscapes of the American West not only operated as a truth claim to assert the veracity of specific historical narratives; the landscapes themselves functioned to add grandeur to the story being told. This process of cinematic mythmaking can be more fully understood by looking at the way *The Covered Wagon* structures these two elements—landscapes and people, or background and foreground—in relation to each other.

LANDSCAPE IS GRAND, SETTLERS ARE ORDINARY

Two powerful visual traditions have been deployed in the service of justifying the colonization of the western United States: the trope of empty space, and the magisterial gaze. The construction of "uninhabited" nature has been a powerful topos in the Western film genre. Functioning as a visual tool to justify colonization in any region, one of the basic ideological functions of landscape representations (whether in painting, photography, or film) is to portray that landscape as empty or unused. As Simmon puts it, in Westerns, "empty land is there for the taking" and "to fill the land is the heroic role."[64] Susan Courtney has shown how the trope of "empty space" continued into the post-WWII era in atomic bomb testing films.[65] The relationship between figure and landscape in *The Covered Wagon* fits this model: vast spaces are depicted while the pioneers trek through them, but otherwise there are no human traces visible.

In a discussion of the "magisterial gaze," art historian Albert Boime analyzes the "view from above" found in the landscape paintings of the Hudson River school, the Rocky Mountain school, and in popular landscape images influenced by these traditions.[66] Such a view confers mastery upon its spectator, and films such as *The Covered Wagon* and *The Big Trail* borrowed this romantic pictorial aesthetic to portray the grandeur of western landscapes in moving pictures. Albert Bierstadt's 1869 painting "The Oregon Trail" (aka "Emigrants Crossing the Plains") is a paradigmatic example of this aesthetic. In its panoramic size and scope, the painting anticipates the cinema screen. Bierstadt depicts his scene from a straight-on view, with settlers and their cattle receding into the distance through a wooded glade at the left. Majestic mountains frame the upper right of the painting, receding into the distance at the center of the frame. As Bierstadt's painting demonstrates, nineteenth-century landscape painters developed the tradition in which grand landscapes dwarf human figures. Cinema brought several new developments to this tradition: the aesthetic of movement, the realism of location shooting, and the dramaturgical principles of melodrama. As much as possible, Cruze and Brown framed the landscapes of Utah similarly in *The Covered Wagon*; they were particularly successful in the film's climactic gorge scene (see figure 27.5). The Baker Ranch site lacked high mountain peaks, however, and Bierstadt's painting was not directly quoted until

Walsh's widescreen film *The Big Trail* seven years later, shot partly on location in the Rocky Mountains of Wyoming.

Unlike a history painting, which is static, *The Covered Wagon* presents its story of white settlement as a series of emblematic episodes. Set against grandiose natural backdrops including an open plain, a rushing river, and sweeping mountains, these human episodes take on the quality of heroic tableaux. The film's setting is grand, but its settler characters are humble "ordinary" people, designed to evoke audience identification with their plainspoken dialogue, Christian morals, and especially their whiteness. The Indigenous people encountered along the way are figured as two-dimensional threats; they speak an untranslated language and are shown to possess little culture and no moral virtue. These are barely drawn, fearsome Indians whose resistance brings them only death; indigeneity in this film, as in most classical Westerns, signifies a generalized, unexplained savagery. As Virgina Wright Wexman observed in a 1996 essay, *The Covered Wagon* "creates its native antagonists as an extension of the hostile landscape which the pioneers must domesticate."[67] The film's promotional campaign made clear that Native American performers in the film were secured to lend authenticity to the production. In this way, both the landscape and Indigenous people were conceptualized through the essentializing logic of "nature" as an unchanging material presence; the white settlers, on the other hand, are constructed as mobile subjects with a culture and a history. The film's belief in Manifest Destiny is matched by its adherence to patriarchal values. Women in the narrative support their fathers, marry the top male suitor, and bear children. The children, for their part, are seen as a means to an end: an intertitle tells us that it's "more important to get these babies across than it is the grown folks—they'll be the real Empire builders."

I intend the term "ordinary" to carry multiple valences of class and culture. Brooks describes the modernity of melodrama as a "*drama* of the *ordinary*," which he contrasts with the dramas of extraordinary characters—gods and monarchs—that once appeared in tragic drama.[68] Melodrama comes into being after the French Revolution and after the demise of traditional notions of the sacred, Brooks argues, in order to tell stories about and for the bourgeoisie, which still hungers for some version of the sacred but whose world is now characterized by "the impossibility of conceiving sacralization other than in personal terms."[69] There is a specifically modern, democratic principle at work in melodrama, Brooks argues. "While its social implications may be variously revolutionary or conservative, it is in all cases radically democratic, striving to make its representations clear and legible to everyone."[70] *The Covered Wagon* is a conservative melodrama whose argument for modern progress comes cloaked in the trappings of nostalgia. Its democratic celebration of settlers as ordinary *white* people was crucial to its success. It is important to note that there were historical African American pioneers who traveled west in the overland migration of the 1840s–60s, but no Black settlers are portrayed in *The Covered Wagon*.

Furthering this sense of the film's democratic appeal, I also aim to conjure the sense of "ordinary" used by Raymond Williams in his famous essay, "Culture Is Ordinary," in which he describes culture as "a whole way of life."[71] For Williams, to say that "culture is ordinary" is to say that culture is everywhere, it is produced by and works for all humans—in contrast to the elitist notion that culture is only produced by the ruling class. In beckoning migrants west with the promise of farmland, settler colonialism defines the settler paradigm as ordinary, democratic, accessible to all—even though this promise is built on violent Indigenous dispossession. This is not precisely how Williams meant the term "ordinary"—he was interested in a progressive, anti-elitist notion of culture, rather than falsely promised democracy. But in *The Covered Wagon*, we can see how an anti-elitist appeal to populist notions of settlers as "ordinary" (in this case meaning white) ends up normalizing the racialized framework of settler ideology. In this way, "ordinary" can also mean folksy, and here it is important to note how *The Covered Wagon* managed to validate rural American values while appealing to diverse audiences in urban and small-town locations. The covered wagon and the automobile it prefigures signify "ordinariness" through the visualization of vehicles. A cover image from *Paramount Pep* in 1923 makes this parallel between covered wagons, cars, and roads explicit (see figure 27.7).

As a period piece, *The Covered Wagon* is an example of modernity representing the past to itself through moving images. Like a history painting, the film condenses a span of time and a complex history into a story of a few characters. Also like a history painting, the film is an ideological statement, celebrating a story of white conquest and Indigenous dispossession through melodramatic characterizations of victims, villains, and heroes. "Herein it is history recounted and made vivid," exclaimed a film reviewer for the New York *Globe*.[72] *The Covered Wagon* is an example of what Daniela Bleichmar and Vanessa R. Schwartz have called "visual history," which refers to history paintings, photographs, illustrations, films, or other visual representations of history: "a pictorial account of the past." Visual history functions not only as an artifact of "past visual evidence"—in this case, a film from 1923 whose narrative events take place in 1848—but also "an active creator of the terms by which viewers came to understand pastness."[73] The film, therefore, tells us a great deal about how American history was conceptualized in the 1920s.

Released as the era of popular auto travel began, two years after the passage of the Federal Highway Act, *The Covered Wagon* looks back to an earlier era of travel through western landscapes with fondness and nostalgia.[74] In the first period of long-distance roadbuilding in the 1920s, as the monumental work of laying in modernity's infrastructure was gearing up, this film about an unpaved trail may have provided reassurance and validation to many viewers. But any glance at today's car commercials verifies that the image of a vehicle gliding through the wilderness retains its enduring appeal.[75] The resilience of the trail topos shows the persistence of cultural interest in—and residual ambivalence about—the settlement of the American West. Just as modern expansion and development—specifically understood via extractive capitalism and the burning of fossil fuels—is now known as a major cause of anthropogenic climate change, settler colonialism is now seen by many as one of several constitutive forces of modernity that have contributed to the various forms of environmental collapse we are facing today. Through cinematic traces left by popular films such as *The Covered Wagon*, we

FIGURE 27.7 Covered wagons and the wagon trail prefiguring the automobile and the road. Cover image of *Paramount Pep*, April 25, 1923.

can examine the gears of this racialized, extractive logic as they were turning, decades before the implications of this violence and environmental degradation began to be understood.

Notes

1. My thanks to Richard Abel, Matt Hauske, and the editors of this volume for their helpful feedback on this essay. Lorenzo Veracini, *The Settler Colonial Present* (New York: Palgrave Macmillan, 2015), 8.
2. J. M. Shute, "An Advance in Art of Modern Sign Design," *Motion Picture News*, May 12, 1923, 2309, 2320.
3. *Exhibitors Trade Review*, April 7, 1923, 949.
4. Other silent-era "trail films" include *Blazing the Trail* (Ince, 1912), *The Argonauts of California* (Kabierske, 1916), *Romance of the Redwoods* (DeMille, 1917), *Wagon Tracks* (Hillyer, 1919), and a lost Tom Mix film called *The Wilderness Trail* (Le Saint, 1919). Sound-era titles include *The Big Trail* (Walsh, 1930), *Wagon Wheels* (Barton, 1934), *The Oregon Trail* (Pembroke, 1930), *Bend of the River* (Mann, 1952), *The Oregon Trail* (Fowler, Jr., 1959), *The Way West* (McLaglen, 1967), and more. Continuing the trope is *The Oregon Trail* video game, which debuted in the 1970s and came packaged as educational software for school computers well into the 2000s.
5. See Sheena Wilson, Adam Carlson, and Imre Szeman, eds., *Petrocultures: Oil, Politics, Culture* (Montreal, Canada: McGill-Queen's University Press, 2017).
6. "Biggest Money Pictures," *Variety*, June 21, 1932, 62.
7. John Tuska, *The Filming of the West* (New York: Doubleday, 1976), 87–97; Kevin Brownlow, *The War, The West, and the Wilderness* (New York: Knopf, 1979), 368–381.
8. Clipping, "The Big Trail," n.s., n.d., n.p., Margaret Herrick Library, Academy of Motion Picture Arts and Sciences (hereafter AMPAS), Chamberlin Scrapbook 17. *The Covered Wagon* was released on DVD and Blu-Ray by Kino Lorber in 2018; *The Big Trail* was released on DVD and Blu-Ray by Twentieth Century-Fox in 2012. At the time of this writing, both films can be found on YouTube.
9. Linda Williams, *Playing the Race Card: Melodramas of Black and White from Uncle Tom to O .J. Simpson* (Princeton, NJ: Princeton University Press, 2001); Peter Brooks, *The Melodramatic Imagination: Balzac, Henry James, Melodrama, and the Mode of Excess* (New Haven, CT: Yale University Press, 1976).
10. Lorenzo Veracini, "Settler Colonialism as a Distinct Mode of Domination," in Edward Cavanagh and Lorenzo Veracini, eds., *The Routledge Handbook of the History of Settler Colonialism* (New York: Routledge, 2017), 2.
11. Patrick Wolfe, "Settler Colonialism and the Elimination of the Native," *Journal of Genocide Research* 8, no. 4 (December 2006): 388.
12. In this essay I use the terms "Native American" and "Native" to refer to the Indigenous peoples of North America. I also use the more broadly defined term "Indigenous," which invokes the conceptual paradigm and political struggles of Indigenous, First Nations, and Aboriginal peoples worldwide. I use the term "Indian" (without scare quotes) when referring to Hollywood portrayals of Native people (e.g., cowboys and Indians), along with established terms such as "Indian Citizenship Act."
13. Wolfe, "Settler Colonialism," 388, italics in original.

14. Patricia Nelson Limerick, *The Legacy of Conquest: The Unbroken Past of the American West* (New York: Norton, 1987).
15. Joanna Hearne, *Native Recognition: Indigenous Cinema and the Western* (Albany: State University of New York Press, 2012); Michelle H. Raheja, *Reservation Reelism: Redfacing, Visual Sovereignty, and Representations of Native Americans in Film* (Lincoln: University of Nebraska Press, 2011); Richard Abel, *Americanizing the Movies and Movie-Mad Audiences, 1910–1914* (Berkeley: University of California Press, 2006); and Scott Simmon, *The Invention of the Western Film: A Cultural History of the Genre's First Half-Century* (Cambridge, UK: Cambridge University Press, 2003). See also Abel's most recent book, *Our Country/Whose Country? Settler Colonialism and Early American Films* (New York: Oxford University Press, 2023).
16. Simmon, *The Invention of the Western Film*, xiii.
17. Peter Limbrick, *Making Settler Cinemas: Film and Colonial Encounters in the United States, Australia, and New Zealand* (New York: Palgrave Macmillan, 2010), 5.
18. On the "nadir" of American race relations see Rayford Logan, *The Negro in American Life and Thought: The Nadir, 1877–1901* (New York: Dial Press, 1954) and Eric Foner, *Reconstruction: America's Unfinished Revolution, 1863–1877* (New York: Harper & Row, 1988).
19. "President Extols 'Covered Wagon,'" *Moving Picture News*, July 21, 1923, 267. Harding's screening included 150 invited guests and featured accompaniment by a twenty-five-piece orchestra sent from the Criterion in New York. "Hardings and Guests See Covered Wagon," *Paramount Pep*, April 18, 1923, 16.
20. R. W. Hatch, "Professor of History Commends 'The Covered Wagon,'" *Morning Telegraph* (NY), May 20, 1923, n.p., *The Covered Wagon* clipping file, AMPAS.
21. Fred, review of *Covered Wagon*, *Variety*, March 22, 1923, n.p., *The Covered Wagon* clipping file, AMPAS.
22. "'Covered Wagon' Breaks Record of Broadway Houses," *Morning Telegraph* (NY), January 20, 1924, n.p., *The Covered Wagon* clipping file, AMPAS.
23. For a sample of the extensive scholarship on *Birth*, see Paul McEwan, *The Birth of a Nation* (London: British Film Institute, 2015); Melvyn Stokes, *D. W. Griffith's* The Birth of a Nation: *A History of "The Most Controversial Motion Picture of All Time"* (New York: Oxford University Press, 2007); Michael Rogin, "'The Sword Became a Flashing Vision': D. W. Griffith's *The Birth of a Nation*," *Representations* 9 (Winter 1985): 150–195.
24. Williams, *Playing the Race Card*, xiii–xiv, italics in original.
25. Ibid., 70.
26. Ibid., 23.
27. Kim TallBear, *Native American DNA: Tribal Belonging and the False Promise of Genetic Science* (Minneapolis: University of Minnesota Press, 2013), 45. For an overview of the history of blood quantum, see TallBear, *Native American DNA*, 55–66.
28. Brooks, *The Melodramatic Imagination*, 5.
29. Matthew Frye Jacobson, *Whiteness of a Different Color: European Immigrants and the Alchemy of Race* (Cambridge, MA: Harvard University Press, 1998), 93.
30. Ibid., 42.
31. Brian Dippie, *The Vanishing American: White Attitudes and U.S. Indian Policy* (Lawrence: University of Kansas Press, 1982), 199.
32. Ibid.

33. Jesse L. Lasky with Don Weldon, *I Blow My Own Horn* (Garden City, NY: Doubleday, 1957), 159.
34. Ibid., 160–161.
35. Wolfgang Schivelbush, *The Railway Journey: The Industrialization of Time and Space in the 19th Century*, trans. Anselm Hollo (Berkeley: University of California Press, 1986), 64.
36. Lasky, *I Blow My Own Horn*, 162.
37. Numerous sources, including Kevin Brownlow, debunk this claim, which was never proven and is probably untrue. There is no authoritative biography of Cruze, though there are numerous accounts of him in the trade press. See, for example, Jim Tully, "A Thousand Dollars a Day!" *Motion Picture Classic*, October 1924, 40, 77–78.
38. Jesse Lasky to Adolph Zukor, September 5, 1922, Adolph Zukor Collection, AMPAS.
39. Lasky, *I Blow My Own Horn*, 164.
40. "Nevadan Claims $3,000,000 Theft: Ely Securities Said Stolen in Salt Lake City," *Nevada State Journal*, September 6, 1924, 1; "Movie Film Starts New 'Dude Ranch,'" *Longmont Daily Times*, April 24, 1925, 3.
41. Paramount theatrical program from Grauman's Egyptian Theatre, 1923, unnumbered page 3, core collection, AMPAS.
42. Douglas S. Wilson, *The Covered Wagon* Program Notes, Toronto Film Society, November 21, 1988, 10.
43. Lasky to Zukor, April 10, 1923, Zukor Collection, AMPAS. In this letter, Lasky recommends the road-show release should be handled "by someone like J. J. McCarthy," who handled Griffith's road shows, but "if McCarthy is not available there are other men of his type." I have been unable to confirm who actually handled *The Covered Wagon*'s road-show release.
44. "Big Plans for 'The Covered Wagon,'" *Paramount Pep*, January 17, 1923, 5.
45. "'The Covered Wagon' Premiere Follows Stupendous Campaign," *Moving Picture World*, March 24, 1923, 460.
46. Paramount theatrical program from the Woods Theatre, Chicago, 1923, 6, Tom B'hend and Preston Kaufmann Collection, AMPAS.
47. "Cruze Starts Big Undertaking," *Paramount Pep*, October 16, 1922, 13.
48. Adam Hull Shirk, "On Location with 'The Covered Wagon,'" *Paramount Pep*, October 23, 1922, 14.
49. Lou Marcus, "'The Covered Wagon' Is on the Way!" *Film Daily*, November 2, 1922, 4.
50. Lois Wilson, "Two Letters from Location," *Picture Play Magazine*, April 1923, 22.
51. Shirk, "On Location," 14.
52. Paramount theatrical program from Grauman's Egyptian, unnumbered page 3.
53. "A Movie of the Prairies," *New York Times*, March 17, 1923, 9.
54. Brownlow, *The War, the West, and the Wilderness*, 368.
55. For an overview of location shooting in the silent era see Jennifer Peterson, "The Silent Screen, 1895–1927," in Joshua Gleich and Lawrence Webb, eds., *Hollywood on Location: An Industry History* (New Brunswick, NJ: Rutgers University Press, 2019), 16–44.
56. Simmon, *The Invention of the Western Film*, 42.
57. Victor Freeburg, *Pictorial Beauty on the Screen* (New York: Macmillan, 1923), 66–67.
58. Kaveh Askari, *Making Movies into Art: Picture Craft from the Magic Lantern to Early Hollywood* (London: British Film Institute, 2015), 169.
59. Paramount theatrical program from Grauman's Chinese Theatre, 1923, core collection, AMPAS.

60. Patrick Adamson, "American History at the Foreign Office: Exporting the Silent Epic Western," *Film History* 31, no. 2 (Summer 2019): 44.
61. Ibid., 48.
62. Linda Nochlin, *Realism* (London: Penguin, 1971), 13.
63. Gleich and Webb, "Introduction," in *Hollywood on Location*, 5.
64. Simmon, *The Invention of the Western Film*, 53, 52.
65. Susan Courtney, *Split-Screen Nation: Moving Images of the American West and South* (New York: Oxford University Press, 2017).
66. Albert Boime, *The Magisterial Gaze: Manifest Destiny and American Landscape Painting c. 1830–1865* (Washington, DC: Smithsonian Institution Press, 1991).
67. Virginia Wright Wexman, "The Family on the Land: Race and Nationhood in Silent Westerns," in Daniel Bernardi, ed., *The Birth of Whiteness: Race and the Emergence of U.S. Cinema* (New Brunswick, NJ: Rutgers University Press, 1996), 145.
68. Brooks, *The Melodramatic Imagination*, 13, italics in original.
69. Ibid., 16.
70. Ibid., 15.
71. Raymond Williams, "Culture Is Ordinary," in Williams, *Resources of Hope: Culture, Democracy, Socialism* (London: Verso, 1989), 3–14.
72. New York *Globe* review quoted in "Paramount's 'The Covered Wagon' Acclaimed by New York Critics," *Moving Picture World*, March 31, 1923, 566.
73. Daniela Bleichmar and Vanessa R. Schwartz, "Visual History: The Past in Pictures," *Representations* 145 (Winter 2019): 3, 5.
74. For a history of roads and automobiles in the US, see Christopher W. Wells, *Car Country: An Environmental History* (Seattle: University of Washington Press, 2012).
75. A few examples: Kia Sportage, "Mountain" (2021), https://www.ispot.tv/ad/tFxG/2021-kia-sportage-mountain-t2; Lincoln, "Comfort in the Extreme: Cold" (2021), https://www.youtube.com/watch?v=Ki6XnR6DkeY; and Chevy Trailblazer, "Middle of Nowhere" (2020), https://www.youtube.com/watch?v=R5xZ1IrPh6o.

CHAPTER 28

SCANDINAVIAN CINEMA, LOCATION, AND THE DISCOURSE OF QUALITY IN 1920

ANNE BACHMANN

THIS chapter considers a juncture in film history around 1920 when Swedish cinema came to define film as art in Scandinavia.[1] Working through notions and practices involving Swedes Victor Sjöström and Mauritz Stiller and the Dane Carl Th. Dreyer, I trace how changing ideals and aesthetics of filmmaking at the time were discussed and executed, with a view to examining how Swedish films from the late 1910s would impact film culture in the other Scandinavian countries. Nature and folklore were central, and while they were by no means new to film, they now became an important criterion for the discussion of feature fiction film in Scandinavia. As a rule, scholars have viewed this period in Scandinavian film culture through the optics of individual national cinemas, and folkloristic or nature elements would seem to confirm the pertinence of the national as a category for making historical sense of the films. However, the films' handling of landscape, nature, ethnography, and folklore is less straightforward than that. I argue that these and other central components in this specific value system, such as literariness, cluster around a sense of "authenticity." Such authenticity may stem from ethnographic or historical aspects, from a perceived depth of character psychology, from fidelity to prestigious literary originals, or from the role nature plays thematically, among other components of this historically specific "prestige" project. Often, authenticity was bound up in the meanings that landscape could convey; surprisingly, stand-in locations could also be lauded as "authentic" under certain circumstances. Moreover, I look at how the national in Scandinavian cinemas at the time might coincide with, coinhabit space with, or be exchanged for something "Nordic," "Scandinavian," or "Northern," as well as the national markers of a different Scandinavian country. As a starting point, I employ Carl Th. Dreyer's 1920 critique of previous Danish cinema and endorsement of the Swedish filmmaking of the time. I locate authenticity first in the literariness of adaptations and transmedia practices associating film with literature and then, as mentioned, in notions about something genuine, worthwhile, or authentic as expressed through ethnography and nature or landscape. In so doing, I seek to point out how the practices around such strivings for the genuine or authentic have been complex and contradictory, with gaps between the ideal and the realized that are sometimes instructive.

In the historiography of Swedish film, scholars have customarily seen Swedish Biograph's strategy of producing fewer, but more thoroughly developed, films from 1916 onward as resulting in a "golden age" of Swedish cinema. Recently, a more sustained critique of this categorization in film history has appeared, although the period's status as a dynamic moment in film culture remains unchanged.[2] Sweden's output as a whole during this time was diverse, but the productions that received the most interest at home and abroad—notably in France—were those characterized by natural scenery, psychological interest, and a weighty sense of literariness that divulged their artistic ambition. The greatest number of these films were directed by Victor Sjöström or Mauritz Stiller, both of whom had made their debut as film directors in 1912. Sjöström and Stiller would continue their careers alongside one another, transitioning from the world of theater to Swedish Biograph, often acting in each other's films, and would both go on to Hollywood in the mid-1920s. Soon, the much-publicized "Swedish style" became a transnational phenomenon, as its influence spread to filmmaking in surrounding countries. Indeed, "Swedish" ideas associated with this style, such as sublime landscapes with a patriotic tinge, turned out to travel easily. In other words, even if these ideas were tied to a specific nation, they were in practice generally applicable to the national cinemas of other Scandinavian countries, in accordance with the general paradox of nationalism. The "Swedish" style heavily influenced the Norwegian and Finnish film industries, both of which up until that time had a limited output.

The Danish film industry, on the other hand, had had enormous success in the recent past. The Danish international triumphs had been accomplished by Nordisk Film Compagni in particular and had typically leaned on the formula of the so-called erotic melodrama. By 1920, the ideals from Sweden prescribing psychological depth rooted in culture and nature were seen by some as a promising path to renewal in place of quicker thrills. Denmark's keenest advocate of the "Swedish style" was the director-to-be Carl Th. Dreyer. Dreyer, like Stiller and Sjöström, would eventually work internationally, becoming particularly active in Germany and France at roughly the same time as the two Swedes went to the US. (The Swedish directors' backgrounds were partly international, too; Sjöström had spent some of his childhood years in America, while Stiller possessed a cosmopolitan profile, courtesy of his Russian-Finnish-Jewish background.)[3] The individual silent films of these three have been read as falling somewhere between European and American practices. Lately, Eivind Røssaak has discussed differences between the Swedish and American edits of Stiller's metafilmic comedy *Thomas Graal's Best Film* (*Thomas Graals bästa film*, 1917), whereas David Bordwell notes Dreyer's exploratory take on American continuity in *The President* (*Præsidenten*, 1919).[4] Much of

Stiller's and Sjöström's early work, however, is shrouded in mystery, owing to a blaze in a Swedish film archive, although considerable progress has been made of late on the films' restoration and research into extant materials.[5]

A journalist and critic before his filmmaking career, Dreyer famously passed strictures on the contemporaneous Danish film in a virulent piece from 1920.[6] Interestingly, Dreyer framed his censorious points about Danish output within a eulogy to Swedish film. He even adopted a Swedish perspective in the text, by describing a perceived antipathy toward Danish film found in what he referred to as the "more discerning" neighboring countries—read: Sweden. Dreyer was indeed right that the concept of Danish film in Sweden at this point evoked notions of clichéd or erotically suggestive popular entertainment, even if it required ignorance or disregard of Danish literary and idealist ambitions to maintain this view.[7] The contrast set up between Danish and Swedish film is instructive, as it mirrors attitudes about art versus entertainment more often found in the European/American binary at the time. In the common Swedish film parlance of the 1910s, criticism leveled at mindless or speculative cinema would be directed as often at Danish film as at American. The erotic melodrama that Dreyer was referring to had thus far been the recipe for success in Danish film, although in Sweden it had been disproportionately censored and treated as morally and artistically inferior.[8] This, in spite of Swedish film production in the early 1910s having taken the Danish cue, producing a string of quite similar films. Judgment was also passed on films from the south of Europe, according to the trope of a "serious" North in contrast with a "lecherous" South. The north/south pattern sheds light on the perceived opposition between the Swedish and Danish cinemas, since they, too, shared the same terms.

The Swedish quality concept quickly swept into neighboring Norway and Finland.[9] However, the pattern of influence proved more complex in Denmark's case. Casper Tybjerg has described how Denmark's Nordisk Film embraced the art film as a business strategy in a manner similar to Swedish Biograph, dismissing established directors in favor of younger ones with other ideas, such as Dreyer; he further demonstrates how several Danish directors turned to other and differently coded Scandinavian markets in the 1920s.[10] At the same time, Tybjerg has also shown that, outside of Dreyer's work, manifestations of Swedish influence in Danish film were irregular or remote.[11] Stephen Larry Larson has observed that even when it comes to Dreyer's most relevant works in this context, not many Danish critics would have associated them with the Swedish ideal.[12] Danish cinema's previous history of world relevance is a meaningful context for its resilience—either in reaction to influence from abroad, or to such influence being acknowledged.

Transmedia and the Quality Concept

Beyond the fastidious production strategy introduced by Swedish Biograph, there were other factors that propelled the Swedish quality concept into being: literary advisors who strengthened cinema's relationship to the higher-ranking literary art; an emphasis on location shooting; and the presence of a censorship system that encouraged quality. Transmedial practices were central to this juncture, serving to connect the film and publishing industries. Bo Florin has traced the relationship of important Swedish films from this period to canonized literature, theater, and painting, and has pointed to a Scandinavian variant of the "photoplay edition" or film-illustrated tie-in book. Common in the US, tie-in books were sometimes novelizations, sometimes original fiction that had been adapted into films. The Swedish take on this kind of transmedia product materialized as "quality" book editions illustrated with production stills.[13] I have elsewhere connected these book editions to contemporaneous innovations in Swedish souvenir film programs, as well as to a turn toward more visually developed film posters, film journals that were higher in (visual) quality, and general magazines that partly relied on glossy film-production stills for visual effect.[14] All of these printed products were part of a visual culture that played up connections between film and other arts and media. Moreover, the link between the souvenir programs and the film-illustrated book editions set issues of literary style into play. For instance, even if most of the programs contained the films' synopses, the programs that were marked out as higher quality by means of layout choices and thickness might have those synopses rendered in a more literary style—even going so far as to emulate the style of the original text in the case of adaptations.[15] Still, the piece of printed matter that went the furthest toward hybridization between book and program did not derive from an adaptation but from an original script. Hjalmar Bergman's novella *Vem dömer?*, based on his own film script, was set in the renaissance and told in the style of a legend. This book was launched as a little volume in time for the opening night of its film adaptation as *Love's Crucible* (*Vem dömer*, 1922) by Victor Sjöström, and in a letter to his publisher, Bergman suggested that the program-vending boys in the cinema should offer the book for sale.[16] In this case, there is a noteworthy convergence between novella, script, and program where they are in a sense thought to be one and the same.

Extant correspondence concerning the film-illustrated book editions reveals changes in attitudes among key personalities toward Swedish cinema's relation to other arts in the mid-1910s. In April 1915, at the publishing company Albert Bonnier, the eponymous publisher, Albert Bonnier, Jr., a descendant of the company's founder, contacted Swedish Biograph's Charles Magnusson about possible film adaptations.[17] Magnusson, despite greenlighting other adaptation projects, dismissed Bonnier's suggestions on the grounds that literary adaptations were damned if they were too filmic, because then they were not faithful enough to the original, but they were equally damned if they were instead too close to the original, because then they were lacking in medium specificity. Mauritz Stiller was less diplomatic two years earlier, proclaiming that cinema had nothing at all to do with literary fiction and that it would be ridiculous to talk about the artistic dramatization of a novel. For Stiller, in the context of a film drama, mere words meant nothing at all.[18]

Sjöstrom's 1916 adaptation of Norwegian author Henrik Ibsen's epic *Terje Vigen* (or *A Man There Was*, an alternative title) is typically mentioned as the first film of the

Swedish "golden age." On a practical basis, the reason is that this was the first production to be allocated considerably more production time and a greater budget as a conscious strategy by the production company, Swedish Biograph. As a measure of its cultural impact, the film was reviewed (and lauded) by a literary critic in a respected newspaper; in other words, a gatekeeper allowed the film into the field of higher cultural value. Although some scholars have pointed to Stiller's *Wolo Czawienko* (*Balettprimadonnan*, 1916) as an earlier harbinger of Swedish ideals of "quality," *Terje Vigen* remains a watershed for its explicit literary associations.[19] The promotional material generated for the film included a small printed program made in Stockholm and distributed during screenings in that city. The booklet contained Ibsen's epic poem "Terje Vigen," which the film builds on and quotes at length. Like the film itself, the booklet reproduced the poem in its original norvagized Danish, instead of commissioning a Swedish translation.

In an obvious way, then, the literary vein of this Swedish quality concept was ambiguously transnational or trans-Scandinavian from the outset, and yet that ambiguity has typically not been foregrounded. For films with an ethnographic interest, as offered by the costumes and scenography in *Terje Vigen*, this is perhaps not so surprising. At least, it is reminiscent of the formation of Sweden's ethnographic museum institutions a few decades earlier (when Sweden and Norway were in a personal union, i.e., the Swedish monarch also ruled Norway). The open-air museum Skansen was planned to contain buildings from all Nordic countries, and its sister museum, the cultural history museum Nordiska museet, was likewise Nordic in scope.

As Eirik Frisvold Hanssen and Anna Sofia Rossholm have pointed out, the literary film frequently fetishized the original literary text (for instance, by not translating any of the source material for *Terje Vigen*, as mentioned).[20] Because the rights to some works of Ibsen had been procured earlier on, it was inevitable that Swedish Biograph would produce an Ibsen adaptation, but *Terje Vigen* initiated a bona fide hunt for originals in the realms of canonized literature. Indeed, works by Nobel laureates became overrepresented in Swedish-produced adaptations in the late 1910s and the 1920s. This practice was in itself trans-Scandinavian, since the majority of these authors came from Scandinavian countries other than Sweden: Henrik Pontoppidan and Karl Gjellerup were from Denmark, while Bjørnstjerne Bjørnson and Knut Hamsun were from Norway. Only Selma Lagerlöf hailed from Sweden.

The shift toward the literary resonated particularly well with Dreyer. When working as a literary advisor for Nordisk Film, Dreyer told a Danish newspaper in 1916 that in cinema, the future order of the day would be adaptation from a novel.[21] On the one hand, the statement illustrates Dreyer's own agenda, which Morten Egholm has covered in depth, but on the other hand, it also illustrates the newspaper's interest in literary adaptation, in line with the newly literature-fevered Scandinavian film climate at the time.[22] On the publishing side, the practice of the quality, film-illustrated novel was transnational, too. The series at Bonnier was inspired by Danish publishing house Gyldendal's similar release of the source text behind Sjöström's Swedish production *The Outlaw and His Wife* (*Berg-Ejvind och hans hustru*, 1918), using production stills from the upcoming film. The source text was the play by the Danish-Icelandic Jóhann Sigurjónsson,

Eyvindur of the Mountains (*Bjærg-Ejvind og hans Hustru*, this ed. 1917), a work that was reminiscent of the Icelandic sagas and well known from Danish stages at the time. The Bonnier company was involved in several transmedial practices involving film culture, from introducing film-related visual culture into journals to producing films themselves in the 1920s, through their subsidiary, Bonnierfilm.[23]

AUTHENTICITY IN ACTUAL LOCATION

Literariness was one vehicle for promoting notions of cultural heritage in cinema; another was landscape. Wilderness, as well as agrarian culture, is immediately noticeable in the films of the Swedish "golden age of cinema," and their usage of landscape has been assessed at length both formally and aesthetically.[24] This section explores notions of heritage and ownership that reside in nature in Swedish as well as other Scandinavian silent film through the prism of location practices and finds an underlying link between nature and heritage. Ways of dealing with landscape and location in film production were contradictory and sometimes surprising, but the discussion around the films uncovers the felt importance of both to the notion of "quality" cinema.

In Scandinavian fiction film, the concept of location went through decisive changes during the 1910s, when film culture appropriated conceptions of nationality, nature, and Nordicness that were already at play in the broader cultural conversation. This marks a shift in the rhetoric of quality toward the notion of the "authentic," roughly understood as something true on a deep level, possibly realistic although not precisely so, but always knowledgeable, reliable, and somehow "worthy" and authoritative. Concepts of authenticity in fiction film at the time were otherwise typically tied to psychological depth, not least in the case of Sjöström. Dreyer scholar Stephen Larry Larson uses the term "lyrical" to capture the perceived depth of films in the Swedish vein.[25] Dreyer picked up on a quality of the authentic when he pointed to the natural rhythm of Swedish films as one reason for their success.[26] Similarly, nature and folklore were also charged with values of the desirably genuine.

By contrast, Mark Sandberg has shown how Danish production practices in the 1910s did not take authenticity into account when it came to film locations.[27] These earlier Danish films attempted a placelessness (or "erasure of site-specificity") that sets off the geographical particularities of the Swedish style. However, such a neat and tidy comparison is too simple. Ideas of national landscape may have been central to how Swedish films were discussed, but regularly, the actual locations where the films were shot were *not* the represented location of the story. Interestingly, such stand-in locations were no secret at all; rather, the landscapes where the films happened to be shot were emphasized for publicity in themselves, for the production value of their beauty or drama. Locations of Sjöström's *Terje Vigen* and *The Outlaw and His Wife* are discussed in this light below. It seems that the desired "authenticity" might have resided in a general striving for an atmosphere of something windswept and rugged rather than a sense that the represented place should be the *actual* place.

We can discern how location was thought of in this era in Sweden through contemporaneous correspondence. For instance, the Swedish ideal of the authentic location in the late 1910s is apparent on the micro level in correspondence between Swedish Biograph and the Swedish consul in Naples in 1918.[28] The consul acted as intermediary when suggesting Swedish Biograph should adapt a screenplay by the Neapolitan writer Salvatore di Giacomo. This idea was particularly apt, the consul opined, as Scandinavians could no longer visit Italy themselves during World War I. Swedish Biograph, however, declined, "since we, to achieve a real and convincing environment, would need to locate some of the takes in Italy, which at the moment is absolutely impossible." Still, Swedish Biograph did not adhere strictly to its own ideal; as *Terje Vigen* and several later big productions demonstrate, that ideal was subject to negotiation. We will consider *Terje Vigen* again shortly, in its capacity as the first and most famous of a series of Swedish-made adaptations based on a text from the Norwegian literary canon. South Norwegian coastal landscape is vital to Ibsen's story and has often been stressed anecdotally as the reason for Sjöström's choice to film the source material, but despite plans to shoot the film in Norway, in the end the setting was represented by proxy: the Stockholm archipelago.

Replacing a landscape actually located in a different Scandinavian country with its representation somewhere within Swedish borders was likewise the practice adhered to during the production of *The Outlaw and His Wife*, where Iceland is the represented location but Abisko in northern Sweden is the actual one. Mauritz Stiller's two pastoral adaptations of Finnish literary originals, *The Song of the Scarlet Flower* (*Sången om den eldröda blomman*, 1919) and *The Rapids of Life* (*Johan*, 1921), perform the same trick. In the two "Finnish" films, river rapids and log drivers were central motifs and reflected a preoccupation with such imagery in Finnish visual culture in general.[29] The two films were shot in northern Swedish landscapes that share the same forestry practices of log driving, so that the filming locations are visually not so different from the represented locations in Finland, a propinquity that abets the masquerade. In the case of *Terje Vigen*, however, the represented location among skerries and reefs on the very tip of southern Norway differs somewhat more from the actual Swedish location on the isle of Öja; certainly, this is the case with the building styles of the houses that form part of the film's visual environment.

A brief comparison with two other Swedish-produced films using actual or represented Norwegian locations may be instructive: Dreyer's comedic seventeenth-century *The Parson's Widow* (*Prästänkan*, 1920), and Rune Carlsten's *A Dangerous Wooing* (*Ett farligt frieri*, 1919), shot in mountain pastures and produced by Swedish Biograph's then-rival, Skandia. The Norwegian location amounts to a trope of sorts in the Swedish lyrical film. Merging the Northern, the Nordic, the Scandinavian, and the national, Swedish productions in Norway and based on Norwegian literary originals are particularly obvious in showing how national and regional identities can be seen as iterations of one another, at times more like a Matryoshka doll and, at others, more like a

Venn diagram. If we were to see the same films through the optics of national cinema history, it might theoretically be possible to isolate Swedish cinema (to take one example) from the implications of transnational activity and meaning-making. In practice, however, the culturally "Swedish" aspects of the films were quite easily exchanged for the "Norwegian," or, typically, the "Danish" for the "Icelandic," for the purposes of playing up Nordic folklore and nature. By the mid-1920s, Danish cinema that was influenced by the Swedish style occasionally emphasized Norwegian locations as well. That was the case in *The House of Shadows* (*Morænen*, A. W. Sandberg, 1924) and *Solskinsdalen* (Emanuel Gregers, 1925). However, in *The Parson's Widow* and *A Dangerous Wooing*, the choice of an authentic location was crucial to the entire project. In this way, the geographical "authenticity" sought after was quite straightforward. *The Parson's Widow* was filmed in an open-air museum, and in that capacity demonstrates how the striving for genuineness took form within an already mediatized and facilitated structure. Such was the case in this instance, with the museum assembling a group of actual, preexisting antiquated buildings, which had been relocated to the museum grounds. The film's sense of fidelity to location and folklore is a subject well covered by Mark Sandberg.[30] Dreyer's aspirations toward location realism, combined with the aims of producers at Swedish Biograph, who were at this point accustomed to a certain type of "folklore" fiction film, resulted in a joint effort of significant ethnographic exactitude. Sandberg picks out the film's striking sense of convergence of the fictional and documentary, which is at work not least in the film's ethnographic detours.

With *The Parson's Widow*, location as the ultimate guarantor of heritage and quality also supports Dreyer's status as a director of film art. *The Parson's Widow*, as well as Dreyer's later, Norwegian-produced *The Bride of Glomdal* (*Glomdalsbruden*, 1926), are symptoms of the direction advocated by Dreyer in his praise of Swedish film in 1920: true-to-life images of characters; atmosphere over technology.[31] Dreyer's ideal of painstaking location authenticity coheres seamlessly with these ideas, whereas previously, such efforts to secure actual locations had not been inherent in conceptions of the literary in Denmark.[32] Particularly in Norway, discussion about the film was informed by a sense of endorsement, often in the form of retelling anecdotes and hearsay concerning the production.[33]

A Dangerous Wooing also featured ethnological interest but could not have been shot in a museum; this story, adapted from Bjørnstjerne Bjørnson, required a dramatic West of Norway setting where a summer farm would be perched on top of a precipice. Therefore, the most authentic aspect of the production was the strenuous conditions endured by the cast and crew while attempting to access this remote locale. For marketing purposes, that behind-the-scenes story seemed highly valuable because of the genuine effort required; the souvenir program details a three-hour non-stop trek (on a road that was actually not a road at all) in the burning heat, plus numerous additional hardships.[34] In silent film culture, the films more likely to function in this way were travelogues, where the demands of filming partly determined the quality of the final product. However, this could also be the case in fiction films dealing with nature in the Swedish style, such as *The Outlaw and His Wife* and also *Terje Vigen*.

Authenticity Discourse in Represented Locations

Discussion of *Terje Vigen* has invited sustained invocations of nature.[35] Nevertheless, the reception of the film first and foremost concerned itself with the source material: critics cited lines from Ibsen's epic poem, provided summaries of its contents, or offered eulogies of its significance and fame. As film historians have often pointed out, the serious press recognition given to this film was a milestone for film culture in Sweden. However, when looking more closely, the attention given to the role of nature lagged somewhat in comparison. One can get the sense from the Swedish press that they only really connected "quality" film to nature afterward, taking cues after the fact that beautiful landscapes could now be a prestige ingredient—however immediate and important sea, cliffs, wind, and waves might be to the film visually. For Sjöström's next film, one year afterward, the press was more prepared and immediately drew on nature as a key reference point for this vein of films. A host of journalists expressed exuberant admiration for the majestic locations in *The Outlaw and His Wife*, with the key term in Swedish being "ståtlig" (grand, splendid, handsome), a term that proceeded to spill over to Victor Sjöström himself, lionizing him and his stature.[36] This time, comments about the film's nature tropes fully overshadowed any mention of the productions of the stage play, even if these were both popular and recent.

When nature and location were in fact mentioned at all in connection with *Terje Vigen*, the ambiguities imparted on the film by its stand-in location were ignored. Through the poem's detailed local geography, the story is inextricably linked to its location in the maritime surroundings of Grimstad in Norway, whereas the film was shot at Landsort on Öja in the Stockholm archipelago. The production process was much publicized, and publicity for the film made much of the location. For instance, reports of a probably lost actuality film shot during filming at Landsort actively linked *Terje Vigen* to this location in a straightforward way, thus giving the actual location primacy over the represented one.[37] Both the Norwegian and the Swedish reception in the press dealt to a considerable degree with concepts of authenticity of the historical or folkloric variety. There was agreement that, excepting a couple of scenes, the illusion held up, even if the location was fake and critics relied on concepts such as veneration and realism.[38] In advance reports, journalists had clearly taken clues about authenticity from the marketing information offered by the company: for instance, that the well-reputed costume designer and theater set-painter had been engaged from Norway to ensure the right touch.[39] Regardless of the degree of felt success, however, the demonstrated willingness to discuss ideals of authenticity is in itself significant, since this very openness characterizes the changed attitude toward locations at this time.

Even so, Swedish film production, too, in its own way, relied substantially on studios, in particular those large studios on the outskirts of Stockholm in Lidingö and later on in Långängen in Stocksund (opened in 1919) and Råsunda (opened in 1920). In other words, the dependence of "golden-age" films on nature and location is relative, and a more accurate description would be that the productions alternated between the location shoots and studio takes, which, for all practical purposes, were equally important. External locations for shooting were ideally not altered in any substantial way; rather, they served as found locations. For the studio takes, usually interiors, a common mode of production for the "national" fiction films involved rebuilding parts of ethnographically correct houses in the studio.[40] In fact, the practice of location substitution, where, for instance, the north of Sweden could be Iceland, may be seen as an alternative "studio" mode of filmmaking. The location swapping was present not only in Sjöström's work but also in Mauritz Stiller's nature-rich literary adaptations for Swedish Biograph and its successor Svensk Filmindustri, including *The Song of the Scarlet Flower* and *The Rapids of Life* and, later, *The Atonement of Gösta Berling* (*Gösta Berlings saga*, 1924).

The terminology Mark Sandberg employs to describe actual and represented locations provides the basis for a history of location practices in Danish film culture.[41] In such a history, notions of correct or ethnological spatiality surface now and then but eventually are stamped by the influence of Swedish ideas. While Dreyer's *Parson's Widow*, shot in Norway in 1920, was a Swedish production, it was also evidently a transnational media event. In Danish film culture, the film marks an occasion where Norwegian folklore, as well as literature, is engaged with most "Swedishly" by someone central to Danish cinema. One newspaper called Dreyer "fully equal to Sjöström and Stiller as regards Nordic peasant films," and some of the shots were "as good as the best from Swedish Biograph."[42] The Danish filmmakers were aligning their films with the Swedish style in order to improve their marketability.

A look at an earlier, non-canonical Danish film production made before the Swedish influence established itself can prove instructive: the rustic narrative *Britta fra Bakken* (*Britta from Bakken*, Vilhelm Glückstadt, 1915) likewise dealt with folklore from a different Scandinavian country but preceded the quest for a lyrical "authenticity" present from *Terje Vigen* onward. In this way, *Britta fra Bakken* can prove useful for tracing developments in the authenticity concept through both academic sources and writings in the press. While it was conceived of entirely in Denmark by Danes, it aimed to create an illusion of Swedishness: the names of the characters were given as Nils Erson, Margit, Gösta, Martha, Britta, Elof, Annie, and Erik. Jan Nielsen, in his extensive catalogue of the Danish production and distribution company Filmfabriken Danmark/Det Skandinavisk-Russiske Handelshus, notes that this two-reeler was promoted as a Swedish film shot on location in the Swedish province Dalarna (or Dalecarlia) but that there is no doubt that the film was shot in Denmark, in the surroundings of Horsens in Jylland.[43] Clearly, geographical authenticity was only a rhetorical value for the film. For once, Sweden, or rather, "Sweden," is reduced to a two-dimensional supplier of folkloric content rather than Swedish producers being "buyers" of such content. As we have seen, Swedish cinema in the years to follow often explicitly used *Norwegian* locations in order to convey a general "Nordicness." In this case from 1915, when Denmark was leading and Sweden following, the power relations are different and the phenomenon is similar, but in a sense inverted. *Britta fra Bakken* deceptively boasted Swedish locations in order to convey a specific "Swedishness." Such a strategy would have been far less likely only a couple of years later.

The scant sources on *Britta fra Bakken* give the impression that the film was lightweight and not very credible in its representation of foreignness. The sense of "authenticity" seems not to have been in demand at all at this point. In this way, superficially similar location practices may become part of significantly different kinds of meaning-making. In the contemporaneous press, some journalists were misled and thought the film was shot in Sweden. The publicity value of a countryside location in tandem with ethnographic content becomes obvious in a review in the theater (and cinema) journal *Masken*: "One sees among other things a succession of enchanting autumn images from those famous districts in the heart of Sweden where the old folk customs and costumes have been maintained right into our time."[44] However, more intriguingly, in other press sources, the countryside images in themselves were complimented despite a realization that they were in fact Danish. The newspaper *Politiken* called the location's bluff but nevertheless went on to cede: "One is given the opportunity to admire an enchanting Danish nature in splendid sunlight, and the film takes form as a succession of very beautiful genre images."[45] These two reviews offer an interesting likeness of wording, despite the completely opposite rendering of facts. In terms of their journalistic practice, these writers do not seem to have simply rewritten the press material, as one may at other times suspect. Rather, the choice of words (enchanting, splendid, beautiful) seems to depend on contemporary newspapers' usual film-writing tropes. Such wording testifies that the visual codes of national or Northern folklore and scenery in *Britta* were likely to be similar to those in early film. At the same time, the two different journalistic accounts of the film, similar in tone but offering divergent accounts of where the film was shot, suggest that the authenticity issue could be interpreted as subjective and emotional rather than actual. As we shall see later, such practices of authenticity would be noticeable within the paradigm of the Swedish ideals.

The Swedish Ideal Takes Root in the Rest of Scandinavia

How, then, can nature be heritage, as the authenticity rhetoric seems to indicate? People are seen as shaped by natural environments, and cultural landscapes as shaped by people who "naturally" belong there. In 1920, an article in a Norwegian film journal written by a Swede addressed the subject of contemporary Swedish film as a self-presentation of sorts. The author (possibly using a pseudonym) contrasted her notion of an overly civilized American cinema as "culture" to the unaffected Swedish rural films as "nature," subsuming under that heading not just wildlife but also farming:

> The fiddle is playing in the pale summer night. People in folk costumes lightly tread the dance. By the cottage's corner stands the old man, looking on. Behold the stern

expression in his face, behold the resolute gaze twinkling in his eye. Behold nature sleeping, how the yellow straws stand in even squares. [. . .] That is *nature*. Then the image changes as if by magic. A furious conductor beats the time for his orchestra with his foot. See the piano, that modern invention, and see the magnificent ballrooms where nicely clad high society whirls in modern dance. See the young man, his listless eyes. That is *culture*. [. . .] This is the difference between Swedish national film art and American film routine. *Nature* is the Swedish and *culture* the American film art.[46]

Dancers in folk costumes and "types" like this old man, then, represented another side to the ideal of authentic and beautiful natural locations: the human activity in these locations, ethnographic practices with primordial overtones. Just as silent actuality films with a touristic interest often seemed to equate folklore and nature, or the ethnographic and the geographic, so, too, did feature films.

In Norway as well as in Sweden, producers believed that nature in domestic film production would ensure export options as well as securing a genuine sense of beauty in their films which, in turn, would act as guarantor for "quality" and "authenticity." The article quoted above ended with a statement of the maxim of the newly established merger, Svensk Filmindustri: " 'Swedish film for national publicity' is the watchword for the new Swedish film trust. The company wishes to, with the aid of film, spread knowledge about Sweden everywhere in the world." As Laura Horak has shown, there had been a turn in Swedish film production toward the international market even before Swedish Biograph's explicit policy of fewer and more expensive films, and when Svensk Filmindustri took over this production line from Swedish Biograph (and also from Skandia, which had emulated Swedish Biograph's strategies), it enlisted the help of the Ministry of Foreign Affairs to facilitate the expansion into foreign markets.[47]

In this respect, ethnographic and geographic qualities combined through "nature" to provide a treasure chest of possible riches from which to draw. The recurrent Swedish film productions taking place on site in Norway and making use of dramatic and visually arresting nature, instead of domestic productions doing the same, was a source of discussion and criticism. Some of the most assertive Norwegian voices practiced this vocabulary, seeing nature as an economic asset to Norwegian film and arguing that the domestic film industry should take note and claim ownership of it.[48] This sense of patriotic annoyance at what was seen as a pillaging of both Norwegian literary originals, as well as picturesque and dramatic natural settings to film them in, is well covered in Norwegian film historiography.[49]

When Norwegian film production did pick up momentum in the 1920s, it heeded this advice to a considerable degree. We have ample evidence of the profound impact that Swedish films had on the growing Norwegian film industry in the 1920s.[50] The Norwegian "national breakthrough" never reached the scope or sophistication of the Swedish movement, but the wave of nationally minded Norwegian films throughout the 1920s relied heavily on images of nature. Most of these films had few interior shots, and *Til sæters* (*To the mountain pasture*, Harry Ivarson, 1924) had none at all: it borrowed from the nature-film mode of production by renouncing electricity for outdoor lighting and camera.[51] In *Til sæters*, which was based on a nineteenth-century musical play, nature was coded, as in many other films: streams or preferably waterfalls were the backdrop for true love, and the mountain pasture was a liminal space for youth regulating their love affairs without the interference of elders. Both in terms of ideas and in light of later film production to come, the Swedish trend had a quick and direct impact on Norwegian filmmaking.

In Denmark, its effect beyond Dreyer was less pervasive. The new idiom from Swedish film culture came to be integrated within a certain repertoire of film discourse, rather than informing the whole of Danish film culture in a dominant way as in Norway. Another difference is that the Swedish style was used in Denmark to criticize other Danish film output. Using terms similar to the opinions soon to be voiced by Dreyer, a 1919 article in the Danish film journal *Filmen* chastised Danish film production and called for Danish films to be made in the Swedish vein. Focusing on location, it connected place to folkloric culture and national character: "Whenever one of our films was to be especially effective, we went to Kullen [a Swedish location] and used the cliffs there as settings, we never made the most of Danish nature, Danish folk songs and the Danish disposition."[52] Nonetheless, the lyrical style was to influence some large productions in revealing ways.

The nature-imbued rhetoric of prestige readily connected to other quality concepts in the Danish silent era. As outlined by Casper Tybjerg, previous discussions of film as art in Denmark had typically been tied to either fine acting by theater performers or to established authors writing directly for the cinema or else making their works available for adaptation.[53] The interests of the literary film in Denmark had historically not been centered on notions of the authentic, whether of location or otherwise. For instance, Holger-Madsen's *Love's Devotee* (*Liebelei/Elskovsleg*, 1914) had transposed Schnitzler's Vienna to Denmark, a move which was mostly praised, due to the dreamy and elegiac qualities of the forest landscapes around Copenhagen.[54] By the time *Terje Vigen* and *The Outlaw and His Wife* reached Denmark, an authenticity idiom as a carrier of cultural prestige was certainly not unknown in Danish film culture, but the examples had been few and far between. When the author and scriptwriter Palle Rosenkrantz described his vision for a filmic history of Denmark, *The Golden Horns*, in 1913 (*Guldhornene*, Kay van der Aa Kühle, 1914), he explained the film's ambitions toward correct historical costume and also toward displaying different parts of Danish nature in this way: "You know that Danish films abroad are enjoying the best of reputations and are sold all over Europe, and so it occurred to me that it might be fun to write a film which gave other countries a true impression of Danish history and Danish nature."[55] In other words, Rosenkrantz's idea was that the current age of international expansion in Danish film was a Trojan horse for slipping in a sense of Danish specificity. At this time, "Danishness" in film practice was normally the non-specific.[56]

In response to the recession occurring during the last stages of World War I, the Danish film industry tried multiple strategies to address the situation, some connected to concepts related to art and some not. The lyrical film emerged among a host of strategies. One strategy entailed making sequels and remakes, such as the string of exotic "maharaja" films starring the Norwegian Gunnar Tolnæs as the eponymous Indian prince.[57] Another was to continue the string of films promoting lofty ideals such as pacifism.[58] Three idealist films by Holger-Madsen at Nordisk Film Compagni typify this strategy, which combined internationalism with literary connotations: the pacifist parable *Peace on Earth* (*Pax Æterna*, 1917); *A Trip to Mars* (*Himmelskibet*, 1918); and the political drama *A Friend of the People* (*Folkets Ven*, 1918), this, too, advocating concord.[59] The latter two films were written by Sophus Michaëlis, whose ideal, in accordance with Nordisk's still unfulfilled need for international markets, was for film to act as a truly international, educational force, "supreme in its national independence."[60] Famously, Nordisk's earlier production policies had traditionally been of an international character in prioritizing cosmopolitan films that could work anywhere. This international inflection would persist to an extent into the 1920s with A. W. Sandberg's string of Dickens adaptations: *Our Mutual Friend* (*Vor fælles Ven*, 1921), *Great Expectations* (*Store Forventninger*, 1922), *David Copperfield* (1922), and *Little Dorrit* (*Lille Dorrit*, 1924). Like the screenplays by the author and poet Michaëlis, the Dickens adaptations were also a new figuration of the Danish literary film, in the wake of the *Autorenfilme* initiated by the Germans.[61]

Finally, as Casper Tybjerg has discussed, the Danish film press eagerly promoted the idea of a national Danish film, expressing inherent "Danishness" in the wake of the national ideas in Swedish as well as Norwegian and, eventually, Finnish film in the same period.[62] This exhortation, however, was only partially fulfilled. Among a handful of films, Tybjerg mainly discusses Carl Th. Dreyer's fairy-tale pastiche *Once upon a Time* (*Der var engang*, 1922). Nevertheless, among Dreyer's films, *Once upon a Time* is not the most Swedish-influenced: on the contrary, that epithet goes to the distinctly un-Danish looks of the previously mentioned *Parsons' Widow* and *The Bride of Glomdal*, both set in Norway.

SONS OF THE SOIL AS A RESPONSE TO *THE OUTLAW AND HIS WIFE*

Dreyer's two Norwegian settings in *The Parson's Widow* and *The Bride of Glomdal* were both actual, not just represented. One way that Danish-produced film mimicked Swedish cinema was by wishing to assign genuine, deep, or psychological qualities to locations in nature-rich films. In Denmark, ideals of authenticity found specific expression in Icelandic and Norwegian landscapes. In resonance with historically colonialist Danish relations to Iceland and to Norway, these two countries were chosen to represent landscape and folklore, as opposed to modernity at home in Denmark. The psychological drama *The House of Shadows* (*Morænen*, A. W. Sandberg, 1924), which I have covered elsewhere, used a Norwegian setting and location for such purposes.[63] When it comes to Icelandic settings, Stiller's Swedish-produced *The Outlaw and His Wife*, shot in the north of Sweden, used very different strategies than the later Danish family saga *Sons of the Soil*, which was actually shot in Iceland (*Borgslægtens Historie*, Gunnar Sommerfeldt 1920).

Along with the Danish-Icelandic *Hadda Padda* from 1924 (Gunnar Robert Hansen and Guðmundur Kamban), *Sons of the Soil* and *The Outlaw and His Wife* partook in a Danish-Icelandic relation. The literary works behind each of the three narratives had been written while their respective Icelandic authors lived in Denmark in the first half of the 1910s. *The Outlaw and His Wife* was an important film to the Danish audience. It had the honor of inaugurating Copenhagen's magnificent Palads-Teater cinema in February 1918, an honor Casper Tybjerg interprets as being primarily due to the owner Sophus Madsen's involvement in the distribution company Dansk-Svensk Film, a collaboration with Charles Magnusson of Svenska Bio.[64] As Tybjerg has pointed out, Madsen later financed Dreyer's nationally minded fairytale variant *Once upon a Time*, a film that referenced Swedish literary adaptations akin to those Madsen had become accustomed to seeing in his theater.[65] This detail illustrates the role of *The Outlaw and His Wife* in influencing Danish films.

When *The Outlaw and His Wife* came out in Sweden, the then popular and well-known original play *Eyvind of the Mountains* (*Bjærg-Ejvind og hans Hustru/Fjalla-Eyvindur*, Jóhann Sigurjónsson, 1911) had only recently departed theater stages in Stockholm.[66] Still, the Swedish reception of the film seldom referenced this.[67] The film had, through its extensive advance publicity, already subsumed the play's place in the public consciousness. Instead, the fixed point for discussion about *The Outlaw and His Wife* was the film's use of nature.[68] The location choices were applauded and their alleged likeness to Icelandic landscape stressed, a key word being "vederhäftighet" (trustworthiness, accuracy). The location was, after all, approved by the play's author, according to an interview in *Politiken* prior to the film's inter-Scandinavian premiere.[69] The playwright Jóhann Sigurjónsson stepped forward as guarantor of the location's felt authenticity when declaring the Swedish region of Lapland had the "same" mountains, views, and clear air as Iceland.[70] As quoted in a Norwegian program booklet, Sigurjónsson also phrased the likeness in a more metaphysical sense: "I have wandered on foot through the most desolate areas of Iceland, he said, and now [in the film] it was as if I recognized every spot. But above all, it was the inner, invisible likeness—that which lies in the soil itself."[71] Establishing the judgment by means of the observations and insights of a lone ramble endows the account with near-spiritual overtones. The imponderable affinity between Lapland and Iceland hidden in the earth's interior can only be understood as a mystical phrasing of Nordic kindredship.

The location Abisko, however, had intrinsic value of its own, primarily the publicity value stemming from its relatively recent establishment as a national park. Just as in the case of *Terje Vigen*, spinoff nature films displayed views from the locations used for shooting current feature films. Motifs from mountainous Abisko, likely taken in connection with the filming of *The Outlaw and His Wife* in the summer of 1917, were marketed with an invocation of that epic.[72] The spinoff practice marked a shared space between travelogue and fiction film, serving, in this case, to promote the new national park, which had been established in 1909. The infrastructure offered by the national park system made filmmaking there an attractive opportunity. Touristic experiences are detailed in travelogues from Abisko, and the travel film's framing of tourists as intermediaries between audience and landscape suggests a didactic function: here is how to experience and appreciate a national park. As a canonized and nationalized piece of landscape, the national park was allocated its place in film culture. The mechanism is not unlike how landscapes in Swedish "quality" films with literary originals were also portrayed in a more didactic spirit in actuality shorts, as was the case with the locations used for *Terje Vigen*.

In a piece from 1920 in the popular journal *Filmen*, the anonymous writer—presumably film censor and assiduous debater Gustaf Berg—commented on the link between travelogues and the practice of screening Swedish nature in fiction films, popularized over the past few years.[73] Moving on to link province and landscape (incidentally, in Swedish, "province" and "landscape" are polysemous homonyms, *landskap*), the writer arrives at *The Outlaw and His Wife*, which is evoked as a "patriotic" film on the grounds of its actual Swedish location, "painted" in moving pictures: "We are used to seeing glorious Swedish paintings being rolled out in every Swedish 'drama.' We are so used to this that we almost feel ever so slightly disappointed when it is not so—such as in *Sir Arne's Treasure* [*Herr Arnes pengar*, Mauritz Stiller 1919]—however good the film may be in other respects. In *The Girl from Marsh Croft* [*Tösen från Stormyrtorpet*, Victor Sjöström 1917], we saw the lakes and mountains of Dalarna, in *The Outlaw and His Wife* the wide empty spaces and foaming streams of Lapland." In this account, then, a key to selling films is through geographical identification according to province. Displacement of represented foreign settings was no (necessary) impediment to this cartography of provinces.

On the other hand, rearrangements within Sweden jeopardized the element of regional authenticity. The text mentions *Sir Arne's Treasure* as a film lacking in nature scenes; in fact it has several striking nature scenes, although these were shot in stand-in locations instead of the story's Marstrand, a location traditionally used by Gothenburg's film-producing company Hasselblads but not by the Stockholm companies. Writing in 1977, film historian Marguerite Engberg actually used *Sir Arne's Treasure* as exemplary of the Swedish deployment of nature, in contrast with Danish film: "However, the ability to make full use of Danish nature and Danish climate dramatically, like Mauritz Stiller could with Swedish nature, for example in *Sir Arne's Treasure* (1919), we unfortunately do not find with Danish silent-film directors."[74] The use of Mauritz Stiller to emblematize nature use is unusual, despite being fully valid.[75] Instead, the figure invoked has traditionally been Victor Sjöström, whose performative embodiment as Terje Vigen and Berg-Ejvind renders him a more apt choice.

If the represented Icelandic location took more of a back seat in *The Outlaw and His Wife*, actual Icelandic locations were given a clear function in Danish films like *Sons of the Soil*. In the cultural relationship between Denmark and Iceland, the Icelandic perspective has been that Icelanders were more serious, with "a broader view and a more deeply-rooted culture."[76] Such a view of the Icelander seems to resonate quite well with the contents of the chosen literary originals for the films set in Iceland and was in this way also passed on to the film adaptations from the Danish side. (Likely, a degree of reciprocity already informed the two-sided understanding of the relation between Icelanders and Danes.) Icelandic scenography, then, diametrically opposed that of the many non-specific drawing-room scenes in the Danish erotic melodramas and could embody the kind of depth and seriousness Dreyer had called for in Danish film. In Sweden, *Sons of the Soil* was received as a "Scandinavian" film, connoting films in the vein of the "Swedish golden age": *Filmbladet* reviewed it in tandem with the Norwegian rural feature film *Kaksen paa Øverland* (*The Bigwig of Øverland*, G. A. Olsen, 1920), thinking these two of a kind, under the headline "Two Scandinavian films."[77] In Denmark, the film was seen as an attempt toward the "Swedish." The cinema Palads-Teater's own publication attempted to frame the film in the same terms employed in the later case of *Morænen*, pronouncing a proud comeback of Nordisk Film, although in this instance specifically from beneath Swedish domination.[78] A critical review in *Københavns Amts Folkeblad* was clear in using Swedish film as the gauge and the film's intended benchmark: "one must remember that this film was supposed to hold its own against the Swedish Selma Lagerlöf films."[79]

Sjöström's usual trademark combination of the artistic and the realistic was commended, and seen as lacking here. What the implications of this stated "realism" were, or more exactly, what they were contrasted with, is not clear. However, if "realism" is interpreted as "authenticity," the reviewer's opinion makes sense in the context of the rest of the review and the overall reception of *Sons of the Soil*. For instance, in the reviewer's mind, the landscape—Sjöström's bearer of authenticity value—did not offer the film anything of value: "And then these dreary Icelandic landscapes, made even more tedious through the work of a single-minded photographer utterly devoid of ideas."[80] Several criticized the photography, particularly the use of silhouette technique, doubtless because the writers regarded it as too much like the old-fashioned genre of the shadow play. "Realism," then, seems here to have consisted of attitude and stylistic freshness; arguably it also touched on concepts of character psychology, vital to critical discussion of the Sjöström films. Framed as external physiognomy, realism-as-psychology made a strong appearance in another review of *Sons of the Soil*. Even if the film was shot in Iceland, its performances still failed to embody a piece of Iceland, as they has been expected to: "There was no trace of Iceland in this priest" was the judgment on Sommerfeldt's own acting contribution.[81] Publicity material, however, underscored authenticity by means of actual location and contrasted it with Nordisk's previous practices: "Once upon a time, it seemed natural to depict a 'heavily crowded Parisian street'—on Amager [in Copenhagen]—an alp landscape out by Lake Damhussøen [also in Copenhagen]. That is no longer possible. Now, cinema sends its ships out on raids to distant lands."[82] Interestingly, the possibility of using local locations as themselves, as, for instance, in Amager, was not an option that sprang to mind. Rather, the distant Iceland, as well as Norway, fit the bill as Denmark's other.

Scandinavian Provinces and the Reification of Ethnographic Content

In the series of Matryoshka dolls incorporating Northern–Nordic–Scandinavian–national, we find the smallest yet—the provincial. One of film culture's continuities with the literary canon resided in ideas about province and nature. Filmic discourse evoked geodeterminist thought that linked personal character to the natural surroundings in which such character was ostensibly formed. Location practices in these cases indicated that Norway and Iceland in particular equaled nature, at home and abroad, and performed a Nordicness "more Nordic" than Denmark's own. The psychology of such nature typically manifested itself in figures like Terje Vigen and Ejvind, as played by Sjöström. Region could play a part in the geodeterminist universe; for instance, the rocky and barren surroundings of *The House of Shadows* functioned as an analogy for the state of local inhabitants' souls, with the story unfolding in Norway's Gudbrandsdalen valley.[83] The Swedish-produced Bjørnson adaptation *A Norway Lass* (*Synnöve Solbakken*, John W. Brunius, 1919), as well as *The Parson's Widow*, had likewise been made on location in Gudbrandsdalen, and awareness of Gudbrandsdalen folk culture was generally high due to the Maihaugen museum, the location of the latter film. In fact, the films from Gudbrandsdalen had made the Norwegian journal *Film og Kino* consider other options for the future, such as the neighboring Østerdalen valley.[84] A few years later, Østerdalen would indeed see filmmaking in this vein, with Dreyer's ethnographically accurate *Bride of Glomdal*.[85]

Such an approach to filmmaking held the promise of enhancing national film culture, both at home and abroad, but first and last was commercial. The social anthropologist Thomas Hylland Eriksen has discussed a specific strain that characterizes commercial or political interests in culture: the tension between the apotheosis of cultural authenticity and an "inevitable" simplification and standardization of form.[86] Hylland Eriksen's discussion gives us a model for understanding the "ownership" rhetoric—of nature and of heritage such as literature—in Scandinavian film culture at this time. As he states, "for culture to be turned into a form of property, a process of externalization and reification of symbols is necessary."[87] Both ownership and commercialization, then, as sometimes conflicting and sometimes conflating forces, rely on the reification of the culture that they invoke. An underlying attitude feeding into the ownership discourse was that both nature and literature, as two kinds of heritage, were limited resources that could be "used up."

If some of these location practices now seem somewhat contrived, the use of province was more organic or intrinsic earlier in the period. One can find a straightforward case in the films based on books by Selma Lagerlöf, directed by either Sjöström or Stiller, where province was definitely played up. Gabriel Bladh has shown how geographical specificity and the idea of "landskap" were central to Selma Lagerlöf's writings and informed "the making of a national Swedish landscape."[88] Particularly, *The Atonement of Gösta Berling* imparted a "backward-looking and romantic" picture of Värmland, looking for identity in the already irrecoverable past.[89] At the time of its writing in the late nineteenth century, folkloristic interest was steered toward the provinces instead of operating at the national level.[90] "Landskap," a long obsolete political delimitation, was again actualized in a body of historical and geographical literature and provincial historical societies, creating a communal-geographical sense of continuity and belonging in a time of rapid change associated with processes of modernity. Naturalistic romanticism was often place-bound, and artists and writers in particular combined the ideas of the anthropocentric, lived-in landscape with landscape as scenery.

The most crucial symbolism of the region was still its capacity as metonym for the native country as a whole. Thus, nature scenes in *The Girl from Marsh Croft*'s Dalarna were abstracted in the film's program booklet to become "unforgettably fair images of our Swedish fatherland, taken in sun and shadow, images of rivers and mountains and enticing lakes."[91] In similar terms, elevating the regional level to the national, *The Sons of Ingmar* (*Ingmarssönerna*, Victor Sjöström, 1919) coaxed even more purple prose out of a reviewer: "One was truly proud to be Swedish during those hours when this incarnation of Swedish character and genuinely Swedish nature was rolled out before one's gaze [. . .] above all, a love for Swedish countryside and Swedish culture emerges, radiant and warming, in every little detail in this great work."[92] In this phrase, there is already a sliding signification at work in the term denoting "countryside," "bygd," the etymology of which is "settlement" but which can or could in Swedish usage mean anything from hamlet, district (perhaps the word's most commonly used sense now), countryside in general ("landsbygd"), or in a lofty idiom, even the entire country, conceived as a fatherland cultivated by ancestors.[93] The element of belonging is particularly obvious in the term "hembygd," meaning "native district" (also sometimes used about urban areas). The reviewer capitalized on this indistinctness of the term and succeeded in hinting at a specific and a generalized geographical level all at once.

A notion of belonging and ownership, then, whether national or more generally Nordic, was built into the use of landscape and region. On the flipside, the opposite also existed in Swedish film culture, namely exclusion; for instance, Swedish censorship authorities had targeted many Danish and continental films as undesirable, Southern, speculative, and irresponsible, in contrast to the desirable, Northern "lyrical" films.[94] Furthermore, if landscape in film adaptations retained the same national and canonical overtones that it possessed in the literary originals, then this not only makes us understand the visual content and touristic appeal of such films, it also situates the "lyrical" film among other quality concepts. In this period, transmedia practices were instrumental in framing and accentuating literary values in film, while transtextual conventions hailing from the actuality film and travelogue provided a context for the feature films' treatment of location. In the case of literature and of literary films, originality was an all-important parameter that, in the case of landscape, became yoked to a corollary concept of authenticity. In light of such a value system, the subjective and contingent nature of this authenticity trait is apparent. Along these lines, we can describe key developments in Scandinavian film aesthetics circa 1920 in terms of notions of genre, authenticity, and originality, as preexisting conceptions of canon, nationality, and nature came into play in film discourse and practice.

Notes

1. The article is based on research for my PhD. See Anne Bachmann, *Locating Inter-Scandinavian Silent Film Culture: Connections, Contentions, Configurations* (PhD diss., Acta Universitatis Stockholmiensis, 2013).
2. See Joel Frykholm, "The Not-So-Golden Age of Swedish Silent Cinema? Historiographies of Isepa (1926–1928)," *Kosmorama* 278 (2020) and Laura Horak, "The Global Distribution of Swedish Silent Film," in Mette Hjort and Ursula Lindqvist, eds., *A Companion to Nordic Cinema* (Oxford, UK: Blackwell, 2016), 465.
3. See, for instance, Laura Horak, "Sex, Politics and Swedish Silent Film: Mauritz Stiller's Feminism Comedies of the 1910s," *Journal of Scandinavian Cinema* 4, no. 3 (2014): 193–208.
4. Eivind Røssaak, "Comedy, Love, Irony: On Mauritz Stiller's *Thomas Graal's Best Film*," *Journal of Scandinavian Cinema* 4, no. 3 (2014): 183–191; David Bordwell, "The Dreyer Generation," 2010, https://www.carlthdreyer.dk/carlthdreyer/about-dreyer/visual-style/dreyer-generation.
5. Jan Olsson, "Stiller at First: A Footnote," *Journal of Scandinavian Cinema* 4, no. 1 (2014): 5–13.
6. Carl Th. Dreyer, "Svensk Film," *Dagbladet*, January 7, 1920.
7. An apt example of press discourse around this is the anonymous press piece "When film counts were rampant. From Copenhagen life," in original: "När filmgrevarne florerade. Ur Köpenhamnslivet," *Skånska Dagbladet*, July 27, 1917. It maliciously reported about the outmoded emphasis on melodrama and high society in the preferred Danish mode of fiction filmmaking.
8. Jan Olsson, "Svart på vitt: film, makt och censur," *Aura* 1, no. 1 (1995): 14–46.
9. See accounts in Anne Marit Myrstad, "National Romanticism and Norwegian Silent Cinema," in Richard Dyer and Ginette Vincendeau, eds., *Popular European Cinema* (London: Routledge, 1992), 181–193; Jaakko Seppälä, "Finnish Film Style in the Silent Era," in Henry Bacon, ed., *Finnish Cinema* (Basingstoke, UK: Palgrave Macmillan, 2016), 51–80.
10. See Tybjerg's essays "Searching for Art's Promised Land: Nordic Silent Cinema and the Swedish Example," in Mette Hjort and Ursula Lindqvist, eds., *A Companion to Nordic Cinema* (Malden, MA: Wiley Blackwell, 2016), 271–290; and "On the Periphery of the 'National Film': Danish Cinematic Border Crossings, 1918–1929," *European Journal of Scandinavian Studies* 45, no. 2 (2015): 168.
11. Tybjerg, "Searching for Art's Promised Land."
12. Stephen Larry Larson, *The Birth, Death, and Re-birth of an Auteur: The Analog to Digital Conversion of Carl Theodor Dreyer's Films* (PhD diss., North Carolina State University, 2015), 98.
13. Bo Florin, *Den nationella stilen: studier i den svenska filmens guldålder* (Stockholm: Aura, 1997).
14. Anne Bachmann, "Souvenirs from the Selma Lagerlöf Silent Film Adaptations: How 'Beautiful' Book Editions and Prestige Cinema Collaborated in Swedish Visual Culture around 1920," *Scandinavica* 51 (2012): 184–207.
15. Ibid.
16. Ibid.

17. Letter to Albert Bonnier from Charles Magnusson, April 7, 1915. The Bonnier Archives.
18. Anon., "Skönlitteraturens biografdramatisering," *Dagens Nyheter*, March 7, 1913.
19. Horak, "The Global Distribution of Swedish Silent Film," 465.
20. Frisvold Hanssen, Eirik and Anna Sofia Rossholm, "The Paradoxes of Textual Fidelity: Translation and Intertitles in Victor Sjöström's Silent Film Adaptation of Henrik Ibsen's *Terje Vigen*," in Laurence Raw, ed., *Translation, Adaptation and Transformation* (New York: Continuum, 2011), 145–161.
21. Anon., "En ny Epoke i Dansk Film," *B. T.*, October 9, 1916.
22. Morten Egholm, *En visionær fortolker af andres tanker: om Carl Th. Dreyers brug af litterære forlæg* (PhD diss., Det Humanistiske Fakultet, Københavns Universitet, Copenhagen, 2009).
23. Other companies in some way involved in both publishing and film in Sweden in the 1920s were Bewefilm, Tullberg Film, Hökerbergs, and Åhlén & Åkerlund. See Eiwor Göterfelt's and Ann-Mari Nilsson's dissertation "Filmproducerande bokförlag i 1920s-talets Sverige: C-uppsats" (PhD diss., Stockholm University, 1981).
24. See Florin, *Den nationella stilen*; John Fullerton, *The Development of a System of Representation in Swedish Film, 1912–1920* (Norwich, UK: University of East Anglia, 1994); and Christopher Oscarson, "*Terje Vigen*, Naturbilder and the Natural History of Film in Sweden," *Journal of Scandinavian Cinema* 3, no. 1 (2013): 69–86.
25. Larson, *Birth, Death, and Re-birth of an Auteur*.
26. See discussion in Claire Thompson, "The Slow Pulse of the Era: Carl Th. Dreyer's Film Style," in Tiago De Luca and Nuno Barradas Jorge, eds., *Slow Cinema* (Edinburgh: Edinburgh University Press, 2016): 47–58.
27. Mark Sandberg, "Location, 'Location': On the Plausibility of Place Substitution," in Jennifer M. Bean, Anupama Kapse, and Laura Horak, eds., *Silent Cinema and the Politics of Space* (Bloomington: Indiana University Press, 2014): 23–46.
28. Correspondence with consul Enrico Cimmino, March 26 and May 14, 1918, Swedish Film Institute, Swedish Biograph, NI G2 for 1917–1918. My translation in this and all other instances.
29. See Jaakko Seppälä, "Finnish Film Style in the Silent Era," in Henry Bacon, ed., *Finnish Cinema: A Transnational Enterprise* (Basingstoke, UK: Palgrave Macmillan, 2016): 51–80.
30. Mark Sandberg, "Mastering the House: Performative Inhabitation in Carl Th. Dreyer's *The Parson's Widow*," in Claire Thompson, ed., *Northern Constellations: New Readings in Nordic Cinema* (London: Norvik Press, 2006).
31. Dreyer, "Svensk Film."
32. Sandberg, "Mastering the House."
33. For instance, local extras were reported to sport their own authentic, homegrown beards. "Felix"; "Filmnyt", *Hjemmenes Vel*, September 16, 1920.
34. Anon., "Hur *Ett farligt frieri* kom till," souvenir program held at the Swedish Film Institute's library, 10.
35. Recently by Oscarson, "*Terje Vigen*, Naturbilder."
36. Mark Sandberg, "The Outlaw and No-Man's Land: The International Circulation of Visual Repertoires in World War I," *European Journal of Scandinavian Studies* 45, no. 2 (2015): 198.
37. Swedish Film Institute's Swedish Biograph collections, 11:45.
38. N., "Berg-Ejvind och hans hustru," *Social-Demokraten*, January 2, 1918; Dagmar Engelhart, "Terje Vigen paa biograf. En kunstnerisk film-sejr," *Morgenbladet*, February 1, 1917; Anon., "Terje Vigen paa film," *Aftenposten*, February 2, 1917.

39. "Filmen Terje Vigen färdig. Den dyrbaraste svenska film, som hittills inspelats," *Svenska Dagbladet*, November 14, 1916.
40. For a discussion showing that "either/or" descriptions of studio and location takes as separate modes of filmmaking can be inaccurate, see Richard Koszarski, "Out on Location: D. W. Griffith and Fort Lee," in Paolo Cherchi Usai, ed., *The Griffith Project*, vol. 12: *Essays on D. W. Griffith* (London: BFI, 2008).
41. Sandberg, "Location, 'Location.'"
42. L.S., "Paladsteatret. Præstekonen," *B.T.*, April 27, 1921. The film was in fact produced by Swedish Biograph's successor, Svensk Filmindustri; possibly, this was not known to the critic.
43. Jan Nielsen, *A/S Filmfabriken Danmark: SRH/Filmfabriken Danmarks historie og produktion* (København, Denmark: Multivers, 2003), 648.
44. Ibid., quoted from *Masken*, August 22, 1915.
45. Ibid., quoted from *Politiken*, August 20, 1915.
46. Ewe Winquist, "Några betraktelser om svensk film," *Filmen og vi* 1, no. 5 (1920): 20–21.
47. Horak, "The Global Distribution of Swedish Silent Film."
48. This was voiced above all in *Filmen og vi* by its editor, Gustav Berg-Jæger. See Gustav Berg-Jæger, "Hvor blir der av den norske filmindustri? Har nordmændene ikke anlæg for at lage film?" *Filmen og vi* 1, no. 1 (December 1919): 4; Anon. (probably Berg-Jæger), "Norsk Film. Hvor længe skal vi vente paa den?," *Filmen og vi* 5, no. 2 (1924): 4.
49. See, for instance, Gunnar Iversen, *Norsk filmhistorie: spillefilmen 1911–2011* (Oslo: Universitetsforl., 2011), 36.
50. Sigurd Evensmo, *Det store tivoli: film og kino i Norge* (Oslo: Gyldendal,] 1992 [1967]), 148. See also Anne Marit Myrstad, "National Romanticism and Norwegian Silent Cinema," in Richard Dyer and Ginette Vincendeau, eds., *Popular European Cinema* (London: Routledge, 1992), 184. In the latter text, the connection between the Swedish and Norwegian developments is described in weaker terms than in Evensmo.
51. The effect was praised in "Norsk film igjen," *Filmavisen* 1, no. 10 (1924): 242–244. When indoor takes were attempted, the reactions were negative. See "Två skandinaviska filmer," *Filmbladet* 7, no. 7 (1921): 127.
52. Anon., "Den Danske Film," *Filmen* 7, no. 7 (1919): 84–86.
53. Casper Tybjerg, "An Art of Silence and Light: The Development of the Danish Film Drama to 1920" (Ph.D. diss., University of Copenhagen, 1996), 75.
54. Leonardo Quaresima, "Wien-Kopenhagen-Wien. Schnitzlers Liebelei und die Nordisk," in Manfred Behn, ed., *Schwarzer Traum und weisse Sklavin: deutsch-dänische Filmbeziehungen 1910–1930* (München, Germany: Edition Text und Kritik, 1994), 98 ff.
55. Nielsen, *A/S Filmfabriken Danmark*, 419. Nielsen quotes from the interview "Palle Rosenkrantz som Filmatiker," *Politiken*, August 5, 1913.
56. As for the Swedish-influenced films, Erik Nørgaard mentions *Struggling Horses* (*Lasse Månsson fra Skaane*, A. W. Sandberg [1923]) as the exemplary film. However, this categorization mostly amounts to the film's story being set in historical times and to its striving to depict costumes correctly. Erik Nørgaard, *Levende billeder i Danmark: Fra "Den gamle biograf" til moderne tider* (Copenhagen: Lademann, 1971), 110.
57. Nørgaard relates the remaking practice to Nordisk's crisis during the war in Nørgaard, *Levende billeder i Danmark: Fra "Den gamle biograf" til moderne tider*, 113.

58. The trend continued from *Ned med Vaabnene!* (*Lay Down Your Arms!*, Holger-Madsen, 1914) and *Verdens Undergang* (*The Flaming Sword/The End of the World*, August Blom, 1916).
59. Casper Tybjerg discusses these three films among others in chapter 12 of "An Art of Silence and Light."
60. "Hr. Sophus Michaëlis udtaler sig om Filmens Kunst," *Filmen* 6, no. 10 (1918): 97.
61. Casper Tybjerg discusses *Autorenfilme* and "art films" more or less in the same breath; see Tybjerg, "An Art of Silence and Light," 206.
62. Casper Tybjerg, "Dreyer and the National Film in Denmark," *Film History* 13, no. 1 (2001): 23–36.
63. Anne Bachmann, "Nordic Landscape Discourse in Scandinavian Silent Cinema: *Morænen*, Nature, and National Character," *Kosmorama*, no. 269 (2017); https://www.kosmorama.org/en/kosmorama/artikler/nordic-landscape-discourse-scandinavian-silent-cinema-moraenen-nature-and.
64. The secondary reason was the film's qualities; see Tybjerg, "An Art of Silence and Light," 247 ff.
65. Tybjerg, "Dreyer and the National Film in Denmark," 30.
66. Anders de Wahl and Harriet Bosse played the two leading parts at Dramaten, premiering on November 19, 1913. It was one of the most played productions that season at thirty-three performances. Lennart Forslund, *Teater i Stockholm 1910–1970* (Umeå, Sweden: Umeå University, 1982), 86.
67. Of course, the play was sometimes mentioned, as in "Colibri & Co.," "Veckans biografpremiärer," *Svenska Dagbladet*, January 2, 1918.
68. The trend was universal, but two clear examples are "Chinoise et Cie," "Biograferna," *Stockholms Dagblad*, January 2, 1918, and N:., "Berg-Ejvind och hans hustru," *Social-Demokraten*, January 2, 1918.
69. Quoted in Swedish translation in "Hos Berg-Eyvinds författare," *Skånska Dagbladet*, January 30, 1918. Similar remarks were also made in Jóhann Sigurjónsson's interviews with the Swedish press, as cited in "Berg-Eyvind och hans hustru," *Filmbladet* 4, no. 1 (1918): 6.
70. Similarly, Selma Lagerlöf "guaranteed" the cartographical suitability of Victor Sjöström's adaptations of her literary originals by assigning suitable locations herself. This was widely mentioned in the reception. See Jan Olsson, "'Den dramatiserande folklivsskildringen i landskapets miljö': Ett receptionscollage över den nationella filmkulturens gränssnitt," in Bjørn Sørenssen, Stig Kulset, Gunnar Iversen, and Kathrine Skretting, eds., *As Time Goes By: festskrift i anledning Bjørn Sørenssens 50-årsdag* (Trondheim, Norway: Tapir, 1996), 99.
71. Norwegian souvenir program held at the National Library of Norway, Småtrykk 792.9.
72. The film is presumably lost. Textual material in Swedish Film Institute, Swedish Biograph 11:14. An existing, similar, and contemporaneous film is *Abisko nationalpark* (Svenska Bio, 1917, censorship identification no. 18399).
73. Anon., "En fosterlandssång i bilder," *Filmen* 3, no. 3 (1920): 10.
74. Marguerite Engberg, *Dansk stumfilm: de store år* (Copenhagen: Rhodos, 1977), 367.
75. Another much-discussed Stiller film that did not comply with the tacit rules of the "regional" paradigm was *Gösta Berlings saga* (Mauritz Stiller, SF 1924).
76. Christina Folke Ax, "The Stranger You Know: Icelandic Perceptions of Danes in the Twentieth Century," in Anne Folke Henningsen, Leila Koivunen, and Taina Syrjämaa, eds., *Nordic Perspectives on Encountering Foreignness* (Turku, Finland: University of Turku, 2010): 23.

77. Anon., "Två skandinaviska filmer," *Filmbladet* 7, no. 7 (1921): 127.
78. Ellen Duurloo, "Den stumme Scene. Af Borgslægtens Historie." Orphan cutting marked September 1920. In the film's file at the DFI.
79. Anon., "Om Borgslægtens Historie," *Paladsteatrets Filmsnyheder*, no. 4 (1920–21): 14–15.
80. Axel K., "Borgslægten," *Københavns Amts Folkeblad*, September 17, 1920. Also cited in Tybjerg, "An Art of Silence and Light," 26.
81. Duurloo, "Den stumme Scene. Af Borgslægtens Historie."
82. Anon., "Om Borgslægtens Historie."
83. Cand. mixi, "Indstuderingen af Laurids-Skands [*sic*] nye Nordlandsfilm 'Moraenen,'" *Vore Damer*, May 31, 1923.
84. "Et sommereventyr paa Maihaugen og et andet i Vaage. To norske bygderomaner spilles for film," *Film og Kino* 6, no. 7 (1920). Unpaginated.
85. The idea to base a film on a story by author Jakob Breda Bull, who was associated with that valley, was outlined as suitable and proper already in the piece in *Film og Kino*.
86. Thomas Hylland Eriksen, "Keeping the recipe: Norwegian folk costumes and cultural capital," *Focaal—European Journal of Anthropology* 44 (2004): 20-34.
87. Ibid., 31.
88. Gabriel Bladh, "Selma Lagerlöf's Värmland: A Swedish Landskap in Thought and Practice," in Michael Jones, ed., *Nordic Landscapes: Region and Belonging on the Northern Edge of Europe* (Minneapolis: University of Minnesota Press, 2008): 220–250.
89. Ibid., 228.
90. Ibid., 222. Bladh cites the ethnologist Mats Rehnberg, who termed the process "the national construction of the provinces" (landskapens nationsbyggande).
91. Souvenir program held at the Swedish Film Institute, Swedish Biograph (in file for advertisements).
92. Review in *Svenska Dagbladet*, quoted in program booklet for *Ingmarssönerna II*. Held at the Swedish Film Institute.
93. See *Svenska Akademiens ordbok*, entry "bygd." One of the encyclopedia's examples of the "fatherland" meaning is the Finnish national anthem by Runeberg ("mer älskad än vår bygd i nord, än våra fäders jord").
94. See Olsson, "Svart på vitt."

CHAPTER 29

RUNNING LATE

The Silent Serial, the Cliffhanger, and the Exigencies of Time, 1914–1920

RUTH MAYER

THERE is much amiss in the storyworlds depicted in the silent film serials of the 1910s and 1920s: natural forces and machines and people keep running out of control and need to be reined in, order disintegrates and has to be reinstalled, plots are hatched and must be rooted out. But perhaps the most consistent problem is a problem of time. What Linda Williams wrote about the melodramatic last-minute-rescue plot applies to the film serial as well: it is always almost too late and still too early for it all to make sense.[1] Film serials are immensely rushed and at the same time marked by delays and deferrals. Moreover, they abound with repetitions. While moving breathlessly from "incident to incident at breakneck speed," as Scott Higgins put it for the sound serial, they do so with an ever-same cast of actors in ever-same parts, facing ever-same predicaments in serial after serial.[2] Thrill and formulaic reiteration constitute the two pivotal features of the film serial, and they should not be seen as opposing forces.[3]

In this essay, I would like to explore the temporal dimensions of serial storytelling in film, taking into account both the structural temporality of the narratives and their engagement with time on the plot level. I argue that it is by tackling temporal constraints and temporal challenges in a manner at variance with the feature film that the film serial comes into its own during the silent period. Even before the cliffhanger—arguably the most efficient means of serial time-management—came to be established as a routine chapter ending in film serials of the late 1910s and after, serials tampered with temporal indices and markers of time in order to ensure continuity while at the same time retaining a sense of novelty and surprise. The core purpose of the cliffhanger—to keep chapters "open" and to generate a sense of audience loyalty, inducing viewers to return in order to see more of the same—is thus acknowledged already in serials with autonomous episodes, as we shall see.[4]

To chart the development in the serial representation and fashioning of time, I will focus on two silent film serials: my main focus will be on the "pre-cliffhanger" serial *The Hazards of Helen* (Kalem, 1914–1917), which I will compare in closing with the cliffhanger serial *A Woman in Grey* (Serico, 1920). While the latter serial exemplifies the workings of sophisticated cliffhanger narration, the former is laid out as a string of episodes featuring one leading character and star. Other successful serials of the 1910s, such as *What Happened to Mary* (Edison, 1912), *The Perils of Pauline* (Pathé, 1914), *Zudora* (Thanhouser, 1914), or *The Exploits of Elaine* (Pathé, 1914), showed more consistency than *The Hazards of Helen* with respect to overarching plot structures, even to the point of introducing some cliffhanger endings. Yet *The Hazards of Helen* merits attention precisely because it makes the most of episodic narration, while sharing with other successful serials of the day an open-ended design. Like *The Perils of Pauline*, whose producers allegedly proclaimed "that they will keep their heroine skipping from one adventure to another as long as the public evinces a liking for her," *The Hazards of Helen* was meant to go on as long as it attracted viewers.[5] These serials thus reel off their stories without a final resolution in mind, and they organize their narration by way of climaxes and surprising turns that may resemble the cliffhanger structure in form but are not necessarily situated at the end of a chapter.

I am interested in the ways in which these two serials address and enact time constraints and practice "appropriations" of time in the form of temporal condensation or prolongation. Both serials engage with novelty and repetition in order to propel their narratives, and both generate storyworlds that are not so much organized in a linear fashion as reliant on narrative principles of sprawl or concrescence. Like so many other serials of the time, they draw heavily on temporally inflected narrative formulas such as the "last-minute rescue" or the chase, and they do so in ways that differ from the practices of the feature film. At the same time, these serials take part in a more pervasive cultural renegotiation of time and temporality, taking issue with the time politics of industrial modernity at large. Before turning to the serials themselves, I shall map out some larger parameters that determine serials' technical and narrative unfolding.

Temporality, Modernity, Seriality

In the first decades of the twentieth century, every major social theorist from Thorstein Veblen to Georg Simmel and Max Weber, from the critics of the Chicago School to Walter Benjamin and Siegfried Kracauer, resorted to the diagnosis of a "temporal disorder" to capture the ailments of modernity.[6] The imagery of a pathological condition prevalent in these contemporaneous assessments is telling: the theorists saw modernity as afflicted with alienation and heteronomy. Time appears as a problem or puzzle to be solved rather than a reliable and computable entity to be factored in. Whereas the nineteenth century can be considered the "century of synchronization," as Michael Gamper and Helmut Hühn have labeled it, capitalizing on the ambition to establish one committing time regime the world over, the twentieth century acknowledges "the manifold character of temporalities."[7]

The idea that temporalities proliferate into a multiplicity of distinct times ("proper times" in the terminology of Gamper and Hühn) that cannot be controlled by means of an overarching system of synchronization or an ordering principle of simultaneity, takes root in the sciences, most notably modern physics. Yet it also registers in other social and cultural fields, affecting the discursive systems of imperial politics, industrial management, the market economy, and many more—including literature and the arts.[8] This transformation also impacts the conceptualization of time in everyday life and the ways in which entertainment cultures address and configure pervasive cultural needs and anxieties.

According to large parts of the established literature, modernist artistic expression split into two major trends regarding the representation of and reflection on time. Writers and artists, these readings suggest, either embraced a resistant aesthetics of stillness and an agenda of "slowing down" in disavowal of the imperative of acceleration, or engaged in celebratory emulations of the spirit of the fast and new.[9] But skepticism and enthusiasm are by no means the only reactive patterns at work at the time. Both avant-garde experiments and commercial mass-cultural media articulate discursive and artistic responses to the conditions of time constraint and stress that disclose the transformations of modernity as practical options rather than dead ends or spectacular ruptures.

Film serials play an important role in this context, and they do so because of their peculiar combination of shortness and seriality. Both the serials with stand-alone episodes and the cliffhanger serials accentuate the structural modularity of their installments, fashioning their narratives as loosely strung and highly flexible arrangements of variable story units. Shelley Stamp points out that there is evidence that "exhibitors may have shown separate episodes [of the cliffhanger serial *The Exploits of Elaine*] in various sequences and arrangements," thus "adapt[ing] the serial format to their own needs."[10] This kind of "creative programming" required narrative structures that relied heavily on repetition and what Umberto Eco identified as the serial principle of the loop.[11]

Like the slapstick film or the newsreel, film serials came to be seen as "minor" cinematic formats from the mid-1910s onward, and in keeping with this placement at the lower end of the spectrum of entertainment culture, they were classified as "shorts" by the trade press of the day.[12] In the course of the 1910s, the one- or two-reel film entered into competition with longer formats, and the feature film established itself as the cinematic norm. For some years, the outcome of this competition was entirely unclear, as contradictory and conflicting "predictions and prognostications" filled the papers of a trade press that tried to make sense of the transformation at work.[13] In the 1920s, film serials and feature films distinguished themselves not only on the grounds of narrative possibility and scope but also with regard to social spaces and everyday practice. Cheap neighborhood theaters, where film serials tended to run, cultivated a different entertainment culture than the big movie palaces where the major feature films of the era were screened. By consequence, different cinematic formats—such as the film serial or the feature film—afforded different practices of viewing and responded to different notions of leisure. The feature film experienced in the movie palace may have promised a luxurious time-out from the ordinary. The film serial, in contrast, embedded and integrated fantastic sights and spectacular displays into everyday routines, and it did so not only by means of its exhibition practice but also on the level of theme and narrative.[14]

The serial-queen films of the 1910s relied on and fine-tuned a complex referential system that linked their stars as public figures to their alter egos on screen, who often bore the same first names or rubbed off their first names on the actors (so that, when Helen Holmes dropped out of The Hazards of Helen, Rose Gibson, who took over the part of Helen, became "Helen Gibson" in turn). An intricate machinery of marketing and promotion busily generated ever-tighter interlinkages between off- and onscreen personas, eventually forging both the stars and the figures into glittering surfaces, athletic "girls complexes" (Mädchenkomplexe), to borrow a term Siegfried Kracauer coined in another context.[15] The star system in the serials (just as in the Hollywood system at large) induced a logic of typecasting and thus had certain actors return over and over again in similar plot constellations and roles. The effect of familiarity arising from this practice was further intensified by the mechanism of formula narration, with its recurrent and recursive diegetic patterns. In consequence, film serials figured as exemplary agents in the paradoxical coalition of familiarization and exaggeration that constitutes the motor of popular seriality.[16]

One immediate and obvious manifestation of this narrative principle that alternates between confirmation and disruption is the cliffhanger ending, which by the 1920s had been established as a staple element of narrative organization in the film serials.[17] The cliffhanger hinges on the logic of repetition—especially once it becomes the standard mode of (not) concluding a chapter—even as it works, at the same time, by claiming exceptional and possibly terminal singularity. It is "the end" that everybody knows is just a new beginning. The last-minute rescue as an exemplary cliffhanger plot contrivance epitomizes this logic, engaging the spectator simultaneously on the level of narrative thrill and on the level of an "operational aesthetic," as it draws attention to the question of how the seemingly impossible is to be achieved "this time," and thus highlights the enmeshing of storytelling routine and medial innovation.[18]

In this respect, the serial implementation of the last-minute rescue clashes with the melodramatic structure of this narrative device, which Linda Williams describes referring to feature films. While both serials and features engage with what Williams characterizes as the modern subject's frustrated insight that "time [. . .] passes too fast," their responses to and enactments of this insight are quite different.[19] Williams shows that the melodramatic feature film addresses the experience of temporal stress by creating pockets of time within or out of the relentless flow of a larger homogeneous time regime: "the spectacular essence of melodrama seems to rest in those moments of temporal prolongation when 'in the nick of time' defies 'too late.'"[20] The melodramatic quest in the silent film, Williams argues, is driven by the desire to restitute an original order and utopian "space of innocence" and to resolve and overcome the chaos and contingency unleashed by the film's ongoing narrative.[21] The melodramatic feature film thus establishes a characteristic time politics predicated on an "immense rhythmic tease": "Actions feel fast and yet the duration of the event is slowed down. We are moved in both directions at once in a contradictory hurry-up and slowdown."[22]

Film serials, however, have no time to waste in their fifteen- to twenty-minute episode or chapter structure, so that action churns on relentlessly and continuously without a return to a peaceful and perfect beginning, and without the teasing alternation of fast- and slow-paced sections characteristic of the melodramatic feature. Rather than lending paradoxical duration to the instant by means of rhythmically edited temporalities, the film serial hurries from one "last minute" to the next, as it were. At the same time, however, the film serial has all the time in the world, unfolding in a panoply of successive episodes, which in the most successful case of *The Hazards of Helen* added up to 119, approximately twenty-four hours of film. As a result, the serial is both immensely rushed and unabashedly long-winded. Where the feature film strives for an integration of fast and slow sequences, the serial thus rigorously separates its "hurry-up" and "slowdown" by enforcing acceleration within the individual episode's narration, while retarding the overall serial flow.

Once the film serials adopt and perfect the machinery of "cliffhanger continuity," they fashion a characteristic rhythmical pattern of their own to contain and direct this exhausting narrative momentum.[23] But even in the transitional period, between 1912 and 1920, when film serials were still making use of a wide range of serial narrative patterns, alternating between episodically closed structures and overarching storylines, they displayed forms of filmic time management that differed notably from the devices and structures explored at the same time by the feature film. Their efforts to come to terms with the exigencies of speed, stress, and time pressure are obviously related to the larger economic, political, social, and cultural transformations of industrial modernity, which involved pervasive reconceptualizations of time and space, establishing the parameters of acceleration and synchronization as forceful cultural imperatives. But the interrelation between the film serial's "proper times" and the larger time regimes of industrial modernity is not one of representation or reflection. It rather takes the guise of a therapeutic intervention—instructing its viewers in techniques of managing time and coping with the lack of it—in view of industrial and cultural acceleration.

Runaway Stories: *The Hazards of Helen*

In his magisterial take on the silent film serial, Ben Singer quotes the synopsis of a Helen Holmes serial of 1916, *The Girl and the Game*, provided by the production company Mutual before the serial had run its course:

> The story to date: Helen Holmes prevents collision of train carrying the father and Storm, saves Storm from death on burning train, recovers accidental duplicate map of railroad cut-off, averting withdrawal of financial support. By desperate leap, Helen

recovers payroll from thieves. Kidnapped by Seagrue, Helen is rescued by Storm and Spike. She brings deputies to prevent death in rival camp's pitched battle. Helen rescues Storm, Rhinelander and Spike from runaway freight car by desperate chase in automobile, ditching car to prevent collision with limited. Rescues Spike from lynching, captures ore thieves. Saves lives of Rhinelander and Storm trapped by mine cave-in, regains money stolen by Segrue's agents. Helen accepts Storm's proposal of marriage. After daring ride, Helen uncouples freight and prevents terrible wreck.[24]

Singer quotes this plot summary to point out the heroine's casual "masculinization" and thus indicate one of the most striking features of the serial queen.[25] Beyond this, Singer reads the synopsis as evidence of the film serial's immersion in and determination by the larger forces of a modern culture of speed and hyperstimulus—that is, by a world subject to a time regime beyond its control. Singer assumes that film serials respond to the impositions of industrial modernity by exhibiting scenarios of steadily increasing stress and relentless acceleration. In contrast, I argue that instead of merely representing time pressure, the serials refashion it, transforming stress from a mundane and annoying experience into a thrilling spectacle. Such a transformation constitutes the entertainment value and pleasure factor of these films: they manage to recode the modern experience, lending significance and heroic weight to the banal, without entirely eliminating the reference to the habitual experiences of labor and leisure. After all, the above plot summary of *The Girl and the Game* also reads like a momentous to-do list, a daunting schedule of responsibilities. It illustrates a plot logic characterized by a succession of challenges that need to be mastered one step at a time—steadily, systematically, and with determination. Satisfaction derives from each mastered task, every single achievement, and not the final outcome or repose. This is the logic of (modern) labor, glossed over and glamorized.

Repetitious routines constitute staple elements of both industrial production and serial narration. In the film serial, they serve to forge a specific mode of spectator engagement and are thus by no means antithetical to entertainment: "rather than enjoying film serials despite their constitutive repetitiveness, spectators may enjoy film serials because of it," writes Ilka Brasch on the serials of the 1910s.[26] She points to the pleasures of close engagement, pattern recognition, and an appreciation of the serials' characteristic operational aesthetic as major constituents of a pleasurable viewing practice of film serials, which hinge upon repetition of scenes and sequences. But there is more to the film serial's correlation of familiar routine with spectacular disruption, or rather, its routinization of the extraordinary (and its inverse, and tacit, glamorization of the routine).

The film serials of the mid-1910s adhered much more rigorously to a modular organization of their episodic structure than did the later silent or sound cliffhanger serials. Flexibility was key in the transitional period, and both the producers and distributors of serials maintained the principle of a random screening order, which was easier to achieve with stand-alone episodes.[27] "Audiences did not go to the theater with the idea that they were seeing part of a whole, nor did they know with certainty that there would be another such film," wrote Raymond Stedman in his foundational 1977 study of the genre.[28] *The Hazards of Helen*, which appeared as a single-reel serial for most of its run, pursues this organizational principle exemplarily, as a sequence of relatively self-contained shorts, all revolving around a working girl facing all sorts of plights and perils (played in most of the first forty-eight films by Helen Holmes, and then later by Helen Gibson), which invariably arise from her professional responsibilities as a train controller and telegraph operator.[29]

Rather than adhere to a strict linearity, the modular format of the early serials follows a more cumulative logic that brings about a diffuse temporality on the level of the narrative. In episode after episode of *The Hazards of Helen*, engines and trains run out of control, time and again threatening to collide, collapse, explode, or derail, as Helen manages, over and over, to ward off the worst in the nick of time. While every film enacts several monumental, life-threatening events and the spectacular means of fending them off, none of these events leaves a trace: at the beginning of each film the heroine starts where she left off last time, with the same or a similar job, the same or similar colleagues, and mostly in the exact-same precarious situation—since her employers will be just as quick as always to discharge her or a hapless colleague when something goes amiss, forcing her to once more take to action in order to get her own or somebody else's job back.

Since the heroine has to be introduced anew in each one of the films, like all film serials *The Hazards of Helen* needed to accommodate a certain degree of redundancy. This is the most obvious reason why Helen never gains much of a backstory or much of a private life in the course of the serial.[30] In this respect, the serial is more formally radical than many other chapter-plays of its day, whether episodic or, like *The Perils of Pauline*, alternating between cliffhanger and episodic endings. Like all transitional films, *The Hazards of Helen* experimented with ways to direct and secure its viewers' attention. This is done prominently by anchoring the narrative in time and space. The time in this case, as in so many other serials (even the later cliffhanger serials and the 1930s sound serials are no exception), is always "now"—Helen has no past, and she has no future, and particularly the latter circumstance ensures her serial survival and recurrence.[31] "Future," particularly for women in the silent film era, tended to mean marriage—and marriage for Helen would have meant the end of her hazards, which are all invariably work-related. Consequently, "the Kalem publicists worked hard at finding new ways to express Helen's determination to stay single."[32] Helen turns down proposal after proposal in the course of the serial. Soon, her reluctance to become engaged no longer needed to be explicated. At the end of episode thirty, "The Human Chain" (1915), she just shakes her head, sadly, as the partner and colleague with whom she just experienced a bout of breathtaking exploits takes both of her hands in his and tries to kiss them. He walks off and away from the camera dejectedly, while she turns back to the screen, facing her audience and the next adventure.

The Hazards of Helen has no interest in romance; it is a serial about work, efficiency, responsibility, and determination. In many respects, the serial thus totalizes the story logic of other popular serial-queen narratives such as *What Happened to Mary*, *The Adventures of Kathlyn* (Selig, 1913), *The Perils of Pauline*, or *The Million Dollar Mystery*

(Thanhouser, 1914), as pinpointed by Shelley Stamp: "virtually all serial heroines are cut adrift from conventional family relationships," which "echo[es] the economic and social autonomy often experienced by women living away from their families for the first time while working in urban centers."[33] Helen's job as an operator—performed, most of the time, alone, but always as part of a larger network of dispatchers, managers, conductors, laborers, and salesmen—serves as a backdrop to an unending series of coincidences, accidents, and moments of happenstance, which Helen takes on stoically, like another round of filing duties or a late lunchbreak. In this professional sphere, Helen is the only woman, and she is made out as an instrument rather than a subject—very much in keeping with Friedrich Kittler's take on the feminization of the profession of the typist and stenographer at the turn of the twentieth century. She can hence be considered a "medium," an "interface," or "relay station" in a larger network, which, in the case of the serial, is not so much concerned with the transfer and processing of information and the organization of discourses but rather reflects the administration and facilitation of often much more material circuits of transportation.[34]

The serial's formulaic action usually starts with an interruption of the flow of information, of wares or of passengers, and often this disruption is associated literally with breaks and ruptures of links. Cords snap, cables tear loose, wires are torn, and consequently, runaway trains abound. In "The Human Chain," for instance, the telegraph line is cut by crooks, and we see Helen's fingers click futilely on the telegraph key. In this and in many other installments, once Helen notices the blockage or disconnection, she takes to action, which means leaving her desk and engaging in a variety of risky stunts. Thus, even though her profession requires her to "ensure the smooth running of the trains" rather than running them herself, she is routinely "given opportunities to literally engineer," as Lynn Kirby pointed out. Kirby reads this plot contrivance as a means for the serial to show a female engineer while not getting involved in cumbersome discussions around emancipation and the New Woman—female self-assertion by circumstance, as it were.[35] This may account for the serial's popularity with female audiences, but it still raises the question of the purpose of this "occasional emancipation." While Helen is all action, she never becomes a self-determined agent. Even outdoors, riding on train roofs and on horseback, racing on motorcycles and jumping from bridges, Helen never acts in her own interest, let alone the interest of "women" more generally. After all, in most of the chapters she is the only woman *of* interest—exceptional, odd, extraordinary.

Indeed, the ordinary and orderly gets short thrift in the serial, as Jennifer Bean has pointed out. What can go wrong in Helen's world does go wrong. Nobody is really in control here, and malfunction or rupture does not mean standstill—the system is too advanced and too complex to break down completely. *The Hazards of Helen*, Bean concludes, "showcases a modern industrial universe on the brink not of progress, but of catastrophe."[36] Bean juxtaposes each film's "radically unbalanced plot, warped in the middle, blasted out of proportion" with its perfunctory ending, "when Helen restores the railway to its proper working order."[37] Bean is right: the thrill of the serial is undeniably predicated on the workings of chaos rather than order. Yet the pleasure of watching hinges just as clearly on the joy of seeing order reinstalled: things are getting done, obstacles removed, dangers averted, one step at a time.

In this respect, *The Hazard of Helen* corresponds closely with the detective serials of the 1910s, which are equally intrigued by the display of chaos and the reassertion of order, as Ilka Brasch has elaborated with respect to *The Exploits of Elaine*.[38] By extension, these serials are obsessed with time and temporality, even though they are strangely "out of time." They exhibit ways of organizing and processing time, creating continuity in the face of all sorts of interruptions but also fashioning pockets of time in a relentless flow or rush. John McGowan points out that among other visual cues such as the "written labels, letters, and telegrams" that are used in lieu of "intrusive caption cards" in *The Hazards of Helen*, the serial makes heavy use of close-ups of clocks.[39] Clocks are regularly shown to communicate a sense of urgency or indicate the simultaneity of actions.

In a DVD commentary on episode thirteen, "Escape on the Fast Freight" (1915), Jennifer Bean points out that the film's temporal logic "can be a bit confusing, but the point of the story is the stress placed on the cause-and-effect situation."[40] But if this film, just like serials of time more generally, invokes the mechanics of cause and effect, it does so in order to highlight the latter. Like the slapstick film, the serial maps a world with very little cause and a whole lot of effect. In keeping with this effect-driven trajectory, the serial's temporal logic is confusing indeed, even though visual markers (such as clocks) and linguistic cues (references to "before" and "after" in diegetic inserts, or, even more dramatically, intertitles such as "Too late") seem to promise otherwise.[41] The enactment of the last-minute-rescue plot and the chase is significantly affected by the persistent blurring of temporal conditions. The serial routinely signals relationships of simultaneity, synchronicity, or sequence that do not really add up. Every so often, its times are severely out of joint.

In this respect, the serial deviates from tendencies in other narrative film formats of the transitional era, in which filmic editing and framing serve to establish a coherent time regime. As Tom Gunning has noted with regard to D. W. Griffith's *The Lonedale Operator* (1911), a film that is often cited as an inspiration for *The Hazards of Helen*: "[t]he systematic order of [the film] extends beyond its narration and becomes part of its diegetic world, the modern environment of similar systematic networks in which time and space are connected through technology, just as Griffith connects them via new patterns of editing."[42] In Griffith's film, modern systems of communication and transportation and new cinematic techniques all serve to create a sense of closure and coherence, invoking "the systematic nature of the modern world."[43] Even though *The Hazards of Helen* draws on the same referential grid of industrial modernity and relies on similar techniques of parallel editing, it fails to establish a comparable overarching spatio-temporal order. It falls apart, not only into episodes that seem to explore alternative versions and options in the working life of Helen but also into segments, plotlines, and incidents *within* individual films. Parallel editing, in particular, does not really manage to fashion a close-knit system of scenes that take place "at the same time" or "meanwhile." Instead, it often tends to enmesh so many simultaneous actions that a larger sense of coherence seems hard to forge or even maintain.

In a reflection on the structures of narration in *The Perils of Pauline*, and thus on a serial of the 1910s that hardly made use of cliffhanger continuity, Shane Denson has addressed the functions of formal and medial discontinuity in the course of serial narration, reflecting on, among other things, film serials' "technique [. . .] of narrating a story in fits and starts, of developing the spatiotemporal continuities of an ongoing tale through the discontinuous structure of discrete chapters."[44] Denson focuses on the deployment of "segments" in the serial narrative, in particular on the diegetic display of cut and torn "lines" (such as the rope securing a hot-air balloon in "Trials by Fire" [1914]) that threaten to bring the narrative to an end. According to Denson, loose ends and the "line segments" they bring about are displayed on the plot level of the serial, but they also inform the serial's narrative structure. Structurally, line segments manifest as standard and recurring elements in the serial narration (the villain's plotting, the chase, the last-minute-rescue)—and like the ropes that hold the air-balloon, these plot contrivances can be cut loose and reassembled, acting as disruptions and interfaces in the larger serial flow. The line segments thus need to be assembled and connected for the narrative to make sense (and to continue), but they also need to be noticeably distinct for the narrative to be processable and enjoyable. As a "hybrid mode," the line segment thus paves the way for the cliffhanger; it constitutes cliffhangers *within* the individual episode as it were: "The serial line segment, which is the formal precondition for the cliffhanger [. . .] generates continuity—posits the inevitability of something 'to be continued'—even in the midst of the discontinuity or uncertainty that attaches to an upheaval of media or their narrative paradigms."[45]

Denson is interested in the media historical situation of the film serial, but his observations can also serve to elucidate the specific temporal logic and the conceptualization of time in the pre-cliffhanger serial, as exemplified in *Hazards of Helen*. Thus, in episode twenty-six, "The Wild Engine" (1915), we witness Helen on a motorcycle trying to chase down a train that needs to be stopped. The ensuing sequence of events, intercut with the shots of Helen's wild chase, involves a collision course between two trains, which are hard to distinguish and impossible to locate in relation to each other, an additional train that is introduced at some point and disappears from the action shortly thereafter, a big freight ship, a drawbridge and its operator, and the railway controllers in their office. All of these scenes alternate; some of them are full of action, others (usually the ones displaying machines or technology, such as the ships or the drawbridge) extremely slow.[46] As a consequence, orientation in space and time is made increasingly difficult—even though all the shots of the controllers' office are dominated by a huge wall clock in the background. Everything is happening right now, in front of our eyes, but we cannot determine the sequentiality or synchronicity of the events. The only time that the two trains that threaten to collide are shown together in a single shot comes shortly after Helen rides with her motorcycle onto the opening drawbridge and shoots out, spectacularly, into the empty air. At this point, it it is physically impossible for her to make it out of the water and back to the rails in time to stop the trains from crashing. She will, though, as always, and precisely because so much is going on in parallel actions, we do not care or wonder how exactly the time of the rescue relates to the rest of the action.

Not all serials are so confusing or sprawling in their use of parallel montage, but many are. Jennifer Bean has demonstrated that episode fifty-eight, "The Wrong Train Order" (1915), offers a panoply of intersecting plots that creates the impression of "vertiginous, overlapping uncertainty," rigorously effacing "the accuracy implied by the time-table with its carefully inked calculation."[47] Instead of cinematically implementing an overarching operative time regime or signaling an ideal melodramatic "utopian time," as does the feature film, the film serial fans out into many different times, presenting them as options and possibilities, variations and versions, rather than facets of one story that can or should be conjoined. The single most important shot in "The Wild Engine" is thus not the one of Helen flagging down the excursion train about to be derailed, which brings the chase to a close, but the earlier one, which proves of no importance for the narrative, when the drawbridge spectacularly catapults Helen on her motorcycle into space. It marks the end of a line segment; it disrupts the serial flow in an exemplary fashion; and, even though it points to the narrative future, eliciting the question "what now?," it perhaps more importantly showcases a perfectly self-contained moment in time: Helen, the character, and Helen, the actor (who was reported to do all her stunts herself), in spectacular and momentous action.

This could be the end of the story, the character, and even the actor, but anybody familiar with this or any other serial of the day would know that it is not. Instead, the shot marks a point at which nothing is certain and everything is possible, in exhilarating, thrilling, melodramatic terms. This is, of course, a cliffhanger, even though the film does not yet know this and does not employ the shot to this purpose. In *The Hazards of Helen*, such "embedded" cliffhangers abound. Like the real cliffhangers, these spectacular peaks in the action punctuate the narrative, creating breaks, pauses, and ruptures that then allow for brief recaps, and sometimes, reboots, of the action. In doing so, they act as a powerful means of narrative organization and temporal management, fashioning anxiety-raising conditions of alienation, stress, or heteronomy into exemplary displays of physical prowess or energetic self-assertion. We shall see that the cliffhanger serial of the 1920s perfects this procedure.

"Not just yet!": *A Woman in Grey*

In many respects, *A Woman in Grey* (1920) seems to be a late serial-queen melodrama. Ruth Hope, the character played by the serial's lead, Arline Pretty, was clearly modeled to recall the Paulines, Helens, Pearls, and Elaines of some years before: she comes across as tough, athletic, outgoing, and independent. But then, the serial of 1920 also borrows from the mystery and the detective serials of the past, in ways that go beyond the genre hybridity of the 1910s. By 1920, film serials had been around for almost a decade, and *A Woman in Grey* attests to the riches of the format's legacy, making use of much that worked in the past in new combinations.[48] But at the same time, *A Woman in Grey* explores new narrative formulas and modes of address, pointing ahead toward the history of serial entertainment in the 1920s and eventually to the serials' reinvention in the sound era. The time politics of the serial remain of key importance, with methods of cross-cutting and parallel editing continuing to play an important role alongside seasoned conventions of last-minute rescues and techniques of narrative retardation (mix-ups, abductions, amnesia, doppelgangers). Yet this cliffhanger serial deploys its temporal markers and techniques in ways that differ from the style of representation in, say, *The Hazards of Helen*.

Like *The Hazards of Helen*, *A Woman in Grey* engages with the (temporal) exigencies of modernity, fashioning constraints into challenges to be managed rather than passively endured. Ben Singer has mapped the serial against the backdrop of an aggressive monopoly capitalism and social Darwinism of the day: "Sensational melodramas like *A Woman in Grey* capture the essence of social atomization and all-against-all antagonism. Everyone is competing with everyone else."[49] Indeed, alliances in this serial are frail, and the protagonist is consistently exposed to attacks on all sorts of fronts. But there is still more at stake in this serial than the representation of a precarious social system, or, rather, perhaps representation is precisely what the serial is *not* about.

Matthias Makropoulos argues that (American) mass culture of the early to mid-twentieth century narrates in patterns that no longer seek closure. Instead, mass-cultural representations figure forth an array of "different possibilities that may enter into relationships of mutual outbidding at times, but always compete with each other."[50] The options that are arranged and laid out in the mass-cultural imaginary need not (and cannot) be "suspended in a final act of ordering, but are kept permanently open."[51] This productivity of mass culture comes to the fore in an aesthetics of acts and numbers, in cartoons and sketches, in shorts and chapters: modules that can be combined flexibly and do not necessarily adhere to an order of linearity or chronological sequence.

The American film serial is a multiplier of options. All its important plot characteristics can be basically rendered as manifestations of a modernist "sense of possibilities," which thrives on the systematic exploration and unfolding of the implications and variations of some core scenarios, as *The Hazards of Helen* exemplifies. The cliffhanger serial takes hold of a somewhat different set of tools to pursue the same goal. The cliffhanger sequence usually points ahead to *one* possible and usually fatal turn of the plot, which the experienced viewer will be quick to dismiss as improbable *because* it is mapped out in the cliffhanger ending. This ending is then complemented by a recapitulating scene at the beginning of the next film, which presents another and newly plausibilized reading of what we have seen before. Conventionally this is done by editing new shots in between those already seen. The new images reorganize our serial knowledge—now what happened no longer comes across as a deadlock but constitutes an interface that discloses further narrative possibilities. At the end of the first chapter of *A Woman in Grey* ("The House of Mystery"), the protagonist is thus thrown from a railway bridge by the villain—her certain death. At the beginning of the following chapter ("The Dagger of Death") we get to see that the woman "really" landed on the container wagon of a train that is just passing by underneath—the train rides on, the narrative continues. Repeating the almost exact same scene with a slight variation thus serves to readjust the viewer's perspective in a process of serial synchronization that is characteristic for the format.

These filmic devices that manifest at the beginning and end of every chapter (and which thus take up considerable time—the two-reel chapters are rarely longer than thirty minutes, after all) are supplemented by a narrative that constantly generates expectations and issues promises. The opening sequence of chapter three, "The Trap of Steel," for instance, dissolves the preceding cliffhanger that showed the protagonist underneath the threatening knife of the villain. Now we see her love interest intervening with a drawn gun, and the following intertitle could serve as the motto of nearly all such serials: "Not just yet . . . Mister!" This mix of deferral and urgency is captured in other intertitles from the serial, too, when the heroine repeatedly asks for patience before revealing who she really is: "Not now, please? I promise you shall soon know everything," or: "My promise will be kept. I'll tell you everything but not here, please," or: "I promise to explain everything to you, Tom, when we meet Saturday." There is, as we will learn later, no real narrative reason to persistently delay the explanation. But the serial logic of unfolding is based on such references to the future, which keep the plot afloat and maintain suspense. "Saturday?" Tom thus repeats confusedly, because he, just like us, has probably lost track of the serial's complicated time scheme, despite (or perhaps because of) the constant promise of orientation.

The confusion is heightened because Ruth is a woman in grey indeed—shadowy, obscure, and vaguely outlined. Though she may well resemble a serial queen of the 1910s in her athletic performance and self-assertion, *A Woman in Grey* clearly deviates from the formulaic narration of the serial-queen melodrama by abandoning the figure's spectacular singularity. A serial queen like Helen emerged as unique in a male world of labor. The woman in grey, by contrast, is quickly complemented by a series of mirroring figures—body doubles, as it were. A similar multiplication of stock characters can be noted in many serials of this later stage, such as *The Trail of the Octopus* (Hallmark, 1919), *The Hope Diamond Mystery* (Kosmik, 1921), *The Power God* (J. Charles Davis, 1925), or *Officer 444* (Goodwill, 1926). The plot of *A Woman in Grey* revolves around a crime committed in the past, which involved three women—one as a victim, one as a perpetrator, and one as a witness. The events are briefly depicted in the first chapter of the serial in a flashback sequence wherein witness and perpetrator wear similar outfits and are shown from a distance. The woman in grey, we quickly learn, is one of the two: but who? And is the convicted perpetrator, who then later escapes from prison, really the perpetrator, and the witness the witness, or is it the other way around? In the serial's narrative present, a female figure mirroring the woman in grey is introduced. She quickly turns out to be an adversary, because the two are in love with the same man. The two women try to get rid of each other, but they are also constantly mixed up with each other and are time and again in similarly precarious situations. As soon as the rival dies, another antagonist enters the scene, who adopts similar mirroring functions in the subsequent course of action.

As with most serials of the day, *A Woman in Grey* makes almost impossible demands on its viewers' concentration and memory: "The plot of *A Woman in Grey*," summarizes Ben Singer, "is incredibly convoluted."[52] But of course, neither this nor any other serial of the time really expected any of its viewers to bear in mind all the ramifications and loops of its complicated plot, let alone process them into an overarching and continuous systemic order. In this respect, *A Woman in Grey* corresponds to *The Hazards of Helen*, which threw synchronicity to the winds when fashioning its parallel tracks of action. In either case, the serial viewer's target competence consisted in the capacity to continuously reconfigure her narrative knowledge in accordance with the status quo of serial narration.

These demands on the spectator's collaboration manifest themselves most impressively in the handling of what we might think of as "serial memory," which is persistently updated throughout the narration. What has been written about the early days of television, when the medium was still exclusively live, may help to understand the principles of storytelling in the cliffhanger film serials. Early television series organized story events according to the principle of "working memory," as Lorenz Engell writes with close reference to Elena Esposito, and they operated exclusively in the present, generating and updating the series' various "pasts" and "futures" in the course of their unfolding.[53] According to Engell, serial storytelling gained a particular significance in this context, since more than other genres, series (or serials) evoke two parallel working memories—one inscribed in the screen events (informed by narrative references to the past, recaps, and repetitions) and one inscribed in the individual viewer (informed by an idiosyncratic mix of personal recollection, attention, expectation, experience, and speculation). These two memories need to be balanced and correlated, in a continuous and constitutive process of organization. Unlike the episodic series, which keeps forgetting, the cliffhanger series remembers as a whole, "but in its individual episodes the conditions—or circumstances—do not remain stable. [. . .] Even the past can be rewritten."[54]

Like the TV series, the cliffhanger film serial works by means of an ongoing process of recurrence and reassurance. *A Woman in Grey* pretends to be interested in the past, but it actually engages in the relentless updating of past knowledge into the diegetic present. In this context, specific viewer memories need to be accommodated to the serial's own memory. This does not only come to the fore in the management of cliffhanger continuity but also in the techniques of mediating memories and recollections in the serial's diegesis. *A Woman in Grey* both highlights and complicates the serial process of actualization and updating by representing all sorts of "images" of the past in disconcertingly similar ways. Usually (and in keeping with the filmic narrative conventions of the time) individual characters' memories of past events are presented by means of diegetic inserts. At times, these inserts literally consist in repetitions of scenes that we have seen before—the second time around often marked as memories by iris shots. But fake memories and mendacious representations are presented in the same way, so that "true" flashbacks and fabrications of the past are depicted side by side with the exact same narrative techniques. The relation between the serial's "own" memory, the memories of individual characters, and wrong and deceitful versions of the past is thus regularly obfuscated to maintain suspense and to keep the story going. The serial's enactment of cliffhanger continuity, finally, drives this operative logic home.

***

The pleasure of watching the "complex TV" series of our days has been traced back to the series' "rewatchability"—that is, to the fact that since the advent of VCR technology, we have had the opportunity to review and "rework" programs into ever more accurate approximations of narrative coherence (or incoherence, when narrative flaws and inconsistencies are discovered).[55] Even the casual viewer of complex TV series is expected to keep track of the narrative by comparing and conceptualizing various and diverging perspectives, time frames, and diegetic layers. Rewatching was only rarely an option for the (original) spectators of film serials. Instead, they were assigned the task of skimming and skipping: impressions needed to be flexibly sampled, weighed, dismissed, and replaced. The picture politics of the cliffhanger then and now epitomize this discrepancy. The recapitulating opening sequence, after all, consists not so much of a reflection and reassessment of the formerly seen but rather of its overwriting and substitution. In consequence, while *A Woman in Grey*, like other serials produced after World War I, seems to be obsessed with the past, its synchronization with the present, and its significance for the future, it is no less presentist in its narrative method than *The Hazards of Helen*. No need to look back or worry about the future, this logic runs: what you see now is all that matters. While there are numerous narrative options at any moment in the serial flow, they are continuously updated and presented like a freshly shuffled fan of cards from which we are asked to take a pick.

At times, this process of reshuffling entails the literal substitution of one version of the past with another—by implementing cheat continuity. Thus, at the ending of chapter eight, "The Drop to Death," the protagonist indubitably falls into a hole which is studded with deadly steel spikes. At the beginning of the next chapter she does not drop but turns around before she loses her grip. Similar inconsistencies can also be found at other transitional points. Obviously such "shifts" can be accommodated from one week to the next and reconciled with the narrative flow. They generate irritations at best, which may lead to doubts in one's own recollections or to consultations with other viewers, and ultimately sustain rather than abort interest in the narrative. In fact, the fake memories or continuity cheats in *A Woman in Grey* should be seen as integral parts of a mass-cultural logic of the possible. The film serial is not only firmly committed to the narrative principle of "what if," but also allows the viewer to pursue this principle in all kinds of dimensions and directions. Serial story-telling is thus rigorously organized with a view to the ending, of the chapter or the serial as a whole; however, at the same time the ending is clearly not the point of the narrative, because eventually it is not very important. Once it has run its course, which usually happens after about fifteen chapters, the cliffhanger serial is over, and it ends wherever we are at this point, with a few hasty explanations and perhaps with a kiss. On the way to this ending, whatever happens happens and nothing really matters; even occasional (and very rare) deaths do not really figure strongly in the serial flow. Characters who disappear are replaced, and when the heroine, as in *A Woman in Grey*, notices in the end that she is the daughter of the man whose money she recovered, this should not be understood as an invocation of the genealogically convoluted meaning-making of classical stage melodrama. It just presents the last loop in the serial's concatenation of episodic elements by means of relations, alternatives, and exclusions: if the heroine is not the murderer, she can be the heir; if the hero falls for the heroine, her friend will turn against her; if you take one step back, you're going to fall into a hole; if you turn around, you're confronting a gun. Every action changes the situation, but the next action may rearrange everything again. Like Ben Singer, I, too, see the serial in a tight conjunction with the reality of its time, but I do not think that the relation is one of representation, but rather of continuous substitution. The sheer flow of serial narration thus appears to be the actual point of the narrative. Its ceaseless production of stories aims to propel them into space, like Helen on her motorbike, to generate spectacular effects and launch other, even more outrageous, chapters, exploring variations of the same. Nothing ever ends.

Notes

1. Linda Williams, "Melodrama Revised," in Nick Browne, ed., *Refiguring American Film Genres: Theory and History* (Berkeley: University of California Press, 1998), 42–88.
2. Scott Higgins, *Matinee Melodrama: Playing with Formula in the Sound Serial* (New Brunswick, NJ: Rutgers University Press, 2016), 35. For the history of film serials see Ilka Brasch, *Film Serials and the American Cinema, 1910–1940: Operational Detection* (Amsterdam: Amsterdam University Press, 2018); Monica Dall'Asta, *Trame spezzate: Archeologia del film seriale* (Bologna, Italy: Le mani, 2009); Ben Singer, *Melodrama and Modernity: Early Sensational Cinema and Its Contexts* (New York: Columbia University Press, 2001); Shelley Stamp, *Movie-Struck Girls: Women and Motion Picture Culture after the Nickelodeon* (Princeton, NJ: Princeton University Press, 2000); and Rafael Vela's excellent overview "With the Parents' Consent: Film Serials, Consumerism, and the Creation of the Youth Audience, 1913–1938" (PhD diss., University of Wisconsin-Madison, 2000). On serial exhibition and distribution practices, see Marina Dahlquist, ed., *Exporting Perilous Pauline: Pearl White and the Serial Film Craze* (Chicago: University of Illinois Press, 2013) and Rudmer Canjels, *Distributing Silent Film Serials: Local Practices, Changing Forms, Cultural Transformation* (New York: Routledge, 2011). On the differences between the serial mode and the feature film, see Ilka Brasch and Ruth Mayer, "Modernity Management: 1920s Cinema, Mass Culture and the Film Serial," *Screen* 57, no. 3 (September 2016): 302–315.
3. See Higgins, *Matinee Melodrama*, 36–38; Brasch, *Film Serials*, 43–80.
4. Therefore, and because the transition from episodic serial storytelling to cliffhanger serials was more gradual and in its consequences less decisive than often claimed, I will also refrain from adopting the terminological distinction of "series" and "serial," which was not consistently in use in the transitional era. Serials in the 1910s took all kind of forms and formats, and even cliffhanger serials were sometimes screened in ways that defied continuity and sequence. See Canjels, *Distributing Silent Film Serials*, 24–38; Stamp, *Movie-Struck Girls*, 110–124.

5. "Washington Man Has New Idea For a Serial Film Story," *Washington Times*, September 17, 1914, quoted in Brasch, *Film Serials*, 115–116.
6. Annemone Ligensa, "Sensationalism and Early Cinema," in Nicolas Dulac, André Gaudreault, and Santiago Hidalgo, eds., *A Companion to Early Cinema* (Malden, MA: Wiley Blackwell, 2012), 163–182; Miriam Hansen, *Cinema and Experience: Siegfried Kracauer, Walter Benjamin, and Theodor W. Adorno* (Berkeley: University of California Press, 2011); Hartmut Rosa, *Social Acceleration: A New Theory of Modernity*, trans. Jonathan Trejo-Mathys (New York: Columbia University Press, 2011 [2005]); Singer, *Melodrama and Modernity*, 59–99; John Urry, "The Sociology of Time and Space," in Bryan Turner, ed., *The Blackwell Companion to Social Theory* (Oxford, UK: Blackwell, 2000), 416–444; and Stephen Kern *The Culture of Time and Space: 1880–1918* (Cambridge, MA: Harvard University Press, 2003 [1983]).
7. Michael Gamper and Helmut Hühn, "Einleitung," in *Zeit der Darstellung: Ästhetische Eigenzeiten in Literatur, Kunst und Wissenschaft* (Hannover, Germany: Werhahn, 2014), 17 (my translation). See also Vanessa Ogle, *The Global Transformation of Time, 1870–1950* (Cambridge, MA: Harvard University Press, 2015).
8. Aleida Assmann, *Ist die Zeit aus den Fugen? Aufstieg und Fall des Zeitregimes der Moderne* (München, Germany: Hanser, 2013); Adam Barrows, *The Cosmic Time of Empire: Modern Britain and World Literature* (Berkeley: University of California Press, 2010); Peter Galison, *Einstein's Clocks, Poincaré's Maps: Empires of Time* (New York: Norton, 2004); Michael Whitworth, *Einstein's Wake: Relativity, Metaphor, and Modernist Literature* (New York: Oxford University Press, 2001); Thomas Vargish and Delo E. Mook, *Inside Modernism: Relativity Theory, Cubism, Narrative* (New Haven, CT: Yale University Press, 1999).
9. Enda Duffy, *The Speed Handbook: Velocity, Pleasure, Modernity* (Durham, NC: Duke University Press, 2009); Mary Anne Doane, *The Emergence of Cinematic Time: Modernity, Contingency, the Archive* (Cambridge, MA: Harvard University Press, 2002); Michael North, *Reading 1922: A Return to the Scene of the Modern* (New York: Oxford University Press, 1999); Cecelia Tichi, *Shifting Gears: Technology, Literature, Culture in Modernist America* (Chapel Hill: University of North Carolina Press, 1987); Andreas Huyssen, *After the Great Divide: Modernism, Mass Culture, Postmodernism* (Basingstoke, UK: Macmillan, 1986).
10. Stamp, *Movie-Struck Girls*, 118.
11. Ibid.; Umberto Eco, "Interpreting Serials," in *The Limits of Interpretation* (Bloomington: Indiana University Press, 1990), 86.
12. See Brasch, *Film Serials*, 16; Brasch and Mayer, "Modernity Management."
13. Rob King, "1914: Movies and Cultural Hierarchy," in Charlie Keil and Ben Singer, eds., *American Cinema of the 1910s: Themes and Variations* (New Brunswick, NJ: Rutgers University Press, 2009), 117. On this phase in cinematic history see also Charlie Keil and Shelley Stamp, "Introduction," and Ben Singer, "Feature Films, Variety Programs, and the Crisis of the Small Exhibitor," in Keil and Stamp, eds., *American Cinema's Transitional Era: Audiences, Institutions, Practices* (Berkeley: University of California Press, 2004), 1–14, 76–102; Charlie Keil, *Early American Cinema in Transition: Story, Style, and Filmmaking, 1907–1913* (Madison: University of Wisconsin Press, 2002); Eileen Bowser, *The Transformation of Cinema, 1907–1915* (Berkeley: University of California Press, 1994).
14. Brasch, *Film Serials*; Brasch and Mayer, "Modernity Management"; Singer, *Melodrama and Modernity*; Stamp, *Movie-Struck Girls*; Nan Enstad, "Dressed for Adventure: Working Women and Silent Movie Serials in the 1910s," *Feminist Studies* 21, no. 1 (1995): 67–90; Kathy Peiss, *Cheap Amusements: Working Women and Leisure in Turn-of-the-Century New York* (Philadelphia, PA: Temple University Press, 1989).

15. Siegfried Kracauer, "Das Ornament der Masse" (1927), in *Das Ornament der Masse: Essays* (Frankfurt a.M., Germany: Suhrkamp, 1963), 50. See also Mark Garrett Cooper, "Pearl White and Grace Cunard: The Serial Queen's Volatile Present," in Jennifer M. Bean, ed., *Flickers of Desire: Movie Stars of the 1910s* (New Brunswick, NJ: Rutgers University Press, 2011), 174–195; Rob King, *The Fun Factory: The Keystone Film Company and the Emergence of Culture* (Berkeley: University of California Press, 2009), chap. 6; Jennifer M. Bean, "Technologies of Early Stardom and the Extraordinary Body," in Jennifer M. Bean and Diane Negra, eds., *A Feminist Reader in Early Cinema* (Durham, NC: Duke University Press, 2002), 404–443; Singer; *Melodrama and Modernity*, 263–287.
16. Frank Kelleter, "Five Ways of Looking at Popular Seriality," in Kelleter, ed., *Media of Serial Narrative* (Columbus: Ohio State University Press, 2017), 7–30; and Ruth Mayer, "In the Nick of Time? Detective Film Serials, Temporality, and Contingency Management, 1919–1926," *Velvet Light Trap* 79 (Spring 2017): 21–35. See also Ruth Mayer, *Serial Fu Manchu: The Chinese Supervillain and the Spread of Yellow Peril Ideology* (Philadelphia, PA: Temple University Press, 2014).
17. On the gradual adoption of a classical film serial structure (with plot recap at the beginning and cliffhanger at the end) in the United States, see Canjels, *Distributing Silent Film Serials*, 16–17; Singer, *Melodrama and Modernity*, 210–211.
18. On the serial's operational aesthetic, see Brasch, *Film Serials*, 43–80. On the medial logic of the alternation of routine and innovation, see Shane Denson, *Postnaturalism: Frankenstein, Film, and the Anthropotechnical Interface* (Bielefeld, Germany: transcript publishing, 2014).
19. Williams, "Melodrama Revised," 74.
20. Ibid.
21. Ibid. On the different modalities of time in the film serial and the feature film, as well as these formats' different mobilizations of melodrama, see Mayer, "In the Nick of Time?"
22. Williams, "Melodrama Revised," 74, 73.
23. Josh Lambert, "'Wait for the Next Pictures': Intertextuality and Cliffhanger Continuity in Early Cinema and Comic Strips," *Cinema Journal* 48, no. 2 (Winter 2009): 10.
24. Quoted in Singer, *Melodrama and Modernity*, 230.
25. Singer, *Melodrama and Modernity*, 231. While the serial-queen genre is arguably the most researched segment of the serial film market of the 1910s, only a fraction of the serial output of the period can be categorized in these terms. The one consistent element characterizing every one of the popular serials from the early 1910s to the late 1920s and into the sound era is, in fact, not a strong heroine but rather a sensational plotline—unfolding in crime, detection, mystery, or adventure contexts, sometimes with serial queens, sometimes without. See Mayer, "In the Nick of Time?"; Singer, *Melodrama and Modernity*, 198.
26. Brasch, "Narrative, Technology, and the Operational Aesthetic in Film Serials of the 1910s," *Literatur in Wissenschaft und Unterricht* 47, nos. 1–2 (2014): 23.
27. Stamp, *Movie-Struck Girls*, 111–112. See also Canjels, *Distributing Silent Film Serials*, 18.
28. Quoted in Canjels, *Distributing Silent Film Serials*, xix.
29. Only fragmentary prints of selected chapters of the serial are still available, all of them one-reelers. However, Richard Braff lists chapter ninety-six as a two-reel film in *The Braff Silent Short Film Working Papers* (Jefferson, NC: McFarland, 2002). See also "The Hazards of Helen," *Progressive Silent Film List*, http://www.silentera.com/PSFL/data/H/HazardsOfHelen1914.html. A 1916 article in *Motion Picture News* announced that "Kalem's 'Hazards'

Will Appear as Two Reelers" (February 5, 677). Whether this change was then actually implemented is unclear. Thanks to Ilka Brasch for alerting me to this.
30. There are some exceptions, especially in later chapters with Helen Gibson. In chapter seventy-six, "The Governor's Special" (1916), Helen is married and tries to prevent her brother's wrongful execution. At this point, elements of family melodrama were making their way into the serial, probably because the producers were running out of scenarios for train disasters. The focus of my analysis will be on the first run of films with Helen Holmes.
31. See also Mark Garrett Cooper's observations on the serial queen's "volatile present." Cooper, "Pearl White and Grace Cunard."
32. John J. McGowan, *J. P. McGowan: Biography of a Hollywood Pioneer* (Jefferson, NC: McFarland, 2005), 71. Shelley Stamp discusses the prominence of similar narrative patterns in other serial-queen chapter-plays of the time in *Movie-Struck Girls*, 125–140.
33. Stamp, *Movie-Struck Girls*, 127.
34. Friedrich Kittler, *Discourse Networks, 1800/1900*, trans. Michael Meteer with Chris Cullens (Stanford, CA: Stanford University Press, 1990 [1985]), 109. See also Tom Gunning, "Systematizing the Electric Message: Narrative Form, Gender, and Modernity in *The Lonedale Operator*," in Keil and Stamp, *American Cinema's Transitional Era*, 15–50.
35. Lynne Kirby, *Parallel Tracks: The Railroad and Silent Cinema* (Exeter, UK: University of Exeter Press, 1997), 114. See also Singer's much-quoted insight that the serial-queen melodramas "may have less to do with an earnest stake in a progressive ideology of female emancipation than with the utter novelty and curiosity value of a spectacle based on the 'category mistake' of a woman [. . .] acting like a man" (*Melodrama and Modernity*, 253).
36. Jennifer Bean, "'Trauma Thrills': Notes on Early Action Cinema," in Yvonne Tasker, ed., *The Action and Adventure Cinema* (New York: Routledge, 2004), 20.
37. Ibid.
38. Brasch, "Narrative, Technology, and the Operational Aesthetic."
39. McGowan, *J. P. McGowan*, 5.
40. DVD commentary for "Escape on the Fast Freight" (1915), on *More Treasures from American Film Archives, 1894–1931* (National Film Preservation Foundation, 2004).
41. Deictic temporal markers are used throughout the serial. The intertitle "Too late" appears in chapter fifty-eight, "The Wrong Train Order" (1915, with Helen Gibson).
42. Gunning, "Systematizing the Electric Message," 26–27. See also Kirby, *Parallel Tracks*, 75–132.
43. Gunning, "Systematizing the Electric Message," 27.
44. Shane Denson, "The Logic of the Line Segment: Continuity and Discontinuity in the Serial-Queen Melodrama," in Robert Allen and Thijs van den Berg, eds., *Serialization in Popular Culture* (New York: Routledge, 2014), 65.
45. Ibid., 75.
46. DVD commentary for "The Wild Engine" (1915), on *More Treasures from American Film Archives, 1894–1931*.
47. Bean, "Trauma Thrills," 21.
48. The first American film serial was the 1912 *What Happened to Mary*, but before that Louis Feuillade had established the format in France, based on an ample tradition of serial narration in print. See Ruth Mayer, "'Never twice the same': Fantômas' Early Seriality," *Modernism/modernity* 23, no. 2 (April 2016): 341–364; Dall'Asta, *Trame spezzate*, 79–118; Vicki Callahan, *Zones of Anxiety: Movement, Musidora, and the Crime Serials of Louis Feuillade* (Detroit, MI: Wayne State University Press, 2005); Robin Walz, *Pulp Surrealism:*

Insolent Popular Culture in Early Twentieth-Century Paris (Berkeley: University of California Press, 2000), 42–58; Tom Gunning, "A Tale of Two Prologues: Actors and Roles, Detectives and Disguises in *Fantômas*, Film and Novel," *Velvet Light Trap* 37 (Spring 1996): 30–36.

49. Singer, *Melodrama and Modernity*, 144.
50. Michael Makropoulos, "Organisierte Kreativität: Überlegungen zur 'Ästhetisierung des Sozialen,'" in Roger Lüdeke, ed., *Kommunikation im Populären: Interdisziplinäre Perspektiven auf ein ganzheitliches Phänomen* (Bielefeld, Germany: transcript publishing, 2011): 31 (my translation).
51. Ibid. (my translation).
52. Singer, *Melodrama and Modernity*, 139.
53. Lorenz Engell, "Erinnern/Vergessen: Serien als operatives Gedächtnis des Fernsehens," in Robert Blanchet et al., eds., *Serielle Formen: Von den frühen Film-Serials zu Quality-TV und Online-Serien* (Marburg, Germany: Schüren, 2011): 115–133; Elena Esposito, *Soziales Vergesssen: Formen und Medien des Gedächtnisses der Gesellschaft* (Frankfurt a.M., Germany: Suhrkamp, 2002).
54. Engell, "Erinnern/Vergessen," 124–125 (my translation).
55. See Felix Brinker, "On the Formal Politics of Narratively Complex Television Series: Operational Self-Reflexivity and Audience Management in *Fringe* and *Homeland*," in Sebastian M. Herrman et al., eds., *Poetics of Politics: Textuality and Social Relevance in Contemporary American Literature and Culture* (Heidelberg, Germany: Universitätsverlag Winter, 2015): 41–62; Jason Mittell, *Complex TV: The Poetics of Contemporary Television Storytelling* (New York: New York University Press, 2015), 170–173.

PART VI
CINEMATIC PUBLICS
Critics, Fans, Communities

CHAPTER 30

THE SILENT FILM CRITICISM OF SIEGFRIED KRACAUER

JOHANNES VON MOLTKE

The Art of Criticism

In late 1930, the leading German trade journal *Film-Kurier* turned a spotlight on film critics. Under the programmatic heading "Kritik ist schöpferische Kunst" ("Criticism Is a Creative Art"), the paper interviewed Germany's leading critics for a series of brief, individual portraits that would be published in six installments from September through December. The articles trace out the different paths that led well-known critics such as Kurt Pinthus and Herbert Ihering to their posts at top journals and newspapers; we learn about the politics of film criticism and are treated to some tricks of the trade (how many cigarettes does it take to turn in a review by the paper's deadline?).

The six-part series begins with Pinthus, "the senior among the film critics in Germany."[1] Casting a retrospective glance at the origins of film criticism in Germany, the Pinthus interview also indexes a persistent ambivalence, characteristic for the early period of film criticism and theory, about how to treat the medium of film, particularly in the context of a trade journal such as the *Film-Kurier*: whether as industry or as art. For in Pinthus's view only the latter would merit the engagement of critics on behalf of the filmgoing audience. Underlying this interview and the series as a whole is a lingering unease about the very definition of the film critic, and indeed of the medium in question. Even as it enters its third decade, the cinema is still clamoring for legitimacy, and film reviewing is still in need of justification—whether through a comparison to the more established role of the theater critic, by invoking the critic's function as educator in visual literacy, or by appeal to received notions of art and aesthetics.

While Pinthus and Ihering remain familiar to scholars of German film as two of the leading critics of the Weimar Republic, other writers featured in the series, such as Heinz Pol, Ernst Blass, and Hans Sahl, have largely been forgotten.[2] The sixth and final installment, however, profiled a figure who would go on to enter the pantheon of film theory: Siegfried Kracauer.[3] To be sure, it is not yet the author of *From Caligari to Hitler* (1947), let alone the much later *Theory of Film* (1960), who graces the page of the *Film-Kurier* on December 13, 1930 (a sketch at the top of the article shows him smoking a pipe and suggests an air of thoughtful, relaxed authority); rather, we are introduced here to Kracauer as the lead critic for the left-liberal *Frankfurter Zeitung* (see figure 30.1). At the time of the interview, the author of the recently published *Salaried Masses* (first serialized in the paper in 1929 and then published as a book in 1930) had just moved from Frankfurt to Berlin to become the cultural editor of the paper's Berlin pages, where he continued, among other things, to publish the film reviews readers had come to expect of him on a near-daily basis. Like other classical film theorists such as Béla Balàzs or Rudolf Arnheim, in other words, Kracauer got his start reviewing films of the silent era; but his decade-long employment by the *Frankfurter Zeitung* sets him apart as a professional critic of longer standing and with a larger corpus of reviews to his name.[4] From 1921 onward, and until his dismissal from the *Frankfurter Zeitung* in the wake of Hitler's rise to power in 1933, Kracauer reviewed multiple films a week, attending every film premiere even if the paper ultimately did not run a review.

Asked by the *Film-Kurier* about the task of the film critic, Kracauer responds with three guidelines: film critics should know something about the technology of film; they should be able to offer a sociological perspective that relates films to their audiences; and they are tasked with delivering aesthetic analyses.[5] And while the film critic should watch indiscriminately, s/he should write selectively: his newspaper, Kracauer notes, tends to publish only on films that provide the opportunity for more general discussion.

In what follows, I attempt to extrapolate the contours of that discussion from Kracauer's reviews of cinema until the advent of sound in Germany in the late 1920s.[6] It is a discussion that is at once intensely topical and implicitly theoretical: the claims that

FIGURE 30.1 Sketch of Siegfried Kracauer in *Film-Kurier* 294, December 13, 1930.

Kracauer advances are historically contingent and yet their relevance transcends the moment in which they were formulated. Occasionally over the course of his career as a film critic, Kracauer will note that the comparatively new medium still lacks a theory.[7] To be sure, it would be an exaggeration to see in his own reviewing practice "the as yet unwritten metaphysics of film" toward which Kracauer gestures in one of his earliest pieces from 1923.[8] And yet, thanks to the meticulous critical edition of Kracauer's collected works in nine volumes (2004–2012), we are today in the fortunate position to be able to extrapolate from the routine work of the film critic the principles of a more theoretical engagement with silent cinema during the 1920s. Reading through the complete sequence of published reviews now available in a three-volume subset of Kracauer's *Werke*, one begins to discern a number of recurring themes that may contribute to our understanding not only of Kracauer's own later, more explicitly theoretical, work but also of the culture of late silent cinema in Germany, including the politics of film criticism and the stakes for defining the medium theoretically.

With the benefit of synoptic hindsight, we can identify the masses, media, and modernity as three main themes of Kracauer's silent film criticism. For his concern here is, first, not with cinema as art, but with cinema as a popular medium whose subject is ultimately *the masses*. Kracauer shares with other writers of the time an assumption about the specificity of cinema, which he locates in its unique abilities to capture movement, illuminate surface phenomena, and address the masses. Second, in demonstrating how the cinema and its technologies thus restructure human perception, the social world, and even our very notion of human life, his reviews ultimately outline a *media theory* for the early twentieth century. Third, as has often been noted, Kracauer's work from the 1920s chronicles and reflects upon the transformations wrought by technology, industrial progress, and urbanization, as well as on concomitant changes in the realm of culture and the arts; his film reviews play a central role in Kracauer's evolving understanding of these shifts and ruptures, and in this sense, they evince an ongoing concern with cinema's place in *modernity*.

Miriam Hansen, whose work remains central for understanding how these concerns with the masses, media, and modernity shaped his overall trajectory as a thinker, once described Kracauer as "a critical intellectual for whom journalism was not a default career but a chance and challenge to engage in writing as a public medium."[9] Given Kracauer's literary ambitions (he was also a novelist), it may thus be worth noting that one gets a clear sense of an emerging stylistic signature from the outset of his critical writing.[10] For film reviewing, as David Bordwell rightly points out, "is not merely a report on current releases but an occasion for a display of the writer's sensibility"; it is, in Phillip Lopate's words, "a literary performance, in the final analysis."[11] Kracauer clearly treated it as such, devoting as much attention to his reviews as he did to his novels. In this respect, the stylistic decisions that he makes take on substantive significance over the course of the 1920s, as an increasingly ironic tone signals his growing impatience with ever-recurring plots, and a preference for the rhetorical figure of chiasmus signals a new dialectical turn in his evolving critique of ideology at the movies.[12] I will return to these issues below but would note again that such insights derive, to a great degree, from the collection of quasi-daily reviews in a critical edition that orders them chronologically and certainly affects the way we now read Kracauer's work. In this sense comparable to anthologies of reviews by other critics—whether James Agee or Pauline Kael, Rudolf Arnheim or Herbert Ihering—the three volumes afford a synoptic view that may have escaped even the most faithful readers of Kracauer's reviews in the *Frankfurter Zeitung*.[13]

"THE FUTURE BELONGS TO THIS TYPE OF FILM": STARS, GENRES, PLOTS

Film history long tended to treat Weimar cinema as a golden era, devoting inordinate attention to a handful of masterworks and a narrowly defined canon of auteurs.[14] Kracauer's reviewing practice forcefully undoes this received image: in his reports on Frankfurt's (and later Berlin's) film scene, we encounter not an art cinema of auteurs but a star- and genre-driven industry of run-of-the-mill storylines and soon-to-be-forgotten commercial fare. We find the future film theorist honing his critical tools not on Robert Wiene, F. W. Murnau, Fritz Lang, or G. W. Pabst, but on popular blockbusters (*Großfilme*) and repeated generic formulas: "And yet another filmed operetta, and yet again with Harry Liedtke, who has a veritable monopoly on charming, noble and level-headed romantic leads. Each time, he wins with the same smile and the same postures that are apparently so irresistible that women never tire of them."[15] Repetition of formulas ensures box-office success. Instead of unique masterworks, we find patterns, stereotypes, genres—a seemingly unending progression of detective films, impostor films (*Hochstaplerfilme*), marriage comedies, city films, street films, history films, adventure films, fairy tales, slapstick, edifying films (*Kulturfilme*). Products of the Weimar-era culture industry, these films trade on sensations but evince little variation; rather, "in the endless sequence of films, a limited number of typical themes recur again and again."[16] Like the recurring "typical roles that run like well-oiled machines these days," these motifs are so evident to Kracauer and repeat so predictably as to become transparent, as if revealing the true scaffolding underneath.[17] As the decade progresses, Kracauer consequently becomes more and more ironic about film plots "with [their] beginnings, middles, and ends," which he recounts reliably but often with more than a hint of impatience—as if to suggest that the truly interesting aspects of cinema are to be located elsewhere.[18] As Lopate rightly suggests, "Working critics have to develop philosophies about 'trash' or 'bad movies' [. . .] and strategies for writing about entertaining junk, either by isolating those gifted cameos or enjoyable moments that rise above the general mediocrity or by employing a variety of ironic, satiric, humorous tones to illuminate the triumph of tripe."[19] Kracauer perfected this art over the course of the 1920s, often invoking kitchen recipes or laboratory instructions to account for the formulaic nature of the decade's favored plots. Thus, the Austrian film *Tragödie einer Frau* (*Tragedy of a Woman*; Desider Kertesz,

1924) is "prepared according to a tried and tested recipe," whose ingredients include an impostor, a woman of loose morals, another woman, and a man caught in the middle. These "principal components are mixed together, entering into a chemical process that yields the expected precipitate."[20] In other instances, Kracauer condenses the details even further, dismissing the construction of plots like that of *Das Spielzeug von Paris* (*Red Heels*; Michael Kertész, 1925) with a couple of deliberately placed indefinite articles: "once again a dancer suffers a fate."[21]

The perpetual recurrence and formulaic nature of these plot motifs becomes an organizing literary device in the well-known series of essays from the period later published in *The Mass Ornament* under the title "The Little Shopgirls Go to the Movies." Each of these texts (which together "caused a sensation in the *Frankfurter Zeitung*," as Adorno recalled almost forty years later) begins with the description of a typical movie plot from the era that today seems composited, if not invented from whole cloth; those descriptions become the basis for the series' vignettes about class, gender, and moviegoing.[22] As become apparent to readers of Kracauer's collected film criticism, however, all of these descriptions have antecedents in specific films Kracauer had previously reviewed. This interchangeability between actual films and the clichés Kracauer seems to construct in "The Little Shopgirls" is precisely the point: Kracauer's critiques derive as much from the cross-section of recurrent fare as from the encounter with individual films.

Crowds, Masses, Audiences

The standardization of cinematic fare finds its equivalent in the standardization of its consumers: the "little shopgirls" are but a gendered subgroup of the masses (themselves often gendered as feminine) that incontrovertibly form the subject of the new medium and of Kracauer's reviews alike.[23] In an approving nod to Balàzs, Kracauer holds that film "represents the masses as no other artform can"; he singles out this fact in numerous reviews, praising the treatment of crowd scenes in epic films such as *Danton* (Dimitri Buchowetzki, 1921), *Die Gezeichneten* (*The Stigmatized*; Carl Theodor Dreyer, 1921), or *Ben-Hur* (Fred Niblo, 1925).[24] These films, he opines, manage to stage their crowds so that the people become the films' protagonist. What is valuable about a film such as *Danton*, he notes already in one of his earliest reviews, "is that it shows the *demos*, that it impressively reveals this large, hulking animal in its cowardice and its reckless daring, in its contempt and its primeval force."[25] The representation of the masses on film will continue to fascinate Kracauer throughout the decade, about which he writes retrospectively in *From Caligari to Hitler*: after the War, "no one could avoid encountering [crowds] on the streets and squares. These masses were more than a weighty social factor; they were as tangible as any individual. A hope to some and a nightmare to others, they haunted the imagination."[26]

This is not just a matter of how crowds get represented in films such as *Danton*, *Battleship Potemkin* (Sergei Eisenstein, 1925), or *Die Weber* (*The Weavers*; Friedrich

Zelnik, 1927). For Kracauer, the masses are the true subject of cinema also in their function as spectators—as the mass audiences that flocked to Berlin's movie palaces, devoting themselves to the "cult of distraction." Here, Kracauer holds, the audience encounters itself "in pure externality"—thus rendering tangible the social order of modernity. For Kracauer the mass is, as Stefan Johnsson rightly observes, "the effect of [a] social contradiction: people had been liberated from old oppressive communities but at the same time enslaved under a new set of abstract social relationships."[27] The cinema of the 1920s is a key site for organizing and making visible this dialectic. For all his ambivalence about the standardization of genre and culture that he observes in the films he reviews, Kracauer vehemently opposes conservative responses that would curtail the new medium or press it into the service of "art." The distracted mass audience gives a clearer, more "sincere" representation of the social than any pretense to art or appeal to "concepts such as personality, inwardness, tragedy, and so on" ever could.[28] This is why he considers Berlin audiences to be acting "in a profound sense [. . .] truthfully when they increasingly shun [. . .] art events (which, for good reason remain caught in mere pretense), preferring instead the surface glamor of the stars, films, revues, and spectacular shows. Here, in pure externality, the audience encounters itself; its own reality is revealed in the fragmented sequence of splendid sense impressions."[29] Accordingly, the audience's laughter "justifies" lowbrow entertainment and historical kitsch. As a critic, Kracauer refuses to dismiss "conventional feelings from 'middlebrow novels,'" contending that after all, "the audience demands to be satisfied."[30]

This commitment to the crowds that he joined as a spectator himself remains surprisingly consistent through Kracauer's career. As he will write twenty years later: "fortunately, all efforts to ennoble the film by dragging it into the sphere of stage and literature aroused the skepticism of film experts and encountered the salutary indifference of the masses."[31] This judgment, at which Kracauer arrives in *From Caligari to Hitler*, certainly has the privilege of hindsight. And yet, it is of a piece with the earlier reviewing practice on which it draws.[32] It is difficult to miss the way in which Kracauer, the "film expert," aligns himself here with the masses, just as he routinely (if often implicitly) took their side as a salaried employee of the *Frankfurter Zeitung* in his film reviews of the 1920s. In those texts, his own skepticism toward artistic pretense joined the masses' indifference toward any attempts to subordinate cinema to traditional notions of art.

Rather than disavow its basis in technology, rationalization, and the masses, Kracauer holds that cinema comes into its own where it lays that basis bare. In this sense, cinema is of a piece with the mass ornament that he describes primarily with reference to other spectacles such as the Tiller Girls, revues, and sporting events. Here, too, there is no turning back, since for Kracauer, modernity's "process leads directly through the center of the mass ornament, not away from it."[33] For the professional film reviewer, writing in the public medium of the newspaper, cinema has a clear diagnostic value precisely in its routinized, standardized form as mass entertainment. From Kracauer's film reviews we can glean a clear sense that the preeminent site for the confrontation with modernity and the mass ornament is the modern medium of cinema, with its formative power to alienate us from our alienated conditions of existence.

Paradigmatic Films: *The Gold Rush, Die Straße, Battleship Potemkin*

That said, a number of individual films do stand out in Kracauer's evaluation—though it is worth noting that these are not necessarily the films we now hold to be masterworks of Weimar cinema: Kracauer has nothing but scorn for Fritz Lang's *Metropolis* (1927), considers *Berlin, Die Sinfonie der Großstadt* (*Berlin, Symphony of a Great City*; Walther Ruttmann, 1927) a "bad disappointment," and barely mentions films by Murnau or Wiene.[34] Instead, as Miriam Hansen has previously noted, the German film that most impresses Kracauer during these years is Karl Grune's *Die Straße* (*The Street*, 1923), to which he in fact devotes multiple reviews.[35] Other paradigmatic films tend to be of foreign origin: repeatedly, Kracauer will refer to Sergei Eisenstein's *Battleship Potemkin* in his effusive praise for Soviet cinema (notably Pudovkin's *Mother* [1926] and *The End of St. Petersburg* [1927]); more generally speaking, Eisenstein's film also figures prominently in Kracauer's own evolving theoretical views of what cinema is, or should be.[36] Similarly, Chaplin's *The Gold Rush* (1925) functions as Kracauer's gold standard for the possibilities of slapstick but also as cinema's ideal response to modernity. The importance of this genre for Kracauer is reflected in the fact that, during his first few years as a critic, he regularly reserves his greatest praise for the American comic shorts that open the evening programs—films featuring Chaplin, Buster Keaton, Harold Lloyd, Roscoe "Fatty" Arbuckle, and others. Their American "tempo" outshines the ponderous predictability of even the most ambitious German *Großfilm*. To the degree that Kracauer's silent film criticism has received any attention in film studies scholarship, commentators have consequently focused largely on these highlights—and justifiably so: the encounters with these standout productions were momentous for Kracauer, as was the sheer physical force of the American shorts. To him, these films typified what cinema was, and references to them recur in subsequent reviews.

It makes sense, then, to speak of a proto-theoretical practice of film reviewing when we already find Kracauer in the 1920s describing slapstick, for example, as particularly *filmgerecht* (film appropriate; for more on this concept, see below).[37] The principle of these films, Kracauer claims, "is always the same: the demonstration of [a universe] devoid of essences and the desperate fight of no-longer real human beings against a mechanized world."[38] Kracauer might have (and certainly did) derive this insight from any number of short comedies he saw before an evening's feature and discussed at the end of the following day's review—but he happens to be referring here specifically to Chaplin's *Laughing Gas* (1914), which accompanied the second of a two-part feature entitled *Die große Unbekannte* (*The Mysterious Woman*; Willi Wolf, 1923). And indeed, the world of surfaces and recalcitrant objects that Chaplin creates in his films is paradigmatic for Kracauer's understanding of the genre, and of cinema more generally—as becomes obvious in his euphoric review of *The Gold Rush*.

Simply entitled "Chaplin," the article describes the director as a poet of the cinema who has tapped the medium's subterranean connections to the utopian powers of fairy tales.[39] To Kracauer, Chaplin's tramp is the very incarnation of the human (*eine Darstellung des Menschlichen*)—but again, it is a distorted, alienated form of humanity that we encounter in the cinema. For the tramp is a human without will, without the drive for self-preservation—without a self. He is *ohnmächtig*: powerless, helpless, unconscious, impotent. "Others have a sense of self and live in human relations; [but the tramp] has lost his Ego (*ihm ist das Ich abhanden gekommen*)."[40] Precisely by virtue of this derealization, of the abyss that opens up where we would expect to find a person's interiority—his soul, his desires, his drives, his very identity—Chaplin becomes a powerful figure of alienation: the tramp reflects back to us the atomized fragments that make up our quotidian existence. He is, in a particularly memorable formulation, "a hole into which everything falls; things that are normally integrated (*verbunden*) shatter into their component parts upon impact down inside him."[41] It is as if Chaplin holds up a distorted mirror to the distortions of the modern world. In this sense, "his powerlessness (*Ohnmacht*) is dynamite."[42]

Even though *The Gold Rush* obviously bears Chaplin's signature, Kracauer's fascination remains as much with the genre as with the figure: the tramp simply crystallizes what slapstick can teach the mass audience about objectification, mechanization, and the very fate of humanity. That cinema can develop this revelatory power in a few isolated instances where a film's design stands out against the mass of generic fare also becomes evident in Kracauer's rapturous praise for *Die Straße*. As Hansen has detailed, Kracauer experienced Karl Grune's film as a revelation of cinema's power to invest objects with agency and to reveal the objectification of humans in modernity. His multiple reviews of the film revolve around Grune's ability to train the medium on surfaces, on outward appearances and the lack of interiority. Life in the film is "devoid of substance, empty like a tin can," consisting only of isolated events that "congeal kaleidoscopically into an ever shifting series of images."[43] Modern life, according to *Die Straße*, is nothing but a "confused assembly, a *tohuwabohu* of reified souls and pseudo-animate objects."[44] The film, in other words, thematizes both the atomization and the anonymity of contemporary, metropolitan existence and as such becomes, in Hansen's words, "a manifesto of metaphysical malaise" that lays bare the conditions of modernity.[45] For it is the task of cinema, Kracauer avers in an earlier review, "to point to genuine reality by exaggerating the irreality of our lives and thereby to ironize their illusory qualities."[46] Precisely by training the camera on surfaces, mute objects, and seemingly meaningless details, film can elevate the hidden, reifying tendencies of modern life to the level of consciousness. This profound theoretical insight continues to resonate, albeit in very different ways, in both of Kracauer's major treatises on film: *From Caligari to Hitler* will anchor Kracauer's (re)interpretation of Weimar cinema precisely in film's power to bring to the fore a period's unconscious "dispositions"; and *Theory of Film* will amplify the importance of objects and surfaces for the medium's realist tendencies.

If *The Gold Rush* and *Die Straße* each in their own way lay bare the antinomies of modernity, Eisenstein's *Battleship Potemkin* points the way forward and accesses a different truth. Kracauer's review on the occasion of the film's Frankfurt premiere is another unalloyed hymn of praise, the record of an affective encounter between Eisenstein's film and a critic who is steeped in very different fare. Against the backdrop of social comedies and sentimental historical films that repress current socio-political conjunctures, Kracauer is palpably awakened by Eisenstein's film. In this, he shares the reaction of other contemporary critics, but he also interprets the film through the lens of his own film aesthetics, his developing interests in what counts as specifically *filmgemäß*, or "film appropriate." Kracauer's take on *Potemkin* is consequently sui generis: he reads it, for example, as a film about surface rather than depth, truth rather than sensationalism, directed by an imagination (*Phantasie*) filled with "indignation, horror, and hope."[47] And, like *Die Straße* and Chaplin's comedies, *Potemkin* is a film about the encounter between humans and objects. As the people and the Odessa Steps "meld into an indissoluble unity," insurrection becomes a matter of people and things: to Eisenstein's imagination, "the individual parts of things count as much as the mutinous soldiers, for mutiny inheres in them, too."[48] In fact, Kracauer raises the stakes even further. What characterizes this revolutionary film above all, in his opinion, is "the natural (*selbstverständlich*) connection between humans and technology."[49] Eisenstein impresses Kracauer because he moves away from the idealist separation of humans and things, spirit and technology. In the eyes of this reviewer, the battleship becomes essentially a cyborg made up of human and non-human actants, where the human and the technological enter into symbiosis, allowing the film to break through the wall of repression erected by routine German and American films to keep reality at bay. "Herr Eisenstein," by contrast, has succeeded "perhaps for the first time in representing a reality through filmic means."[50]

The Gold Rush, *Die Straße*, and *Potemkin* are doubtless extraordinary films that give Kracauer pause in his daily routine as a critic. Along with a handful of actors and directors whom he values—among them Werner Krauß, Fritz Kortner, Pola Negri, Lil Dagover, Jackie Coogan, Ludwig Berger, and Ernst Lubitsch—Chaplin, Grune, and Eisenstein help Kracauer to articulate an incipient theory of film. By the same token, and as I suggested above, these exceptional films and directors only gain their contours against the ground of the regular offerings at the movie theaters. Taken together, the hundreds of silent films that Kracauer reviewed during the Weimar Republic provide the material from which he derives theoretical insights that will carry through all the way to the major books on cinema—*From Caligari to Hitler* and *Theory of Film*—that he writes much later in the United States.

"*FILMGEMÄSS*": TOWARD A MEDIA THEORY OF FILM

To identify these early theoretical intuitions, one might simply track Kracauer's evaluation of individual films for what is—and what is not—*filmgemäß*. Few terms recur more regularly over the course of the decade than variations on this adjective, a composite of Kracauer's own devising that denotes what he considers "film appropriate," adequate to film, or simply filmic: in accordance with what film can—and consequently should—do. The frequent use of *filmgemäß*, *filmgerecht*, and *filmisch*, in other words, indexes an emerging theory of medium specificity. It does so both by affirmation, when Kracauer isolates aspects of films that he considers particularly cinematic, and by negation, whenever he finds particular works that betray the "spirit of film (*Geist des Films*)."[51] In this sense, Kracauer joins an aesthetic discourse that dates back at least to Gotthold Ephraim Lessing's *Laokoon* (1766) and which deduces aesthetic norms from a medium's possibilities—a "should" from a "can." Significantly, however, Kracauer develops this discourse in *social* terms as much as on the aesthetic plane, as we have already seen in his emphasis on the masses: far less concerned than other contemporary critics to integrate the cinema into an established notion of the arts (of which Arnheim's *Film als Kunst* from 1932 would be the paradigmatic example), Kracauer instead investigates the specific ability of the medium to intervene in modernity by rendering it sensible on a mass scale.

In a review of recent publications on film in which he again bemoans the fact that "there is not even an aesthetic theory of film even though such a theory could exist," Kracauer develops some fundamental claims about the specificity of the medium and the guiding historical assumptions of its theory. Film, he avers, "is restricted to the representation (*Abbildung*) of the visible world and is based on a technical procedure from which its boundaries and freedoms must be derived. [. . .] Not every type of content is to be found in every art form at every time – idealist aesthetics are historically blind."[52] Accordingly, as early as 1923 we find Kracauer reviewing a Shakespeare adaptation as "strictly against the spirit of film: instead of visible, disjointed movement there are mental transitions and superfluous interconnections, instead of grotesque surfaces there is false spiritual depth, instead of surprising improvisation there are carefully prepared scenes. In other words: no genuine piece of film but bad theater and brilliant revue."[53] At one point in a column on the misguided artistic pretensions of the *Kulturfilm*, Kracauer even imagines the instructive value of a film museum, yet to be established, for "counter-examples" from which one might derive a sense of cinema's limits: the boundaries of what is *filmgemäß*.[54] Visitors to such a museum would presumably learn to distinguish film from what it is not and should not be, according to Kracauer: it is not just literature with some moving images added, nor is it theater; nor, moreover, can genuine, successful cinema rely on plot alone. Instead, Kracauer speaks of the construction of films in terms of pointillism and mosaics.[55] "Authentic films draw their power not from the overall action that can be put into words, but from the tension with which they charge their tiny image units."[56] This slightly enigmatic notion of the medium's constituent units (*Bildeinheiten*) derives from a fundamentally cinephilic disposition on Kracauer's part—the tendency to privilege and even revel in isolated moments rather than the manifest content or narrative of a given film.[57] By the same token, it also begins to suggest an aesthetic stance that favors atomization over totality, fragments over wholes. In a review of Manfred Noa's 1924 film *Helena*, which he critiques as a misguided attempt to translate the verbal and spiritual world of myth into moving images, Kracauer makes this aesthetic principle explicit: the object of film, he writes, "is merely the mute exterior aspect of the world, it fulfills its mission in representing actions that are pieced together much like the film strip. A series of momentary images, an aggregate of punctual events: that is truly the world of film."[58]

This normative claim contains a second aspect of Kracauer's film aesthetics: the focus on exteriority, surface, and movement. Contrary to Balàzs's rather more romantic, "physiognomic" approach, Kracauer holds that silent film can access interiority and "the soul" only insofar as "it can be deciphered completely in the stirring of the exterior world (*im bewegten Außen*)."[59] As a visual medium, film is beholden to surfaces: it "demands the surface, drastic situations that exhaust themselves in the optical realm, and rapid progression."[60] One senses here again the importance of slapstick for Kracauer's incipient theorization of the medium, which tends to generalize the genre's emphasis on the sheer exuberance of movement and favors a type of comedy that "has withdrawn entirely to the surface."[61] By contrast, soul, mind, thought, and spirit—that is, the classical *loci* of interiority—are *filmgerecht* only in their external manifestations, their reverberations in the material world. Or in their absence, as in the case of the stonefaced Buster Keaton who, like Chaplin, becomes for Kracauer a prototype for the kind of character around whom silent film gravitates. His enthusiastic review of *The General* (1926), praises Keaton's portrayal of a character "lost in thoughtlessness," a figure who leaves viewers wondering about the "whereabouts of his mind."[62]

As our earlier discussion of Chaplin also suggests, moreover, another of Kracauer's aesthetic tenets concerns film's ability to foreground and animate the mute object world. "Since humans are silent beings on the screen, *things* obtain tongues like nowhere else. For the first time perhaps they speak. Film brings the 'small lives' of things to the surface and integrates them into the world of symbols."[63] The slapstick comedians' stumbles, their often unwelcome encounters with all manner of objects, become reminders of a more general affinity of film for the material world. In a characteristic chiasmus (I will return to the importance of this rhetorical figure shortly), Kracauer celebrates those films in which "humans behave like things and things themselves appear to be animated."[64] This crossover, which Hansen identifies as the characteristic "chiastic relation between the living and the mechanical, animate and inanimate" in Kracauer's Weimar writings more generally, becomes explicit, uncanny, and indeed terrifying when the wires cross and we can no longer distinguish between humans and objects—as in *The Chess Player* (*Le Joueur d'Échecs*; Raymond Bernard, 1927), the first film Kracauer reviews in 1927. He considers the automata featured in the film a cinematic conceit par excellence. The actors who portray the mechanical figures embody the chiastic relation between humans and technology that characterizes the medium itself: one gets the impression, writes Kracauer, "that the human actors who impersonate the mechanical inhabitants of [the protagonist's] mansion were in fact automata who had become human in turn."[65] Kracauer clearly admires the way in which the film carefully choreographs this equivocation, right through the final showdown between a Russian intruder and an army of mechanical soldiers. The concluding paragraph of Kracauer's review merits quoting in full since it gestures toward the broader theory of the medium that he had been developing as film critic at the *Frankfurter Zeitung*. In this final scene, Kracauer writes, *The Chess Player*

> meets a reality that is fully [the film's] own. The automaton that the film can engage because it shares its identity wins out over the human being, and nothing any longer evades mechanical exteriority. What is invisible is negated by colorful visibility, no other world seems to exist beside the one given up to the lenses [of the camera]. The power of objects over objectified humans, one of the great themes of American slapstick (*Filmgroteske*), has become demonically personified in the deformations of the automata.[66]

There is an undeniable post-humanist strain to this type of *filmgerecht* reality (in his later books, this is what Kracauer will label "camera reality"): as a medium, cinema outruns its human inventors and their intentions, becoming a mechanical agent in its own right and dispensing with the trappings, if not of humans themselves, then certainly of humanism. Automata are its ideal subjects because they dislodge the last remnants of idealism—replacing humanist notions of interiority, soul, will, and subjectivity with cold, "demonic" objects. As a mechanical, photographic medium, film consequently intimates a world from which humans are absent, a motif that will become central to Kracauer's later film theory.

In this sense, we might begin to think of the latter, and of the reviews that fueled it, as an inquiry into the medium's power to reshape the very categories we use to describe notions of experience, aesthetics, and media. The chess-playing automaton of *Le Joueur d'échecs* becomes emblematic in this sense. Hand-cranked like a camera, operated by a human actor, it confounds the relation between humans and technology to such a degree that the viewer can no longer discern the individual contributions of each. Following this model case, cinema itself becomes a sort of artificial intelligence that rethinks the human as an object among others. Although Kracauer was certainly alive to other medial configurations of his time and certainly attuned, for example, to the sounds of modernity—whether via the radio or as "screams in the street"—it was the visual configurations of silent cinema that for him constituted the medial a priori of modernity.

Chiasmus: The Politics of Kracauer's Film Criticism

Kracauer's impatience with both the industry and the audience clearly grows over time. By 1927, he is already lambasting the former for its lack of moral compass: most films are set in a safely contained past, whereas the industry increasingly loses its "courage," Kracauer suggests, "in direct proportion to their proximity to the present."[67] One year later he summarily dismisses "our average productions" as "miserable," and the end of 1928 finds him looking back at the year's fare with disdain: "stupid, false, and often mean."[68] By 1930, he has clearly lost all patience whatsoever. When he reviews a film entitled *Das lockende Ziel* (*The Beckoning Destination*, 1930), directed by Max Reichmann and featuring the popular tenor Richard Tauber, who also produced the film, Kracauer cuts down the entire plot with the curt observation that it is "baby blue, like the tenor"—in other words: pure kitsch.[69] Toward the end of the review, exasperation gives way to searching self-reflection: "Do I take the film too seriously?" Kracauer asks. His answer once more underlines the task of the film critic and points to the paucity of politically engaged reviewers: "Because hardly anyone seriously engages with the unparalleled rawness of such machinations, they can be produced over and over again. Because almost nobody stands up to them, their production ruins both conscience and art."[70]

Around the same time, while the deepening economic crisis engulfed the world and Germany's first experiment with democracy began to erode, Kracauer begins to speak explicitly of "political reaction" on screen.[71] As Ufa falls in line with reactionary politics under Alfred Hugenberg and Ludwig Klitzsch and the Nazis seize power, Kracauer's film criticism clearly takes on a new political edge that points forward, in intriguing and still uncharted ways, to the wholesale indictment of Weimar cinema in *From Caligari to Hitler*. At the same time, a careful reading of the texts we have been discussing reveals the ways in which this political stance derives from a decade of film reviewing. Over that period, Kracauer honed forms of ideological critique that were no less trenchant for being somewhat less directly stated than from 1930 onward. During the 1920s, this critique is encoded instead in asides, in ironic turns of phrase, and especially in one recurrent rhetorical figure to which I alluded above: the chiasmus.

Chiasmatic structures abound in Kracauer's reviews, where they fulfill a variety of functions from stylistic flourish or gentle irony to poison-penned critique and outright political positioning. At times, a glancing observation is rhetorically heightened by chiasmatically inverting a pair of terms—such as Kracauer's praise for Mary Pickford's ability as an actress to "laugh under tears and cry even while laughing."[72] Other instances probe more deeply into the aesthetic structure of particular films such as Ludwig Berger's Cinderella adaption *Der velorene Schuh* (*The Lost Shoe*, 1923), which succeeds because it "does not reinterpret the fairy tale realistically, but rather draws reality into the realm of the fairy tale."[73] But there is something more systematic about Kracauer's turn to chiasmus, which has to do with the relation of film and reality—and, by extension, with the political.

An excursion to the Ufa studio grounds, about which Kracauer reports in the essay "Calico World" (later included in *The Mass Ornament*), helps to illustrate the structural force of this rhetorical figure. Even to enter the grounds involves reversing a habitual figure-ground relationship: Kracauer asks his readers right away to imagine the studios as "a desert within an oasis." The ensuing piece, which appears impressionistic at first, is carefully designed to show how the natural world and the "papier-mâché world" of cinema cross over into each other. Describing the props and activities in the studio in ways that disenchant the medium of film and mediate its powers of enchantment through his own figurative language, Kracauer engages in a constant short-circuiting of authenticity and fakery, the objectivity of the camera lens (*Objektiv* in German) and its powers of deception. For "when it comes to deception, the heart and soul appreciate authenticity," he writes.[74] Consequently the two sides of cinematic illusion—its technical fabrication and the tromp-l'oeil effect that hides the conditions of production—meet on the grounds of the studios: "everything guaranteed unnatural and everything exactly like nature."[75]

Kracauer frequently deploys chiasmus to convey precisely this interlacing of illusion and reality—whether he is describing Abel Gance's Napoleon (who "appears real when his face congeals into a mask"), or whether he is discussing the appearance of the French Riviera on film (which "appears as a colorful film image in reality, [but] loses its make-up when it appears on film, and transforms back into pure nature").[76]

But what is ultimately at stake in Kracauer's chiasmatic flourishes are the politics of the medium, and the medium as a precondition of politics. As a rhetorical figure, chiasmus permits the critic to condense his critique of ideology into a pithy phrase, as when he concludes a review by referring, once again, to its spectators: "the same audience that the film has mocked, applauds it unsuspectingly."[77] When viewers applaud a film that mocks those same viewers, ideology has crept into the equation. That same sense of false consciousness pervades the plots of countless films Kracauer reviews, and again, the inverse reciprocity of chiasmatic rhetoric shines through in his descriptions: the film *Der Liebeskäfig* (*The Love Cage*; Erich Schönfelder, 1925), for example, spends its time treating "the inner conflicts of people who dispose of enough time and money to experience such conflicts."[78] The issue for Kracauer is not simply that film peddles ideological images of reality. He claims instead that reality itself has already become filmic ("Monte Carlo [. . .] already appears as a film scene in the original"), and is prefigured by the medium in which it then finds representation.[79] In the process, reality is so fully mediated that it is canceled out: the Riviera, which in real life looks like footage from a color film, looks natural only on the screen.

The transformative power of film thus has the potential to work in two directions at once: it can reinforce the ideological construction of a world that always already looks like a film image, but it can also reveal the sham appearance of a world in which people have the time and money to experience inner conflicts. Precisely because cinema in a sense medially prefigures our perception of everyday life, it also harbors the potential to refresh and redirect that perception. The very technology of cinema, after all, relies heavily on fragmentation and montage, thus providing unprecedented possibilities for representing the fragmented world of modernity. And yet, Kracauer concludes, films generally assemble the "mosaic" of individual scenes, props, and devices into illusions of wholeness. "Instead of leaving the world in its fragmented state, one reconstitutes a world out of these pieces. The objects that have been liberated from the larger context [in the 'calico world' of the studios] are now reinserted into it, their isolation effaced and their grimace smoothed over."[80]

Against this backdrop, we can further refine our assessment of what makes the films of Chaplin, Grune, or Eisenstein so exceptional in Kracauer's eyes. Whereas the broad swath of genre films that he reviews during the 1920s profoundly shapes his diagnosis of modernity, these exceptions point the way out of the closed circuit of total mediation. They tap the potential that any film harbors by dint of its technological basis. It is no accident that this key insight, too, is often figured chiasmatically. One recalls, for example, the encounter in *Die Straße* with "reified souls and pseudo-animate objects"— a chiasmus that is perhaps more immediately apparent in the original German (*verdinglichte Seelen und scheinwache Dinge*). By the same token, it is in a paradigmatic film like *The Gold Rush* that Kracauer finds humans and objects to cross in a way that directs us out of modernity's dehumanizing forcefield: the tramp, he contends, is "a human without a surface, [he is] a hole. But from this hole shines forth what is purely human."[81] It is as if the film medium, for Kracauer, becomes the site for a chiasmatic crossing between humanity and the forces of modernity that exert pressure on the very notion of what it means to be human. And a film like *The Gold Rush* can catalyze that process by both acknowledging the dehumanizing tendencies of modernity and celebrating modernity—through film, its crucial medium—for its ability to produce a new, decentered notion of the human.[82]

REDEEMING THE DIN OF THE URBAN STREET: THE TRANSITION TO SOUND

When the *Film-Kurier* published its portrait of Kracauer in late 1930, the conversion to sound was in full swing even in Germany (where the transition was belated relative to the technological advances in the United States). Kracauer's most recent review at the time had been published a few days before in the *Frankfurter Zeitung*: it was devoted to Lewis Milestone's *All Quiet on the Western Front* (1930). Sketching the politics of the film's distribution in Germany, where the war ministry had protested against its release but was overruled by the film censorship office, Kracauer applauds the film's "extraordinary fidelity to reality" and its consequent power to unravel the continuing idealist glorification of war in Germany.[83] At the same time, he critiques both Milestone's film and the equally famous book by Erich-Maria Remarque on which it was based. For Kracauer, neither had gone far enough. Failing to analyze the causes for war, the film's anti-war stance merely scratches the surface and ultimately withdraws into a "highly questionable neutrality."[84]

All Quiet on the Western Front was of course a sound film, which reached Germany in a dubbed version—leading Kracauer to complain, like many other critics around the time, that the advent of sound was threatening the internationality of silent cinema. At the same time, however, Kracauer explicitly lauded the "imbrication of the most varied hellish sounds" through which the "old-fashioned thunder of battle" found expression on film.[85] This is not a critic who, like his colleague Rudolf Arnheim, would flatly dismiss the sound film as a debasement of the art of cinema. Instead, as sound irrevocably entered German theaters from the late 1920s onward, Kracauer remained open to the medial shift and developed a nuanced response that laid the basis for a differentiated assessment and theorization of the "talkies." Although these developments fall outside of the parameters of this article, in concluding we may mark the theoretical import of Kracauer's response to the advent of sound by briefly considering the first review that he devotes to the matter.

Entitled "Tonbildfilm" (Sound-Image Film), the review is devoted to the first screening of two "talking films" in Frankfurt on October 11, 1928. Both were by well-known directors: one was an advertising film for radio by Walther Ruttmann, titled *Tönende Welle* (*Sound Wave*, 1928); the other was directed by one of the pioneers of silent film in Germany, Max Mack, whose *Ein Tag Film* (*A Day of Film*, 1928) self-reflexively stages the goings-on in a film studio. Kracauer's review intimates his own incredulity at the technological advance that makes the sound film possible. To him, the filmstrip that records an optical soundtrack under the "Tri-Ergon" patent (later sold to Fox in the US) is nothing short of mysterious. But Kracauer welcomes this mystery with notable openness: "nobody can begin to fathom what sound-image film (*Tonbildfilm*) will mean to us in the future, once the invention has been technically perfected and aesthetically mastered."[86] Kracauer does, however, foresee a direction for that development, which in his assessment tends toward increasing realism, "the complete representation of human reality." But just as he developed criteria for the medium specificity of silent cinema (the emphasis on surfaces, exteriority, mute objects), so does he now intimate a use of sound that corresponds to the possibilities of cinema and distinguishes it from theater. The most important sonic developments, he holds, will not involve spoken language; rather, "the possibilities of sound film lie much more in the representation and shaping of a reality that has never been perceived by any previous means, a reality to which the stage has not yet been able to give voice." As in the later *All Quiet* review, Kracauer here already thinks of the brute sounds of human activity—if not on the battlefield, then in modern metropolitan space. "Sound film will only come into its own when it taps an existence that was unknown prior to its arrival, the sounds and noises around us that had never before communicated with our visual impressions and always escaped our senses." And in keeping with the valorization of urban streets in his silent film criticism, Kracauer again nominates the street as containing this untapped potential. If sound film is able to capture and convey the din (*Getöse*) of the street, it will match the accomplishment that Kracauer had attributed to silent film over the preceding decade: "just as the earlier film technology had the task of rendering the life of light and shadow available to consciousness, so does it fall to the new technical possibilities to redeem the unintended din of the street so that it might intervene in our world." The fortuitous continuum of material existence and its redemption through film—these are motifs that we associate with Kracauer's late work, and with his *Theory of Film* in particular. Here, in a review that marks the transition from silent to sound, we find them articulated in the context of the author's daily practice as a critic attuned to the modernity of the still-developing medium.

Notes

1. All translations by the author, unless otherwise indicated. "Kritik ist schöpferische Kunst (1): Kurt Pinthus," in *Film-Kurier* 229, September 27, 1930.
2. The editor of a lastingly influential anthology of expressionist poetry (*Menschheitsdämmerung* [Berlin: Rowohlt, 1920]), Pinthus also remains well known to scholars of German film as the author of *Das Kino-Buch* (Leipzig, Germany: Kurt Wolff, 1914), an early attempt at establishing a high-minded authors' cinema (*Autorenfilm*). Similarly, Herbert Ihering, who was featured in the fourth installment of the series, is still famous today as one of the leading film and—especially—theater critics of the Weimar Republic. "Kritik ist schöpferische Kunst (4): Herbert Ihering," in *Film-Kurier* 259, November 1, 1930; see also *Herbert Ihering: Filmkritiker* (Munich, Germany: Edition text + kritik, 2011). While Blass died relatively forgotten in 1939, like Pol and Sahl he occupied an important position in the journalistic landscape of the late Weimar Republic. Pol and Sahl, by contrast, went on to fashion fascinating careers in their own right in US exile. Pol managed to escape Nazi Germany via Prague and Paris to New York, where he went on to publish in *The Nation*, the *New York Times*, and elsewhere. Sahl similarly made it to the United States, where he published in the German-Jewish journal *Der Aufbau* and made a career for himself as a poet and foreign correspondent. On his film reviews from the 1920s, see *Hans Sahl: Filmkritiker* (Munich, Germany: Edition text + kritik, 2012); "Kritik ist schöpferische Kunst (2): Ernst Blaß," in *Film-Kurier* 236, October 4, 1930; "Kritik ist schöpferische Kunst (3): Heinz Pol," in *Film-Kurier* 243, October 11, 1930; "Kritik ist schöpferische Kunst (5): Hans Sahl," in *Film-Kurier* 265, November 8, 1930.
3. "Kritik ist schöpferische Kunst (6): Siegfried Kracauer," in *Film-Kurier* 294, December 13, 1930.
4. Although Kracauer's film criticism was more ephemeral at the time than his magisterial contributions to film theory, or even the essayistic writings collected in *The Mass Ornament: Weimar Essays* (ed. and trans. Thomas Y. Levin [Cambridge, MA: Harvard University Press, 1995]), his standing as the Weimar era's leading film critic was recently reconfirmed with the inauguration of a "Siegfried Kracauer Award for Film Criticism," bestowed annually for the best German-language film review. See https://www.vdfk.de/kategorie/siegfried-kracauer-preis-fuer-filmkritik.
5. Kracauer reprises the latter two themes at other points in his career as a critic and theorist, notably in a later piece on "The Task of the Film Critic," published in the *Frankfurter Zeitung* on May 23, 1932. See Anton Kaes, Martin Jay, Edward Dimendberg, eds. *The Weimar Republic Sourcebook* (Berkeley: University of California Press, 1995), 634-635.
6. Kracauer's first review of sound films is dated October 12, 1928, and immediately offers a number of highly intriguing perspectives on the new technology, to which I return at the conclusion of this essay. See his review of *Tönende Welle* (*Sound Wave*; Walther Ruttmann, 1928) and *Ein Tag Film* (*A Day of Film*; Max Mack, 1928), "Tonbildfilm," in Inka Mülder-Bach with Sabine Biebl and Mirjam Wenzel, eds., *Werke* 6.2, (Frankfurt a.M., Germany: Suhrkamp, 2004), 122–125.

7. "There is as yet no aesthetics of film," Kracauer notes in a 1925 article, "Schünzel als dummer Hans" (review of *Dear Hahn im Korb* [*The Rooster in the Basket*; Georg Jacoby, 1925]) in *Werke* 6.1, 170. It is worth noting that, at the time Kracauer made this claim, Béla Balàzs had already published, if not an "aesthetics of film," then at least an influential set of theoretical reflections on the medium; however, Kracauer would not review Balàzs's *Der sichtbare Mensch* (*Visible Man*) until two years later. See "Bücher vom Film" (Books on Film) in *Werke* 6.1, 370–374. In addition, efforts at theorizing the new medium were well under way in other national and linguistic contexts, of course. In the Anglophone world, Vachel Lindsay's *The Art of the Moving Picture* (1915) and Hugo Münsterberg's *The Photoplay* (1916) are generally considered to have laid the groundwork for the development of film theory.
8. "Wetter und Retter" (review of *Die närrische Wette des Lord Aldini* [Luigi Romano, 1923] and *Jimmy Aubrey als Beschützer der Unschuld* [orig. title/date unknown]), in *Werke* 6.1, 43–44.
9. Miriam Hansen, *Cinema and Experience: Siegfried Kracauer, Walter Benjamin, Theodor W. Adorno* (Berkeley: University of California Press, 2012), 5.
10. On the relation between Kracauer's novels and his film theory, see Johannes von Moltke, "Theory of the Novel: The Literary Imagination of Classical Film Theory," *October* 144 (Spring 2013): 49-72.
11. David Bordwell, *The Rhapsodes: How 1940s Critics Changed American Film Culture* (Chicago, IL: University of Chicago Press, 2016), 1; Phillip Lopate, *American Movie Critics: An Anthology from the Silents until Now* (New York: Library of America, 2006), xxiii.
12. Hansen similarly points out that Kracauer's reviews from the 1920s—especially of literary or theatrical adaptations, mythological or historical spectacles, and "society films"—are written "in the key of ironically amused to caustic critique." Hansen, *Cinema and Experience*, 13.
13. See James Agee, *Agee on Film: Criticism and Comment on the Movies* (New York: McDowell/Obolensky, 1958); various collections of Pauline Kael's reviews (as, for example, *I Lost It at the Movies* [Boston, MA: Little and Brown, 1965]); Rudolf Arnheim, *Film Essays and Criticism* (Madison: University of Wisconsin Press, 1997); Herbert Ihering, *Herbert Ihering: Filmkritiker*. It is worth pointing out that the volumes of Kracauer's film criticism stand apart from such anthologies (some of them published by the authors themselves during their lifetimes) in terms of comprehensiveness and the accompanying critical apparatus.
14. For a comparatively late and already highly reflexive contribution to this trend, see Noah Isenberg, ed., *Weimar Cinema: An Essential Guide to Classic Films of the Era* (New York: Columbia University Press, 2009). For a collection of essays exemplifying the many revisions and differentiations now under way, see Christian Rogowski, ed., *The Many Faces of Weimar Cinema: Rediscovering Germany's Filmic Legacy* (Rochester, NY: Camden House, 2010).
15. "Der Bettelstudent" (review of *Der Bettelstudent* [*The Pauper Student*; Jakob and Luise Fleck, 1927]), *Werke* 6.2, 11.
16. Kracauer, "The Little Shopgirls Go To the Movies," *The Mass Ornament*, 294.
17. "Die Bräutigame der Babette Bomberling" (review of *Die Bräutigame der Babette Bomberling* [*The Husbands of Babette Bomberling*; Victor Janson, 1927]), *Werke* 6.1, 327.
18. "Die Veilchen der Kaiserin" (review of *Violettes Impériales* [*Imperial Violets*; Henry Roussell, 1923]), *Werke* 6.1, 176.

19. Lopate, *American Movie Critics*, xxi.
20. "Tom Mix" (review of *Teeth*; John Blystone, 1924), *Werke* 6.1, 189.
21. "Das Liebesleben einer Tänzerin" (review of *Das Spielzeug von Paris*), *Werke* 6.1, 172.
22. Theodor W. Adorno, "The Curious Realist," in *New German Critique* 54 (Autumn 1991): 168.
23. On the changing definitions of the masses during the Weimar Republic, see Stefan Johnsson, *Crowds and Democracy: The Idea and Image of the Masses from Revolution to Fascism* (New York: Columbia University Press, 2013).
24. "Bücher vom Film," 371.
25. "Großfilm 'Danton'" (review of *Danton*), *Werke* 6.1, 11.
26. Kracauer, *From Caligari to Hitler: A Psychological History of the German Film* (Princeton, NJ: Princeton University Press, 2004), 54.
27. Johnsson, *Crowds and Democracy*, 156.
28. Kracauer, "The Cult of Distraction," in *The Mass Ornament*, 326.
29. Ibid.
30. "Volk in Not" (review of *Volk in Not* [*A People in Distress*; Wolfgang Neff, 1925]), *Werke* 6.1, 272.
31. Kracauer, *From Caligari to Hitler*, 19.
32. On the relation of *From Caligari to Hitler* to Kracauer's earlier writings, see Leonardo Quaresima, "Introduction," in Kracauer, *From Caligari to Hitler*.
33. Kracauer, "The Mass Ornament," in *The Mass Ornament*, 86.
34. "Wir schaffens" (review of *Berlin, Die Sinfonie der Großstadt*), *Werke* 6.1, 411.
35. Hansen, *Cinema and Experience*, 9–11.
36. "The fact that films as a whole reaffirm the ruling system was demonstrated by the excitement over *Potemkin*. It was perceived to be different and was aesthetically endorsed, but only for its meaning to be repressed." Kracauer, "The Little Shopgirls," 291.
37. In a note on a Fatty Arbuckle film, "an amusing bit of nonsense, *filmgerecht* and improbable from start to finish." "Der Kaufmann von Venedig" (review of *Der Kaufmann von Venedig* [*The Merchant of Venice*; Peter Paul Felner, 1923]), *Werke* 6.1, 39.
38. "Die große Unbekannte [Teil II]" (review of *Die große Unbekannte*), *Werke* 6.1, 69.
39. "Chaplin" (review of *The Gold Rush*), *Werke* 6.1, 269–270. In an earlier review, referring to John G. Blystone's *The Huntsman* (1920), Kracauer had already averred that "traits of the fairy tale are contained in all of these grotesques." "Aus der Inflationszeit" (review of *Der Bankkrach unter den Linden* [*The Bank Crash of Unter den Linden*; Paul Merzbach, 1925]), *Werke* 6.1, 190.
40. "Chaplin," 269.
41. Ibid.
42. Ibid., 270.
43. "Ein Film" (Review of *Die Straße*), in *Werke* 6.1, 56.
44. Ibid., 57.
45. Hansen, *Cinema and Experience*, 9.
46. "Wetter und Retter," 43.
47. "Die Jupiterlampen brennen weiter: Zur Frankfurter Aufführung des Potemkin-Films" (review of *Battleship Potemkin*), *Werke* 6.1, 235.
48. Ibid., 236.
49. Ibid.

50. Ibid., 235.
51. "U. T.-Lichtspiele" (review of *Die grüne Manuela* [*Green Manuela*; E. A. Dupont, 1923]), *Werke* 6.1, 34.
52. "Der Kaufmann von Venedig," 38.
53. Ibid.
54. "Die Kulturfilmgemeinde Frankfurt," *Werke* 6.1, 179–182.
55. "Calico-World," *Mass Ornament*, 287.
56. "Die Jagd nach dem Glück" (review of *Die Jagd nach dem Glück* [*Chasing Happiness*; Rochus Gliese, 1930]), *Werke* 6.2, 363.
57. Hansen, by contrast, reads this spectatorial disposition backward in time, seeing in it traits of "a pre-classical moviegoer" invested in an aesthetics of astonishment rather than of narrative continuity. See Hansen, *Cinema and Experience*, 15.
58. "Der Mythos im Großfilm" (Review of *Helena*; Manfred Noa, 1923/24), *Werke* 6.1, 80.
59. "Niddy Impekoven im Film" (review of *Armes kleines Mädchen* [*Poor Little Girl*; Ulrich Kayser, 1924]), *Werke* 6.1, 104.
60. "Ein Seefilm" (review of *Eld Ombord* [*Fire on Board*; Victor Sjöström, 1922/23]), *Werke* 6.1, 187.
61. "Eine Film-Vexierposse" (review of *Seine Frau, die Unbekannte* [*His Unknown Bride*; Benjamin Christiansen, 1923]); Kracauer's reference here is to one of the Hallroom Boys shorts distributed in German under the title *Fix und Fax als Luftschiffer* (possibly *High Flyers*; Alfred Stanell, 1922), *Werke* 6.1, 40.
62. "Buster Keaton im Krieg" (review of *The General*; Buster Keaton and Clyde Bruckman, 1926), *Werke* 6.1, 340.
63. "Bücher vom Film," 371.
64. "Ägypten im Film" (review of *The Desert Sheik*; Tom Terriss, 1924), *Werke* 6.1, 91.
65. "Der Schachspieler" (review of *Le joueur d'échecs*), *Werke* 6.1, 285–286.
66. Ibid., 286.
67. "The Little Shopgirls," 293.
68. "Ein Zirkusfilm" (review of *Manege*; Max Reichmann, 1927), *Werke* 6.2, 15; "Film 1928," *The Mass Ornament*, 151.
69. "Oh du himmelblauer See..." (review of *Das lockende Ziel*), *Werke* 6.2, 352.
70. Ibid., 353.
71. "Berliner Notizen" (review of *Der Walzerkönig* [*The Waltz King*; Manfred Noa, 1930] and *Flight* [Frank Capra, 1929]), *Werke* 6.2, 356.
72. "Ladenmädchen spielen Kino" (review of *My Best Girl* [Sam Taylor, 1927]), *Werke* 6.2, 20.
73. "Der verlorene Schuh" (review of *Der verlorene Schuh*), *Werke* 6.1, 52.
74. "Calico-World," 283.
75. Ibid., 281.
76. "Der Napoleon-Film" (review of *Napoleon*; Abel Gance, 1927), *Werke* 6.1, 420; "Osterspaziergang auf der Leinwand" (Easter Walk on Screen), *Werke* 6.1, 223.
77. "Ein Zirkusfilm" (review of *Der Dumme August des Zirkus Romanelli* [*The Fool in the Romanelli Circus*; Georg Jacoby, 1926]), *Werke* 6.1, 260.
78. "Im goldenen Liebeskäfig" (review of *Der Liebeskäfig*), *Werke* 6.1, 216.
79. "Die Spielerin" (review of *Die Spielerin* [*The Player*; Graham Cutts, 1927]), *Werke* 6.1, 415.
80. "Calico-World," 287.
81. "Chaplin," 269.

82. This is arguably the constellation Hansen has in mind when she refers to film as the "medium of a disintegrating world" in *Cinema and Experience*, 3–39.
83. "Im Westen nichts Neues" (review of *All Quiet on the Western Front*; Lewis Milestone, 1930), *Werke* 6.2, 428.
84. Ibid., 427.
85. Ibid., 428.
86. This and all remaining quotes from "Tonbildfilm," 124.

CHAPTER 31

THE DECLINE OF MIDDLEBROW TASTE IN CELEBRITY CULTURE

The First Fan Magazines

SUMIKO HIGASHI

Selling Middlebrow Culture: Stewardship

When Florence Turner, the Vitagraph Girl, was mobbed by crowds during a personal appearance in Jersey City in 1910, her popularity registered more than brisk box-office business.[1] Writing about the emergence of such personalities, Warren Susman argues that "somewhere in the middle of the first decade of the twentieth century, there rapidly developed another vision of self [. . .] and an awareness of significant change in the social order."[2] Among the forces effecting this transformation were modern personalities displacing Protestant character, middlebrow taste signifying proper social class, and the leisure industry thriving under consumer capitalism. As cheap amusement, the movies attracted immigrant workers as well as the proletarianized lower middle class. Aspiring girls and women earning scant wages were enthralled with personalities like Florence Turner, who used a chafing dish at her table and claimed kinship with British painter J. M. W. Turner. Capitalizing on such class dynamics, J. Stuart Blackton, an entrepreneur who co-founded Vitagraph in Brooklyn (1897), legitimized movies as middlebrow culture. As a matter of fact, he exploited well-known classics to validate a "novelty amusement" by marketing it as an accessible, but reputable, product. Adaptations of *Treasure Island* (1908), *Romeo and Juliet* (1908), and *Francesca da Rimini* (1910), as well as historical films like *The Life of Moses* (1909) and *Becket* (1910), enhanced the studio's reputation.[3] As an entrepreneur, however, Blackton founded a magazine that unwittingly illustrated the ease with which middlebrow taste—itself a product of commerce—could be debased in a modern celebrity culture.[4] Within a short period of time, an emphasis on film as an uplifting literary narrative gave way to publicity about glamorous stars and lifestyles. *Motion Picture Story Magazine* (*MPSM*), which began in February 1911, was retitled *Motion Picture Magazine* (*MPM*) in March 1914.[5] The elimination of the word "story" from its moniker signified vast differences in the social class and cultural consumption of its readers; that is to say, lower-class females focused on stargazing were more dynamic fans than middle-class subscribers intent on proper self-making.

Blackton, a former lecturer who showed film on the Lyceum circuit of churches, schools, and clubs, was among the middlebrow entrepreneurs displacing the Brahmin elect as cultural stewards.[6] Such a transition exemplifies what Janice Radway, following Pierre Bourdieu, labels as "class fracture" among an elite with conflicting responses to a standardized mass market.[7] Commodore, as he was called after hobnobbing with Oyster Bay patricians, was a social climber who rewrote his English patrimony to include Eton credentials. The *Blue Book Magazine* labeled him "A New Belasco," as he claimed that "the successful pictures of the future will come from the pens of the great playwrights and authors." And the players, he added, "must be actors with stage experience, having personality" as well as refinement.[8] Vitagraph represented the highest standards in the US—at least until D. W. Griffith's tenure at Biograph—and was even better known in Europe.[9] As members of the monopolistic Motion Picture Patents Company (MPPC), a trust formed in 1908, both studios achieved excellence.

Attempting to gain publicity as well as legitimacy, Blackton was as innovative a publisher as he was a filmmaker when he printed storyized versions of MPPC films in *MPSM*. Such a recycling of narrative in a magazine addressed to an aspiring audience, rather than circulating in-house, yielded additional revenue. A storyization by a bestselling author, moreover, could improve a mediocre or even a poor film release.[10] While translating film into literary narrative, Blackton was also promoting visual culture in a consumer society enthralled with spectacle. As sacrosanct Arnoldian high culture—"the best that has been thought and said"—was being debased in a market economy, he asserted that "moving pictures are the books of the masses." Despite claims that *MPSM* could "stand alone on the quality of its art and literature," early issues exemplified middlebrow taste: literary adaptations; biblical, historical, and frontier themes; biographies of well-known figures; sentimental domestic melodramas; Middle Eastern and Oriental exoticism; and occasional comedies.[11] Poetry was inserted between storyizations. As for the personalities, their photos appeared in a "Gallery of Picture Players" in the front, but unlike coverage in *Photoplay*, which promoted performers in its earliest issues, publicity about them was scant. Cast lists of the films in which they appeared were infrequent.

What was the nature of the middlebrow reading experience during these transformative years in the Progressive Era? And why was literature published for educated consumers so easily debased in modern celebrity culture? Around the turn of the century, as Christopher Wilson argues, middlebrow magazines like the *Saturday Evening Post* and *Ladies' Home Journal*, unlike highbrow *Harper's*, *Scribner's*, and the *Atlantic*, ceased to address "the gentle reader" and transformed reading so that it was no longer an "inner and contemplative" process. Rather, mass-market publications naturalized a realistic, but illusory, world reinforcing vicarious experience and a prefabricated response. An appealing consumer rhetoric that had saturated a sales economy now pervaded representations of the public and private spheres for middle- and lower-class readers.[12] Signifying this marketing strategy was Norman Rockwell's illustration of folksy American life on *Saturday Evening Post* covers; the first appeared in 1916. Such appeals to middlebrow taste, essentially anti-intellectual, suited *MPSM* because it recycled film narrative as plot summaries in sentimental prose and poetic stanzas. Storyizations would not interest the most literate readers, but they stimulated reading and filmgoing as related forms of moviegoing consumption. And as part of a marketplace with interpenetrating levels of taste, they reproduced canonical texts while denoting the higher exchange value of middlebrow products. Film adaptations enhanced interest in Scott, Dickens, Thackeray, and Stevenson, as well as Shakespeare and Dante, but readers turned to "Chambers, Glynn, McGrath, and the rest" for contemporary works. A full-page ad for an annual *MPSM* subscription, costing $1.50, showcased "celebrated writers" like Rex Beach, Montanye Perry, and Will Carleton, who legitimized movies with storyized versions. Beach was the bestselling author of *The Spoilers* (1906), a novel about the Alaskan frontier that was recycled in stage and screen versions.[13] Authors like him who wrote for middlebrow magazines that privileged gossip columns, celebrity profiles, practical advice, popular science, and timely stories appealed to passive and voyeuristic readers. Within such a context, the publication of the first fan magazines signified that the line between middlebrow and lowbrow culture could indeed be tenuous. *MPSM* was more literary than *Photoplay*, a humbler rival founded six months later in Chicago to advertise independent exchanges and players, but in less than three years after it became *MPM*, it compromised its mission of validating narrative in favor of stargazing for its female readers.

A close reading of the July 1911 issue of *MPSM* characterizes Blackton's stewardship in cultivating a middlebrow sensibility among readers. An ad, the cover reproduces a long shot of actors as American cavalry and Mexicans on the Texas border in the Méliès production *The Honor of the Flag*. Underneath are the lines: "STORIES FROM THE WORLD'S BEST PHOTOPLAYS, BEAUTIFULLY ILLUSTRATED TO CHARM[,] INSTRUCT AND ENTERTAIN." All magazine covers copied trade paper *Moving Picture World* (*MPW*) by showing dramatic scenes of a film that was not initially storyized in the contents in an intertextual relay promoting releases. *MPSM* was dependent on MPPC manufacturers, as they were called, to provide movies and stills for storyizations. The "Gallery of Picture Players," which displayed eleven photos of stars, including Florence Turner, was followed by seventeen "Photoplay Stories" of film releases, four "Poems," and six "Special Articles." D. W. Griffith's storyized film "Enoch Arden" would be best known today, but the director and players, unlike the author Montanye Perry and an attribution to Tennyson's poem, went unmentioned. The educational and commercial value of literary narrative was unquestioned. Storyizations followed middlebrow conventions and exemplified dense plots often set in exotic locales and historical periods, well-delineated characters, and moralistic closure.

A Pathé Frères melodrama about the genteel middle class titled "The Stepsisters," for example, was storyized by Louis Reeves Harrison, later a writer for *MPW*. Advertised in *MPSM*'s back pages, this trade paper had published brief profiles of "Picture Personalities" and artless plot synopses that the fan magazine translated into literary storyizations. Written in purple sentimental prose to heighten emotional and moral fervor, the storyization of "The Stepsisters" was meant to appeal to female readers.[14] A scheming fortune hunter named Sophie provides for herself and her daughter by marrying an upstanding widower who has a daughter of his own. As Harrison moralizes:

> Idleness is woman's curse. The desire [. . .] to lay all the burden of disagreeable or enforced work upon men, lies deep in the nature of woman. Having the means [. . .] of using money only for self-indulgence, she [. . .] will vent whatever is meanly critical or otherwise odious in her nature upon the man [. . .] denying himself to make her happy.[15]

Upon her husband's death, Sophie learns that his estate has been bankrupted, but his loving daughter, unlike her own, anticipates marriage to an earnest and prosperous young man. What female fan would not have been pleased by such a resolution? Also storyized in the issue were a few non-fiction Essanay films like "Wild Animals in Captivity" and "Life at Hull House/Chicago's Melting Pot." An editor commended the latter for "demonstrating the best methods of converting large numbers of foreign people into useful American citizens." Such non-fiction, which was not storyized for very long, was included in the early issues to affirm the educational value of film. As a way to solicit input regarding such storyizations, a "Cash Prize Contest" offered eighty-five prizes totaling $250 to readers expressing their preferences. At first addressing literate subscribers, the staff, seemingly unaware of lower levels of literacy among moviegoers, later announced that writing and spelling were unimportant and that thousands from all walks of life had posted letters. Women, interestingly, outnumbered men by two to one.[16]

As this close reading shows, *MPSM* and later *MPM* under Blackton and his managing editor Eugene V. Brewster, a Princeton graduate, articulated a Progressive ethos undergirded by Protestant morality for urban masses. Assimilating unprecedented immigration from southern and eastern Europe was a troublesome issue. A series of melodramas sponsored by civic organizations to warn immigrant girls at Ellis Island about prostitution and white slavery was commended. But a contest titled "What Improvement in Motion Pictures Is Needed Most?" had prompted a reader to protest that he had had "more than enough of the morbid drama dealing with the sex problem and the human fiend."[17] Readers usually wrote to demand more authenticity and realism. *The Battle Cry of Peace* (1915), an eight-part serial written and produced by Blackton himself, was exemplary in preaching pacifism while warfare ravaged the Old World. A storyized version was serialized not only in *MPM* but also in *Motion Picture Supplement*, a spin-off that was advertised in September 1915 and retitled *Motion Picture Classic* at the end of the year. Circulation for its third issue reached 205,000, a figure yet to rival *MPM* at 292,000 in mid-year. Any reader following the melodrama would have had to purchase both magazines.[18] An example of lower-middlebrow taste, the story was written in a florid sentimental style and demonized rapacious Germans:

> How kind, how wise the Creator when, with all the blessings of memory and knowledge with which human beings were endowed, He, in His infinite wisdom, withheld from them the power to . . . solve the question of even tomorrow! How merciful that big, generous, tender-hearted John . . . could not *know* the abyss of terror which yawned at the feet of those he loved best in all the world![19]

Constituting the abyss was an invasion of barbaric Huns who had crossed the Atlantic to besiege Manhattan and threaten American womanhood. Among those enthused about an overwrought portrayal fueling debate about pacifism and American entry into the war—foreign policy issues dividing Progressive reformers—was former president Theodore Roosevelt, a bellicose internationalist.

Consistent with a middlebrow mission, *MPSM* and *MPM* constructed film as a legitimate art with a social function that advanced the Progressive agenda. Announcing that fifteen million persons attended the movies daily, an editorial touted the benefit of exposure to "travel, enlightenment, instruction and moral lessons, combined with entertainment." Robert Grau, a frequent contributor until his death a few years later, aptly titled his book *Theatre of Science: A Volume of Progress and Achievement in the Motion Picture* (1914). Another writer predicted that the unwieldy term "motion picture" would be replaced by the colloquialism "movies." Censorship was a frequently discussed controversial issue. Reverend William Sheafe Chase asserted that the "moral and psychological" well-being of children required a watchdog. But Frank Dyer, president of General Film Company, countered that manufacturers would make "decent and elevating films" to ensure profit. A monthly department written in a superior tone, "Musings of 'The Photoplay Philosopher'" argued that censorship would prohibit viewing Shakespeare and other classics but later criticized "a mania for unrefined sensationalism."[20] Articles about film production were informative and showed photographs of location shooting at dangerous sites and on battlefields. And reports spotlighted movie studios like Essanay and Lubin and personalities like Thomas H. Ince and "Southern gentleman" D. W. Griffith. Brewster himself wrote articles about Thomas A. Edison and the origin of motion pictures, the evolution of pictorial art leading to the magic lantern, and a series about emotions, facial expressions, and film acting.[21] *MPSM* and *MPM*, in sum, represented middlebrow discourse grounded in Progressive Era issues, didacticism, and moral values. But "Musings of 'The Photoplay Philosopher,'" surely a custodial voice, was discontinued about a year after the magazine's moniker was changed, and reports about the industry declined in favor of publicity about the stars for female readers.

Among the most blatant stereotyped expressions of Progressive Era social hierarchy and cultural stewardship were the cartoons depicting class, ethnicity, and race.[22] A drawing of an urban neighborhood in September 1912 showed a church, movie theater, school, office, and factory to emphasize the influence of the film industry on local institutions. Another pictured a respectable couple with children entering a theater next to a dingy saloon. The caption read, "A practical solution to the liquor problem." Drawings illustrating "The Two Signs," a poem about the saloon and photoplay, juxtaposed crime and jail against family, religion, and patriotism. "A Safe and Sane Fourth of July" was the caption of a cartoon that depicted well-dressed patrons, including a veteran with medals pinned to his chest, watching a filmed parade. And an ad in the February 1913 issue announced that a "Happy Wife" would share a remedy that had curbed her husband's drinking.[23] At the time, class, ethnicity, and religion were conflated in constructing industrial workers, especially the Irish and Italians, as the urban Other. As Roy Rosenzweig argues regarding such class dynamics, the white native-born Protestant upper and middle classes waged temperance campaigns to reform raucous workers expressing their virility in rum shops.[24] Working-class wives, on the other hand, seldom enjoyed such leisure.

Aside from characterizing manual workers as degenerate drunks, cartoons also represented race relations. A few perpetuated racist stereotypes of cannibalistic Africans and squinting pigtailed Chinese. Such caricatures were intertextually related to storyizations with subservient or suspicious characters labeled Japs and Chinamen who could not speak grammatical English. Racist characterizations in the movies had, in fact, prompted a contest entrant to suggest that Westerns show fewer "massacres of Indians by superhuman cowboys."[25] A decade later, the social structure privileging whiteness was buttressed by the Immigration Act (1924), which established quota systems based on country of origin and excluded racialized Asians. Divided by race, ethnicity, and religion, the lower classes nevertheless proved resistant to Progressive Era reformers. Although movie theaters eventually displaced saloons and mixed-sex leisure became more common, lower-class reception of middlebrow culture as a model for self-making was unremarkable. Still, the Americanization of masses of spectators, especially females, through stargazing as a site of products and performance was an affirmation of middle-class values.[26] Consumption, an essential practice in the formation and social reproduction of an old propertied middle class, became vital for individuals affirming their personal identities and social status in urban America.

Despite a growing fan base that was indifferent to middlebrow taste, *MPSM* and *MPM*, unlike *Photoplay*, held frequent and varied contests to solicit reader input. As opposed to cartoons depicting unequal class, ethnic, and race relations, contests expressed gender identification insofar as working-class females had become vocal starstruck fans.[27] Girls and women were enthusiastic in following the players and seizing opportunities to single out their favorites and articulate opinions. As consumers of cheap newspaper serials and dime-novel fiction, they explained their votes for the best storyizations in a series of contests. A Colorado entrant did select the "beautiful story of Esther" as a poetic film that acquainted the reader with "a masterpiece of literature," but she was an exception. Winning contestants among the top five chose "A Republican Marriage," a titillating romance by Montanye Perry about a muscular blacksmith who goes to the guillotine with a noblewoman loved from afar. *MPSM* continued to address literate readers with contests like "The Great Mystery Play" that required them to decode a scenario about a missing diamond and study motives to identify culprits. Among the judges representing the "world's best thought and action"—a phrase recalling Arnoldian high culture—were Blackton, Brewster, and *MPW* writer Epes Winthrop Sargent.[28] But a "Popular Player Contest" that focused on the stars was conducted with such hoopla that monthly tallies were posted opposite ads on the back pages. Contestants, who were at first fixated on romantic male leads, expressed their appreciation in prose or verse:

> There is one to whom I would give first prize,
> It is he with such expressive eyes,
> Whose every movement is full of grace,
> And the pleasant smile upon his face
> Holds all spellbound who come to see
> The prince of actors, Francis X. B.[29]

Appearing in the July 1912 issue were the photos of five winning players who had collectively garnered 1.5 million votes: Maurice Costello, E. Delores Cassinelli, Mae Hotely, Francis X. Bushman, and Gilbert M. Anderson.[30] Cassinelli was an attractive woman who could be cast in glamorous roles, but Hotely was a middle-aged character actress. All the male winners, on the other hand, were typecast as romantic personalities.

A second "Popular Player Contest" asked readers to vote separately for a male and a female personality. As the contest drew to a close in late 1913, *MPSM* updated tallies for 250 players and claimed that clerks counting "cart-loads of ballots" would occupy the entire second floor. Seven million votes were cast! Allowing for readers repeatedly sending in coupons worth ten votes, this result was still a whopping number. Significantly, all the winners were actors playing romantic male leads: Romaine Fielding, Earle Williams, J. Warren Kerrigan, Carlyle Blackwell, Francis X. Bushman, G. M. Anderson, and Arthur Johnson. Among the female stars, only Alice Joyce and Muriel Ostriche scored impressive numbers. *MPSM* reported that many players were at a disadvantage because they were unknown while others benefited from advertising. Some manufacturers were ambivalent about publicity and remained impervious to the economics of an emerging star system. The continuing popularity of male, as opposed to female, personalities was notable. According to *MPSM*, male actors who portrayed a "heroic lover, or brave soldier, or gallant prince" were more beloved than those cast in "thankless parts" as villains or comics.[31] Clearly, women and girls were enthralled with masculine heroics rather than identified with feminine stars embodying a beauty culture—an ambivalent form of bisexuality that would soon be rendered conventional in a consumer culture. Although dime novels signified the powerlessness of women in patriarchal households untouched by gentility, lower-class females also read serialized fiction stressing physicality and violence that, unlike genteel literature, translated into cinematic cliffhangers. Stars like Pearl White, who played daredevil heroines in sex-role reversals, were among the first to win loyal female fans and endorse fetishized goods like diamond jewelry.[32] She embodied both masculine aggression and feminized consumption. As strong independent women with agency, lower-class heroines like White became dazzling modern personalities. After the war, the so-called New Woman, whose boyish silhouette dictated a revolution in fashion, would embody a more willful upper-class femininity based on performance and products.

Attempting to offset the voice of female fans in popularity contests with a more thoughtful competition that required brainstorming, *MPM* launched a challenge titled "What Improvement in Motion Pictures Is Needed Most?" Such a contest did elicit more response from men rather than women, by a margin of two to one. The winning male contestant expressed middlebrow values by advocating "a higher standard of literary and dramatic taste for both the scenario writer and the producer." Directors in the evolving central producer system were not considered as important as writers in legitimizing film as art. A "Great Artist Contest" was run concurrently with a screenwriting competition so that literate fans could not only vote for their favorites but also write parts for them in a one- or two-reeler. A galaxy of rising stars in feature films, however, was becoming the main attraction. Asked to vote for "distinguished" players "in specific roles," readers chose Earle Williams in *The Christian* (1914) over Henry Walthall in *The Birth of a Nation* (1915). Among the female players, voluptuous soprano Geraldine Farrar in *Carmen* (1915) polled slightly ahead of petite ingenues Marguerite Clark in *Wildflower* (1914) and Mary Pickford in the first *Tess of the Storm Country* (1914). Another "Popular Player Contest" in 1917 was significant because "Little Mary" triumphed over heartthrob Francis X. Bushman when separate votes were no longer cast for a male and a female personality.[33] An astonishing success, Pickford signified the ascent of female stars as ingenues in feature films rather than as daredevils in cliffhanger serials. Maurice Costello, who won the first "Popular Player Contest" in 1912, was also adored by female fans clamoring for details about his personal life, but he failed to make the transition from one-reelers to features.[34]

As shown by their response to numerous contests, starstruck girls and women did influence both the magazine and film industry. The emerging star system, however, was not only a response to their clamorous reception but also the result of distribution and exhibition changes leading to standardized features. According to Eileen Bowser, among the top exchanges, General Film and Mutual distributed 295 one- and two-reelers, compared to Paramount's twenty feature films and Alliance's nine, in December 1914. As *MPSM* announced early in that year, the fans themselves voted in favor of shorts over features by 2,053 to 1,572. Unquestionably, fan magazines were influential in the promotion of film releases by circulating storyized versions. Although *MPM* published approximately 160 storyizations from 1915 to 1917, only 40 percent were about features. *Photoplay*'s tally for the same period, however, was significantly higher at 59 percent and presaged the future. The MPPC and its distributor General Film Company, whose products *MPSM* and *MPM* initially advertised, were more invested in short programs.[35] Debate in the trade papers affirmed that William N. Selig and Carl Laemmle still preferred shorts, but Alex E. Beyfuss of the California Motion Picture Association predicted a trend toward multi-reel films. A most significant merger, therefore, was the formation of Famous Players-Lasky, with Paramount as distributor, in a "$12,500,000 Combine" in 1916.[36]

As features became more technically advanced in a streamlined industry, the decline of literary narrative as an index of middlebrow culture occurred in proportion to the rise of stars. *MPM* published only four storyizations, including Cecil B. DeMille's *Joan the Woman*, a Progressive Era historical pageant with Geraldine Farrar, in December 1916. But the issue included full-page photos of Farrar, Mary Miles Minter, and Valeska Suratt, as well as Chawlie [sic] Chaplin cartoons and a Fay Tincher paper-doll cutout. Myrtle Stedman was shown wearing appropriate fashion on the golf course, and Nona Thomas shared a recipe for cream and maraschino chocolates. Stars like Cleo Madison, Douglas Fairbanks, Olga Grey, Louise Fazenda, Francis X. Bushman, and Anita King were also publicized, while Mabel Normand was shown adding a feminine touch to her new studio.[37] Such a complete reversal of the magazine's middlebrow mission—not to mention Blackton's departure from Vitagraph in 1917—signified the ascendance of popular culture expressing the taste of female readers. A six-month series titled "Breaking into the Movies in California" began in the next issue to assure adulatory fans that they too could reach for the stars.

SELLING FEMALE STARS: CONSUMPTION

Any consideration of *MPM* evolving into a fan magazine that followed trends set by *Photoplay*, which was initially cheaper, slapdash, and lowbrow, requires a close reading of changes in players' publicity. At first notices were scant. The first issue of *MPSM* briefly acknowledged Miss Clara Williams, a horsewoman in "plays of the West"; Lottie Briscoe, an actress known for her "pleasing personality"; and Maurice Costello, a "genius" in Vitagraph's *A Tale of Two Cities* (1911).[38] The "Gallery of Picture Players" began to include colored inserts of popular stars like Costello in issues for subscribers only. "Answers to Inquiries," which began as three pages in August 1911, was retitled several times and became the largest department, as inquisitive fans mailed an avalanche of queries. Capitalizing on high volume, the editors alternated a page of answers with a page of ads and thus constructed an intertext promoting consumerism. (Ad stripping, the practice of stacking numerous ads for cheap products on the back pages where stories ended, was not initiated until 1914.) "Chats with the Players" began as portraits of Miss Florence Lawrence and Mr. John E. Halliday at Lubin in December 1911 and was subsequently expanded. Anticipating gossip columns, "Greenroom Jottings: Little Whispers from Everyone in Playerdom" appeared in July 1912 to report that Miss Lottie Pickford was joining the Kalem Company. Publicity was increased in a retitled *MPM* in October 1914 with "Brief Biographies of Popular Players" and "How I Became a Photoplayer" (later "How I Got In"), as well as lengthier interviews with Alice Joyce and Harold Lockwood. Such notices, however, remained secondary to the storyizations and appeared, like the articles about the industry, in the middle or back of the magazine.

Stars on *MPSM* and *MPM* covers that enhanced spectator identification were among the most visible signs of their ascent, but in contrast to *Photoplay*'s practice, they appeared rather gradually. A few portraits of female players like Alice Joyce and Anna Nilsson began to replace movie still covers even before *MPSM* became *MPM*. As Charlie Keil argues, photographs were essential in differentiating stars from their screen roles and establishing them as bankable personalities.[39] But cover portraits of players like Mary Pickford and Ruth Stonehouse did not appear regularly until the end of 1914. As a matter of fact, *MPM* continued to exemplify middlebrow culture by reproducing oil paintings on three successive covers in that year and offered signed copies for twenty-five cents. Art appealing to the middle-class tourist gaze included scenes of a ship on the high seas and a street in exotic Mexico. The clipper on the July cover was part of an intertexual relay that included a poem titled "The Pirates," storyizations of "Cast Adrift in the South Seas" and "Neptune's Daughter," starring swimmer Annette Kellerman, and an ad for a sixty-dollar cruise.[40] As part of the social reproduction of the old propertied middle class, travel to sites like Cairo and Pompeii was not only exotic but educational. A painting of a demure French country girl holding a daisy on *MPM*'s August cover, however, could not compete with *Photoplay* displaying Florence La Badie wearing a short bathing costume and dipping a shapely leg at the seashore. After promoting middlebrow art, *MPM* resumed its practice of displaying stars as alluring cover commodities. But unlike *Photoplay*, which rarely accorded male personalities the limelight, its roster included Charlie Chaplin, Romaine Fielding, William S. Hart, Carlyle Blackwell, Harold Lockwood, and Wallace Reid. As a publication unfettered by middlebrow values, *Photoplay* was quicker to capitalize on the demographics of female fans identifying with commodified stars and buying fetishized goods. The seductive picture of Florence La Badie at the beach was reproduced on the back cover of its September issue to advertise a pink complexion soap.[41]

Signifying the ascent of glamorous female personalities and a corresponding decline in middlebrow storyizations were changes in the table of contents. Separate sections with title listings had been identifiably fiction or non-fiction. "Photoplay Stories" or storyizations, as opposed to "Special Articles and Departments" about the industry, remained privileged in the front of the magazine. A few months after *MPSM* became *MPM*, however, all the titles in the July 1914 issue were listed under the single heading "Photoplay Stories and Special Articles." *MPM* proved more innovative in this respect than *Photoplay*, which did not construct its entire content as a single promotional intertext until February 1915. But such intertextuality must have confused readers, accustomed to fiction and non-fiction sections, because descriptive lines were added under the titles in subsequent issues. A brief reversion to separate headings occurred in 1916, but not for long. The "Gallery of Photoplayers," a section that had always appeared first in the table of contents to identify portraits of stars on succeeding pages, was next merged with all the storyizations and articles. Snappy pieces like "Favorite Recipes of Favorite Players" and "Edna Mayor's Latest Gowns" began to appear in the front–a practice begun by *Photoplay*. Shorter storyizations, reduced to a half dozen, were now interspersed among publicity stories, articles, monthly departments, ads, and ad stripping. Such intertextuality created an advertising bonanza made possible by the construction of a dream world essential to the marketing of goods. A portal to the stars,

MPM provided fans lacking economic and cultural capital with compensatory experience in the form of publicity stories, gossip columns, photographs, drawings, and ads for magical goods.[42] Serial heroines like Mary Fuller, Kathlyn Williams, and Marguerite Snow routinely endorsed facial soap for "velvety skin."[43] After the war, a beauty culture based on an identification with stars embodying femininity in their use of cosmetics, fashion, and décor became big business.[44]

As fan magazines focused on a constellation of female stars, alluring players like Florence La Badie embodied the role of consumption in constructing femininity. Working-class girls had been reared by immigrant mothers resistant to Americanization, but they sought, in a generational shift, to redefine their identities at mixed-sex leisure sites. Although they lacked economic and cultural capital, they still bought affordable goods. During pre-war years beset with a Victorian legacy, stars personified a spectrum of social types that were typically yet ambiguously feminine. As a contrast to petite ingenues, modern women were energetic in displaying their physicality. Ruth Roland, the Kalem Girl, was a comedienne and serial heroine who loved the outdoors and managed to be extremely girlish and boyishly athletic at the same time. Ruth Stonehouse, the "Pavlova of the Movies," was a classical dancer and "an all-around sportswoman." Assuming significance in constructing such feminine types, especially in terms of upward social mobility, was a semiotics of fashion. According to Janice Radway, a detailed description of apparel and accessories was coded by genre conventions so that readers could envision their favorites.[45] Although *MPM* did not match *Photoplay*'s coverage of fashion until 1917, an earlier report about Vitagraph's designer specified that "the gowns of the leading women must conform to their individuality." Gladys Hulette, for example, modeled a dress of "black Chantilly lace over black satin" and a wrap of "black chiffon velvet trimmed with Russian sable." An even earlier piece about "Dame Fashion and the Movies" noted that the "ladies of the Vitagraph, Lubin, Pathé, Mutual, Essanay, and other companies" in society dramas were a big attraction in "wardrobes cost[ing] […] hundreds and sometimes thousands of dollars." Another story reported that Margaret Gibson, who modeled a purple and white silk bathing suit in a contest, was studying the tango because "society people" danced at Los Angeles hotels and beach resort pavilions. And Marguerite Clark was represented as a paper doll that could don cut-outs of a flaring coat and a brimmed hat with folding tabs.[46] The use of a child's toy to enhance identification and to promote fashion was clever indeed.

As important as fashion in publicity about the stars, who were themselves commodities, were tours of elegant homes that at first exemplified middlebrow taste. Writing about "What a Home Means to Me," Ruth Roland celebrated real-estate values. After years spent on the road, she was luxuriating in "a place of friendship, of peace; a place to think in, to express one's personality in, to be joyous in, to cultivate […] the beautiful and the true." She enjoyed a large fireplace in a living room with a seaside view; a modern kitchen and a dining room with silver place settings; blue larkspur walls with artwork by Corot and Burne-Jones; a table stacked with books by Dickens, Kipling, and Twain; a piano as well as a Victrola to play Puccini and foxtrots; and a garden with lavender and pink roses.[47] Such elegance signified that genteel middle-class refinement required more than a modicum of good taste. And the necessity for costly goods showed how easily middlebrow culture could be co-opted under consumer capitalism. As reported by writers touring palatial estates, many stars flaunted what Thorsten Veblen condemned as conspicuous consumption and leisure among the nouveaux riche.[48] A voyeuristic survey of "Country Homes of Illustrious Players: Intimate Peeps at Their Vacation-Retreats" reported that Ralph W. Ince enjoyed summers in a Brightwaters mansion with a billiard room, an adjoining sleeping porch, a tennis court, and dog kennels. And he sailed a yacht. Pearl White rented a Bayswater summer house with three stories and a large garage, where she tinkered in overalls with her new car and enjoyed the morning air and swimming. She embodied in her leisure pursuits the daring cliffhanger heroine whom she played on screen without a stunt double.[49]

As compulsive shoppers uninhibited by middlebrow restraint, female stars reinforced sex stereotypes, but reports about their response to automobiles, which recalled the popularity of bicycles in a previous era, signaled a redefinition of femininity. Women buying and driving expensive cars were still consumers remaking their personal identities and social relations in the material world. But what could be construed as a form of commodity fetishism was also a sign of changing sex roles. The influence of lowbrow entertainment on high-end consumption, moreover, was not insignificant. Stars were behaving like daredevil heroines in working-class serials and assuming masculine characteristics projected onto shiny gadgets. As Bernarr Macfadden had earlier observed in *The Power and Beauty of Superb Womanhood*, physically vigorous women could develop "muscular strength to an equal degree with man."[50] And unlike elite neurasthenic men outpaced by rapid change, they responded enthusiastically to modern technology. An outdoors woman, Edith Storey, built a bungalow and described her forty-mile commute to the Vitagraph studio in Brooklyn as "a delightful morning constitutional." Also "fond of motoring," Helen Holmes owned three cars, including a "low-hung, wicked-looking white racer," that she repaired herself. Stars were also behind the wheel in Los Angeles, the city with the most "private cars per capitum [sic] in the United States." Chauffeurs were dismissed because "after the grind and perils of picture work, auto driving... [is] as easy as running a sewing-machine." Myrtle Gonzalez scoffed at "simply looking pretty at the steering wheel" and wore a "mechanician's overalls" to work on her car. She was madcap.[51] A symbol of modernity, the automobile represented personal autonomy, self-reliance, and freedom. Women were among the first motorists to venture out West, write popular travel literature, and pave the way for a booming tourist industry.[52] As future decades unfolded, car ownership became an envied sign of success, stimulated consumption and leisure pursuits on an unprecedented scale, and radically transformed social mores. A serial star like Helen Holmes, who drove a roadster with abandon in the 1910s, signified change—not the least of which was the construction of her own subjectivity. Admittedly a product of consumption denoting a privileged social class, the rebellious New Woman had arrived in fan magazine pages.[53]

Selling Aspiration: Advertisements

Stars were subject to commodification and reification, but their high exchange and signifying value enabled them to accumulate fashion, real estate, and roadsters. Fans, however, faced more limited options. As David Huyssen argues, the fault lines in the "economic, social and political landscape" of the Progressive Era deepened so that "inequality between rich and poor became more, not less, acute." And as social historians point out, working-class families with an average income of $800 a year could neither rely on a regular paycheck nor advance into the middle class until 1945. Although most fan magazine readers were working-class, as Kathryn Fuller-Seeley concludes, their numbers still represented a source of revenue at a time when a national system of advertising was emerging.[54] After *MPSM* became *MPM*, eight pages of ads appeared before the table of contents, and the "Classified Advertisements" section (later "The Opportunity Market") as well as ad stacking in the back migrated to the front. Advertisers, assured that they could reach "millions attending the photoplay everyday," began to promote commodities with symbolic value, grooming and health care products, and job opportunities. Women, even those with a scant income, constituted an important demographic group of buyers. Advertising trade journal *Printers' Ink* and local newspapers read by white middle-class wives, who were addressed as family purchasing agents, had been promoting a woman's page in the news. A correlation between increased female subscription and greater advertising revenue was noted in the news business in the 1910s.[55] As a magazine with an expanding female, albeit ethnic working-class, fan base, *MPM* was well positioned to exploit a promising market but slower to do so than rival *Photoplay*.

A close reading of ads in what Raymond Williams calls a magic system validating goods with personal and social meaning illustrates the power of advertising. Shoppers were persuaded that commodities enabled them to become alluring and socially prominent personalities. Why else were goods desirable? Given that products circulated "in a highly organized and professional system of magical inducements and satisfactions," magic coexisted with technology and mass production. Advertising, "the official art of modern capitalistic society," sustained consumption as both aspiration and unending practice. The magic system, however, obscured the reality of commodities signifying human desires that ultimately could not be met without structural change.[56] Consumers themselves, moreover, were objectified and defined in terms of their cultural capital. Such contradictions may be observed in aspirational class-based advertising in *MPSM* and *MPM*. At first *MPSM* appealed to lower- and middle-class readers who desired respectability. Leisure remained suspect, according to Protestant tenets, but travel was educational so that ads promoted Niagara Falls hotels, cruise lines, and *Burton Holmes Travelogues*. Also important was a middlebrow library denoting "intelligent discrimination": Dickens, George Eliot, Balzac, Washington Irving, Eugène Sue, and Walter Scott. Goods symbolizing refinement included Waterman pens, Kodak cameras ($15), gold-tone pocket watches, diamond rings, Edison phonographs ($15–$200), and upright pianos. A number of these products, as well as an ocean voyage, oil paintings, and bound volumes, were awarded in the "Great Cast Contest." An ambitious reader could even send for the plans of a Gustave Stickley Craftsman's house and build it for $900. Assuredly a sign of comfort, Travelers' life insurance costing fifty-one cents a day became a marketable, if expensive, product.[57]

As evident in the ads, *MPSM* and *MPM*, which initially sanctified middlebrow culture, began to address lower-class fans without prospects but anxious to become socially mobile like the stars. At first the magazines capitalized on a fledgling but thriving movie business by encouraging hopeful readers to become screenwriters. The Photoplay Clearing House, a marketing organization affiliated with Vitagraph in Brooklyn, solicited manuscripts "of every description" to revise, type, and sell for a commission. A clever writer like Louella Parsons at Essanay was singled out as a role model for females who, in fact, had few professional options. And a profusion of ads like one titled "Ideas Wanted for Photoplays" boldly claimed, "Your chance to succeed is as good as anybody's." Such promotions, however, were manipulative and inflated expectations. Particularly revealing were ads addressed to ordinary males who had few resources but did indeed read fan magazines at the time and coveted well-paying jobs. The International Correspondence Schools urged them to "break away from the ranks of the untrained" and qualify for manual and non-manual positions: plumber and steam fitter, concrete construction worker, surveyor, bookkeeper, advertising man, etc. Self-made men were reassuringly characterized as individuals who could succeed like others "with no more natural ability." The American Correspondence School of Law claimed that legally trained men could earn $5,000–$20,000 a year. Such salaries were unlikely. The Franklin Institute in Rochester, New York, was more realistic and advertised a postal service job at $800 to $1,800 a year.[58] Ads, in sum, assumed that the educational level of gullible readers was as low as their expectations were high.

A sign of anxiety in an urban society with abundant consumer goods but limited mobility, *MPSM* ads, reinforced by pseudo-science and magic, urged readers to radiate health and well-being. After all, this was an era when Theodore Roosevelt pursued a strenuous life and rebelled against over-civilization and neurasthenia among wealthy repressed men. Anxiety about exhaustion of the physical self as well as financial reserves was a vague but widespread response to rapid technological change. What T. J. Jackson Lears analyzes as a shift from a Protestant to a secular idiom in pursuit of self-renewal among the elite filtered down to the masses in less sophisticated terms.[59] Bernarr Macfadden, whose enterprise published *True Story* and would acquire *Photoplay*, advertised *Physical Culture*, headquartered in the Triangle Building, as a primer on male bodybuilding in both *MPSM* and *MPM*. Douglas E. (Electricity) Fairbanks preferred California to Broadway because he enjoyed vigorous outdoor life. The Swoboda System of Conscious Evolution promised readers that they would become "thoroughly well, virile, and energetic." Addressed to married couples, a book titled *Sex Force* trumpeted "The Vital Power." Weak, nervous, and thin women could rehabilitate themselves with Dr. James P. Campbell's complexion wafers. Anticipating a pervasive beauty culture, in which females would become obsessed with their bodies, an ad for a hand massager preached, "To Be Beautiful Is a Woman's Duty." Beauty might be the product of artifice, but it had to appear natural. An ad for Pompeian Massage Cream, endorsed by Mary Pickford, labeled make-up as artificial and stressed a natural complexion. As for fashion, the Charles William Stores advertised the latest New York apparel, and Bellas Hess and Company published a mail order catalog.[60]

At a time when genteel middle-class women emerged in the public sphere to frequent sumptuous department stores with plate glass windows and colorful bazaars, shopping, which had once been a male prerogative, became essential to self-making. Standing opposite privileged white women at the sales counter, however, were ethnic working-class women with less income, education, and taste. Significantly, a change in the nature of female employment was occurring in the 1910s so that sales jobs, as opposed to those in garment and textile factories and domestic households, increased. Salesgirls remained at the bottom of the social ladder, however, and endured harsh working conditions and subservience to middle-class consumers. Clerical work, cashiering, and bookkeeping would become more common white-collar jobs in the next decade. Unsurprisingly, ads promoted typewriters from the latest Royal at $75 to rebuilt machines at $6. The Monarch Light Touch promised that a woman's work would become "cleaner cut, more accurate, more rapid." Aimed at grammar and high school graduates with an education, *The Girl Who Earns Her Own Living* was a manual that offered "practical and ethical" advice. But working-class women were transient workers in unskilled and semi-skilled jobs who could not earn a living wage and were reputed to be immoral. Approximately half the female labor force in New York earned less than eight dollars a week at this time. As for salesgirls, they were subject to various forms of incentive payments tied to selling products. Admittedly, marriage was still an economic option for working-class females, but a correspondence school ad affirmed that a wife's happiness was a function of her husband's earning power. A distraught spouse asserts, "You've simply got to earn more money—QUICKLY."[61] Divorce rates, especially among middle-class wives, rose with increasing urbanization and consumption. But as the failed companionate marriage movement showed in the following decades, easier access to divorce and contraception—let alone reforming traditional wedded life—provoked widespread resistance.[62] Such dismal conditions in the lives of masses of women accounted for the appeal of romantic movies, glamorous stars, and gossipy fan magazines.

Conclusion: *MPSM* and *MPM* versus *Photoplay*

A close examination of *MPSM*, *MPM*, and *Photoplay* as the earliest fan magazines promoting the film industry results in a study in contrasts. Blackton's entrepreneurial ambition was a sign of the times. The stewardship of middlebrow culture, based on the social uses of art, was a part not only of Progressive class, ethnic, and gender relations but also of monopolistic industry practices. As magazines advertising MPPC films, *MPSM* and early *MPM* tutored lower-class fans in the reception of film as a legitimate art with educational value. A perusal of the earliest issues shows page after page of recycled but uplifting narrative. Admittedly, storyizations, which became only slightly less literary over time, were soon eclipsed by trivial stories about the stars in order to attract female readers. *Photoplay*'s earlier promotion of film personalities, on the other hand, set a template with which we are all too familiar today. A less promising slapdash magazine, it was founded in Chicago in 1911 to advertise the independent exchanges, printed on cheaper paper, and cost only ten cents. It was not nationally circulated for six months and survived near-bankruptcy and a four-month hiatus in 1913 and yet another reorganization in 1915.

Attempting to increase circulation and advertising by becoming respectable, *Photoplay* adapted *MPSM* and *MPM* middlebrow conventions like literary storyizations and captioned stills. At the same time, however, it appealed to lower-class female readers with storyized films as romance fiction and exciting serials featuring glamorous career women. A color-tinted illustration in a series titled "Peggy Roche: Saleslady" showed a well-dressed and coiffed heroine engaging in foreign intrigue while wearing high heels on a submarine deck. Sexual awakenings, wild adventures, and exotic locales were de rigueur in texts that would today be labeled bodice rippers and chick lit.[63] As a hybrid publication with varying levels of taste in stories, articles, and departments, *Photoplay*, especially under James R. Quirk, evolved into a more imaginative magazine for female readers than its staid rival. And it was more savvy about marketing as it reinforced commodity fetishism and constructed an alluring dream world obscuring unequal social relations. Acquiring commodities endowed with magic, however, became an unending ritual. Since the pleasure of indulging in goods was momentary, an endless cycle of "getting and spending" resulted in what Colin Campbell describes as a state of "longing and a permanent unfocused dissatisfaction."[64] As early fan magazines constructing mass consumer psychology, *Photoplay* and *MPM* were competitors on trajectories that were at first divergent but then converged to form a celebrity culture as the basis of modern consumption.

Was *Photoplay*'s scenario of lower-class fans who lacked capital and agency but still bought fetishized goods to identify with stars inevitable in a modern celebrity culture? Was *MPM*'s more restrained version of such commodification less problematic? What were the prospects, in other words, of sustaining middlebrow culture as a bulwark against celebrities and consumer capitalism in the first half of the twentieth century? A focus on *MPSM* and early *MPM* provides a view of such a cultural formation as it responded to what Janice Radway analyzes as issues of massification and standardization in a democracy. Arnoldian high culture, not to mention modernism and the avant-garde, might be inaccessible for the aspiring classes, but middlebrow taste might well be within their reach. As Henry Canby, who moved from the *Yale Review* and *Saturday Review of Literature* to the Book-of-the-Month Club, affirmed in the next decade, "false jewels, and rayon, and Books of Etiquette need not necessarily indicate anything more deplorable than an untrained taste." The uneducated could be taught to pursue "rationality, beauty, and truth."[65] What could be more transformative for a struggling individual than becoming successful while the existing social structure remains intact? Aesthetics as a sign of what Pierre Bourdieu labels distinction need not be a permanent marker denoting social class. But class, ethnicity, and religion were conflated in the Progressive Era to define manual workers as the unassimilable Other. And middlebrow culture, itself commoditized, required economic capital. Advice literature recommended that the middle class, which enjoyed an income of $1,200 to $5,000 a year, acquire a suburban home, apparel, travel experience, and books. Despite inflationary pressures, this self-conscious class was advised to distinguish itself from the ostentatious rich as well as the ethnic immigrant poor. Social reproduction, which defined the old propertied middle class, thus remained a function of class formation and structure. An individual's taste, as Bourdieu argues in defining habitus, was the product of family upbringing, education, and aesthetics that differentiated homogeneous yet stratified classes.[66] But a growing new middle class of managerial employees in governmental bureaucracies and corporations would sustain middlebrow culture until the advent of television. As for working-class families, they would not enjoy higher incomes until the first mass-consumption society was built in sprawling suburbs after World War II. Significantly, the sheer number of working- and lower-middle-class housewives would then influence the aesthetics of mass production design and marketing.[67] Such a development was anticipated by the demographics of early fan magazine readership because gender proved to be as significant as class and ethnicity in influencing consumer behavior.

As long as cultural arbiters like Blackton and Brewster sanctioned middlebrow taste for aspiring manual and proletarianized non-manual workers, they had a role to play. Storyizations affirmed the didactic value of narrative in white Protestant middle-class society as an uplifting context for self-making. What these entrepreneurs failed to anticipate in introducing a new yet familiar narrative to the earliest fan magazines, however, was the rapidly growing feminization of movie fandom. *Photoplay*'s early history showed that ethnic working-class females consuming publicity stories and romance fiction required less mediation. As a matter of fact, the demographics of such consumers ensured that mass merchandising, especially products endorsed by celebrities, appealed to lowbrow taste. And glamorous movie stars embodying conspicuous consumption provided yearning readers with compensatory experience. Such class dynamics were essential to the fantasies exploited by advertisers to sell commodities. Why limit the aspiration of lower-class women to middlebrow taste when consumption required limitless daydreaming? Also diminishing the relevance of cultural stewardship was the sheer number of urban masses rendering its survival, in an interpenetrating and contested space between high and low, problematic. As cultural forms signifying a pre-war world receding into the past, *MPSM* and early *MPM* represented a brief period when film was marketed as a middlebrow product. Such a strategy assumed more continuity than change under consumer capitalism. Despite Blackton remaining on the masthead as president of the Motion Picture Publishing Company until June 1918, the magazine had been replicating *Photoplay*'s practice of defining femininity as consumerism for several years. A story about Pearl White, for example, portrayed her as "an ordinary young girl" who disliked fancy costumes, yet she was photographed wearing a sumptuous full-length coat trimmed with yards of sable.[68] Aspiring readers who lacked capital but identified with enviable personalities were emboldened to daydream, become self-indulgent, and purchase cheap goods signifying glamour. As the twentieth century progressed, starstruck fans ensured the dominance of celebrity culture and enshrined consumption as an obsessive ritual in contemporary life.

Notes

1. F. H. Richardson, "A Vitagraph Girl Night," *Moving Picture World* (*MPW*) (December 31, 1910): 1521. A version of this essay was delivered as a keynote at Women and the Silent Screen VIII, University of Pittsburgh, September 2015. A sequel including part of the keynote, "Adapting Middlebrow Taste to Sell Stars, Romance, and Consumption: Early Photoplay," appears in *Feminist Media Histories* 3, no. 4 (Fall 2017): 121–161. I thank Mark Lynn Anderson for inviting me to WSS VIII and the Cecil B. DeMille Estate for partly funding expenses.
2. Warren Susman, "'Personality'" and the Making of Twentieth-Century Culture," *Culture As History: The Transformation of American Society in the Twentieth Century* (New York: Pantheon, 1984), 274. See also Richard deCordova, *Picture Personalities: The Emergence of the Star System in America* (Urbana: University of Illinois Press, 1990), 50–117.
3. Unidentified clipping, Florence Turner clip file, Library and Museum of the Performing Arts, Lincoln Center (hereafter LMPA); William Basil Courtney, "History of Vitagraph," *Motion Picture News* (*MPN*) (March 28, 1925): 1313, 1317 (serialized history). The term "middlebrow" was coined in 1925.
4. See Sumiko Higashi, "Vitagraph Stardom: Constructing Personalities for 'New' Middle-Class Consumption," in Vicki Callahan, ed., *Reclaiming the Archive: Feminism and Film History* (Detroit, MI: Wayne State University Press, 2009), 264–288.
5. *MPSM* (*MPSM*) and *Motion Picture Magazine* (*MPM*) are online, but not all issues are extant, complete, or in chronological order. A run of hard copies with some missing issues is available at the Margaret Herrick Library, Academy of Motion Picture Arts and Sciences, Beverly Hills.
6. Courtney, "Vitagraph," *MPN* (February 14, 1915): 661.
7. Janice Radway, *A Feeling for Books: The Book-of-the-Month Club, Literary Taste, and Middle-Class Desire* (Chapel Hill: University of North Carolina Press, 1997), part 2. See Joan Shelley Rubin, *The Making of Middlebrow Culture* (Chapel Hill: University of North Carolina Press, 1992), Introduction.
8. "A New Belasco," *Blue Book* (June 1914): 246–247, in J. Stuart Blackton clip file, LMPA; Don Dewey, "Man of a Thousand Faces," *American Film* (November 1990): 44–50, in J. Stuart Blackton clip file, LMPA.
9. Eileen Bowser, *The Transformation of Cinema, 1907–1915* (Berkeley: University of California Press, 1994), 105. See William Uricchio and Roberta Pearson, *Reframing Culture: The Case of the Vitagraph Quality Films* (Princeton, NJ: Princeton University Press 1993).
10. Since *MPSM* and *Photoplay* used "storyized by," I coin the term "storyization" to avoid using "adaptation," implying a screen version of a literary work.
11. Editorial, *MPSM* (October 1911): unnumbered page.

12. Christopher Wilson, "The Rhetoric of Consumption: Mass-Market Magazines and the Demise of the Gentle Reader, 1850–1920," in Richard Wightman Fox and T. J. Jackson Lears, eds., *The Culture of Consumption: Critical Essays in American History, 1880–1980* (New York: Pantheon Books, 1983), 39–64.
13. William Lord Wright, "Literature and Filmland," *MPSM* (October 1913): 117; Ad, *MPSM* (July 1912): 153; Henry Albert Phillips, "How I Came to Write for the Motion Pictures," *MPM* (May 1915): 95–98.
14. On purple prose, see Maryan Wherry, "More Than a Love Story: The Complexities of the Popular Romance," in Christine Berberich, ed., *The Bloomsbury Introduction to Popular Fiction* (New York: Bloomsbury, 2015), 65–66.
15. Louis Reeves Harrison, "The Stepsisters," *MPSM* (July 1911): 27–32.
16. Harold Aurelius Heltberg, "Life at Hull House," *MPSM* (July 1911): 79–89; Peter Wade, "Wild Animals in Captivity," *MPSM* (July 1911): 91–93; "The Cash Prize Contest," *MPSM* (July 1911): 129–131.
17. Geraldine Ames, "Saving Immigrant Girls with 'Movies,'" *MPM* (December 1914): 92; "What Improvement in Motion Pictures Is Needed Most?" *MPM* (November 1914): 119.
18. Ad for *Supplement*, *MPM* (September 1915): 155; Ad, *MPM* (June 1915): 166; "Editorial Announcements," *MPM* (November 1915): 2.
19. J. Stuart Blackton, "The Battle Cry of Peace," *MPM* (December 1915): 78.
20. Editorial, *MPSM* (October 1911): unnumbered page; William Lord Wright, "'Movies' or Not 'Movies,'" *MPM* (April 1915): 119; "The Great Debate: Shall the Plays Be Censored?" *MPM* (April 1914): 73–74; "Musings of 'The Photoplay Philosopher,'" *MPSM* (March 1912): 137; *MPM* (April 1914): 117.
21. Eugene V. Brewster, "Thomas A. Edison," *MPSM* (January 1914): 55–63, 146; Eugene V. Brewster, "Moving Picture Toys," *MPM* (June 1914): 89–96; Eugene V. Brewster, "Expressions of the Emotions," *MPM* (July 1914): 107–114 (first in a series with same title); *MPM* (August 1914): 101–109; *MPM* (September 1914): 97–102; *MPM* (October 1914): 113–119; *MPM* (December 1914): 111–114.
22. On defining the middle class in terms of social reproduction as opposed to the working class in terms of relations of production, see Stuart M. Blumin, *The Emergence of the Middle Class: Social Experience in the American City, 1760–1900* (New York: Cambridge University Press, 1989), chap. 1.
23. Cartoons, *MPSM* (September 1912): 147, 155; Beatrice Howard, "The Two Signs," *MPM* (October 1914): 31; "July 4th," *MPM* (August 1915): 100; Ad, *MPSM* (February 1913): 173.
24. Roy Rosenzweig, *Eight Hours for What We Will: Workers and Leisure in an Industrial City, 1870–1920* (New York: Cambridge University Press, 1983), chap. 2; Mark Pittenger, "A World of Difference: Constructing the 'Underclass' in Progressive America," *American Quarterly* 49 (March 1997): 26–65.
25. Cartoons, *MPM* (February 1916): 164; *MPM* (May 1916): 154; "What Improvement in Motion Pictures Is Needed Most?" *MPM* (April 1914): 121.
26. See Andrew R. Heinze, *Adapting to Abundance: Jewish Immigrants, Mass Consumption, and the Search for American Identity* (New York: Columbia University Press, 1990), 18.
27. See Shelley Stamp, *Movie-Struck Girls: Motion Picture Culture after the Nickleodeon* (Princeton, NJ: Princeton University Press, 2000); Richard Abel, *Americanizing the Movies and "Movie Mad" Audiences* (Berkeley: University of California Press, 2006), chap. 6; Diana Anselmo-Sequeira, "Screen Struck: The Invention of the Movie Fan Girl," *Cinema Journal* 55, no. 1 (Fall 2015): 1–28.

28. "The Cash Prize Contest," *MPSM* (July 1911): 130; "The Cash Prize Contest," *MPSM* (October 1911): 141–142 (listed in September, not October, contents); "The Great Mystery Play," *MPSM* (November 1912): 80; "The Great Mystery Play," *MPSM* (April 1913): 80.
29. "Popular Player Contest," *MPSM* (May 1912): 135.
30. "Popular Player Contest Winners," *MPSM* (July 1912): 34.
31. "Popular Player Contest," *MPSM* (October 1913): 109–112.
32. Michael Denning, *Mechanic Accent: Dime Novels and Working-Class Culture in America* (New York: Verso, 1987), chap. 10; Ben Singer, "Female Power in the Serial-Queen Melodrama: The Etiology of An Anomaly," *Camera Obscura* 22 (January 1990): 90–112; Ad for diamonds, *MPM* (November 1916): 161.
33. "What Improvement in Motion Pictures Is Needed Most?" *MPM* (April 1914): 121–122; *MPM* (December 1914): 126; "Great Artist Contest," *MPM* (August 1914): 121; "Screen Masterpieces," *MPM* (May 1916): 179; "Here Are the Winners of the Great Popular Player Contest," *MPM* (February 1917): 126–128.
34. Maurice Costello scrapbook, Robinson Locke Collection, Series II Scrapbooks 1720–1947, v. 85, LMPA; Higashi, "Vitagraph Stardom," 266–275.
35. Bowser, *Transformation*, chap. 12; "Statistics Report," *MPSM* (January 1914): 154; Michael Quinn, "Distribution, the Transient Audience, and the Transition to the Feature Film," *Cinema Journal* 40, no. 2 (Winter 2001): 35–56. A list of storyizations was checked against titles in *American Film Institute Catalog of Motion Pictures Produced in the United States Feature Films 1911–1920*, ed. Patricia King Hanson and Alan Gevinson (Berkeley: University of California Press, 1988) to identify features.
36. William N. Selig, "Present Day Trend in Film Lengths," and Carl Laemmle, "Doom of Long Features Predicted," *MPW* (July 11, 1914): 181, 185; "Short Films the Best," *New York Dramatic Mirror* (July 28, 1915): 22; "Famous Players and Lasky in $12,500,000 Combine," *MPN* (July 15, 1916): 223.
37. Roberta Courtlandt, "A Voiceless Prima Donna," *MPM* (December 1916): 97–99; Mosgrove Colwell, "Candy and the Movies," *MPM* (December 1916): 94–96.
38. The February 1911 issue was replicated with more material in March.
39. Charlie Keil, "Studio Girls: Female Stars and the Logic of Brand Names," in Sofia Bull and Astrid Soderbergh Widding, eds., *Not So Silent: Women in Cinema before Sound* (Stockholm: Acta Universitatis Stockholmiensis, 2010), 280.
40. Covers, *MPM* (July, August, September 1914); Ad for paintings, *MPM* (August 1914): 168; George Wildey, "The Pirates," *MPM* (July 1914): 78; Gladys Hall, "Cast Adrift in the South Seas," *MPM* (July1914): 51; Walter H. Bernard, "Neptune's Daughter," *MPM* (July 1914): 57; Ad for cruise, *MPM* (July 1914): 6
41. Cover, *Photoplay* (August 1914); Ad for soap, *Photoplay* (September 1914): back cover.
42. On compensatory experience, see Don Slater, *Consumer Culture and Modernity* (Cambridge, UK: Polity Press, 1997), 105; Fredric Jameson, "Reification and Utopia in Mass Culture," *Social Text* 1 (1979): 130–148; Janice Radway, *Reading the Romance: Women, Patriarchy and Popular Literature* (Chapel Hill: University of North Carolina Press, 1984), chaps. 3, 4, 5.
43. Ad for soap, *MPM* (November 1915): back cover.
44. On identification, see Jackie Stacey, *Star Gazing: Hollywood Cinema and Female Spectatorship* (New York: Routledge, 1994); Rachel Moseley, *Growing Up with Audrey Hepburn: Text, Audience, Resonance* (Manchester, UK: Manchester University Press, 2002).

45. Jean Darnell, "Ruth Roland, 'The Kalem Girl,'" *MPM* (August 1914): 84–85; Jean Darnell, "Ruth Stonehouse and Dancing," *MPM* (December 1914: 88; Radway, *Reading the Romance*, 193–195.
46. Therese Lavoisier, "The Latest Fashion in Moving Pictures," *MPM* (July 1915): 117–120; William Lord Wright, "Dame Fashion and the Movies," *MPM* (September 1914): 108–110; Grace Lavender, "Margaret Gibson Wins First Prize for Having Prettiest Bathing Suit," *MPM* (September 1914): 128; J. Argens, "Paper Cut-Outs of Popular Players," *MPM* (November 1916): 135.
47. Ruth Roland, "What a Home Means to Me," *MPM* (November 1915): 91–93.
48. Thorstein Veblen, *The Theory of the Leisure Class* (New York: 1899; repr. Viking, 1967), chaps. 3, 4.
49. Robert F. Moore, "Where They Live," *MPM* (November 1916): 35–41; Lillian May, "Country Homes of Illustrious Players," *MPM* (June 1917): 45–49.
50. Bernarr Macfadden, *The Power and Beauty of Superb Womanhood* (New York: Physical Culture Publishing Co., 1901), quoted in John Higham, *Writing American History* (Indianapolis: Indiana University Press, 1970), 83.
51. Peter Wade, "Their Homes on Wheels," *MPM* (April 1916): 89–95; Roberta Courtlandt, "Feminine Fads and Fancies," *MPM* (January 1917): 39.
52. Peter J. Blodgett, ed., *Motoring West: Automobile Pioneers 1900–1909*, vol. 1 (Norman: University of Oklahoma Press, 2015), 49.
53. On the New Woman not being so new, see Sumiko Higashi, "The New Woman and Consumer Culture: Cecil B. DeMille's Sex Comedies," in Jennifer Bean and Diane Negra, eds., *A Feminist Reader in Early Cinema* (Durham, NC: Duke University Press, 2002), 298–300.
54. David Huyssen, *Progressive Inequality: Rich and Poor in New York, 1890–1920* (Cambridge, MA: Harvard University Press, 2014), 2, 6; Kathy Peiss, *Cheap Amusements: Working Women and Leisure in Turn-of-the-Century New York* (Philadelphia, PA: Temple University Press 1986), 12; Susan Porter Benson, *Household Accounts: Working Class Family Economies in the Interwar United States* (Ithaca, NY: Cornell University Press, 2007), Introduction; Kathryn Fuller-Seeley, *At the Picture Show: Small-Town Audiences and the Creation of Movie Fan Culture* (Washington, DC: Smithsonian, 1996), 166. Fuller-Seeley traces the development of *MPM* and *Photoplay*, especially its female readership, in separate chapters in a chronological survey ending in the 1920s.
55. "Facts of Interest to the Advertiser," *MPM* (March 1914): unnumbered page; Julie A. Golia, "Courting Women, Courting Advertisers: The Woman's Page and the Transformation of the American Newspaper, 1895–1935," *Journal of American History* 103 (December 2016): 606–628.
56. Raymond Williams, "Advertising the Magic System," *Problems in Materialism and Culture* (New York: Verso, 1980), 170–195.
57. Ads for hotel, travelogue, books, pen, *MPSM* (March 1911): 121–136; Ad for cruise, *MPSM* (August 1912): 153; Ad for cameras, *MPSM* (August 1911): back cover; Ad for watches, *MPSM* (January 1914): back cover; Ad for diamonds, *MPM* (December 1916): 155; Ad for phonograph, *MPSM* (March 1912): back cover; Ad for piano, *MPM* (April 1914): 145; "Great Cast Contest," *MPM* (November 1915): 123; Ad for Craftsman's, *MPSM* (October 1911): 150; Ad for insurance, *MPSM* (October 1911): 151.
58. Photoplay Clearing House, *MPSM* (August 1913): unnumbered page; Edwin M. La Roche, "A New Profession for Women," *MPM* (May 1914): 84; "Ideas Wanted for Photoplays,"

MPM (February 1916): 165; Ads for correspondence school, *MPSM* (May 1911): 135; *MPM* (April 1915): 155; *MPM* (December 1915): 145; Ad for law, *MPSM* (February 1914): unnumbered page; Ad for postmen, *MPM* (December 1914): 177. In February 1916, actress Rose Tapley began writing "The Answer Lady" with Agony Aunt advice and more detailed, but fewer, answers to queries about stars.

59. T. J. Jackson Lears, *No Place of Grace: Antimodernism and the Transformation of American Culture 1860–1920* (New York: Pantheon, 1981), Preface. See also Anna Katharina Schaffner, *Exhaustion: A History* (New York: Columbia University Press, 2015).

60. Ad for *Physical Culture, MPSM* (July 1913): 163; Carl W. Seitz, "Douglas E. (Electricity) Fairbanks," *MPM* (December 1916): 67; Ad for Swoboda, *MPM* (March 1915): 2–3; Ad for book, *MPM* (May 1915): 160; Ad for wafers, *MPSM* (December 1912): 163; Ad for massage, *MPSM* (February 1914): 153; Ad for Pompeian, *MPSM* (January 1912): 168; Ad for fashion, *MPM* (October 1914): 8; Ad for catalog, *MPM* (March 1915): 155. On the female body, see Joan Jacobs Brumberg, *The Body Project: An Intimate History of American Girls* (New York: Random House, 1997), xvii–xx.

61. Ad for typewriters, *MPSM* (March 1912): 165; *MPM* (April 1914): 173; Ad for Monarch, *MPSM* (August 1911): 159; Ad for book, *MPSM* (April 1913): 151; Ad about wife, *MPM* (November 1914): 161.

62. Susan Porter Benson, *Counter Cultures: Saleswomen, Managers, and Customers in American Department Stores 1890–1940* (Urbana: University of Illinois Press, 1988), chap. 4; Peiss, *Cheap Amusements,* 52; Rebecca L. Davis, "Not Marriage at All but Simple Harlotry: The Companionate Marriage Controversy," *Journal of American History* 94, no. 4 (March 2008): 1137–1163.

63. Victor Rousseau, "Peggy Roche," *Photoplay* (May 1917): 61.

64. Colin Campbell, *The Romantic Ethic and the Spirit of Modern Consumerism* (London: Blackwell, 1987), 47.

65. Cited in Radway, *A Feeling for Books,* 241–242.

66. Daniel Horowitz, *The Morality of Spending: Attitudes toward the Consumer Society in America, 187–1949* (Baltimore, MD: Johns Hopkins University Press, 1985), chaps. 6, 7; Pierre Bourdieu, *Distinction: A Social Critique of the Judgment of Taste,* trans. Richard Nice (Cambridge, MA: Harvard University Press, 1984), parts 2, 3. Janice Radway interprets Bourdieu's distinction between the grande landed and petite shopkeeping bourgeoisie as "class fracture" that, in the US, is culturally expressed as highbrow versus middlebrow art; see Radway, *A Feeling for Books.*

67. See Sumiko Higashi, *Stars, Fans, and Consumption in the 1950s: Reading* Photoplay (New York: Palgrave Macmillan, 2014).

68. Arthur Pollock, "The Pastimes of a Motion Picture Actress," *MPM* (February 1916):138. As of this writing, Meghan Markle has become the latest royal celebrity whose clothes and accessories are publicized to empty inventories. See Vanessa Friedman, "The Greatest Influencer of All," *New York Times,* April 16, 2018, D1, 4.

CHAPTER 32

THE MANY GENDERS AND SEXUALITIES OF AMERICAN AND EUROPEAN SILENT CINEMA

LAURA HORAK

THE camera follows two sets of legs in skirts as they enter a lively Parisian dance hall, then tilts up to reveal a woman and a male soldier in a kilt. In a subsequent shot in the same dance hall, the camera tracks dizzyingly through a succession of odd couples engendered by the Great War—a wealthy woman handing a wad of cash to a young man; a woman caressing another woman's cheek; a man and woman who turn to stare at the female couple; and a woman throwing her drink in a man's face. We halt at the face of a drunken young American soldier, Jack (Buddy Rogers). Later on, Jack mistakes his old friend Mary (Clara Bow) for a man due to her Women's Army Corps uniform. At the film's tragic conclusion, Jack embraces fellow soldier and former rival David (Richard Arlen) as he dies, and kisses him on the mouth (see figure 32.1). Holding David's head in his arms, Jack declares: "You know there's nothing in the world that means so much to me as your friendship." David responds: "I knew it—all the time—."

The film was *Wings* (1927), a $2 million Paramount super-production that won the first Oscar for Best Picture. Today these scenes of gender confusion and same-sex intimacy look deliberately queer and trans. What were they doing in one of the most expensive productions of the silent era?

Many people today assume that same-sex desire and diverse gender expressions were absent from cinema until the 1950s and 60s and that silent cinema was exclusively heteronormative. Others, like gay activist Vito Russo, have described gay and lesbian representation in silent cinema as perpetuating derogatory anti-gay stereotypes like the sissy.[1] However, alternative genders and sexualities were everywhere in US and European silent cinema, and they were incredibly varied. Furthermore, gay and lesbian directors

FIGURE 32.1 Jack (Buddy Rogers) kisses his dying friend David (Richard Arlen) in *Wings* (1927).

and actors worked in US and European film industries, and many were quite open about their sexuality to their film-world peers and—using certain codes—to fans as well. Representations of alternative genders and sexualities on- and offscreen did not simply reflect anti-gay attitudes; instead, they participated in the dynamic construction of modern sexual and gender categories.

One reason that this prevalence and variety may be difficult to recognize now is that many forms of same-sex eroticism and cross-gender performance that we would label "queer" or "trans" today were accepted as part of middle- and upper-class social norms in the early twentieth century. At that time, some artists, authors, and educators praised same-sex passion as a higher form of love than that between a man and a woman.[2] In single-sex environments such as boarding schools and the military, passionate attachments were expected and even encouraged. What's more, cross-gender casting, gender-disguise comedies, and accidental same-sex desire had long been common on stage. It should therefore be no surprise that the passionate same-sex loves of schoolgirls and soldier boys and the many-gender hijinks of the stage all show up in silent cinema. Just as literary scholar Sharon Marcus has used "surface reading" to reveal the variety of passionate relations between women in Victorian literature and popular culture, we can find alternative expressions of gender and sexuality on the surface of films of this period—in the narratives, casting, costumes, makeup, and gags.[3]

However, some forms of gender and sexuality did go against middle- and upper-class social norms. While passionate relationships between feminine women or between masculine older and younger men in single-sex environments were largely accepted, new categories of identity popularized by sexologists, like sexual invert, homosexual, transvestite, and pseudohermaphrodite were not. However, these types still showed up in silent cinema, but through coded behaviors, styles, and language. We can uncover these kinds of meanings by reconstructing the codes—a limp wrist, a prancing walk, flowers such as violets and lavender, face powder on men, monocles on women, etc. These types of signs communicated one meaning to the "wise" and another to everyone else. Thus, films and writings about film stars yield additional alternative genders and sexualities when we use contemporaneous codes to read the texts "in depth." Silent films represented alternative genders and sexualities that were considered completely mainstream but also those considered deviant and transgressive.

In this essay, I argue that US and European silent cinema was a varied and complex field of genders and sexualities in which same-sex relationships and alternative gender expressions were not necessarily opposed to middle- and upper-class social norms.[4] Cinema often mobilized respectable cultural forms such as theater, dance, and literature to convey same-sex eroticism and cross-gender behavior, and these representations helped associate cinema with high-class entertainment forms. We can see this in the dance films of early cinema and the genteel comedies and dramas of the 1910s and 1920s. The high-culture framework seems to have saved even relatively explicit films from censure. Conversely, when slapstick comedies represented same-sex desire and cross-gender behavior, censors expressed their concern, although a lot of this content still got through. However, when two German *Aufklärungfilme* (Enlightenment films) advocated directly for sexual minorities in 1919, they revealed the limit to how explicitly and positively same-sex desire and cross-gender expression could be expressed in cinema. The press also framed and communicated information about stars' sexuality and gender to the public through the trope of the cosmopolitan European artist as part of the development of modern stardom.

Older, activist approaches to gay and lesbian representation in silent cinema like Vito Russo's *Celluloid Closet* consider gender and sexuality to be stable categories and film to reflect or perhaps intensify negative stereotypes about gays and lesbians.[5] This scholarship often champions "positive" representations and dismisses male effeminacy and female mannishness as homophobic slander. However, we now recognize that being a sissy man or butch woman is not necessarily a bad thing, and that gender variance is not only part of a genealogy of queerness but also of transness. There has also been a tendency, particularly in celebrity biographies but also in film scholarship, to fight over whether a particular actor was "actually" gay or whether a particular scene is "actually" queer.

More recent scholarship takes a more productive history-of-sexuality approach to silent cinema.[6] This approach acknowledges that gender and sexuality are not static but in constant flux and that the 1910s and 1920s were a time of great change. Consumer capitalism, mass migration, urbanization, the rise of sexology, and the proliferation of new forms of popular culture were changing the meanings and implications of what it meant to be a "man" or a "woman"; shifting the rules of courtship, marriage, and reproduction; and popularizing new forms of sexual identity. Cinema was part of these negotiations and debates. This approach recognizes that categories and articulations of gender and sexuality were not necessarily the same in the early twentieth century as today and that some very queer-seeming behaviors were part of accepted middle-class social norms. As lesbian film scholar Susan Potter writes: "To presume, at least before critical work commences, the sexual opacity of early cinema is to start from the position that the past is different from the present, particularly in terms of sexual subjectivity but not to accede to a homophobic denial of the historical existence of same-sex desire or queer ways of living and being."[7] Literary scholar Sharon Marcus's study of relationships between women in Victorian literature, fashion magazines, and life writing exemplifies the power of a history-of-sexuality approach. She reveals how many types of passionate same-sex relationships have been obscured by researchers' attachment to more recent identity categories like "lesbian" and by the conviction that passion between women was inherently opposed to middle-class norms.[8]

Rather than weigh in on whether a particular star is or isn't gay, this newer wave of scholarship examines how and why these debates get established in the first place. Film scholar Mark Lynn Anderson in particular has criticized the tendency of celebrity biographers to reduce sexuality to "the truth of the individual," to assume "an individual is heterosexual until proven otherwise," and to discount "queer reception as [not being] culturally significant."[9]

While history-of-sexuality silent film scholarship often consists of specific case studies, this essay takes a broader view, to consider silent cinema across the United States and Europe and from early to late silent cinema. Although this broad approach risks lifting representations out of the complex webs of discourse that made them meaningful, these are sometimes necessary risks in order to get a sense of how film genres and stardoms functioned across different times and places. Bringing the existing scholarship together with my research on US and Swedish silent cinema allows me to analyze how transnational silent film genres enabled alternative gender and sexual expressions and how the popular press borrowed selectively from these representations to present lesbian and gay directors and actors to the public.

Finding terms to describe sexual and gendered behaviors, styles, and desires from the early twentieth century that are different from today's concepts of sexual orientation and gender identity presents a challenge. While my interest in this research is informed by my investments in today's queer and trans communities, I try to avoid naming the representations I am studying as simply "queer" or "trans" because those terms can make it harder to recognize the differences between then and now. Instead, I will try to describe the phenomena without labeling them or implying that they were considered deviant, through phrases like same-sex eroticism, passionate relationships, and alternative genders and sexualities. I will also discuss the terms available at the time and what they meant. When I describe historical figures like Mauritz Stiller and Greta Garbo, I have chosen to use the terms lesbian and gay, which did exist at the time, rather than other terms that were as likely to have been used back then (e.g., homosexual, Sapphist, or sexual invert) because the former are more legible for today's readers.[10]

THE INVENTION OF CINEMA AND SPREAD OF SEXOLOGY

The invention of cinema in the 1890s coincided with the popularization of the new science of sexology—attempts by European and North American scientists to categorize, name, and theorize the diversity of human sexual practices and gender expressions.[11] Cinema helped spread models of gender and sexuality articulated by sexologists but also drew on older models that sexology hoped to displace. From the beginning, filmmakers wanted to draw as large an audience as possible, and spectacular presentations of sexuality in all its forms were sure sellers. Filmmakers may also have hoped to exploit contemporary debates over "pathological" sexualities occurring in literature, theater, and the popular press. A succession of scandals in Europe and the United States made alternative sexual practices a topical and thrilling subject. These included the 1892 Alice Mitchell murder trial in Memphis and the Oscar Wilde trials in London, which have received scholarly attention, but also the lesser-known Danish Sexual Morality Scandal in 1906–1907, the Swedish Santesson Affair in 1907, and the German Harden-Eulenburg Affair in 1907–1909.[12] In the world of entertainment, Sholem Asch's 1907 Yiddish play *The God of Vengeance* about love between women at a brothel was produced all over Europe and in New York in the 1910s and 1920s; a Swedish novel inspired by a male prostitute's real-life diary was published in 1916; and a British MP accused dancer Maud Adams of inspiring a "cult of the clitoris" through her Salome performances in 1918.[13]

While we might suppose that discussions of same-sex eroticism were confined to the elite spheres of medicine and law, these examples show that plays, novels, and newspapers were regularly presenting the most scandalous versions of same-sex attraction, such as love murders, libel trials, the experiences of sex workers, and pathological forms of fan devotion. Because cinema reached such large, diverse audiences and had a strong, sensuous appeal, censors enforced stricter moral standards on film than on plays, novels, and newspapers. Nevertheless, cinema, too, participated in the proliferation of diverse genders and sexualities.

Scholars have described a shift in Europe and the United States from a "sodomy" model in the late-nineteenth century—religious and legal frameworks focused on sinful and criminal *acts*—to a "homosexuality" model in the early twentieth century—medical and scientific frameworks focused on classifying pathological *individuals*.[14] French philosopher Michel Foucault famously argued that sexologists invented the homosexual as a "species" with the publication of Carl von Westphal's article on "inversion of the sexual instinct" in 1870.[15] Sexologists like von Westphal named people who expressed feelings, desires, dress, or behavior that were atypical of their assigned gender "sexual inverts." This concept conflated gender identity and sexual object choice.

However, sexologists did not invent the idea of a type of person defined by sexual practice, and their conceptualizations of gender and sexuality were not the only ones vying for purchase. People with atypically sexed bodies, gender identities, and sexual practices had long existed and went by a variety of names, including *tribades, lesbians, sodomites, hermaphrodites, female husbands, men-women, Sapphists, androgynes, pansies,* and *fairies*.[16] However, sexologists and sex reformers introduced new vocabularies and theories of sexuality and gender to European and American publics. Reformers like German writer Karl Heinrich Ulrichs and, later, British socialist Edward Carpenter worked to create a political movement to fight for the rights and freedoms of this newly recognized class of people.[17] Some sexologists, including Magnus Hirschfeld from Germany and Havelock Ellis from England, joined the reformers' cause to argue that alternative expressions of gender and sexuality were part of natural human variation and associated with positive contributions to society.[18] Sexologists and reformers coined terms like *homosexual, transvestite, sexual invert, Eonist* (a synonym for sexual invert), and *Urning* (a name for men who love men), and the terms were adopted across many European languages. By the 1910s, a variety of slang and underworld terms were also in widespread use among English-speakers, including *queer, gay,* and *bulldyker*.[19] Far from being "a love that dare not speak its name," as Oscar Wilde famously put it, by the first decades of cinema, there were many different names to describe an array of genders and sexualities.

Cross-dressing was also part of mainstream entertainment culture. While men had played all the roles on stage in times and places when women were banned from theater (as in Elizabethan England), in the early twentieth century men continued to play female characters in university theatricals, minstrel shows, and British Christmas pantomimes, while women also played male roles in many of the same types of performance idioms.[20] Comedies of errors such as Shakespeare's *Twelfth Night* (ca. 1601–1602) and the enormously popular *Charley's Aunt* (1892) also regularly presented characters who disguised their genders and participated in accidental same-gender kisses and embraces. These traditions were taken up in different ways by a variety of transnational silent film genres.

Early Cinema Dance Films

From the beginning, cinema drew widely from existing traditions such as dance, theater, and opera. Film could offer versions of more high-priced entertainments to audiences across class. One example was early films of women dancing together, with one woman taking the role of the male partner "en travesti," as was common in nineteenth-century European ballet and operetta.[21] Examples include: *Gavotte* (France, 1898), *Au bal de flore* (*At the Flowers' Ball*, France, 1900), and *Skilda tiders danser* (*Dances through the Ages*, Sweden, 1909).[22] The Swedish film *Dances through the Ages* is typical of these types of films. In the film, popular operetta performer Rosa Grünberg wears a black tailcoat and trousers and approaches Emma Meissner, who wears a white dress. Grünberg bows to Meissner and proffers her hand. The two twirl together in a lively "Boston waltz," grinning and nodding to each other as they dance (see figure 32.2). The women are playacting as a romantic male-female couple. One Stockholm critic was delighted with Grünberg's impersonation of genteel masculinity, writing: "the cavalier, Miss Grünberg, invites his lady to dance in the most manly way, while she expectantly awaits his arrival."[23]

Film scholars have questioned how to interpret these types of dances. Alison McMahan argues that the female couples in Alice Guy-Blaché's dance films were primarily intended to titillate male spectators, while Susan Potter argues that the films likely appealed to female spectators as well but in indeterminate, inchoate ways. She states that the "playful erotics" of Alice Guy's *Gavotte* (1898) "are inherently fleeting and multilayered, countering any effort to resolve them or fix them into any one definitive interpretation or experience."[24] Likely the films titillated male *and* female spectators. The women performers radiate pleasure, suggesting that desire and eroticism were part of this practice, which proved such a long-standing convention on the stage.[25]

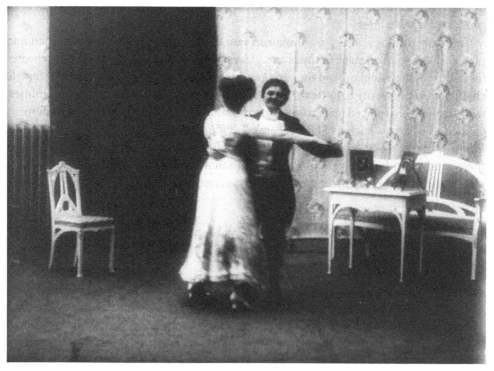

FIGURE 32.2 Rosa Grünberg (in black tailcoat) and Emma Meissner (in white dress) dance a Boston waltz in *Dances through the Ages* (1909). Courtesy of the Swedish Film Institute.

Men also sometimes danced together in early cinema, though it was less common than women doing so. These films were not part of upper-class performance traditions so much as a bleed-over of the social traditions of all-male environments such as the military, men's schools, sailing ships, and ranches. The most well-known film example is *Dickson Experimental Sound Film* (1894–95), in which two employees from Thomas Edison's laboratory dance in each other's arms as another man plays a violin in front of a recording horn.[26] The music played on the violin was "The Song of the Cabin Boy" from an 1877 comic opera, directly referencing these types of all-male environments.[27] A recently rediscovered Lumière actuality *Danse au bivouac* (1896) depicts a group of French soldiers dancing in couples. While Vito Russo claims *Dickson Experimental Sound Film* as an early gay film, film scholars Wheeler Winston Dixon and Shane Brown have argued that the dance was part of normal male homosociality and would not have been considered gay at the time.[28] However, these traditions do not necessarily discount potential feelings of eroticism and desire between the dancers, which were also an accepted part of men's homosocial worlds, as Jonathan Ned Katz has shown.[29] The fact that it became less common to see men dancing in each other's arms in films after the early 1900s (and then only in comedies like Harold Lloyd's *Sailor-Made Man* [1921]) suggests that the behavior became more associated with deviance over the course of the silent era.

GENTEEL CROSS-DRESSING COMEDIES OF THE 1910S AND 1920S

Because comedy generates humor from inverting and distorting cultural norms, playing on taboo subjects, and ridiculing outliers, it proved a rich genre for expressions of alternative genders and sexualities. Comedies could sometimes get away with transgressive representations because of their ambivalence (e.g., is the film laughing with or at a gender-inverted character?), and because audiences were often required to complete the joke by interpreting gestures, expressions, costumes, and wordplay, making transgressive meanings deniable. Drawing on long-standing theatrical traditions, genteel silent comedies of the 1910s and 1920s presented scenarios of gender disguise, which offered myriad opportunities for same-sex flirtation. These films were a variation on the comedy-of-errors genre. Usually, due to some external motivation, one or more characters disguise themselves as another gender, and the disguise is convincing to other characters but not to viewers. As Chris Straayer and Annette Kuhn have pointed out, the humor in these films arises through disjunctions between viewer and character knowledge, contradictions between bodies and clothing, and accidental same-sex eroticism, including kisses.[30] Humor was also generated through the acting feat of switching quickly between male and female characterizations and the anxiety of getting found out.

Popular British cross-dressing stage comedies such as *Twelfth Night, As You Like It* (1599), and *Charley's Aunt* were adapted to short and feature silent film in the US, UK,

Italy, and Sweden in the 1910s and 1920s.[31] Adapting these plays and similar scenarios to cinema was part of the effort to legitimize the new medium by associating it with respectable entertainment.[32] In the United States, director D. W. Griffith also made genteel cross-dressing two-reel comedies at the Biograph Company, such as *The Woman from Mellon's* (1910), in which a young man (Billy Quirk) disguises himself as a female detective and flirts with his fiancée's father to win the man's blessing for their marriage, and *Taming a Husband* (1910), in which a young woman (Dorothy West) disguises herself as a man and woos her female friend in order to rekindle her friend's husband's love.[33] Furthermore, Broadway's most famous female impersonator, Julian Eltinge, made a series of gender-disguise film comedies between 1914 and 1925; unlike the central disguise in most cross-dressing comedies, Eltinge's is utterly persuasive.[34] While unconvincing disguises act as sight gags and intensify the appearance of same-sex intimacy, Eltinge's transformation has the potential to astonish the audience, convincing them not to believe their own eyes when it comes to gender performance.

Cross-dressed women often provided opportunities for expressions of male same-sex desire. In Ernst Lubitsch's feature-length *Ich möchte kein Mann sein* (*I Don't Want to Be a Man*, Germany, 1918), a male tutor (Curt Goetz) repeatedly kisses a boy he meets at a nightclub on the mouth during their shared carriage ride home, not realizing that the boy is actually his female tutee (Ossi Oswalda) in disguise. Conversely, in the two-reel Asta Nielsen comedy *Zapatas Bande* (*Zapata's Band*, Germany, 1914), a young woman tries to hug, kiss, and run away with the male bandit who has snuck into her bedroom at night, not realizing that the bandit is actually a female actress (Nielsen) in disguise.

The most baroque variation of the gender disguise comedy was Vitagraph's feature-length *A Florida Enchantment* (1914).[35] The film was adapted from a novel and play of the same name about magic seeds with the power to change one's sex overnight. Because the film portrays sexual inversion quite literally, including women flirting, kissing, and dancing together, and a coquettish, effeminate man, one might think it would have aroused the censors' ire; however, its class status seems to have saved it from concern. The film's star, Sydney Drew, was the standard-bearer for polite farce in the film industry of the 1910s. Thus, the film's high-class status was established by the reputation of its star, but also its location (an elite Florida resort), upper-class milieu, high production values, the reputation of the source work and production company, and its overall stylistic similarities to theatrical gender-disguise comedies.

SAME-SEX RELATIONSHIPS IN DRAMAS OF THE 1910S AND 1920S

Silent film dramas, including many adaptations from literature and theater, presented amorous relationships cultivated in single-sex environments like boarding schools or the military, as well as those between artists and apprentices. Some relationships were structured around age and power differences, as between teacher and student or artist and apprentice, while others were between fellow students, roommates, or soldiers of the same age. Familial love was sometimes a cover for other types of deep attachment. However, ardent same-sex attachments were not necessarily seen as contradicting a person's "normal" development and eventual marriage. Thus, the relationships could be erotic but not considered deviant.

One of the earliest cinema love stories between two men is the Swedish film *Vingarne* (*The Wings*, 1916). The film was adapted from the 1902 novel *Mikaël* by gay Danish novelist Herman Bang and was filled with art historical and literary references—framing the same-sex devotion within established representational traditions. In the film, an artist, Claude Zoret (Eigil Eide), comes across a beautiful youth, Eugene Mikael (Lars Hanson), painting outside. Zoret takes the youth on as his apprentice, model, and adopted son. Mikael poses for Zoret, who creates a nude sculpture of the boy reaching upward to an eagle that stretches its wings around him (see figure 32.3). As film scholar Richard Dyer points out, the statue references the Greek myth of Ganymede, a Trojan boy who drew the affection of Zeus and who has long symbolized love between an older and younger man.[36] However, in the film, the faithless Mikael has an affair with a countess and sells his copy of the sculpture to pay her debts. When he discovers Mikael's faithlessness, Zoret runs out to his version of the sculpture and drops dead at its feet. Mikael has a vision of his master's demise and leaves the countess, repenting his foolhardy ways.

The author Herman Bang's homosexuality was well known in Scandinavia. According to Scandinavian studies scholar Oliva Gunn, "the press outed Bang in more and less explicit terms over the years, and he more than once fled Denmark in fear of homophobic persecution. For example, following the *sædelighedsskandalen* (decency scandal) of 1906—during which time the press referred to him as the typical homosexual and as a murderer-by-means-of-perversity—he moved to Berlin."[37] The film was created by gay Finnish-Swedish director Mauritz Stiller and his friend, the gay Swedish writer and set designer Axel Esbensen. Stiller and Esbensen added a "frame story" before and after the main narrative in which Stiller plays himself coming across the real-life statue Vingarne (created by Swedish artist Carl Milles), then Bang's novel, and then the aspiring actor Nils Asther. In the frame story, Stiller decides to adapt Bang's novel to film using Milles's sculpture as the central prop and casts Asther as Mikael (though he ends up replacing Asther with Lars Hanson). After the interior story ends, the actors, director, and Asther all go watch the finished film in the concluding frame. It was an open secret in Stockholm that Asther was one of Stiller's "boys," and Asther later admitted that "One evening, Mauritz Stiller came up [to my apartment] with me and inaugurated me in the art of loving and enjoying my own sex," but, he added, "This was not anal sex."[38] Esbensen, too, was known to be gay; he had been arrested by Stockholm police for picking up two young men in a park and taking them home with him to have sex.[39]

Considering its topic and the reputation of its makers, it may surprise us today that *Vingarne* was received warmly in Sweden. Censors approved the film for audiences over age fifteen and critics praised the film's main story, though many criticized the

FIGURE 32.3 Mikael (Lars Hanson, right) poses for Zoret (Eigil Eide, left) in a Swedish film program for Mauritz Stiller's *The Wings* (1916). Courtesy of the Swedish Film Institute.

frame story.[40] One Stockholm critic wrote that "the drama itself [. . .] stands at a truly artistic level. And the novel's delicate subject has not been vandalized."[41] Critics were even more approving in Denmark. A solid twenty-eight copies of the film were sold abroad, including seven each to Germany and Russia, five to Austria, and copies to Finland, the UK, the Netherlands, Switzerland, Spain, Hungary, Argentina, Brazil,

Chile, Cuba, and the United States.[42] Part of the film's strategy to win widespread acceptance was to frame Zoret and Mikael's relationship as that between father and son. Though Milles's sculpture clearly represents Ganymede and Zeus, the film's original intertitles describe the sculpture as representing Icarus, the son of Daedalus who flew too close to the sun in the wings made by his father. This misdirection is an example of how silent films communicated one meaning to the "wise" and another to everyone else. Danish director Carl Theodor Dreyer adapted the novel to film once more in 1924 but downplayed the eroticism of the men's relationship even further.

Feature-length American films of the late 1920s often presented passionate relationships between men in the contexts of college and the battlefield. These friendships between masculine men were valorized as a higher type of connection than desire between men and women. Film historian Shane Brown presents examples such as *Brown of Harvard* (1926) and *The Collegians* shorts from Universal (1926–1929), as well as *Behind the Front* (1926), *Two Arabian Knights* (1927), and the part-talkie *Noah's Ark* (1928).[43] Here we come full circle to *Wings*. In this film, Jack and David are initially rivals who fight over the same girl. But when they are stationed together overseas during the Great War, they learn to love and trust each other. The film's central tragedy is that when Jack learns that David has been shot down, he shoots several German planes in revenge, unwittingly shooting down the very plane David had stolen from the enemy in order to return to his friend. Having accidentally killed David in the very act of trying to avenge him, Jack caresses and kisses David's face, then tenderly carries his body away.

Drawing on cultural historian Anthony Rotundo's work on nineteenth-century male romantic friendships, Brown describes these relations as "a kind of same-sex relationship which, while not sexual, often featured physical gestures such as kissing and caressing and even the sharing of a bed."[44] While these types of romantic friendships were indeed accepted and even valorized as part of middle- and upper-class culture, we cannot necessarily conclude that they were not also erotic or even sexual. Historian Jonathan Ned Katz has documented many examples of passionate "love between men" in the nineteenth and early twentieth century that included erotic touching and sex that did not preclude marrying, having children, and being admired pillars of society.[45] As George Chauncey has shown in *Gay New York*, deviance was defined more in terms of "pansy" self-presentation than in terms of sexual object choice.

Silent films also explored passionate relationships between women at single-sex schools. One well-known example is Dorothy Arzner's *The Wild Party* (US, 1929).[46] Similarly, *Norrtullsligan* (1929), a Swedish film adapted from the memoir of a famous woman journalist, represents intimacy between professional working women who live together in the big city. Four young professional women throw a party where they don togas and dance and pose together. At one point, a roomful of girls lies on one another's stomachs and interweaves their legs. Interestingly, only the one really masculine woman in attendance (a labor organizer) abstains from these antics. Later in the film, one roommate embraces and kisses another who is mourning the perfidy of her sweetheart. Like the male romantic friendships, the women's close and sometimes erotic relationships don't preclude their interest in and eventual marriage to men.

However, a handful of late 1920s feature films from Europe and the United States do offer a future for mannish women who choose to live with other women rather than marrying a man. For example, in *The Girl in Pants* (*Flickan i frack*, Sweden, 1926), adapted from a novel by gay Swedish author Hjalmar Bergman, Katja (Magda Holm) is rejected by her father for wearing her brother's tailcoat to a high school graduation party. She runs away to a country estate inhabited by "a wild horde of learned women" presided over by a mannish woman with an Eton crop, monocle, cigar and cane (see figure 32.4).[47] While Katja eventually gets back together with her beau, the country estate offers a glimpse of a different kind of future. Likewise, in *La Princesse Mandane* (France, 1928), directed by lesbian filmmaker Germaine Dulac, the princess of the title abandons her castle in the company of a mannishly dressed female friend rather than the leading man. More tragically, in *Der Büchse der Pandora* (*Pandora's Box*, 1929), the dapper Countess Augusta Geschwitz (Alice Roberts) falls for Lulu (Louise Brooks), who exploits and then brushes aside her affection.[48] In *The Crystal Cup* (US, 1927), a young woman adopts masculine garb and swears off men, reminding the critic at *Photoplay* of a lesbian play recently challenged on Broadway, even though the protagonist eventually ends up with a man.[49]

FIGURE 32.4 "Wild horde of learned women" in *The Girl in Pants* (1926). Lotten Brenner (Anna-Lisa Baude-Hansen) stands behind Dr. Karolina Willman (Lotten Ohlson), who reads a telegram. © AB Svensk Filmindustri (1926). Photography: Ragnar Westfelt, Archive still: The Swedish Film Institute.

Similar to gender-disguise comedies, some European and American dramas also used gender disguise to represent same-sex attraction. In Asta Nielsen's *Hamlet* (Germany, 1921), Nielsen plays Hamlet as a girl disguised as a boy for the sake of the throne, who is in love with her friend Horatio and embarrassed by Ophelia's attentions. In an even more complicated example, *Der Geiger von Florenz* (*The Violinist of Florence*, aka *Impetuous Youth*, Germany, 1926), an artist and his sister fight for the attentions of a young man they have picked up on the side of the road, who is actually a girl in disguise, Renée (Elisabeth Bergner). At one point the artist tells the boy, "Sometimes I think you are a girl—and often I wish you were." When the boy asks "What would you do if I were a girl?" he answers: "I think I should want to marry you." However, when the sister realizes that the boy is a girl, she places her hand on one of Renée's breasts and promises not to divulge Renée's secret, then the two women kiss on the lips (see figure 32.5). This film lingers on the prospect of apparent same-sex desire and erotic touch longer than most.

Big-budget American prestige dramas like *Four Horsemen of the Apocalypse* (1921), *Manslaughter* (1922), and *Wings* included same-sex eroticism in sequences set either in Ancient Rome or in contemporary Parisian dance halls. Effeminate male "eunuchs" were also common fixtures in silent film depictions of Antiquity, as in D. W. Griffith's *Judith of Bethulia* (1913)—characters that historian Susan Stryker points to as being part

FIGURE 32.5 Renée (Elizabeth Bergner) and the artist's sister (Grete Mosheim) kiss once the sister has agreed not to reveal Renée's gender in *The Violinist of Florence* (1926).

of a genealogy of trans representation in cinema.[50] Alla Nazimova's reputedly all-gay production of Oscar Wilde's *Salomé* (US, 1922) takes this association of sexual decadence and the ancient world to its furthest point. While unbound sexualities of the ancient world and Parisian nightclubs exceeded middle-class norms, the films cordoned off these sexualities to distinct times and places.

SAME-SEX EROTICISM AND GENDER INVERSION IN SLAPSTICK COMEDY

While early dance films, genteel comedies, and film dramas presented forms of same-sex attraction and cross-gender behavior that were part of high-culture traditions, slapstick comedies drew from working-class comedy conventions and reveled in less acceptable forms of gendered and sexual behavior. In early comedies, male performers regularly played comic women's roles, which presented audiences with assigned-male bodies performing womanhood and kisses and hugs between male actors. Examples include *Women's Rights* (UK, 1899), *Aunt Sallie's Wonderful Bustle* (UK, 1901), *Le Rembrandt de la rue Lepic* (France, 1911), *L'infaillible Baume* (*The Infallible Balm*, France, 1912), and *A Busy Day* (US, 1914). In the United States, popular stage female impersonator Gilbert Sarony appeared in a series of comedies for Edison and Lubin, culminating in *Meet Me at the Fountain* (US, 1904), in which Sarony's "old maid" character wins the hand of a nobleman by beating out a hoard of women chasing after him.

Like genteel comedies, slapstick often featured scenarios of gender disguise. American slapstick performers like Fatty Arbuckle, Charlie Chaplin, Harold Lloyd, Stan Laurel, and Mabel Normand repeatedly disguise their gender, usually to sneak into a single-sex environment or trick a love interest's busybody parent. The gender-disguise scenarios in slapstick comedies tend to involve more physical contact than their genteel comedy equivalents: slapstick offers more kissing, more sitting on laps and falling on top of each other, and more pinching and poking of butts. And characters in slapstick films more often react with shock or consternation to apparent same-sex couples, which may have endorsed a homoerotic interpretation. For example, in *Behind the Screen* (1916), when Chaplin kisses Edna Purviance while she is disguised as a boy, his boss reacts with visible shock, then acts out stereotypical "pansy" gestures as a kind of accusation. He struts across the set with an arched back and demonstratively limp wrist, then brushes one index finger against the other in a "for shame" gesture. This reaction makes the homoerotic reading of the scene clear, while genteel comedies more often used forms of suggestion and connotation that remained deniable.

Another arena for expressing alternative sexualities in slapstick films was male friendship. An early, quite suggestive example appears in Griffith's single-reel comedy *Pranks* (1909). While the film's main gag is that naughty boys switch the clothes of a male-female couple as they swim, forcing them to don the other's clothing, at one point the protagonists run past two men lying on the grass in a secluded area of a park. The men, played by Billy Quirk and Henry B. Walthall, jump up in surprise and make a series of swishy gestures, suggesting that they have been caught in a surreptitious rendezvous.[51] The gestures are similar to those of Chaplin's boss in *Behind the Screen*, suggesting that these were recognized codes. I have not found examples of friendships between women that are played for laughs in the same way, perhaps because women's passionate relationships with each other were not yet as pathologized as men's were or because female same-sex desire was associated with drama rather than comedy.

Film scholar Scott Balcerzak argues that American male comedy duos often queered masculine relationships by pairing a straight man with a hysterical feminized man or by forming a "queer unit," as with Laurel and Hardy.[52] He argues that Laurel and Hardy, who began making films together in 1927, were "the most overtly queer of on-screen buddies" and that they repeatedly "blur[red] the socially dictated line [separating] the homosocial and the homoerotic."[53] For example, in their silent short *Liberty* (1929), Laurel and Hardy play escaped convicts who accidentally don each other's pants. They keep trying to find a place to exchange pants—in an alley, behind a truck, etc.—but are repeatedly caught with their pants down. The onlookers' shocked reactions suggest that the men may be suspected of trying to find a place for a tryst. Two early sound shorts elaborate their close relationship—in *Their First Mistake* (1932) they raise a baby together, while in *Twice Two* (1933) they play their own twin sisters and pretend to be each other's wives. As Balcerzak puts it, this gag morphs "the homosocial . . . into the homosexual [. . .] since the image of the 'female' comedians paired with the male comedians only suggests a bizarre fantasy version of the male couple already established on screen."[54] Balcerzak argues that even the less overt Laurel and Hardy films queer male homosociality.

Gender-inverted comic types were also common in slapstick comedies of the 1910s and 1920s, likely drawing from the popularity of pansy and lesbian nightclub performers. Effeminate men, or "pansies," were the most common. For example, in the Hal Roach Studios' *The Soilers* (US, 1923), a parody of the Western drama *The Spoilers* (US, 1923), an effeminate cowboy's increasing feyness is one of the film's running jokes. The cowboy (George Rowe) walks into a room where the film's protagonist Bob Canister (Stan Laurel) and the evil Smacknamara (James Finlayson) argue over a land claim, rests one hand on his hips, then arches his back and walks primly through the scene while reading a magazine. He appears again after Canister's and Smacknamara's argument has devolved into a brawl, walking cheerfully in, holding arms up with wrists crooked. He lifts Canister's head to grab a piece of paper from the desk and prances out the door, back arched and wrists still bent. Once he leaves, the brawlers stare at the door for several moments before resuming their fight. Later, the brawlers crash through this door into a bedroom where the effeminate cowboy files and admires his nails then skips away. At the film's end, the cowboy leans out of a window (see figure 32.6), stretching his arms toward Canister, and cries: "My hero!" Canister dismisses him with a wave, so the spurned cowboy picks up a flowerpot, delicately smells the flower, then drops it on Canister head. The cowboy's admiring gesture and words to Canister are the "topper" of this particular gag, which relies on the comic disjuncture between the masculine cowboy ideal and the

FIGURE 32.6 Fey cowboy (George Rowe) yells "My hero!" in *The Soilers* (1923). Courtesy of UCLA Film & Television Archive.

cowboy's effeminacy. The gag also brings to the surface the repressed homoeroticism of male-dominated spaces like frontier mining towns. *The Soilers*' effeminate cowboy is typical of the pansy comic type, which also appears in films like *Battling Bruisers: Some Boxing Buffoonery* (UK, 1925) and *Irene* (US, 1926). In US films, this type was often associated with Europeans, the upper class, New York City, and certain professions like dressmakers and hairdressers. Some films also present the labor of transforming male "mollycoddles" into red-blooded American men through frontier living, such as *Algie the Miner* (US, 1912) and *The Mollycoddle* (US, 1920).

Just as some films showed sissyish men who had to toughen up on the frontier, a cycle of American films portrayed boyish frontier girls learning to adjust to the mores of the big city, such as Mabel Normand in *Mickey* (US, 1918) and Fay Tincher in *Rowdy Ann* (US, 1919). Though *Mickey* ends with heterosexual romance, in *Rowdy Ann*, the cowgirl Ann heroically breaks up a male-female couple, saving a wealthy girl from a swindler, and the film ends with Ann's pillow fight with two friends at their boarding school. Tincher herself lived with a female partner for many years, according to Steve Massa, so perhaps she had something to do with the film's lack of heterosexual resolution.[55] Other films, from *Kärlek och journalistisk* (*Love and Journalism*, Sweden, 1916) to *The Clinging Vine* (US, 1926), portrayed mannish professional women in big cities who fail to achieve their professional goals due to their unwillingness to flirt with men or else lament their lack of a love life.

While censors showed little concern for high-class presentations of same-sex desire and alternative gender expressions—and even praised some of them—they did worry about the slapstick presentation of feminine and cross-dressing men.[56] In the 1910s, the National Board of Review of Motion Pictures in New York released a series of recommendations in the 1910s warning against the comedic portrayal of "sexual perversion." A 1914 bulletin advised that "scenes of action between men and women or among members of the same sex [. . .] which stimulate sexual thoughts are distasteful to the rank and file of the American public."[57] An undated bulletin that aimed to keep slapstick comedies free from "smut" and "nauseating vulgarity" stated that "comedies based on the antics of a pervert and invert or any picture which involves degeneracy will be condemned altogether."[58] In 1916, the Board released a "Special Bulletin" specifically aimed at "sexual perversion" in comedy. Because the Board had observed a "growing tendency on the part of directors who are in search of comedy elements is to make use of characters portraying **sexual perversion** as a groundwork for comedy situations," they told producers: "**In accordance with a resolution passed by The National Board, you are hereby notified that any picture given over entirely to the comedy presentation of the sexual pervert will be condemned and that any part of a picture in which such a character is shown with intention to burlesque will be eliminated** [bold in original]."[59]

While the Board did not explain what counted as a "sexual pervert," we can get a sense of what they meant by examining the cuts that they recommended. The most common were performances of male effeminacy. For example, the Board recommended that Triangle Komedy's *A Film Exposure* (1917) "shorten the scene [. . .] where the butler meets the owner of the house to a flash so as to do away with part of the butler's effeminate manner" and eliminate the scene where the butler "speaks to the pugilist in an effeminate manner." On the Keystone Film Company's *Maggie's First False Step* (1917), the Board wrote: "In connection with the scene where the big man of effeminate type is in the store[,] change the subtitle 'Gentleman's Kimonas [*sic*] Please' to read 'Young Men's Suits Please'" and "Eliminate the scene in which the big effeminate man appears with the others of the same type in the Department Store when he gives them ornaments for their button holes." The reference to "Gentlemen's Kimonos" suggested an association between sexual perversion and Orientalism. The Board also objected to the cross-dressed kissing scene in Chaplin's *Behind the Screen*, but not to the kiss itself, rather to the boss's reaction to it. They recommended to "eliminate the action of the fat man imitating a sissified character. This cut should be made from the point where he shakes his finger at Chaplin and the girl [until] that part where he switches [swishes] up and down the room." While that section still appears in the copies of the film that circulate today, an intertitle that the Board wanted cut (in which the boss exclaims "Oh! Mercy") does not. It is clear from these recommendations, and from the Board's frustration when the recommendations were ignored, that effeminate and "sissified" men were a staple of American slapstick comedies, despite censor concern.[60]

While the Board did not generally object to cross-dressing per se, they did sometimes recommend that scenes in which a cross-dressed man engaged in sexualized activity with another man be eliminated. For example, for L-KO's *A Gambler's Gambol* (1916), they recommended: "Eliminate the scene [. . .] showing the gambler's wife (a man dressed as a woman) sitting on top of the other men counting the money." For Vitagraph's *Turks and Troubles* (1917), they told the producer to reduce to a flash "the scene which shows one man holding the other in his lap in the supposition that he is a woman" and "those parts of the dance in which the man masquerading as a woman wiggles his body suggestively." The Board was particularly concerned about a scene in the Selig comedy *A Trip to Chinatown* (US, 1917) in which a "swordsman [. . .] puts his finger in his mouth as a degenerate." As with the reference to "Gentlemen's Kimonos," sexual degeneracy is here associated with fantastical Orientalism.[61] Producers regularly disregarded the Board's prohibitions, so we can assume that these types of gags continued to appear in these and other films. When the Motion Pictures Producers and Distributors of America issued their "Don'ts and Be Carefuls" a decade later, they banned "any inference [i.e., implication] of sex perversion." In 1930, the Production Code adopted the same policy.[62] The constant work of these censors to try and eliminate representations of "sex perversion" demonstrates just how persistent the representations were. Comedy was the perfect genre for flouting taboos related to alternative genders and sexualities, because these meanings could be either denied or else dismissed through ridicule.

Advocating for Sexual and Gender Minorities in German "Enlightenment" Films

Only two films that I know of campaigned directly and explicitly for the rights of gay and intersex people during the silent era. They did this by combining a high-culture appeal to science and a low-culture approach of sensationalist melodrama. These films seem to only have been possible to make in Germany during the short period after the war when censorship was temporarily abolished (November 1918–June 1920).[63] In 1917, film director Richard Oswald began directing a series of sexual hygiene films, also called *Aufklärungsfilmer* or "Enlightenment" films, that used melodramatic plots to explore pressing public health issues such as sex work, sexually transmitted disease, drug use, abortion, and homosexuality. While critics denounced the films as prurient bids for cash that glamorized bad behavior, Jill Suzanne Smith has shown that the films' messaging was in line with the platform of the League for the Protection of Mothers and Sex Reform and that Oswald often partnered with its members.[64] In 1918 Oswald began working with sexologist Magnus Hirschfeld on a series of films. Their first was *Sinful Mothers (Penal Code S218)* (1918) on the dangers of back alley abortions. Hirschfeld and Oswald released two films the next year—*Prostitutionen* (*Prostitution*, 1919), criticizing state control over sex work, and *Anders als die Andern* (*Different from the Others*, 1919), calling for the abolition of Paragraph 175, which outlawed male homosexuality.[65]

Different from the Others was sponsored by Hirschfeld's Scientific-Humanitarian Committee, founded in 1897, which campaigned for the rights of homosexuals, transvestites, and intersex people. The film was released to the general public in May 1919, two months before the opening of Hirschfeld's Institute for Sexology in Berlin.[66] It tells the story of a violinist, Paul Körner (Conrad Veidt), who takes a young male student, Kurt Sivers (Fritz Schulz), under his wing and is blackmailed by a former lover, Franz Bollek (Reinhold Schünzel), until he commits suicide. The film includes depictions of a nightclub full of same-sex couples dancing together. At one point, Hirschfeld (playing himself) delivers an illustrated lecture arguing that homosexuality is part of natural human variation. The film ends with Hirschfeld proclaiming "Through knowledge to justice!" and the image of a brush striking out Paragraph 175. (Unfortunately, people continued to be prosecuted under Paragraph 175 until 1957 in East Germany and 1969 in West Germany.) Though popular at the box office, it inspired significant controversy and pushback from police censorship boards and politicians and was banned when new federal censorship laws were put into place in 1920.

At the same time as *Different from the Others*, Hirschfeld worked with directors Julius Rode and Paul Legband on *Aus eines Mannes Mädchenjahren* (*A Man's Girlhood*, 1919). The film was adapted from the memoir of one of Hirschfeld's patients, Karl M. Baer, an intersex person assigned female at birth who eventually demanded to live as a man and was able to change his legal sex designation.[67] German actress Erika Glässner played the title role. Unfortunately, the film is considered lost. The distributor described *A Man's Girlhood* as a tragedy that would lead viewers to sympathize with the protagonist's plight: "Erika Glässner embodies pseudohermaphroditism in a self-effacing manner of characterization. She portrays the unfortunately afflicted boy/girl in gripping scenes, as a poor creature of indeterminate sex—scenes that capture all the tragedy of sexual intermediacy."[68] The film does not seem to have provoked censors as *Different from the Others* did, perhaps because audiences read it within the tradition of women disguising themselves as men in order to seek work.

Different from the Others and *A Man's Girlhood* seem to be alone in the silent era in their depiction of unquestionably homosexual and intersex protagonists, embrace of sexology, and direct demands for political reform. While they were not screened as widely as the comedies and dramas discussed previously, they demonstrate that direct and sympathetic representations of alternative sexual and gender identities occurred in film as far back as the 1910s.

Alternative Genders and Sexualities Offscreen

Just as cinema frequently represented same-sex desire and cross-gender expression through high-culture frameworks, newspapers and magazines often presented film workers' sexual identities through the trope of the cosmopolitan European artist, a strategy that informed the "wise" while leaving naïve readers in the dark. As in contemporary theater and the arts, many of the people involved in making movies had same-sex lovers and some expressed their gender in atypical ways. Many of the films described above were authored, at least in part, by lesbian and gay directors, authors, and actors. The press communicated the sexualities of film workers to audiences through established codes that were also being used in film, so audiences were encountering cinema's alternative genders and sexualities both on- and offscreen.

As film historian Richard deCordova has shown, the drive to uncover secrets is part of the structure of stardom, especially sexual secrets.[69] However, during the 1920s, many stars' alternative sexualities were essentially open secrets that were communicated by the mainstream press to readers through established codes.[70] Contemporary European art circles were understood to include "bohemian" genders and sexualities, such as, for example, the gender fluidity of Claude Cahun, Gluck, and Marcel Duchamp (aka Rrose Sélavy) and the social circles of lesbian icons Natalie Barney and Gertrude Stein. When people from these European art milieux entered filmmaking, bohemian genders and sexualities entered too. Writer-director Germaine Dulac is one example. Dulac sported a fashionable, masculine look and wore her hair in a short Eton crop. Film historian Tami Williams has shown that Dulac's female lovers were instrumental to her career: dancer Stasia Napierkowska introduced Dulac to filmmaking and acted in her films; Irène Hillel-Erlanger started a production company with Dulac that made six features and several journalistic shorts; and Marie-Anne Colson-Malleville, who lived with Dulac from 1922 until Dulac's death in 1942, worked as a directorial assistant and wrote songs that Dulac adapted to film.[71] According to Williams, Dulac's relationships were well known.

Likewise, in Sweden, director Mauritz Stiller's relationships with young men like Asther were part of his image as a cosmopolitan dandy and artist (see figure 32.7). He was part of a circle of queer artists in Stockholm and Berlin that included his collaborator Axel Esbensen. One gay man in Stockholm who had been arrested for having sex with a man lamented in his diary that even though Stiller's "guilt" was "ten thousand times greater than mine," the lucky director seemed to be able to get away with anything.[72] In 1925, a yearbook of Swedish film personalities declared Stiller to be "Cinema's [Oscar] Wilde."[73] Cultivating a public persona as elegant cosmopolitan allowed Stiller to parlay his homosexuality, as well as his Jewishness and foreignness, into assets for the Swedish film industry, a small national film industry looking toward a global market.[74] In Europe, same-sex desire and fashionable androgyny were associated with contemporary art circles and helped filmmakers tie their craft to art.

Interestingly, there seems to have been a professional masculine look shared by lesbian film directors transnationally in the 1920s and 1930s. Germaine Dulac (see figure 32.8a) in France, Dorothy Arzner (see figure 32.8b) in the United States, Tazuko Sakane (see figure 32.8c) in Japan, and Esther Eng (see figure 32.8.d) in Hong Kong and the United States all sported short, slicked-back hair, blazers, and buttoned-down shirts.[75] Their masculine style was associated with modern professional women (as seen, for example, in the ultra-mannish look of Leatrice Joy in *The Clinging Vine*) but was also common among professional and artistic lesbians. Their masculine style and relationships with

FIGURE 32.7 Portrait of Mauritz Stiller. Courtesy of the Photo Archive at the Swedish Film Institute.

women do not seem to have hindered their careers—on the contrary, they were some of the few women directors in industries that had become dominated by men. Perhaps their masculine gender presentations helped them be considered "one of the boys"?

In the United States, same-sex desire and fashionable androgyny were associated with Europe. Many of the lesbian and gay European actors brought to Hollywood, such as Greta Garbo, Marlene Dietrich, and Alla Nazimova, were promoted in these terms. For example, profiles of Garbo noted that she often wore trousers and men's clothing, did not like dresses or shopping, and didn't want to get married. At first, Garbo's eccentricities were interpreted as characteristics of a working-class Swedish immigrant. However, as she was increasingly spotted with close women friends, such as Lilyan Tashman, Gigi d'Orsay, Mercedes de Acosta, and Salka Viertel, journalists began to speculate more explicitly about her sexuality. One *Photoplay* writer reported that Garbo's favorite flowers were "pansies and violets" and that "a bunch of violets was almost always to be

FIGURE 32.8 Germaine Dulac (top left): rights reserved, courtesy of Cinémathèque français. Dorothy Arzner (top right): courtesy of the BFI National Archive. Tazuko Sakane (bottom left): Sakane stands in between Takehisa Shin (left) and Tōkichi Ishimoto (right) at Daiichi Eiga, courtesy of the Museum of Kyoto. Esther Eng (bottom right): courtesy of S. Louisa Wei and Sally Ng—for more on Eng, watch *Golden Gate Girls* (2014).

found at the head of her bed."[76] These types of flowers were well-known codes for lesbianism. In 1933, Garbo's sound film, *Queen Christina*, cowritten by Viertel, aligned Garbo's eccentricities with those of the notorious trouser-wearing, woman-loving Swedish monarch.[77]

Male stars like Rudolph Valentino were promoted as irresistible ladies' men but also interpreted as "pink powder puff" threats to American masculinity.[78] However, studios also promoted all-American actors like "wisecracker" William Haines as gay. Film historian Ron Gregg has shown that "[B]oth Haines and the studio [MGM] tried to expand Haines' star appeal by signaling his homosexuality through codes that would have been intelligible to a sophisticated urban audience."[79] Profiles of Haines noted his sensitive nature, close relationship with his mother, interest in interior decorating (he created the "Hollywood Regency" style of interior decoration), and lack of interest in sports.[80] Haines sometimes mimicked pansy performers and female impersonators in his film performances.[81] While Garbo's house was described as very masculine, Haines's house was described as extremely feminine.[82] Film archivist Brett L. Abrams shows that the press used similar codes to describe actors Ramon Novarro and Alla Nazimova.[83]

There was eventually a backlash to these publicity strategies and filmic representations of alternative genders and sexualities. In 1933, the Screen Writers' Guild and the Writers' Branch of the Academy declared a "War on Filth."[84] Will Hays, head of the new Production Code Administration, lamented that "This slant they have taken out there [in Hollywood] on homosexuality and Lesbianism has about ruined us."[85] The open secrets of the 1920s shifted to a regime of actual secrets, though the structure of stardom continued the ceaseless drive to uncover them. However, during the silent era, the varied field of gender and sexuality was found in press descriptions of actors and directors, not only onscreen.

Conclusion

From the 1890s through the early 1930s, silent cinema represented a varied and diverse field of genders and sexualities, participating in the shifting definitions and possibilities of such categories over these volatile years. Silent cinema presented alternative genders and sexualities such as passionate same-sex relationships and cross-dressing through high-culture frameworks, often adapting existing literature and theater, whereas slapstick treaded in more taboo territory with parodic performances of effeminate pansies and cross-dressing that leads to sexualized same-sex physical encounters. Only a couple of films dared to advance outright pleas for the acceptance of homosexual and intersex people. Lesbian and gay actors and directors were responsible for some of these representations, their sexualities "open secrets" associated with European artistic social circles that were sometimes even promoted by studios and fan magazines.

In this essay, I have focused primarily on films and film workers from the United States, Sweden, and Germany, but this picture would be enriched by attention to other places, as well as to how these films and stars traveled and how they were received and understood in different places. It would also be fascinating to explore how these representations influenced filmgoers, through additional research in scrapbooks, diaries, and contemporary descriptions of the behaviors of fans.

The realization that fantasies of gender malleability, effeminate men and masculine women, and many kinds of same-sex love were present on the screen already during the silent era demonstrates that gender and sexual diversity have long had a central place in our cultural imaginations and entertainment culture. The differences in how genders and sexualities were understood in the early twentieth century compared to now demonstrate that other ways of organizing and understanding these core aspects of our existence are possible and that we can help transform them through audiovisual media.

Notes

1. Vito Russo, *The Celluloid Closet: Homosexuality in the Movies* (New York: Harper & Row, 1981), 3–61.
2. See, for example, Jonathan Ned Katz, *Love Stories: Sex Between Men Before Homosexuality* (Chicago, IL: University of Chicago Press, 2013); Martha Vicinus, *Intimate Friends: Women Who Loved Women, 1778–1928* (Chicago, IL: Chicago University Press, 2004).
3. Sharon Marcus, *Between Women: Friendship, Desire, and Marriage in Victorian England* (Princeton, NJ: Princeton University Press, 2007); Stephen Best and Sharon Marcus, "Surface Reading: An Introduction," *Representations* 108, no. 1 (November 1, 2009): 1–21, https://doi.org/10.1525/rep.2009.108.1.1.
4. Chris Berry, S. Louisa Wei, Johan Nordström, Michael Raine, and Romit Dasgupta have described same-sex eroticism in East Asian silent films such as *Daigaku no wakadanna* (*The Boss's Son at College*, Japan, 1933), *Fukujusō* (*The Scent of Pheasant's Eye*, Japan, 1935), and *Dalu* (*The Big Road*, China, 1935). See Chris Berry, "Asian Values, Family Values," *Journal of Homosexuality* 40, no. 3–4 (May 2001): 211–31; S. Louisa Wei, "Finding Voices Through Her Images: *Golden Gate Girls* as an Attempt in Writing Women Filmmakers' History," *Feminist Media Histories* 2, no. 2 (April 2016): 32–46; Johan Nordström, "Otome Shirizu Sono Ichi Hanamonogatari Fukujoso," Le Giornate del cinema muto database, 2013 (http://www.cinetecadelfriuli.org/gcm/ed_precedenti/screenings_recorden.php?ID=6999); Michael Raine, Letter to Laura Horak, "Re: Japanese Lesbian Involved in Silent Cinema?," July 31, 2017; Romit Nasgupta, "Queer Imaginings and Traveling of 'Family' across Asia," in *Queering Migrations Towards, From, and Beyond Asia*, eds. Hugo Córdova Quero, Joseph N. Goh, and Michael Sepidoza Campos (New York: Palgrave Macmillan, 2014), 99–112. And Rielle Navitski has described representations of male same-sex eroticism in Latin American silent films such as *El Puño de Hierro* (*The Iron Fist*, Mexico, 1927) and *Morfina* (*Morphine*, Brazil, 1928). See Rielle Navitski, *Public Spectacles of Violence: Sensational Cinema and Journalism in Early Twentieth-Century Mexico and Brazil* (Durham, NC: Duke University Press, 2017), 115. However, these areas fall outside the scope of this chapter.
5. Russo, *The Celluloid Closet*.
6. For example: Siobhan Somerville, *Queering the Color Line: Race and the Invention of Homosexuality in American Culture* (Durham, NC: Duke University Press, 2000); Ronald Gregg, "Gay Culture, Studio Publicity, and the Management of Star Discourse: The Homosexualization of William Haines in Pre-Code Hollywood," *Quarterly Review of Film and Video* 20, no. 2 (January 1, 2003): 81–97; Mark Lynn Anderson, *Twilight of the Idols: Hollywood and the Human Sciences in 1920s America* (Berkeley: University of California Press, 2011); Xinyi Zhao, "So Queer Yet So Straight: Japan's First Female Director(s)" (Women and the Silent Screen IX, Shanghai, 2017); Susan Potter, *Queer Timing: The Emergence of Lesbian Sexuality in Early Cinema* (Urbana: University of Illinois Press, 2019); Kiki Loveday, "Sister Acts: Victorian Porn, Lesbian Drag, and Queer Reproduction," *Framework: The Journal of Cinema and Media* 60, no. 2 (Fall 2019): 201–226.
7. Potter, *Queer Timing*, 9.
8. Marcus, *Between Women*.
9. Anderson, *Twilight of the Idols*, 74.
10. Two drawbacks to using the terms "lesbian" and "gay" is that they erase the elements of gender variance associated with sexual inversion at the time and also the bisexual or

pansexual behaviors of many of these figures (though bisexual meant something else at the time and pansexual had not yet been coined).
11. Lucy Bland and Laura Doan, eds., *Sexology Uncensored: The Documents of Sexual Science* (Chicago, IL: University of Chicago Press, 1998).
12. Lisa Duggan, *Sapphic Slashers: Sex, Violence, and American Modernity* (Durham, NC: Duke University Press, 2000); Greger Eman, "1907: Det Homosexuella Genombrottet," in Göran Söderström et al., eds., *Sympatiens Hemlighetsfulla Makt: Stockholms Homosexuella 1860–1960* (Stockholm: Stockholmia förlag, 1999), 149–164.
13. The 1923 Broadway production of *The God of Vengeance* was recently the subject of an award-winning Broadway play, *Indecent*. The Swedish novel was Martin Koch's *Guds vackra värld, en historia om rätt och orätt*. Kaier Curtin, *We Can Always Call Them Bulgarians: The Emergence of Lesbians and Gay Men on the American Stage* (Boston, MA: Alyson Publications, 1987); Greger Eman, "Homosexualitet i Kulturdebatten," in Göran Söderström et al., eds., *Sympatiens Hemlighetsfulla Makt*, 165–180; Jodie Medd, "'The Cult of the Clitoris': Anatomy of a National Scandal," *Modernism/modernity* 9, no. 1 (January 2002): 21–49.
14. George Chauncey, *Gay New York: Gender, Urban Culture, and the Makings of the Gay Male World, 1890–1940* (New York: Basic Books, 1994); Jens Rydström, *Sinners and Citizens: Bestiality and Homosexuality in Sweden, 1880–1950* (Chicago, IL: University of Chicago Press, 2003).
15. Michel Foucault, *The History of Sexuality: An Introduction*, vol. 1, trans. Robert Hurley (New York: Vintage Books, 1978), 43.
16. Chauncey, *Gay New York*; Leila Rupp, *Sapphistries: A Global History of Love Between Women* (New York: New York University Press, 2009); Jack Halberstam, *Female Masculinity* (Durham, NC: Duke University Press, 1998).
17. Karl Heinrich Ulrichs, *Forschungen über das Räthsel der mannmännlichen Liebe*, 1864; Edward Carpenter, *Homogenic Love and Its Place in a Free Society* (London: Redundancy Press, 1908).
18. Magnus Hirschfeld, *Die Transvestiten: ein Untersuchung über den erotischen Verkleidungstrieb: mit umfangreichem casuistischen und historischen Material* (Berlin: Alfred Pulvermacher, 1910); Havelock Ellis and John Addington Symonds, *Sexual Inversion* (London: Wilson and Macmillan, 1897).
19. Chauncey, *Gay New York*; Rupp, *Sapphistries*.
20. Men also played women's roles in some forms of theater in Japan, China, and India; women played men's roles in Japan's Takarazuka Revue.
21. Lynn Garafola, "The Travesty Dancer in Nineteenth-Century Ballet," *Dance Research Journal* 17/18 (October 1, 1985): 35–40, https://doi.org/10.2307/1478078.
22. Ballet and *féerie* films like *Don Quichotte* (France, 1904), *Le Langage des Fleurs* (*The Language of Flowers*, France, 1904), *Porcelaines tendres* (*Tender Porcelains*, France, 1909), and *Cagliostro* (France, 1910) also include dancing female couples.
23. "Divorna På Biografduken," *Aftonbladet*, October 21, 1909. My translation. For more on this film, see Laura Horak, "Cross-Dressing and Transgender Representation in Swedish Cinema, 1908–2017," *European Journal of Scandinavian Studies* 47, no. 2 (2017): 380, https://doi.org/10.1515/ejss-2017-0025.
24. Potter, *Queer Timing*, 58.

25. Trans media scholar Eliza Steinbock argues that George Méliès's trick films featuring cuts that transform men into women and vice versa "provide a view of gender that is based on montage and assembly" that contributed to the emergence of "diverse conceptualizations for trans embodiments and identities" in the early twentieth century. It would be well worth researching the reception of these films to flesh out this fascinating claim. Eliza Steinbock, *Shimmering Images: Trans Cinema, Embodiment and the Aesthetics of Change* (Durham, NC: Duke University Press, 2019), 40, 27; see also 36–42.
26. This film was made as a test rather than a product to be distributed.
27. Daniel Eagan, *America's Film Legacy: The Authoritative Guide to the Landmark Movies in the National Film Registry* (New York: Continuum, 2010), 3.
28. Russo, *The Celluloid Closet*; Wheeler W. Dixon, *Straight: Constructions of Heterosexuality in the Cinema* (Albany: State University of New York Press, 2003), 53; Shane Brown, *Queer Sexualities in Early Film: Cinema and Male-Male Intimacy* (London: I. B. Tauris, 2016).
29. Katz, *Love Stories*.
30. Chris Straayer, "Redressing the 'Natural': The Temporary Transvestite Film," in *Deviant Eyes, Deviant Bodies: Sexual Re-Orientations in Film and Video* (New York: Columbia University Press, 1996), 42–78; Annette Kuhn, "Sexual Disguise in Cinema," in *The Power of the Image: Essays on Representation and Sexuality* (London: Routledge and Kegan Paul, 1985), 48–75.
31. See, for example, *Twelfth Night* (US, 1910), *La zia di Carlo* (Italy, 1911), *As You Like It* (US, 1912), *Charley's Aunt* (US, 1925), *Charleys tant* (Sweden, 1926), and *As You Like It* (UK, 1929).
32. William Uricchio and Roberta Pearson, *Reframing Culture: The Case of the Vitagraph Quality Films* (Princeton, NJ: Princeton University Press, 1993).
33. Laura Horak, "Cross-Dressing in Griffith's Biograph Films: Humor, Heroics, and Edna 'Billy' Foster's Good Bad Boys," in Charlie Keil, ed., *A Companion to D.W. Griffith* (West Sussex, UK: Wiley-Blackwell, 2018), 289–290.
34. The only Eltinge films known to survive at this time are the cross-dressing comedy *Madame Behave* (US. 1925); the dramas *An Adventuress* (1920) and *Maid to Order* (1931); and *How Molly Malone Made Good* (US, 1915), in which Eltinge plays himself in a brief cameo.
35. R. Bruce Brasell, "A Seed for Change: The Engenderment of 'A Florida Enchantment,'" *Cinema Journal* 36, no. 4 (Summer 1997): 3–21; Somerville, *Queering the Color Line*, 39–76; Laura Horak, *Girls Will Be Boys: Cross-Dressed Women, Lesbians, and American Cinema, 1908–1934* (New Brunswick, NJ: Rutgers University Press, 2016), 93–117; Potter, *Queer Timing*, 63–79.
36. Richard Dyer, "Sweden 1916: Taking Off," in *Now You See It: Studies on Lesbian and Gay Film*, 2nd ed. (London: Routledge, 2003), 8–22.
37. Olivia Gunn, "Love Thy Fatherland as Thyself: Patriotism and Passing in Herman Bang," *Scandinavian Studies* 85, no. 2 (August 29, 2013): 185, https://doi.org/10.1353/scd.2013.0014. See also Niels Nyegaard, "Heteronormative Foundations of Modern Citizenship in Early-Twentieth-Century Denmark," *NORA—Nordic Journal of Feminist and Gender Research* 25, no. 1 (January 2, 2017): 4–18, https://doi.org/10.1080/08038740.2017.1306580.
38. Nils Asther, *Narrens Väg* (Stockholm: Carlsson, 1988), 31.

39. Göran Söderström, "Privatperson Stiller Och Hans Krets," in Göran Söderström et al., eds., *Sympatiens Hemlighetsfulla Makt*, 327–331.
40. "Vingarne: Drama i 4 Akter (1916) – Svensk Filmdatabas," accessed January 4, 2019, http://www.svenskfilmdatabas.se/sv/item/?type=film&itemid=3405.
41. Elin Brandell (Regan), "Vingarna-Ett Sensationellt Svenskt Filmdrama," *Dagens Nyheter*, September 5, 1916, *Vingarne* clipping file, SFI.
42. "Vingarne."
43. Brown, *Queer Sexualities in Early Film*, 81–142.
44. Ibid., 84.
45. Katz, *Love Stories*.
46. Andrea Weiss, *Vampires and Violets: Lesbians in Film* (New York: Penguin Books, 1993); Judith Mayne, *Directed by Dorothy Arzner* (Bloomington: Indiana University Press, 1994); Susan Potter, "Mobilizing Lesbian Desire: The Sexual Kinaesthetics of Dorothy Arzner's *The Wild Party*," *Screen* 52, no. 4 (January 12, 2011): 442–460, https://doi.org/10.1093/screen/hjr036.
47. "Flickan i Frack: En Sommarlätt Filmhistoria— (1926)—Svensk Filmdatabas," accessed January 4, 2019, http://www.svenskfilmdatabas.se/sv/item/?type=film&itemid=3616.
48. For the US reception of this film, see Horak, *Girls Will Be Boys*, 173–175.
49. "The Shadow Stage," *Photoplay*, October 1927.
50. From interview with Stryker in Sam Feder, *Disclosure* (Netflix, 2020).
51. Horak, "Cross-Dressing in D. W. Griffith's Biograph Films," 286–287.
52. Scott Balcerzak, *Buffoon Men: Classic Hollywood Comedians and Queered Masculinity* (Detroit, MI: Wayne State University Press, 2013), 139–163, 169–172.
53. Ibid., 143.
54. Ibid., 150.
55. Steve Massa, *Slapstick Divas: The Women of Silent Comedy* (Albany, GA: BearManor Media, 2017), 239–240.
56. When the Production Code was instituted in the early 1930s, censors turned their attention to female same-sex eroticism in genteel dramas and comedies like *Queen Christina*, *Sylvia Scarlett*, and *Cavalcade*. Horak, *Girls Will Be Boys*, 169–223.
57. National Board of Review of Moving Pictures, "Bulletin 10" (New York, October 1, 1914), 10, National Board of Review of Moving Pictures, Box 171, New York Public Library, Manuscripts & Archives Division.
58. National Board of Review of Moving Pictures, "Special Bulletin on Motion Picture Comedies" (New York, n.d.), National Board of Review of Moving Pictures, Box 171, New York Public Library, Manuscripts & Archives Division.
59. National Board of Review of Moving Pictures, "Special Bulletin to Motion Picture Producers" (New York, n.d.), National Board of Review of Moving Pictures, Box 171, New York Public Library, Manuscripts & Archives Division.
60. National Board of Review of Moving Pictures, "Reviews and Reports of Correspondents" (New York, n.d.), National Board of Review of Moving Pictures, Boxes 155–158, New York Public Library, Manuscripts & Archives Division.
61. Ibid.
62. Jon Lewis, "Appendix," in *Hollywood v. Hardcore: How the Struggle Over Censorship Saved the Modern Film Industry* (New York: NYU Press, 200), 301-316.

63. James D. Steakley, "Cinema and Censorship in the Weimar Republic: The Case of *Anders Als Die Andern*," *Film History* 11, no. 2 (June 1999): 189, 192.
64. Bund für Mutterschutz und Sexualreform. Its members included "the feminist activist Helene Stöcker, the psychoanalyst Sigmund Freud, the writer Frank Wedekind, and sexologists Iwan Bloch and Magnus Hirschfeld." See Jill Suzanne Smith, "Richard Oswald and the Social Hygiene Film: Promoting Public Health or Promiscuity?," in Christian Rogowski, ed., *The Many Faces of Weimar Cinema: Rediscovering Germany's Filmic Legacy* (Rochester, NY: Camden House, 2010), 23–24.
65. Smith, "Richard Oswald and the Social Hygiene Film," 15.
66. Ibid., 25.
67. N. O. Body, *Aus Eines Mannes Mädchenjahren* (Berlin: G. Riecke Nachf., 1907); N. O. Body, *Memoirs of a Man's Maiden Years*, trans. Deborah Simon (Philadelphia: University of Pennsylvania Press, 2009). On the film, see "Aus Eines Mannes Mädchenjahren," FilmPortal.de, accessed February 8, 2017, http://www.filmportal.de/film/aus-eines-mannes-maedchenjahren_f6cd676a2f7f4aa0b1bd2ce511a1b9a9. The script was written by Beate Schach and Karl Grüne. Grüne went on to direct *Marquis d'Eon, der Spion der Pompadour* (1929), one of two German films about the historical Chevalier d'Eon, who lived as both man and woman and whose name British sexologist Havelock Ellis appropriated as an English-language term for transvestism ("Eonism").
68. As quoted in "Bei Der UFA Machte Man Das so . . . : Kino—Das Grosse Traumgeschäft," *Der Spiegel*, October 11, 1950, http://www.spiegel.de/spiegel/print/d-44450783.html. Translation by Nicholas Baer.
69. Richard deCordova, *Picture Personalities: The Emergence of the Star System in America* (Urbana: University of Illinois Press, 1990), 98.
70. In the 1900s and 1910s lesbian and gay film actors in the United States didn't seem to have been subjected to any particular press scrutiny or speculation. See Edith Storey and Fay Tincher, as well as the actors described in Anthony Slide, "The Silent Closet," *Film Quarterly* 52, no. 4 (1999): 24–32.
71. Tami Williams, *Germaine Dulac: A Cinema of Sensations* (Urbana: University of Illinois Press, 2014).
72. Söderström, "Privatperson Stiller Och Hans Krets," 330.
73. Teddy Nyblom, ed., "Mauritz Stiller-Filmens Wilde," in *Film Och Filmfolk*, Våra Nöjens Bokserie (Stockholm, 1925).
74. Laura Horak, "Artist, Cosmopolitan, Homosexual, Jew: Mauritz Stiller and *Vingarne* (1916)" (Society of Cinema and Media Studies, Seattle, 2014).
75. Xinyi Zhao, "Tazuko Sakane," Women Film Pioneers Project, https://wfpp.columbia.edu/pioneer/tazuko-sakane/ July 21, 2017; S. Louisa Wei, "Esther Eng," Women Film Pioneers Project, https://wfpp.columbia.edu/pioneer/esther-eng/ August 15, 2014. Sakane named Dorothy Arzner and Leontine Sagan as inspirations. She even tried to make a Japanese version of Sagan's *Mädchen in Uniform* (*Girls in Uniform*, 1931), but her studio refused. Zhao, "So Queer Yet So Straight."
76. Rilla Page Palmborg, "Chapter Two of The Private Life of Greta Garbo," *Photoplay*, October 1930, 142.
77. For more on Garbo's reception in the United States, see Laura Horak, "Queer Crossings: Greta Garbo, National Identity, and Gender Deviance," in Jennifer M. Bean, Anupama Kapse, and Laura Horak, eds., *Silent Cinema and the Politics of Space* (Bloomington: Indiana University Press, 2014), 270–294.

78. Gaylyn Studlar, "'Optic Intoxication': Rudolph Valentino and Dance Madness," in *This Mad Masquerade: Stardom and Masculinity in the Jazz Age* (New York: Columbia University Press, 1996), 150–198; Anderson, *Twilight of the Idols*.
79. Gregg, "Gay Culture, Studio Publicity, and the Management of Star Discourse," 82.
80. Ibid., 89.
81. Ibid., 91.
82. On queerness and profiles of Hollywood star houses, see Brett L. Abrams, *Hollywood Bohemians: Transgressive Sexuality and the Selling of the Movieland Dream* (Jefferson, NC: McFarland, 2008), 113–158.
83. Ibid., 98–101, 121–126.
84. "Writers War on Filth," *Hollywood Reporter*, February 27, 1933.
85. Will H. Hays, "Reaffirmation Necessary to Avoid Emergency and Legislation and Anti-Movie Editorials," January 5, 1933, MDDPA Digital Archive, https://web.archive.org/web/20221112222432/http://mppda.flinders.edu.au/records/914.

CHAPTER 33

ART, ANTI-ART, AND POETIC CINEMA
Revisiting Un Chien andalou *(Luis Buñuel, 1929)*

BREIXO VIEJO

But venom must be fought with venom, and cinema with cinema.
    Luis Buñuel, "Quand la chair succombe," 1927[1]

Un Chien andalou, though a subjective drama developed as a poem, is nonetheless a film of social consciousness.
    Jean Vigo, "Vers un cinéma social," 1930[2]

It is never the image that goes too far, but always reality.
    Amos Vogel, *Film as a Subversive Art*, 1974[3]

WEST Hollywood, August 17, 1946. The Spanish filmmaker Luis Buñuel, aged forty-six, has been unemployed for ten months; his last job as a dubbing producer for Warner Brothers ended when the studio decided to terminate the operations of the Spanish Dubbing Unit in early November 1945. Married, with two sons, without savings, and the lease of his 5642 Fountain Avenue home about to expire, Buñuel has now been living in exile for ten years (he fled Madrid in September 1936 after the outbreak of the Civil War, first to Paris, and then, two years later, to the United States). Life is passing fast. The last time he directed a film, he was thirty-three. His three "short" pictures—*Un Chien andalou* (1929), *L'Âge d'or* (1930), and *Las Hurdes, tierra sin pan* (1933)—total only 110 minutes of screen time: a few reels hidden in the back of a dark cupboard. As he writes to an old friend, describing his inability to find directing work in his adult years, "Buñuel is dead."[4]

In this context, the director surely was surprised to get a phone call that summer from Frank Stauffacher, the curator of the "Art in Cinema Series" at the San Francisco Museum of Art. Stauffacher was organizing a program of experimental films and wanted Buñuel to contribute an essay on *Un Chien andalou* for the series catalogue. As he wrote in a letter dated August 28:

> *Un Chien andalou* is scheduled for November 29, the last night in the series. [...] We will need some kind of an analysis of it. There are plenty of analyses available for reprinting, but they are all personal and they are all different, and according to your own word, they are all not correct. Such being the case, we feel wrong in reprinting a false interpretation of this film. A few paragraphs from you would be worth more than ten pages of pretentious analysis.[5]

Buñuel now had a chance to amend those "false" interpretations: following Stauffacher's request, he sat down at his desk and wrote the two-page "Notes on the Making of *Un Chien andalou*."[6]

Buñuel's contribution to the San Francisco Museum of Art catalogue proves essential today in understanding some of his original intentions; paradoxically, it also marks the beginning of a common miscategorization of the film. By placing Buñuel's work in the series, Stauffacher "framed" it as a perfect example of "experimental cinema," which, as he wrote in the catalogue's preface, "has never really had anything to do with money [...It] exists on the back of the commercial film."[7] Stauffacher's curatorial choices, in fact, established a canon of silent avant-garde films that, for better or worse, later became official—furthering the misrepresentation of Buñuel as a confined artist indifferent to social impact or commercial success. The curator's selection—early works by Viking Eggeling and Hans Richter, Fernand Léger's *Ballet mécanique* (1924), Walter Ruttmann's *Berlin, Die Sinfonie der Großstadt* (1927), etc.—has persisted in most histories of early experimental film; Buñuel's *Un Chien andalou* has insidiously been there, too, as "the most famous avant-garde film," with its "romantic moon" and "no logical progression," "filled with metaphors" and "hallucinatory confections."[8]

However, if we read Buñuel's "Notes" for Stauffacher, what do we *really* find? Historically, he writes in the first paragraph,

> this film represents *a violent reaction* against what was at that time called "avant-garde cinema," which was directed exclusively to the artistic sensibility and to the reason of the spectator, with its play of light and shadow, its photographic effects, its preoccupation with rhythmic montage and technical research, and at times in the direction of the display of a perfectly conventional and reasonable mood. To this avant-garde cinema group belonged Ruttmann, Alberto Cavalcanti, Man Ray, Dziga Vertov, René Clair, Germaine Dulac, Joris Ivens. [...] In *Un Chien andalou*, the filmmaker takes his place for the first time on a purely *poetical-moral* plane. [...] The result is a film *deliberately anti-plastic, anti-artistic*, considered by traditional canons.[9]

How did it happen, then, that the "anti-artistic" *Un Chien andalou* became a landmark of film art? Was Buñuel's work—cowritten by the Catalan painter Salvador Dalí—as "anti-plastic" as he claimed? If it represented a "violent reaction" against all kind of avant-garde films (the Surrealist works of Dulac and Ray included), what were the connections of *Un Chien andalou* to the Hollywood movies that Buñuel and Dalí admired so much? And how should we approach today a film whose ultimate purpose was, according to Buñuel again, nothing less than "a desperate and passionate appeal to murder"?[10]

This chapter studies the conception, production, and exhibition of *Un Chien andalou* in order to reassess its relevance in the history of world cinema during the last years of the silent period. My main argument is that Buñuel's film needs to be reconsidered as a work of conflicting forces (the artistic, the anti-artistic, the poetical) that co-exist *on equal terms*. Previously published studies favoring one force at the expense of the others do little justice to the aesthetic complexity of the film.[11] In this sense, my goal is to take *Un Chien andalou* out of the "margins" of the history of experimental film and to relocate it at the core of our current narrative of silent cinema. By doing so, I intend to reactivate the (often neutralized) subversive element of Buñuel's masterpiece—for *Un Chien andalou* remains one of the most important political films of the silent era.[12]

Art Film: Buñuel and the European Avant-Gardes

Buñuel's interest in artistic experimentation started early on. Throughout the 1920s, before directing *Un Chien andalou*, he undertook several projects as a writer, stage director, film programmer, film critic, screenwriter, and assistant director—projects that, one way or another, were strongly influenced by the interwar European avant-gardes.[13] The film is, in fact, the culmination of a creative journey that started years before its commercial release in October 1929. Without a genealogical study of the preparation of *Un Chien andalou*, one can't understand to what extent the avant-garde (partially) infused the writing and making of Buñuel's first work.

As a student at the Universidad Central in Madrid from 1917 to 1924, Buñuel learned about Cubism, Futurism, and Dadaism.[14] He read Apollinaire's *L'Enchanteur pourrissant* (1909), André Gide's *La Porte étroite* (1909), and the early works of Jean Cocteau.[15] With his friends at the Residencia de Estudiantes—not only Federico García Lorca and Salvador Dalí, but also Pepín Bello, Rafael Alberti, and Guillermo de Torre—he joined several literary circles, including the weekly Saturday night gathering at Café Pombo, just off Puerta del Sol, organized by the avant-garde writer Ramón Gómez de la Serna. "We loaned one another books and foreign journals," Buñuel later recalled.[16] "We were very influenced by the French and we looked to other horizons. We were, excuse the word, avant-gardists."[17]

Young Buñuel wanted to become an experimental writer. His early poems and short stories fully reflect the influence of Gómez de la Serna and Ultraism, a hybrid Dada-Futurist movement founded in Madrid in the fall of 1918—when the Ultraist manifesto was written—and whose members included de Torre, Jorge Luis Borges, Juan Chabás, and Pedro Garfias.[18] Chabás and Garfias co-edited the short-lived journal *Horizonte* (1922–23), where Buñuel published two early short stories, "Instrumentación" and "Suburbios," in Ultraist style—that is, deprived of sentimentality and full of visual associations aimed at shocking the readers.[19]

This aesthetic would, of course, nourish *Un Chien andalou*. In fact, some of Buñuel's writings of the 1920s present "images" later incorporated in his Surrealist film: in "Diluvio," an unpublished text dated 1925, "the entire city [...] found itself powerless against the deluge, which fell *in slow motion as in dreams*"; in "El arco iris y la cataplasma" (February 1929), Buñuel asks "how many Marists can fit on a footbridge? [...] Would it be impolite of me to vomit a piano on [deaf-mute children] from my balcony?"; and in "Palacio de Hielo" (January 1929), he writes "When Napoleon's soldiers entered Zaragoza, VILE Zaragoza, they found nothing but wind blowing through the deserted streets. Alone in a puddle croaked the eyes of Luis Buñuel. Napoleon's soldiers finished them off with bayonets."[20] The slow motion, the Marist brothers, the piano, the cut eye, the presence of Buñuel himself as a "character": any viewer familiar with *Un Chien andalou* immediately recognizes these motifs.

Shortly after moving to Paris in January 1925, Buñuel frequented various gatherings of Spanish artists—he met Pablo Picasso and Juan Gris—and planned to publish a book of poems, which he eventually envisioned under the title *El perro andaluz*.[21] He often attended theater and opera productions and started to consider a career as a dramatist and stage director. In April of 1926, he worked as *regisseur* for the premiere of Manuel de Falla's opera *El retablo de Maese Pedro* (1923) at the Royal Concertgebouw of Amsterdam, and, a few months later, co-wrote with Bello *Hamlet (Tragedia cómica)* a short play in four acts, which was staged at the basement of the Café Select in Montparnasse in the summer of 1927 (Buñuel played the role of Hamlet).[22] The piece was a parody of melodramatic theater and included some experimental dramatic "techniques"—absurd dialogue, lack of continuity, flexibility of space and time—that, again, would reappear in *Un Chien andalou*.[23]

Buñuel's interest in cinema took off in Paris. He was a moviegoer in Madrid—"we loved the American comedians: Ben Turpin, Fatty [Arbuckle], the Keystone Bathing Beauties, Buster Keaton, Harold Lloyd, Harry Langdon"—but now filmmaking became his professional goal.[24] In the French capital, he went to the movies up to three times a day: "Thanks to a press pass I'd inveigled out of a friend, I saw private screenings of American films in the morning at the Salle Wagram; during the afternoon, I went to a neighborhood theatre; and, in the evenings, to the Vieux Colombier or the Studio des Ursulines."[25] Among the films that made strong impressions on him were F. W. Murnau's *Der letzte Mann* (1924), Sergei M. Eisenstein's *Bronenosets Potyomkin* (1925), and, "above all, Fritz Lang's movies," *Der müde Tod* (1921) and *Die Nibelungen* (1924).[26] When he saw *Der müde Tod* at the Vieux Colombier, "I suddenly knew that I too wanted to make movies."[27]

The young writer with some stage experience was now ready to enter the film world, first as a programmer and critic, later as a screenwriter and assistant director. Buñuel's work as a Paris-based curator of avant-garde cinema for the Spanish cine-clubs was, in fact, pioneering. He selected the titles, managed the rentals, and even traveled to Madrid to introduce some of the screenings, both at the Residencia de Estudiantes (from May 1927 to December 1928) and at the Cineclub Español (from December 1928 to May 1929).[28] "Coming from Paris," Alberti remembered, "Buñuel discovered for us a type of cinema that was unknown in Spain, because such films were neither commercial nor accepted by the general public."[29] The Spanish press described it as "the newest avant-garde cinema."[30]

A quick look at the list of films Buñuel selected for the Madrid cine-clubs shows to what extent he knew and appreciated French experimental films. His selection for the Residencia session of May 21, 1927, for example, included the dream sequence of Renoir's *La fille de l'eau* (1924), Clair's *Entr'acte* (1924), and Cavalcanti's *Rien que les heures* (1926). The March 1928 screening at the Cineclub Español featured Dulac's *La Coquille et le clergyman* (1927) and Epstein's *La Glace à trois faces* (1927). Other programs in the fall of 1928 and spring of 1929 included Marcel L'Herbier's *Feu Mathias Pascal* (1925), Man Ray's *L'Étoile de mer* (1928), and Eugène Deslaw's *Les nuits électriques* (1928).[31]

Unfortunately, no transcription of Buñuel's presentations has survived (the title of his March 1928 lecture was "Cinematógrafo: Algunos ejemplos de sus modernas tendencias" [The Cinematograph: Some Examples of its Modern Tendencies]), but we do know that he personally liked Dulac's film—scripted by Antonin Artaud—and publicly praised Cavalcanti's. "I really enjoyed *La Coquille et le clergyman*," he would later say, "I found it was an excellent film."[32] On *Rien que les heures*, he wrote: "Nothing but the hours. No loves, no hatreds, no denouement with a final kiss. [. . .] This is among the most fully realized of the so-called scriptless films. 'Visual' music[,] subjective cinema."[33] Besides this appreciation for Dulac's and Cavalcanti's art films, Buñuel wrote to Bello in November 1927 that *Feu Mathias Pascal* was an "extraordinary and ingenious" film.[34] Nonetheless, it was *Entr'acte*, co-scripted by Clair and Francis Picabia, which inspired him the most: "An excellent film [. . .] where dreams and 'unrealized events in our minds,' as Picabia himself said, were essential."[35]

As a film programmer, Buñuel learned the wide spectrum of film techniques used by these avant-garde cineastes: fast and slow motion, reverse action, split screen, superimpositions, extreme close-ups, handheld camera, animated stop motion, rapid crosscutting to create multiple points of views, jump cuts to break space-time continuity, etc. He became intimately familiar with Renoir's visual metamorphoses in *La fille de l'eau* (e.g. the rope that becomes a snake) and with L'Herbier's use of double exposure to visualize the doppelgänger in *Feu Mathias Pascal* (where Pierre Batcheff, the main actor of *Un Chien andalou*, plays an important part). There is a link indeed between the character that tears apart the film screen and is kicked in the face in *Entr'acte* and Buñuel's famous sliced eye in *Un Chien andalou*.

While programming for the cine-clubs, Buñuel also started writing film reviews for *Cahiers d'Art*, the Paris art journal founded by Christian Zervos in 1926, and for *La Gaceta Literaria*, the literary bi-weekly initiated by Ernesto Giménez Caballero in Madrid in 1927. From January 1927 to May 1929, Buñuel contributed several texts to both journals—incluing reviews of Erich von Stroheim's *Greed* (1924), Lang's *Metropolis* (1927), Abel Gance's *Napoléon* (1927), and Carl Th. Dreyer's *La Passion de Jeanne d'Arc* (1928).[36] Some of these essays, again, focused on the importance of the avant-garde film, which Buñuel described in January of 1927 as "the purest expression of the present age."[37] (Even when reviewing non-experimental films, Buñuel often admired their experimental aspects: Stroheim's expressionistic lighting, Lang's "indifference" to plot, Dreyer's extreme camera angles). As his first biographer José Francisco Aranda pointed out, Buñuel's film criticism was influenced by the theories of French Impressionists such as Epstein and Dulac and their emphasis on cinematic specificity.[38] "Today," Buñuel wrote in December 1927, "cinema has at its disposal an almost perfect language of signs."[39] His own seminal articles on *photogénie* and *découpage*, as we will see, would inform the conception of *Un Chien andalou* only a few months later.[40]

Buñuel the film critic, however, wanted to transcend the limitations of his profession by becoming a film director: as he wrote to Bello in November 1927, "in spite of [my] success as a critic, I am not, God forbid, a critic! I would rather have my own work criticized by others."[41] Since funding for his first film was secured by Buñuel's mother, who gave him 25,000 pesetas to direct a short picture, the first step was writing a script.[42] After a frustrated attempt at collaborating with Lorca, Buñuel managed to develop two screenplays: one written on his own, a biopic of Francisco de Goya commissioned by the Aragonese Government in September 1926, and the second, a script that Buñuel asked Gómez de la Serna to craft in May 1927, *El mundo por diez céntimos* (later known as *Caprichos*).[43]

Although these scripts were never filmed, *Goya* presented the idea of *amour fou* between the painter and his muse the Duchess of Alba, and *Caprichos* had an episodic, gag-based structure that anticipates *Un Chien andalou* (Buñuel said it was "like a newspaper, with different sections: the news, the dramas, the court reports").[44] The script of *Goya*, in fact, includes some framing and editing choices that would reappear in the script of *Un Chien andalou*—such as a shot of the moon and clouds and the use of a jump cut in the dream of a character named Primorosa, when she is in her room and, suddenly, leans on a rock in the middle of an arid landscape.[45]

Avant-garde literature inspired Buñuel as a poet, dramatist, and screenwriter, and film criticism and programming enriched his understanding of cinema as an original audiovisual form, but he only ascended to the profession of *metteur en scène* through his work as an apprentice of Jean Epstein. Altough Buñuel later minimized the influence of Epstein, he learned film techniques from him and his sister Marie, both as a student at their Académie du Cinéma in Paris (in late 1925/early 1926) and as an assistant director on *Mauprat* (February 1926) and *La Chute de la maison Usher* (February 1928), both directed by Epstein. Marie's uncredited assistance in editing *Un Chien andalou*, in fact, has often been overlooked.[46]

Mauprat and *La Chute de la maison Usher*, two examples of the 1920s Impressionist school of French cinema, include oneiric sequences in which Epstein displayed an arsenal of experimental techniques: extreme close-ups, double exposures, jump cuts, hand-held subjective camera, and use of *flou* (blur filter)—all techniques later used in *Un Chien andalou*. Buñuel's two other experiences as an assistant director during that period—on Feyder's *Carmen* in the spring of 1926 and for Henri Étiévant and Mario Nalpas's Josephine Baker film, *La Sirène des tropiques*, in the summer of 1927—were less influential, but *La Sirène des tropiques* put him in contact again with Batcheff and the cinematographer Albert Duverger (who also photographed *Mauprat*), two of his closest collaborators on *Un Chien andalou*.

The script of *Un Chien andalou* was co-written with Dalí, "in complete harmony," at Dalí's house in Figueres in January 1929.[47] By then, Buñuel knew about the difficulties of entering the film industry (as witness the two failed projects *Goya* and *Caprichos*) to the extent of conceding to Dalí the importance of having a "plan of attack" to impress the Parisian intelligentsia in general, and the Surrealist group in particular.[48] They needed to create a work, in his own words, "without precedent in the history of cinema."[49] As Buñuel later explained to his friend Max Aub, "We were searching for some sort of equilibrium between the rational and the irrational, an equilibrium which would be both unstable and invisible, in order to understand the incoherent, to join dream and reality, the conscious and the unconscious—avoiding any sort of symbolism."[50]

The first draft of *Un Chien andalou* included very clear indications of the film techniques that Buñuel ultimately used in the film, shot in two weeks in Paris and Le Havre in early April 1929.[51] These included the *plano americano* ("American shot," i.e., medium-long shot) of the man riding the bicycle; the *gros plan* or close-up of the striped box; the *fondu enchaîné* or dissolve between the man and the box; the iris and *plongeon* (high-angle shot) of the androgynous woman moving the severed hand with a stick; and the *flou* and slow motion in the section featuring the doppelgänger.[52] Buñuel's early Ultraist techniques were also incorporated: the lack of reaction in the face of an emotional event (the "complete lack of expression" of the male character after falling off the bicycle); the evocative sexual imagery ("a stream of blood-flecked saliva runs out of the corner of the man's mouth onto the naked breasts of the young woman"); and the shocking visual associations (the breasts that become buttocks; the shot of a hand covered in ants that dissolves to the armpit of the young woman and dissolves again to the "undulating spines of a sea urchin").[53]

Some of these aesthetic features make *Un Chien andalou* an avant-garde film. In fact, one of the key characteristics of what is considered "experimental cinema" today is continuously present in Buñuel's masterpiece: spatial and temporal flexibility, highlighted by the "chronological" position of the five intertitles ("Once upon a time . . . ," "Eight years later," "At three o'clock in the morning," "Sixteen years before," and "In the Spring"), as well as by the use of match and jump cuts breaking the space-time continuum (the man who begins to fall in the room ends up falling in the forest; the woman who opens the door of the room is on the beach when she closes it). Thus, it is not coincidental that, shortly after its first special screening at the Studio des Ursulines on June 6, 1929, *Un Chien andalou* was received as "the most important example of avant-garde cinema."[54]

Yet the study of Buñuel's creative activities in the 1920s does not only reveal to what extent the avant-garde permeated the making of *Un Chien andalou*. It also shows an ongoing conflict between experimentation and commercialism in the director's mind.[55] For Buñuel's interest in commercial cinema—Hollywood melodramas, popular comedies, scientific newsreels—and his defense of the "anti-artistic film" were equally vital for him at that point. "Traditional ideas about art applied to film seems to me monstrous," he stated in early 1929. "Whether we are talking about a film or a car. It is the artist who sullies the purest objects of our time."[56]

ANTI-ART FILM: BUÑUEL AND COMMERCIAL CINEMA

When did this anti-artistic drive in Buñuel develop, and how exactly did it influence the making of *Un Chien andalou*? What was the purpose of that "violent reaction" against the avant-gardes, as Buñuel put it to Stauffacher? If *Un Chien andalou* is a work of conflicting forces, as I have argued, where are its commercial elements to be found?

Buñuel had liked American commercial cinema since he was a student in Madrid, and, as a critic, often endorsed Hollywood films: he praised the use of the close-up by D. W. Griffith, venerated the acting style of stars like Adolphe Menjou, and admired Fred Niblo's *Camille* (1926), von Stroheim's *The Merry Widow* (1925), and Ernst Lubitsch's *Lady Windermere's Fan* (1925).[57] At the end of 1927, he started to explore the contrast between Hollywood film and avant-garde cinema: "A 'cine-drama,' if wisely directed and fully realized, is in the end more novel, more unusual than one of the so-called 'visual symphony' films," he wrote—indirectly criticizing the mannerisms of Ruttmann's *Berlin*.[58]

The exploration of this conflict, in fact, would often reappear in Buñuel's film activities of 1928 and 1929 and would play a vital role in the making of *Un Chien andalou*. For example, while reviewing Buster Keaton's *College* (1927) for *Cahiers d'Art* in December 1927, he argued that the film's technical achievements were actually greater than those of Gance's *Napoléon*.[59] In June 1928, he further elaborated:

> [A film] is composed of segments [. . .] which, taken as such, separately and arbitrarily, are utterly banal, divested of logical meaning, of psychology, of literary transcendence. In literature, a lion or an eagle can represent many things, but on the screen there are only two animals and nothing else, even if for Abel Gance they might symbolize ferocity, courage, or imperialism. That is why so many intelligent people, so many pitiful "art aficionados" are mistaken when they denounce the superficiality of American cinema, without considering that it was the first to realize that the great cinematic truths have no common denominator with those of literature and

the theater. Why do they keep calling for metaphysics in cinema and failing to recognize that in a well-made film, the act of opening a door or seeing a hand—an enormous monster—pick up an object can encompass an authentic and novel beauty?[60]

By the end of 1928, Buñuel firmly believed it was the Hollywood studio system that really understood the power of film. In the movies, what seemed "banal" and "superficial" was actually "the great cinematic truth." For him, now, there was no need to emulate the grandiloquent dramatic traditions of the nineteenth century, nor, for that matter, the innovations of abstract art of the twentieth. He perfectly sensed that commercial cinema was, to use a term later coined in film studies, "psychoanalysis in reverse" (a hand on the screen is, of course, an enormous monster).[61] That is why the pictures with Ben Turpin and Harry Langdon were "purer than all the avant-garde efforts to date," why Josef von Sternberg's *Underworld* (1927) and W. S. Van Dyke's *White Shadows in the South Seas* (1928) were much better than the grand European films in the style of *Napoléon*.[62]

Buñuel's intellectual admiration for Hollywood was, of course, hardly unique. The French Surrealist group, which accepted the Spanish director as a member right after the premiere of *Un Chien andalou* in June 1929, had been writing about the lyrical magnetism of American cinema since the end of World War I.[63] "Charlot sentimental" and "Charlot mystique," Louis Aragon's early poems on Chaplin, were published in 1918, and his essay "On décor," also written that year, claimed that "the best of American films enable a screen poetry to be redeemed from the farrago of theatrical adaptations."[64] André Breton, Philippe Soupault, Benjamin Péret, Robert Desnos, Paul Éluard, and Georges Sadoul all also wrote with veneration about American movies throughout the 1920s.[65]

Most important, cinema offered the Surrealists a perfect medium for their theories. "At the time when we were inventing Surrealism," Soupault recalled, "cinema was for us an immense discovery."[66] As is known, Breton believed "pure psychic automatism" expressed "the real mechanism of thought" beyond the control of scientific, aesthetic, and moral imperatives.[67] The main goal of Surrealism was to radically transform individuals by reaching a superior state of consciousness (a "superior reality" or *surréalité*) where the division between fantasy and reality existed no more, where wakefulness and sleep merged.[68] Automatism was the method to deactivate the repressive "rational" mind in order to liberate the unconscious, and silent cinema had a fundamental role to play in achieving that goal. For, as Jean Goudal pointed out in his article "Surréalisme et cinéma" (1925), language and literature depended too much on rational linguistic codes.[69] The concept of the "mental image" in literature lacked the *surréalité* of the percept of the "visual image" in film.

Buñuel's growing appreciation for Hollywood must also be seen through this Surrealist lens. Like the members of the Paris circle, what he found in commercial movies was a "primal transubstantiation of the material world."[70] By fully adhering to the principles of Breton's group in the summer of 1929 ("my connection with the Surrealists determined the course of my life"), he could remain true to his admiration for American cinema.[71] At the same time, their aesthetic credo nurtured his rebellion against experimentalism in film: "My adoption of Surrealism meant my distance—for a long time—from the so-called avant-garde."[72] He now had the support of Breton's circle, who repudiated experimental filmmakers' *mystique de l'expression*, to use Desnos's phrasing, and the "box of tricks[,] the endless abuses, the monotonous harping on what had once been the freshest and most brilliant ideas," as Surrealist Jacques Brunius put it.[73]

At the beginning of 1929, while pre-producing *Un Chien andalou*, Buñuel was not only following Surrealism closely but also conceptualizing with Dalí their new theory about cinema as an anti-art form. Anti-artistic filmmakers, for the two young Spaniards, were those who rejected the standards of traditional art, with its stress on "originality," authorship, and sentimentalism—what Buñuel and Dalí described as "the putrid."[74] Both concepts, *putrefacto* and *anti-artístico*, first hypothesized—half jokingly—at the Residencia, took intellectual shape in different texts published by Dalí and Buñuel from 1927 to 1929. For example, in "Sant Sebastià" (July 1927), Dalí contrasted the romantic art of the nineteenth century with the empirical anti-art of his own time: mannequins, automobiles, ocean-liners, Fox newsreels, and, of course, the movies of Menjou and Tom Mix.[75] Transcendental artists were *putrefactes*; Buster Keaton, the anti-artist par excellence, "pure poetry."[76] In "Film-arte, film-antiartístico," another text by Dalí—dedicated to Buñuel and published in *La Gaceta Literaria* in December 1927—he further argued: "The anti-artistic filmmaker ignores art; he shoots in a pure manner, obeying only the technical requirements of his apparatus."[77]

When Dalí interviewed Buñuel for the Catalan journal *L'Amic de les Arts* in early 1929, he asked him: "Are you interested in art?" Buñuel bluntly replied: "Not at all, I am immunized against typhoid."[78] By then, Buñuel's admiration for the scientific documentaries of Jean Painlevé and his defense of the commercial cinema was stronger than ever.[79] "True cinema will emerge mechanically in Europe *only if* a real film industry is established," he said.[80] Artistic experimentation was now the archenemy of true cinema, for "the purest emotion [in film] does not have to be sought in the world of invented forms."[81] Directors trying to reproduce on screen the style of abstract art, such as Eggeling and Richter, missed the most important element in filmmaking: the magical objectivity of the camera lens. "The possibilities of cinema are to be found in that unlimited fantasy which is born of things in themselves," Dalí wrote.[82] No place, thus, for artistic invention: merely documenting the world of facts would reveal the world of fantasy.

This was a fundamental postulate *Un Chien andalou* was to put into practice: the importance of filming in a non-personal, automatic manner. As Dalí revealed shortly after its premiere, *Un Chien andalou* presented a "simple noting down, recording of facts [. . .] made apart from any aesthetic intention."[83] In this respect, the documentary quality of the shot of the sliced eye should not be disregarded. As Joan Minguet has suggested, it is very likely that Dalí had seen the medical newsreels on cataract surgery by the ophthalmologist Ignacio Barraquer in Barcelona, which were distributed as part of the Medical Gaumont film series in the early 1920s.[84] Buñuel's well-known passion for entomology also manifests itself in *Un Chien andalou*, in the images of the hand with the Guadarrama red ants and the shots of the *Acherontia atropos* skull butterfly.[85] Simply photographing an insect—another "enormous monster"—was enough to confront the pretentious metaphysics of art.

Buñuel's anti-artistic position not only reflected a theoretical inclination; for practical purposes, the production of *Un Chien andalou* was commercially oriented from beginning to end. Unlike experimental short films of the period, Buñuel's two-reeler had a high budget, featured professional actors (Batcheff and Simone Mareuil), and was shot by a salaried crew with 35mm equipment at the Billancourt studios. On June 12, 1929, a week after the film's special premiere at the Ursulines, the Spanish director was delighted to sell the world exhibition rights to Pierre Braunberger, co-owner of the Cinéma du Panthéon.[86] And, a few days later, he gladly signed a twelve-week deal, starting on October 1, with Jean Mauclaire, the manager of Studio 28, a four hundred-seat theater in Montmartre where *Un Chien andalou* would play as support to an early Hollywood detective film, *The Cop* (1929).[87]

Sharing the bill with a commercial feature rather than with avant-garde films definitely contributed to the financial success of *Un Chien andalou*. Although its exact box-office revenue is still unknown, the film did well enough in the first months to break even.[88] By February 1930, the *New York Times* reported, Studio 28 was still playing it to full capacity.[89] If, as Buñuel later said, the picture "had a successful eight-month run," that clearly indicates some economic achievement, to which several "one night only" screenings must have also contributed.[90] The Viscounts of Noailles paid a thousand francs for a private show in their Paris residence, and similar fees were likely charged for a number of 1929 screenings in European and South American capitals. When Aranda wrote "few non-commercial films have had a more triumphant run," he was obviously overlooking Buñuel's commercial vocation.[91]

Formally, Buñuel wanted to tell a love story, with a beginning, a middle, and an end—although not precisely in that order, to use Jean-Luc Godard's famous expression. It is evident that the main narrative develops between a prologue ("Once upon a time") and an epilogue ("In the Spring"), which are used as such. A revision of the boy-meets-girl trope, *Un Chien andalou* is not only very much plot-focused but also—like a Hollywood slapstick film—carefully organized by "gags," Buñuel's own term for moments of levity, humor, and surprise.[92] Perfectly understandable when seen independently, each gag follows the standard shot pattern popularized by Hollywood (establishing shot, medium shot, close-up of main character, reverse shot of what this character is seeing, etc.), and respects conventions of camera position, framing, and lighting. An average shot length of 4.5 seconds emulates Hollywood's fast cutting.[93] Use of fade-ins and outs to separate sequences, adherence to the 180-degree rule in the "dialogue" scenes between Batcheff and Mareuil, and invisible editing within each sequence stand in stark contrast to the discontinuous techniques and non-linear narratives of avant-garde cinema.[94] All these characteristics demonstrate to what extent Buñuel closely followed the Hollywood template of editing, in its particulars, if expressly not in spirit.

A common misperception about *Un Chien andalou* is to believe it recreates a dream full of symbolism and without logical order. But Buñuel often reiterated that the film was *not* a dream: "Although I availed myself of oneiric elements, the film is not the description of a dream. On the contrary, the environment and characters are of a realistic type."[95] As he wrote to Stauffacher, using capital letters, "NOTHING, in the film,

SYMBOLIZES ANYTHING."[96] Regarding the hypothetical absence of continuity, he said to Aub:

> [T]he lack of a logical inference in *Un Chien andalou* is total non-sense. If that were the case, I should have edited the film sequences as flashes, by throwing the different gags into various hats, and pasting the sequences together at random. [. . .] When the dying man falls in the garden, he caresses the naked back of a statue of a woman; the absurdity would be for this second shot to precede the former. We used our dreams—this is not new—to express something. But not to present gibberish.[97]

If the film delighted the Surrealists, it was perhaps partly due to these Hollywood elements. Unlike *La Coquille et le clergyman*, rejected by the group in a highly publicized controversy, Breton was quick to sing the praises of *Un Chien andalou*, claiming "*C'est un film surréaliste!*"[98] The group saw in the film the same exaltation of *amour fou* they found in Frank Borzage's *7th Heaven* (1927); the melodramatic intensity they discovered in gangster films; and the humorous contempt for marriage they found in slapstick comedies (Buñuel's ending directly refers to the last shot of the married couple in the grave in Keaton's *College*).[99] In this respect, Dalí's observation to Buñuel after seeing *L'Âge d'or* a year later is especially eloquent: "I really loved it. *It looks like a Hollywood movie.*"[100] Yet that enthusiasm cannot detract from the fact that the film put the "look" of Hollywood conventions in the service of upending them.

Buñuel's evident admiration for American cinema and his position as an anti-artist helped maintain a febrile tension between experimentation and commercialism in his early career. These two tendencies co-exist in *Un Chien andalou*: understanding the film only as a sui generis example of commercial cinema would be as misguided as seeing it solely as an avant-garde work. Buñuel was "firmly convinced that people [could not] stand the upside-down houses and car wheels passing by" of experimental films, but he also believed that cinema could be something more than "just frivolous entertainment."[101] All the Hollywood conventions he followed in *Un Chien andalou* were metamorphosed when coming into contact with the avant-garde techniques he also used throughout the film. Let's not forget that, when Buñuel had the chance to work for Metro-Goldwyn-Mayer in California at the end of 1930, he described the studio system as a "marvelous organization at the service of the worst kind of imbecility."[102] In fact, it was only through the amalgamation of these two modes of representation (the artistic and the commercial) that Buñuel was able to create a third one.

Poetic Film: *Un Chien andalou* and Subversive Cinema

Buñuel, of course, was neither the first nor the only filmmaker to explore a midpoint between commercialism and independence in the 1920s. But he was unique in finding in that midpoint a platform for what he called "poetic" film. He often used the terms "poetry" and "poetic" to describe what he considered true cinema. In an interview published while he was preparing *Un Chien andalou*, he declared: "I believe that the cinema is the most appropriate instrument to express the great poetry (*la gran poesía*) of our time and the only one that has been able to universally establish certain visual truths."[103] But what did he exactly mean when he said "poetry" and "truth"?

"Poetic cinema" meant that films should not merely focus on plot nor follow only a logic of cause and effect but also explore, with intensity and honesty, other, non-logical functions of the mind. The premises for story construction of nineteenth-century novels and plays—psychological motivation, causality, drive toward overcoming obstacles and achieving goals, etc., constantly incorporated by Hollywood—were not good enough for poetic films.[104] Cinema had unique, non-linguistic qualities that determined its own specificity. "The four main Pillars that support the great temple of Cinematics," Buñuel called them: the close-up, camera angles, lighting, and—the most fundamental—editing (what, at that time, he named *segmentación* or *composición*).[105] The rhythmic combination of these four elements in a silent movie constituted cinema's lyrical character, its "*poetical-moral* plane."[106]

Two early theoretical essays of Buñuel—one, "Del plano fotogénico" (1927), addressing Epstein's concept of *photogénie*; the other, "*Découpage* o segmentación cinegráfica" (1928), on script technique—are indispensable for an understanding of *Un Chien andalou* as a poetic film. In these two theoretical texts, Buñuel followed Epstein and defended cinema as a purely visual, "intelligent instrument," capable of incorporating and eventually overcoming traditional literary structures.[107] "Through segmentation, the script or the written assemblage of visual ideas ceases to be literature and becomes cinema," he wrote. "*¡Pensar en imágenes; sentir con imágenes!*" ("Think with images, feel with images!")[108] Visual "purity," however, was not the only requirement for a film to be poetic. Buñuel acknowledged, for instance, that some Hollywood melodramas worked *visually* but were nonetheless still sentimental "trash."[109]

Influenced by Breton's concept of automatism, Buñuel believed that movies had to reproduce the way the mind really perceived and imagined the world. For cinema, despite the power of the "objective" camera, was ultimately not a realistic medium but a mental one: reality was radically transformed in the editing and screening rooms. Through the silent, enlarged, two-dimensional, monochrome photographic projection (the young Buñuel adamantly rejected color and sound), cinema transfigured objects on the screen; through the spatial-temporal flexibility of montage, it surpassed the constraints of physical logic.[110] In this sense, Buñuel's vision aligned with the Surrealists' concept of cinema. For poetic cinema to exist, it needed *both* to be purely visual *and* to reject the dictates of the rational (that is, instrumental) mind.

Indeed, for the Surrealists, it was this tension between the "fidelity" of photography and the "infidelity" of montage that qualified cinema to unite the conscious and unconscious on the very same plane.[111] Soupault celebrated how films ignored "natural laws;"

Breton, their "power to disorient" (*pouvoir de dépaysement*); Artaud, the "physical intoxication" they caused among moviegoers.[112] In Buñuel's own words:

> [S]eated comfortably in a dark movie theatre, dazzled by a light and movement that exert an almost hypnotic power over him, attracted by the interest of the human face and ultra rapid changes of location[,] by virtue of such hypnagogic inhibition, the moviegoer loses a high percentage of his intellectual faculties. [. . . Cinema] is the finest instrument there is for expressing the world of dreams, of the emotions, of instinct. Because of the way it works, the mechanism for producing film images is, of all the means of human expression[,] the one which best imitates the functioning of the mind.[113]

This concept of poetic cinema, this proto-Deleuzian "the brain is the screen" understanding of film, developed by Buñuel in Paris in 1927 and 1928, took form in *Un Chien andalou* through the clash of artistic and commercial elements.[114]

Like the Surrealists, Buñuel was particularly impressed by psychoanalysis and the works on sexuality by Sigmund Freud. "My discovery of Freud took place in 1921, when I first read *Psychopathology of Everyday Life* [1901]," he told Aranda.[115] By the time he prepared *Un Chien andalou*, he had already internalized the fundamental tenet of psychoanalysis—that much of our mental life is unknown to us due to our repression of conflicting memories, motivations, and desires. Freud's *Unbewusstsein* (unconsciousness) reigned over us. When describing *Un Chien andalou* in 1939, Buñuel admitted that it "amalgamated Freud's discoveries with the aesthetics of Surrealism."[116] The plot of the film—the psychological obstacles a couple encounters in consummating sexual desire—is "Freudian" indeed, and it develops through processes of "condensation and displacement."[117] The main characters, Buñuel added, were "animated by impulses, the primal sources of which are confused with those of irrationalism, which, in turn, are those of *poetry*."[118]

Although the director never "psychoanalyzed" his film, he left the door open for Freudian interpretations. As he wrote, the characters in *Un Chien andalou* "react enigmatically, in as far as a pathological psychic complex can be enigmatic."[119] And, again in 1946, after indicating to Stauffacher that nothing in the film symbolized anything, he added: "The only method of investigation of the [film's] symbols would be, perhaps, psychoanalysis."[120] Psychoanalytical readings of *Un Chien andalou* indeed proliferated among critics after 1950, once the film was internationally rereleased in art houses.[121] For François Piazza, it symbolized man's castration complex vis-à-vis the woman; for Pierre Renaud, it visualized the struggle of the male protagonist with his homosexual inclinations; for Fernando Césarman, it was the perfect illustration of the Oedipal conflict where "a man and a woman, dominated by forbidden sexual impulses, try to meet and solve their incestuous conflict."[122] The slitting of the eye, in this sense, has been variously interpreted as a reenactment of the primal scene, Oedipal self-infliction, sexual cruelty against women, and "an extended linguistic pun."[123]

The problem with "psychoanalyzing" the film, however, involves a common misinterpretation of the Surrealists' reading of Freud. Buñuel, Breton, and his peers were sympathetic to psychoanalysis, indeed, but with one fundamental difference. As Paul Hammond has indicated:

> [W]hile Freud underlined the materialism of the dream—its origins in everyday life; the secret, parallel activity of unconscious thought during waking; the squirreling away of material for use when asleep—the Surrealists sought to extend the process the other way, to complete the circle. They wanted everyday life to be emphatically and consciously permeated by the dream, by its scabrous language, its transgressive remodeling of normative constraints. [. . .] The Surrealists [transferred] mental disorder into poetic illumination, social negative into ontological positive.[124]

Poetic cinema was thus psychoanalysis in reverse *and* upside down. For Buñuel not only described but also *celebrated* the world of the unconscious mind. Rather than an illustration of Freudianism, *Un Chien andalou* should be understood as a revision—if not a critique—of Freud's ideas. Here Buñuel *reveres* desire as a productive force, thus surpassing the Freudian insistence on the role of repression in the governance of irrational drives: rather than sublimating, repressing, or simply recognizing primordial instincts, the filmmaker uncovers, often with humor, the tremendous creative potential of these forces.[125] Desire, in *Un Chien andalou*, has no limits, and overpowers any Freudian "reality principle."

Once again, there is a proto-Deleuzian aspect to the film, insofar as its Surrealist examination of Freud anticipates a critique that would receive its fullest development in later philosophical studies of psychoanalysis, such as Gilles Deleuze and Félix Guattari's influential *Capitalism and Schizophrenia* (1980).[126] In fact, Deleuze and Guattari help unlock one further dimension to Buñuel's notion of poetic cinema: its transgressive potential. If, as *Capitalism and Schizophrenia* notoriously claimed, "*la production désirante*" (desiring production) is, at the same time, transformative social production—"there is only desire and the social, and nothing else"—then Buñuel's celebration of unconsciousness certainly is political.[127] His famous description of *Un Chien andalou* as "a desperate and passionate appeal to murder" (i.e., revolt) should not be seen then as an empty provocation but rather as a formative expression of a power that Buñuel, again anticipating Deleuze, came to think of as anti-fascist.[128]

"A film of social consciousness," Vigo called *Un Chien andalou* in June 1930. By then, Buñuel had finished his second Surrealist work, *L'Âge d'or*, whose commercial release was later boycotted by the far-right Action française and the Ligue antisémitique in December 1930 (and then indefinitely banned by the French state police).[129] This boycott, including the vandalization of Studio 28 where *L'Âge d'or* premiered, marked the beginning of Buñuel's "Red Years," as Gubern and Hammond have eloquently called the period of his career in the 1930s, when he joined the Communist Party and turned to social documentary with *Las Hurdes, tierra sin pan*.[130] Undoubtedly, with the advance of fascisms across Europe, *Un Chien andalou* was received more politically than before, either as a tool for social change, as Vigo claimed, or as a sign of "intellectual anarchism, meaningless and inconsequential," as film historian Carl Vincent dismissively described it.[131] Censorship boards that expurgated a couple of shots in the 1929 original release now completely banned it for its "sadistic dreams."[132]

But the political commitment existed in *Un Chien andalou* from its very inception. Buñuel, who had "sympathized with the anarchists" since the mid-1920s and was radicalized in the last years of Primo de Rivera's dictatorship from 1928 to 1930, actually charged his first film with political ideas (Brunius wrote that the film caused the "dissolution of the avant-garde" precisely because it called for "the resurgence of [political] content").[133] Today it is virtually impossible not to think of the film politically: the subversive representation of taboo subjects such as transvestism, androgyny, and physical mutilation; the exposure of sexual harassment and impotence; the substitution of heroic figures for protagonists full of human flaws; the absence of a happy ending and thereby the lack of restitution of social order—all visibly reflect Buñuel's highly political discourse. The critique of the bourgeoisie and the Catholic church could not be more explicit than in the famous sequence when Batcheff drags priests, pianos, and rotten donkeys behind him.

Some readers of the leading Surrealist journal—which, significantly, changed its name from *La Révolution Surréaliste* to *Le Surréalisme au service de la révolution* in June 1930—had already detected this political predisposition in Breton's circle.[134] Walter Benjamin, who was living in Paris at that time, wrote that the "most particular task" of Surrealism was to defend at all costs "every manifestation of radical intellectual freedom [. . .] *for the revolution*."[135] Buñuel's later description of films as "small weapons" that "may still be useful for exposing the fascist potential that lies at the heart of capitalism" takes us back to his attraction to Communist causes in the early 1930s.[136] Indeed, it was this commitment to the anti-fascist ideas of the Association des Écrivains et Artistes Révolutionnaires that ultimately made his friendship with Dalí untenable—and what caused the traumatic breakdown of the entire Surrealist group in 1932.

Un Chien andalou also exerted its influence by instigating a tradition of what might be termed "unpleasurable" filmmaking. As Ado Kyrou pointed out in 1953, "we are faced with the first film in the history of cinema which, against all the rules, was made so that the average viewer could not bear to watch it. *Un Chien andalou* is the first unattractive film."[137] For cinema to become a weapon against the patriarchal institutions of state, church, and family (*L'Âge d'or, Las Hurdes*) it first had to radically confront its own ideological complicities (*Un Chien andalou*). Cinema's hypnagogic power, Buñuel wrote, could be captivating or "brutalizing."[138] The abundance of shock images and the refusal of a single artistic style in *Un Chien andalou* have been interpreted as Buñuel's rejection of cinema in general. (American scholar Martin Jay, for instance, has written that the very act of damaging the eye should be seen in a larger tradition of anti-ocularcentrism in French culture, depriving the eye of "its spiritualizing, elevating function.")[139] But this is only partially true.

"Venom must be fought with venom," Buñuel wrote, "and *cinema with cinema*."[140] The plan of constructing *Un Chien andalou* as a film *not to be liked* was not an attempt to destroy all practices of filmmaking but "to subvert the dominant regime of cinematic pleasure."[141] For Buñuel only believed in film that did not believe in film: that is, too, what made *Un Chien andalou* political—its anti-seductiveness. The director's own reactions to the posterior neutralization of his first work's counter-hypnotic power should be read in this context: "This film has no intention of attracting nor pleasing the spectator," he wrote in 1946. "Indeed, on the contrary, it attacks him, to the degree that he belongs to a society with which Surrealism is at war."[142] Those who, by then, still missed Buñuel's political commitment and simply considered him a provocateur, clearly forgot that "it is never the image that goes too far, but always reality" (needless to say, *Un Chien andalou*, *L'Âge d'or*, and *Las Hurdes* did not invent—but denounced—sexual depravity, filicide, and hunger).

Conclusion

Un Chien andalou needs to be reconsidered today as a work of conflicting forces. Rather than trying to reconcile its tensions, we should acknowledge how the clash of art and anti-art, and the Surrealist critique of Freudian thought, made the film so relevant, aesthetically and politically speaking. For Buñuel's picture is not a curiosity of the avant-garde but a seminal work that was at once conversant with, yet also antagonistic toward, some of the most relevant strains of cinema from this period. It was this that Robert Desnos seems to have perceived in *Un Chien andalou* when he counted it among the most important works of silent cinema, together with Eisenstein's *Bronenosets Potyomkin*, Chaplin's *The Gold Rush* (1925), and Stroheim's *The Wedding March* (1928). "Nothing is revolutionary but outspokenness," Desnos wrote. "Lies and insincerity are characteristic of all reactionaries. And it is this frankness that now allows us to place on the same footing *Un Chien andalou*."[143]

"Truthfulness" here should not be seen only as an aesthetic but also as a political category. Buñuel himself envisioned the filmmaker as a truth-teller under constant self-scrutiny.[144] *Un Chien andalou*, he wrote in 1939:

> is of universal value, although it may seem disagreeable to certain groups of society which are sustained by puritanical moral principles. When I made the film, I was absolutely sure that it was going to be a failure; but I didn't care because I had the conviction that it expressed something until then never said in motion pictures. Above all, it was *sincere*.[145]

Rephrasing Vigo, I argue that *Un Chien andalou* is a film of social consciousness *precisely* because it develops as a truthful poem about unconscious desire. What was once described as a contradiction ("the paradox of *Un Chien andalou* is that the author tries to create a poetic object that is at the same time an object of revolt"), is in fact Buñuel's greatest achievement.[146]

As the quintessence of poetic cinema in the silent period, *Un Chien andalou* is a political artifact because it presents the social power of *production désirante* while resisting artistic propaganda and depoliticized cinema at the same time. It is a film about desire—and about the role desire would play in an "anti-capitalist society," to use again a Deleuzian term. Buñuel definitively took his place on a "purely poetical-moral plane" when he used cinema as a tool of truth-telling against the mendacities of the status quo. Needless to say, his fellow Surrealists did not see a conflict between poetry and political commitment; quite the opposite. As Buñuel later recalled, "Surrealists fought [. . .] against social inequality, the exploitation of man by man, the deadening influence of religion, the brutality of colonial militarism. [. . .] The real purpose of Surrealism was not to create a literary, artistic, or even philosophical movement, but to explode the social order, to transform life itself."[147]

NOTES

1. Luis Buñuel, "Quand la chair succombe (par Victor Fleming)," *Cahiers d'Art* 2, no. 10 (November 1927): 6.
2. Jean Vigo, "Vers un cinéma social," lecture delivered on June 14, 1930, published in *Ciné-Club* 5 (February 1949): 1.
3. Amos Vogel, *Film as a Subversive Art* (London: Weidenfeld and Nicolson, 1974), 266.
4. Buñuel to Ricardo Urgoiti, January 30, 1939, in Jo Evans and Breixo Viejo, eds., *Luis Buñuel: A Life in Letters* (London: Bloomsbury, 2019), 150.
5. Frank Stauffacher to Buñuel, August 28, 1946, in Scott MacDonald, ed., *Art in Cinema: Documents toward a History of the Film Society* (Philadelphia, PA: Temple University Press, 2006), 29–30.
6. Buñuel, "Notes on the Making of *Un Chien andalou*," in Stauffacher, ed., *Art in Cinema* (San Francisco, CA: Museum of Art, 1947), 29–30.
7. Stauffacher and Richard Foster, "Introductory Notes," in Stauffacher, ed., *Art in Cinema*, 2.
8. Sheldon Renan, *The Underground Film* (New York: Dutton, 1967), 67; David Curtis, *Experimental Cinema* (London: Studio Vista, 1971), 22; Stephen Dwoskin, *Film Is* (London: Peter Owen Publishers, 1975), 15; P. Adams Sitney, *Visionary Film* (New York: Oxford University Press, 1974), 15; Standish Lawder, *The Cubist Cinema* (New York: New York University Press, 1975), 174.
9. Buñuel, "Notes on the Making of *Un Chien andalou*," 29 (emphasis added).
10. Buñuel, "*Un Chien andalou*," *La Révolution Surréaliste* 12 (December 15, 1929): 34.
11. For a summary of partial interpretations of the film since its premiere in 1929, see Román Gubern, *Proyector de luna: La generación del 27 y el cine* (Barcelona, Spain: Anagrama, 1999), 419–422.
12. Needless to say, this is not the first attempt to consider *Un Chien andalou* in its full complexity: my analysis is indebted to the numerous studies on Buñuel by José Francisco Aranda, Gubern, Paul Hammond, Ian Gibson, and Agustín Sánchez Vidal.
13. Ian Gibson's *Luis Buñuel: La forja de un cineasta universal, 1900–1938* (Madrid: Aguilar, 2013) is the best biography of Buñuel up until his American exile.
14. Buñuel, *My Last Sigh* (New York: Knopf, 1983), 59; quotes from this English version have been revised when they differed too much from the original French edition.

15. Buñuel describes his early readings in Max Aub, ed., *Luis Buñuel, novela* (Granada, Spain: Ediciones del Vigía, 2013), 97, and in José de la Colina and Tomás Pérez Turrent, eds., *Objects of Desire: Conversations with Luis Buñuel* (New York: Marsilio Publishers, 1992), 9.
16. Buñuel, *My Last Sigh*, 59.
17. Buñuel, in Colina and Turrent, *Objects of Desire*, 9.
18. "Ultra. Un manifiesto de la juventud literaria," *Cervantes* 3, no. 1 (January 1919): 2–3. Buñuel's first printed text, "Una traición incalificable" (An Unspeakable Betrayal), was published in *Ultra* 23 (February 1922): 4. This and other early texts have been collected in English in *An Unspeakable Betrayal: Selected Writings by Luis Buñuel* (Berkeley: University of California Press, 2000).
19. Both "Instrumentación" (Orchestration) and "Suburbios" (Suburbs)—published in *Horizonte* 2 (November 1922): 4, and *Horizonte* 4 (January 1923): 9—are included in *An Unspeakable Betrayal*, 6–10.
20. Buñuel, "Deluge," *An Unspeakable Betrayal*, 22 (emphasis added), first published as "Diluvio" in Sánchez Vidal, ed., *Luis Buñuel: Obra literaria* (Zaragoza, Spain: Heraldo de Aragón, 1982), 101–102; "The Rainbow and the Poultice," *An Unspeakable Betrayal*, 55, first sent as a story to Bello in a letter dated February 10, 1929 (*A Life in Letters*, 34–37); and "Palace of Ice," *An Unspeakable Betrayal*, 60, first published as "Palacio de hielo" in *Helix* 4 (May 1929): 5.
21. The book, initially titled *Polismos*, was never published.
22. Buñuel, "Hamlet," *An Unspeakable Betrayal*, 65–76; the final draft held in Filmoteca Española, Madrid, is dated July 6, 1927.
23. An early story by Buñuel, "Por qué no uso reloj"—in *Alfar* 29 (May 1923): 280–281—quoted Albert Einstein and joked about the relativity of time.
24. Buñuel, in Max Aub, ed., *Conversations with Buñuel* (Jefferson, NC: McFarland, 2017), 35; this is the English version, trans. and ed. Julie Jones, of Aub's *Conversaciones con Buñuel* (Madrid: Aguilar, 1985).
25. Buñuel, *My Last Sigh*, 87.
26. Buñuel writes "mais par-dessus tout les films de Fritz Lang," in *Mon dernier soupir* (Paris: Laffont, 1982), 106.
27. Buñuel, *My Last Sigh*, 88.
28. See Buñuel's letters to León Sanchez Cuesta in April 1927, in *A Life in Letters*, 15–16.
29. Rafael Alberti, in *Conversaciones con Buñuel*, 285.
30. Miguel Pérez Ferrero, "Films de Vanguardia," *La Gaceta Literaria* 11 (June 1, 1927): 8.
31. A study of the programming of these Madrid cine-clubs can be found in Gubern, *Proyector de luna*, 260–327.
32. Buñuel, in *Luis Buñuel, novela*, 127.
33. Buñuel, "A Night at the Studio des Ursulines," *An Unspeakable Betrayal*, 97; the original review, "Una noche en el Studio des Ursulines," was published in *La Gaceta Literaria* 2 (January 15, 1927): 6.
34. Buñuel to Bello, November 8, 1927, *A Life in Letters*, 23.
35. Buñuel, in *Luis Buñuel, novela*, 126, where he added: "I think [*Entr'acte*] is the film that resembles *Un Chien andalou* the most" (126).
36. Buñuel reviewed *Greed* in "Una noche en el Studio des Ursulines," 6; see also his "Metrópolis," *La Gaceta Literaria* 9 (May 1, 1927): 6; "Napoléon, par Abel Gance," *Cahiers d'Art* (*Feuilles volantes*) 3 (May 1927): 3; and "Juana de Arco," *La Gaceta Literaria* 43 (October 1, 1928): 3.

37. Buñuel, "A Night at the Studio des Ursulines," 96.
38. José Francisco Aranda, *Luis Buñuel: Biografía crítica* (Barcelona, Spain: Lumen, 1969), 64.
39. Buñuel, "Fred Niblo's *Camille*," in *An Unspeakable Betrayal*, 105; originally published as "La Dama de las Camelias," *La Gaceta Literaria* 24 (December 15, 1927): 4.
40. Buñuel, "The Cinematic Shot" and "*Découpage*, or Cinematic Segmentation," in *An Unspeakable Betrayal*, 125–130 and 131–135; first published as "Del plano fotogénico," *La Gaceta Literaria* 7 (April 1, 1927): 6, and "Découpage o segmentación cinegráfica," *La Gaceta Literaria* 43 (October 1, 1928): 1.
41. Buñuel to Bello, November 8, 1927, in *A Life in Letters*, 23.
42. The final budget of *Un Chien andalou* was 130,000 francs (*Luis Buñuel, novela*, 127), a bit less than 25,000 pesetas, the equivalent of $300,000 today (adjusted for inflation).
43. See the 1926 letter and two postcards from Buñuel to Lorca, in *A Life in Letters*, 6–11, as well as the two original drafts of *Goya* held at Filmoteca, and Gómez de la Serna's short stories "Caprichos" in *La Gaceta Literaria* 21 (November 1, 1927): 3 and 24 (November 15, 1927): 7.
44. Buñuel, in *Conversations with Buñuel*, 37.
45. The Goya script is the subject of Auro Berardi, ed., *Goya 1926. Il pittore e la duchessa* (Venice, Italy: Marsilio, 1994).
46. Buñuel said to Aub that, after the shooting was finalized in April 1929, "I didn't know anything about montage, so I went to learn how to do it with Marie Epstein" (*Luis Buñuel, novela*, 126).
47. Buñuel, in *Luis Buñuel, novela*, 130.
48. Buñuel to Dalí, June 24, 1929, in *A Life in Letters*, 44.
49. Buñuel to Bello, February 10, 1929, in *A Life in Letters*, 35.
50. Buñuel, in *Luis Buñuel, novela*, 130.
51. All references to the film come from the digitally restored version of *Un Chien andalou* supervised by Ferrán Alberich, released on DVD by the Filmoteca in 2009, using negatives of the Cinémathèque française, Paris, Cinémathèque Royale de Belgique, Brussels, and the Museum of Modern Art, New York.
52. The first version, "¡Vaya Marista!," and the second version, "El perro andaluz—Découpage," were both typewritten in Spanish and are reproduced as facsimiles in *Un perro andaluz: ochenta años después*, exh. cat. (Madrid: La Fábrica Editorial, 2009), 129–181; the third and final version was originally published in French as "*Un Chien andalou*" in *La Revue du cinéma* 5 (November 15, 1929): 2–16. For an English translation of the first and third versions, see Buñuel, *L'Âge d'or and Un Chien andalou* (London: Lorrimer, 1968), 85–116.
53. Quotes taken from Buñuel and Dalí, "¡Vaya Marista!" 1–3.
54. Program of eighth session (December 8, 1929), Cineclub Español, Filmoteca.
55. For an analysis of this conflict in Buñuel's career, see Evans and Viejo, "Introduction," *A Life in Letters*, xxxiii–xliii.
56. Buñuel, in an interview with Dalí, published as "Luis Buñuel," *L'Amic de les Arts* 4, no. 31 (March 31, 1929): 16.
57. Buñuel writes on Griffith, von Stroheim, and Lubitsch in "The Cinematic Shot," 125–129; see also his "Variations on Adolphe Menjou's Mustache," in *An Unspeakable Betrayal*, 112–115, originally published as "Variaciones sobre el bigote de Menjou," *La Gaceta Literaria* 35 (June 1, 1928): 4; and "Fred Niblo's *Camille*," 103.
58. Buñuel, "Fred Niblo's *Camille*," 104.

59. Buñuel, "Buster Keaton's *College*," in *An Unspeakable Betrayal*, 110–111; originally published as "Sportif par amour (par Buster Keaton)," *Cahiers d'Art* 10 (1927): 6–7.
60. Buñuel, "Variations on Adolphe Menjou's Mustache," 114–115.
61. See Leo Lowenthal, *An Unmastered Past* (Berkeley: University of California Press, 1987), 186.
62. The quote comes from Buñuel, "The Comic in Cinema," *An Unspeakable Betrayal*, 123; von Sternberg and van Dyke's movies are listed among Buñuel's ten favorite films in *Sight and Sound* 22, no. 1 (July–September 1952): 18.
63. Surrealism was "officially" established in 1924, when the magazine *La Révolution Surréaliste* (1924–1929) and André Breton's first *Manifeste du Surréalisme* (Paris: Éditions du Sagittaire, 1924) were published, yet many of its ideas were already introduced in *Littérature*, the journal co-founded by Breton in March of 1919.
64. Louis Aragon, "Charlot sentimental," *Le Film* 105 (March 18, 1918): 11, and "Charlot mystique," *Nord-Sud* 15 (May 1918): n.p., are collected in Alain and Odette Virmaux, eds., *Les surréalistes et le cinéma* (Paris: Seghers, 1976), 119–120. His essay "Du décor"—originally published in *Le Film* 131 (September 16, 1918): 8–10—is translated in Paul Hammond, ed., *The Shadow and Its Shadow: Surrealist Writings on the Cinema* (San Francisco, CA: City Lights, 2000), 50–54, 52.
65. Georges Sadoul, "Souvenirs d'un témoin," *Études cinématographiques* 38–39 (Winter 1965): 10–28.
66. Jean-Marie Mabire, "Entretien avec Philippe Soupault," *Études cinématographiques* 38–39 (Winter 1965): 29.
67. Breton, "Entretien avec Judith Jasmin," *Premier Plan*, February 27, 1961, reproduced at www.andrebreton.fr/es/work/56600100158870.
68. Breton, "Manifesto of Surrealism" (1924), in *Manifestoes of Surrealism* (Ann Arbor: University of Michigan Press 1972), 1–48.
69. Jean Goudal, "Surréalisme et cinéma," *Revue hebdomadaire*, February 21, 1925, 343–357; the English version is "Surrealism and Cinema," in *The Shadow and Its Shadow*, 84–94.
70. Hammond, "Available Light," *The Shadow and Its Shadow*, 7.
71. Buñuel, *My Last Sigh*, 105.
72. Buñuel, *Mon dernier soupir*, 123.
73. Desnos, "Cinéma d'avant-garde," *Documents* 7 (December 1929): 385; Jacques Brunius, "Experimental Film in France," in Roger Manvell, ed., *Experiment in the Film* (London: Grey Walls Press, 1949), 60.
74. For the idea of *putrefacto*, see Sánchez Vidal, *Buñuel, Lorca, Dalí: El enigma sin fin* (Barcelona, Spain: Planeta, 1988), 81–91.
75. Dalí, "Sant Sebastià," *L'Amic de les Arts* 16 (July 31, 1927): 52–54; the English translation is "Saint Sebastian," in Haim Finkelstein, ed., *The Collected Writings of Salvador Dalí* (Cambridge, UK: Cambridge University Press, 1998), 19–23.
76. Right after mentioning Keaton, Dalí writes "Heus ací la Poesia Pura, Paul Valéry!" ("Sant Sebastià," 53).
77. Dalí, "Art Film, Antiartistic Film," in *The Collected Writings of Salvador Dalí*, 54, first published as "Film-arte, film-antiartístico," *La Gaceta Literaria* 24 (December 15, 1927): 4.
78. Dalí, "Luis Buñuel," 16.
79. See Buñuel's letters to Painlevé, August 27, 1929, and June 5, 1930, in *A Life in Letters*, 48, 69.
80. Dalí, "Luis Buñuel," 16.
81. Dalí, "Art Film, Antiartistic Film," 56 (emphasis added).

82. Ibid., 55.
83. Dalí, "*Un Chien andalou*" (1929), in *The Collected Writings of Salvador Dalí*, 134; originally published in *Mirador*, October 24, 1929, 6.
84. Joan M. Minguet Batllori, *Salvador Dalí, cine y surrealism(s)* (Barcelona, Spain: Parsifal, 2003), 92–94.
85. For Buñuel's passion for entomology, see *My Last Sigh*, 217, the scorpion sequence in *L'Âge d'or*, and, of course, *Las Hurdes, tierra sin pan*.
86. Gibson, *Luis Buñuel*, 341.
87. Gubern and Hammond, *The Red Years of Luis Buñuel* (Madison: University of Wisconsin Press, 2012), 14.
88. Juan Luis Buñuel, in conversation with the author in Paris, September 15, 2015.
89. Morris Gilbert, "Parisian Cinema Chatter," *New York Times*, February 9, 1930, X6.
90. Buñuel, *My Last Sigh*, 108, where he remembers getting eight thousand francs in total from Mauclaire.
91. Aranda, *Luis Buñuel*, 86.
92. Buñuel described his early scripts with Dalí as "lists of gags" in *My Last Sigh*, 114, and discussed the essential traits of the gag in *Conversaciones con Buñuel*, 70.
93. Average shot length has been calculated from the 2009 restored version, which runs at 18 frames per second.
94. Paul Rotha praised the film's "fluid continuity that was amazing in its swift transference of thought," in *The Film Till Now* (London: Jonathan Cape, 1930), 62.
95. Buñuel, "Auto-Biography of Luis Buñuel," July 28, 1939, quoted in Aranda, *Luis Buñuel*, 74.
96. Buñuel, "Notes on the Making of *Un Chien andalou*," 30.
97. Buñuel, in *Luis Buñuel, novela*, 131.
98. Breton's response is recorded in James Bigwood, "Cinquante ans de cinéma dalinien," in *Salvador Dalí: rétrospective 1920–1980*, exh. cat. (Paris: Centre Georges Pompidou, 1979), 345. On the controversy, see Virmaux, *The Seashell and the Clergyman* (Paris: Paris expérimental, 2009).
99. Sadoul, "Souvenirs d'un témoin," 13.
100. Buñuel, in *Luis Buñuel, novela*, 244 (emphasis added).
101. Buñuel to Dalí, June 24, 1929, and to Pierre Lherminier, March 1963, in *A Life in Letters*, 44 and 350, respectively.
102. Buñuel to Charles de Noailles, December 2, 1930, in *A Life in Letters*, 77.
103. Buñuel, interviewed by Luis Gómez Mesa, "La generación del cine y los deportes," *Popular Film* 128 (January 10, 1929): 4.
104. For a detailed assessment of Hollywood's dependency on nineteenth-century literary traditions, see part 1 of David Bordwell, Janet Staiger, and Kristin Thompson, *The Classical Hollywood Cinema: Film Style and Mode of Production to 1960* (New York: Columbia University Press, 1985).
105. Buñuel, "A Night at the Studio des Ursulines," 96.
106. Buñuel, "Notes on the Making of *Un Chien andalou*," 29 (emphasis added).
107. Buñuel, "The Cinematic Shot," 128.
108. Buñuel, "*Découpage*, or Cinematic Segmentation," 133, 134.
109. Buñuel wrote that Victor Fleming's *The Way of All Flesh* (1927), "although technically perfect, is, ultimately, a counterfeit [. . .] completely infected with sentimental typhus" ("Quand la chair succombe," 6).
110. Buñuel, "The Cinematic Shot," 128.

111. Hammond, "Available Light," 24.
112. Soupault, "Note I sur le cinéma," *Sic* 25 (January 1918), reproduced in *Les surréalistes et le cinéma*, 205; André Breton, "Comme dans un bois," *L'Age du Cinéma* 4-5 (August-November 1951): 27; Artaud, "Sorcellerie et cinéma," originally written in July 1927, in *Œuvres* (Paris: Gallimard, 2004), 256.
113. Buñuel, "The Cinema, Instrument of Poetry," in *The Shadow and Its Shadow*, 112–113 and 114; the original text, presented as a lecture in 1954, synthesizes the concept of cinema that Buñuel had in 1929.
114. Gilles Deleuze, "Le cerveau, c'est l'écran," *Cahiers du Cinéma* 380 (February 1989): 25–32.
115. Aranda, *Luis Buñuel*, 33.
116. Buñuel, "Auto-Biography of Luis Buñuel," quoted in Aranda, *Luis Buñuel*, 74.
117. Brunius, "Experimental film in France," 100.
118. Buñuel, "Auto-Biography of Luis Buñuel," quoted in Aranda, *Luis Buñuel*, 74 (emphasis added).
119. Ibid.
120. Buñuel, "Notes on the Making of *Un Chien andalou*," 30.
121. Braunberger commercialized *Un Chien andalou* internationally during the 1950s; Jean Gaborit and Jacques Maréchal purchased the exploitation rights for Les Grandes Films Classiques in 1960 (*A Life in Letters*, 306–307).
122. François Piazza, "Considérations sur le *Chien andalou*," *Psyché* 27–28 (January–February 1949): 147–156; Pierre Renaud, "Un Symbolisme au second degrée," *Études cinématographiques* 22–23 (Spring 1963): 147–157; Fernando Césarman, *El ojo de Buñuel: Psicoanálisis desde una butaca* (Barcelona, Spain: Anagrama, 1976), 85–86.
123. Martin Jay, *Downcast Eyes: The Denigration of Vision in Twentieth-Century French Thought* (Berkeley: University of California Press, 1993), 258.
124. Hammond, "Available Light," 9, 11.
125. Steven Kovács, *From Enchantment to Rage: The Story of Surrealist Cinema* (Rutherford, NJ: Fairleigh Dickinson University Press, 1980), 206.
126. Deleuze and Guattari's *Capitalism and Schizophrenia* was published in two volumes in 1972 and 1980; for the English translations, see *Anti-Oedipus* (Minneapolis: University of Minnesota Press, 1983) and *A Thousand Plateaus* (Minneapolis: University of Minnesota Press, 1997).
127. Deleuze and Guattari, *Anti-Oedipus*, 29, where they add: "Dalí's method of critical paranoia assures the explosion of a desiring-machine within an object of social production" (31).
128. See the similarity with Joan Miró's 1927 anti-fascist concept of "the assassination of painting," as discussed in Maurice Raynal, *Anthologie de la peinture en France de 1906 à nous jours* (Paris: Montaigne, 1927), 34.
129. See Gibson's chapter on *L'Âge d'or*, in his *Luis Buñuel*, 347–433.
130. Gubern and Hammond, *The Red Years of Luis Buñuel*, 3–5.
131. Carl Vincent, *Histoire de l'art cinématographique* (Brussels: Éditions du Trident, 1938), 213.
132. In 1929, the French Ministère de l'Instruction Publique asked Buñuel to remove the two shots of the priests for the film's commercial release; by 1935, the film's exhibition was prohibited in Switzerland due to "its total incoherence and sadistic dreams" (letter from Zoltán Mohos to Buñuel, February 9, 1935, Filmoteca).
133. Buñuel, in *Objects of Desire*, 7; Brunius, "Experimental film in France," 98 and 104.

134. Following Breton's advice, Buñuel disallowed the publication of the script of *Un Chien andalou* by the mainstream *Revue du Cinéma* and only authorized the version published in *La Révolution Surréaliste* (see *A Life in Letters*, 51).
135. Walter Benjamin, "Surrealism: Last Snapshot of the European Intelligentsia" (February 1929), in *Reflections* (New York: Schocken Books, 1986), 177–192; the quotes come from pages 185 and 189 (emphasis added).
136. Buñuel, in Carlos Fuentes, "Luis Buñuel: el cine como libertad," *Casa con dos puertas* (México City: Mortiz, 1970), 214.
137. Ado Kyrou, *Le Surréalisme au cinema* (Paris: Arcanes, 1953), 212.
138. Buñuel, "The Cinema, Instrument of Poetry," 113.
139. Jay, "The Disenchantment of the Eye," 259.
140. Buñuel, "Quand la chair succombe," 6 (emphasis added).
141. Linda Williams, *Figures of Desire: A Theory and Analysis of Surrealist Film* (Berkeley: University of California Press, 1981), 41
142. Buñuel, "Notes on the Making of *Un Chien andalou*," 30.
143. Desnos, "Cinéma d'avant-garde," 386.
144. In "Pesimismo" (1980), Buñuel wrote, "I am always on the side of those who search for the truth, but I drop them as soon as they think they have found it," in Pedro García Buñuel, ed., *Recordando a Luis Buñuel* (Zaragoza, Spain: Ayuntamiento de Zaragoza, 1985), 172.
145. Buñuel, "Auto-Biography of Luis Buñuel," quoted in Aranda, *Luis Buñuel*, 74 (emphasis added).
146. Frédéric Grance, "*Un Chien andalou*," in Carlos Rebolledo, *Luis Buñuel* (Paris: Éditions Universitaires, 1964), 15.
147. Buñuel, *Mon dernier soupir*, 105–106.

CHAPTER 34

CODA

Silent Film after Sound

DONNA KORNHABER

Since the debut of the Academy Awards in 1929, only two silent films have won its top honor: *Wings* (dir. William Wellman, 1927)—the very first such awardee—and, eighty-three years later, *The Artist* (2011), director Michel Hazanavicius's mostly silent homage to an era and mode of filmmaking that supposedly vanished long ago. The presence of silent film at both ends of the Academy's first century speaks to a level of persistence in the form that cuts against the standard narrative of silent film's early twentieth-century demise. Hollywood has long put forward stories of obsolescence and replacement in depictions of the transition from silent to sound-era filmmaking, a viewpoint repeated in the intertitle cards of *The Artist* with its mantra of "Out with the old, in with the new." Yet the irony of this statement is that *The Artist* itself is part of a pair of movements in contemporary filmmaking that together seek to demonstrate the continued commercial and artistic viability of storytelling without dialogue or sound. Some of these films, like *The Artist*, broadcast their connections to the silent era, wearing their cinephilia and antiquarianism proudly. Others practice a more subtle form of continuity, eliminating or limiting dialogue or sound in ways that re-engage the challenges of silent filmmaking without carrying the markers of that age. All of them reject the premise of silent film's desuetude, redefining the form as part of cinema's continuous present or even using it to point toward new aesthetic possibilities for its future.

Such later-day silent films are for the most part recent enough and their filmmakers diffuse enough in their geographies, styles, and goals that they have received only limited critical attention as a group; neither do they practice under any common terminology or frameworks, leaving critics to devise their own. Robert Klepper has suggested the phrase "post-era silents" to cover the whole of silent cinematic practice after 1931, while Paul Flaig and Katherine Groo offer the more expansive terminology of "new silent cinema" to encompass those contemporary films that foreground their affinity to silent-era cinema.[1] While useful, such terms run the risk of identifying silent film exclusively with its historical manifestations prior to the 1930s and thus channeling considerations of later silent cinema primarily through the lens of its connection to the specific practices of that era—presuming any later instances to be at least partly revivalist in motivation. In fact, the films in question often approach inaudibility as an artistic *choice* and are more interested in the aesthetics or even the politics of silence than its historicity.

The contours of this approach were perhaps best foreseen by one of the earliest theoretical respondents to the sound transition. In his 1933 essay "The Complete Film," Rudolph Arnheim lamented that "the development of the silent film was arrested possibly forever when it had hardly begun to produce good results," yet he also harbored hope that silent filmmaking would continue as an aesthetic mode even into the age of sound's dominance.[2] Arnheim differentiates between films without sound or dialogue, films with sound but limited dialogue (which he calls simply "sound films"), and films with sound, dialogue, and color (which he terms "'complete' films"—insofar as they complete a certain drive toward total verisimilitude), and he posits that all three might together become part of cinema's future. He specifically argues of silent and (non-dialogue) sound films that "aesthetically these categories of film could and should exist along with mechanically complete reproduction," believing that the rise of the "'complete' film" with its default and often unthinking use of sound, dialogue, and color "would probably have an excellent influence on the other—the real—film forms, by forcing them to advance along their own lines."[3] In many ways, the story of silent film after sound is not only the story of filmmakers returning to the stylistics of silent-era cinema but also the story of Arnheim's tentative predictions slowly and incrementally coming to fruition, as individual filmmakers have chosen to engage with silence as a contemporary expressive mode.

In this essay, I wish to consider silent film after sound in its broadest scope, encompassing both the instances of pastiche, recovery, and revival on which Klepper, Flaig, and Groo primarily focus and those examples of silent film being employed as an artistic choice absent historical signifiers along the lines predicted by Arnheim. I use Flaig and Groo's terminology of "new silent cinema" for the former, indicating films that make an elective connection to historical silent film practice. For the latter, I adapt Donald Crafton's terminology of an "alternative silent cinema," used in his case to describe Charlie Chaplin's failed attempts to continue silent cinema as a viable filmmaking form beyond the advent of sound in the early 1930s.[4] In my usage, I expand the term to encompass films that would later accept Chaplin's challenge of filmmaking absent dialogue or sound as an alternative mode of contemporary sound-era practice without foregrounding any connection to silent film's past. Artistically, such films touch on what Susan Sontag describes as a foundational feature of modern and avant-garde art across media, wherein "silence exists as a decision"—one that in the case of film was historically foreclosed and that such filmmakers self-consciously seek to recuperate for the cinema.[5] In contrast, the "new silent cinema" is as interested in the historical markers of silent film as the aesthetics of silence itself. Its project is inherently referential and ultimately as much about cultural memory as artistic form—particularly in the investigation of cultural memory as a means of understanding the present anew. Together, I argue, these two strands of filmmaking constitute a viable, if largely unacknowledged, continuation of silent film practice well past the point of its supposed historical end.[6] Though their aims may differ, in both cases the turn to silence is a choice that is carefully calibrated to speak volumes.

Finding the End of Silent Film

From one perspective, the era of silent film came to a clear end in the year 1929, with *The Kiss* (dir. Jacques Feyder, 1929) often counted as the last major Hollywood film produced and released without extensive synchronized sound. Even Chaplin, whose *City Lights* (1931) and *Modern Times* (1936) maintained key elements of silent film production after most other filmmakers had abandoned the form, made a point of employing elements of synchronized sound throughout both pictures. From another perspective, it is almost impossible to say exactly when silent films exited the cultural sphere. Internationally, the end of silent filmmaking was a rolling transition that continued to unfold for more than a decade after the introduction of Vitaphone sound technology circa 1926. While most European countries made a definitive switch from silent to sound production by the first years of the 1930s, at least two major international film markets were much slower in that change. The Soviet Union continued to produce silent films until as late as 1935, even as the nation's leading filmmakers had resolved to adopt sound production in a statement from 1928.[7] (Even then, filmmakers like Sergei Eisenstein often preferred to shoot silently and add sound and dialogue in post-production.) And silent film production was especially resilient in Japan, which had developed a highly refined system of live narration during silent film exhibition using *benshi* performers—a tradition that continued in pockets into the 1940s.

Even in the United States, the transition to sound was far less clear-cut than Hollywood production choices alone would indicate. This is an argument William Drew has persuasively put forward in *The Last Silent Picture Show*, where he documents the remarkable persistence of silent film exhibition practices in America across the 1930s. As Drew notes, the full adoption of sound required both a change in production technologies and a revamping of exhibition spaces across the country, and by the year 1930 only about two-thirds of the nation's estimated 14,500 cinemas had been upgraded to accommodate sound; nearly five thousand theaters nationwide would continue to exhibit silent films over some portion of the 1930s.[8] In the case of rural cinemas, many continued to run back-catalogue silent films for years until they could afford to change their equipment. Elsewhere, the decision to continue exhibiting silent films followed the demands of local audiences. This was often the case with theaters that catered to specific immigrant and ethnic populations, where the assortment of older silent films to be shown from home nations far outnumbered the few new sound films those countries had just begun to produce and so created a corresponding lag in sound exhibition. For different reasons, theaters catering to urbane cosmopolitan audiences also saw a continuing demand for silent films even after Hollywood's mass-market shift. Many of the earliest sound-era films were static and visually awkward, encumbered by the need for muting devices that immobilized the camera and for microphones placed carefully (and sometimes conspicuously) within the mise-en-scène.[9] In contrast, the mobile camera of the late silent era seemed to represent a peak of filmic artistry, and certain viewers continued to seek out the visual pleasures of the silent film even in the midst of sound's ascendancy, such that dedicated revival theaters in New York City and Los Angeles persisted in exhibiting silent films for an audience of "sophisticates," in the language of contemporary news reports, throughout much of the 1930s.[10] For nearly a decade, then, silent and sound film were synchronous forms.

Golden-Era Hollywood and the Idea of Silent Film

It is in this context that we can begin to understand the recurrent self-historicization in a number of sound-era films depicting the recently closed epoch of the silents. During the decades of Hollywood's Golden Era from the 1930s to the 1950s, it was not uncommon for films to dramatize the medium's transition. As Drew records, many in the film industry at the time insisted that silent cinema "come to be regarded as part of history"—specifically a "linear" history "in which film evolved from primitivism to the technical refinements of Griffith and other pioneers" and culminated in sound as the inevitable fulfillment of that trajectory. This perspective countered that of contemporary critics who "saw the advent of sound as an extrastylistic force," a situation wherein "businessmen's desire for a technological novelty made technique regress," as David Bordwell describes.[11] Such is the case with *Hollywood Cavalcade* (dir. Irving Cummings, 1939), whose main story beats carefully follow a standard narrative of film's necessary evolution, embedding in the career of one fictional filmmaker nearly the entire story of the silent screen, from Keystone shorts to Griffithian epics, all leading inevitably to the ascendancy of sound. In fact, the key encounter with synchronization staged within the film is rendered, quite literally, religious, with the film featuring long excerpts from *The Jazz Singer*'s nearly forgotten scenes of Jewish liturgical song.

For a film replete with cameos of iconic performers of the silent era—and helmed by a filmmaker who started directing pictures in 1921—*Hollywood Cavalcade* is remarkably unreliable in its rendering of that age. The centerpiece of the film's depiction of silent cinema comes in a ten-minute sequence dedicated entirely to showcasing a Keystone-style one-reel short entitled *Help! Murder! Police!* Directed not by Cummings but by Malcolm St. Clair, a silent-era actor and director who got his start working with Mack Sennett in the late 1910s, the short is both a loving homage to silent slapstick and a deliberate update. Marked by extensive use of interior sets, crisp three-point lighting, ubiquitous but unobtrusive editing, and even rear projection for an exterior chase (though others are in fact filmed outdoors), the film-within-a-film is a strange exercise in transposing the tropes of the Keystone Cops into Golden-Era visual standards. Most egregiously, the film is even layered with synchronized sound effects throughout—a hallmark of slapstick reissues of the 1930s but an absolute anachronism within the film's transitional-era timeline, the variety and omnipresence of the synchronized effects far exceeding the kind of live sound effects used in some forms of silent-era exhibition. It is as though audiences could not be expected to tolerate the actual conditions of silent film even for a span of ten minutes, never mind the fact that a good portion of that audience had undoubtedly sat through a great number of those silent films a mere decade before. The film-within-a-film was meant to be a high point of *Hollywood Cavalcade*, and it generally functioned, as Rob King has extensively shown, as an origin point for the view of slapstick as "an anachronistic vehicle for old-time reminiscence," even "nostalgia's fast track."[12] The very texture of St. Clair's short, wholly indebted to classical stylistics and the technology of synchronized sound, speaks to silent film as both beloved and also irretrievably ancient, something that can only be approached in modern translation.

Cavalcade is comparatively subtle in its ribbing of silent-era technique, but no such nuance would be at work in other early sound-era recollections of silent-era film. "Don't laugh at these early picture pioneers," declares the narrator in the 1934 Vitaphone short "Old Silent Days," part of the *Movie Memories* series, speaking over an unidentified still image of what he (erroneously) claims to be "the first set for the first silent drama," presuming that the mere depiction of silent-era filmmaking will provoke immediate laughter. This same presumption undergirds the sound-era comedy *Merton of the Movies* (dir. Robert Alton, 1947), a vehicle for vaudeville and radio star Red Skelton and a relentless travesty of silent film stylistics. Here Skelton plays a cinema usher with delusions of stardom tricked into thinking he is performing a dramatic role when he has actually been cast in a comedy centered on his risible pantomimic acting. Voice-over narration early in the film explains that the action is set in 1915, when motion pictures were in their "infancy," their muteness figured as both inherently temporary and inescapably juvenile. That the world of silent film might ever produce a serious work of cinema is rendered an obvious absurdity.

Merton of the Movies is hardly canonical, but it shares an ideology of cinema's evolution with a far more acclaimed film: Hollywood's Golden-Era musical *Singin' in the Rain* (dirs. Gene Kelly and Stanley Donen, 1952). The film is marked by much of the same nostalgia that King identifies in other sound-era depictions of silent film in general and silent film comedy in particular, yet this nostalgia goes hand-in-hand with a baseline assumption of inferiority that informs the movie's story. Much of that story actually turns on the supposed artistic insufficiency of silent film, the attempt to render the film's silent-style melodrama *The Dueling Cavalier* as a vacuous talking picture being an open disaster until the filmmakers fully embrace the potential of sound-era film and transform their project into *The Dancing Cavalier*—replete with the showstopping "Broadway Melody" number, as visually and musically vibrant as the silent-era sequences were dramatically inert. There is a place for the legacy of silent film within the sound-era world of *Singin' in the Rain*, but it is one that depends on the elaboration and transformations only afforded by sound.

One can discern this ideology of improvement and replacement perhaps most clearly in the dynamics of the much-beloved musical number "Make 'Em Laugh," performed by Donald O'Connor playing funnyman Cosmo Brown. Unfolding on a movie set during the early days of sound in 1927, O'Connor's romp offers a master class in the tenets of silent-to-sound evolution. For nearly half the runtime of the song, O'Connor ceases all musicality and instead performs a show-stopping series of elaborate physical comedy routines as the music continues behind him, including a long bit with a mannequin, a series of acrobatic prat falls, and two backflips off the scenery. Having started from a form which only sound-era film can allow—the vibrant, toe-tapping song-and-dance number—O'Connor transitions into a routine no different in its fundamentals than that which might be seen in any number of silent-era comedies. Yet this slapstick turn is bookended by his elaborate song-and-dance sequence, which depends on the synchronization of voice and music that only the sound era can achieve. The supposed components of silent film—rendered here as cinematographically static, narratively torpid, and diegetically manic—still have a place within the world of cinema. But that place, so *Singin' in the Rain* posits, must be contained inside the supposedly more spectacular, more narratively developed, and more evolved world—what Arnheim might derisively call the more "complete" world—of the sound-era film itself.

Counter-narratives: Chaplin and Brooks

For all their differences, films like *Hollywood Cavalcade*, *Merton of the Movies*, *Singin' in the Rain*, and other self-referential Hollywood products of the era like *Sunset Boulevard* (dir. Billy Wilder, 1950) set a tone for the cinematic treatment of silent film that would hold sway for much of the later classical era. Though they vary in the acidity of their critiques and the degree to which their treatment of silent film is interlaced with nostalgia, the common denominator among these films is a belief in the stylistic insufficiency of the silent motion picture and a shared conviction in the aesthetic advancement represented by the transition to sound. So ubiquitous was this perspective in Golden-Era studio films that it can be difficult to remember just how much such views were originally in dialogue with an isolated but important counter-narrative regarding the nature and the legacy of silent film. Chaplin, Hollywood's lone holdout against sound film throughout the 1930s, was the standard-bearer of this view. In an editorial for the *New York Times* tied to the release of *City Lights* in 1931, he made his case plain: "Because the silent or nondialogue picture has been temporarily pushed aside in the hysteria attending the introduction of speech by no means indicates that it is extinct or that the motion picture screen has seen the last of it."[13]

For many commentators, the nature of Chaplin's long resistance to sound filmmaking is defined by his ultimate acquiescence with *The Great Dictator* in 1940, rendering *City Lights* (1931) and *Modern Times* (1936) more the delayed holdovers of an artist resistant to change than the principled execution of Chaplin's bold claims. Yet Chaplin's intent was real, if short-lived: prior to the release of *City Lights*, he predicted a "strong market for inaudible pictures" and planned for a time to open a new studio dedicated to producing other such films beyond his own.[14] Even if those plans were never realized, his argument for silent film's continued vitality in the face of sound—akin to the argument put forward by Arnheim in his call for silent films to be allowed to "advance along their own lines"—is evidenced in his films of the 1930s themselves. Though not directly meta-filmic in the manner of *Hollywood Cavalcade* and its descendants, Chaplin's final films before turning to sound would be inexorably committed to demonstrating and exploring the unique aesthetic possibilities of silent filmmaking, offering an enduring testament to the power of the form.

The fundamental narrative dynamics of *City Lights*, the work many consider to be Chaplin's masterpiece, turn on the fact of the film's "inaudibility." That is, *City Lights* is not just a silent picture but a picture that depends on silence for both its story and its core thematics. The relationship between Chaplin's Tramp and the blind Flower Girl (Virginia Cherrill) who becomes the object of his affections is directly inverse to that between the Tramp and the audience itself. The film's viewers can plainly see the Tramp before them on screen, but—as always—they cannot hear him in any way. In contrast, the Flower Girl is entirely blind to the Tramp but smitten by his voice and convinced by a series of aural miscues (both inadvertent and deliberate) that he is a figure of great wealth and clout. Their relationship is forever inaccessible to us: we cannot know by what means the Tramp has beguiled one of the few figures in the world of the film to pay him any notice. Likewise, the Flower Girl is immune to what we know of the Tramp, fooled by what she hears and oblivious to how he appears. The film turns on questions of hearing and sight, and Chaplin asks his audience to hold the differences between those two realities forever in their minds as the story unfolds—a direct affront to the ideology of Arnheim's "complete" film, wherein sound and visuals are always meant to act as one. *City Lights* tells a story the specific contours of which would be irreplicable in the world of audio-visual convergence that the sound era was then demanding, and as such it stands as a testament to the possibilities of storytelling that exist beyond such demands.

Modern Times, which moved Chaplin incrementally closer to the conditions of sound filmmaking, would explore such possibilities in a very different vein. Though the strategies Chaplin developed in his selective use of sound and dialogue throughout the film are numerous, one especially salient aspect of his approach (and one that would again be largely irreplicable under the conditions of sound-era filmmaking as they existed at the time) was the careful connection he draws between dialogue and power, both in its inclusion and excision from the film. The question of who is given a voice is a pivotal one in *Modern Times*, wherein the metaphorical voicelessness of the downtrodden Tramp is rendered literal in a world of radios, screens, and voice recorders that bark orders at his character without any chance of reciprocity. Tellingly, the only moments of comprehensible spoken dialogue that the film includes are filtered through a technological device and connected in some way to the levers of power and capital from which Chaplin's Tramp is ostracized. From a boss issuing orders from a bathroom wall monitor to an automatic sales machine making a hard pitch to a radio advertisement broadcast at a particularly uncomfortable moment, the intrusion of dialogue into Chaplin's film is designed to emphasize the isolation and powerlessness of the Tramp in the face of modernity. When the Tramp does at last "speak" within the final portion of the film, he in fact does not speak at all but rather sings in a nonsense language that carries no authority and communicates no definitive meaning. In a world of default blanket speech, the stark differences that Chaplin creates between those who can speak within his film and those who cannot would be incommunicable. The film's fundamental reliance on the techniques of silent cinema liberate Chaplin from the conventional uses of dialogue: if stories might still be told silently, Chaplin argues, then dialogue could come to function not narratively but thematically and new realms of artistic possibility might become available.[15]

The lingering memory of films like *City Lights* and *Modern Times* stands in the background of the arguments put forward by films from *Hollywood Cavalcade* to *Singin' in the Rain*. It is not just that Chaplin continued making silent films after the transition to sound; rather, he found ways of making silent films that actively depended on the absence (or highly selective use) of sound to tell their stories. Crafton is not wrong to label Chaplin's attempts an "alternative silent cinema," seeing in his work of the 1930s an effort to build a new direction for silent film defined against the ascendency of sound, but he is perhaps too quick to conclude that this project ultimately came to naught. It would take decades, but Chaplin's work in this vein would, at the very end of his lifetime, see a profound echo in the filmmaking of one of his avowed inheritors—Mel Brooks, who, in the 1970s, would for the first time in fifty years use the machinery of the Hollywood studio system to produce an argument for silent film's continued vitality. "I really felt a closeness to Chaplin and to Keaton," Mel Brooks would later say of the two filmmakers who inspired his film *Silent Movie* and whom he described as being his "mentors."[16]

Released in 1976, *Silent Movie* serves as an ideological stress test of modern Hollywood's relationship to silent cinema. Having established himself as a bankable comic auteur with the back-to-back successes of *Blazing Saddles* and *Young Frankenstein* (both 1974), Brooks approached the creation of *Silent Movie* as a deliberate challenge: would his prior success be enough to afford him permission to attempt that most supposedly unbankable of forms? The question is knowingly disingenuous, as the film is in fact born of Brooks's unstinting admiration for silent-era comedy—likewise for the great many contemporary celebrities, from Burt Reynolds to Paul Newman to Liza Minnelli, who all agreed to appear in the film at cut-rate wages out of admiration both for Brooks and for silent film itself. Yet despite the film's origins in Brooks's avowed silent-era cinephilia, the picture never approaches the condition of pastiche. In fact, the true subject of the film is the Golden-Era ideology of silent film deficiency—the idea that any film without diegetic sound and dialogue can be funny only in its failings—rather than the specific comic style of the silent clowns Brooks so admired.

Silent Movie was no failure at all: it received positive to glowing reviews and performed respectably at the box office, a feat that can be attributed to Brooks's central proposition that silent comedy could be recuperated as a modern filmmaking form rather than rehearsed as a series of well-worn stereotypes and clichés. Though he nods to the silent era in his constant playing with various film speeds and his echoes of certain Buster Keaton gags—as well as the inclusion of all dialogue on intertitle cards (save for Marcel Marceau's single spoken line)—he largely approaches the construction of a silent film as a *modern* filmmaking challenge, shooting in color in a 1970s-standard 1.85:1 aspect ratio, shaping the story with screenwriter Barry Levinson, and crafting the look of the film with cinematographer Paul Lohmann, fresh off of Robert Altman's *Nashville* (1975). Taking a page from Chaplin's films of the 1930s, Brooks also works to build a soundtrack of comic effects evocative of those that often accompanied re-releases and revivals of silent film in the sound era. It was an effort that went beyond simple cartoonishness, the film's soundscape being the creation of an expert sound team that included Don Hall from *The Towering Inferno* (dir. John Guillermin, 1974) and Michael Galloway, who would go on to help create the legendary sound effects for *Star Wars* (dir. George Lucas, 1977).

What Brooks conducted, in other words, was an experiment in what might happen if Hollywood took seriously the proposition of making silent films again. *Silent Movie* behaves like a transmission from some alternate historical timeline where silent film was allowed to persist and develop as a filmmaking form in its own right alongside the sound picture, just as Arnheim had once hoped and Chaplin had twice attempted. As with all of Brooks's work, how one responds to the humor is ultimately a matter of taste, but the film can neither be said to be antiquated in its form nor stunted in its comedy. It is, as Brooks hoped and intended it to be, a declaration of the continued viability of silent filmmaking—in the realm of comedy at least—although one that also acknowledges the seeming impossibility of the restitution of that form. In a particularly ingenious conceit, the film diegetically depicts a process of creation roughly analogous to the film's actual production conditions. Told by his producer within the film that "slapstick is dead," Brooks's filmic alter ego responds that he will ensure success by getting "the biggest stars in Hollywood to be in the movie," which is in fact the exact strategy he used to win a greenlight for *Silent Movie* itself. The approach is premised on the unrepeatability of the stunt, with no star likely to risk his or her career on a full-time return to silent filmmaking. It is at once a test of the viability of silent filmmaking and a simultaneous admission that the conditions to support such efforts will probably never be forthcoming again.

In fact, Brooks's work would not mark a belated end to silent film production as he himself envisioned; instead, it would, in many ways, foretell a new beginning. Brooks's Hollywood-backed production was undoubtedly a rarity: the timing of his exercise at the end of the experimental New Hollywood period and just before the consolidations of the Blockbuster Era would be fortuitous. Brooks won studio support for his exploits at the very moment when Hollywood was rethinking old orthodoxies and looking for new voices. Yet if *Silent Movie* remains the only full-length film of its sort backed by a major Hollywood studio since 1929 (Chaplin's sound-era silent features being independently produced outside the major studio system), the viability of Brooks's proposition that silent filmmaking could still be successfully reconstituted even at feature length would be repeatedly revisited outside the domains of American studio production over the last decades of the twentieth century. Ultimately, the alternative silent cinema that Crafton saw in Chaplin's final silent films was not so much abandoned as displaced—actively argued against by Golden-Era films intent on establishing a singular narrative of silent film's sound-era fulfillment and yet actively picked up again almost as soon as that narrative had lost its dominant hold. The alternative silent cinema was in this way not so much defeated as rendered dormant: as soon as the conditions allowed for such experimentation to re-emerge, it almost immediately did.

Alternative Silent Cinema

Of course, the precise nature of those conditions has varied substantially according to the geographies and temporalities of the films in question. One of the greatest difficulties in analyzing the later-day manifestations of the alternative silent cinema is the sheer diversity represented by the form. Experiments in silent filmmaking that seek to move the medium forward rather than recalling the historical tropes associated with silent-era film have emerged the world over, created by individual filmmakers who sometimes share little in terms of background, industrial conditions, or artistic intent. What they share instead is a belief in the viability of silent filmmaking and an interest in its applicability to specialized cases of storytelling, ones wherein a default application of sound would substantially change if not altogether negate the intended meanings of the work. Though most of these films still maintain some degree of diegetic sound and musical scoring, their use of dialogue and even noise is consistently minimized, eliminated, or strategically and selectively deployed. In this way, these films constitute a belated inheritance of Chaplin's efforts from the 1930s, joining him in probing the ways in which silence can become reimagined in the era of sound.

For some in this tradition, this probing is primarily aesthetic: a means of using silence as a tool of cinematic *poesis*. Such is the case in what is one of the earliest instances of the alternative silent cinema, which emerged in one of the countries where silent filmmaking persisted the longest: Japanese director Kaneto Shindo's *Hadaka no shima* (*The Naked Island*). Released in 1960, just eight years after *Singin' in the Rain* and less than twenty years after silent film production finally ceased in Japan in the 1940s, the film is set on a remote island and follows the daily routines of an isolated family eking out an existence under punishing conditions. The film straddles a line between quasi-documentarian realism and existential parable—a study in the human struggle to get through each day wherein language is not so much eliminated from the film as it is rendered unnecessary and redundant, disappearing on its own. The family members, following the same harsh routine year after year, have little cause to speak to one another in words, though there is no shortage of understanding between them. Shindo takes the added step of minimizing diegetic sounds as well, incorporating certain noises from nature but mostly turning the film's audio track over to Hikaru Hayashi's famed modernist score. In a bold reversal of the treatment of silent filmmaking within much sound-era work, *The Naked Island* actively wonders at the very purpose of incorporating sound into film. In a key moment of meta-filmic reflection, the film's central family encounters a television in a shop window of a town that they are visiting and stares aghast as a woman in a black unitard dances to a 1960s-era pop soundtrack. The pairing of music and movement is of course one of the most important additions to the cinema with the coming of sound—the climax of Hazanavicius's *The Artist* turns on this very element—but here it is figured as something almost incomprehensible, an obvious triviality compared to the somber work of daily life. In contrast to this dance and everything it represents in the world of modern filmmaking, Shindo's film functions primarily as a contemplative tone poem, a study in the stillness and sobriety that silence makes possible.

If silence for Shindo is most valuable in its thematic resonances, for Spanish director José Luis Guerín it is a powerful tool for narrative and characterological development, as in his 2007 film *Dans la ville de Sylvia* (*In the City of Sylvia*). Here the deep isolation of the film's central character is self-imposed as a condition of psychology rather than being a product of culture and geography, as in Shindo's work. Guerín's story follows a young man known only as Él, or Him (Xavier Lafitte), as he travels through the streets of Strasbourg, France, searching for a woman named Sylvia he once met briefly in a bar. Alone in a city where he seems to know no one, Él's experience is nearly wordless. Guerín dampens both the diegetic sound and limited dialogue to almost imperceptible levels as he washes the film in a lush soundtrack. He luxuriates in extremely long takes of point-of-view shots where Él studies the women of the city looking for Sylvia and then latches on to one passerby in particular, following her at length. The film is a case study in the male gaze, Él's long looks being ostensibly chaste but also inescapably prurient, with the women serving as little more than objects of attention for his visual fixation—or, in the case of the woman he believes to be Sylvia, an actual object of obsession. The ambiguity of Él's situation and psychological condition gives the film an underlying tension that remains unresolved: Él seems to be a romantic on a quixotic mission to recapture a lost chance for love, but he is also a completely isolated obsessive engaging in a prolonged act of stalking. For Guerín, the near-silence of the film is a tool for probing and exposing without ever fully answering the question of Él's psychological state, a condition of longing in which love and madness come dangerously close together. To force Él to talk would inevitably be to come closer to answering the questions that Guerín purposefully does not want to pose overtly, instead preferring to let them reverberate in the background of his story: Who is this man? Where does he come from? What are his intentions? How dangerous might he be? To pose such enquiries would be to change the film: its silence is constitutive to the very distance that makes it so enveloping and confounding.

As different as their films might be, for Shindo and Guerín alike, Chaplin's *City Lights* stands as an important filmic precursor, demonstrating how silence can actively enable new storytelling. Yet for other films of the alternative silent cinema, the questions of dialogue and power that animate *Modern Times* prove more central. Here it is not the aesthetics of silence so much as the politics of silence that is vital to the function of the film's story: the vehicle of silent film stands, as it did for Chaplin, as a potent tool for exploring the conditions of those who have been silenced, cast out, and shut off from the sociability of sound. One sees these dynamics directly in the masterful work of an explicit Chaplin inheritor, the African American filmmaker and performer Charles Lane, whose independently financed 1989 film *Sidewalk Stories* offers a retelling of Chaplin's *The Kid* set amid the 1980s-era homeless population of New York City. *Sidewalk Stories* is open about its debt to the era of silent film, and cinephiles can revel in Lane's adaptation of individual gags from Chaplin's work: a scene in a homeless shelter bed where Lane must hide with his ward that recalls a similar bit in *The Kid*, or a comedic fight with an adversary as big as Chaplin's old heavy Eric Campbell. But the film is also far from a museum piece, eschewing homage and focusing instead on the silence of modern social isolation. The central conceit of the film (born from an incident in which Lane struck up a conversation with a homeless man on the New York City subway) is that the experience of homelessness can be in itself an experience of prolonged silence, one wherein the normal flow of conversation is unavailable or avoided. The silence of Lane's film is thus diegetically rather than formally motivated. Fearful of those around him, Lane's Tramp-like character avoids most conversation; fearful of him, most people around him do the same. The silence of the film is a sympathetic choice even more than it is a technical or stylistic one, an attempt to convey via the structure of the film itself something of the daily conditions of its lonesome but good-hearted protagonist, an evocation of Chaplin's humanistic spirit as much as his stylistics.

For the Ukranian director Myroslav Slaboshpytskyi, the silence of social isolation need not be an individual affair as it is for Lane. In his 2014 film *Plemya (The Tribe)*, he explores a community brought together by their shared condition of silence. Set in a Ukrainian boarding school for the deaf with all dialogue delivered in unsubtitled Ukrainian sign language, *The Tribe* is a dark tale of criminality and violence among a subclass segregated from the rest of society and subsequently forgotten or ignored. For Slaboshpytskyi, the near-total silence of the film, which deliberately mutes almost all diegetic sound, is not a stylistic marker but an act of envelopment in the world as it is aurally experienced by the characters in this story, while the lack of subtitles places the audience at a remove from these characters' lives that roughly parallels their own distance from wider society. The director's slow revelation of this approach during the opening minutes of the film is masterful in its introduction of silence as an approximate experience of the characters' deafness. Tracking behind the main character as he arrives at the school for his first day, Slaboshpytskyi's camera remains outside the grounds of the school at first, watching in long shot through glass doors as an assembly unfolds in the interior courtyard of the building. A throng of students waves tiny bells in the air, producing only the dimmest of sounds. In the background, we see a student marching back and forth with a tuba, but still there is no sound. As the assembly ends and the students rush silently into the hallway before us, gesturing to one another in sign language, the full scope of Sloboshpytskyi's approach becomes clear, and we understand the spectatorial position in which we have been placed. As in silent-era cinema, the characters in Sloboshpytskyi's story are able to converse with one another, but we in the audience who do not know Ukrainian sign language are entirely isolated from those communications and forced to view them at a distance. Likewise, we are separated from the sonic world of the film; as in Chaplin's films of the 1930s, only select and isolated sounds are provided, sounds that can occasionally orient us in the story but also serve to reinforce our sense of separation. The approach is at once empathetic and alienating, a window into a world few viewers will have seen before and a reminder of just how different that world is from our own lived experience.

New Silent Cinema

The work of the alternative silent cinema is ultimately the work of highly individualized, singular experimentation with the artistic possibilities of silence. What these varied experiments share is what Arnheim put forward just a few years after the coming of synchronization: the conviction that silent films be allowed to "advance along their own lines," finding those corners of cinematic storytelling that can only be explored absent sound. (Arnheim even predicted that such films would come to exist without intertitles, leaving dialogue entirely to the "'complete' film," just as these alternative silent films do.)[17] In contrast, the new silent cinema seeks a return to the stylistics of silent-era filmmaking, intertitles and all. Its mandate is not just pure revivalism, however. Rather, the new silent cinema posits a level of continuity between self-consciously antiquated cinematic forms and contemporary cinematic conditions—"refusing or ignoring Hollywood's over-determined separation of old and new," as Flaig and Groo describe.[18] Whereas the alternative silent cinema seeks to forge a new path forward for silent film after sound, the new silent cinema offers promises of return, deliberately undoing Golden-Era tropes even to the degree of wondering whether silent film itself might be the ultimate fulfillment of sound's own potential trajectory of development and decline.[19]

To understand this aspect of the new silent cinema's purpose is to recognize the historical compression of this filmmaking trend. Examples of the alternative silent cinema span the latter half of the twentieth century and beyond, ranging from Shindo's experiments in 1960, still in the shadow of the Hollywood Golden Era's global reach, to Sloboshpytskyi's experiments of 2014. The films connected to the new silent cinema, in contrast, generally date from the turn of the millennium forward. To appreciate why, we can profitably examine one of the earliest and most internationally prominent examples of the form, Finnish director Aki Kaurismäki's 1999 film *Juha*, filmed in black-and-white with intertitle cards in a manner deliberately evocative of silent-era film. Kaurismäki's antiquarianism is of a very unusual type. His source text, a well-known

Finnish novel from 1911, is set in the eighteenth century, but Kaurismäki's silent adaptation resets the tale to the present day—rendering it both anachronistic in form and contemporary in content at one and the same time. His work is actually the fourth cinematic adaptation of the source novel, and the temporalities of those previous three adaptations are important to understanding the film's function as a work of new silent cinema. The first adaptation came in 1920 in a Swedish production directed by Mauritz Stiller, a Finn, while the second came in 1937 in the first few years of Finland's turn to sound; the third appeared in 1956 and was the country's first color film. In this way, *Juha* has served as a milestone for the Scandinavian cinema's major transitions over the twentieth century: from silent film to sound film to color film. In creating the *second* silent adaptation of the story, Kaurismäki has effectively cycled back to the beginning of this trajectory, pointing toward a connection between the conditions of the work's first adaptation and its latest iteration—at once its most antiquated and also most contemporary rendition.

At its heart, the new silent cinema always posits such historical convergences. The dynamics of this updated historical form cannot be understood apart from the processes of transformation that such films allude to and explore, reengaging Golden-Era tropes about silent film's obsolescence and replacement and applying them to the era of sound film in a new moment of technological revolution—the age of digital cinema. First established in the 1990s, digital filmmaking as a replacement for the use of film stock reached widespread prominence around the turn of the millennium, quickly becoming the default production and exhibition format by the new century's second decade. "It was," as Bordwell writes of this moment, "the biggest upheaval in film exhibition since synchronized sound."[20] The emergence of the new silent cinema is historically and thematically intertwined with the growth of digital filmmaking technology. Whether shot digitally or on film, and whether consciously engaged with questions of the digital revolution or not, the new silent cinema was born of a new period of anxiety in film history and is arguably inseparable from the conditions of this change. The turn to historical revival is at least partly a condition of industrial déjà vu—a recognition of the way in which the existential questions of the silent-to-sound transition so troubling to figures like Arnheim and so confidently answered by films of the Golden-Era studios had once again become vital. As David Rodowick writes, digital film "has loosed its anchors from both substance and indexicality," indicating that the very nature of what it means to make or watch a film may yet forever change.[21] André Gaudreault and Philippe Marion observe as much in *The End of Cinema?*, writing that "Lines are moving, boundaries are constantly shifting, and the classical media have lost many of their bearings. [. . .] What remains of cinema in what cinema is in the process of becoming? Or rather: what remains of *what we thought*, just yesterday, *cinema was* in what cinema is in the process of becoming?"[22] If the alternative silent cinema demands a space for new forms of silent film experimentation in the face of sound-era hegemony, the new silent cinema turns to old techniques of silent film construction as one means of probing how much longer the hegemony of cinema itself might reasonably last, at least as the form has been understood since the rise of synchronization and the advent of what Arnheim perhaps preemptively called "the complete film."

In this sense, Hazanavicius's *The Artist*, arguably the most well known of all contemporary silent films, is meant to be evocative of profound changes under way in cinema and those yet to come, deploying its cinephilia as a bulwark against worry and a reminder of the tremendous changes the film industry has already weathered and withstood. Made in homage to certain stylistics of the classical silent era, from the visual invention of its storytelling to its much-touted 1.33:1 Academy ratio, the film also vitally reiterates a narrative of industrial self-improvement that could have been borrowed directly from *Hollywood Cavalcade*, a depiction of silent film acting remarkably resonant with *Merton of the Movies*, and an ending taken almost directly from the reels of *Singin' in the Rain*—reinforcing a historical view of silent film's demise that most films in the new silent cinema tradition are at pains to complicate or dispute. "Out with the old, in with the new. Make way for the young! That's life!" says sound-era starlet Peppy Miller (Bérénice Bejo) in the film, echoing the characters of *Hollywood Cavalcade* in her insistence on rendering as a matter of artistic evolution a change that was historically determined and commercially driven. So complete is this supposed transformation that George Valentin (Jean Dujardin), a leading film star at the start of the story, is seen as laughable in his performances only months after the transition begins, performing to empty cinemas and eliciting chuckles from younger film fans now suddenly enamored of sound. "People are tired of old actors mugging at the camera to be understood," Peppy declares. Valentin's artistic redemption comes only after his acceptance of the new filmmaking reality, transforming in the film's conclusion from a dramatic lead to a smiling song-and-dance man as though he had actually taken Cosmo Brown's advice from *Singin' in the Rain*.

Ultimately, *The Artist* is a studio-friendly modern silent film: a deeply elegiac piece that also offers the same old justifications for the inevitability of silent film's demise that Hollywood had been selling for much of the twentieth century. One sees this dynamic especially in the trans-temporal nature of the film's cinephilia. Much was made in the press at the time of the film's release about Hazanavicius's inclusion of filmic references that far exceeded his silent-era focus, with Hitchcock heroine Kim Novak even taking out a full-page ad in *Variety* decrying the film's misplaced allusions to *Vertigo*. Yet, in a sense, such out-of-period references are entirely in keeping with the ideology of progress at the heart of *The Artist*'s rendition of film history. As in *Hollywood Cavalcade*, the silent film is here best understood not as an autonomous artistic mode cut off from further development due to the commercial decisions of 1927–1929, but as a generative point for sound-era filmic evolutions, the seed from which the full flowering of the talking picture eventually grew. If we can see sound-era Hitchcock within the germ of the silent-era film—or Orson Welles or John Ford or Federico Fellini, to name just a few of the film's other scattered citations—that is because these sound-era auteurs represent what the silent film was meant to become. *The Artist*'s meta-filmic focus—relatively distinctive among examples of the new silent cinema but entirely in keeping with the construction of Golden-Era films about the silent-to-sound transition—is thus vital to the film's reassurances. The film industry will survive ongoing transitions because the film industry has survived past transitions; the cinema will continue to evolve and grow because the cinema has always done so. In an era of increasing concern over the future of film and the long-term implications of the digital transition, *The Artist* answers with reassurances born of the story Hollywood has long told itself about its first major technological revolution.[23]

In many ways, the new silent cinema is always concerned with dynamics of change. At its heart, it offers a deliberate rewriting of film history, one wherein the past is made actively present again, altering the very narrative of film's supposed evolution. This, too, is a means of confronting the anxieties of cinema's new transformations, mitigating the terror of obsolescence by reveling in the medium's newfound continuities, demonstrating that what is seen as past need not be regarded as lost. One sees this celebratory aspect in one of the more visually exuberant examples of the new silent cinema, Spanish director Pablo Berger's 2012 film *Blancanieves* (*Snow White*), which offers a retelling of the Snow White tale reset in 1920s Andalusia, with the titular Blancanieves here figured as a virtuosic matador. Set to a vibrant flamenco score and filmed in sumptuous black-and-white, Berger's film is unabashed in its silent-era cinephilia. From the severe close-ups of Theodor Dreyer's *La Passion de Jeanne d'Arc* (1928) to the rapid-fire editing of the Soviet montage school to the precise pictorialism of Maurice Tourneur in works like *The Blue Bird* (1918), the citations built into *Blancanieves* reveal it to be as much a silent film about silent film as *The Artist* is a silent film about sound. In a pivotal scene where Blancanieves masters a bull merely by sighing and turning away from it, Berger unfurls a veritable highlight reel of such period techniques, all carefully designed to place us in a position of awe—not only at her performance in the ring but at the athleticism of the filmmaking itself. In its superabundance of allusions and citations, Berger's creation is a twenty-first century celebration of century-old cinematic forms.

This same sense of reverie stands at the heart of the work of Canadian avant-garde filmmaker Guy Maddin, perhaps the most famous and consistent practitioner of contemporary silent filmmaking. Within Maddin's work, the trend toward pastiche in the new silent cinema is brought to an absolute fever pitch. He is remarkably fluent in the stylistics of silent film across a variety of genres and temporal periods: whereas most contemporary silent film evocations tend toward broadness, Maddin's work is marked by its specificity. His lengthy oeuvre includes manic Soviet montage-style films like *The Heart of the World* (2000), *benshi* narration in *Brand Upon the Brain!* (2006), and works like *The Forbidden Room* (2015) that build on the tradition of adventure serials, spanning both the silent and early sound periods.

The ultimate question at the heart of much of Maddin's sui generis work is whether the exultant practice of pastiche can also serve as a means of serious personal expression, or, put another way, whether turning eagerly to the past can also tell us something new about our present. A gifted imitator, Maddin is also committed to the auteurist project of memoiristic self-expression. *My Winnipeg* (2007), perhaps his most famous work, is both a docu-fictional account of his experiences growing up in Canada and an experiment in filmic collage, with portions evoking everything from silent Soviet propaganda films to silent-era travelogues to the city symphony films of the 1920s. It is easy to enjoy the most imitative aspects of Maddin's work as a kind of gifted forgery; yet Maddin demands that we also recognize the personal markings embedded in these imitative acts. His project—historical and personal, imitative and original—is in many ways distinct from the more standard forms of storytelling seen in other reaches of the new silent cinema. But it shares with them a reverence for displaced modes of filmmaking and a belief that an active engagement with the past can lead to important insights into present conditions, even to a collapsing of distinctions between the two. For Maddin, silent film remains vibrant because it offers him the best way to understand himself, echoing the way in which all new silent cinema attempts to grapple with modern filmmaking's anxious present through a deliberate excavation of its past.

Silent Film's New Beginning

In an interview from 1925, just months before the release of the first Vitaphone short, Chaplin said of silent film "We're only just beginning," insisting that "our medium is new, that we are young at the game."[24] Chaplin would soon know how wrong he was. For much of the twentieth century, silent film would become the very emblem of cinema's past, the transition to sound being, as Drew observes, the effective origin point of the modern concept of film history: silent film *was* that history, the supposedly archaic form against which cinema's present might forever be defined.[25] Yet such distinctions have long been suspect. Every decade since the birth of cinema has in fact seen the production of silent films somewhere in the world—the form has always been part of cinema's present. What the alternative silent cinema and the new silent cinema both offer above all else is an acknowledgment of this fact. For all their manifold differences and for all of the individual aims and concerns of the filmmakers encompassed by these trends, where the alternative silent cinema and the new silent cinema converge is in the belief that the hard distinctions between cinema's supposed past and its presumed future have long been, as Flaig and Groo say, "overdetermined." Nearly every turn to silent filmmaking after 1929 has at least in part evinced the same request: that silent film be allowed to begin again and to regard itself as new. Even this most seemingly antiquated of forms is not yet finished. Silent film is ultimately, like all film, still emerging.

Notes

1. Robert K. Klepper, *Silent Films, 1877–1996: A Critical Guide to 646 Movies* (Jefferson, NC: McFarland, 1999): 545; Paul Flaig and Katherine Groo, eds., *New Silent Cinema* (New York: Routledge, 2016).
2. Rudolph Arnheim, "The Complete Film," in *Film as Art* (Berkeley: University of California Press, 1957), 154–160; 154.
3. Ibid., 160.
4. Donald Crafton, *The Talkies: American Cinema's Transition to Sound, 1926–1931* (Berkeley: University of California Press, 1999), 17.

5. Susan Sontag, "The Aesthetics of Silence," in *Styles of Radical Will* (New York: Farrar, Straus, and Giroux, 1966), 9.
6. This essay will only concern feature-length, live-action narrative filmmaking and will rely only on select examples—the total universe of both "alternative silent cinema" and "new silent cinema" far exceeding what can be covered in these pages. If one also accounts for the realms of short-form narrative, animation (especially short-form animation), documentary, and experimental film, the instances in each category grow even greater. Short-form live-action filmmaking, both narrative and experimental, has long had a particularly robust relationship to silent film, with dialogue-less or even fully silent films being produced regularly in this tradition. In the case of short-form animation, the genealogy leading back to the silent era is nearly unbroken, with dialogue-less or sound-less animated shorts being common throughout the history of the form. One sees this especially in the attention surrounding *The Triplets of Belleville* (2003) or the opening act of Pixar's *Wall-E* (2008), which include no dialogue or extremely limited dialogue, respectively, and which echo short-form animation's long history of silent storytelling. For one of the few accountings of contemporary silent film, see Klepper, whose chronology extends until 1996.
7. See Sergei Eisenstein, V. I. Pudovkin, G. V. Alexandrov, and Dziga Vertov, "A Statement on Sound (USSR, 1928)," in Scott MacKenzie, ed., *Film Manifestos and Global Cinema Cultures: A Critical Anthology* (Berkeley: University of California Press, 2014), 566-568.
8. William M. Drew, *The Last Silent Picture Show: Silent Films on American Screens in the 1930s* (Lanham, MD.: Scarecrow Press, 2010), 63.
9. On the cinematographic limitations of early sound cinema, see David Bordwell, "The Introduction of Sound," in David Bordwell, Janet Staiger, and Kristin Thompson, *The Classical Hollywood Cinema: Film Style and Mode of Production to 1960* (New York: Columbia University Press, 1985), 306.
10. Drew, *Last Silent Picture Show*, 72.
11. Ibid., xi, 173; David Bordwell, *On the History of Film Style* (Cambridge, MA: Harvard University Press, 1997), 43.
12. Rob King, *Hokum!: The Early Sound Slapstick Short and Depression-Era Mass Culture* (Berkeley: University of California Press, 2017), 195.
13. Charlie Chaplin, "Pantomime and Comedy," *New York Times* (January 25, 1931), X6.
14. Crafton, *The Talkies*, 374.
15. For further analysis of Chaplin's work, see Donna Kornhaber, *Charlie Chaplin, Director* (Evanston, IL: Northwestern University Press, 2014).
16. Dan Lyberger, "Believing in Make-Believe: An Interview with Mel Brooks," *The Keaton Chronicle* (Autumn 1997), 1.
17. See Arnheim, "The Complete Film," 160.
18. Flaig and Groo, *New Silent Cinema*, 15.
19. One recalls here Mary Pickford's observation that "it would have been more logical if silent pictures had grown out of the talkie instead of the other way round." See Anne O'Hare McCormick, "Searching for the Mind of Hollywood: An Inquiry into the Influences Molding the Vast Flow of Motion Pictures," *New York Times Magazine* (December 13, 1931), 21.
20. David Bordwell, *Pandora's Digital Box: Films, Files, and the Future of Movies* (2012), www.davidbordwell.net.

21. D. N. Rodowick, *The Virtual Life of Film* (Cambridge, MA: Harvard University Press, 2009), 9.
22. André Gaudreault and Philippe Marion, *The End of Cinema? A Medium in Crisis in the Digital Age*, trans. Timothy Barnard (New York: Columbia University Press, 2015), 2.
23. For a further analysis, see Donna Kornhaber, "Hollywood's Recurring Dream: Myth and Fantasy in *The Artist*," *Bright Lights Film Journal* 77 (August 2012), https://brightlightsfilm.com/hollywoods-recurring-dream-myth-and-fantasy-in-the-artist/.
24. Robert Nichols, "Future of the Cinema: Mr. Charles Chaplin," *Times* [London] (September 3, 1925): 13.
25. See Drew, *Last Silent Picture Show*, x.

Index

For the benefit of digital users, indexed terms that span two pages (e.g., 52–53) may, on occasion, appear on only one of those pages.

Figures are indicated by *f* following the page number

Abadie, A. C., 194
Abbott, Edith, 365
Abbott, Grace, 361–62, 365
Abbott, Robert S., 152
Abel, Richard, 483, 511, 574
Abi and Rabi (1930), 10
abortion, 8–9, 375–77, 378–89, 390–91.
    See also birth control films
Abrams, Brett L., 706–7
Abramson, Ivan, 379
Académie des Beaux Arts (France), 225–26
Academy Awards, 738
Academy of Medicine (France), 321, 322
Academy of Motion Picture Arts and Sciences
    (AMPAS), 415, 434, 440–41, 452–53, 454
Academy of Science (France), 312, 314
accidental technology, 80–84
Acosta, Mercedes de, 705–6
Acres, Birt, 194–95
Across Asia's Snows and Deserts (Morden), 345*f*
Acteurs Japonais: Excercice de la perruque
    (1897), 126
Actor-Network-Theory, 9–10
Adams, Maud, 433n.74, 688
Adamson, Patrick, 584–85
Addams, Jane, 355, 360–61
Add Hoyt's Minstrels. *See* Hoyt's Minstrels
Ader, Clément, 106
adoption, 386–87
Adorno, Theodor, 4–5
advertising
    and African American cinema, 135*f*, 141–43,
        144, 150*f*, 154n.18
    for Animatoscope, 176, 183n.59

background of national campaigns, 481–84
for cameras, 83*f*
and chase comedy genre, 186, 198–99
and Children's Bureau films, 365, 366–67
and Chinese cinema, 170
for copy technologies, 86, 86*f*
and film distribution systems, 464, 467,
    470–71, 515–16
Hanff-Metzger's campaign for Paramount,
    489–94, 491*f*, 493*f*
H. E. Lesan's campaign for
    Paramount, 484–88
and Hollywood service sector, 424–25, 426,
    427, 428, 432*f*
and middlebrow culture, 674–76, 677
Paramount Week, 494–98, 497*f*
and popular science films, 298
and promotion of female film stars, 670–73
and reproductive politics in cinema, 376–
    79, 378*f*, 380*f*, 381, 383–84, 385*f*, 387, 388*f*
Aestheticism, 231–32, 237
"The Aesthetic Upheaval in France"
    (Wilson), 242
African Americans. *See* Black Americans
African Hunt (1910), 333
L'Âge d'or (1930), 714, 725
Agee, James, 643–44
agency system, 462–63
"The Age of Birth Control," 375–76
Agfa, 431, 563
agrarian culture and settings, 599
Agricultural College of North Dakota, 294–95
agricultural extension system, 531–35
Aitken, Harry and Roy, 466–67, 472–73, 474

Akeley, Carl F., 297–98
Akeley cameras, 297–98, 298f, 299
Alabama Polytechnic Institute, 533–34
Albert Bonnier (publishing company), 597
Alberti, Rafael, 716
Alco, 464–65
Algie the Miner (1912), 699–700
Ali No-Rouze (Moghaddam pseudonym), 555
Allied Film Laboratories Association, 426–27
Allison and Hadaway, 422
All Quiet on the Western Front (1930), 655–57
alternating shots, 214. *See also* editing
alternative genders, 703–7. *See also* gender and sexual identities
alternative silent cinema, 739–40, 745, 746–50
Altman, Rick, 292
Altman, Robert, 746
Alton, Robert, 742
Alvarez, Max, 463–64
Amateur Dramatic Club of Shanghai, 167
Amateur Minstrel Club, 140
ambimodern framework, 519–20n.8
American Cinematographer, 241, 423–24, 427–28, 432f
American Correspondence School of Law, 675
American Federation of Sex Hygiene, 382
American Film Laboratories, 425
American International Corporation, 514–15
Americanism, 515–16
American Medical Association, 362
American Museum of Natural History (AMNH), 8–9, 292, 297–98, 332–33, 334–35, 339, 344–45, 346–47, 348
American Mutoscope & Biograph Co., 4, 34, 185–86, 187, 189–91, 193, 196–99, 200, 234–35, 528, 663, 691–92
American Society of Cinematographers (ASC), 427–28, 429
American Sunday Magazine, 486
American Telephone & Telegraph Co. (AT&T), 530–31, 531f, 539
America's Answer (1918), 511, 512–13
L'Amic de les Arts, 723
Amiel, Denys, 252, 257–58
Anders als die Andern (*Different from the Others*, 1919), 702–3
Anderson, Benedict, 48–49

Anderson, Gilbert M., 668–69
Anderson, Mark Lynn, 687
Anderson, Thom, 26–27
Andrew, Nell, 266, 273–74
Andrews, Roy Chapman, 334, 335, 346
Andriopoulos, Stefan, 7
Andriot, Lucien, 233
androgyny, 705–6. *See also* gender and sexual identities
Anger, Lou, 450–51
"Animated Pictures" (Barr), 284–85, 286f
animation
 animated cartoons, 294–95
 animated pictures/photography, 99–100, 290–91, 292–93, 299
 and ontology of cinema, 162–63
 and parallel histories of film and television, 42
 time-lapse animated photography, 287–88
Animatoscope, 176, 183n.59
animism, 60
Anna Boleyn (1920), 248n.64
L'Annonce faite à Marie (1912), 255
Anschütz, Ottomar, 19, 25, 28
Antelope Island, 580–81
anti-art, 715–16, 721–25, 730
anti-capitalism, 731
anti-fascism, 729
Anti-Piracy Warning, 85f
Antoine, André, 227, 233, 235–36, 251–52, 254–56
Antoine's Théâtre, 259–60
apparatus theory, 2
Appleton & Company, 580–81
The Arab (1924), 239
Arabesque (1929), 271–72, 273f
Aragon, Louis, 722
Aranda, José Francisco, 719
Arapahoe Indians, 585f
Arbuckle, Roscoe "Fatty," 414, 444, 647, 698, 717–18
Archer Brothers, 467
Arenera and Victor (dance duo), 146
Argand lamps, 20–21
Argosy (production company), 574
Aristotelian ontology, 159
Arlen, Richard, 684, 685f

Armat, Thomas, 33–34, 35
Arnheim, Rudolf, 643–44, 649–50, 655–56, 739, 743, 744, 750, 751
Arnoldy, Édouard, 110–11, 112
Arquilliere, Alexandre, 269
L'Arroseur arrosé (1895), 192, 208
Artaud, Antonin, 252, 274, 726–27
Artcraft films, 495
Art Deco style, 241–42, 243–44
art films, 55, 716–21
artificial darkness, 174
Artificial Darkness (Elcott), 185
"Art in Cinema Series," 715
"Art in the Motion Pictures" (Griffith), 406–7
The Artist (2011), 738, 748, 752–53
Art Nouveau, 243–44
Arzner, Dorothy, 583*f*, 695, 704–5, 706*f*
Asano, Shirō, 116–17
Asch, Sholem, 688
Asian Americans, 578
Askari, Kaveh, 10–11, 227–28, 237–39, 583
assimilation policies, 576
Associated Motion Picture Advertisers, 483
Associated Negro Press (ANP), 149, 151
Association des Écrivains et Artistes Révolutionnaires, 729
Astor House Hotel, 170, 176
astronomical photography, 291
asynchrony, 547–48, 549–50, 551–53, 554, 555–57, 560–64, 566
As You Like It (Shakespeare), 691–92
L'Atalante (1934), 263
Athletics and Football (Shearman), 187–89
At Jolly Coon-ey Island, 134
The Atonement of Gösta Berling (*Gösta Berlings saga*, 1924), 602–3
At the Foot of the Flatiron (1903), 193
Au bal de flore (*At the Flowers' Ball*, 1900), 689–90
Audiovisions (Zielinski), 43
Aufklärungfilme (Enlightenment films), 686, 702
Aunt Sallie's Wonderful Bustle (1901), 698
Aus eines Mannes Mädchenjahren (*A Man's Girlhood*, 1919), 703

authenticity and Swedish cinema, 594–95, 599–601, 602–4, 605, 606, 607–8, 609, 610, 611, 612–13
automata, 652
automatism, 726
automobiles, 295–97, 298, 462–63, 571–72, 573, 588–90, 589*f*
Autour d'une cabine (1894), 26–27
avant-garde cinema
  and anti-art film, 721, 722–23, 724, 725
  and art direction, 237
  and art film, 716–21
  and Bunuel's *Un chien andalou*, 715–16, 730
  counter-cinema, 3
  and film distribution systems, 509
  and lighting design, 231–32
  and middlebrow culture, 677–78
  and modernity thesis, 3
  and poetic film, 729
  and post-silent era silent film, 739–40, 753
  and Symbolist influences, 251, 252, 253, 254–55, 256, 259–60, 263
  and Synthetist influences, 274
  and temporal dimensions of film, 620
The Avenging Conscience (1914), 237, 464–65, 468
Une avenue à Tokyo (1898), 125

Bab, Julius, 56
Bachmann, Anne, 10–11
backlots, 409–11, 432–33
Baer, Karl M., 703
Baetens, Jan, 103, 104, 109
Baine, Harry, 448–49, 454
Baker, Josephine, 720
Baker, Tarkington, 488
Baker Ranch, 580–81, 586–87
Balázs, Béla, 162–63, 651, 658n.7
Balcerzak, Scott, 699
ballet, 260, 560–61
Ballets Russes, 260
Ballin, Hugo, 237, 240–41
Balshofer, Fred J., 86, 436n.27
Bandbox Theater, 376–77
Bang, Herman, 693
Bangville Police (1913), 197–98
Bank of Italy, 450

banks and banking systems, 404, 410–11, 440, 511–12, 514–15, 527, 531, 538
Bantu Educational Kinema Experiment (BEKE), 537, 538–39
Barney, Natalie, 704
Baroncelli, Jacques de, 257
Barr, J. Miller, 284–85, 287–88, 290–93, 299
Barraquer, Ignacio, 723
Barsam-Tollar Mechanical Works, 431, 432f
Barthes, Roland, 162–63, 371–72n.14
basquity, 371–72n.14
Bassermann, Albert, 55, 56, 61, 65
Bataille, Félix-Henri "Henry," 251–52, 257, 258
Bathing Beauties (Keystone), 717–18
The Battle Cry of Peace (1915), 665–66
Battleship Potemkin (*Bronenosets Potyomkin*, 1925), 269, 645–46, 647, 648–49, 717–18, 730
"The Battles in the Blood," 314–18, 315f
Battling Bruisers: Some Boxing Buffoonery (1925), 699–700
Baude-Hansen, Anna-Lisa, 696f
Baudelaire, Charles, 258–59, 550–51
Bauer, Felice, 56
Baxter & Wray, 116–17
Bazin, André, 34, 162–63, 230–31
Beach, Rex, 663–64
Beale, C. W., 19–20
Bean, Jennifer, 625–26, 628
beauty culture, 671–72, 675–76
Beaux-Arts style, 225–26, 241–42
Becker, Jérôme, 348
Becket (1910), 662–63
Beerbohm-Tree, Herbert, 471
Behind the Front (1926), 695
Behind the Screen (1916), 698–99, 701
Beijing Opera, 167, 170, 173–74, 182n.45
Bejo, Bérénice, 752
Belasco, David, 235–36
Belgian International African Association Third Expedition to Africa, 348
Bell, Alexander Graham, 46–47
Bell, George, 389
Bell, Joshua A., 346
Bellas Hess and Company, 675–76
La Belle Dame sans merci (*The Beautiful Merciless Woman*, 1921), 258, 263–65, 266, 268f

Belle Époque period, 251–52, 253–54, 262, 274
Bell & Howell Camera Co., 335, 431, 432f
Bello, Pepín, 716, 717, 719
Bell Telephone, 289–90, 301–2n.23
Benelli, Sam, 257
Ben-Hur (1925), 242, 645
Benjamin, Walter, 4–5, 12, 39–40, 64, 65, 162–63, 517–18, 519
benshi performers, 740, 753
Berger, Ludwig, 653
Berger, Pablo, 753
Die Bergkatze (1921), 248n.64
Bergman, Hjalmar, 596–97, 696
Bergner, Elisabeth, 697, 697f
Bergson, Henri, 95
Berlin, Symphony of a Great City (*Berlin, Die Sinfonie der Großstadt*, 1927), 647, 721
Bernard, Jean-Jacques, 257–58
Bertellini, Giorgio, 9, 10–11
Beserer Films, 362–63
The Best-Fed Baby (1925), 361, 368, 369–70
Better Baby contests, 363
Better Films Movement, 361–62, 368
Beyfuss, Alex E., 669
Beyond Adventure (Andrews), 334
Bierstadt, Albert, 586–87
The Big Parade (1925), 449
Big "T" Film Corporation, 468
The Big Trail (1930), 572, 586–87
Billboard, 143–44, 146, 147, 389
Biograph. *See* American Mutoscope & Biograph Co.
Biograph Bulletin, 186, 188f, 192–94, 198–99
biological race theory, 576. *See also* racial identity and racism
biomechanical acting, 558
Bird, Robert, 256
Birth (1917), 377–78, 378f
Birth Control (1917), 364–66, 388f
birth control films, 8–9, 375–91. *See also* abortion; contraception; eugenics
The Birth of a Nation (1915), 132, 294, 406–7, 466–68, 516, 574–75, 579, 582–83, 669
The Birth of Tragedy (Nietzsche), 255
birth registration/certification initiatives, 358–59, 367–68

bisexuality, 668–69, 708–9n.10, *See also* gender and sexual identities
Bismarck, Otto von, 48–49
Bitzer, Billy, 203n.41, 229, 230, 232–33
Bjørnson, Bjørnstjerne, 598, 601
Black Americans, 130–53, 573–74, 575, 578, 587. *See also* Black press; Black theatrical comedy
black-and-white film, 750–51
Black Box Theater, 387–88
Black Maria studio, 99–100
Black Narcissus (1929), 149
Black Patti's Troubadours, 134, 135
Black press, 151–52
The Black Stork (1917), 364
Black theatrical comedy, 130–48, 149–53
Blackton, J. Stuart, 662–63, 676–77, 678–79
Blackwell, Carlyle, 668–69, 670–71
Blair Camera Company, 30
Blancanieves (*Snow White*, 2012), 753
Blasco Ibáñez, Vicente, 243–44
Blass, Ernst, 641–42, 657n.2
Blazing Saddles (1974), 745–46
Bleichmar, Daniela, 588
Bloch, Ernst, 4–5
Bloch, Marc, 505
Blockbuster Era, 746–47
Blood and Sand (1922), 239–40
blood quantum, 576
Bloom Film Labs, 427
Bluebeard's Eighth Wife (1924), 495–96
The Blue Bird (1918), 227, 236–39, 241, 248n.64, 255, 753
Blue Book Magazine, 663
Board of Trade (UK), 536
bohemianism, 704
Boime, Albert, 586–87
Le Bois sacré cher aux arts et aux muses (Puvis de Chavannes), 237–39
Bonnard, Pierre, 260
Bonnier, Albert, Jr., 597
booking practices, 471. *See also* distribution
Book-of-the-Month Club, 677–78
book tours, 345–46, 345f
Boorstin, Daniel, 517
Bordwell, David, 207, 208–10, 227–28, 595–96, 643–44, 751

Borges, Jorge Luis, 717
Borzage, Frank, 400–1, 402f, 725
Bosworth Productions, 481–82
Bottomore, Stephen, 520–21nn.16–17
Boulevard Theater, 253–54
Bourdieu, Pierre, 484, 663, 677–78
Le Bourreau turc (*Decapitation in Turkey*, 1904), 96
Bow, Clara, 684
Bowser, Eileen, 2, 366–67
Brand Upon the Brain! (2006), 753
Brasch, Ilka, 626
Braun, Marta, 18
Braunberger, Pierre, 724
Bray, J. R., 294–95
Bray Educational Pictures, 362–63
Breast Feeding (pamphlet), 369–70
Brecht, Bertolt, 112
Breckinridge, Sophonisba, 365
Bren, Frank, 170–71, 176, 183n.59
Brenon, Herbert, 239–40
Breton, André, 722, 725, 726–27, 728
Brewster, Ben, 2–3, 217–18, 464, 521n.19, 678–79
Brewster, Eugene V., 665–66
bricolage, 547–50, 551–52, 556–57, 560–62, 564
The Bride of Glomdal (*Glomdalsbruden*, 1926), 601
Brilliant Film Manufacturing Company, 425
Briscoe, Lottie, 670
British-American Concession, 167
British Association for the Advancement of Science, 289–90
British Broadcasting Corporation, 536
British Commonwealth, 535–36
British Council, 536
British imperialism and colonialism, 511–12, 527–28, 535–40
Britta fra Bakken (*Britta from Bakken*, 1915), 603–4
broadcasting, 43–44, 448, 449
Broadway, 154n.18
Broken Blossoms (1919), 229, 230, 231–32
Bronenosets Potyomkin. See Battleship Potemkin (1925)
Brooklyn Institute, 30–31
Brooks, Louise, 696

Brooks, Mel, 745
Brooks, Peter, 572–73, 575, 578, 587
Broome, George W., 154n.18
Broome, Louise, 389–90
Brown, Clarence, 234–35, 586–87
Brown, Cosmo, 743
Brown, Harry, 138
Brown, Karl, 582–83
Brown, Shane, 691, 695
Brownlow, Kevin, 233, 375–76, 572, 581–82
Brown of Harvard (1926), 695
Brulatour, Jules, 422, 426
Brunius, Jacques, 722–23
Brunton, Robert, 237
Buck and Bubbles, 149, 150*f*, 151, 152–53
Buckland, Wilfred, 228–29, 235–36
Bull, Lucien, 25
Buñuel, Luis, 714–31
    and anti-art film, 721–25
    and avant-garde film, 716–21
    and subversive cinema, 725–30
Burbank, California, 432–33
Bureau of Animal Industry, 532–33
Bureau of Commercial Economics, 298
Burlesdon Hall, 240–41
burlesque, 131, 137–38, 147
Burlesque on Carmen (1915), 229
Burris, Jim, 143
Burzil Pass, 337, 338
Der Büsche der Pandora (*Pandora's Box*, 1929), 696
Bushman, Francis X., 668–69, 670
A Busy Day (1914), 698
The Butler (1916), 130, 140
Buxton, R. C., 495–96
Buyū gi Genji, 125–26
"By Coolie and Caravan" (Morden), 347
By the Law (1926), 558

Caddoo, Cara, 387
Cahiers d'Art, 719, 721
Cahun, Claude, 704
Caldwell, John, 427–28
"Calico World" (Kracauer), 653
California Motion Picture Association, 669
The Call, 382–83
Calloway, Cab, 152–53

calotypes, 22
cameramen, 428
camera obscura, 20–21
Camera Work (Stieglitz), 226–27, 229–30
Camille (1921), 241–42
Camille (1926), 721
Campbell, Colin, 677
Campbell, Eric, 749
Campbell, James P., 675–76
Campbell, William, 333
"Camp Cruze," 580–81, 583*f*
Canby, Henry, 677–78
Cantonese Opera, 170, 173, 182n.45
Canudo, Ricciotto, 253
capitalism, 513–14, 519n.7, 526–28, 529, 530–31, 534–39, 540
Capitalism and Schizophrenia (Deleuze and Guattari), 728
Carleton, Will, 663–64
Carlsten, Rune, 600–1
Carlyle, Thomas, 519
Carmen (1915), 228–29, 239–40, 669
Carmen (1926), 720
Carnegie Institute, 537–38
Carpenter, Edward, 689
Carré, Ben, 235–37, 243
Carroll, Noel, 17
cartoons, 667–68
Cassinelli, E. Delores, 668
casting couch scandals, 405–6
Catelain, Jacques, 265*f*
Cavalcanti, Alberto, 715, 718
Celles qui s'en font (1930), 271
Celluloid Closet (Russo), 686
celluloid films, 23–24, 27–28, 29–33, 34, 44, 56, 103, 284–85, 291–92
Cendrillon/Cinderella (1899), 72, 73*f*
censorship, 406–8, 408*f*, 511, 596–97, 666, 701–2
Central Casting Bureau, 399–400
Chabás, Juan, 717
chain-store strategy, 482–83
Chalice of Sorrow (1916), 228, 239–40
Chamber of Commerce (Hollywood), 446–47
Chamber of Commerce (Los Angeles), 407
Chamisso, Adalbert von, 62
Chang (1927), 333, 346

Les chansons illustrées, 107f
Chaplin, Charlie
    and anti-art film, 722
    and Bunuel's *Un chien andalou*, 730
    and Children's Bureau films, 368–69
    and distribution, 511, 512–13
    and gender inversion in slapstick comedy, 698–99, 701
    and Grauman's theaters, 444, 445f, 447–48
    and Kracauer's film criticism, 647–49, 651–52, 655
    and lighting design, 229
    and middlebrow culture, 670
    and modernity themes, 242
    and *Photoplay*'s promotion of film stars, 670–71
    and post-silent era silent film, 739–40, 743–47, 749–50, 754
    and race issues in cinema, 134–35
Chapman, Rose Woodallen, 382
character-centered narratives, 217. *See also* narrative structure of films
Charles William Stores, 675–76
Charley's Aunt (1892), 689, 691–92
Charvet, Maurice, 176, 177
Chase, William Sheafe, 666
chase comedy, 184–200
chase narratives, 560. *See also* chase comedy; narrative structure of films
"Chats with the Players" (magazine column), 670
Chauncey, George, 695
Chavannes, Puvis de, 227
The Cheat (1915), 228
Chenault, Lawrence, 137
Cherchi Usai, Paolo, 520n.16, 521n.18
Cherrill, Virginia, 744
Chess Fever (1925), 557–58
The Chess Player (*Le Joueur d'Échecs*; 1927), 652
Le Cheval emballé (1907), 197–98
chiasmus/chiasmatic structures, 643–44, 651–55
Chicago American Giants, 140
Chicago Defender, 131, 139–40, 141–42, 144–45, 148, 151, 152, 387–89
Chicago Exposition, 47–48
"Chicago Letter" column, 130–32

Chicago School, 3
Chicago's South Side, 131
Chicago Tribune, 376–77, 377f, 485–86
The Chicken Thief (1904), 200
Un Chien andalou (1929), 714–16, 717, 718–21, 722, 723–31
chikudō shaei (phonographic projection), 120–21
Children's Bureau (US), 354–58, 359–64, 365–70, 372n.29, 372–73n.30, 373n.31, 374n.45
Children's Year, 366, 367–68
Children Who Labor (1912), 362
China, 303n.40, 338, 541n.15, 708n.4, 709n.20
    first film screenings in, 160, 176–78
    and magic lantern shows, 174–75
    and photography, 165, 166–67, 168f, 169f
    and screen as mode of spatiality, 171–72, 174
    and theatrical entertainment, 166, 167–71, 173–74
    See also Beijing Opera; Cantonese Opera; Chinese terminology for film; Shanghai
"The Chinese and Some of Their Customs" (Ibn Fadlan), 338
Chinatown (Los Angeles), 453–54
Chinese Opera, 182n.45
Chinese photo studios, 166–67
Chinese terminology for film, 160–65
Chirurgie fin de siècle (1901), 363–64
Choreutoscope, 19–20
Christening and Launching Kaiser Wilhelm's Yacht "Meteor" (1902), 74–75
The Christian (1914), 669
Christian missionaries, 174
Christie Comedies, 149
chronophotography, 22–26, 34, 41–42
Chun, Wendy, 43–44
La Chute de la maison Usher (1928), 719–20
La Cigarette, 257, 259
"Cinema across Media" rubric, 5–6
Cinema and Experience: Siegfried Kracauer, Walter Benjamin, and Theodor W. Adorno (Hansen), 5, 643–44, 647, 648, 651–52
Cinema before Cinema (Tosi), 291–92
Cinéma du Panthéon (Paris), 724
Cinema Equipment Co., 431, 432f
Cinema Law (Cohn), 59, 66
cinema of attractions, 10, 204, 313–14

cinema of narrative integration, 10. *See also* narrative structure of films
Cinema Props Co., 431, 432*f*
Cinema Studio Supply Corp., 423–24, 432*f*
Cinématographe, 24, 32–34, 46–47, 97, 99–100, 103, 120–21, 124, 160–61, 183n.59, 192, 287
Cineograph, 82, 83*f*, 99
circulation of media, 77, 80–81, 82–84. *See also* distribution
City Civil Service Commission, 407
City Lights (1931), 740, 743, 744, 745, 749
civic efficiency, 366, 374n.48
civic moralism, 399–400
Civil Rights Act (Illinois), 144–45
civil rights law (US), 144–45
Civil Service Commission (Los Angeles), 407
Civil Service Commission (US), 365–66
Clair, René, 263, 274, 715, 718
Clark, James L., 334–35, 336*f*, 338, 339, 351n.28, 351n.31. *See also* Morden-Clark Central Asiatic expedition
Clark, Marguerite, 669, 672
The Classical Hollywood Cinema (Bordwell, Staiger, and Thompson), 227–28
Claudel, Paul, 251–52, 255, 257–58, 259
Cleveland Gazette, 136
Cleveland Plain Dealer, 383–84
cliffhanger structure, 618–19, 620, 621, 622, 623–24, 627, 628–30, 631–33, 633n.4. *See also* narrative structure of films
Clifford, James, 348
climate change, 588–90
The Clinging Vine (1926), 700, 704–5
clock imagery, 626, 627
Clorindy, Or, The Origin of the Cake Walk (musical), 134, 154n.18
close-up shots, 105, 231, 339–40, 341–43, 342*f*, 346, 368–69, 448, 533–34, 560–61, 563, 626, 718, 720, 721, 724, 726, 753
cloud computing, 75
Clunas, Craig, 164–65
Clune Labs, 428
Coburn, Alvin Langdon, 234–35
coded behaviors, 672, 684–85, 686, 698–99, 703–4, 705–7
Cody, Hal, 449
Cohn, Georg, 57–58, 59–61, 65, 66

Cole, Bob, 133–36
collectivization, 534
College (1927), 721
The Collegians (1926–1929), 695
Collins, Rube, 533–34
Colombia, 530
Colonial Advisory Committee on Native Education (UK), 537
Colonial Films Committee (UK), 537
colonialism
    British imperialism and colonialism, 511–12, 527–28, 535–40
    colonial goods, 551
    and *The Covered Wagon*, 569–72
    and film distribution systems, 511–12
    and imperial power of cinema, 527–28
    and location shooting as truth claim, 579–80, 581–82
    post-colonial studies, 573–74
    settler colonialism, 573–74, 576, 577–78, 579–80, 581–82, 587–90
    settler colonial studies, 573–74
    and settler melodrama, 573–74, 576, 578
Colonial Office (UK), 536, 537–38
color film, 4, 32, 420–21, 654, 750–51
Colson-Malleville, Marie-Anne, 704
Columbia Phonographs, 489
Columbia Pictures, 430, 563
Comandon, Jean, 305, 308–9, 308*f*, 310–20, 321–22, 323, 326–27, 328n.10
Comédie-Française, 254
comedy verité sitcoms, 199
comic strips, 185–87
comic types, 197
Commercial Raw Stock Company, 431, 432*f*
Commercial Traders, 429
Committee on Public Information (CPI), 511, 512–13
communism, 519, 728–29
Comolli, Jean-Louis, 230–31
comparative media approach, 12, 75–76, 80, 87. *See also* historiography of film; integrated history of the media; intermediality
"The Complete Film" (Arnheim), 739, 744, 750, 751
Congress (US), 358, 365–66, 371n.4, 530
Connick, H. D. H., 514–15

The Conquering Power (1921), 237, 239, 240–42
conservatism, 375–76, 382, 388–89, 390–91, 645–46
Consolidated Film Industries, 429–30, 431
conspicuous consumption, 484, 672–73
Constantini, Lilian, 271, 273*f*
Constitution (US), 77
consumerism, 484, 518, 549–50, 551–52, 571–72, 670–73, 676–79
contraception, 375–76, 381–82, 383, 384, 386–91. *See also* birth control films
contre-jour ("against daylight") photography, 232–35, 247n.39
Cook, Will Marion, 134, 142–43, 144–45, 154n.18
Coolidge, Calvin, 518
Coolus, Romain, 257
"coon songs," 147–48
Cooper, Madeline "Kinky Doo," 140
Cooper, Mark Garrett, 403–4
Cooper, Merian C., 333
Cooter, Roger, 308–9
The Cop (1929), 724
Copperbelt (Africa), 537–39
copying technologies, 7, 72–87
copyright issues
   and chase comedy genre, 193–94, 202n.31
   and copying technologies, 87
   digital media as key to early cinema, 78–79, 80–81
   early cinema as key to digital media, 81–84
   and historical background of film piracy, 72–75, 76–77
   and media archaeology approach, 7
   and Megaupload raid, 84–87
   and "right to one's own image," 56–57, 58
Copyright Office (US), 78–79
La Coquille et le clergyman (*The Seashell and the Clergyman*, 1927), 252, 274, 718
Corfin, Michael, 253–54
Corot, Jean-Baptiste-Camille, 235–36
corporatization, 455
cosmetics industry, 671–72, 675–76
cosmopolitanism, 703–4
Costello, Maurice, 668, 669, 670
Cotton, William, 237
Cotton States Exposition, 33–34

Council for Cultural Affairs (Japan), 117
counter-cinema, 3
Courtney, Susan, 586
Court of Appeals (US), 74–75
Couvreur, André, 316–17
The Covered Wagon (1923), 569–73, 570*f*, 571*f*, 582*f*, 583*f*, 584*f*
Coward, Noël, 546–47
Cowling, Herford Tynes, 334–35
Craft, Pliny P., 467–70, 478–79n.44
Crafton, Donald, 739–40, 745, 746–47
Craftsmen, 425–26, 429
Cramer-Brownell, Kathryn, 518
The Creation of the Media: Political Origins of Modern Communications (Starr), 288–89
Creco, Inc., 431, 432*f*
Creel, George, 512–13
Criterion Theatre (New York), 569–71, 570*f*
"Criticism Is a Creative Art" (*Film-Kurier* series), 641
Cronyn, Thoreau, 412–13
cross-dressing, 689, 691–92. *See also* gender and sexual identities
Crouse and Davidge, 428
Crust, Kevin, 440
Cruze, James, 572, 580–81, 582–83, 585*f*, 586–87
Cryer, George, 447–48
Cry of the Children (1911), 362
The Crystal Cup (1927), 696
Cubism, 547–48, 716
Culter, Richard, 490–94, 491*f*
cultural impact of cinema
   cultural hegemony, 511–12, 518
   cultural mobilization, 511
   cultural significance of Hollywood, 399
   cultural stewardship, 662–70
   and mass culture, 5–6
   and middlebrow culture, 662–73, 674–79
   and modernity/modernism, 3–5, 505–7, 509
   and stereotypes, 336–37
cultural series concept, 95–96, 97–104, 105–12, 184–87, 191–92, 194, 195–96, 199–200
"Culture Is Ordinary" (Williams), 587–88
Culver City, 432–33
Cummings, Irving, 741
The Curtain Pole (1908), 197–98
Curtis, Scott, 8–9

cut-ins, 206–7, 209–10, 211–12, 215–17. *See also* editing
cyberlockers, 78, 80–84, 86–87

Dadaism, 263, 274, 716, 717
"Daedeleum," 19
Daguerre, Louis, 22
daguerreotype, 22, 165
Daleyme, Tania, 268*f*
Dalí, Salvador, 716, 720, 723, 725
Dana, Viola, 444
dance, 562*f*, 686, 689–91, 705–7
Dances through the Ages (1909), 689–90, 690*f*
dandyism, 546–47, 549–57, 560–61, 563–66
A Dangerous Wooing (*Ett farligt frieri*, 1919), 600–1
Dan'gui teahouse (Shanghai), 167, 173, 174
Daniels, William, 243–44
Danish cinema, 594–96, 597–601, 603–4, 606–8, 609–10, 612–13
Danse au bivouac (1896), 691
Danse japonaise II: Harusame (Veyre), 124–25
Dans la ville de Sylvia (*In the City of Sylvia*, 2007), 748
Danton (1921), 645–46
A Daring Daylight Burglary (1903), 186
"Darktown Birmingham" stories, 149
Darktown Follies, 149
Darwin, Charles, 255
D'Auray, Jacques, 235
Davidge, Roy, 431
Davis, Andrew Jackson, 45
Davis, H. O., 407–8, 473
Davis, John Merle, 537–38
Dawes Act, 578
Dawley, Alan, 534–35
A Day in Baby's Life (1915), 360
Débussy, Claude, 255, 258–59, 270–71
"Décadisme," 237
Decatur Herald, 495–96
Decherney, Peter, 82
The Decline of Sentiment (Jacobs), 240–41
deCordova, Richard, 704
"*Découpage* o segmentación cinegráfica" (Buñuel), 726
De Kuyper, Eric, 253–55
De Land, Fred, 301–2n.23

Deleuze, Gilles, 728, 731
Delft school, 234
Delluc, Louis, 252, 253, 263, 266
"Del plano fotogénico" (Buñuel), 726
Demenÿ, Georges, 24–25, 28
de Meyer, Adolphe, 229–30
DeMille, Cecil B., 227, 228–29, 239–40, 241, 242–43, 401–4, 414–15, 444, 447–48, 454, 481–82, 557, 670
DeMille, William C., 454
democratic values, 515–16, 587–88
demographic trends, 411–12, 674, 678–79
Denis, Maurice, 249n.71, 260, 262
Denson, Shane, 627
Department of Agriculture (US), 359–60, 526, 530–32, 534–35, 539
Department of Commerce and Labor (US), 8–9, 354–55, 357–58, 512–13
Department of Justice (US), 84
Department of State (US), 512–13, 523n.45
Department of the Treasury (US), 511, 523n.45
depth of field, 205–7, 210, 211*f*, 212–14, 213*f*, 230–31. *See also* staging
Dermoz, Germaine, 269, 270*f*, 279n.61
Descartes, René, 19
"Descriptions of Positions of Camera in Taking Views for Complainant's 'Personal' Photograph," 193
desegregation, 142–44
Deslandes, Jacques, 18
Deslaw, Eugene, 718
Desmond, William, 444
Desnos, Robert, 722–23, 730
Desnoyers, Marcelo, 233, 235
Desperate Poaching Affray (1903), 186
Desprès, Suzanne, 252, 254–55, 261*f*, 269
de Torre, Guillermo, 716–17
Detroit Free Press, 485–86
Deutsches Theater, 55
developing machines, 424, 430
Dewey, John, 374n.48
Dianshizhai Pictorial, 175
Dicke, Thomas, 462–63
Dickson, Antonia, 78–79
Dickson, William Kennedy Laurie, 29–31, 33–34, 78–79

Dickson Experimental Sound Film (1894–1895), 691
Dictionnaire historique et pittoresque du théâtre et des arts qui s'y rattachent (Pougin), 97, 98f
Diderot, Denis, 255–56
Dietrich, Marlene, 705–6
diffusionist model of science popularization, 308–9
digital filmmaking, 75, 78–87, 751
Digital Millennium Copyright Act (DMCA), 85
Dillenbeck, Arthur O., 495
Dinet, Étienne, 239
Dippie, Brian, 578
discrimination, 144–45
Disney, 80–81
dispositif, 111, 171–75
Disque 957 (1929), 271–72
distribution, 460–76, 478–79n.44, 479n.48. See also agency system; franchise system; state-rights system,
District of Columbia, 365–66
division of labor, 518
divorce rates, 676
Dixon, Thomas, 406–7
Dixon, Wheeler Winston, 691
Doane, Mary Ann, 185, 194–95, 202–3n.33
documentary film, 104, 357–58, 371–72n.14, 526–27, 528, 529, 530, 532, 533–35, 536, 540. See also expedition films; Morden-Clark Central Asiatic expedition
Domestic Industrial Exposition (Japan), 122
Domitor, the International Society for the Study of Early Cinema, 10, 520n.16
Donaldson, Orren M., 414
Donen, Stanley, 742–43
Donisthorp, Wordsworth, 28
Donjeck River expedition, 334–35
Doré, Gustave, 233–34
Dorothy Vernon of Haddon Hall (1924), 414–15
d'Orsay, Gigi, 705–6
Dotcom, Kim (Kim Tim Jim Vestor), 75, 80, 84–87, 86f
The Double: A Psychoanalytic Study (Rank), 63
double exposure, 62, 718, 720
doubles trope, 55, 56, 57, 59–64, 66

Doyen, Eugène Louis, 314, 329n.23
Dressler, Marie, 146–48
Drew, Sydney, 692, 754
Drew, William, 740–41
Dreyer, Carl Theodor, 594–96, 598–99, 600–1, 603, 606, 607–8, 609–10, 611, 645, 695, 719, 753
Druick, Zoe, 371–72n.14
dry-plate photography, 22, 23–24, 32
Du Bois, W. E. B., 149
Duboscq, Louis Jules, 19–20
Duchamp, Marcel, 263, 704
Duenschmann, Hermann, 55–56, 64, 66
Dujardin, Jean, 752
Dulac, Albert, 254, 262–63, 704
Dulac, Germaine, 706f
    avant-garde cinema, 715–16, 718, 719
    and same-sex relationships on film, 696
    sexuality, 704–5
    and Symbolist influences, 252, 253, 254–55, 256–65
    and Synthetist influences, 266–73, 268f, 270f, 272f, 273f, 274, 279n.61
Dunbar, Paul Laurence, 134, 154n.18
Duncan, F. Martin, 313–14
Duncan, Isadora, 237–39
duping, 72–77
DuPont, 425–26, 431
Duverger, Albert, 720
DVDs, 75
Dwan, Allan, 240–41
Dyer, Frank, 666
Dyer, Richard, 693

"The Earliest Japanese Movie" (Yoshirō), 116–17
"early cinema" label, 505, 506, 508–9, 510
Eastman, George, 23–24, 28, 29–30, 425, 447–48
Eastman Kodak, 30, 335, 420, 424, 425–26
Eastman Service Building, 431, 432f
Eckhardt, Joseph, 82
Éclair (film production company), 233, 313–14
L'École des Beaux-Arts, 237
École du Silence, 257–58
ecological ontology, 178–79
economic globalization, 539, 542n.26

economic impact of cinema, 401–3, 409–13
Edema camera, 335
Edinburgh International Film Festival, 2
Edison, Thomas A., 18, 28–31, 32–33, 34, 35, 44–45, 47–48, 72, 78–79, 99–100, 103, 666, 691
Edison Company
   and chase comedy genre, 186, 192, 193
   and Children's Bureau films, 359–60, 362
   and Cinématographe, 33–34
   and copying technologies, 74–75, 76, 78–79, 81–82, 85–86, 87
   and early moving images, 29–30
   exhibitions in Japan, 120–21
   and gender inversion in slapstick comedy, 698
   and imperial power of cinema, 528, 529f, 530f
Edison Kinetoscopic Records (1893), 78–79
Edison v. Lubin, 74–75, 76, 78–79, 81–82
editing, 205–7, 216f, 559, 560–61, 626, 726, 741–42. *See also* alternating shots; cut-ins; intrascene cutting; montage; non-continuity editing; parallel editing
educational films, 518, 702
Eggeling, Viking, 715, 723
Egginton, William, 171–72
Egholm, Morten, 598–99
Ehrlich, Paul, 312–13, 324–27, 326f
Eichberg, Henning, 189, 191–92
Eide, Eigil, 693, 694f
Eidoloscope, 33–34
eiga (projected pictures), 120
Eisenstein, Sergei M., 39–40, 534, 557–58, 647, 648–49, 717–18, 730, 740
Elcott, Noam, 185
El Dorado (1921), 231–33, 239–40, 263–65, 265f
elections, 518
Electrical Tachyscope, 19–20
Electrician and Mechanic, 294
electric lights, 20–21. *See also* lighting sources and design
Electric Theatre Supply Company, 468–69
Electrotachyscope, 19
Eliot, Charles William, 382, 515–16
Elite Café, 140
Elizabethan theater, 689

Ellington, Duke, 152–53
Ellis, Carlyle, 361–62, 366–70
Ellis, Havelock, 689
Elsaesser, Thomas, 6–7, 39, 40–41, 50, 78–79, 80, 112, 127, 163–64
Eltinge, Julian, 691–92
Éluard, Paul, 722
The Emergence of Cinematic Time (Doane), 185
Emerick, Charles F., 288–89
Empire Marketing Board (EMB), 526, 535–37
L'Emprise, 254
L'Enchanteur pourrissant (Apollinaire), 716
The End of Cinema? (Gaudreault and Marion), 110, 751
End of St. Petersburg (1927), 647
Eng, Esther, 704–5, 706f
Engell, Lorenz, 631
Enlighten Thy Daughter (1917), 378–81, 380f
Enoch Arden (1911), 664
en plein air filming, 231–32
Entr'acte (1924), 263, 718
environmental damage, 588–90
episodic structure, 623–24. *See also* serial films
Epstein, Jean, 259, 266, 718, 719
Epstein, Marie, 719
Erbograph, 429
Erlanger, Camille, 254
Erlanger Opera House (Cleveland), 383–84
Ernst, Wolfgang, 6, 39, 43–44, 184–85
The Error of Omission (1912), 362–63
Esbensen, Axel, 693, 704
The Escaped Lunatic (1904), 185–86, 187, 192–96, 196f
"Escape on the Fast Freight" (1915), 626
Esposito, Elena, 631
Essanay (film production company), 675
ethnic minorities, 510
ethnography, 58–59, 333, 348
Étiévant, Henri, 720
L'Étoile de mer (1928), 718
Ettela'at, 563
Eugenic Film Company, 377–78
eugenics, 364, 386–88. *See also* birth control films
Eugénie Grandet (Balzac), 239, 241–42
Ewers, Hanns Heinz, 55
exchange men, 471

Exhibitors Herald, 384, 385*f*, 444–45, 445*f*, 447–48, 452*f*, 495–96
Exhibitor's Trade Review, 449, 571*f*
expedition films, 8–9
experimental film, 715. *See also* avant-garde cinema
exploitative dimensions of cinema, 364, 405
The Exploits of Elaine (1914), 619, 620, 626
Explorers Club, 334–35, 339–40, 345*f*, 345–46, 350n.21
exposure times, 22
The Extraordinary Adventures of Mr. West in the Land of the Bolsheviks (1924), 558
extras, 151, 294, 402*f*
eyelines, 205, 212, 213–14, 213*f*
Eyemo camera, 339
Eyvindur of the Mountains (*Bjarg-Ejvind og hans Hustru,* 1917), 598–99

Fabian, Johannes, 332–33, 346–47
Fairbanks, Douglas, 240–41, 414–15, 444, 445*f*, 451–52, 454, 473–74, 511, 546, 670, 675–76
fairy play, 8, 96, 97, 185
fake memories, 632–33
Falla, Manuel de, 717
"Fallen Women, Rising Stars, New Horizons" (Hansen), 4
The Fall Guy (1921), 130
Famous Players-Lasky (FPL), 228, 401, 403, 443, 445–46, 465–66, 473–74, 475, 481–82, 490, 514–15, 569–71, 579, 669
fan magazines, 662–79
Fantastic Voyage (1966), 316
Faraday, Michael, 19
Faraday Wheel, 19
Farnum, Dustin, 444
Farrar, Geraldine, 229, 669, 670
fascism, 519
Faust (Goethe), 65, 167–70
Fay, Jennifer, 343
Fazenda, Louise, 670
F. B. Film Laboratories, 436n.27
Federal Bureau of Investigation (FBI), 84–85, 85*f*
federal films, 359–60

Federal Highway Act (US), 588–90
Federal Trust and Savings Bank of Hollywood, 451–52
féerie. *See* fairy play
Fellini, Federico, 752–53
feminism, 2–3, 365, 389
La Femme de nulle part (1922), 263
Fenton, Ernest, 468–69
Ferber, Edna, 546–47
festive running, 187–92
Fetchit, Stepin, 151
La Fête espagnole (1919), 252, 266, 267*f*, 268*f*
Feu Mathias Pascal (1925), 718
Feyder, Jacques, 720, 740
Fielding, Romaine, 668–69, 670–71
Field Museum (Chicago), 335
La Fièvre (1921), 263
Le Figaro, 322
The Fighting Trail (1917), 571–72
Figures de cire (1914), 233
Figures in an Interior (Vuillard), 264*f*
file-hosting services, 85
La fille de l'eau (1924), 717–18
Film als Kunst (Arnheim), 649–50
"Film Archives and Audiovisual Techniques/The Methodology of Film History" (FIAF congress), 2, 39–40
Film as a Subversive Art (Vogel), 714
Filmcraft Labs, 428
film criticism
    and film publics, 11
    and film's transition to sound, 655–57
    and media theory of film, 649–52
    origins in *Film-Kurier,* 641–44
    politics of Kracauer's criticism, 652–55
    and standardization of film audience, 645–46
    and Weimar cinema, 644–45
The Film Daily, 450–51, 452
A Film Exposure (1917), 701
filmgemäß, 649–52
filmgerecht, 651
Film History as Media Archaeology (Elsaesser), 127
The Filming of the West (1976), 572
Film-Kurier, 641–44, 642*f*, 655

film labs and processing
   and background of West Coast technology service companies, 422–24
   and the Hollywood service corridor, 431–34
   and proximity to Hollywood, 427–31
   rise of independent laboratories, 424–27
finance for filmmaking. *See* banks and banking systems
Finlayson, James, 699–700
Finnish cinema, 595–96, 600, 607
First Amendment, 290, 406
First International Berkeley Conference on Silent Cinema, 5–6, 201n.4
First National, 474–75, 485, 488, 489, 495
First National Month, 495
first-run advertising, 484–85
first-run theater circuits, 485
fixed release schedule, 478–79n.44
Flaherty, Robert, 333, 339
Flaig, Paul, 738–40, 750, 754
La Flamme (1910), 258
The Flatiron (1905), 234
Fleischer, Richard, 316
Fleming, J. A., 301–2n.23
flexible-roll film, 28, 30
Flinn, John C., 580–81
flipbooks, 18, 19
Florey, Robert, 241–42
A Florida Enchantment (1914), 692
Florin, Bo, 596–97
The Fly Pest (1910), 362–63
fokoli, 553
Folco, Alice, 255
folklore and Swedish cinema, 594–95, 599, 600–1, 602, 603–5, 606, 607–8, 611–12
fondu enchaîné, 720
A Fool There Was (1915), 205–7, 208–9, 209f, 211–12
Forbidden Adventure (1931), 333
The Forbidden Room (2015), 753
Ford, John, 572–73, 574, 752–53
Fordism, 191–92
Ford Model T, 571–72
foreground staging, 208–9, 209f. *See also* staging
Forsberg, Laura, 316–17
Forsman, John, 146

Fort, Paul, 259–60
For Those Unborn (1914), 364
Forty-Niners, 576–77
"Forty Years of the Negro on the Stage," 137–38
Foster, William (cameraperson), 427, 428
Foster, William (journalist and film producer)
   and American musical theater, 132–33, 134, 135–39
   featured in "Chicago Letter" column, 130–32
   in Hollywood, 149–53
   moving picture venture, 139–48
Foster Photo Play Film Company, 130, 140
Foucault, Michel, 6, 39, 110–11, 688–89
The Four Horsemen of the Apocalypse (1921), 225, 226f, 228, 229–30, 233–36, 237, 238f, 239–44, 246n.25, 697–98
The Fourth Estate, 490
Fox, Charles Donald, 375, 397–98, 398f, 402f
Fox Film Corporation, 430, 432–33, 438n.62. *See also* West Coast Theaters
Fox-Talbot, William Henry, 22
Fox Week, 495
framing conventions, 204–5, 206–13, 214–17, 218–21, 235–36
La Française, 254–55
France
   ciné-clubs in, 253
   and cinematic avant-garde, 251–74
   and debates about film as art, 253
   Hollywood films in, 523n.43
   impact of WWI on film industry, 511–12
   and the "invention" of cinema, 99
   and Japonisme trend, 125–26
   and modernist theater, 251–52, 255, 276n.22
   and modernity, 242
   popularity of Swedish films in, 595–96
   role in construction of Panama Canal, 542n.24
   science films in, 313–14
   and scientific research, 319–20, 324
   and serial films, 636–37n.48
France Films, 381
Francesca da Rimini (1910), 662–63
franchise system, 461–76
   product franchising, 462–64, 465, 466, 470, 474–75, 476
   system franchising, 462–63

Francis, Corinne, 146
Francis, David, 2
Francis, Ève, 252, 255, 257–58, 265, 265f, 266, 268f
Franco-Prussian War (1871), 48
Frankfurter Zeitung, 11, 641–42, 643–44, 645, 646, 651–52, 655
Frankfurt School, 4–5
Franklin, Sidney, 243
Franklin Institute, 675
Frazer, James George, 58–59
Freeburg, Victor, 229–30, 583, 584f
French New Wave, 274
French Revolution, 587
Fresnault-Deruelle, Pierre, 104
Freud, Sigmund, 63, 727–28, 730
Friedberg, Anne, 39–40
Friedrich, Caspar David, 232–34
Friese-Greene, William, 28–29
From Bud to Blossom (1910), 291–92
From Caligari to Hitler (Kracauer), 641–42, 645, 646, 648, 649, 653
From the Field to the Cradle (1911), 362–63
Fuchun teahouse (Shanghai), 173, 174
Fujikan Theater (Asakusa, Japan), 123
Fuller, Loïe, 259, 262
Fuller, Mary, 671–72
Fuller-Seeley, Kathryn, 494, 674
La Fumée noire (1919), 263
Futurism, 260, 716, 717

La Gaceta Literaria, 719, 723
Gade, Sven, 239–40
Gaines, Jane, 7, 347
Galili, Doron, 7
gallery exhibits, 344
"Gallery of Photoplayers" (*Photoplay* column), 671–72
Galloway, Michael, 746
A Gambler's Gambol (1916), 701–2
A Game of Checkers/ A Game of Draughts (Vuillard), 264f
Gamper, Michael, 619–20
Gance, Abel, 233, 654, 719, 721
Garbo, Greta, 243–44, 687–88, 705–7
La Gardienne (Regnier), 278n.53
Garelick, Rhonda, 550

Garfias, Pedro, 717
Garson, Harry I., 467–70, 478–79n.44
gaslight, 173–74. *See also* lighting sources and design
Gastou, Paul, 312–13
Gates, Eleanor, 237–39
Gaudio, Tony, 243–44
Gaudreault, André, 2, 7, 10, 17, 34, 49–50, 109, 111, 119, 184, 186–87, 191–92, 520n.16, 751
Gauguin, Paul, 260
Gaumont Film Company, 117–18, 231–32, 313–14, 363–64, 559, 723
Gavotte (1898), 689–90
Gaycken, Oliver, 8–9, 291–92
Gay New York (Chauncey), 695
Der Geiger von Florenz (*The Violinist of Florence*, aka *Impetuous Youth*, 1926), 697, 697f
gender and sexual identities
  advocating for minority rights, 702–3
  alternative identities offscreen, 703–7
  background in cinema, 684–88
  cross-dressing comedies, 691–92
  and dance films, 689–91
  female stars and consumerism, 670–73
  gender and sexual inversion, 686, 687–89, 691, 692, 698–702, 708–9n.10
  and middlebrow culture, 667–69
  and runaway stories, 624–25
  same-sex relationships in dramatic films, 692–98
  in slapstick comedy, 698–702
  and spread of sexology, 688–89
The General (1926), 651
General Electric, 420
General Federation of Women's Clubs, 363, 368
General Film Company (GFC), 460–61, 463–65, 467, 470–72, 666, 669
General Strike of 1926, 536
General Theory of Magic (Mauss), 63
generic Western portals, 161, 162
genres, 644–45
Gentlemen Prefer Blondes (1925), 241–42
Georgie, Florence, 194
Gerbier, Laurent, 102, 109–10

German cinema, 425–26, 641–44, 647, 648–49, 655–57, 702. *See also* Kracauer, Siegfried; Weimar cinema
Gérôme, Jean-Léon, 237
Gerow, Aaron, 117–18, 120, 121, 123
Die Gezeichneten (*The Stigmatized*, 1921), 645
G. Gennert Camera, 422
The Ghost in the Garret (1931), 495–96
Giacomo, Salvatore di, 600
Giannini, A.P., 450
Gibson, Helen, 623–24
Gibson, Margaret, 672
Gibson, Rose, 621
Gide, André, 716
Gignoux, Régis, 314, 316–18, 319, 327
Gigolo (Vahidi), 546–66, 548f
gigolos, 546–48, 564–66
Gillespie, John, 235–36, 237
Gilpin, Charles, 137, 152–53
Gipsy Blood (1918), 239–40
Girel, Constant, 124–25, 126
The Girl and the Game (1916), 622–23
The Girl in Pants (*Flickan i frack*, 1926), 696, 696f
"girls complexes" (*Mädchenkomplexe*), 621
The Girl Who Earns Her Own Living (manual), 676
Gish, Dorothy, 495–96
Gitelman, Lisa, 45–46
Gjellerup, Karl, 598
La Glace à trois faces (1927), 718
A Glance at the Great Inventions of the Twentieth Century (Plessner), 46–47, 49
Glässner, Erika, 703
Gleich, Joshua, 585–86
Glick, Elisa, 550–51
global networks, 10
Globe Theatre (San Francisco), 443–44
Gluck, Alma, 704
The Goats (performance group), 139–40
Godard, Jean-Luc, 112, 724
The God of Vengeance (play), 688
Goebel, James, 367–68
Goethe, Johann Wolfgang von, 65
Goetz Curt, 692
The Golden Bough (Frazer), 58–59
The Golden Chance (1915), 228

The Gold Rush (1925), 647, 648–49, 655, 730
gold rush migrants, 443, 576–77
Gold Standard, 527
Goldwyn, Samuel, 403–4
Goldwyn Week, 495
Gomery, Douglas, 482–83
Gómez de la Serna, Ramón, 716–17, 719
Gonzalez, Myrtle, 673
Goodbar, Edward, 140
Good Hunting (Clark), 335, 336–37
Good Neighbor diplomatic policy, 518
Google, 80–81
Gordon, Linda, 386–87
Gordon, Nathan, 485
Gorky, Maxim, 49
Goss, Foster, 427–28, 429–30
gossip columns, 670
Goudal, Jean, 722
Gould, George, 377
Goya, Francisco de, 719
Grady, Lottie, 130, 140–41, 141f, 142, 144, 148
gramophones, 43, 563–64
Grand Hotel (1932), 455
Grand Hotel (Tehran), 554
Granville-Barker, Harley, 236–37
Grass (1925), 346
Gratacap, L. P., 292
Grau, Robert, 666
Grauman, David, 443
Grauman, Sidney "Sid" Patrick, 414–15, 440–42, 441f, 443–49, 445f, 447f, 450–54, 452f, 455–56
Grauman's Chinese Theater (Los Angeles), 440–42, 444–45, 451–52, 453–54, 455–56
Grauman's Egyptian Theatre (Los Angeles), 414–15, 440–42, 444–45, 446–49, 447f, 450–51, 455–56, 584–85
Grauman's Greater Hollywood Theater, Inc., 450–51
Grauman's Metropolitan Theatre (Los Angeles), 445–46, 448
"Great Artist Contest" (magazine contest), 669
The Great Art of Light and Shadow (Kircher), 20–21
"A Great Big Girl Like Me" (song), 147
The Great Dictator (1940), 744
Great Kanto Earthquake, 126

"The Great Mystery Play" (magazine contest), 667–68
Great Northern Theater (Chicago), 134
Great Salt Lake, 580
Greco-Roman Revival style, 237
Greed (1924), 719
Green, J. Ed., 137
"Greenroom Jottings: Little Whispers from Everyone in Playerdom" (gossip column), 670
Gregg, Ron, 706–7
Grey, Olga, 670
Grierson, John, 526, 529, 536
Grieveson, Lee, 9, 10–11, 518
Griffith, D. W.
  and art direction, 237
  and the Beaux-Arts tradition, 225–26
  and chase comedy genre, 197–98, 200, 203n.41
  and Children's Bureau films, 365–66
  and commercial cinema, 721
  and creation of Hollywood myth, 406–8
  and cross-dressing comedies, 691–92
  and film distribution systems, 464–65, 466–67, 471, 473, 516
  and film history, 1
  and gender inversion in slapstick comedy, 698–99
  and Grauman's theaters, 444, 453
  and lighting design, 229, 230
  and middlebrow culture, 663, 664, 666
  and modernity thesis, 4, 626
  and post-silent-era silent film, 741
  and race issues in cinema, 132
  and same-sex relationships on film, 697–98
  and shot composition, 232–33, 234–35
Griffiths, Alison, 8–9, 292
Gris, Juan, 717
Groo, Katherine, 738–40, 750, 754
Die große Unbekannte (*The Mysterious Woman*, 1923), 647
Großfilm, 647
Grünberg, Rosa, 689–90, 690f
Grune, Karl, 647, 648
Guangzhou, 173
Guantanamo Bay, Cuba, 528–29
Guattari, Félix, 728

Guerín, José Luis, 748–49
Guillermin, John, 746
gunboat diplomacy, 530
Gunn, Oliva, 693
Gunning, Tom, 2, 3–4, 7, 10, 39–40, 119, 185–86, 202–3n.33, 505, 520n.16, 626
Guy-Blaché, Alice, 187, 363–64, 690
Gyldendal's (publishing company), 598–99
Gynt, Emma, 270–71, 272f

Haas, Willy, 62
Hadaka no shima (*The Naked Island*, 1960), 747–48
Haines, William, 706–7
Hale, Alan, 575–76
Hall, Arthur C. A., 382
Hall, Don, 746
Halliday, John E., 670
Hal Roach Studios, 699–700
Hamlet (1921), 697
Hamlet (*Tragedia cómica*), 717
Hammond, Paul, 728
Hampton, Benjamin B., 1, 484–85, 512
Hamsun, Knut, 598
The Hand That Rocks the Cradle (1917), 364, 389–91, 390f
Hanff, Joseph A., 489
Hanff-Metzger, Inc., 489–95, 496–98
Hansen, Miriam, 3, 4, 5–6, 517–18, 643–44, 647, 648, 651–52
Hanson, Lars, 693, 694f
Hanson, Robert, 140
Hans Roberts & Co. (vaudeville team), 146
Hanssen, Eirik Frisvold, 598
Harden-Eulenburg Affair, 688
Harding, Warren, 574–75
Harlem, 142
Harper's Bazaar, 229–30
Harris, Mildred, 446–47
Harrison, Louis Reeves, 383, 665
Hart, Lizzie, 140
Hart, William S., 444–45, 473–74, 670–71
Harvard College Observatory, 291
Harvey, David, 527–28
Harvey Do Vora Trio, 146
Harvey's Motion Picture Exposure Meter, 423–24

Hasinoff, Erin L., 346
Hassan, Charles F., 146
Hatami, Ali, 552–53
Hawaii, 565–66
Hayakawa, Sessue, 444
Hayashi, Hikaru, 747–48
Hays, Will, 414, 453, 513, 523n.45, 707
Hazanavicius, Michel, 738, 748, 752–53
The Hazards of Helen (1914-1917), 619, 621, 622–31, 632
Hearne, Joanna, 574
The Heart of the World (2000), 753
Hearts Are Trumps (1920), 235–36, 237
Hebdige, Dick, 549
hegemony. *See* cultural impact of cinema
Heidegger, Martin, 159–60, 163, 179n.3
Helena (1924), 650–51
H. E. Lesan (advertising firm), 481–82, 484–88, 487f, 489–90, 496–98
Help! Help! (1912), 197–98
Helping Negroes to Become Better Farmers and Homemakers (ca. 1921), 533–35
Help! Murder! Police! (1914), 741
Herbert, Stephen, 18
heroic tableaux, 587
Her Sister from Paris (1925), 243, 244f
"Hertzian Wave Wireless Telegraphy" (Fleming), 301–2n.23
Hexter, S. M., 467
Heyl, Henry, 19–20
Hide and Seek (1913), 197–98
Higashi, Sumiko, 11–12
Higgins, Scott, 618
high-speed cinematography, 306–7
High Toned (1929), 149, 152–53
highway system, 588–90
Hillel-Erlanger, Irene, 255, 266
Hipple, J. E., 376
Hiromeya (exhibitor), 116–17
Hirschfeld, Magnus, 689, 702–3
Hise, Gregory, 413
"His Honor: The Barber" (vaudeville sketch), 148
"His Master's Voice" slogan, 563
Histoire generale du cinema, L'Invention du cinema, 1837-1897 (Sadoul), 1, 18
Histoire(s) du cinéma (1988-1998), 112

historical frames, 74–77
historiography of film, 126–27. *See also* "Cinema across Media" rubric; comparative media approach; historical frames; integrated history of the media; intermediality; periodization
A History of the Movies (Hampton), 1
Hobart, Mark, 333
Hodge, Marguerite V., 121–22
Hodkinson, W. W., 465–66, 473–74, 481–82
Hoffmann, E. T. A., 62
Hogan, Ernest, 154n.18
Holden, Delos, 186–87
An Holland Smock to run for, by any Woman born in this County: the best Woman in three Heats (Collet), 190f
Holly Leaves, 399–400, 413, 414–15
Hollywood, California, 4, 9–10, 397–415, 420–34
 annexation of, 399
 dichotomous perception of, 413
 Golden Era of, 741–43, 750–51
 "Hollywood" name, 415
 Hollywood Regency style, 706–7
 "Hollywood" sign, 411
 and real-estate development, 440–56
 service corridor, 431–34, 432f
Hollywood Art Association, 414–15
Hollywood Boulevard Association, 448–49, 454
Hollywood Business Men's Club, 413
Hollywood Cavalcade (1939), 741–42, 743–44, 745, 752–53
Hollywood Hotel, 446
Hollywood magazine, 415
Hollywood Olympic Club, 451–52
Hollywood on Location (Gleich and Webb), 585–86
Hollywood-Pioneer Lumber Co., 431
Hollywood Saga, 454
Holm, Magda, 696
Holmes, E. Burton, 333, 426
Holmes, Helen, 621, 622–24, 673
homelessness, 749
Honest Crooks (1929), 149
Hong Kong, 160–62, 164–65, 166–67, 170–71, 173, 175, 176, 183n.59

INDEX

Hong Kong Daily Press, 176
The Honor of the Flag (1911), 664
Hoover, Herbert, 518
The Hope Diamond Mystery (1921), 630
Hopper, DeWolf, 471
Horace Bushnell Memorial Hall, 345–46
Horak, Jan-Christopher, 1
Horak, Laura, 11–12, 605
horizontal integration, 443
Horizonte (journal), 717
Horkheimer, H. M., 407–8
Horne, Jennifer, 8–9
Horner, William, 19
Horsley, William, 426, 427, 430, 433
Hotaling, Arthur D., 73–74
Hotel Holding Co., 450–51
Hotely, Mae, 668
Hough, Emerson, 579, 581
The House of Shadows (*Moranen*, 1924), 600–1
The House Without Children (1919), 383–87, 385f
Housman, Lawrence, 236–37
How a French Nobleman Got a Wife through the New York Herald "Personal" Columns (1904), 186–87, 191, 192, 193–95, 196–97, 198–99, 200
Howe, Lyman H., 333, 366–67
"How Shall I Tell My Child?" (column), 382
Hoyt, Eric, 474
Hoyt's Minstrels, 146–47
Huang, Dequan, 170
Hubert, Henri, 63
Hudson River School, 233–34, 586–87
Hugenberg, Alfred, 653
Hughes Bill, 417n.26
Hühn, Helmut, 619–20
Huhtamo, Erkki, 6, 39, 111
Hulette, Gladys, 672
Hull, Matthew S., 372n.15
Hull-House, 355, 356–57, 360–61
Hulsey, E. H., 467, 474–75, 476
"The Human Chain" (1915), 624, 625
Hunting, Tony, 146
Las Hurdes, tierra sin pan (1933), 714, 728–29
Huxley, Julian, 537
Huygens, Christian, 20–21
Huyssen, David, 674

hyaloscope, 47–50

Ibn Fadlan, Ahmad, 338
Ibsen, Henrik, 251–52, 253, 255, 257–58, 260, 262, 263–65, 597–98, 600, 602
Icelandic cinema, 598–99, 600–1, 602–3, 607–8, 609–10, 611
Ichikawa, Danjurō IX, 116, 117–18, 119f, 120, 120f, 122–23
Ichikawa Danjurō (Kamiyama), 118
Ich möchte kein Mann sein (*I Don't Want to Be a Man*, 1918), 692
Ihering, Herbert, 641–42, 643–44, 657n.2
ikiningyō (papier-mâché dolls), 121
Illinois Record, 136–37
Illustrated London News, 305, 306f, 307–9, 322–23, 327
imagined community (Anderson), 48–49
Immigration Act of 1924 (US), 578, 667
Imperial Economic Committee (UK), 536
imperialism, 344, 510, 519n.7, 526–40
Important Cultural Property (*jūyō bunkazai*), 116, 117
Impressionism
  and art direction, 235–36
  avant-garde cinema, 719, 720
  and the Beaux-Arts tradition, 225–27
  and lighting design, 229–32
  and Symbolist influences, 252, 256–62, 263, 265, 276n.22, 277n.41
  and Synthetist influences, 266, 274
incandescent lights, 439n.74, See also lighting sources and design
Ince, Ralph W., 672–73
Ince, Thomas H., 232–33, 397, 403, 406, 407–8, 444, 466–67, 473, 666
Inceville, 403
indexicality, 199, 343
indexical realism, 122, 346–47
Indianapolis Freeman, 131, 132, 133, 136, 137–38, 139, 148
Indian Citizenship Act (US), 578
Indigenous North Americans, 573–74, 587, 588
Industrial Revolution, 527
L'infaillible Baume (*The Infallible Balm*, 1912), 698

Infant Care (Chidren's Bureau pamphlet), 357–59
infant mortality, 354, 356–57, 358, 363, 366, 367–68
L'Inferno (1911), 233–34
influenza pandemic (1918), 511
Ingagi (1930), 333
Ingram, Rex, 225–26, 230–32, 235–36, 241, 243, 249n.67
Inhospitable Worlds (Fay), 343
L'Inhumaine (1923), 263, 265, 265f
innervation, 5
Inoue, Takejirō, 122, 124
"The 'Inside' of Moving Pictures" (*Popular Electricity* article), 294
Institute for Serotherapy, 325–26
Institute for Sexology, 702–3
institutional cinema, 10
integrated history of media, 43. See also comparative media approach; historiography of film; intermediality
intellectual property doctrine, 80. See also copyright issues
Interior with Worktable, aka The Suitor (Vuillard), 264f
intermediality, 7–8, 38–41. See also comparative media approach; historiography of film; integrated history of media
International Correspondence Schools, 675
International Federation of Film Archives (FIAF), 1, 2, 520–21n.17
International Harvester Company, 362, 534–35
International Photographer, 432f
internet, 106
intersex identity, 703. See also gender and sexual identities
intertitles, 321, 576, 738, 746, 750–51
Intimacy (Vuillard), 263, 264f
intraracial audience, 133
intrascene cutting, 206–7, 210. See also editing
Une invasion de Macrobes (Couvreur), 316–17
invention of cinema, 17–18, 103
L'Invitation au voyage (1927), 258–59, 260, 263–65, 270–71, 272f
Ioka Theater (Exeter, US), 496
Iran, 10, 546–66

Irene (1926), 699–700
Irie, Yoshirō, 116–17
The Iron Horse (1924), 584–85
Irwin, Will, 512–13
Ishimoto, Tōkichi, 706f
The Italian (1915), 232–33
Itier, Alphonse Eugène Jules, 165
Ivan Film Productions, 378–79
Ivens, Joris, 715

J'accuse (1919), 233
Jack and the Beanstalk (1902), 74–75
Jacknis, Ira, 343, 348
Jackson, Peter, 336–37
Jacobs, Ken, 187–89
Jacobs, Lea, 240–41
Jacobson, Matthew Frye, 578
Jacques-Dalcroze, Émile, 237–39
Jafar Khan Has Returned from the West (play), 549–50, 552–56, 561
James, William, 285–87
Jameson, Fredric, 4–5, 10–11
Japanese cinema, 116–27, 740, 747–48
Japanese terminology for film, 120–21
La Japonaise (Camille Monet in Japanese Costume) (Monet), 125–26
"Japonisme," 124–26, 127
Japonisme and the Birth of Cinema (Miyao), 124
Jasper, Gertrude, 278n.53
Jay, Martin, 729
Jazz Age, 242
The Jazz Singer (1927), 741
Jenkins, C. Francis, 33–34, 35, 284–85
Jesse L. Lasky Productions, 481–82
Jesuit missionaries, 20–21
Jewish moguls, 404
jidō genga (automatic phantom picture), 120–21
jidō gentō (automatic magic lantern), 120–21
jidō shashin (automatic photography), 120–21
Jin'gui teahouse (Shanghai), 173
Joan the Woman (1916), 670
Johnson, Arthur, 668–69
Johnson, Lewis M., 176, 177
Johnson, Martin, 333
Johnson, Noble, 152

Johnson, Osa, 333
Johnson, Billy, 133
Johnston, William A., 482–83
John the Baptist, 62–63
Jones, Juli (William Foster's pen name), 131, 138. *See also* Foster, William (journalist and film producer)
Jones, Sissieretta, 134
Jordan, David Starr, 301n.10
Joseph in the Land of Egypt (1914), 205–7, 214–15
Josephson, Matthew, 240–41
Jourdain, Francis, 263
Jourdain, Frantz, 262–63
Le Journal, 322
The Journey to the West (Wu), 173–74
Joy, Leatrice, 704–5
Joyce, Alice, 668–69, 670–71
Les Joyeux Microbes (1909), 559, 561–62
J. P. Morgan & Co., 511–12, 514, 531, 534–35
Judith of Bethulia (1913), 697–98
Juha (1999), 750–51

Kabuki, 116, 117, 118, 119–20, 122–24, 125, 126, 127. *See also Maple Viewing (Momijigari*, 1899)
Kabukiza Theater, 117–18, 122, 124
Kael, Pauline, 643–44
Kaempffert, Waldemar, 293
Kafka, Franz, 56, 61, 65
Kahn, Otto, 514, 517
Kaiser Wilhelm's Yacht Meteor Entering the Water (1902), 193
Kalatozov, Mikhail, 341–42
Kalmus, Herbert, 420–21, 432, 433
Kamiyama, Akira, 118, 123–24
Kaplan, Amy, 510
Kapoor, Raj, 564–66
Kärlek och journalistisk (*Love and Journalism*, 1916), 700
Käsebier, Gertrud, 232–33
katsudō genga (moving phantom picture), 120–21
katsudō shashin (moving photography), 120–21
Katz, Jonathan Ned, 691, 695
Kaurismäki, Aki, 750–51

Kawaura, Kenichi, 124
Kazakh people, 339
Kazuichi, Araki, 120–21
Keating, Patrick, 227–28, 229–30, 233–34, 241, 246n.22, 427–28
Keaton, Buster, 186, 343, 647, 651, 717–18, 721, 723, 745, 746
Keil, Charlie, 9–10, 204, 205, 222, 521n.19, 670–71
Kellerman, Annette, 670–71
Kelley, Emmett, 134–35
Kelley, Florence, 365
Kelly, Gene, 742–43
Kelly, Kitty, 376–77
Kemble, William H., 467, 468, 469–70, 476
Kennedy, J. J., 471–72
Kent, S. R., 580–81
Kepler, Johannes, 19
Kerrigan, J. Warren, 575–76, 668–69
Kessel and Baumann, 471–72
Kessler, Frank, 111
Kettaneh, F. A., 562–63
Keyssner, Hugo, 56–58, 65
Keystone Film Company, 197–99, 295–97, 464–65, 466–67, 469–70, 473, 701, 741–42. *See also* Bathing Beauties (Keystone)
Khachikian, Samuel, 568n.42
KHJ (radio station), 448
The Kid (1921), 368–69, 749
Kimdotcom: Caught in the Web (2017), 87
kimonos, 125–26
"kine-attractography," 10
Kinemacolor, 291–92
kinematograph and kinematography, 99–100, 104, 105, 106–8, 107f, 110–12, 184, 288
Kinetograph, 29–30, 32–33, 34, 78–79, 99–100
Kinetophone, 47–48
Kinetoscope, 29–35, 46–47, 78–79, 99–100, 103, 120–21, 287, 563–64
King, Anita, 670
King, Rob, 8, 295–97, 470–71, 741–42
King's College, 305, 307–8, 324, 326–27
Kingsley, Grace, 446–47
Kinkikan Theater, 123, 126
Kinodrome, 156n.82
Kino Eye (1924), 558
Kirby, Lynn, 625

Kircher, Athanasius, 20–21
Kirmani, Bahram, 555, 564–65
Kirschenbaum, Matthew, 43–44
The Kiss (1929), 740
A Kiss from Mary Pickford (1927), 557–58
kitsch, 645–46, 652–53
Kittler, Friedrich, 6, 43, 45–46, 62–63, 624–25
Kleine, George, 313–14
Kleines Theater, 236–37
Klepper, Robert, 738–40
"Klieg" lights, 228, 442, 449. *See also* lighting sources and design
Klitzsch, Ludwig, 653
Klöckner, Albert, 63–64, 65
Knapp, Bettina L., 256
Knox, Elwood, 137
KNX (radio station), 449
Kodak. *See* Eastman Kodak
Kohler, Josef, 57
Konishi Honten Company, 116–17
Kornhaber, Donna, 12
Kosmos Labs, 428
Koster and Bial's Music Hall (New York), 34
Kracauer, Siegfried, 4–5, 11, 162–63, 343, 621, 641–57, 642f
　critique of paradigmatic films, 647–49
　and film's transition to sound, 655–57
　and media theory of film, 649–52
　and origins of film criticism, 641–44
　politics of film criticism, 652–55
　and standardization of film audience, 645–46
　and Weimar cinema, 644–45
Kramer, Holton, 263–65
Krasner, David, 134–35
"Kritik ist schöpferische Kunst" (*Film-Kurier* series), 641
Kuhn, Annette, 691
Kuhn, Loeb & Co., 511–12, 514
Kuleshov, Lev, 558–59, 560–61
kulturfilm, 341–42
Kunsky, John H., 488, 492–94
Kunst-or Autorenfilm, 56
Kyōkanonko musume ninin Dōjōji (*Dōjōji: A Lover's Duet*, 1899), 122
Kyoto dentō hatsudensho no kaji (*The Fire at Kyoto Electric Company*, 1908), 123

Kyrgyz people, 339
Kyrou, Ado, 729

LaBadie Florence, 670–71
labor issues in cinema, 399–400, 536, 537–38
Lacan, Jacques, 57
La Croix, Paul, 146
Ladd-Taylor, Molly, 356
Ladies' Home Journal, 382–83, 486, 663–64
Lady Windermere's Fan (1925), 721
Laemmle, Carl, 403–4, 425, 485–86, 669
Lafayette Players, 142–43
Lafayette Theater (New York), 142, 153
La Fontaine, Henri, 106
Lagerlöf, Selma, 598
Lahue, Kalton, 467, 471–72, 473–74
Landecker, Hannah, 291–92
land management, 413
landscape painting, 585–87
landscapes, 572–73
　empty space trope of, 586–90
　Italianate landscapes, 233–34
　and landscape painting, 585–87
　and magisterial gaze, 586
Lane, Charles, 749
Lang, Fritz, 644–45, 647, 717–18, 719
Langdon, Harry, 717–18, 722
Lange, André, 49–50
"lantern of fear," 21. *See also* magic lanterns
lantern plays, 170, 173. *See also* magic lanterns
lantern slides, 28, 175, 345f
Laokoon (1766), 649–50
Larson, Stephen Larry, 596, 599
LaSalle Theater (Chicago), 387–88
Lasky, Blanche, 443
Lasky, Jesse L., 401–4, 406, 407, 409, 443, 444, 447–48, 451–52, 574–75, 579–81, 583, 585f. *See also* Famous Players-Lasky (FPL)
Lasky lighting, 229. *See also* lighting sources and design
Lasky Productions, 401–3, 425
The Last Laugh (1924). *See Der letzte Mann* (1924)
last-minute-rescue plot, 197–98, 618, 619, 621–23, 626, 627, 628–29. *See also* narrative structure of films
The Last of the Mohicans (1920), 233–34

The Last Silent Picture Show (Drew), 740–41
Latham, Ella, 362, 368, 372–73n.30
Latham family, 33–34
Lathrop, Julia C., 354–57, 358–63, 365–66, 373–74nn.44–45, 374n.47
Latin American modernity, 505–6, 508
Latour, Bruno, 9–10
Laughing Gas (1914), 647
Laurel, Stan, 698, 699–700
Laurel and Hardy, 699
Law, Kar, 170–71, 176, 183n.59
Law for the Protection of Cultural Properties (Japan), 116
Lawrence, Florence, 485–86, 670
Lawrie, Lee, 227, 235–36, 237
Lay (Vuillard), 263
League for the Protection of Mothers and Sex Reform, 702
Lears, T. J. Jackson, 675–76
Leavitt, Michael, 134
Leblanc, Georgette, 252, 255, 265, 265f
Le Bon, Gustave, 11
Leezer, John, 428
Le Forestier, Laurent, 109, 313–14
The Legacy of Conquest (Limerick), 574
Legband, Paul, 703
Lehrman, Henry, 197–98
Leitz (German manufacturing firm), 312
lenses, 21, 28
Le Prince, Louis, 28, 31, 33
Lessig, Lawrence, 76–77, 81, 82, 86–87
Lessing, Ephraim, 649–50
Der letzte Mann (1924), 717–18
Levaditi, Constantin, 305, 307f, 308–9, 310, 318, 319–24, 325–27
Levinson, Barry, 746
Lévy-Bruhl, Lucien, 59–60
Lewis, Cary B., 137
L'Herbier, Marcel, 231–32, 239–40, 252, 253, 259, 263, 266, 718
Liberty (1929), 699
Liberty Bonds Campaigns, 511
Liberty Theater (Illinois), 495–96
Der Liebeskäfig (*The Love Cage*, 1925), 654
Liedtke, Harry, 644–45
Life of an American Fireman (1903), 2
The Life of Charlie (compilation film), 557

The Life of Moses (1909), 662–63
lighthouses, 45–46
lighting sources and design, 20–21, 173–74, 209–10, 228–32, 245–46n.15, 423, 424. *See also* electric lights; gaslight; incandescent lights; "Klieg" lights; Lasky lighting; limelight; Mole-Richardson Lighting Co.; Rembrandt lighting
Limbrick, Peter, 574
limelight, 20–21. *See also* lighting sources and design
Limerick, Patricia Nelson, 574
"Limits of Experimentation in Hollywood" (Thompson), 227–28
Lincoln Motion Picture Company, 132, 152
Lindau, Paul, 55
linguistic barriers, 511
Lippmann, Walter, 516–17
lithography, 165
The Little American (1917), 511
"The Little Shopgirls Go to the Movies" (Kracauer), 645
L-KO Kompany, 701–2
Lloyd, Harold, 647, 691, 698, 717–18
Lobato, Roman, 82–84
location shooting, 239, 257, 573–90
    and Swedish cinema, 596–97, 599–601, 602–4
    and wagon-trail trope, 569–73
Das lockende Ziel (*The Beckoning Destination*, 1930), 653
Lockwood, Harold, 670–71
Loew, Marcus, 485
logos, 486
Lohmann, Paul, 746
Loiperdinger, Martin, 18
Les lois de l'imitation (Tarde), 11
Londe, Albert, 25
London, Jack, 443, 481–82
The Lonedale Operator (1911), 626
lone-wolf expeditions, 349n.4
The Long vs. The Short Haul: Mother's Milk Best for Baby (1915), 362–63
Loos, Anita, 241–42
López, Ana M., 505–7, 508, 511, 518
Lorca, Federico García, 716, 719
The Lor Girl (*Dokhtar-e Lor:* 1933), 568n.42

Lorna Doone (1922), 240–41
Lorrain, Claude, 233–34, 235–36
Los Angeles Aqueduct, 410
Los Angeles, California, 397–98, 399, 409–13. See also Hollywood, California
Los Angeles Herald, 407–9, 408f
Los Angeles Realtor, 412
Los Angeles Times, 241, 377–78, 378f, 407, 409–10, 412–13, 440, 444–45, 447–48, 453–54
The Lost Child (1904), 185–86, 196–200
Louis Theater (Paris), 167–70
The Love Light (1921), 247n.44
"A Love Lozenger" (1913), 146
Love's Crucible (*Vem dömer*, 1922), 596–97
lowbrow entertainment, 645–46
Lu, Sheldon, 341
Lubin, Siegmund, 72–73, 80, 82, 83f, 85–86, 87, 192
Lubin Company, 72–73, 75, 76, 78–79, 80, 81–82, 83f, 85–86, 87, 698
Lubinville, 424
Lubitsch, Ernst, 186, 239–40, 243, 248n.64, 249n.72, 692, 721
Lugné-Poë, Aurélien, 251–52, 254–55, 256, 257–62, 261f, 263–65, 269, 270–71, 274
Lumholtz, Carl, 349n.4
Lumière brothers, 18, 24, 28–29, 34, 103, 160–61, 563. See also Cinématographe
Lumière Company, 32, 33–34, 72, 124, 160–61, 162–63
luminous projections, 100–2
Luna Park, 561–62
Lusk, Norbert, 240–41
Lyceum Theater (Shanghai), 167, 176–77
Lyles, Aubrey, 137
Lynch, Stephen A., 473–74

Mabuchi, Akiko, 125–26
MacCann, Richard Dyer, 359–60
MacDonald, Margaret I., 388–89
Macfadden, Bernarr, 673, 675–76
Mack, Max, 55, 656–57
Mackintosh-Smith, Tim, 338
Maddin, Guy, 753–54
Madison, Cleo, 670
Madison Avenue advertising forms, 483

Maeterlinck, Maurice, 236–39, 251–52, 255, 256, 257–58, 260, 265, 270–72
Maggie's First False Step (1917), 701
magic lanterns, 666
  and celluloid film, 27, 28
  Cinématographe, 34
  and "cultural series" concept, 101f, 106–8, 111–12
  and development of motion picture, 24
  and early moving images, 31–32
  and film in China, 160–61, 162–64, 165, 167, 171–75, 176, 177–78
  and lantern plays, 170, 173
  and lantern slides, 28, 175, 345f
  and ontology of cinema, 174–75
  and projection technology, 19–22
  and recording of time, 29
Magnusson, Charles, 597
Mai, Sylvia, 268f
Majestic (production company), 364, 464–65, 466–67, 468, 471, 478n.29
Majestic Building (Chicago), 145f
Majestic Theater (Montana), 495–96
Majestic Theatre (Chicago), 131, 144–46, 147, 148, 153, 156n.82
Majestic Theatre (Los Angeles), 377–78
Making Movies into Art: Picture Craft from the Magic Lantern to Early Hollywood (2014), 227–28
Making Settler Cinemas (Limbrick), 574
Makropoulos, Matthias, 629
Malinowski, Bronislaw, 340–41
Mallarmé, Stéphane, 237–39, 256, 258–60
Mallet-Stevens, Robert, 263, 265
Mallinckrodt (chemical works), 425–26
Malraux, André, 557
Maltby, Richard, 485
Manabu, Ueda, 118
Manet, Édouard, 225–26
Maniac Chase (1904), 198–99
Manifest Destiny, 569–71, 574–75, 577, 587, 588
Mannoni, Laurent, 18, 20–21, 23–24, 25
Manovich, Lev, 162–63
Man Ray, 263, 715, 716, 718
Mantle, Robert Burns, 241
The Man Who Learned (1910), 362–63
Man with a Movie Camera (1929), 561–62

Maple Viewing (*Momijigari*, 1899), 116–27, 119*f*
Marceau, Marcel, 746
Marcus, Sharon, 685, 686–87
Marey, Étienne-Jules, 19, 22–25, 28, 30, 32
Marinescu, Gheorghe, 25
Marion, Frank, 186–87, 191, 200
Marion, Philippe, 7, 49–50, 109, 184–85, 751
marketing, 463–64. *See also* advertising
The Mark of Zorro (1920), 239–40
Marozzi, Jason, 344
The Marriage Circle (1924), 243
Marsh, Maude, 449
Martí Pérez, José Julián, 528–29
Mary (Nabokov), 65–66
Marzola, Luci, 9–10, 413
Masken (journal), 604
Massa, Steve, 700
mass audience for cinema, 5–6, 11, 518, 643–44, 645–46, 648, 649–50
The Mass Ornament (Kracauer), 645
"The Mass Problem in Art: On the Essence and Value of Reproduction (Film and Radio)" (Klöckner), 63–64
"The Mass Production of the Senses" (Hansen), 4
Mastbaum, Stanley, 488
The Master Builder (Ibsen), 260, 262, 263
Mathews, Albert P., 289–90
Le Matin, 322
Matisse, Henri, 262–63
Matsumoto, Kōshirō VII, 118
Matuszewski, Bolesław, 49
Mauclair, Camille, 259–60
Mauclaire, Jean, 724
Mauprat (1926), 719–20
Mauss, Marcel, 63, 484
Maxwell, William H., 146
May, Bruno, 60
May, Lary, 9–10, 441–42
Mayer, Louis B., 450–52
Mayer, Ruth, 10–11
Mayne, Judith, 202–3n.33
McCoy, T. J., 585*f*
McCutcheon, Wallace, 185–87, 191, 193, 200
McGowan, John, 626
McKenna, Denise, 9–10, 442
McKernan, Luke, 18

McLuhan, Marshall, 39
McMahan, Alison, 690
McQuade, James S., 130–31, 143–44
Mécanisme de la phagocytose des trypanosomes, phénomene de l'accolement (1910), 321–22
Mechanical Research Laboratories, 432*f*
media archaeology, 50
  and chase comedy genre, 184–86, 194, 195–96, 199–200
  and copying technologies, 77, 80
  and "cultural series" concept, 105, 110–11, 112
  described, 6–7, 39–41
  and intermediality, 7
  and ontology of cinema, 159, 160, 163, 178, 179
  and parallel histories of film and television, 42–44
  and recording and transmission technology, 44–46
media theory, 643–44, 649–52
"medium sensitivity" (Tsivian), 316–17
medium specificity, 579–80
Meek, Otto, 580
Meek's Cutoff (2011), 571–72
Meet Me at the Fountain (1904), 186, 698
Meftahi, Ida, 560–61
Megaupload Ltd., 75, 82–87, 85*f*, 86*f*
Meighan, Thomas, 444
Meissner, Emma, 690*f*
Meiyū Onoe Kikugorō no sōshiki (*Great Actor Onoe Kikugorō's Funeral*, 1903), 122
Méliès, Gaston, 73–74
Méliès, Georges, 95–96, 97, 184–85, 710n.25
Méliès Company, 72, 103, 111, 162–63, 560–61, 664
Melnick, Ross, 9–10
melodrama, 197, 365–66, 587, 596
  and advocacy for sexual and gender minorities, 702
  settler melodrama, 573–78
  and silent serial films, 618, 621–22, 628–29, 630, 632–33
Melodrama and Modernity (Singer), 3
Menjou, Adolphe, 721, 723
Menzies, William Cameron, 239–40, 243
Merchants and Manufacturing Association (Los Angeles), 409

Merritt, Russell, 478–79n.44
The Merry Widow (1925), 721
Merton of the Movies (1947), 742–43, 752
Mesnil, Félix, 319–20
Messages d'Orient, 555
Metchnikoff, Élie, 314, 324–27, 325f
Metro-Goldwyn-Mayer (MGM), 430, 432–33, 706–7
Metropolis (1927), 239, 647, 719, 722
Metropolitan Opera, 106
Metro Week, 495
Metz, Christian, 2, 5
Metzger, George P. (Hanff-Metzger), 489
Meyer, Mendel (Meyer & Holler), 450–51
Meyer & Holler (architects), 450
Meyers, J. L., 495–96
Micheaux, Oscar, 132, 133
Mickey (1918), 700
microcinematography, 305–7, 310–12, 313f, 314–16, 322–23
microphones, 740–41
microscopes, 559–60, 559f
middlebrow culture
  and advertising industry, 674–76
  comparison of early fan magazines, 676–79
  and cultural stewardship, 662–70
  and promotion of consumerism, 670–73
migration, 411–12, 418n.45, 573
Mikaël (Bang), 693
Milestone, Lewis, 655
military recruitment films, 298
Miller, Arthur, 245n.14
Miller, Flournoy, 137
Miller, Henri, 271
Miller, Peter N., 335–36
Milles, Carl, 693
A Million and One Nights (1926), 1
"Million Dollar" Theater (Los Angeles), 444–46, 445f, 447, 448
Milne, Peter, 389–90
mimesis, 5
Mimosa, 563
Minguet Joan, 723
Ministry of Education, Culture, Sports, Science, and Technology (Japan), 116, 117
Ministry of Foreign Affairs (Norway), 605
Minneapolis Tribune, 497f

Minnelli, Liza, 745–46
minstrelsy, 134–35, 146–47, 148, 154n.18
Minter, Mary Miles, 444, 670
The Miracle of Life (1915), 376–77, 383
Mirrors of Hollywood (Fox), 397–98, 398f, 399–401, 402f, 412, 413
mirror-stage theory, 57
Mirtel, Héra, 258
mise-en-scène, 252, 257, 263, 363–64, 585–86, 740–41. *See also* staging
misemono (sideshow entertainments), 121, 123, 127
missionaries, 20–21
Mitchell, Abbie, 144–45, 146
Mitchell Camera, 431
Mitman, Gregg, 345–46
Mix, Tom, 723
model theaters (Triangle Film Corp.), 467
Modern Industry and the African (Davis), 537–38
modernity and modernism
  alternative modernities, 505–6
  "ambimodern" framework, 519–20n.8
  "cultural" and "acultural" formulations of, 505–7
  cultural modernity, 505–7, 509
  and dandyism in Iranian cinema, 546–48, 549–50, 551–53, 555–56, 560–62, 562f, 563–64
  and film distribution systems, 517–19
  and geopolitics, 510–14
  and Kracauer's film criticism, 643–44, 645–46, 647, 648–50, 652, 654–55, 656–57
  modernist camerawork, 562f
  modernity thesis, 2–5, 10–11
  and perceptions of Paris, 241–42
  and periodization, 508–9
  and popular science films, 283–84, 287, 290
  and public opinion, 514–17
  and temporality in silent serial films, 619–22, 629–30
  vernacular modernism, 4, 517–18
Modern Mechanics, 294, 295–97, 299
Modern Times (1936), 740, 744–45, 749
Moghaddam, Hasan, 552–53, 554–56, 564–65
Mokuami, Kawatake, 117
Mole, Peter, 433

Mole-Richardson Lighting Co., 431, 433, 439n.74
The Mollycoddle (1920), 699–700
Molteni (magic lantern manufacturer), 101f
Moltke, Helmuth von, 48–49
Monet, Claude, 125–26
Mongolia, 336–37, 343, 344, 345–46, 347, 349n.5
monopoly rights, 81
Monsen, Frederick, 333
Monsieur Beaucaire (1924), 414–15
montage, 61, 557–58, 559–60, 561–62, 628, 654, 710n.25, *See also* editing
Montana, Bull, 237
Moon, Krystyn, 134–35
Moonshiners (1904), 200
Morad, Habibolla, 556–57, 558
"The Moral Equivalent of War" (James), 285–87
Morden, William J., 334–35, 345f, 351n.31, *See also* Morden-Clark Central Asiatic expedition
Morden African Expedition, 334–35
Morden-Clark Central Asiatic expedition
  background of scientific expeditions, 332–33
  film footage as visual small talk, 340–43, 342f
  funding and logistics, 334–37, 336f, 349n.14, 350n.15
  gallery and museum exhibits, 344–46, 345f
  hunt for *ovis poli*, 337–40, 340f, 345, 351nn.41–42
  legacy of, 346–48
Moreno, Antonio, 239–40
Morgan, J. P., 334
Morse, Samuel, 45
Mort du Soleil (1921), 260
Moscow Film Academy, 557–58
Moses, Isaac S., 381
Mosheim, Grete, 697f
Mother (1926), 647
"The Motion Picture" (Kahn), 515–16
Motion Picture Classic, 240–41, 665–66
Motion Picture Conservation Association, 405, 406, 407, 417n.24
Motion Picture Directors Association (MPDA), 405–6, 409

Motion Picture Magazine (*MPM*), 295, 383, 662–64, 665–66, 667–68, 669–72, 674–75, 676–79
Motion Picture News, 235, 237, 444–45, 482–83, 488
Motion Picture Patents Company (MPPC), 663, 664, 669, 676–77
Motion Picture Producers and Distributors of America (MPPDA), 485, 512–13, 523n.45, 701–2
Motion Picture Producers Association (MPPA), 405, 406–9, 417n.24
Motion Picture Protective Organization, 405, 406, 417n.24
Motion Picture Story Magazine (*MPSM*), 662–66, 667–69, 670–72, 674–79
Motion Picture Supplement, 665–66
Motography, 381, 383
Motts, Robert T., 137
The Mountain of Flames (lantern play), 173–74
Movie Memories (series), 742
movie moguls, 404–5
Moving Picture World (*MPW*), 130, 131, 143–44, 235–36, 245n.3, 295, 381, 425, 472, 474–75, 580–81, 664–65, 667–68
Mr. Haji, the Movie Actor (1934), 549–50, 552–53, 555–65, 559f, 566, 568n.42
Der müde Tod (1921), 717–18
Muir, John, 579–80
Mundaneum, 106, 114n.24
El mundo por diez céntimos (*Caprichos*, 1927), 719
Münsterberg, Hugo, 63
mural decoration, 237–39
Murnau, F. W., 644–45, 717–18
Murray, Mae, 444
Murzat Pass, 337
Musée Grévin, 25–26, 29
The Muses of Inspiration (Puvis de Chavannes), 237–39
museum-sponsored expeditions
  background of, 332–33
  funding and logistics, 334–37, 336f, 349n.14, 350n.15
  gallery and museum exhibits, 344–46
  hunt for *ovis poli*, 337–40, 340f, 345, 351nn.41–42
  legacy of, 346–48

Music (Vuillard), 263, 264f
"Musings of 'The Photoplay Philosopher'" (column), 666
"La Musique du Silence" (Dulac), 257–58, 271–72
Musser, Charles, 2, 18, 33–34, 39–40, 185–86, 528, 529
Mutermilch, Stefan, 320–21, 323
Mutoscope, 31–32
Mutual Film Corporation, 460, 464–65, 466–67, 470–71, 485–86, 622
Mutual Film Corporation v. Industrial Commission of Ohio, 8–9, 406
Muybridge, Eadweard, 18, 22–24, 26–27, 29, 30, 33, 41–42, 288, 290–91
Myers, Amos, 235
Mythologies (Barthes), 371–72n.14
My Winnipeg (2007), 753–54

Nabi painters, 259, 262, 263, 273–74
Nabokov, Vladimir, 65–66
Naficy, Hamid, 553, 554
Nagauta Ikioijishi (*Long Song: Vigorous Lion*, ca. 1899), 116–17
Nakamura, Ganjirō I, 122, 126
Nakamura, Utaemon IV, 117
Nakaza Theater (Osaka), 122
Nalpas, Mario, 720
Nanny Goats (performance group), 139–40
Nanook of the North (1922), 333, 339, 343
Naoyuki, Kinoshita, 121
Napierkowska, Stasia, 271, 704
Napoléon (1927), 719, 721, 722
narrative structure of films, 26–27, 208, 217
    character-centered narratives, 217
    chase narratives, 186–96, 203n.41, 560
    cinema of narrative integration, 10
    cliffhanger structure, 618–19, 620, 621, 622, 623–24, 627, 628–30, 631–33, 633n.4
    double plotline structure, 577
    last-minute-rescue plot, 197–98, 618, 619, 621–23, 626, 627, 628–29
    narrational conventions, 204
    narrativization of space, 205–6
Nashville (1975), 746
USS *Nashville*, 530

National Association of the Motion Picture Industry (US), 512–13
National Board of Censorship for Better Films (US), 362–63
National Board of Review of Motion Pictures (US), 701–2
National Child Labor Committee (US), 354–55, 362
National Congress of Mothers (US), 354–55
National Council of Defense (US), 363
national dance (*raqs-e melli*), 560–61
National Film Archive (Japan), 116–17, 118
National Film Registry (US), 572
National Geographic Society (US), 332
nationalism, 191–92, 511, 595, 599
National Theater (San Francisco), 443–44
Native Americans, 569–71, 575, 577, 578, 587
Natural History (magazine), 333, 338
"Naturalism on the Stage" (Zola), 255
The Natural Law (1917), 381
nature and Naturalism
    and authenticity on location shooting, 599, 600–1
    and ethnographic content in Swedish cinema, 611–12
    and influence of Swedish cinema, 594–96, 602–6, 607–9, 611–13
    and Symbolist influences, 251–52, 254–57, 258, 260, 263–65
    and Synthetist influences, 271, 274
Naulty, J. R., 467
Navy (US), 529
Naylor, Hazel Simpson, 383
Naylor, T. W., 19–20
Nazimova, Alla, 241–42, 697–98, 705–7
Negri, Pola, 239–40
Negro Players, 142–43
Neoclassicism, 225–26
Netflix, 86
New Film History, 1–2, 5, 6, 10
New French Extremism, 274
New Hollywood period, 746–47
Newman, Paul, 745–46
New Pekin Theater (Chicago), 137
New Republic, 375, 516
new sensorium, 517–18
new silent cinema, 738–40, 750–54

"A New Source of History" (Matuszewski), 49
newspaper journalism, 483, 484–85. *See also* advertising
newsreels, 511, 620–21
New Stagecraft, 227, 236–37
New Testament, 62–63
New Womanhood, 365, 366, 625, 668–69, 673
The New World (1917), 364
New York Age, 141*f*, 142, 143
New York Amsterdam News, 149
New York Athletic Club, 187
New York City Department of Education, 350n.15
New York Clipper, 147, 193
New York Dramatic Mirror, 381
New Yorker, 241–42
New York Globe, 588
New York Motion Picture Company, 466–67
New York Sun, 135*f*
New York Telegram, 495
New York Times, 230, 240–41, 344, 446, 581–82, 724, 743
New York World, 186–87
Die Nibelungen (1924), 717–18
Niblo, Fred, 239–40, 447–48, 451–52, 453, 721
Nibur, Benjamin, 142, 143
Nichols, George, 197–98
nickelodeons, 287–88, 313–14, 443
Nickolaus, John M., 430, 433
Nicodemi, Dario, 257, 277n.37
Nielsen, Asta, 692, 697
Niépce, Nicéphore, 22
Nietzsche, Friedrich, 255
Nilsson, Anna, 670–71
Nipkow, Paul, 41–42
Noa, Manfred, 650–51
Noah's Ark (1928), 695
Nobel Prizes, 324, 325–27
Nochlin, Linda, 585–86
"Nocturnes" (Whistler), 229–30
non-continuity editing, 119–20. *See also* editing
non-fiction films, 518. *See also* documentary film
non-theatrical film, 8
Norden, Martin F., 375–76, 388–89
Nordic identity, 599

Nordicness, 603–4
Nordisk Film Compagni, 595–96, 598–99
Normand, Mabel, 670, 698, 700
Norrtullsligan (1929), 695
North-China Herald, 176
Northern Rhodesia, 537–39
Norwegian cinema, 595, 596, 597–98, 600–1, 602, 603–4, 605–8, 609–10, 611
Notcutt, Leslie Alan, 537
"Notes on the Development of Telephone Service" (De Land), 301–2n.23
Notre Dame (Coburn), 234–35
Novak, Kim, 752–53
Novarro, Ramon, 239, 706–7
Les nuits électriques (1928), 718

Obey, André, 252
The Obstacle Course (1906), 187
OCFH (One Click File Host), 79
O'Connor, Donald, 743
October Revolution, 2–3
Officer 444 (1926), 630
Oganezov, Konstantin, 341–42
Ohanian, Ovanes, 10, 549, 551, 556–58, 559–61, 559*f*, 562–63, 564–65
Ohlson, Lotten, 696*f*
Okajima, Hisashi, 116–17
Okanesarashi (*Exposing Clothes to the Sun*, ca. 1899), 116–17
The Old and the New (1929), 534
Old Testament, 62–63
O'Leary, Liam, 235
Olympic Games, 191–92
Omega watches, 562–64
O. M. McAdoo's Minstrels, 154n.18
Onoe, Kikugorō V, 116, 117–18, 120*f*, 122–23
On the Origin of Species (Darwin), 255
ontology, 159–60, 161, 162–63, 178, 179n.3
open-booking model, 475–76
Open Door diplomatic policy (US), 526–27
open-market commodities, 551
Opium War, 164–65, 182n.55
optics, 20–21, 34
Oregon Trail, 569–71, 575–76, 581–82, 584–85, 586–87
The Oregon Trail (Bierstadt), 586–87

Orientalism, 116–17, 125, 126, 239, 454, 663, 701–2
Orpheum Theater, 469
Osaka Asahi Shinbun, 122
Osaka dai 5 kai hakurankai no jikkyō (*Report of the Fifth Domestic Industrial Exposition*, 1903), 122
Osborn, Henry Fairfield, 334, 345, 349n.5
Ostriche, Muriel, 668–69
Oswald, Richard, 702
Oswalda, Ossi, 692
L'Otage (Claudel), 257–58
The Other (1913), 55–56, 57, 61
Otherness, 575
Otlet, Paul, 106
Our Children (1919), 361–62, 366, 367–68, 367f
The Outlaw and His Wife (*Berg-Ejvind och hans hustru*, 1918), 598–600, 601, 602
ovis poli sheep, 337–40, 340f, 345, 351nn.41–42

Pabst, G. W., 644–45
Pacific Film Labs, 427
pacifism, 666
Painlevé, Jean, 723
painted scenery plays (*huajingxi*), 170
painting (*hua, hui*), 164–65
pamphlets, 354, 356–59, 361–62, 363, 366–67, 368–70
Panama Canal, 526, 528–29, 530, 531
Panama-Pacific International Exposition, 359–60, 530–31, 536, 539
Panama Papers, 542n.26
Pandora's Box (*Der Büchse der Pandora*, 1929), 696
Paoli, Raoul, 269
paper technology, 372n.15
parallel editing, 626. *See also* editing
Paramount-Artcraft films, 445–46, 492–94
Paramount Pep, 580–81, 584–85, 587–88, 589f
Paramount Pictures, 239–40, 430, 460–61, 465–67, 470–71, 473–74, 512–13, 569–71, 669
  baby-themed films, 365
  and background of national advertising, 481–84
  Hanff-Metzger's advertising campaign, 489–94, 491f, 493f
  H. E. Lesan's advertising campaign, 484–88, 487f

Paramount Progress, 486
Paramount-Publix theaters, 482–83
Paramount Week (advertising campaign), 494–98, 497f
Parikka, Jussi, 6
Paris Exposition Universelle, 123–24, 126
Paris qui dort (1923), 274
Park Theatre (New York), 378–79, 389
Parnaland, Ambroise-François, 329n.23
Parsons, Louella, 443, 675
The Parson's Widow (*Prästänkan*, 1920), 600–1, 603
La Passion de Jeanne d'Arc (1928). *See The Passion of Joan of Arc* (1928)
The Passion of Joan of Arc (1928), 719, 753
Pasteur Institute, 305, 319–21, 324, 325–26
pastiche, 607, 739–40, 745–46, 753–54
Pastime Theater (Chicago), 144, 153
patents, 18, 19, 30, 299, 656–57
paternalism, 405–6
Pathé Frères, 72, 123, 149–53, 150f, 158n.116, 197–98, 305, 310–12, 311f, 313–14, 321, 485–86, 563–64, 665
Pathé Weekly, 144
Patrick, George Thomas White, 288
patriotism, 489, 511
Paul, William, 482–83
peep-hole machines, 31–32, 47–48, 111
peer-to-peer sharing, 80–81
Pekin Stock Company, 140–41, 142–43, 148
Pelléas et Mélisande (Debussy), 255
Péret, Benjamin, 722
Perfect 10 v. Megaupload, 84
The Perils of Pauline (1914), 619, 624–25, 627
periodization, 505, 507, 508–9, 517, 566. *See also* historiography of film
Pernick, Martin S., 364
Perret, Léonce, 232–33
Perry, Montanye, 663–64, 667–68
Pershing's Crusaders (1918), 512–13
Persian-language sound films, 564–65
Personal (1904), 185–86
personality rights (*Persönlichkeitsrecht*), 56–57
Peters, John Durham, 44–45, 78
Peterson, Jennifer, 10–11, 292
Petro, Patrice, 2–3
phagocytosis, 305, 314–16, 319–27

Phantasmagoria ghost shows, 21
Phantoscope, 34, 35, 284–85
Phenakistiscope, 19–20, 21, 22, 24–25, 26, 27, 28, 29, 162–63, 287
phenomenology, 159, 179n.3
phonograph, 28–30, 33, 45–46, 47–48
Phonoscope, 24–25
The Phonoscope, 83f
photography and photographic techniques, 19–20, 42, 58–61, 117–18, 119–22, 123–25, 126, 127, 161, 166, 175, 413, 585–86
    in China, 165, 168f
    and *contre-jour* effects, 232–35, 247n.39
    and development of moving pictures, 22–25
    Griffith article on, 245n.3
    and magic lantern shows, 21
    and *Popular Science Monthly*'s approach to moving pictures, 290–93
photomicrography, 291–92
photo picture (*yinghua*), 161, 162–63
Photoplay (magazine), 241, 404, 516, 663–64, 666–68, 669, 670–72, 674, 675–79, 696, 705–6
The Photoplay: A Psychological Study (Münsterberg), 63
Photoplay Clearing House, 675
photoplays, 55
Physical Culture, 675–76
Piazza, François, 727
Picabia, Francis, 263
Picasso, Pablo, 717
Pickering, Edward C., 291
Pickford, Lottie, 670
Pickford, Mary, 233, 247n.44, 365–66, 414–15, 444, 445f, 451–52, 453, 454, 481–82, 486, 511, 512–13, 653, 669, 670–71, 675–76
Pictorial Beauty on Screen (Freeburg), 229–30, 583, 584f
Pictorial Composition and the Critical Judgment of Pictures (Poore), 234
Pictorial Effect in Photography (Robinson), 234
pictorialism, 225–32, 240–44
"Pictorialism and the Picture" (Griffith), 245n.3
"picture" in Chinese cinema, 159, 160, 161–63, 164–66, 167, 175, 177, 179

The Picture of Dorian Gray (Wilde), 550–51
Picture Play Magazine, 581
Pindère, Etienne, 269
Pinthus, Kurt, 641–42, 657n.2
piracy
    copying technology as accidental technology, 80–84
    digital media as key to early cinema, 77–79
    early cinema as key to digital media, 79–80
    historical background of print duping, 72–77
    lessons of, 87
    and Megaupload raid, 84–87
placedness, 506, 507, 509
Plaindealer, 136
plano americano ("American shot"), 720
plan (shot), 104–5
Plateau, Joseph, 19
Platt Amendment, 528–29
"play" in Chinese cinema, 159, 161–62, 164, 165–71, 173–74, 178–79. *See also yingxi* (shadow play)
Playing the Race Card (Williams), 575
Plemya (*The Tribe*, 2014), 749–50
Plessner, Maximilian, 46–50
plot structures, 577, 628. *See also* narrative structure of films
poesis, cinematic, 747–48
poetic cinema, 725–30
Poetic Realism, 274
Pogany, Willy, 490–92
Point Four Program, 565–66
point-of-view shots, 217–18
Pol, Heinz, 641–42
political economy, 9
political influence of cinema, 518. *See also* cultural impact of cinema; propaganda value of cinema
Politiken (Danish newspaper), 604
Polo, Marco, 336–37, 347, 351n.28
Polytechnic Institute and Reading Rooms (Shanghai), 174–75
Polytechnic Institution (London), 21
Pompeian Massage Cream, 675–76
Pompeii Buffet and Café, 140
Pontoppidan, Henrik, 598
Poore, Henry Rankin, 234

The Poor Little Rich Girl (Gates), 237–39
Popular Electricity, 294, 295–97, 299
popularization of sciences, 291–92, 307–10, 313–14, 316–19, 323, 327
Popular Mechanics, 291–92, 295–97, 299
"Popular Player Contest" (magazine contest), 667–69
Popular Science Monthly, 8, 283–84
    and advances in motion pictures, 284–90, 285f, 286f, 298f, 301n.10, 302n.28
    and influence of photography on film, 290–93
    "Motion Pictures" section, 295, 295f
    and popularization of science, 293–95, 295f, 296f, 299
    and state of film in 1916, 295–98
La Porte étroite (Gide), 716
Porter, Edwin S., 2, 186–87, 198–99
Porter, Michael, 421
portrait (*xiaoxiang*), 165
Portrait de Lugné-Poë (Vuillard), 261f
portraiture, 164–65, 166–67
postfilmic technologies, 50
Post Office Savings Bank (1935), 538
Potter, Susan, 686–87, 690
Pougin, Arthur, 97, 98f
Poverty Row distributors, 461–62, 476
Powell, Paul, 149, 151, 158n.116
The Power and Beauty of Superb Womanhood (Macfadden), 673
The Power God (1925), 630
Pozzi, Samuel, 316
Pranks (1909), 698–99
Praxinoscope, 19–20, 25–27
Prayer in the Mosque of Amor Cairo (Gérôme), 239
pregnancy. *See* birth control films
pre-marital sex, 381. *See also* birth control films
premier plan (staging term), 105
premiers of films, 440–42, 444–45, 446–49, 450–51, 453, 455–56, 584–85, 596–97
Prenatal Care (Children's Bureau pamphlet), 357–58, 368–69
The President (*Prasidenten*, 1919), 595–96
Pretty, Arline, 628–29
Pride of the Clan (1916), 233

primitive cinema, 39–40
La Princesse Mandane (1928), 260, 268f, 269, 696
Printers' Ink, 674
printing press, 519
prior restraint, 8
Prisoner of Zenda (1922), 240–42
Pritchard, Walter, 368, 369–70
Private Sex Advice to Women for Young Wives and Those Who Expect to be Married (pamphlet), 386
Production Code, 510, 701–2, 707
Progressive Era and progressivism, 666
    and Children's Bureau films, 354–55, 361, 364, 365, 368, 374n.48
    and inequality issues, 674
    and Los Angeles land values, 411
    and middlebrow culture, 663–64, 665–67, 670, 676–78
    and reproductive politics in cinema, 375
Projecting-Phenakistiscope, 19–20
projection, 19–22, 42
    and Cinématographe, 32–34
    and the hyaloscope, 47–48
    and technical advances, 285f
prologues to film premieres, 441–42, 444–45, 446, 447–48, 449, 450–51, 455
propaganda value of cinema, 21, 356–57, 358, 359, 362, 367–68, 389–90, 512–13, 516, 526, 534–35, 536, 540, 731, 753–54
Prospect Theatre (Brooklyn), 378–79
Prostitutionen (*Prostitution*, 1919), 702
Pruess Lake, 580
Prunella (1918), 227, 236–39
Prunella, or, Love in a Dutch Garden (Housman), 236–37
psychoanalysis, 727–28
Psychologie des foules (Le Bon), 11
"The Psychology of Crazes" (Patrick), 288
"The Psychology of Relaxation" (Patrick), 288
Psychopathology of Everyday Life (Freud), 727
publicity and public relations, 481–86, 488, 490, 580–81, 585f. *See also* advertising
public opinion, 514–19
Public Opinion (Lippmann), 516
publics, 11. *See also* mass audience for cinema
public works programs, 410

The Pulse of Life (1917), 235
Pumfrey, Stephen, 308–9
Die Püppe (1919), 186
Purdue Film Conference, 2
Pure Film Movement, 120
Purviance, Edna, 444, 698
putrefacto (aesthetic concept), 723
Puvis de Chavannes, Pierre, 237–39

Qarun's Treasure (*Ganj-e Qarun*, 1965), 568n.42
Les quatre âges de Pierrot (song), 108f
Queen Christina (1933), 706f
queerness, 685, 686, 687–88. See also gender and sexual identities
The Question (1916), 384–86
Quinn, Michael, 460–61, 464–65, 470–71
Quirk, Billy, 691–92, 698–99
Quirk, James R., 677
Qur'an, 338
Qustanian, Asia, 560–61

Rabinovitz, Lauren, 40
"The Race Problem in the United States" (Washington), 285–87
racial identity and racism
 and Black theatrical comedy, 130–31
 and Children's Bureau films, 364, 367–68
 and *The Covered Wagon*, 572, 573–78, 587–88
 and film distribution systems, 516–17
 and imperial power of cinema, 538–39
 and legal issues of image rights, 58–59
 and middlebrow culture, 667–68
 and museum-sponsored expedition films, 344
 race filmmaking, 132–33, 152–53
 race shows, 138
 "race suicide" trope, 376–77, 386–88
 racialized comedy, 143
 segregation and desegregation, 142–45
 and Southern culture, 152
 and voting rights, 392n.11
Le Radical, 322
Radiguet & Massiot company, 101f
Radway, Janice, 663, 672, 677–78
Raff and Gammon, 35

Raheja, Michelle, 574
The Railroad Porter (1913), 130, 131, 132–33, 140, 143, 144, 148
Rainey, Paul J., 333
Ramsaye, Terry, 1, 403–4
Ramses (magician), 146
Rank, Otto, 63
Raphael, 235–36
RapidShare, 82–84
The Rapids of Life (Johan, 1921), 600, 602–3
RCA, 563
Rea, Christopher, 166
Read, Robert, 476
The Reader (Vuillard), 263
real estate business, 413, 414–15, 432–33, 440–41, 442, 448
Realism, 230–31, 547, 585–86
Realty Board (Los Angeles), 407, 409
rear projection, 741–42
Rebellato, Dan, 255, 256
receptor theory, 324–25, 326–27
das Recht am eigenen Bilde. See "right to one's own image" doctrine
Das Recht des Kinematographen (May), 60
recording technologies, 38–39, 44–46
reenactment, 197
Reformed Beijing Opera (*gailiang jingju*), 170
Reformed New Opera (*gailiang xinxi*), 170
Reich, Jacqueline, 560
Reichardt, Kelly, 571–72
Reichmann, Max, 653
Reid, Wallace, 229, 444, 670–71
Reinhardt, Max, 55, 227, 236–37
Rekabtalaei, Golbarg, 551–52
Reliance (production company), 430
Remarque, Erich-Maria, 655
Rembrandt, 230–31
Le Rembrandt de la rue Lepic (1911), 698
Rembrandt lighting, 228, 229, 245–46n.15, *See also* lighting sources and design
Renaissance, 230–31
Renaud, Pierre, 727
Renoir, Jean, 718
Repas en famille (1897), 124–25
repetition, 623. See also time and temporal frameworks
repoussoir effects, 234, 235–36, 239, 243

reproductive politics. *See* birth control films
Republic (processing lab), 425–26
"A Republican Marriage" (Perry), 667–68
Republican Motherhood, 365
El retablo del Maese Pedro (Falla), 717
Le Rêve (Puvis de Chavannes), 237–39
Revell, Nellie, 443, 448–49
revisionism, 1, 2–3, 5, 6, 10, 39–40, 126–27, 165
La Révolution Surréaliste, 729
rewatchability, 632
Reynaud, Émile, 18, 19, 25–27, 29, 32, 33, 41–42, 100
Reynolds, Burt, 745–46
Reynolds, Glen, 538–39
Rialto Theatre (Los Angeles), 445–46, 448
Rialto Theatre (New York), 444
Richter, Hans, 715, 723
Rien que les heures (1926), 718
"right to one's own image" doctrine, 56–66
Riis, Thomas, 134
Ripley, William Z., 285
Ritchie, Henry, 433, 439n.74
Rivera, Primo de, 729
RKO, 430
Roach, Hal, 444
road movies, 572
roadshow releases, 580–81, 584–85
Robert, Étienne-Gaspard, 111–12
Roberts, Alice, 696
Robertson, George S., 289–90
Robida, Albert, 42
Robin Hood (1922), 240–41, 414–15, 447–48
Robinson, Frederick Cayley, 237–39
Robinson, Henry Peach, 234, 245–46n.15
Rockwell, Helen, 381, 382–83
Rockwell, Norman, 490–92, 493f, 663–64
Rocky Mountain School, 586–87
Rode, Julius, 703
Rodowick, David, 751
Rogers, Buddy, 684, 685f
Rogers, Maureen, 461, 465–66
Rogers, T. F., 143
Roget, Peter Mark, 19
Roland, Ruth, 672–73
Roman d'un Mousse (1913), 232–33
Romanticism, 62, 225–26

"Romanticism— Psychoanalysis— Film" (Kittler), 62–63
Romeo and Juliet (1908), 662–63
Romersholm (Ibsen), 257–58
Rongfang Photography Studio, 168f
Roosevelt, Franklin D., 518
Roosevelt Hotel (Hollywood), 440–41, 450–53, 452f, 454, 455–56
Roosevelt, Theodore, 333, 335, 666, 675–76
Rose-France (1918), 231–32, 265
Rosenzweig, Roy, 666–67
Rosher, Charles, 229–30, 243
Rosita (1923), 239–40
Røssaak, Eivind, 595–96
Rossell, Deac, 18, 28
Rossholm, Anna Sofia, 598
Rothacker, Watterson, 426–27
Rothafel, Samuel "Roxy," 443
Rotundo, Anthony, 695
Rough Sea at Dover (1895), 194–95
Roundhay Garden Scene (1888), 28
Rowdy Ann (1919), 700
Rowe, George, 699–700, 700f
Rowlandson, Thomas, 190f
Royal Geographical Society (UK), 332
Royal Institute of Public Health (UK), 322
Le Royaume des fées (*The Kingdom of Fairies*, 1903), 96, 97, 184–85
Roy Davidge Film Laboratories, 432f
Rube and Mandy at Coney Island (1903), 561–62
Une rue à Tokyo [II] (1898), 125
Rural Sports: Smock Racing (Rowlandson), 190f
Russell, Sylvester, 136; 139, 151
Russell Sage Foundation, 362–63
Russo, Vito, 684–85, 686, 691
Ruttmann, Walther, 656–57, 715, 721

Sabin, F. E., 495–96
Sadoul, Georges, 1, 18, 722
safari films, 333. *See also* expedition films
Safavi, Mirahmad, 560
Sahl, Hans, 641–42
Sailor-Made Man (1921), 691
Saint-Gaudens, Augustus, 235–36
Sakane, Tazuko, 704–5, 706f

Salaried Masses (Kracauer), 641–42
Salomé (1922), 697–98
Salon d'A utomne, 262–63
Salon des Indépendants, 262
Salt, Barry, 226–28, 231–33, 246n.25, 249n.72
Salt for Svanetia (1930), 341–42
same-sex relationships, 687–88, 698–702. *See also* gender and sexual identities
Sandberg, Mark, 599–601, 603
Sandow, Eugene, 78–79
San Fernando Valley, 432–33
San Francisco Museum of Art, 715
Sanger, Margaret, 375, 382–83, 388–91, 388*f*
Santa Monica Boulevard, 431
Santesson Affair, 688
"Sant Sebasti" (Dalí), 723
Sargeant, John Singer, 237
Sargent, Epes Winthrop, 667–68
Sarkisova, Oksana, 341–42
Sarony, Gilbert, 698
satire, 148, 269, 550, 553, 554, 555, 644–45
Saturday Evening Post, 149, 481–82, 485–86, 487*f*, 490, 491*f*, 493*f*, 663–64
Saturday Review of Literature, 677–78
Saxe Brothers, 488
scandals, 399–400, 405–6, 688, 693
Scaramouche (1923), 241–42
Schaefer, Eric, 364
Schallert, Edwin, 454, 455
Schenck, Joseph, 440–41, 450–52, 455
Schivelbusch, Wolfgang, 579
Schmitz, Kevin, 75
Schoedsack, Ernest B., 333
Schönfelder, Erich, 654
Schub, Esfir, 557–58
Schulz, Fritz, 702–3
Schünzel, Reinhold, 702–3
Schwalbe, Harry, 468–69, 474–75, 476
Schwartz, Vanessa R., 39–40, 588
"Science and Morality" (Mathews), 289–90
Scientific American, 41–42, 293, 299
scientific filmmaking, 8–9. *See also* popularization of sciences
Scientific-Humanitarian Committee (Germany), 702–3
Scientific Monthly, 293
Scott, Allen J., 431

screens, 21, 171–72, 173–75, 177, 178–79
Screen Writers' Guild, 707
The Seashell and the Clergyman. *See La Coquille et le clergyman* (1927)
Second Impressionist Exhibition, 125
Secord, Anne, 308–9
Seeley, George, 237
segregation and desegregation, 142–45. *See also* racial identity and racism
Seitz, John F., 228, 231, 233, 241, 243
Sélavy, Rrose (Duchamp pseudonym), 704
seleno-photographic method, 48
Selig, William N., 669
Selig Zoo, 410–11
Selznick International Pictures, 403
Sembat, Georgette, 262–63
Sembat, Marcel, 262–63
Sennett, Mack, 147, 189, 197–98, 203n.41, 444, 466–67, 471–72, 473, 741–42
Séparation des soeurs xiphopages Doodica et Radica (1902), 329n.23
Sepenta, Abdolhussein, 563–64
Sequin, Pierre, 28
serial films, 618–19
  and *Hazards of Helen*, 622–28
  serial queen genre, 621, 623, 624–25, 628–29, 630, 635n.25
  and temporality, 619–22
  and *A Woman in Grey*, 628–33
service corridor of Hollywood, 431–34, 432*f*
set design and construction, 424.
  See also staging
settlement houses, 360–61. *See also* Hull-House
settler colonialism. *See* colonialism
The Settler Colonial Present (Veracini), 569
settler melodramas. *See* melodrama
Seurat, Georges, 260
Seven Chances (1925), 186
7th Heaven (1927), 725
sewing machines, 462–63
sexology, 688–89, 702
sexual hygiene films, 702
sexuality. *See* gender and sexual identities
sexually transmitted diseases, 364
"shadow" in Chinese cinema, 159, 160, 161–62, 163, 164, 165, 171–75, 178–79. *See also yingxi* (shadow play)

Shah, Mohammad Reza, 551–52, 556–57
Shakespeare, William, 650–51, 689
Shanghai, 4, 160–61, 164–65, 167, 170–71, 173–75, 176–77, 178
"Shanghai-style Beijing Opera" (*haipai jingju*), 170
shashin butō (photographic dance), 120–21
shashin katsudō (photographic movement), 120–21
Shearman, Montague, 187–89
sheet music, 108*f*
The Sheik (1921), 239
Shenbao (Shanghai newspaper), 170, 173–74
Sheppard-Towner Act (US), 356
Sherwood, George, 345
Shibata, Tsunekichi, 116, 117–18, 122, 125, 126
Shimabara tayū no dōchū (*A Geisha's Walk*, 1908), 123
Shin, Takehisa, 706*f*
Shindo, Kaneto, 747–48, 749
Shinn, Everett, 237
Shin Shakkyō (*kabuki* play), 126
Shipp, Jesse A., 142–43
Shirk, Adam Hull, 580–81
Shoecraft, Joe, 140
Shore Acres (1920), 230
Shubert, Lee, 451
Shustari, Abu al-Hasan al-, 342
Der sichtbare Mensch (*Visible Man*), 658n.7
side-chain theory. *See* receptor theory
Sidewalk Stories (1989), 749
signal stations, 45–46
Sigurjónsson, Jóhann, 598–99
"silent cinema" label, 507, 508–9
Silent Movie (1976), 745–47
Silk Road, 335–36
Simba (1928), 333
Simmon, Scott, 574, 586
Sinful Mothers (*Penal Code S218*) (1918), 702
Singapore, 170
Singer, Ben, 3, 460–61, 506–7, 622, 629, 630–31, 632–33
Singin' in the Rain (1952), 455, 742–43, 745, 752
La Sirène des tropiques (1927), 720
A Sixth Part of the World (1926), 341–42
Sjöström, Victor, 253, 594–600, 602–3, 609, 610–12

Skandia (production company), 600–1, 605
Skilda tiders danser (*Dances through the Ages*, 1909), 689–90, 690*f*
Skladanowsky, Max, 28–29, 33–34
Sklar, Robert, 9–10
Slaboshpytskyi, Myroslav, 749–51
slapstick comedy, 620–21, 626, 647, 651–52, 698–702, 741–42, 743, 746
slavery, 527–28, 573–74
slides, 20–21. *See also* magic lanterns
Sloan, Kay, 375–76, 388–89
small-gauge film stock, 283
small talk, visual, 340–43, 342*f*
Smart Set Company, 140–41, 144, 148
Smith, Chris, 143
Smith, Jill Suzanne, 702
Smith & Aller (DuPont dealers), 431, 432*f*
"The Smock Race, at Finglas" (Ward), 189–91
Smythe, William E., 411
Snow, Marguerite, 671–72
social change, 506–7, 672
social consciousness, 730
social Darwinism, 629
social governance, 517–18
social issue films, 364
social media, 104, 106
social mobility, 672
social reproduction, 677–78
social sciences, 357–58
Society of Motion Picture Engineers (SMPE), 421–22, 423, 429, 434
The Soilers (1923), 699–700, 700*f*
Solskinsdalen (1925), 600–1
The Song of the Scarlet Flower (*Sangen om den eldröda blomman*, 1919), 600, 602–3
Sontag, Susan, 550–51, 739–40
Sony v. Universal Pictures ("Betamax" case), 81–82
sound film, 564–65, 655–57, 691
Soupault, Philippe, 722, 726–27
La Souriante Madame Beudet (1923), 252, 258–59, 260, 263–65, 269, 270*f*
Southern California, 397–98, 518
Southern Enterprises, 473–74
Southwestern Triangle Film Corporation, 468
souvenir film programs, 596–97
Soviet cinema, 560–61, 563–64, 740

INDEX

space and spatial relationships, 204–5, 208, 213–14
  and hierarchies of knowledge, 219
Spanish-American War, 528–29, 530f
Spanish Civil War, 714
The Spanish Dancer (1923), 239–40
Specht, Charles, 232–33
Spehr, Paul, 2, 18, 30, 78–79
Das Spielzeug von Paris (*Red Heels*, 1925), 644–45
The Spoilers (1923), 663–64, 699–700
Spoor, George, 156n.82
The Sports and Pastimes of the People of England (Strutt), 189–91
The Squaw Man (1914), 440–41
Stafford, Barbar, 179
staging, 205–7, 208–15, 218–19, 221–22, 235–36, 560–61. *See also* depth of field; foreground staging; mise-en-scène; *premier plan* (staging term); set design and construction
Staiger, Janet, 227–28, 424
stained-glass windows, 21
Stamp, Shelley, 8–9, 364, 521n.19, 624–25
Stampfer, Simon, 19
Standard Exhibition Contract, 485
Standard Film Labs, 428–30, 433
Standard Oil, 531
Stanford, Leland, 22–23
Starr, Kevin, 412, 414–15
Starr, Paul, 288–90
Star Wars (1977), 746
state rights system, 464–69, 470, 472, 474, 475, 476. *See also* distribution
Stauffacher, Frank, 715
St. Clair, Malcolm, 741–42
Stedman, Raymond, 623–24
Steichen, Edward, 229–30, 232–33, 234
Stein, Gertrude, 704
Steinbock, Eliza, 710n.25
"The Stepsisters" (Harrison), 665
stereoscopic moving pictures, 50, 75, 229, 231, 233, 287, 302n.28
stereotypes, 133, 197, 644–45, 667, 673, 684–85
Stern, Ernst, 236–37
Sternberg, Josef von, 722
Stevens, Augustus, 131

Stewart, Anita, 446–47
Stewart, Jacqueline, 148, 387
Stieglitz, Alfred, 229–30, 232–33, 234
Stiller, Mauritz, 243–44, 594–96, 597–98, 600, 602–3, 607–8, 609, 611–12, 687–88, 693, 694f, 704, 705f, 750–51
still photography, 339–40. *See also* photography and photographic techniques
St. Louis Post Dispatch, 314–18, 315f
Stolen by Gypsies (1905), 198–99
Stonehouse, Ruth, 670–71, 672
storage media, 7
Storey, Edith, 673
The Story of Paramount (booklet), 486
The Story of the Lost Mirror Image (Hoffmann), 62
Stout, George W., 471–72
Straayer, Chris, 691
Strand Theatre (New York), 443–44, 494
The Strange Story of Peter Schlemihl (Chamisso), 62
Die Straße (*The Street*, 1923), 647, 648–49, 655
Strauven, Wanda, 40
stroboscopic effects, 19, 21–22, 26, 30–31
Stroheim, Erich von, 241, 243–44, 719, 721, 730
Strong, Anna, 362
"The Struggle for Equality in the United States" (Emerick), 288–89
Struss, Karl, 232–33
Strutt, Joseph, 189–91
The Student of Prague (1913), 55, 57, 61–66
Studio 28 (Paris), 724, 728–29
Studio Basic Agreement, 399–400
studio photography, 166–67, 168f, 169f
studio system, 397–98
Sturtevant, Victoria, 148
subject-ego distinction, 57, 61
subsequent-run bookings, 467–68, 478–79n.44
subversive cinema, 725–30
Suggestions for Visitors to County Poorhouses and to Other Public Charitable Institutions (Lathrop), 356–57
Summer Babies (1911), 362–63
A Summer Idyl (1910), 245n.3
Sumurun (1920), 236–37, 239–40

794 INDEX

Sun Babies (1926), 361, 368, 369–70
Sunset Boulevard (1950), 743
Sunset Magazine, 412
Supreme Court (US), 8–9, 81–82
Suratt, Valeska, 670
Surrealism, 274, 547–48, 722–23, 725, 726–27, 728–30, 731
Le Surréalisme au service de la révolution, 729
Susman, Warren, 662–63
Suzanne Després (Vuillard), 261f
Svensk Filmindustri, 602–3, 605
Swanson, Gloria, 495–96
swashbucklers, 241–42
Swedish Biograph, 595, 596–98, 600–1, 602–3, 605
Swedish filmmaking, 594–96
  authenticity and location shooting, 599–601
  authenticity and represented locations, 602–4
  folklore and Swedish cinema, 594–95, 599, 600–1, 602, 603–5, 606, 607–8, 611–12
  and reification of ethnographic content, 611–13
  and *Sons of the Soil* (1920), 607–10
  Swedish ideal in Scandinavia, 604–7
  and Swedish quality concept, 596–99, 604–7
Sweet, Blanche, 364
Switzerland, 564–65
Swoboda System of Conscious Evolution, 675–76
Symbolism, 226–27, 231–32, 236–39, 242–43, 251–52, 254–65, 266, 269–71, 272–74, 278n.53
Symbolist Theater, 259–60
sympsychograph, 301n.10
Synthetism, 259, 260, 263, 266–74
Szalkolczai, Arpal, 199

taboo subjects, 691. *See also* gender and sexual identities
Taft, William, 354–55
Ein Tag Film (*A Day of Film*, 1928), 656–57
Taiping Rebellion, 167
A Tale of Two Cities (1911), 670
talkies. *See* sound film
TallBear, Kimberly, 576
Talmadge, Constance, 243, 444
Talmadge, Norma, 451–52
Talmadge, Richard, 560
Taming a Husband (1910), 691–92
Tanaka, Junichirō, 122
Tang, Leah, 82–84
Tarde, Gabriel, 11
Tarzan of the Apes (1918), 426
Tashman, Lilyan, 705–6
Tauber, Richard, 653
Taurog, Norman, 333
Taylor, Charles, 10–11, 506–7, 509
teahouses, 160–61, 167, 170, 172–74
Technical World, 299
Technicolor Motion Picture Corporation, 420, 421, 431, 432, 433–34
technology and technological development of cinema, 6–7, 162, 420–22, 432f, 434, 506–7, 513–14, 579, 648–49
  as background of copyright infringement, 75–77
  copying technology as "accidental technology," 80–84
  digital media as key to early cinema, 77–79
  early cinema as key to digital media, 79–80
  and the Hollywood service corridor, 420–34, 432f
  and invention of cinema, 17–18
  lessons of piracy, 87
  and Megaupload raid, 84–87
  and ontology, 159–60, 161, 162–63, 178, 179n.3
  and post-silent era silent film, 751
  producing moving images, 18–20
  and proximity to Hollywood, 427–31
  rise of independent laboratories, 424–27
  technological spectacle, 295–97
  technology of magic, 63
  and transmission technologies, 44–46, 50
Teddy Roosevelt in Africa (1910), 333
Tehran, 551–52, 564–65
telegraph, 29–30, 43, 44–47
Tel-Electric Player Pianos, 489
telephones, 38–39, 42–43, 44, 45–47, 530–31
television, 38–39, 41–44, 46–48, 49–50, 631–32
temporality. *See* time and temporal frameworks
The Temptress (1926), 243–44

Tenebrism, 230–31
Terje Vigen (Ibsen), 597–98, 599–600, 601, 602, 603–4, 606, 608–9, 611
Tess of the Storm Country (1914), 205–8, 215–16, 216*f*, 669
Thalhammer, Karl, 422–24
Thanhouser "Big Productions" series, 214–15
Thanhouser Corporation, 362
Theater of Ideas, 257–58
Theater of Silence, 257–58, 271
Theater of the Unexpressed, 257–58
theater's influence on cinema, 251–52, 253–62
Théâtre d'Art, 259–60
Théâtre de l'Oeuvre, 256, 259–60
Theatre of Science: A Volume of Progress and Achievement in the Motion Picture (Grau), 666
Théâtre Optique, 25–27, 29, 100
"Le Théâtre ou les théâtres" (De Kuyper), 254–55
Théâtrophone, 106
Their First Mistake (1932), 699
Thèmes et Variations (1929), 271, 273*f*
Theory of Film (Kracauer), 641–42, 648, 656–57
"This Is Practical Censorship" (cartoon), 407–8, 408*f*
Thomas, Nona, 670
Thomas Graal's Best Film (*Thomas Graals bästa film*, 1917), 595–96
Thomas H. Ince Studios, 403
Thompson, Kristin, 226–28, 229–30, 243, 510, 512–13
three-strip color process, 421. *See also* color film
Three Women (1924), 243
Tichi, Cecelia, 356–57
Tillie's Punctured Romance (1914), 147, 464–65
time and temporal frameworks, 10–11, 202–3n.33
    exposure times, 22
    and repetition, 623
    and serial films, 618–22
    time-image, 162–63
    time-lapse imagery, 287–88, 306–7, 313–14
Times Square, 484–85, 569–71
Tincher, Fay, 670, 700

Tinting and Toning (Kodak guide), 424
Toberman, Charles E., 440–41, 446–48, 450–52, 452*f*
Tom, Tom, the Piper's Son (1905), 187–89, 188*f*
Tonalism, 225–26
"Tonbildfilm" (Kracauer), 656–57
Tönende Welle (*Sound Wave*, 1928), 656–57
Tongqing teahouse (Shanghai), 170, 174
Topeka Capital, 495–96
Tosi, Virgilio, 291–92
Totem and Taboo (Freud), 63
totems, 484
Toulet, Emmanuelle, 520n.16
Tourneur, Maurice, 226–28, 233–39, 241–42, 243–44, 249n.72, 753
The Towering Inferno (1974), 746
trade organizations, 399
Traffic in Souls (1913), 205–7, 211–14, 213*f*, 217–18, 219–22, 220*f*
"Tragedy in Everyday Life" (Maeterlinck), 260
Tragödie einer Frau (*Tragedy of a Woman*, 1924), 644–45
trail films, 572, 575
The Trail of the Octopus (1919), 630
Transactions of the Society of Motion Picture Engineers, 233–34
Transcendentalists, 579–80, 723
transcontinental railroad, 527
trans identities, 685, 686, 687–88. *See also* gender and sexual identities
transitional era of US filmmaking, 10, 204, 517, 521n.19
transmission technologies, 50
Trans-Siberian Railroad, 336–37
travel photography, 292
Treasure Island (1908), 662–63
treaty ports (in China), 164–65, 167, 173, 528–29
Tremont Film Laboratories Corp., 431, 432*f*
The Trey o' Hearts (1914), 294
Triangle Distributing, 473–74, 478–79n.44
Triangle Film Corporation, 433, 461, 466–76
Triangle Komedy, 701
"A Trip around Iceland" (travel photography series), 292
tripods, 423
A Trip to Chinatown (1891), 134

A Trip to Chinatown (1917), 701–2
A Trip to Coontown (1898), 133–37
A Trip to Mars (1903), 72–73
A Trip to the Moon (1902), 72–74, 87
Troop Ships for the Philippines (1918), 528, 530f
Tropical Hookworm (1936), 538
True Story (magazine), 675–76
Truman, Harry, 565–66
"The Truth About Hollywood" (Cronyn), 412–13
Trypanosoma lewisi, 314–16
trypanosomes, 305, 314–17, 319–22, 320f, 323–24, 326–27
"Trypanosomes and Their Harmful Effects" (Mesnil), 319–20
Tsivian, Yuri, 316–17
Tsubouchi Memorial Theater Library, 116–17
tu (picture), 164–65
Tucker, Sophie, 443
Turks and Troubles (1917), 701–2
Turner, Florence, 662–63, 664
Turner & Dahnken, 485, 488
Turpin, Ben, 717–18, 722
Tuska, John, 572
Tuskegee Institute, 533–34
Twelfth Night (Shakespeare), 689, 691–92
The Twentieth Century (Robida), 42
Twice Two (1933), 699
Two Arabian Knights (1927), 695
two-color process, 420–21
two-selves pictures (*erwotu*), 166–67
Two Wrestlers (puppet play), 121
Tybjerg, Casper, 596, 606, 607, 608
typewriters, 43

Uchatius, Franz, 19–20
uchikake (kimono style), 125
Ueda, Manabu, 122–23
Ufa studio, 653–54
Ulrichs, Karl Heinrich, 689
Ultraism, 717, 720
Unbewusstsein (Freud), 727
The Unborn (1916), 376–77, 377f, 384–88
"The Uncanny" (Freud), 63
Uncle Tom's Cabin (1903), 74–75, 74f
Uncle Tom's Cabin (Stowe), 575
underwater filming, 295–97

Underworld (1927), 722
Ungar, Arthur, 450–51
Union Pacific Railroad, 580–81
The Unique (San Francisco theater), 443
United Artists, 450, 451
United Artists Theatre Circuit Inc. (UATC), 451, 454, 455
Universal-Bluebird, 233
Universal City, 410–11, 425, 432–33
Universal Joy Week, 495
Universal Pictures, 81, 430, 460, 488
University of Chicago, 3
University of Pennsylvania, 23–24
"The Unseen World" (series), 313–14
Urban, Charles, 291–92, 313–14
Uricchio, William, 42–43
U.S. Battleship "Indiana," (1918), 528, 529f
U.S. Cruiser "Raleigh," (1918), 528
USDA. *See* Department of Agriculture (US)
Use of Motion Pictures In Agricultural Extension Work (USDA publication), 532–33, 533f
US Navy, 529
USS Nashville, 530
Utagawa, Kuniyoshi, 125–26

Valenti, Jack, 87
Valentino, Rudolph, 239–40, 241–42, 515–16, 706–7
van den Broek, John, 233
Van Dyke, W. S., 722
Vanity Fair (magazine), 229–30, 241–42
Vanta Clothing Company, 362
Van Trees, James, 429–30
Variety, 146, 156n.82, 381, 389, 425–26, 440–41, 450–51, 514, 752–53
Vasey, Ruth, 510, 512
Vasudevan, Ravi, 338
vaudeville, 34, 137–39, 142, 144, 146, 147, 148, 149, 150f, 185–86, 443–44
VCRs, 49–50, 632
Veblen, Thorstein, 484, 672–73
Veidt, Conrad, 702–3
Der velorene Schuh (*The Lost Shoe*, 1923), 653
Vem dömer? (Bergman), 596–97
Veracini, Lorenzo, 569
Verkade, Jan, 260

Vermeer, Johannes, 234
vernacular modernism, 4, 517–18
Verne, Jules, 269, 316–17
vertical integration, 443, 482–83
Vertov, Dziga, 341–42, 557–58, 561–62, 715
Veyre, Gabriel, 124–25
Victorian literature, 685, 686–87
Victorian microscopic culture, 316–17
videotape recorder (VTR), 81–82
Vidor, King, 572–73
Viejo, Breixo, 11–12
La Vierge Folle (1910), 258
Viertel, Berthold, 63
Viertel, Salka, 705–6
Vigo, Jean, 263, 714, 728–29, 730
villains, 630
Vincent, Carl, 728–29
Vingarne (*The Wings*, 1916), 693–95, 694f, 697–98
Virilio, Paul, 82–84
The Visiting Nurse (1911), 362–63
"A Visit to Nassau" (travel photography series), 292
"Visualization" (Dulac), 257–58
Vitagraph, 72, 571–72, 662–63, 670, 672, 673, 675–76, 692, 701–2
Vitaphone, 740, 742, 754
Vitascope, 34–35, 79, 120–21
Vogel, Amos, 714
Vogue, 229–30
von Moltke, Johannes, 11
von Westphal, Carl, 688–89
voting rights, 392n.11
Vuillard, Edouard, 259–60, 261f, 262–65
Vuillermoz, Émile, 231–32, 253
Vulliamy, Ed, 531

wagon-trail trope, 569–73
Wald, Lilian, 365
Walker, George, 131
Walkowitz, Rebecca, 549–50
Waller, Greg, 8, 461, 530–31
Wall Street, 517–18
Walsh, Raoul, 572–73
Walthall, Henry B., 669, 698–99
Walton, Lester, 142
Wang Tao, 165

Wanted— A Nurse (1906), 198–99
The War, the West, and the Wilderness (1979), 572
"War and the Fifth Estate" (Lippmann), 516
War Catalogue films (Edison), 528, 529, 529f
Ward, James, 189–91
Warner, Michael, 11
Warner Brothers, 430, 432–33, 714
Warner's Features, 465–66
Washington, Booker T., 285–87
Washington Monument, 298–99
Wasson, Haidee, 9
The Way of Herodotus (Marozzi), 344
Webb, Lawrence, 585–86
Weber, Anne-Katrin, 43–44
Die Weber (*The Weavers*, 1927), 645–46
Weber, Lois, 8–9, 364, 384–86, 389–90, 390f, 427, 444
The Wedding March (1928), 730
Wegener, Paul, 62
Weimar cinema, 641–42, 644–45, 647, 648, 649, 651–52, 653, 657n.2. *See also* German cinema
Weiss, Nancy Pottishman, 365–66
Weitzel, Edward, 381
Welby Cook, Harry, 176, 178
welfare services and advocacy, 354–56, 361–62, 364. *See also* Progressive Era and progressivism
Well Born (1923), 361, 368–69, 369f
Welles, Orson, 752–53
Wells, David Ames, 285
Werke (Kracauer), 642–43
West, Dorothy, 691–92
West, George R., 166–67
West, Mary Mills, 357
West Coast Theaters, 448, 450, 455. *See also* Fox Film Corporation
Western Electric, 531f
Western gaze, 346–47
Western Import, 474
Western-style painting (*xifahua*), 165
Western Vaudeville Managers' Association, 144
wet collodion process, 22
Wexman, Virgina Wright, 587

"What Every Girl Should Know" (article series), 382–83
"What Every Mother Should Know, or How Six Little Children Were Taught the Truth" (article series), 382–83
"What Happened" films, 194–95, 199, 202–3n.33
What Happened to Mary (1912), 619
"What Improvement in Motion Pictures Is Needed Most?" (magazine contest), 665–66, 669
What the World Should Know (1916), 364
When Tom Went to Work (1915), 360, 362
Where Are My Children? (1916), 8–9, 364, 384–86, 387
While Paris Sleeps (1920), 241–42
Whistler, James McNeill, 229–31, 235–36
White, Clarence, 232–33, 237
White, Pearl, 668–69, 672–73, 678–79
White, Walter, 149
White and Black (*Sepid o Siah*, 1954–1957), 546, 564–65, 566n.9
white-collar occupations, 418n.45
whiteface, 134–35
White Shadows in the South Seas (1928), 722
Wholesale Supply Company, 431, 432f
Wid's Daily, 377–78, 445–46
Wiene, Robert, 644–45
Wilde, Cornel, 546, 547–48
Wilde, Oscar, 555, 688, 689, 697–98, 704
Wilder, Billy, 743
Wilder, Kelley, 290–91
Wildflower (1914), 669
The Wild Party (1929), 695
Wiley, Hugh, 149
Williams, Bert, 131, 140–41, 144, 152–53
Williams, Clara, 670
Williams, Earle, 668–69
Williams, George, 131
Williams, Kathlyn, 671–72
Williams, Linda, 572–73, 575, 618, 621–22
Williams, Raymond, 185, 519n.7, 587–88, 674–75
Williams, Spencer, 149, 152–53
Williams, Tami, 704
Williams and Walker Company, 140
Williamson, Colin, 40

Williams & Stevens (burlesque comedians), 137–38
Wills, Louis L., 146
Wilson, Christopher, 663–64
Wilson, Edmund, 242, 515–16
Wilson, James, 359–60
Wilson, Lois, 575–76, 581
Wilson, Woodrow, 511, 513, 574–75
Wingate, Jesse, 577
Wings (1927), 684, 685f, 738
The Wings (1916). See *Vingarne* (*The Wings*, 1916)
Winik, Hyman, 474
Winn, J. Emmett, 534
The Wishing Ring (1914), 205–7, 210–12, 211f, 217–19
Within Our Gates (1920), 132
Wm. Horsley Laboratories, Inc., 432f
Wolfe, Patrick, 573–74
Wolo Czawienko (*Balettprimadonnan*, 1916), 597–98
The Woman from Mellon's (1910), 691–92
A Woman in Grey (1920), 619, 628–33
A Woman of Paris (1923), 242–43
women's civic organizations, 354, 358, 363, 365, 370
Women's Home Companion, 365
Women's Million Club, 406–7
Women's Progress movement, 259
Women's Rights (1899), 698
Wong, Anna May, 451
Won Through Merit (1915), 365–66
Woolf, Edgar Allan, 146
Woolwine, Claire, 405
"working memory" (concept), 631
"The Work of Art in the Age of Its Technological Reproducibility" (Benjamin), 4–5, 64
The World According to Hollywood (Vasey), 510
The World's Advance (magazine), 293, 294, 295–97
World War I, 9, 253, 257, 489, 508–9, 510–14, 516–19, 521n.19, 535–36, 600, 645, 684, 695
World War II, 539, 677–78
Wright, William, 183n.59
Writers' Branch (Hollywood), 707
Wue, Roberta, 175
Wyckoff, Alvyn, 228

X-ray photography, 301n.10
Xu Garden (Shanghai), 160–61, 176

Yale Review, 677–78
Yale School of Fine Arts, 235–36
Yasumoto, Kamehachi, 121
Yates, Herbert, 430
Yeaton, G. W., 496
Yeh, Emilie Yueh-yu, 161–63, 165, 170, 172, 177
Yen Yung Kiung, 174–75
Yi, Gu, 165
yingxi (shadow play), 160–62, 163–64, 165, 167, 173, 175. *See also* "shadow" in Chinese cinema
YMCAs, 140, 161, 170–71
Yokota shōkai, 123
Yokoyama, Akio, 125–26
Yoshizawa Shōten (production/distribution company), 122, 124

Young Frankenstein (1974), 745–46
Young Iran Society, 553
Yukon Territory, 334–35

Zapatas Bande (*Zapata's Band*, 1914), 692
Zervos, Christian, 719
Zhang Deyi, 167–70
Zielinski, Siegfried, 6, 42–43, 50
Žižek, Slavoj, 2–3
Zoetrope, 19, 24–25, 26, 27, 29, 30–31, 162–63, 287
Zola, Émile, 255–56
Zoöpraxiscope, 24, 27, 41–42
Zudora (1914), 619
Zukor, Adolph, 443, 466, 473–74, 481–82, 485, 512–13, 514–15, 580–81
Zwarich, Jennifer, 359–60